WINCHESTER
EASTLEIGH
SOUTHAMPTON
ROMSEY
PETERSFIELD
HAVANT
FAREHAM
GOSPORT
PORTSMOUTH
PORTSEA ISLAND
HAYLING ISLAND
HORNDEAN
NEWPORT
RYDE
COWES
VENTNOR
New Alresford
Bishop's Waltham
Wickham
Emsworth
Bosham
Waterlooville
Cowplain
Southsea
Lee-on-the-Solent
Hythe
Fawley
Netley
Hamble
Titchfield
Portchester
Bembridge
Shanklin
THE SOLENT
SPITHEAD
SOUTHAMPTON WATER
Portsmouth Harbour
Langstone Harbour
Chichester Harbour
FOREST OF BERE
ISLE OF WIGHT
Bracklesham Bay
DUNNOSE
FORELAND
E N
PORTSMOUTH to
Cherbourg 5-9 hrs
Le Havre 6-8 hrs
St Malo 6-11 hrs
Caen 6 hrs
5 0 miles 5 10
10 5 0 kilometres 5 10 15
4 centimetres to 10 kilometres (one grid square)
1 Kilometre = 0·6214 mile
1 mile = 1·61 kilometre
CW01638678

COUNTY
STREET ATLAS

SOUTH HAMPSHIRE

Ordnance Survey

COUNTY STREET ATLAS

PHILIP'S

SOUTH HAMPSHIRE

3½ INCHES TO 1 MILE

1st edition

COUNTY STREET ATLAS

SOUTH HAMPSHIRE

First Edition published 1991 by

Ordnance Survey and George Philip Ltd
Romsey Road
Maybush
Southampton SO9 4DH

George Philip Ltd
59 Grosvenor Street
London W1X 9DA

ISBN 0 540 05611 1 (George Philip)
ISBN 0 319 00242 X (Ordnance Survey)

Printed in Great Britain by
Butler & Tanner Ltd, Frome and London

CONTENTS

Key to map pages	vi-vii
Administrative boundaries	viii
Street maps	1-217
Index explanation and abbreviations	219
Index of towns, villages and rural localities	220
Index of street names	221-253

KEY TO MAP SYMBOLS

British Rail Station

London Transport Station

Private Railway Station

Bus or Coach Station

Police Station
(may not be open 24hrs)

Hospital with Casualty Facilities
(may not be open 24hrs)

Post Office

Place of Worship

Important Building

P Parking

120 Adjoining page indicator

Motorway and Dual Carriageway

Main or through road

A27(T) Road numbers (Dept of Transport)

Gate and obstruction to traffic
(restrictions may not apply at all times and to all vehicles)

Footpath
Bridleway

The representation in this atlas of a road, track or path is no evidence of the existence of a right of way.

Amb Sta	Ambulance Station	Liby	Library
Coll	College	Mus	Museum
FB	Foot Bridge	Sch	School
F Sta	Fire Station	TH	Town Hall
LC	Level Crossing		

The large letters and numbers around the edge of the maps form the referencing system.
An explanation of how to use the system for locating the position of street names appears on page **219**.

The small numbers identify the 1 kilometre National Grid lines.

Scale of Maps is 3½ inches to 1 mile (1 : 18103)

0 ¼ ½ ¾ 1 Mile

0 250m 500m 750m 1 Kilometre

KEY TO MAP PAGES

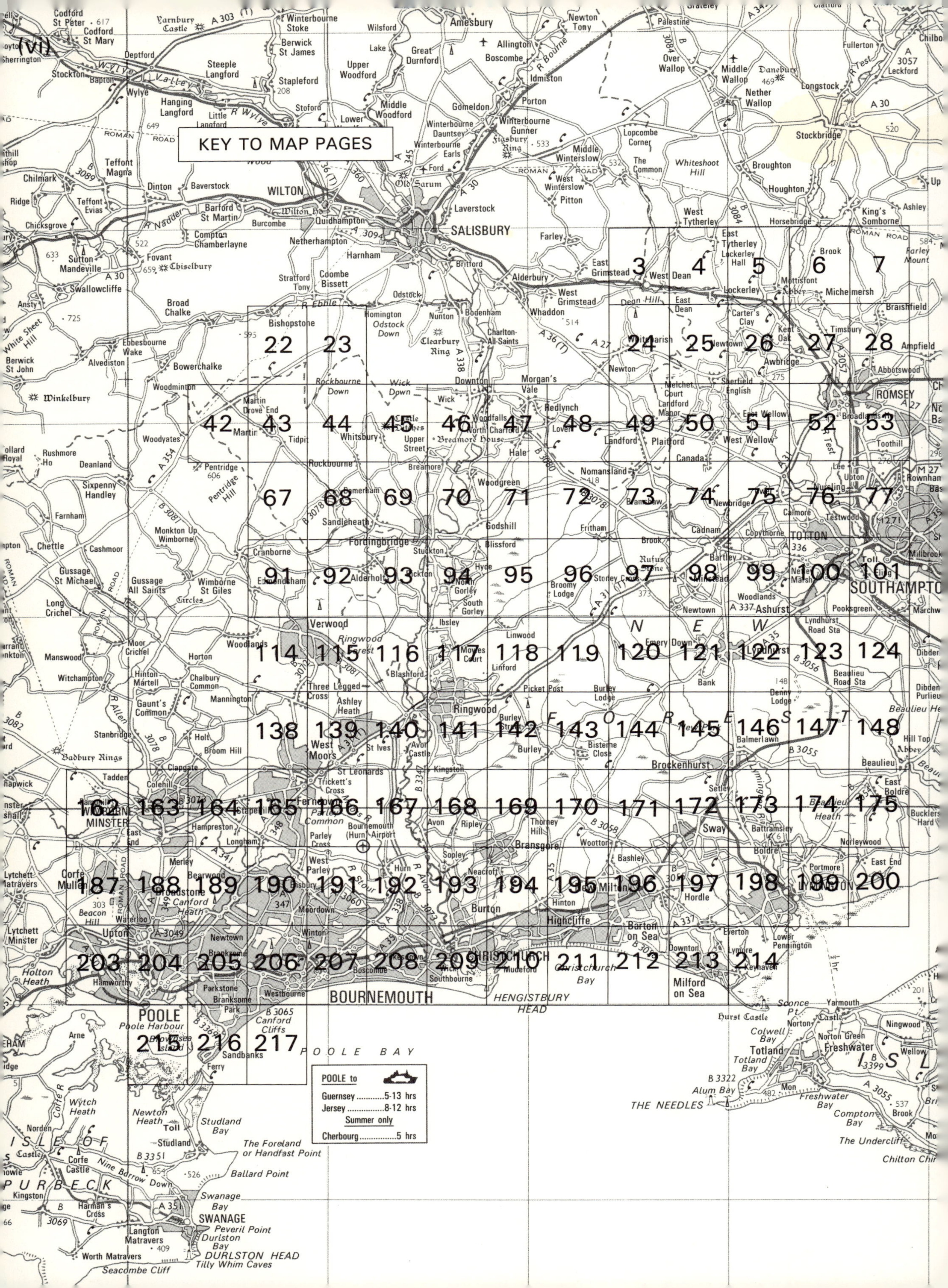

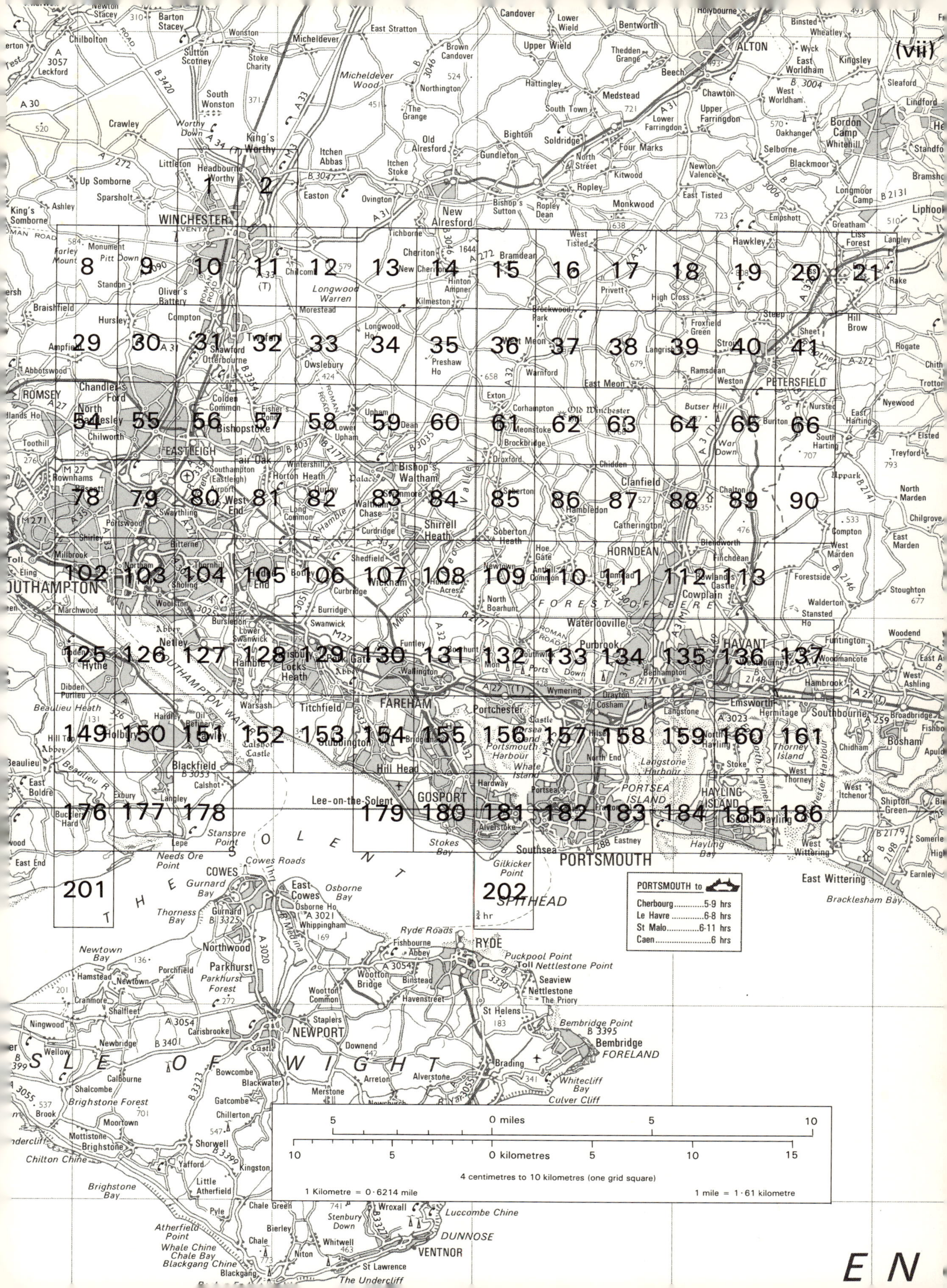
WINCHESTER
EASTLEIGH
ROMSEY
SOUTHAMPTON
FAREHAM
GOSPORT
PORTSMOUTH
PETERSFIELD
ALTON
HAVANT
HORNDEAN
NEWPORT
COWES
RYDE
VENTNOR
I S L E O F W I G H T
T H E S O L E N T
SPITHEAD
1
2
8
9
10
11
12
13
14
15
16
17
18
19
20
21
29
30
31
32
33
34
35
36
37
38
39
40
41
54
55
56
57
58
59
60
61
62
63
64
65
66
78
79
80
81
82
83
84
85
86
87
88
89
90
102
103
104
105
106
107
108
109
110
111
112
113
125
126
127
128
129
130
131
132
133
134
135
136
137
149
150
151
152
153
154
155
156
157
158
159
160
161
176
177
178
179
180
181
182
183
184
185
186
201
202
PORTSMOUTH to
Cherbourg............5-9 hrs
Le Havre.............6-8 hrs
St Malo..............6-11 hrs
Caen.........................6 hrs
5
0 miles
5
10
10
5
0 kilometres
5
10
15
4 centimetres to 10 kilometres (one grid square)
1 Kilometre = 0·6214 mile
1 mile = 1·61 kilometre
E N

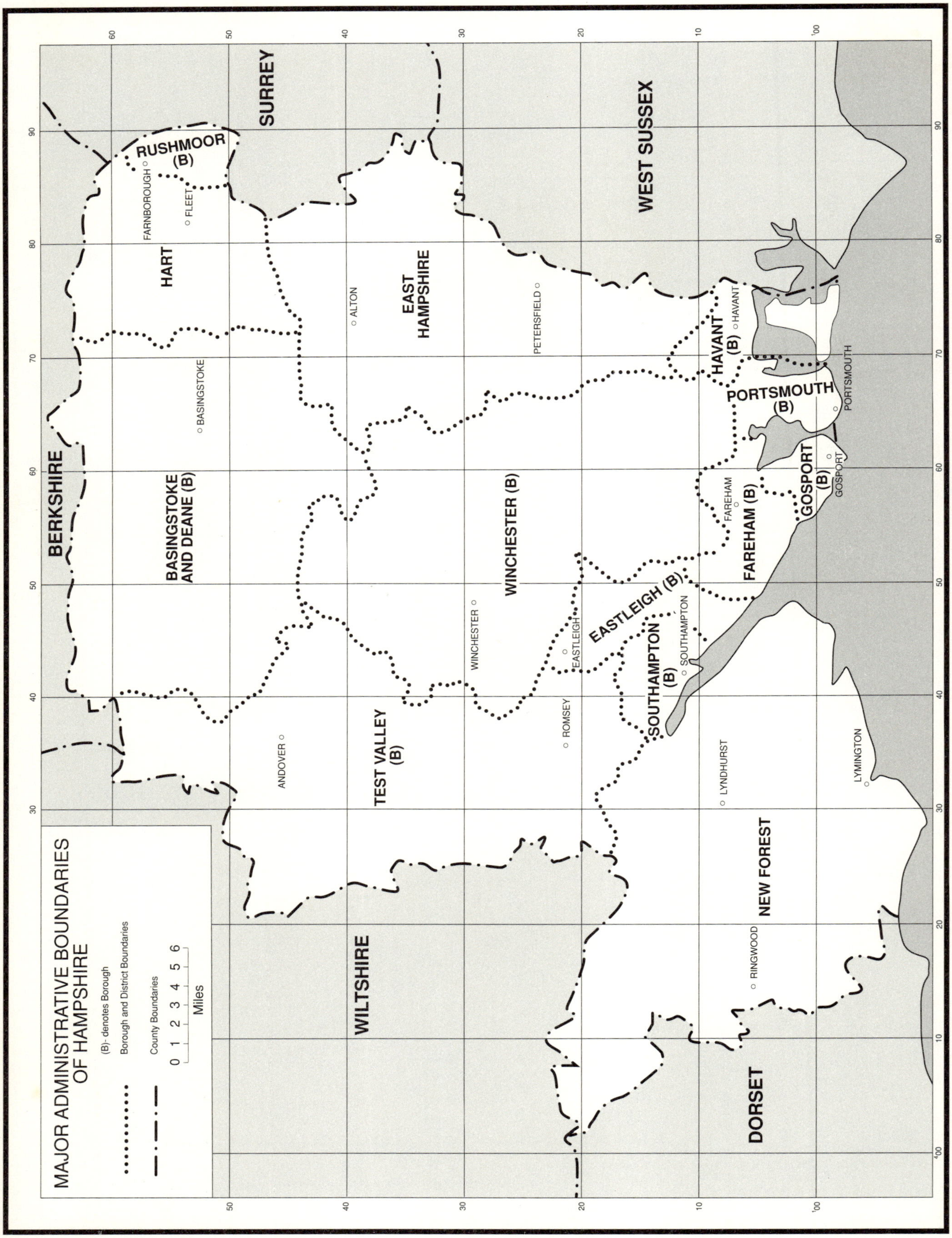

MAJOR ADMINISTRATIVE BOUNDARIES OF HAMPSHIRE
(B)- denotes Borough
Borough and District Boundaries
County Boundaries
0 1 2 3 4 5 6
Miles
BERKSHIRE
SURREY
WEST SUSSEX
WILTSHIRE
DORSET
RUSHMOOR (B)
FARNBOROUGH
FLEET
HART
BASINGSTOKE
BASINGSTOKE AND DEANE (B)
EAST HAMPSHIRE
ALTON
PETERSFIELD
WINCHESTER (B)
WINCHESTER
TEST VALLEY (B)
ANDOVER
ROMSEY
EASTLEIGH (B)
EASTLEIGH
SOUTHAMPTON (B)
SOUTHAMPTON
HAVANT (B)
HAVANT
PORTSMOUTH (B)
PORTSMOUTH
FAREHAM (B)
FAREHAM
GOSPORT (B)
GOSPORT
NEW FOREST
LYNDHURST
LYMINGTON
RINGWOOD

not continued, see key diagram

2

10

not continued, see key diagram

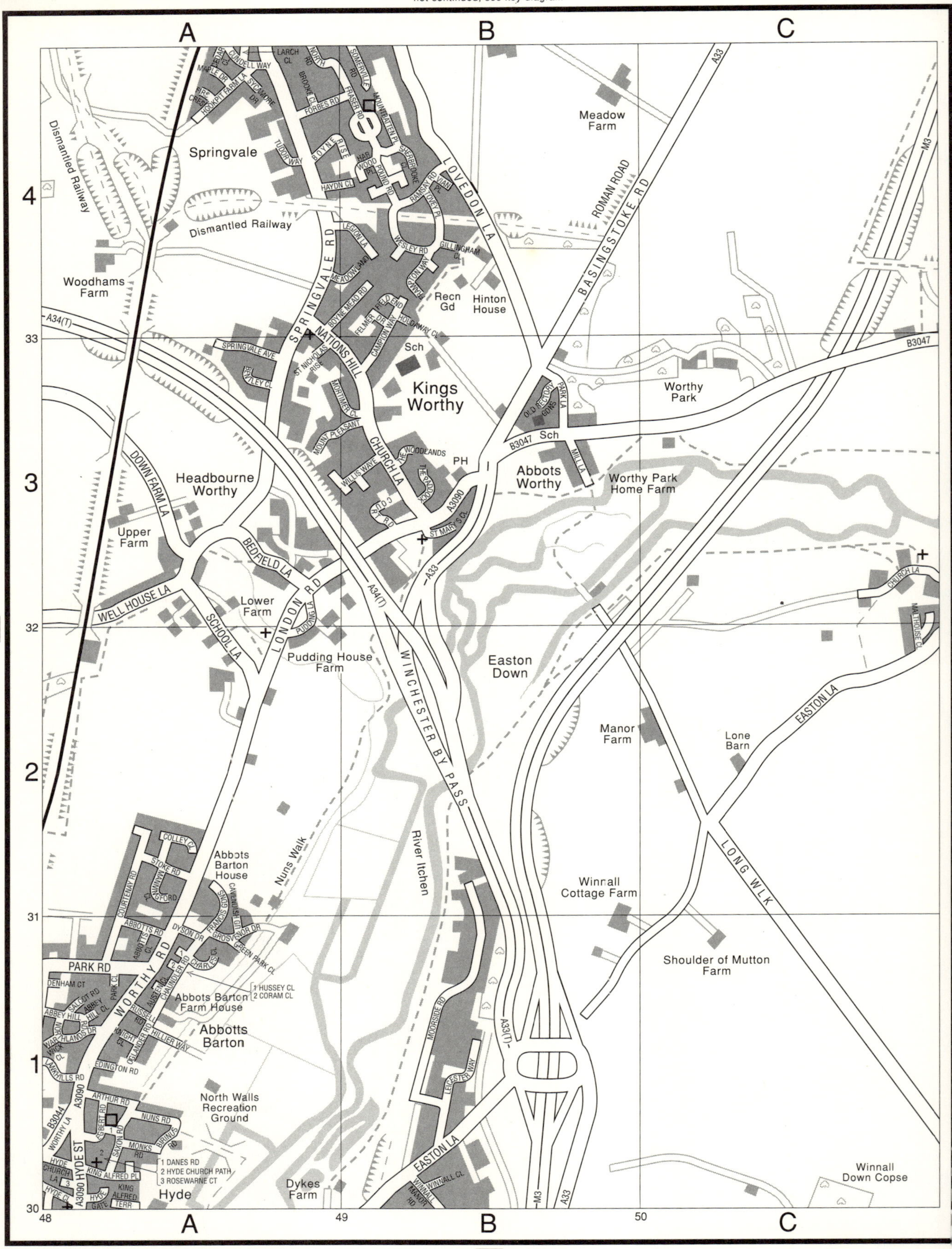

1

11

not continued, see key diagram

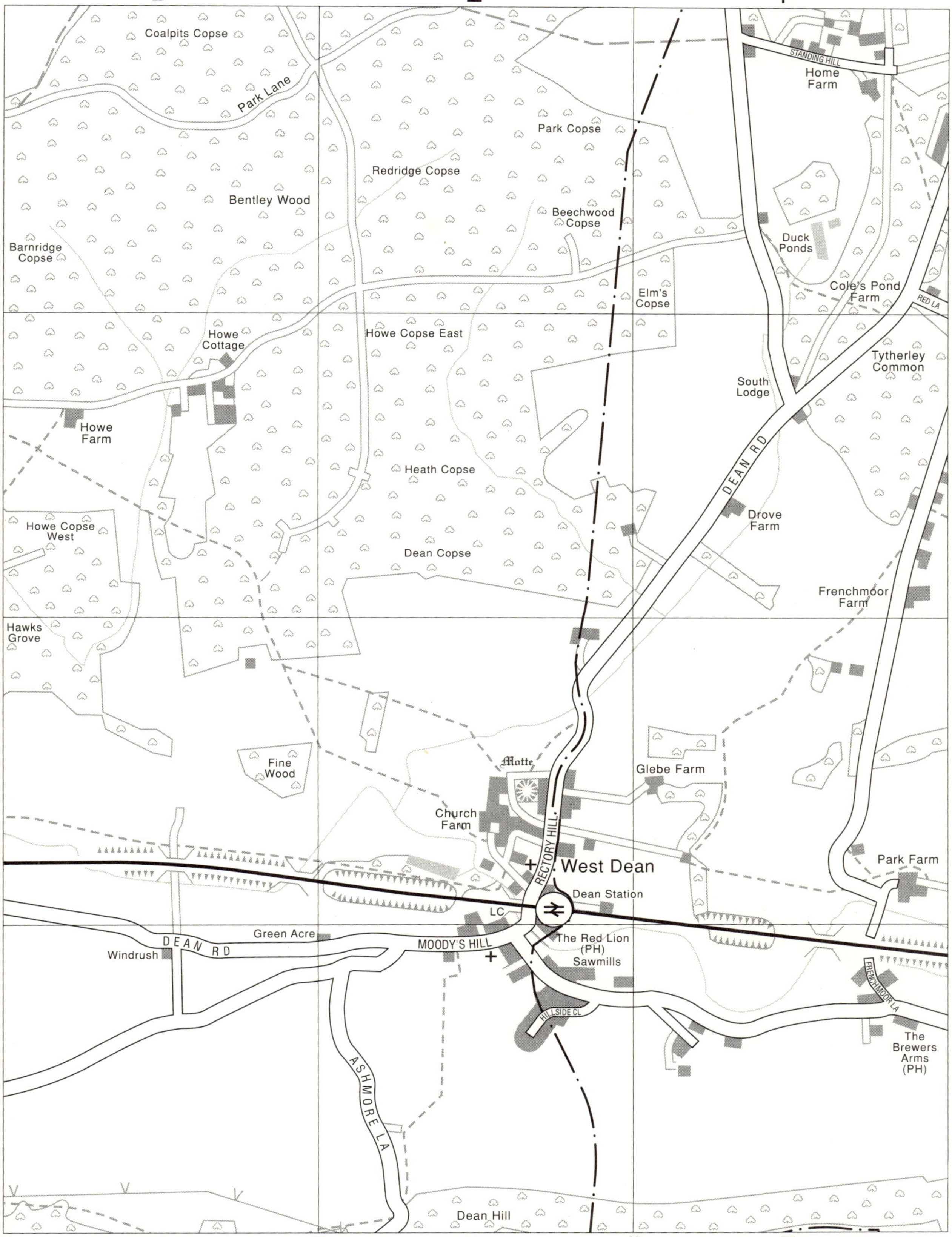

4

24

not continued, see key diagram

3

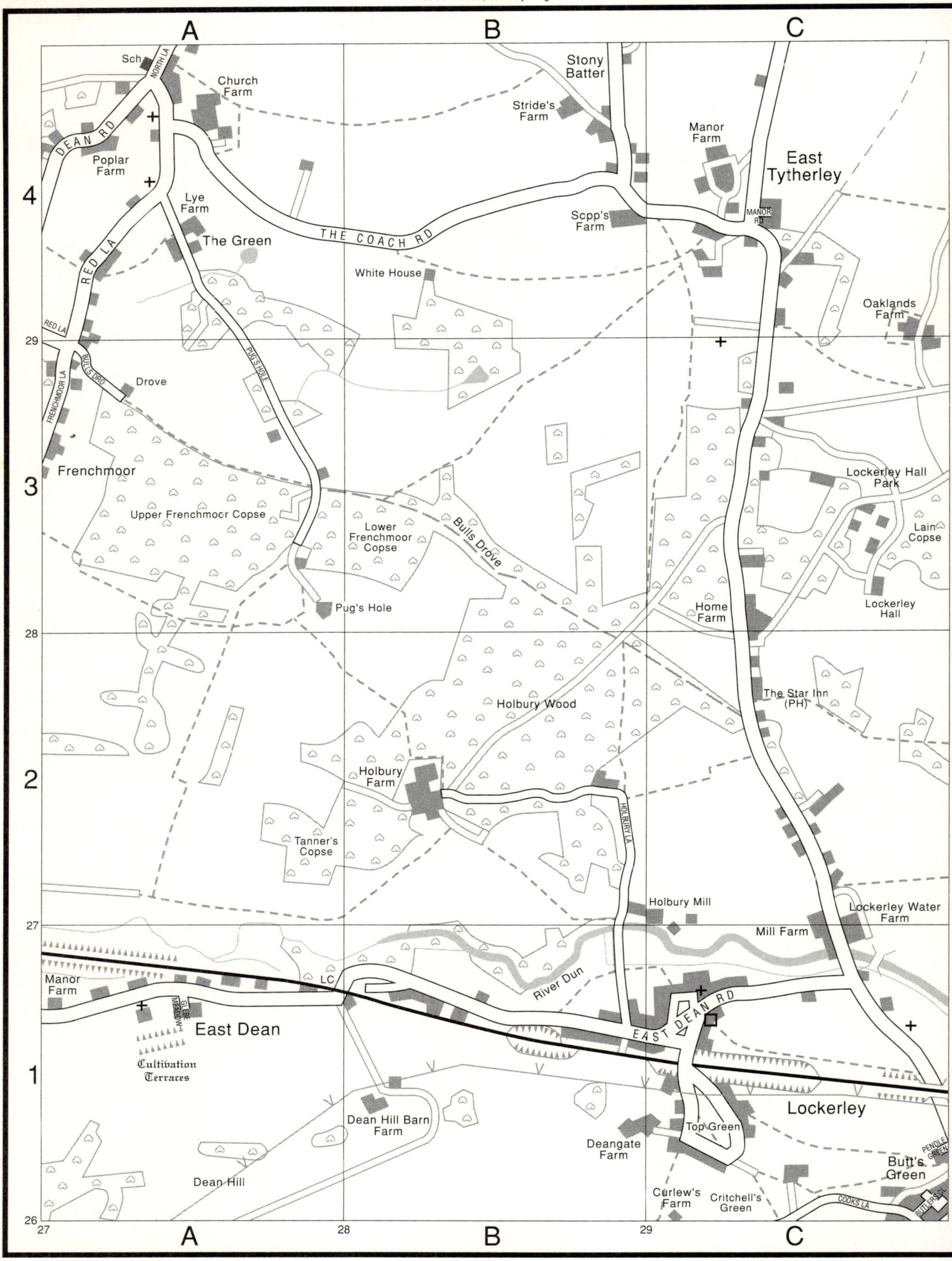

not continued, see key diagram

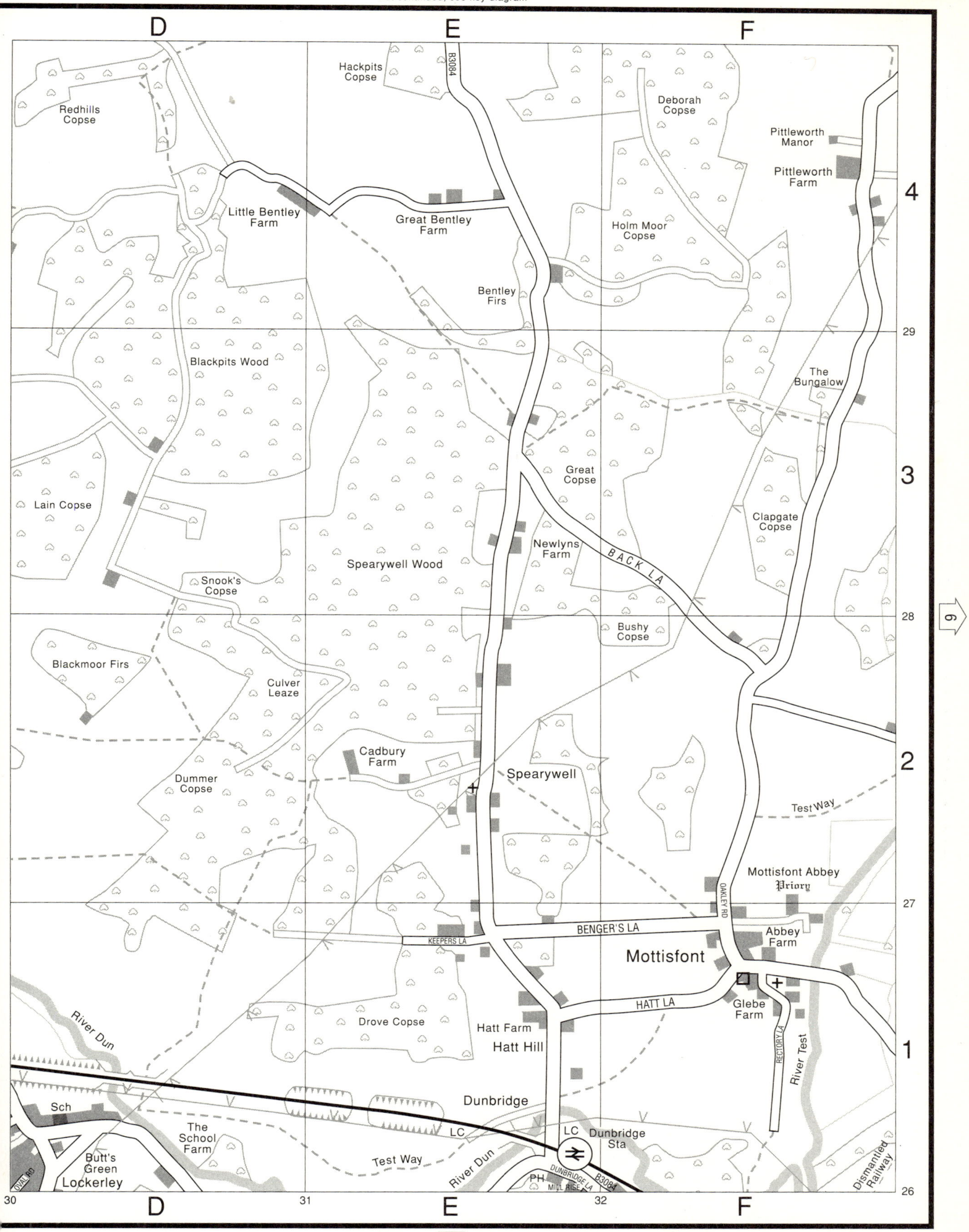

not continued, see key diagram

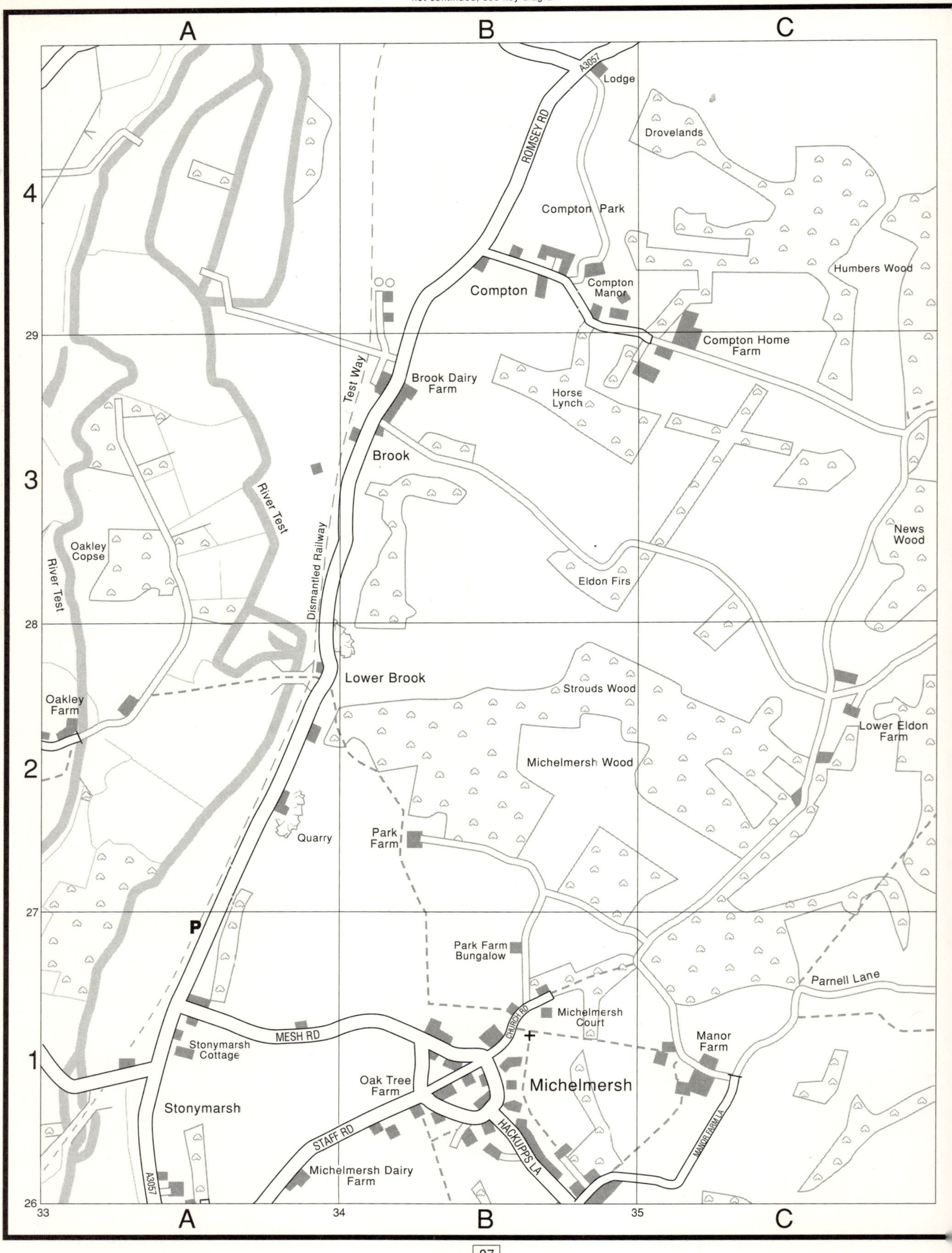

5

27

not continued, see key diagram

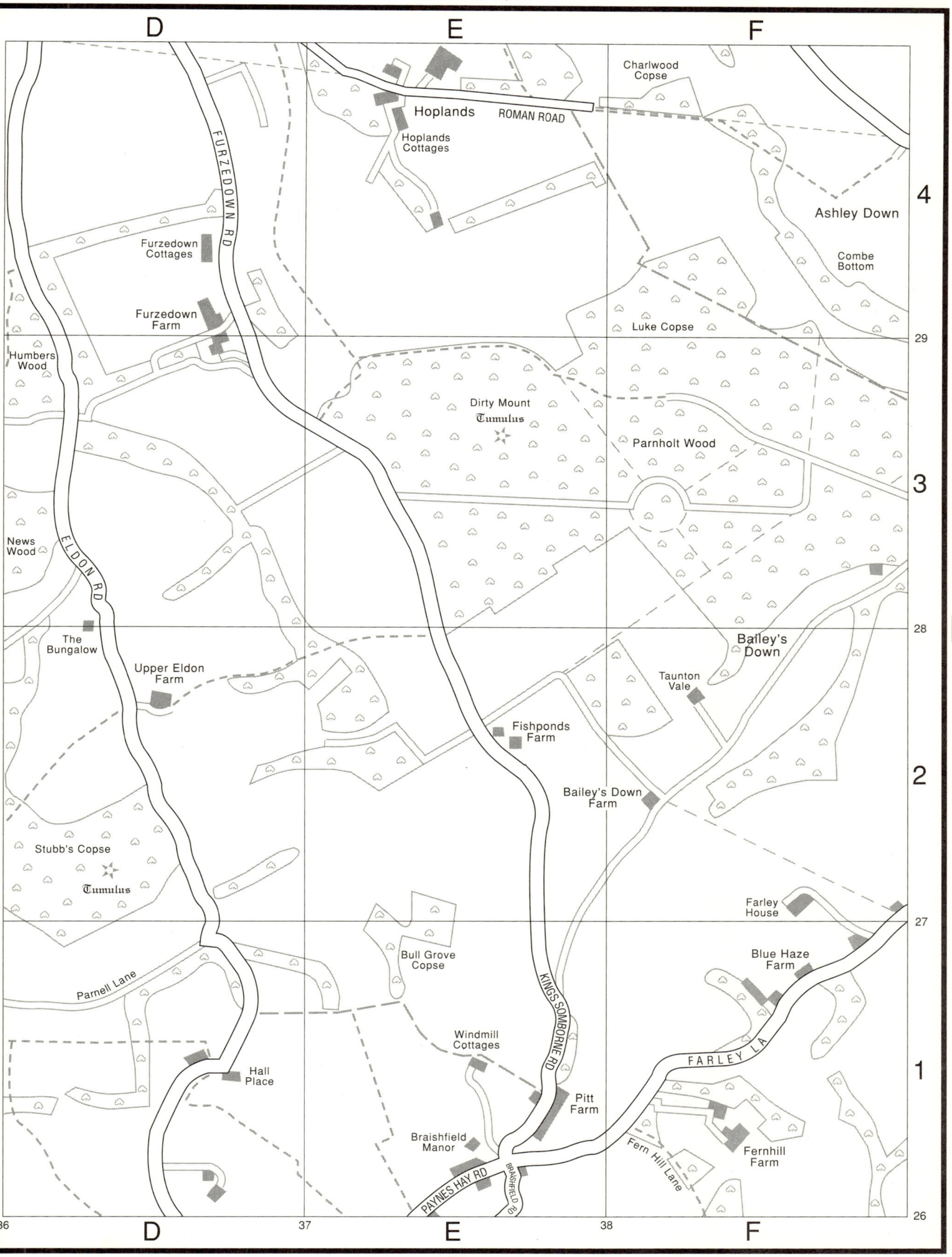

8

28

not continued, see key diagram

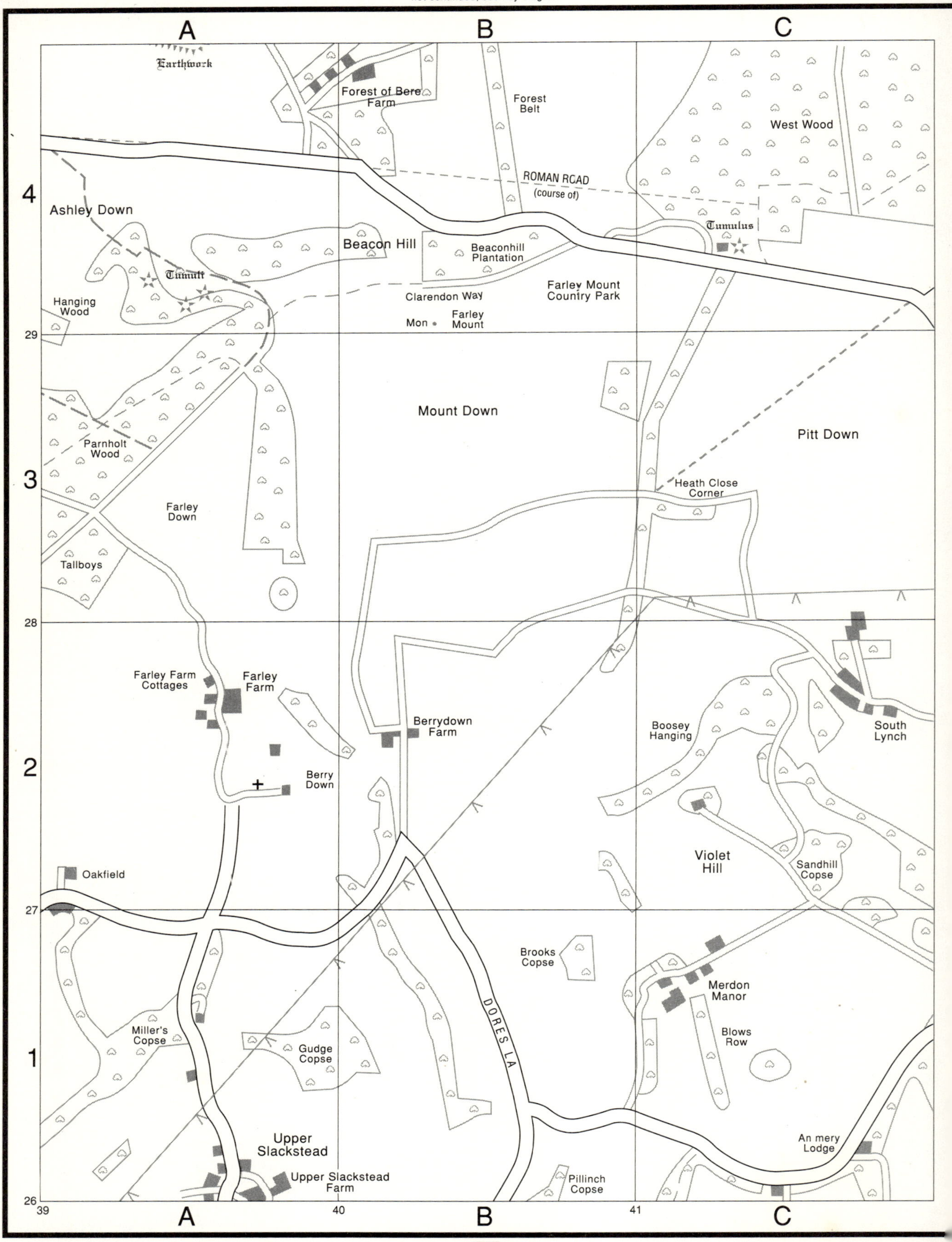

7

not continued, see key diagram

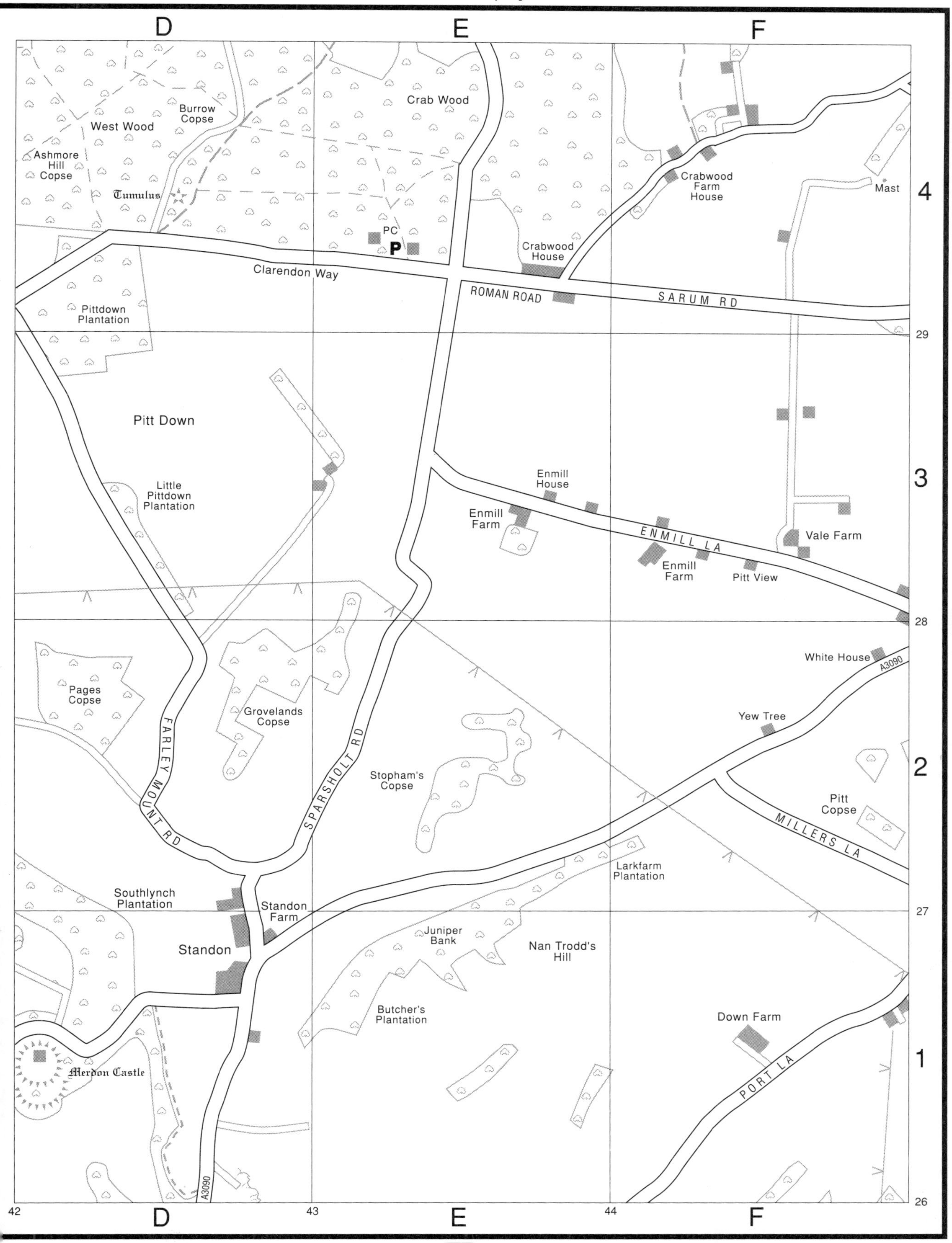

10

30

1

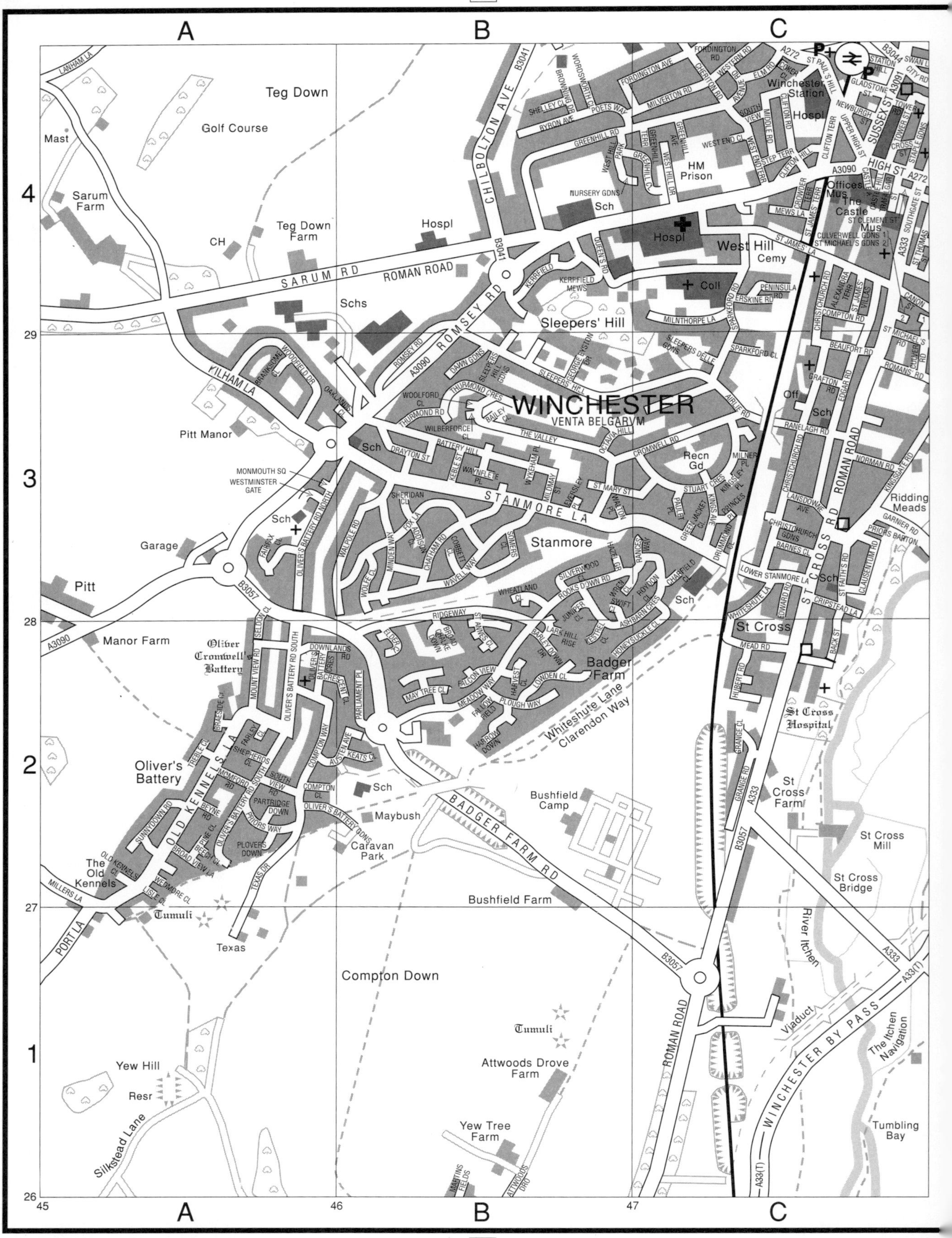

A
B
C
Teg Down
Golf Course
Mast
Sarum Farm
Teg Down Farm
CH
Hospl
SARUM RD
ROMAN ROAD
Schs
CHILBOLTON AVE
B3041
Winchester Station
HM Prison
Sch
Hospl
West Hill
Cemy
Coll
Sleepers' Hill
Offices
Mus
The Castle
HIGH ST
A3090
A272
SUSSEX ST
UPPER HIGH ST
ROMSEY RD
WINCHESTER
VENTA BELGARVM
Pitt Manor
KILHAM LA
MONMOUTH SQ
WESTMINSTER GATE
Sch
Garage
Pitt
A3090
B3057
Manor Farm
Oliver Cromwell's Battery
STANMORE LA
Stanmore
Recn Gd
ROMAN ROAD
ST CROSS RD
Ridding Meads
Off
Sch
St Cross
Badger Farm
Whiteshute Lane
Clarendon Way
St Cross Hospital
Oliver's Battery
OLD KENNELS LA
Sch
Maybush
Caravan Park
BADGER FARM RD
Bushfield Camp
Bushfield Farm
St Cross Farm
St Cross Mill
St Cross Bridge
River Itchen
The Old Kennels
MILLERS LA
PORT LA
Tumuli
Texas
Compton Down
A333
A33(T)
WINCHESTER BY PASS
Viaduct
The Itchen Navigation
Tumuli
Attwoods Drove Farm
Yew Hill
Resr
Silkstead Lane
Yew Tree Farm
Tumbling Bay
4
3
2
1
29
28
27
26
45
46
47

9

31

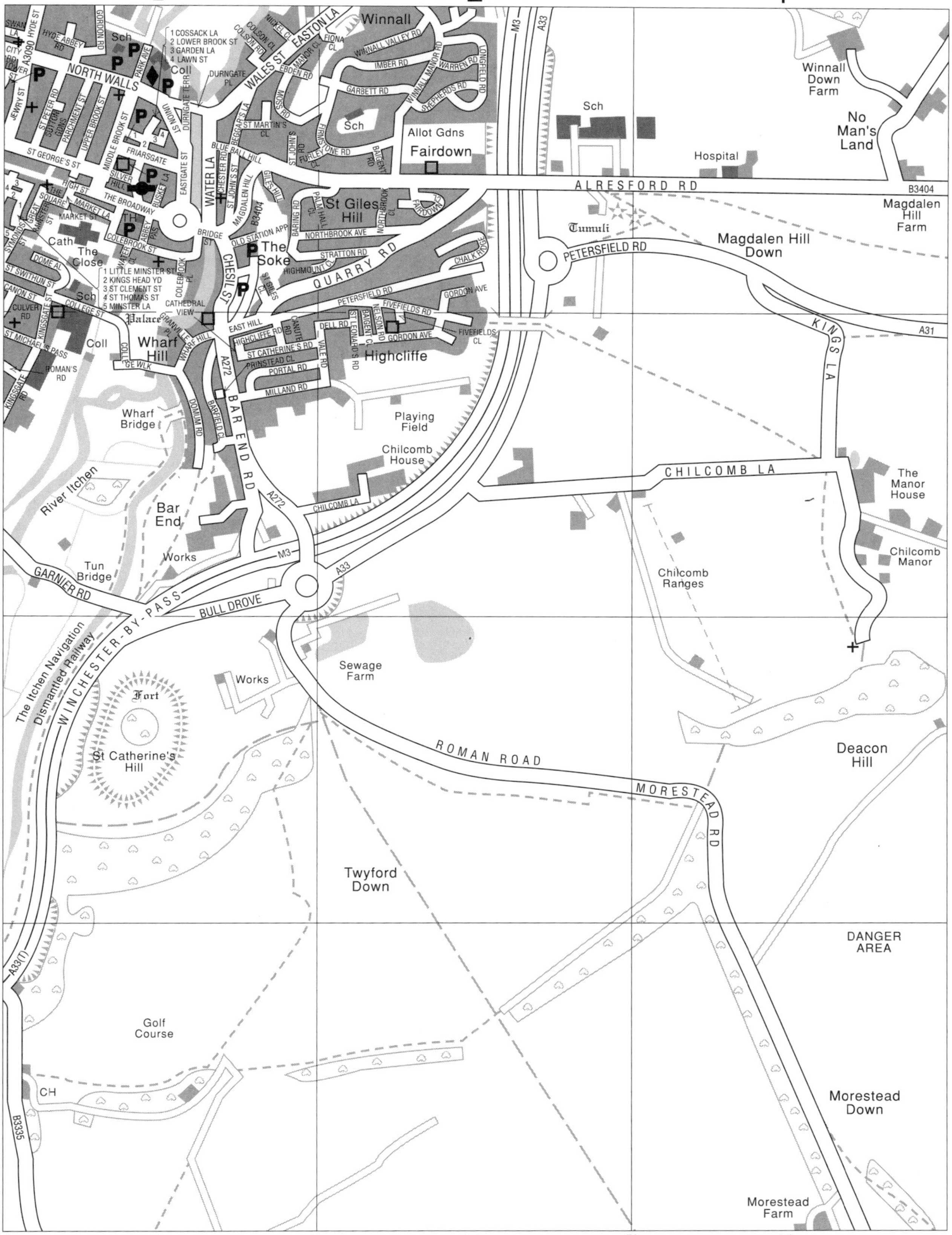
2
32
12
D
E
F
4
3
2
1
29
28
27
26
48
49
50
Winnall
Winnall Down Farm
No Man's Land
Sch
Hospital
Allot Gdns
Fairdown
St Giles Hill
The Soke
ALRESFORD RD
B3404
Magdalen Hill Farm
Tumuli
Magdalen Hill Down
PETERSFIELD RD
QUARRY RD
KINGS LA
A31
NORTH WALLS
Coll
Cath
The Close
Palace
Wharf Hill
Highcliffe
Playing Field
Chilcomb House
Wharf Bridge
River Itchen
Bar End
Works
Tun Bridge
GARNIER RD
BULL DROVE
WINCHESTER-BY-PASS
M3
A33
A272
CHILCOMB LA
The Manor House
Chilcomb Manor
Chilcomb Ranges
Sewage Farm
Fort
St Catherine's Hill
The Itchen Navigation
Dismantled Railway
ROMAN ROAD
MORESTEAD RD
Deacon Hill
Twyford Down
DANGER AREA
Golf Course
CH
B3335
A33(T)
Morestead Down
Morestead Farm
1 COSSACK LA
2 LOWER BROOK ST
3 GARDEN LA
4 LAWN ST
1 LITTLE MINSTER ST
2 KINGS HEAD YD
3 ST CLEMENT ST
4 ST THOMAS ST
5 MINSTER LA

not continued, see key diagram

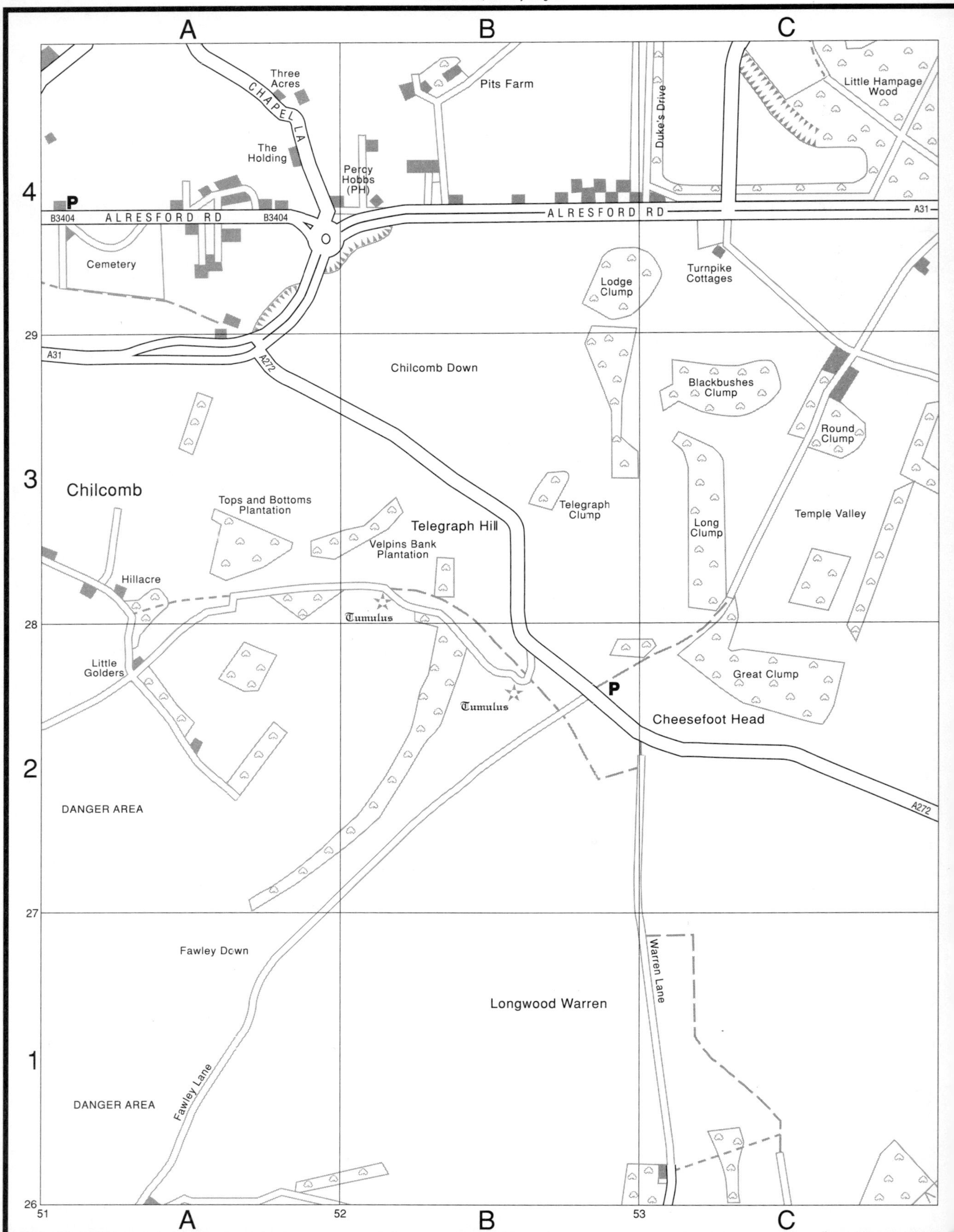

11

33

not continued, see key diagram

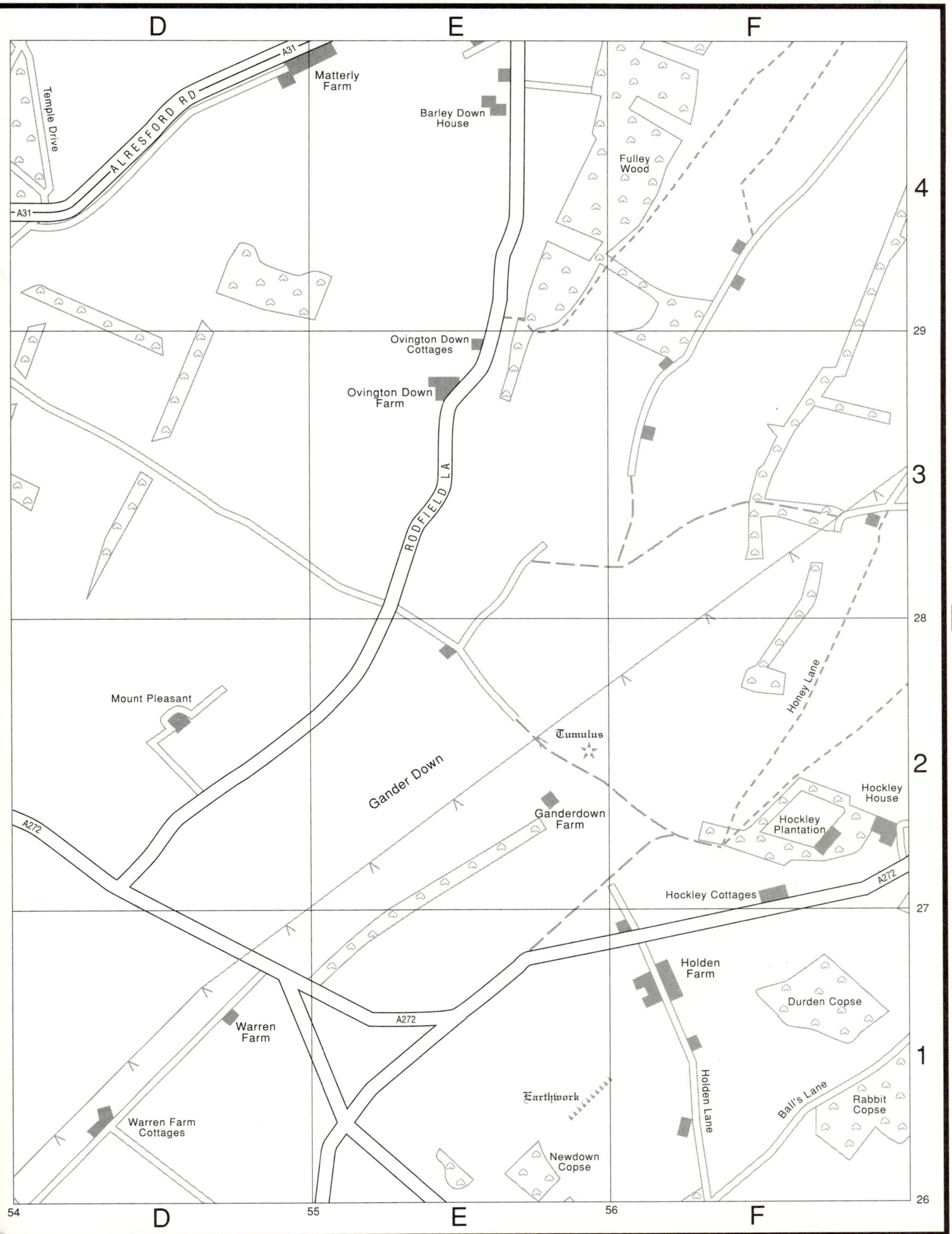

14

34

not continued, see key diagram

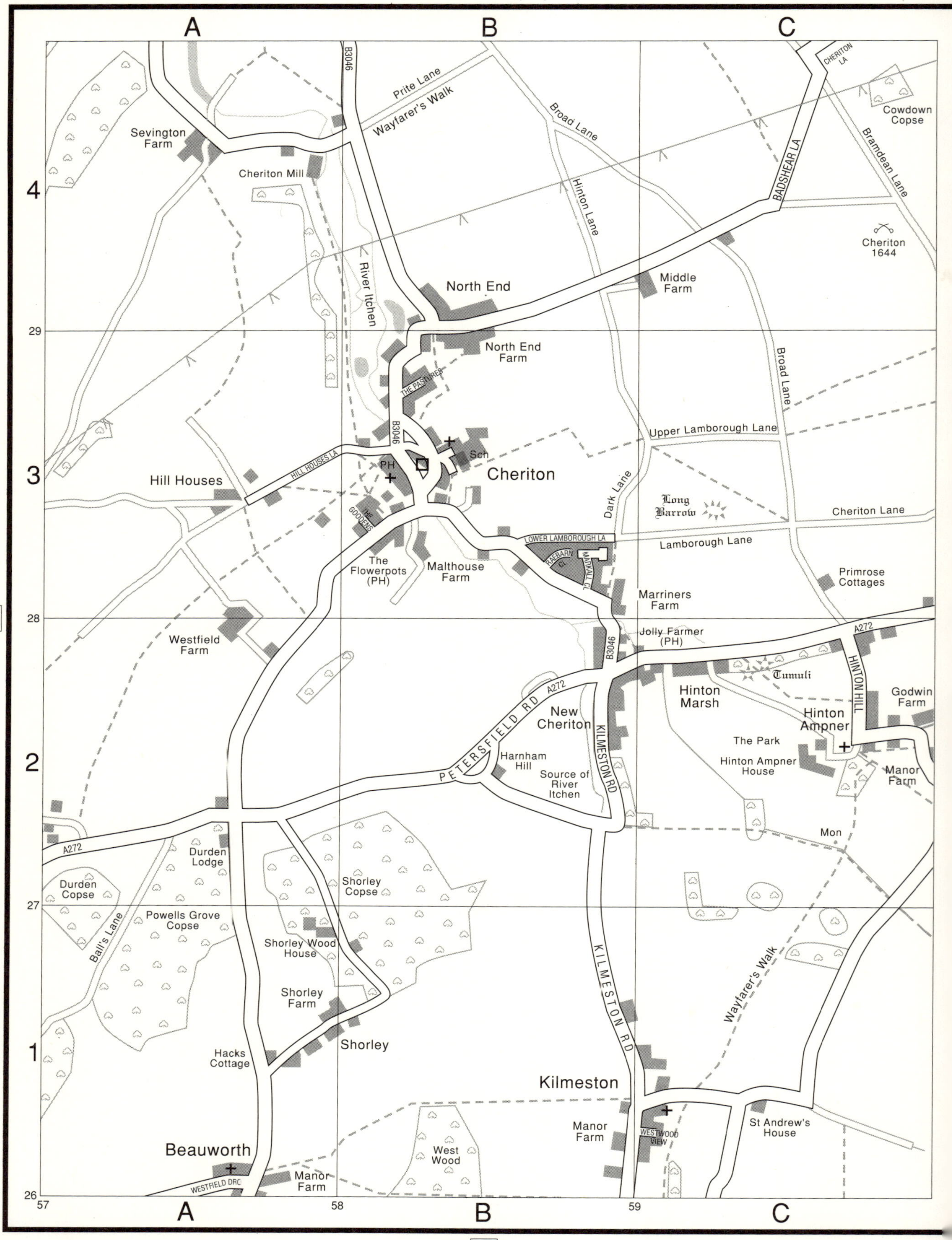

13

35

not continued, see key diagram

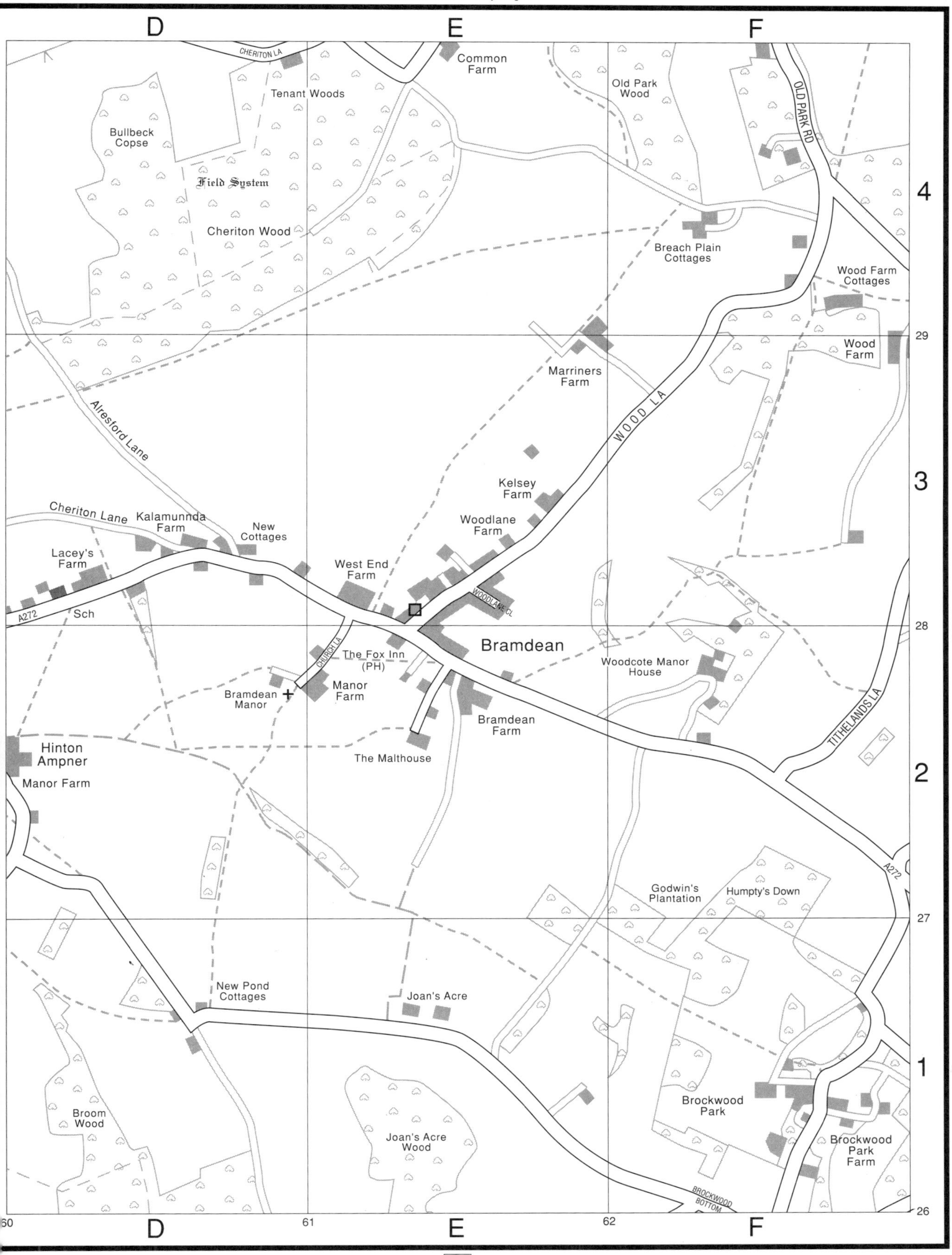

16

36

not continued, see key diagram

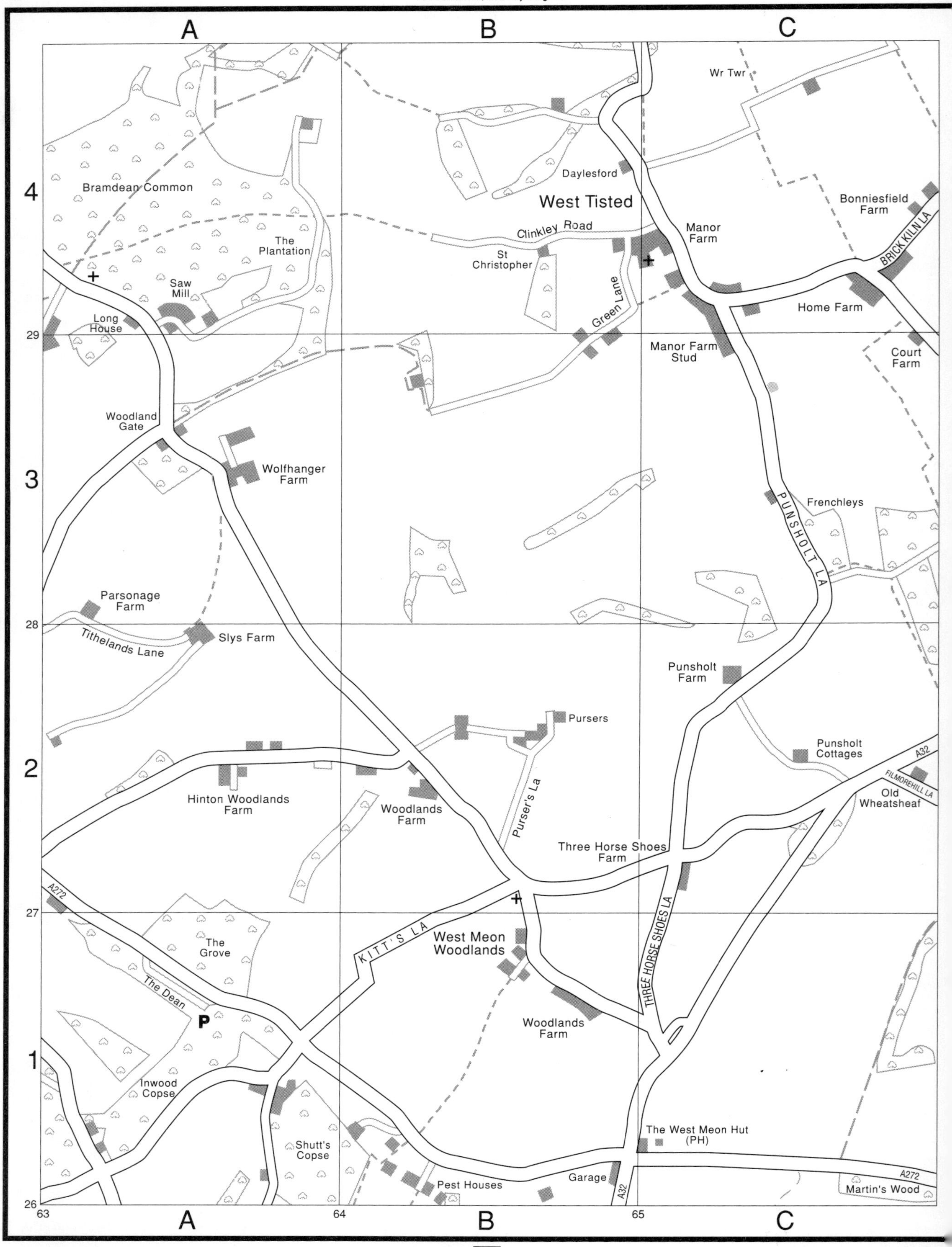

15

37

not continued, see key diagram

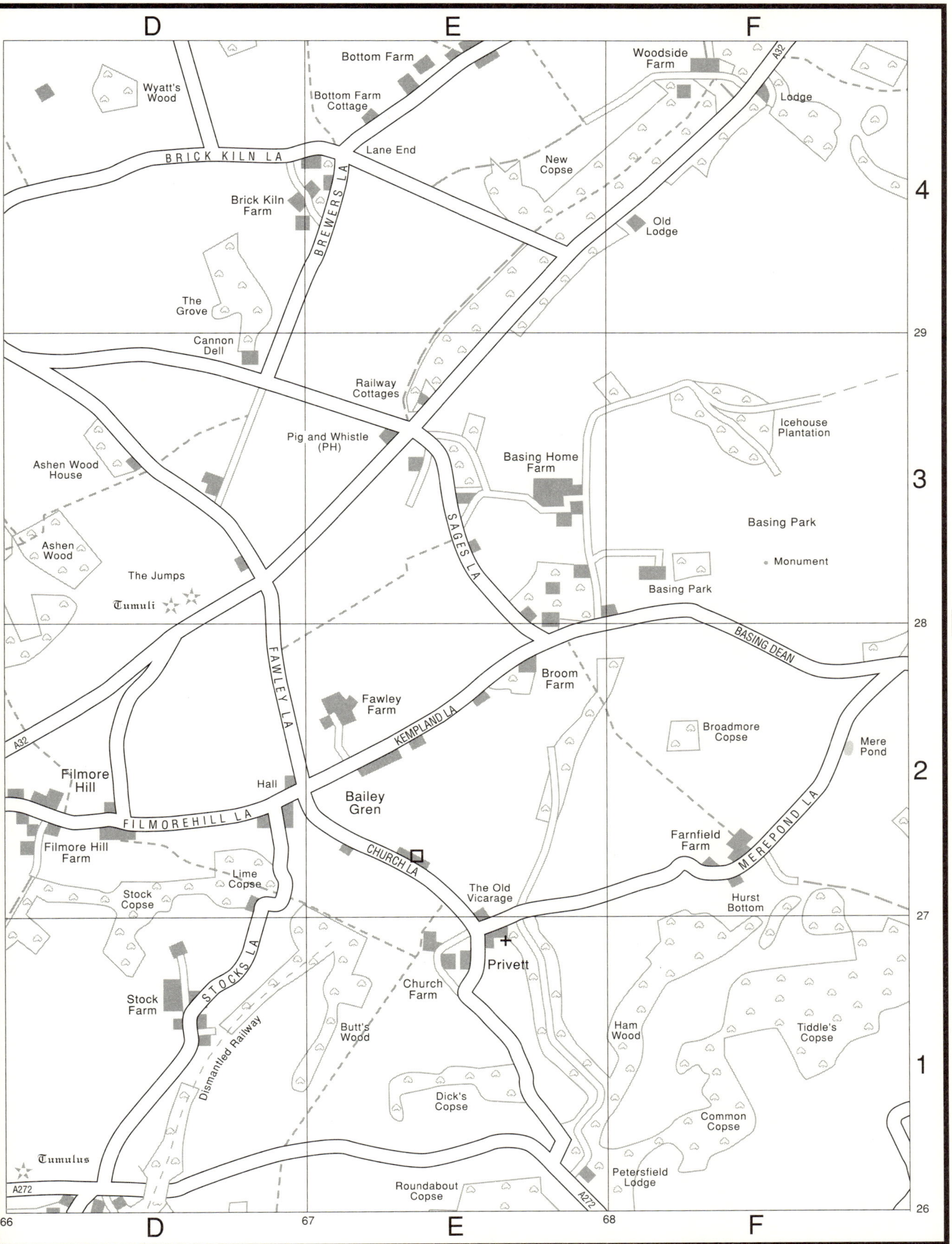

D E F

18

38

not continued, see key diagram

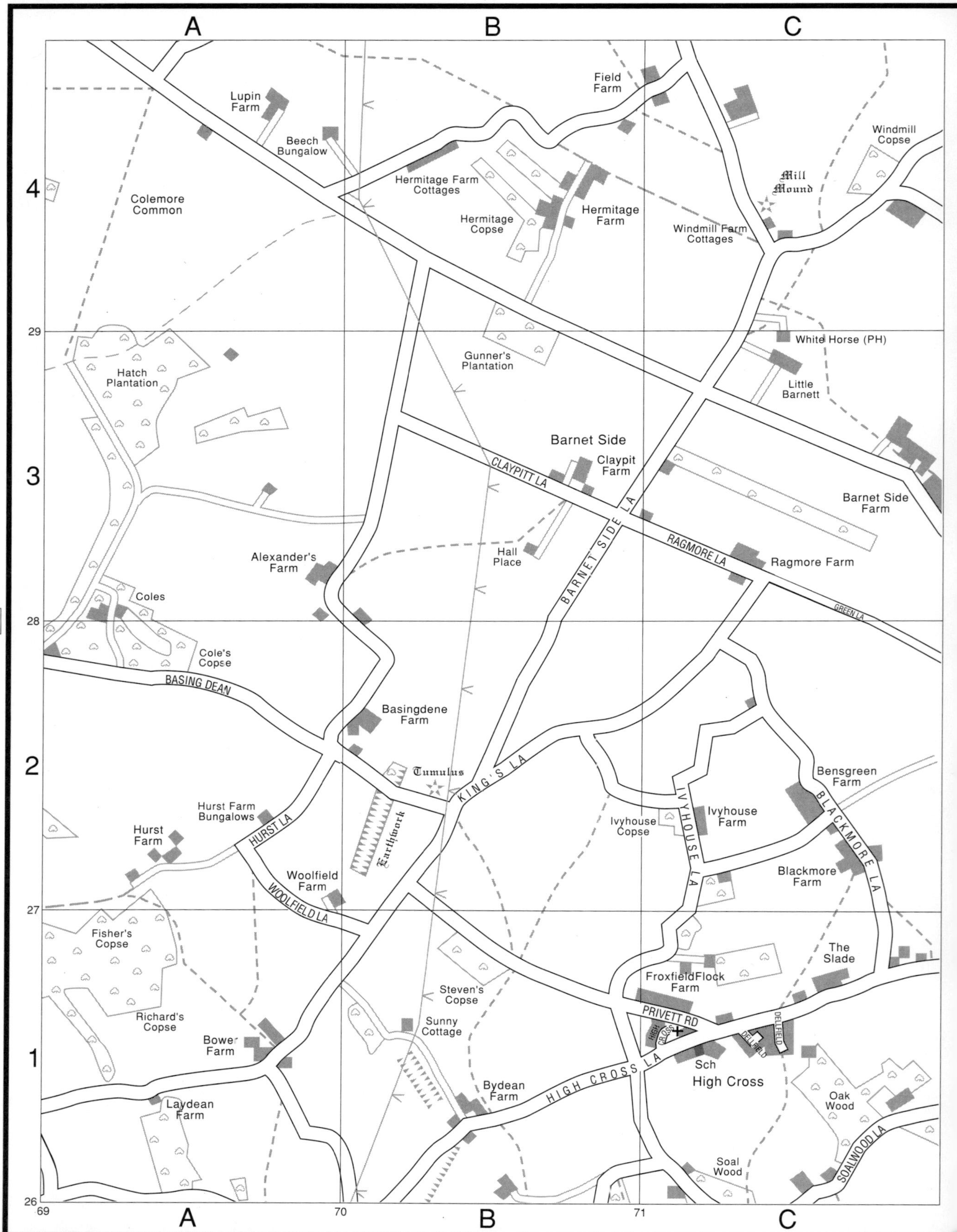

17

39

not continued, see key diagram

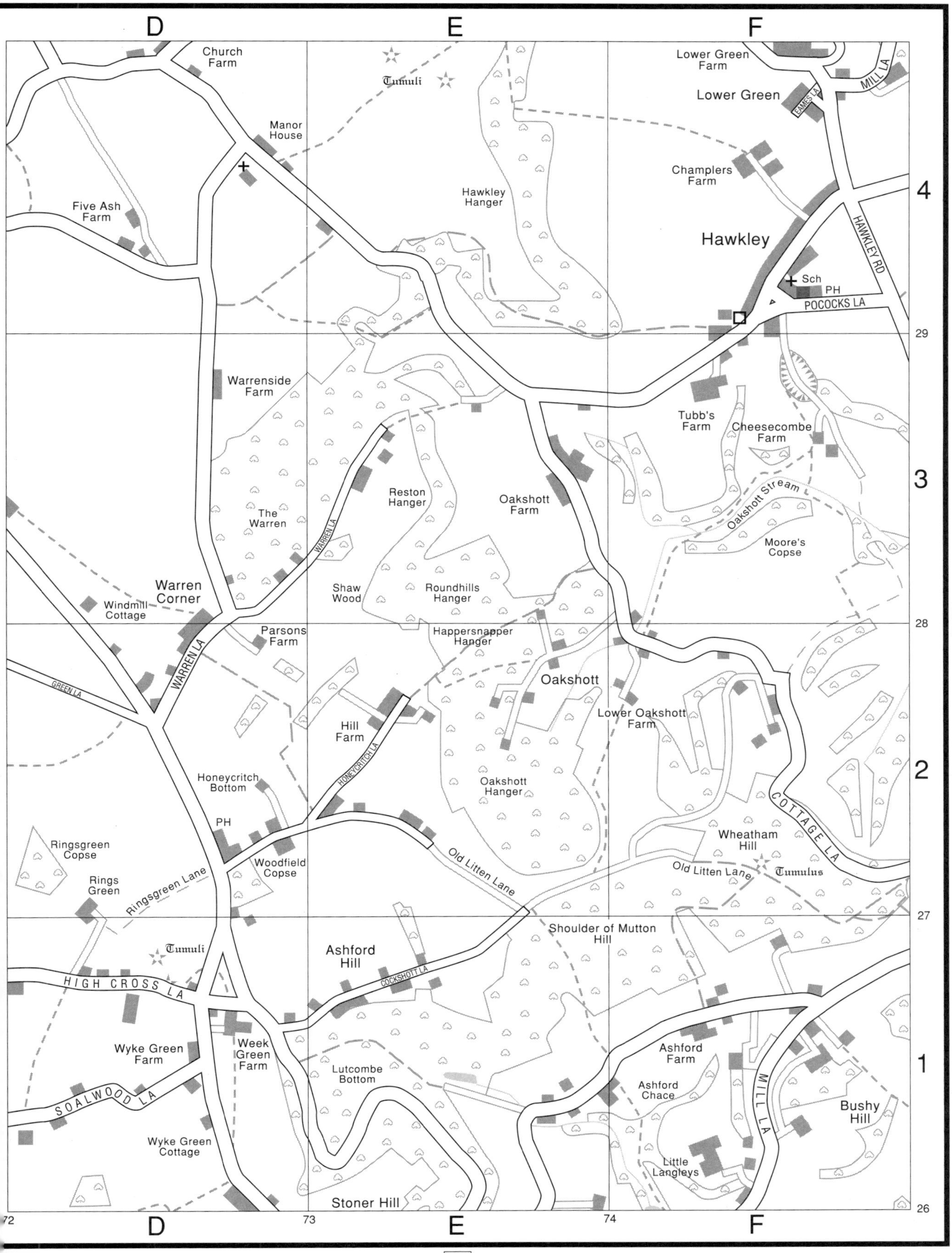

20

not continued, see key diagram

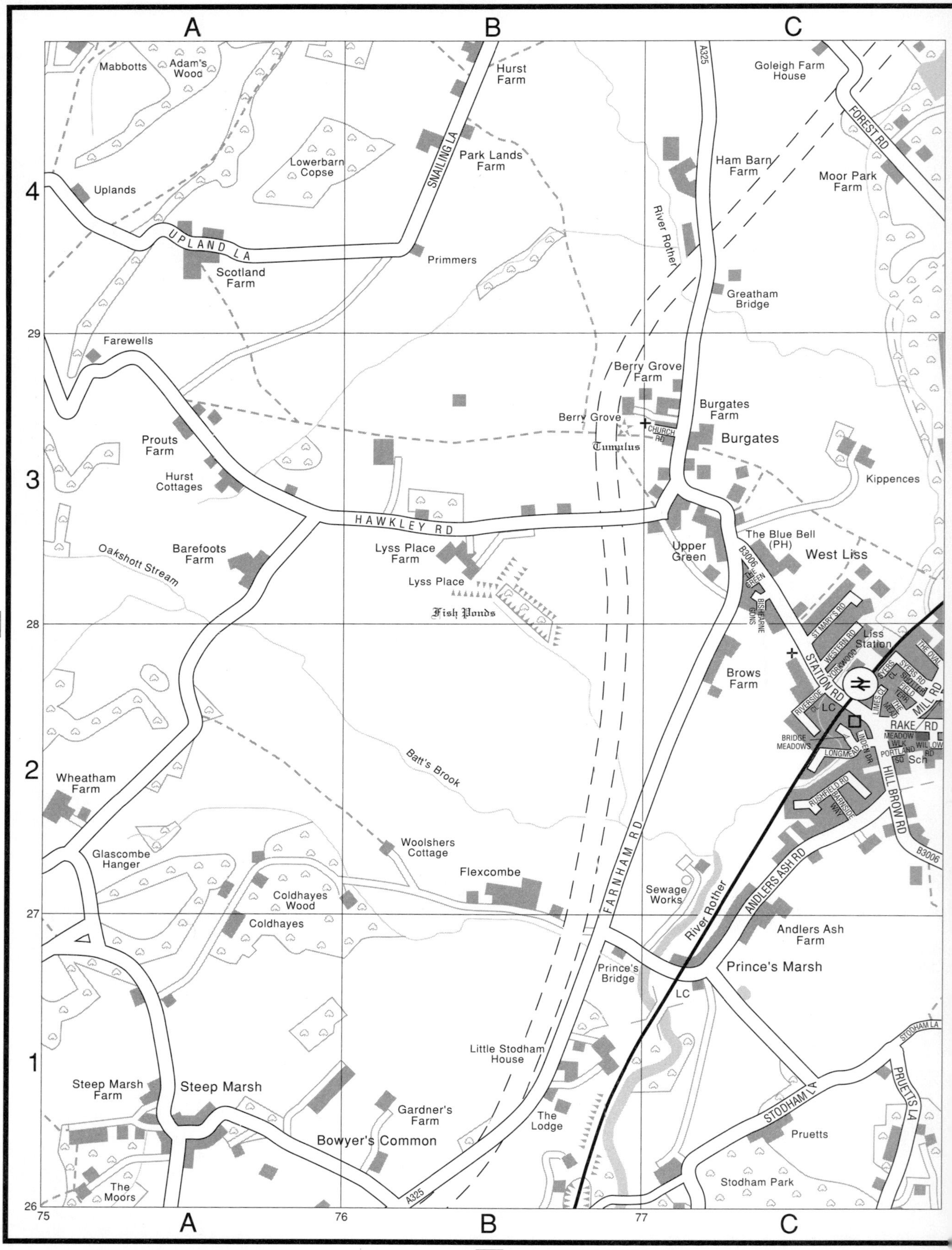

19

41

not continued, see key diagram

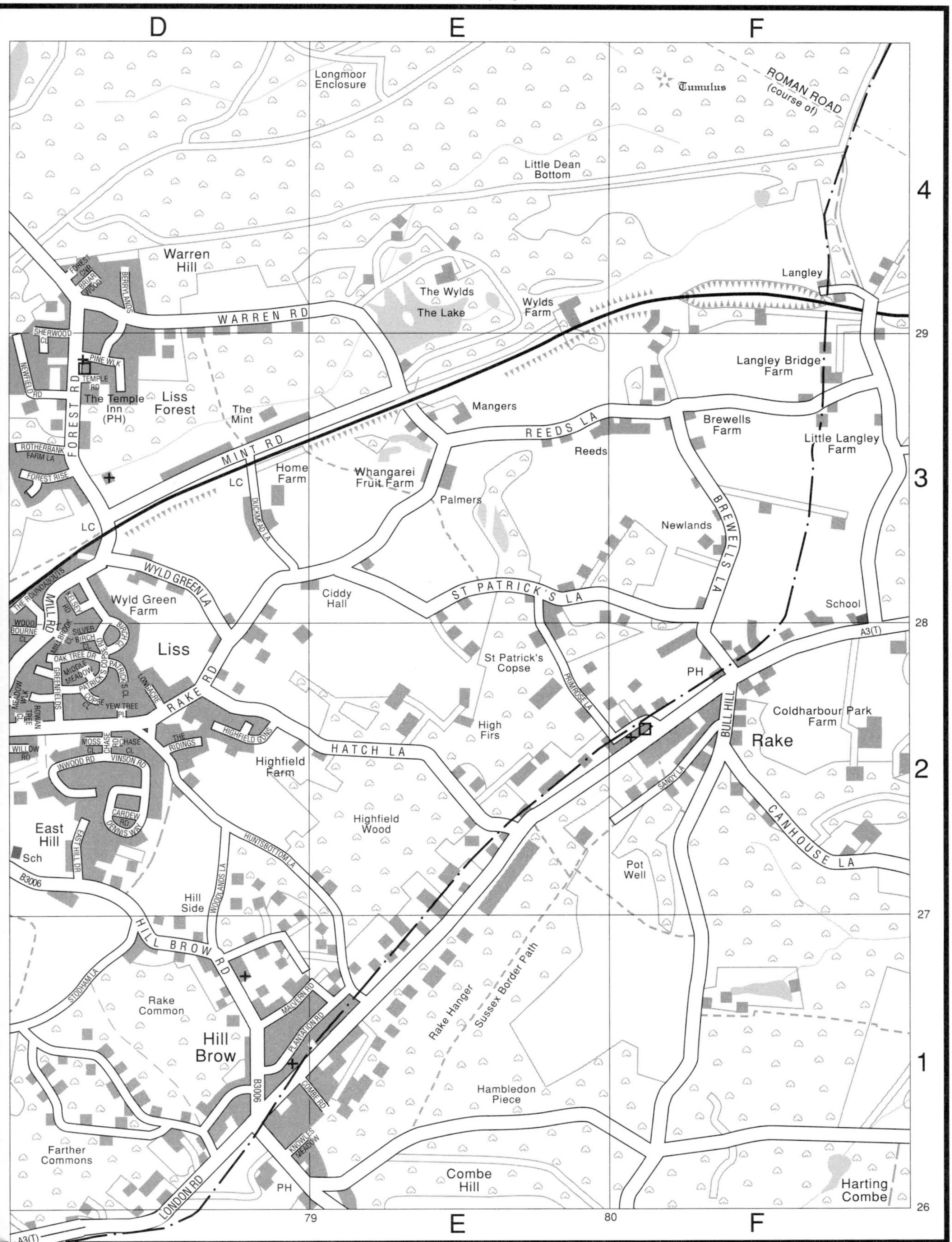

not continued, see key diagram

not continued, see key diagram

not continued, see key diagram

not continued, see key diagram

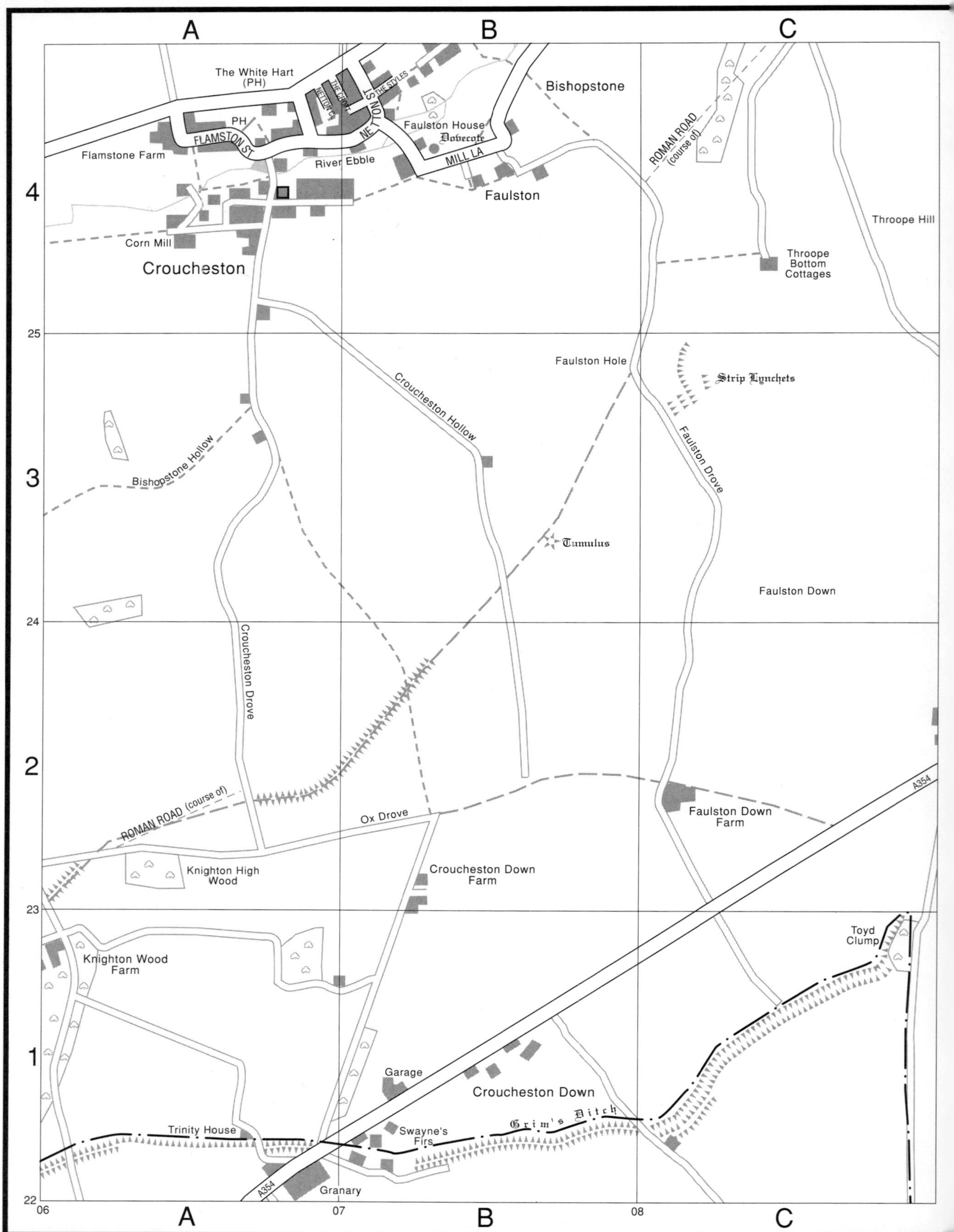

43

not continued, see key diagram

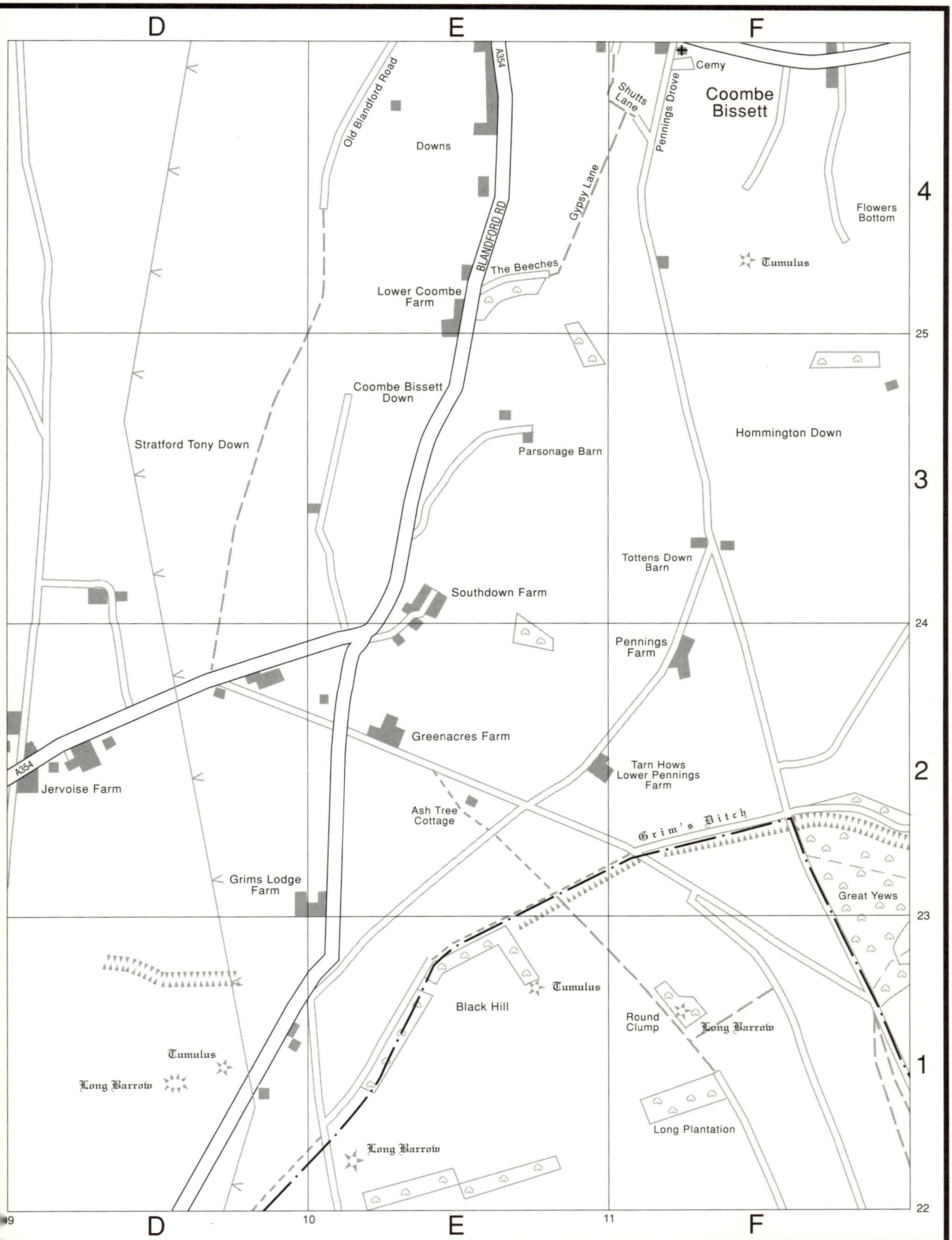

not continued, see key diagram

44

3

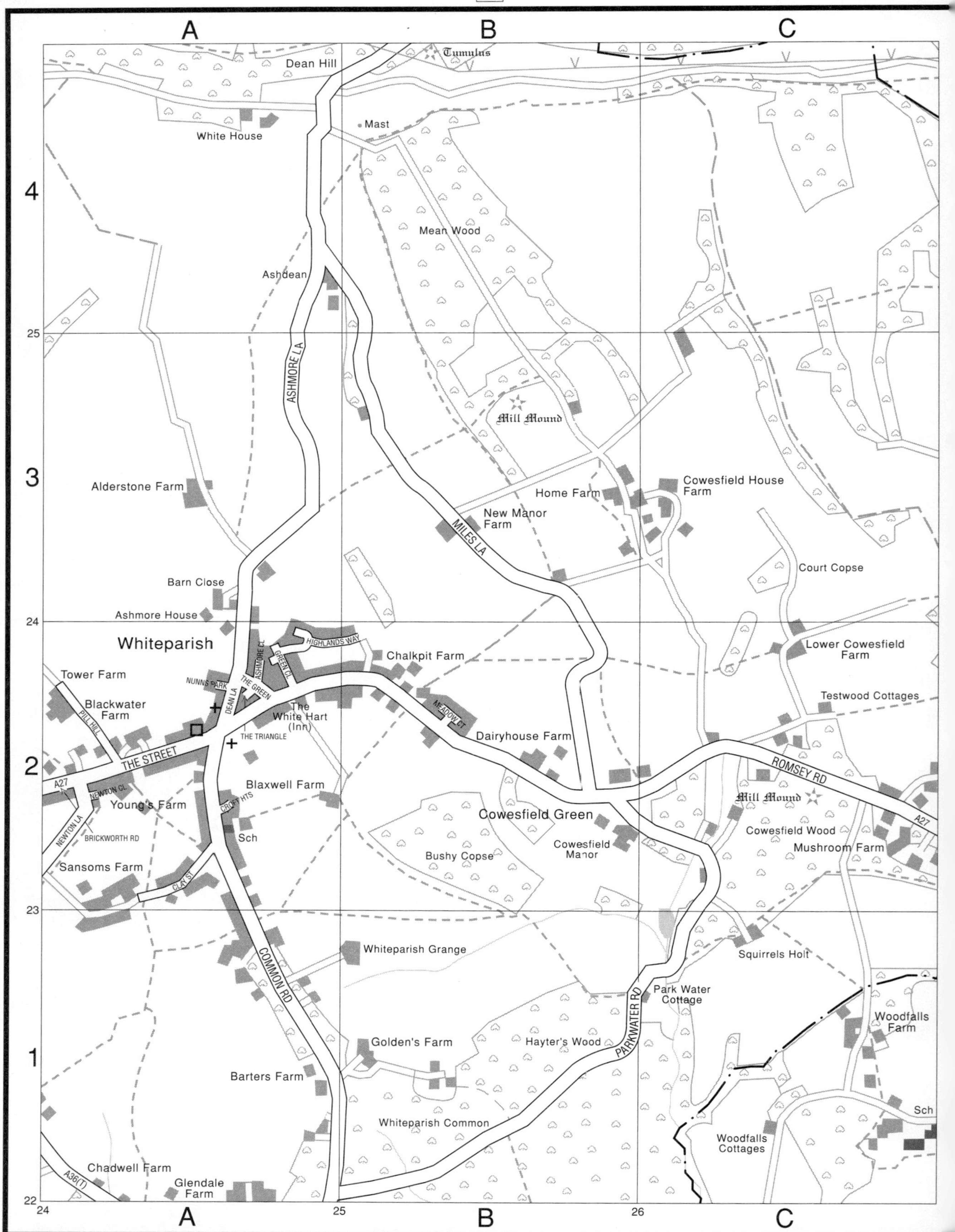

49

not continued, see key diagram

4

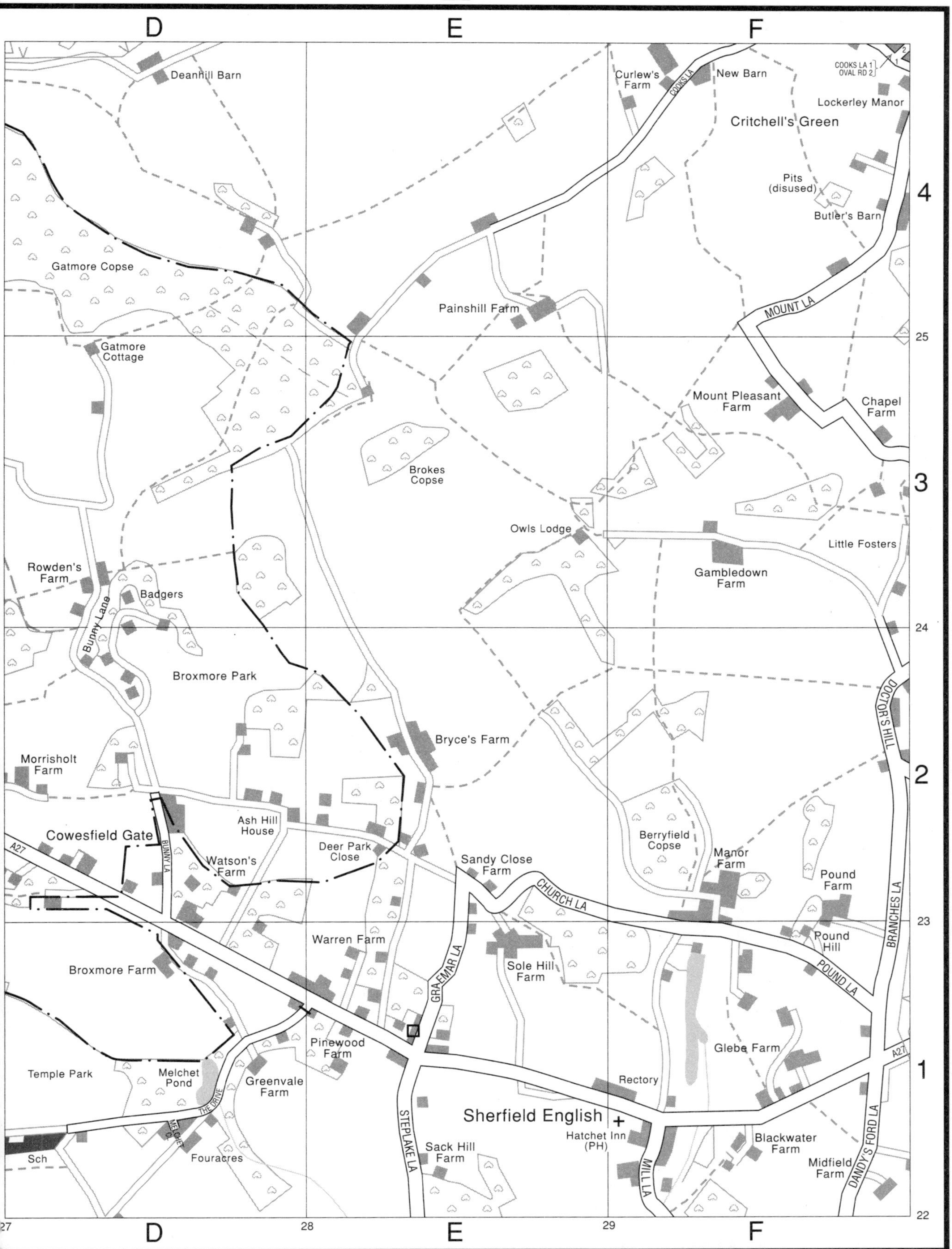
D
E
F
Deanhill Barn
Curlew's Farm
COOKS LA
New Barn
COOKS LA 1
OVAL RD 2
Lockerley Manor
Critchell's Green
Pits (disused)
Butler's Barn
4
Gatmore Copse
Painshill Farm
MOUNT LA
25
Gatmore Cottage
Mount Pleasant Farm
Chapel Farm
Brokes Copse
3
Owls Lodge
Little Fosters
Gambledown Farm
Rowden's Farm
Badgers
Bunny Lane
24
Broxmore Park
DOCTOR'S HILL
Bryce's Farm
Morrisholt Farm
2
Ash Hill House
Cowesfield Gate
A27
BUNNY LA
Watson's Farm
Deer Park Close
Sandy Close Farm
Berryfield Copse
Manor Farm
Pound Farm
CHURCH LA
23
Warren Farm
Pound Hill
BRANCHES LA
Broxmore Farm
Sole Hill Farm
GRAEMAR LA
POUND LA
Pinewood Farm
Glebe Farm
A27
1
Temple Park
Melchet Pond
Greenvale Farm
Rectory
THE DRIVE
STEPLAKE LA
Sherfield English
Hatchet Inn (PH)
MELCHET CL
Sack Hill Farm
Blackwater Farm
MILL LA
Midfield Farm
DANDY'S FORD LA
Sch
Fouracres
27
28
29
22

26

50

5

25

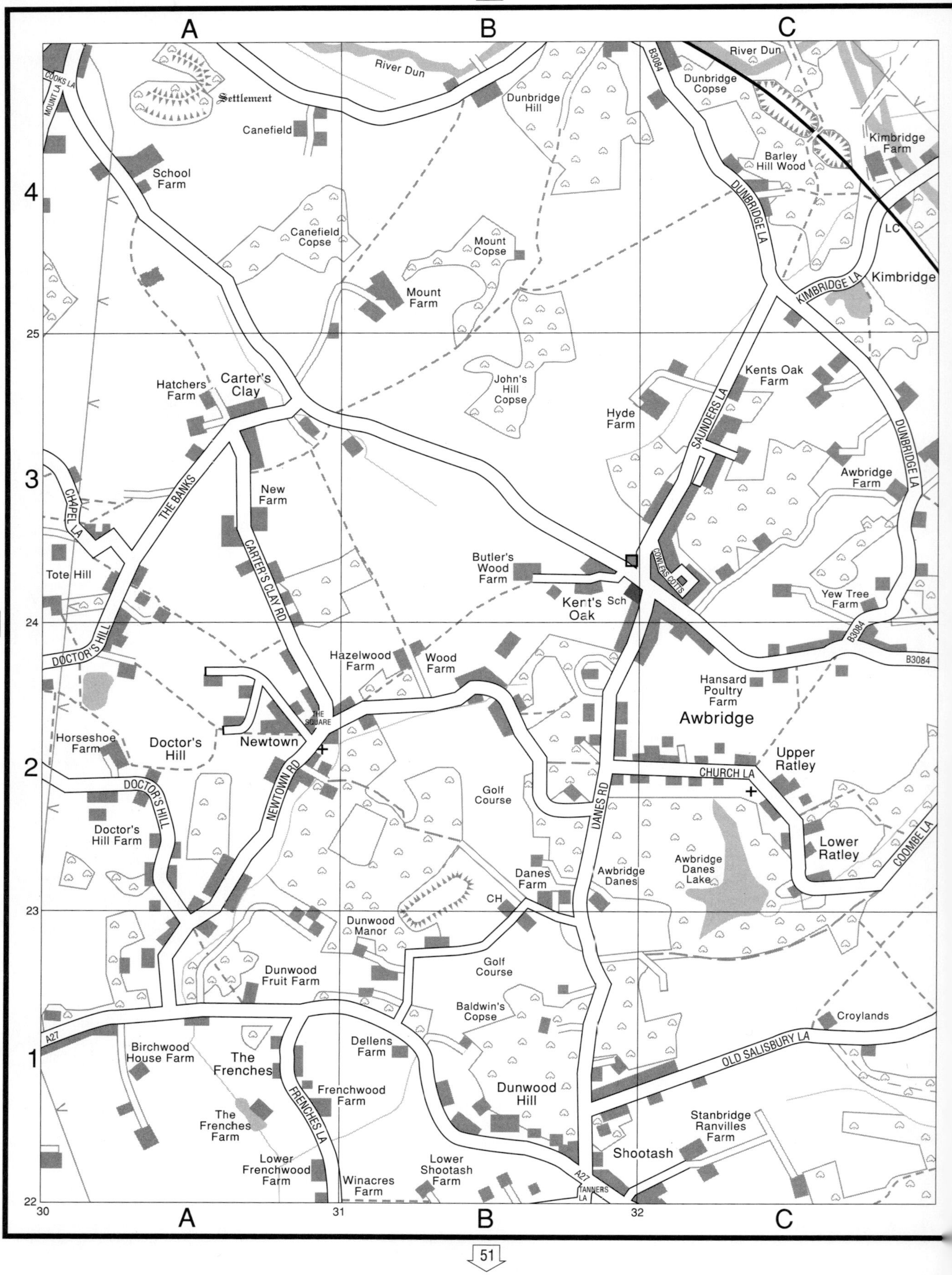
A
B
C
4
3
2
1
25
24
23
22
30
31
32
River Dun
Settlement
Canefield
School Farm
Canefield Copse
Dunbridge Hill
Mount Copse
Mount Farm
John's Hill Copse
Dunbridge Copse
Barley Hill Wood
Kimbridge Farm
Kimbridge
KIMBRIDGE LA
LC
B3084
DUNBRIDGE LA
COOKS LA
MOUNT LA
Hatchers Farm
Carter's Clay
Kents Oak Farm
Hyde Farm
SAUNDERS LA
New Farm
THE BANKS
CHAPEL LA
CARTER'S CLAY RD
Tote Hill
Butler's Wood Farm
Kent's Oak
Sch
COWLEAS COTTS
Awbridge Farm
Yew Tree Farm
DOCTOR'S HILL
Hazelwood Farm
Wood Farm
THE SQUARE
Newtown
Doctor's Hill
Horseshoe Farm
Hansard Poultry Farm
Awbridge
Upper Ratley
CHURCH LA
Golf Course
NEWTOWN RD
DANES RD
Doctor's Hill Farm
Awbridge Danes
Awbridge Danes Lake
Lower Ratley
COOMBE LA
Danes Farm
CH
Dunwood Manor
Dunwood Fruit Farm
Golf Course
Baldwin's Copse
Croylands
A27
Birchwood House Farm
The Frenches
Dellens Farm
OLD SALISBURY LA
Frenchwood Farm
FRENCHES LA
Dunwood Hill
The Frenches Farm
Stanbridge Ranvilles Farm
Shootash
Lower Frenchwood Farm
Winacres Farm
Lower Shootash Farm
TANNERS LA

51

6

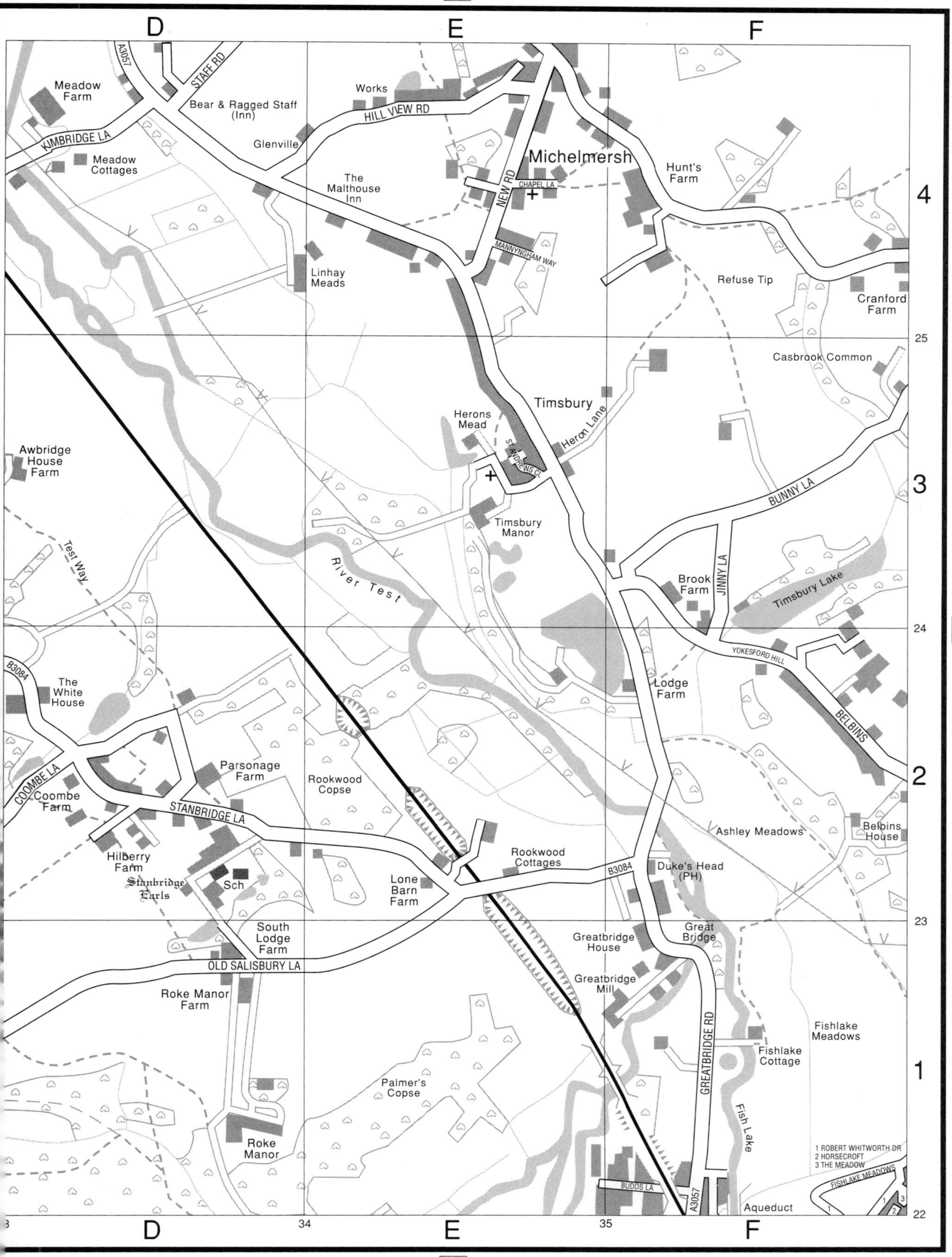
D
E
F
Meadow Farm
A3057
STAFF RD
Bear & Ragged Staff (Inn)
Works
HILL VIEW RD
Glenville
KIMBRIDGE LA
Meadow Cottages
Michelmersh
Hunt's Farm
NEW RD
CHAPEL LA
The Malthouse Inn
4
MANNYNGHAM WAY
Linhay Meads
Refuse Tip
Cranford Farm
25
Casbrook Common
Timsbury
Heron Lane
Herons Mead
ST ANDREWS CL
Awbridge House Farm
3
BUNNY LA
Timsbury Manor
Test Way
River Test
Brook Farm
JINNY LA
Timsbury Lake
24
YOKESFORD HILL
B3084
The White House
Lodge Farm
BELBINS
2
COOMBE LA
Coombe Farm
Parsonage Farm
Rookwood Copse
STANBRIDGE LA
Ashley Meadows
Belbins House
Hilberry Farm
Rookwood Cottages
Duke's Head (PH)
Stanbridge Earls
Sch
Lone Barn Farm
23
South Lodge Farm
Greatbridge House
Great Bridge
OLD SALISBURY LA
Greatbridge Mill
Roke Manor Farm
GREATBRIDGE RD
Fishlake Meadows
Fishlake Cottage
1
Palmer's Copse
Fish Lake
Roke Manor
1 ROBERT WHITWORTH DR
2 HORSECROFT
3 THE MEADOW
FISHLAKE MEADOWS
BUDDS LA
A3057
Aqueduct
22
34
35

28

52

7

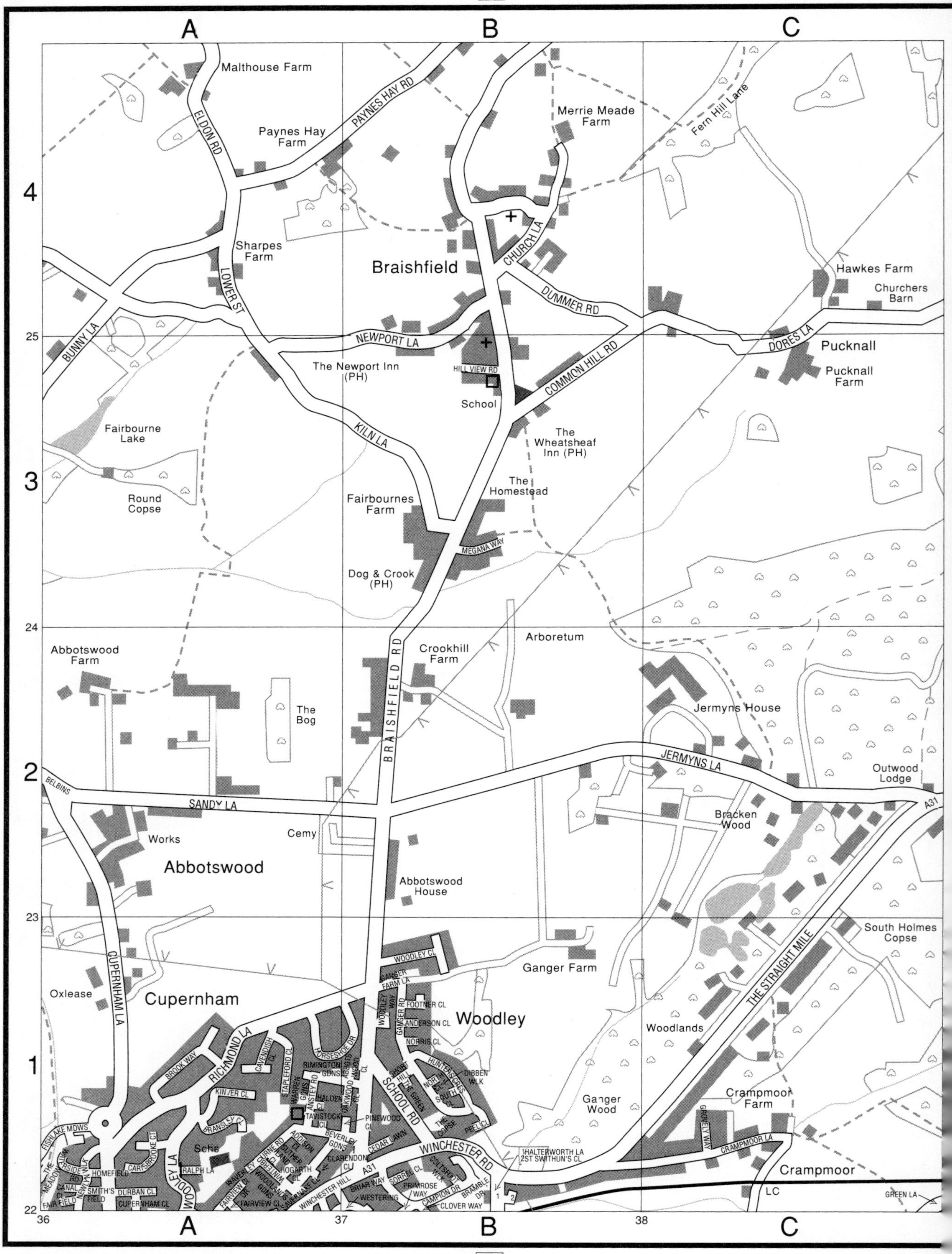
A
B
C
Malthouse Farm
Paynes Hay Farm
PAYNES HAY RD
ELDON RD
Merrie Meade Farm
Fern Hill Lane
Sharpes Farm
LOWER ST
Braishfield
CHURCH LA
DUMMER RD
Hawkes Farm
Churchers Barn
BUNNY LA
NEWPORT LA
DORES LA
Pucknall
Pucknall Farm
The Newport Inn (PH)
HILL VIEW RD
School
COMMON HILL RD
Fairbourne Lake
KILN LA
The Wheatsheaf Inn (PH)
The Homestead
Round Copse
Fairbournes Farm
MEGANA WAY
Dog & Crook (PH)
Arboretum
Abbotswood Farm
Crookhill Farm
BRAISHFIELD RD
The Bog
Jermyns House
JERMYNS LA
Outwood Lodge
BELBINS
SANDY LA
A31
Bracken Wood
Works
Cemy
Abbotswood
Abbotswood House
South Holmes Copse
WOODLEY CL
Ganger Farm
THE STRAIGHT MILE
Oxlease
CUPERNHAM LA
Cupernham
FOOTNER CL
ANDERSON CL
Woodley
NORRIS CL
Woodlands
RICHMOND LA
BROOK WAY
CAVENDISH PL
HORSESHOE DR
RIMINGTON GDNS
HUNTERS CRES
DIBBEN WLK
SCHOOL RD
KINVER CL
STAPLEFORD CL
HALDEN CL
TAVISTOCK CL
PINEWOOD CL
Ganger Wood
Crampmoor Farm
GROVELY WAY
CRAMPMOOR LA
Crampmoor
BRANSLEY CL
Schs
ADDISON CL
BEVERLEY GDNS
CLARENDON CL
CEDAR LAWN
WINCHESTER RD
HALTERWORTH LA
ST SWITHUN'S CL
FISHLAKE MDWS
CARISBROOKE CL
HOMEFIELD
RALPH LA
HOGARTH CL
WINCHESTER HILL
SORREL CL
COTSWOLD WLK
BRAMBLE DR
PRIMROSE WAY
WESTERING
CAMPTON DR
CLOVER WAY
CANAL
SMITH'S FIELD
DURBAN CL
CUPERNHAM CL
FAIRVIEW DR
FAIRVIEW CL
LC
GREEN LA
36
37
38
22
23
24
25
1
2
3
4

27

53

8

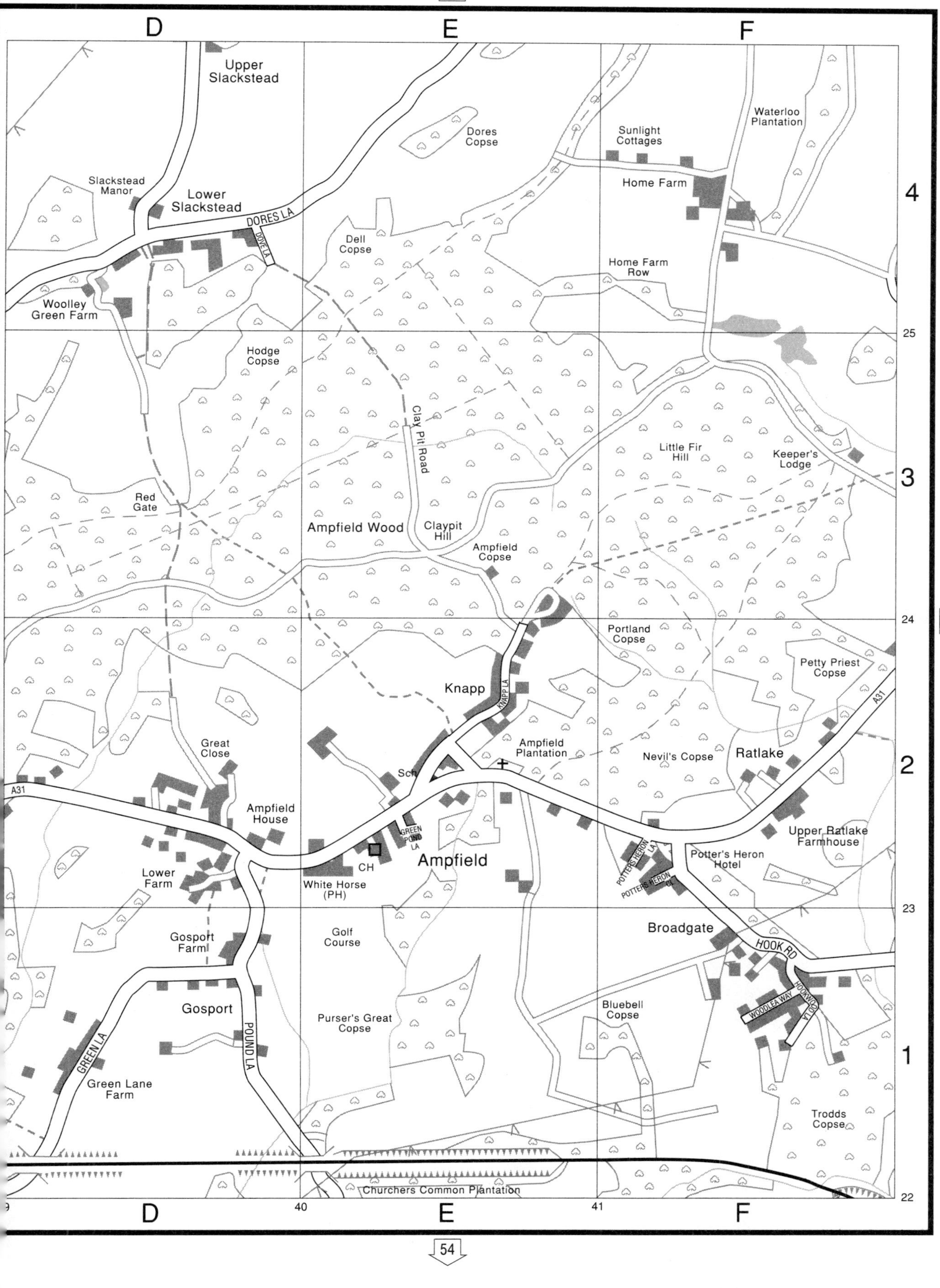
D
E
F
Upper
Slackstead
Dores
Copse
Sunlight
Cottages
Waterloo
Plantation
Slackstead
Manor
Lower
Slackstead
DORES LA
DOVE LA
Home Farm
4
Dell
Copse
Home Farm
Row
Woolley
Green Farm
25
Hodge
Copse
Clay Pit Road
Little Fir
Hill
Keeper's
Lodge
3
Red
Gate
Ampfield Wood
Claypit
Hill
Ampfield
Copse
24
Portland
Copse
Petty Priest
Copse
Knapp
KNAPP LA
A31
Great
Close
Ampfield
Plantation
Nevil's Copse
Ratlake
2
Sch
A31
Ampfield
House
GREEN
POND
LA
Upper Ratlake
Farmhouse
CH
Ampfield
POTTERS HERON LA
Potter's Heron
Hotel
Lower
Farm
White Horse
(PH)
POTTERS HERON CL
23
Broadgate
HOOK RD
Gosport
Farm
Golf
Course
Gosport
POUND LA
Purser's Great
Copse
Bluebell
Copse
WOODLEA WAY
HOOKWOOD LA
GREEN LA
1
Green Lane
Farm
Trodds
Copse
Churchers Common Plantation
22
9
40
41
D
E
F

30

54

9

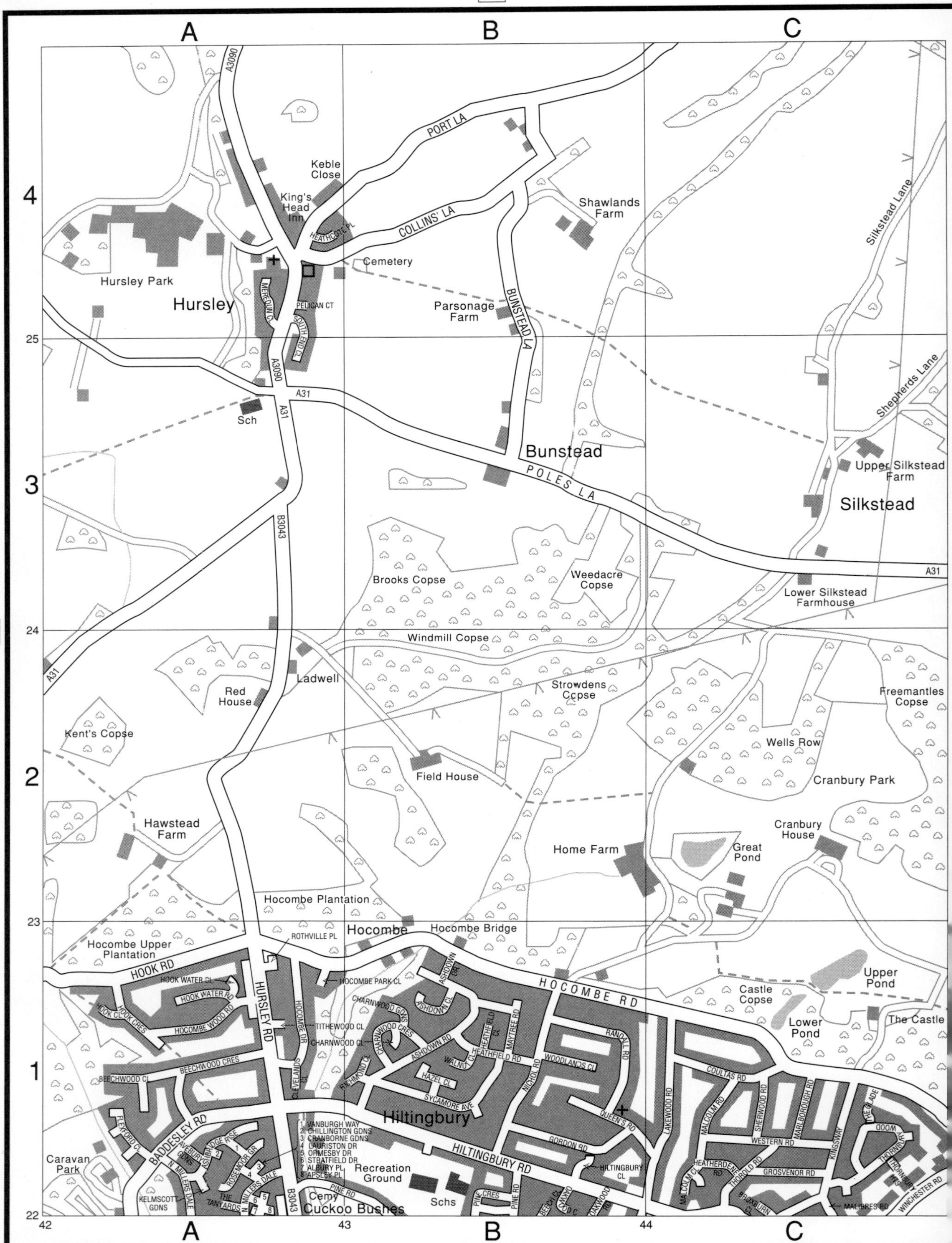
A
B
C
4
3
2
1
25
24
23
22
42
43
44
A3090
PORT LA
Keble Close
King's Head Inn
HEATHCOTE PL
COLLINS' LA
Shawlands Farm
Silkstead Lane
Hursley Park
Hursley
Cemetery
PELICAN CT
SOUTH END CL
Parsonage Farm
BUNSTEAD LA
A31
Sch
Shepherds Lane
Bunstead
POLES LA
Upper Silkstead Farm
Silkstead
B3043
Brooks Copse
Weedacre Copse
Lower Silkstead Farmhouse
Windmill Copse
Ladwell
Red House
Strowdens Copse
Freemantles Copse
Kent's Copse
Wells Row
Field House
Cranbury Park
Hawstead Farm
Cranbury House
Home Farm
Great Pond
Hocombe Plantation
Hocombe
Hocombe Bridge
ROTHVILLE PL
Hocombe Upper Plantation
HOOK RD
HOOK WATER CL
HOOK WATER RD
HOCOMBE PARK CL
ASHDOWN DR
HOCOMBE RD
Castle Copse
Upper Pond
HOOK CL
HOOK CRES
HOCOMBE WOOD RD
HURSLEY RD
HOCOMBE DR
TITHEWOOD CL
CHARNWOOD GDNS
CHARNWOOD CRES
CHARNWOOD CL
ASHDOWN CL
HEATHFIELD CL
MAYTREE RD
RANDALL RD
Lower Pond
The Castle
BEECHWOOD CRES
BEECHWOOD CL
CLEVELAND CT
RICHMOND CL
ASHDOWN RD
WALNUT CL
HEATHFIELD RD
WOODLANDS CL
HAZEL CL
SYCAMORE AVE
NICHOL RD
COULTAS RD
LAKEWOOD RD
MALCOLM RD
SHERWOOD RD
MARLBOROUGH RD
KINGSWAY
THE GLADE
QUEEN'S RD
Hiltingbury
WESTERN RD
FLEXFORD CL
BADDESLEY RD
AVEBURY GDNS
ASHBRIDGE RISE
ROSEMOOR GR
1 VANBURGH WAY
2 CHILLINGTON GDNS
3 CRANBORNE GDNS
4 LAURISTON DR
5 ORMESBY DR
6 STRATFIELD DR
7 ALBURY PL
8 APSLEY PL
HILTINGBURY RD
GORDON RD
HILTINGBURY CL
HEATHERDENE RD
THOROLD RD
GROSVENOR RD
Caravan Park
N MILLERS DALE
THE TANYARDS
Recreation Ground
PINE RD
Cemy
Cuckoo Bushes
Schs
PINE CRES
OAKWOOD RD
BROXBURN CL
MALIBRES RD
WINCHESTER RD
KELMSCOTT GDNS
THORNBURY WOOD
A31

29

55

10

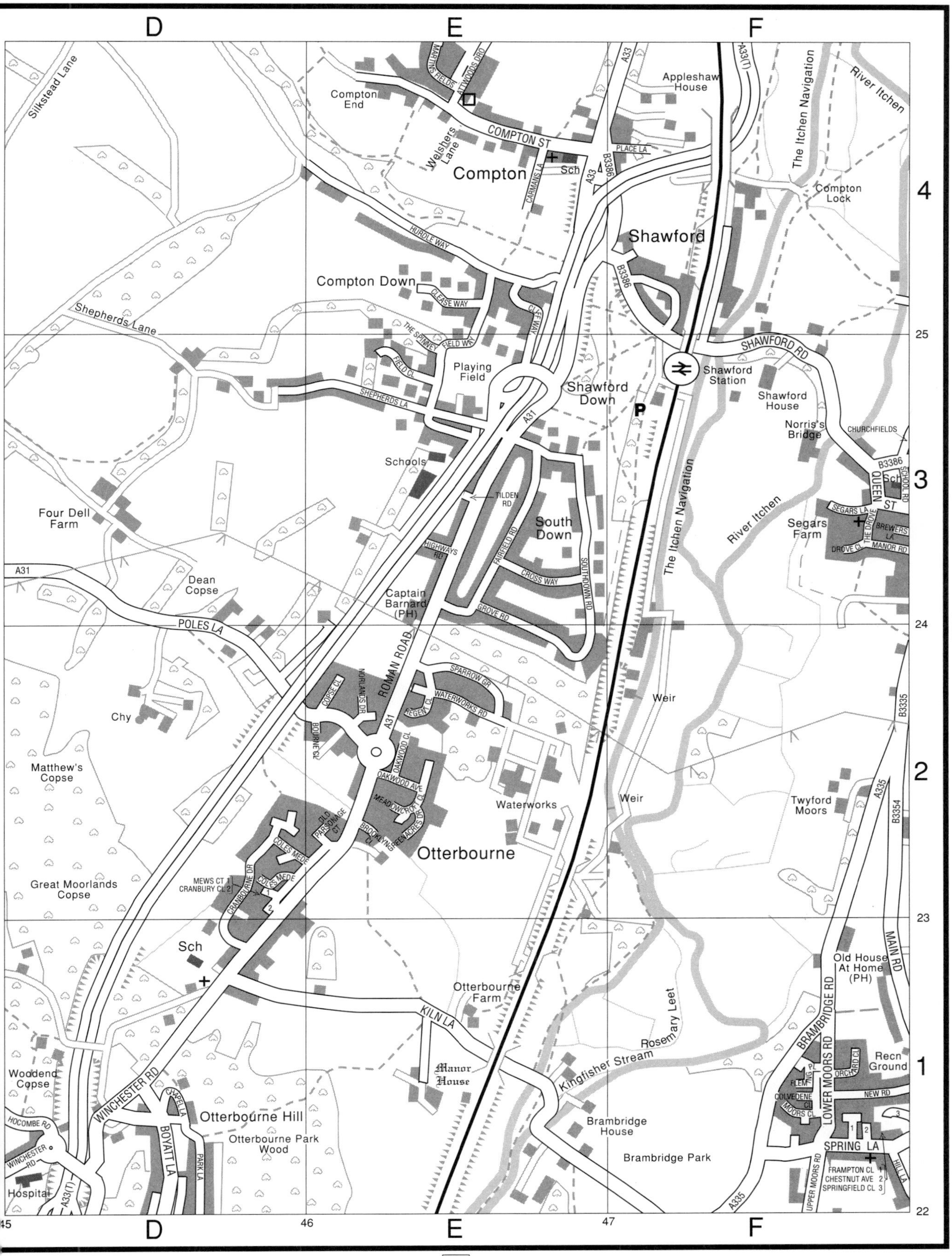
D
E
F
Silkstead Lane
Compton End
MARTINS FIELDS
ATTWOODS DRO
COMPTON ST
Welshers Lane
Compton
CARMANS LA
Sch
A33
B3386
PLACE LA
Appleshaw House
A33(T)
The Itchen Navigation
River Itchen
Compton Lock
HURDLE WAY
Shawford
Compton Down
CLEASE WAY
CLIFF WAY
THE SPINNEY
FIELD WAY
FIELD CL
Shepherds Lane
Playing Field
SHEPHERDS LA
Shawford Down
SHAWFORD RD
Shawford Station
Shawford House
Norris's Bridge
CHURCHFIELDS
A31
Schools
TILDEN RD
South Down
FAIRFIELD RD
HIGHWAYS RD
CROSS WAY
SOUTHDOWN RD
B3386
QUEEN ST
Sch
SCHOOL RD
SEGARS LA
Segars Farm
BREWERS LA
THE DROVE
DROVE CL
MANOR RD
Four Dell Farm
Dean Copse
Captain Barnard (PH)
GROVE RD
POLES LA
ROMAN ROAD
NORLANDS DR
COPSE CL
SPARROW GR
REGENT CL
WATERWORKS RD
Weir
Chy
BOURNE CL
OAKWOOD CL
Matthew's Copse
OAKWOOD AVE
MEADOWCROFT CL
GREENACRES DR
BROOKLYN CL
OLD PARSONAGE CT
COLES MEDE
Waterworks
Weir
Twyford Moors
A335
B3354
B3335
Otterbourne
Great Moorlands Copse
MEWS CT 1
CRANBURY CL 2
CRANBOURNE DR
Sch
Otterbourne Farm
Old House At Home (PH)
MAIN RD
KILN LA
Rosemary Leet
Kingfisher Stream
Manor House
BRAMBRIDGE RD
LOWER MOORS RD
ORCHARD CL
Recn Ground
ELM
COLVEDENE CL
MOORS CL
NEW RD
Woodend Copse
WINCHESTER RD
CHAPEL LA
Otterbourne Hill
BOYATT LA
PARK LA
Otterbourne Park Wood
HOCOMBE RD
WINCHESTER RD
Hospital
A33(T)
Brambridge House
Brambridge Park
SPRING LA
FRAMPTON CL 1
CHESTNUT AVE 2
SPRINGFIELD CL 3
UPPER MOORS RD
HILL LA
A335
4
3
2
1
25
24
23
22
45
46
47

32

56

11

31

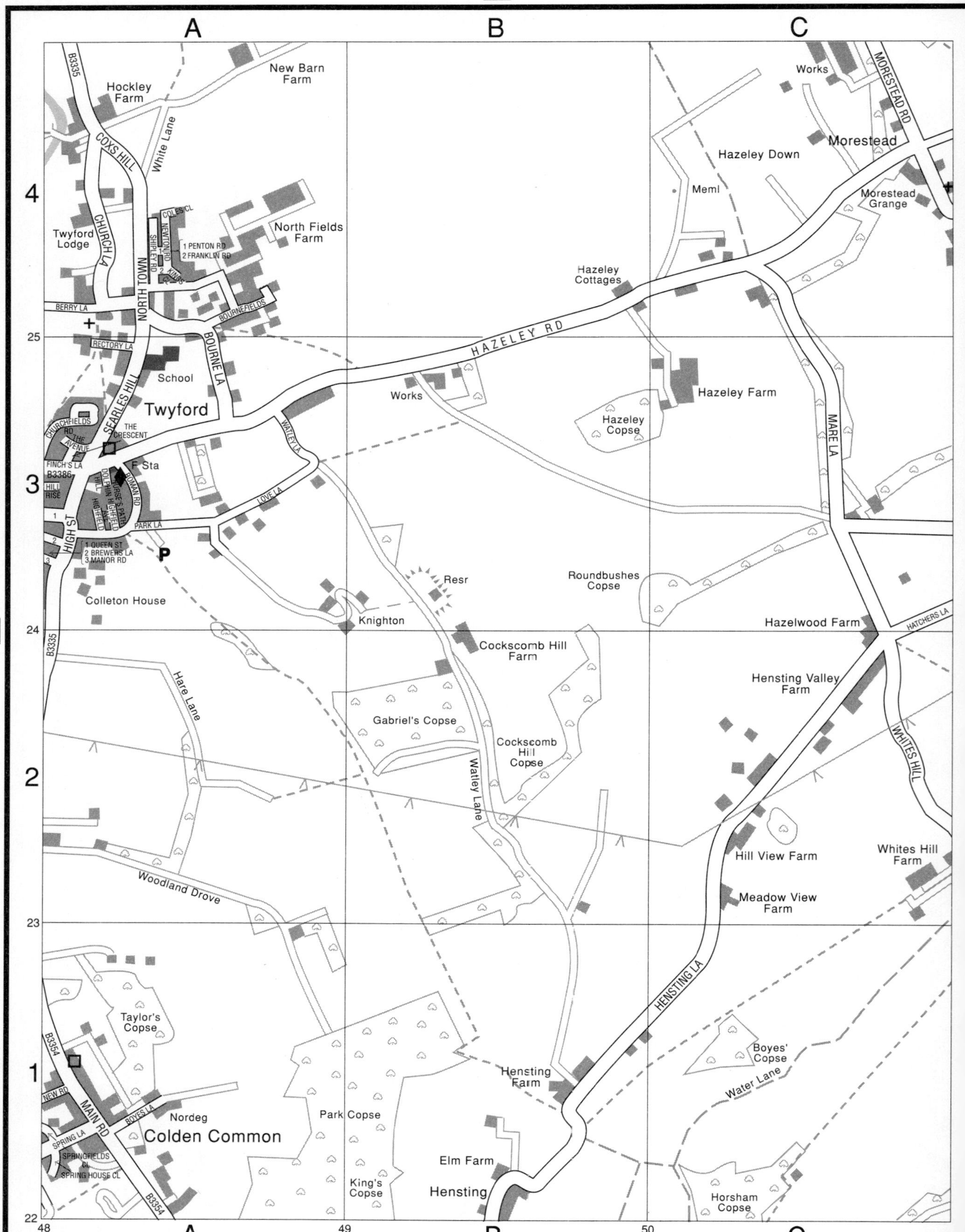
A
B
C
4
3
2
1
25
24
23
22
48
49
50
New Barn Farm
Hockley Farm
B3335
COXS HILL
White Lane
Works
MORESTEAD RD
Morestead
Hazeley Down
Meml
Morestead Grange
Twyford Lodge
CHURCH LA
NORTH TOWN
COLES CL
NEWTOWN RD
SHIPLEY RD
1 PENTON RD
2 FRANKLIN RD
KINGS
North Fields Farm
Hazeley Cottages
BERRY LA
BOURNEFIELDS
RECTORY LA
BOURNE LA
HAZELEY RD
SEARLES HILL
School
Twyford
Works
Hazeley Farm
Hazeley Copse
MARE LA
CHURCHFIELDS RD
THE AVENUE
THE CRESCENT
FINCH'S LA
B3386
HILL RISE
F Sta
WATLEY LA
ROMAN RD
DOLPHIN HILL
HIGHFIELD
LOVE LA
PARK LA
HIGH ST
1 QUEEN ST
2 BREWERS LA
3 MANOR RD
P
Resr
Roundbushes Copse
Colleton House
Knighton
Hazelwood Farm
HATCHERS LA
Cockscomb Hill Farm
Hensting Valley Farm
Hare Lane
Gabriel's Copse
Cockscomb Hill Copse
Watley Lane
WHITES HILL
Hill View Farm
Whites Hill Farm
Woodland Drove
Meadow View Farm
HENSTING LA
Taylor's Copse
B3354
Boyes' Copse
Hensting Farm
Water Lane
NEW RD
MAIN RD
BOYES LA
Nordeg
Colden Common
Park Copse
SPRING LA
SPRINGFIELDS CL
SPRING HOUSE CL
Elm Farm
King's Copse
Hensting
Horsham Copse

57

12

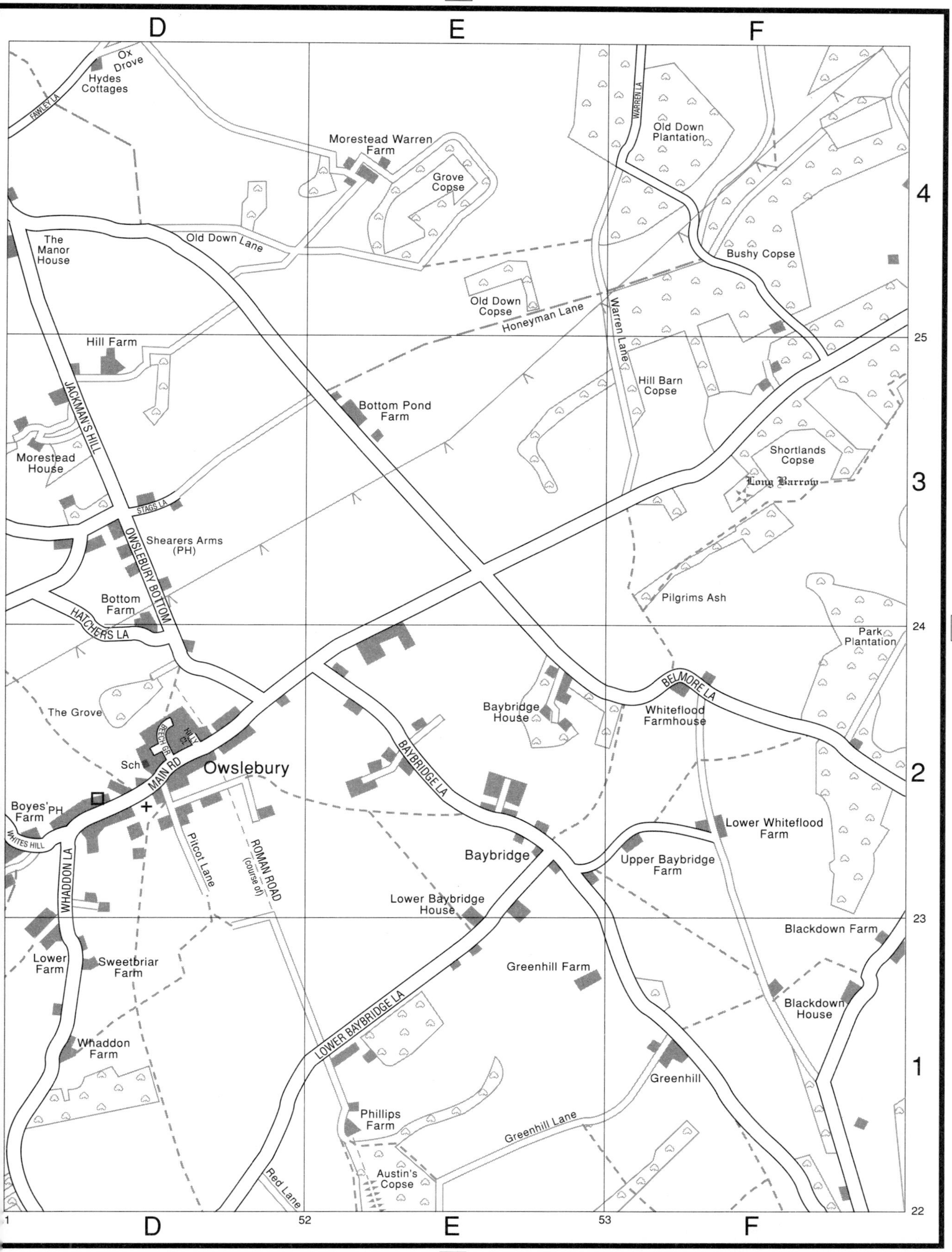
D
E
F
Ox Drove
Hydes Cottages
FAWLEY LA
Morestead Warren Farm
Grove Copse
WARREN LA
Old Down Plantation
4
The Manor House
Old Down Lane
Bushy Copse
Old Down Copse
Honeyman Lane
Warren Lane
Hill Farm
25
JACKMAN'S HILL
Hill Barn Copse
Bottom Pond Farm
Morestead House
Shortlands Copse
Long Barrow
3
STAGS LA
OWSLEBURY BOTTOM
Shearers Arms (PH)
Bottom Farm
Pilgrims Ash
HATCHERS LA
24
Park Plantation
BELMORE LA
The Grove
Baybridge House
Whiteflood Farmhouse
BEECH GR
HILLY CL
Sch
MAIN RD
Owslebury
BAYBRIDGE LA
2
Boyes' Farm
PH
WHITES HILL
WHADDON LA
Pitcot Lane
ROMAN ROAD (course of)
Lower Whiteflood Farm
Baybridge
Upper Baybridge Farm
Lower Baybridge House
23
Blackdown Farm
Lower Farm
Sweetbriar Farm
Greenhill Farm
LOWER BAYBRIDGE LA
Blackdown House
Whaddon Farm
1
Greenhill
Phillips Farm
Greenhill Lane
Austin's Copse
Red Lane
22
52
53
D
E
F

34

58

13

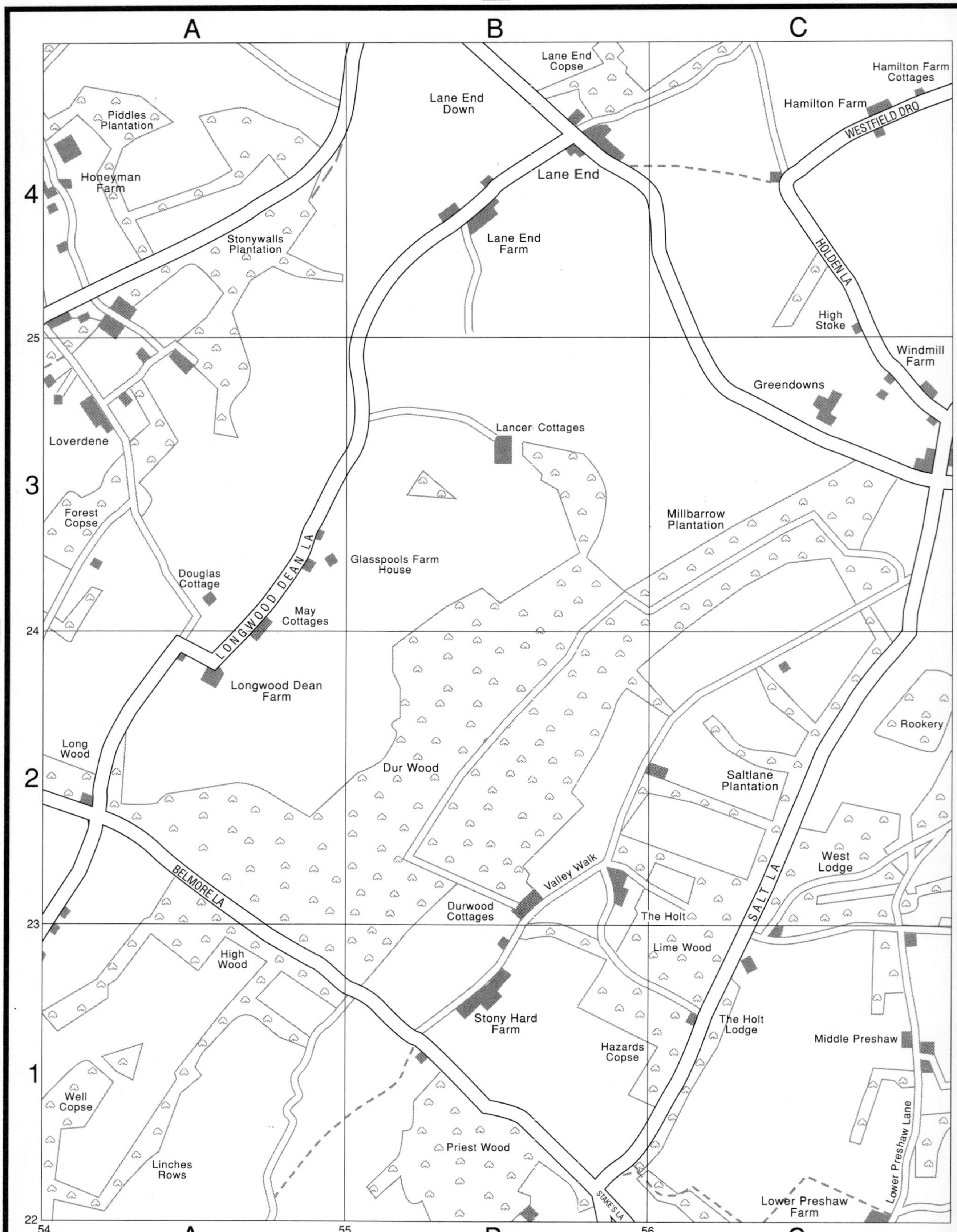
A
B
C
Lane End Copse
Hamilton Farm Cottages
Hamilton Farm
WESTFIELD DRO
Lane End Down
Piddles Plantation
Honeyman Farm
Lane End
4
Lane End Farm
HOLDEN LA
Stonywalls Plantation
High Stoke
25
Windmill Farm
Greendowns
Lancer Cottages
Loverdene
3
Forest Copse
Millbarrow Plantation
LONGWOOD DEAN LA
Glasspools Farm House
Douglas Cottage
May Cottages
24
Longwood Dean Farm
Rookery
Long Wood
Dur Wood
Saltlane Plantation
2
BELMORE LA
Valley Walk
West Lodge
SALT LA
Durwood Cottages
The Holt
23
High Wood
Lime Wood
Stony Hard Farm
The Holt Lodge
Middle Preshaw
Hazards Copse
1
Well Copse
Lower Preshaw Lane
Priest Wood
Linches Rows
STAKE'S LA
Lower Preshaw Farm
22
54
55
56
A
B
C

33

59

14

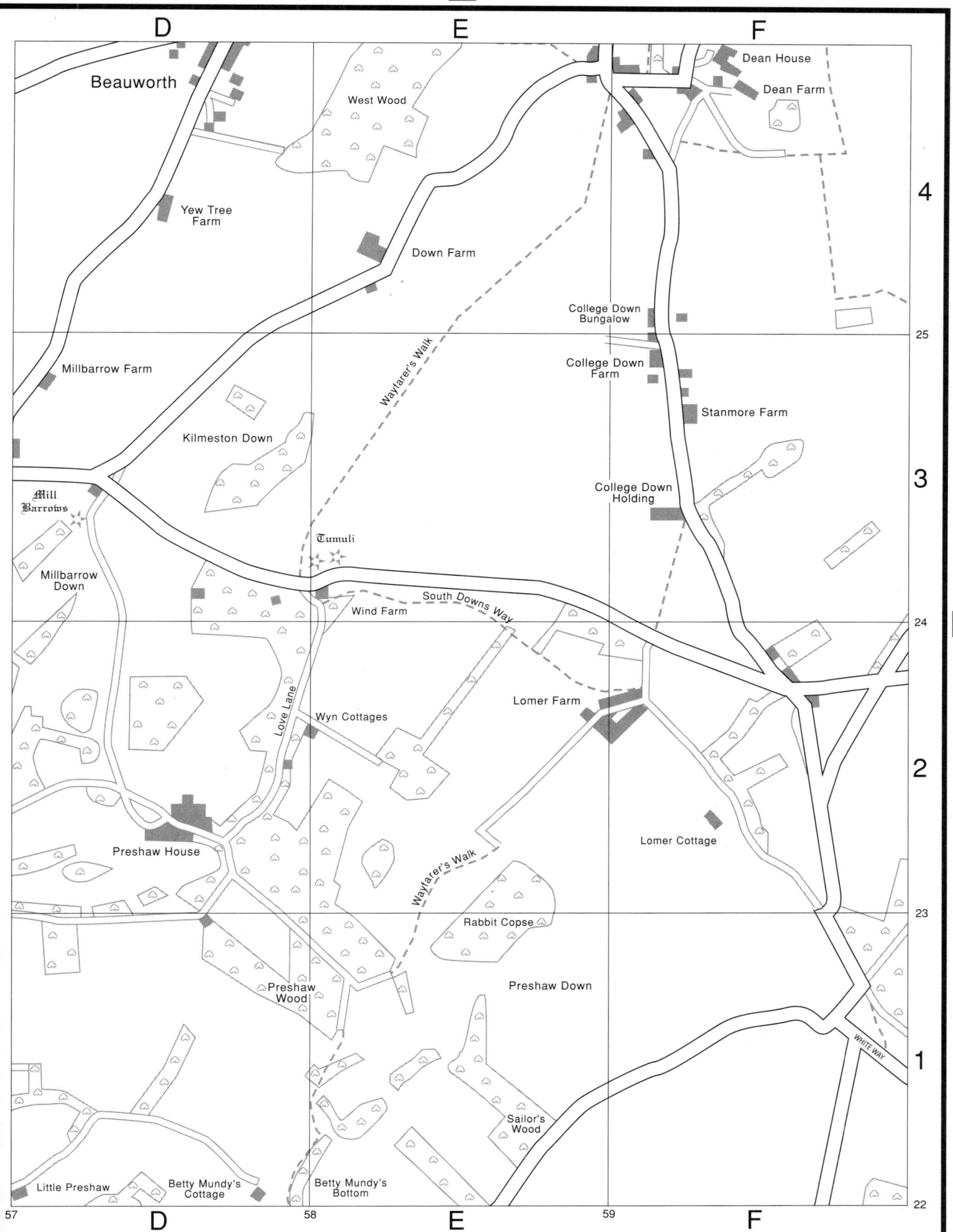
D
E
F
Beauworth
West Wood
Dean House
Dean Farm
Yew Tree Farm
Down Farm
College Down Bungalow
Millbarrow Farm
College Down Farm
Stanmore Farm
Kilmeston Down
Wayfarer's Walk
College Down Holding
Mill Barrows
Tumuli
Millbarrow Down
South Downs Way
Wind Farm
Lomer Farm
Love Lane
Wyn Cottages
Preshaw House
Lomer Cottage
Wayfarer's Walk
Rabbit Copse
Preshaw Wood
Preshaw Down
WHITE WAY
Sailor's Wood
Little Preshaw
Betty Mundy's Cottage
Betty Mundy's Bottom
4
3
2
1
25
24
23
22
57
58
59
D
E
F

36

60

15

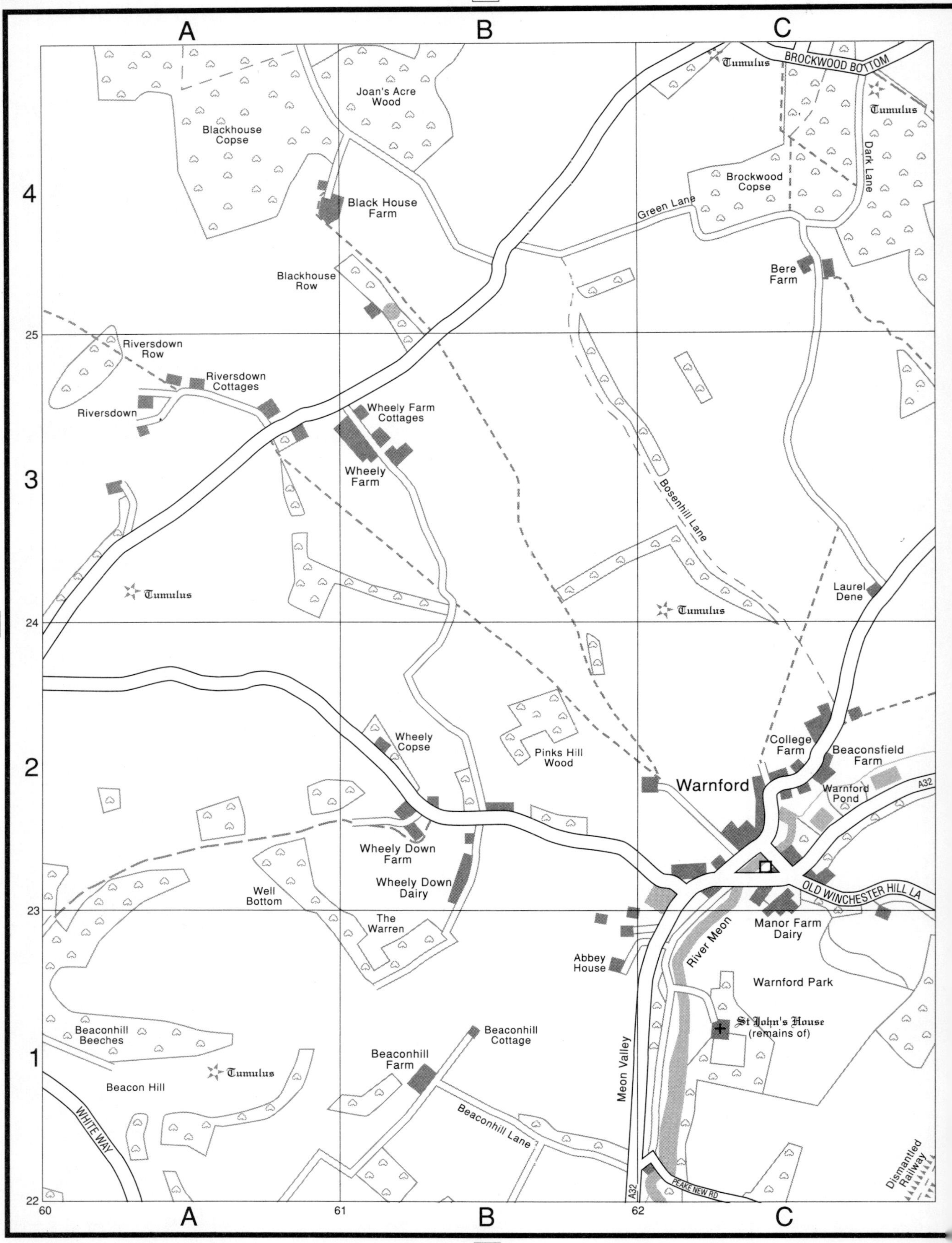

A
B
C
4
3
2
1
25
24
23
22
60
61
62
Joan's Acre Wood
Blackhouse Copse
Black House Farm
Tumulus
BROCKWOOD BOTTOM
Tumulus
Brockwood Copse
Dark Lane
Green Lane
Bere Farm
Blackhouse Row
Riversdown Row
Riversdown Cottages
Riversdown
Wheely Farm Cottages
Wheely Farm
Bosenhill Lane
Tumulus
Tumulus
Laurel Dene
Wheely Copse
Pinks Hill Wood
College Farm
Beaconsfield Farm
Warnford
Warnford Pond
A32
Wheely Down Farm
Wheely Down Dairy
Well Bottom
The Warren
OLD WINCHESTER HILL LA
Manor Farm Dairy
River Meon
Abbey House
Warnford Park
St John's House (remains of)
Beaconhill Beeches
Beaconhill Cottage
Beaconhill Farm
Tumulus
Beacon Hill
Meon Valley
WHITE WAY
Beaconhill Lane
Dismantled Railway
A32
PEAKE NEW RD
A
B
C

35

61

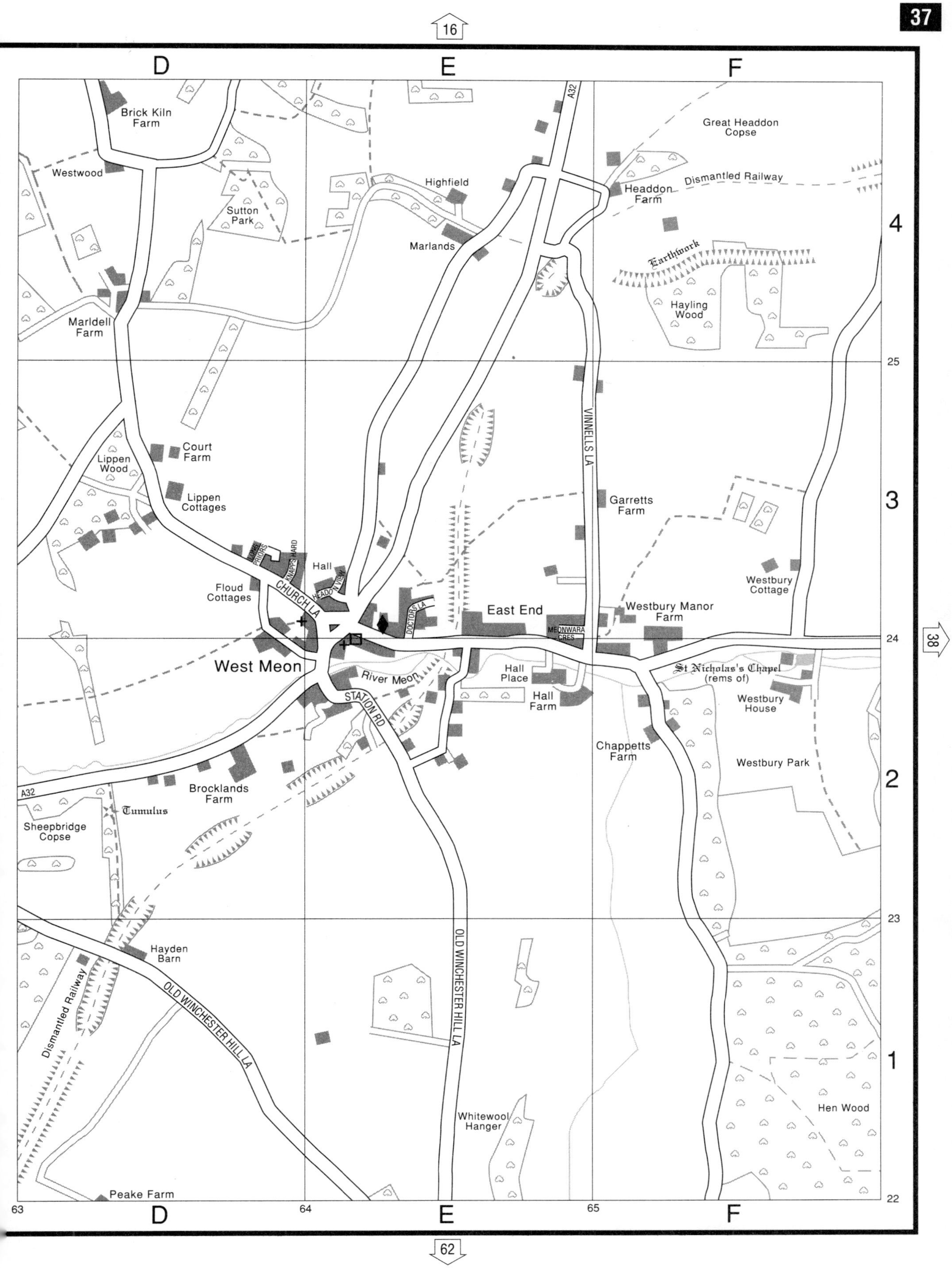
16
D
E
F
Brick Kiln Farm
Westwood
Sutton Park
Highfield
Marlands
A32
Great Headdon Copse
Dismantled Railway
Headdon Farm
Earthwork
Hayling Wood
Marldell Farm
Court Farm
Lippen Wood
Lippen Cottages
VINNELLS LA
Garretts Farm
LOWER PRIORS
KNAPPS HARD
Hall
HEADON VIEW
CHURCH LA
Floud Cottages
DOCTORS LA
East End
Westbury Manor Farm
Westbury Cottage
MEONWARA CRES
West Meon
River Meon
STATION RD
Hall Place
Hall Farm
St Nicholas's Chapel (rems of)
Westbury House
Chappetts Farm
Westbury Park
A32
Brocklands Farm
Tumulus
Sheepbridge Copse
Hayden Barn
Dismantled Railway
OLD WINCHESTER HILL LA
OLD WINCHESTER HILL LA
Whitewool Hanger
Hen Wood
Peake Farm
4
3
2
1
25
24
23
22
38
63
64
65
D
E
F
62

17

37

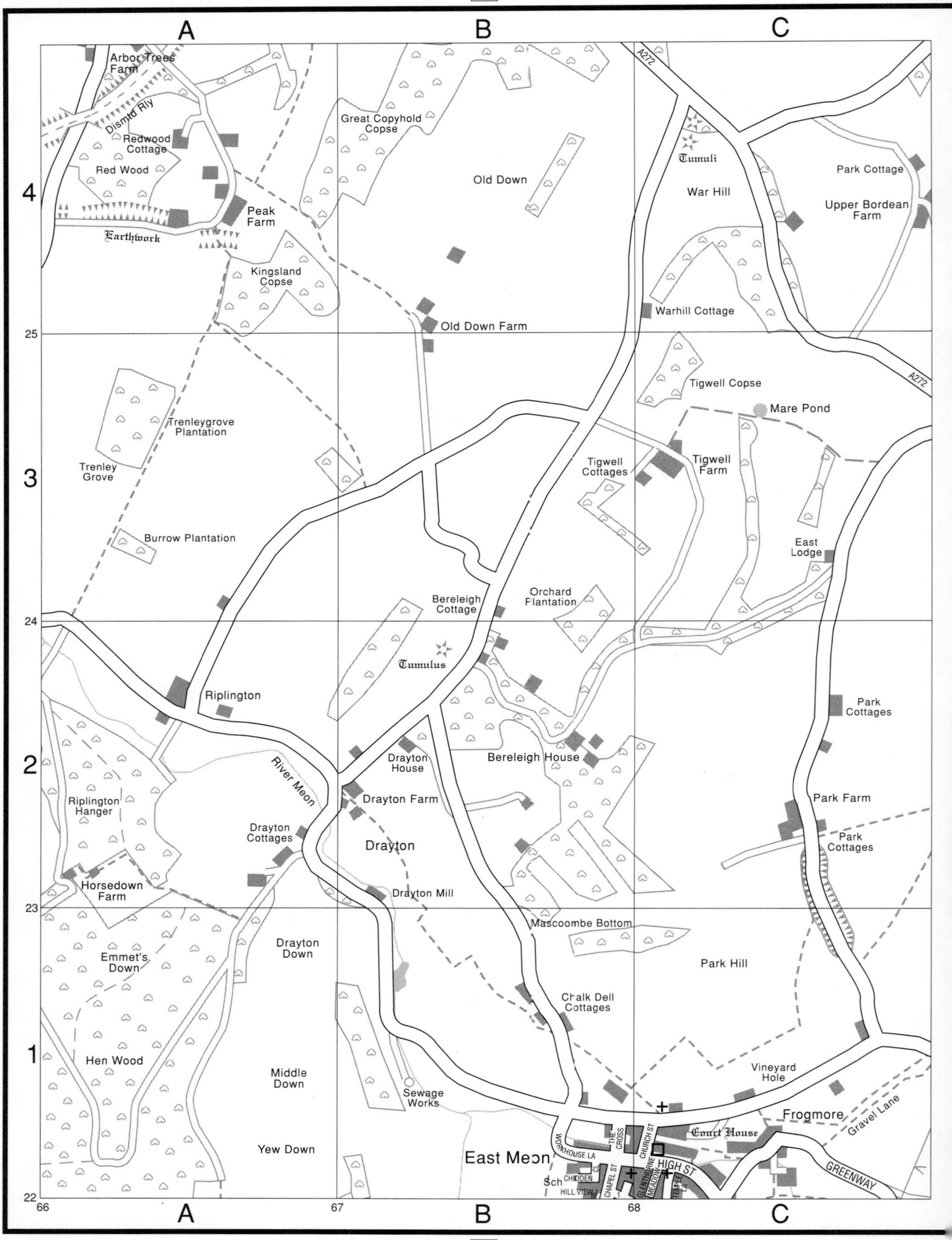
A
B
C
4
3
2
1
25
24
23
22
66
67
68
Arbor Trees Farm
Dismtd Rly
Redwood Cottage
Red Wood
Peak Farm
Earthwork
Kingsland Copse
Great Copyhold Copse
Old Down
Old Down Farm
A272
Tumuli
War Hill
Park Cottage
Upper Bordean Farm
Warhill Cottage
Tigwell Copse
Mare Pond
Trenleygrove Plantation
Trenley Grove
Burrow Plantation
Tigwell Cottages
Tigwell Farm
East Lodge
Orchard Flantation
Bereleigh Cottage
Tumulus
Riplington
Park Cottages
Bereleigh House
Drayton House
River Meon
Riplington Hanger
Drayton Farm
Park Farm
Drayton Cottages
Drayton
Horsedown Farm
Drayton Mill
Mascoombe Bottom
Drayton Down
Emmet's Down
Park Hill
Chalk Dell Cottages
Hen Wood
Middle Down
Vineyard Hole
Sewage Works
Frogmore
Gravel Lane
Court House
Yew Down
East Meon
WORKHOUSE LA
THE CROSS
CHURCH ST
HIGH ST
GREENWAY
Sch
CHIDDEN CL
CHAPEL ST
GLENTHORNE MEADOW
TEMPLE LA
HILL VIEW

63

18

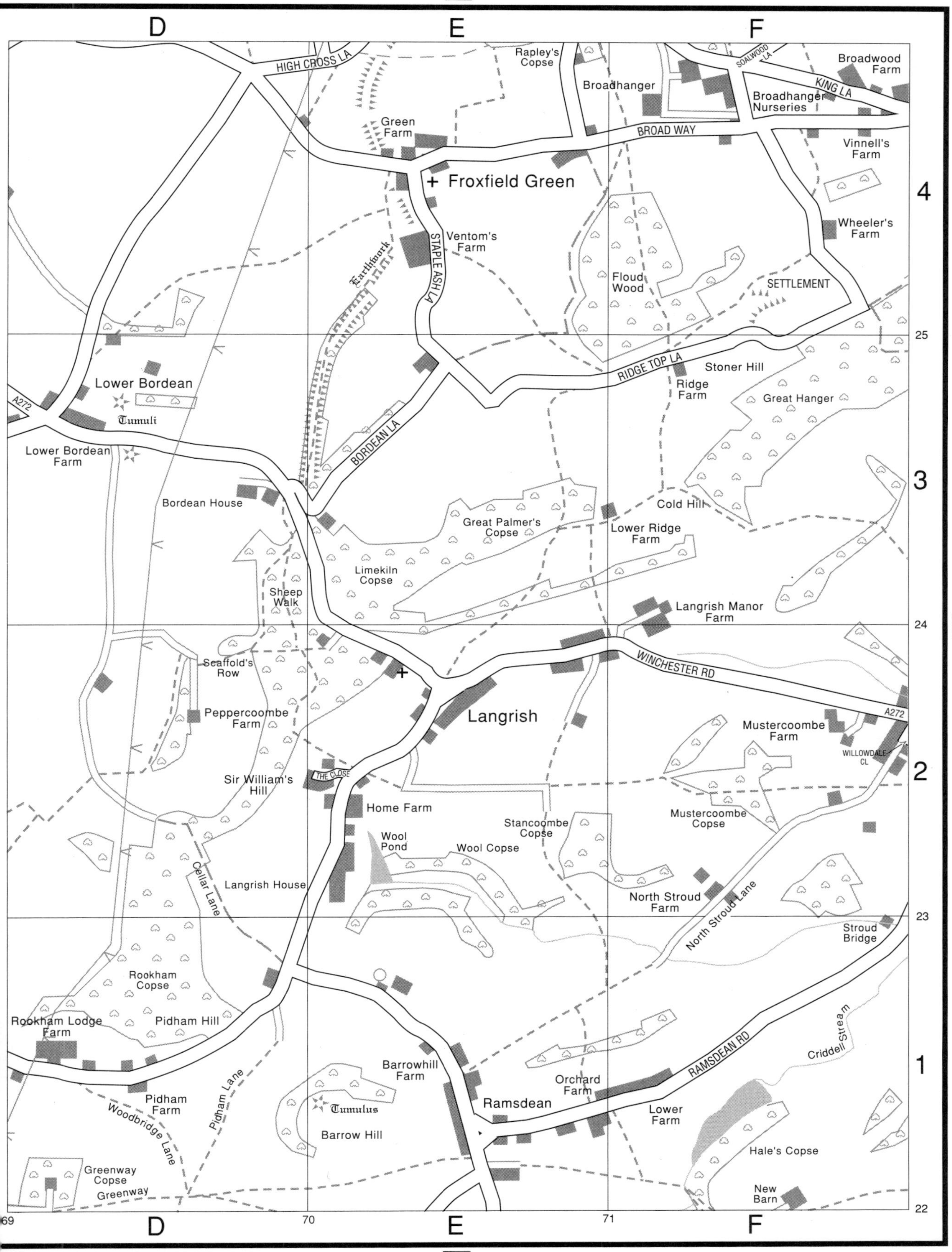

D
E
F
HIGH CROSS LA
Rapley's Copse
Broadhanger
SOALWOOD LA
Broadwood Farm
KING LA
Broadhanger Nurseries
Green Farm
BROAD WAY
Vinnell's Farm
Froxfield Green
4
Wheeler's Farm
Ventom's Farm
Earthwork
STAPLE ASH LA
Floud Wood
SETTLEMENT
25
RIDGE TOP LA
Stoner Hill
Lower Bordean
Ridge Farm
A272
Great Hanger
Tumuli
BORDEAN LA
Lower Bordean Farm
3
Bordean House
Cold Hill
Great Palmer's Copse
Lower Ridge Farm
Limekiln Copse
Sheep Walk
Langrish Manor Farm
24
Scaffold's Row
WINCHESTER RD
Peppercoombe Farm
Langrish
A272
Mustercoombe Farm
WILLOWDALE CL
2
Sir William's Hill
THE CLOSE
Home Farm
Stancoombe Copse
Mustercoombe Copse
Wool Pond
Wool Copse
Cellar Lane
Langrish House
North Stroud Farm
North Stroud Lane
23
Stroud Bridge
Rookham Copse
Rookham Lodge Farm
Pidham Hill
Criddell Stream
Barrowhill Farm
RAMSDEAN RD
1
Orchard Farm
Pidham Farm
Pidham Lane
Ramsdean
Lower Farm
Woodbridge Lane
Tumulus
Barrow Hill
Hale's Copse
Greenway Copse
Greenway
New Barn
22
69
70
71

40

64

19

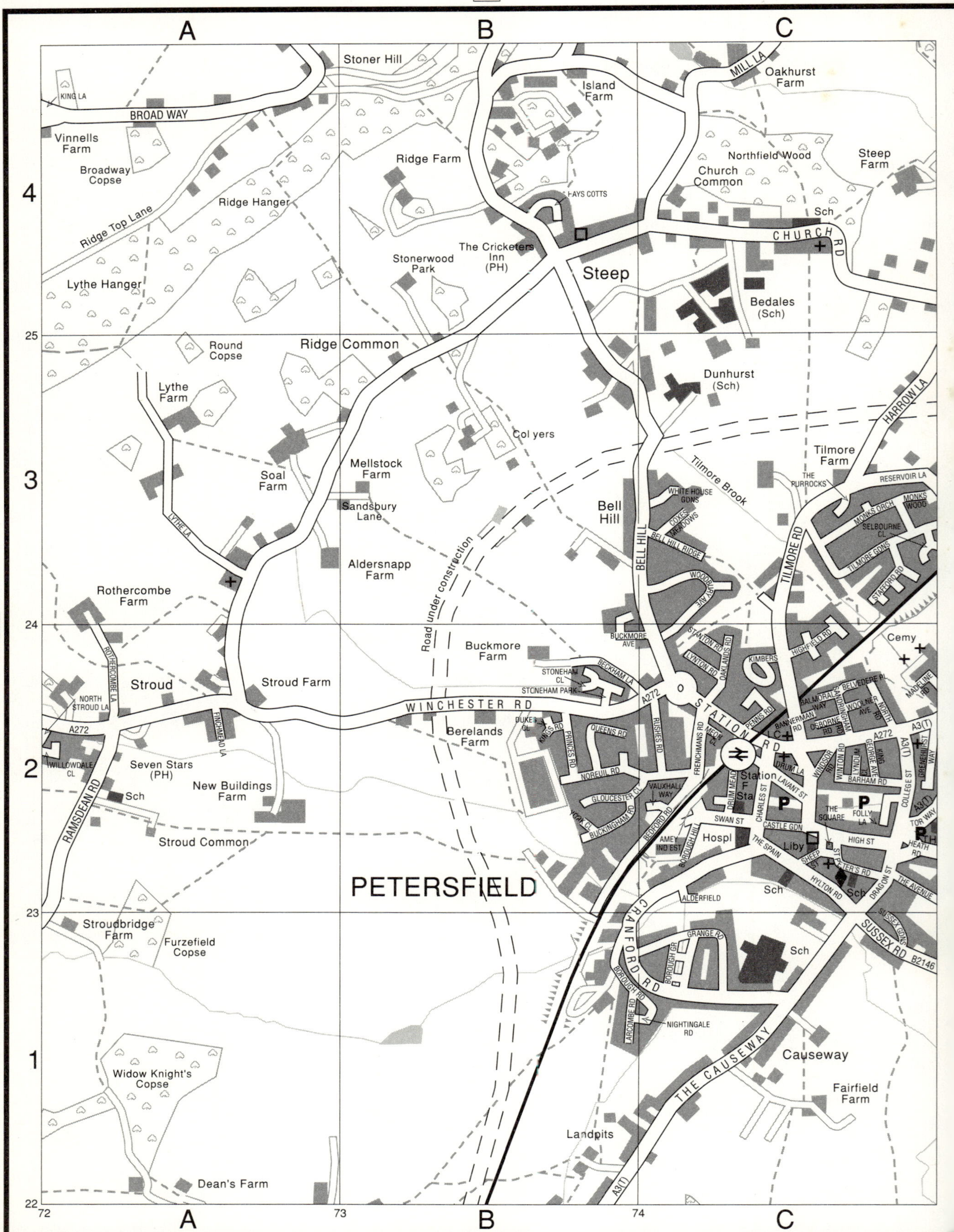
A
B
C
4
3
2
1
25
24
23
22
72
73
74
Stoner Hill
KING LA
BROAD WAY
Vinnells Farm
Broadway Copse
Ridge Hanger
Ridge Top Lane
Lythe Hanger
Island Farm
MILL LA
Oakhurst Farm
Ridge Farm
Northfield Wood
Church Common
Steep Farm
FAYS COTTS
Sch
CHURCH RD
The Cricketers Inn (PH)
Stonerwood Park
Steep
Bedales (Sch)
Round Copse
Ridge Common
Dunhurst (Sch)
Lythe Farm
HARROW LA
Col yers
Tilmore Farm
Mellstock Farm
Soal Farm
Tilmore Brook
THE PURROCKS
RESERVOIR LA
Sandsbury Lane
Bell Hill
WHITE HOUSE GDNS
COXES MEADOWS
BELL HILL RIDGE
MONKS ORCH
MONKS WOOD
SELBOURNE CL
TILMORE GDNS
TILMORE RD
STAFFORD RD
LYTHE LA
Aldersnapp Farm
Road under construction
BELL HILL
WOODBURY AVE
Rothercombe Farm
BUCKMORE AVE
STANTON RD
LYNTON RD
KIMBERS
OAKLANDS RD
HIGHFIELD RD
Cemy
Buckmore Farm
ROTHERCOMBE LA
Stroud
Stroud Farm
NORTH STROUD LA
STONEHAM CL
BECKHAM LA
STONEHAM PARK
A272
STATION RD
BELVEDERE PL
MADELINE RD
WINCHESTER RD
BALMORAL WAY
SANDRINGHAM RD
WOOLNER AVE
NORTH RD
A272
FINCHMEAD LA
DUKES CL
KINGS RD
Berelands Farm
QUEENS RD
RUSHES RD
PENNS RD
BANNERMAN RD
OSBORNE RD
A3(T)
GREENHURST WAY
WILLOWDALE CL
Seven Stars (PH)
PRINCES RD
NOREUIL RD
FRENCHMANS RD
MEON CL
DRUM LA
WINDSOR RD
WINTON RD
LYNDUM PL
GEORGE ST
KING RD
BARHAM RD
COLLEGE ST
Station
Sta
Sch
New Buildings Farm
GLOUCESTER CL
VAUXHALL WAY
DRUM MEAD
CHARLES ST
LAVANT ST
THE SQUARE
FOLLY LA
A3(T)
TOR WAY
RAMSDEAN RD
YORK CL
BUCKINGHAM RD
BEDFORD RD
SWAN ST
CASTLE GDN
HIGH ST
HEATH RD
Stroud Common
AMEY IND EST
BOROUGH HILL
Hospl
THE SPAIN
Liby
SHEEP ST
ST PETER'S RD
PETERSFIELD
ALDERFIELD
Sch
HYLTON RD
Sch
DRAGON ST
THE AVENUE
Stroudbridge Farm
Furzefield Copse
CRANFORD RD
GRANGE RD
Sch
SUSSEX GDNS
SUSSEX RD
B2146
BOROUGH GR
BOROUGH RD
ARCOMBE RD
NIGHTINGALE RD
Causeway
THE CAUSEWAY
Fairfield Farm
Widow Knight's Copse
Landpits
Dean's Farm
A3(T)

39

65

20

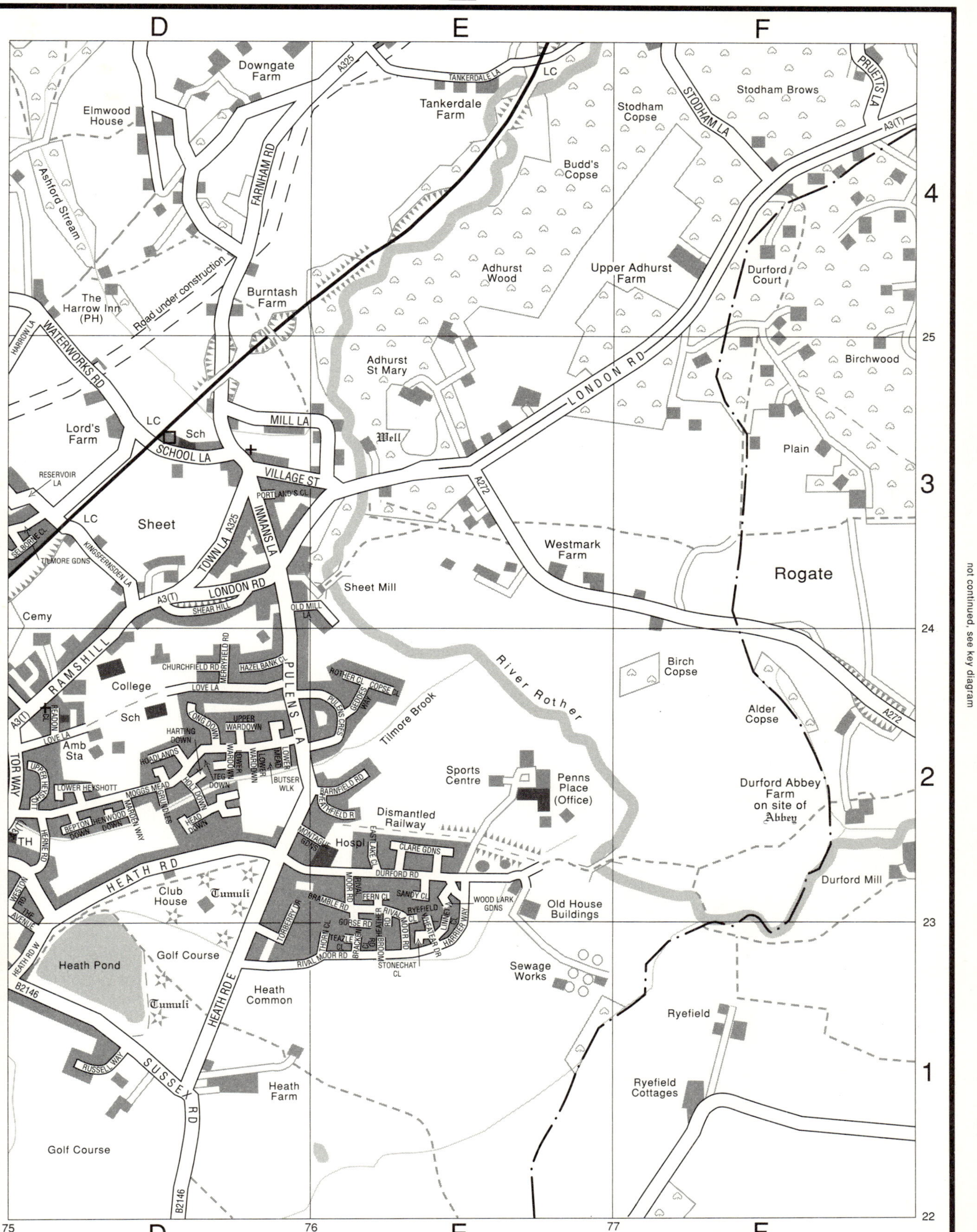

D
E
F
Downgate Farm
Elmwood House
A325
Tankerdale Farm
TANKERDALE LA
LC
Stodham Copse
STODHAM LA
Stodham Brows
PRUETTS LA
A3(T)
Ashford Stream
FARNHAM RD
Budd's Copse
4
Road under construction
The Harrow Inn (PH)
Burntash Farm
Adhurst Wood
Upper Adhurst Farm
Durford Court
HARROW LA
WATERWORKS RD
Adhurst St Mary
LONDON RD
Birchwood
25
Lord's Farm
LC
Sch
MILL LA
Well
SCHOOL LA
VILLAGE ST
Plain
RESERVOIR LA
PORTLAND'S CL
A272
3
LC
Sheet
INMANS LA
TOWN LA
SELBORNE CL
TILMORE GDNS
KINGSFERNSDEN LA
Westmark Farm
Rogate
Sheet Mill
A3(T)
LONDON RD
SHEAR HILL
OLD MILL LA
Cemy
24
RAMSHILL
CHURCHFIELD RD
MERRYFIELD RD
HAZELBANK CL
River Rother
Birch Copse
College
LOVE LA
ROTHER CL
COPSE CL
PULENS LA
PULENS CRES
GEDDES WAY
A3(T)
READON CL
Sch
LONG DOWN
UPPER WARDOWN
Tilmore Brook
Alder Copse
A272
LOVE LA
Amb Sta
HARTING DOWN
TOR WAY
UPPER HEYSHOTT
ROADLANDS
WARDOWN
LOWER WARDOWN
LOWER MEAD
TEG DOWN
BUTSER WLK
Sports Centre
Penns Place (Office)
2
Durford Abbey Farm on site of Abbey
LOWER HEYSHOTT
MOGGS MEAD
HOLT DOWN
BARNFIELD RD
BEPTON DOWN
HENWOOD DOWN
MARDEN WAY
GRUDDIES
HEAD DOWN
HEATHFIELD R
Dismantled Railway
TH
HERNE RD
MONTAGUE GDNS
Hospl
EAST LAKE CL
CLARE GDNS
HEATH RD
DURFORD RD
Durford Mill
WESTON RD
THE AVENUE
Club House
Tumuli
BRAMBLE RD
MOOR RD
RIVAL
FERN CL
SANDY CL
RYEFIELD CL
WOOD LARK GDNS
Old House Buildings
23
HEATH RD W
TORBERRY DR
HORN CL
GORSE RD
TEAZLE CL
HEATHER RD
BROOM RD
LINNET CL
HARRIER WAY
WHEATEAR DR
RIVAL MOOR RD
STONECHAT CL
Golf Course
Heath Pond
Sewage Works
HEATH RD E
Heath Common
Tumuli
B2146
Ryefield
RUSSELL WAY
SUSSEX RD
1
Heath Farm
Ryefield Cottages
Golf Course
B2146
22
75
76
77
D
E
F
not continued, see key diagram

66

not continued, see key diagram

not continued, see key diagram

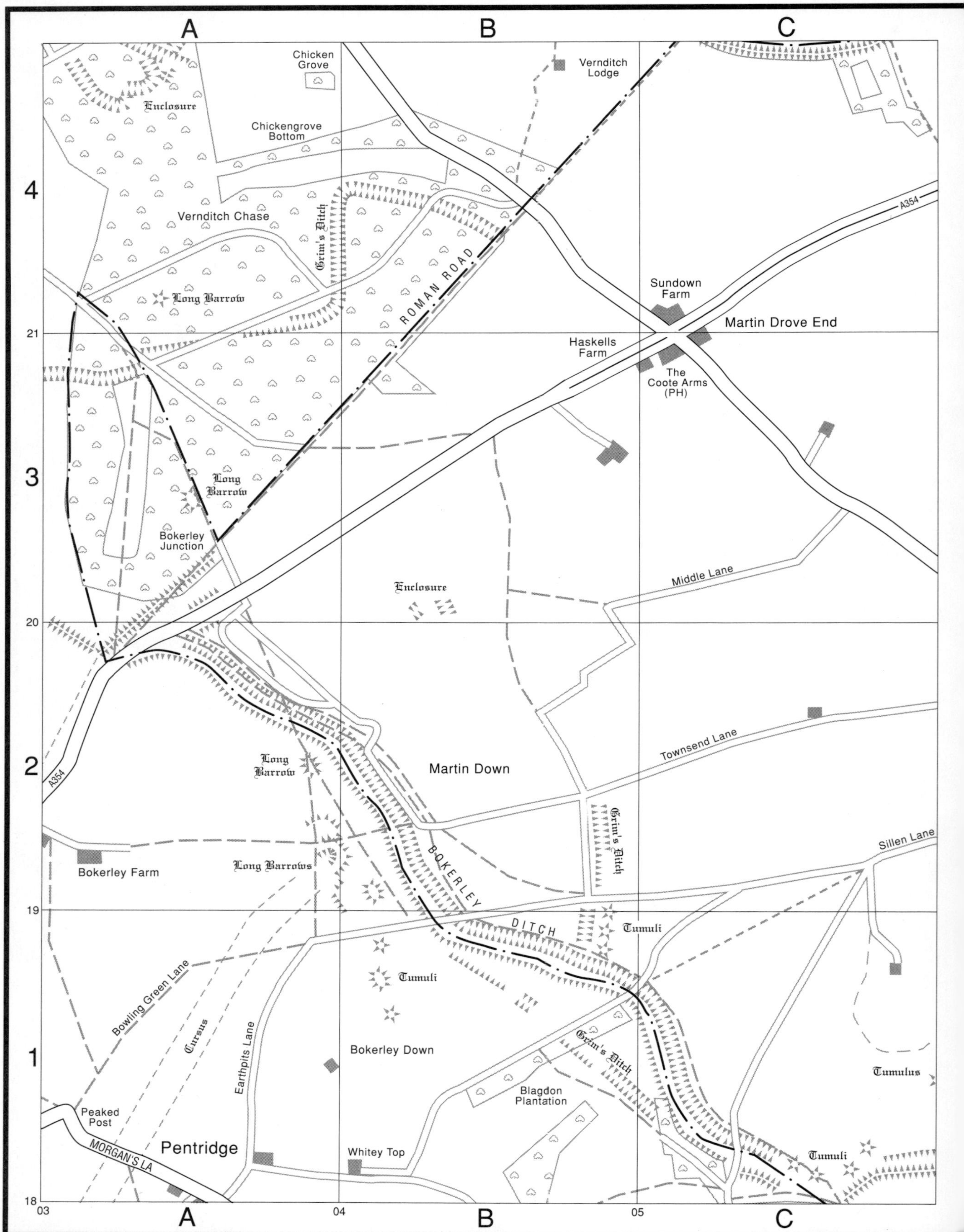

not continued, see key diagram

22

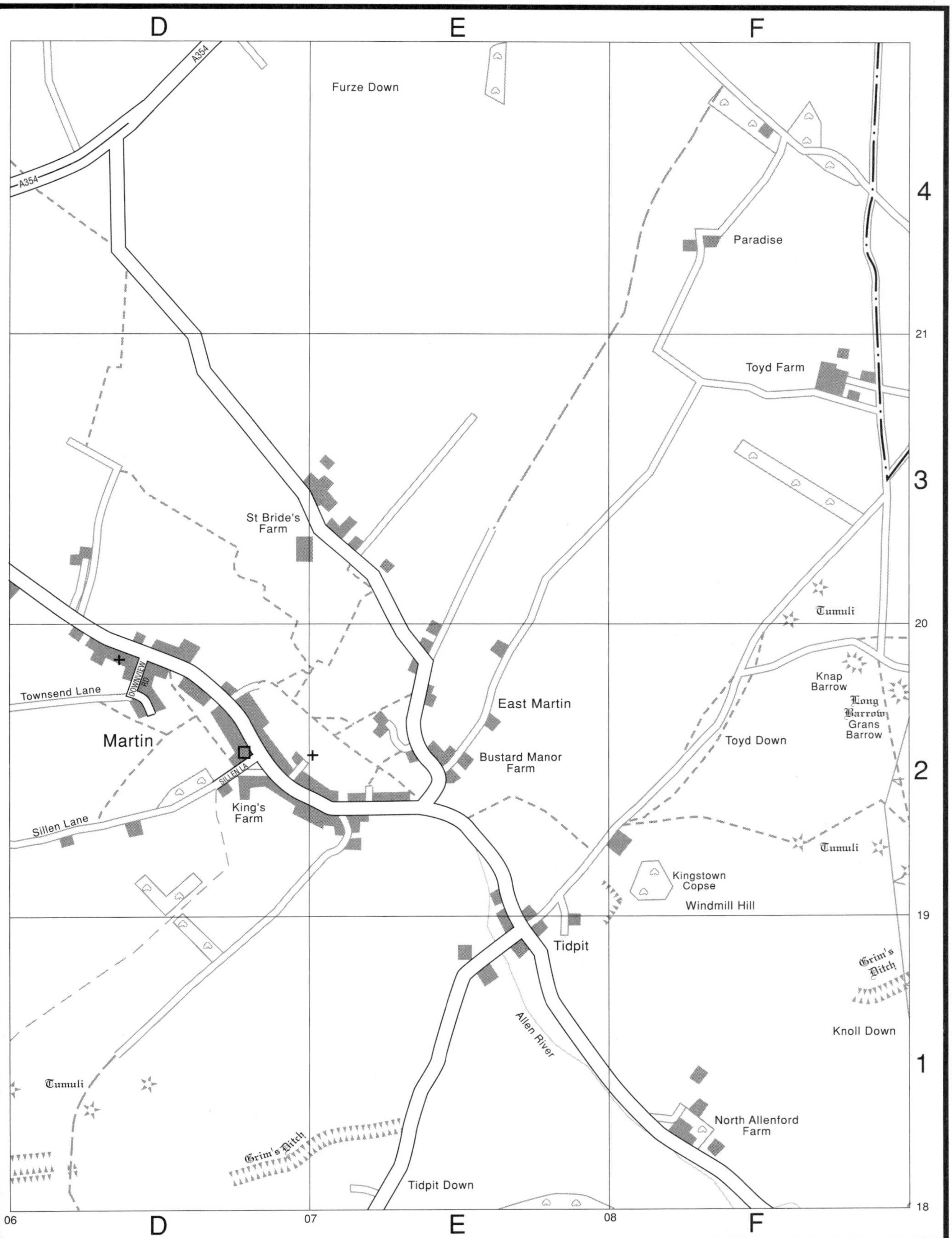
D
E
F
A354
Furze Down
Paradise
Toyd Farm
St Bride's Farm
Tumuli
Knap Barrow
Long Barrow
Grans Barrow
East Martin
Townsend Lane
DOWNVIEW RD
Martin
Bustard Manor Farm
Toyd Down
SILLEN LA
Sillen Lane
King's Farm
Kingstown Copse
Windmill Hill
Tidpit
Grim's Ditch
Allen River
Knoll Down
North Allenford Farm
Tidpit Down
4
3
2
1
21
20
19
18
06
07
08

44

67

23

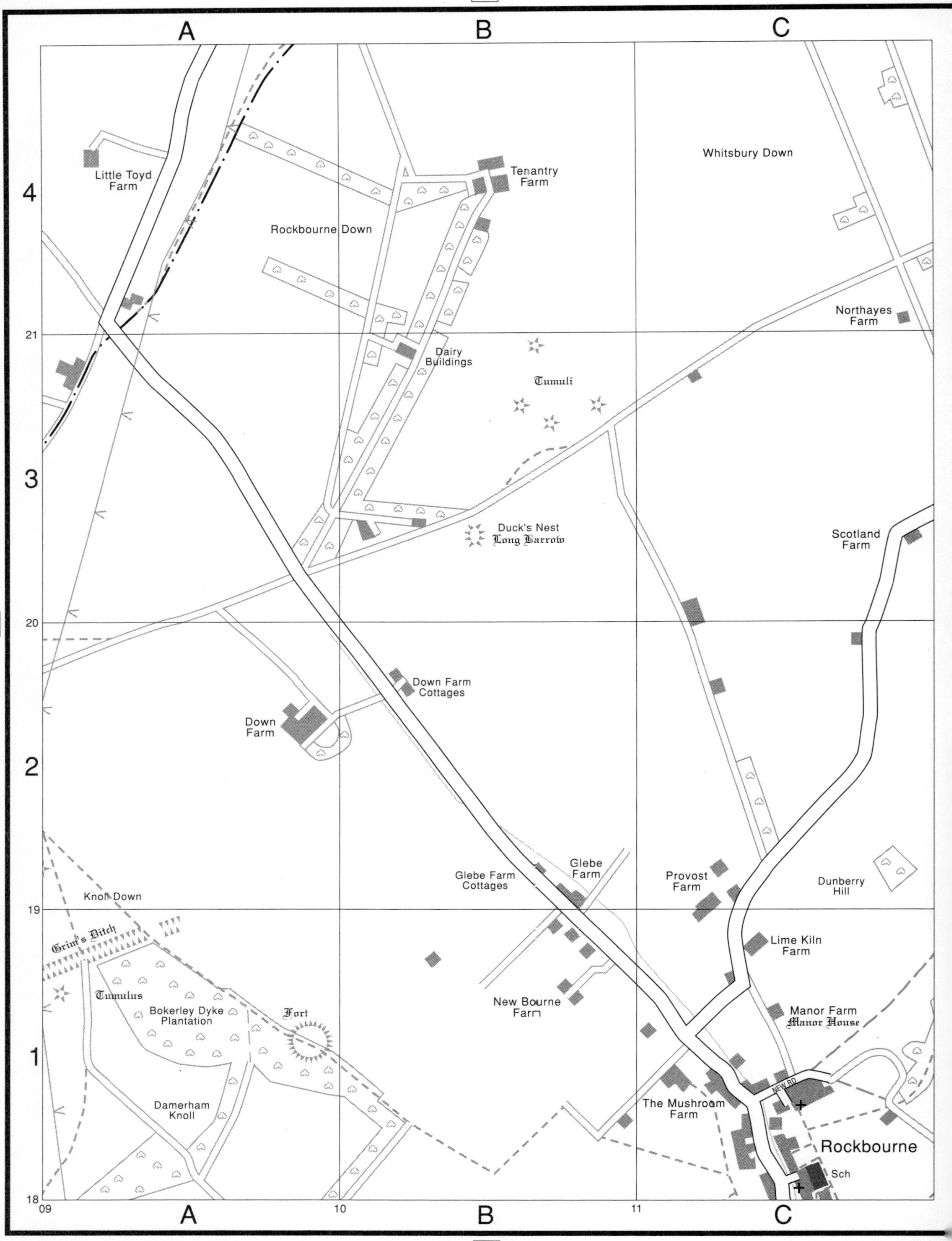
A
B
C
4
3
2
1
21
20
19
18
09
10
11
Little Toyd Farm
Rockbourne Down
Tenantry Farm
Whitsbury Down
Northayes Farm
Dairy Buildings
Tumuli
Duck's Nest
Long Barrow
Scotland Farm
Down Farm Cottages
Down Farm
Glebe Farm Cottages
Glebe Farm
Provost Farm
Dunberry Hill
Knoll Down
Grim's Ditch
Lime Kiln Farm
Tumulus
Bokerley Dyke Plantation
Fort
New Bourne Farm
Manor Farm
Manor House
NEW RD
Damerham Knoll
The Mushroom Farm
Rockbourne
Sch

43

68

not continued, see key diagram

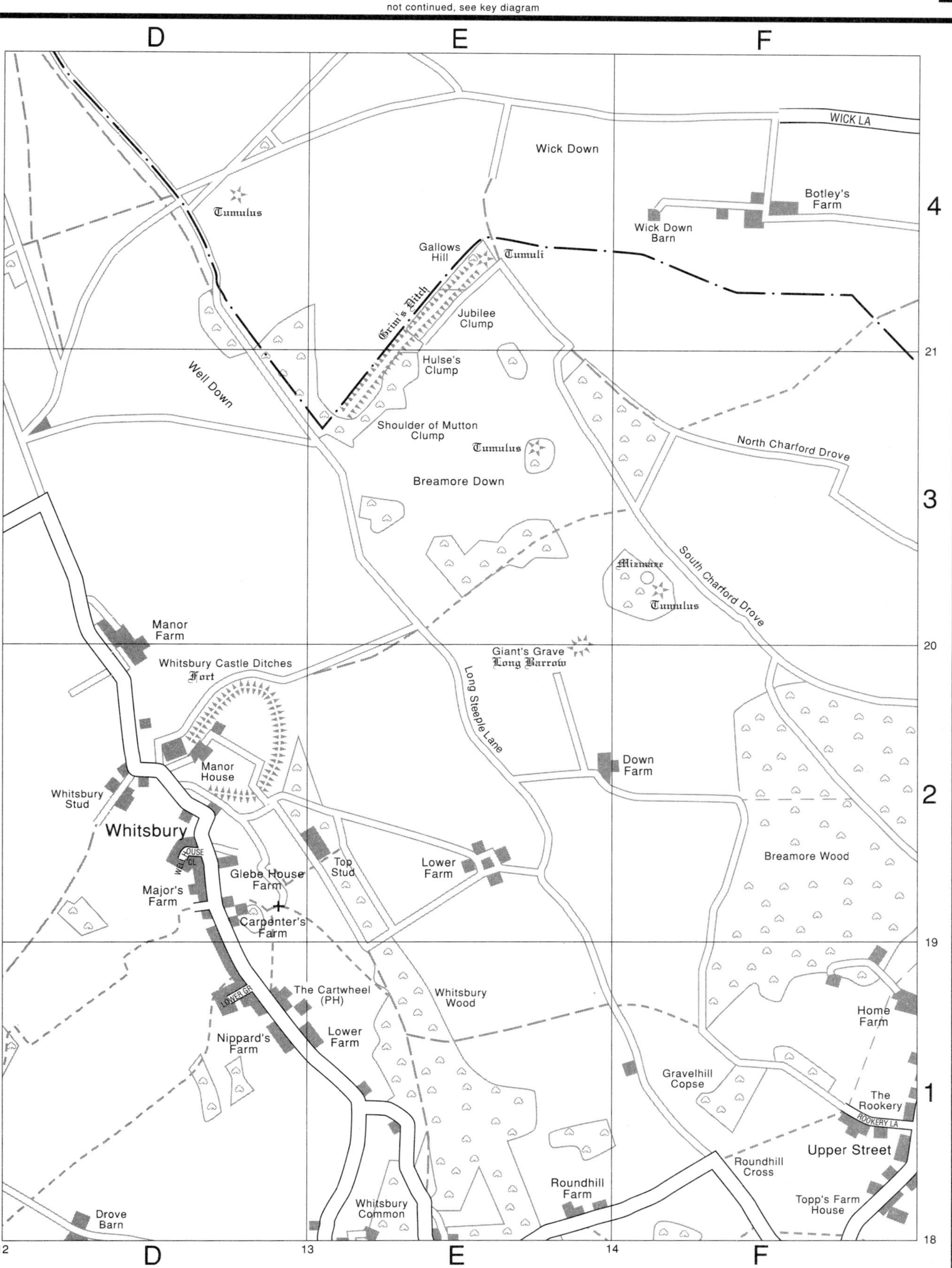

46

69

not continued, see key diagram

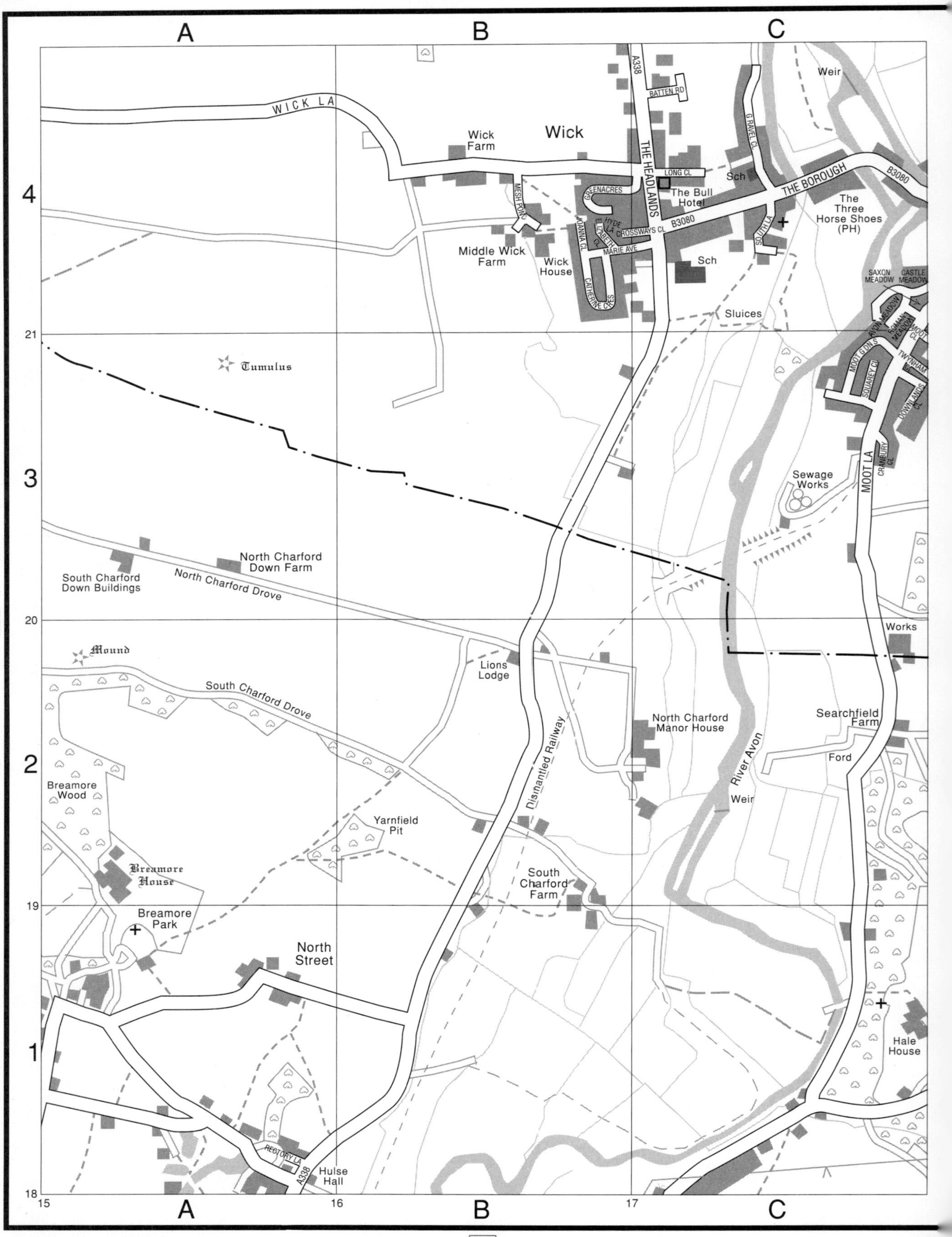

45

70

not continued, see key diagram

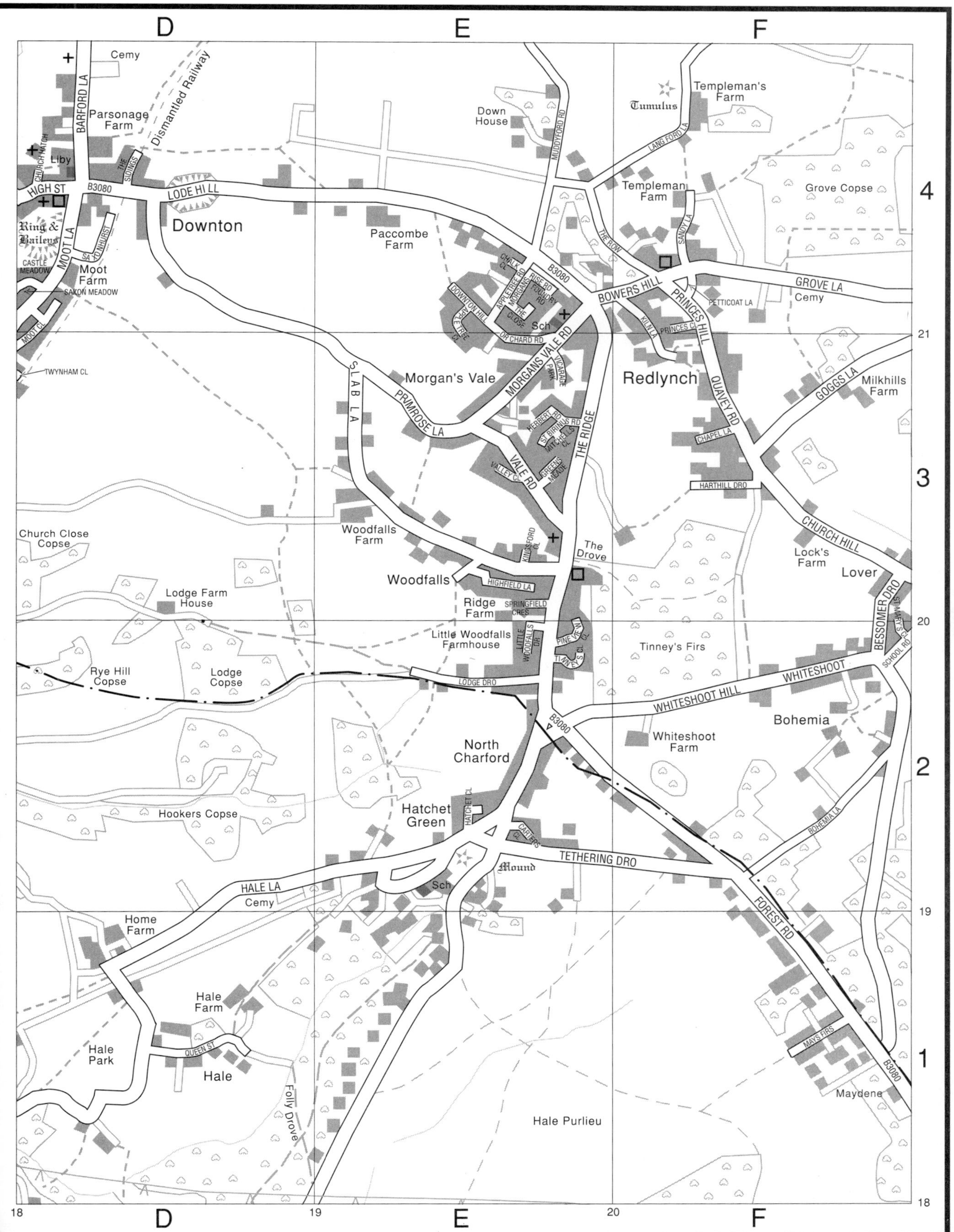

48

not continued, see key diagram

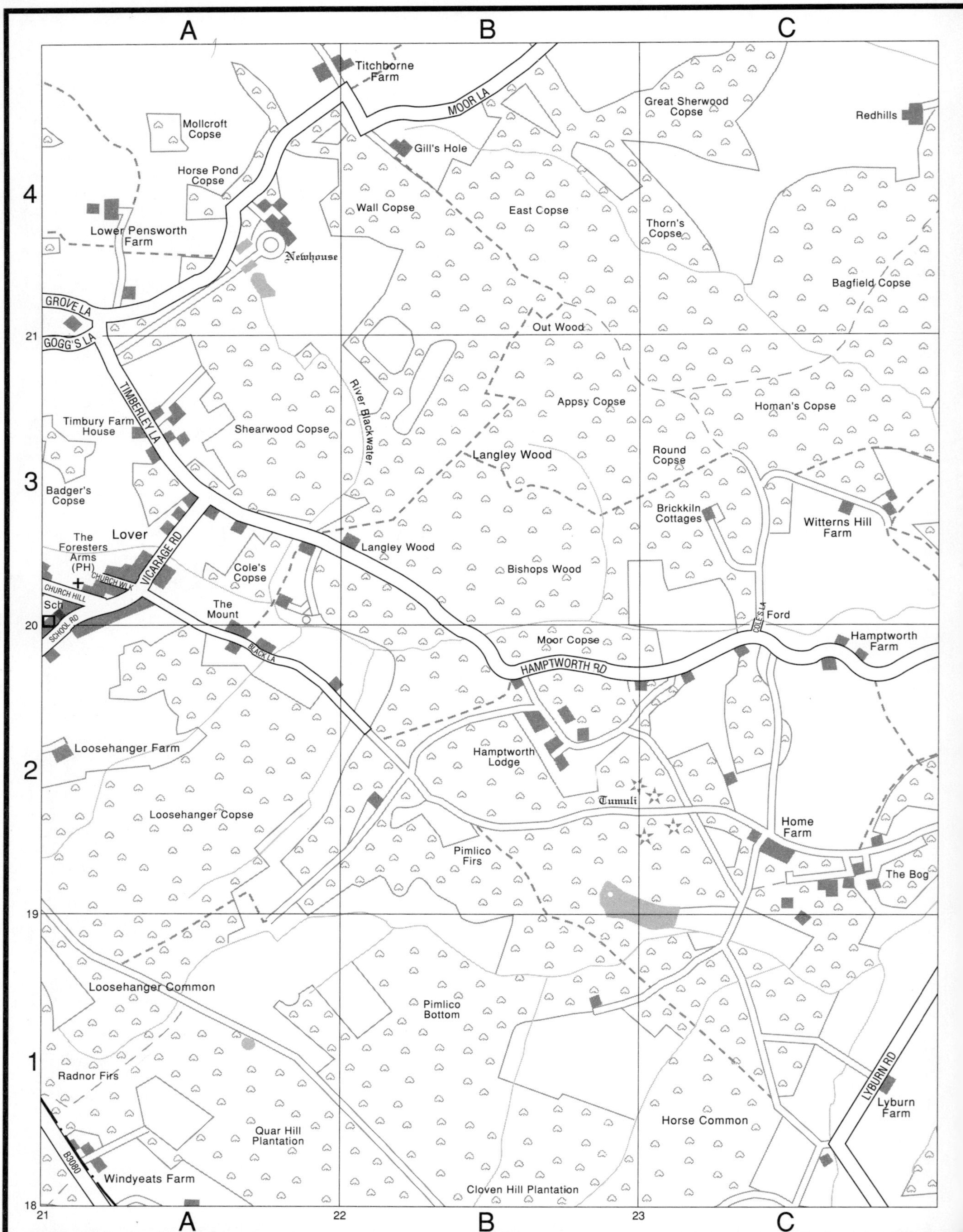

47

72

24

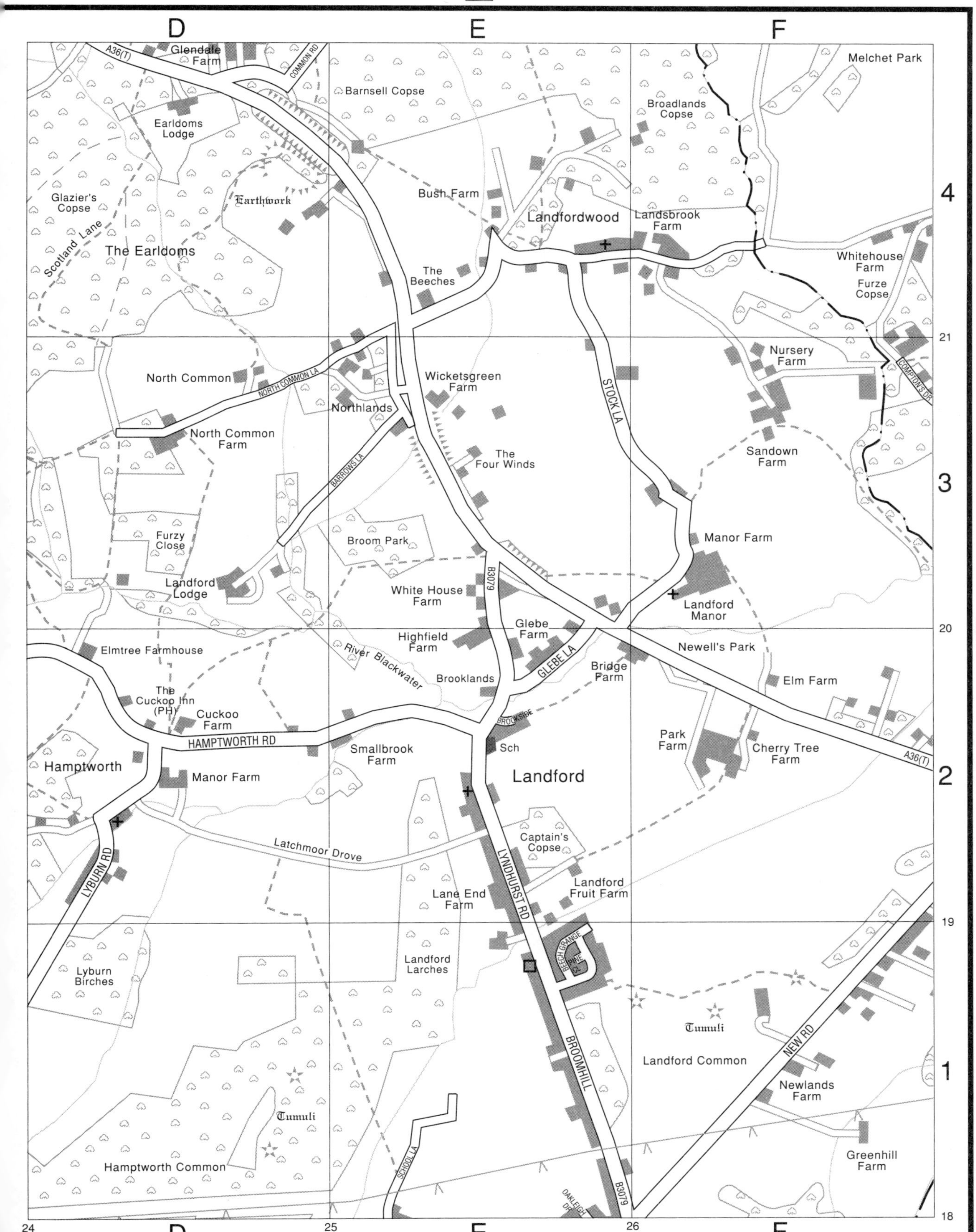
D
E
F
Glendale Farm
COMMON RD
A36(T)
Barnsell Copse
Melchet Park
Earldoms Lodge
Broadlands Copse
Glazier's Copse
Earthwork
Bush Farm
Landfordwood
Landsbrook Farm
4
Scotland Lane
The Earldoms
The Beeches
Whitehouse Farm
Furze Copse
21
Nursery Farm
North Common
NORTH COMMON LA
Wicketsgreen Farm
COMPTON'S DR
Northlands
STOCK LA
North Common Farm
The Four Winds
Sandown Farm
BARROWS LA
3
Broom Park
Furzy Close
Manor Farm
B3079
Landford Lodge
White House Farm
Landford Manor
Glebe Farm
20
Highfield Farm
Newell's Park
Elmtree Farmhouse
River Blackwater
GLEBE LA
Bridge Farm
Brooklands
Elm Farm
The Cuckoo Inn (PH)
Cuckoo Farm
BROOKSIDE
HAMPTWORTH RD
Park Farm
Smallbrook Farm
Sch
Cherry Tree Farm
A36(T)
Hamptworth
Manor Farm
Landford
2
Captain's Copse
Latchmoor Drove
LYBURN RD
LYNDHURST RD
Landford Fruit Farm
Lane End Farm
19
BEECH GRANGE
PINE CL
Lyburn Birches
Landford Larches
Tumuli
NEW RD
BROOMHILL
Landford Common
1
Newlands Farm
Tumuli
SCHOOL LA
Greenhill Farm
Hamptworth Common
OAKLEIGH DR
B3079
18
24
25
26
D
E
F

50

73

25
49
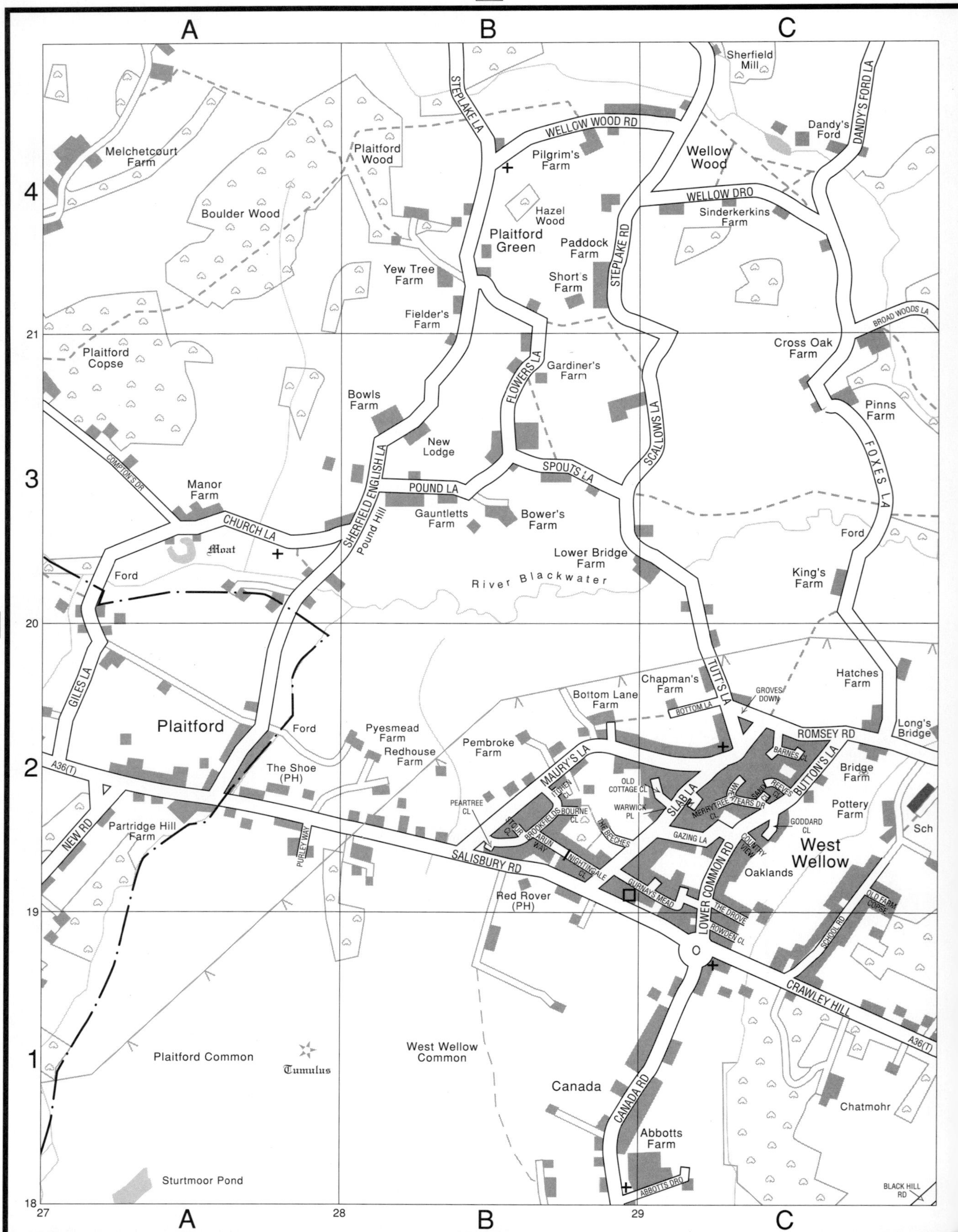

A
B
C
4
3
2
1
21
20
19
18
27
28
29
Melchetcourt Farm
Boulder Wood
Plaitford Wood
Steplake La
Wellow Wood Rd
Pilgrim's Farm
Hazel Wood
Plaitford Green
Paddock Farm
Short's Farm
Steplake Rd
Sherfield Mill
Wellow Wood
Dandy's Ford
Dandy's Ford La
Wellow Dro
Sinderkerkins Farm
Yew Tree Farm
Fielder's Farm
Broad Woods La
Cross Oak Farm
Plaitford Copse
Bowls Farm
Flowers La
Gardiner's Farm
Pinns Farm
New Lodge
Scallows La
Foxes La
Compton's Dr
Manor Farm
Sherfield English La
Pound La
Spouts La
Gauntletts Farm
Bower's Farm
Church La
Pound Hill
Moat
Ford
Lower Bridge Farm
River Blackwater
King's Farm
Giles La
Tutt's La
Chapman's Farm
Bottom Lane Farm
Groves Down
Bottom La
Hatches Farm
Long's Bridge
Romsey Rd
Plaitford
Pyesmead Farm
Redhouse Farm
Pembroke Farm
Maury's La
Barnes Cl
Button's La
Bridge Farm
A36(T)
The Shoe (PH)
Old Cottage Cl
Slab La
Merrytree Cl
Whitfears Dr
Reeves Cl
Sandy Cl
Pottery Farm
Itchen Cl
Peartree Cl
Bourne Cl
Warwick Pl
Goddard Cl
Sch
New Rd
Partridge Hill Farm
Purley Way
Stour Cl
Brookfields
Arun Way
The Beeches
Gazing La
Country View
West Wellow
Salisbury Rd
Nightingale Cl
Lower Common Rd
Oaklands
Gurnays Mead
The Drove
Rowden Cl
Old Farm Copse
Red Rover (PH)
School Rd
Crawley Hill
A36(T)
Plaitford Common
Tumulus
West Wellow Common
Canada
Canada Rd
Chatmohr
Abbotts Farm
Abbotts Dro
Sturtmoor Pond
Black Hill Rd

74

26

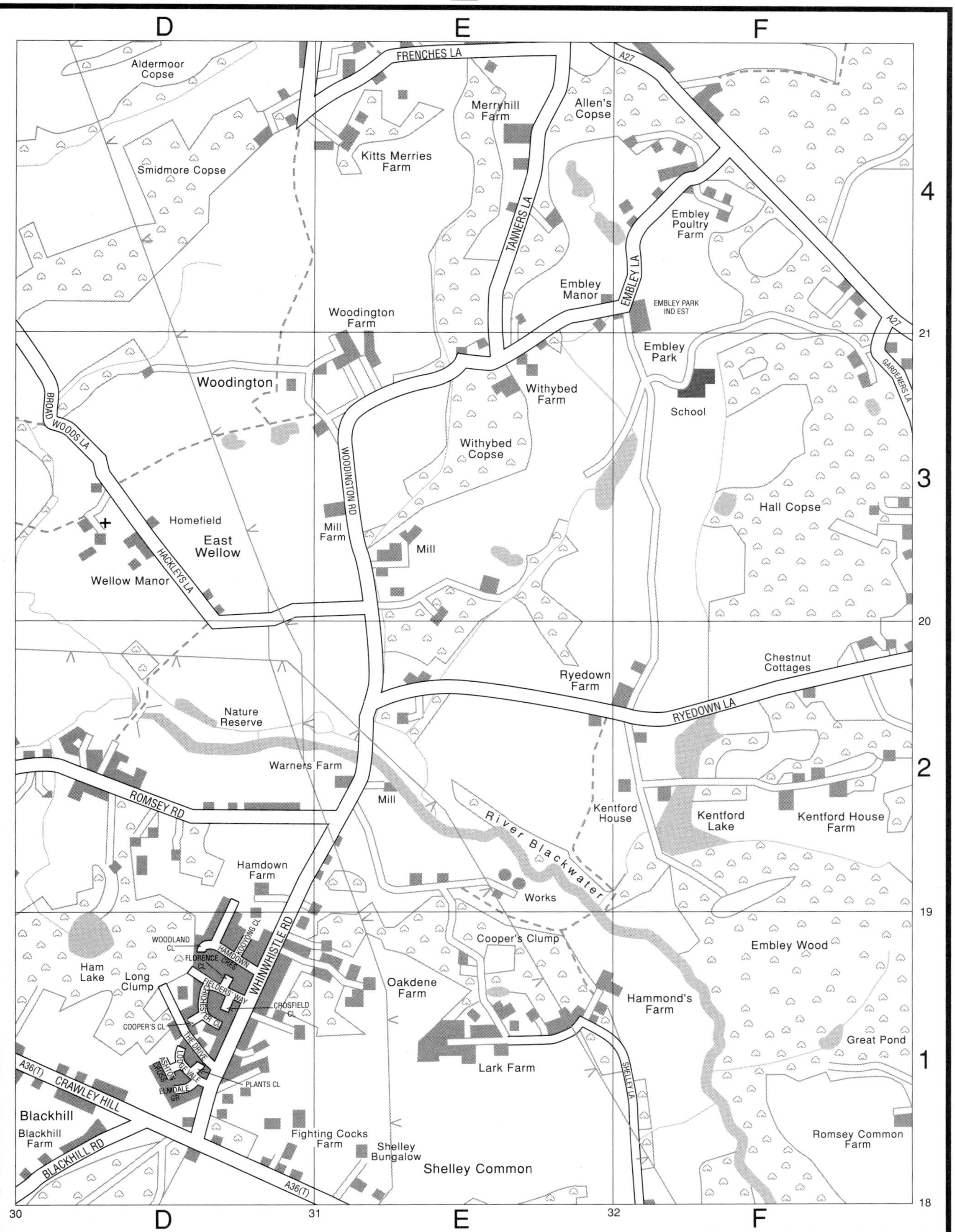

D
E
F
Aldermoor Copse
FRENCHES LA
A27
Merryhill Farm
Allen's Copse
Kitts Merries Farm
Smidmore Copse
4
TANNERS LA
Embley Poultry Farm
Embley Manor
EMBLEY LA
EMBLEY PARK IND EST
A27
Woodington Farm
21
Embley Park
GARDENERS LA
Woodington
BROAD WOODS LA
Withybed Farm
School
Withybed Copse
WOODINGTON RD
3
Hall Copse
Homefield
East Wellow
Mill Farm
Mill
HACKLEYS LA
Wellow Manor
20
Chestnut Cottages
Ryedown Farm
RYEDOWN LA
Nature Reserve
2
Warners Farm
Mill
ROMSEY RD
River Blackwater
Kentford House
Kentford Lake
Kentford House Farm
Hamdown Farm
Works
19
WHINWHISTLE RD
Cooper's Clump
Embley Wood
WOODLAND CL
KOOYONG CL
HAMDOWN CRES
FLORENCE CL
Ham Lake
Long Clump
FIELDERS' WAY
CHICHESTER CL
CROSFIELD CL
Oakdene Farm
Hammond's Farm
COOPER'S CL
THE DRIVE
Great Pond
1
A36(T)
CRAWLEY HILL
ASHTON CROSS
LODGE VALE
ELMDALE GR
PLANTS CL
Lark Farm
SHELLEY LA
Blackhill
Blackhill Farm
BLACKHILL RD
Fighting Cocks Farm
Shelley Bungalow
Romsey Common Farm
Shelley Common
A36(T)
18
30
31
32
D
E
F

52

75

27

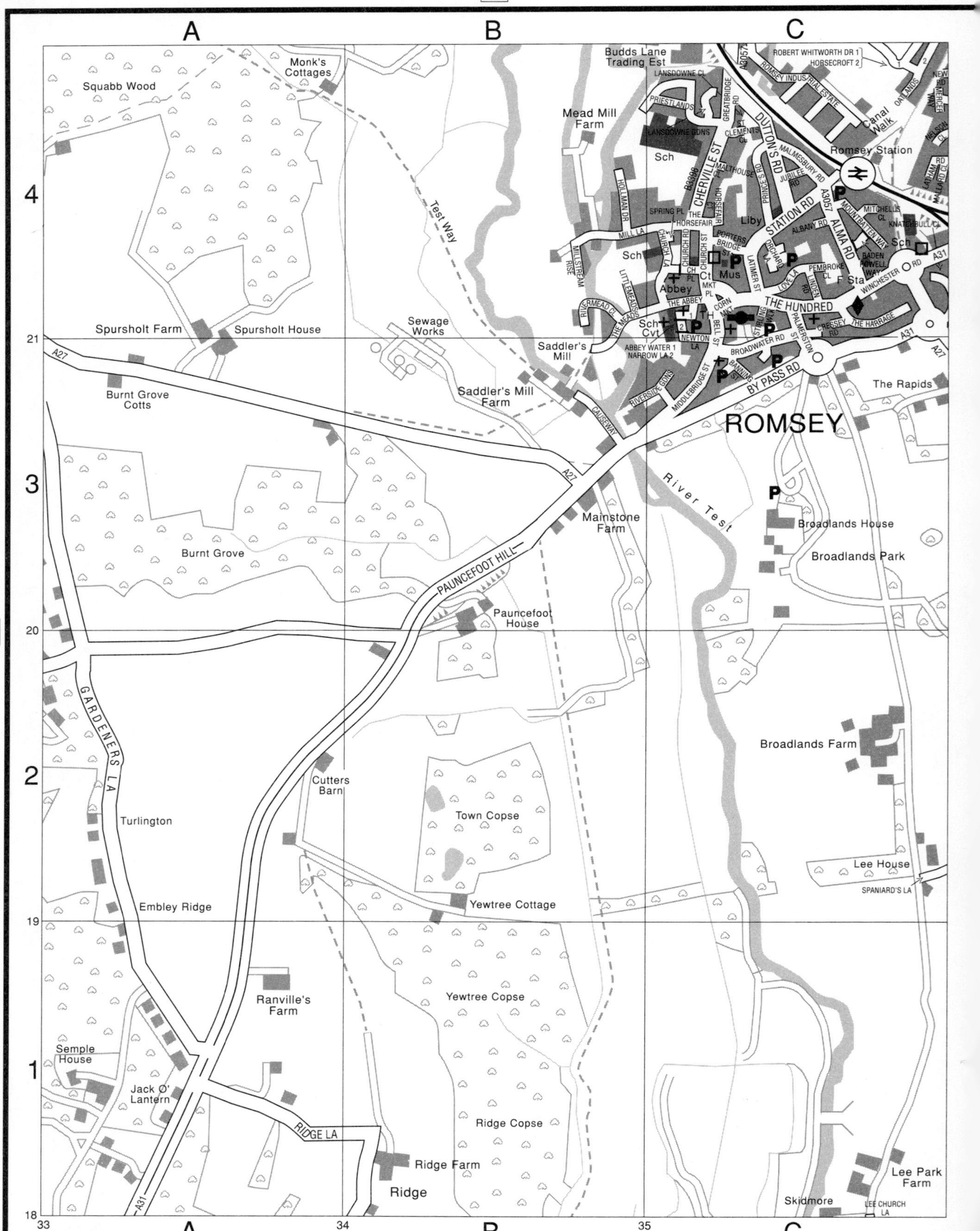
A
B
C
4
3
2
1
21
20
19
18
33
34
35
Squabb Wood
Monk's Cottages
Budds Lane Trading Est
Mead Mill Farm
Romsey Station
Canal Walk
Sch
Liby
Test Way
Abbey
Mus
Ct
F Sta
Spursholt Farm
Spursholt House
Sewage Works
Saddler's Mill
Saddler's Mill Farm
Burnt Grove Cotts
ROMSEY
The Rapids
River Test
Mainstone Farm
Broadlands House
Broadlands Park
Burnt Grove
PAUNCEFOOT HILL
Pauncefoot House
GARDENERS LA
Broadlands Farm
Cutters Barn
Town Copse
Turlington
Lee House
SPANIARD'S LA
Embley Ridge
Yewtree Cottage
Ranville's Farm
Yewtree Copse
Semple House
Jack O' Lantern
RIDGE LA
Ridge Copse
Ridge Farm
Ridge
Lee Park Farm
Skidmore
LEE CHURCH LA
A27
A31
A3057
B3398
THE HUNDRED
BY PASS RD
STATION RD
DUTTON'S RD
CHERVILLE ST
ALMA RD
THE HARRAGE
CAUSEWAY
BROADWATER RD
PALMERSTON ST
MIDDLEBRIDGE ST
RIVERSIDE GDNS
HOLLMAN DR
MILL LA
MILLSTREAM RISE
THE MEADS
ROMSEY INDUSTRIAL ESTATE
ROBERT WHITWORTH DR 1
HORSECROFT 2

51

76

28

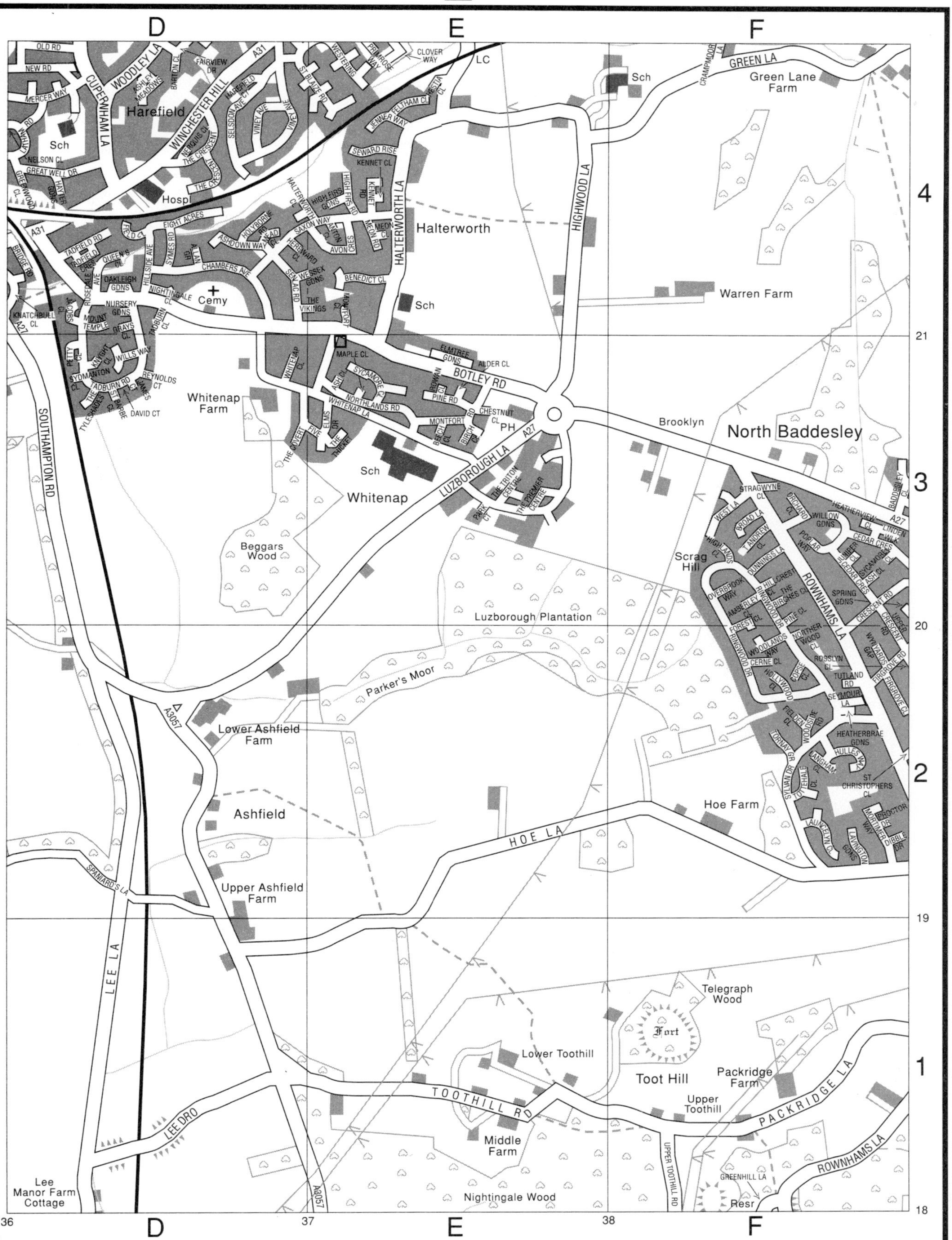

D
E
F
4
3
2
1
21
20
19
18
36
37
38
OLD RD
NEW RD
MERCER WAY
CUPERNHAM LA
WOODLEY LA
ASHLEY MEADOWS
BARTON CL
FAIRVIEW DR
A31
WINCHESTER HILL
SELSDON AVE
VINEY AVE
ST BLAIZE RD
WESTERING
PRIMROSE WAY
CLOVER WAY
LC
Harefield
Sch
NELSON CL
GREAT WELL DR
GREENWOOD CL
HAYTER GDNS
THE CRESCENT
Hospl
JENNER WAY
FELTHAM CL
SEWARD RISE
KENNET CL
HIGH FIRS RD
HIGH FIRS GDNS
HALTERWORTH CL
HALTERWORTH LA
Halterworth
HIGHWOOD LA
Sch
GREEN LA
CRAMPMOOR LA
Green Lane Farm
EIGHT ACRES
A31
BRIDGE RD
TADFIELD RD
QUEEN'S CL
SYMES RD
HOLYBORNE RD
ASHDOWN WAY
SAXON WAY
AVON CRES
HILLSIDE AVE
CHAMBERS AVE
OAKLEIGH GDNS
NIGHTINGALE AVE
Cemy
WESSEX GDNS
BENEDICT CL
THE VIKINGS
MONTFORT CL
Sch
Warren Farm
KNATCHBULL CL
A27
NURSERY GDNS
MOUNT TEMPLE
GRAYS CL
TADBURN CL
WILLS WAY
SYDMANTON CL
TADBURN RD
REYNOLDS CT
DAVID CT
TYLESHADES
ST BARBE CL
ELMTREE GDNS
ALDER CL
MAPLE CL
SYCAMORE CL
BOTLEY RD
PINE RD
CHESTNUT CL
NORTHLANDS RD
WHITENAP LA
WHITENAP CL
MONTFORT CL
BEECH CL
BIRCH CL
PH
A27
Whitenap Farm
SOUTHAMPTON RD
THE COVERT
FIVE ELMS DR
THE THICKET
Sch
LUZBOROUGH LA
THE TRITON CENTRE
THE PREMIER CENTRE
PARK CT
Whitenap
Brooklyn
North Baddesley
STRAGWYNE CL
WEST LA
BROAD LA
ORCHARD CL
HEATHERVIEW CL
WILLOW GDNS
A27
LINDEN WLK
BADDESLEY
HIGHLANDS CL
ANDREW CL
POPLAR WAY
CEDAR CRES
JUNIPER CL
SYCAMORE CL
Scrag Hill
Beggars Wood
DUNNINGS LA
ROWNHAMS LA
OVERBROOK WAY
HILLCREST CL
THE BIRCHES CL
SPRING GDNS
CRESCENT RD
UPPER CRESCENT RD
AMBERLEY CL
RINGWOOD DR
PINE CL
Luzborough Plantation
FOREST CL
WOODLANDS WAY
NORTHERWOOD CL
ROSSLYN CL
TUTLAND RD
FIRGROVE RD
FIRGROVE CL
CERNE CL
HOLLYWOOD CL
COPSE CL
SEYMOUR LA
Parker's Moor
A3057
Lower Ashfield Farm
FIELDEN CL
WOODSIDE RD
HEATHERBRAE GDNS
TORNAY GR
LANGHAM CL
HULLES WAY
ST CHRISTOPHERS CL
SYLVAN DR
TOTEHALE CL
Ashfield
Hoe Farm
HOE LA
LAUNCELYN CL
LAVINGTON GDNS
MORTIMER WAY
PROCTOR DR
DIBBLE DR
SPANIARD'S LA
Upper Ashfield Farm
LEE LA
Telegraph Wood
Fort
Lower Toothill
Toot Hill
Packridge Farm
TOOTHILL RD
Upper Toothill
PACKRIDGE LA
LEE DRO
Middle Farm
UPPER TOOTHILL RD
ROWNHAMS LA
GREENHILL LA
A3057
Lee Manor Farm Cottage
Nightingale Wood
Resr

54

77

29

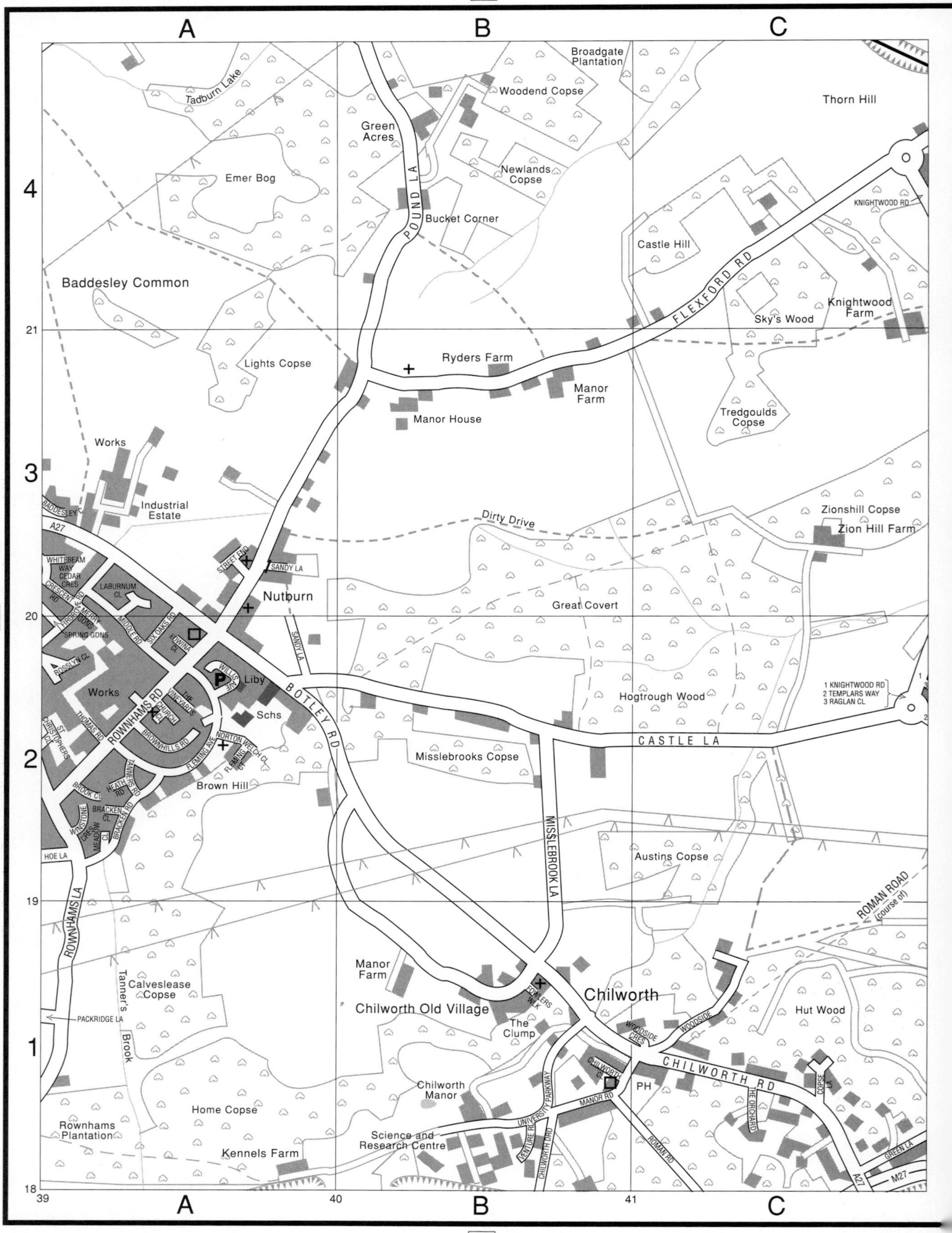

A
B
C
4
3
2
1
21
20
19
18
39
40
41
Tadburn Lake
Broadgate Plantation
Woodend Copse
Thorn Hill
Green Acres
Emer Bog
Newlands Copse
POUND LA
Bucket Corner
KNIGHTWOOD RD
Castle Hill
Baddesley Common
FLEXFORD RD
Knightwood Farm
Sky's Wood
Lights Copse
Ryders Farm
Manor Farm
Manor House
Tredgoulds Copse
Works
Industrial Estate
BADDESLEY CL
A27
Dirty Drive
Zionshill Copse
Zion Hill Farm
WHITEBEAM WAY
CEDAR CRES
CRESCENT RD
LABURNUM CL
STREET END
SANDY LA
Nutburn
Great Covert
MERRY GDNS
FIRGROVE RD
MIDDLE RD
SIX OAKS RD
EDWINA CL
SPRING GDNS
ROSSLYN CL
WILLIS AVE
Liby
SANDY LA
BOTLEY RD
Hogtrough Wood
1 KNIGHTWOOD RD
2 TEMPLARS WAY
3 RAGLAN CL
Works
ROWNHAMS RD
THE VINEYARDS
CHURCH CL
Schs
ST CHRISTOPHERS CL
THOMAS RD
BROWNHILLS RD
NORTON WELCH CL
CASTLE LA
FLEMING AVE
FLEMING CL
Misslebrooks Copse
TANNERS RD
HEATH RD
BROOK CL
Brown Hill
BRACKEN CL
WINSTONE CRES
MEADOW CL
BRACKEN RD
MISSLEBROOK LA
HOE LA
Austins Copse
ROWNHAMS LA
ROMAN ROAD (course of)
Manor Farm
Calveslease Copse
Tanner's Brook
Chilworth Old Village
FOWLERS WLK
Chilworth
Hut Wood
PACKRIDGE LA
The Clump
WOODSIDE CRES
WOODSIDE
CHILWORTH CL
CHILWORTH RD
Chilworth Manor
PH
COPSE LA
THE ORCHARD
Home Copse
UNIVERSITY PARKWAY
MANOR RD
Rownhams Plantation
Science and Research Centre
VENTURE RD
CHILWORTH DRO
ROMAN RD
Kennels Farm
GREEN LA
A27
M27

53

78

30

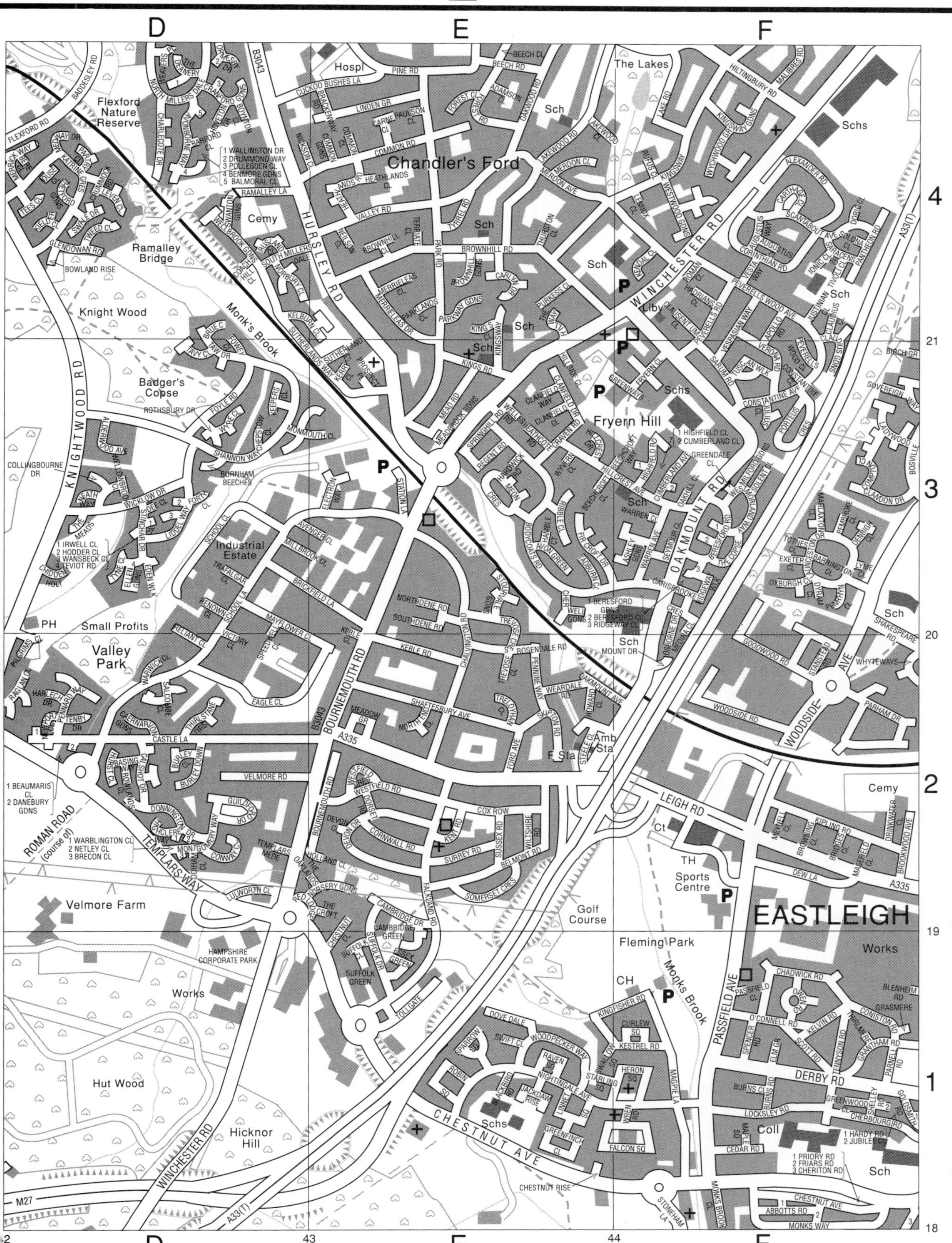

Chandler's Ford
EASTLEIGH
Flexford Nature Reserve
Ramalley Bridge
Knight Wood
Badger's Copse
Monk's Brook
Industrial Estate
Small Profits
Valley Park
Velmore Farm
Hampshire Corporate Park
Works
Hut Wood
Hicknor Hill
Fryern Hill
The Lakes
Golf Course
Fleming Park
Monks Brook
Sports Centre
KNIGHTWOOD RD
HURSLEY RD
WINCHESTER RD
BOURNEMOUTH RD
OAKMOUNT RD
CHESTNUT AVE
TEMPLARS WAY
PASSFIELD AVE
LEIGH RD
DERBY RD
CASTLE LA
ROMAN ROAD (course of)
WOODSIDE AVE
M27
A33(T)
A335
B3043
1 WALLINGTON DR
2 DRUMMOND WAY
3 POLLESDEN CL
4 BENMORE GDNS
5 BALMORAL CL
1 IRWELL CL
2 HODDER CL
3 WANSBECK CL
4 TEVIOT RD
1 BEAUMARIS CL
2 DANEBURY GDNS
1 WARBLINGTON CL
2 NETLEY CL
3 BRECON CL
1 HIGHFIELD CL
2 CUMBERLAND CL
1 BERESFORD GDNS
2 BERESFORD CL
3 RIDGEWAY CL
1 HARDY RD
2 JUBILEE CL
1 PRIORY RD
2 FRIARS RD
3 CHERITON RD
D
E
F
4
3
2
1
21
20
19
18
43
44

56

79

31

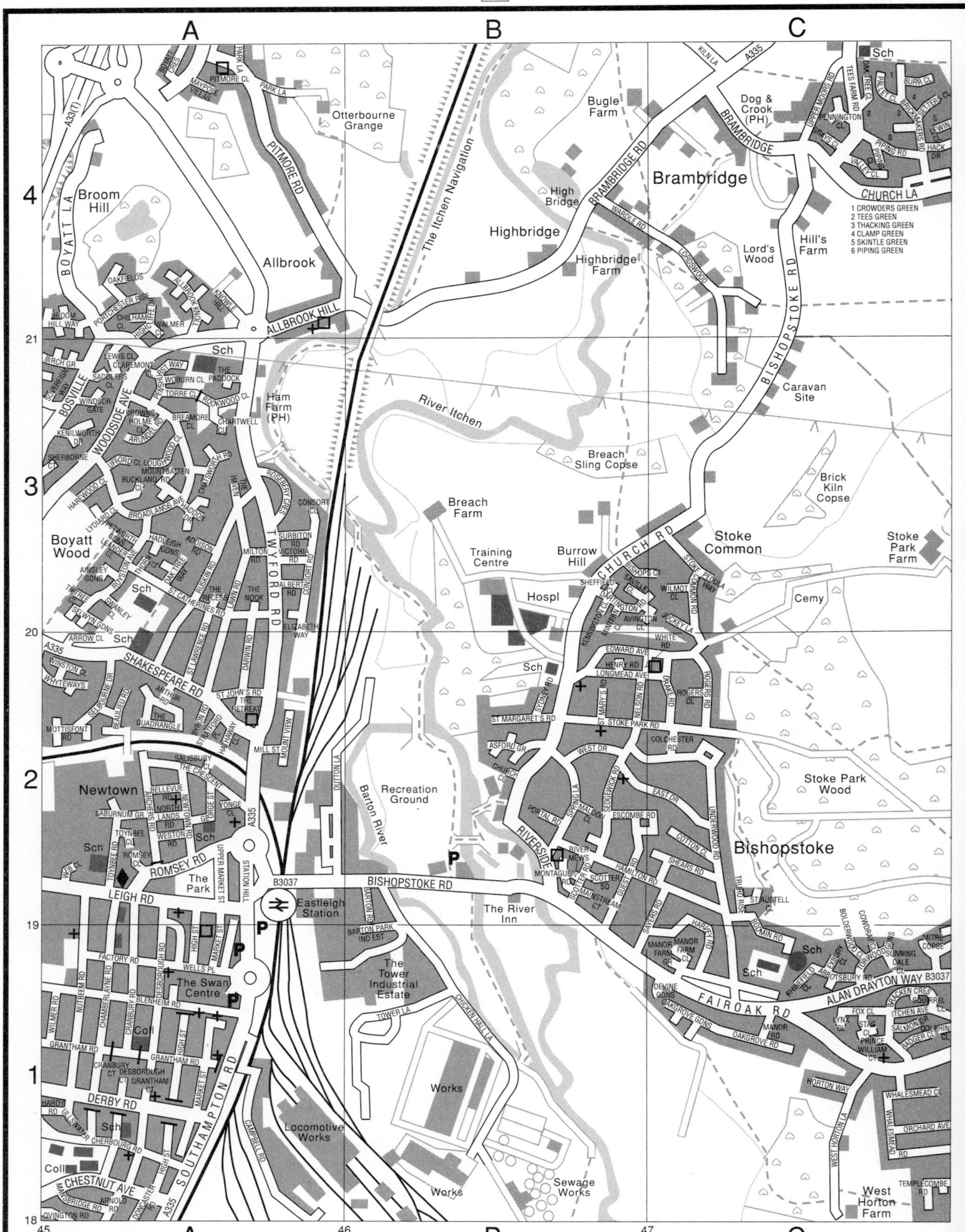

A
B
C
4
3
2
1
21
20
19
18
45
46
47
Broom Hill
Allbrook
Otterbourne Grange
Bugle Farm
Dog & Crook (PH)
Brambridge
High Bridge
Highbridge
Highbridge Farm
Lord's Wood
Hill's Farm
1 CROWDERS GREEN
2 TEES GREEN
3 THACKING GREEN
4 CLAMP GREEN
5 SKINTLE GREEN
6 PIPING GREEN
The Itchen Navigation
River Itchen
Ham Farm (PH)
Caravan Site
Breach Sling Copse
Brick Kiln Copse
Breach Farm
Training Centre
Burrow Hill
Stoke Common
Stoke Park Farm
Hospl
Cemy
Boyatt Wood
Sch
Newtown
Recreation Ground
Barton River
Stoke Park Wood
Bishopstoke
The Park
Eastleigh Station
The River Inn
The Swan Centre
Coll
The Tower Industrial Estate
Works
Locomotive Works
Sewage Works
West Horton Farm
BOYATT LA
PITMORE RD
ALLBROOK HILL
BRAMBRIDGE RD
BRAMBRIDGE
CHURCH LA
BISHOPSTOKE RD
WOODSIDE AVE
TWYFORD RD
SHAKESPEARE RD
CHURCH RD
STOKE COMMON RD
RIVERSIDE
BISHOPSTOKE RD
B3037
A335
A33(T)
LEIGH RD
ROMSEY RD
SOUTHAMPTON RD
DERBY RD
CHESTNUT AVE
FAIR OAK RD
ALAN DRAYTON WAY
OAKGROVE RD
CHICKEN HALL LA
TOWER LA
WEST HORTON LA

55

80

32

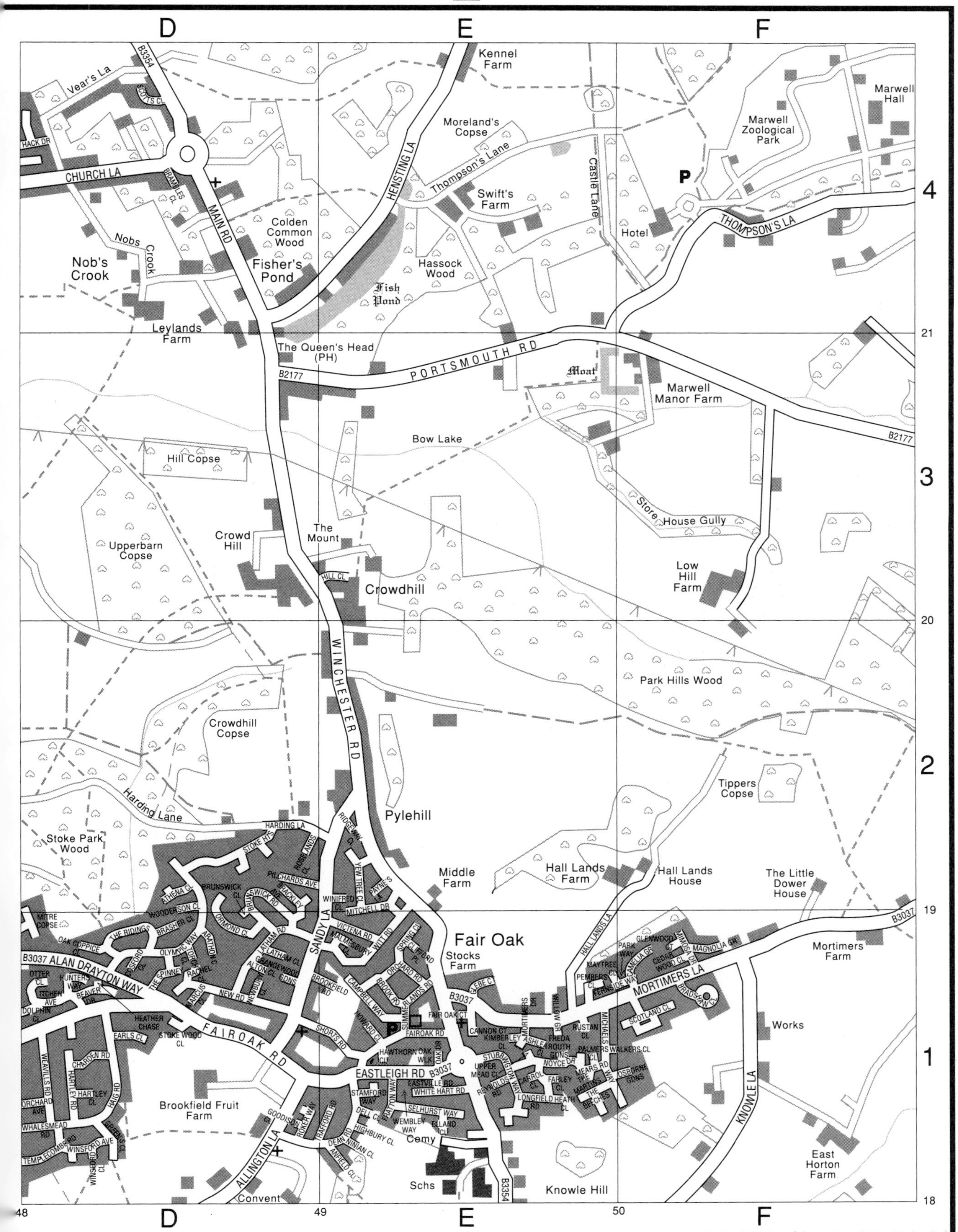
D
E
F
Kennel Farm
Marwell Hall
Marwell Zoological Park
Moreland's Copse
Thompson's Lane
Castle Lane
Hotel
THOMPSON'S LA
Year's La
B3354
CHURCH LA
HACK DR
MAIN RD
Nobs Crook
Nob's Crook
Colden Common Wood
Fisher's Pond
HENSTING LA
Swift's Farm
Hassock Wood
Fish Pond
Leylands Farm
The Queen's Head (PH)
PORTSMOUTH RD
B2177
Moat
Marwell Manor Farm
Bow Lake
Hill Copse
Store House Gully
Upperbarn Copse
Crowd Hill
The Mount
HILL CL
Crowdhill
Low Hill Farm
WINCHESTER RD
Park Hills Wood
Crowdhill Copse
Harding Lane
HARDING LA
Tippers Copse
Pylehill
Stoke Park Wood
Middle Farm
Hall Lands Farm
Hall Lands House
The Little Dower House
Fair Oak
Stocks Farm
SANDY LA
Mortimers Farm
MORTIMERS LA
HALL LANDS LA
B3037
B3037 ALAN DRAYTON WAY
FAIROAK RD
Works
Brookfield Fruit Farm
EASTLEIGH RD
ALLINGTON LA
Cemy
Schs
Convent
Knowle Hill
KNOWLE LA
East Horton Farm
48
49
50
18
19
20
21
1
2
3
4

58

81

33

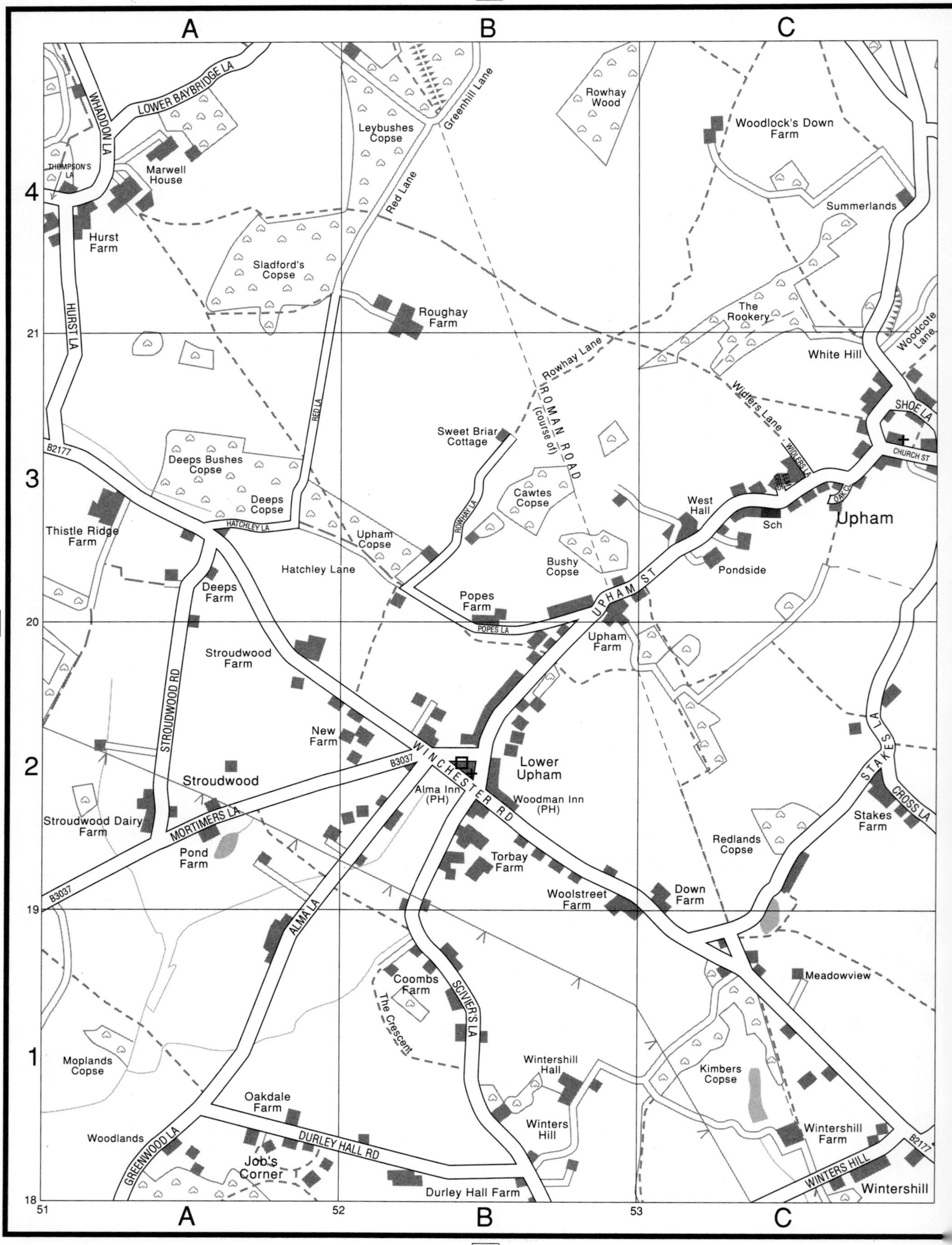

A
B
C
4
3
2
1
21
20
19
18
51
52
53
LOWER BAYBRIDGE LA
WHADDON LA
THOMPSON'S LA
Marwell House
Hurst Farm
HURST LA
Leybushes Copse
Greenhill Lane
Red Lane
Rowhay Wood
Woodlock's Down Farm
Summerlands
Sladford's Copse
Roughay Farm
The Rookery
Woodcote Lane
White Hill
Rowhay Lane
ROMAN ROAD (course of)
Widlers Lane
SHOE LA
CHURCH ST
RED LA
B2177
Sweet Briar Cottage
Deeps Bushes Copse
Deeps Copse
HATCHLEY LA
Thistle Ridge Farm
Cawtes Copse
ROWHAY LA
WIDLERS LA
ELM CRES
OAK CL
West Hall
Sch
Upham
Upham Copse
Hatchley Lane
Bushy Copse
Pondside
Deeps Farm
Popes Farm
POPES LA
UPHAM ST
Upham Farm
Stroudwood Farm
STROUDWOOD RD
New Farm
WINCHESTER RD
B3037
Stroudwood
Lower Upham
Alma Inn (PH)
Woodman Inn (PH)
STAKES LA
CROSS LA
Stroudwood Dairy Farm
MORTIMERS LA
Pond Farm
Redlands Copse
Stakes Farm
Torbay Farm
B3037
Woolstreet Farm
Down Farm
ALMA LA
Coombs Farm
The Crescent
SCIVIER'S LA
Meadowview
Moplands Copse
Wintershill Hall
Kimbers Copse
Oakdale Farm
Winters Hill
Wintershill Farm
Woodlands
GREENWOOD LA
DURLEY HALL RD
Job's Corner
B2177
WINTERS HILL
Wintershill
Durley Hall Farm

57

82

34

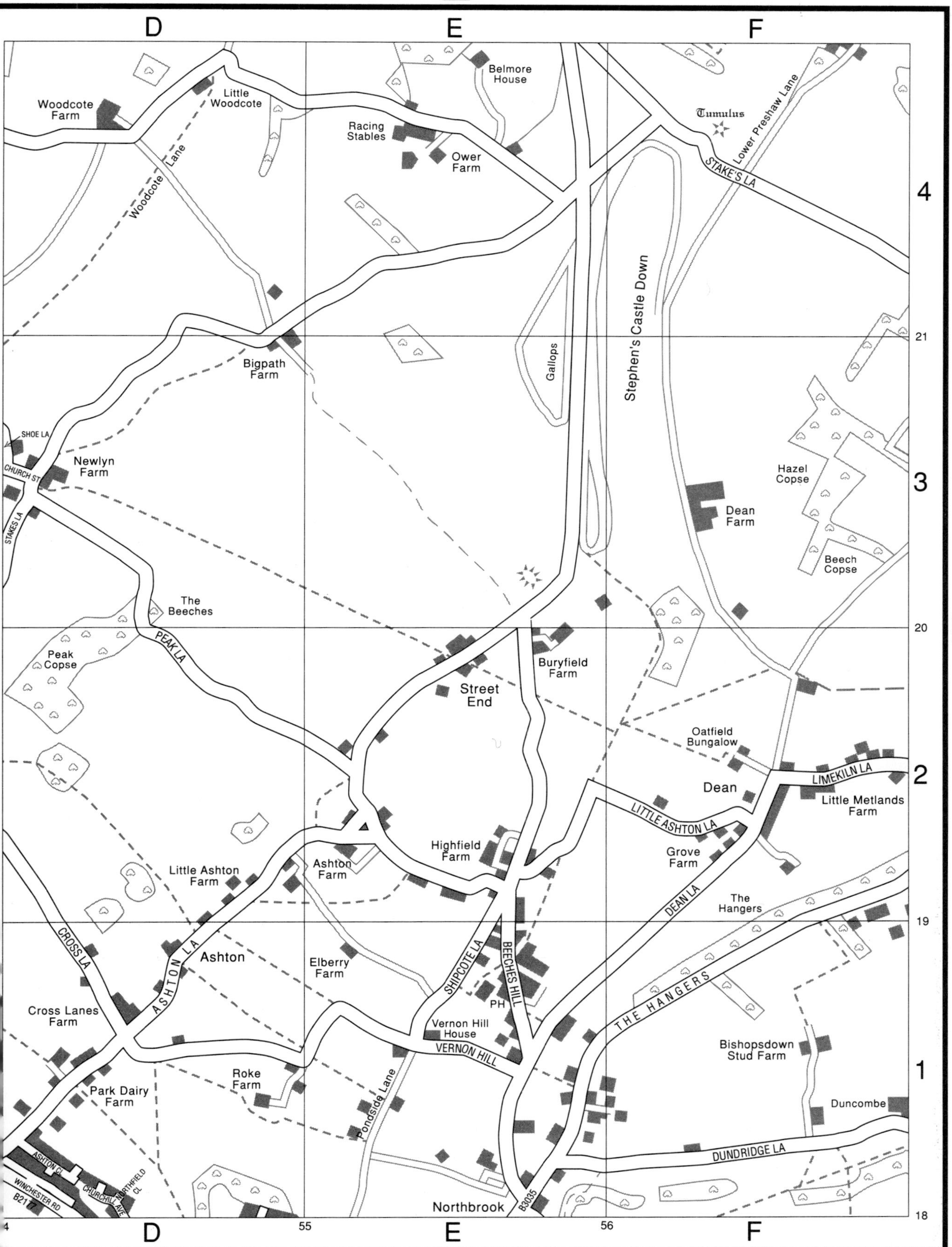
D
E
F
Woodcote Farm
Little Woodcote
Woodcote Lane
Belmore House
Racing Stables
Ower Farm
Tumulus
Lower Preshaw Lane
STAKE'S LA
4
21
Bigpath Farm
Gallops
Stephen's Castle Down
SHOE LA
CHURCH ST
Newlyn Farm
STAKES LA
3
Hazel Copse
Dean Farm
Beech Copse
The Beeches
20
Peak Copse
PEAK LA
Buryfield Farm
Street End
Oatfield Bungalow
Dean
LIMEKILN LA
2
Little Metlands Farm
LITTLE ASHTON LA
Grove Farm
Highfield Farm
Ashton Farm
Little Ashton Farm
DEAN LA
The Hangers
19
CROSS LA
ASHTON LA
Ashton
Elberry Farm
SHIPCOTE LA
BEECHES HILL
PH
THE HANGERS
Cross Lanes Farm
Vernon Hill House
VERNON HILL
Bishopsdown Stud Farm
1
Roke Farm
Park Dairy Farm
Pondside Lane
Duncombe
DUNDRIDGE LA
ASHTON CL
NORTHFIELD CL
CHURCHILL AVE
WINCHESTER RD
B2177
B3035
Northbrook
18
4
55
56

60

83

35

59

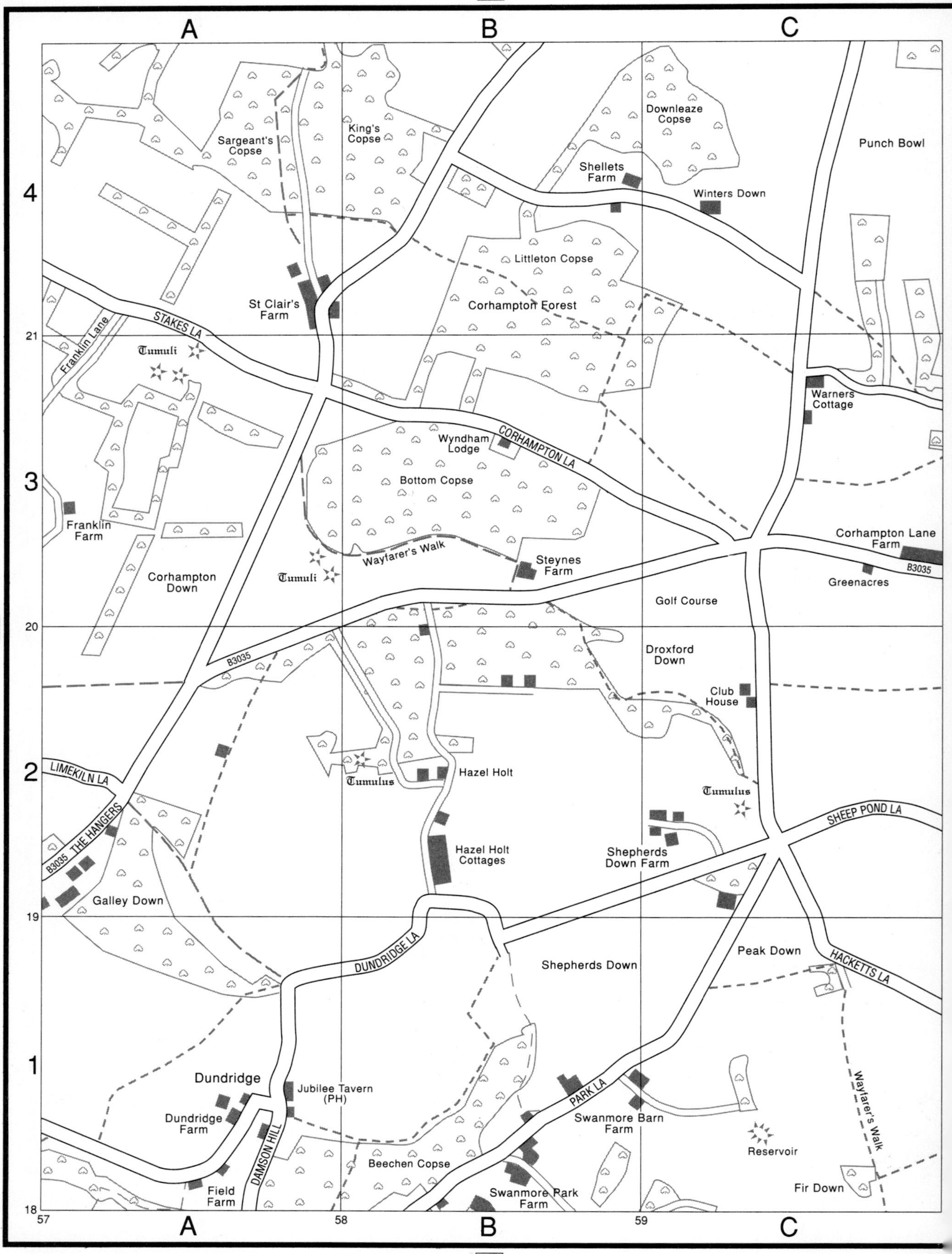

A
B
C
4
3
2
1
21
20
19
18
57
58
59
Sargeant's Copse
King's Copse
Downleaze Copse
Punch Bowl
Shellets Farm
Winters Down
Littleton Copse
St Clair's Farm
Corhampton Forest
STAKES LA
Franklin Lane
Tumuli
Warners Cottage
Wyndham Lodge
CORHAMPTON LA
Bottom Copse
Franklin Farm
Corhampton Lane Farm
Wayfarer's Walk
Steynes Farm
B3035
Greenacres
Corhampton Down
Tumuli
Golf Course
Droxford Down
B3035
Club House
LIMEKILN LA
Hazel Holt
Tumulus
Tumulus
SHEEP POND LA
B3035 THE HANGERS
Hazel Holt Cottages
Shepherds Down Farm
Galley Down
DUNDRIDGE LA
Peak Down
HACKETTS LA
Shepherds Down
Dundridge
Jubilee Tavern (PH)
PARK LA
Wayfarer's Walk
Dundridge Farm
Swanmore Barn Farm
DAMSON HILL
Reservoir
Beechen Copse
Field Farm
Swanmore Park Farm
Fir Down

84

36

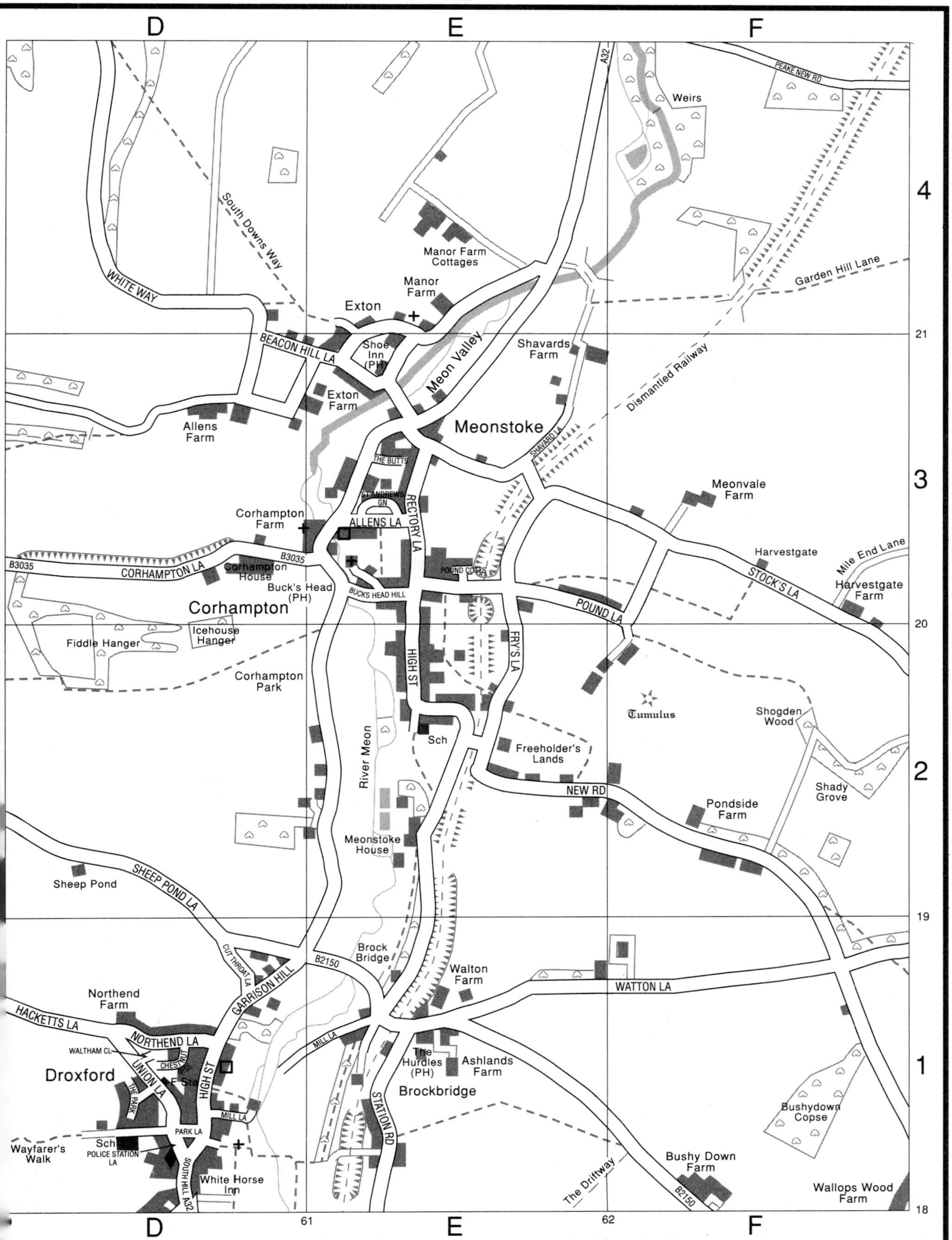
D
E
F
4
3
2
1
21
20
19
18
61
62
Weirs
PEAKE NEW RD
A32
South Downs Way
WHITE WAY
Manor Farm Cottages
Manor Farm
Exton
Garden Hill Lane
Dismantled Railway
BEACON HILL LA
Shoe Inn (PH)
Meon Valley
Shavards Farm
Exton Farm
Allens Farm
Meonstoke
SHAVARD LA
THE BUTTS
ST ANDREWS GN
RECTORY LA
Meonvale Farm
Corhampton Farm
ALLENS LA
Harvestgate
Mile End Lane
B3035
CORHAMPTON LA
Corhampton House
POUND COTTS
STOCK'S LA
Harvestgate Farm
Buck's Head (PH)
BUCKS HEAD HILL
Corhampton
POUND LA
Icehouse Hanger
Fiddle Hanger
HIGH ST
FRY'S LA
Corhampton Park
Tumulus
Shogden Wood
Sch
River Meon
Freeholder's Lands
NEW RD
Shady Grove
Pondside Farm
Meonstoke House
Sheep Pond
SHEEP POND LA
CUT THROAT LA
Brock Bridge
B2150
GARRISON HILL
Walton Farm
WATTON LA
Northend Farm
HACKETTS LA
NORTHEND LA
WALTHAM CL
MILL LA
The Hurdles (PH)
Ashlands Farm
Droxford
UNION LA
CHESTNUT
F Sta
HIGH ST
THE PARK
Brockbridge
MILL LA
Bushydown Copse
PARK LA
STATION RD
Sch
Wayfarer's Walk
POLICE STATION LA
Bushy Down Farm
SOUTH HILL A32
White Horse Inn
The Driftway
B2150
Wallops Wood Farm

62

85

37

61

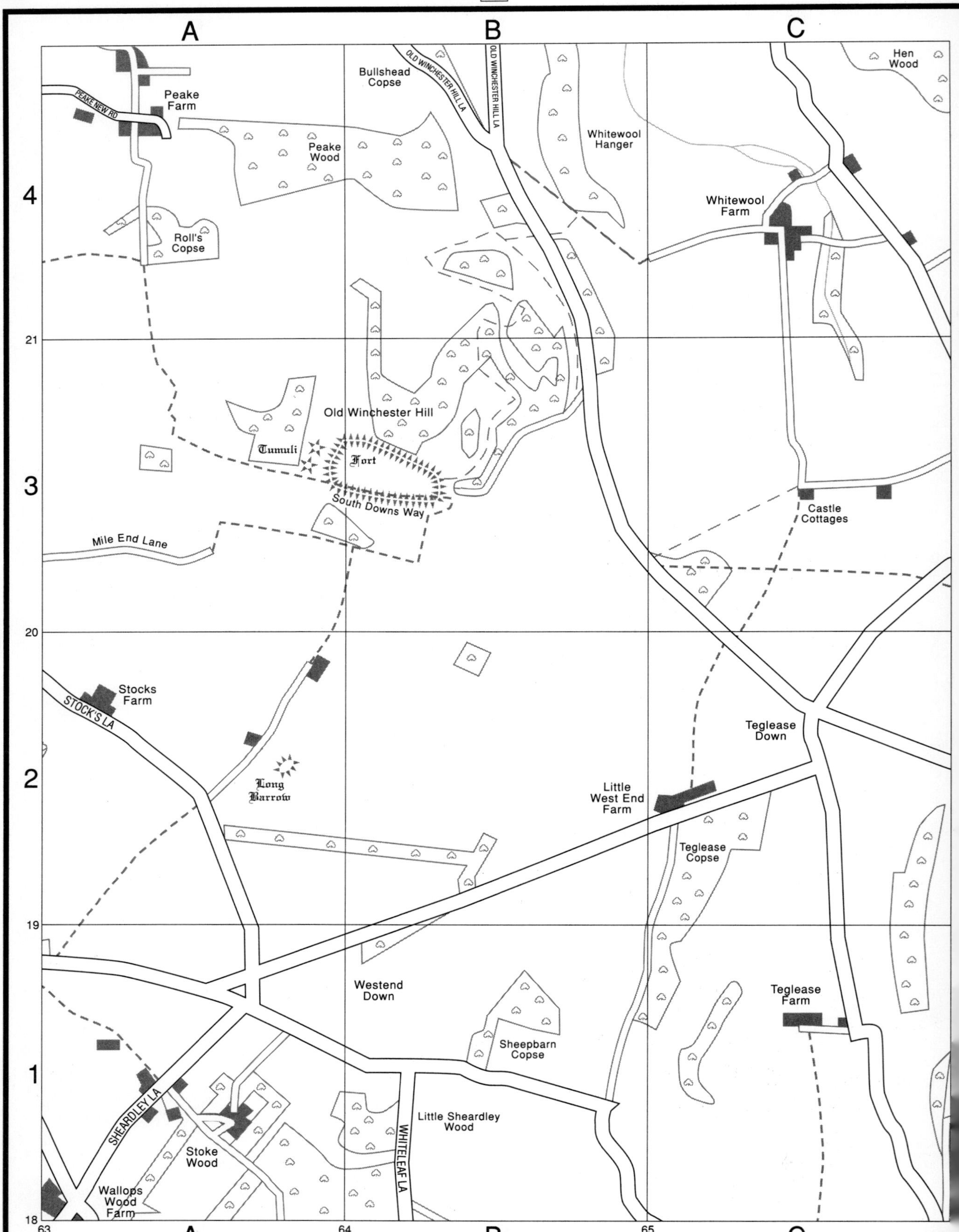
A
B
C
4
3
2
1
21
20
19
18
63
64
65
PEAKE NEW RD
Peake Farm
Bullshead Copse
OLD WINCHESTER HILL LA
OLD WINCHESTER HILL LA
Hen Wood
Peake Wood
Whitewool Hanger
Whitewool Farm
Roll's Copse
Old Winchester Hill
Tumuli
Fort
South Downs Way
Mile End Lane
Castle Cottages
Stocks Farm
STOCK'S LA
Teglease Down
Long Barrow
Little West End Farm
Teglease Copse
Westend Down
Teglease Farm
Sheepbarn Copse
SHEARDLEY LA
Little Sheardley Wood
WHITELEAF LA
Stoke Wood
Wallops Wood Farm

86

38

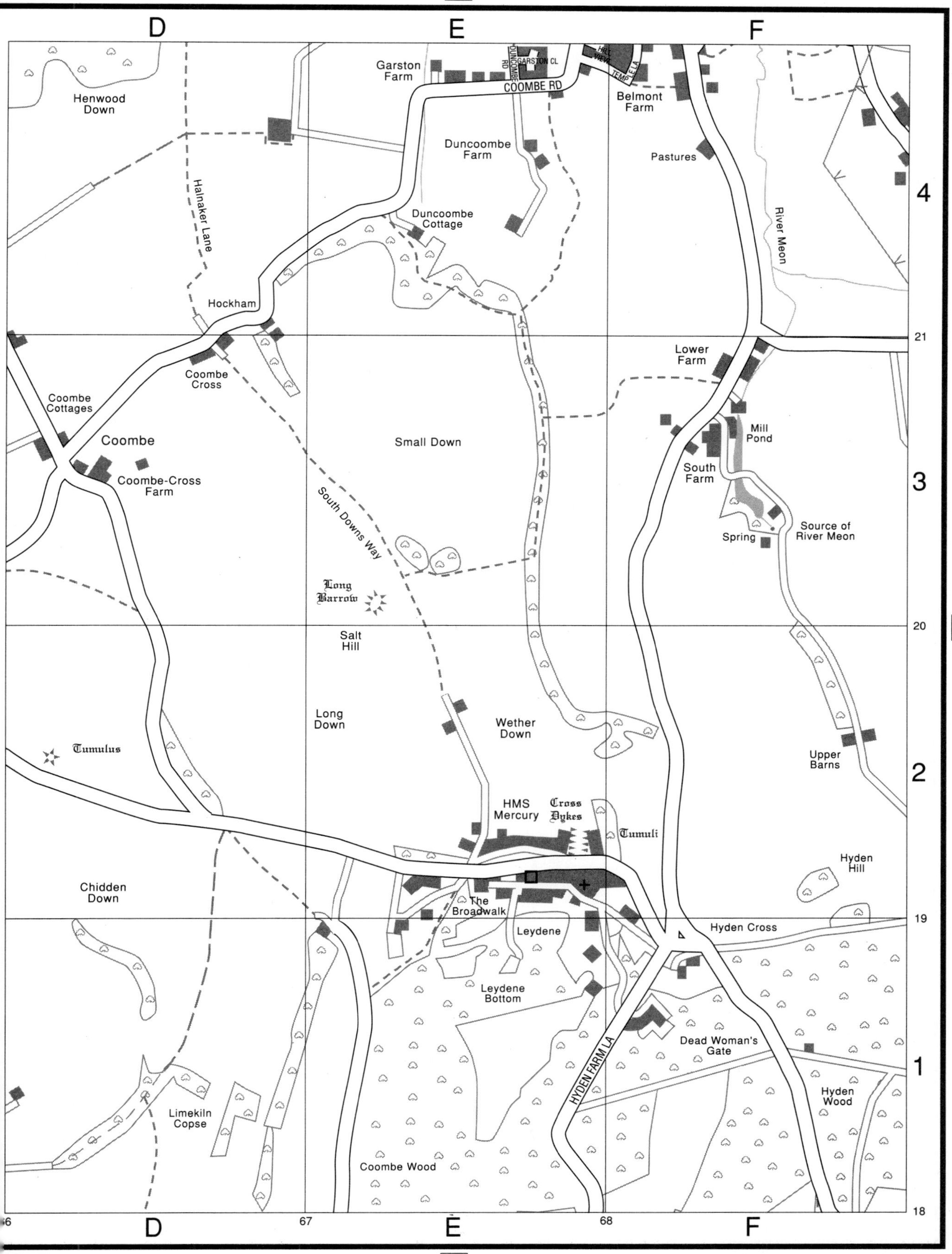
D
E
F
Henwood
Down
Garston
Farm
DUNCOOMBE RD
GARSTON CL
COOMBE RD
HILL VIEW
TEMPLE LA
Belmont
Farm
Duncoombe
Farm
Pastures
Halnaker Lane
Duncoombe
Cottage
River Meon
4
Hockham
21
Lower
Farm
Coombe
Cross
Coombe
Cottages
Coombe
Small Down
Mill
Pond
Coombe-Cross
Farm
South
Farm
3
South Downs Way
Source of
River Meon
Spring
Long
Barrow
Salt
Hill
20
Long
Down
Wether
Down
Tumulus
Upper
Barns
2
HMS
Mercury
Cross
Dykes
Tumuli
Hyden
Hill
Chidden
Down
The
Broadwalk
Leydene
Hyden Cross
19
Leydene
Bottom
Dead Woman's
Gate
HYDEN FARM LA
1
Hyden
Wood
Limekiln
Copse
Coombe Wood
18
66
67
68
D
E
F

64

87

39

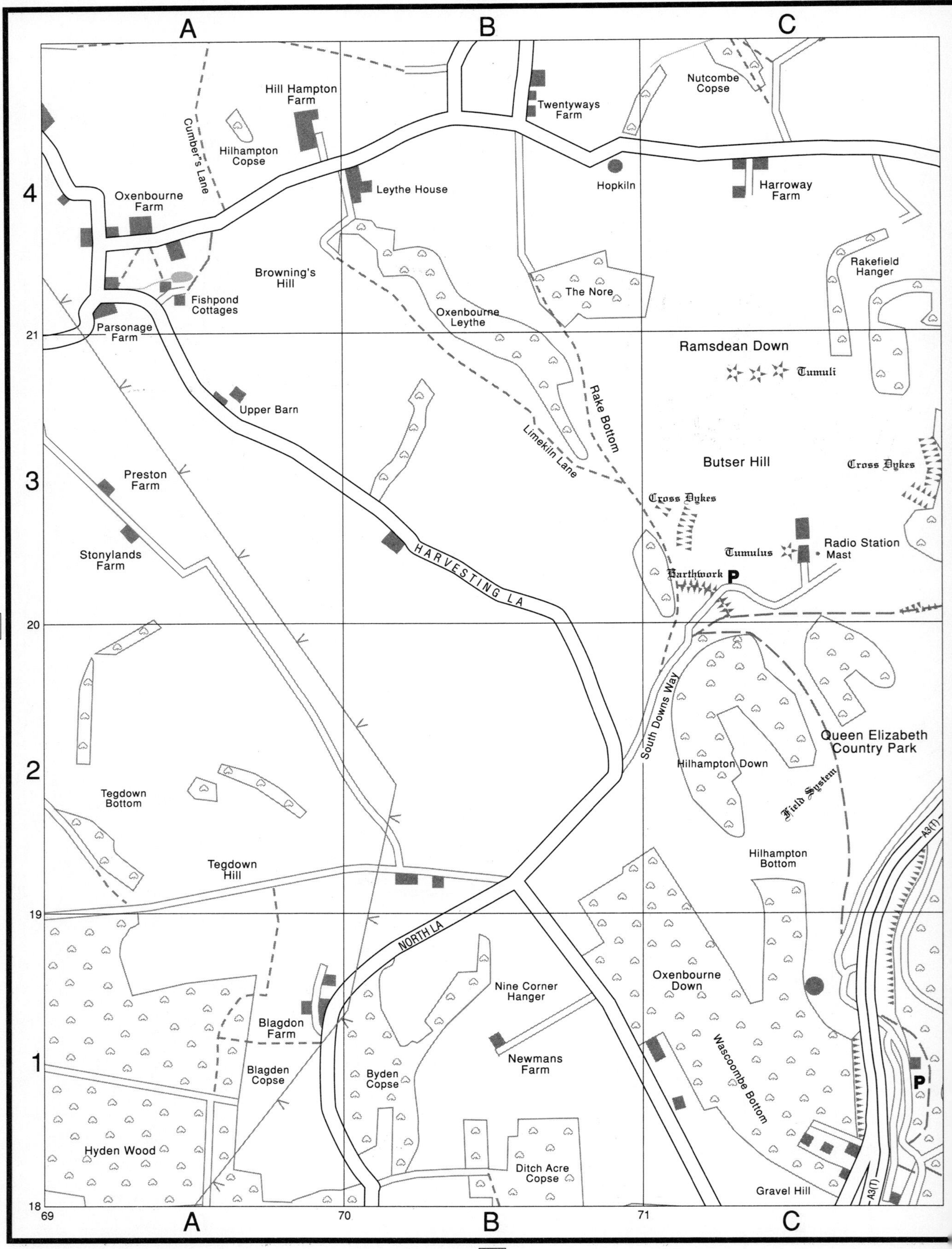
A
B
C
4
3
2
1
21
20
19
18
69
70
71
Hill Hampton Farm
Cumber's Lane
Hilhampton Copse
Twentyways Farm
Nutcombe Copse
Hopkiln
Harroway Farm
Oxenbourne Farm
Leythe House
Browning's Hill
Fishpond Cottages
Parsonage Farm
The Nore
Rakefield Hanger
Oxenbourne Leythe
Ramsdean Down
Tumuli
Upper Barn
Rake Bottom
Limekiln Lane
Butser Hill
Cross Dykes
Preston Farm
Stonylands Farm
HARVESTING LA
Tumulus
Radio Station Mast
Earthwork
P
South Downs Way
Hilhampton Down
Queen Elizabeth Country Park
Field System
Tegdown Bottom
Tegdown Hill
Hilhampton Bottom
A3(T)
NORTH LA
Nine Corner Hanger
Oxenbourne Down
Blagdon Farm
Blagden Copse
Newmans Farm
Wascombe Bottom
Byden Copse
Hyden Wood
Ditch Acre Copse
Gravel Hill

63

88

40

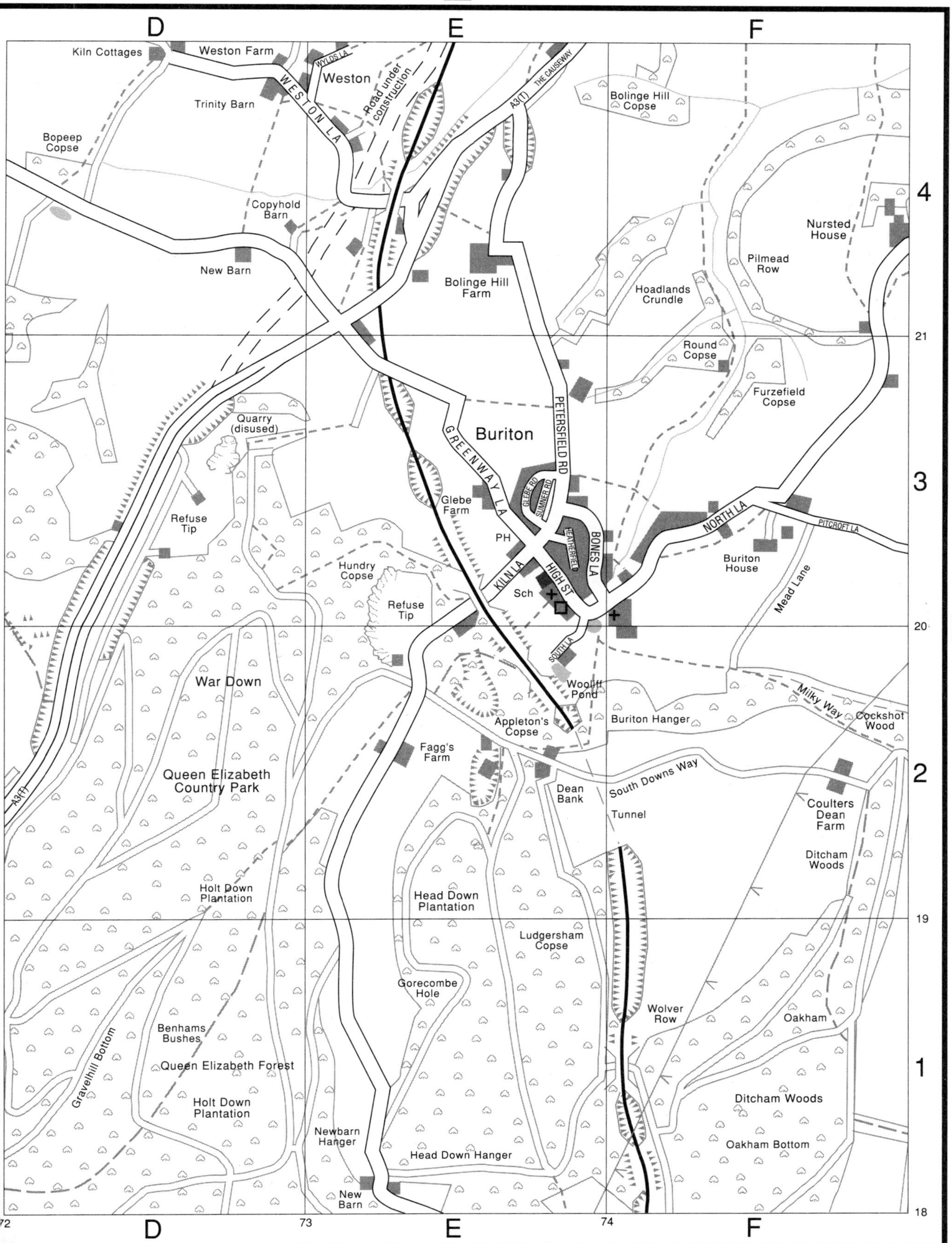
D
E
F
Kiln Cottages
Weston Farm
WYLDS LA
Weston
Road under construction
A3(T)
THE CAUSEWAY
WESTON LA
Trinity Barn
Bolinge Hill Copse
Bopeep Copse
4
Copyhold Barn
Nursted House
New Barn
Pilmead Row
Bolinge Hill Farm
Hoadlands Crundle
21
Round Copse
Furzefield Copse
Quarry (disused)
PETERSFIELD RD
GREENWAY LA
Buriton
3
GLEBE RD
SUMNER RD
Glebe Farm
Refuse Tip
NORTH LA
HEATHERFIELD
BONES LA
PITCROFT LA
PH
Hundry Copse
Buriton House
KILN LA
HIGH ST
Mead Lane
Sch
Refuse Tip
20
SOUTH LA
War Down
Woolff Pond
Milky Way
Cockshot Wood
Appleton's Copse
Buriton Hanger
Fagg's Farm
2
Queen Elizabeth Country Park
Dean Bank
South Downs Way
Coulters Dean Farm
A3(T)
Tunnel
Ditcham Woods
Holt Down Plantation
Head Down Plantation
19
Ludgersham Copse
Gorecombe Hole
Wolver Row
Oakham
Benhams Bushes
Gravelhill Bottom
1
Queen Elizabeth Forest
Ditcham Woods
Holt Down Plantation
Newbarn Hanger
Oakham Bottom
Head Down Hanger
New Barn
18
72
73
74
D
E
F

99

89

41

65

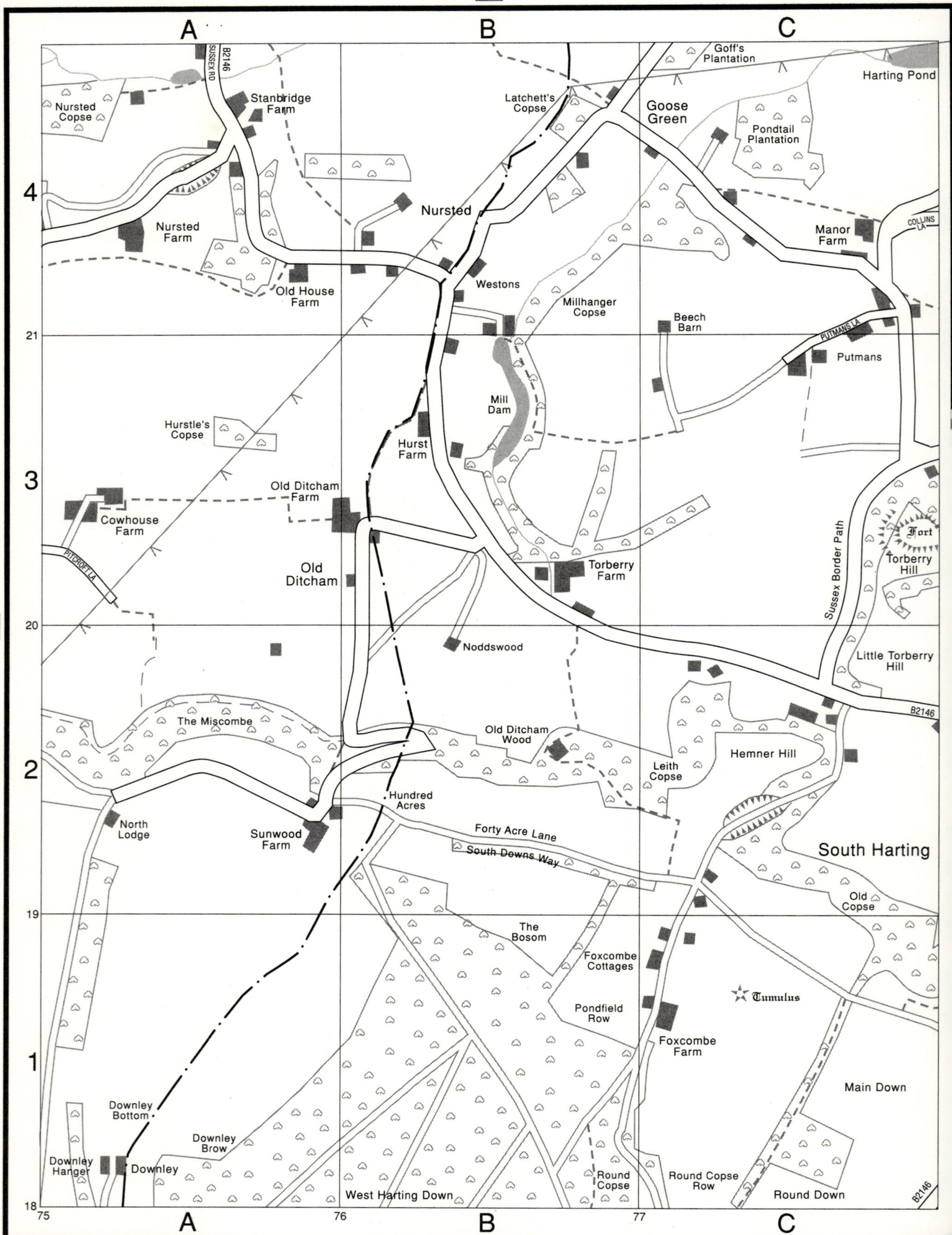
A
B
C
4
3
2
1
21
20
19
18
75
76
77
B2146
SUSSEX RD
Goff's Plantation
Harting Pond
Nursted Copse
Stanbridge Farm
Latchett's Copse
Goose Green
Pondtail Plantation
Nursted
Nursted Farm
Manor Farm
COLLINS LA
Old House Farm
Westons
Millhanger Copse
Beech Barn
PUTMANS LA
Putmans
Mill Dam
Hurstle's Copse
Hurst Farm
Old Ditcham Farm
Cowhouse Farm
Fort
Torberry Hill
Sussex Border Path
PITCROFT LA
Old Ditcham
Torberry Farm
Noddswood
Little Torberry Hill
The Miscombe
Old Ditcham Wood
Hemner Hill
Leith Copse
Hundred Acres
North Lodge
Sunwood Farm
Forty Acre Lane
South Downs Way
South Harting
Old Copse
The Bosom
Foxcombe Cottages
Tumulus
Pondfield Row
Foxcombe Farm
Main Down
Downley Bottom
Downley Brow
Downley Hanger
Downley
Round Copse
Round Copse Row
Round Down
West Harting Down

90

43

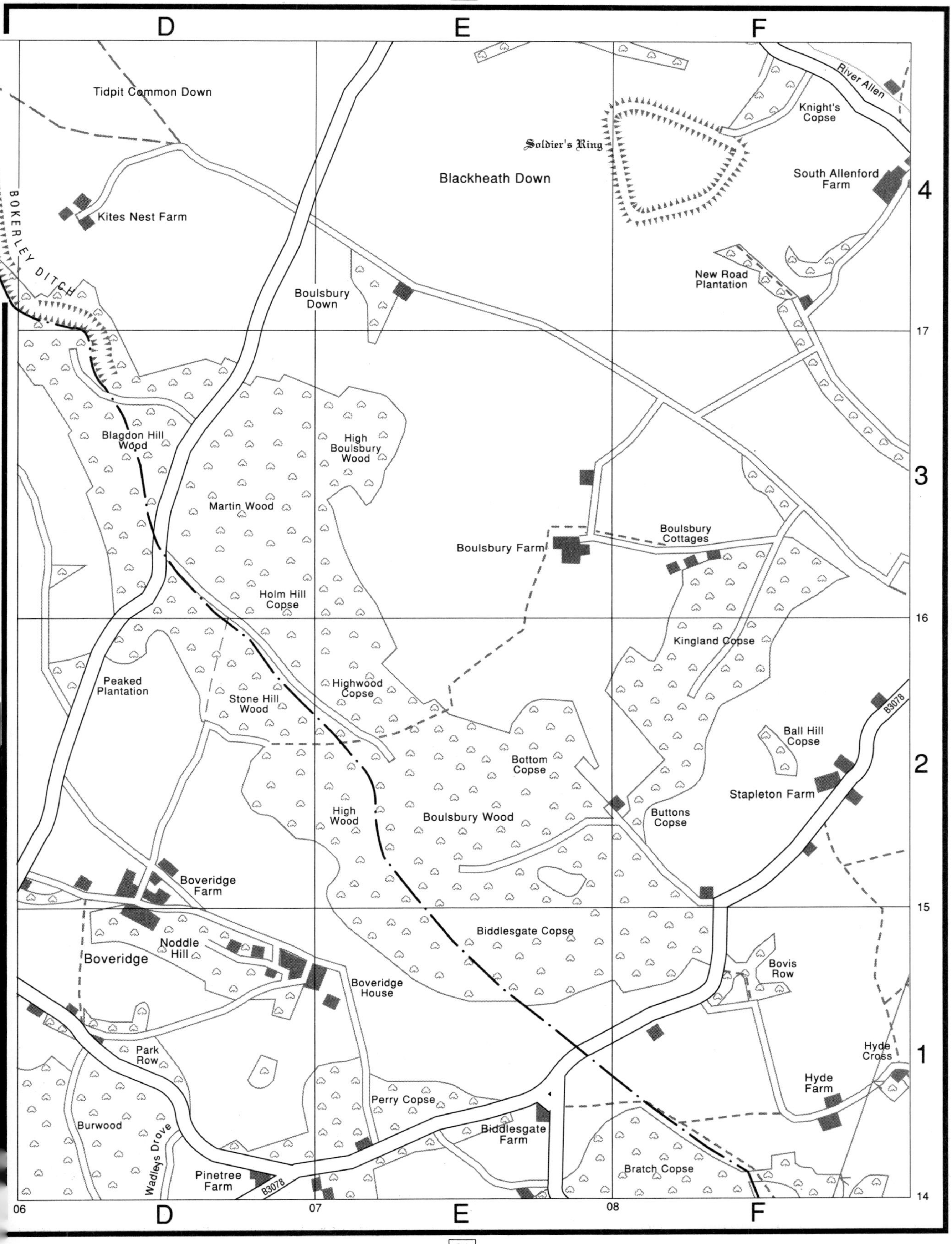
D
E
F
Tidpit Common Down
Kites Nest Farm
BOKERLEY DITCH
Boulsbury Down
Blackheath Down
Soldier's Ring
Knight's Copse
River Allen
South Allenford Farm
New Road Plantation
4
17
Blagdon Hill Wood
High Boulsbury Wood
Martin Wood
3
Boulsbury Farm
Boulsbury Cottages
Holm Hill Copse
16
Kingland Copse
Peaked Plantation
Stone Hill Wood
Highwood Copse
B3078
Ball Hill Copse
Bottom Copse
2
Stapleton Farm
High Wood
Boulsbury Wood
Buttons Copse
Boveridge Farm
15
Biddlesgate Copse
Noddle Hill
Boveridge
Boveridge House
Bovis Row
Park Row
Hyde Cross
1
Hyde Farm
Perry Copse
Burwood
Wadleys Drove
Biddlesgate Farm
Pinetree Farm
B3078
Bratch Copse
14
06
07
08
D
E
F

69

91

44

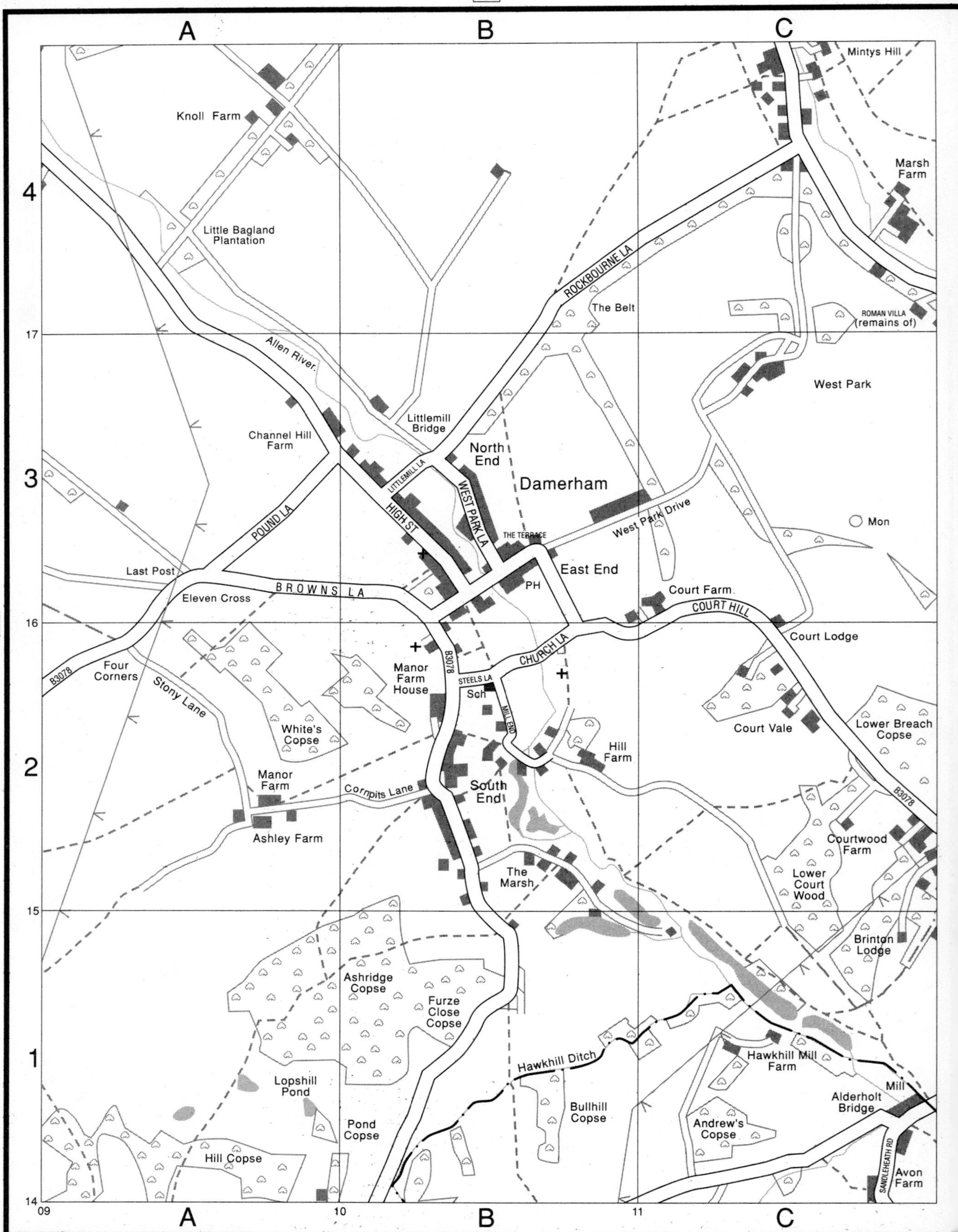
A
B
C
4
3
2
1
17
16
15
14
09
10
11
Knoll Farm
Mintys Hill
Marsh Farm
Little Bagland Plantation
ROCKBOURNE LA
The Belt
ROMAN VILLA (remains of)
Allen River
West Park
Littlemill Bridge
Channel Hill Farm
North End
LITTLEMILL LA
WEST PARK LA
HIGH ST
Damerham
POUND LA
THE TERRACE
West Park Drive
Mon
Last Post
East End
PH
BROWNS LA
Eleven Cross
Court Farm
COURT HILL
Court Lodge
B3078
Four Corners
Manor Farm House
CHURCH LA
STEELS LA
Sch
MILL END
Stony Lane
White's Copse
Court Vale
Lower Breach Copse
Hill Farm
Manor Farm
Cornpits Lane
South End
Ashley Farm
Courtwood Farm
Lower Court Wood
The Marsh
Brinton Lodge
Ashridge Copse
Furze Close Copse
Hawkhill Ditch
Hawkhill Mill Farm
Mill
Alderholt Bridge
Lopshill Pond
Bullhill Copse
Pond Copse
Andrew's Copse
Hill Copse
SANDLEHEATH RD
Avon Farm

67

92

45

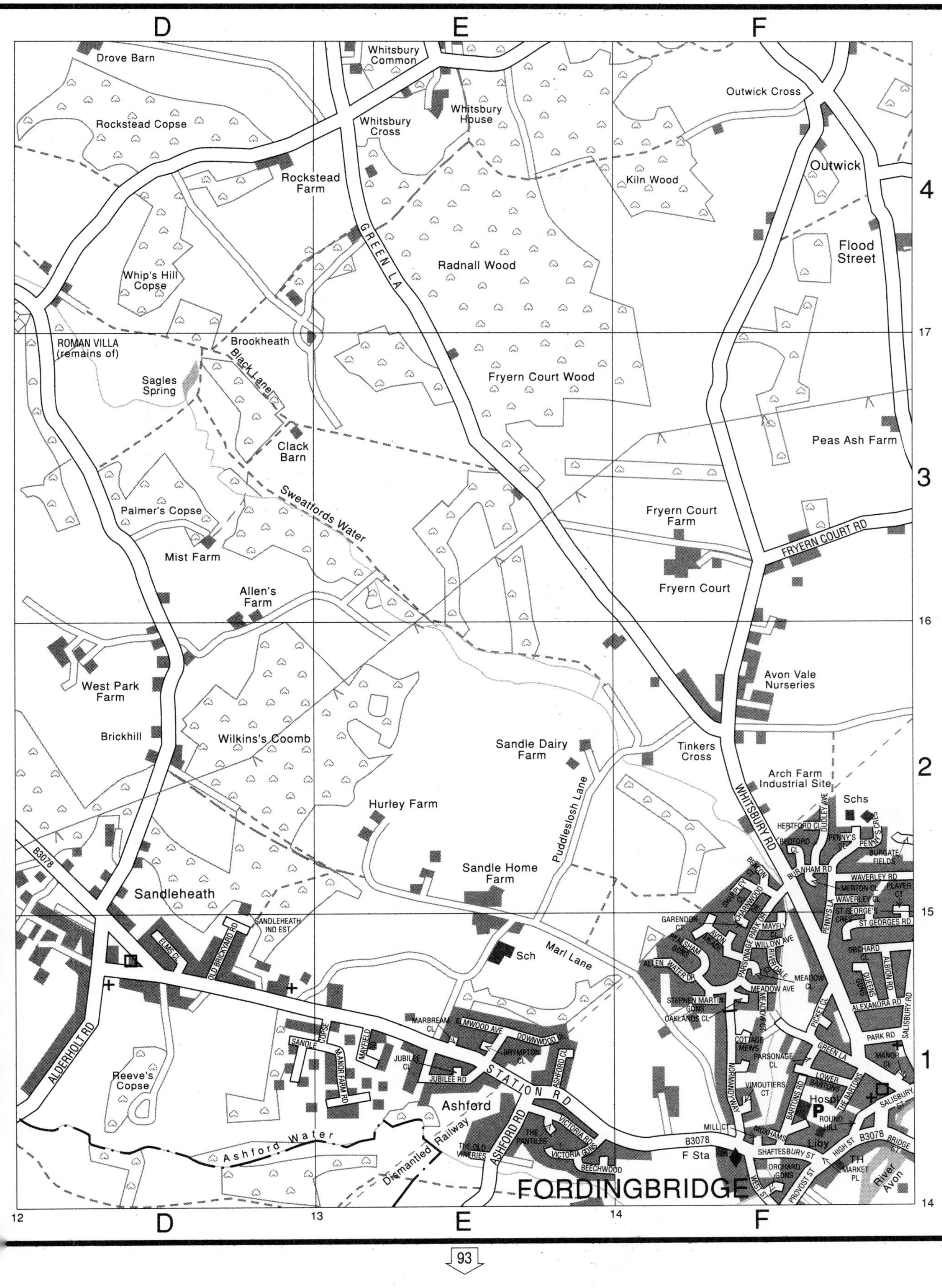
D
E
F
Drove Barn
Whitsbury Common
Rockstead Copse
Whitsbury Cross
Whitsbury House
Outwick Cross
Outwick
Rockstead Farm
Kiln Wood
4
Flood Street
GREEN LA
Radnall Wood
Whip's Hill Copse
17
ROMAN VILLA (remains of)
Brookheath
Black Lane
Sagles Spring
Fryern Court Wood
Peas Ash Farm
Clack Barn
3
Sweatfords Water
Palmer's Copse
Fryern Court Farm
FRYERN COURT RD
Mist Farm
Fryern Court
Allen's Farm
16
West Park Farm
Avon Vale Nurseries
Brickhill
Wilkins's Coomb
Sandle Dairy Farm
Tinkers Cross
2
Arch Farm Industrial Site
Schs
Hurley Farm
Puddleslosh Lane
WHITSBURY RD
B3078
Sandle Home Farm
Sandleheath
15
SANDLEHEATH IND EST
ELMS CL
OLD BRICKYARD RD
Sch
Marl Lane
ALDERHOLT RD
SANDLE COPSE
MANOR FARM RD
MAYFIELD RD
JUBILEE CL
JUBILEE RD
MARBREAM CL
ELMWOOD AVE
DOWNWOOD CL
BRYMPTON CL
ASHFORD CL
STATION RD
Reeve's Copse
Ashford
ASHFORD RD
VICTORIA RD
VICTORIA GDNS
THE PANTILES
THE OLD VINERIES
BEECHWOOD
Dismantled Railway
Ashford Water
B3078
F Sta
FORDINGBRIDGE
HERTFORD CL
BEDFORD CL
DUDLEY AVE
PENNY'S CT
PENNY'S CRES
BURGATE FIELDS
BURNHAM RD
WAVERLEY RD
MERTON CL
WAVERLEY CL
PLAYER CT
ST GEORGE'S CRES
ST GEORGES RD
PENNYS LA
BEACON
SHAPLEY CL
CHARNWOOD CL
GARENDON CT
AVON MEAD
MAYFLY CL
WILLOW AVE
PENSHAM GDNS
ALLEN WATER DR
PARSONAGE PARK DR
RIVERDALE
MEADOW CL
MEADOW AVE
ORCHARD CL
QUEENS GDNS
ALBION RD
ALEXANDRA RD
SALISBURY RD
STEPHEN MARTIN GDNS
OAKLANDS CL
MEADOW CT
PICKET CL
PARK RD
COTTAGE MEWS
PARSONAGE CL
GREEN LA
MANOR CL
1
NORMANDY WAY
VIMOUTIERS CT
LOWER BARTONS
BARTONS RD
THE BARTONS
Hospl
P
ROUND HILL
MILL CT
MONHAMS
SALISBURY ST
Liby
B3078
BRIDGE ST
HIGH ST
SHAFTESBURY ST
TH
MARKET PL
ORCHARD GDNS
WEST ST
PROVOST ST
River Avon
14
12
13
14
D
E
F

70

93

46

69

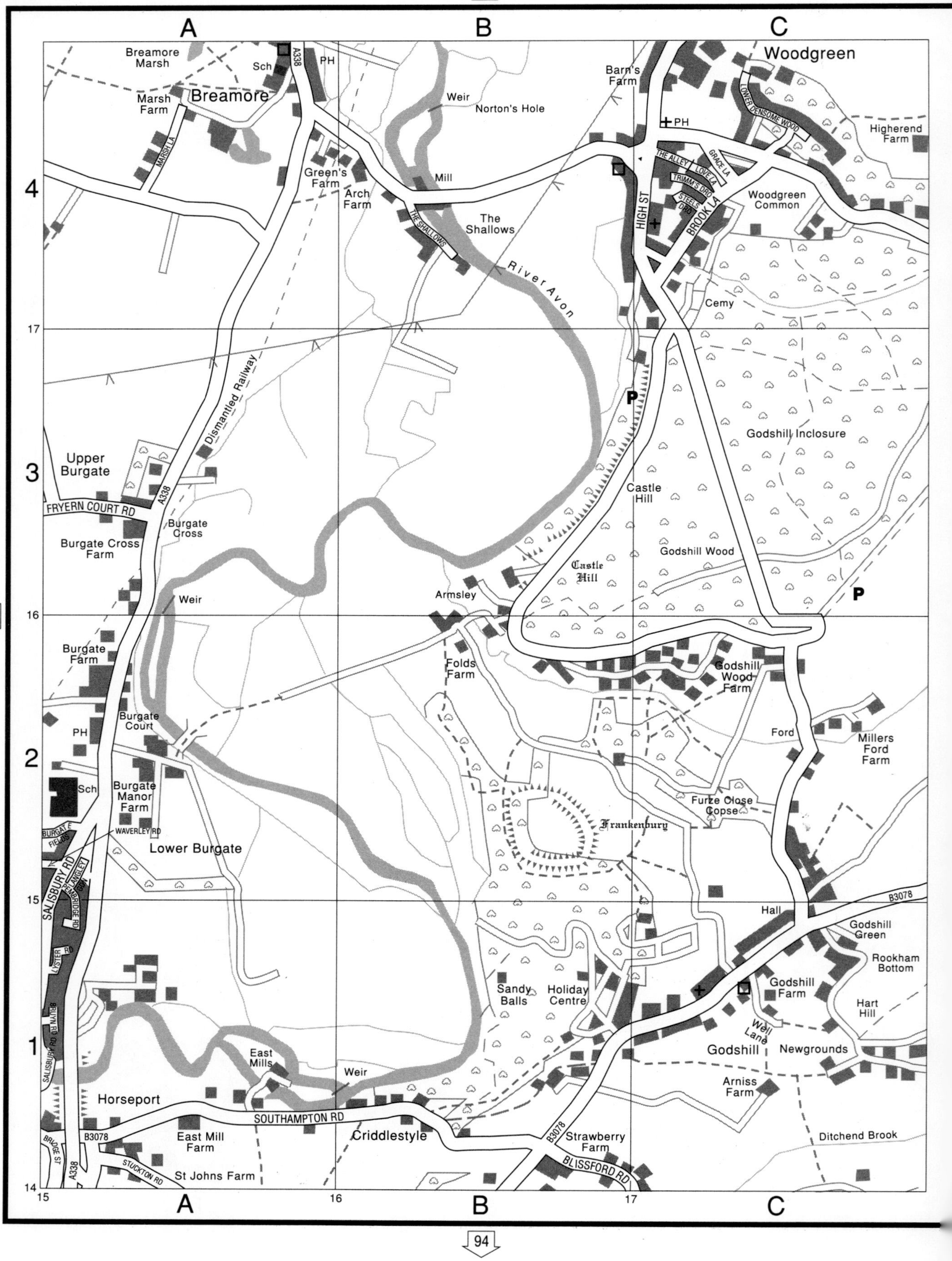
A
B
C
Woodgreen
Breamore Marsh
Sch
A338
PH
Barn's Farm
Marsh Farm
Breamore
Weir
Norton's Hole
PH
Lower Densome Wood
Higherend Farm
The Alley
Love La
Grace La
Trimm's Dro
Steels Dro
Green's Farm
Mill
Arch Farm
4
High St
Brook La
Woodgreen Common
Marsh La
The Shallows
The Shallows
River Avon
Cemy
17
Dismantled Railway
P
Godshill Inclosure
Upper Burgate
3
Castle Hill
A338
Fryern Court Rd
Burgate Cross
Burgate Cross Farm
Godshill Wood
Castle Hill
P
Armsley
Weir
16
Burgate Farm
Folds Farm
Godshill Wood Farm
Burgate Court
PH
Ford
Millers Ford Farm
2
Sch
Burgate Manor Farm
Furze Close Copse
Frankenbury
Burgate Fields
Waverley Rd
Lower Burgate
Salisbury Rd
Pembridge Rd
15
B3078
Hall
Godshill Green
Lyster Rd
Rookham Bottom
Sandy Balls
Holiday Centre
Godshill Farm
Hart Hill
Well Lane
1
Godshill
Newgrounds
East Mills
Weir
Arniss Farm
Horseport
Southampton Rd
B3078
Criddlestyle
East Mill Farm
B3078
Strawberry Farm
Ditchend Brook
Bridge St
Stuckton Rd
St Johns Farm
Blissford Rd
A338
14
15
16
17

94

47

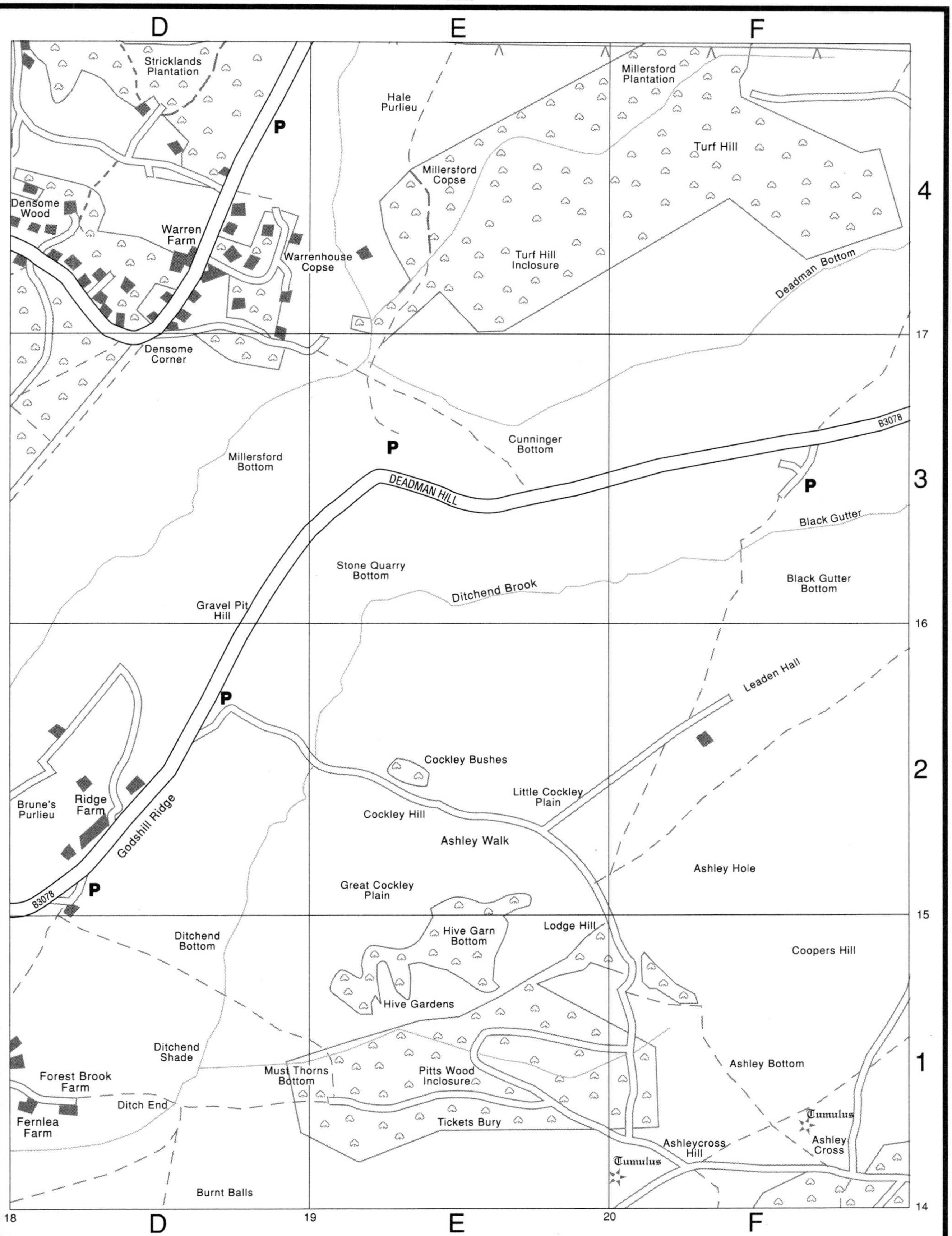

D
E
F
Stricklands Plantation
Hale Purlieu
Millersford Plantation
Turf Hill
Millersford Copse
Densome Wood
Warren Farm
Warrenhouse Copse
Turf Hill Inclosure
Deadman Bottom
Densome Corner
17
B3078
Cunninger Bottom
Millersford Bottom
DEADMAN HILL
Black Gutter
Stone Quarry Bottom
Black Gutter Bottom
Ditchend Brook
Gravel Pit Hill
16
Leaden Hall
Cockley Bushes
Little Cockley Plain
Brune's Purlieu
Ridge Farm
Cockley Hill
Ashley Walk
Godshill Ridge
Ashley Hole
B3078
Great Cockley Plain
15
Ditchend Bottom
Hive Garn Bottom
Lodge Hill
Coopers Hill
Hive Gardens
Ditchend Shade
Ashley Bottom
Forest Brook Farm
Must Thorns Bottom
Pitts Wood Inclosure
Ditch End
Fernlea Farm
Tickets Bury
Tumulus
Ashley Cross
Ashleycross Hill
Tumulus
Burnt Balls
14
18
19
20
4
3
2
1

72

95

48

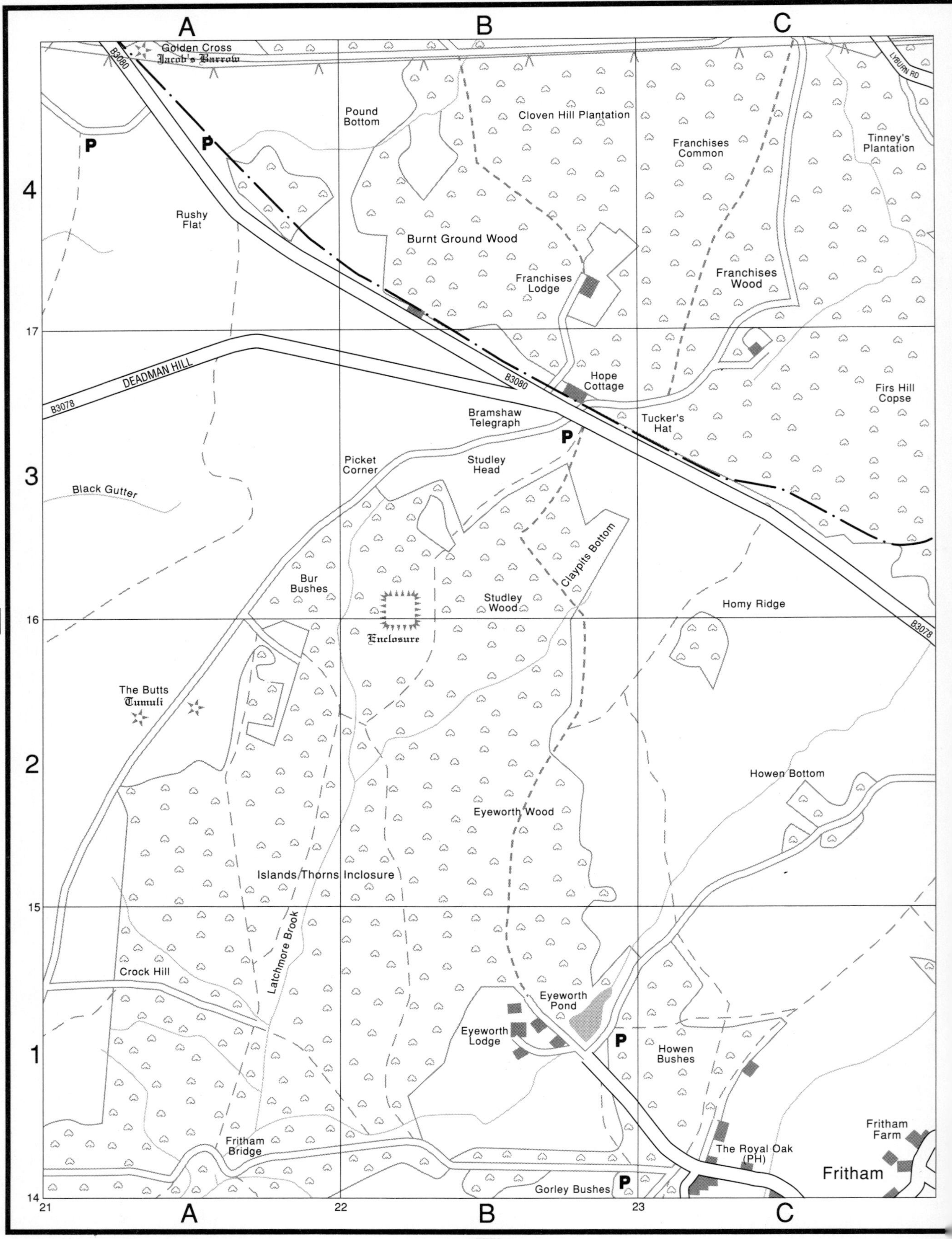
A
B
C
Golden Cross
Jacob's Barrow
B3080
LYBURN RD
Pound Bottom
Cloven Hill Plantation
Franchises Common
Tinney's Plantation
4
Rushy Flat
Burnt Ground Wood
Franchises Lodge
Franchises Wood
17
DEADMAN HILL
B3078
B3080
Hope Cottage
Firs Hill Copse
Bramshaw Telegraph
Tucker's Hat
Picket Corner
Studley Head
3
Black Gutter
Claypits Bottom
Bur Bushes
Studley Wood
Homy Ridge
16
Enclosure
B3078
The Butts
Tumuli
2
Howen Bottom
Eyeworth Wood
Islands Thorns Inclosure
15
Latchmore Brook
Crock Hill
Eyeworth Pond
Eyeworth Lodge
1
Howen Bushes
Fritham Bridge
Fritham Farm
The Royal Oak (PH)
Fritham
Gorley Bushes
14
21
22
23
A
B
C

71

96

49

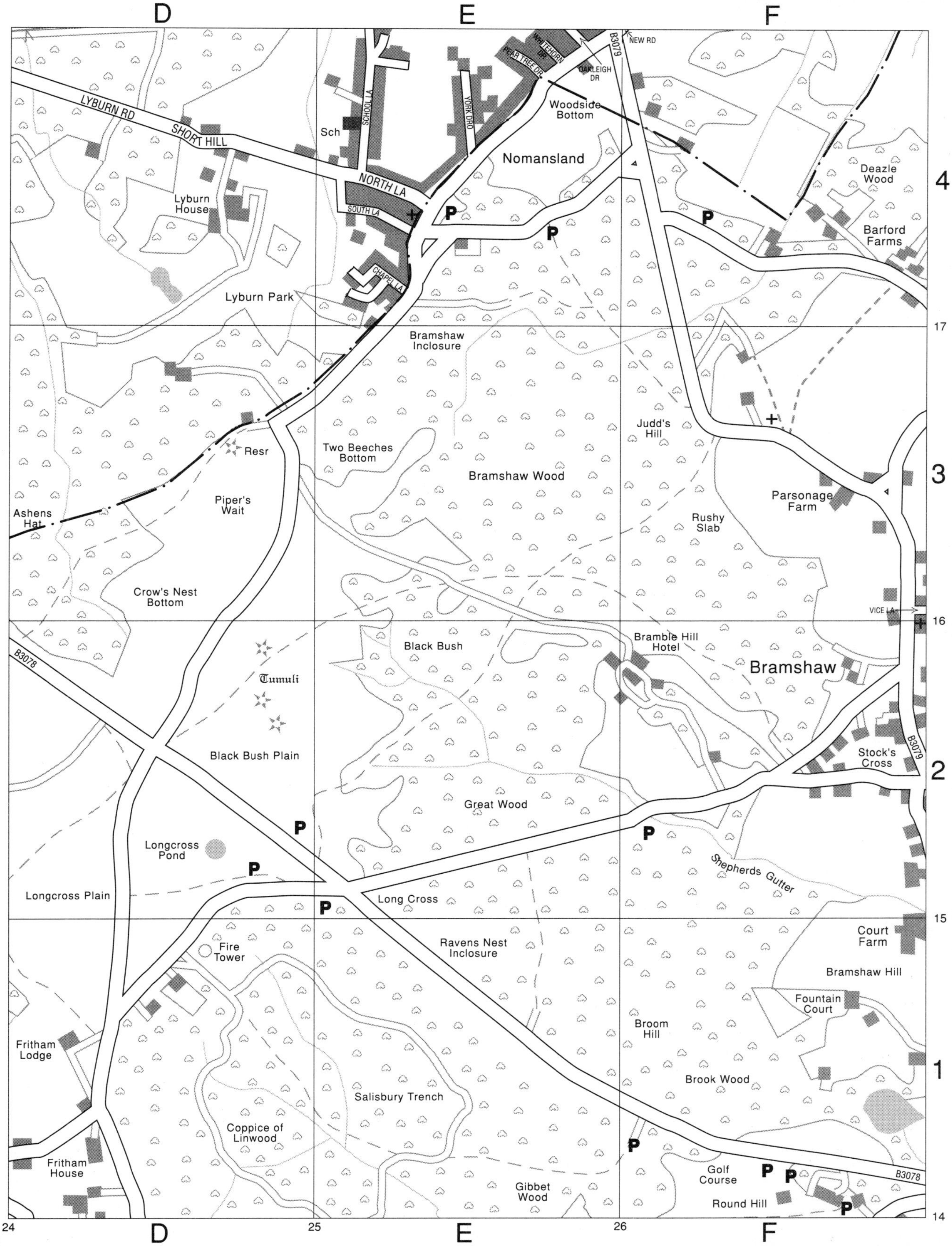
D
E
F
LYBURN RD
SHORT HILL
Sch
SCHOOL LA
YORK DRO
WHITEHORN DR
PEAR TREE DR
OAKLEIGH DR
B3079
NEW RD
Woodside Bottom
Nomansland
NORTH LA
SOUTH LA
CHAPEL LA
Lyburn House
Lyburn Park
Deazle Wood
Barford Farms
4
17
Bramshaw Inclosure
Judd's Hill
Resr
Two Beeches Bottom
Bramshaw Wood
Parsonage Farm
3
Piper's Wait
Ashens Hat
Rushy Slab
Crow's Nest Bottom
VICE LA
16
B3078
Black Bush
Bramble Hill Hotel
Bramshaw
Tumuli
Black Bush Plain
Stock's Cross
2
Great Wood
Longcross Pond
Shepherds Gutter
Longcross Plain
Long Cross
15
Court Farm
Fire Tower
Ravens Nest Inclosure
Bramshaw Hill
Fountain Court
Fritham Lodge
Broom Hill
1
Brook Wood
Salisbury Trench
Coppice of Linwood
Fritham House
Golf Course
Gibbet Wood
Round Hill
14
24
25
26

74

97

50

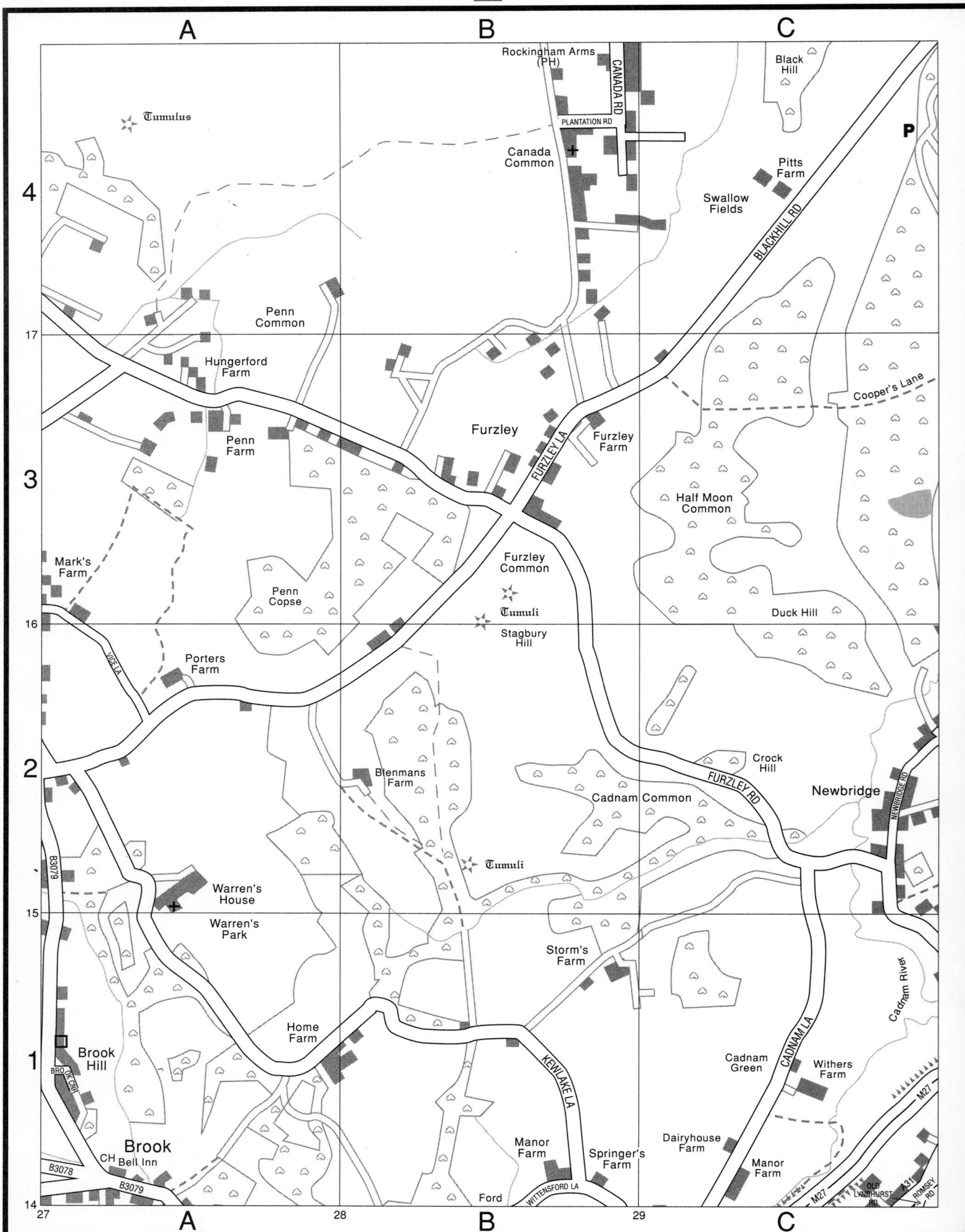
A
B
C
4
3
2
1
17
16
15
14
27
28
29
Rockingham Arms (PH)
CANADA RD
PLANTATION RD
Canada Common
Black Hill
P
Pitts Farm
Swallow Fields
BLACKHILL RD
Tumulus
Penn Common
Hungerford Farm
Penn Farm
Furzley
FURZLEY LA
Furzley Farm
Cooper's Lane
Half Moon Common
Mark's Farm
Penn Copse
Furzley Common
Tumuli
Stagbury Hill
Duck Hill
VICE LA
Porters Farm
Blenmans Farm
Crock Hill
FURZLEY RD
Cadnam Common
Newbridge
NEWBRIDGE RD
B3079
Tumuli
Warren's House
Warren's Park
Storm's Farm
Cadnam River
Home Farm
Brook Hill
KEWLAKE LA
CADNAM LA
Cadnam Green
Withers Farm
M27
Dairyhouse Farm
Manor Farm
Springer's Farm
Manor Farm
Brook
CH
Bell Inn
B3078
B3079
Ford
WITTENSFORD LA
OLD LYNDHURST RD
A31
ROMSEY RD

73

98

51

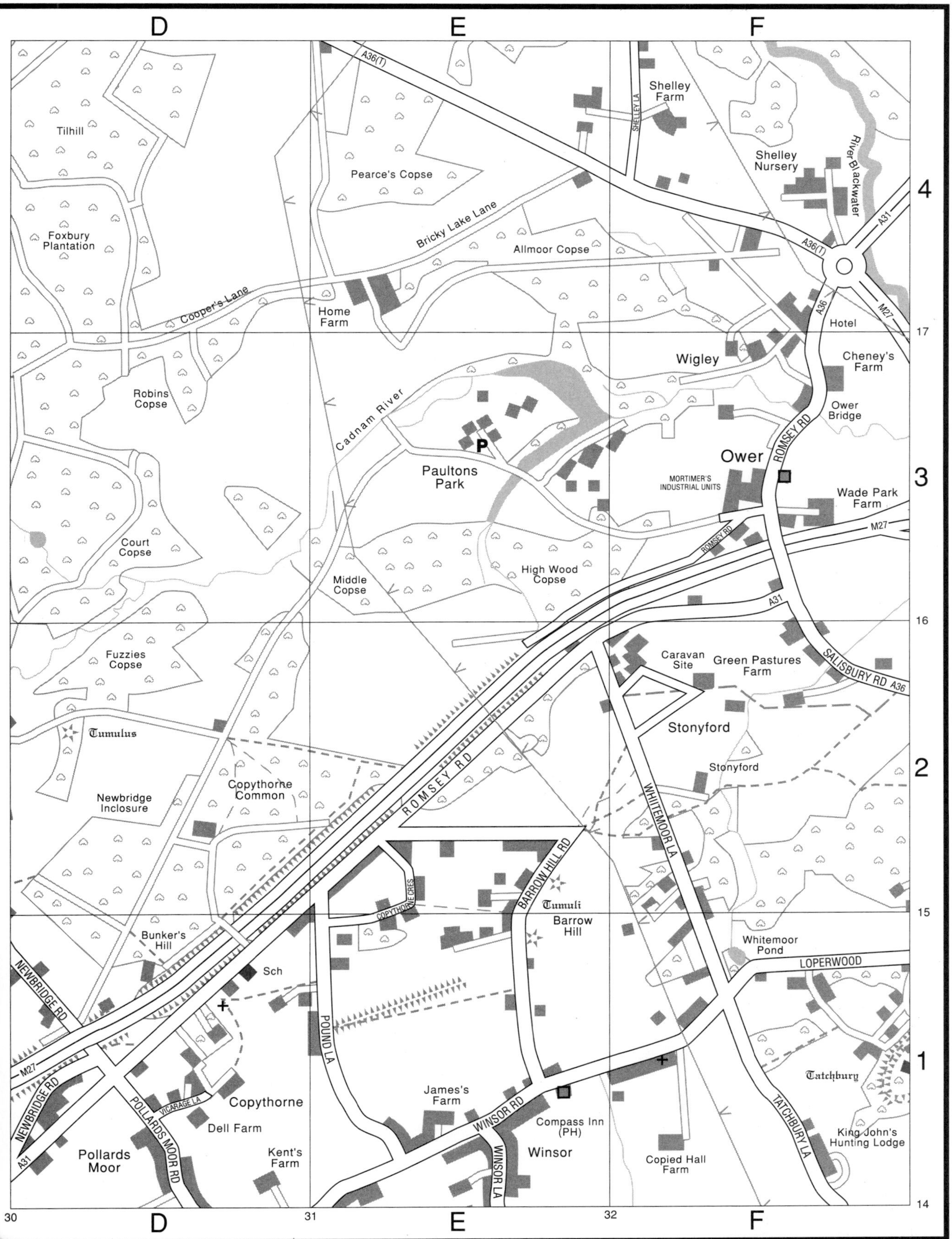
D
E
F
Tilhill
Foxbury Plantation
Pearce's Copse
Bricky Lake Lane
Allmoor Copse
A36(T)
Shelley Farm
SHELLEY LA
Shelley Nursery
River Blackwater
A31
A36
M27
Hotel
Cooper's Lane
Home Farm
Wigley
Cheney's Farm
Robins Copse
Cadnam River
P
Paultons Park
Ower
Ower Bridge
ROMSEY RD
MORTIMER'S INDUSTRIAL UNITS
Wade Park Farm
Court Copse
Middle Copse
High Wood Copse
Fuzzies Copse
Caravan Site
Green Pastures Farm
SALISBURY RD
Tumulus
Stonyford
Copythorne Common
Newbridge Inclosure
WHITEMOOR LA
BARROW HILL RD
COPYTHORNE CRES
Tumuli
Barrow Hill
Bunker's Hill
Sch
Whitemoor Pond
LOPERWOOD
NEWBRIDGE RD
POUND LA
Tatchbury
King John's Hunting Lodge
TATCHBURY LA
James's Farm
Copythorne
VICARAGE LA
POLLARDS MOOR RD
Dell Farm
WINSOR RD
Compass Inn (PH)
Winsor
WINSOR LA
Kent's Farm
Pollards Moor
Copied Hall Farm
4
3
2
1
17
16
15
14
30
31
32

76

99

52

75

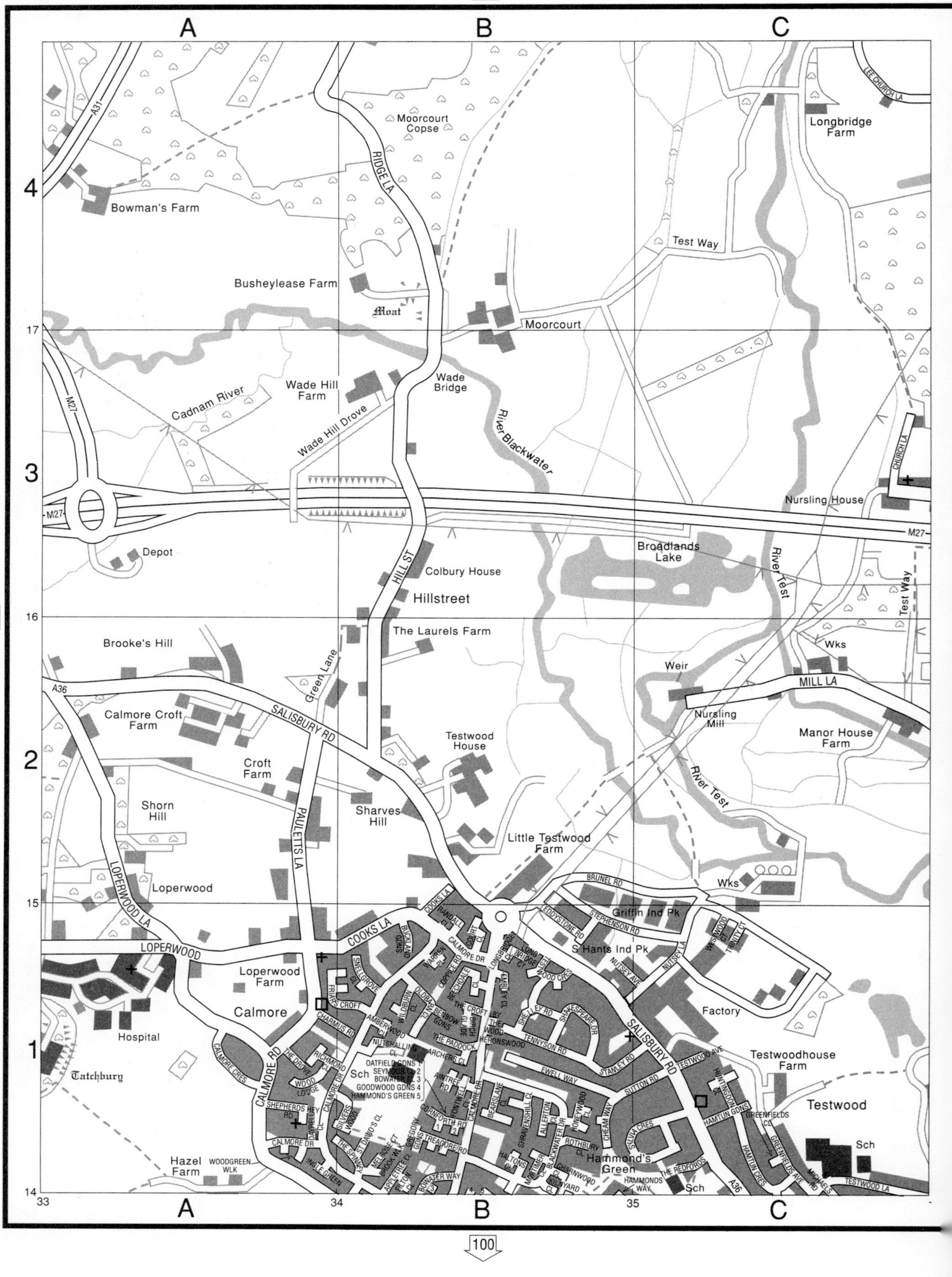
A
B
C
4
3
2
1
17
16
15
14
33
34
35
Moorcourt Copse
Longbridge Farm
LEE CHURCH LA
A31
RIDGE LA
Bowman's Farm
Test Way
Busheylease Farm
Moat
Moorcourt
Wade Hill Farm
Wade Bridge
Cadnam River
M27
Wade Hill Drove
River Blackwater
CHURCH LA
Nursling House
Broadlands Lake
River Test
Depot
Colbury House
HILL ST
Hillstreet
Test Way
The Laurels Farm
Brooke's Hill
Wks
Weir
MILL LA
A36
Green Lane
Calmore Croft Farm
SALISBURY RD
Nursling Mill
Testwood House
Manor House Farm
Croft Farm
River Test
Shorn Hill
PAULETTS LA
Sharves Hill
Little Testwood Farm
LOPERWOOD LA
Loperwood
Wks
BRUNEL RD
COOKS LA
Griffin Ind Pk
STEPHENSON RD
LOPERWOOD
EDDYSTONE RD
S Hants Ind Pk
Loperwood Farm
NUTSEY AVE
NUTSEY LA
Calmore
Factory
Hospital
CALMORE RD
SALISBURY RD
TENNYSON RD
Testwoodhouse Farm
Tatchbury
Sch
OATFIELD GDNS 1
SEYMOUR CL 2
BOWATER CL 3
GOODWOOD GDNS 4
HAMMOND'S GREEN 5
TESTWOOD AVE
Testwood
EWELL WAY
STANLEY RD
SUTTON RD
HAMTUN GDNS
GREENFIELDS CL
Sch
Hammond's Green
THE REDFORDS
HAMMONDS WAY
Sch
A36
Hazel Farm
WOODGREEN WLK
TESTWOOD LA

100

53

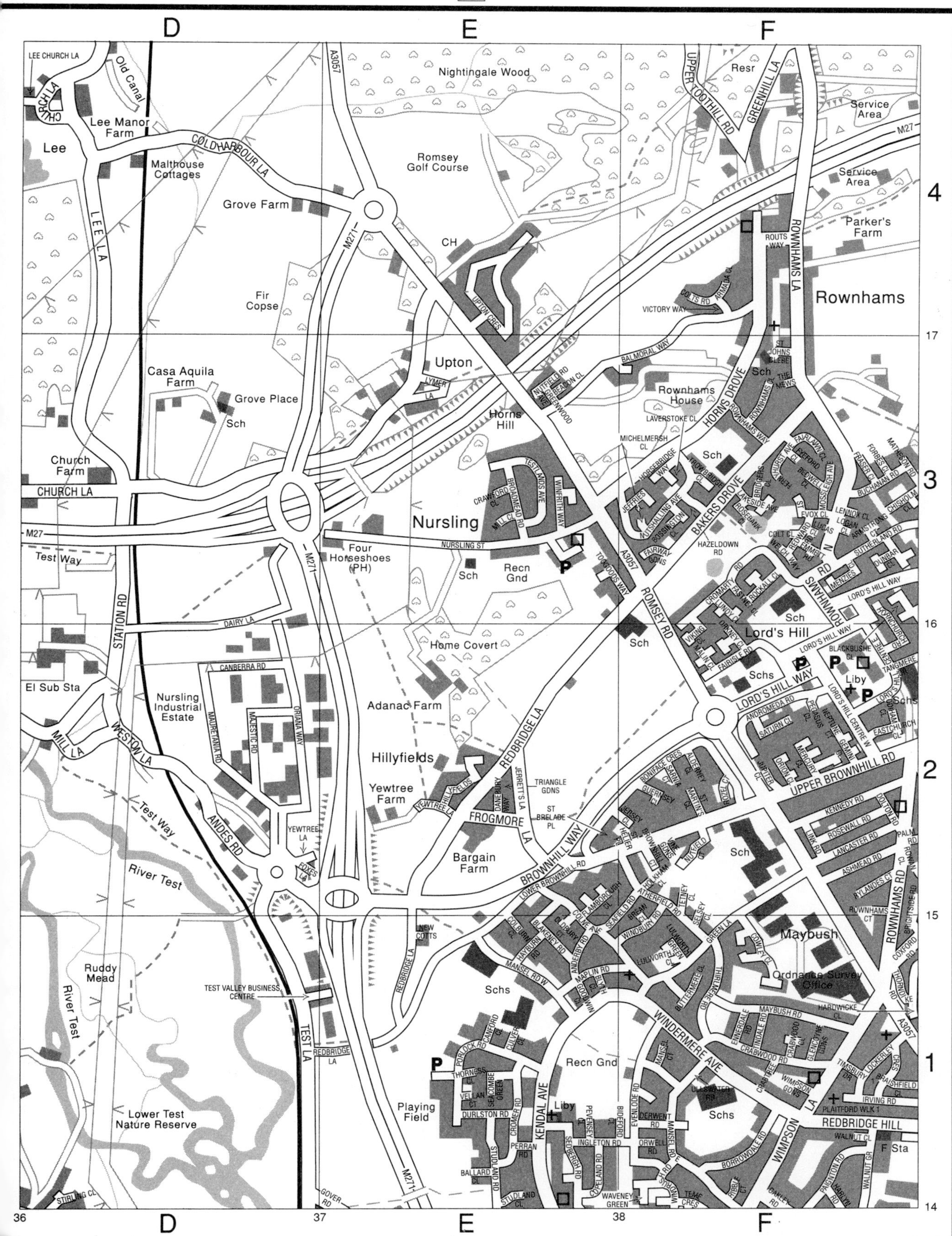
D
E
F
LEE CHURCH LA
CHURCH LA
Old Canal
Lee Manor Farm
Lee
COLDHARBOUR LA
Malthouse Cottages
Grove Farm
A3057
Nightingale Wood
Romsey Golf Course
UPPER TOOTHILL RD
GREENHILL LA
Resr
Service Area
M27
Service Area
Parker's Farm
4
LEE LA
M271
CH
UPTON CRES
ROUTS WAY
ROWNHAMS LA
Rownhams
COLTS RD
ARMADA CL
VICTORY WAY
Fir Copse
17
Casa Aquila Farm
Grove Place
Sch
Upton
LYMER LA
NUTFIELD RD
BEACON CL
GREENWOOD AVE
BALMORAL WAY
ST JOHNS GLEBE
THE MEWS
Sch
ROWNHAMS CL
Rownhams House
LAVERSTOKE CL
HORNS DROVE
ROWNHAMS WAY
Horns Hill
MICHELMERSH CL
Church Farm
CHURCH LA
TESTLANDS AVE
BROADMEAD RD
CRAWFORD CL
MILL CL
WINFRITH WAY
HORSEBRIDGE WAY
JEFFERIES CL
NUTSHALLING AVE
BOSSINGTON CL
TROWBRIDGE CL
BAKERS DROVE
ROSEBANK CL
LAKESIDE AVE
BRIDGERS CL
Sch
FAIRLAWN CL
EXFORD DR
BEDWELL CL
MOSSLEIGH AVE
FORBES CL
FRASER CL
MATHESON RD
BUCHANAN RD
CHISHOLM
3
Nursling
M27
NURSLING ST
Four Horseshoes (PH)
Sch
Recn Gnd
TO WOODS WAY
A3057
FAIRWAY GDNS
HAZELDOWN RD
EVOX CL
LENNOX CL
LOGAN CL
ARMSTRONG CT
SUTHERLAND RD
DUNBAR CL
MENZIES CL
LUCAS CL
EMMETT RD
WELCH WAY
COLT CL
ROWNHAMS RD
LORD'S HILL WAY
Test Way
CROMARTY RD
FASTNET CL
ROCKALL CL
LUNDY CL
ORKNEY CL
VIKING CL
MALIN CL
FAIRISLE RD
Sch
Lord's Hill
STATION RD
DAIRY LA
ROMSEY RD
Sch
16
Home Covert
LORD'S HILL WAY
BLACKBUSHE CL
Liby
TANGMERE
El Sub Sta
CANBERRA RD
Nursling Industrial Estate
MAURETANIA RD
MAJESTIC RD
ORIANA WAY
Adanac Farm
REDBRIDGE LA
Schs
LORD'S HILL WAY
LORD'S HILL CENTRE W
ANDROMEDA RD
PEGASUS CL
NEPTUNE CL
SATURN CL
MERCURY CL
GEMINI CL
EASTCHURCH CL
Schs
MILL LA
WESTON LA
Hillyfields
DANEBURY WAY
JERRETT'S LA
TRIANGLE GDNS
BONIFACE CRES
ALDERNEY CL
SARNIA CL
GUERNSEY CL
ST MARTINS CL
ROZEL CT
JUPITER CL
ORION CL
UPPER BROWNHILL RD
2
KENNEDY RD
DOLTON RD
Test Way
Yewtree Farm
HILLYFIELDS
YEWTREE LA
FROGMORE LA
ST BRELADE PL
BROWNHILL WAY
JERSEY CL
HELIER CL
BROWNHILL CL
VINE GDNS
NUTFIELD CT
Sch
LINK RD
ROSEWALL RD
LANCASTER RD
PALM RD
ANDES RD
YEWTREE LA
FOXES LA
River Test
Bargain Farm
BROWNHILL RD
LOWER BROWNHILL RD
FLAMBOROUGH CL
HOLKHAM CL
ATHERFIELD RD
TETNEY CL
SEAFIELD RD
BREAN CL
SELSEY CL
ASHMEAD RD
RYLANDES CT
ROWNHAMS CT
BRIGHTSIDE RD
15
NEW COTTS
COLBURN CL
BLAKENEY RD
CLOVELLY RD
COLNE AVE
WINDBURY RD
LULWORTH GREEN
GREEN LA
COWLEY CL
Maybush
ROWNHAMS RD
COXFORD CL
Ruddy Mead
REDBRIDGE LA
HAYBURN RD
ANDERBY RD
MAPLIN RD
LULWORTH CL
THIRLMERE RD
BUTTERMERE CL
Ordnance Survey Office
TEST VALLEY BUSINESS CENTRE
MANSEL RD W
Schs
WINDERMERE AVE
MAYBUSH RD
HARDWICKE CL
A3057
River Test
TEST LA
REDBRIDGE LA
CANFORD CL
CULVER CL
MANSEL CT
ENNERDALE RD
TINDALE RD
CRABWOOD RD
GLENCOYNE GDNS
TIMSBURY DR
LOCKERLEY CRES
PORLOCK RD
THORNESS CL
SEACOMBE GREEN
VELLAN CT
Recn Gnd
EVENLODE RD
ULLSWATER RD
WIMPSON GDNS
HAILSHFIELD CL
IRVING RD
1
P
Playing Field
DURLSTON RD
CROMER RD
KENDAL AVE
Liby
PEVENSEY CL
BIDEFORD CL
DERWENT RD
Schs
PLAITFORD WLK 1
REDBRIDGE HILL
Lower Test Nature Reserve
PERRAN RD
SEDBERGH RD
INGLETON RD
ORWELL RD
MANSEL RD
WIMPSON LA
WALNUT CL
F Sta
STUDLAND RD
COPELAND RD
BORROWDALE RD
PAIGNTON RD
WALNUT GR
BALLARD CL
STIRLING CL
GOVER RD
M271
STUDLAND CL
WAVENEY GREEN
TEME CRES
RIBBLE CT
DAKLEY RD
14
36
37
38
D
E
F

78

101

54

77

A
B
C
4
3
2
1
17
16
15
14
39
40
41
M27
A27
A33
A35
A3035
A3057
Chilworth Common
Chilworth Tower
Dymer's Wood
Tanner's Brook
Lord's Wood
Castle Hill
Chilworth Ring
Golf Course
CH
Sports Centre
Schs
Sch
Hospl
Cemy
Holly Brook
Aldermoor
Coxford
Shirley Warren
Conv
Upper Shirley
Coll
Univ
Cutthorn
Resr
Southampton Common
Coronation Ave
The Lake
Cemetery Lake
Cowherds (PH)
LORD'S HILL WAY
ALDERMOOR RD
LORDSWOOD RD
COXFORD RD
WINCHESTER RD
WARREN AVE
OLIVE RD
ROMSEY RD
BURGESS RD
BASSETT AVE
CHILWORTH RD
THE AVENUE
HILL LA
ST JAMES'S RD
ANGLESEA RD
GOLF COURSE RD
BASSETT ROW
REDBRIDGE HILL

102

55

D
E
F
4
3
2
1
17
16
15
14
42
43
44
Home Wood
Fred Woolley House
North Stoneham
Golf Course
Park Pond
Shrubbery Pond
Park Farm
Doncaster Drove
Monks Brook
Hotel
Stoneham Park
CH
Southampton Parkway Station
Airport
Works
Crem
Bassett Green
Sch
Bassett
Schs
Swaythling Station
Swaythling
White Swan (PH)
PH
Liby
Univ
Mans Bridge
The Itchen Navigation
Woodmill
Riverside Park
Hampton Park
Highfield
River Itchen
Wks
Coll
Westwood Park
Portswood
Bitterne Park
Cobden Bridge
WINCHESTER RD
M27
A33(T)
A27
A335
A35
A3035
NUTWOOD
BIRCH RD
STONEHAM LA
STONEHAM WAY
WIDE LA
CHERITON RD
TICHBORNE RD
BASSETT GREEN RD
BURGESS RD
LANGHORN RD
THOMAS LEWIS WAY
UNIVERSITY RD
HIGHFIELD LA
WELBECK AVE
SHAFTESBURY AVE
PORTSWOOD RD
ST DENYS RD
MANSBRIDGE RD
WOODMILL LA
FOREST HILLS DR
WITTS HILL
WESSEX LA
ETHELBURT AVE
CARNATION RD
DAFFODIL RD
LABURNUM RD
BLUEBELL RD
HONEYSUCKLE RD
TULIP RD
HAREFIELD RD
HARRISON RD
MAYFIELD RD
BROADLANDS RD
GRANBY GR
SIRDAR RD
KITCHENER RD
CASTLE RD
WELLINGTON RD
CHURCH LA
MONKS WOOD CL
BASSETT WOOD RD
GLEN EYRE DR
GLENWOOD AVE
COPPERFIELD RD
VIOLET RD
SALISBURY RD
HIGHFIELD AVE
WESTWOOD RD
WINN RD
LEIGH RD
BLENHEIM AVE
WESTBOURNE CRES
OAKMOUNT AVE
ABBOTTS WAY
BROOKVALE RD
RUSSELL PL
OSBORNE RD
BELMONT RD
KENT RD
PRIORY RD
NURSERY RD
RIVER VIEW RD
MANOR FARM RD
OAK TREE RD
ASH TREE RD
DIMOND RD
COPSEWOOD RD
DELL RD
HILLSIDE AVE
APPLETON RD
BOND RD
THOROLD RD
PARKLANDS
DELL WHARF
COBDEN AVE
ST CATHERINE'S RD
CORNWALL RD
HALSTEAD RD
NORWICH RD
DOWNTON RD
KINGSDOWN WAY
RIVER WLK
MOAT HILL
PORTSWOOD RD
WOODCOTE RD
HIGH RD
PARKVILLE RD
RAYNERS GDNS
FLEMING RD
MEAD CRES
OLIVER RD
ROBERT CECIL AVE
ITCHENSIDE CL
MEADOWSIDE CL
ITCHEN VIEW
ALFRED ROSE CT
FRIARS WAY
WALNUT AVE
STONEHAM CEMETERY RD
HOWARD CL
Sch
Sch
Schs
Schs
Sch
Sch

80

103

56

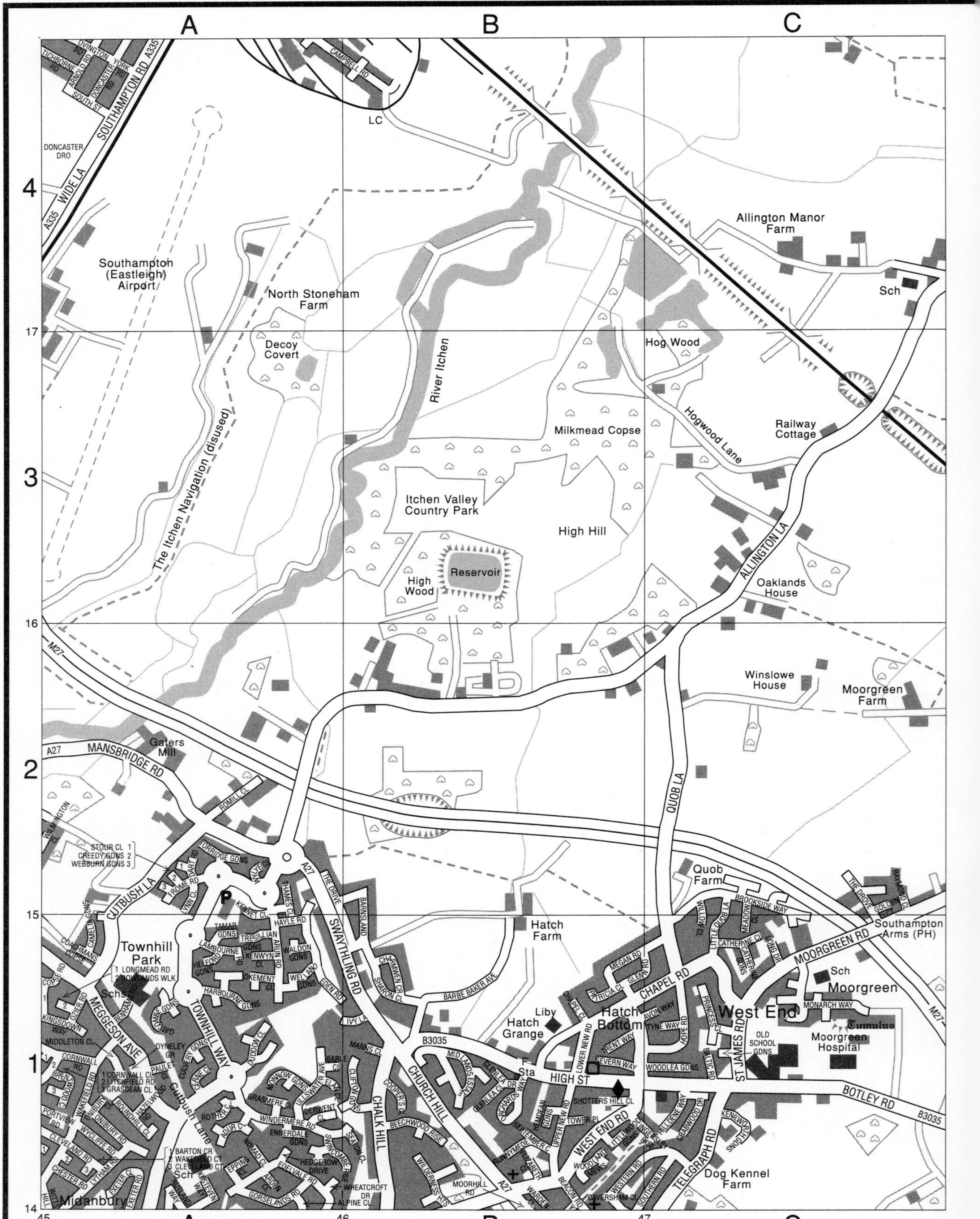

A
B
C
4
3
2
1
17
16
15
14
45
46
47
SOUTHAMPTON RD A335
WIDE LA
A335
DONCASTER DRO
TICHBORNE RD
OVINGTON RD
ARNOLD RD
DONCASTER RD
YORK RD
SOUTH ST
CAMPBELL RD
LC
Southampton (Eastleigh) Airport
North Stoneham Farm
Decoy Covert
The Itchen Navigation (disused)
River Itchen
Hog Wood
Allington Manor Farm
Sch
Milkmead Copse
Hogwood Lane
Railway Cottage
Itchen Valley Country Park
High Hill
Reservoir
High Wood
ALLINGTON LA
Oaklands House
Winslowe House
Moorgreen Farm
M27
A27
MANSBRIDGE RD
Gaters Mill
QUOB LA
WILMINGTON CL
ROMILL CL
STOUR CL 1
CREEDY GDNS 2
WEBBURN GDNS 3
CUTBUSH LA
TORRIDGE GDNS
FROME RD
LYNN CL
KENNET CL
THAMES CL
HAYLE RD
THE DRIVE
BARNSLAND
SWAYTHLING RD
Quob Farm
BROOKSIDE WAY
THE DROVE
RAYMOND CL
GOLDEN CT
Southampton Arms (PH)
MOORGREEN RD
Sch
Moorgreen
MONARCH WAY
Tumulus
Moorgreen Hospital
OLD SCHOOL GDNS
West End
Hatch Farm
Townhill Park
1 LONGMEAD RD
2 ROWLANDS WLK
Schs
TAMAR GDNS
TRESILLIAN GDNS
LAMBOURNE
KENWYN CL
WALDON GDNS
ARUN RD
HELFORD GDNS
OKEMENT CL
WELLAND GDNS
EDEN RD
HARBOURNE GDNS
CH
SHARON CL
BARBE BAKER AVE
COACHMANS COPSE
CAMELIA GDNS
COPSE RD
KINGSDOWN WAY
MEGGESON AVE
MIDDLETON CL
CORNWALL RD
BRENDON
1 CORNWALL CL
2 LITCHFIELD RD
3 GRASDEAN CL
TOWNHILL WAY
DYNELEY GR
PAULET
CULVERY GDNS
DUDDON CL
IVY LA
MANNS CL
BABLE CL
MONNOW GDNS
ULLSWATER AVE
CLIFTON GDNS
COOPER'S CL
CHURCH HILL
CHALK HILL
BRASMERE CL
WINDERMERE RD
DERWENT CL
ENNERDALE GDNS
ADUR CL
ROTHER CL
Cutbush Lane
HAZELWOOD
PORTVIEW RD
UNIBURY
ONIBURY RD
WYCLIFFE RD
BOUNDHILL CL
CLEVELAND RD
CHESTER RD
LYTHAM RD
EXETER CL
EXETER RD
1 BARTON CR
2 WAKEFIELD CT
3 CLEVELAND CT
Sch
Midanbury
HILL
NOMAD CL
EPPING CL
ARDEN CL
EDELVALE RD
HEDGEROW DRIVE
SWINCOMBE RISE
SEATON CL
GORSELANDS RD
WHEATCROFT DR
ALPINE CL
BEECHWOOD RISE
WILDERNESS HTS
MOORHILL RD
B3035
MIDLANDS EST
GLENLEA CL
GLENLEA DR
ORCHARDS WAY
Sta
HIGH ST
Hatch Grange
Liby
Hatch Bottom
LOWER NEW RD
UPPER NEW RD
TRENT WAY
SEVERN WAY
TYNE WAY
AVON WAY
HOPE RD
SHOTTERS HILL CL
TOWER PL
WEST END RD
SEPTEMBER CL
HEMDEAN GDNS
RUNNYMEDE
ELIZABETH
WOODLAND MEWS
BEACON CL
WARDEN CL
CAVERSHAM CL
WESTERN RD
SOUTHERN RD
TELEGRAPH RD
GRABWOOD DR
HILLDENE WAY
KENILWORTH GDNS
Dog Kennel Farm
WOODLEA GDNS
BALTIC RD
ST JAMES RD
PRINCESS CL
CHAPEL RD
CHAPEL CL
PATRICIA CL
GLEN RD
MEGAN RD
WILLOW CL
LITTLE QUOB LA
MEADOW CL
CATHERINE CL
LONG DR
BOTLEY RD
B3035
M27

79

104

57

D
E
F
Lake Farm
Quobleigh Pond
Whitetree Farm
Greenwood Farm
Durley Copse
Lapstone Farm
The Lapstone (PH)
Firtree Farmhouse
ALLINGTON LA
BOTLEY RD
KNOWLE LA
The Cockpit Farm
GREENWOOD LA
FIRTREE LA
Foxholes Farm
Horton Heath
DURLEY RD
The Old Rectory
Hearts Copse
Chalcroft Farm
Sch
Church Croft Farm
CHURCH LA
Brigadier Gerard (PH)
Beech Corner
BURNETTS LA
BLIND LA
SNAKEMOOR LA
Snakemoor Farm
Little Snakemoor Farm
STAPLEFORD LA
Denham's Corner
B3342
B3354
Little Moorgreen Farm
BUBB LA
Jacksons Farm
Croft House
WINCHESTER RD
The Firs
SHAMBLEHURST LA
Berrywood Farm
MOORGREEN RD
Hedge End Station
Park Farm
Braxells Farm
Golf Course
Long Common
Dowd's Farm
Shamblehurst Lane (Path)
Moorlands
TOLLBAR WAY
M27
Pear Tree (PH)
Boorley Green
MADDOXFORD LA
Nelson Business Park
Herald Industrial Estate
SOLENT INDUSTRIAL EST
HEDGE END BUSINESS CENTRE
BOTLEY RD
WATERLOO IND EST
NAVIGATORS WAY
CHICHESTER CL
WALKER GDNS
LOCKE RD
CUDWORTH MEAD
DRUMMOND RD
STIRLING CRES
ELLIOT RISE
BEATTIE RISE
MAUNSELL WAY
GILES CL
BILLINGTON GDNS
REPTON GDNS
WATKIN RD
ST LAWRENCE CL
STROUDLEY WAY
WOODHOUSE LA
WINCHESTER ST
CROWS NEST LA
KESTREL CL
HAVEN CROFT
FALCON WAY
OATLANDS RD
PEAR TREE CL
MADDOXFORD WAY
CHAPEL DRO
FIR TREE CL
ANGELICA GDNS
BURNETTS FIELDS
BURNETTS GDNS
CENTAURY GDNS
VALERIAN CL
ROSEBAY
MEADOWSWEET WAY
ST ANDREWS PARK
CAMPION CL
CHERRY DROVE
DUMPERS DROVE
THE DROVE
HERALD RD
FLANDERS RD
48
49
50
14
15
16
17
1
2
3
4

82

58

81

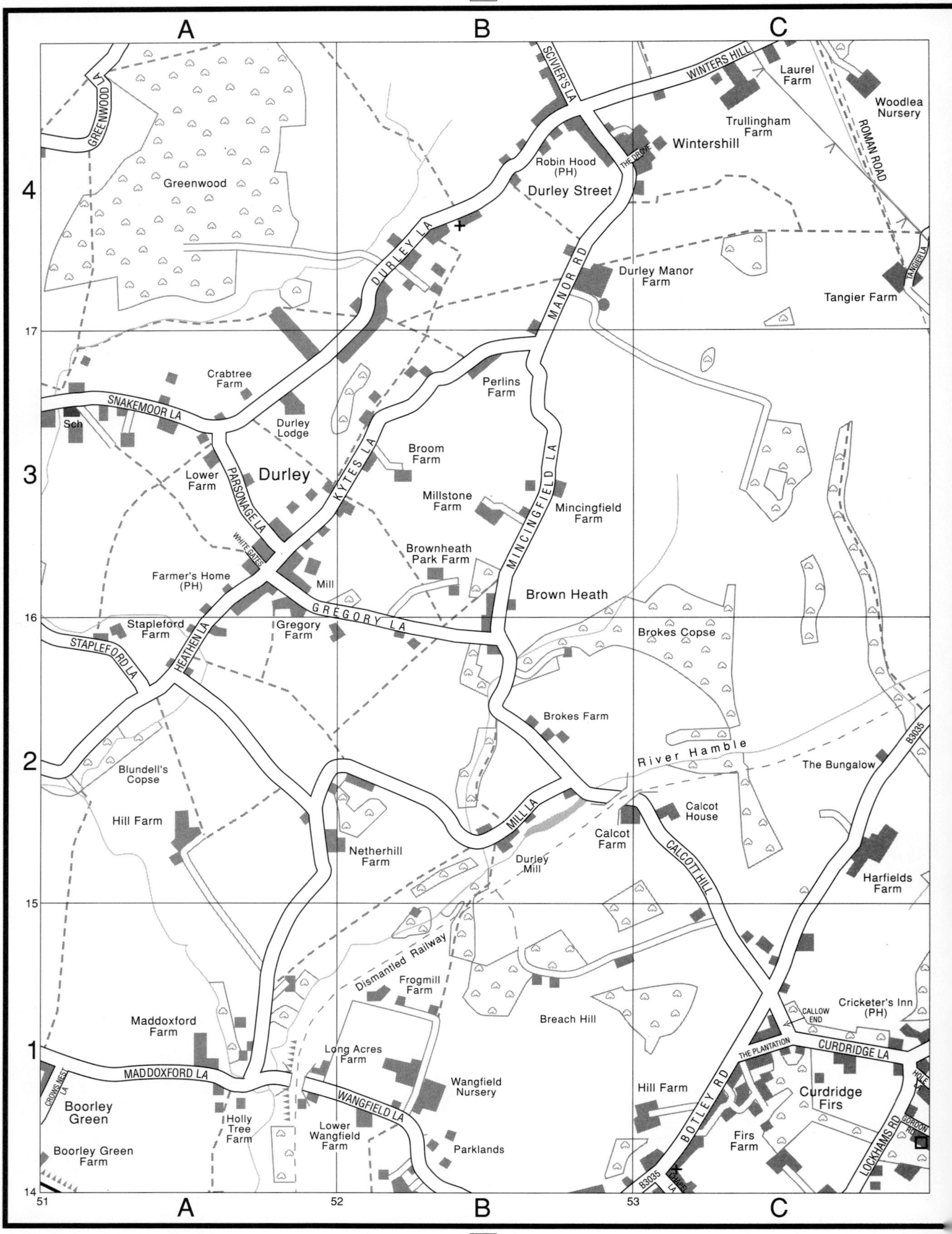
A
B
C
4
3
2
1
17
16
15
14
51
52
53
GREENWOOD LA
Greenwood
SCIVIERS LA
WINTERS HILL
Laurel Farm
Woodlea Nursery
Trullingham Farm
ROMAN ROAD
Wintershill
THE DROVE
Robin Hood (PH)
Durley Street
DURLEY LA
MANOR RD
Durley Manor Farm
TANGIER LA
Tangier Farm
Crabtree Farm
SNAKEMOOR LA
Sch
Durley Lodge
Perlins Farm
Broom Farm
Lower Farm
PARSONAGE LA
Durley
KYTES LA
Millstone Farm
MINCINGFIELD LA
Mincingfield Farm
WHITE GATES
Brownheath Park Farm
Farmer's Home (PH)
Mill
Brown Heath
Stapleford Farm
Gregory Farm
GREGORY LA
Brokes Copse
STAPLEFORD LA
HEATHEN LA
Brokes Farm
River Hamble
B3035
The Bungalow
Blundell's Copse
Hill Farm
MILL LA
Calcot House
Calcot Farm
Netherhill Farm
Durley Mill
CALCOTT HILL
Harfields Farm
Dismantled Railway
Frogmill Farm
Breach Hill
Cricketer's Inn (PH)
CALLOW END
Maddoxford Farm
THE PLANTATION
CURDRIDGE LA
Long Acres Farm
MADDOXFORD LA
Wangfield Nursery
Hill Farm
Curdridge Firs
HOLE LA
CROWS NEST LA
WANGFIELD LA
BOTLEY RD
GORDON RD
Boorley Green
Holly Tree Farm
Lower Wangfield Farm
Firs Farm
LOCKHAMS RD
Boorley Green Farm
Parklands
B3035
CHAPEL LA

106

59

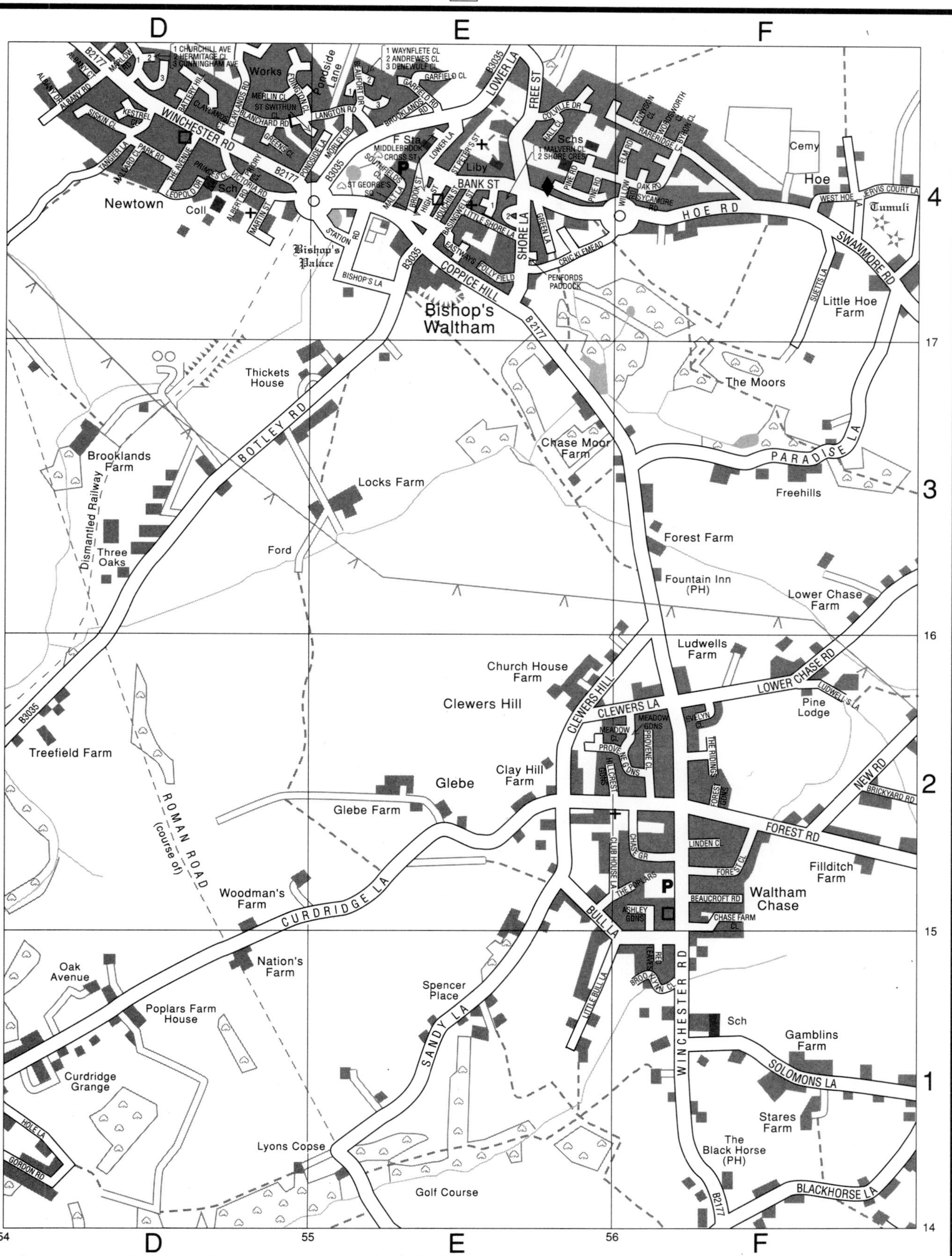

D
E
F
Newtown
Coll
Sch
Works
Pondside Lane
F Sta
Liby
Schs
Cemy
Hoe
Tumuli
Bishop's Palace
Bishop's Waltham
WINCHESTER RD
B2177
B3035
BANK ST
LOWER LA
FREE ST
SHORE LA
HOE RD
SWANMORE RD
COPPICE HILL
BISHOP'S LA
STATION RD
1 CHURCHILL AVE
2 HERMITAGE CL
3 CUNNINGHAM AVE
1 WAYNFLETE CL
2 ANDREWES CL
3 DENEWULF CL
1 MALVERN CL
2 SHORE CRES
PENFORDS PADDOCK
Little Hoe Farm
The Moors
Thickets House
BOTLEY RD
Brooklands Farm
Dismantled Railway
Three Oaks
Ford
Locks Farm
Chase Moor Farm
PARADISE LA
Freehills
Forest Farm
Fountain Inn (PH)
Lower Chase Farm
Ludwells Farm
Church House Farm
Clewers Hill
CLEWERS LA
LOWER CHASE RD
Pine Lodge
Treefield Farm
ROMAN ROAD (course of)
Glebe
Glebe Farm
Clay Hill Farm
NEW RD
FOREST RD
Fillditch Farm
Waltham Chase
Woodman's Farm
CURDRIDGE LA
BULL LA
Oak Avenue
Nation's Farm
Spencer Place
SANDY LA
Poplars Farm House
WINCHESTER RD
Sch
Gamblins Farm
SOLOMONS LA
Curdridge Grange
Stares Farm
The Black Horse (PH)
HOLE LA
GORDON RD
Lyons Copse
Golf Course
BLACKHORSE LA
17
16
15
14
4
3
2
1
54
55
56

84

60

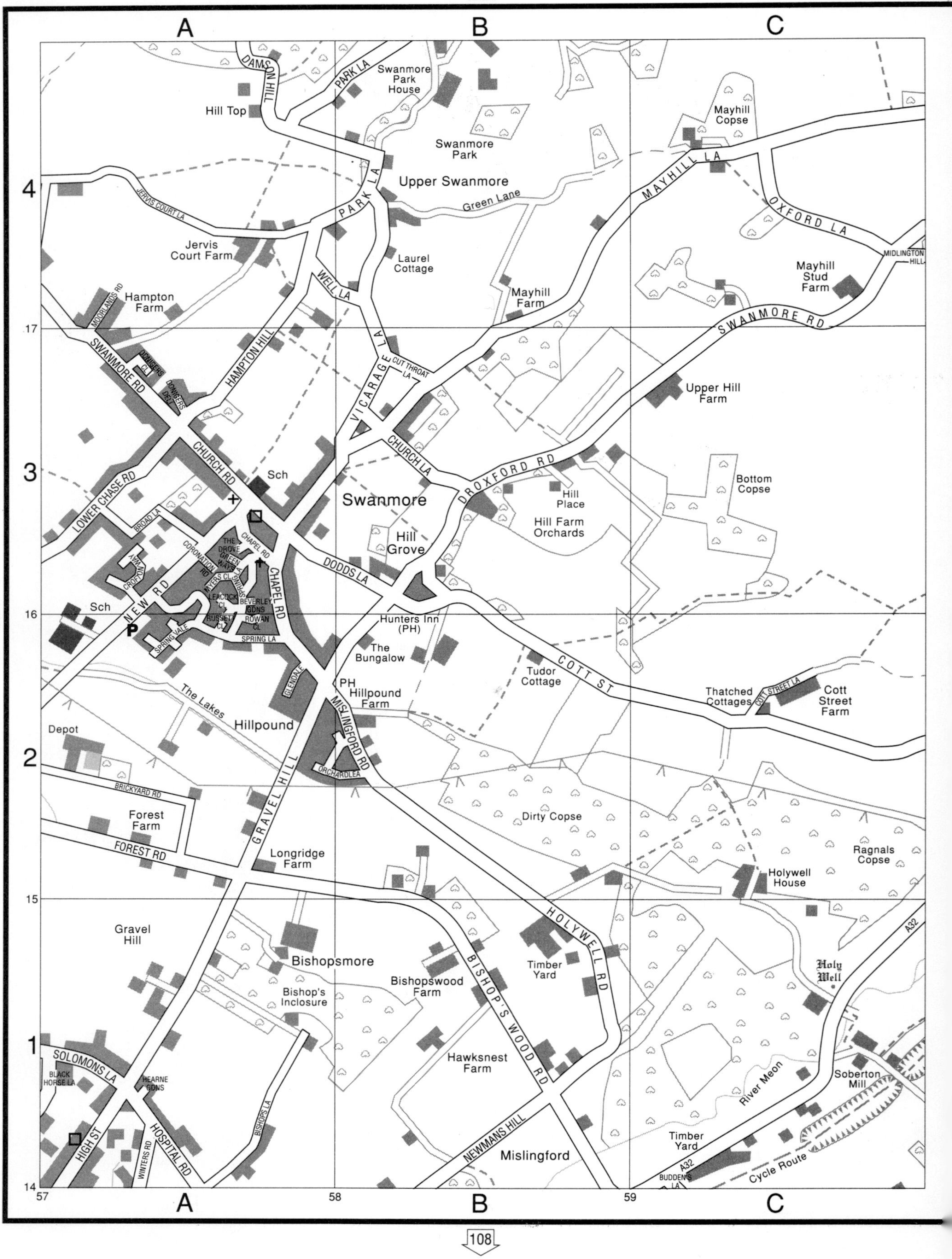
A
B
C
4
3
2
1
17
16
15
14
57
58
59
Hill Top
DAMSON HILL
PARK LA
Swanmore Park House
Swanmore Park
Upper Swanmore
Green Lane
Mayhill Copse
MAYHILL LA
OXFORD LA
MIDLINGTON HILL
Mayhill Stud Farm
SWANMORE RD
JERVIS COURT LA
Jervis Court Farm
Hampton Farm
MOORLANDS RD
WELL LA
Laurel Cottage
Mayhill Farm
HAMPTON HILL
DONIGERS CL
DONIGERS DELL
SWANMORE RD
VICARAGE LA
CUT THROAT LA
Upper Hill Farm
CHURCH RD
CHURCH LA
DROXFORD RD
Hill Place
Hill Farm Orchards
Bottom Copse
Sch
Swanmore
Hill Grove
LOWER CHASE RD
BROAD LA
CORONATION RD
THE DROVE
GREEN WAY
CHAPEL RD
MYERS CL
LEACOCK CL
BEVERLEY GDNS
ROWAN CL
RUSSETT CL
SPRING LA
SPRING VALE
CROFTON WAY
NEW RD
Sch
P
DODDS LA
Hunters Inn (PH)
The Bungalow
Tudor Cottage
COTT ST
Thatched Cottages
COTT STREET LA
Cott Street Farm
GLENDALE
PH
Hillpound Farm
MISLINGFORD RD
The Lakes
Hillpound
Depot
BRICKYARD RD
ORCHARDLEA
Forest Farm
FOREST RD
GRAVEL HILL
Longridge Farm
Dirty Copse
Holywell House
Ragnals Copse
Gravel Hill
Bishopsmore
Bishop's Inclosure
Bishopswood Farm
BISHOP'S WOOD RD
HOLYWELL RD
Timber Yard
Holy Well
A32
Hawksnest Farm
River Meon
Soberton Mill
SOLOMONS LA
BLACK HORSE LA
HEARNE GDNS
HIGH ST
HOSPITAL RD
WINTERS RD
BISHOPS LA
NEWMANS HILL
Mislingford
Timber Yard
BUDDEN'S LA
Cycle Route

83

108

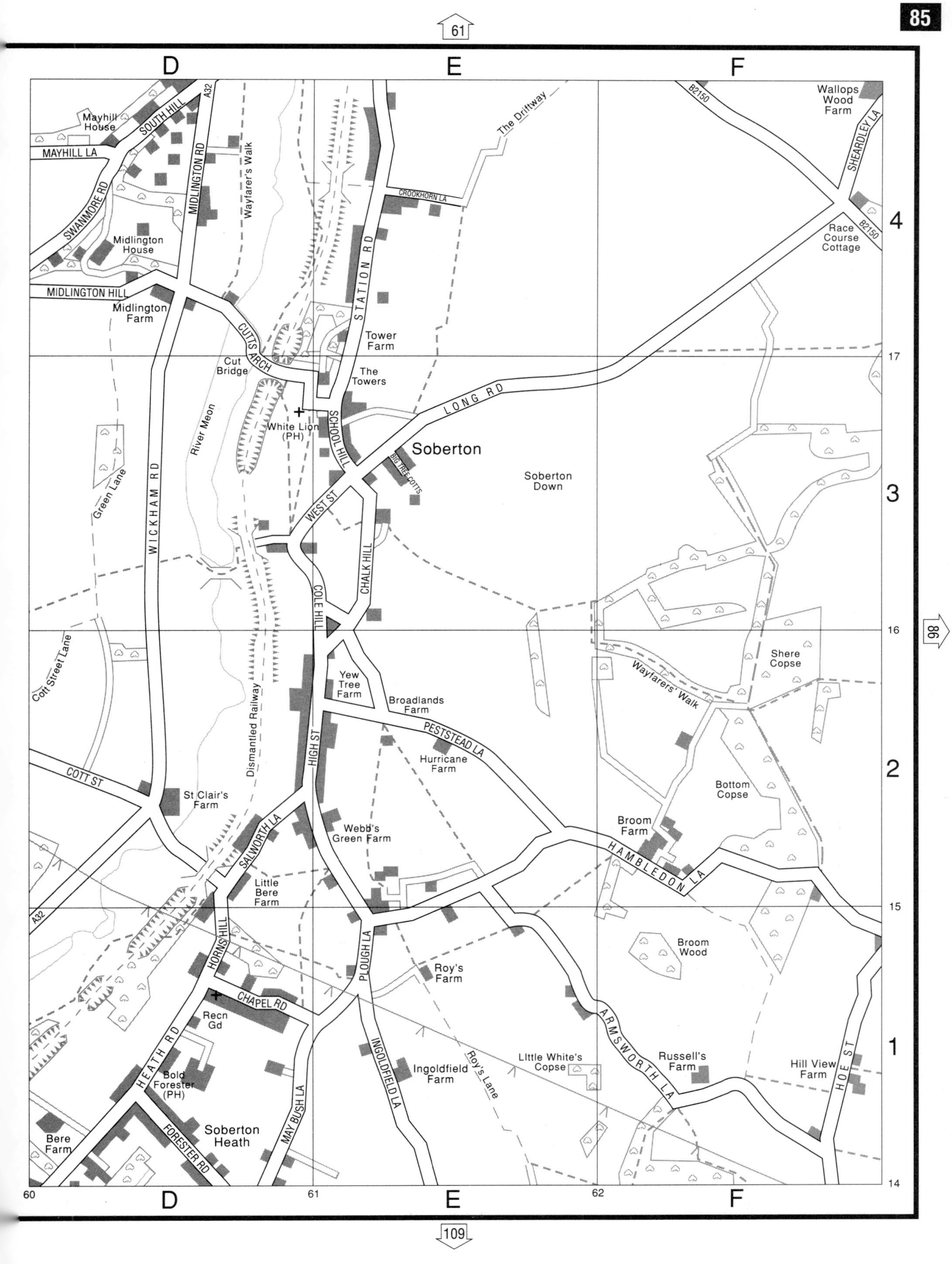
61
D
E
F
Mayhill House
MAYHILL LA
SOUTH HILL
A32
SWANMORE RD
MIDLINGTON RD
Wayfarer's Walk
Midlington House
MIDLINGTON HILL
Midlington Farm
CUTTS ARCH
Cut Bridge
STATION RD
Tower Farm
The Towers
The Driftway
CROOKHORN LA
B2150
Wallops Wood Farm
SHEARDLEY LA
Race Course Cottage
4
17
LONG RD
White Lion (PH)
SCHOOL HILL
River Meon
Soberton
BIG TREE COTTS
Soberton Down
WEST ST
3
Green Lane
WICKHAM RD
CHALK HILL
COLE HILL
16
98
Cott Street Lane
Yew Tree Farm
Broadlands Farm
Shere Copse
Wayfarers' Walk
Dismantled Railway
PESTSTEAD LA
HIGH ST
Hurricane Farm
COTT ST
St Clair's Farm
2
Bottom Copse
Broom Farm
SALWORTH LA
Webb's Green Farm
HAMBLEDON LA
Little Bere Farm
15
A32
HORNS HILL
PLOUGH LA
Broom Wood
Roy's Farm
CHAPEL RD
Recn Gd
ARMSWORTH LA
1
HEATH RD
INGOLDFIELD LA
Ingoldfield Farm
Roy's Lane
Little White's Copse
Russell's Farm
Hill View Farm
HOE ST
Bold Forester (PH)
Soberton Heath
MAY BUSH LA
FORESTER RD
Bere Farm
14
60
61
62
109

62

85

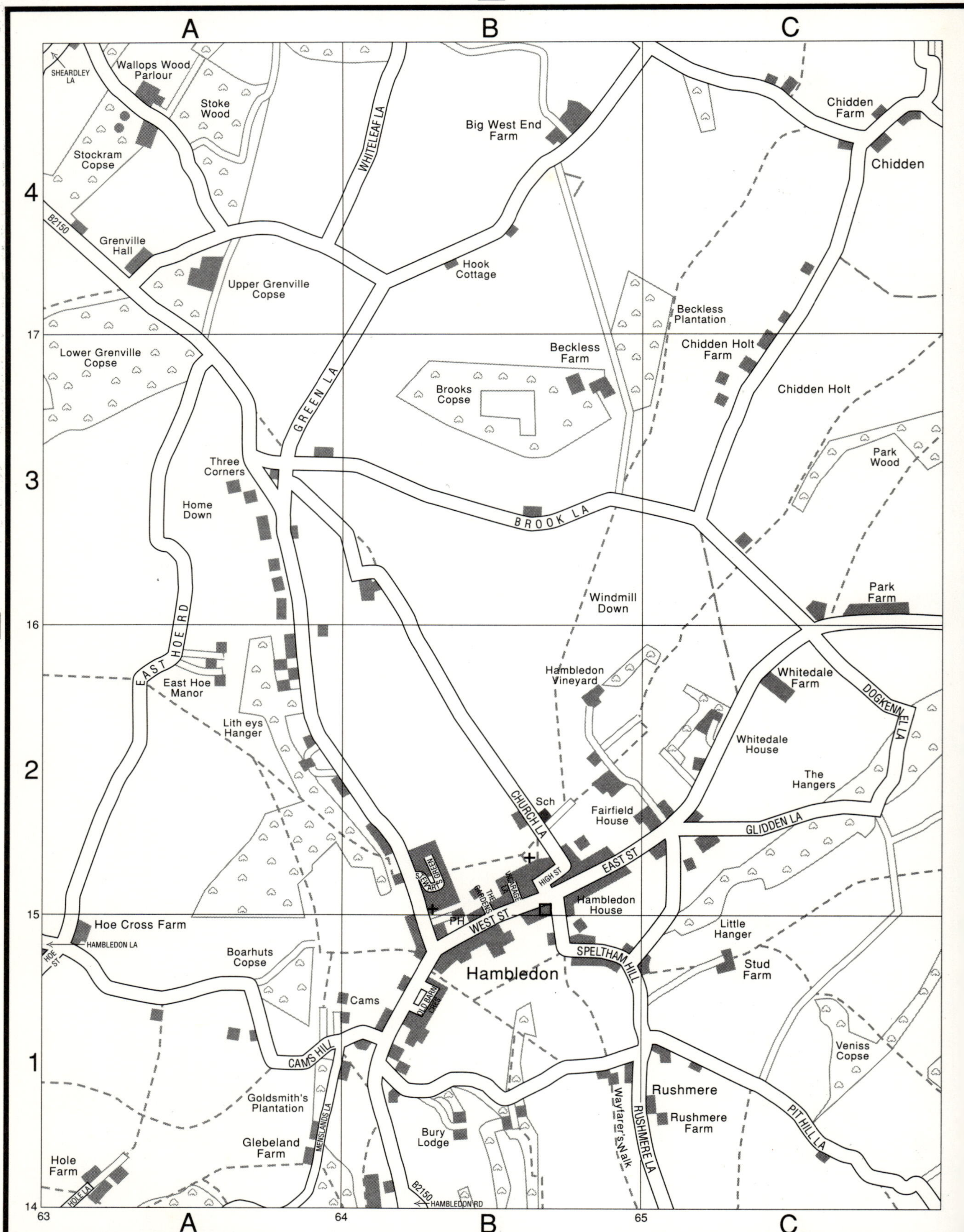
A
B
C
SHEARDLEY LA
Wallops Wood Parlour
Stoke Wood
Stockram Copse
WHITELEAF LA
Big West End Farm
Chidden Farm
Chidden
4
B2150
Grenville Hall
Upper Grenville Copse
Hook Cottage
Beckless Plantation
17
Lower Grenville Copse
Beckless Farm
Chidden Holt Farm
Brooks Copse
Chidden Holt
GREEN LA
Park Wood
3
Three Corners
Home Down
BROOK LA
Windmill Down
Park Farm
16
EAST HOE RD
East Hoe Manor
Hambledon Vineyard
Whitedale Farm
DOGKENNEL LA
Lith eys Hanger
Whitedale House
2
The Hangers
CHURCH LA
Sch
Fairfield House
GLIDDEN LA
EAST ST
HIGH ST
STEWARTS GREEN
THE GARDENS
VICARAGE LA
Hambledon House
15
Hoe Cross Farm
PH
WEST ST
Little Hanger
HAMBLEDON LA
HOE ST
Boarhuts Copse
SPELTHAM HILL
Stud Farm
Hambledon
Cams
OLD BARN CRES
Veniss Copse
1
CAMS HILL
Goldsmith's Plantation
Rushmere
Wayfarer's Walk
RUSHMERE LA
Rushmere Farm
PITHILL LA
MENSLANDS LA
Bury Lodge
Glebeland Farm
Hole Farm
HOLE LA
B2150
HAMBLEDON RD
14
63
64
65

110

63

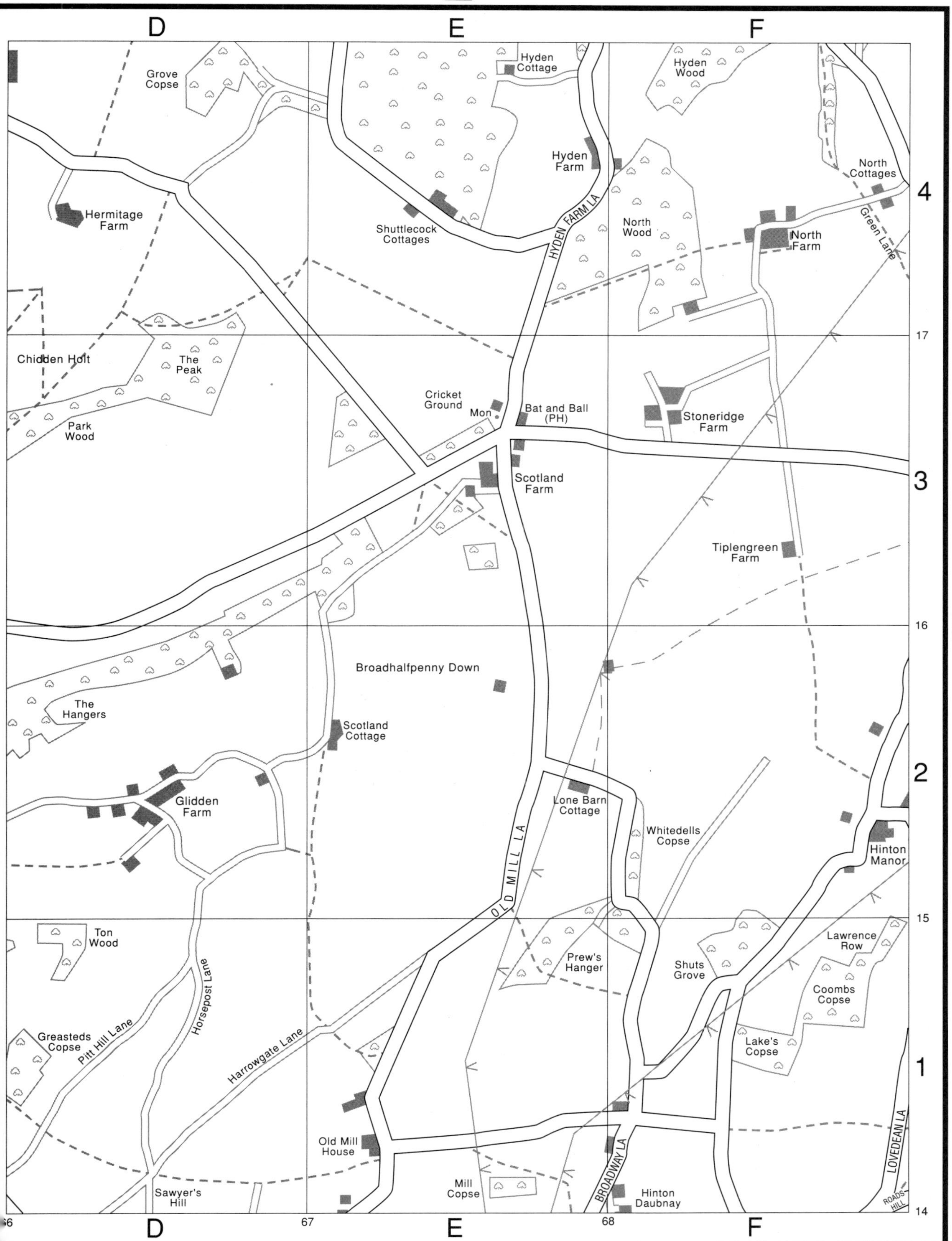
D
E
F
Grove Copse
Hyden Cottage
Hyden Wood
Hyden Farm
North Cottages
Hermitage Farm
Shuttlecock Cottages
HYDEN FARM LA
North Wood
North Farm
Green Lane
4
17
Chidden Holt
The Peak
Park Wood
Cricket Ground
Mon
Bat and Ball (PH)
Stoneridge Farm
Scotland Farm
3
Tiplengreen Farm
16
Broadhalfpenny Down
The Hangers
Scotland Cottage
2
Glidden Farm
Lone Barn Cottage
Whitedells Copse
Hinton Manor
OLD MILL LA
15
Ton Wood
Prew's Hanger
Shuts Grove
Lawrence Row
Coombs Copse
Horsepost Lane
Greasteds Copse
Pitt Hill Lane
Harrowgate Lane
Lake's Copse
1
Old Mill House
LOVEDEAN LA
Mill Copse
BROADWAY LA
Hinton Daubnay
Sawyer's Hill
ROADS HILL
14
66
67
68
D
E
F

88

111

64

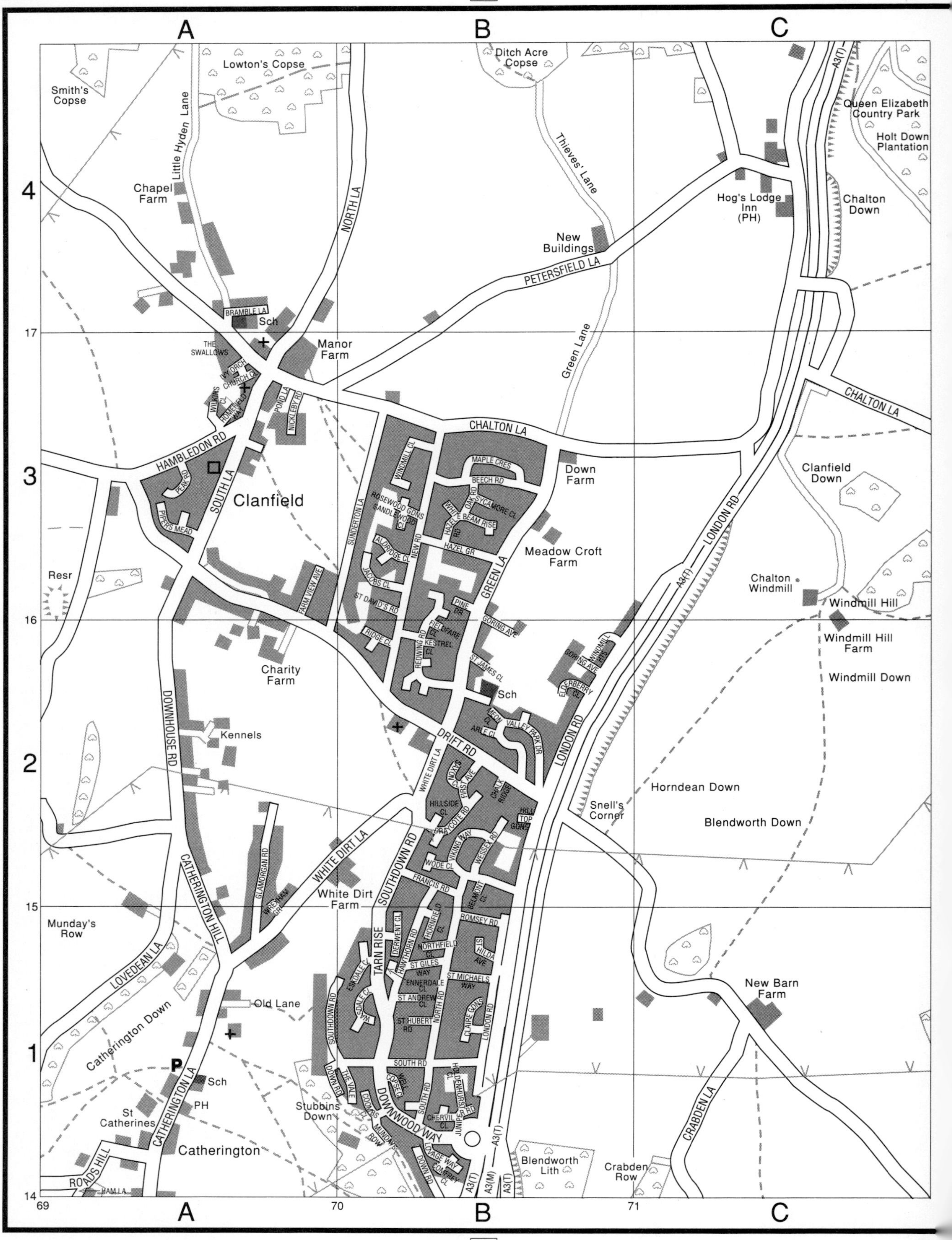
A
B
C
4
3
2
1
17
16
15
14
69
70
71
Smith's Copse
Lowton's Copse
Ditch Acre Copse
Little Hyden Lane
Queen Elizabeth Country Park
Holt Down Plantation
Chapel Farm
NORTH LA
Thieves' Lane
Hog's Lodge Inn (PH)
Chalton Down
New Buildings
PETERSFIELD LA
A3(T)
BRAMBLE LA
Sch
THE SWALLOWS
Manor Farm
Green Lane
IVY ORCH
CHURCH CL
WILKINS CL
HOMEFIELD
POND LA
NICKLEBY RD
CHALTON LA
HAMBLEDON RD
MAPLE CRES
Down Farm
BEECH RD
Clanfield Down
PEAK RD
SOUTH LA
Clanfield
WINDMILL CL
ROSEWOOD GDNS
SANDLEWOOD CL
OAK RD
SYCAMORE CL
WHITE BEAM RISE
HAZEL RD
LONDON RD
PIPERS MEAD
SUNDERTON LA
ALDRIDGE CL
NEW RD
HAZEL GR
GREEN LA
Meadow Croft Farm
Resr
JACOBS CL
FARIA VIEW AVE
ST DAVID'S RD
PINE DR
Chalton Windmill
Windmill Hill
RIDGE CL
FIELDFARE CL
KESTREL CL
REDWING RD
GORING AVE
WINDMILL HTS
Windmill Hill Farm
Charity Farm
ST JAMES CL
ELDERBERRY CL
Windmill Down
Sch
MEON CL
ARLE CL
VALLEY PARK DR
Kennels
DOWNHOUSE RD
DRIFT RD
WHITE DIRT LA
FIRST AVE
CHALK RIDGE
HILLSIDE CL
HILL TOP GDNS
Snell's Corner
Horndean Down
Blendworth Down
CATHERINGTON HILL
GLAMORGAN RD
WHITE DIRT LA
SOUTHDOWN RD
VIKING WAY
WESSEX RD
WODE CL
FRANCIS RD
BELMONT CL
WREXHAM GR
White Dirt Farm
Munday's Row
TARN RISE
DERWENT CL
HAWTHORN RD
NORTHFIELD CL
ROMSEY RD
ST HILDA AVE
LOVEDEAN LA
ESKDALE CL
ST GILES WAY
ENNERDALE CL
ST MICHAELS WAY
New Barn Farm
Old Lane
ST ANDREW CL
WASDALE CL
ST HUBERT RD
NORTH RD
CLAIRE GDNS
LONDON RD
Catherington Down
SOUTHDOWN RD
SOUTH RD
P
Sch
CATHERINGTON LA
DOWN RD
THE VALE
COPSE CL
WELL CL
HOLDENHURST CL
PH
St Catherines
Stubbins Down
DOWNWOOD WAY
CHERVIL CL
JUNIPER RD
CRABDEN LA
Catherington
LOVAGE WAY
COMFREY CL
DOWN RD
Blendworth Lith
Crabden Row
ROADS HILL
HAM LA
A3(M)

87

112

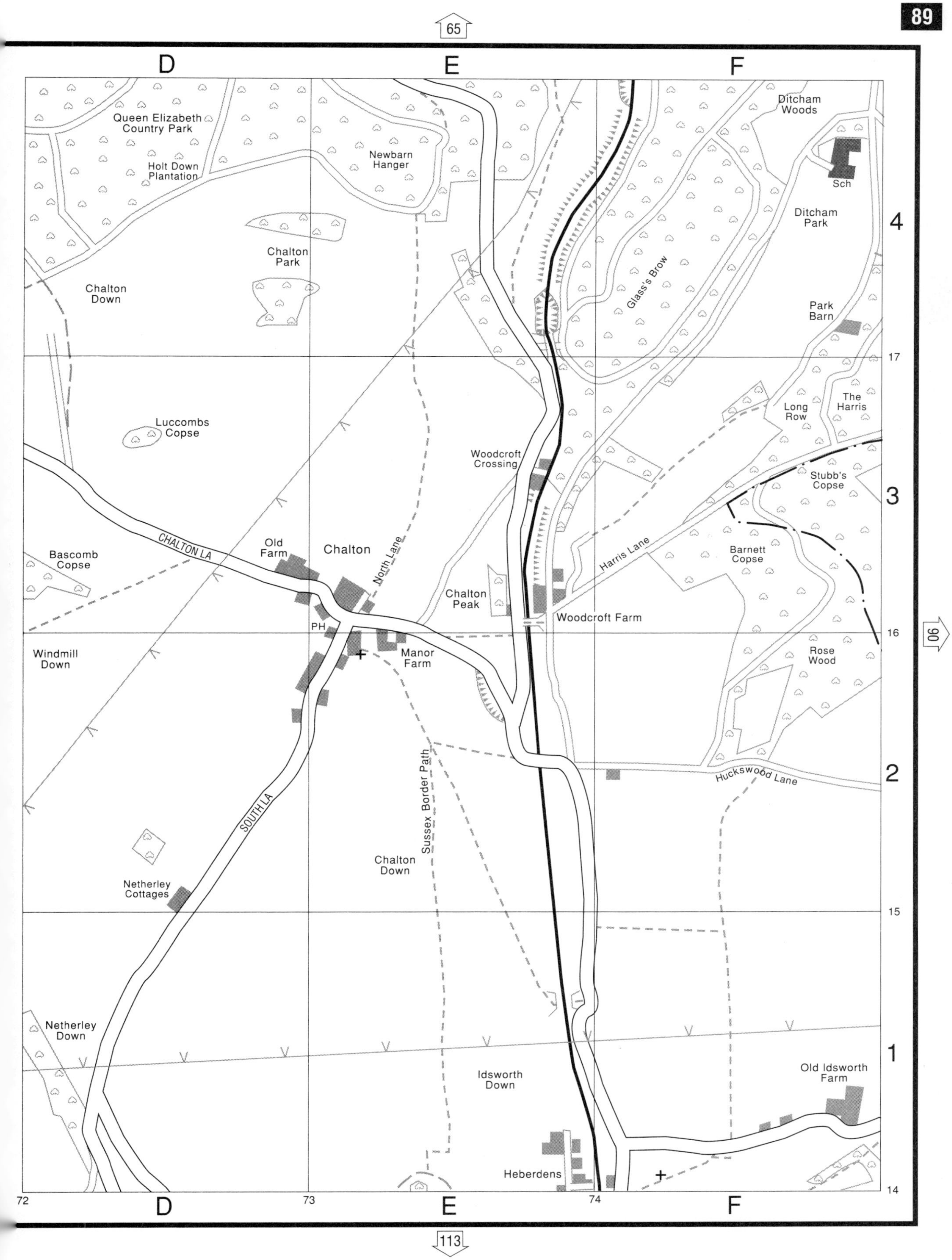
65
D
E
F
Queen Elizabeth
Country Park
Holt Down
Plantation
Newbarn
Hanger
Ditcham
Woods
Sch
Ditcham
Park
4
Chalton
Park
Chalton
Down
Glass's Brow
Park
Barn
17
Luccombs
Copse
Long
Row
The
Harris
Woodcroft
Crossing
Stubb's
Copse
3
CHALTON LA
Old
Farm
Chalton
North Lane
Bascomb
Copse
Harris Lane
Barnett
Copse
Chalton
Peak
Woodcroft Farm
PH
16
90
Windmill
Down
Manor
Farm
Rose
Wood
Sussex Border Path
2
Huckswood Lane
SOUTH LA
Chalton
Down
Netherley
Cottages
15
Netherley
Down
1
Idsworth
Down
Old Idsworth
Farm
Heberdens
14
72
73
74
D
E
F
113

66

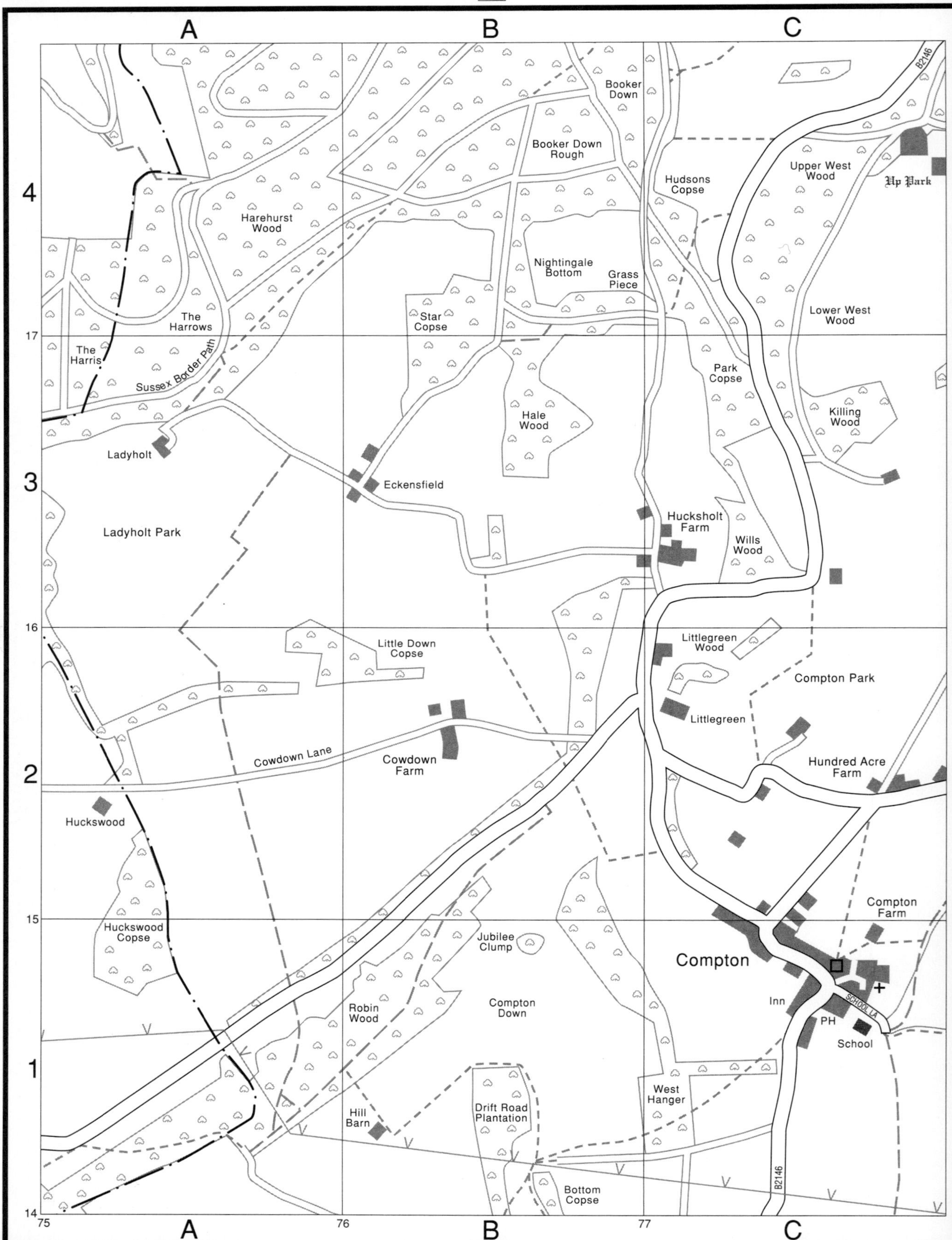

89

not continued, see key diagram

67

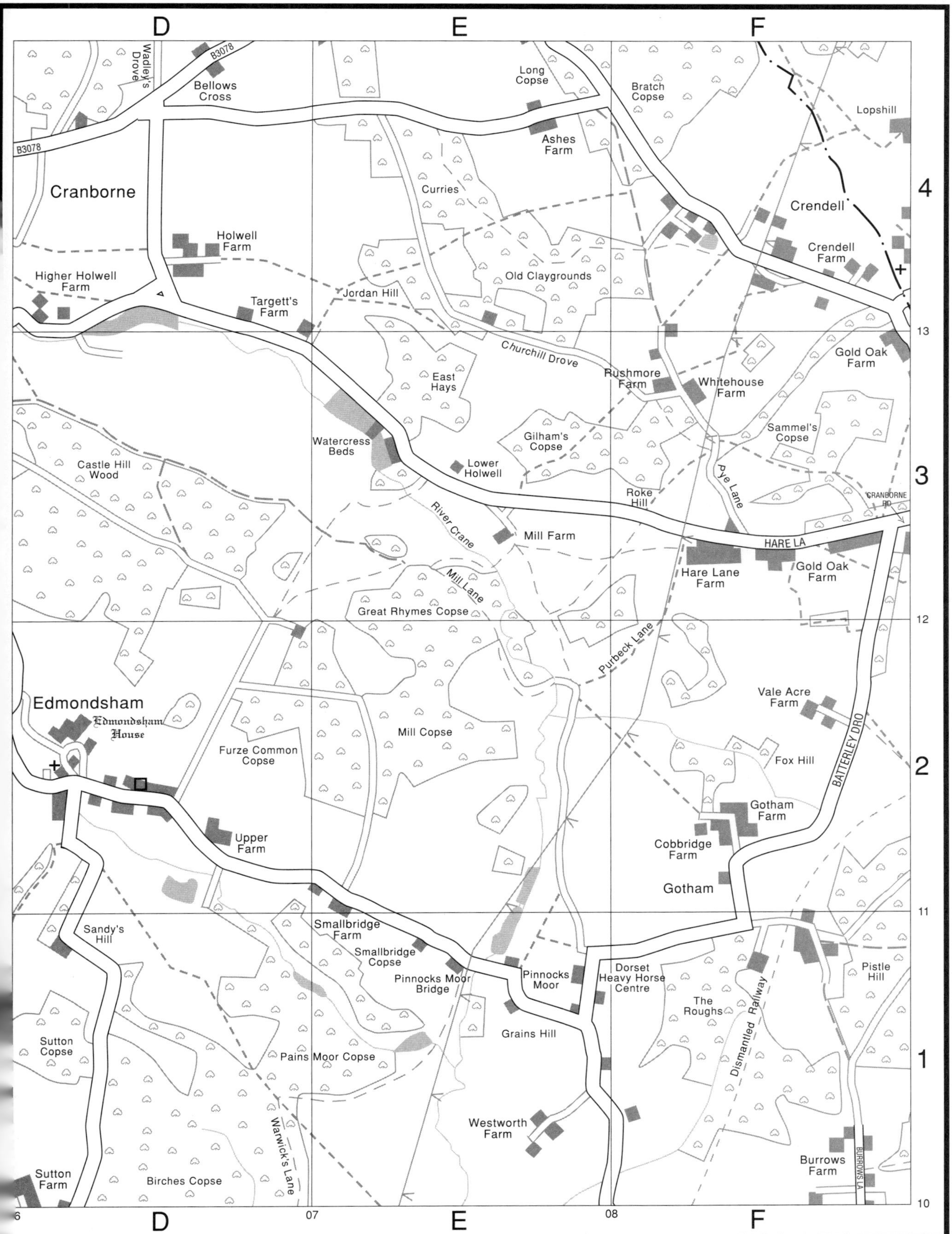
D
E
F
B3078
Wadley's Drove
Bellows Cross
Long Copse
Bratch Copse
Lopshill
Ashes Farm
Cranborne
Curries
Crendell
Holwell Farm
Crendell Farm
Higher Holwell Farm
Old Claygrounds
Jordan Hill
Targett's Farm
Churchill Drove
Gold Oak Farm
East Hays
Rushmore Farm
Whitehouse Farm
Watercress Beds
Gilham's Copse
Sammel's Copse
Castle Hill Wood
Lower Holwell
Pye Lane
Roke Hill
CRANBORNE RD
River Crane
Mill Farm
HARE LA
Hare Lane Farm
Gold Oak Farm
Mill Lane
Great Rhymes Copse
Purbeck Lane
Vale Acre Farm
Edmondsham
Edmondsham House
Mill Copse
Furze Common Copse
Fox Hill
BATTERLEY DRO
Gotham Farm
Upper Farm
Cobbridge Farm
Gotham
Sandy's Hill
Smallbridge Farm
Smallbridge Copse
Pinnocks Moor Bridge
Pinnocks Moor
Dorset Heavy Horse Centre
Pistle Hill
The Roughs
Dismantled Railway
Grains Hill
Sutton Copse
Pains Moor Copse
Westworth Farm
Warwick's Lane
Burrows Farm
BURROWS LA
Sutton Farm
Birches Copse
4
3
2
1
13
12
11
10
06
07
08

92

114

68

91

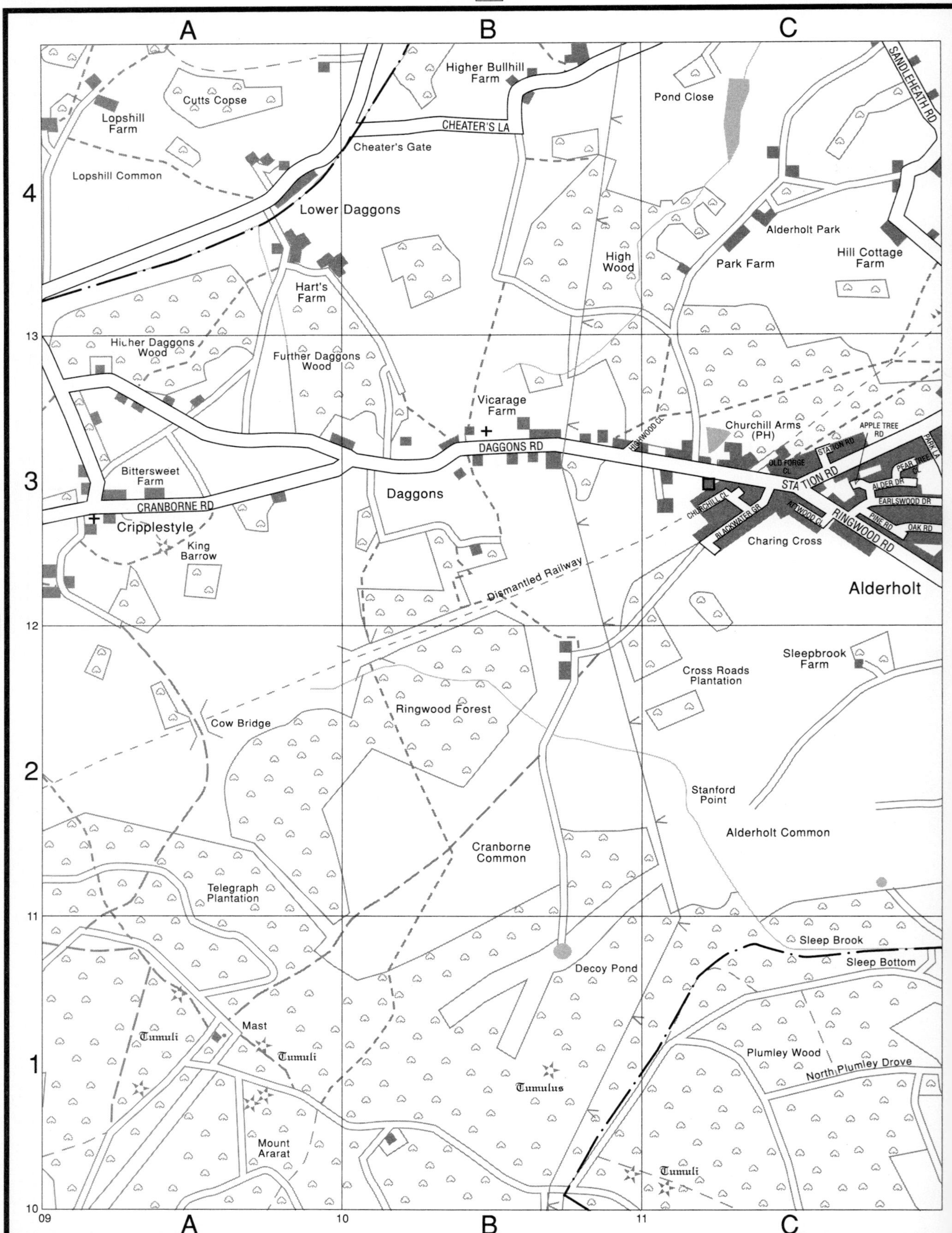
A
B
C
4
3
2
1
13
12
11
10
09
Higher Bullhill Farm
Cutts Copse
Lopshill Farm
Pond Close
SANDLEHEATH RD
CHEATER'S LA
Cheater's Gate
Lopshill Common
Lower Daggons
Alderholt Park
High Wood
Park Farm
Hill Cottage Farm
Hart's Farm
Hicher Daggons Wood
Further Daggons Wood
Vicarage Farm
Churchill Arms (PH)
APPLE TREE RD
HIGHWOOD CL
DAGGONS RD
STATION RD
OLD FORGE CL
PARK LA
PEAR TREE CL
ALDER DR
EARLSWOOD DR
Bittersweet Farm
Daggons
CRANBORNE RD
CHURCHILL CL
BLACKWATER GR
ATTWOOD CL
RINGWOOD RD
PINE RD
OAK RD
Cripplestyle
King Barrow
Charing Cross
Dismantled Railway
Alderholt
Sleepbrook Farm
Cross Roads Plantation
Ringwood Forest
Cow Bridge
Stanford Point
Alderholt Common
Cranborne Common
Telegraph Plantation
Sleep Brook
Sleep Bottom
Decoy Pond
Mast
Tumuli
Tumuli
Plumley Wood
North Plumley Drove
Tumulus
Mount Ararat
Tumuli

115

69

D
E
F
Hill Farm
Dismantled Railway
SANDLEHEATH RD
Home Farm
Bowerwood House
ASHFORD RD
BOWERWOOD RD
WEST ST
DIAMOND CL
BROOK TERR
Mus
CHURCH FARM
MULBERRY GDNS
CHURCH ST
PADSTOW PL
BUSHELLS FARM
4
FORDINGBRIDGE RD
New Farm
SANDLEHEATH RD
Padstow Farm
Sewage Works
Weir
Highfield Farm
Midgham Wood
Salisbury Arms Farm
Bonfire Hill
Cross Farm
13
Wolvercrate Copse
STATION RD
Hilbury Copse
Camel Green
Hillbury Farm
Midgham Farm
Sch
Bickton
3
Midgham Long Copse
Bickton Farm
HILLBURY RD
River Avon
RINGWOOD RD
12
Oak Tree Farm
Sleepbrook Farm
Drove End Farm
Alderholt Common
East Moor Copse
NORTH END LA
Warren Park Farm
2
LOMER LA
Whitefield Bottom
HARBRIDGE DRO
Bleakhill Farm
Bleak Hill
North End Farmhouse
Plumley Wood
11
Cobley Wood Farm
Harbridge Green
CHURCHFIELD LA
Cobley Hill
1
North Plumley Farmhouse
KENT LA
Kent
Hamer Copse
Hamer
Kent Hill
Harbridge
Harbridge House
10
2
13
14
D
E
F

94

116

70

93

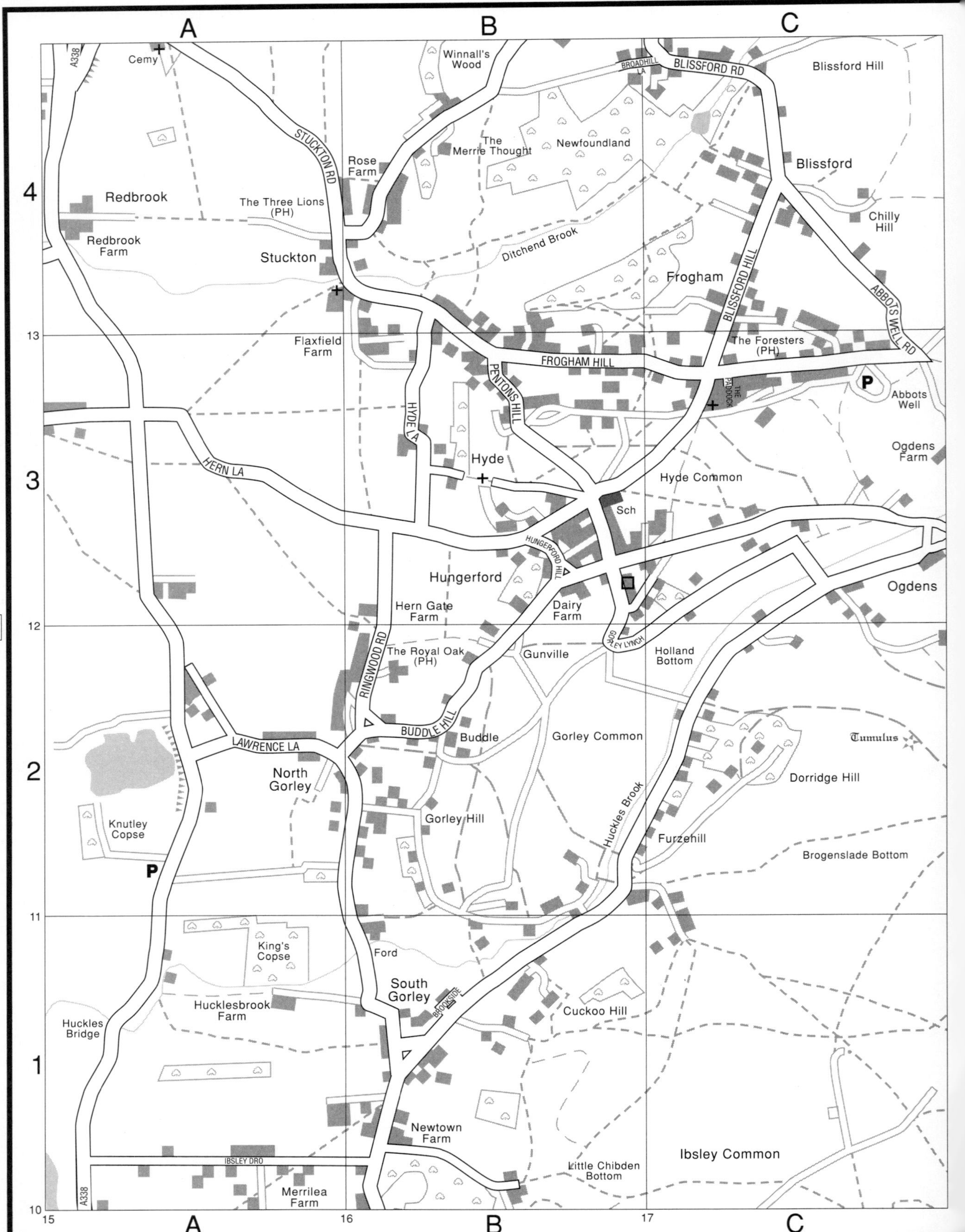
A
B
C
A338
Cemy
Winnall's Wood
BROADHILL LA
BLISSFORD RD
Blissford Hill
STUCKTON RD
Rose Farm
The Merrie Thought
Newfoundland
Blissford
4
Redbrook
The Three Lions (PH)
Chilly Hill
Redbrook Farm
Ditchend Brook
Stuckton
Frogham
BLISSFORD HILL
ABBOTS WELL RD
13
Flaxfield Farm
The Foresters (PH)
FROGHAM HILL
PENTONS HILL
THE PADDOCK
HYDE LA
Abbots Well
Ogdens Farm
Hyde
3
HERN LA
Hyde Common
Sch
HUNGERFORD HILL
Hungerford
Ogdens
Hern Gate Farm
Dairy Farm
12
RINGWOOD RD
GORLEY LYNCH
The Royal Oak (PH)
Gunville
Holland Bottom
BUDDLE HILL
Buddle
Gorley Common
Tumulus
LAWRENCE LA
2
North Gorley
Dorridge Hill
Knutley Copse
Gorley Hill
Huckles Brook
Furzehill
Brogenslade Bottom
11
King's Copse
Ford
South Gorley
BROOKSIDE
Hucklesbrook Farm
Cuckoo Hill
Huckles Bridge
1
Newtown Farm
Ibsley Common
IBSLEY DRO
Little Chibden Bottom
Merrilea Farm
A338
10
15
16
17
A
B
C

117

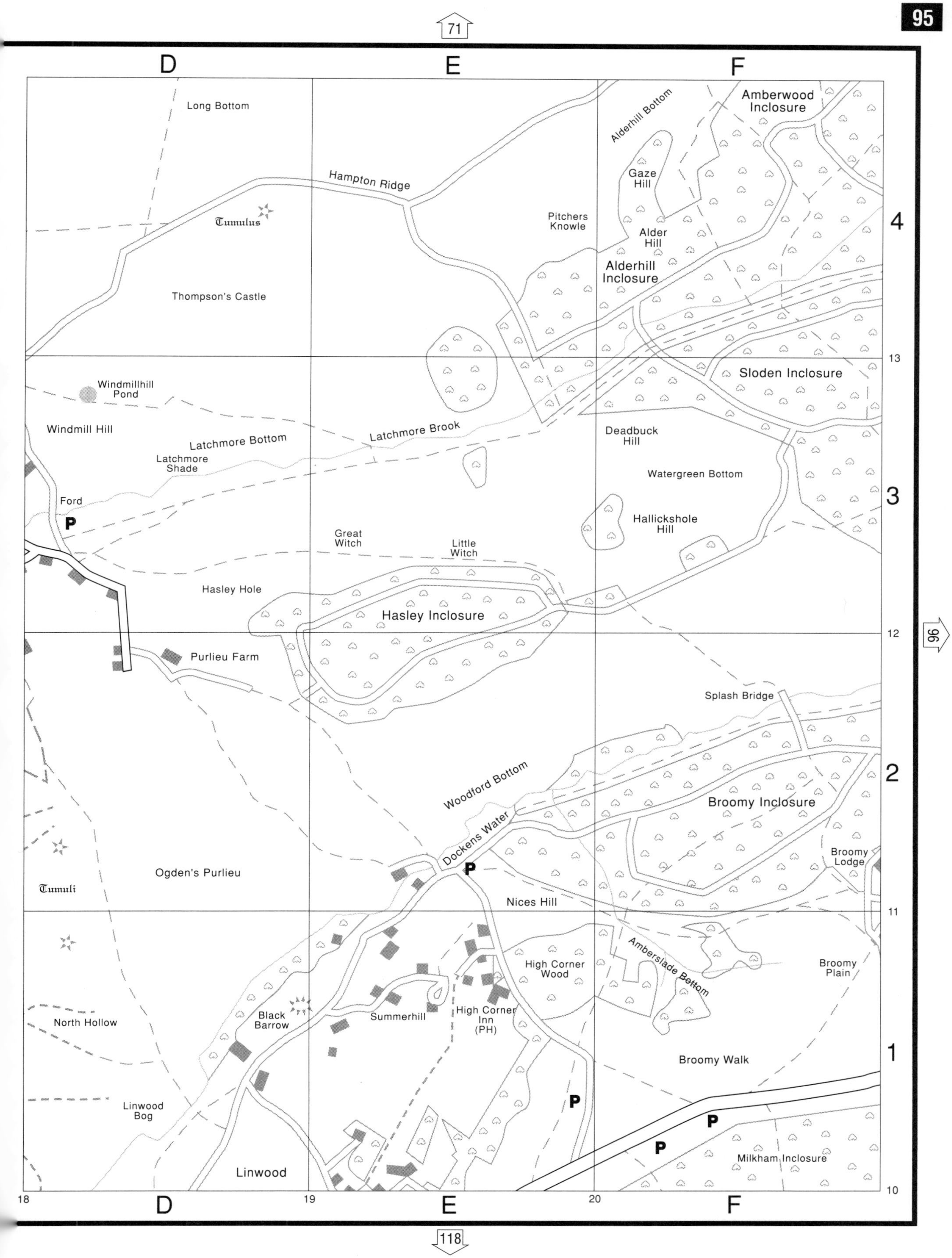
71
D
E
F
Long Bottom
Hampton Ridge
Tumulus
Thompson's Castle
Alderhill Bottom
Amberwood Inclosure
Gaze Hill
Pitchers Knowle
Alder Hill
Alderhill Inclosure
4
13
Windmillhill Pond
Windmill Hill
Latchmore Bottom
Latchmore Shade
Latchmore Brook
Sloden Inclosure
Deadbuck Hill
Watergreen Bottom
Ford
P
3
Great Witch
Little Witch
Hallickshole Hill
Hasley Hole
Hasley Inclosure
12
96
Purlieu Farm
Splash Bridge
Woodford Bottom
2
Broomy Inclosure
Dockens Water
P
Broomy Lodge
Ogden's Purlieu
Tumuli
Nices Hill
11
High Corner Wood
Ambersiade Bottom
Broomy Plain
Black Barrow
Summerhill
High Corner Inn (PH)
North Hollow
Broomy Walk
1
P
P
P
Linwood Bog
Milkham Inclosure
Linwood
10
18
19
20
D
E
F
118

72

95

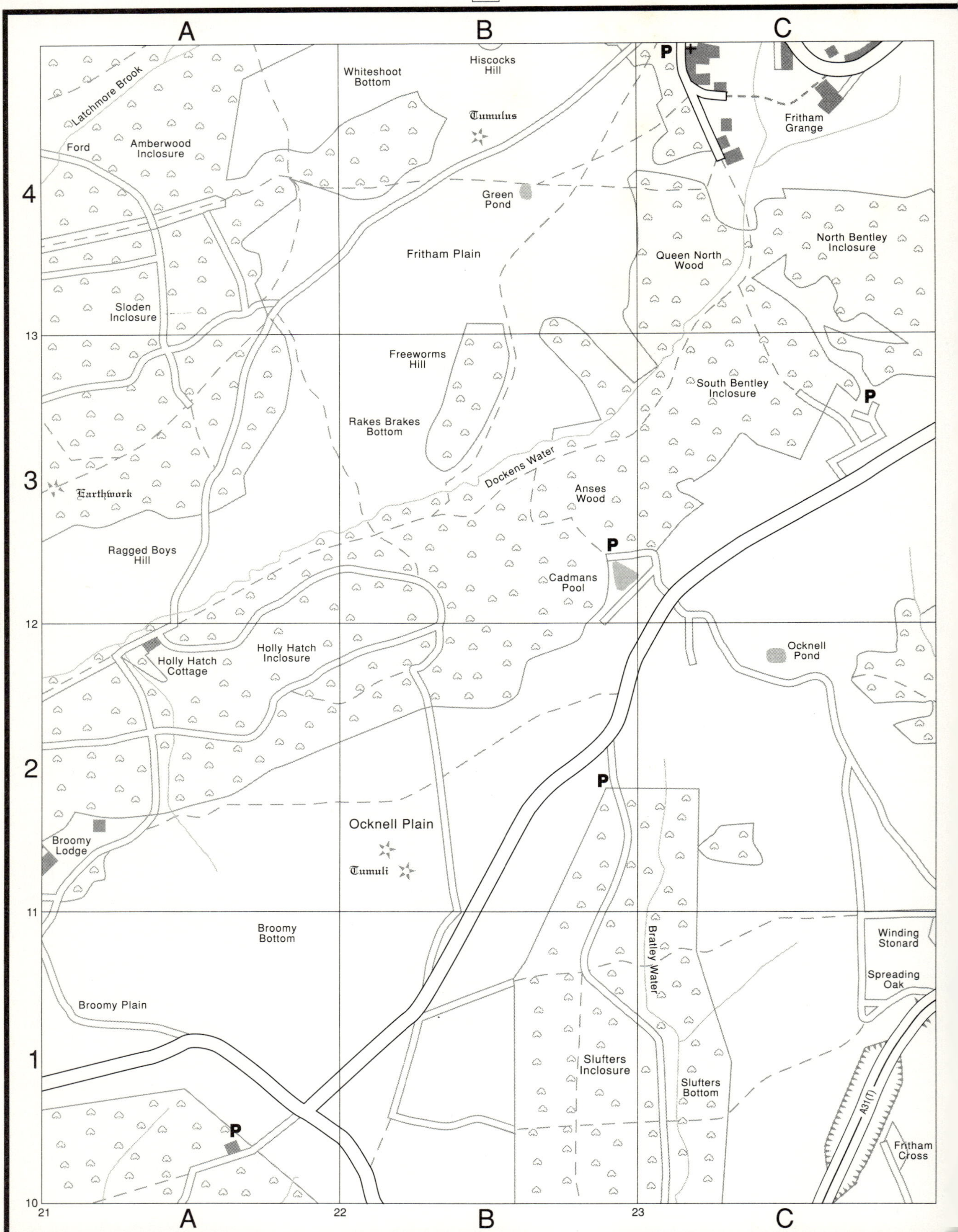
A
B
C
Whiteshoot Bottom
Hiscocks Hill
Latchmore Brook
Tumulus
Fritham Grange
Ford
Amberwood Inclosure
Green Pond
4
Fritham Plain
Queen North Wood
North Bentley Inclosure
Sloden Inclosure
13
Freeworms Hill
South Bentley Inclosure
Rakes Brakes Bottom
Dockens Water
3
Earthwork
Anses Wood
Ragged Boys Hill
Cadmans Pool
12
Ocknell Pond
Holly Hatch Cottage
Holly Hatch Inclosure
2
Ocknell Plain
Broomy Lodge
Tumuli
11
Broomy Bottom
Bratley Water
Winding Stonard
Spreading Oak
Broomy Plain
1
Slufters Inclosure
Slufters Bottom
A31(T)
Fritham Cross
10
21
22
23

119

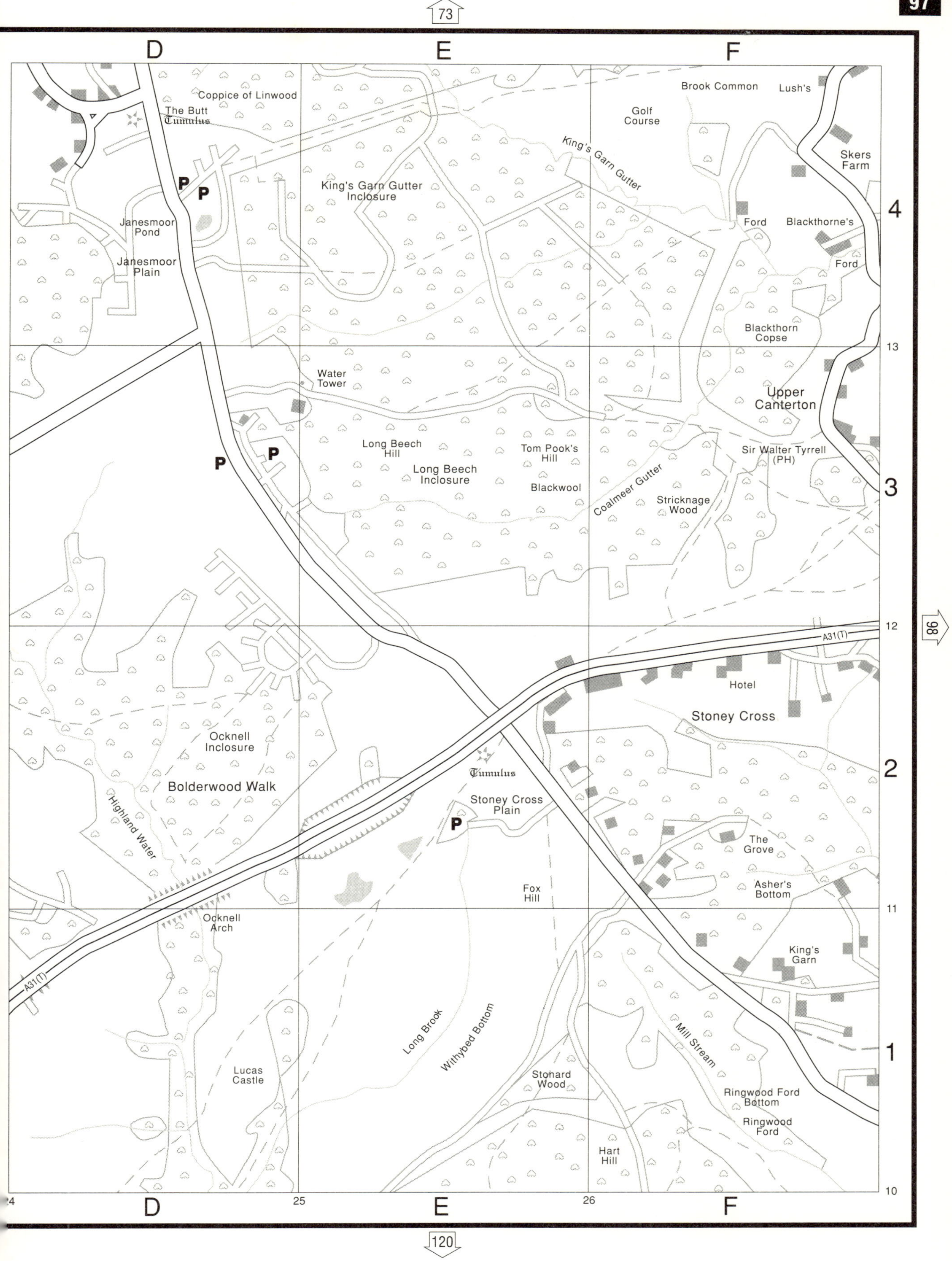
73
D
E
F
Coppice of Linwood
The Butt
Tumulus
Brook Common
Lush's
Golf
Course
King's Garn Gutter
Skers
Farm
P
P
King's Garn Gutter
Inclosure
Janesmoor
Pond
Janesmoor
Plain
Ford
Blackthorne's
Ford
4
Blackthorn
Copse
13
Water
Tower
Upper
Canterton
P
P
Long Beech
Hill
Long Beech
Inclosure
Tom Pook's
Hill
Blackwool
Coalmeer Gutter
Sir Walter Tyrrell
(PH)
Stricknage
Wood
3
12
98
A31(T)
Hotel
Stoney Cross
Ocknell
Inclosure
Tumulus
2
Bolderwood Walk
Highland Water
Stoney Cross
Plain
P
The
Grove
Asher's
Bottom
Fox
Hill
11
Ocknell
Arch
King's
Garn
A31(T)
Long Brook
Withybed Bottom
Mill Stream
1
Lucas
Castle
Stonard
Wood
Ringwood Ford
Bottom
Ringwood
Ford
Hart
Hill
10
24
25
26
D
E
F
120

74

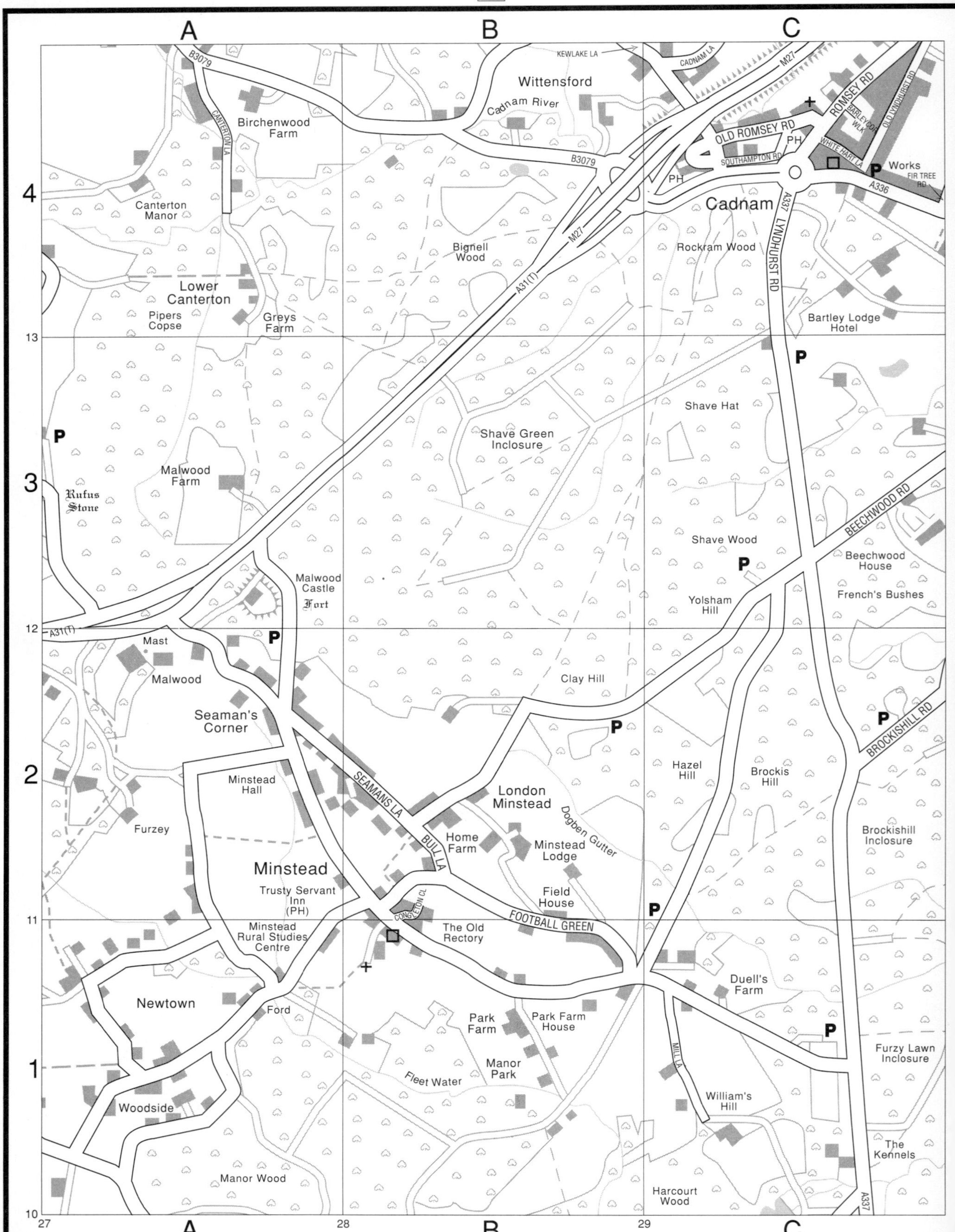
A
B
C
Wittensford
Cadnam River
KEWLAKE LA
CADNAM LA
M27
ROMSEY RD
OLD LYNDHURST RD
BARLEYCOM WLK
OLD ROMSEY RD
PH
WHITE HART LA
SOUTHAMPTON RD
Works
FIR TREE RD
A336
Cadnam
A337
LYNDHURST RD
B3079
CANTERTON LA
Birchenwood Farm
Canterton Manor
Bignell Wood
Rockram Wood
Lower Canterton
Pipers Copse
Greys Farm
A31(T)
Bartley Lodge Hotel
Shave Hat
Shave Green Inclosure
Malwood Farm
Rufus Stone
Shave Wood
BEECHWOOD RD
Beechwood House
French's Bushes
Malwood Castle
Fort
Yolsham Hill
Mast
Malwood
Clay Hill
Seaman's Corner
BROCKISHILL RD
Minstead Hall
SEAMANS LA
London Minstead
Hazel Hill
Brockis Hill
Dogben Gutter
Furzey
BULL LA
Home Farm
Minstead Lodge
Brockishill Inclosure
Minstead
Trusty Servant Inn (PH)
Field House
CONGLETON CL
FOOTBALL GREEN
Minstead Rural Studies Centre
The Old Rectory
Duell's Farm
Newtown
Ford
Park Farm
Park Farm House
Furzy Lawn Inclosure
MILL LA
Manor Park
Fleet Water
William's Hill
Woodside
The Kennels
Manor Wood
Harcourt Wood
4
3
2
1
13
12
11
10
27
28
29
P

97

121

75

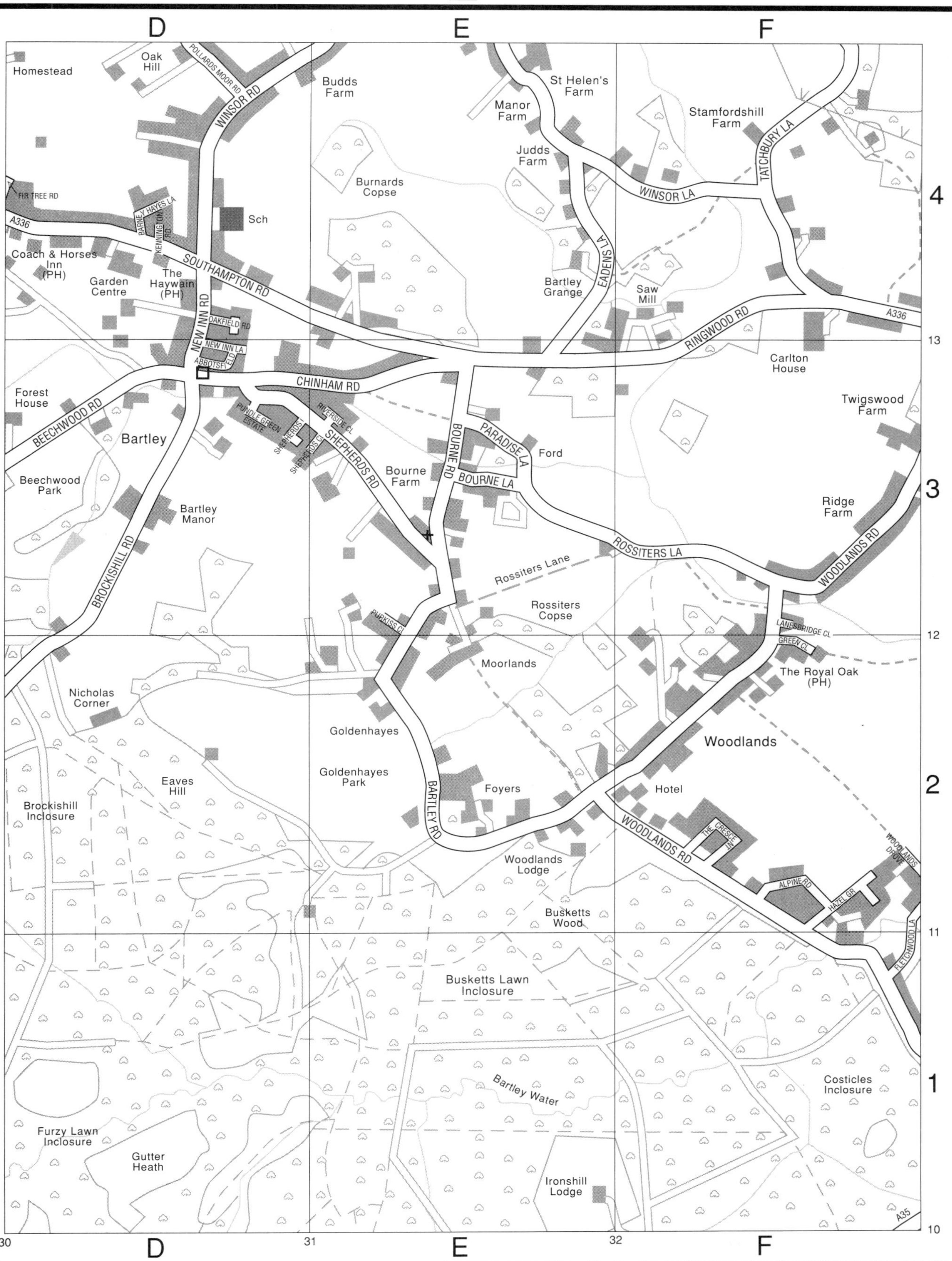
D
E
F
Homestead
Oak Hill
POLLARDS MOOR RD
WINSOR RD
Budds Farm
St Helen's Farm
Manor Farm
Stamfordshill Farm
TATCHBURY LA
Judds Farm
Burnards Copse
WINSOR LA
FIR TREE RD
BARNEY HAYES LA
KENNINGTON RD
Sch
A336
Coach & Horses Inn (PH)
SOUTHAMPTON RD
Garden Centre
The Haywain (PH)
NEW INN RD
Bartley Grange
EADENS LA
Saw Mill
OAKFIELD RD
NEW INN LA
ABBOTSFIELD
RINGWOOD RD
A336
Carlton House
Forest House
CHINHAM RD
BEECHWOOD RD
PUNDLE GREEN ESTATE
RIVERSIDE CL
SHEPHERDS CL
SHEPHERDS RD
BOURNE RD
PARADISE LA
Ford
Twigswood Farm
Bartley
Beechwood Park
Bourne Farm
BOURNE LA
Bartley Manor
Ridge Farm
ROSSITERS LA
Rossiters Lane
WOODLANDS RD
BROCKISHILL RD
Rossiters Copse
PURKISS CL
LANESBRIDGE CL
GREEN CL
Moorlands
The Royal Oak (PH)
Nicholas Corner
Goldenhayes
Woodlands
Eaves Hill
Goldenhayes Park
Brockishill Inclosure
Foyers
Hotel
BARTLEY RD
WOODLANDS RD
THE CRESCENT
WOODLANDS DROVE
Woodlands Lodge
ALPINE RD
HAZEL GR
Busketts Wood
FLETCHWOOD LA
Busketts Lawn Inclosure
Bartley Water
Costicles Inclosure
Furzy Lawn Inclosure
Gutter Heath
Ironshill Lodge
A35
30
31
32
13
12
11
10
4
3
2
1

100

122

76

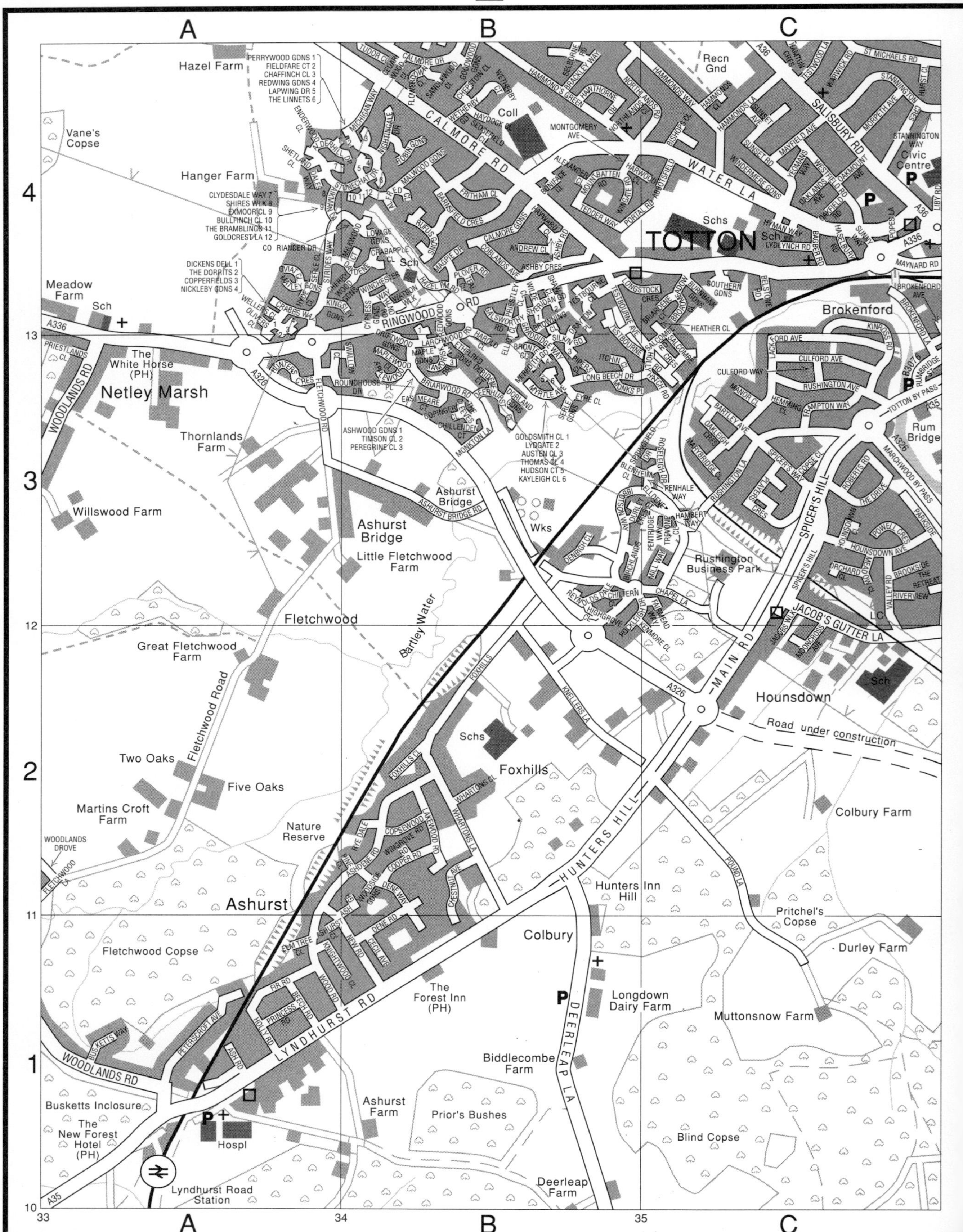
A
B
C
Hazel Farm
PERRYWOOD GDNS 1
FIELDFARE CT 2
CHAFFINCH CL 3
REDWING GDNS 4
LAPWING DR 5
THE LINNETS 6
Vane's Copse
Hanger Farm
CLYDESDALE WAY 7
SHIRES WLK 8
EXMOOR CL 9
BULLFINCH CL 10
THE BRAMBLINGS 11
GOLDCREST LA 12
CORIANDER DR
DICKENS DELL 1
THE DORRITS 2
COPPERFIELDS 3
NICKLEBY GDNS 4
Meadow Farm
Sch
A336
The White Horse (PH)
Netley Marsh
WOODLANDS RD
Thornlands Farm
Willswood Farm
CALMORE RD
RINGWOOD RD
Coll
MONTGOMERY AVE
WATER LA
Recn Gnd
TOTTON
Schs
SALISBURY RD
Civic Centre
Brokenford
HEATHER CL
ASHWOOD GDNS 1
TIMSON CL 2
PEREGRINE CL 3
GOLDSMITH CL 1
LYDGATE 2
AUSTEN CL 3
THOMAS CL 4
HUDSON CT 5
KAYLEIGH CL 6
Ashurst Bridge
ASHURST BRIDGE RD
Little Fletchwood Farm
Wks
Rushington Business Park
SPICER'S HILL
TOTTON BY PASS
Rum Bridge
A326
JACOB'S GUTTER LA
Fletchwood
Great Fletchwood Farm
Bartley Water
Fletchwood Road
Two Oaks
Five Oaks
Martins Croft Farm
WOODLANDS DROVE
Nature Reserve
Schs
Foxhills
Hounsdown
Road under construction
Colbury Farm
MAIN RD
HUNTERS HILL
Hunters Inn Hill
Pritchel's Copse
Durley Farm
Ashurst
Fletchwood Copse
Colbury
The Forest Inn (PH)
Longdown Dairy Farm
Muttonsnow Farm
LYNDHURST RD
WOODLANDS RD
DEERLEAP LA
Biddlecombe Farm
Busketts Inclosure
The New Forest Hotel (PH)
Hospl
Ashurst Farm
Prior's Bushes
Blind Copse
Lyndhurst Road Station
Deerleap Farm
A35
33
34
35
10
11
12
13
1
2
3
4

99

123

77

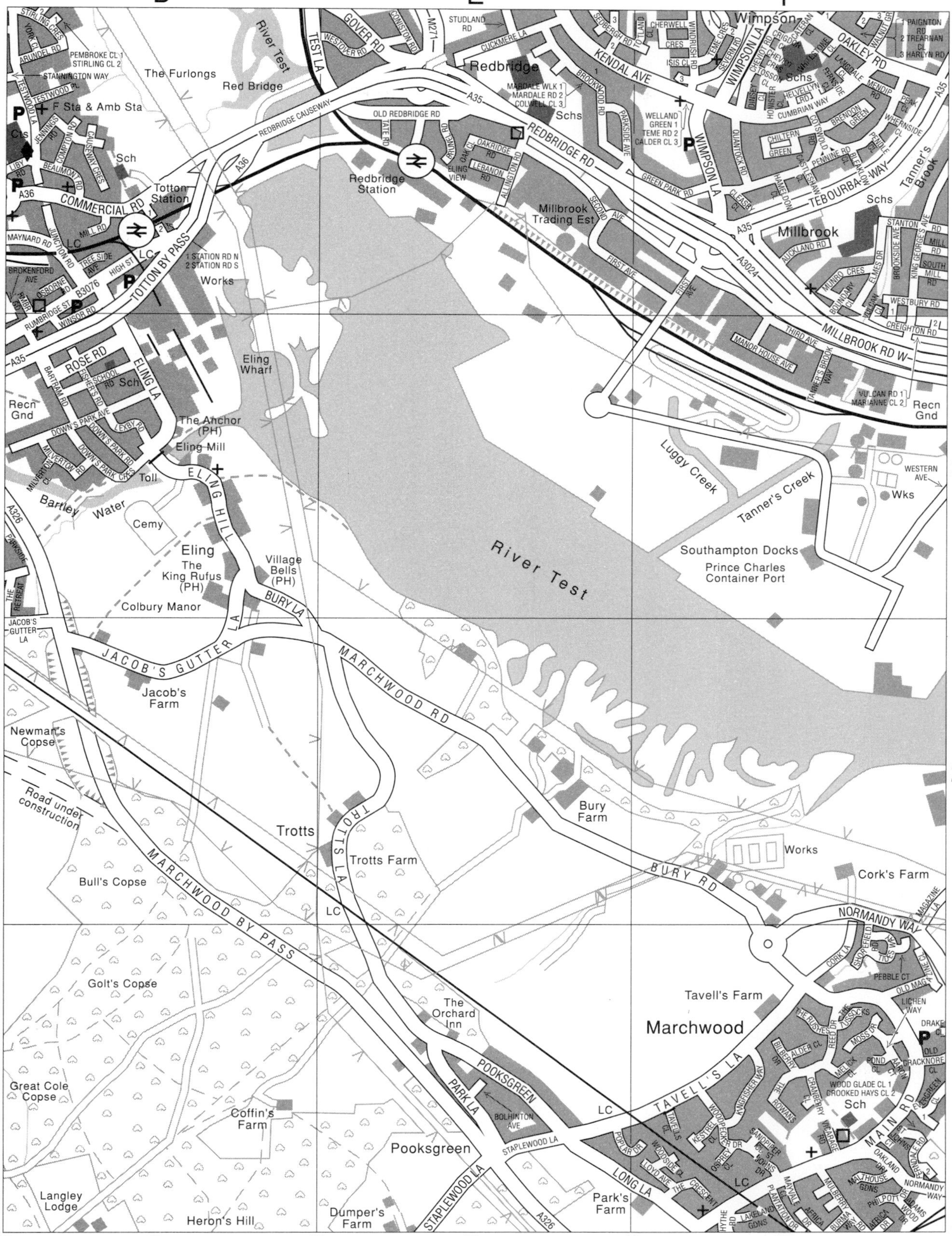

D
E
F
River Test
The Furlongs
Red Bridge
Redbridge
Wimpson
TEST LA
GOVER RD
WESTOVER RD
CONISTON RD
M271
STUDLAND RD
CUCKMERE LA
KENDAL AVE
WIMPSON LA
OAKLEY RD
PAIGNTON RD
2 TREARNAN CL
3 HARLYN RD
PEMBROKE CL 1
STIRLING CL 2
STANNINGTON WAY
TESTWOOD LA
F Sta & Amb Sta
REDBRIDGE CAUSEWAY
A35
OLD REDBRIDGE RD
MARDALE WLK 1
MARDALE RD 2
COLWELL CL 3
Schs
REDBRIDGE RD
BROOKWOOD RD
PARKSIDE AVE
WELLAND GREEN 1
TEME RD 2
CALDER CL 3
QUANTOCK RD
CHILTERN GREEN
CUMBRIAN WAY
MENDIP RD
BRENDON GREEN
PENNINE RD
TEBOURBA WAY
Tanner's Brook
Sch
Totton Station
A36
COMMERCIAL RD
MILL RD
Redbridge Station
OAKRIDGE RD
LEBANON RD
ALLINGTON RD
ELING VIEW
GREEN PARK RD
Millbrook Trading Est
SECOND AVE
Schs
Millbrook
A35
A3024
MAYNARD RD
JUNCTION RD
LC
TREE SIDE AVE
HIGH ST
TOTTON BY PASS
1 STATION RD N
2 STATION RD S
Works
FIRST AVE
AUCKLAND RD
MUNRO CRES
BROOKSIDE AVE
KING GEORGE'S AVE
STANTON RD
WESTBURY RD
CREIGHTON RD
BROKENFORD AVE
OSBORNE RD
RUMBRIDGE ST
WINSOR RD
B3076
13
MILLBROOK RD W
THIRD AVE
MANOR HOUSE AVE
TANNER'S BROOK WAY
ROSE RD
BARTRAM RD
ELING LA
SCHOOL RD
Sch
Eling Wharf
Recn Gnd
DOWN'S PARK AVE
LEXBY RD
DOWN'S PARK RD
DOWN'S PARK CRES
MILVERTON RD
The Anchor (PH)
Eling Mill
VULCAN RD 1
MARIANNE CL 2
Recn Gnd
Toll
ELING HILL
Luggy Creek
Tanner's Creek
WESTERN AVE
Wks
3
Bartley Water
Cemy
A326
Eling
The King Rufus (PH)
Village Bells (PH)
River Test
Southampton Docks
Prince Charles Container Port
THE RETREAT
BURY LA
Colbury Manor
12
JACOB'S GUTTER LA
JACOB'S GUTTER LA
MARCHWOOD RD
Jacob's Farm
Newman's Copse
2
Road under construction
Bury Farm
Trotts
TROTTS LA
Trotts Farm
Works
Cork's Farm
BURY RD
Bull's Copse
MARCHWOOD BY PASS
LC
NORMANDY WAY
MAGAZINE LA
11
CORK LA
PEBBLE CT
OLD MAGAZINE CL
Golt's Copse
Tavell's Farm
The Orchard Inn
Marchwood
LICHEN WAY
DRAKE CL
THE RUSHES
REED DR
THE TUSSOCKS
MOSS DR
POND CL
ALDER CL
BILBERRY DR
CRACKNORE CL
POOKSGREEN
TAVELL'S LA
WOODPECKER DR
KINGFISHER WAY
THE ROWANS
CRANBERRY CL
WOOD GLADE CL 1
CROOKED HAYS CL 2
Sch
1
Great Cole Copse
PARK LA
BOLHINTON AVE
Coffin's Farm
LC
STAPLEWOOD LA
Pooksgreen
POPLAR DR
WOODSIDE CL
LLOYD AVE
THE CRESCENT
KESTREL CL
OSPREY CL
SANDPIPER CL
LC
VICARAGE RD
MAIN RD
OAKLAND DR
MALTHOUSE GDNS
NORMANDY WAY
FERNDALE RD
STAPLEWOOD LA
LONG LA
Park's Farm
Langley Lodge
Heron's Hill
Dumper's Farm
A326
HYTHE RD
LAKELAND GDNS
PLANTATION DR
MAYVALE
MULBERRY
AFRICA DR
PHILPOTT DR
10
36
37
38
D
E
F

102

124

78

101

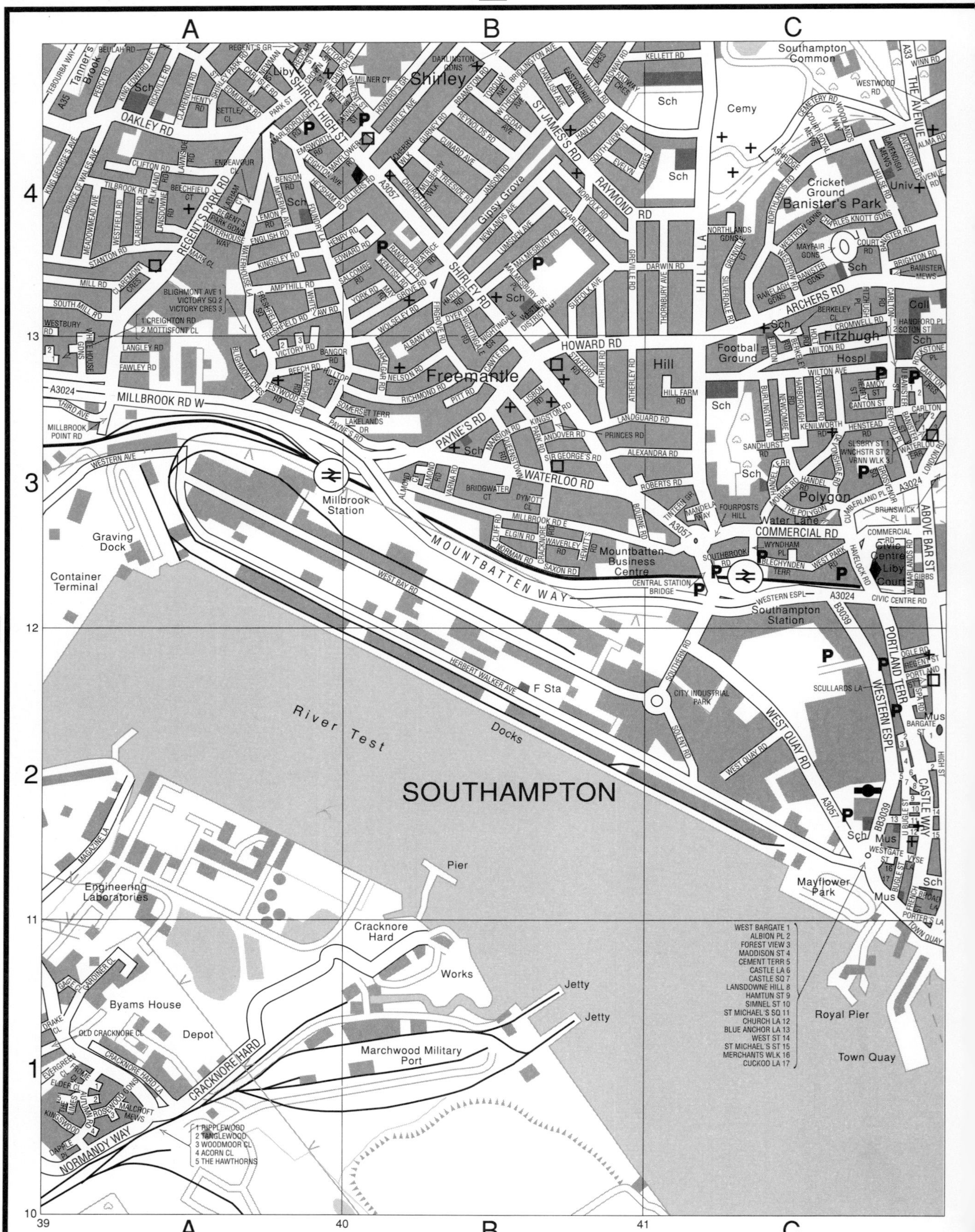
A
B
C
4
3
2
1
13
12
11
10
39
40
41
SOUTHAMPTON
Shirley
Freemantle
Hill
Fitzhugh
Polygon
Banister's Park
Southampton Common
Cemy
Cricket Ground
Football Ground
Tanner's Brook
Gipsy Grove
Millbrook Station
Southampton Station
Graving Dock
Container Terminal
Mountbatten Business Centre
CITY INDUSTRIAL PARK
River Test
Docks
F Sta
Pier
Cracknore Hard
Works
Jetty
Jetty
Byams House
Depot
Marchwood Military Port
Engineering Laboratories
Mayflower Park
Royal Pier
Town Quay
Civic Centre
Liby
Court
Univ
Hospl
Coll
Mus
Sch
Water Lane
MILLBROOK RD W
MOUNTBATTEN WAY
WESTERN AVE
WEST BAY RD
HERBERT WALKER AVE
WESTERN ESPL
COMMERCIAL RD
WEST QUAY RD
SOUTHERN RD
SOLENT RD
PORTLAND TERR
OAKLEY RD
REGENT'S PARK RD
SHIRLEY HIGH ST
SHIRLEY RD
HOWARD RD
WATERLOO RD
PAYNE'S RD
RAYMOND RD
ST JAMES'S RD
HILL LA
ARCHERS RD
THE AVENUE
ABOVE BAR ST
CASTLE WAY
CRACKNORE HARD
NORMANDY WAY
A3024
A3057
A33
A35
B3039
WEST BARGATE 1
ALBION PL 2
FOREST VIEW 3
MADDISON ST 4
CEMENT TERR 5
CASTLE LA 6
CASTLE SQ 7
LANSDOWNE HILL 8
HAMTUN ST 9
SIMNEL ST 10
ST MICHAEL'S SQ 11
CHURCH LA 12
BLUE ANCHOR LA 13
WEST ST 14
ST MICHAEL'S ST 15
MERCHANTS WLK 16
CUCKOO LA 17
1 RIPPLEWOOD
2 TANGLEWOOD
3 WOODMOOR CL
4 ACORN CL
5 THE HAWTHORNS
BLIGHMONT AVE 1
VICTORY SQ 2
VICTORY CRES 3
1 CREIGHTON RD
2 MOTTISFONT CL

125

79

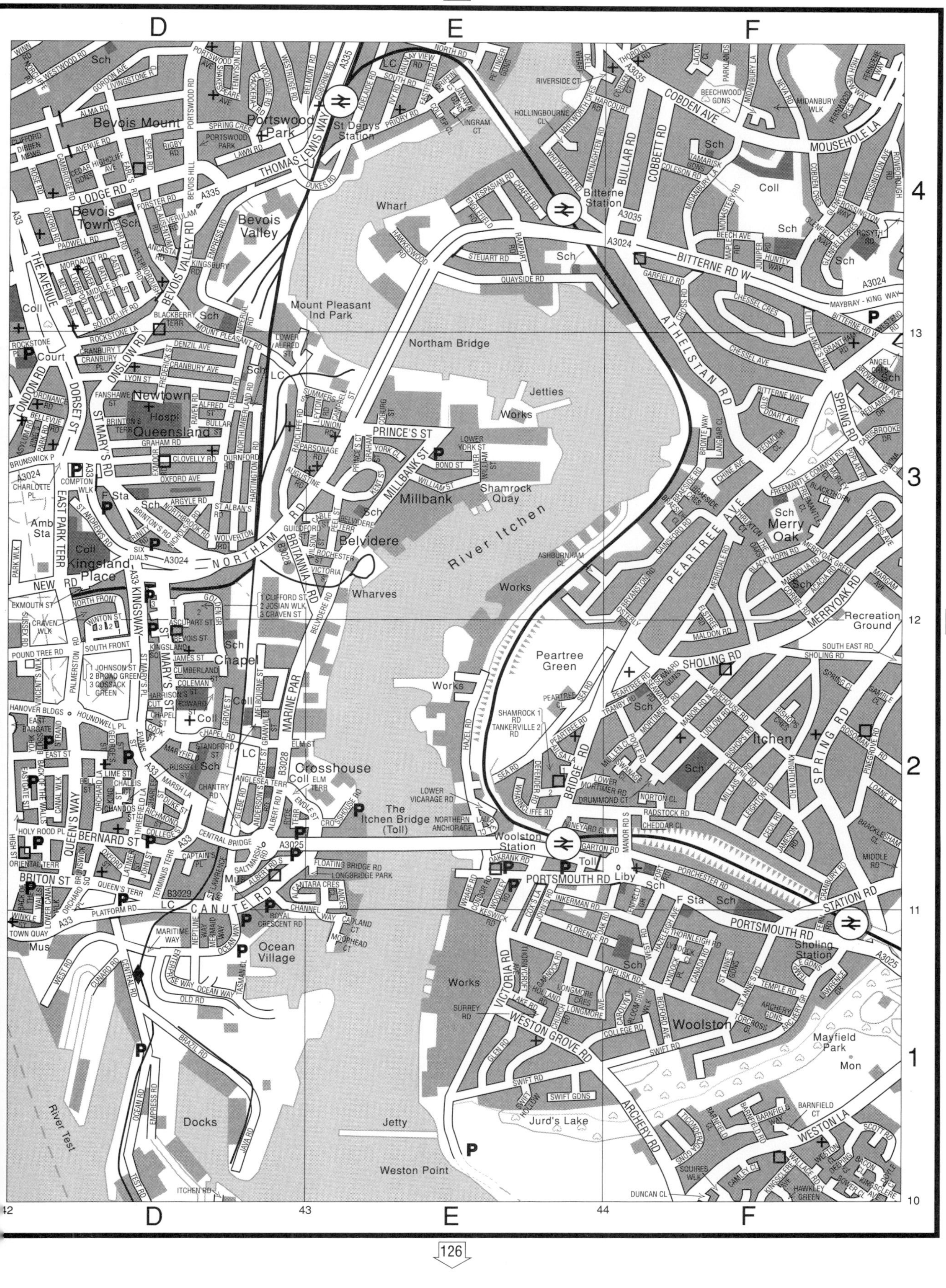

104

126

80

103

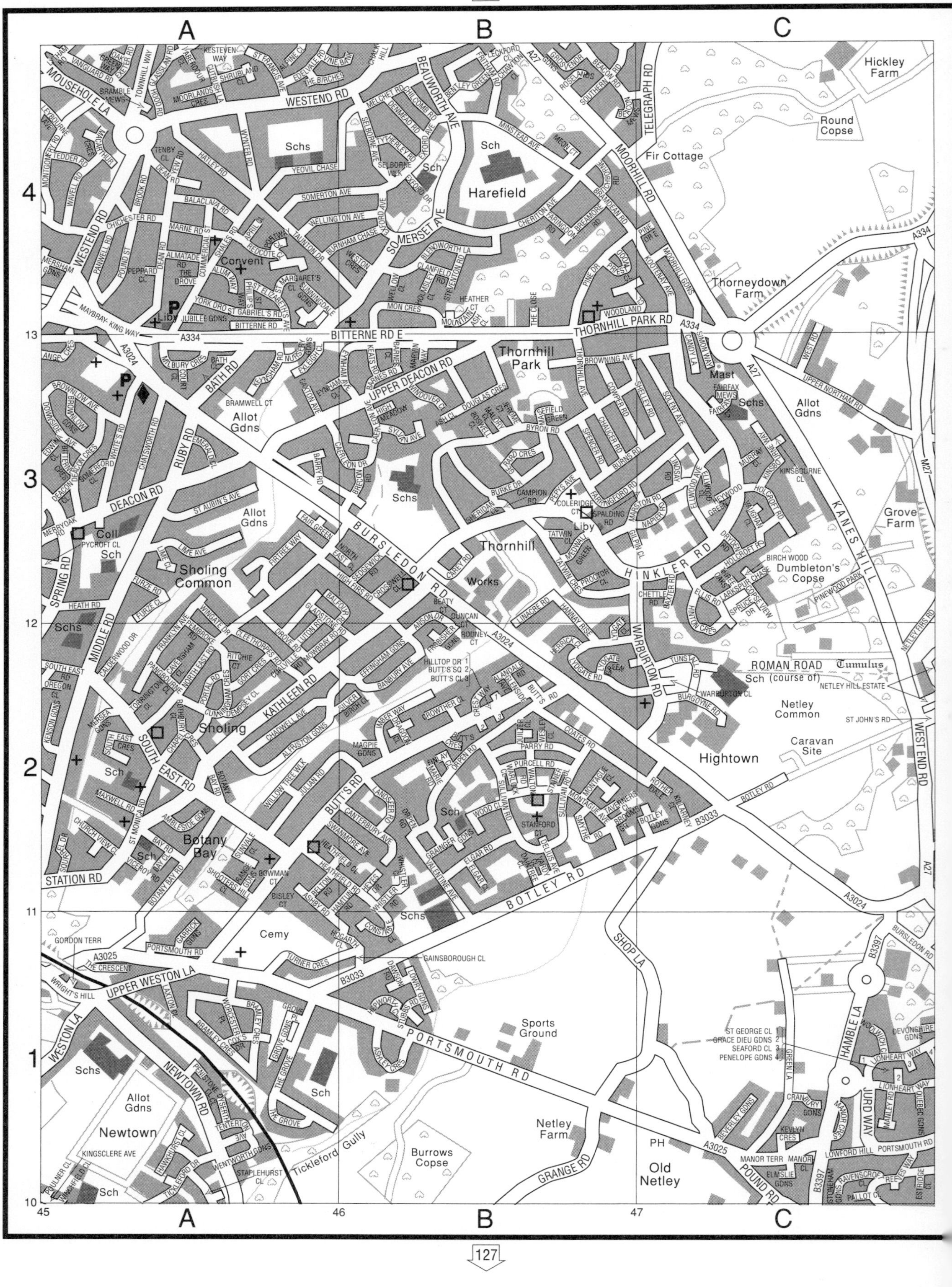
A
B
C
4
3
2
1
13
12
11
10
45
46
47
Hickley Farm
Round Copse
Fir Cottage
Schs
Sch
Harefield
Convent
Liby
Thorneydown Farm
Thornhill Park
Mast
Allot Gdns
Coll
Sholing Common
Thornhill
Works
Dumbleton's Copse
Grove Farm
Netley Common
Caravan Site
Hightown
ROMAN ROAD
Tumulus
Sch (course of)
Sholing
Botany Bay
Cemy
Sports Ground
Netley Farm
Burrows Copse
Tickleford Gully
Old Netley
PH
Newtown
WESTEND RD
MOUSEHOLE LA
BEAULWORTH AVE
SOMERSET AVE
MOORHILL RD
TELEGRAPH RD
THORNHILL PARK RD
BITTERNE RD E
MAYBRAY KING WAY
A334
A3024
A27
M27
KANES HILL
UPPER DEACON RD
DEACON RD
BURSLEDON RD
HINKLER RD
WARBURTON RD
MIDDLE RD
SOUTH EAST RD
BOTLEY RD
B3033
A3025
PORTSMOUTH RD
UPPER WESTON LA
WESTON LA
NEWTOWN RD
SHOP LA
GRANGE RD
POUND RD
HAMBLE LA
JURD WAY
WEST END RD
B3397
STATION RD
SPRING RD
KATHLEEN RD
BUTT'S RD
RUBY RD
BATH RD
NETLEY HILL ESTATE
ST JOHN'S RD
HILLTOP DR 1
BUTT'S SQ 2
BUTT'S CL 3
ST GEORGE CL 1
GRACE DIEU GDNS 2
SEAFORD CL 3
PENELOPE GDNS 4

127

81

D
E
F
Waterloo Industrial Estate
Royal London Park
TOLLBAR WAY
CHARLES WATTS WAY
1 FOWLERS RD
2 FORSYTHIA CL
B3035
GRANGE RD
ROSE CL
LOCKE RD
MISSENDEN ACRES
NAVIGATOR'S WAY
Botleigh Grange Hotel
WOODHOUSE LA
WINCHESTER ST
B3354
HOLMESLAND LA
Wildern
Schs
WILDERN LA
GRANGE RD
A334
LAKE FARM CL
TAPLIN DR
BERRYWOOD GDNS
DOWNSCROFT GDNS
COLTSFOOT CL
GOLLYCROFT MEAD
TURNPIKE WAY
Wildern Farm
A334
M27
B3036
HOLMESLAND WLK 1
LIME WLK 2
SYCAMORE WLK 3
CHESTNUT WLK 4
Holmesland
Broadway Farm
4
PH
BROAD OAK
A334 HIGH ST
Sch
Recn Gd
Broadoak
Caravan Site
LOWER NORTHAM RD
B3033
MARVIN WAY
MARVIN CL
ORCHARD CT
MARLS RD
OSTERLEY CL
BLOSSOM CL
DOBBETT WAY
Botley
13
Southbrook Farm
GOODLANDS VALE
FOUNTAIN CT 1
LITTLE PARK CL 2
UPPER NORTHAM RD
B3036
ST JOHN'S CENTRE
FERRYBRIDGE GREEN
SPEGGS WLK
KINGS COPSE AVE
HORNBEAM CL
Sch
1 GENTO CL
2 TAMELLA RD
3 MONTROSE CL
SOVEREIGN DR
TUDOR MEADOWS
WHEATSHEAF CT
UPPER NORTHAM CL
CLOVER WAY
MALLOW RD
OAK TREE GDNS
CHAPEL DRO
ALLOTMENT RD
B3033
FREEGROUNDS AVE
MELBOURNE GDNS
VALERIAN RD
VERRENA WAY
MAPLETON RD
HOBB LA
BROOK LA
Fir Tree Farm
3
NETLEY FIRS RD
RESERVOIR LA
CHURCH LA
GRANADA RD
Liby
RUSTAN CL
WESTBURY CT
FREEGROUNDS RD
LARKSPUR GDNS
LINDEN GDNS
BERRY CL
CRUSADER RD
NOBLE RD
PRECOSA RD
1 SENGANA CL
2 ABRAHAM CL
Hatts Copse Farm
Gould Copse
Manor Lodge
VICARAGE DR
ST JOHN'S RD
PRETORIA RD
ALEXANDRA RD
ALBERT RD
BURSLEDON RD
CONISTON GDNS
TANHOUSE LA
DUKE RD
HAVENDALE
FERNDALE
TICKNER CL
AMBLESIDE
NETLEY FIRS RD
Cemy
DOWNLAND PL
Sch
KINGS COPSE RD
Hedge End
FOORD RD
UPPER ST HELENS RD
STOCKHOLM DR
BERGEN CRES
12
106
Manor Farm (Mus)
P
Netley Hill
B3033
HEATH HOUSE CL
HEATHHOUSE LA
METUCHEN WAY
CRANBOURNE PARK
THURMELL WLK
ROMAN ROAD (course of)
Tanhouse Lane
Sunday's Hill
Piland's Copse
Kings Copse Farm
Bursledon Common
2
PEEWIT HILL CL
PYLANDS LA
PEEWIT HILL
Dodwell Farm
DODWELL LA
Upper Hamble Country Park
P
P
P
P
P
P
Dock Copse
A27
A3024
11
Hoe Moor House
River Hamble
WINDMILL LA
Windmill
1 GRIFFON CL
2 DILIGENCE CL
3 PHOENIX CL
BURSLEDON RD
A27
Catland Copse
Hospl
PROVIDENCE HILL
1
Swanwick Wood
Lowford
P
PORTSMOUTH RD
OAKHILL
OAKHILL CL
BLUNDELL LA
Brixedone Farm
LOWFORD HILL
SCHOOL RD
LONG LA
REDCROFT LA
P
Claypits
BURSLEDON HTS
BRIDGE RD
A27
1 SHERLEY GREEN
2 CUMMINS GREEN
Works
M27
COAL PARK LA
Lynwood
NEW RD
10
48
49
50
D
E
F

128

82

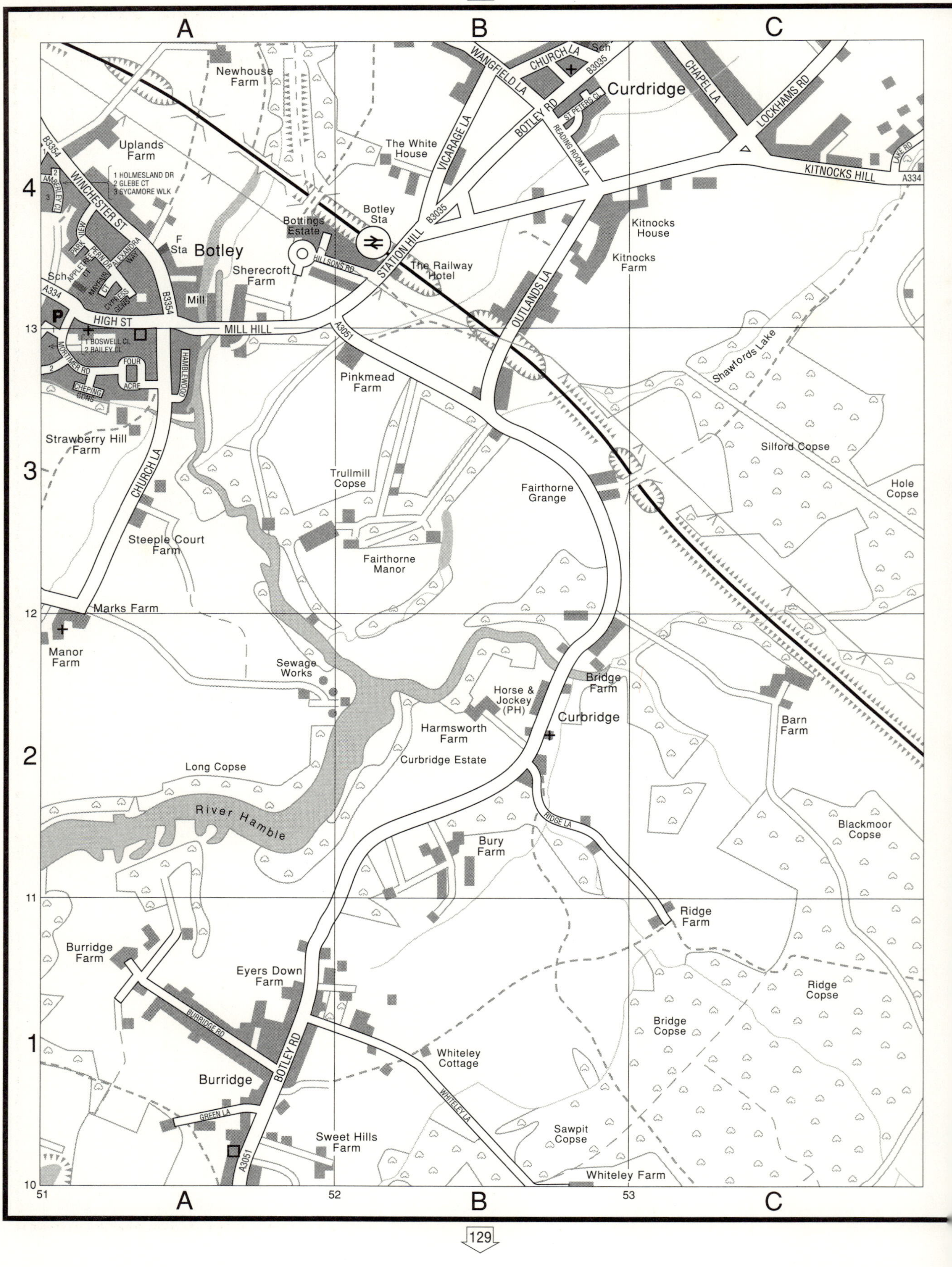
A
B
C
Newhouse Farm
Curdridge
Sch
CHURCH LA
WANGFIELD LA
B3035
BOTLEY RD
ST PETERS CL
READING ROOM LA
CHAPEL LA
LOCKHAMS RD
LAKE RD
KITNOCKS HILL
A334
Uplands Farm
The White House
VICARAGE LA
B3354
WINCHESTER ST
1 HOLMESLAND DR
2 GLEBE CT
3 SYCAMORE WLK
Botley Sta
Bottings Estate
B3035
Kitnocks House
Kitnocks Farm
F Sta
Botley
Sherecroft Farm
HILLSONS RD
STATION HILL
The Railway Hotel
OUTLANDS LA
Sch
A334
Mill
HIGH ST
MILL HILL
A3051
1 BOSWELL CL
2 BAILEY CL
MORTIMER RD
FOUR ACRE
HAMBLEWOOD
CHEPING GDNS
Pinkmead Farm
Shawfords Lake
Strawberry Hill Farm
Silford Copse
Trullmill Copse
Fairthorne Grange
Hole Copse
CHURCH LA
Steeple Court Farm
Fairthorne Manor
Marks Farm
Manor Farm
Sewage Works
Bridge Farm
Horse & Jockey (PH)
Curbridge
Harmsworth Farm
Barn Farm
Curbridge Estate
Long Copse
River Hamble
RIDGE LA
Blackmoor Copse
Bury Farm
Ridge Farm
Burridge Farm
Eyers Down Farm
Ridge Copse
BURRIDGE RD
Bridge Copse
Whiteley Cottage
BOTLEY RD
Burridge
WHITELEY LA
GREEN LA
Sweet Hills Farm
Sawpit Copse
A3051
Whiteley Farm
4
13
3
12
2
11
1
10
51
52
53

105

129

83

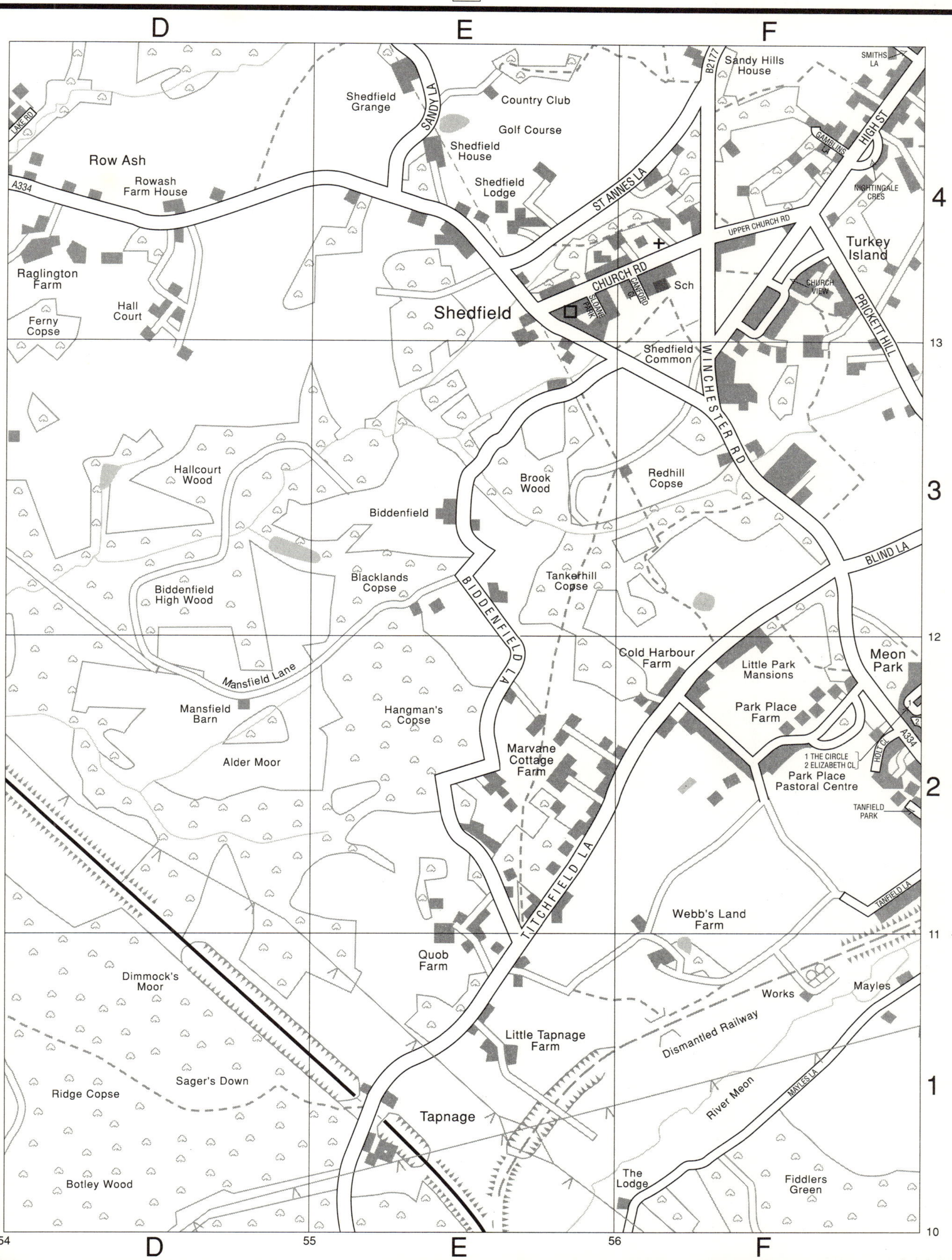
D
E
F
Sandy Hills House
SMITHS LA
Shedfield Grange
SANDY LA
Country Club
Golf Course
Shedfield House
Shedfield Lodge
B2177
GAMBLINS LA
HIGH ST
NIGHTINGALE CRES
LAKE RD
Row Ash
Rowash Farm House
A334
ST ANNES LA
UPPER CHURCH RD
Turkey Island
Raglington Farm
Hall Court
Ferny Copse
CHURCH RD
SLOANE PARK
CANFORD CL
Sch
CHURCH VIEW
PRICKETT HILL
Shedfield
Shedfield Common
WINCHESTER RD
4
13
Hallcourt Wood
Brook Wood
Redhill Copse
Biddenfield
3
Biddenfield High Wood
Blacklands Copse
Tankerhill Copse
BLIND LA
BIDDENFIELD LA
12
Mansfield Lane
Cold Harbour Farm
Little Park Mansions
Meon Park
Mansfield Barn
Hangman's Copse
Park Place Farm
A334
Alder Moor
Marvane Cottage Farm
1 THE CIRCLE
2 ELIZABETH CL
HOLT CL
Park Place Pastoral Centre
2
TANFIELD PARK
TITCHFIELD LA
TANFIELD LA
Webb's Land Farm
11
Dimmock's Moor
Quob Farm
Works
Mayles
Little Tapnage Farm
Dismantled Railway
Sager's Down
Ridge Copse
River Meon
MAYLES LA
1
Tapnage
The Lodge
Fiddlers Green
Botley Wood
10
54
55
56
D
E
F

108

130

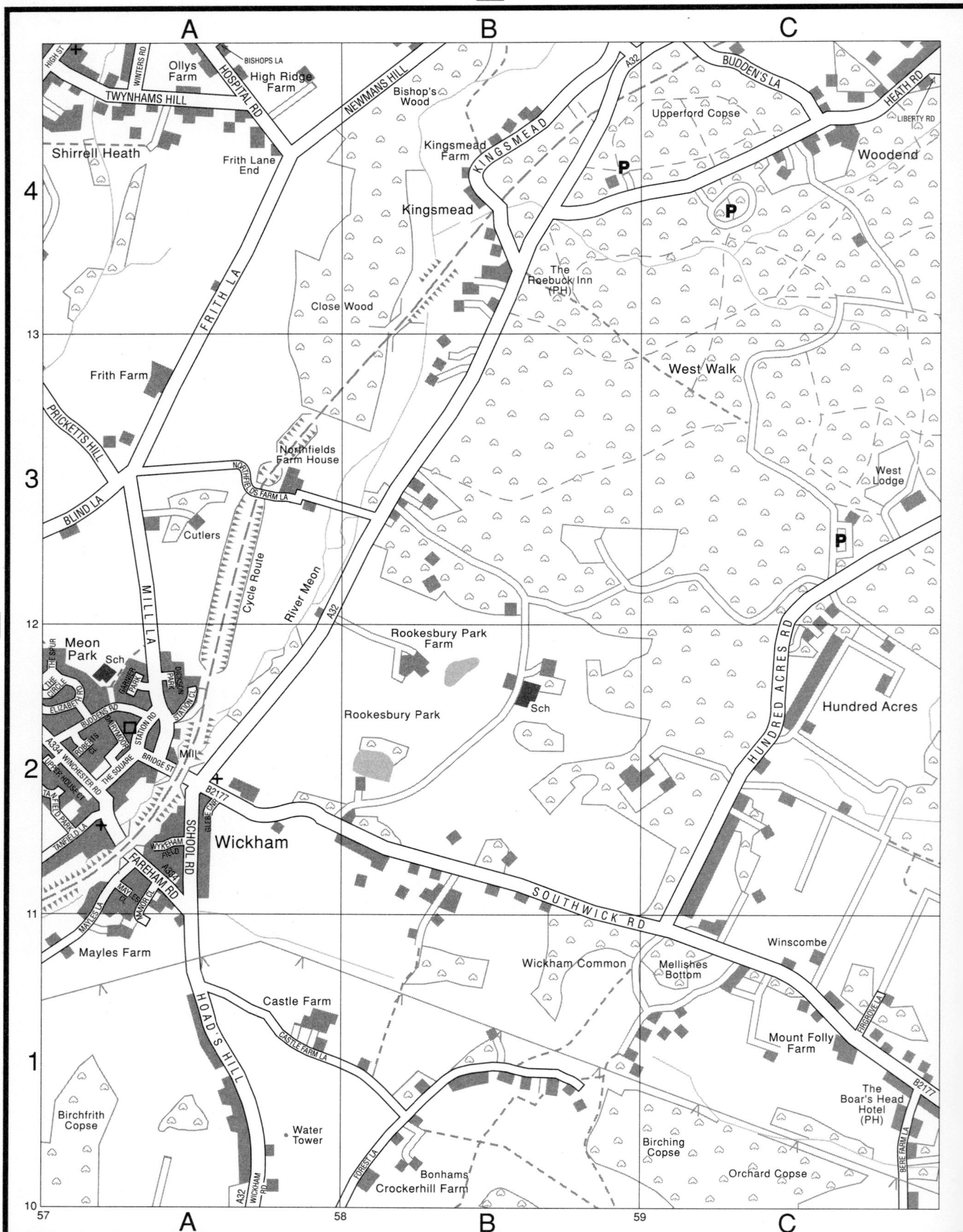
84
A
B
C
Ollys Farm
High Ridge Farm
Bishop's Wood
Shirrell Heath
Frith Lane End
Kingsmead Farm
Upperford Copse
Woodend
Kingsmead
The Roebuck Inn (PH)
Close Wood
Frith Farm
West Walk
Northfields Farm House
West Lodge
Cutlers
Cycle Route
River Meon
Rookesbury Park Farm
Meon Park
Sch
Rookesbury Park
Hundred Acres
Mill
Wickham
Mayles Farm
Wickham Common
Mellishes Bottom
Winscombe
Castle Farm
Mount Folly Farm
The Boar's Head Hotel (PH)
Birchfrith Copse
Water Tower
Birching Copse
Orchard Copse
Bonhams
Crockerhill Farm
TWYNHAMS HILL
HOSPITAL RD
NEWMANS HILL
KINGSMEAD
BUDDEN'S LA
HEATH RD
LIBERTY RD
FRITH LA
PRICKETTS HILL
BLIND LA
NORTHFIELDS FARM LA
MILL LA
HUNDRED ACRES RD
SOUTHWICK RD
SCHOOL RD
FAREHAM RD
HOAD'S HILL
CASTLE FARM LA
FOREST LA
BERE FARM LA
FIRGROVE LA
A32
A334
B2177
107
131
57
58
59
10
11
12
13
1
2
3
4

85

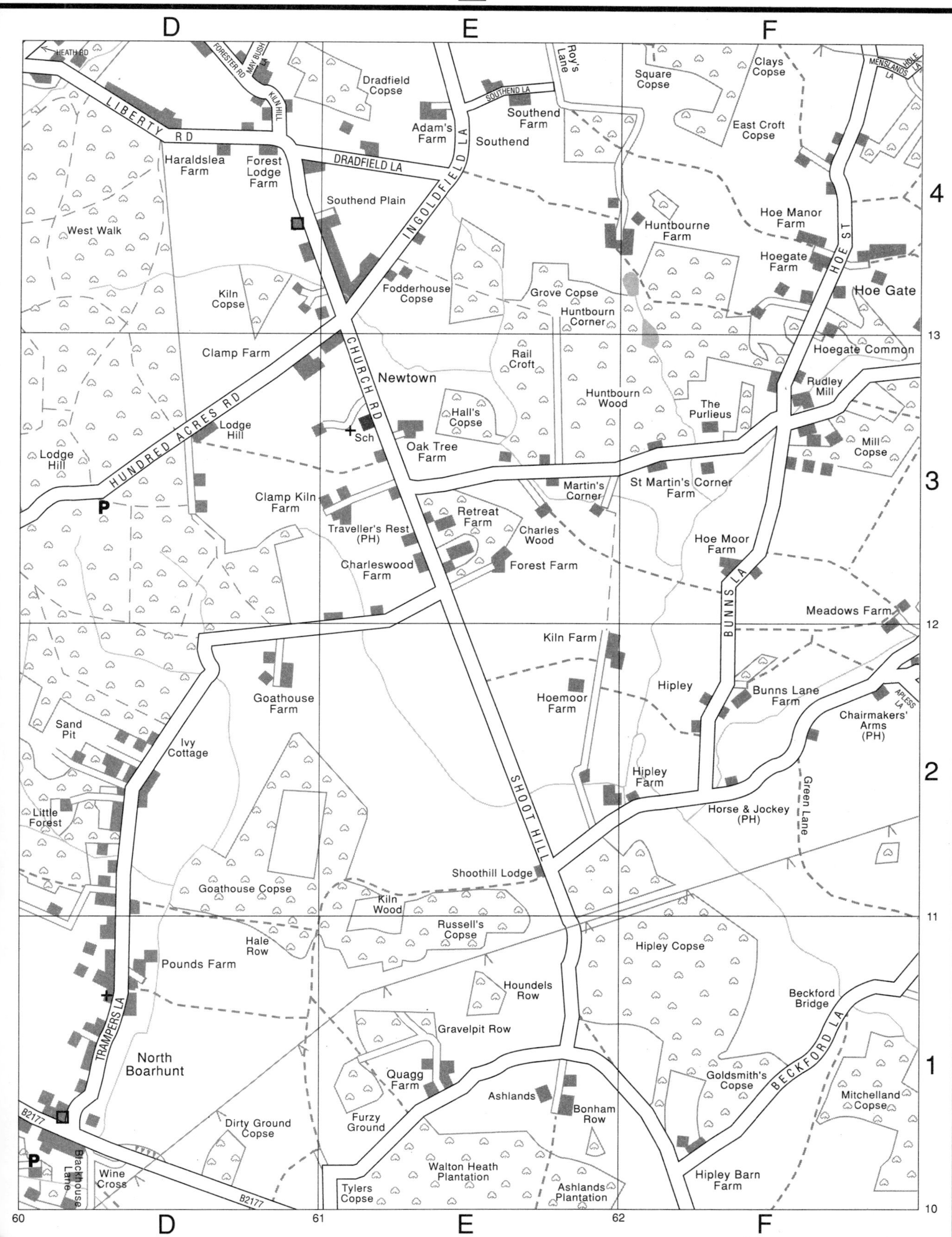
D
E
F
HEATH RD
FORESTER RD
MAY BUSH LA
KILN HILL
LIBERTY RD
Dradfield Copse
Roy's Lane
Square Copse
Clays Copse
MENSLANDS LA
HOLE LA
SOUTHEND LA
Southend Farm
Adam's Farm
Southend
East Croft Copse
Haraldslea Farm
Forest Lodge Farm
DRADFIELD LA
INGOLDFIELD LA
Southend Plain
4
Hoe Manor Farm
Huntbourne Farm
West Walk
Hoegate Farm
HOE ST
Kiln Copse
Fodderhouse Copse
Grove Copse
Huntbourn Corner
Hoe Gate
13
Clamp Farm
Rail Croft
Hoegate Common
CHURCH RD
Newtown
Rudley Mill
Huntbourn Wood
HUNDRED ACRES RD
Hall's Copse
The Purlieus
Lodge Hill
Sch
Lodge Hill
Oak Tree Farm
Mill Copse
3
Martin's Corner
St Martin's Corner Farm
P
Clamp Kiln Farm
Retreat Farm
Traveller's Rest (PH)
Charles Wood
Hoe Moor Farm
Charleswood Farm
Forest Farm
BUNNS LA
Meadows Farm
12
Kiln Farm
Hipley
Goathouse Farm
Hoemoor Farm
Bunns Lane Farm
APLESS LA
Sand Pit
Chairmakers' Arms (PH)
Ivy Cottage
2
Green Lane
SHOOT HILL
Hipley Farm
Horse & Jockey (PH)
Little Forest
Shoothill Lodge
Goathouse Copse
Kiln Wood
11
Russell's Copse
Hale Row
Hipley Copse
Pounds Farm
Houndels Row
Beckford Bridge
TRAMPERS LA
Gravelpit Row
North Boarhunt
BECKFORD LA
1
Quagg Farm
Goldsmith's Copse
Ashlands
Mitchelland Copse
Bonham Row
B2177
Dirty Ground Copse
Furzy Ground
P
Blackhouse Lane
Wine Cross
Walton Heath Plantation
Hipley Barn Farm
Tylers Copse
Ashlands Plantation
B2177
60
D
61
E
62
F
10

110

132

86

109

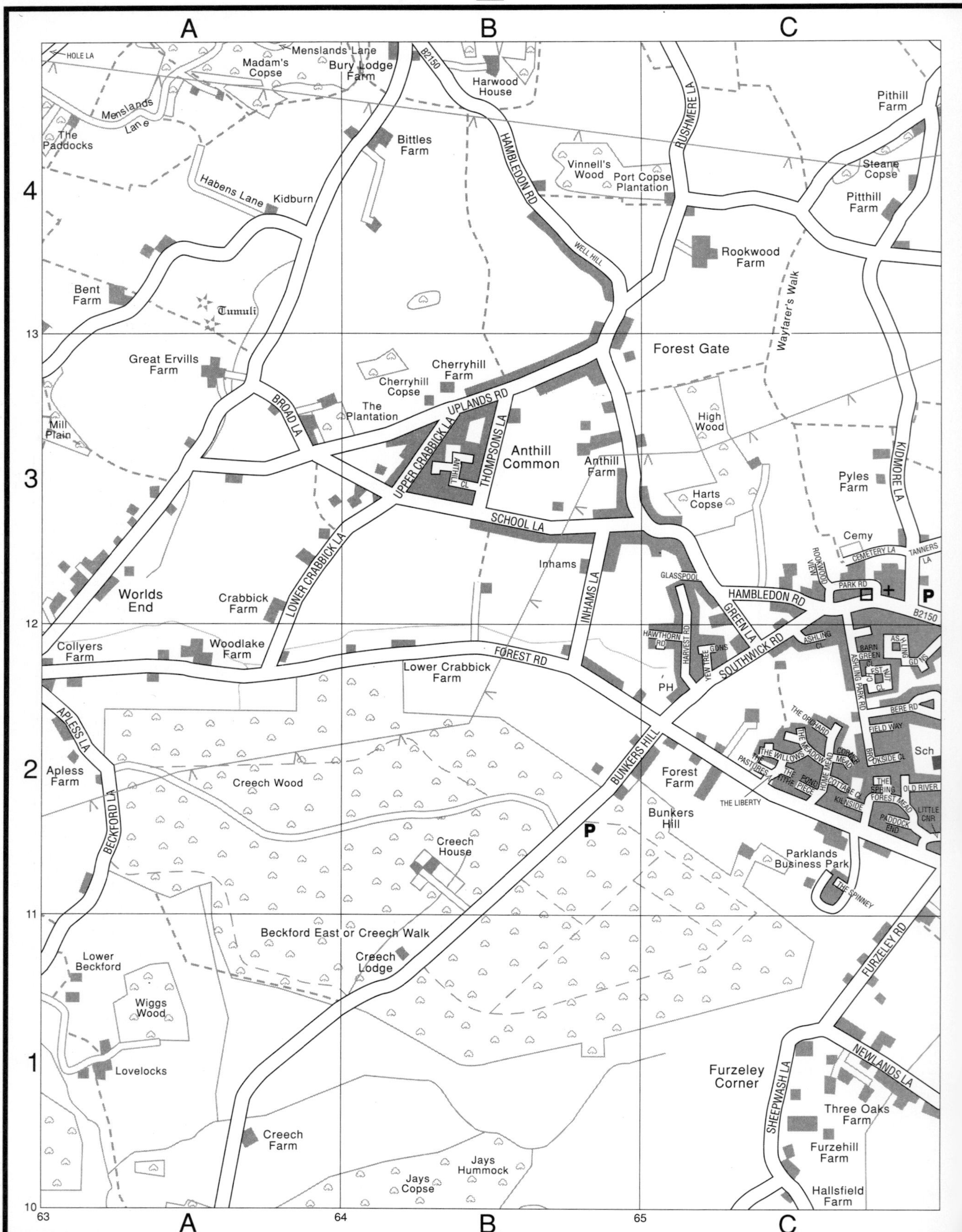
A
B
C
4
3
2
1
13
12
11
10
63
64
65
HOLE LA
Menslands Lane
Madam's Copse
Bury Lodge Farm
B2150
Harwood House
RUSHMERE LA
Pithill Farm
Menslands Lane
The Paddocks
Bittles Farm
HAMBLEDON RD
Vinnell's Wood
Port Copse Plantation
Steane Copse
Pitthill Farm
Habens Lane
Kidburn
WELL HILL
Rookwood Farm
Bent Farm
Tumuli
Wayfarer's Walk
Forest Gate
Great Ervills Farm
Cherryhill Farm
Cherryhill Copse
BROAD LA
UPLANDS RD
The Plantation
High Wood
Mill Plain
Anthill Common
THOMPSONS LA
ANTHILL CL
UPPER CRABBICK LA
Anthill Farm
KIDMORE LA
Pyles Farm
Harts Copse
SCHOOL LA
Cemy
CEMETERY LA
TANNERS LA
ROOKWOOD VIEW
Inhams
GLASSPOOL
PARK RD
LOWER CRABBICK LA
Worlds End
Crabbick Farm
INHAMS LA
HAMBLEDON RD
GREEN LA
P
B2150
HAWTHORN RD
HARVEST RD
YEW TREE GDNS
SOUTHWICK RD
ASHLING CL
BARN GREEN CL
ASHLING GDNS
ASHLING PARK RD
CHESTNUT CL
Collyers Farm
Woodlake Farm
FOREST RD
Lower Crabbick Farm
PH
BERE RD
THE ORCHARD
FIELD WAY
APLESS LA
THE WILLOWS
THE MEADOW
CORNER MEAD
BROOKSIDE CL
Sch
THE PASTURES
THE POND
THE PIECE
HOME MEAD
COTTAGE CL
THE SPRING
OLD RIVER
FOREST MEAD
Apless Farm
Creech Wood
BUNKERS HILL
Forest Farm
KILNSIDE
THE LIBERTY
LITTLE CNR
PADDOCK END
BECKFORD LA
P
Bunkers Hill
Creech House
Parklands Business Park
THE SPINNEY
Beckford East or Creech Walk
Lower Beckford
Creech Lodge
FURZELEY RD
Wiggs Wood
Lovelocks
Furzeley Corner
NEWLANDS LA
SHEEPWASH LA
Three Oaks Farm
Creech Farm
Furzehill Farm
Jays Hummock
Jays Copse
Hallsfield Farm

133

87

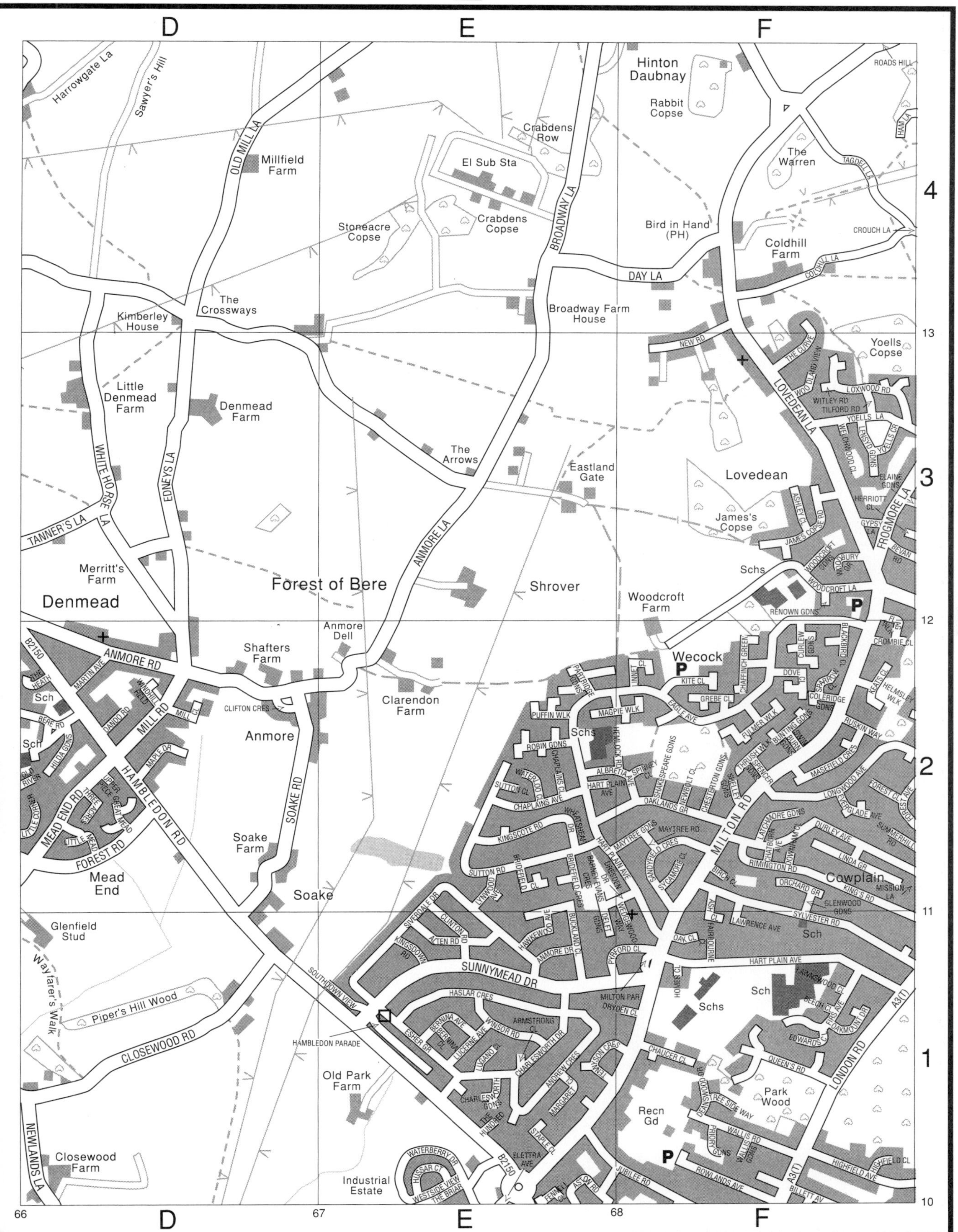

D
E
F
Hinton Daubnay
Rabbit Copse
Harrowgate La
Sawyer's Hill
Crabdens Row
El Sub Sta
Millfield Farm
OLD MILL LA
The Warren
ROADS HILL
HAM LA
TAGDELL LA
Stoneacre Copse
Crabdens Copse
BROADWAY LA
Bird in Hand (PH)
Coldhill Farm
CROUCH LA
COLDHILL LA
DAY LA
The Crossways
Kimberley House
Broadway Farm House
NEW RD
THE CURVE
Yoells Copse
Little Denmead Farm
Denmead Farm
LOVEDEAN LA
WOODLAND VIEW
LOXWOOD RD
WITLEY RD
TILFORD RD
YOELLS LA
The Arrows
WHITE HORSE LA
EDNEYS LA
Eastland Gate
Lovedean
ELAINE GDNS
HERRIOTT CL
TANNER'S LA
James's Copse
ASHLEY CL
JAMES COPSE RD
GYPSY LA
FROGMORE LA
BEVAN RD
Merritt's Farm
ANMORE LA
Forest of Bere
Shrover
Schs
WOODCROFT LA
Woodcroft Farm
Denmead
RENOWN GDNS
P
Anmore Dell
CROMBIE CL
B2150
ANMORE RD
Shafters Farm
Wecock
CURLEW GDNS
BLACKBIRD CL
KITE CL
GREBE CL
DOVE CL
KEATS CL
HELMSLEY WLK
MARTIN AVE
WINDHILL FIELD
CLIFTON CRES
Clarendon Farm
PARTRIDGE GDNS
LINNET CL
CHAFFINCH GREEN
Sch
DANDO RD
MILL RD
MILL CL
PUFFIN WLK
MAGPIE WLK
EAGLE AVE
FULMER WLK
COLERIDGE GDNS
BERE RD
Anmore
ROBIN GDNS
Schs
RUSKIN WAY
HILDA GDNS
MAPLE DR
HAMBLEDON RD
CHAPLAINS CL
HEMLOCK RD
SHAKESPEARE GDNS
BUNTING GDNS
MASEFIELD CRES
WATERLOO CL
ALBRETIA AVE
SPINNEY CL
NEWBOLT CL
CHESTERTON GDNS
THRUSH WLK
SUTTON CL
HART PLAIN AVE
LONGWOOD AVE
FOREST CL
SOAKE RD
CHAPLAINS AVE
OAKLANDS GR
SHELLEY GDNS
SPENCER DR
EVERGLADE AVE
MEAD END RD
WHEATSHEAF DR
MILTON RD
LATCHMORE GDNS
DURLEY AVE
SUMMERHILL RD
KINGSCOTE RD
MAYTREE GDNS
MAYTREE RD
FOREST RD
LITTLE MEAD
Soake Farm
SANDYFIELD CRES
CHATBURN AVE
DOWNHAM CL
RIMINGTON RD
LINDA GR
Mead End
SUTTON RD
BRIDEFIELD CL
BRIDEFIELD CRES
DRESDEN DR
SYCAMORE CL
BIRCH CL
ORCHARD GR
Cowplain
MISSION LA
KING'S RD
Soake
GLENWOOD GDNS
Glenfield Stud
SIVERDALE DR
CLINTON RD
HAWKEWOOD AVE
BUCKLAND CL
DELFT GDNS
ASH CL
FAIRBOURNE CL
LAWRENCE AVE
SYLVESTER RD
Sch
KINGSDOWN RD
ALTEN RD
ANMORE DR
PYRFORD CL
OAK CL
HART PLAIN AVE
SUNNYMEAD DR
LAMBSWOOD CL
Wayfarer's Walk
SOUTHDOWN VIEW
HOMER CL
Sch
MILTON PAR
DRYDEN CL
Schs
BEECH CL
A3(T)
Piper's Hill Wood
HASLAR CRES
ARMSTRONG CL
EDWARDS CL
OAKMOUNT DR
CLOSEWOOD RD
HAMBLEDON PARADE
ESHER GR
WINSOR RD
LUCERNE AVE
CHARLESWORTH DR
CHAUCER CL
QUEEN'S RD
LONDON RD
Old Park Farm
CHARLESWORTH GDNS
ANDREW CRES
GOODSTREE SIDE WAY
Park Wood
Recn Gd
NEWLANDS LA
THE HUNDRED
STAPLE CL
WALLIS RD
PRIORY GDNS
Closewood Farm
WATERBERRY DR
HUSSAR CT
WESTSIDE VIEW
THE BRIAR
Industrial Estate
ELETTRA AVE
JUBILEE RD
ASTON RD
ROWLANDS AVE
HIGHFIELD AVE
HIGHFIELD CL
BILLETT AV
4
3
2
1
13
12
11
10
66
67
68

112

134

88

111

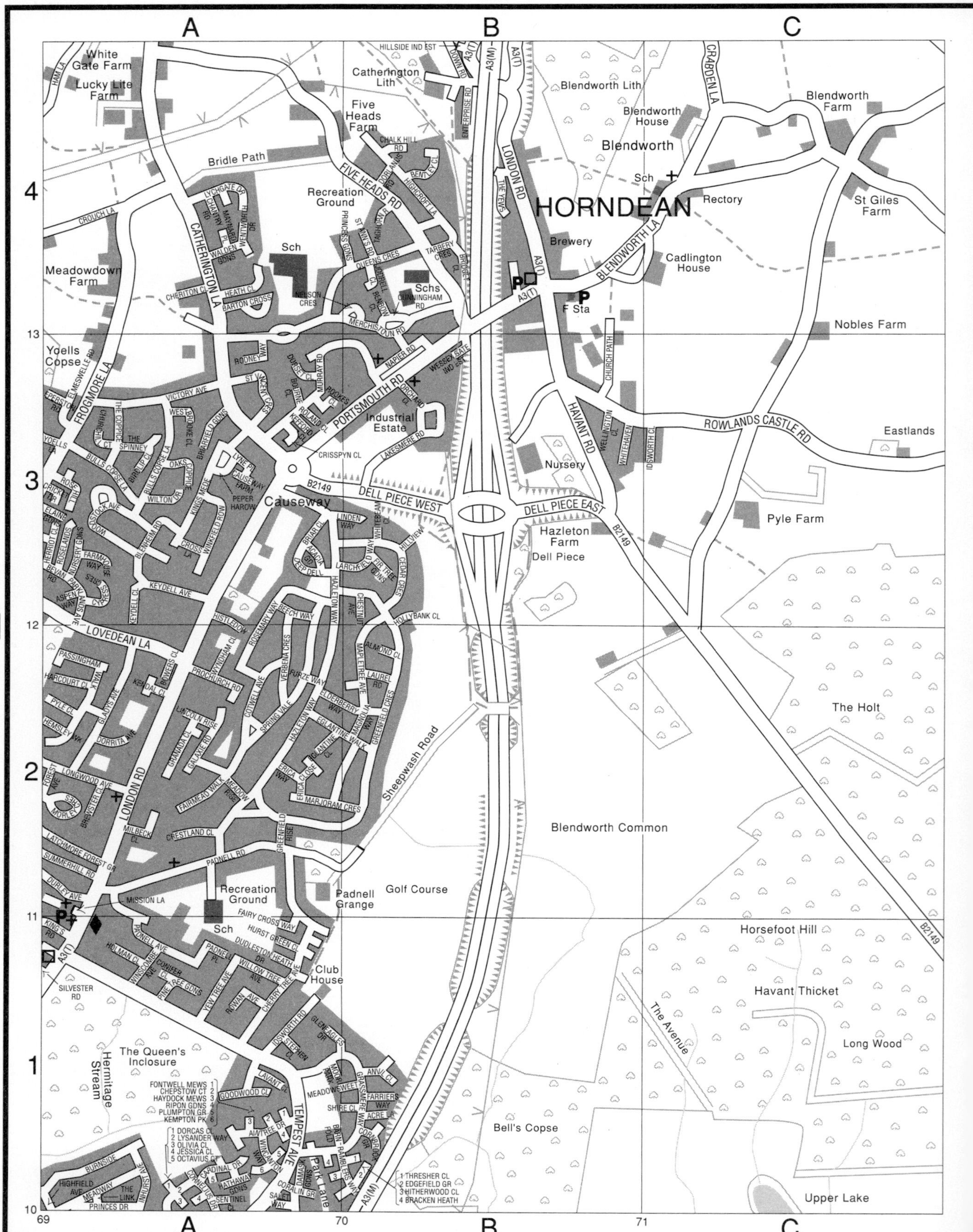
A
B
C
4
3
2
1
13
12
11
10
69
70
71
HORNDEAN
White Gate Farm
Lucky Lite Farm
Catherington Lith
Five Heads Farm
Blendworth Lith
Blendworth House
Blendworth Farm
Blendworth
Bridle Path
Recreation Ground
Sch
Rectory
St Giles Farm
Brewery
Cadlington House
Meadowdown Farm
Schs
F Sta
Nobles Farm
Yoells Copse
Industrial Estate
Eastlands
Nursery
Causeway
Pyle Farm
Hazleton Farm
Dell Piece
The Holt
Sheepwash Road
Blendworth Common
Recreation Ground
Golf Course
Padnell Grange
Club House
Horsefoot Hill
Havant Thicket
The Queen's Inclosure
Hermitage Stream
The Avenue
Long Wood
Bell's Copse
Upper Lake
Park Lane
HILLSIDE IND EST
CRABDEN LA
LONDON RD
ENTERPRISE RD
CHALK HILL RD
FIVE HEADS RD
CROUCH LA
CATHERINGTON LA
BLENDWORTH LA
HIGHCROFT LA
BENTLEY CL
QUEENS CRES
TARBERY CRES
CUNNINGHAM RD
MERCHISTOUN RD
NAPIER RD
HEATH CL
BARTON CROSS
CHERITON CL
NELSON CRES
RODNEY WAY
ST VINCENT CRES
VICTORY AVE
FROGMORE LA
ELMESWELLE RD
PORTSMOUTH RD
WESSEX GATE IND EST
CHURCH PATH
HAVANT RD
ROWLANDS CASTLE RD
WELLINGTON CL
WHITEHAVEN
IDSWORTH CL
LAKESMERE RD
CRISSPYN CL
B2149
DELL PIECE WEST
DELL PIECE EAST
A3(T)
A3(M)
KINGS MEDE
WINKFIELD ROW
PEPER HAROW
WILTON DR
BULLS COPSE LA
KEYDELL AVE
LOVEDEAN LA
HISTLEDOWN
LINDEN WAY
HAZLETON WAY
LARCHFIELD WAY
CEDAR CRES
HOLLYBANK CL
ROSEMARY WAY
BEECH WAY
CHESTNUT AVE
VERBENA CRES
ALMOND CL
MAPLETREE AVE
FURZE WAY
ELDERBERRY WAY
EGLANTINE WALK
GREENFIELD CRES
PROCHURCH RD
WYNDHAM CL
LINCOLN RISE
GRANADA CL
GALAXIE RD
SPRING VALE
FAIRMEAD WALK
MEADOW RISE
MARJORAM CRES
ERICA CLOSE
GREENFIELD RISE
CRESTLAND CL
MILBECK CL
PADNELL RD
LONGWOOD AVE
DORRITA AVE
PASSINGHAM WALK
HARCOURT CL
PYLE CL
HEMSLEY WK
LATCHMORE FOREST GR
SUMMERHILL RD
DURLEY AVE
MISSION LA
FAIRY CROSS WAY
HURST GREEN CL
DUDLESTON HEATH DR
WILLOW TREE AVE
CHERRY TREE AVE
ROWAN AVE
YEW TREE AVE
PINE TREE GDNS
CONIFER AVE
WINSCOMBE AVE
HOLMAN CL
PADNELL AVE
SILVESTER RD
IDSWORTH RD
GLENEAGLES DR
LAVANT DR
GOODWOOD CL
TEMPEST AVE
MEADOWSWEET
GRASSMERE WAY
FARRIERS WAY
ANVIL CL
SHIRE CL
ACRE LA
RAMBLERS WAY
CORALIN GR
SENTINEL CL
CARDINAL DR
HATHAWAY GDNS
BURNSIDE
HIGHFIELD AVE
MEADWAY
THE LINK
PRINCES DR
INHURST AVE
FONTWELL MEWS 1
CHEPSTOW CT 2
HAYDOCK MEWS 3
RIPON GDNS 4
PLUMPTON GR 5
KEMPTON PK 6
1 DORCAS CL
2 LYSANDER WAY
3 OLIVIA CL
4 JESSICA CL
5 OCTAVIUS CT
1 THRESHER CL
2 EDGEFIELD GR
3 HITHERWOOD CL
4 BRACKEN HEATH

135

89

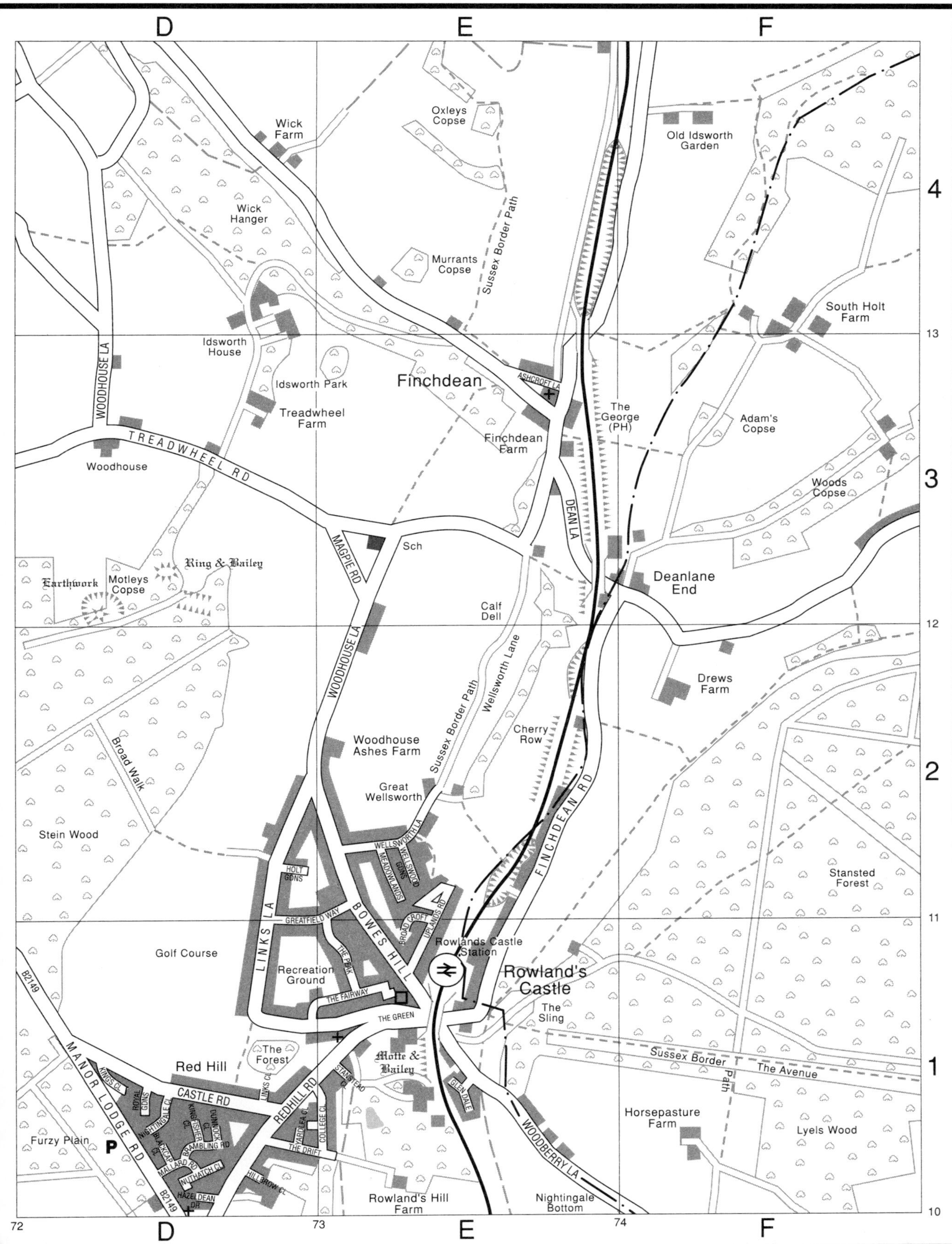
D
E
F
Wick Farm
Oxleys Copse
Old Idsworth Garden
Wick Hanger
Murrants Copse
Sussex Border Path
South Holt Farm
Idsworth House
Idsworth Park
Finchdean
ASHCROFT LA
The George (PH)
Adam's Copse
WOODHOUSE LA
Treadwheel Farm
Finchdean Farm
TREADWHEEL RD
Woodhouse
Woods Copse
DEAN LA
MAGPIE RD
Sch
Ring & Bailey
Earthwork
Motleys Copse
Deanlane End
Calf Dell
Drews Farm
Wellsworth Lane
Broad Walk
Woodhouse Ashes Farm
Cherry Row
Great Wellsworth
FINCHDEAN RD
Stein Wood
WELLSWORTH LA
MEADOWLANDS
WELLSWOOD GDNS
HOLT GDNS
Stansted Forest
GREATFIELD WAY
BOWES HILL
BROAD CROFT
UPLANDS RD
LINKS LA
Golf Course
Rowlands Castle Station
Recreation Ground
THE PEAK
Rowland's Castle
THE FAIRWAY
THE GREEN
The Sling
B2149
The Forest
Motte & Bailey
Sussex Border Path
The Avenue
Red Hill
CASTLE RD
LINKS CL
REDHILL RD
STANSTEAD CL
GLEN DALE
KINGS CL
ROYAL GDNS
NIGHTINGALE CL
KINGFISHER CL
DUNNOCK CL
FAIRLEA CL
COLLEGE CL
Horsepasture Farm
MANOR LODGE RD
BLACKCAP CL
BRAMBLING RD
Lyels Wood
Furzy Plain
P
MALLARD RD
NUTHATCH CL
THE DRIFT
WOODBERRY LA
HILLBROW CL
HAZELDEAN DR
B2149
Rowland's Hill Farm
Nightingale Bottom
4
3
2
1
13
12
11
10
72
73
74
not continued, see key diagram

136

91

not continued, see key diagram

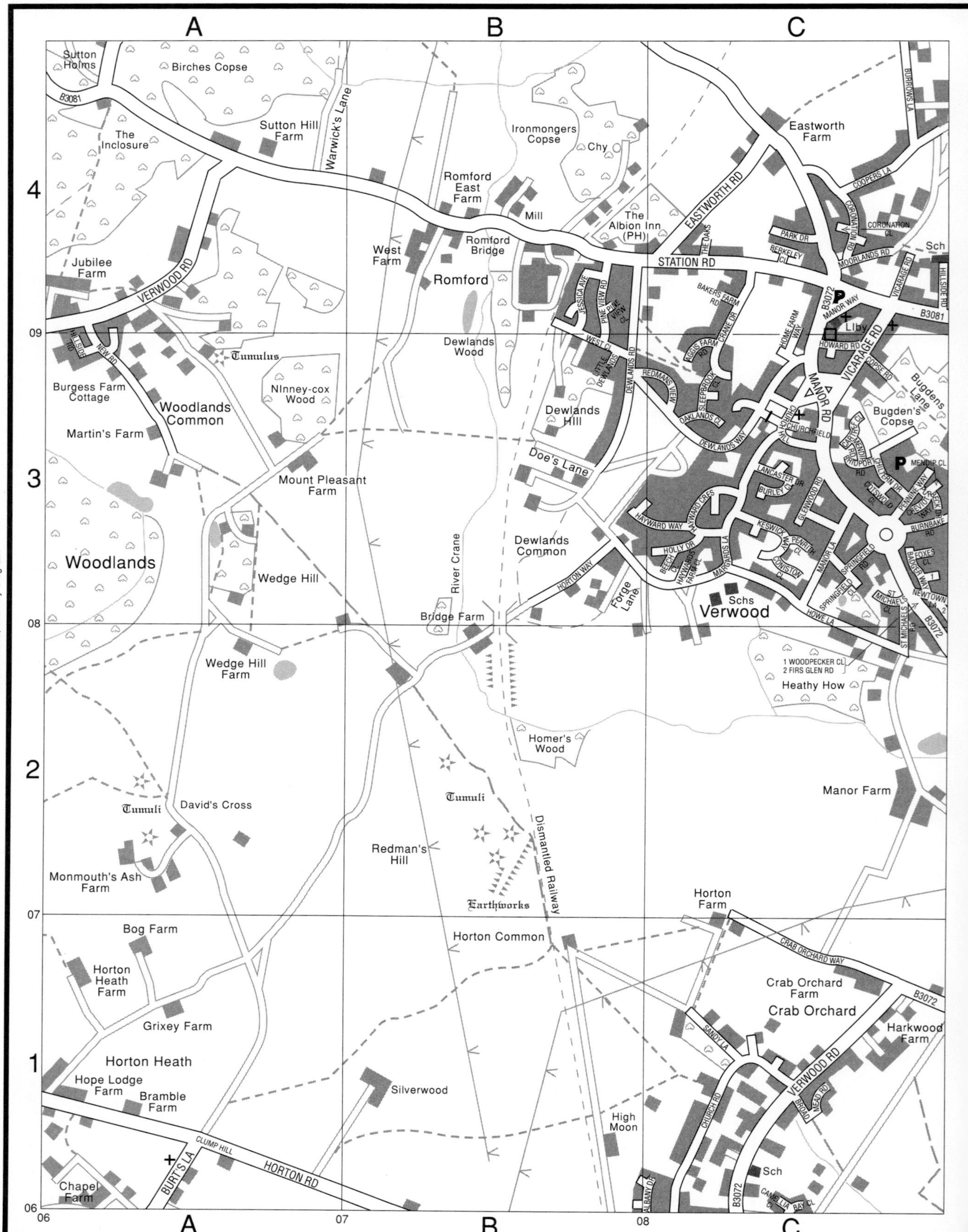

138

92

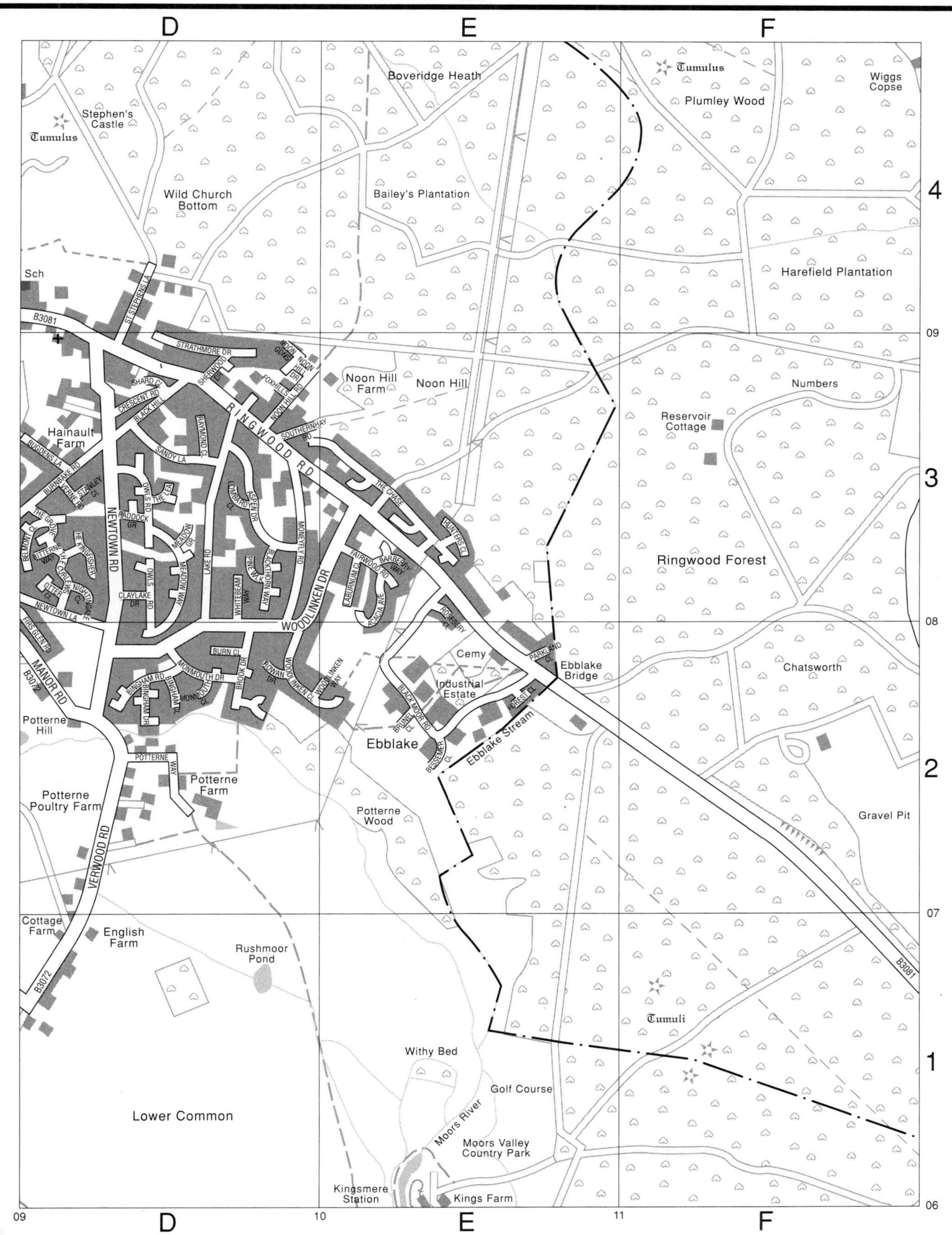
D
E
F
Boveridge Heath
Tumulus
Plumley Wood
Wiggs Copse
Stephen's Castle
Tumulus
Wild Church Bottom
Bailey's Plantation
4
Harefield Plantation
Sch
B3081
ST STEPHENS LA
STRATHMORE DR
NOON GDNS
NOON HILL DR
SHERWOOD DR
FOXHILLS
NOON HILL RD
SHARD CL
CRESCENT RD
BLACK HILL
Noon Hill Farm
Noon Hill
Numbers
09
RINGWOOD RD
SOUTHERNHAY RD
Reservoir Cottage
Hainault Farm
BUGDENS LA
BURNBAKE RD
VERNE RD
STANLEY CL
SANDY LA
RAYMOND CL
LOMBARDY CL
ASPEN DR
THE CHASE
3
THE GROVE
NEWTOWN RD
OWLS RD
THE LEA
PADDOCK GR
MEADOW GR
MONEYFLY RD
HUNTERS CL
BELMONT CL
BITTERNE WAY
THE KINGFISHER
THE CURLEWS
OTTER CL
NIGHTINGALE CL
NEWTOWN LA
LAKE RD
MEADOW WAY
CLAYLAKE DR
WHITEBEAM WAY
PINE WLK
BLACKTHORN WAY
WOODLINKEN DR
FAIRWOOD RD
BARBERRY WAY
LABURNUM CL
ACACIA AVE
Ringwood Forest
ROSEBERY CL
08
FIRS GLEN RD
MANOR RD
B3072
BURN CL
MONMOUTH DR
BINGHAM RD
BINGHAM DR
BINGHAM CL
MONMOUTH CL
BROOK DR
ROWAN DR
WOODLINKEN CL
WOODLINKEN WAY
Cemy
PARKLAND CL
Ebblake Bridge
Industrial Estate
BLACKMOOR RD
BRUNEL CL
FOREST CL
Chatsworth
Potterne Hill
Ebblake
Ebblake Stream
BESSEMER CL
POTTERNE WAY
Potterne Farm
2
Potterne Poultry Farm
Potterne Wood
Gravel Pit
VERWOOD RD
07
Cottage Farm
English Farm
Rushmoor Pond
B3081
B3072
Tumuli
Withy Bed
1
Golf Course
Lower Common
Moors River
Moors Valley Country Park
Kingsmere Station
Kings Farm
06
09
10
11

116

139

93

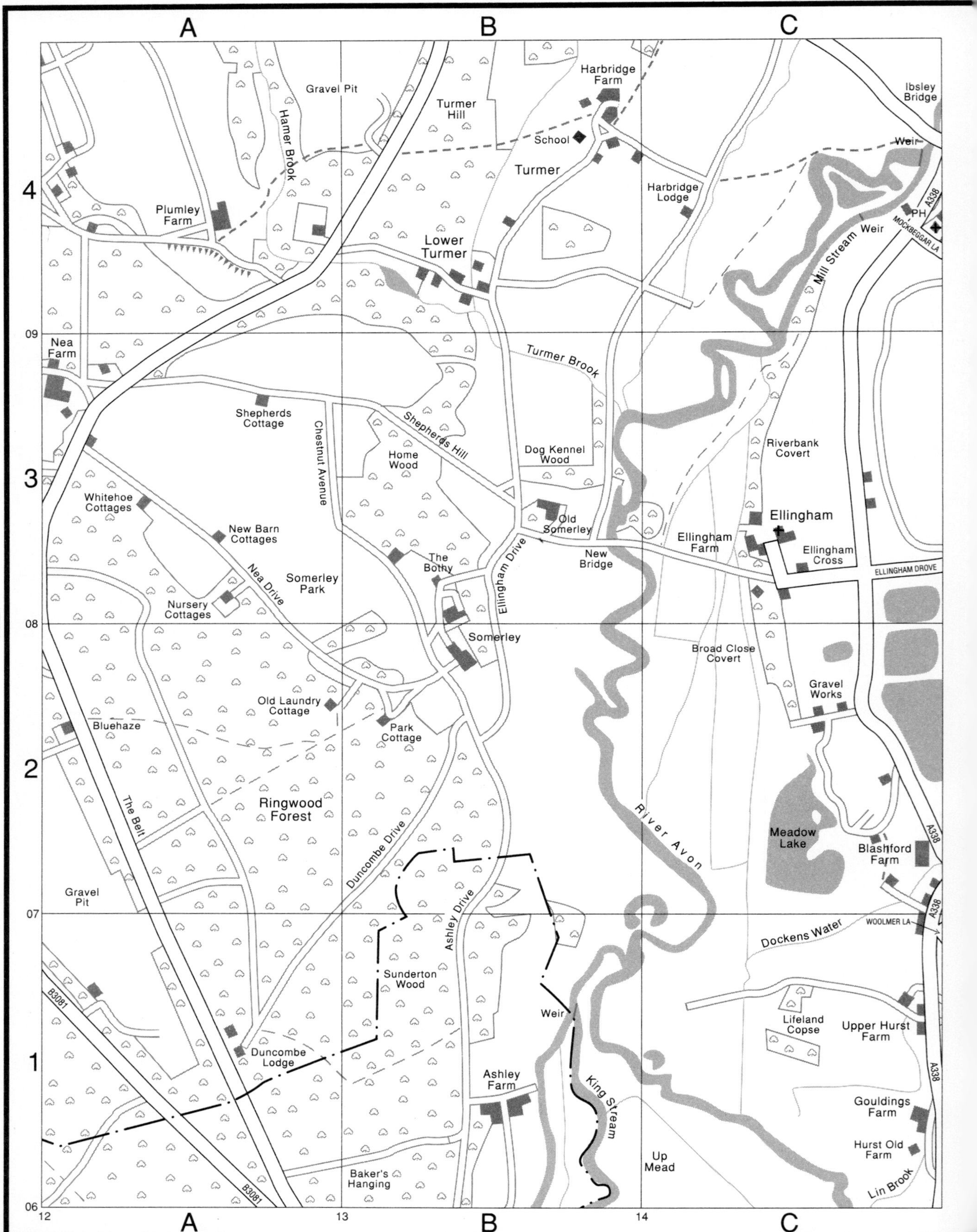
A
B
C
4
3
2
1
09
08
07
06
12
13
14
Gravel Pit
Hamer Brook
Turmer Hill
Harbridge Farm
School
Turmer
Ibsley Bridge
Weir
Harbridge Lodge
Plumley Farm
Lower Turmer
PH
A338
MOCKBEGGAR LA
Mill Stream
Nea Farm
Turmer Brook
Shepherds Cottage
Chestnut Avenue
Shepherds Hill
Home Wood
Dog Kennel Wood
Riverbank Covert
Whitehoe Cottages
New Barn Cottages
Old Somerley
Ellingham
Ellingham Farm
Ellingham Cross
New Bridge
The Bothy
Ellingham Drive
ELLINGHAM DROVE
Nea Drive
Somerley Park
Nursery Cottages
Somerley
Broad Close Covert
Old Laundry Cottage
Gravel Works
Bluehaze
Park Cottage
Ringwood Forest
The Belt
Duncombe Drive
River Avon
Meadow Lake
Blashford Farm
Gravel Pit
Ashley Drive
Dockens Water
WOOLMER LA
Sunderton Wood
Weir
Lifeland Copse
Upper Hurst Farm
B3081
Duncombe Lodge
Ashley Farm
King Stream
Gouldings Farm
Hurst Old Farm
Up Mead
Baker's Hanging
Lin Brook
115

140

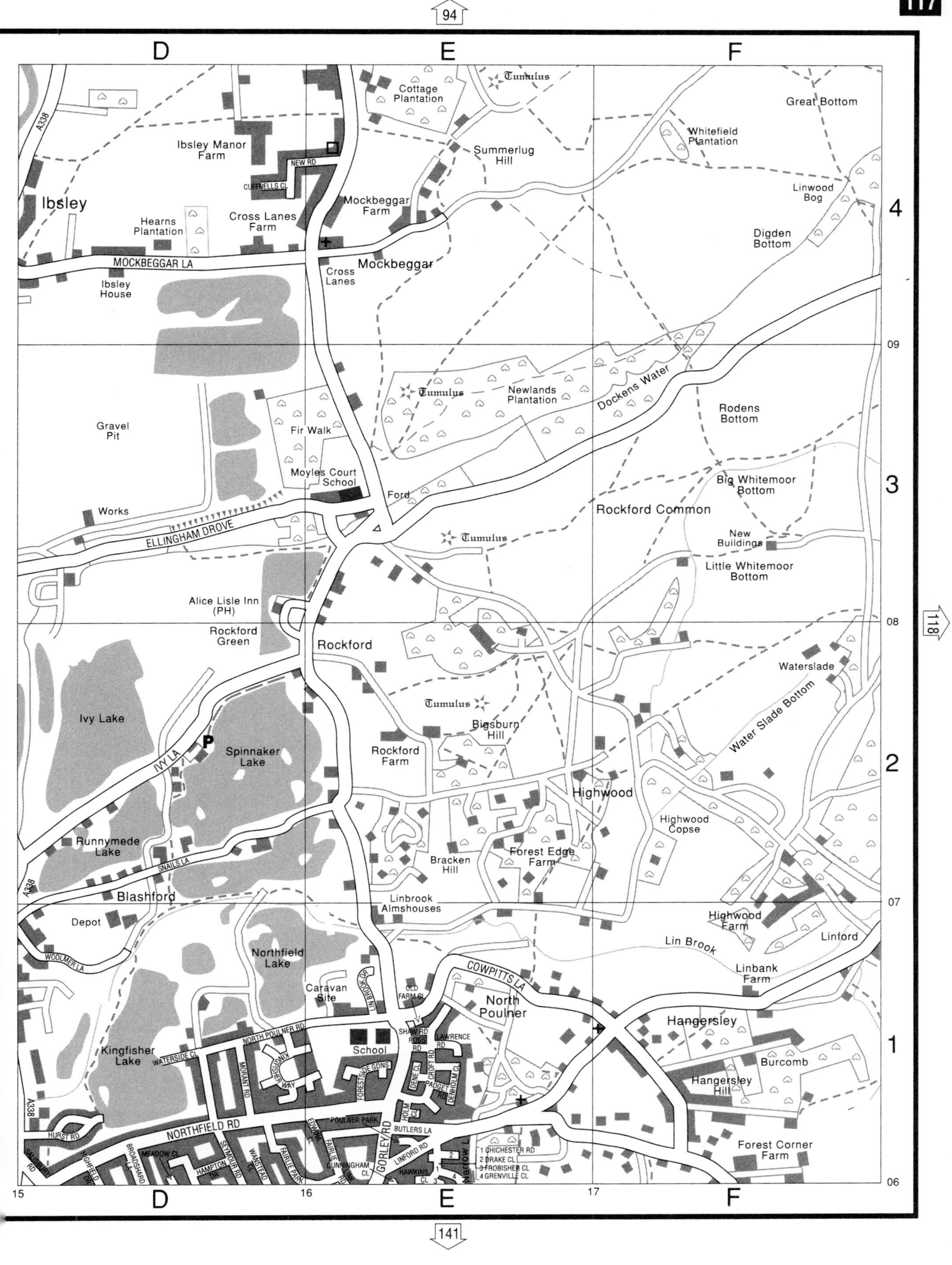
94
D
E
F
Tumulus
Cottage Plantation
Great Bottom
Whitefield Plantation
Summerlug Hill
Ibsley Manor Farm
NEW RD
CUFFNELLS CL
A338
Ibsley
Mockbeggar Farm
Linwood Bog
Hearns Plantation
Cross Lanes Farm
Digden Bottom
4
MOCKBEGGAR LA
Mockbeggar
Cross Lanes
Ibsley House
09
Tumulus
Newlands Plantation
Dockens Water
Rodens Bottom
Gravel Pit
Fir Walk
Moyles Court School
Big Whitemoor Bottom
3
Works
Ford
Rockford Common
ELLINGHAM DROVE
Tumulus
New Buildings
Little Whitemoor Bottom
Alice Lisle Inn (PH)
08
118
Rockford Green
Rockford
Waterslade
Tumulus
Water Slade Bottom
Ivy Lake
Bigsburn Hill
Spinnaker Lake
IVY LA
Rockford Farm
2
Highwood
Highwood Copse
Runnymede Lake
Bracken Hill
Forest Edge Farm
SNAILS LA
A338
Blashford
Linbrook Almshouses
07
Depot
Highwood Farm
Linford
Lin Brook
WOOLMER LA
Northfield Lake
COWPITTS LA
Linbank Farm
Caravan Site
LINBROOK DR
OLD FARM CL
North Poulner
Hangersley
NORTH POULNER RD
SHAW RD
ROSS RD
LAWRENCE RD
1
Kingfisher Lake
WATERSIDE CL
School
Burcomb
KINGFISHER WAY
MORANT RD
FORESTSIDE GDNS
DENE CL
CROFT RD
DENHOLM CL
PADGET RD
Hangersley Hill
A338
HOLM CL
POULNER PARK
HURST RD
NORTHFIELD RD
EDWINA CL
GORLEY RD
BUTLERS LA
Forest Corner Farm
SALISBURY RD
HIGHFIELD RD
BROADSHARD LA
MEADOW CL
HAMPTON DR
SEYMOUR RD
WANSTEAD CL
FAIRLIE PARK
FAIRLIE
CUNNINGHAM CL
LINFORD RD
HAWKINS CL
Narrow L
1 CHICHESTER RD
2 DRAKE CL
3 FROBISHER CL
4 GRENVILLE CL
06
15
16
17
141

95

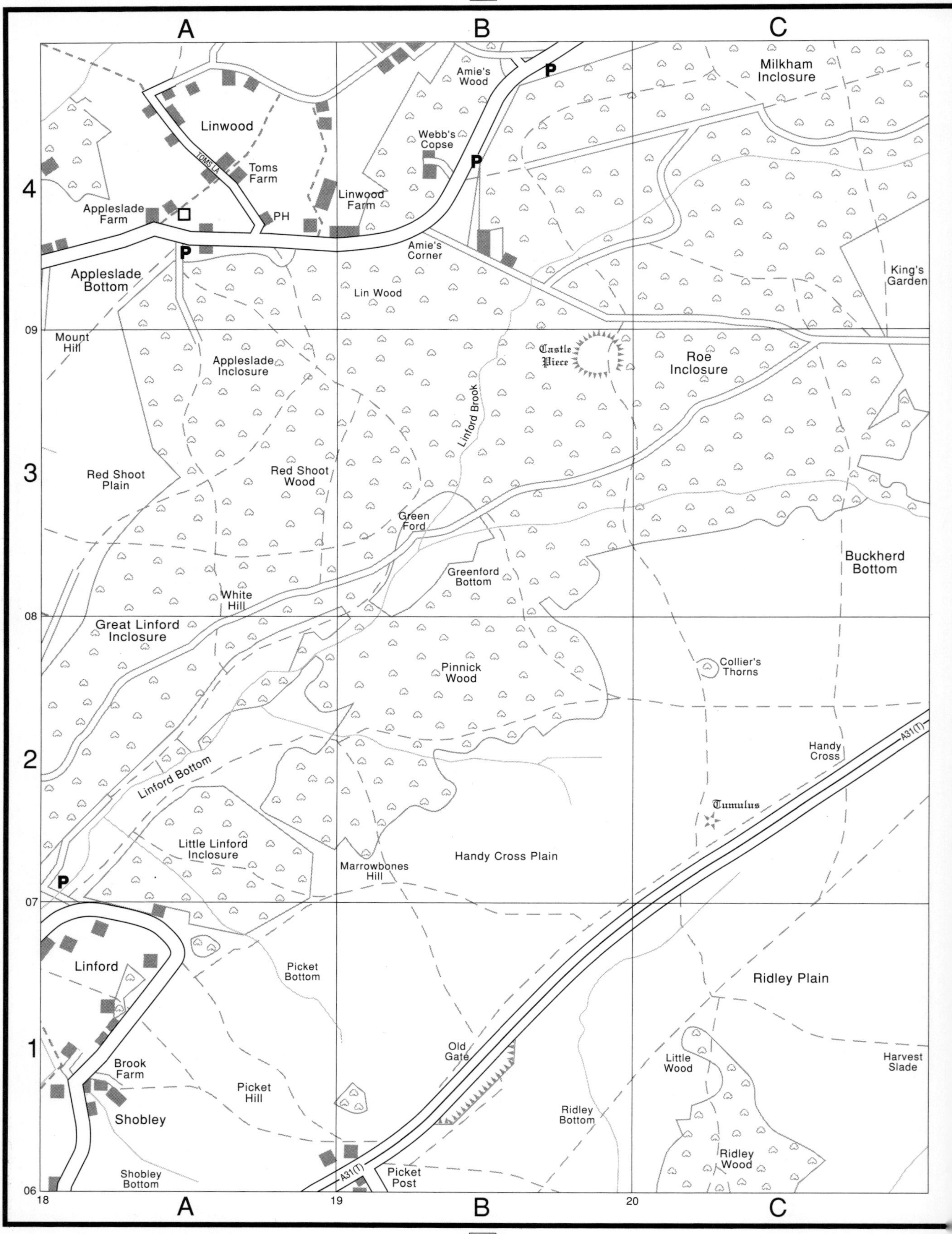

A
B
C
4
3
2
1
09
08
07
06
18
19
20
Milkham Inclosure
Amie's Wood
Linwood
Toms Farm
TOMS LA
Webb's Copse
Linwood Farm
Appleslade Farm
PH
Amie's Corner
Appleslade Bottom
King's Garden
Lin Wood
Mount Hill
Castle Piece
Roe Inclosure
Appleslade Inclosure
Linford Brook
Red Shoot Plain
Red Shoot Wood
Green Ford
Buckherd Bottom
Greenford Bottom
White Hill
Great Linford Inclosure
Collier's Thorns
Pinnick Wood
A31(T)
Handy Cross
Linford Bottom
Tumulus
Little Linford Inclosure
Handy Cross Plain
Marrowbones Hill
Linford
Picket Bottom
Ridley Plain
Old Gate
Harvest Slade
Little Wood
Brook Farm
Picket Hill
Shobley
Ridley Bottom
Ridley Wood
Shobley Bottom
Picket Post

117

142

96

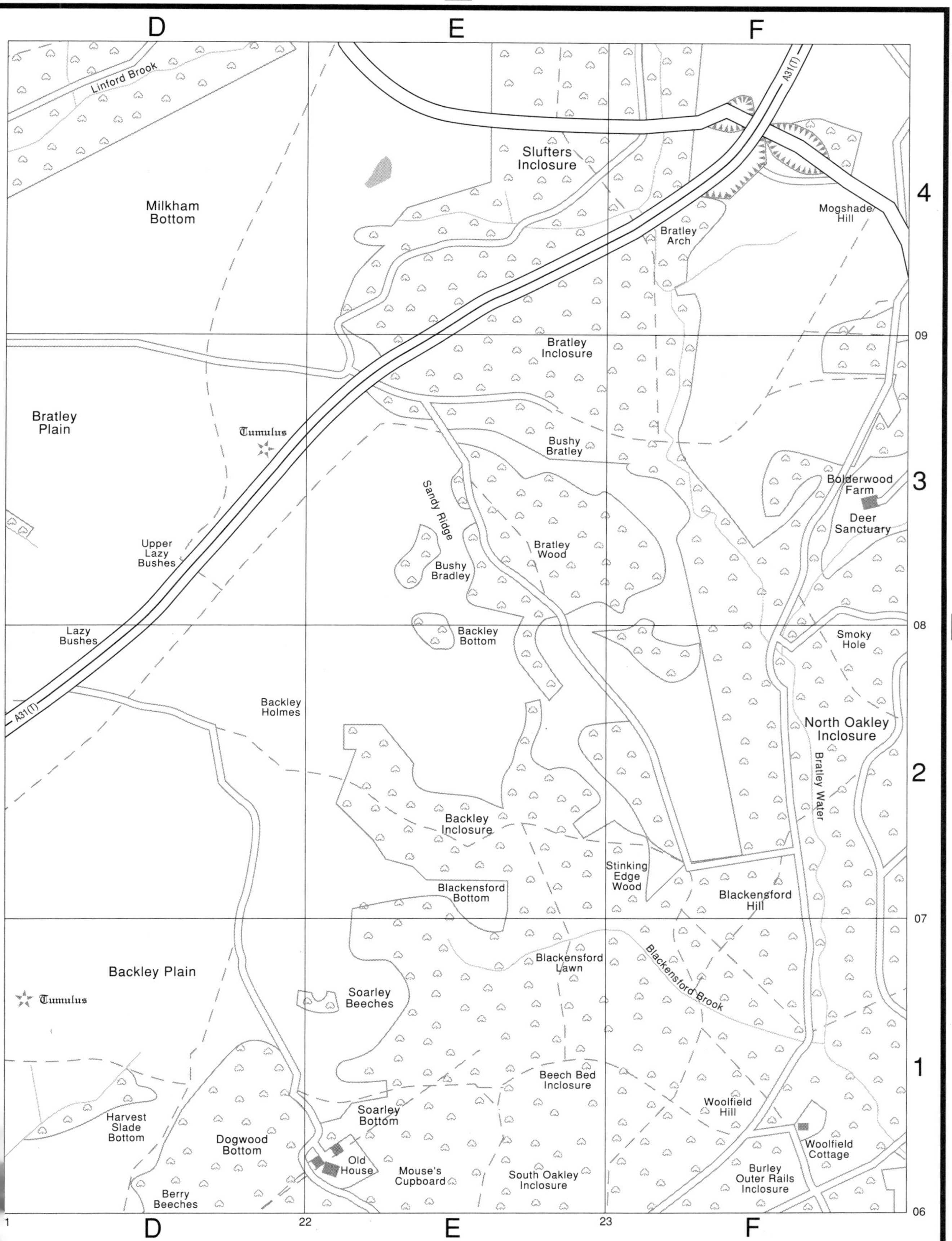
D
E
F
Linford Brook
Slufters Inclosure
A31(T)
Milkham Bottom
Mogshade Hill
Bratley Arch
4
09
Bratley Inclosure
Bratley Plain
Tumulus
Bushy Bratley
Sandy Ridge
Bolderwood Farm
3
Deer Sanctuary
Bratley Wood
Upper Lazy Bushes
Bushy Bradley
Lazy Bushes
Backley Bottom
08
Smoky Hole
Backley Holmes
North Oakley Inclosure
Bratley Water
2
Backley Inclosure
Stinking Edge Wood
Blackensford Hill
Blackensford Bottom
07
Blackensford Lawn
Blackensford Brook
Backley Plain
Tumulus
Soarley Beeches
1
Beech Bed Inclosure
Harvest Slade Bottom
Soarley Bottom
Woolfield Hill
Dogwood Bottom
Woolfield Cottage
Old House
Mouse's Cupboard
South Oakley Inclosure
Burley Outer Rails Inclosure
Berry Beeches
06
1
22
23
D
E
F

120
143

97

119

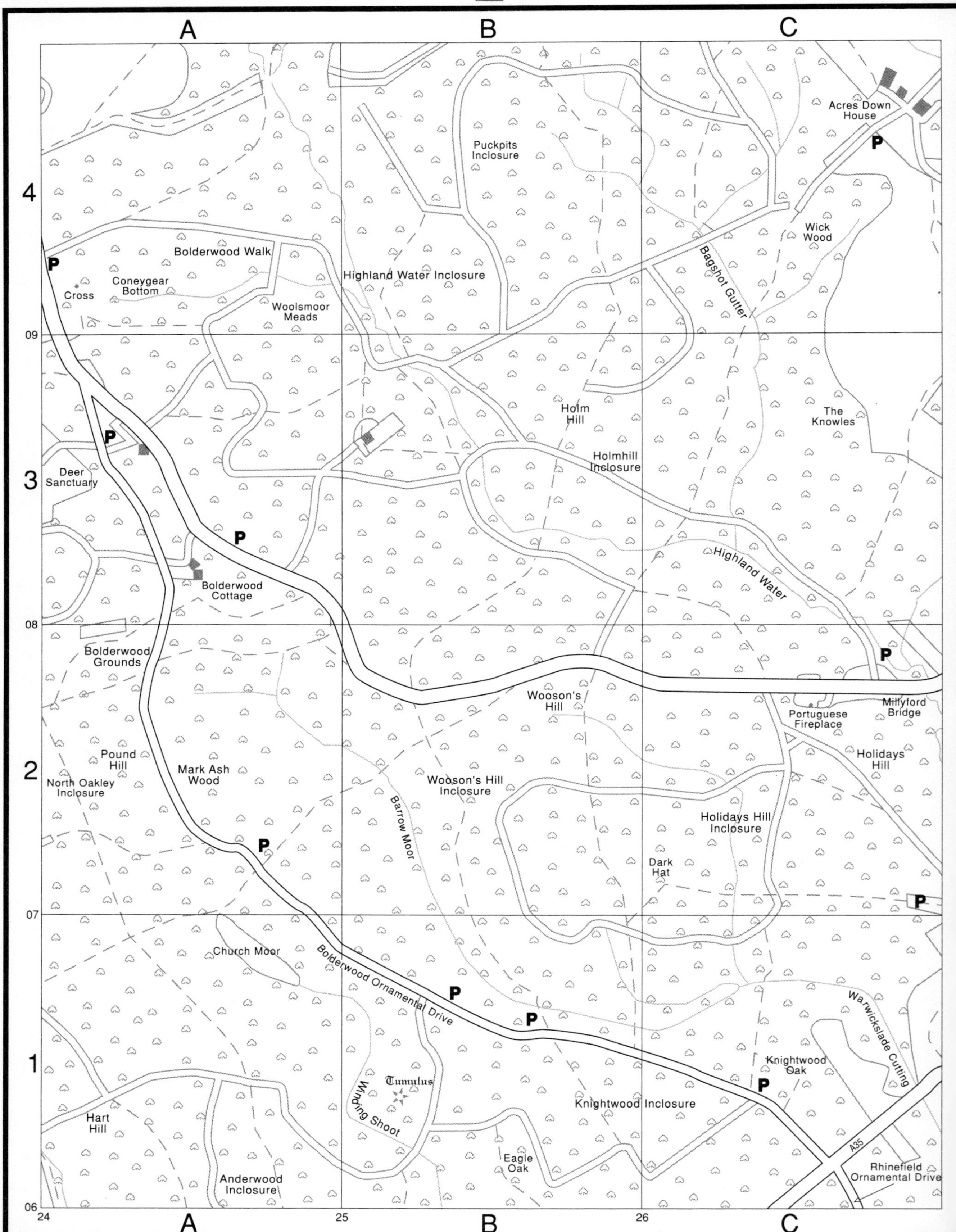
A
B
C
4
3
2
1
09
08
07
06
24
25
26
Acres Down House
Puckpits Inclosure
Wick Wood
Bolderwood Walk
Coneygear Bottom
Cross
Highland Water Inclosure
Bagshot Gutter
Woolsmoor Meads
Holm Hill
The Knowles
Holmhill Inclosure
Deer Sanctuary
Highland Water
Bolderwood Cottage
Bolderwood Grounds
Wooson's Hill
Portuguese Fireplace
Millyford Bridge
Pound Hill
Mark Ash Wood
North Oakley Inclosure
Wooson's Hill Inclosure
Holidays Hill
Barrow Moor
Holidays Hill Inclosure
Dark Hat
Church Moor
Bolderwood Ornamental Drive
Warwickslade Cutting
Knightwood Oak
Tumulus
Winding Shoot
Knightwood Inclosure
Hart Hill
Eagle Oak
A35
Rhinefield Ornamental Drive
Anderwood Inclosure

144

98

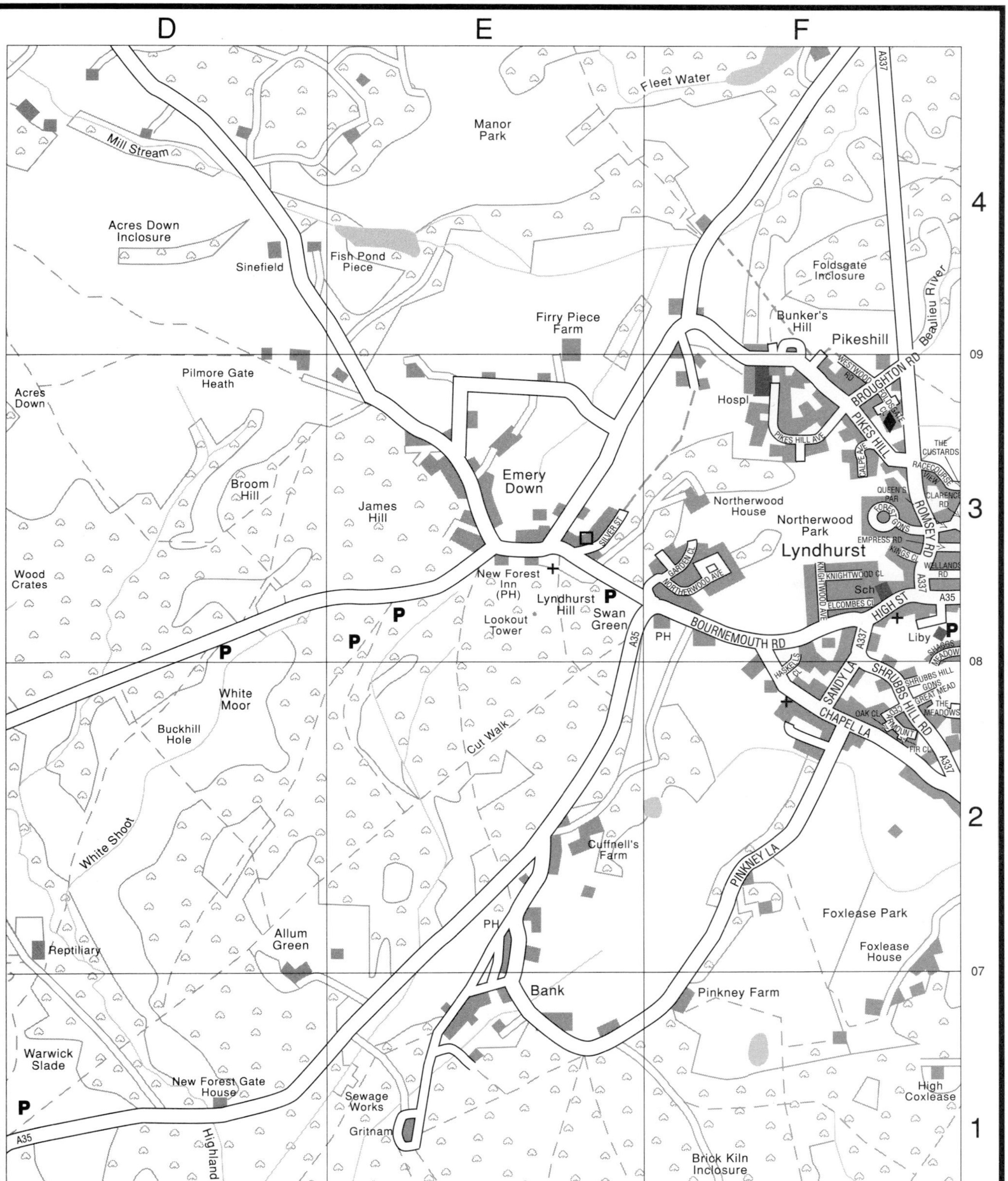

D
E
F
Fleet Water
Manor Park
Mill Stream
Acres Down Inclosure
Sinefield
Fish Pond Piece
Foldsgate Inclosure
Beaulieu River
A337
Firry Piece Farm
Bunker's Hill
Pikeshill
Pilmore Gate Heath
Acres Down
Hospl
WESTWOOD RD
BROUGHTON RD
PIKES HILL
PIKES HILL AVE
CALPE AVE
THE CUSTARDS
RACECOURSE VIEW
Broom Hill
James Hill
Emery Down
Northerwood House
Northerwood Park
QUEEN'S PAR
CLARENCE RD
ROMSEY RD
FOREST GDNS
EMPRESS RD
KINGS CL
Lyndhurst
SILVER ST
GARDEN CL
NORTHERWOOD AVE
KNIGHTWOOD CL
WELLANDS RD
Sch
A35
Wood Crates
New Forest Inn (PH)
Lyndhurst Hill
Swan Green
Lookout Tower
P
PH
BOURNEMOUTH RD
ELCOMBES CL
KNIGHTWOOD AVE
HIGH ST
Liby
White Moor
Buckhill Hole
Cut Walk
HASKELLS CL
SANDY LA
SHRUBBS HILL RD
SHRUBBS HILL GDNS
GREAT MEAD
THE MEADOWS
CHAPEL LA
OAK CL
FIR CL
White Shoot
Cuffnell's Farm
PINKNEY LA
Foxlease Park
Foxlease House
Allum Green
Reptiliary
PH
Bank
Pinkney Farm
Warwick Slade
New Forest Gate House
Sewage Works
Gritnam
High Coxlease
Highland Water
Brick Kiln Inclosure
Gritnam Wood
4
3
2
1
09
08
07
06
27
28
29

122

145

99

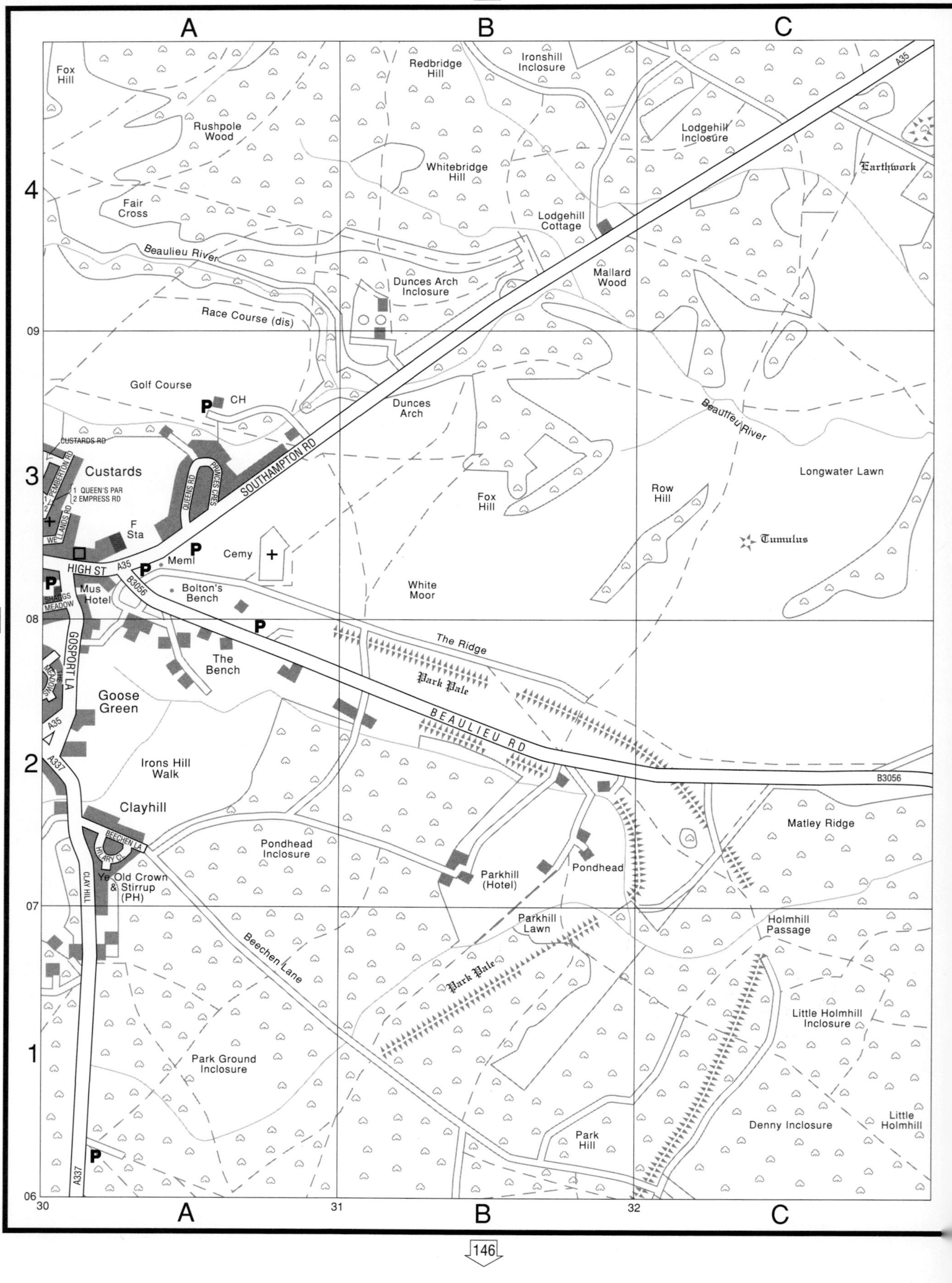
A
B
C
Fox Hill
Rushpole Wood
Redbridge Hill
Ironshill Inclosure
Lodgehill Inclosure
A35
Earthwork
Whitebridge Hill
Fair Cross
Lodgehill Cottage
Beaulieu River
Mallard Wood
Dunces Arch Inclosure
Race Course (dis)
09
Golf Course
CH
P
Dunces Arch
Beaulieu River
CUSTARDS RD
PEMBERTON RD
Custards
1 QUEEN'S PAR
2 EMPRESS RD
WILLANDS RD
QUEENS RD
PRINCES CRES
SOUTHAMPTON RD
Longwater Lawn
Fox Hill
Row Hill
F Sta
Tumulus
Cemy
HIGH ST
A35
Meml
B3056
Bolton's Bench
White Moor
Mus
Hotel
SHAGGS MEADOW
08
The Ridge
GOSPORT LA
The Bench
Park Pale
Goose Green
A35
BEAULIEU RD
A337
Irons Hill Walk
B3056
Clayhill
Matley Ridge
BEECHEN LA
HILARY CL
Pondhead Inclosure
Ye Old Crown & Stirrup (PH)
Parkhill (Hotel)
Pondhead
CLAY HILL
07
Parkhill Lawn
Holmhill Passage
Beechen Lane
Park Pale
Little Holmhill Inclosure
Park Ground Inclosure
Little Holmhill
Denny Inclosure
Park Hill
A337
06
30
31
32
1
2
3
4

121

146

100

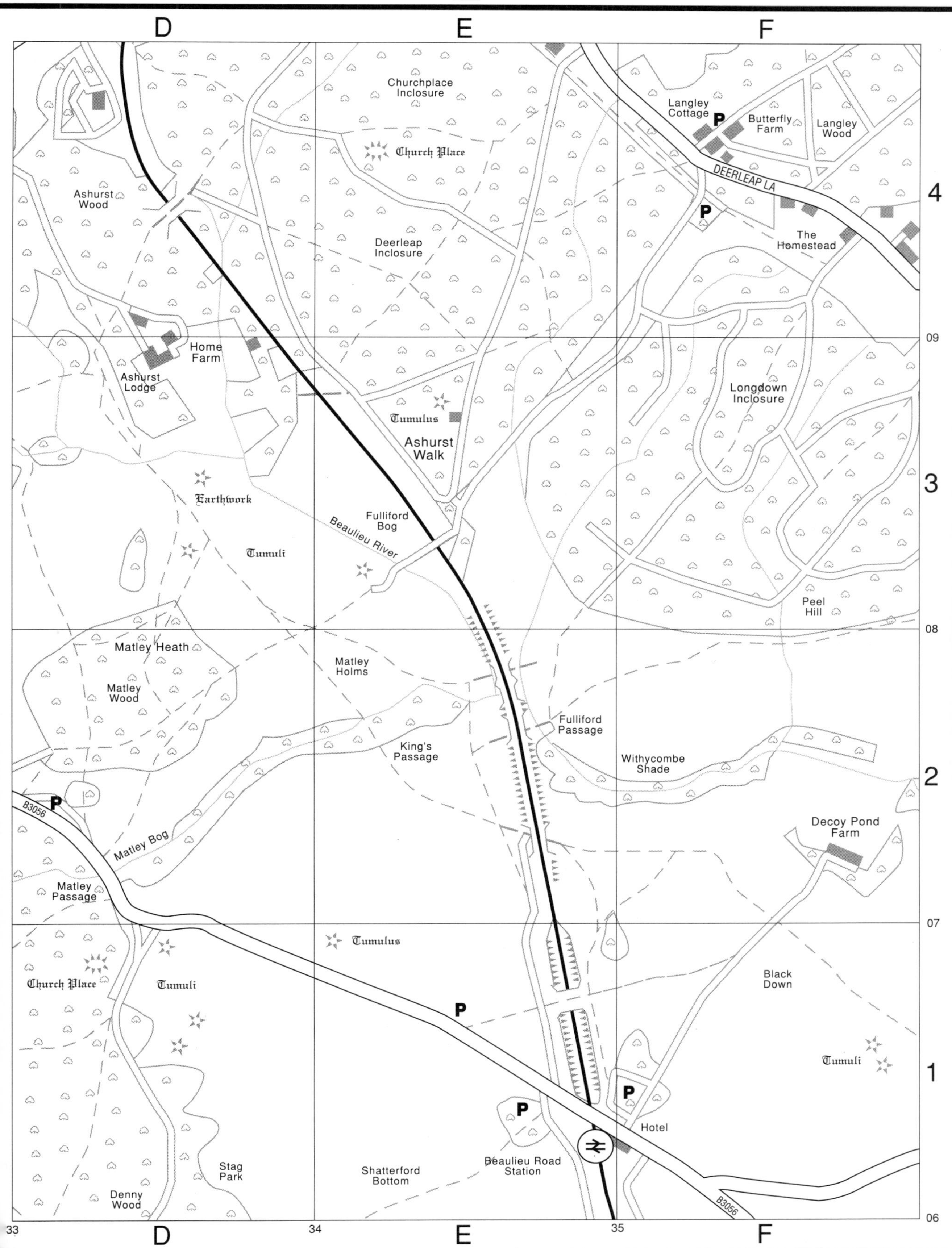
D
E
F
Churchplace Inclosure
Church Place
Langley Cottage
Butterfly Farm
Langley Wood
DEERLEAP LA
Ashurst Wood
Deerleap Inclosure
The Homestead
4
Home Farm
Ashurst Lodge
09
Longdown Inclosure
Tumulus
Ashurst Walk
3
Earthwork
Fulliford Bog
Beaulieu River
Tumuli
Peel Hill
08
Matley Heath
Matley Wood
Matley Holms
Fulliford Passage
King's Passage
Withycombe Shade
2
B3056
Matley Bog
Decoy Pond Farm
Matley Passage
07
Tumulus
Church Place
Tumuli
Black Down
Tumuli
1
Hotel
Stag Park
Shatterford Bottom
Beaulieu Road Station
Denny Wood
B3056
06
33
34
35
D
E
F

124

147

101

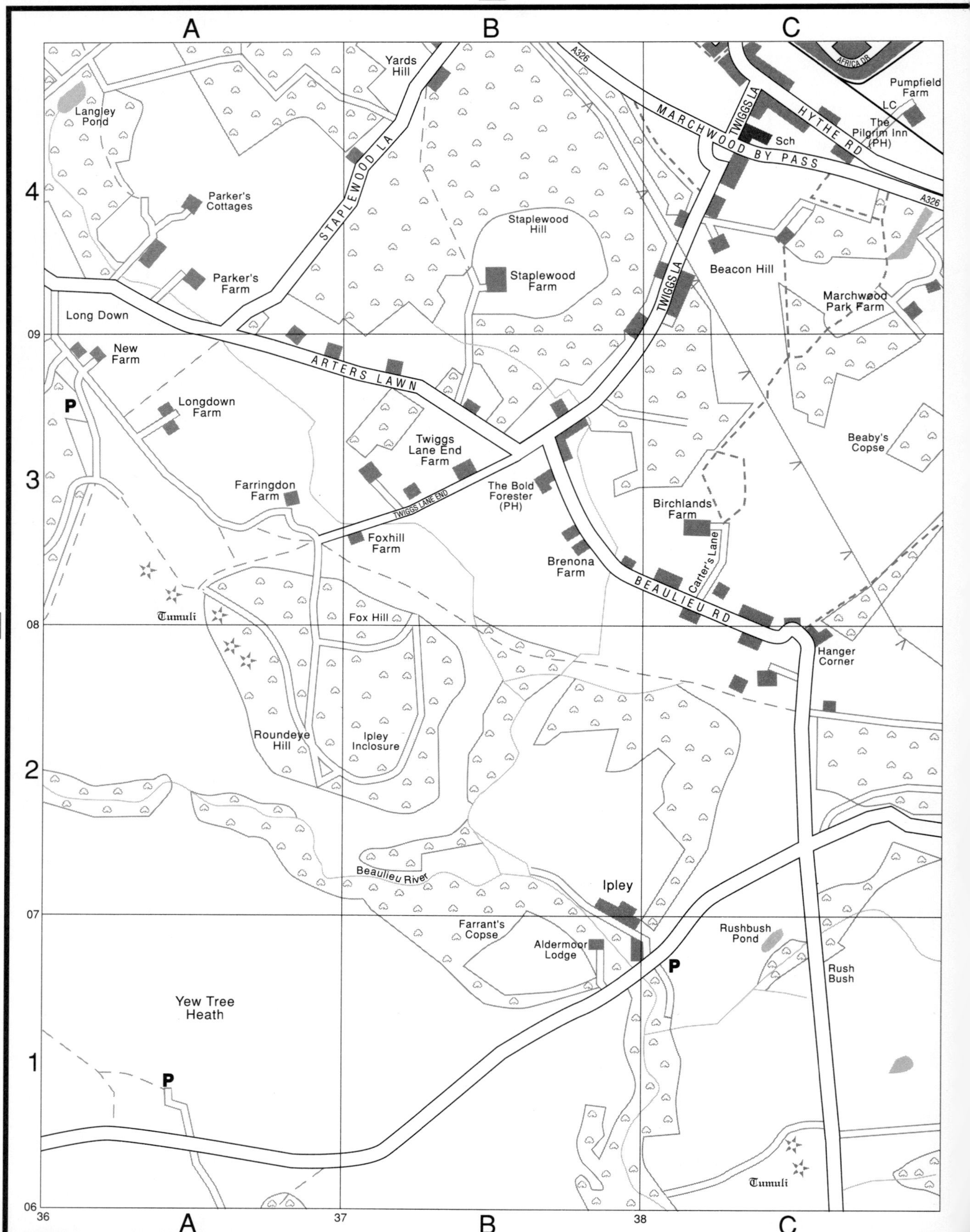
A
B
C
4
3
2
1
09
08
07
06
36
37
38
Yards Hill
Langley Pond
Parker's Cottages
Parker's Farm
Long Down
New Farm
Longdown Farm
STAPLEWOOD LA
Staplewood Hill
Staplewood Farm
ARTERS LAWN
Twiggs Lane End Farm
TWIGGS LANE END
Farringdon Farm
Foxhill Farm
Tumuli
Fox Hill
Roundeye Hill
Ipley Inclosure
Beaulieu River
Farrant's Copse
Aldermoor Lodge
Ipley
Yew Tree Heath
A326
MARCHWOOD BY PASS
TWIGGS LA
HYTHE RD
Sch
AFRICA DR
Pumpfield Farm
LC
The Pilgrim Inn (PH)
Beacon Hill
Marchwood Park Farm
Beaby's Copse
The Bold Forester (PH)
Birchlands Farm
Carter's Lane
Brenona Farm
BEAULIEU RD
Hanger Corner
Rushbush Pond
Rush Bush
P

123

148

102

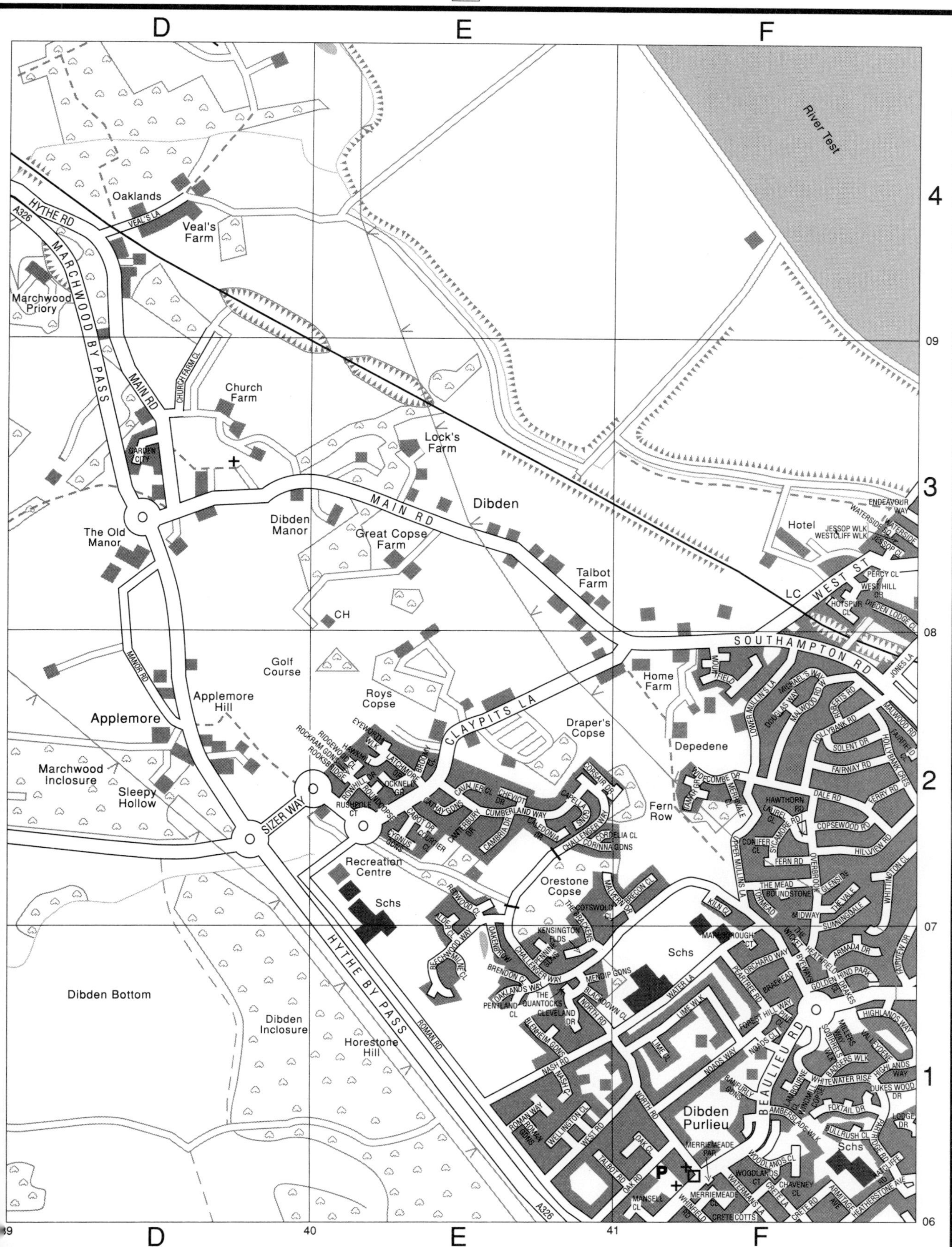
D
E
F
4
3
2
1
09
08
07
06
39
40
41
River Test
Oaklands
HYTHE RD
A326
VEAL'S LA
Veal's Farm
MARCHWOOD BY PASS
Marchwood Priory
MAIN RD
CHURCH FARM CL
Church Farm
GARDEN CITY
Lock's Farm
Dibden
MAIN RD
The Old Manor
Dibden Manor
Great Copse Farm
Talbot Farm
Hotel
ENDEAVOUR WAY
WATERSIDE
JESSOP WLK
WESTCLIFF WLK
JESSOP CL
LC
WEST ST
PERCY CL
WEST HILL DR
HOTSPUR CL
DIBDEN LODGE CL
CH
SOUTHAMPTON RD
JONES LA
MANOR RD
Golf Course
Home Farm
Applemore Hill
Applemore
Roys Copse
CLAYPITS LA
Draper's Copse
Depedene
Marchwood Inclosure
Sleepy Hollow
SIZER WAY
EYEWORTH WLK
LATCHMORE DR
BROOMY CL
CAVALIER CL
CHEVIOT DR
CORSAIR DR
CUMBERLAND WAY
CAPELLA GDNS
CALEDONIA DR
CAMBRIA DR
CANTERBURY DR
CATHAY GDNS
CABOT DR
COURTIER CL
CYGNUS GDNS
RUSHPOLE CT
CHALLENGER WAY
CORDELIA CL
CORINNA GDNS
Fern Row
WIDECOMBE DR
HAWTHORN RD
LAUREL CL
SYCAMORE RD
CONIFER CL
FERN RD
DALE RD
FERRY RD
COPSEWOOD RD
HILLVIEW RD
FAIRWAY RD
SOLENT DR
HOLLYBANK RD
HOLLYBANK CRES
MALWOOD RD
ROBERTS RD
DOUGLAS WAY
MICHAEL'S WAY
LOWER MULLIN'S LA
UPPER MULLINS LA
Recreation Centre
Orestone Copse
Schs
REDWOOD CL
ALDER CL
BEECHWOOD WAY
OAKENBROW
BRENDON CL
OAKLANDS WAY
PENTLAND CL
THE QUANTOCKS
CLEVELAND DR
KENSINGTON FLDS
THE COTSWOLDS
MALVERN DR
BRECON CL
MENDIP GDNS
BLACKDOWN CL
NORTH RD
WATER LA
KILN CL
MARLBOROUGH CT
Schs
THE MEAD
BOUNDSTONE
ORMEAD
OVERBROOK
GLENSIDE
THE VALE
SUNNINGDALE
MIDWAY
ARMADA DR
GOLDEN HIND PARK
DRAKES CL
WHITTINGTON CL
FAIRVIEW DR
ORCHARD WAY
PEARTREE RD
BRAEHEAD
FOREST HILL WAY
HIGHLANDS WAY
VALLEY SIDE
MILLERS WAY
SQUIRRELS WALK
BADGERS WLK
WHITEWATER RISE
DUKES WOOD DR
FOXTAIL DR
LODGE DR
BULLRUSH CL
PARTRIDGE RD
Dibden Bottom
Dibden Inclosure
Horestone Hill
HYTHE BY PASS
ROMAN RD
A326
LIME WLK
LIME CL
NOADS WAY
NOADS CL
BEAULIEU RD
BAINFURLY GDNS
NASH RD
NASH CL
ROMAN WAY
ROMAN GDNS
WELLINGTON CL
WEST RD
OAK CL
TALBOT RD
OAK RD
Dibden Purlieu
MERRIEMEADE PAR
P
WOODLANDS CL
WOODLANDS CT
CHAVENEY CL
CRETE LA
CRETE RD
WATERMANS LA
MERRIEMEADE CL
MANSELL CL
WHINFIELD RD
CRETE COTTS
ARMITAGE AVE
HEATHERSTONE AVE
Schs
AMBERSLADE WLK

126

149

103

125

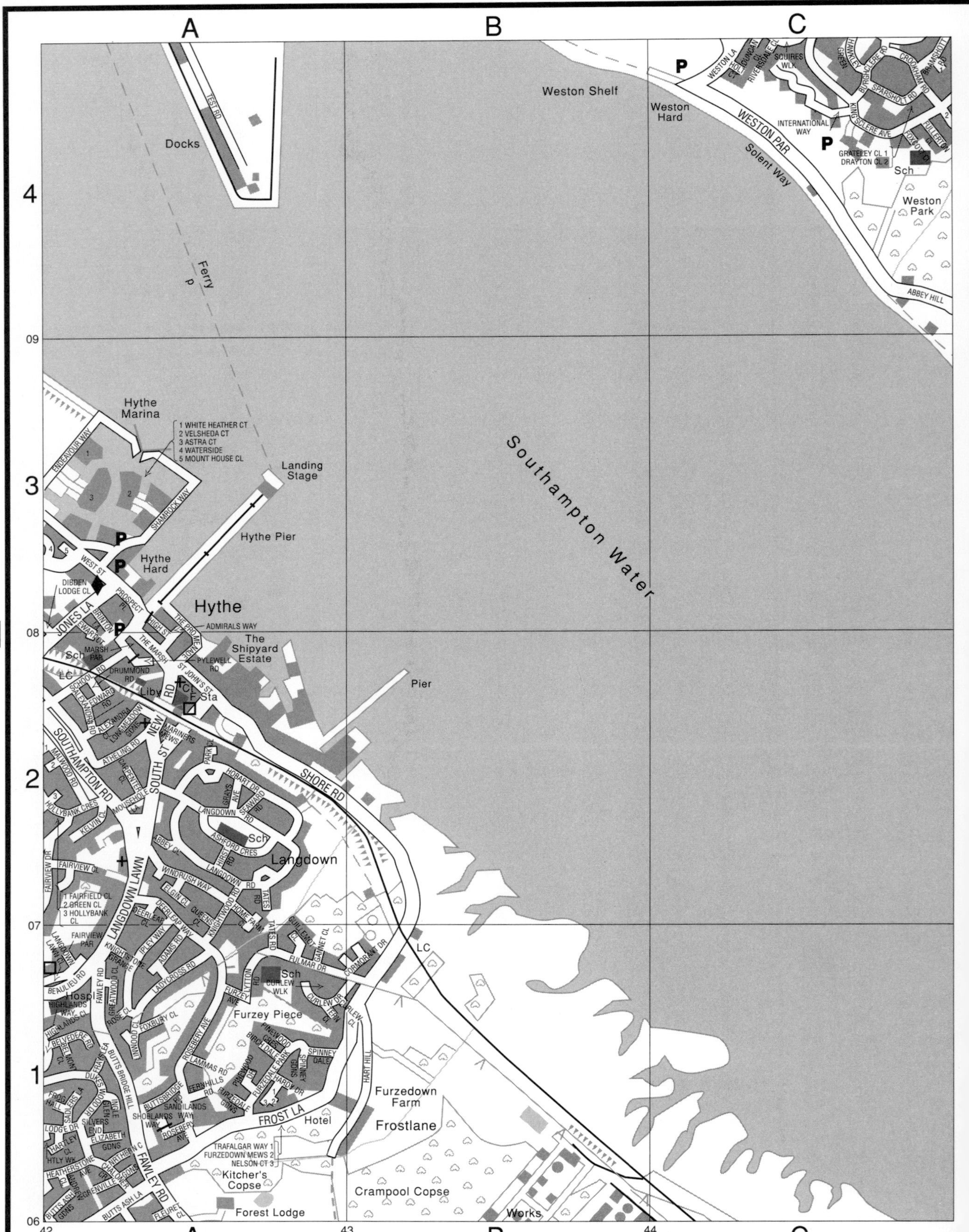

A
B
C
4
3
2
1
09
08
07
06
42
43
44
Docks
TEST RD
Ferry
Weston Shelf
Weston Hard
WESTON LA
RIVERSDALE CL
SQUIRES WLK
INTERNATIONAL WAY
WESTON PAR
Solent Way
KINGSCLERE AVE
SPARSHOLT RD
CROOKHAM RD
BURGHCLERE RD
HAWKLEY GREEN
GRATELEY CL 1
DRAYTON CL 2
FULLERTON CL
FOXCOTT CL
Sch
Weston Park
ABBEY HILL
Hythe Marina
ENDEAVOUR WAY
1 WHITE HEATHER CT
2 VELSHEDA CT
3 ASTRA CT
4 WATERSIDE
5 MOUNT HOUSE CL
SHAMROCK WAY
Landing Stage
Hythe Pier
Hythe Hard
Hythe
Southampton Water
WEST ST
DIBDEN LODGE CL
JONES LA
PROSPECT PL
HIGH ST
THE PROMENADE
ADMIRALS WAY
The Shipyard Estate
MARSH PAR
THE MARSH
PYLEWELL RD
ST JOHN'S ST
DRUMMOND RD
Sch
LC
Liby
NEW RD
F Sta
Pier
SOUTHAMPTON RD
ALEXANDRA RD
EDWARD RD
ATHELING RD
MARINERS MEWS
SOUTH ST
SHORE RD
HOBART DR
GRAYS AVE
SEAWARD RD
LANGDOWN RD
ASHFORD CRES
Sch
Langdown
HOLLYBANK CRES
KELVIN CL
MOUSEHOLE LA
ABBEY CL
FAIRVIEW DR
FAIRVIEW CL
WINDRUSH WAY
ELGIN CL
LANGDOWN LAWN
1 FAIRFIELD CL
2 GREEN CL
3 HOLLYBANK CL
DEERLEAP WAY
QUEENS CL
KNIGHTWOOD RD
HOME FARM CL
TATES RD
FAIRVIEW PAR
IPLEY WAY
ADAMS RD
GUILLEMOT CL
GANNET CL
CORMORANT DR
FULMAR DR
LC
KNIGHTSTONE GRANGE
LADYCROSS RD
Sch
CURLEW WLK
CURLEW DR
FURZEY AVE
Hospl
HIGHLANDS WAY
BEAULIEU RD
FAWLEY RD
GREATWOOD CL
ROSE CL
FOXBURY CL
Furzey Piece
ROSEBERY AVE
FINEWOOD CRES
BIRCHDALE RD
SPINNEY DALE
HART HILL
BELVEDERE RD
BUTTS BRIDGE HILL
AMMAS RD
FERN HILLS RD
PINEWOOD
HARDY DR
Furzedown Farm
FROG HALL
SADLERS LA
BUTTSBRIDGE RD
SANDILANDS WAY
SHOBLANDS WAY
FROST LA
Hotel
Frostlane
LODGE DR
SILVERS END
ELIZABETH GDNS
ROSEBERY AVE
TRAFALGAR WAY 1
FURZEDOWN MEWS 2
NELSON CT 3
HEATHERSTONE AVE
GRENVILLE
Kitcher's Copse
Crampool Copse
BUTTS ASH LA
FLEURET CL
Forest Lodge
Works

150

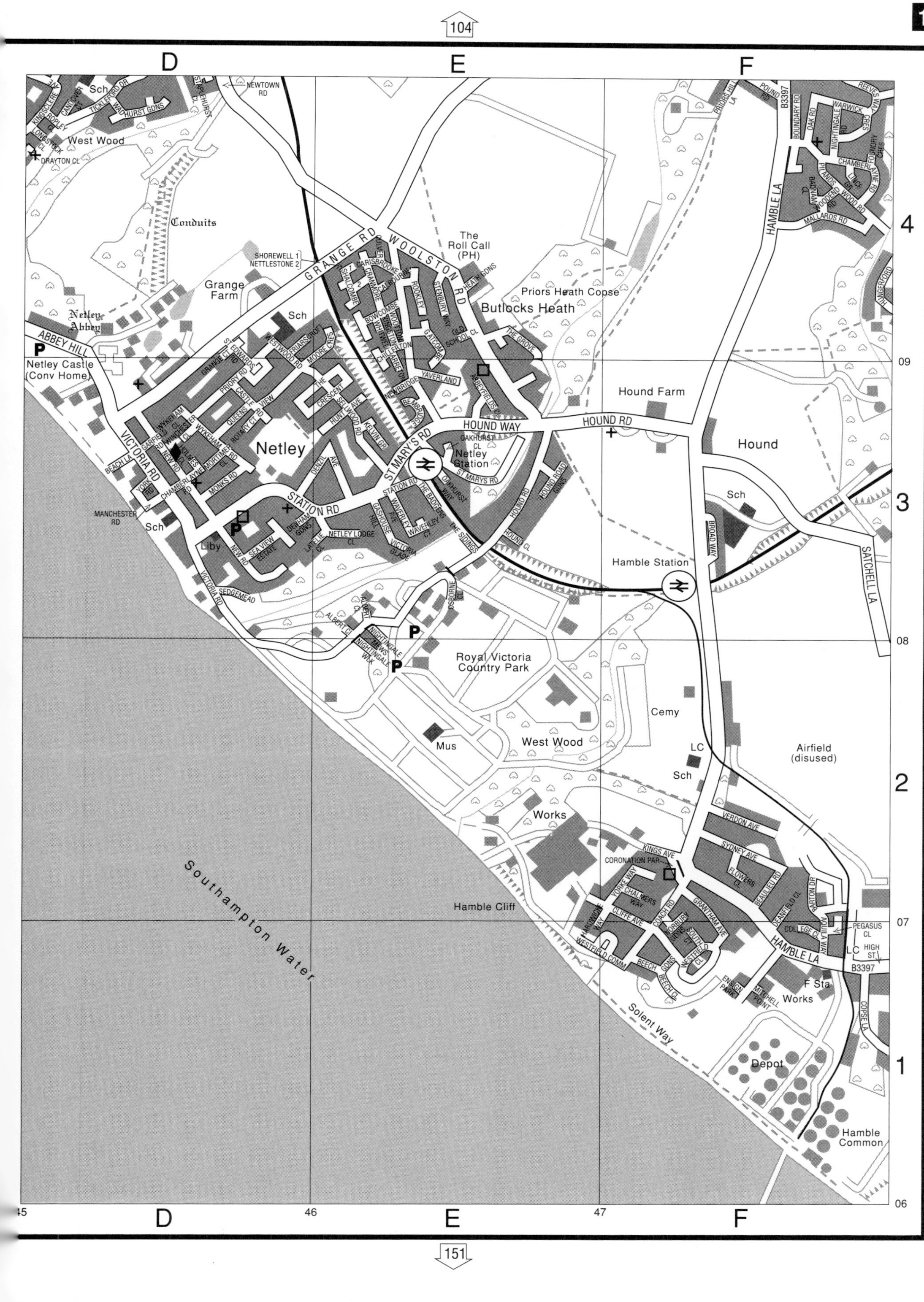
104
D
E
F
4
3
2
1
09
08
07
06
45
46
47
128
151
Netley
Butlocks Heath
Hound
West Wood
Conduits
Grange Farm
Netley Abbey
Netley Castle (Conv Home)
The Roll Call (PH)
Priors Heath Copse
Hound Farm
Netley Station
Hamble Station
Royal Victoria Country Park
Mus
Cemy
Airfield (disused)
Works
Hamble Cliff
Depot
Hamble Common
Southampton Water
Solent Way
GRANGE RD
WOOLSTON RD
HOUND WAY
HOUND RD
ST MARY'S RD
STATION RD
VICTORIA RD
ABBEY HILL
HAMBLE LA
SATCHELL LA
B3397
Sch
Liby
LC
F Sta

105

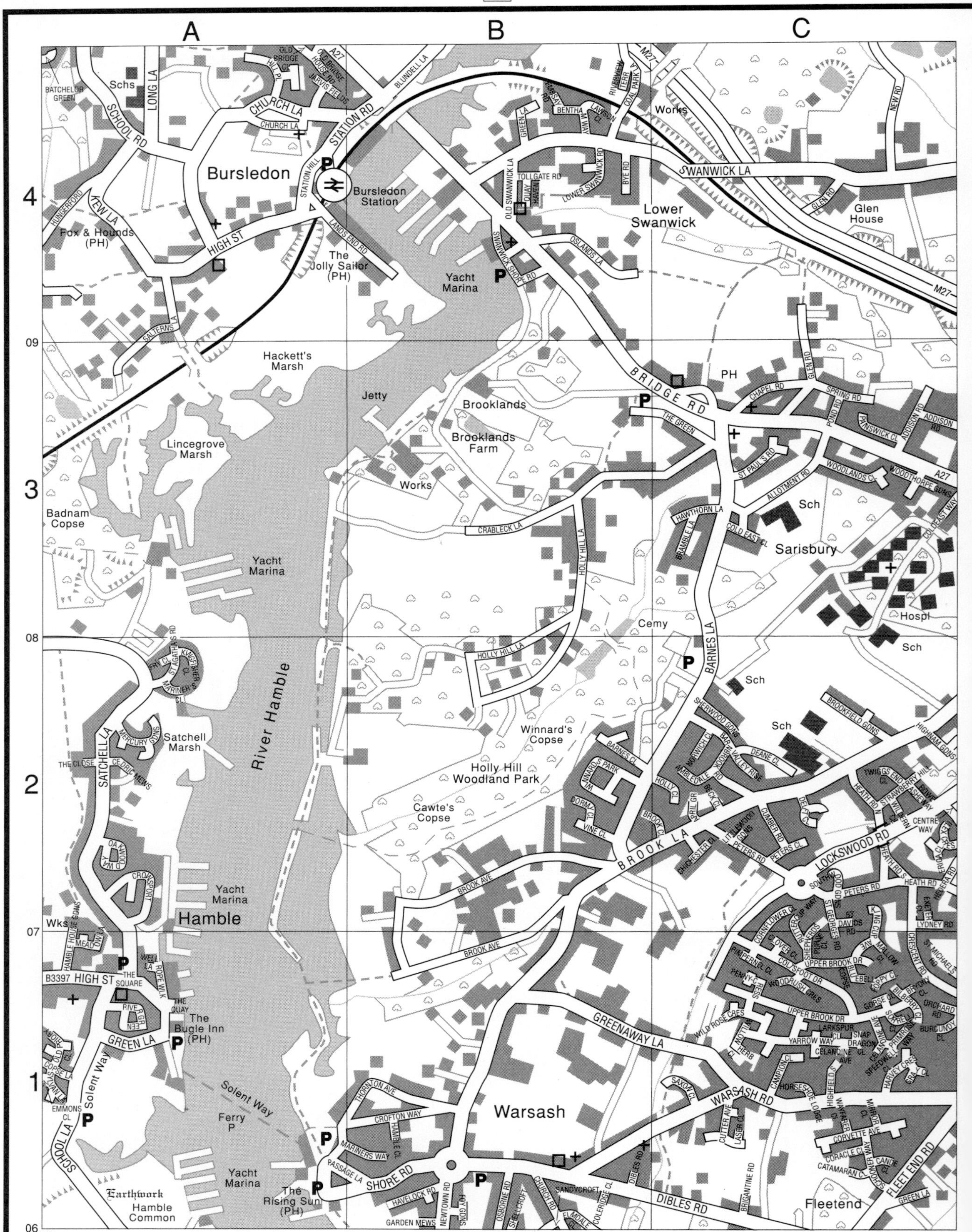

A
B
C
4
3
2
1
09
08
07
06
48
49
50
Bursledon
Schs
Bursledon Station
Fox & Hounds (PH)
The Jolly Sailor (PH)
Yacht Marina
Lower Swanwick
Works
Glen House
Hackett's Marsh
Jetty
Brooklands
Brooklands Farm
Lincegrove Marsh
Badnam Copse
Works
PH
Sch
Sarisbury
Hospl
Cemy
Sch
River Hamble
Satchell Marsh
Winnard's Copse
Holly Hill Woodland Park
Cawte's Copse
Hamble
Wks
The Bugle Inn (PH)
Solent Way
Ferry
Warsash
The Rising Sun (PH)
Earthwork
Hamble Common
Fleetend
SCHOOL RD
LONG LA
CHURCH LA
STATION RD
HIGH ST
SWANWICK LA
BRIDGE RD
CRABLECK LA
HOLLY HILL LA
BARNES LA
BROOK LA
BROOK AVE
LOCKSWOOD RD
GREENAWAY LA
WARSASH RD
SHORE RD
DIBLES RD
FLEET END RD
SATCHELL LA
GREEN LA
SCHOOL LA
B3397 HIGH ST
A27
M27

127

152

106

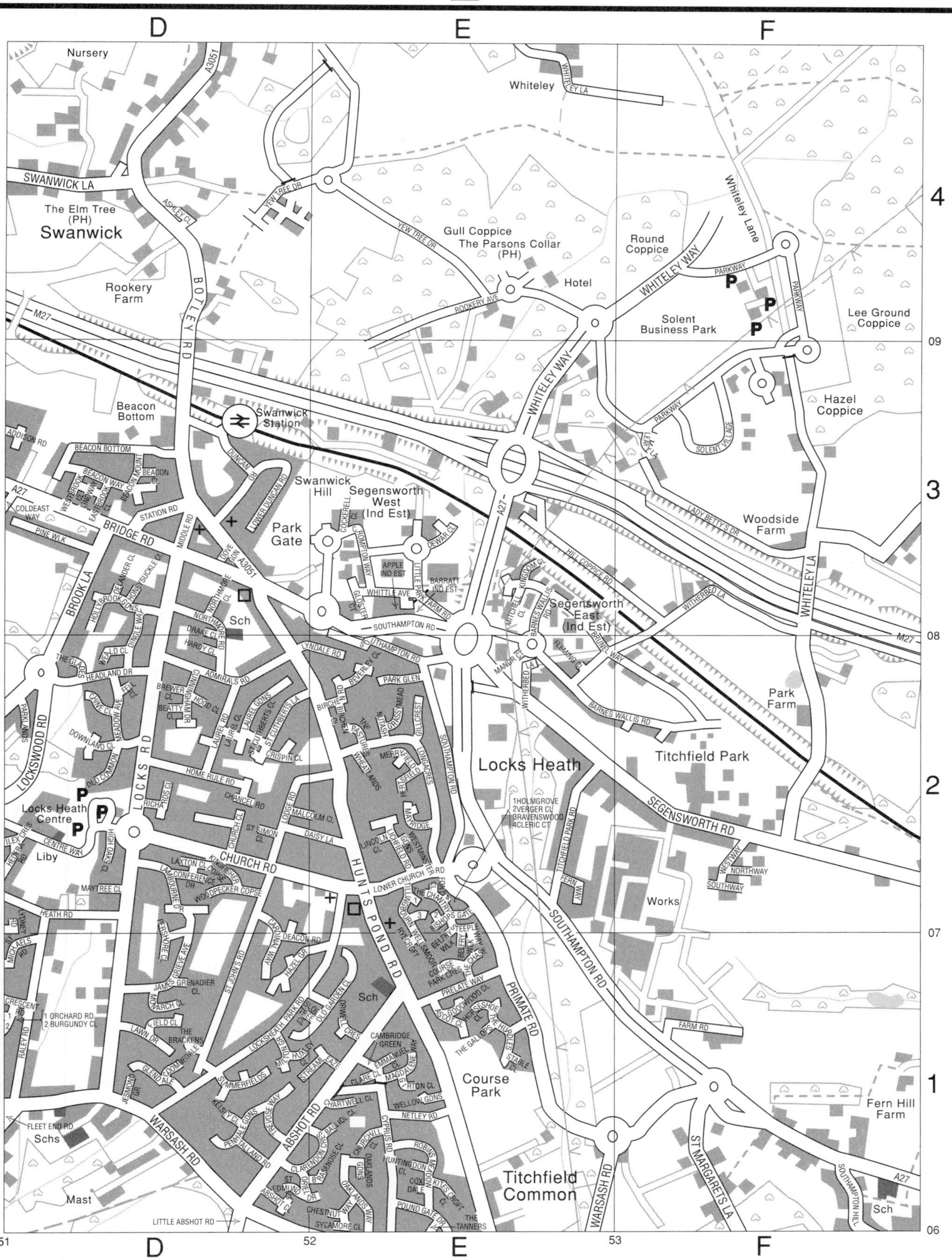
D
E
F
4
3
2
1
09
08
07
06
51
52
53
Nursery
Whiteley
Whiteley Lane
Swanwick
The Elm Tree (PH)
Rookery Farm
Gull Coppice
The Parsons Collar (PH)
Hotel
Round Coppice
Solent Business Park
Lee Ground Coppice
Hazel Coppice
Beacon Bottom
Swanwick Station
Swanwick Hill
Segensworth West (Ind Est)
Park Gate
Apple Ind Est
Barratt Ind Est
Segensworth East (Ind Est)
Woodside Farm
Park Farm
Titchfield Park
Locks Heath
Locks Heath Centre
Liby
Sch
Works
Course Park
Titchfield Common
Fern Hill Farm
Schs
Mast
SWANWICK LA
BOTLEY RD
M27
A27
A3051
WHITELEY WAY
PARKWAY
SOLENT VILLAGE
LADY BETTY'S DR
HILL COPPICE RD
WITHERBED LA
WHITELEY LA
BRIDGE RD
SOUTHAMPTON RD
BARNES WALLIS RD
SEGENSWORTH RD
LOCKS RD
BROOK LA
LOCKSWOOD RD
CHURCH RD
HUNTS POND RD
WARSASH RD
ST MARGARETS LA
PRIMATE RD
ABSHOT RD
LITTLE ABSHOT RD
FLEET END RD
SOUTHAMPTON HILL
1 HOLMGROVE
2 VERGER CL
3 RAVENSWOOD
4 CLERIC CT
1 ORCHARD RD
2 BURGUNDY CL

130

107

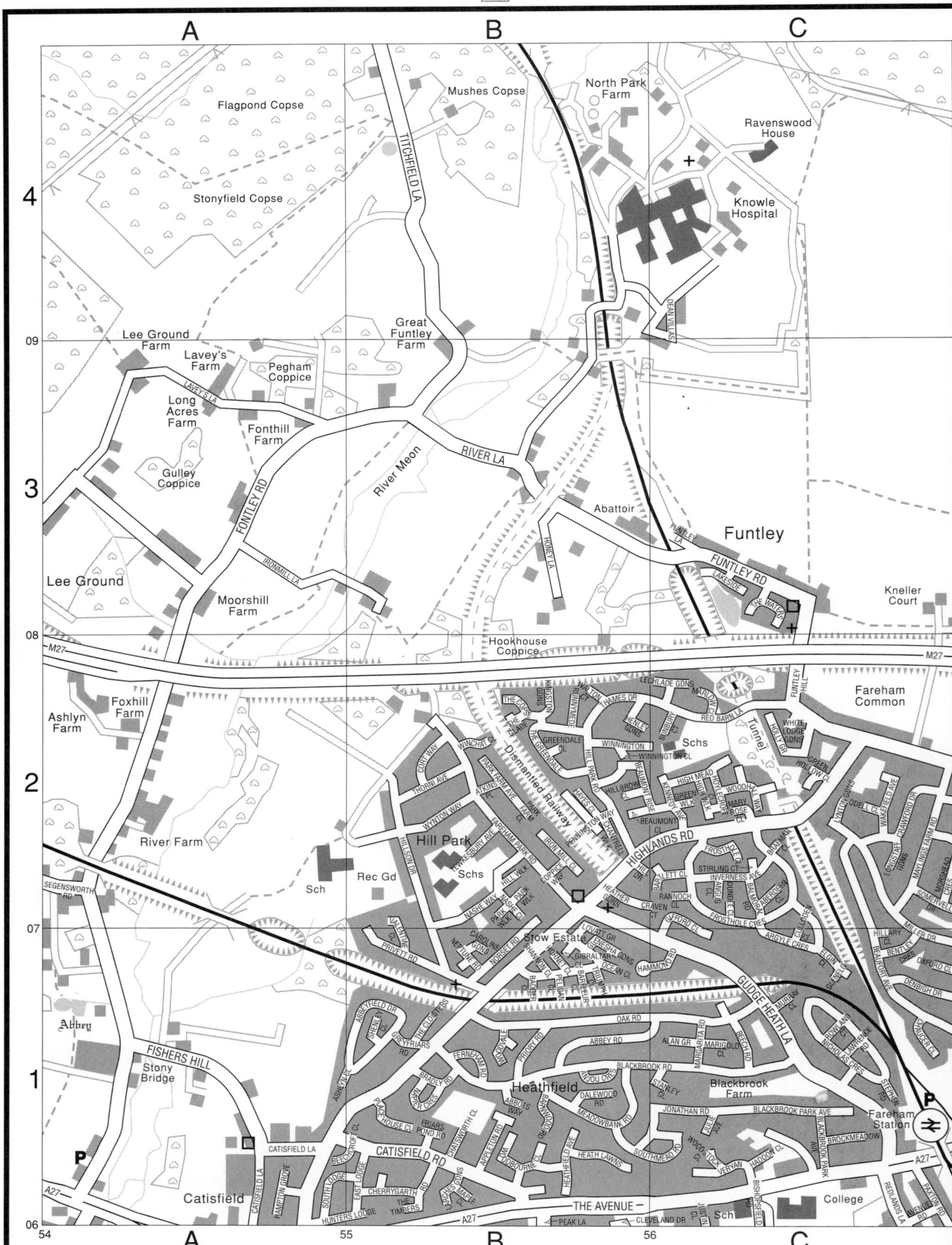
A
B
C
Flagpond Copse
Mushes Copse
North Park Farm
Ravenswood House
Stonyfield Copse
Knowle Hospital
TITCHFIELD LA
DEAN VILLAS
Lee Ground Farm
Great Funtley Farm
Lavey's Farm
Pegham Coppice
LAVEY'S LA
Long Acres Farm
Fonthill Farm
RIVER LA
River Meon
Gulley Coppice
FONTLEY RD
Abattoir
Funtley
FUNTLEY LA
HONEY LA
IRONMILL LA
FUNTLEY RD
LAKESIDE
THE WATERS
Lee Ground
Moorshill Farm
Kneller Court
Hookhouse Coppice
M27
LECHLADE GDNS
THAMES DR
RED BARN LA
FUNTLEY HILL
Fareham Common
Foxhill Farm
Ashlyn Farm
Schs
Tunnel
HOLLY GR
WHITE LODGE GDNS
GREENDALE CL
WINNINGTON
WINNINGTON CL
Dismantled Railway
GREEN HOLLOW CL
HIGH MEAD
HILLBROW CL
BEAUMONT RISE
BEAUMONT CL
MARY ROSE CL
WOODHALL WAY
HIGHLANDS RD
Hill Park
Schs
Rec Gd
Sch
River Farm
HILLSON DR
SEGENSWORTH RD
STIRLING CT
INVERNESS AVE
RANNOCH CL
FROSTHOLE CRES
ARGYLE CRES
HEATHER GDNS
CRAVEN CT
GIFFORD CL
Stow Estate
GIBRALTAR CL
OCEAN CL
HAMMOND RD
PRIVETT RD
GUDGE HEATH LA
OAK RD
ABBEY RD
ALAN GR
MARGARITA RD
MARIGOLD CL
BEECH RD
Abbey
FISHERS HILL
Stony Bridge
BLACKBROOK RD
Heathfield
DALEWOOD RD
Blackbrook Farm
JONATHAN RD
BLACKBROOK PARK AVE
Fareham Station
BROCKMEADOW
CATISFIELD LA
CATISFIELD RD
HEATH LAWNS
SOUTHMEAD RD
A27
Catisfield
THE AVENUE
PEAK LA
CLEVELAND DR
Sch
College
REDLANDS LA
LYNTON GDNS
WAKEFIELD AVE
CRAWFORD DR
HILLARY CL
BEAUFORT AVE
DENBIGH DR
OXFORD CL
54
55
56
09
08
07
06
4
3
2
1

129

154

108

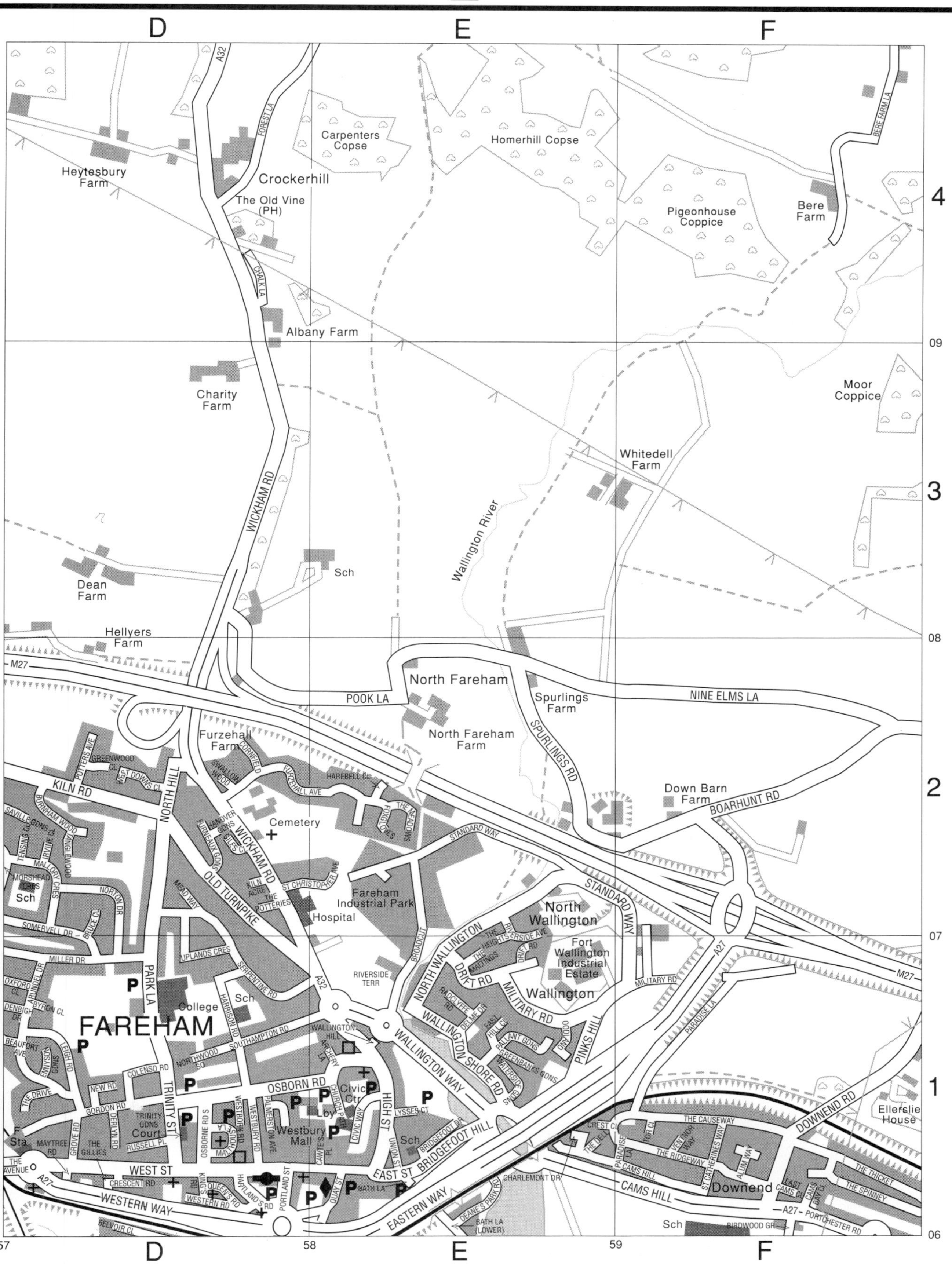
D
E
F
4
3
2
1
09
08
07
06
57
58
59
Heytesbury Farm
Crockerhill
The Old Vine (PH)
Carpenters Copse
Homerhill Copse
Pigeonhouse Coppice
Bere Farm
BERE FARM LA
FOREST LA
A32
CHALK LA
Albany Farm
Charity Farm
Moor Coppice
Whitedell Farm
Wallington River
WICKHAM RD
Sch
Dean Farm
Hellyers Farm
M27
POOK LA
North Fareham
North Fareham Farm
Spurlings Farm
NINE ELMS LA
SPURLINGS RD
Down Barn Farm
BOARHUNT RD
Furzehall Farm
GREENWOOD CL
POTTERS AVE
KILN RD
NORTH HILL
SWALLOW WOOD
FURZEHALL AVE
HAREBELL CL
THE MEADOWS
FOXGLOVES
Cemetery
STANDARD WAY
OLD TURNPIKE
ST CHRISTOPHER AVE
Fareham Industrial Park
Hospital
THE POTTERIES
KILN ACRE
MEAD WAY
North Wallington
Fort Wallington Industrial Estate
NORTH WALLINGTON
DRIFT RD
Wallington
MILITARY RD
BROADCUT
RIVERSIDE TERR
SAVILLE GDNS
BURNHAM WOOD
TENSING CL
IRVINE CL
ANGLESWOOD
MALLORY CRES
MORSHEAD CRES
NORTON DR
SOMERVELL DR
BRUCE CL
MILLER DR
OXFORD CL
ARUNDEL DR
BYRON CL
DENBIGH DR
PARK LA
UPLANDS CRES
SERPENTINE RD
College
FAREHAM
HARRISON RD
SOUTHAMPTON RD
NORTHWOOD SQ
WALLINGTON HILL
ARCHERY LA
WALLINGTON WAY
WALLINGTON SHORE RD
PINKS HILL
MILITARY RD
PARADISE LA
A27
BEAUFORT AVE
LEIGH RD
COLENSO RD
NEW RD
TRINITY ST
OSBORN RD
Civic Ctr
Lby
Westbury Mall
HIGH ST
LYSSES CT
THE DRIVE
GORDON RD
DERLYN RD
TRINITY GDNS
Court
RUSSELL PL
WESTBURY RD
PALMERSTON AVE
CIVIC WAY
UNION ST
BRIDGEFOOT DR
BRIDGEFOOT HILL
Sta
MAYTREE RD
GROVE RD
THE GILLIES
THE AVENUE
WEST ST
CRESCENT RD
QUEEN'S RD
WESTERN RD
HARTLAND'S RD
PORTLAND ST
QUAY ST
BATH LA
EAST ST
WESTERN WAY
EASTERN WAY
BELVOIR CL
CHARLEMONT DR
DEANE'S PARK RD
BATH LA (LOWER)
CREST CL
THE DELL
TOR CL
THE CAUSEWAY
THE RIDGEWAY
ST CATHERINES WAY
ALUM WAY
DOWNEND RD
Downend
CAMS HILL
EAST CAMS CL
CAMS BAY CL
THE THICKET
THE SPINNEY
PORTCHESTER RD
BIRDWOOD GR
Ellerslie House

132

155

109

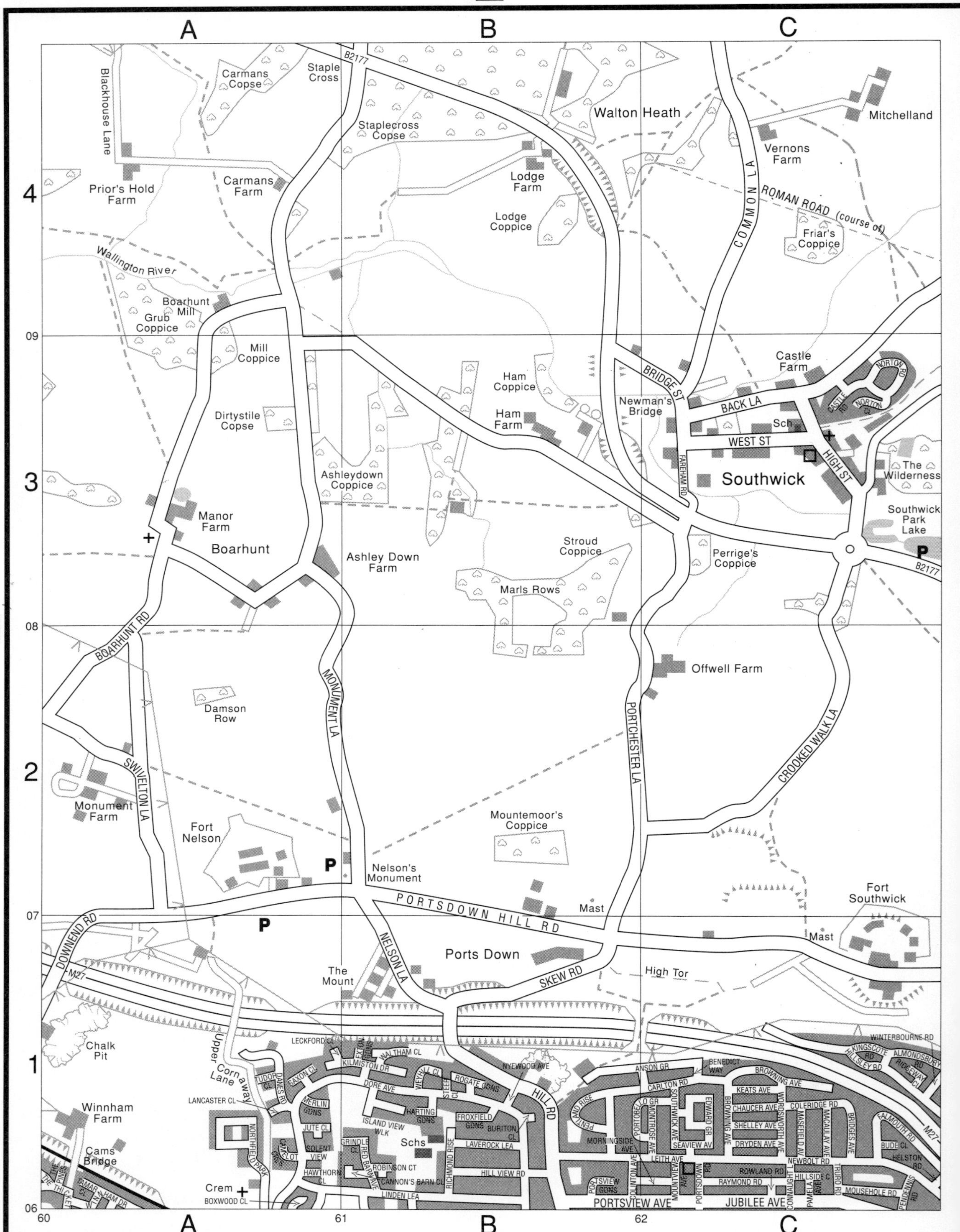
A
B
C
4
3
2
1
09
08
07
06
60
61
62
B2177
Staple Cross
Carmans Copse
Blackhouse Lane
Staplecross Copse
Walton Heath
Mitchelland
Vernons Farm
Prior's Hold Farm
Carmans Farm
Lodge Farm
Lodge Coppice
COMMON LA
ROMAN ROAD (course of)
Friar's Coppice
Wallington River
Boarhunt Mill
Grub Coppice
Mill Coppice
Ham Coppice
BRIDGE ST
Castle Farm
NORTON RD
Newman's Bridge
BACK LA
CASTLE RD
NORTON CL
Dirtystile Copse
Ham Farm
Sch
WEST ST
HIGH ST
FAREHAM RD
Southwick
The Wilderness
Ashleydown Coppice
Manor Farm
Boarhunt
Ashley Down Farm
Stroud Coppice
Perrige's Coppice
Southwick Park Lake
P
Marls Rows
BOARHUNT RD
Offwell Farm
MONUMENT LA
Damson Row
PORTCHESTER LA
CROOKED WALK LA
SWIVELTON LA
Monument Farm
Fort Nelson
Mountemoor's Coppice
Nelson's Monument
Fort Southwick
PORTSDOWN HILL RD
Mast
DOWNEND RD
NELSON LA
Ports Down
High Tor
The Mount
SKEW RD
M27
Chalk Pit
Upper Cornaway Lane
LECKFORD CL
WALTHAM CL
KILMISTON DR
NYEWOOD AVE
BENEDICT WAY
ANSON GR
BROWNING AVE
WINTERBOURNE RD
KINGSCOTE RD
ALMONDSBURY RD
HILLSLEY RD
RIDGEWAY CL
SAXON CL
TUDOR CL
DANES RD
DORE AVE
WEYHILL CL
STEEP CL
ROGATE GDNS
HILL RD
CARLTON RD
KEATS AVE
LANCASTER CL
MERLIN GDNS
HARTING GDNS
PENTLAND RISE
PORTOBELLO GR
SOUTHWICK AVE
EDWARD GR
CHAUCER AVE
WORDSWORTH AVE
COLERIDGE RD
Winnham Farm
NORTHFIELD PARK
JUTE CL
ISLAND VIEW WLK
FROXFIELD GDNS
BURITON CL
SHELLEY AVE
MASEFIELD AVE
MACAULAY AVE
BRIDGES AVE
FALMOUTH RD
Schs
LAVEROCK LEA
MORNINGSIDE AVE
MONTROSE AVE
SEAVIEW AV
DRYDEN AVE
Cams Bridge
CAMELOT CRES
SOLENT VIEW
GRINDLE CL
RED BARN AVE
RICHMOND RISE
LEITH AVE
NEWBOLT RD
BUDE CL
HELSTON RD
ROBINSON CT
HAWTHORN CL
CANNON'S BARN CL
HILL VIEW RD
ROWLAND RD
HILLSIDE C
TRURO RD
Crem
BOXWOOD CL
LINDEN LEA
PORTSVIEW GDNS
COLINTON AVE
MOUNTVIEW AVE
PORTSDOWN RD
RAYMOND RD
CONNAUGHT LA
PAMELA AVE
MOUSEHOLE RD
PENDENNIS RD
PORTSVIEW AVE
JUBILEE AVE
THE THICKET
TAMAR
HAM DR

131

156

110

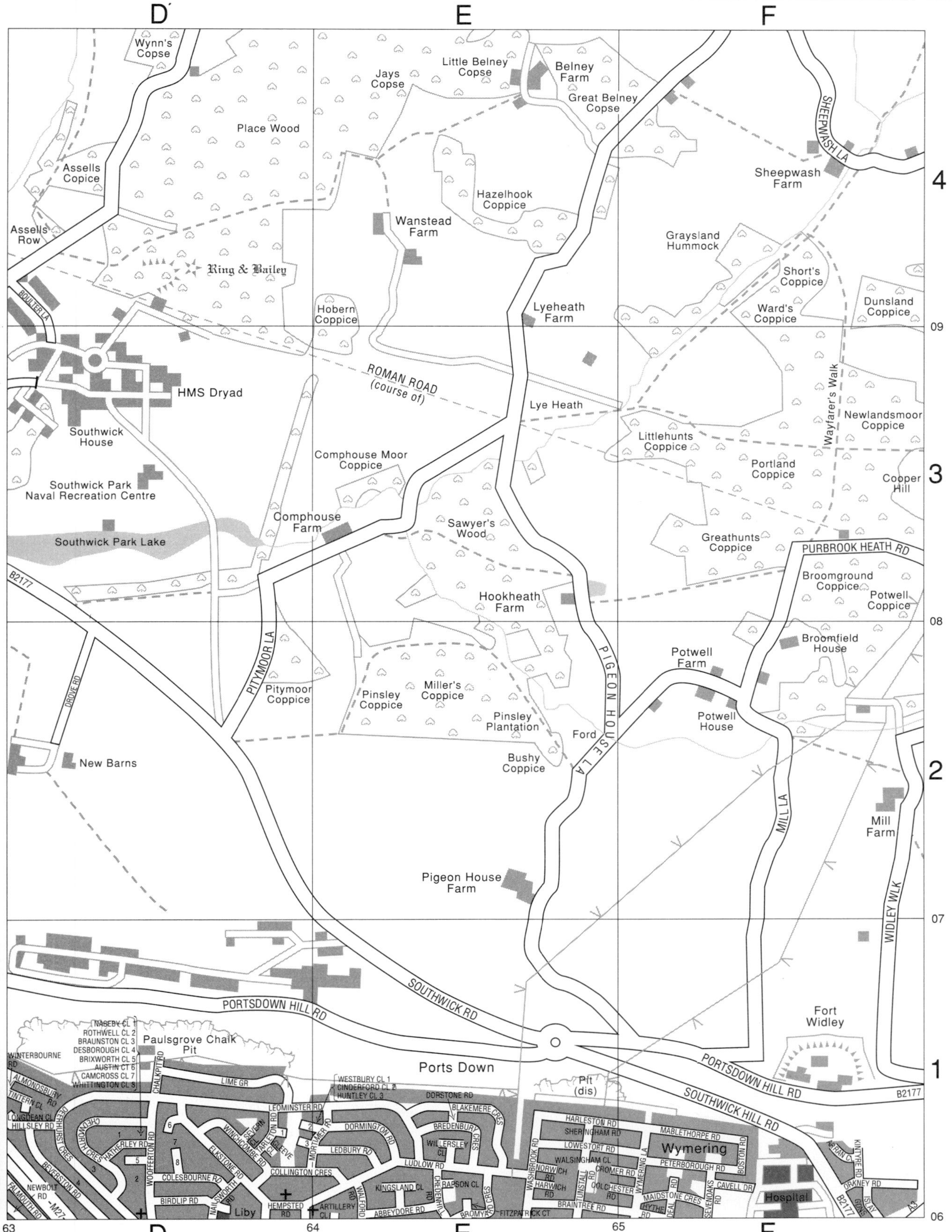

D
E
F
Wynn's Copse
Little Belney Copse
Belney Farm
Jays Copse
Great Belney Copse
Place Wood
SHEEPWASH LA
Assells Copice
Hazelhook Coppice
Sheepwash Farm
4
Assells Row
Wanstead Farm
Graysland Hummock
Ring & Bailey
Short's Coppice
BOULTER LA
Lyeheath Farm
Ward's Coppice
Dunsland Coppice
Hobern Coppice
09
ROMAN ROAD (course of)
HMS Dryad
Lye Heath
Wayfarer's Walk
Newlandsmoor Coppice
Southwick House
Littlehunts Coppice
Comphouse Moor Coppice
Portland Coppice
Cooper Hill
3
Southwick Park Naval Recreation Centre
Comphouse Farm
Sawyer's Wood
Southwick Park Lake
Greathunts Coppice
PURBROOK HEATH RD
B2177
Broomground Coppice
Hookheath Farm
Potwell Coppice
08
Broomfield House
PITYMOOR LA
Potwell Farm
DROVE RD
Pitymoor Coppice
Miller's Coppice
Pinsley Coppice
PIGEON HOUSE LA
Potwell House
Pinsley Plantation
Ford
New Barns
Bushy Coppice
2
MILL LA
Mill Farm
Pigeon House Farm
WIDLEY WLK
07
SOUTHWICK RD
PORTSDOWN HILL RD
Fort Widley
NASEBY CL 1
ROTHWELL CL 2
BRAUNSTON CL 3
DESBOROUGH CL 4
BRIXWORTH CL 5
AUSTIN CT 6
CAMCROSS CL 7
WHITTINGTON CL 8
Paulsgrove Chalk Pit
WINTERBOURNE RD
CHALKPIT RD
Ports Down
1
PORTSDOWN HILL RD
ALMONDSBURY RD
LIME GR
WESTBURY CL 1
CINDERFORD CL 2
HUNTLEY CL 3
Pit (dis)
SOUTHWICK HILL RD
B2177
TINTERN CL
DORSTONE RD
LONGDEAN CL
LEOMINSTER RD
BLAKEMERE CRES
HARLESTON RD
HILLSLEY RD
DORMINGTON RD
SHERINGHAM RD
MABLETHORPE RD
BREDENBURY CRES
LOWESTOFT RD
WILLERSLEY CL
Wymering
LEDBURY RD
WALSINGHAM CL
HATHERLEY RD
LUDLOW RD
CROMER RD
PETERBOROUGH RD
COLLINGTON CRES
NORWICH RD
HARWICH RD
KINGSLAND CL
RAPSON CL
COLCHESTER RD
CAVELL DR
COLESBOURNE RD
MAIDSTONE CRES
KINTYRE RD
ORKNEY RD
NEWBOLT RD
BIRDLIP RD
BRAINTREE RD
Hospital
HEMPSTED RD
ARTILLERY CL
Liby
ABBEYDORE RD
BROMYARD CRES
FITZPATRICK CT
M27
A3
63
64
65
06

134

157

111

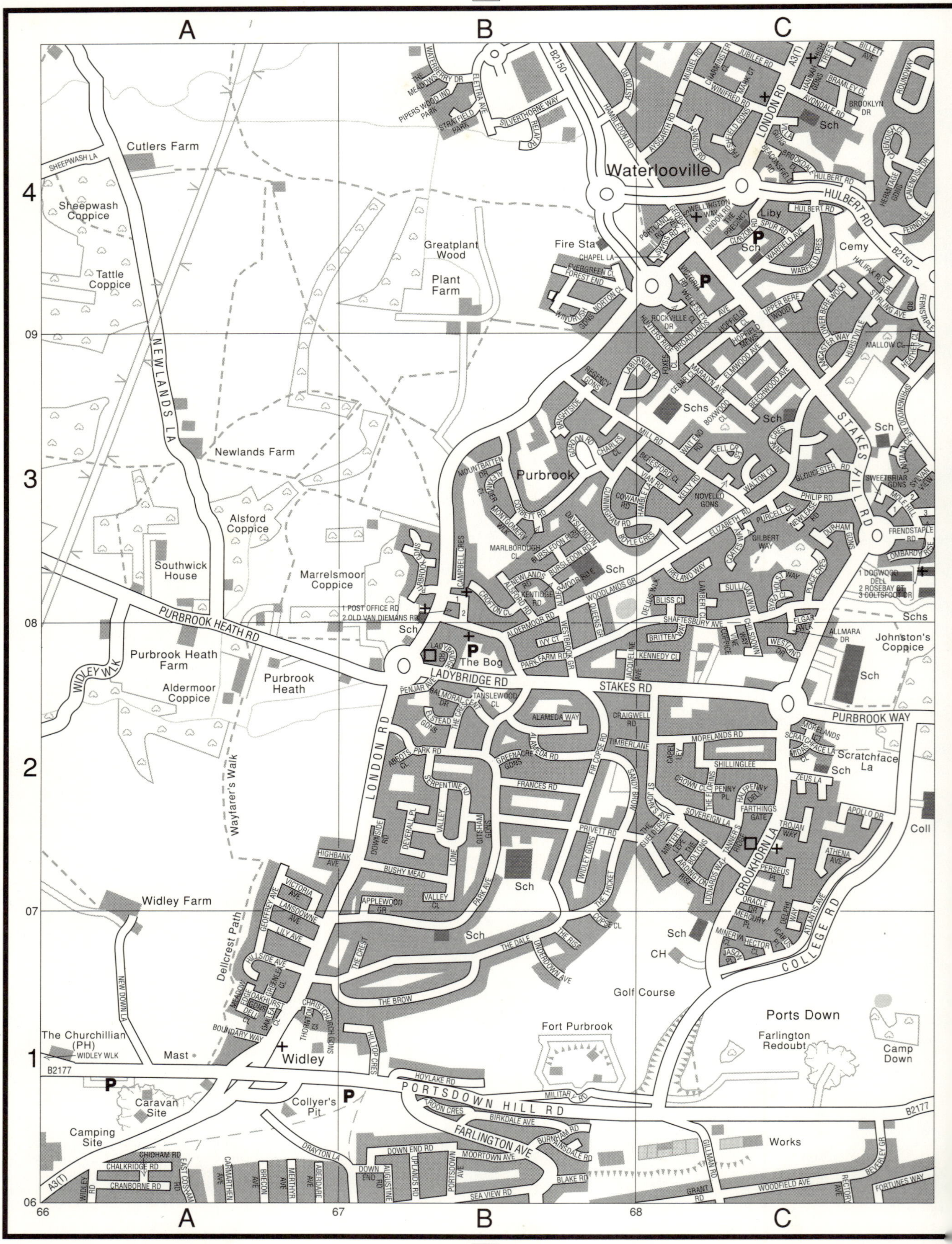

A
B
C
4
3
2
1
09
08
07
06
66
67
68
Waterlooville
Purbrook
Widley
Cutlers Farm
SHEEPWASH LA
Sheepwash Coppice
Tattle Coppice
NEWLANDS LA
Newlands Farm
Southwick House
Alsford Coppice
Marrelsmoor Coppice
Greatplant Wood
Plant Farm
PURBROOK HEATH RD
Purbrook Heath Farm
Aldermoor Coppice
Purbrook Heath
WIDLEY WLK
Waytarer's Walk
Widley Farm
Dellcrest Path
NEW DOWN LA
The Churchillian (PH)
Mast
B2177
Caravan Site
Camping Site
Collyer's Pit
A3(T)
CHIDHAM RD
CHALKRIDGE RD
CRANBORNE RD
EAST COSHAM RD
CARMARTHEN AVE
BRECON AVE
MERTHYR AVE
ABERDARE AVE
DRAYTON LA
DOWN END RD
UPLANDS RD
AUGUSTINE RD
PORTSDOWN AVE
MOORTOWN AVE
SEA VIEW RD
BLAKE RD
FARLINGTON AVE
BIRKDALE AVE
TROON CRES
BURNHAM RD
SUNNINGDALE RD
PORTSDOWN HILL RD
MILITARY RD
HOYLAKE RD
HILLTOP CRES
GILLMAN RD
GRANT RD
WOODFIELD AVE
RECTORY RD
BEVERLEY GR
FORTUNES WAY
Works
Fort Purbrook
Golf Course
Ports Down
Farlington Redoubt
Camp Down
COLLEGE RD
CH
Sch
THE BROW
BOUNDARY WAY
CHRISTCHURCH GDNS
THORNTON CL
HILLSIDE AVE
LILY AVE
LANSDOWNE AVE
VICTORIA AVE
GEOFFREY AVE
HIGHBANK AVE
LONDON RD
APPLEWOOD GR
BUSHY MEAD
VALLEY CL
DOWNSIDE RD
DEVERALL PL
SERPENTINE RD
GITSHAM GDNS
PARK AVE
THE CREST
THE DALE
UNDERDOWN AVE
THE RISE
COPSE CL
THE THICKET
WIDLEY GDNS
PRIVETT RD
FRANCES RD
GREENACRE GDNS
ALAMEDA RD
ALAMEDA WAY
FIR COPSE RD
TIMBERLANE
CRAIGWELL RD
SANDY BROW
ST JOHNS AVE
THE BUILDERS
MINTERS LEPE
THE BOLTONS
ARDINGTON RISE
TANNERS RIDGE
CROOKHORN LA
PERSEUS PL
ORACLE DR
MERCURY PL
HECTOR CL
MINERVA DR
JASON WAY
ICARUS PL
DELPHI WAY
ATLANTIS AVE
ATHENA AVE
APOLLO DR
TROJAN WAY
ZEUS LA
Scratchface La
Coll
MORELANDS RD
MORELANDS CT
SCRATCHFACE LA
MIDAS CL
SHILLINGLEE
CROWN CL
THE FLORINS
PENNY PL
HALFPENNY DELL
FARTHINGS GATE
SOVEREIGN LA
CAPEL LEY
PURBROOK WAY
STAKES RD
STAKES HILL RD
LADYBRIDGE RD
PENJAR AVE
BALMORAL DR
TANSLEWOOD CL
ELSTEAD GDNS
ABBOTS CL
PARK RD
The Bog
P
Johnston's Coppice
ALLMARA DR
Schs
1 DOGWOOD DELL
2 ROSEBAY CT
3 COLTSFOOT DR
LOMBARDY RISE
FRENDSTAPLE RD
WESTLAND DR
ELGAR WLK
CHILSDOWN WAY
VINE COPPICE
BRITTEN WAY
KENNEDY CL
JACQUELINE AVE
SHAFTESBURY AVE
BLISS CL
LAMBERT CL
SULLIVAN WAY
BYRD CL
HOLST WAY
PLACE CRES
WESTBROOK GR
PARK FARM RD
IVY CT
ALDERMOOR RD
QUEENS GR
WOODLANDS GR
DELIUS WLK
IRELAND WAY
1 POST OFFICE RD
2 OLD VAN DIEMANS RD
CAMPBELL CRES
CROFTON CL
KENTIDGE RD
ALSFORD RD
NEWLANDS RD
MARLBOROUGH CL
BURSLEDON RD
MONTGOMERY WLK
CORBETT RD
ALEXANDER CL
MOUNTBATTEN DR
DAYSLONDON RD
CUNNINGHAM RD
COWAN RD
HAMBLE LA
BOYLE CRES
BERESFORD CL
VIAN RD
KELLY RD
NOVELLO GDNS
ELIZABETH RD
COATES WAY
GILBERT WAY
PURCELL CL
NEWLEASE RD
DURHAM GDNS
PHILIP RD
GLOUCESTER RD
WALTON CL
ANNE CRES
BELL CRES
WAIT END RD
BOXWOOD CL
MILL RD
CHARLES CL
GORDON RD
BRIGHTSIDE
REGENCY GDNS
LABURNUM RD
CEDAR CL
MARALYN AVE
ELMWOOD AVE
BEECHWOOD AVE
HOPFIELD CL
HOPFIELD MEWS
FOXES CL
HUNTERS RIDE
BROADLANDS AVE
ROCKVILLE DR
WELLESLEY CL
VICTORIA RD
WINDRUSH GDNS
NORTON CL
FOREST END
EVERGREEN CL
CHAPEL LA
Fire Sta
Liby
Cemy
B2150
HULBERT RD
WARFIELD AVE
WARFIELD CRES
UPPER BERE WOOD
LOWER BERE WOOD
LANCASTER WAY
HURSTVILLE DR
STIRLING AVE
HALIFAX RISE
FERNSTAPLE RD
MALLOW CL
HEATHER CL
SPRINGWOOD AVE
SWEETBRIAR GDNS
SYLVAN VIEW
MOLE HILL
FERNDALE
HERMITAGE GDNS
CAVENDISH DR
ROUNDWAY
BILLETT AVE
BRAMLEY CL
BROOKLYN DR
AVONDALE RD
HANNAH GDNS
HIGH TREES
JUBILEE RD
CHARMINSTER CL
MURIEL RD
WINIFRED RD
MARK CT
ASTON RD
HAMBLEDON RD
AYSGARTH RD
ARNSIDE RD
FREDERICK RD
VILLA GDNS
BEACONSFIELD RD
BROOKDALE CL
SPUR RD
CURZON RD
THE PRECINCT
LONDON RISE
WELLINGTON WAY
PORTLAND RD
GEORGES RD
LEWIS RD
SILVERTHORNE WAY
RELAY RD
STRATFIELD PARK
PIPERS WOOD IND PARK
ELETTRA AVE
WATERBERRY DR
THE MEADOWS

133

158

112

D
E
F
4
3
2
1
09
08
07
06
69
70
71
Bell's Copse
Dunsbury Hill Farm
The Avenue
Beech Wood
Deerslaughter Plain
TEGLEASE GREEN
Gammon's Hill
1 UPTON CL
2 ABBAS GREEN
3 STRATFIELD GDNS
4 HAWSTEAD GREEN
5 BICKTON WLK
6 EASTOVER CT
7 ST DENYS WLK
8 OXENWOOD GREEN
9 HARVESTGATE WLK
The Lake
Thicket Lawn
HULBERT RD
1 BROADMEADOWS LA
2 THE HASSOCKS
Hermitage Stream
B2150
PARK LA
MIDDLE PARK WAY
Neville's Park
Great Copse
Sch
Schs
Bushy Lease
PARK HOUSE FARM WAY
DUNSBURY WAY
1 ANGELICA CT
2 MONTANA CT
3 PRIMROSE CT
4 LOBELIA CT
5 HONEYSUCKLE CT
Simond's Hill
Amb Sta
Leigh Park
HAVANT
PURBROOK WAY
STOCKHEATH RD
BEDHAMPTON WAY
BARNCROFT WAY
Stockheath
STOCKHEATH LA
Coll
Littlepark Wood
Liby
PETERSFIELD RD
Recn Gd
SCRATCHFACE LA
NEW RD
TH
CIVIC CENTRE
Cts
ELMLEIGH RD
BEDHAMPTON RD
B2149
Havant Station
Camp Down
PORTSDOWN HILL RD
B2177
Bedhampton
Bedhampton Halt
WEST ST
ROMAN ROAD
Hospl
Sta
ELM LA
EAST ST
Works
THE TANNERIES INDUSTRIAL ESTATE
Brockhampton
Old Mill House
PARK RD N
PARK RD S
SOLENT RD
A3(M)

136

159

113

A
B
C
4
3
2
1
09
08
07
06
72
73
74
Gipsies Plain
Durrants
Mays Coppice Farm
Hammond's Land Coppice
School
Sewage Works
Sandpit Roundell
Shuffles Plantation
Blackbush Copse
Sussex Border Path
Southleigh Forest
Leigh Park Gardens
Barton's Copse
Hospl
Holly Lodge
Hollybank House
Hemsley House
East Leigh House
Southleigh Park
Home Farm
Locks Farm
Southleigh Farm
Factories
Nursery
Denvilles
Manor Farm
EMSWORTH
HAVANT
Warblington Halt
Emsworth Station
Mus
WHICHERS GATE RD
DURRANTS RD
PROSPECT LA
PETERSFIELD RD
WAKESFORD WAY
MIDDLE PARK WAY
BARTONS RD
COMLEY HILL
EMSWORTH COMMON RD
WOODBERRY LA
LONG COPSE LA
HOLLYBANK LA
HORNDEAN RD
SOUTHLEIGH RD
EAST LEIGH RD
NEW LA
CROSSLAND DR
MARTIN RD
STANBRIDGE RD
DOWNLEY RD
FARRINGDON RD
SOUTHLEIGH RD
FIFTH AVE
FOURTH AVE
THIRD AVE
SECOND AVE
FIRST AVE
GLENLEIGH PARK
EAST ST
EMSWORTH RD
NEW BRIGHTON RD
NORTH ST
VICTORIA RD
WASHINGTON RD
A27(T)
B2149
B2148
B2147
1 KEN BERRY CT
2 HOUGHTON CL
3 SYDMONTON CT
4 FOUR MARKS GREEN
5 WYEFORD CL
6 ITCHEN RD
7 AVINGTON GREEN
8 SOLDRIDGE CL
9 HEDGE END WLK
10 TIPTOE GREEN
11 MONXTON GREEN
12 SHALDON RD
13 BLACKMOOR WLK
14 BURLEY CL
15 WOODHAY WLK
16 TYTHERLEY GREEN
17 FREEFOLK GREEN
18 SUMMERLANDS WLK
19 PENWOOD GREEN
20 HAZELEY GREEN
21 ASHE RD
22 KITWOOD GREEN
1 FURZEDOWN CRES
2 HILTINGBURY AVE
3 CURDRIDGE CL
4 WITCHAMPTON CL
1 BARWELL GR
2 PANTON CL
3 GODWIN CL
4 ALLENDALE AVE
1 TAVISTOCK GDNS
2 LUARD CT
3 THE GARDENS

135

160

not continued, see key diagram

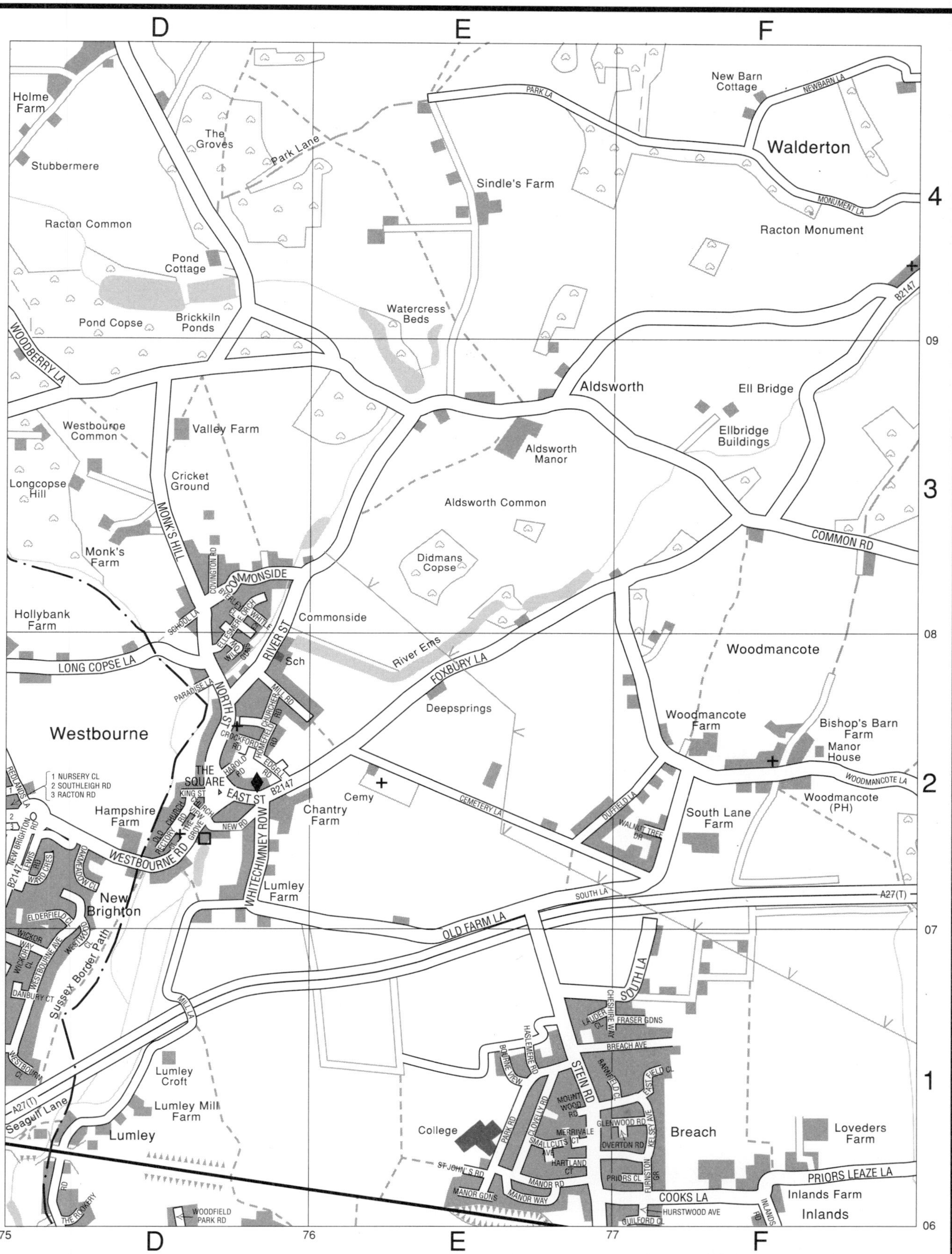

not continued, see key diagram

114

not continued, see key diagram

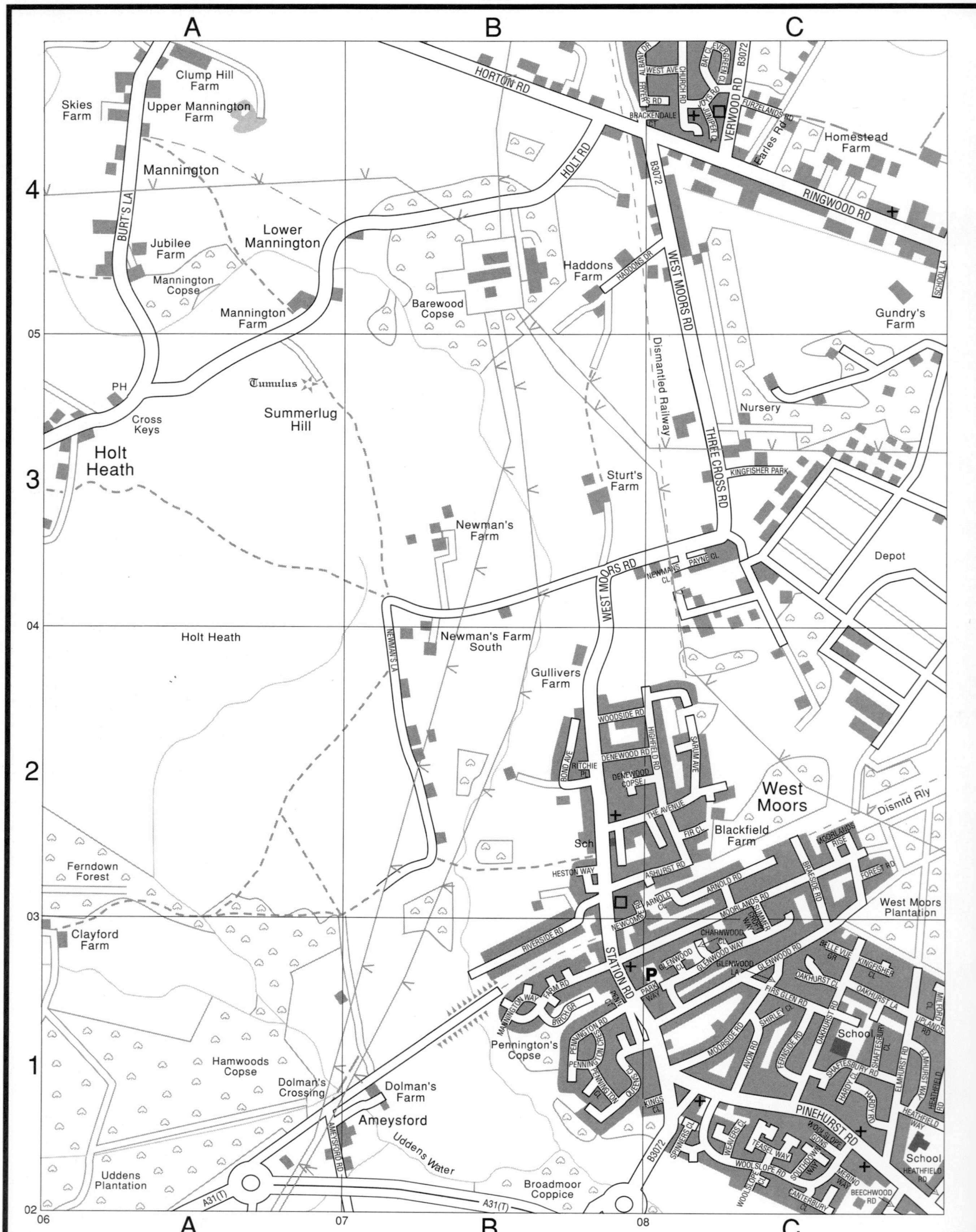

165

115

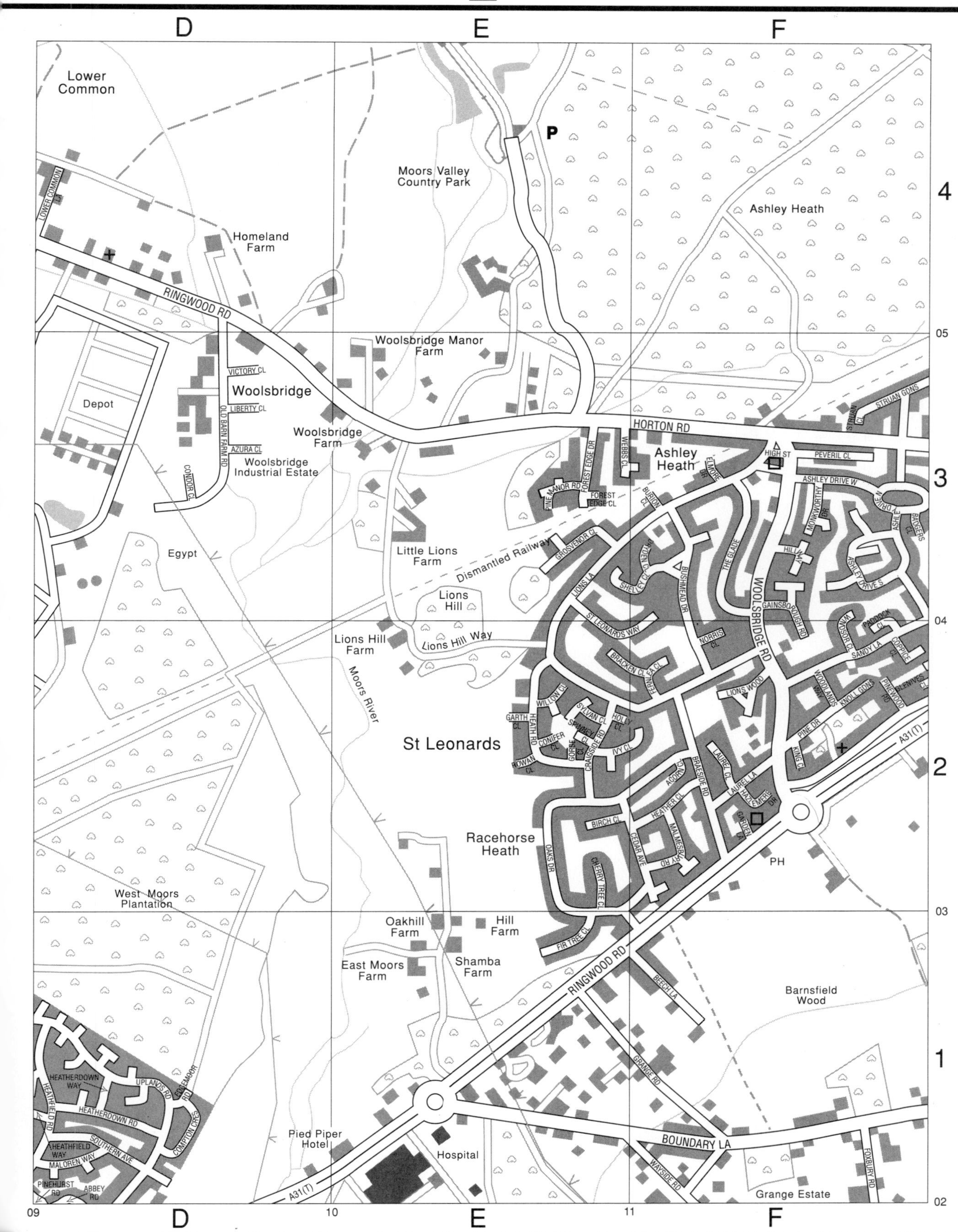
D
E
F
Lower Common
Moors Valley Country Park
P
Ashley Heath
Homeland Farm
RINGWOOD RD
LOWER COMMON RD
Woolsbridge Manor Farm
VICTORY CL
Woolsbridge
LIBERTY CL
OLD BARN FARM RD
AZURA CL
CONDOR CL
Depot
Woolsbridge Farm
Woolsbridge Industrial Estate
HORTON RD
WEBBS CL
FOREST EDGE DR
PINE MANOR RD
FOREST EDGE CL
Ashley Heath
ELMORE DR
HIGH ST
PEVERIL CL
STRUAN GDNS
STRUAN CL
ASHLEY DRIVE W
MONKWORTHY DR
ASHLEY DRIVE N
BADGERS CL
BURTON CL
GROSVENOR CL
Egypt
Little Lions Farm
Dismantled Railway
LIONS LA
SHELLEY CL
BUSHMEAD DR
THE GLADE
WOOLSBRIDGE RD
HILL WAY
ASHLEY DRIVE S
GAINSBOROUGH RD
Lions Hill
Lions Hill Way
Lions Hill Farm
ST LEONARDS WAY
NORRIS CL
BRACKEN CL
PADDOCK CL
SANDY LA
COPPICE CL
WOODLANDS
LIONS WOOD
KNOLL GDNS
PINEWOOD RD
GLENIVES CL
Moors River
WILLOW CL
SYLVAN CL
HOLLY CL
GARTH CL
HEATH RD
CONIFER CL
SPINNEY CL
GORSE CL
CRAIGSIDE RD
IVY CL
ROWAN CL
St Leonards
LAUREL CL
LAUREL LA
HAZELMERE DR
BRAESIDE RD
ACORN CL
PINE DR
KING CL
A31(T)
HEATHER CL
BIRCH CL
GARDEN LA
MALMESBURY RD
CEDAR AVE
Racehorse Heath
OAKS DR
CHERRY TREE CL
PH
West Moors Plantation
Oakhill Farm
Hill Farm
FIR TREE CL
East Moors Farm
Shamba Farm
RINGWOOD RD
BEECH LA
Barnsfield Wood
GRANGE RD
HEATHERDOWN WAY
UPLANDS RD
EDGEMOOR RD
HEATHFIELD RD
HEATHERDOWN RD
COMPTON CRES
SOUTHERN AVE
HEATHFIELD WAY
MALOREN WAY
PINEHURST RD
ABBEY RD
Pied Piper Hotel
Hospital
BOUNDARY LA
WAYSIDE RD
FOXBURY RD
Grange Estate
A31(T)
4
3
2
1
05
04
03
02
09
10
11
D
E
F

140

166

116

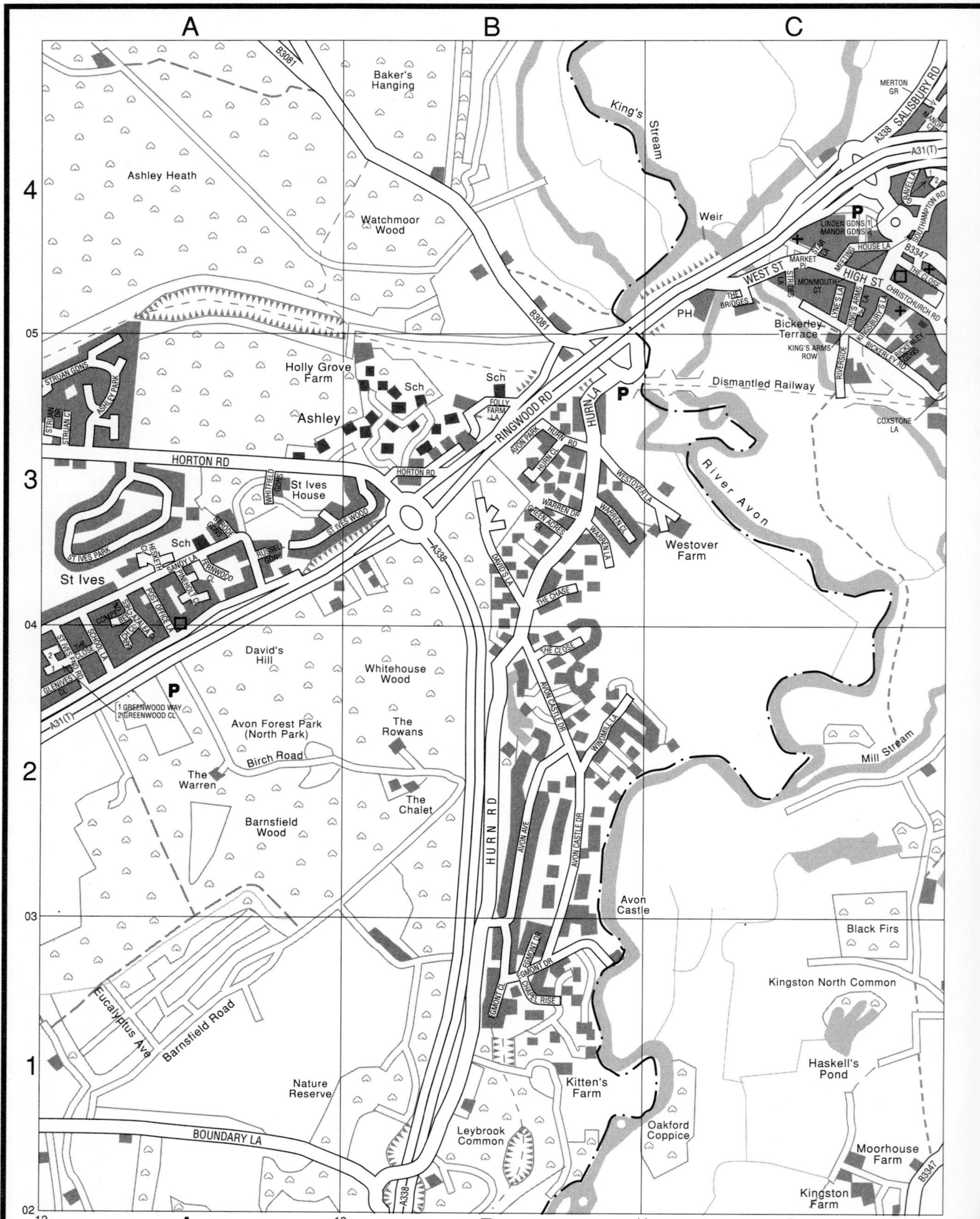
A
B
C
4
3
2
1
05
04
03
02
12
13
14
Baker's Hanging
B3081
King's Stream
MERTON GR
A338 SALISBURY RD
A31(T)
Ashley Heath
Watchmoor Wood
Weir
LINDEN GDNS 1
MANOR GDNS 2
MEETING HOUSE LA
MARKET PL
WEST ST
HIGH ST
MONMOUTH CT
THE BRIDGES
PH
B3347
THE CLOSE
CHRISTCHURCH RD
Bickerley Terrace
KING'S ARMS ROW
RIVERSIDE
BICKERLEY RD
Dismantled Railway
COXSTONE LA
Holly Grove Farm
Sch
Ashley
STRUAN GDNS
ASHLEY PARK
STRUAN DR
STRUAN CT
FOLLY FARM LA
RINGWOOD RD
HURN LA
AVON PARK
HURN CL
HURN RD
HORTON RD
St Ives House
WHITEFIELD GDNS
ST IVES WOOD
WESTOVER LA
River Avon
WARREN DR
GREEN ACRES CL
WARREN CL
WARREN LA
Westover Farm
ST IVES PARK
STRODE GDNS
Sch
HESKETH CL
SANDY LA
FERNWOOD CL
RUSSELL GDNS
St Ives
PINEHOLT CL
POST OFFICE LA
A338
DAVID'S LA
THE CHASE
SCHOOL LA
THE CLOSE
ST IVES END LA
GLENIVES CL
David's Hill
Whitehouse Wood
THE CLOSE
AVON CASTLE DR
WINDMILL LA
1 GREENWOOD WAY
2 GREENWOOD CL
A31(T)
Avon Forest Park (North Park)
The Rowans
Birch Road
The Warren
The Chalet
Mill Stream
Barnsfield Wood
HURN RD
AVON AVE
AVON CASTLE DR
Avon Castle
Black Firs
EGMONT DR
EGMONT CL
CHAPEL RISE
Kingston North Common
Eucalyptus Ave
Barnsfield Road
Haskell's Pond
Nature Reserve
Kitten's Farm
BOUNDARY LA
Leybrook Common
Oakford Coppice
Moorhouse Farm
B3347
Kingston Farm

139

167

117

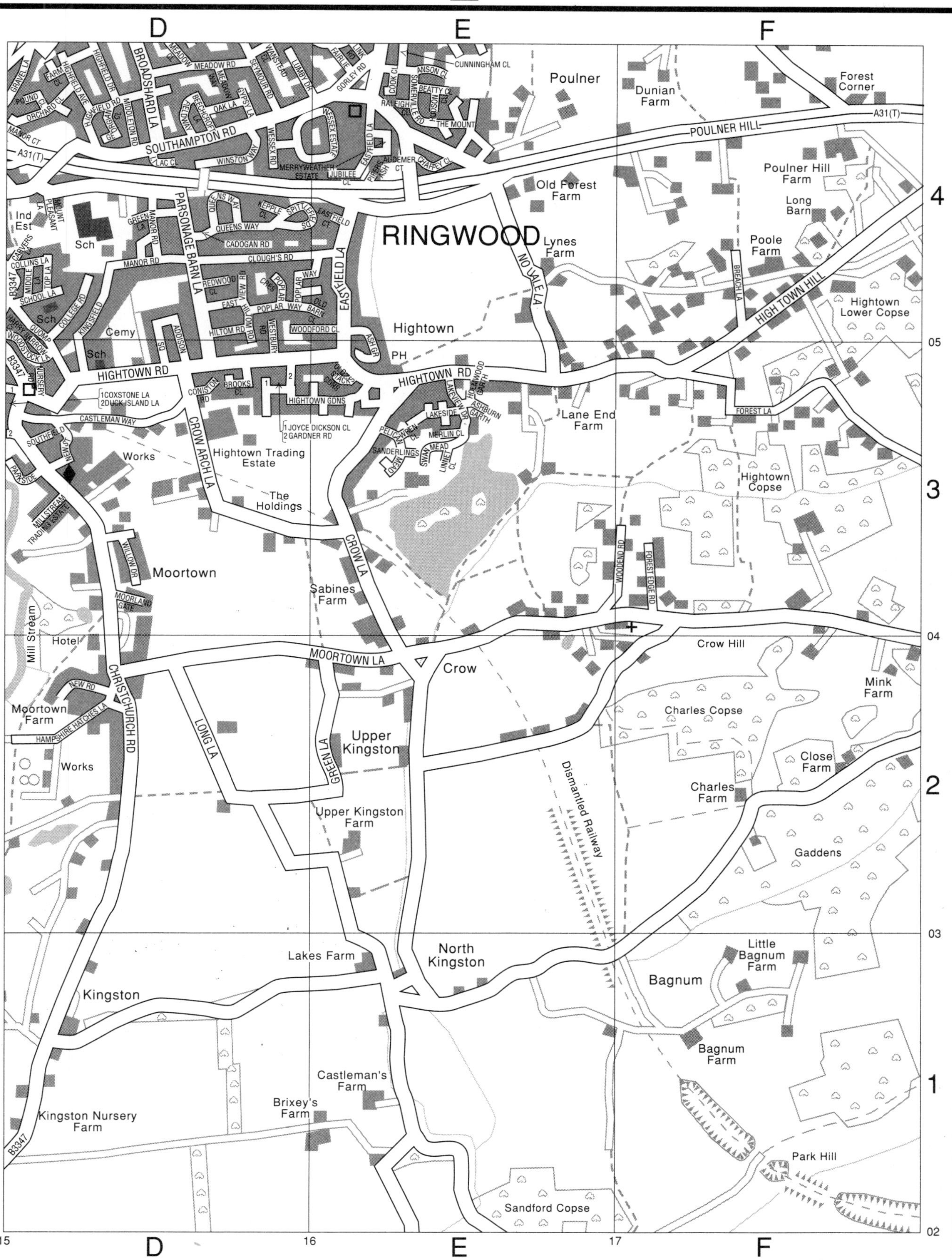
D
E
F
RINGWOOD
Poulner
Dunian Farm
Forest Corner
A31(T)
POULNER HILL
Poulner Hill Farm
Long Barn
Old Forest Farm
Lynes Farm
Poole Farm
HIGH TOWN HILL
BREACH LA
Hightown Lower Copse
Hightown
PH
HIGHTOWN RD
FOREST LA
Lane End Farm
Hightown Copse
Hightown Trading Estate
The Holdings
Works
Moortown
Sabines Farm
CROW LA
CROW ARCH LA
WOODEND RD
FOREST EDGE RD
Crow Hill
Mink Farm
Crow
MOORTOWN LA
Charles Copse
Close Farm
Charles Farm
Upper Kingston
Upper Kingston Farm
LONG LA
GREEN LA
Dismantled Railway
Gaddens
Mill Stream
Hotel
Moortown Farm
HAMPSHIRE HATCHES LA
CHRISTCHURCH RD
Works
Lakes Farm
North Kingston
Little Bagnum Farm
Bagnum
Bagnum Farm
Kingston
Castleman's Farm
Brixey's Farm
Kingston Nursery Farm
B3347
Park Hill
Sandford Copse
SOUTHAMPTON RD
BROADSHARD LA
PARSONAGE BARN LA
EASTFIELD LA
MANOR RD
CLOUGH'S RD
QUEENS WAY
CADOGAN RD
POPLAR WAY
WOODFORD CL
HILTOM RD
ASH GR
CASTLEMAN WAY
1 COXSTONE LA
2 DUCK ISLAND LA
1 JOYCE DICKSON CL
2 GARDNER RD
HIGHTOWN GDNS
NORTH LA
Ind Est
Sch
Cemy
4
3
2
1
05
04
03
02
15
16
17

142

168

118

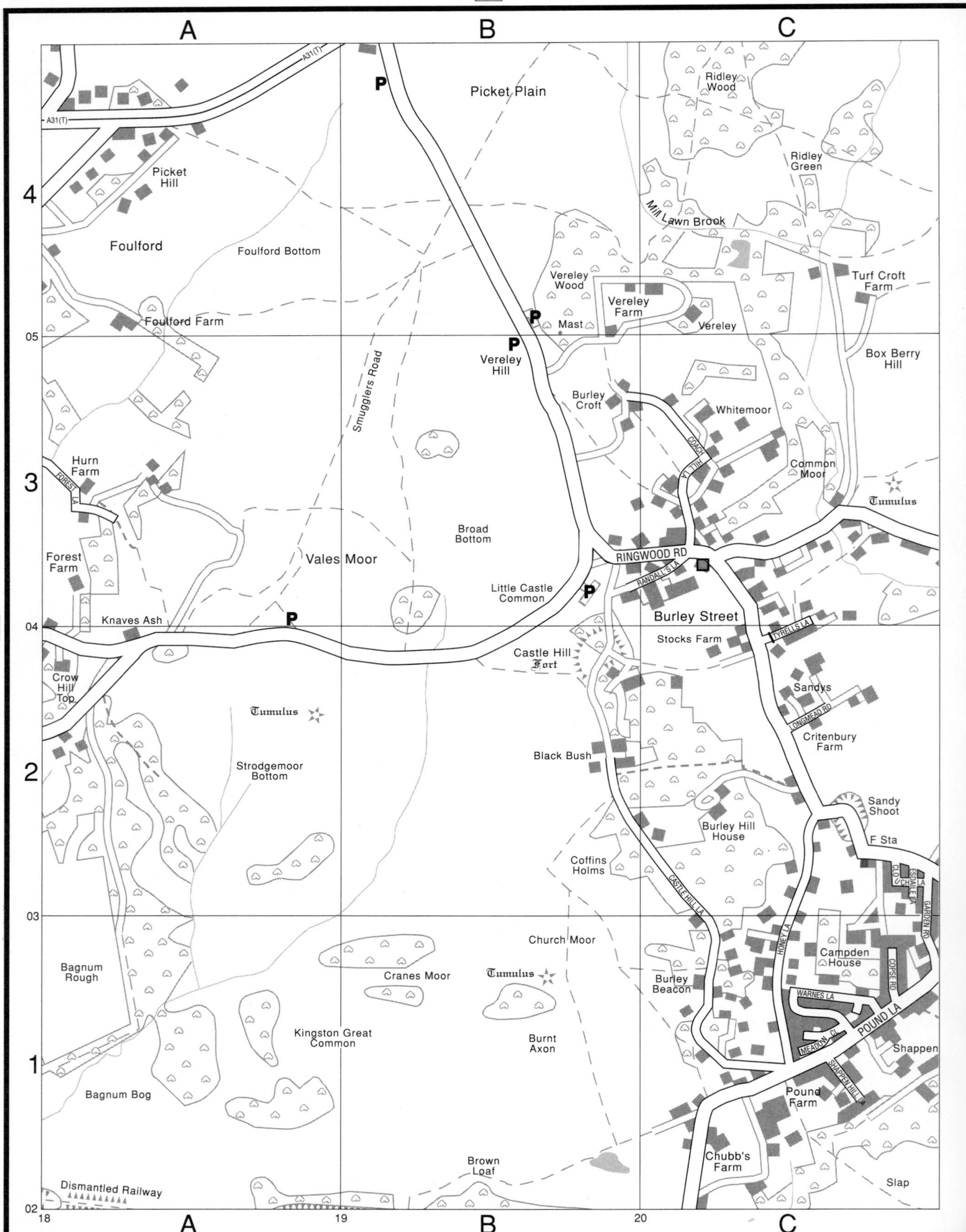
A
B
C
A
B
C
4
05
3
04
2
03
1
02
18
19
20
A31(T)
Picket Plain
Ridley Wood
Ridley Green
Picket Hill
Foulford
Foulford Bottom
Mill Lawn Brook
Vereley Wood
Vereley Farm
Turf Croft Farm
Foulford Farm
Mast
Vereley
Box Berry Hill
Vereley Hill
Smugglers Road
Burley Croft
Whitemoor
COACH HILL LA
Hurn Farm
FOREST LA
Common Moor
Tumulus
Broad Bottom
RINGWOOD RD
RANDALL'S LA
Forest Farm
Vales Moor
Little Castle Common
Knaves Ash
Burley Street
TYRELLS LA
Stocks Farm
Castle Hill Fort
Crow Hill Top
Sandys
Tumulus
LONGMEAD RD
Critenbury Farm
Black Bush
Strodgemoor Bottom
Sandy Shoot
Burley Hill House
F Sta
Coffins Holms
CASTLE HILL LA
GARDEN RD
HONEY LA
Church Moor
Campden House
COPSE RD
Bagnum Rough
Cranes Moor
Tumulus
Burley Beacon
WARNES LA
POUND LA
Kingston Great Common
Burnt Axon
MEADOW CL
Shappen
SHAPPEN HILL LA
Bagnum Bog
Pound Farm
Chubb's Farm
Brown Loaf
Slap
Dismantled Railway

141

169

119

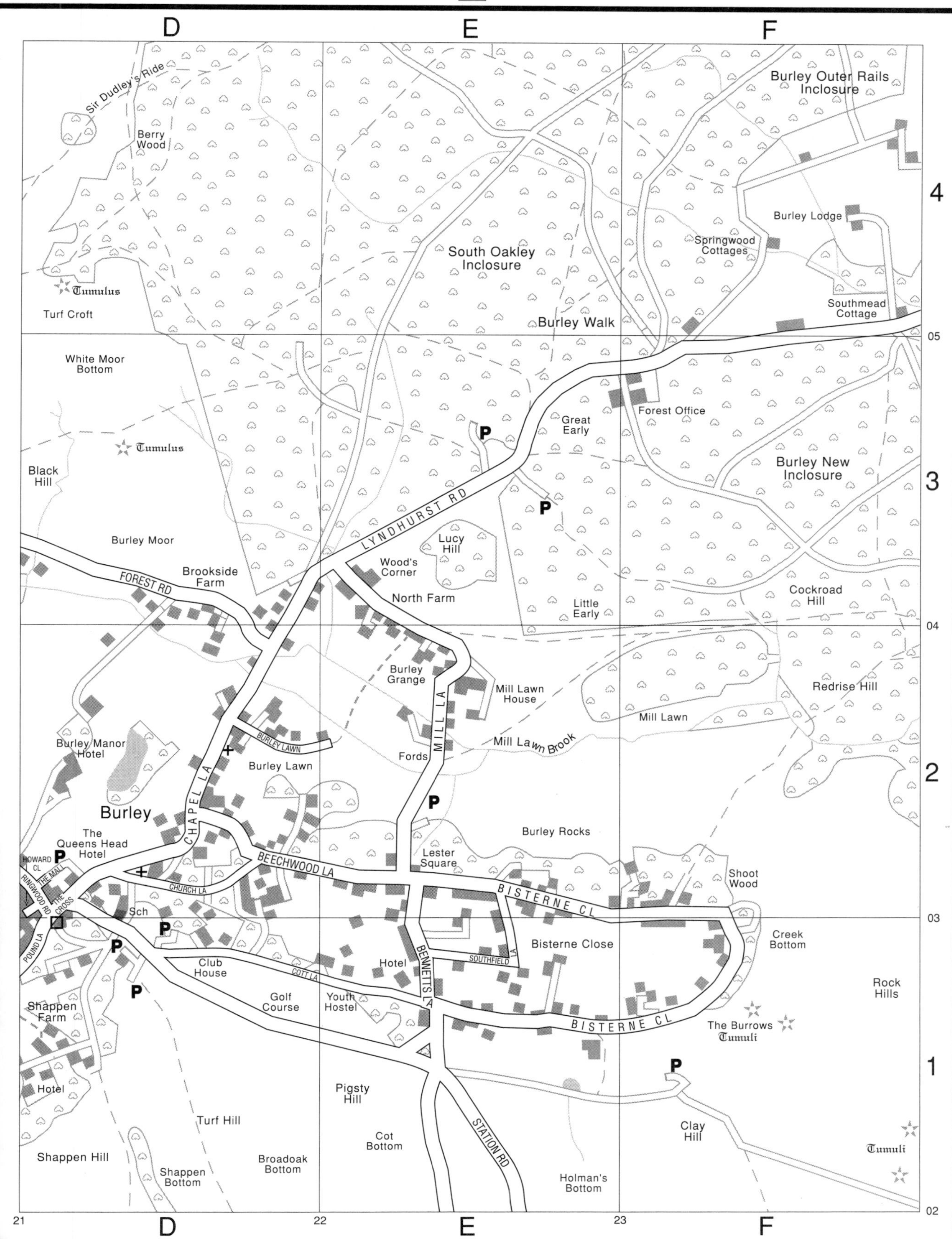
D
E
F
Sir Dudley's Ride
Berry Wood
Burley Outer Rails Inclosure
Burley Lodge
Springwood Cottages
South Oakley Inclosure
Tumulus
Turf Croft
Southmead Cottage
Burley Walk
White Moor Bottom
Forest Office
Great Early
Tumulus
Black Hill
Burley New Inclosure
LYNDHURST RD
Lucy Hill
Burley Moor
Wood's Corner
Brookside Farm
FOREST RD
North Farm
Cockroad Hill
Little Early
Burley Grange
Mill Lawn House
Redrise Hill
Mill Lawn
MILL LA
Mill Lawn Brook
BURLEY LAWN
Burley Manor Hotel
Burley Lawn
Fords
CHAPEL LA
Burley
Burley Rocks
The Queens Head Hotel
HOWARD CL
THE MALL
RINGWOOD RD
THE CROSS
Lester Square
BEECHWOOD LA
Shoot Wood
CHURCH LA
BISTERNE CL
Sch
POUND LA
Creek Bottom
Bisterne Close
Club House
SOUTHFIELD LA
Hotel
BENNETTS LA
COTT LA
Rock Hills
Golf Course
Youth Hostel
Shappen Farm
BISTERNE CL
The Burrows
Tumuli
Hotel
Pigsty Hill
Clay Hill
Turf Hill
STATION RD
Cot Bottom
Shappen Hill
Tumuli
Broadoak Bottom
Shappen Bottom
Holman's Bottom
4
05
3
04
2
03
1
02
21
22
23
P

144

170

120

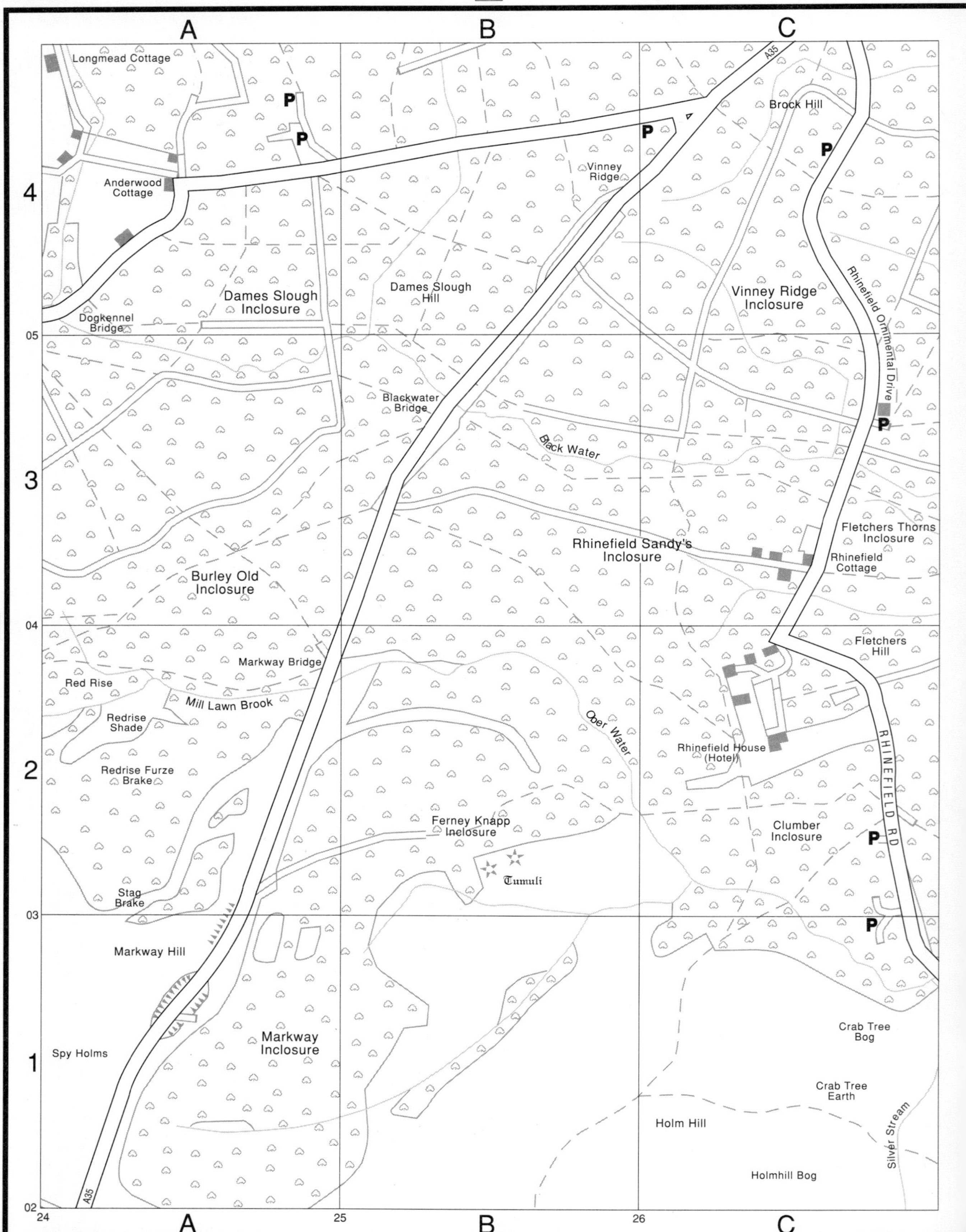
A
B
C
Longmead Cottage
Anderwood Cottage
Brock Hill
Vinney Ridge
A35
Dames Slough Inclosure
Dames Slough Hill
Vinney Ridge Inclosure
Rhinefield Ornamental Drive
Dogkennel Bridge
Blackwater Bridge
Black Water
Fletchers Thorns Inclosure
Rhinefield Sandy's Inclosure
Rhinefield Cottage
Burley Old Inclosure
Fletchers Hill
Markway Bridge
Red Rise
Mill Lawn Brook
Redrise Shade
Ober Water
Rhinefield House (Hotel)
RHINEFIELD RD
Redrise Furze Brake
Ferney Knapp Inclosure
Clumber Inclosure
Tumuli
Stag Brake
Markway Hill
Markway Inclosure
Crab Tree Bog
Spy Holms
Crab Tree Earth
Holm Hill
Silver Stream
Holmhill Bog
4
3
2
1
05
04
03
02
24
25
26

143

171

121

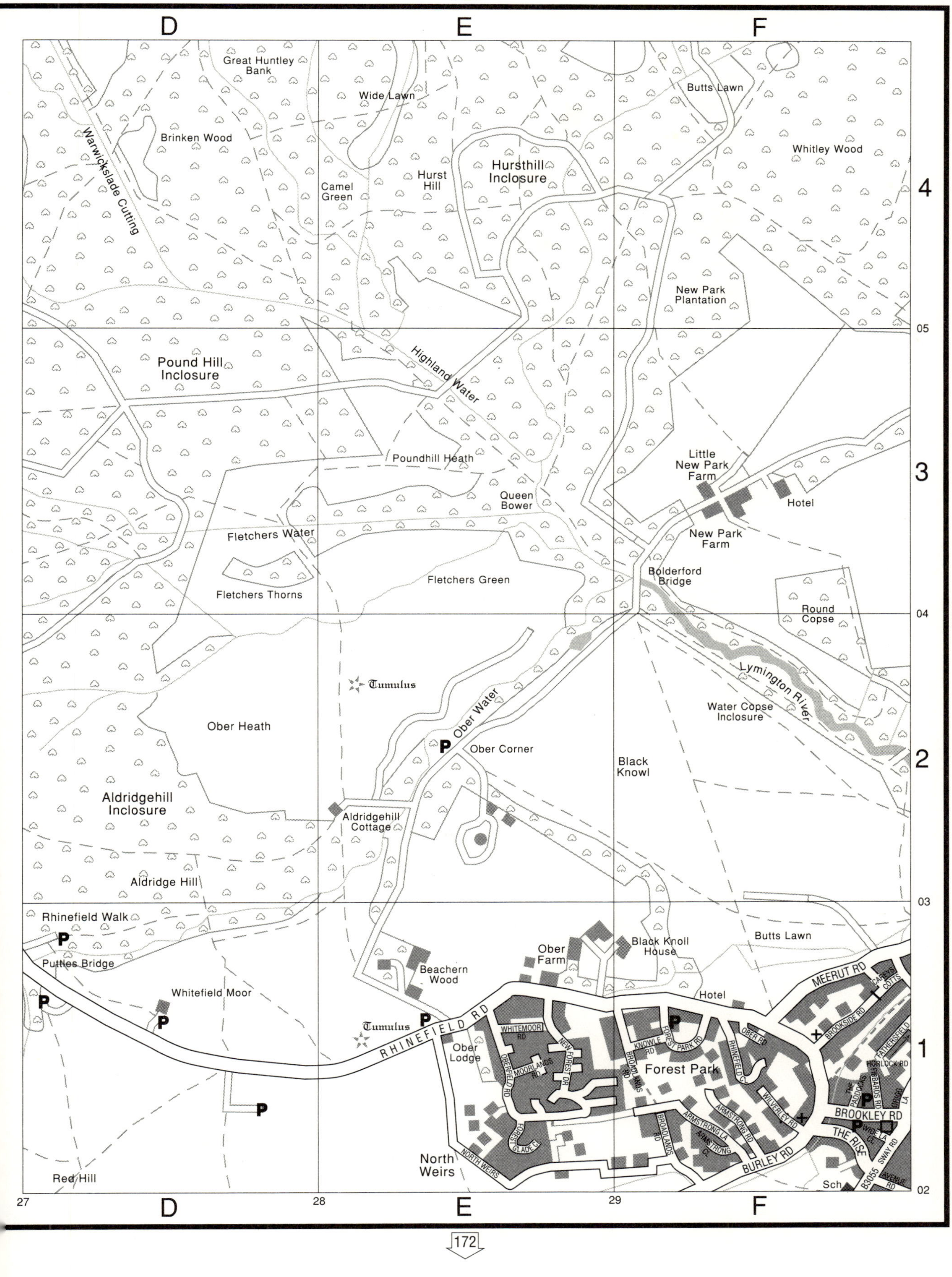
D
E
F
4
05
3
04
2
03
1
02
27
28
29
Great Huntley Bank
Wide Lawn
Butts Lawn
Brinken Wood
Warwickslade Cutting
Hurst Hill
Camel Green
Hursthill Inclosure
Whitley Wood
New Park Plantation
Pound Hill Inclosure
Highland Water
Poundhill Heath
Little New Park Farm
Hotel
Queen Bower
New Park Farm
Fletchers Water
Fletchers Thorns
Fletchers Green
Bolderford Bridge
Round Copse
Tumulus
Lymington River
Water Copse Inclosure
Ober Heath
Ober Water
P
Ober Corner
Black Knowl
Aldridgehill Inclosure
Aldridgehill Cottage
Aldridge Hill
Rhinefield Walk
Puttles Bridge
Whitefield Moor
Beachern Wood
Ober Farm
Black Knoll House
Butts Lawn
Hotel
MEERUT RD
CAREYS COTTS
BROOKSIDE RD
FATHERSFIELD
HORLOCK RD
RHINEFIELD RD
WHITEMOOR RD
NEW FOREST DR
MOORLANDS RD
OBERFIELD RD
Ober Lodge
KNOWLE RD
FOREST PARK RD
OBER RD
BROADLANDS RD
RHINEFIELD CL
Forest Park
WILVERLEY RD
ARMSTRONG RD
ARMSTRONG LA
ARMSTRONG CL
BROOKLEY RD
THE PADDOCKS
EBBARDS RD
BRIGG LA
WIDE LA CL
THE RISE
SWAY RD
FOREST GLADE CL
NORTH WEIRS
North Weirs
BURLEY RD
Sch
B3055
AVENUE RD
Red Hill

146

172

122

145

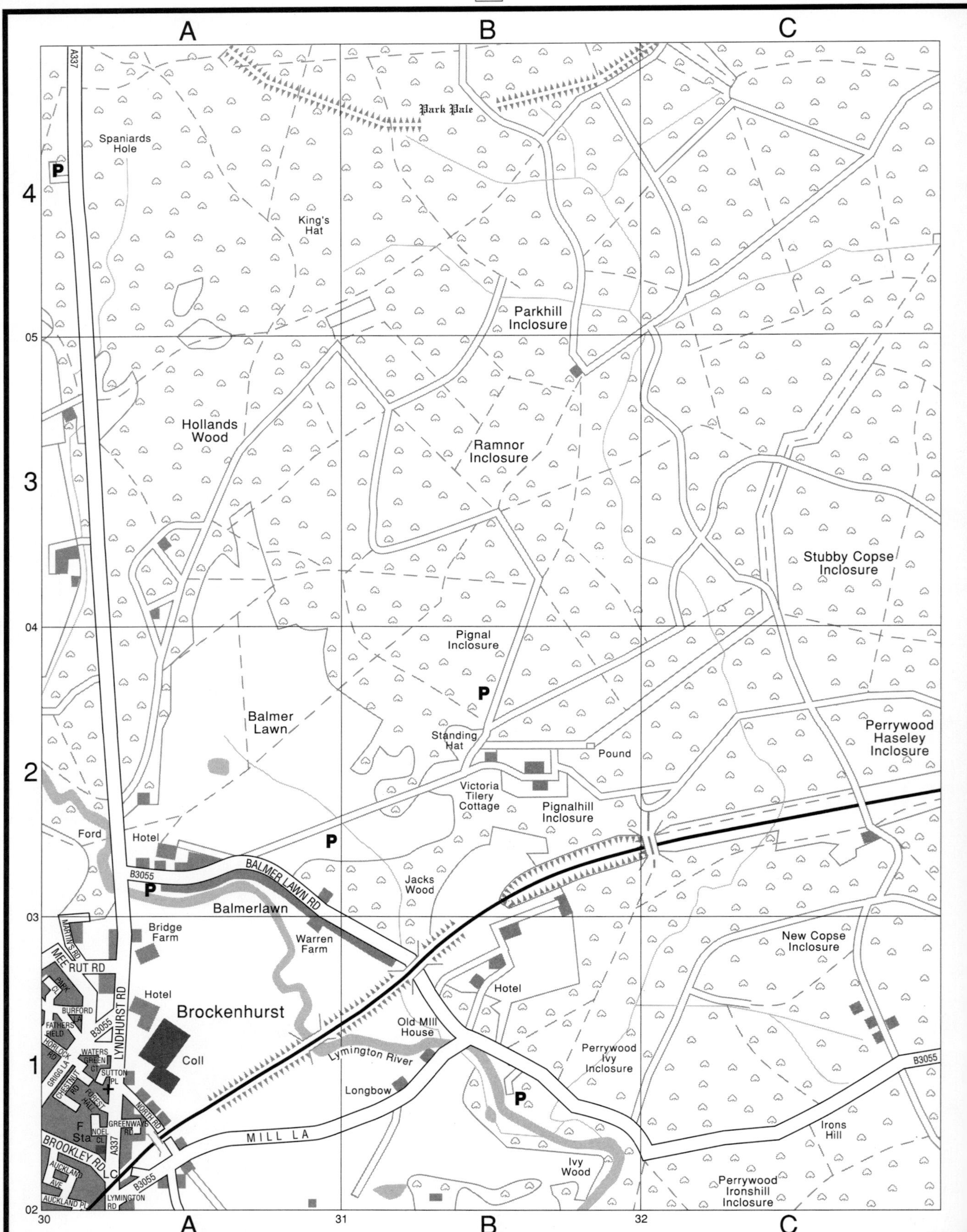
A
B
C
4
3
2
1
05
04
03
02
30
31
32
A337
Spaniards Hole
King's Hat
Park Pale
Parkhill Inclosure
Hollands Wood
Ramnor Inclosure
Stubby Copse Inclosure
Pignal Inclosure
Balmer Lawn
Standing Hat
Pound
Perrywood Haseley Inclosure
Victoria Tilery Cottage
Pignalhill Inclosure
Ford
Hotel
B3055
BALMER LAWN RD
Balmerlawn
Jacks Wood
Bridge Farm
Warren Farm
New Copse Inclosure
MARTIN'S RD
MEERUT RD
PARK CL
BURFORD LA
FATHERS FIELD
HORLOCK RD
GRIGG LA
CHESTNUT RD
WATERS GREEN CT
SUTTON PL
FOREST HALL
NORTH RD
GREENWAYS RD
NOEL CL
LYNDHURST RD
Hotel
Brockenhurst
Coll
F
Sta
BROOKLEY RD
LC
AUCKLAND AVE
AUCKLAND PL
LYMINGTON RD
Old Mill House
Lymington River
Longbow
MILL LA
Perrywood Ivy Inclosure
Irons Hill
Ivy Wood
Perrywood Ironshill Inclosure

173

123

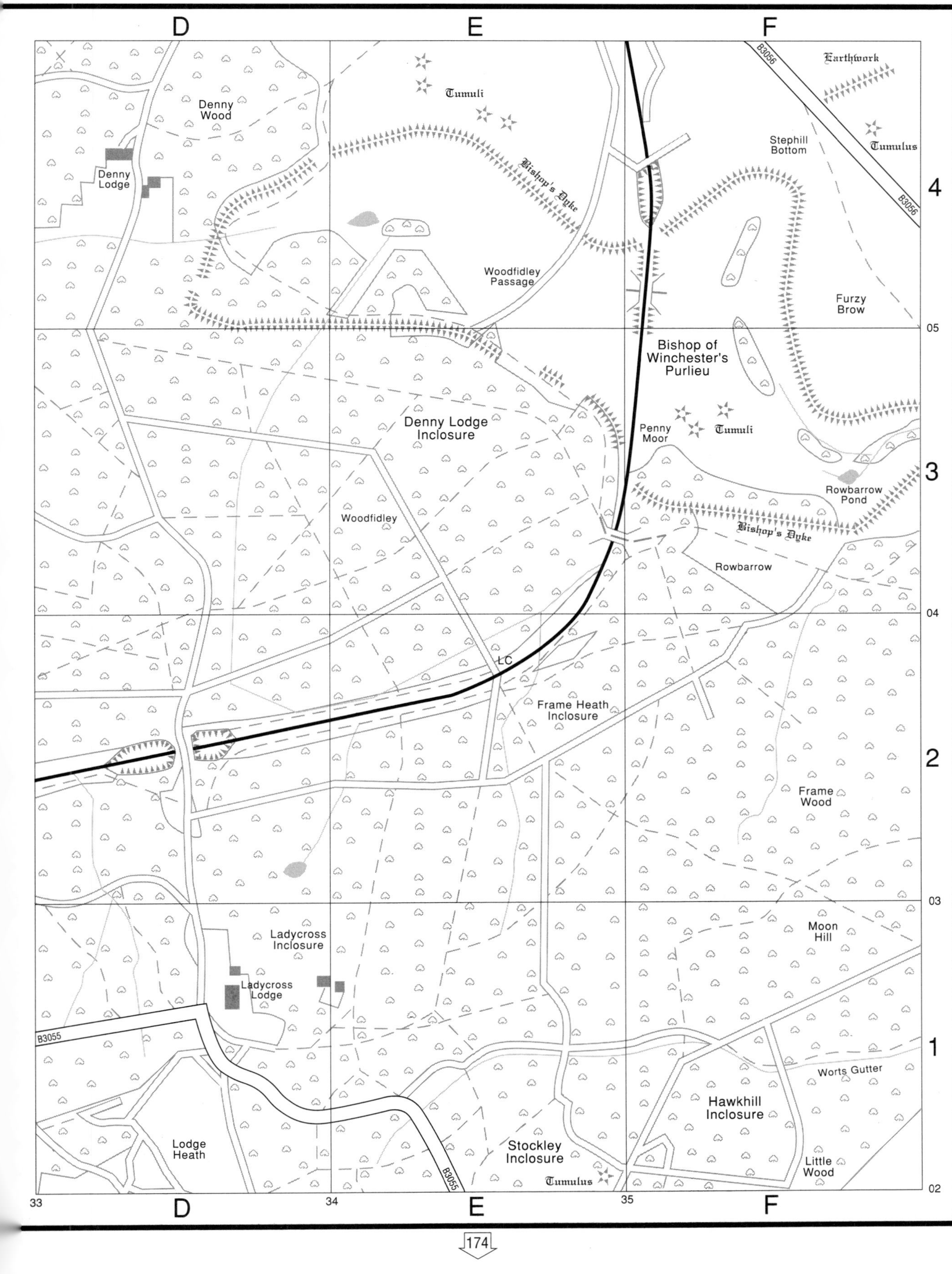

D
E
F
Denny Wood
Denny Lodge
Tumuli
Bishop's Dyke
Earthwork
Tumulus
Stephill Bottom
B3056
Woodfidley Passage
Furzy Brow
Bishop of Winchester's Purlieu
Denny Lodge Inclosure
Penny Moor
Tumuli
Rowbarrow Pond
Woodfidley
Bishop's Dyke
Rowbarrow
LC
Frame Heath Inclosure
Frame Wood
Moon Hill
Ladycross Inclosure
Ladycross Lodge
B3055
Worts Gutter
Hawkhill Inclosure
Lodge Heath
Stockley Inclosure
Tumulus
Little Wood
B3055
4
3
2
1
05
04
03
02
33
34
35

148

174

124

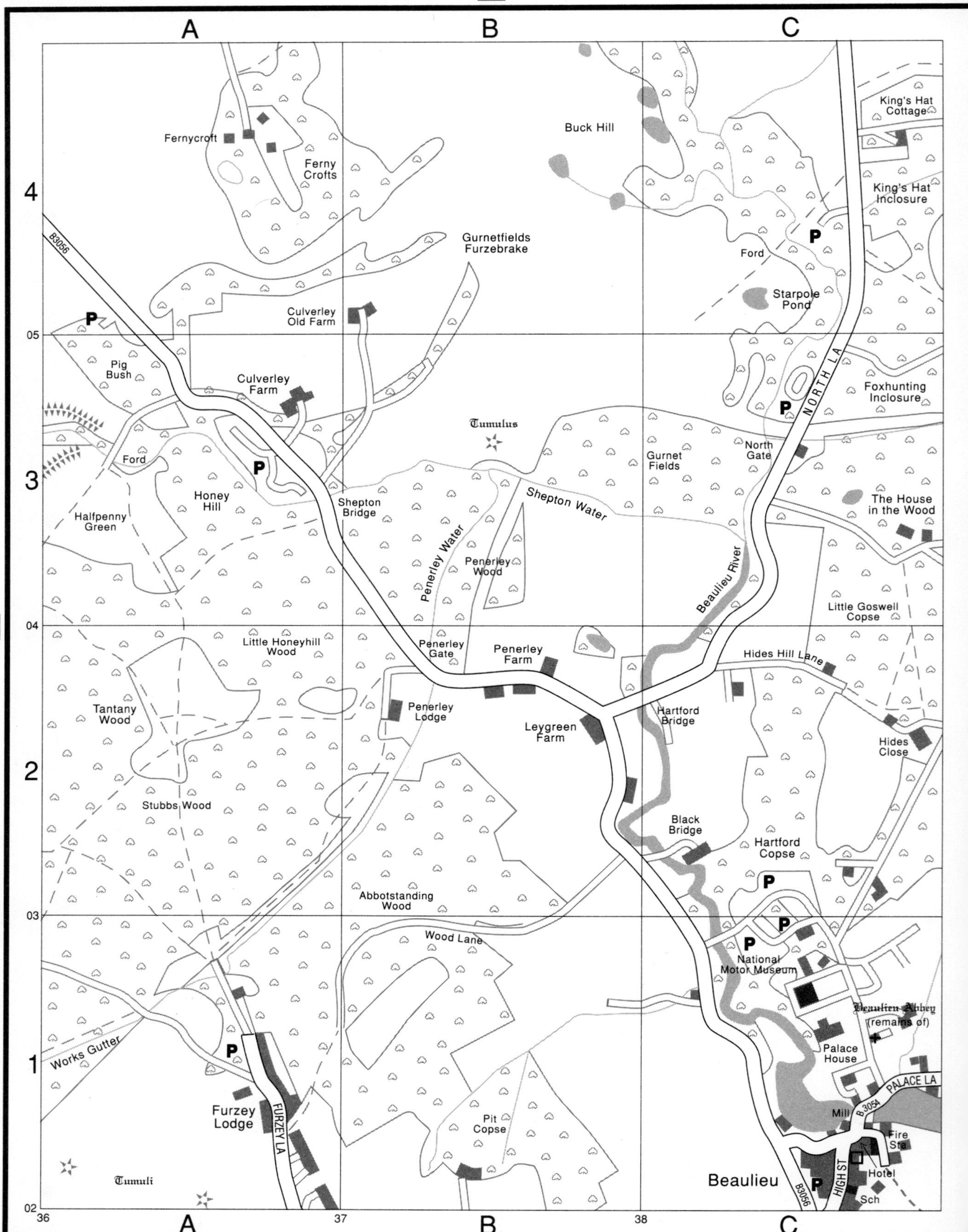
A
B
C
4
3
2
1
05
04
03
02
36
37
38
Fernycroft
Ferny Crofts
Buck Hill
King's Hat Cottage
King's Hat Inclosure
Gurnetfields Furzebrake
B3056
Ford
Starpole Pond
Culverley Old Farm
Pig Bush
Culverley Farm
NORTH LA
Foxhunting Inclosure
Tumulus
North Gate
Gurnet Fields
Ford
Honey Hill
Shepton Bridge
Shepton Water
The House in the Wood
Halfpenny Green
Penerley Water
Penerley Wood
Beaulieu River
Little Goswell Copse
Little Honeyhill Wood
Penerley Gate
Penerley Farm
Hides Hill Lane
Tantany Wood
Penerley Lodge
Leygreen Farm
Hartford Bridge
Hides Close
Stubbs Wood
Black Bridge
Hartford Copse
Abbotstanding Wood
Wood Lane
National Motor Museum
Beaulieu Abbey (remains of)
Works Gutter
Palace House
PALACE LA
Furzey Lodge
FURZEY LA
Pit Copse
Mill
B 3054
Fire Sta
HIGH ST
Hotel
Tumuli
Beaulieu
B3056
Sch
P

147

175

125

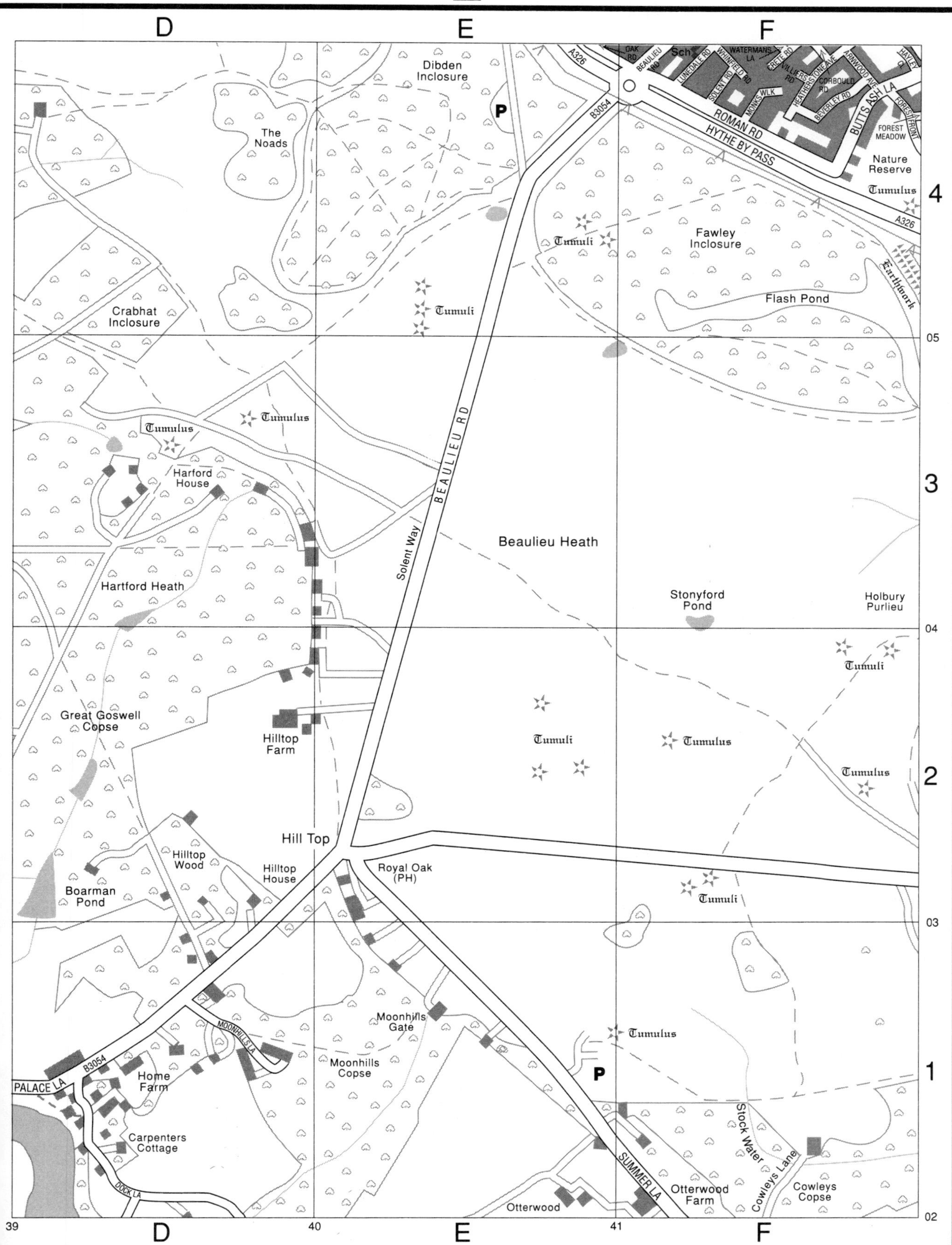
D
E
F
OAK RD
BEAULIEU RD
Sch
LUNEDALE RD
WHINFIELD RD
SOLENT RD
WATERMANS LA
CRETE RD
VILLIERS RD
MONKS WLK
HEATHERSTONE AVE
CORBOULD RD
ARNWOOD AVE
BEVERLEY RD
HAYLEY CL
BUTTS ASH LA
FOREST FRONT
FOREST MEADOW
ROMAN RD
HYTHE BY PASS
A326
B3054
Dibden Inclosure
P
The Noads
Nature Reserve
Tumulus
4
Tumuli
Fawley Inclosure
Earthwork
Flash Pond
Tumuli
Crabhat Inclosure
05
Tumulus
Tumulus
Harford House
BEAULIEU RD
3
Solent Way
Beaulieu Heath
Hartford Heath
Stonyford Pond
Holbury Purlieu
04
Tumuli
Great Goswell Copse
Hilltop Farm
Tumuli
Tumulus
Tumulus
2
Hill Top
Hilltop Wood
Hilltop House
Royal Oak (PH)
Boarman Pond
Tumuli
03
Moonhills Gate
MOONHILLS LA
Tumulus
B3054
1
PALACE LA
Home Farm
Moonhills Copse
P
Stock Water
Carpenters Cottage
SUMMER LA
Cowleys Lane
Cowleys Copse
DOCK LA
Otterwood Farm
Otterwood
39
40
41
02
D
E
F

150

176

126

149

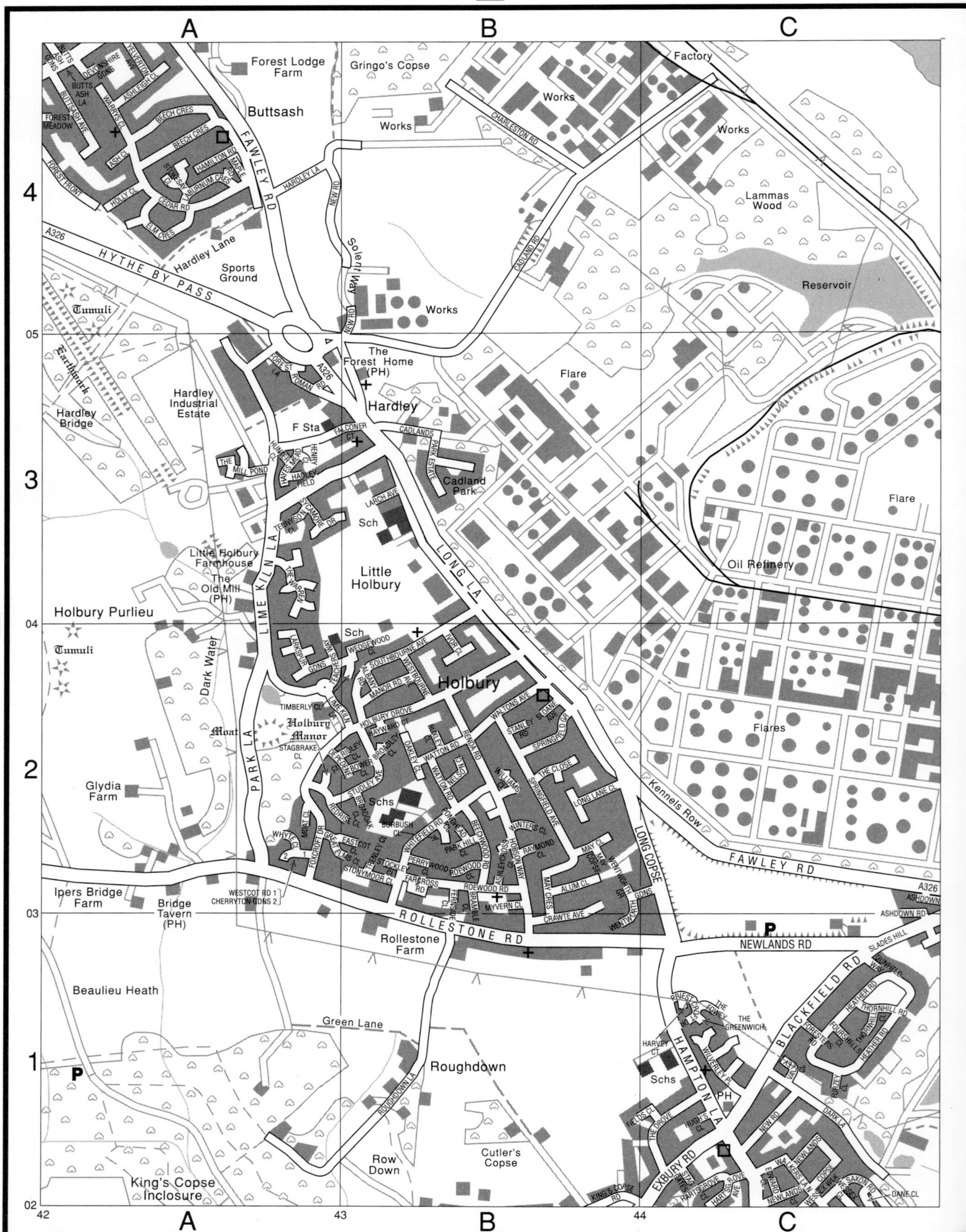
A
B
C
4
3
2
1
05
04
03
02
42
43
44
Forest Lodge Farm
Gringo's Copse
Factory
Works
Buttsash
Lammas Wood
Reservoir
Hardley Lane
Sports Ground
HYTHE BY PASS
A326
FAWLEY RD
Solent Way
Tumuli
Earthwork
The Forest Home (PH)
Hardley
Hardley Industrial Estate
Hardley Bridge
F Sta
Flare
Cadland Park
Sch
Little Holbury Farmhouse
The Old Mill (PH)
Little Holbury
Oil Refinery
Holbury Purlieu
LONG LA
LIME KILN LA
Dark Water
Holbury
Holbury Manor
Moat
Flares
PARK LA
Glydia Farm
Schs
Kennels Row
LONG COPSE
Ipers Bridge Farm
Bridge Tavern (PH)
ROLLESTONE RD
NEWLANDS RD
Rollestone Farm
Beaulieu Heath
Green Lane
Roughdown
HAMPTON LA
BLACKFIELD RD
PH
Row Down
Cutler's Copse
King's Copse Inclosure
EXBURY RD

177

127

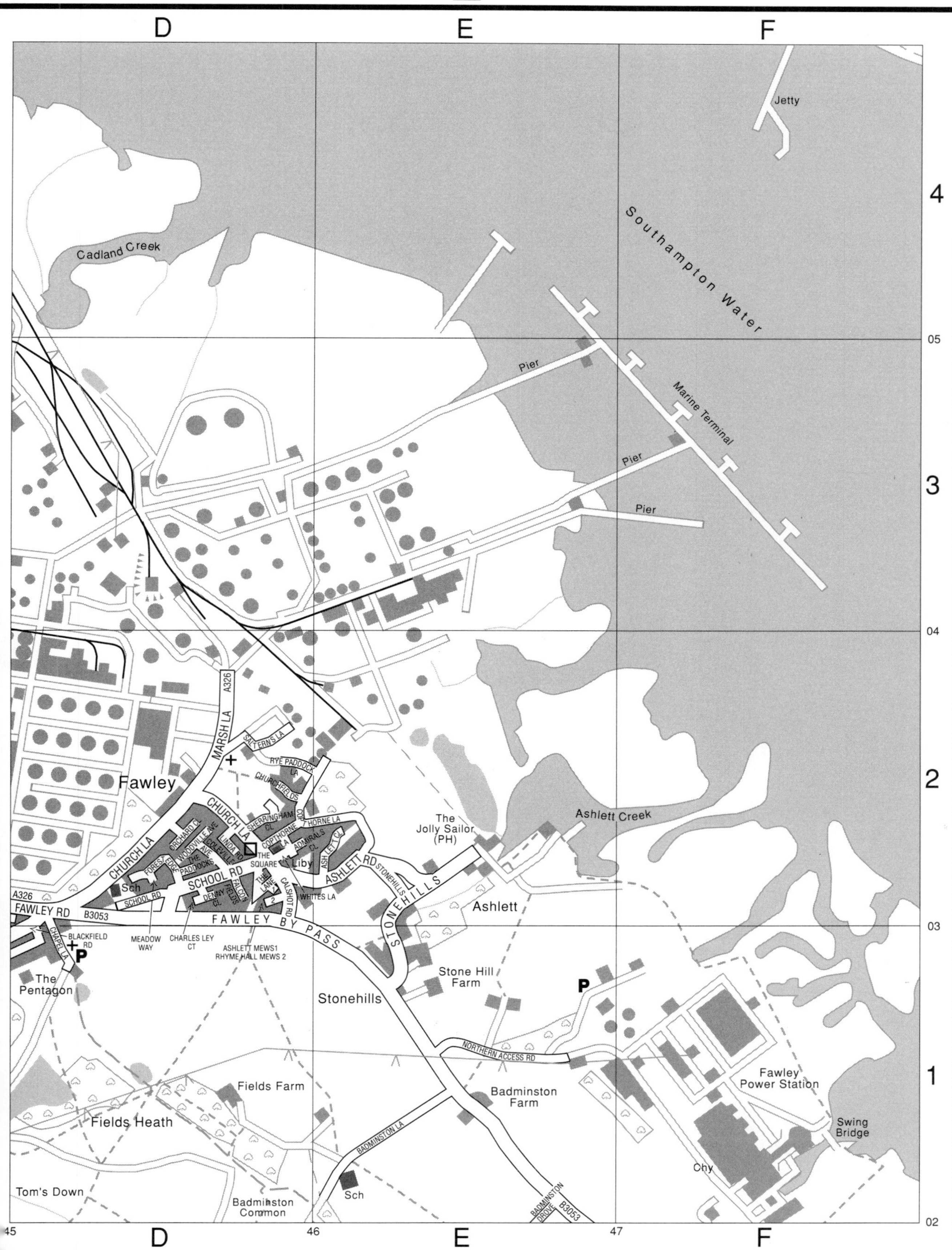
D
E
F
4
05
3
04
2
03
1
02
45
46
47
Jetty
Southampton Water
Cadland Creek
Marine Terminal
Pier
Pier
Pier
Fawley
Ashlett Creek
The
Jolly Sailor
(PH)
Ashlett
Stone Hill
Farm
Stonehills
Fawley
Power Station
Swing
Bridge
Chy
Badminston
Farm
Fields Farm
Fields Heath
Tom's Down
Badminston
Common
Sch
Sch
The
Pentagon
Liby
MARSH LA
A326
A326
SALTERNS LA
RYE PADDOCK
LA
CHURCHFIELDS
CHURCH LA
CHURCH LA
SHERRINGHAM
CL
COPTHORNE
LA
HORNE LA
ADMIRALS
CL
ASHLETT CL
ORCHARD CL
WOODVILLE AVE
COLEVILLE AVE
LINDA RD
THE PADDOCKS
FOREST EDGE
THE
SQUARE
SCHOOL RD
SCHOOL RD
DENNY
CL
FIELDS
FALCON
THE LANE
CALSHOT RD
WHITES LA
ASHLETT RD
STONEHILLS
STONEHILLS
FAWLEY RD
B3053
FAWLEY BY PASS
CHAPEL LA
BLACKFIELD
RD
MEADOW
WAY
CHARLES LEY
CT
ASHLETT MEWS1
RHYME HALL MEWS 2
NORTHERN ACCESS RD
BADMINSTON LA
BADMINSTON
DROVE
B3053
P
P

152

178

128

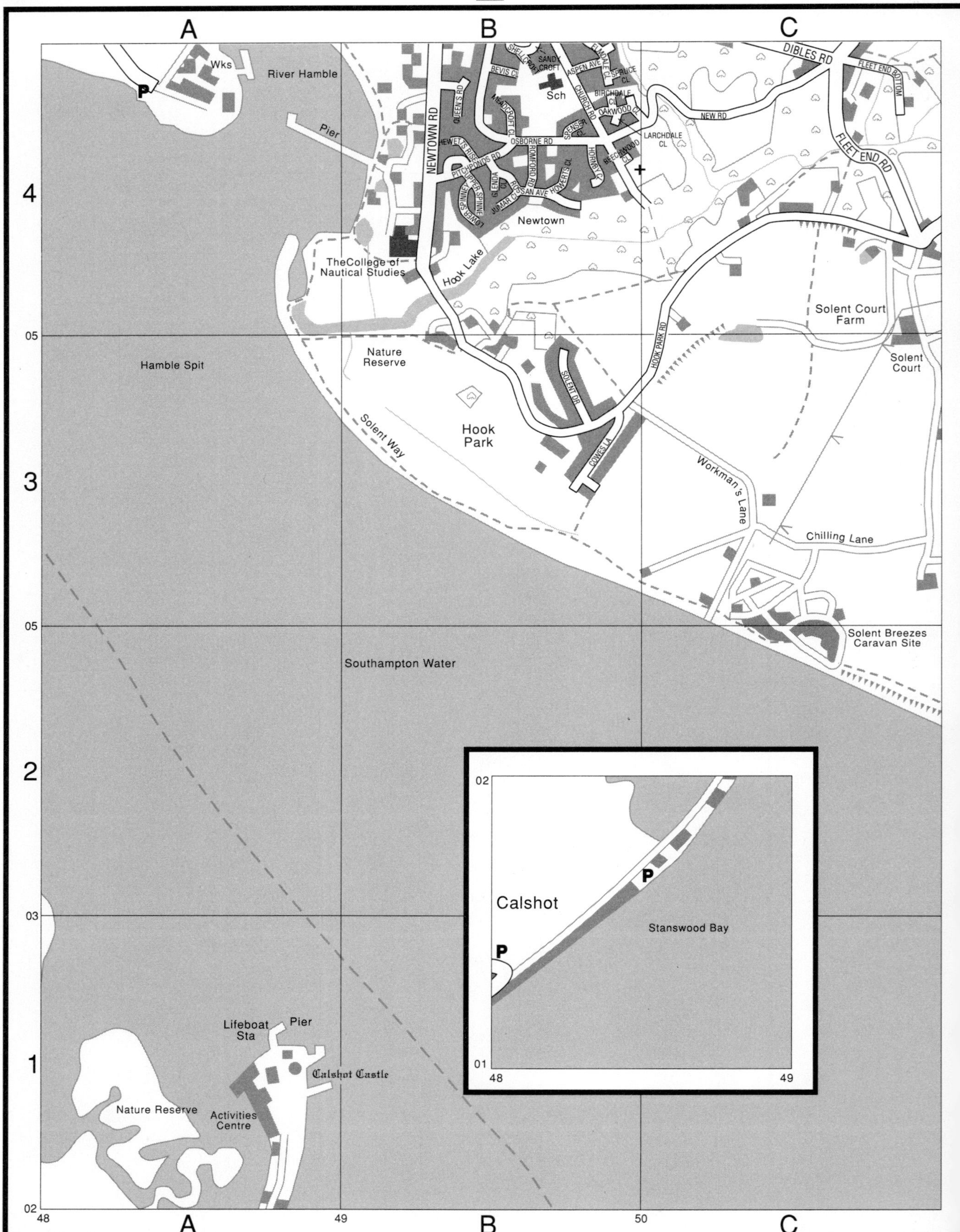

A
B
C
Wks
River Hamble
Pier
NEWTOWN RD
QUEEN'S RD
BEVIS CL
SANDY CROFT
ASPEN AVE
SPRUCE CL
Sch
BIRCHDALE CL
OAKWOOD CL
CHURCH RD
MEADCROFT CL
OSBORNE RD
SPENSER CL
LARCHDALE CL
BEECHWOOD CL
HORNBY CL
HEWETTS RISE
PITCHPONDS RD
ROMFORD RD
HOWERTS CL
RUSSAN AVE
GLENDA CL
JUMAR CL
UPPER SPINNEY
LOWER SPINNEY
Newtown
DIBLES RD
FLEET END BOTTOM
NEW RD
FLEET END RD
TheCollege of Nautical Studies
Hook Lake
HOOK PARK RD
Solent Court Farm
Hamble Spit
Nature Reserve
Solent Court
SOLENT DR
Hook Park
Solent Way
COWES LA
Workman's Lane
Chilling Lane
Solent Breezes Caravan Site
Southampton Water
Calshot
Stanswood Bay
P
Lifeboat Sta
Pier
Calshot Castle
Nature Reserve
Activities Centre
4
3
2
1
05
05
03
02
01
48
49
50

151

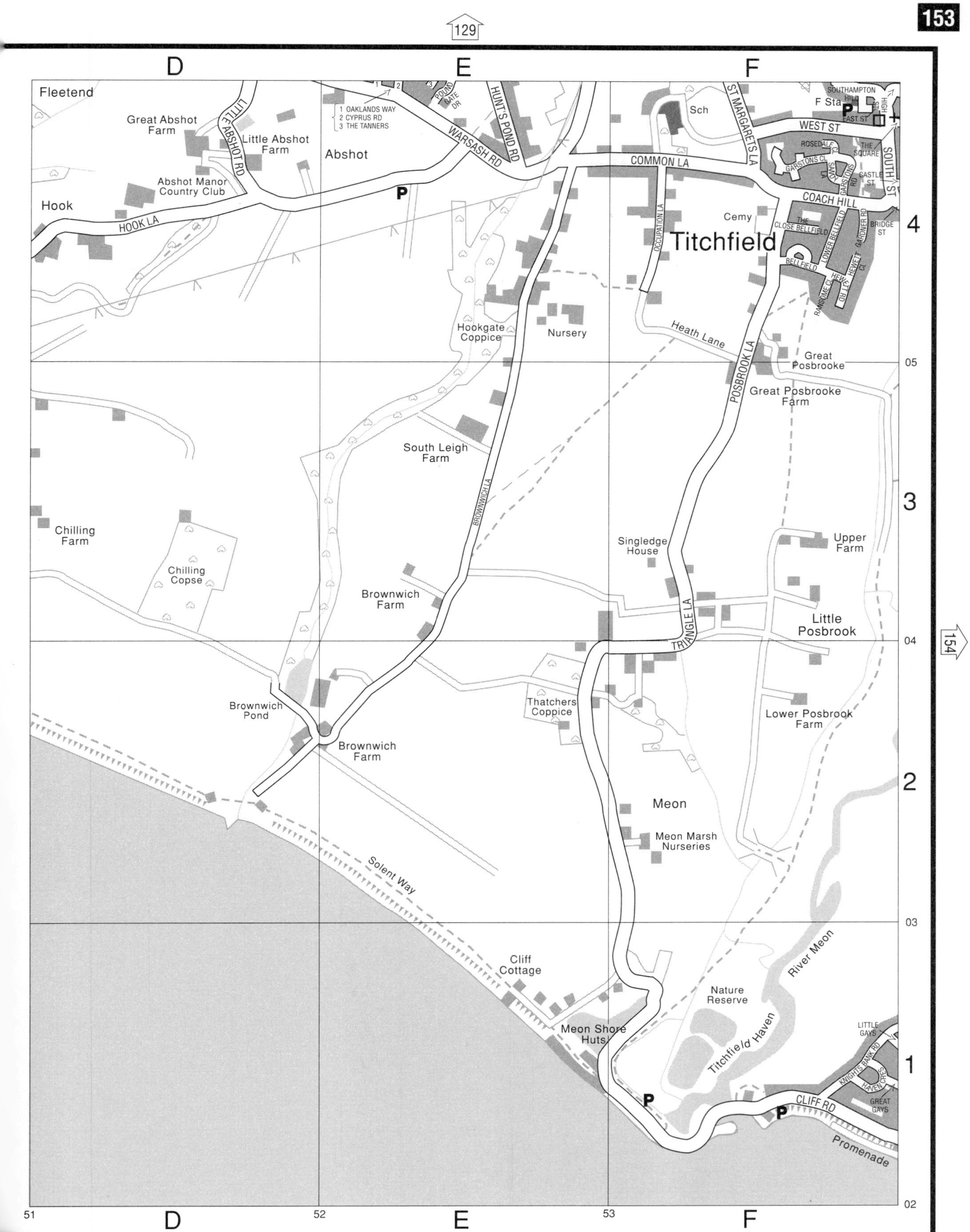
129
D
E
F
Fleetend
Great Abshot Farm
LITTLE ABSHOT RD
Little Abshot Farm
Abshot
1 OAKLANDS WAY
2 CYPRUS RD
3 THE TANNERS
POUND GATE DR
WARSASH RD
HUNT'S POND RD
Abshot Manor Country Club
Hook
HOOK LA
P
Sch
ST MARGARETS LA
SOUTHAMPTON HILL
F Sta
HIGH
EAST ST
WEST ST
ROSEDALE
THE SQUARE
SOUTH ST
GARSTONS CL
GARSTONS RD
CASTLE ST
COMMON LA
COACH HILL
OCCUPATION LA
Cemy
THE CLOSE
BELLFIELD
LOWER BELLFIELD
GARDNER RD
BRIDGE ST
HEWETT CL
RANSOME CL
HEWETT RD
Titchfield
4
Hookgate Coppice
Nursery
Heath Lane
POSBROOK LA
Great Posbrooke
Great Posbrooke Farm
05
South Leigh Farm
BROWNWICH LA
3
Chilling Farm
Chilling Copse
Singledge House
Upper Farm
Brownwich Farm
TRIANGLE LA
Little Posbrook
04
154
Thatchers Coppice
Lower Posbrook Farm
Brownwich Pond
Brownwich Farm
2
Meon
Meon Marsh Nurseries
Solent Way
03
Cliff Cottage
River Meon
Nature Reserve
Meon Shore Huts
Titchfield Haven
LITTLE GAYS
KNIGHTS BANK RD
HAVEN CRES
1
CLIFF RD
GREAT GAYS
Promenade
51
52
53
02

130

A
B
C
4
3
2
1
05
04
03
02
54
55
56
Titchfield Industries
Mast
Hollam Farm
BRIDGE ST
Schs
ROWAN WAY
PEAK LA
Oxleys Coppice
RANVILLES LA
LONGFIELD AVE
West End
Sch
Hollam Hill Farm
TITCHFIELD RD
Ranvilles Farm
Crofton Farm Dairy
River Meon
OAKCROFT LA
Crofton Manor Farm
Cemy
Newlands Farm
HMS Collingwood
STROUD GREEN LA
TANNERS LA
CUCKOO LA
MAY'S LA
Stubbington
Wireless Station Mast
Sch
Works
Meon View Farm
OLD ST
Liby
Peel Common
Park Lane
BELLS LA
GOSPORT RD
B3334
STUBBINGTON LA
CROFTON LA
Hill Head
Schs
HMS Daedalus Airfield
HILL HEAD RD
Seafield Park
SEAFIELD PARK RD

153

179

131
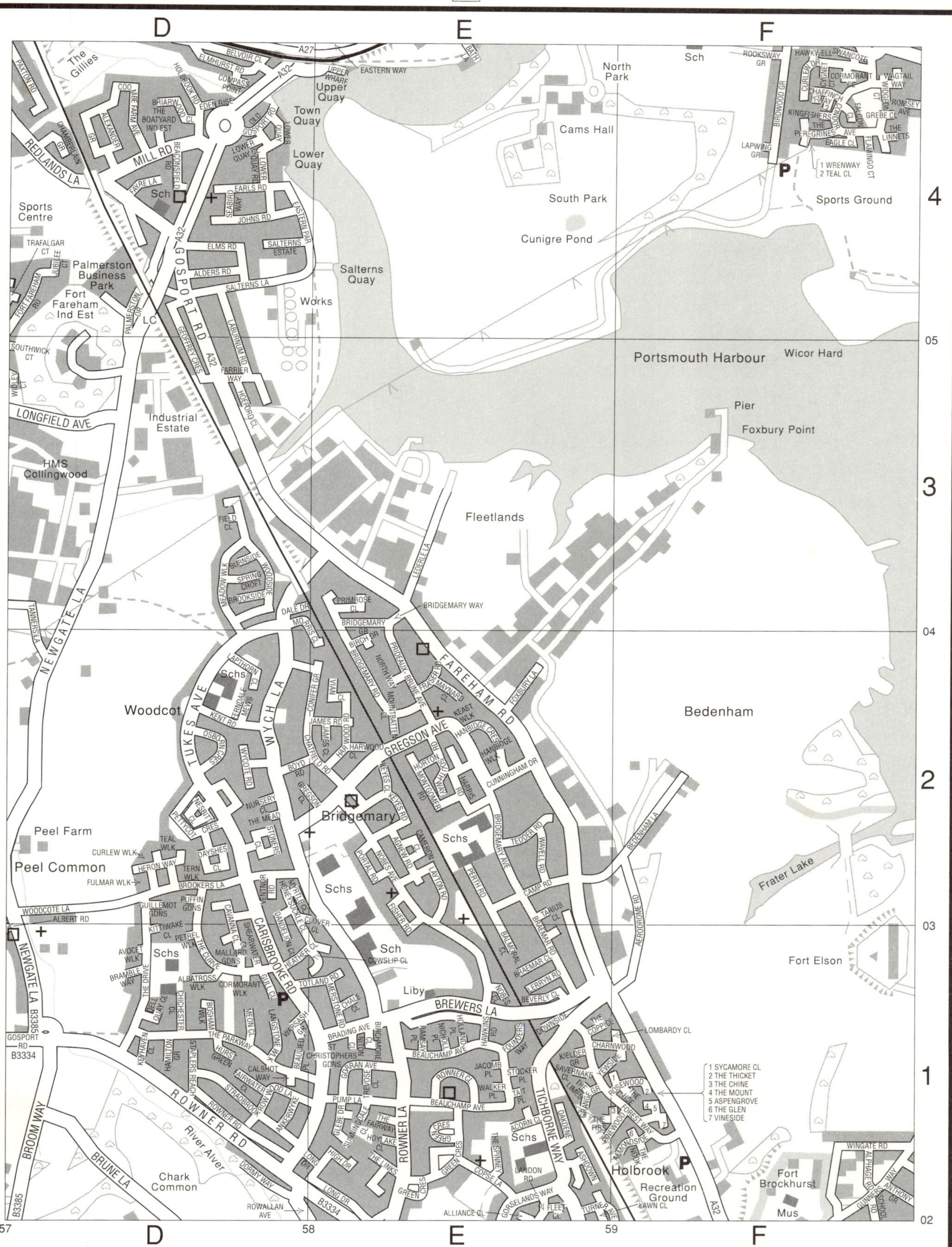
D
E
F
4
3
2
1
05
04
03
02
57
58
59
The Gillies
North Park
Sch
Upper Quay
Town Quay
Lower Quay
Cams Hall
South Park
Cunigre Pond
Sports Ground
Sports Centre
Palmerston Business Park
Fort Fareham Ind Est
Salterns Quay
Works
Portsmouth Harbour
Wicor Hard
Pier
Foxbury Point
Industrial Estate
HMS Collingwood
Fleetlands
Woodcot
Bedenham
Schs
Bridgemary
Peel Farm
Peel Common
Frater Lake
Fort Elson
Liby
Chark Common
River Alver
Holbrook
Recreation Ground
Fort Brockhurst
Mus
A27
A32
B3334
B3385
MILL RD
GOSPORT RD
REDLANDS LA
LONGFIELD AVE
NEWGATE LA
FAREHAM RD
GREGSON AVE
WYCH LA
TUKES AVE
CARISBROOKE RD
BREWERS LA
ROWNER RD
ROWNER LA
TICHBORNE WAY
BROOM WAY
BRUNE LA
BRIDGEMARY WAY
CUNNINGHAM DR
BEDENHAM LA
AERODROME RD
WOODCOTE LA
ALBERT RD
BEAUCHAMP AVE
LONG DR
1 SYCAMORE CL
2 THE THICKET
3 THE CHINE
4 THE MOUNT
5 ASPENGROVE
6 THE GLEN
7 VINESIDE
1 WRENWAY
2 TEAL CL
156
180

132

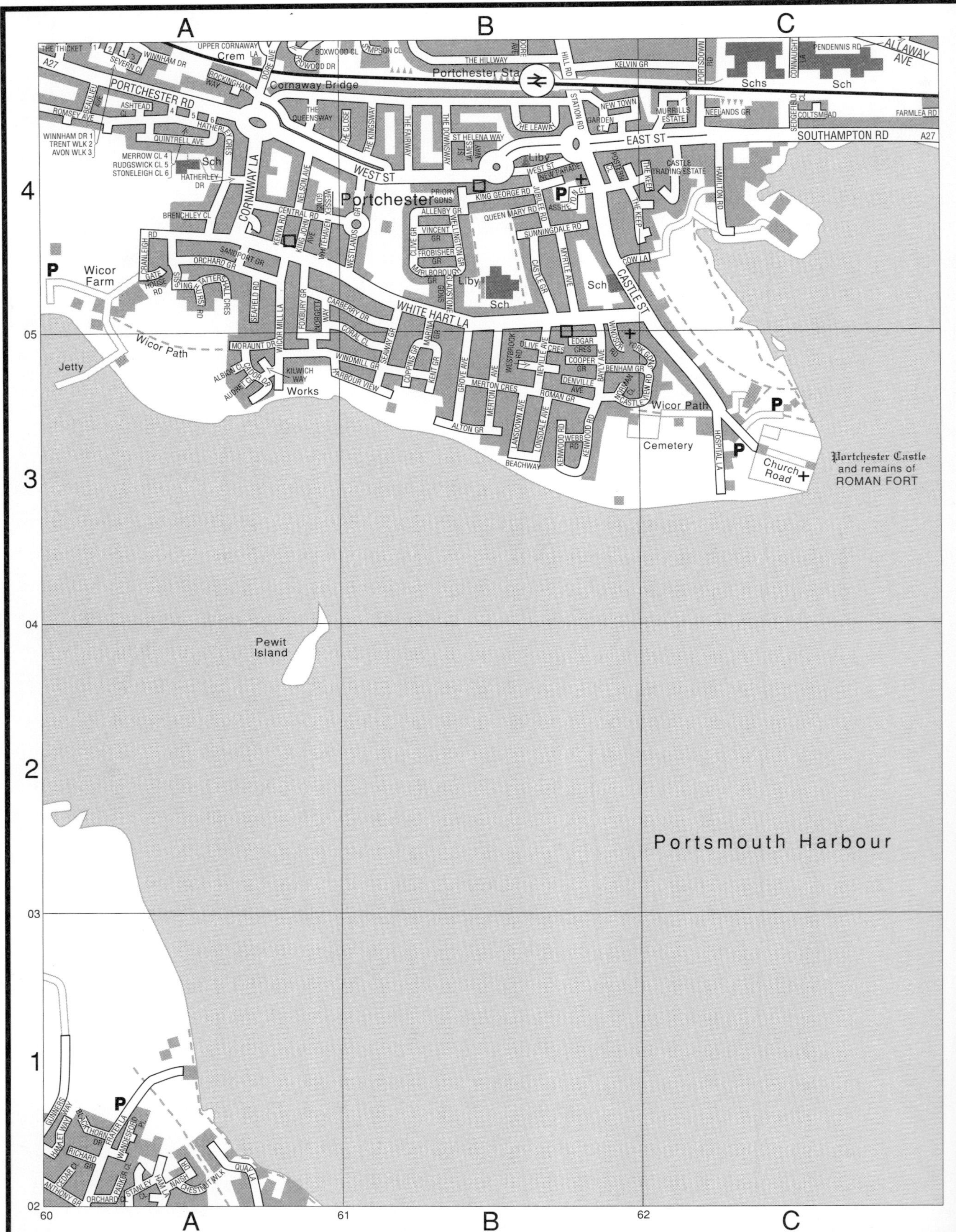
A
B
C
THE THICKET
SEVERN CL
WINNHAM DR
UPPER CORNAWAY LA
Crem
DORE AVE
BOXWOOD CL
SIMPSON CL
BOXWOOD DR
THE HILLWAY
DORE AVE
HILL RD
KELVIN GR
PORTSDOWN RD
CONNAUGHT LA
PENDENNIS RD
ALLAWAY AVE
A27
ROCKINGHAM WAY
Portchester Sta
Cornaway Bridge
Schs
Sch
PORTCHESTER RD
BEAULIEU AVE
ASHTEAD CL
ROMSEY AVE
WINNHAM DR 1
TRENT WLK 2
AVON WLK 3
MERROW CL 4
RUDGSWICK CL 5
STONELEIGH CL 6
QUINTRELL AVE
HATHERLEY CRES
HATHERLEY DR
Sch
THE QUEENSWAY
THE CLOSE
THE KINGSWAY
THE FAIRWAY
THE DOWNSWAY
ST HELENA WAY
ST JAMES WAY
THE LEAWAY
STATION RD
NEW TOWN
GARDEN CT
MURRILLS ESTATE
NEELANDS GR
SEDGEFIELD CL
COLTSMEAD
FARMLEA RD
EAST ST
SOUTHAMPTON RD
A27
CORNAWAY LA
WEST ST
Liby
WEST ST
NEW PARADE
POSTERN CL
THE KEEP
CASTLE TRADING ESTATE
HAMILTON RD
4
BRENCHLEY CL
NELSON AVE
Portchester
PRIORY GDNS
KING GEORGE RD
JUBILEE RD
ASSHETON CT
CENTRAL RD
KENYA RD
KING JOHN AVE
WHITEHAVEN
WESSEX GDNS
WESTLANDS GR
ALLENBY GR
QUEEN MARY RD
VINCENT GR
WELLINGTON GR
SUNNINGDALE RD
CLIVE GR
FROBISHER GR
MARLBOROUGH GR
GLADSTONE GDNS
THE KEEP
COW LA
CRANLEIGH RD
SANDPORT GR
ORCHARD GR
P
Wicor Farm
GATE HOUSE RD
SISSINGHURST RD
TATTERSHALL CRES
SEAFIELD RD
FOXBURY GR
NORGETT WAY
CARBERRY DR
Liby
Sch
CASTLE GR
MYRTLE AVE
Sch
CASTLE ST
WHITE HART LA
05
Wicor Path
Jetty
MORAUNT DR
WICOR MILL LA
CORAL CL
SEAWAY GR
MARINA GR
COPPINS GR
KENT GR
GROVE AVE
WESTBROOK RD
OLIVE CRES
EDGAR CRES
COOPER GR
DENVILLE AVE
NEVILLE AVE
BAYLY AVE
WINDSOR RD
YORK GDNS
BENHAM GR
NORMAN CL
NEW RD
CASTLE
ALBION CL
AUDRET CL
TUDOR DR
KILWICH WAY
Works
WINDMILL GR
HARBOUR VIEW
MERTON AVE
MERTON CRES
ROMAN GR
Wicor Path
ALTON GR
LANSDOWN AVE
LONSDALE AVE
KENWOOD RD
WEBB RD
KENWOOD RD
P
Cemetery
HOSPITAL LA
P
Church Road
Portchester Castle
and remains of
ROMAN FORT
BEACHWAY
3
04
Pewit Island
2
Portsmouth Harbour
03
1
P
GUNNERS WAY
HAMLET WAY
BLACKHORN DR
FRIATER LA
WANDESFORD PL
RICHARD GR
CEDAR CL
ANTHONY GR
PARKER CL
STANLEY CL
HAM LA
NAISH
CHESTNUT WLK
QUAY LA
ORCHARD GR
02
60
61
62
A
B
C

155

133

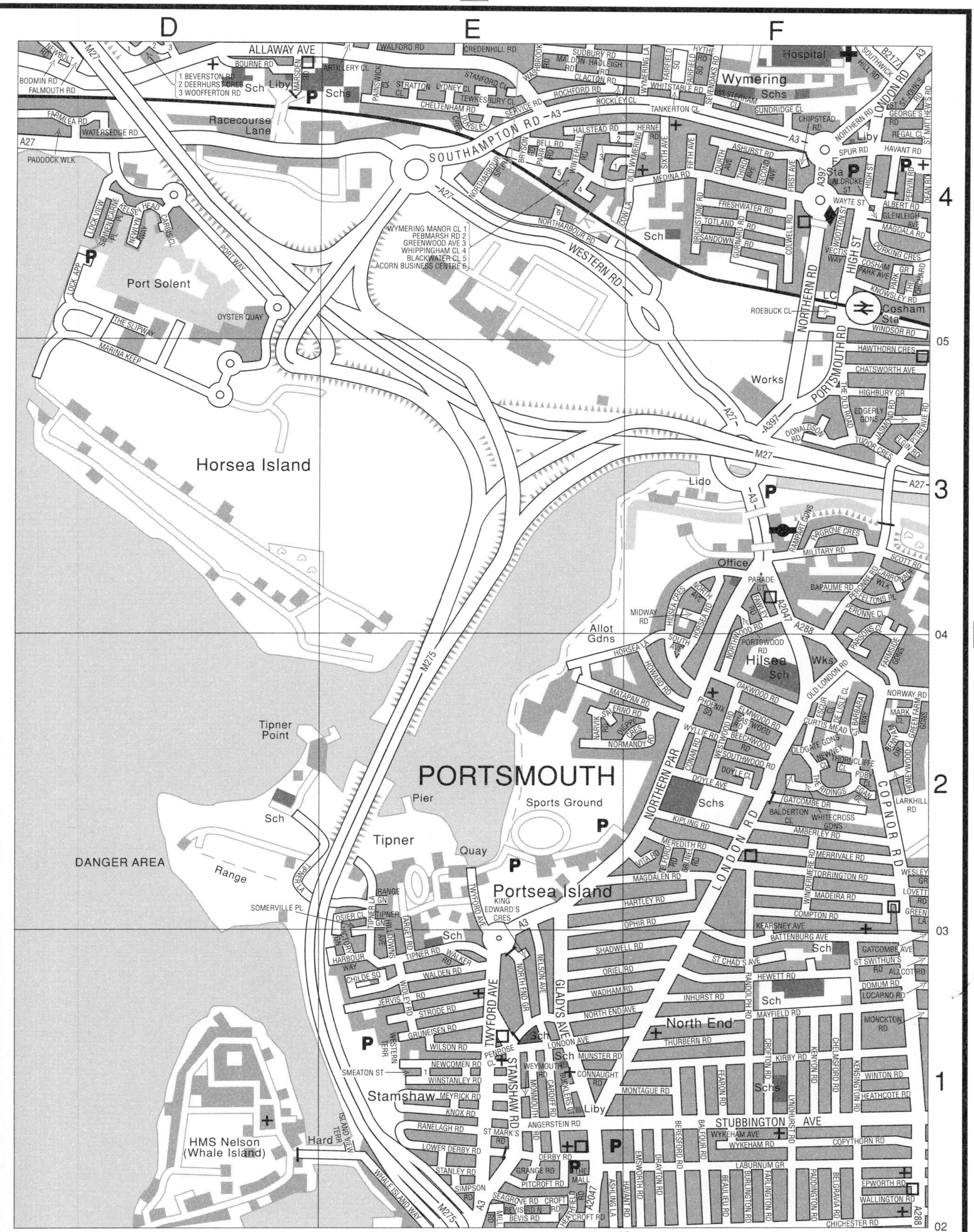
D
E
F
4
3
2
1
05
04
03
02
63
64
65
PORTSMOUTH
Horsea Island
Port Solent
Wymering
Hilsea
Portsea Island
Tipner
North End
Stamshaw
HMS Nelson
(Whale Island)
Tipner Point
DANGER AREA
Range
Racecourse Lane
Cosham Sta
Sports Ground
Allot Gdns
Lido
Hospital
Works
Pier
Quay
Hard
M27
M275
A27
A3
A397
A2047
A288
SOUTHAMPTON RD
WESTERN RD
NORTHERN RD
PORTSMOUTH RD
HIGH ST
LONDON RD
COPNOR RD
NORTHERN PAR
STUBBINGTON AVE
TWYFORD AVE
STAMSHAW RD
GLADYS AVE
ALLAWAY AVE
NORTHARBOUR RD
OYSTER QUAY
THE SLIPWAY
MARINA KEEP
PORT WAY
MILITARY RD
HORSEA LA
TIPNER LA
WHALE ISLAND WAY
1 BEVERSTON RD
2 DEERHURST CRES
3 WOOFFERTON RD
WYMERING MANOR CL 1
PEBMARSH RD 2
GREENWOOD AVE 3
WHIPPINGHAM CL 4
BLACKWATER CL 5
ACORN BUSINESS CENTRE 6

158

182

134

157

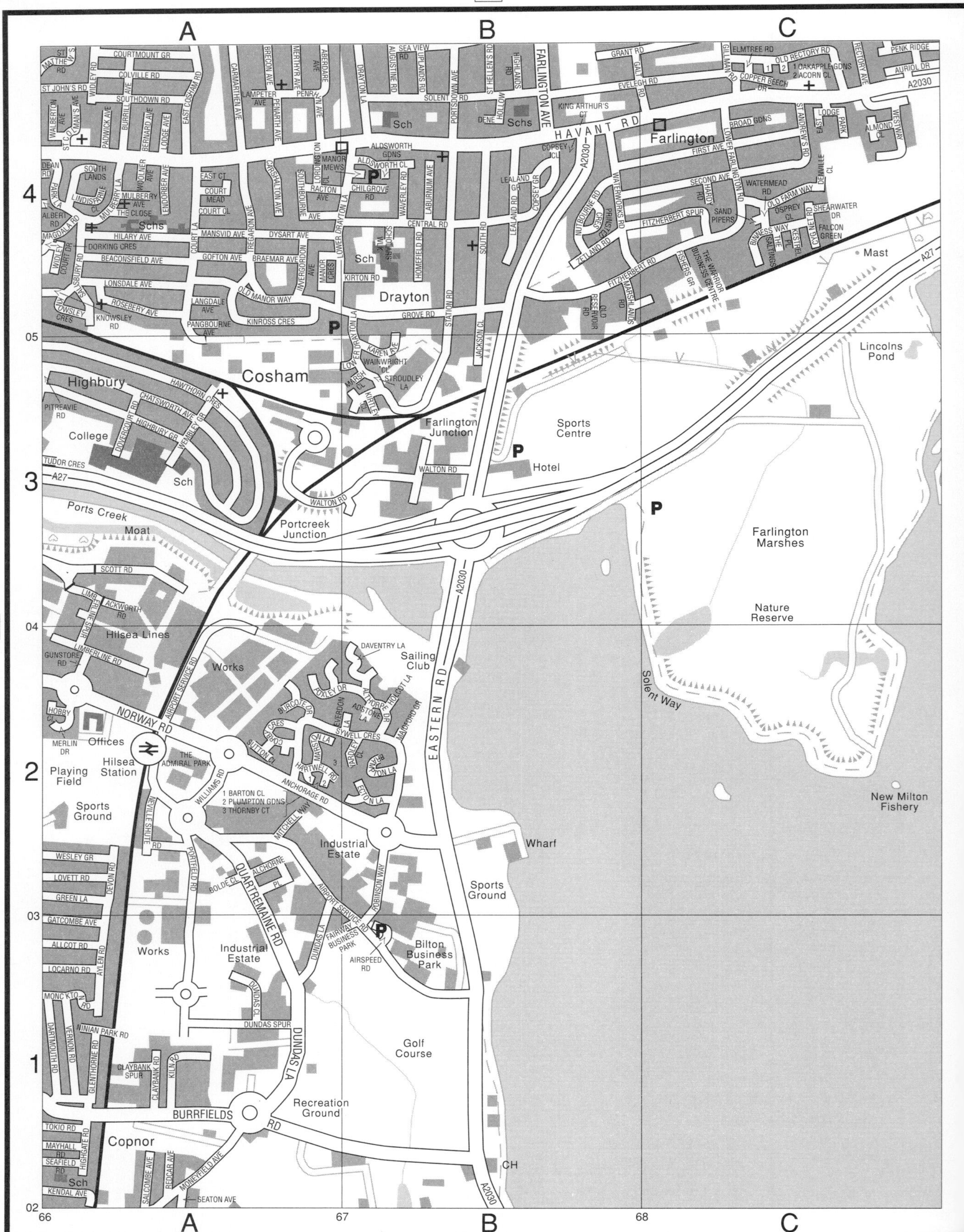
A
B
C
4
3
2
1
05
04
03
02
66
67
68
COURTMOUNT GR
COLVILLE RD
SOUTHDOWN RD
ST JOHN'S RD
ST MATTHEW'S RD
WIDLEY RD
EAST COSHAM RD
CARMARTHEN AVE
BRECON AVE
MERTHYR AVE
ABERDARE AVE
LAMPETER AVE
PENARTH AVE
DRAYTON LA
AUGUSTINE RD
SEA VIEW RD
UPLANDS RD
PORTSDOWN AVE
SOLENT RD
ST HELEN'S RD
HIGHLANDS RD
DENE HOLLOW
FARLINGTON AVE
GRANT RD
EVELEGH RD
ELMTREE RD
GILLMAN RD
OLD RECTORY RD
1 OAKAPPLE GDNS
2 ACORN CL
COPPER BEECH DR
RECTORY AVE
PENK RIDGE
AURIOL DR
A2030
KING ARTHUR'S CT
HAVANT RD
Farlington
BROAD GDNS
ST ANDREW'S RD
LODGE
EAST PARK
WESTWAY
ALMOND CL
FIRST AVE
SECOND AVE
LOWER FARLINGTON RD
WATERMEAD RD
OLD FARM WAY
DENVILLE CL
OSPREY CL
SHEARWATER DR
FALCON GREEN
BINNESS WAY
THE SALTINGS
KESTREL PL
CYGNET RD
FITZHERBERT SPUR
SAND PIPERS
HARDY RD
WATERWORKS RD
NUTBOURNE RD
PRINSTED CRES
ZETLAND RD
FITZHERBERT RD
FISHERS GR
THE WARRIOR BUSINESS CENTRE
MARSHLANDS RD
OLD RESERVOIR RD
COPSEY CL
COPSEY GR
LEALAND GR
LEALAND RD
Mast
A27
Sch
Schs
WALBERTON AVE
ST COLMAN'S AVE
PADWICK AVE
BURRILL AVE
BERNARD AVE
LODGE AVE
DEAN RD
PARK LA
ALBERT RD
SOUTH LANDS
LINDISFARNE CL
MULBERRY LA
MULBERRY AVE
WOOLNER AVE
THE CLOSE
ENDORBER AVE
EAST CT
COURT MEAD
COURT CL
COURT LA
MAGDALA RD
HILARY AVE
DORKING CRES
BEACONSFIELD AVE
LONSDALE AVE
WIDLEY COURT DR
SALISBURY RD
ROSEBERY AVE
KNOWSLEY CRES
KNOWSLEY RD
MANSVID AVE
GOFTON AVE
TREGARON AVE
DYSART AVE
BRAEMAR AVE
CARSHALTON AVE
SOUTHBOURNE AVE
LORDINGTON CL
MANOR MEWS
ALDSWORTH GDNS
ALDSWORTH CL
RACTON AVE
CHILGROVE RD
WAVERLEY RD
LABURNUM AVE
CENTRAL RD
SOUTH RD
HOMEFIELD RD
SCHOLARS WLK
LOWER DRAYTON LA
INVERGORDON AVE
MANOR CRES
KIRTON RD
OLD MANOR WAY
LANGDALE AVE
PANGBOURNE AVE
KINROSS CRES
GROVE RD
STATION RD
JACKSON CL
Drayton
Cosham
KAREN AVE
WAINWRIGHT CL
STROUDLEY LA
MARSH CL
KIRTLEY CL
Highbury
HAWTHORN CRES
CHATSWORTH AVE
HIGHBURY GR
DOVERCOURT RD
WEMBLEY GR
PITREAVIE RD
College
TUDOR CRES
Farlington Junction
WALTON RD
Sports Centre
Hotel
Lincolns Pond
Ports Creek
Moat
Portcreek Junction
Farlington Marshes
Nature Reserve
Solent Way
SCOTT RD
LIMBERLINE SPUR
ACKWORTH RD
Hilsea Lines
GUNSTORE RD
LIMBERLINE RD
AIRPORT SERVICE RD
Works
DAVENTRY LA
Sailing Club
HOLCOT LA
ALTHORPE DR
FOXLEY DR
BURCOTE DR
EVERDON LA
ADSTONE LA
SYWELL CRES
MAIDFORD GR
CORBY CRES
SUTTON CL
MARSTON LA
YARDLEY CL
BRIXWORTH CL
HARTWELL RD
ECTON LA
EASTERN RD
HOBBY CL
MERLIN DR
NORWAY RD
Offices
Hilsea Station
THE ADMIRAL PARK
WILLIAMS RD
ANCHORAGE RD
1 BARTON CL
2 PLUMPTON GDNS
3 THORNBY CT
MITCHELL WAY
Playing Field
Sports Ground
NEVILLE SHUTE RD
PORTFIELD RD
Industrial Estate
Wharf
WESLEY GR
LOVETT RD
GREEN LA
DEVON RD
GATCOMBE AVE
ALLCOT RD
LOCARNO RD
AYLEN RD
MONCKTON RD
QUARTREMAINE RD
BOLDE CL
ALCHORNE PL
ROBINSON WAY
DUNDAS LA
FAIRWAY BUSINESS PARK
AIRSPEED RD
Bilton Business Park
Sports Ground
New Milton Fishery
DUNDAS CL
DUNDAS SPUR
NINIAN PARK RD
DARTMOUTH RD
VERNON RD
GLENTHORNE RD
CLAYBANK SPUR
CLAYBANK RD
KILN RD
Golf Course
Recreation Ground
BURRFIELDS RD
TOKIO RD
MAYHALL RD
SEAFIELD RD
HIGHGATE RD
KENDAL AVE
Copnor
SALCOMBE AVE
REDCAR AVE
MONEYFIELD AVE
SEATON AVE
CH

135

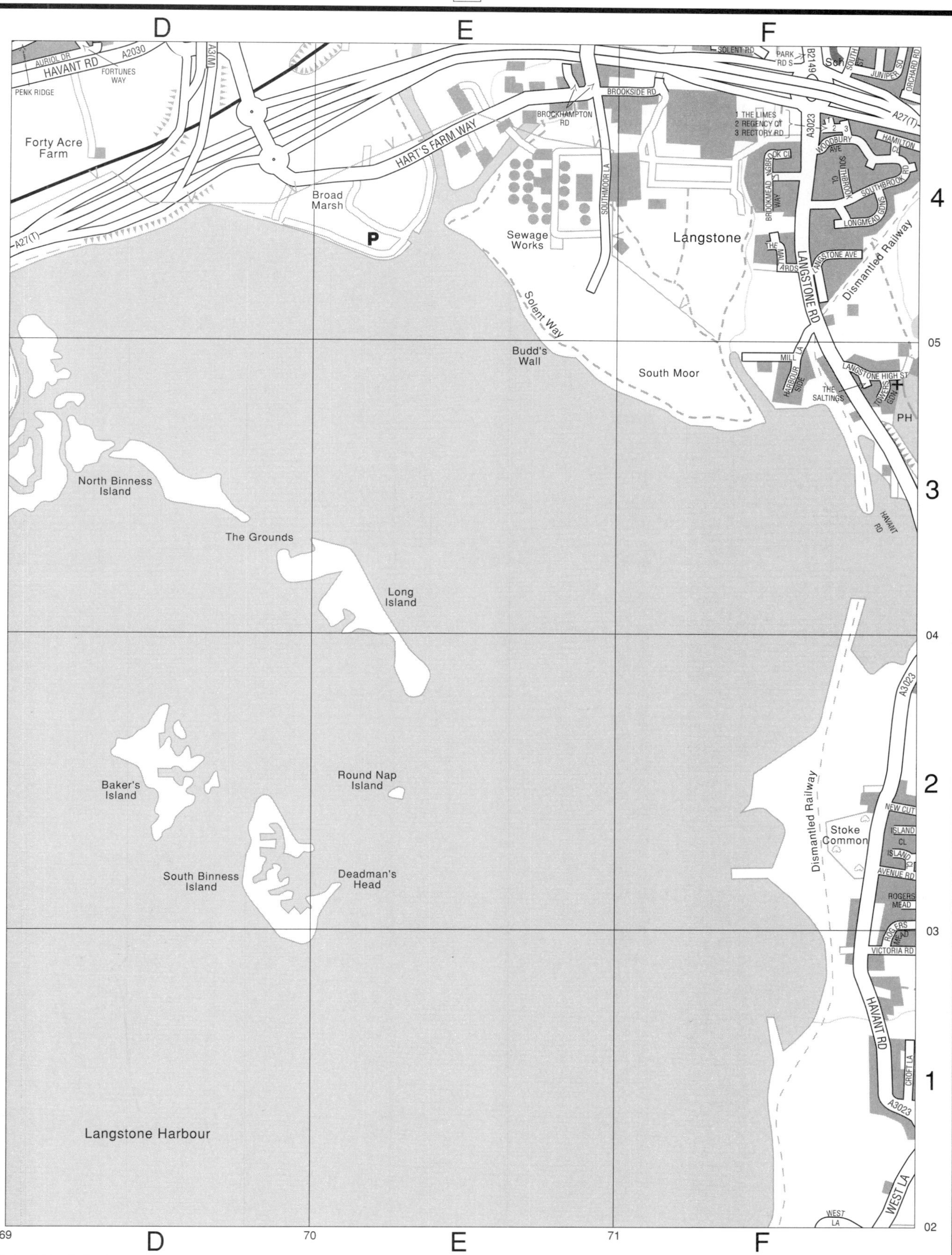

D
E
F
HAVANT RD
AURIOL DR
A2030
FORTUNES WAY
PENK RIDGE
A3(M)
Forty Acre Farm
A27(T)
Broad Marsh
P
HART'S FARM WAY
BROCKHAMPTON RD
BROOKSIDE RD
SOLENT RD
PARK RD S
B2149
Sch
SOUTH ST
JUNIPER SQ
ORCHARD RD
1 THE LIMES
2 REGENCY CT
3 RECTORY RD
A3023
WOODBURY AVE
HAMILTON CL
SOUTHBROOK CL
SOUTHBROOK RD
LONGMEAD GDNS
BROOKMEAD WAY
Sewage Works
SOUTHMOOR LA
Langstone
THE MALLARDS
LANGSTONE AVE
LANGSTONE RD
Dismantled Railway
Solent Way
Budd's Wall
South Moor
MILL LA
HARBOUR SIDE
LANGSTONE HIGH ST
THE SALTINGS
TOWERS GDN
PH
North Binness Island
The Grounds
Long Island
HAVANT RD
Baker's Island
Round Nap Island
South Binness Island
Deadman's Head
Dismantled Railway
Stoke Common
NEW CUT
ISLAND CL
ISLAND
AVENUE RD
ROGERS MEAD
VICTORIA RD
HAVANT RD
CROFT LA
A3023
Langstone Harbour
WEST LA
4
3
2
1
05
04
03
02
69
70
71

160

184

136

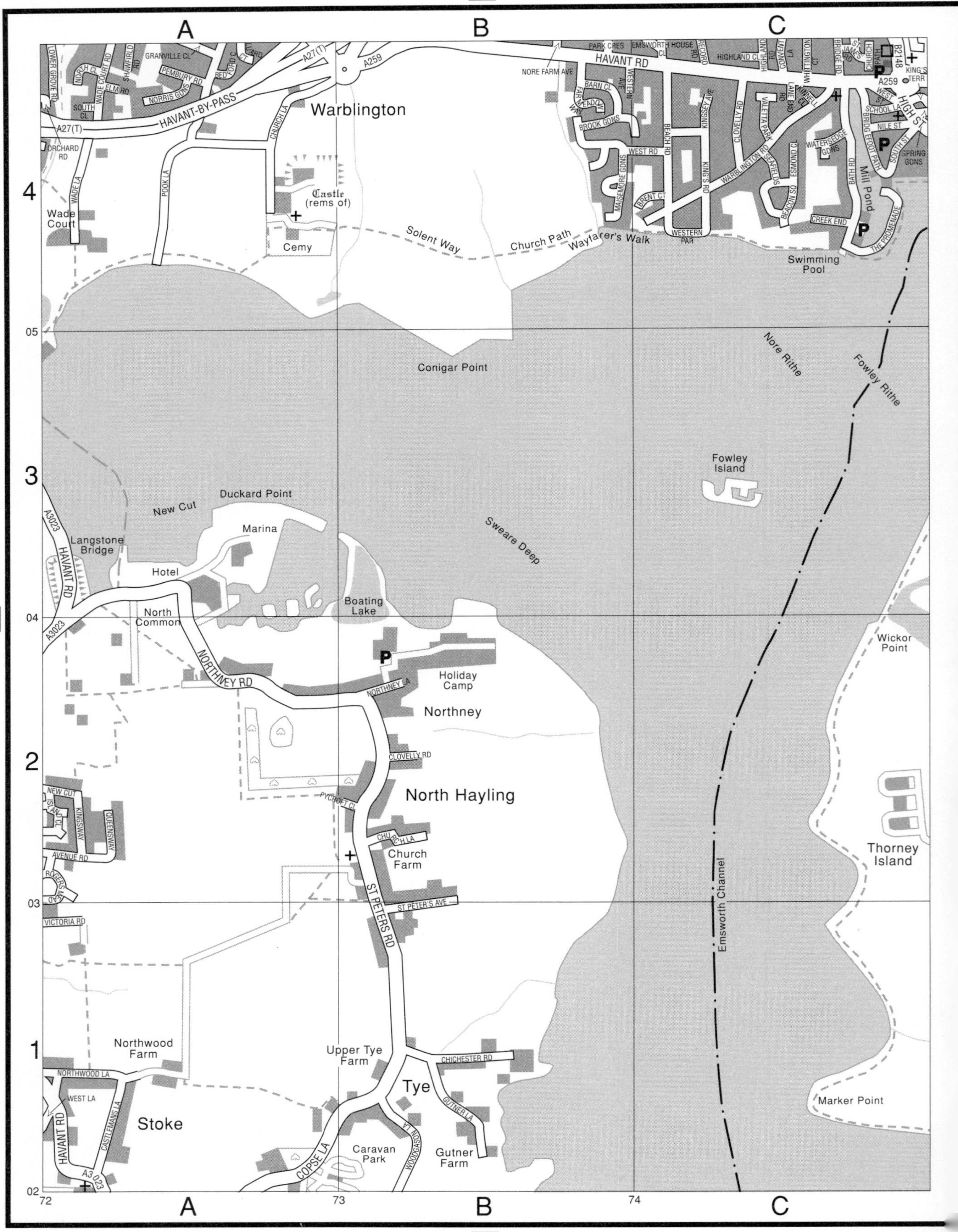
A
B
C
4
3
2
1
05
04
03
02
72
73
74
Warblington
HAVANT-BY-PASS
A27(T)
A259
HAVANT RD
PARK CRES
EMSWORTH HOUSE CL
NORE FARM AVE
HIGHLAND CL
GRANVILLE CL
PEMBURY RD
NORRIS GDNS
LOWER GROVE RD
NORTH CL
WADE COURT RD
ELM RD
SOUTH CL
ORCHARD RD
WADE LA
POOK LA
CHURCH LA
Wade Court
Castle (rems of)
Cemy
Solent Way
Church Path
Wayfarer's Walk
BARN CL
BROOK GDNS
WEST RD
MAISEMORE GDNS
BRENT CT
BEACH RD
KINGSEY AVE
KING'S RD
CLOVELLY RD
VALETTA PARK
WARBLINGTON RD
SEAFIELDS
BEACON SQ
ESMOND CL
LANE END
WATERSEDGE GDNS
BATH RD
Mill Pond
CREEK END
THE PROMENADE
WESTERN PAR
SCHOOL LA
NILE ST
SOUTH ST
SPRING GDNS
HIGH ST
KING'S TERR
B2148
Swimming Pool
Conigar Point
Nore Rithe
Fowley Rithe
Fowley Island
New Cut
Duckard Point
Marina
Sweare Deep
A3023
HAVANT RD
Langstone Bridge
Hotel
Boating Lake
North Common
NORTHNEY RD
NORTHNEY LA
Holiday Camp
Northney
CLOVELLY RD
North Hayling
PYCROFT CL
CHURCH LA
Church Farm
ST PETER'S AVE
ST PETERS RD
NEW CUT
KINGSWAY
QUEENSWAY
AVENUE RD
ROGERS MEAD
VICTORIA RD
Wickor Point
Thorney Island
Emsworth Channel
Northwood Farm
NORTHWOOD LA
WEST LA
CASTLEMANS LA
Stoke
Upper Tye Farm
Tye
CHICHESTER RD
GUTNER LA
Gutner Farm
Caravan Park
COPSE LA
WOODGASTON LA
Marker Point

159

185

137

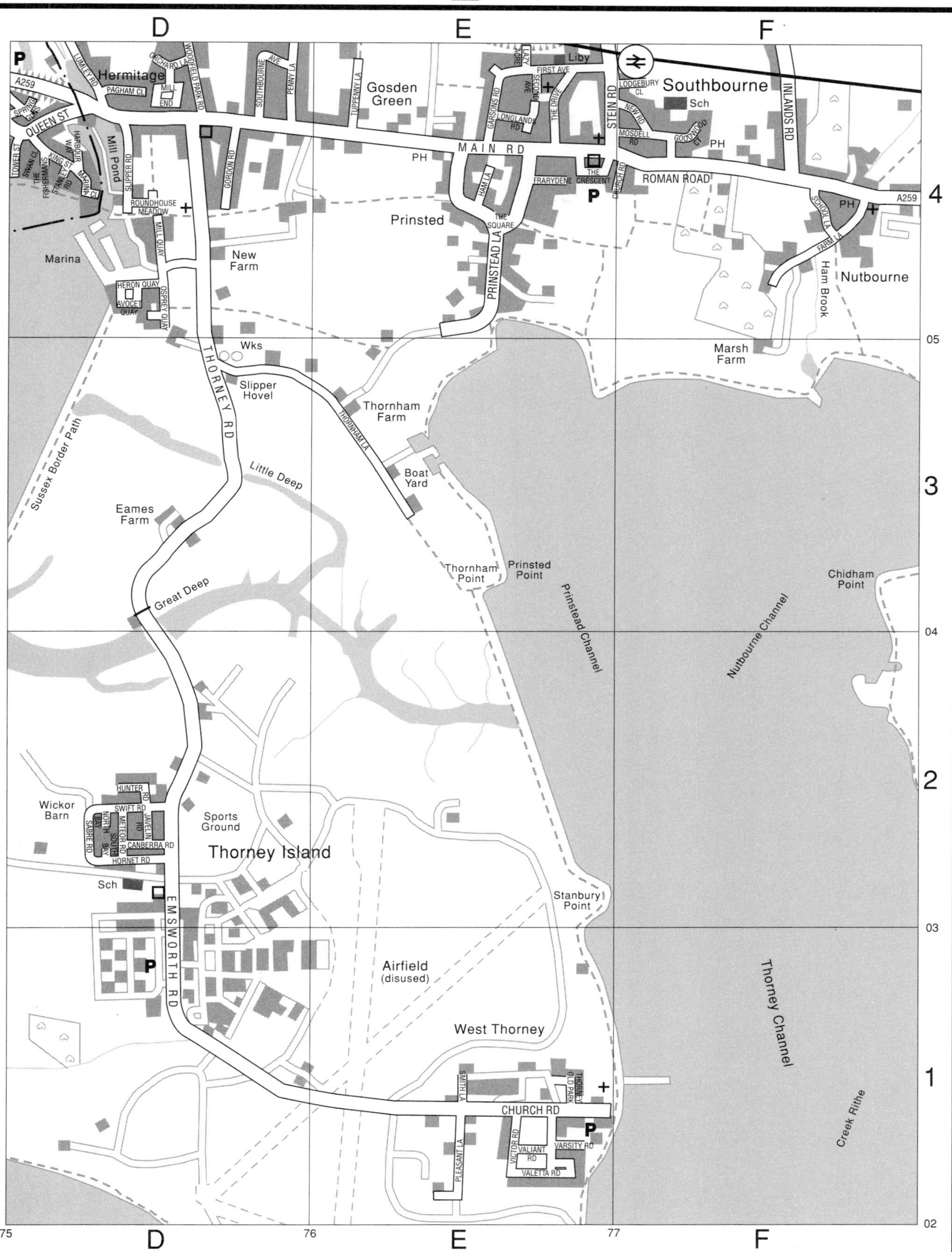

not continued, see key diagram

186

not continued, see key diagram

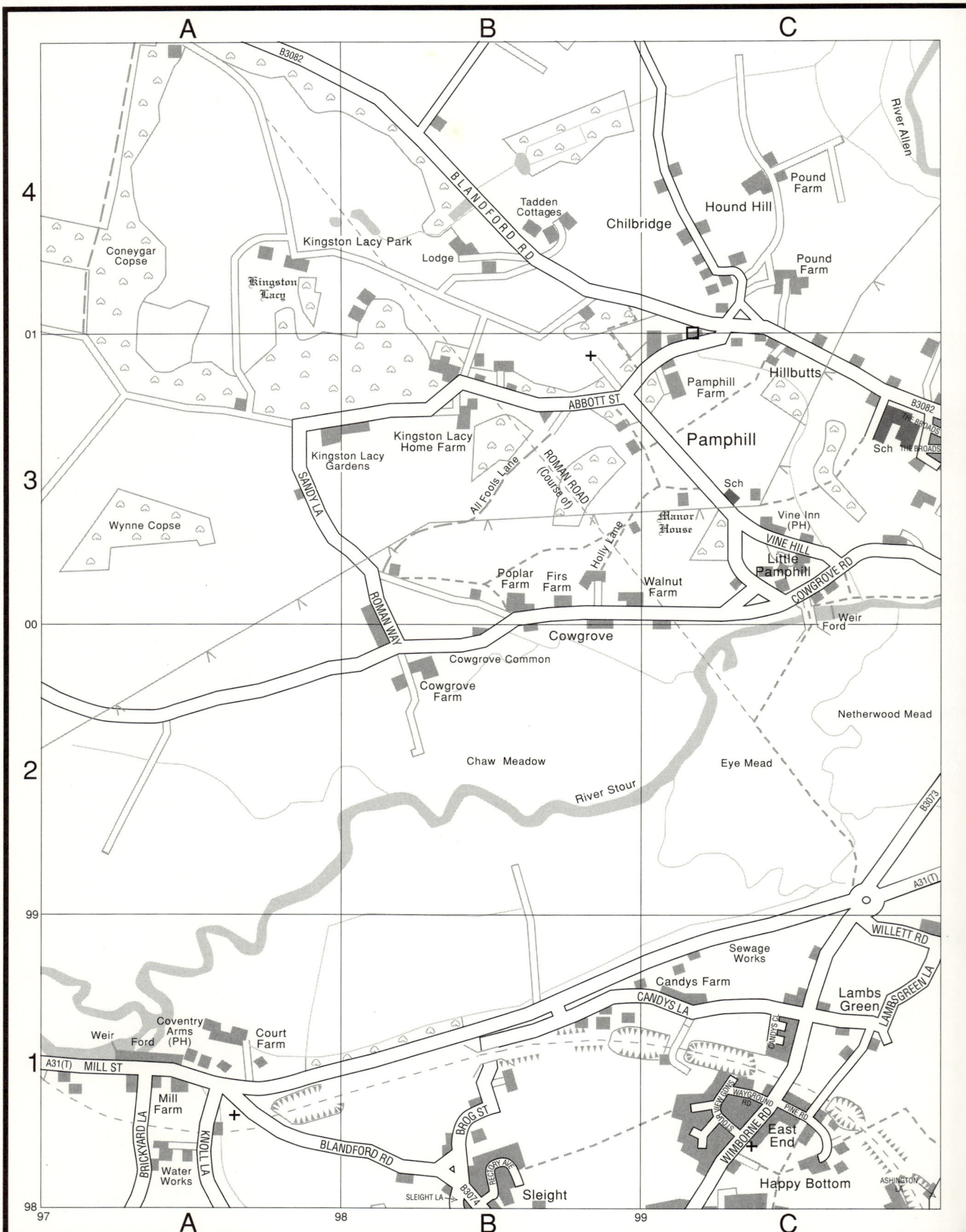

not continued, see key diagram

not continued, see key diagram

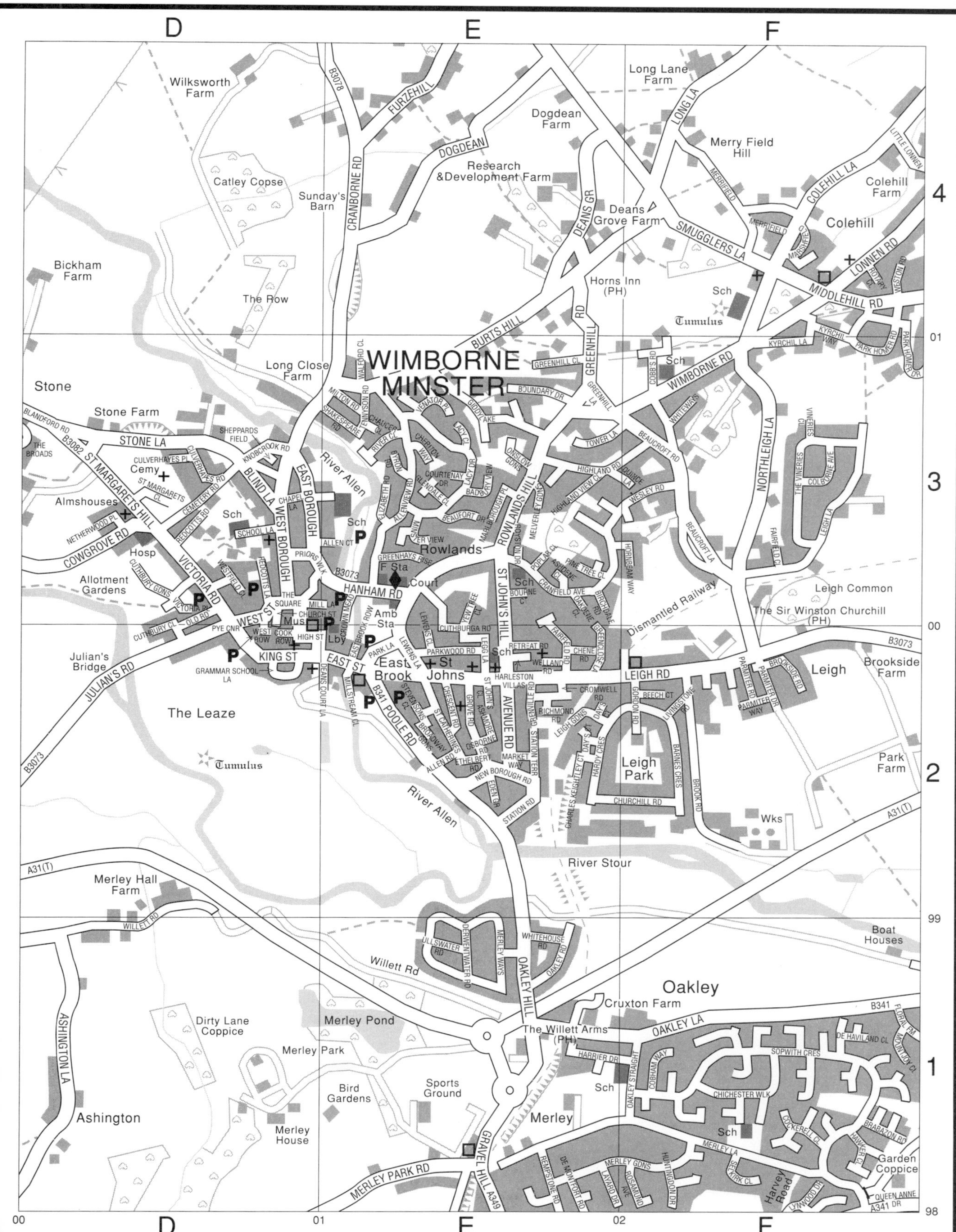

164

188

not continued, see key diagram

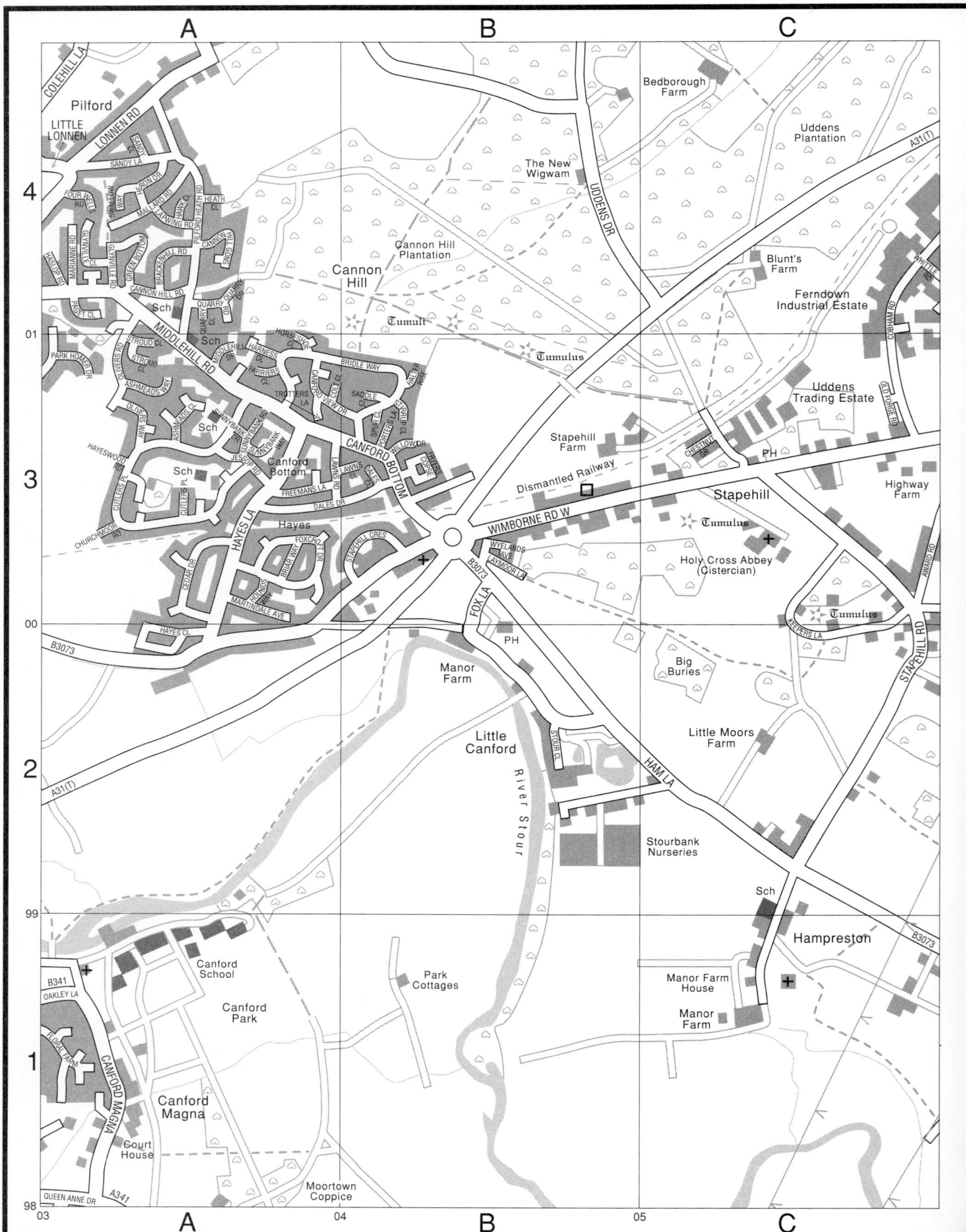

163

138

D
E
F
Uddens Plantation
A31(T)
COBHAM RD
TELFORD RD
Ferndown Industrial Estate
HAVILAND RD
WHITTLE RD
BRICKYARD LA
ST JAMES RD
AWARD RD
PADDOCK CL
FOREST VIEW DR
FOREST WAY
LEESON DR
KINGSWAY
STONECHAT CL
NUTHATCH CL
BUNTING RD
DUNNOCK CL
SISKIN CL
HILLTOP RD
KESTREL
HILLTOP CL
CURLEW CL
LARKS RISE
LARKS CL
BRACKEN RD
CLAY FORD AVE
CLAYFORD AVE
RED OAKS CL
BRACKEN RD
COPPICE AVE
WARREN WLK
PRUNUS CL
PRUNUS DR
LABURNUM CL
HILL VIEW RD
PH
PINE GLEN AVE
AMESFORD RD
HILL CREST AVE
PINE CL
RYAN CL
RYAN GDNS
ELFIN DR
THE LAURELS
JUNIPER CL
CEDAR WAY
REDWOOD DR
MAPLE DR
LARCH WAY
WILLOW WAY
HAZEL DR
ROBINSWOOD DR
PINEWOOD RD
BEAUFOYS AVE
BEAUFOYS CL
QUEENSWOOD DR
QUEENS RD
PINEWOOD GDNS
HEATHER WAY
HEATHER DR
EVERGLADES CL
HIGH TREES WLK
LYNWOOD CL
WEST MOORS RD
B3072
Uddens Water
Cemy
A31(T)
MARTINS CL
MARTINS DR
MARTINS WAY
STEWARTS WAY
GARDEN WLK
Gladelands Mobile Home Park
WOODLAND WLK
A347
FORD CL
Trickett's Cross
AMEYS LA
PICKARD RD
TURBARY RD
LOCKYERS DR
TRICKETTS LA
STAPLEHURST AVE
FAIRWAYS
GREENSOME DR
GLENEAGLES CL
DUGDELL CL
WIMBORNE RD E
MONKTON CL
WHINCROFT CL
WHINCROFT DR
POMONA CL
BRAMLEY RD
MALBOURNE RD
MAYFIELD DR
MAYFIELD CL
MAYFIELD WAY
RUSSET CL
STANFIELD RD
CARTER CL
Tumulus
CHERRY GR
School
Playing Field
Ferndown
CHURCH RD
WESTWOOD AVE
SOUTHWOOD AVE
PENROSE RD
ALBERT RD
VICTORIA RD
VICTORIA GDNS
GLENDALE AVE
WOODSIDE RD
EASTWOOD AVE
WOODSIDE CL
GREENWOOD AVE
PRINCES RD
MANOR CL
APPLETREE GR
PRINGLES CL
PRINGLES DR
ORCHARD CL
CARROLL AVE
LIBRARY RD
P
PENNY'S WLK
Liby
B3072
A347
Fire Sta
ST MARY'S RD
SPINNEYS LA
Schools
MOUNTBATTEN DR
A348
RINGWOOD RD
Golf Course
CRAIGWOOD DR
GOLF LINKS RD
Great Barrow
Tumulus
BRABOURNE AVE
LONGACRE DR
FERNLEA CL
FERNLEA AVE
LEA GDNS
FERN BARROW
CHANDER CL
MELBURY CL
WOODACRE GDNS
DUDSBURY CRES
OLD PINES CL
DUDSBURY AVE
SHERBORNE DR
WINCOMBE DR
STALBRIDGE DR
DORSET AVE
MORDEN AVE
THE GROVE
ST GEORGE'S DR
CLIFTON GDNS
Pompey's Corner
The Roughs
Pompeys Lane
Tumuli
Big Copse
CH
EVENING GLADE
Hotel
Parley Common
HEATH FARM CL
HEATH FARM RD
HEATH FARM WAY
MONSAL AVE
GLENMOOR RD
SHERWOOD AVE
LOCKSLEY DR
MATLOCK RD
DARLEY RD
WOLLATON RD
WOLLATON CRES
Sch
DUNEDIN CL
DUNEDIN DR
ST JUST CL
ANGEL LA
Coneygar Lane
PH
GORSELANDS CT
NEW RD
ALDRIDGE RD
LONE PINE DR
DANE DR
Beacon Farm
B3073
HAM LA
GLISSONS
HIGH MEAD
Holmwood
Holmwood Park
PLECY CL
BERKLEY AVE
BELMORE WAY
EBOR CL
CRESTA GDNS
LONE PINE WAY
LONE PINE DR
FITZPAIN RD
FITZPAIN CL
CAMMEL RD
CAMMEL CL
ELLESFIELD DR
MANSFIELD CL
DRUIDS CL
WIGHT WLK
MAG'S BARROW
WINNARDS CLOSE
Ralph's Barrow
Belle Vue Barrow
HADRIAN CL
BELLE VUE WLK
CRESCENT WLK
HEATHLANDS AVE
HIGH MEAD LA
PH
Dudsbury Hill
LINDEN CL
LINDEN RD
BURNBRAE RD
DUDSBURY RD
MEADOW CL
GALLOWS DR
CHINE WLK
Mag's Barrow
West Parley
BRIERLEY AVE
BIRCH AVE
CONIFER CL
OAKLAND WLK
Parley Wood
GREEN LA
CHRISTCHURCH RD
Hillamsland
Longham
Dudsbury
YOLLINCH CL
OAK CL
DENE WLK
A347
PARLEY CL
A348
Longham Farm
PH
4
3
2
1
01
00
99
98
06
07
08

166

190

139

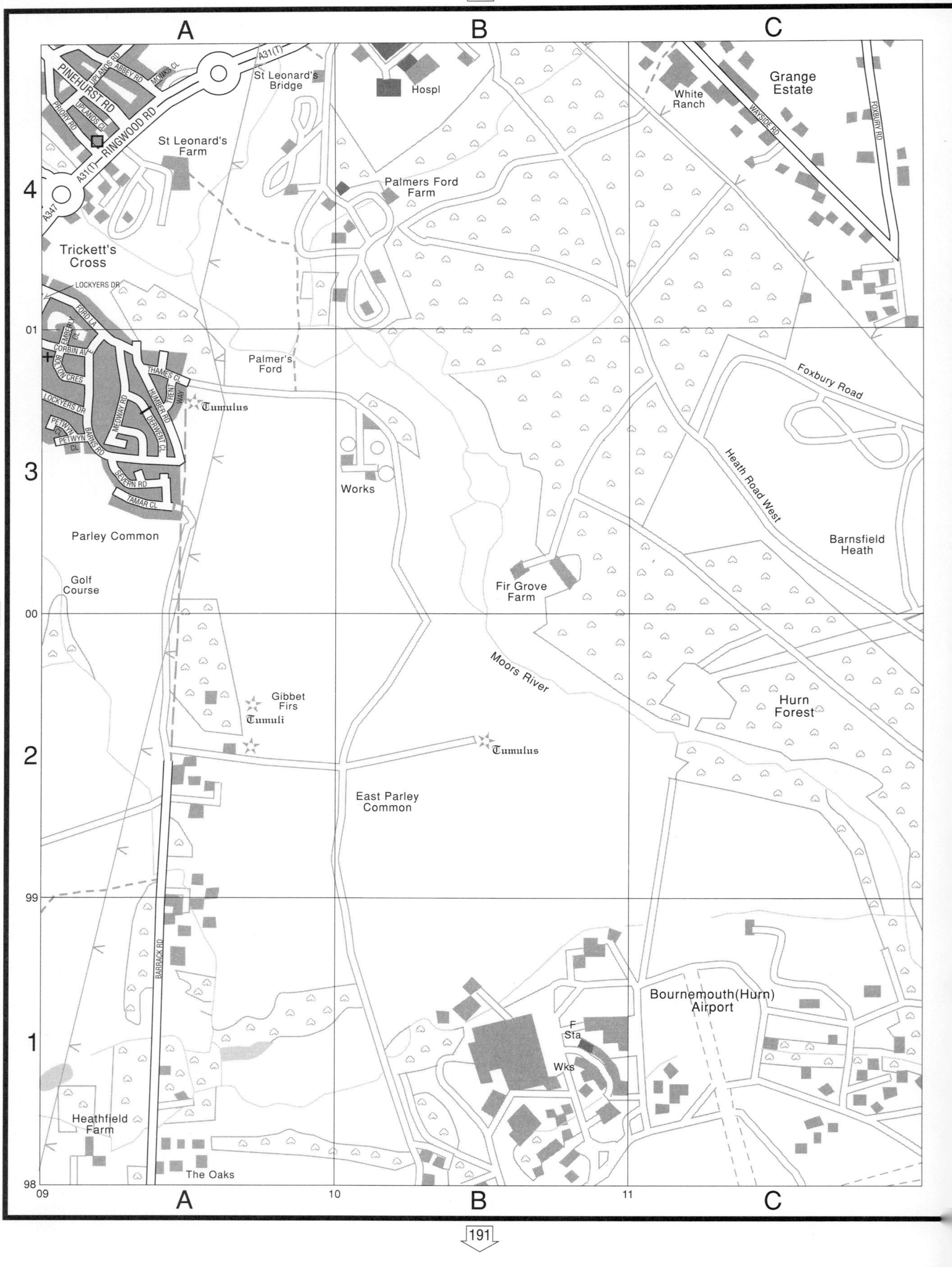
A
B
C
St Leonard's Bridge
Hospl
Grange Estate
White Ranch
PINEHURST RD
UPLANDS RD
ABBEY RD
MONKS CL
A31(T)
RINGWOOD RD
PRIORY RD
UPLANDS CL
A31(T)
A347
St Leonard's Farm
Palmers Ford Farm
WAYSIDE RD
FOXBURY RD
4
Trickett's Cross
LOCKYERS DR
FORD LA
CORBIN AV
BOLTON CRES
LOCKYERS DR
PETWYN CL
BARNS RD
MEDWAY RD
HUMBER RD
DERWENT CL
THAMES CL
TRENT WAY
SEVERN RD
TAMAR CL
01
Palmer's Ford
Tumulus
Foxbury Road
Heath Road West
3
Works
Parley Common
Barnsfield Heath
Golf Course
Fir Grove Farm
00
Moors River
Gibbet Firs
Tumuli
Hurn Forest
2
Tumulus
East Parley Common
99
BARRACK RD
Bournemouth(Hurn) Airport
1
F Sta
Wks
Heathfield Farm
The Oaks
98
09
10
11
A
B
C

165

191

140

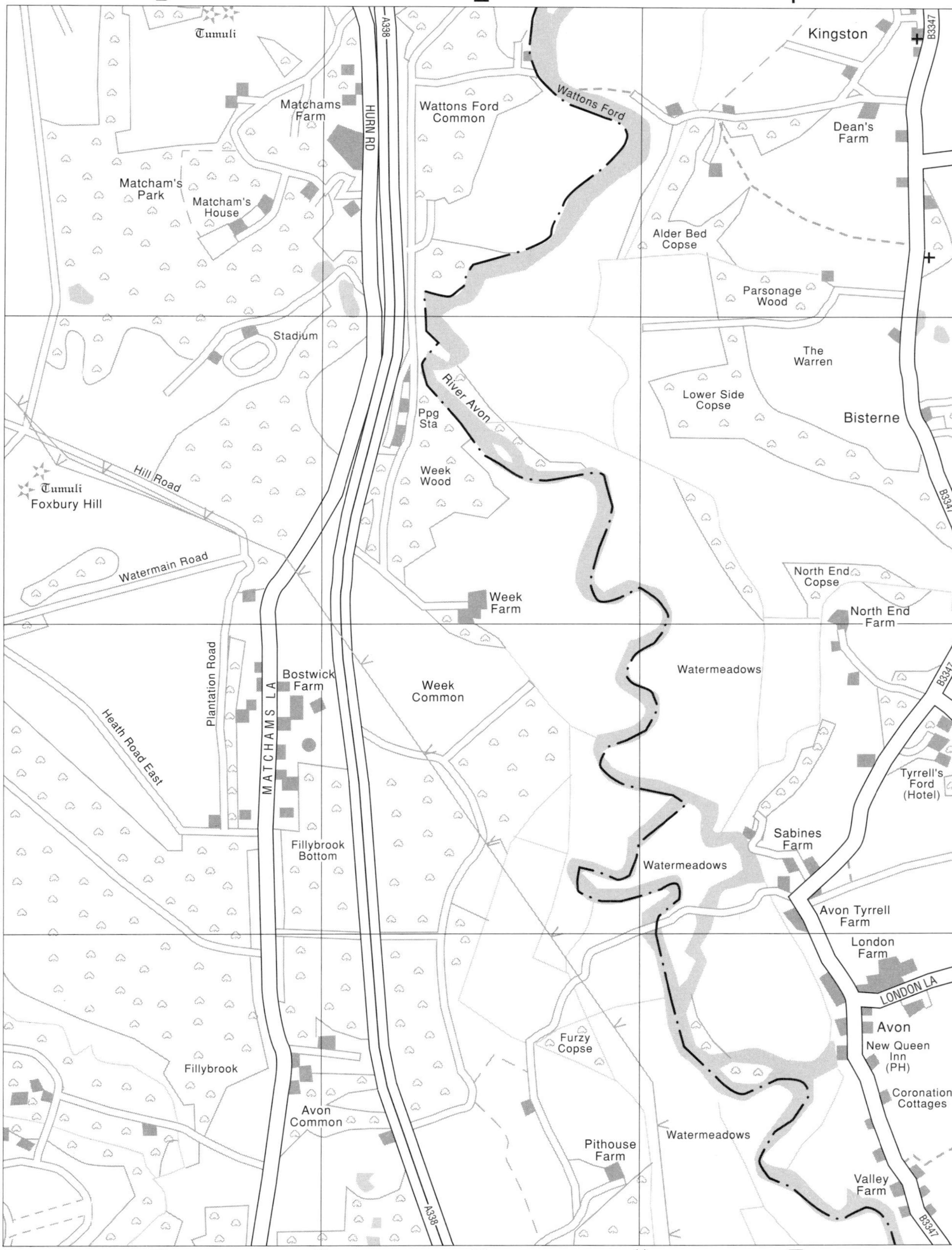
D
E
F
Tumuli
Matchams Farm
Matcham's Park
Matcham's House
HURN RD
A338
Wattons Ford Common
Wattons Ford
Kingston
B3347
Dean's Farm
4
Alder Bed Copse
Parsonage Wood
01
Stadium
The Warren
Lower Side Copse
Bisterne
River Avon
Ppg Sta
Week Wood
Hill Road
Tumuli
Foxbury Hill
3
Watermain Road
North End Copse
Week Farm
North End Farm
00
Watermeadows
Plantation Road
Bostwick Farm
Week Common
Heath Road East
MATCHAMS LA
2
Tyrrell's Ford (Hotel)
Sabines Farm
Fillybrook Bottom
Watermeadows
Avon Tyrrell Farm
99
London Farm
LONDON LA
Avon
Furzy Copse
New Queen Inn (PH)
Fillybrook
1
Coronation Cottages
Avon Common
Watermeadows
Pithouse Farm
Valley Farm
98
12
13
14

168

192

141

167

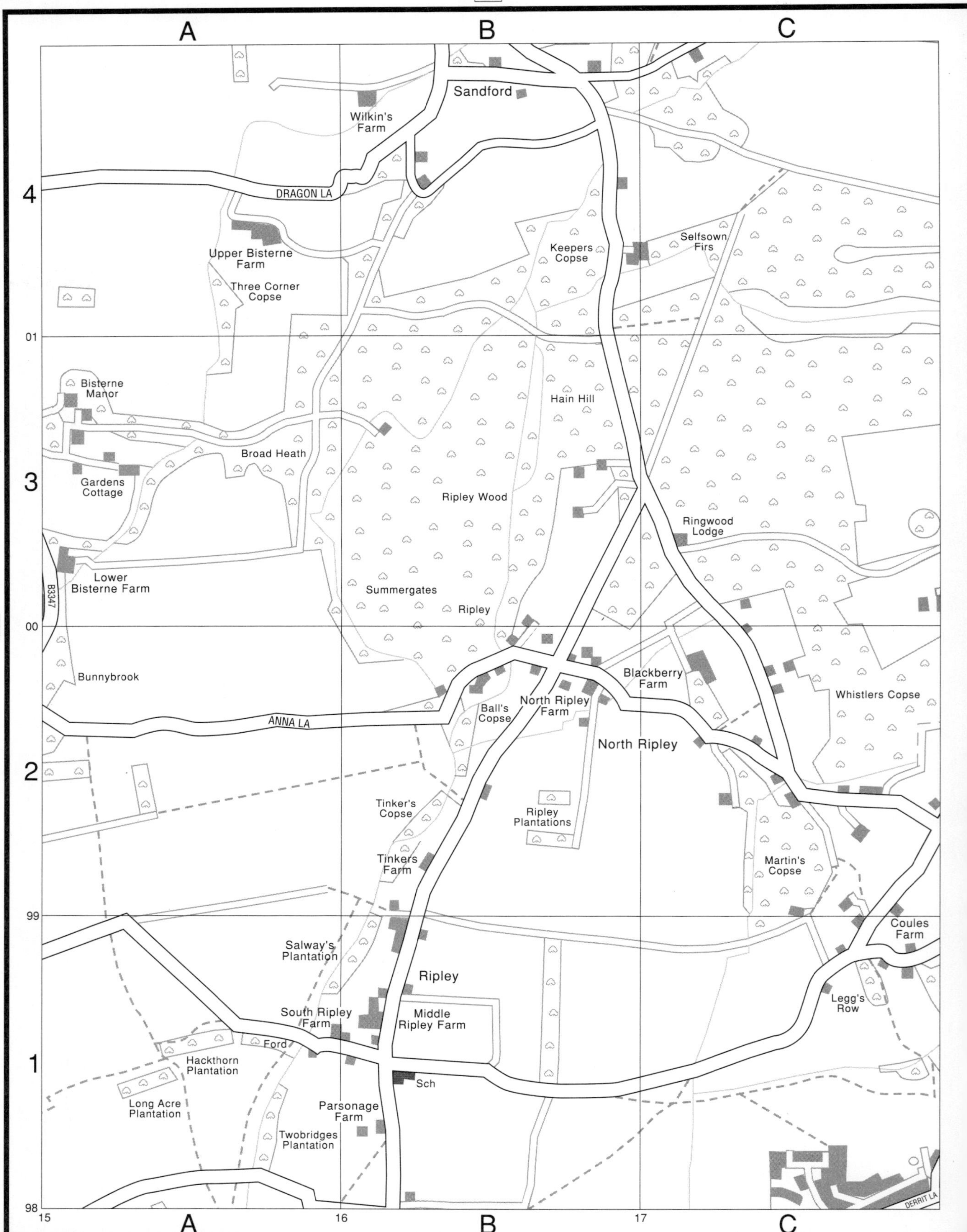
A
B
C
4
01
3
00
2
99
1
98
15
16
17
Sandford
Wilkin's Farm
DRAGON LA
Upper Bisterne Farm
Three Corner Copse
Keepers Copse
Selfsown Firs
Bisterne Manor
Hain Hill
Broad Heath
Gardens Cottage
Ripley Wood
Ringwood Lodge
Lower Bisterne Farm
B3347
Summergates
Ripley
Bunnybrook
Blackberry Farm
Whistlers Copse
North Ripley Farm
Ball's Copse
ANNA LA
North Ripley
Tinker's Copse
Ripley Plantations
Tinkers Farm
Martin's Copse
Coules Farm
Salway's Plantation
Ripley
Legg's Row
South Ripley Farm
Middle Ripley Farm
Ford
Hackthorn Plantation
Sch
Long Acre Plantation
Parsonage Farm
Twobridges Plantation
DERRIT LA

193

142

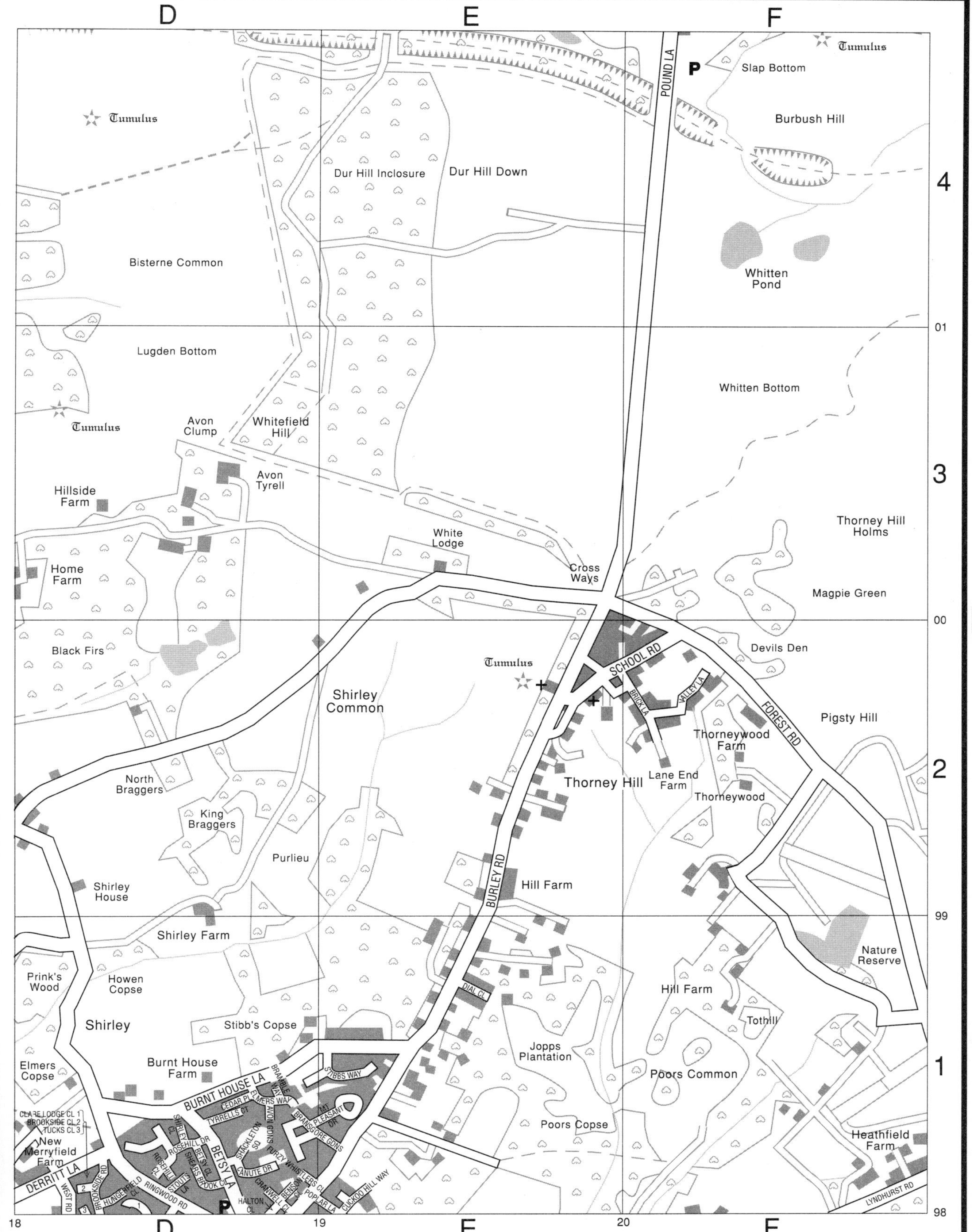
D
E
F
Tumulus
Slap Bottom
POUND LA
Burbush Hill
Tumulus
Dur Hill Inclosure
Dur Hill Down
4
Bisterne Common
Whitten Pond
01
Lugden Bottom
Whitten Bottom
Tumulus
Avon Clump
Whitefield Hill
3
Avon Tyrell
Hillside Farm
Thorney Hill Holms
White Lodge
Home Farm
Cross Ways
Magpie Green
00
Black Firs
Tumulus
SCHOOL RD
Devils Den
BRICK LA
VALLEY LA
Shirley Common
FOREST RD
Pigsty Hill
Thorneywood Farm
North Braggers
Thorney Hill
Lane End Farm
2
Thorneywood
King Braggers
Purlieu
BURLEY RD
Shirley House
Hill Farm
99
Shirley Farm
Nature Reserve
Prink's Wood
Howen Copse
DIAL CL
Hill Farm
Shirley
Stibb's Copse
Tothill
Jopps Plantation
Elmers Copse
Burnt House Farm
1
Poors Common
BURNT HOUSE LA
STIBBS WAY
BRAMBLE WAY
CEDAR PL
PLUMERS WAY
TYRRELLS CT
MT PLEASANT DR
BRANSGORE GDNS
CLARE LODGE CL 1
BROOKSIDE CL 2
TUCKS CL 3
New Merryfield Farm
SHIRLEY CL
ROSEHILL DR
BETSY LA
SHACKLETON SQ
AVON GDNS
FURZY WHISTLERS CL
Poors Copse
Heathfield Farm
DERRITT LA
CANUTE DR
CRANWELL
WEST RD
BROOKSIDE RD
HUNGERFIELD
RINGWOOD RD
HALTON CL
POPLAR LA
CUCKOO HILL WAY
LYNDHURST RD
98
18
19
20
D
E
F

170

194

143

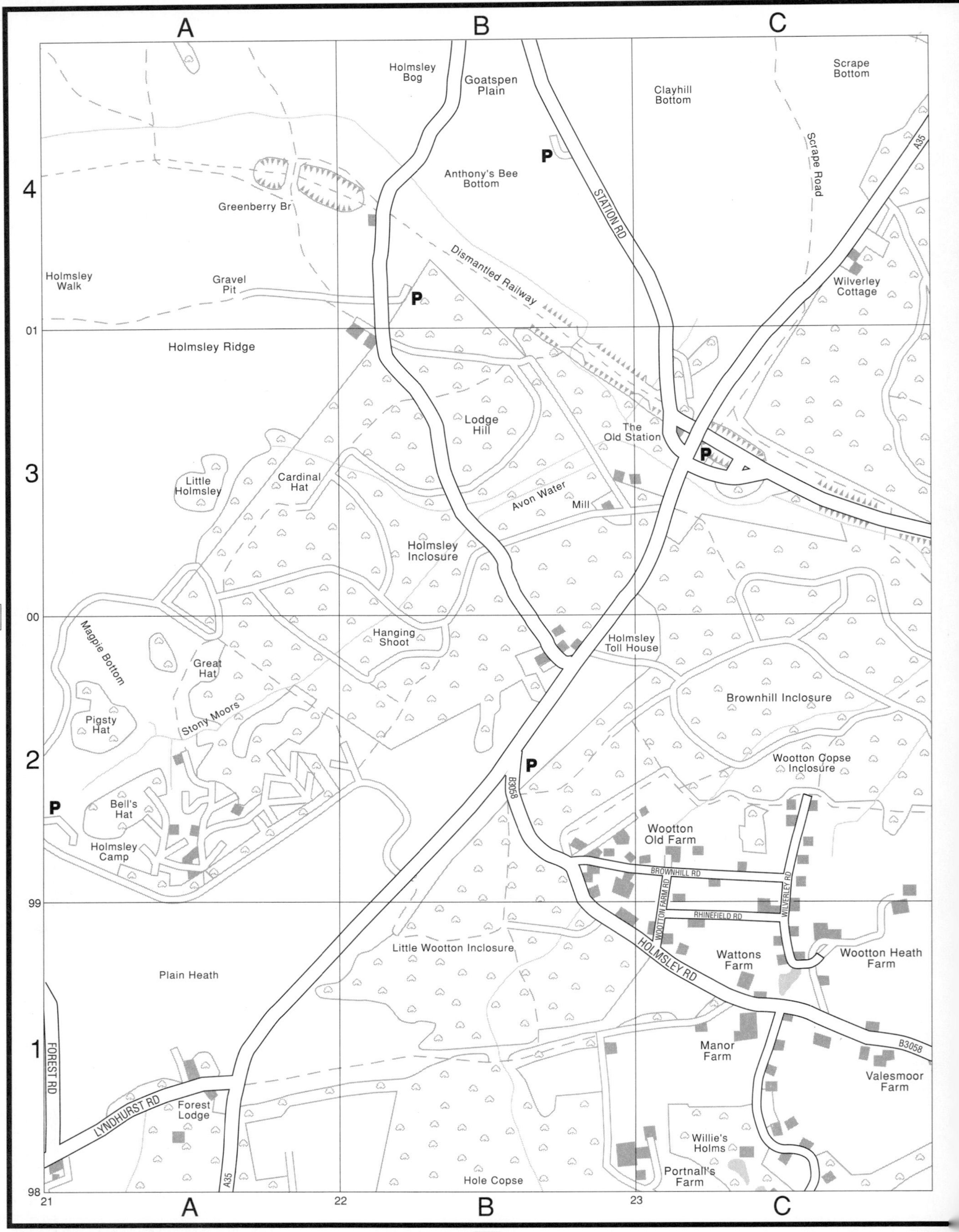
A
B
C
4
3
2
1
01
00
99
98
21
22
23
Holmsley Bog
Goatspen Plain
Clayhill Bottom
Scrape Bottom
Scrape Road
A35
Anthony's Bee Bottom
STATION RD
Greenberry Br
Dismantled Railway
Holmsley Walk
Gravel Pit
Wilverley Cottage
Holmsley Ridge
Lodge Hill
The Old Station
Little Holmsley
Cardinal Hat
Avon Water
Mill
Holmsley Inclosure
Magpie Bottom
Hanging Shoot
Holmsley Toll House
Great Hat
Brownhill Inclosure
Pigsty Hat
Stony Moors
Wootton Copse Inclosure
B3058
Bell's Hat
Wootton Old Farm
Holmsley Camp
BROWNHILL RD
WOOTTON FARM RD
WILVERLEY RD
RHINEFIELD RD
HOLMSLEY RD
Little Wootton Inclosure
Wattons Farm
Wootton Heath Farm
Plain Heath
FOREST RD
Manor Farm
B3058
Valesmoor Farm
LYNDHURST RD
Forest Lodge
Willie's Holms
Portnall's Farm
A35
Hole Copse
P

169

195

144

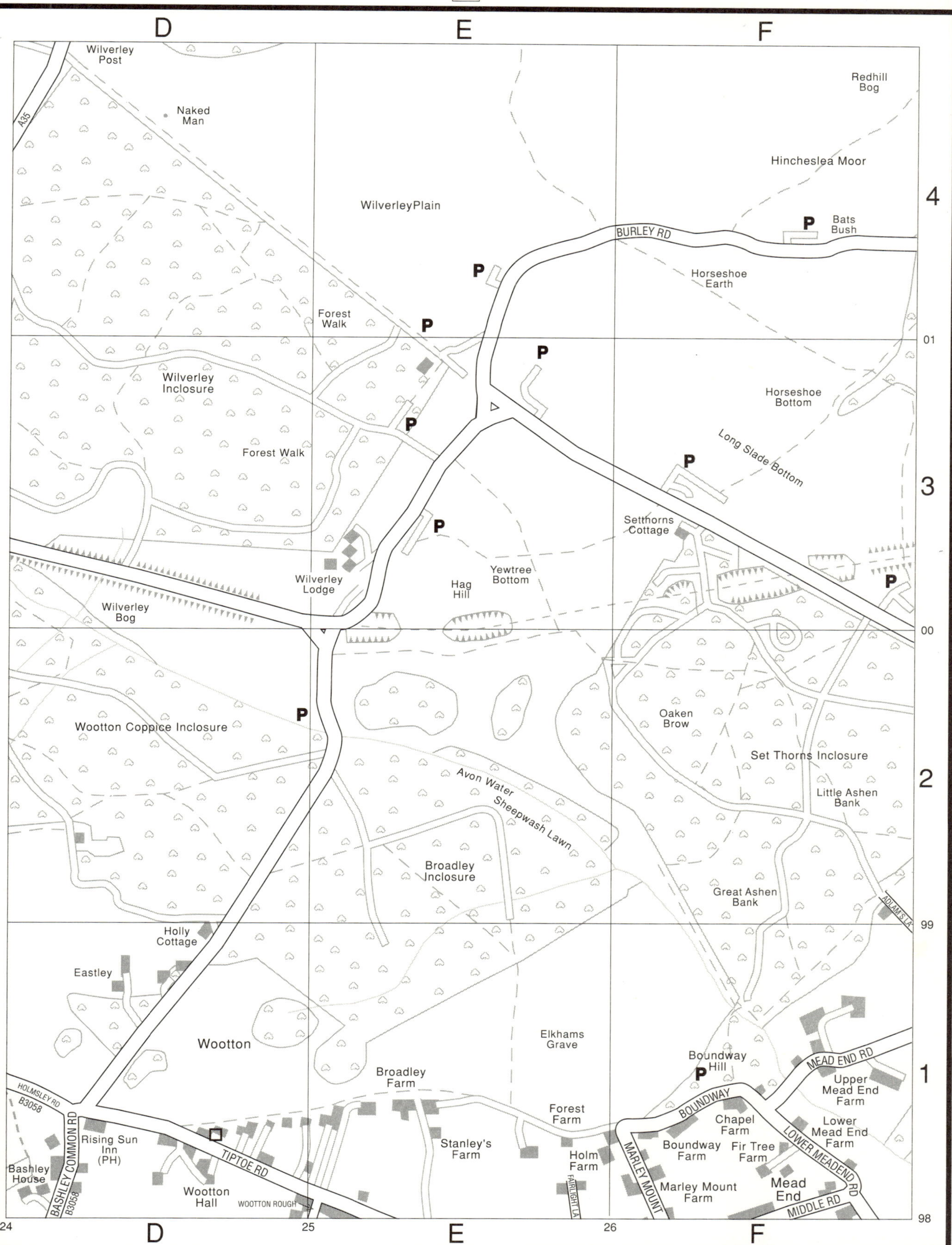
D
E
F
Wilverley Post
Naked Man
A35
Redhill Bog
Hinchesléa Moor
WilverleyPlain
4
BURLEY RD
Bats Bush
Horseshoe Earth
Forest Walk
01
Wilverley Inclosure
Horseshoe Bottom
Long Slade Bottom
Forest Walk
3
Setthorns Cottage
Wilverley Lodge
Hag Hill
Yewtree Bottom
Wilverley Bog
00
Oaken Brow
Wootton Coppice Inclosure
Set Thorns Inclosure
Avon Water
Sheepwash Lawn
2
Little Ashen Bank
Broadley Inclosure
Great Ashen Bank
ADLAM'S LA
99
Holly Cottage
Eastley
Elkhams Grave
Wootton
Boundway Hill
MEAD END RD
1
Upper Mead End Farm
Broadley Farm
BOUNDWAY
HOLMSLEY RD
B3058
Forest Farm
Chapel Farm
Lower Mead End Farm
Rising Sun Inn (PH)
Stanley's Farm
Boundway Farm
Fir Tree Farm
LOWER MEADEND RD
Bashley House
TIPTOE RD
Holm Farm
MARLEY MOUNT
Mead End
BASHLEY COMMON RD
B3058
Wootton Hall
WOOTTON ROUGH
FAIRLIGHT LA
Marley Mount Farm
MIDDLE RD
24
25
26
98
D
E
F

172

196

145

171

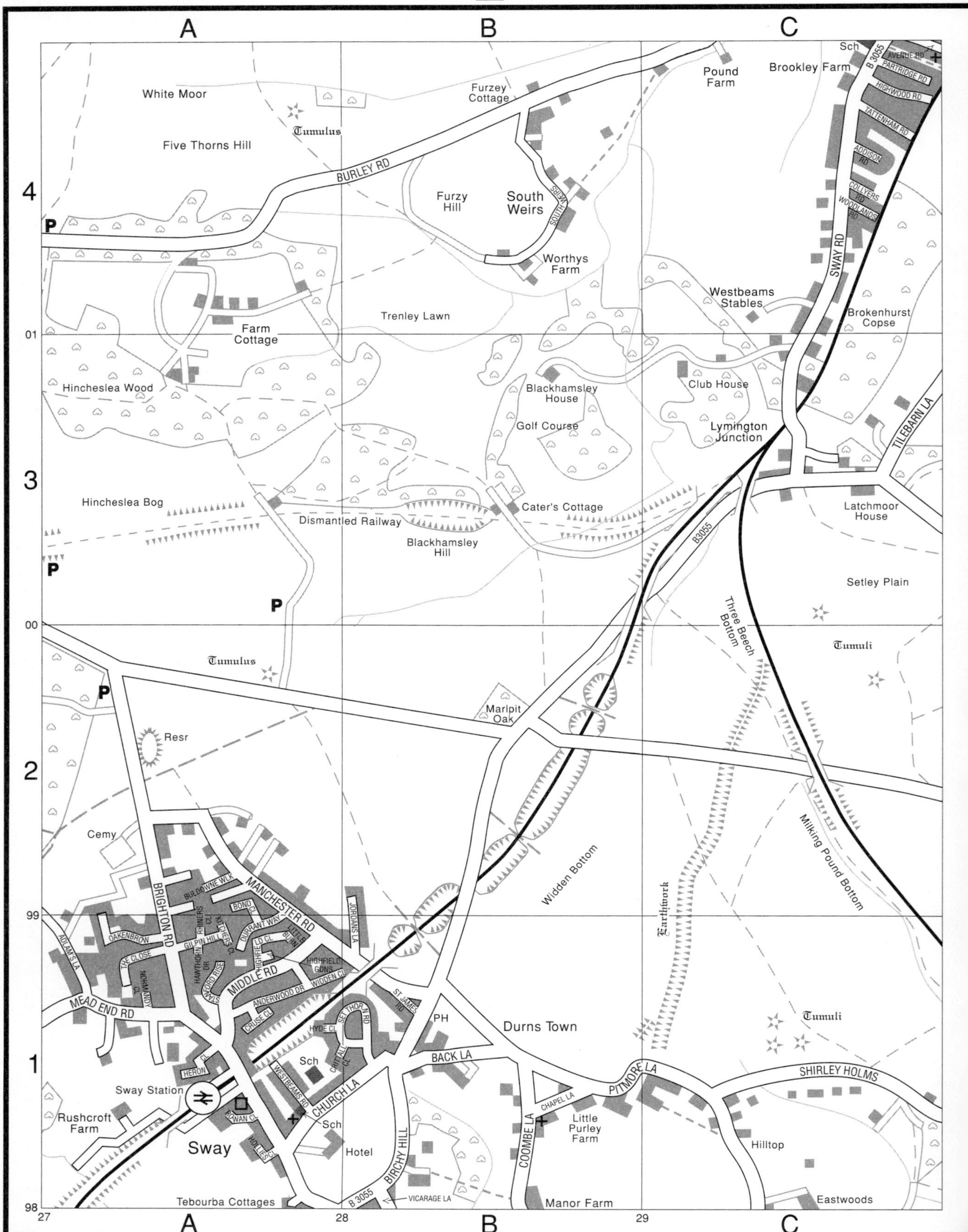
A
B
C
4
3
2
1
01
00
99
98
27
28
29
White Moor
Five Thorns Hill
Tumulus
Furzey Cottage
Pound Farm
Brookley Farm
Sch
B 3055
AVENUE RD
PARTRIDGE RD
HIGHWOOD RD
TATTENHAM RD
ADDISON RD
COLLYERS RD
WOODLANDS RD
BURLEY RD
Furzy Hill
South Weirs
SOUTH WEIRS
Worthys Farm
P
Trenley Lawn
Farm Cottage
Westbeams Stables
SWAY RD
Brokenhurst Copse
Hincheslea Wood
Blackhamsley House
Club House
Golf Course
Lymington Junction
TILEBARN LA
Hincheslea Bog
Dismantled Railway
Cater's Cottage
Blackhamsley Hill
Latchmoor House
B3055
Setley Plain
Three Beech Bottom
Tumuli
Tumulus
Marlpit Oak
Resr
Cemy
Widden Bottom
Milking Pound Bottom
Earthwork
BRIGHTON RD
BULDOWNE WLK
MANCHESTER RD
BOND CL
JORDANS LA
DURRANT WAY
OAKENBROW
GILPIN HILL
LITTLE BURN
THE CLOSE
ADLAM'S LA
HAWTHORN DR
STANFORD RISE
MIDDLE RD
HIGHFIELD GDNS
WIDDEN CL
NORMANDY CL
MEAD END RD
ANDERWOOD DR
CRUSE CL
ST JAMES RD
HYDE CL
SELTHORN RD
PH
Durns Town
Tumuli
Sch
BACK LA
PITMORE LA
SHIRLEY HOLMS
HERON CL
Sway Station
CHURCH LA
WESTBEAMS RD
Rushcroft Farm
ROWAN CL
Sch
CHAPEL LA
Little Purley Farm
Hilltop
Sway
HOLLIES CL
Hotel
BIRCHY HILL
COOMBE LA
Tebourba Cottages
B 3055
VICARAGE LA
Manor Farm
Eastwoods

197

146

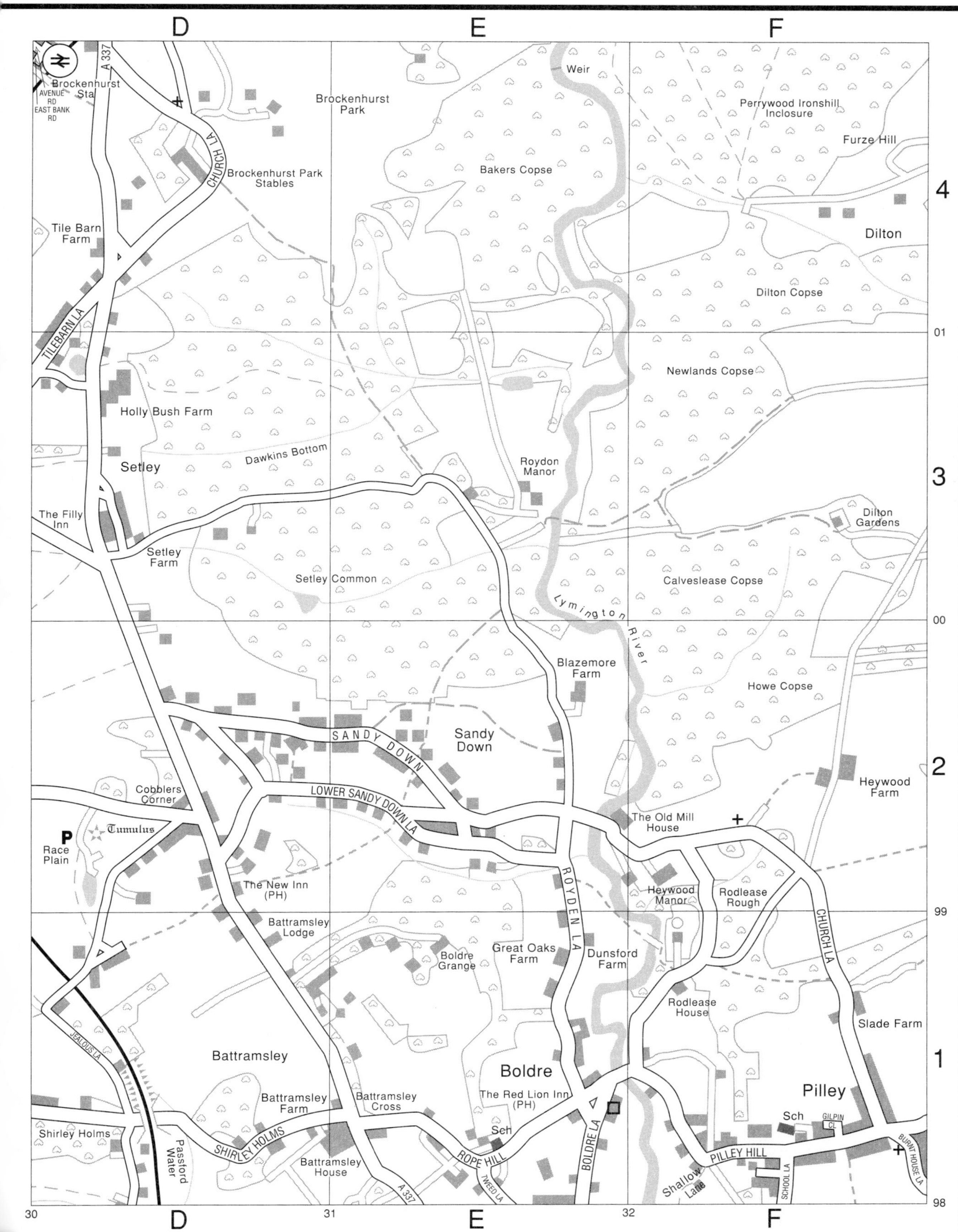
D
E
F
Brockenhurst Sta
AVENUE RD
EAST BANK RD
A 337
Brockenhurst Park
Weir
Perrywood Ironshill Inclosure
Furze Hill
CHURCH LA
Brockenhurst Park Stables
Bakers Copse
4
Tile Barn Farm
Dilton
Dilton Copse
TILEBARN LA
01
Newlands Copse
Holly Bush Farm
Dawkins Bottom
Roydon Manor
Setley
3
The Filly Inn
Dilton Gardens
Setley Farm
Setley Common
Calveslease Copse
Lymington River
00
Blazemore Farm
Howe Copse
SANDY DOWN
Sandy Down
2
Heywood Farm
Cobblers Corner
LOWER SANDY DOWN LA
The Old Mill House
P
Tumulus
Race Plain
The New Inn (PH)
ROYDEN LA
Heywood Manor
Rodlease Rough
CHURCH LA
99
Battramsley Lodge
Boldre Grange
Great Oaks Farm
Dunsford Farm
Rodlease House
Slade Farm
JEALOUS LA
Battramsley
Boldre
1
Pilley
Battramsley Farm
Battramsley Cross
The Red Lion Inn (PH)
Sch
GILPIN CL
Shirley Holms
SHIRLEY HOLMS
Passford Water
Sch
ROPE HILL
BOLDRE LA
PILLEY HILL
BURNT HOUSE LA
Battramsley House
TWEED LA
A 337
Shallow Lane
SCHOOL LA
98
30
31
32
D
E
F

174

198

147

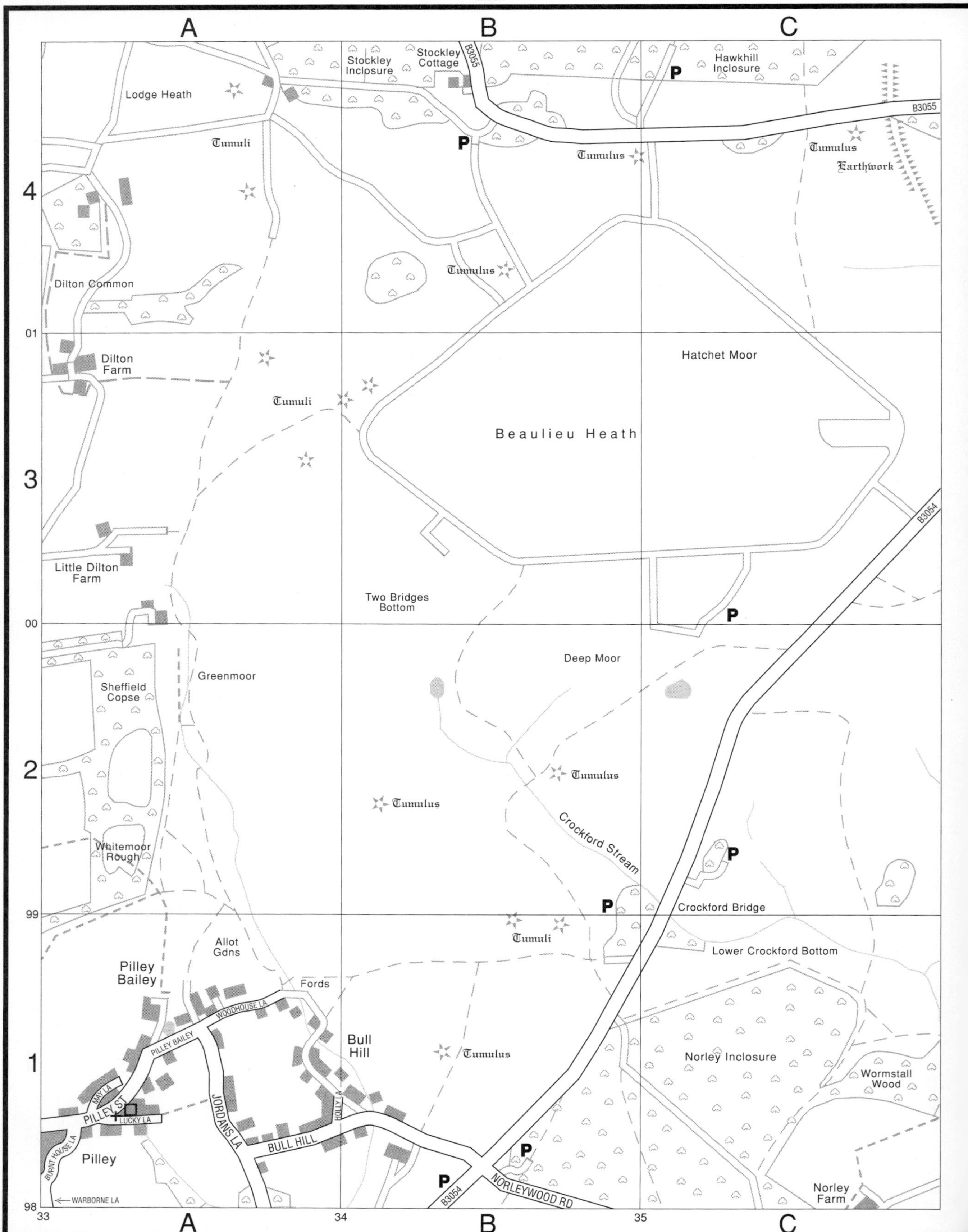

A
B
C
4
3
2
1
01
00
99
98
33
34
35
Lodge Heath
Stockley Inclosure
Stockley Cottage
B3055
Hawkhill Inclosure
P
Tumuli
Tumulus
Earthwork
Dilton Common
Dilton Farm
Hatchet Moor
Beaulieu Heath
B3054
Little Dilton Farm
Two Bridges Bottom
Deep Moor
Greenmoor
Sheffield Copse
Whitemoor Rough
Crockford Stream
Crockford Bridge
Lower Crockford Bottom
Allot Gdns
Pilley Bailey
Fords
Bull Hill
WOODHOUSE LA
PILLEY BAILEY
MAY LA
PILLEY ST
LUCKY LA
JORDANS LA
HOLLY LA
BULL HILL
BURNT HOUSE LA
Pilley
WARBORNE LA
NORLEYWOOD RD
Norley Inclosure
Wormstall Wood
Norley Farm

173

199

148
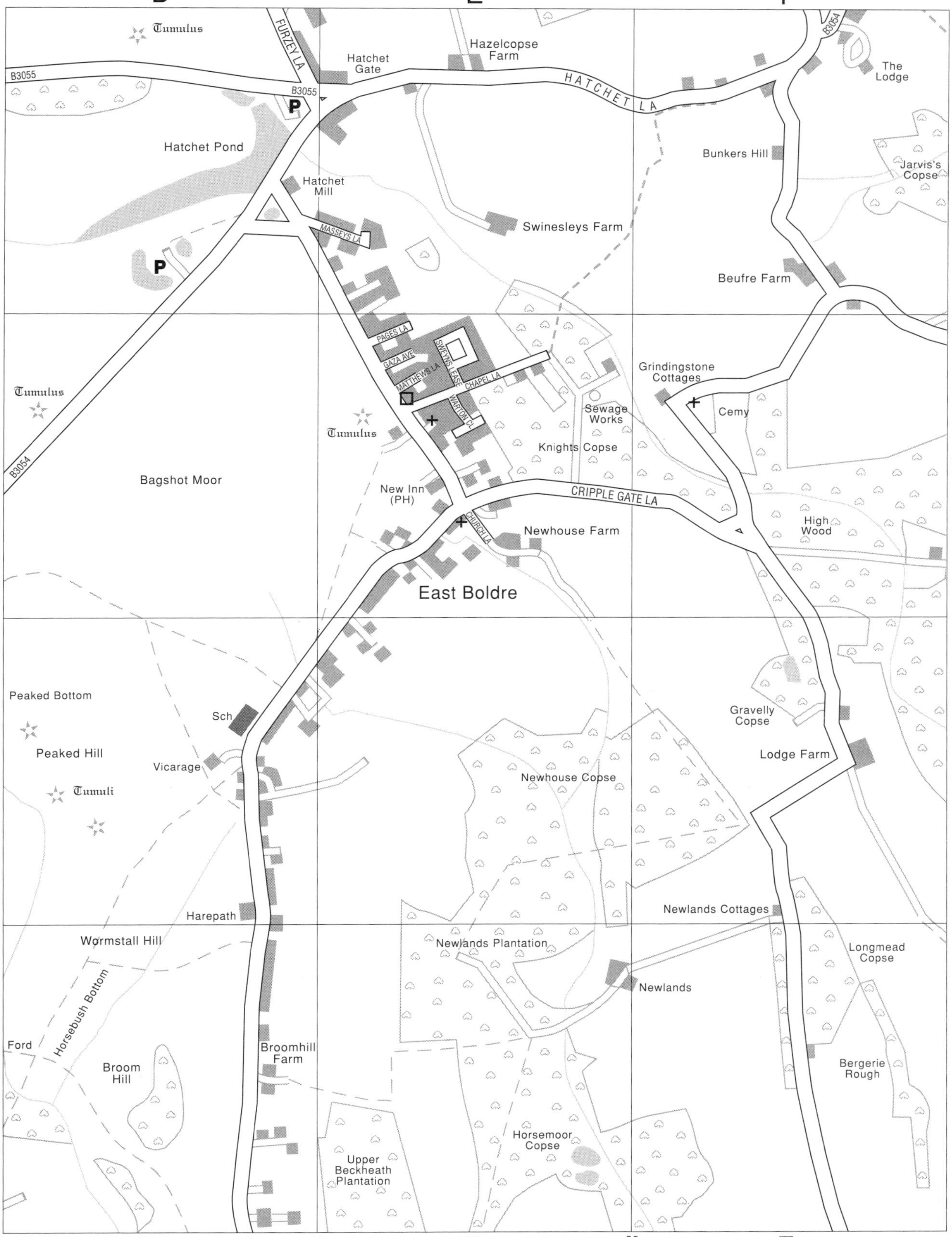

D
E
F
Tumulus
FURZEY LA
Hatchet Gate
Hazelcopse Farm
B3054
The Lodge
B3055
B3055
HATCHET LA
Hatchet Pond
Bunkers Hill
Jarvis's Copse
4
Hatchet Mill
Swinesleys Farm
MASSEYS LA
Beufre Farm
01
PAGES LA
GAZA AVE
SWEYNS LEASE
MATTHEWS LA
CHAPEL LA
Grindingstone Cottages
Tumulus
WARWICK CL
Sewage Works
Cemy
Tumulus
Knights Copse
B3054
3
Bagshot Moor
New Inn (PH)
CRIPPLE GATE LA
CHURCH LA
High Wood
Newhouse Farm
East Boldre
00
Peaked Bottom
Sch
Gravelly Copse
Peaked Hill
Lodge Farm
Vicarage
2
Newhouse Copse
Tumuli
Harepath
Newlands Cottages
99
Wormstall Hill
Newlands Plantation
Longmead Copse
Horsebush Bottom
Newlands
Ford
Broomhill Farm
Broom Hill
Bergerie Rough
1
Horsemoor Copse
Upper Beckheath Plantation
98
36
37
38
D
E
F

176
200

149

175

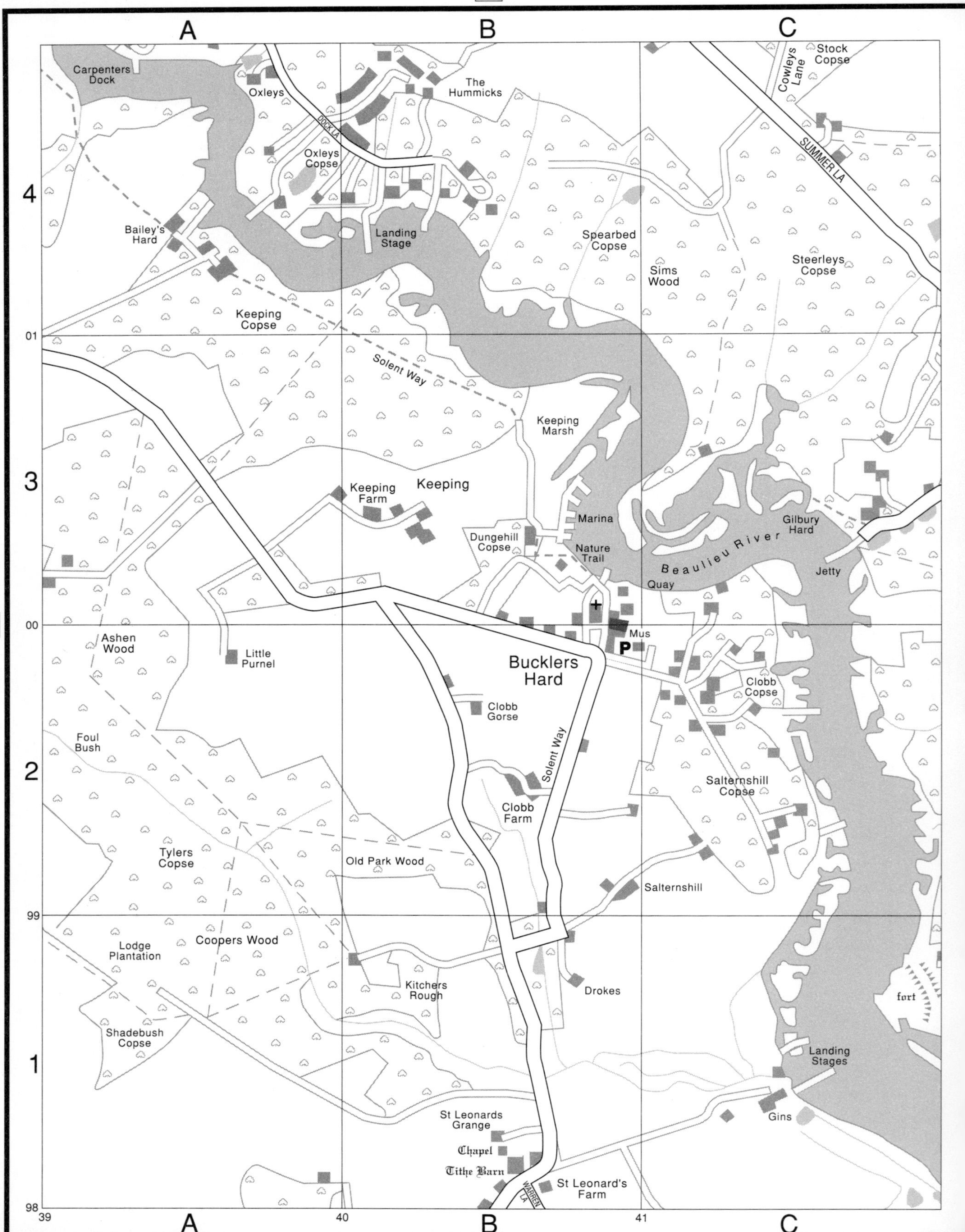
A
B
C
4
3
2
1
01
00
99
98
39
40
41
Carpenters Dock
Oxleys
The Hummicks
DOCK LA
Oxleys Copse
Bailey's Hard
Landing Stage
Spearbed Copse
Sims Wood
Stock Copse
Cowleys Lane
SUMMER LA
Steerleys Copse
Keeping Copse
Solent Way
Keeping Marsh
Keeping Farm
Keeping
Marina
Gilbury Hard
Dungehill Copse
Nature Trail
Beaulieu River
Jetty
Quay
Mus
P
Ashen Wood
Little Purnel
Bucklers Hard
Clobb Copse
Clobb Gorse
Foul Bush
Solent Way
Salternshill Copse
Clobb Farm
Tylers Copse
Old Park Wood
Salternshill
Lodge Plantation
Coopers Wood
Kitchers Rough
Drokes
fort
Shadebush Copse
Landing Stages
Gins
St Leonards Grange
Chapel
Tithe Barn
WARREN LA
St Leonard's Farm

201

150

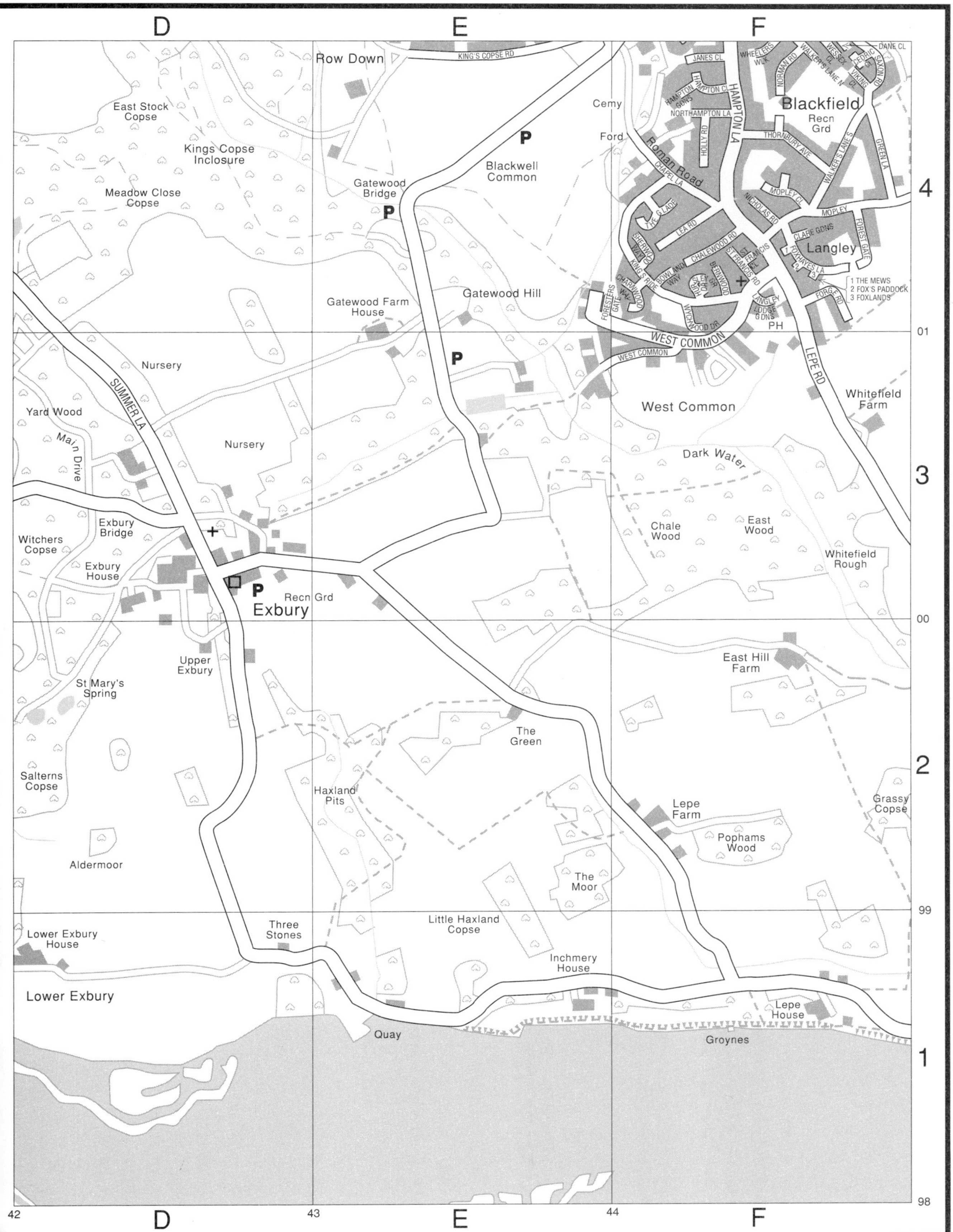

178

not continued, see key diagram

151

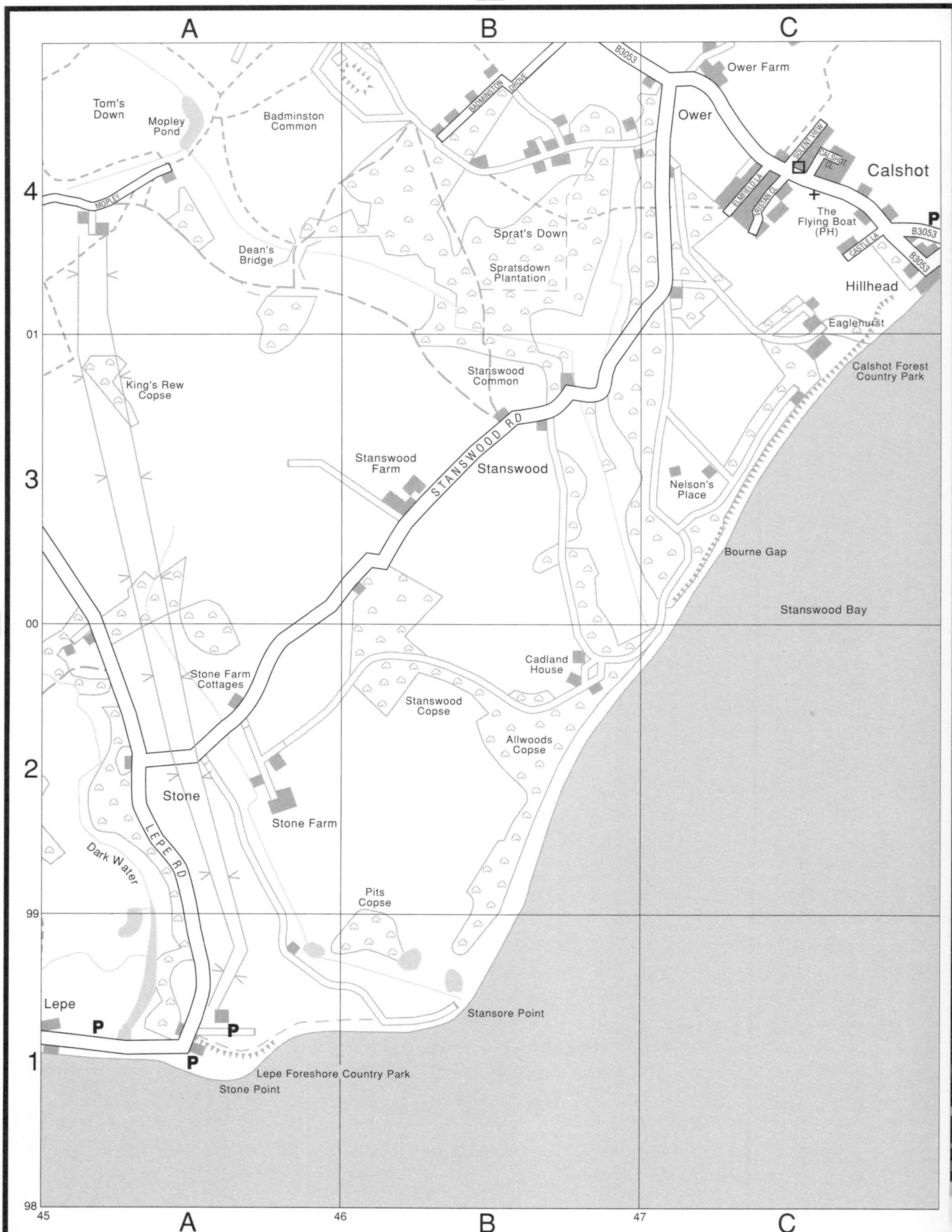

177

not continued, see key diagram

154

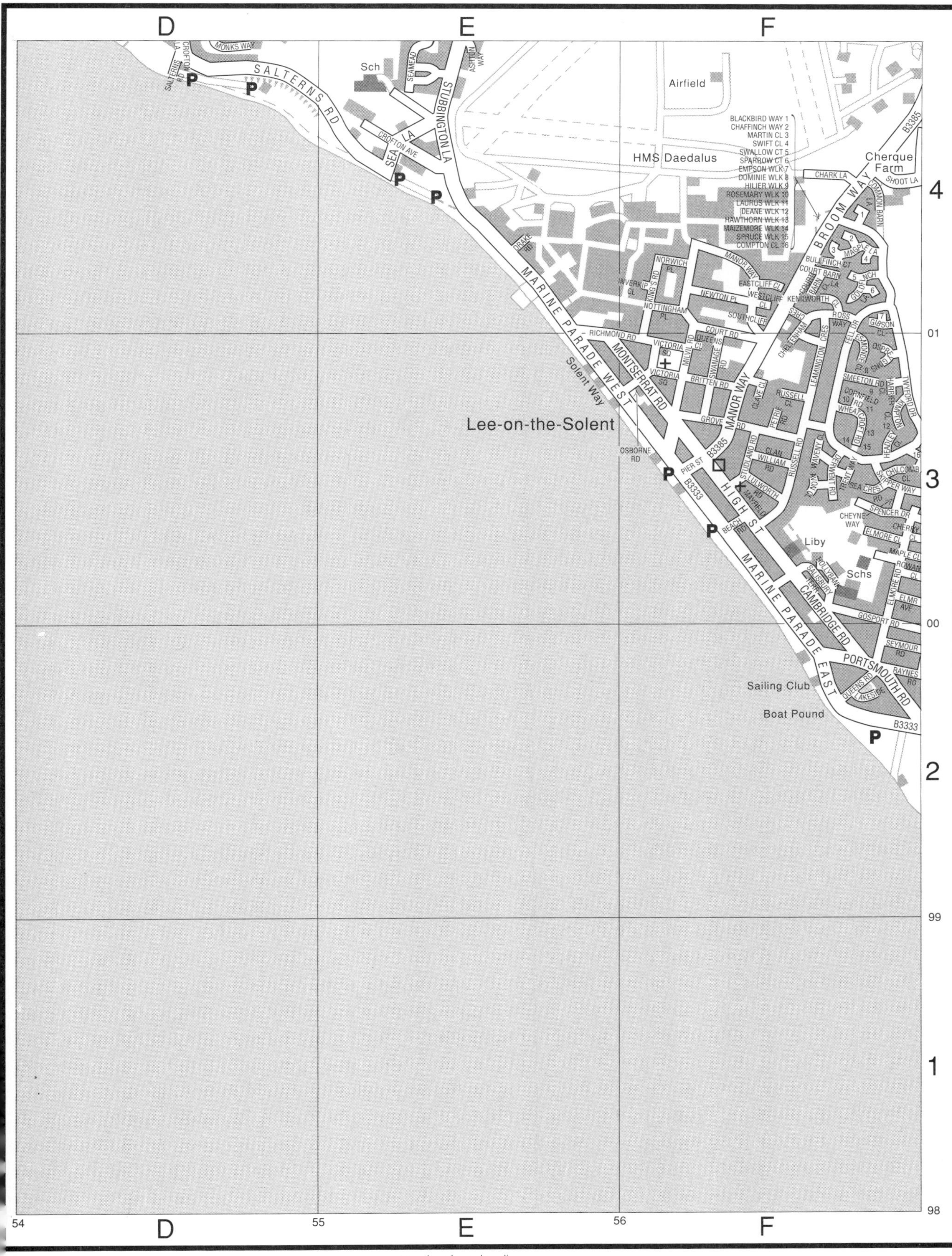

180

not continued, see key diagram

155

179

not continued, see key diagram

156

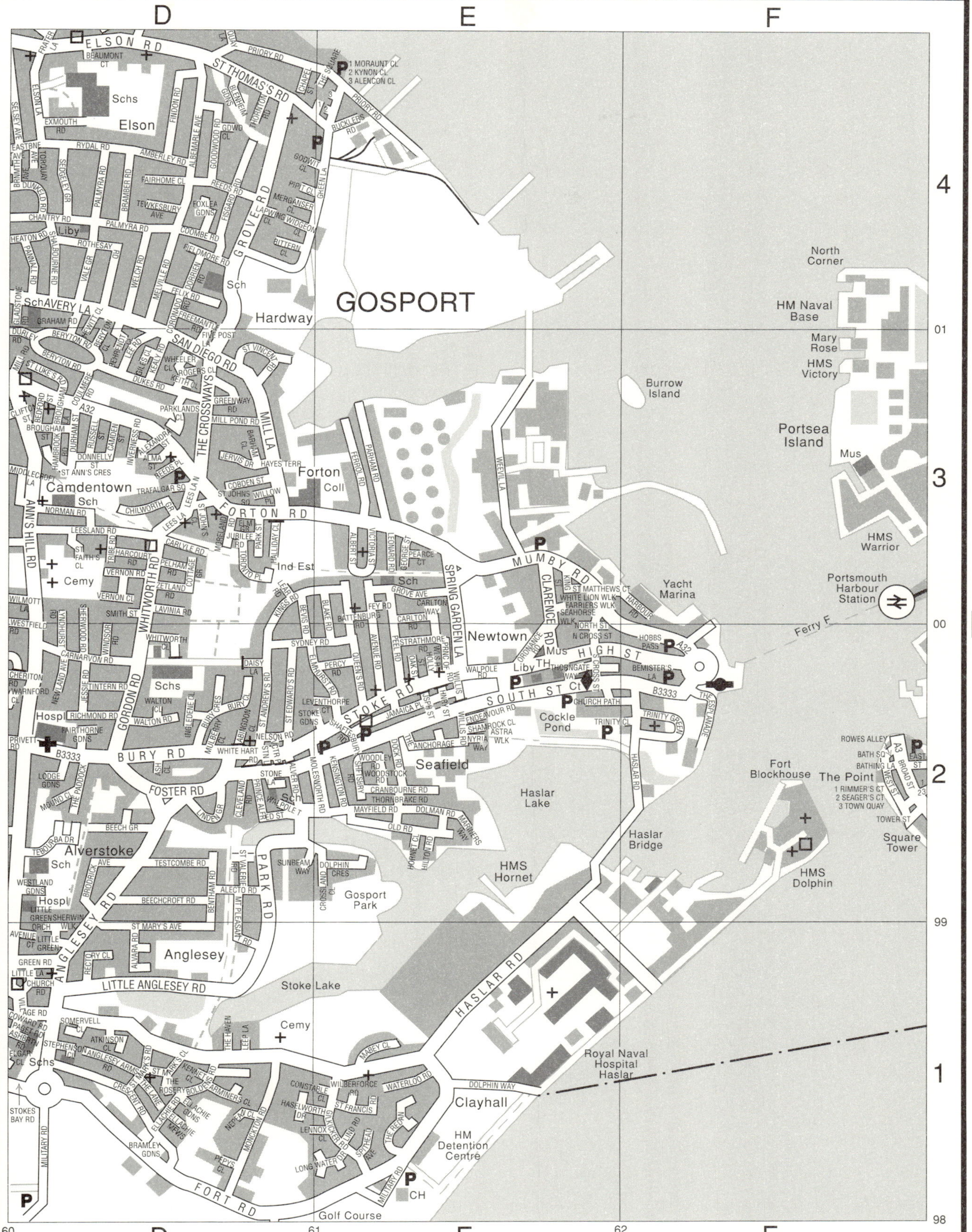
D
E
F
GOSPORT
Elson
Schs
Hardway
Forton
Coll
Camdentown
Sch
Cemy
Ind Est
Newtown
Seafield
Cockle Pond
Haslar Lake
Haslar Bridge
HMS Hornet
Alverstoke
Hospl
Anglesey
Gosport Park
Stoke Lake
Clayhall
HM Detention Centre
Royal Naval Hospital Haslar
Golf Course
North Corner
HM Naval Base
Mary Rose
HMS Victory
Burrow Island
Portsea Island
Mus
HMS Warrior
Portsmouth Harbour Station
Yacht Marina
Ferry
Fort Blockhouse
The Point
Square Tower
HMS Dolphin
ELSON RD
ST THOMAS'S RD
PRIORY RD
GROVE RD
SAN DIEGO RD
THE CROSSWAYS
MILLLA
FORTON RD
MUMBY RD
HIGH ST
SOUTH ST
STOKE RD
BURY RD
FOSTER RD
ANGLESEY RD
LITTLE ANGLESEY RD
PARK RD
HASLAR RD
FORT RD
MILITARY RD
ANN'S HILL RD
WHITWORTH RD
GORDON RD
SPRING GARDEN LA
CLARENCE RD
THE ESPLANADE
DOLPHIN WAY
WATERLOO RD
B3333
A32
A3
4
3
2
1
01
00
99
98
60
61
62

182

202

157

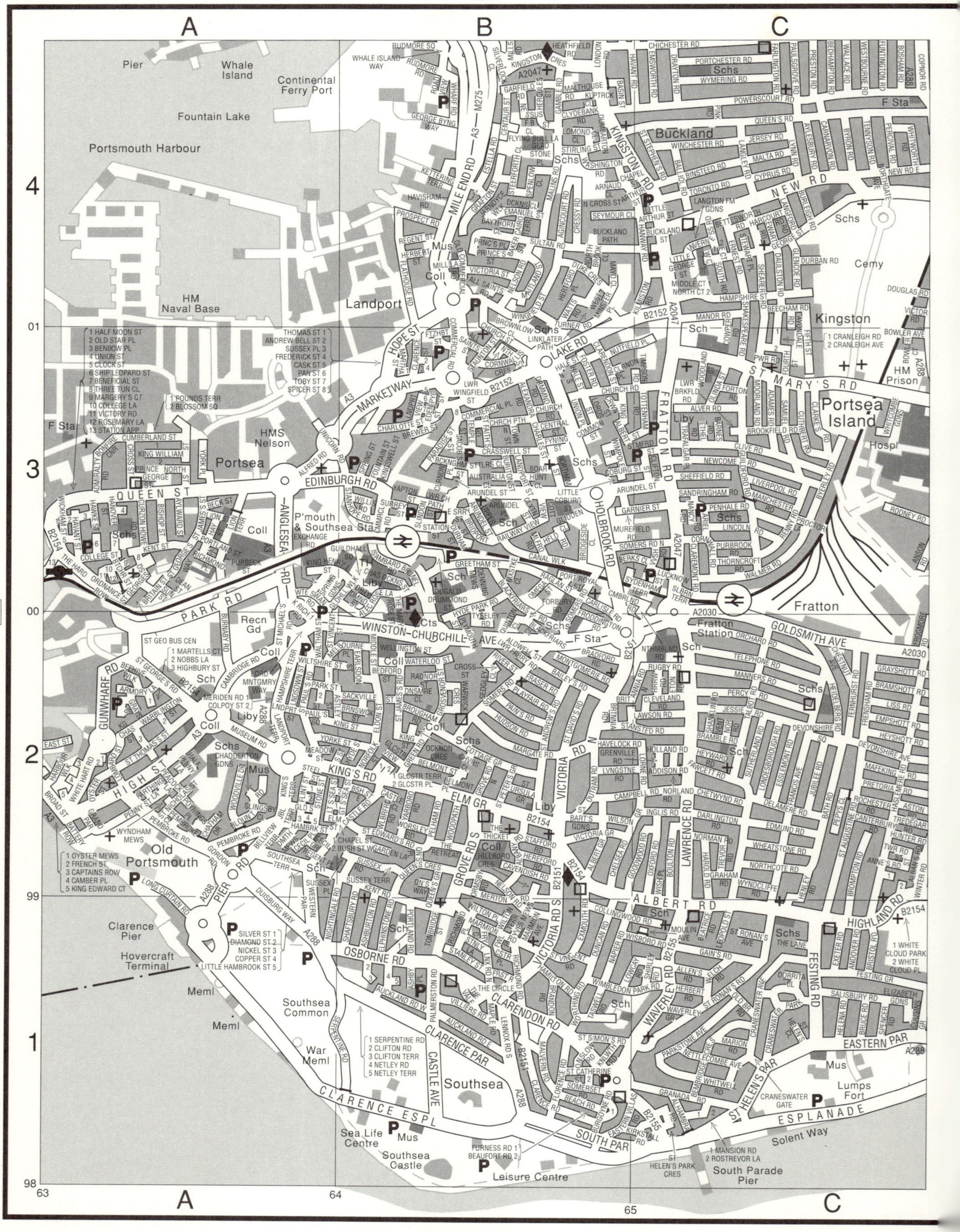
A
B
C
Pier
Whale Island
Continental Ferry Port
Fountain Lake
Portsmouth Harbour
HM Naval Base
Landport
Portsea
HMS Nelson
P'mouth & Southsea Sta
Buckland
Kingston
Portsea Island
HM Prison
Hospl
Cemy
Fratton
Fratton Station
Old Portsmouth
Clarence Pier
Hovercraft Terminal
Southsea Common
Southsea
Sea Life Centre
Southsea Castle
Leisure Centre
South Parade Pier
Lumps Fort
Solent Way
Recn Gd
MILE END RD
KINGSTON RD
FRATTON RD
NEW RD
ST MARY'S RD
LAKE RD
QUEEN ST
EDINBURGH RD
MARKETWAY
PARK RD
ANGLESEA RD
WINSTON CHURCHILL AVE
GOLDSMITH AVE
HOLBROOK RD
VICTORIA RD N
VICTORIA RD S
ALBERT RD
LAWRENCE RD
HIGH ST
KING'S RD
ELM GR
GROVE RD S
CLARENDON RD
OSBORNE RD
CLARENCE PAR
CLARENCE ESPL
CASTLE AVE
SOUTH PAR
ESPLANADE
ST HELEN'S PAR
EASTERN PAR
HIGHLAND RD
FESTING RD
WAVERLEY RD
PIER RD
GUNWHARF RD
A3
A288
A2030
A2047
B2154
B2151
B2152
01
00
99
98
1
2
3
4
63
64
65

181

158

D
E
F
Golf Course
Great Salterns Lake
Great Salterns Quay
A2030
Portsea Island
Baffins
Baffins Pond
Sch
Liby
TANGIER RD
Solent Way
SWORD SANDS RD
EASTERN RD
KESWICK AVE
MONEYFIELD AVE
MONEYFIELD LA
CONISTON AVE
SIDMOUTH AVE
SEATON AVE
TEIGNMOUTH RD
COLLIS RD
MANOR PARK AVE
STATION RD
MARTIN RD
PAIGNTON AVE
EASTBOURNE RD
STAPLETON RD
COPNOR RD
A288
DOVER RD
FOLKESTONE RD
CHESTERFIELD RD
LYNTON GR
RIPLEY GR
IDSWORTH RD
COBDEN AVE
NORTHOVER RD
WESTOVER RD
SILCHESTER RD
HIGHGROVE RD
STANLEY AVE
ALGIERS RD
COLEBROOK AVE
COOPER RD
DUDLEY RD
MILTON RD
ST PIRAN'S AVE
CHASEWATER AVE
WHITECLIFFE AVE
CHILCOTE RD
NEVILLE RD
HAYLING AVE
JENKINS GR
CEDAR GR
EBERY GR
BAFFINS RD
KIMBOLTON RD
LICHFIELD RD
SUNNINGDALE RD
ASCOT RD
Schs
LAKESIDE AVE
WALLISDEAN RD
MYRTLE GR
MARINA GR
STRIDE AVE
TAMWORTH RD
WALSALL RD
CHESLYN RD
LANGSTONE RD
PRIORSDEAN AVE
PETWORTH RD
ROMSEY AVE
SHORE AVE
EASTERN AVE
SALTERNS AVE
Hospl
Cemy
Wks
Fratton Ind Est
ANSON RD
RODNEY RD
VERNON MEWS
MILTON LA
A2030 VELDER AVE
HERON CL
CURLEW PATH
MALLARD RD
PLOVER REACH
WARREN AVE
MARINERS WLK
THE HAVEN
MOORINGS WAY
REVENGE CL
SEAGULL CL
GODWIT RD
SCHOONER WAY
SOVEREIGN CL
SOVEREIGN DR
SANDERLING RD
WHIMBREL CL
DUNLIN CL
REDWING CT
MAYFLOWER DR
WAYFARER CL
ATALANTA CL
Coll
BONCHURCH RD
EDGEWARE RD
BLENDWORTH RD
EASTON RD
CROFTON
SHELFORD RD
MAYLES RD
CHURCH VIEW
MEON RD
FROGMORE RD
SPECKS LA
ALVERSTONE RD
VERNON AVE
MAYLANDS AVE
CARISBROOKE RD
RUSKIN RD
APSLEY RD
CLAYDON AVE
PRIORY CRES
Liby
POSBROOKE RD
WESTON AVE
CATISFIELD RD
HOLLAM RD
Schs
Milton
Sch
BROOM SQ
BROOM CL
FURZE LA
LONGSHORE WAY
WATERLOCK GDNS
SEAWAY CRES
A2030 GOLDSMITH AVE
MILTON PARK AVE
CORMORANT AVE
EASTNEY RD
LOCKSWAY RD
MERYL RD
TOWPATH MEAD
Poly
GRAYSHOTT RD
BRAMSHOTT RD
LISS RD
EMPSHOTT RD
WINTER RD
CLOVELLY RD
ESSEX RD
WIMBORNE RD
WOODMANCOTE RD
EVANS RD
HEYSHOTT RD
TEDDINGTON RD
MAFEKING RD
DEVONSHIRE AVE
MIDDLESEX RD
SUFFOLK RD
GLASGOW RD
CANAL WLK
MELROSE CL
BERNEY RD
MAURICE RD
DUNBAR RD
KINGSLEY RD
MILFORD CT
TRIMMER
Allot Gdns
Bransbury Park
GODIVA LAWN
TORRIDGE CT
WAKE LAWN
LIGHTFOOT LAWN
Marina
FERRY RD
EASTLAKE HTS
LUMSDEN RD
FINCH RD
GIBRALTAR RD
FORT CUMBERLAND RD
Fort Cumberland
Landing Stage
Ferry (F)
IRB Sta
The Ferry Boat Inn (PH)
THE KENCH
CH
Golf Course
PRETORIA RD
EASTFIELD RD
WESTFIELD RD
MAXWELL RD
TREDEGAR RD
LANDGUARD RD
REGINALD RD
HUNTER RD
HATFIELD RD
METHUEN RD
OLIVER RD
CLEGG RD
HELLYER RD
Schs
ALMA TERR
PRINCE ALBERT RD
BRANSBURY RD
RINGWOOD RD
FORDINGBRIDGE RD
MINSTEAD RD
BRITANWOOD RD
EASTNEY FARM RD
CADNAM RD
HENDERSON RD
COCKLESHELL GDNS
HALLIDAY CRES
Eastney
MELVILLE RD
B2154 HIGHLAND RD
LIDDIARD GDNS
DRIFTWOOD GDNS
ESPLANADE GDNS
Eastney Barracks
Mus
KIMBERLEY RD
WAINSCOT RD
COLLINS RD
LINDLEY AVE
TOKAR ST
KASSASSIN ST
ADAIR RD
CROMWELL RD
WORSLEY ST
ST GEORGE'S RD
FESTING GR
NETTLESTONE RD
CULVER RD
SELSEY AVE
MARINE CT
COUSINS GR
BURBIDGE GR
BRADING AVE
EASTERN PAR
A288
ESPLANADE
Solent Way
4
3
2
1
01
00
99
98
66
67
68

184

159

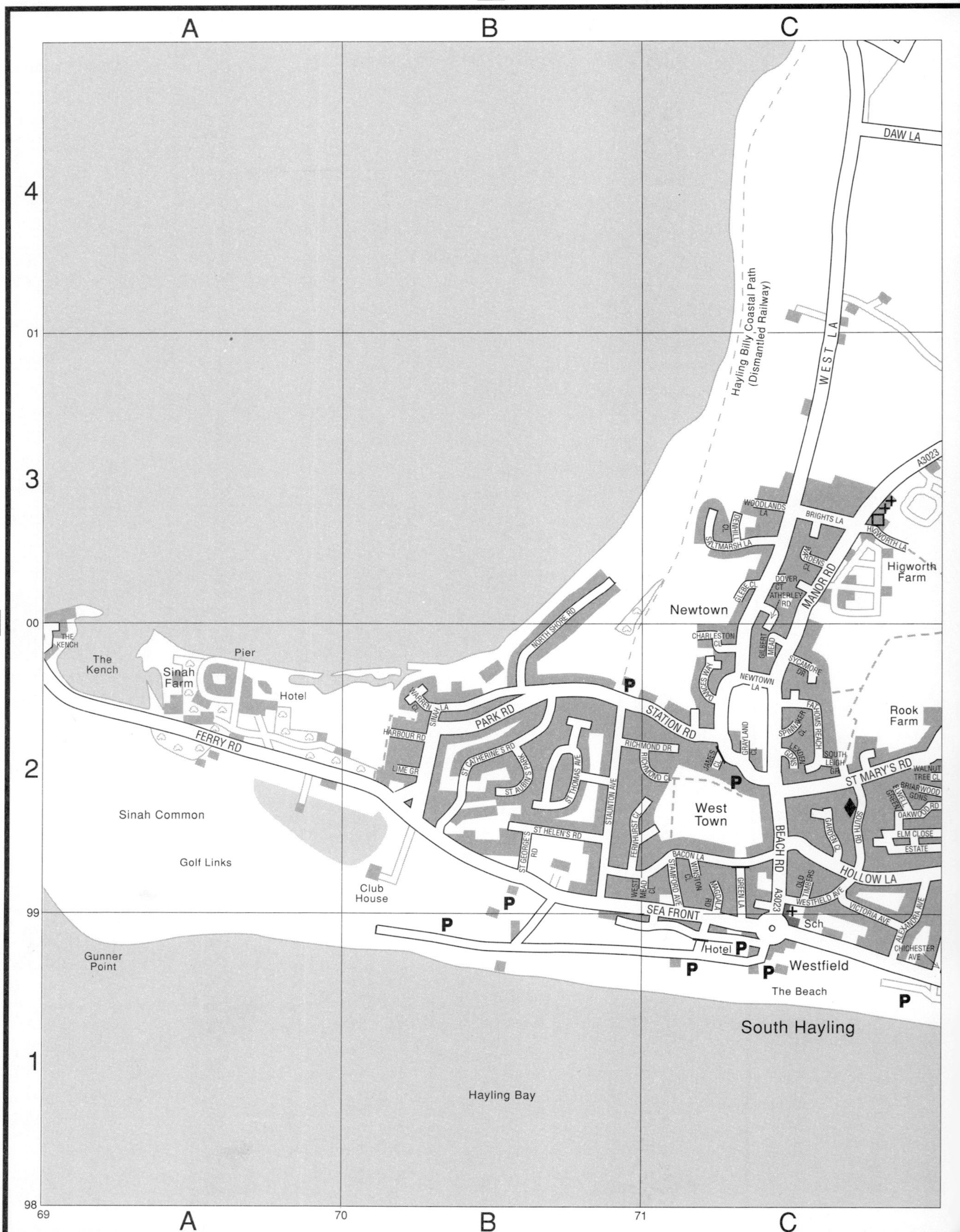
A
B
C
4
3
2
1
01
00
99
98
69
70
71
DAW LA
WEST LA
Hayling Billy Coastal Path
(Dismantled Railway)
A3023
WOODLANDS LA
BRIGHTS LA
HIGWORTH LA
Higworth Farm
SALTMARSH LA
WARDENS CL
DOVER CT
ATHERLEY RD
GLEBE CL
MANOR RD
Newtown
CHARLESTON CL
GILBERT MEAD
SYCAMORE DR
NEWTOWN LA
NORTH SHORE RD
THE KENCH
The Kench
Pier
Sinah Farm
Hotel
WARREN CL
SINAH LA
PARK RD
STATION RD
FATHOMS REACH
Rook Farm
HARBOUR RD
FERRY RD
RICHMOND DR
RICHMOND CL
GRAYLAND CL
SOUTH LEIGH GR
ST MARY'S RD
LIME GR
ST CATHERINE'S RD
ST AUBIN'S PARK
ST THOMAS AVE
STAUNTON AVE
JAMES CL
WALNUT TREE CL
BRIARWOOD GDNS
OAKWOOD RD
ELM CLOSE ESTATE
Sinah Common
West Town
FERNHURST CL
BEACH RD
SOUTH RD
GARDEN CL
ST HELEN'S RD
ST GEORGE'S RD
Golf Links
BACON LA
WINSTON CL
STAMFORD AVE
MAGDALA RD
GREEN LA
OLD TIMBERS
HOLLOW LA
WEST MEAD CL
WESTFIELD AVE
VICTORIA AVE
ALEXANDRA AVE
Club House
P
SEA FRONT
A3023
Sch
Hotel
CHICHESTER AVE
Gunner Point
Westfield
The Beach
South Hayling
Hayling Bay

183

160

D
E
F
4
3
2
1
01
00
99
98
72
73
74
Fleet
A3023
COPSE LA
YEW TREE RD
DAW LA
Caravan Park
HAYLING ISLAND
Verner Common
HAVANT RD
The Maypole (PH)
MILL RYTHE LA
Emsworth Channel
Manor House
Schs
Pound Marsh
Holiday Village
A3023
MANOR RD
Middle Marsh
REST-A-WYLE AVE
POUND LEA
KINGS RD
LULWORTH CL
CHURCH RD
Sch
KATRINA GDNS
DUNDONALD CL
Tournerbury Farm
Tourner Bury Marsh
EASTWOOD CL
Gable Head
TOURNERBURY LA
Tourner Bury Wood
Tourner Bury fort
POPLAR GR
BEECH GR
LABURNUM GR
HAWTHORNE GR
LEGION RD
ST MARY'S RD
F Sta
Sch
PALMERSTON RD
Sch
CHERRYWOOD GDNS
Liby
Tourner Bury Plantations
FIR TREE RD
LINDEN GR
ELM GR
ST LEONARD'S AVE
ST MARGARETS RD
SPENCER CL
GOLDRING CL
MY LORDS LA
OAK WOOD RD
ELM CL ESTATE
Mengham House
My Lord's Pond
Selsmore
HOLLOW LA
MENGHAM RD
MENGHAM LA
Mengham
OSPREY DR
SIMMONDS GREEN
SALTERNS CL
SALTERNS LA
MARINE WLK
RAMSAY RD
SELSMORE RD
Yacht Harbour
CHICHESTER AVE
YADHURST CL
SEA GROVE AVE
MENGHAM AVE
WEBB LA
NORTH CRES
WHITEHORN RD
BLACKTHORN DR
BLACKTHORN RD
ILEX WLK
SELSMORE AVE
SEA VIEW RD
NORMAN RD
CHANDLERS CL
Holiday Village
GRAND PAR
BOUND LA
ORCHARD RD
SEA FRONT ESTATE
MANOR WAY
THE SANDERLINGS
WEBB CL
WYBORN CL
RAILS LA
FISHERY LA
FORELAND CT
MARSHALL RD
Boating Lake
FISHERMANS WLK
Sea View
SEA FRONT
HAROLD RD
ST ANDREW'S RD
Sch
ST HERMANS RD
Eastoke
EASTOKE AVE
HASLEMERE GDNS
ITCHENOR RD
EARNLEY RD
SELSEY CL
WITTERINGS RD
SIDLESHAM CL
PAGHAM GDNS
BRACKLESHAM RD
SEAFARERS WLK
Coastguard Lookout
BEMBRIDGE DR
THE GLADE
CULVER DR
MEATH CL
THE STRAND
ROWIN CL
BURGESS CL
BIRDHAM RD
HAVEN RD
WEST HAYE RD
CREEK RD
NUTBOURNE RD
SANDY POINT RD
CORONATION RD
BOSMERE RD
TRELOAR RD
Hayling Bay
Prom
WINSOR CL
SOUTHWOOD RD
WHEATLANDS AVE
WHEATLANDS CL
ESTATE
SANDY BEACH

186

161

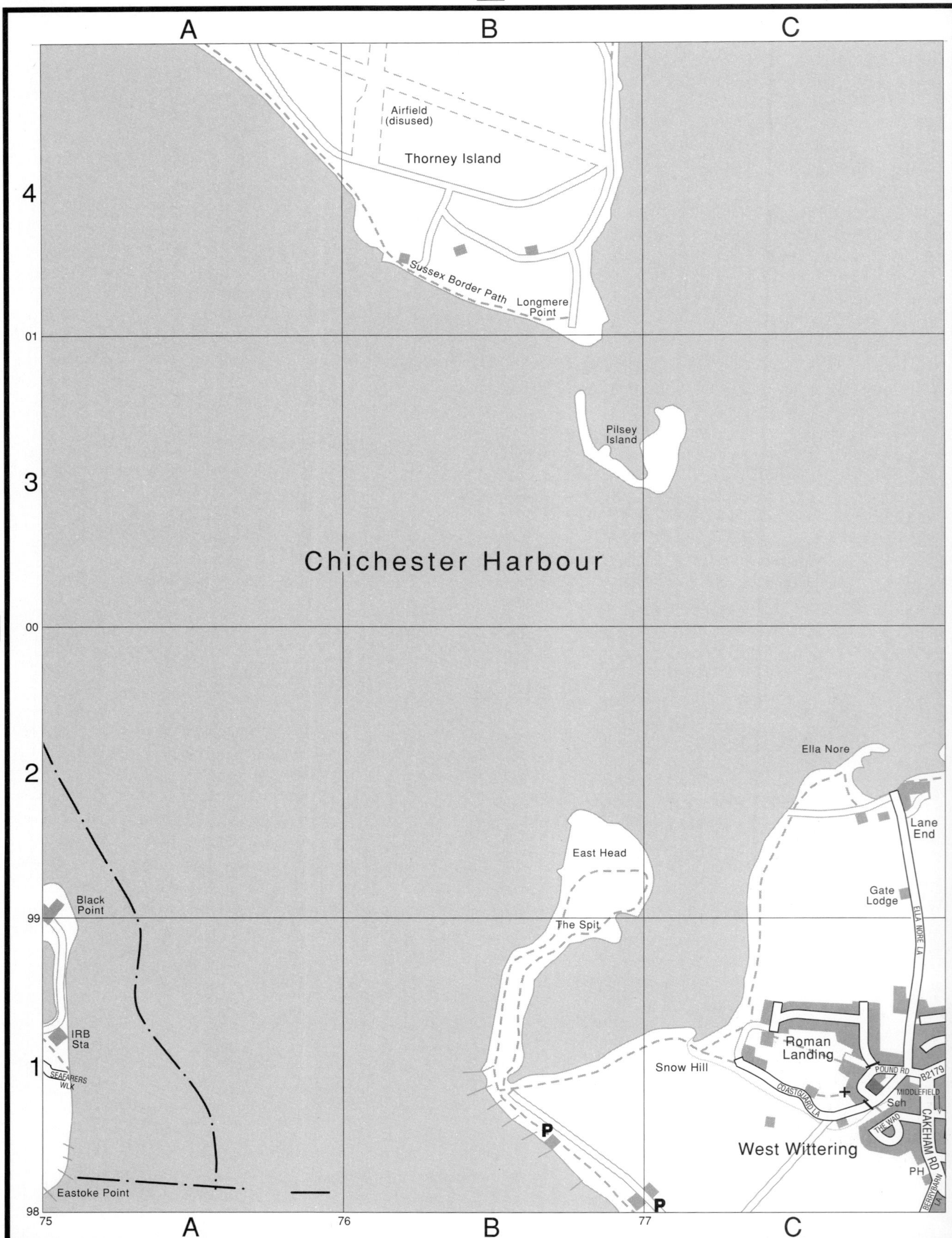

not continued, see key diagram

162

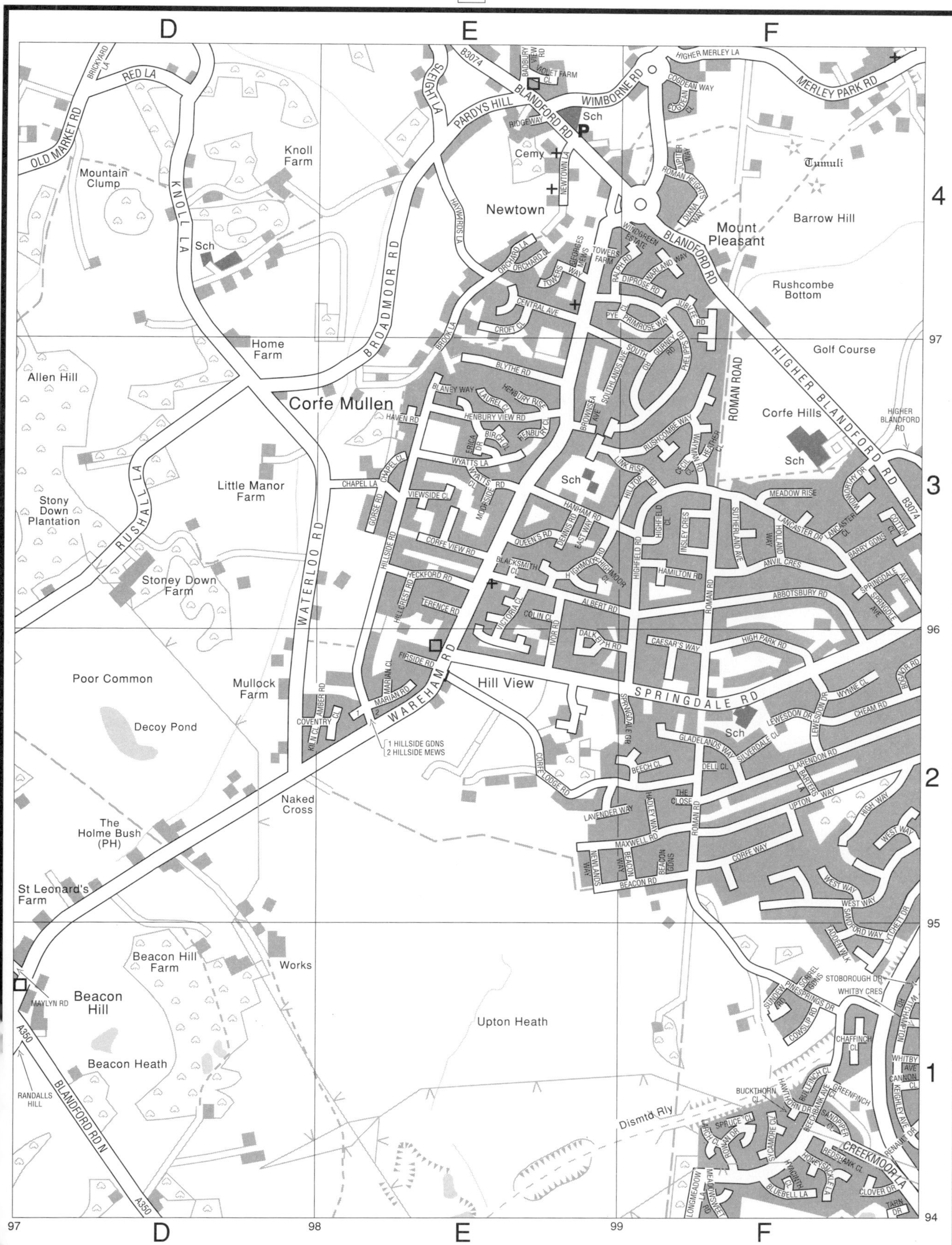
D
E
F
4
3
2
1
97
96
95
94
98
99
Red La
Brickyard La
Old Market Rd
Knoll La
Knoll Farm
Mountain Clump
Sch
Home Farm
Allen Hill
Broadmoor Rd
Sleight La
Pardys Hill
Blandford Rd
B3074
Badbury View Rd
Violet Farm Cl
Ridgeway
Wimborne Rd
Sch
Cemy
Newtown La
Newtown
Haywards La
Higher Merley La
Merley Park Rd
Cogdean Way
Cogdean Cl
Jupiter Way
Roman Heights
Diana Way
Tumuli
Barrow Hill
Mount Pleasant
Blandford Rd
Windgreen Estate
Rushcombe Bottom
Towers Farm
Orchard La
Orchard Cl
Towers Way
Georges Mews
Ralph Rd
Warland Way
Diprose Rd
Central Ave
Croft Cl
Pye Cl
Primrose Way
Jubilee Rd
Brook La
South Rd
Gurney Rd
Phelipps Rd
Southlands Ave
Golf Course
Higher Blandford Rd
Roman Road
Blythe Rd
Blaney Way
Henbury Rise
Laurel Cl
Corfe Mullen
Haven Rd
Henbury View Rd
Erica Dr
Birch Cl
Henbury Cl
Brownsea Ave
Rushcombe Way
Wayman Rd
Heather Cl
Corfe Hills
Sch
Wyatts La
Wyatts Cl
Chapel Cl
Chapel La
Viewside Cl
Moorside Rd
Link Rise
Hilltop Rd
Cecil Cl
Sch
Meadow Rise
Woodworthy Dr
Little Manor Farm
Rushall La
Stony Down Plantation
Waterloo Rd
Gorse Rd
Hillside Rd
Corfe View Rd
Queen's Rd
Dennis Rd
East Way
Hanham Rd
Highfield Cl
Insley Cres
Sutherland Ave
Holland Way
Lancaster Rd
Lancaster Cl
Barry Gdns
Cotton Cl
Anvil Cres
Blacksmith Cl
Highmoor Rd
Highmoor Cl
Highfield Rd
Hamilton Rd
Springdale Ave
Stoney Down Farm
Heckford Rd
Terence Rd
Hillcrest Rd
Victoria Cl
Colin Cl
Albert Rd
Roman Rd
Abbotsbury Rd
Ivor Rd
Dalkeith Rd
Caesar's Way
High Park Rd
Firside Rd
Marian Cl
Marian Rd
Wareham Rd
Hill View
Springdale Rd
Springdale Gr
Wynne Cl
Cheam Rd
Poor Common
Mullock Farm
Decoy Pond
Amber Rd
Coventry Cl
Kiln Cl
1 Hillside Gdns
2 Hillside Mews
Corfe Lodge Rd
Gladelands Way
Sch
Lewesdon Dr
Silverdale Cl
Beech Cl
Dell Cl
Clarendon Rd
Barters La
Upton Way
High Way
West Way
Naked Cross
The Holme Bush (PH)
The Close
Lavender Way
Hadley Way
Maxwell Rd
Newlands Way
Beacon Way
Beacon Gdns
Beacon Rd
Corfe Way
St Leonard's Farm
Sandford Way
Lytchett Dr
Lydden Wlk
Beacon Hill Farm
Works
Beacon Hill
Maylyn Rd
A350
Stoborough Dr
Whitby Cres
Sundew Rd
Sorrel Gdns
Pinesprings Dr
Cowslip Rd
Witchampton Rd
Upton Heath
Chaffinch Cl
Whitby Ave
Cannon Cl
Keighley Ave
Beacon Heath
Randalls Hill
Blandford Rd N
Buckthorn Cl
Hawthorn Dr
Bullfinch Cl
Greenfinch
Beechbank Ave
Sandpiper Cl
Renault Dr
Dismtd Rly
Spruce Cl
Larch Cl
Rowan Dr
Sycamore Cl
Hyacinth Cl
Redshank Cl
Honeysuckle La
Creekmoor La
Longmeadow La
Meadowsweet Rd
Bluebell La
Clover Dr
Tarn Dr

188

203

163

187

A
B
C
4
97
3
96
2
95
1
94
00
01
02
MERLEY PARK RD
Higher Merley Farm
Rose Lawn Coppice
Tumuli
Golf Course
Dismantled Railway
The Delph
A349
A341
DE MONTFORT RD
MIMOSA AVE
LYNWOOD DR
LONGESPEE RD
REMPSTONE RD
DELPH RD
IVY RD
EGDON DR
MONTACUTE WAY
QUEEN ANNE DR
HARVEY RD
Pound Close
Big Covert
BLACKWATER DR
ARROWSMITH LA
ARROWSMITH RD
Long Coppice
Arrowsmith House
Tumuli
Tumulus
Arrowsmith Coppice
GRAVEL HILL
Dunyeat's Hill
WOODLEAZE CL
MERRIFIELD DR
GREENSLEEVES AVE
MERRIFIELD AVE
UPPER GOLF LINKS RD
LOWER GOLF LINKS RD
Cemy
Crem
Tumuli
Sch
BIRKDALE RD
ST ANDREWS RD
BIRKDALE CT
BANSTEAD RD
FAIRVIEW RD
FAIRVIEW DR
FAIRVIEW CRES
WENTWORTH DR
GOLF LINKS RD
MOOR RD
BOOKDALE CL
SPRINGDALE RD
HIGHER BLANDFORD RD
B3074
STATION APP
Sch
Liby
DUNYEATS RD
TUDOR RD
MACAULAY RD
WESTHEATH RD
KIRKWAY
RIDGEWAY
LAUREL DR
WATER TOWER RD
ASHWOOD DR
BOGNOR RD
ASCOT RD
CHEAM RD
CLARENDON RD
UPTON WAY
WEST WAY
GRANGE RD
HEYSHAM RD
SELBY CL
SCARBOROUGH RD
Broadstone
Canford Heath
Longfleet Drive
Tumuli
WESTCROFT PARK
WHITCHURCH AVE
BADBURY CL
TURNWORTH CL
LOWER BLANDFORD RD
Playing Field
WALLACE RD
BENRIDGE CL
BEECH WOOD CL
SYDNEY RD
LYTCHETT DR
BARNRD
STEEPLETON RD
FONTMELL RD
THORN RD
EDGARTON RD
STEEPLE CL
WINTERSHAYES CL
WESTHAM CL
HARCOMBE CL
WHITECROSS CL
PORTESHAM WAY
HOLWELL CL
WILLWOOD CL
DENHAM CL
FURZEBROOK CL
PILSDON DR
CORSCOMBE CL
OVERCOMBE CL
TARRANT CL
BETTISCOMBE CL
HAWKCHURCH GDNS
MARSHWOOD AVE
Lodge Hill
Sch
COGDEANE RD
TOLLERFORD RD
STOURPAINE RD
SANDHILLS CL
NORTHBROOK RD
MISSION RD
PICKERING CL
YORK RD
LYTHAM RD
RIBBLE CL
Hillbourne
YORK CL
HILLBOURNE RD
NORTHBROOK RD
STOBOROUGH DR
KITCHENER CRES
EDWINA DR
CHETWODE WAY
WETHERBY CL
Schs
HASTINGS RD
GOUGH CRES
CLYDE RD
METHUEN RD
ALLENBY CL
ALLENBY RD
OKEFORD RD
GREENHAYS
A349
Sch
Darby's Corner
HASLER RD
BERE CL
CLAYFORD CL
HALSTOCK CRES
CHEDINGTON CL
WALDITCH GDNS
CULLIFORD CRES
ROWBARROW CL
PIMPERNE CL
KNOWLTON RD
B3074
CHALDON RD
MAPPERTON CL
PUDDLETOWN CRES
BEAMINSTER RD
ARMSWELL CL
REDCLIFFE RD
THORNCOMBE CL
P
WHITBY CRES
SKIPTON CL
WHITBY AVE
CANNON CL
COVENTRY CRES
RENAULT DR
MEAD CL
RUGBY RD
RUGBY RD
WAVELL AVE
GORT RD
ROBERTS RD
PLUMER RD
HILARY RD
LAMB CL
MILNE RD
THE PARADE
MARSHAL RD
DENISON RD
APSLEY CRES
CAVAN CRES
FRENCH RD
UNDERWOOD CL
B3074
TERENCE AVE
GENEVA AVE
PLANTATION RD
A349—WATERLOO RD
HOLNEST RD
WAYTOWN CL
STINSFORD RD
SANDYHURST CL
COWLEY RD
CANFORD HEATH RD
Sch
Canford Heath
SHERBORN CRES
HERSTONE CL
BOVINGTON CL
ADASTRAL RD
Haymoor Bottom
WARBURTON RD
BEAMISH RD
VERITY CRES
LYNN RD
Works
SOPERS LA
Waterloo
Sch

204

164
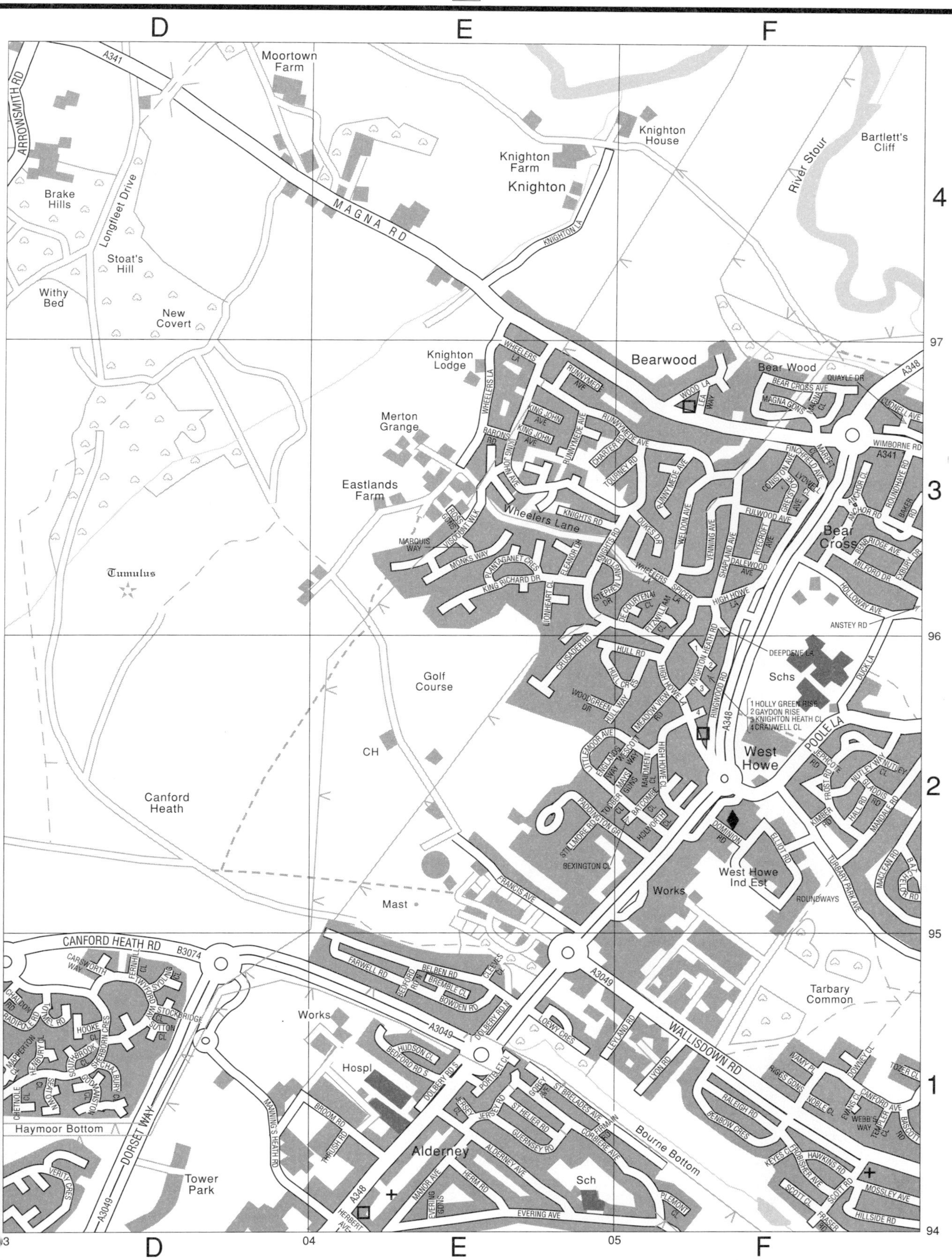
D
E
F
4
3
2
1
97
96
95
94
04
05
A341
ARROWSMITH RD
Moortown Farm
Knighton House
Knighton Farm
Knighton
Bartlett's Cliff
River Stour
Brake Hills
Longfleet Drive
MAGNA RD
KNIGHTON LA
Stoat's Hill
Withy Bed
New Covert
Knighton Lodge
Bearwood
Bear Wood
QUAYLE DR
BEAR CROSS AVE
MAGNA GDNS
A348
WHEELERS LA
RUNNYMEDE AVE
WOOD LA
LEA WAY
Merton Grange
KING JOHN AVE
BARONS RD
CHARTER RD
TOURNEY RD
FINCHFIELD AVE
WIMBORNE RD
CONISTON AVE
GREYSTOKE AVE
Eastlands Farm
Wheelers Lane
KNIGHTS RD
DUKES DR
WELDON AVE
VENNING AVE
SHAPLAND AVE
RYECROFT AVE
FULWOOD AVE
ANCHOR CL
ANCHOR RD
ROUNDHAYE RD
BAKER RD
Bear Cross
MARQUIS WAY
VISCOUNT WLK
MONKS WAY
PLANTAGENET CRES
ELEANOR DR
KING RICHARD DR
DALEWOOD AVE
BEN RIDGE AVE
MILFORD DR
EXBURY DR
Tumulus
LIONHEART CL
STEPHEN DR
DE COURTENAI CL
FITZWILLIAM CL
SPICER LA
HIGH HOWE LA
HOLLOWAY AVE
ANSTEY RD
CRUSADER RD
HULL RD
HULL CRES
KNIGHTON HEATH RD
DEEPDENE LA
Golf Course
Schs
DUCK LA
WOODGREEN DR
HULL WAY
MEADOW VIEW RD
RINGWOOD RD
1 HOLLY GREEN RISE
2 GAYDON RISE
3 KNIGHTON HEATH CL
4 CRANWELL CL
POOLE LA
CH
LITTLEMOOR AVE
ENGLANDS WAY
WESCOTT WAY
MAIDMENT CL
HIGH HOWE CL
West Howe
JEPHCOTE RD
FROST RD
NUTLEY WAY
NUTLEY CL
GLADDIS RD
Canford Heath
PADDINGTON GR
BATCOMBE CL
HOLWORTH CL
DOMINION RD
KIMBER RD
HALL RD
MANDALE RD
STILLMORE RD
BEXINGTON CL
ELLIOT RD
West Howe Ind Est
MACLEAN RD
BATCHELOR RD
FRANCIS AVE
Works
ROUNDWAYS
TURBARY PARK AVE
Mast
CANFORD HEATH RD
B3074
CARSWORTH WAY
FERNHILL CL
TWYFORD WAY
SYDLING CL
FARWELL RD
BELBEN RD
BREMBLE CL
BOWDEN RD
BEDFORD RD N
CLEEVES CL
A3049
Tarbary Common
STOCKBRIDGE
SUTTON CL
HOOKE CL
SHERBORN CRES
Works
HUDSON CL
BEDFORD RD S
DOLBERY RD N
DOLBERY RD S
LOEWY CRES
LEYLAND RD
WALLISDOWN RD
LYON RD
NAMY PL
RIGGS GDNS
DOWNEY CL
TOZER CL
Hospl
PORTELET CL
GOREY AVE
ST BRELADES AVE
JERSEY RD
ST HELIER RD
CANFORD AVE
NOBLE CL
EVANS CL
WEBB'S WAY
TEMPLER CL
BASCOTT RD
RALEIGH RD
BENBOW CRES
CHALDON RD
CHETNOLE CL
SEATOWN CL
DORSET WAY
MANNING'S HEATH RD
BROOM RD
THRUSH RD
GUERNSEY RD
CORBIERE AVE
FIRMAIN RD
Bourne Bottom
KEYES CL
FROBISHER AVE
HAWKINS RD
Haymoor Bottom
Alderney
ALDERNEY AVE
HERM RD
MANOR AVE
EVERING GDNS
Sch
SCOTT CL
SCOTT RD
MOSSLEY AVE
VERITY CRES
Tower Park
A348
HERBERT AVE
EVERING AVE
PLEMONT CL
FRASER RD
HILLSIDE RD
3
196
205

165

189

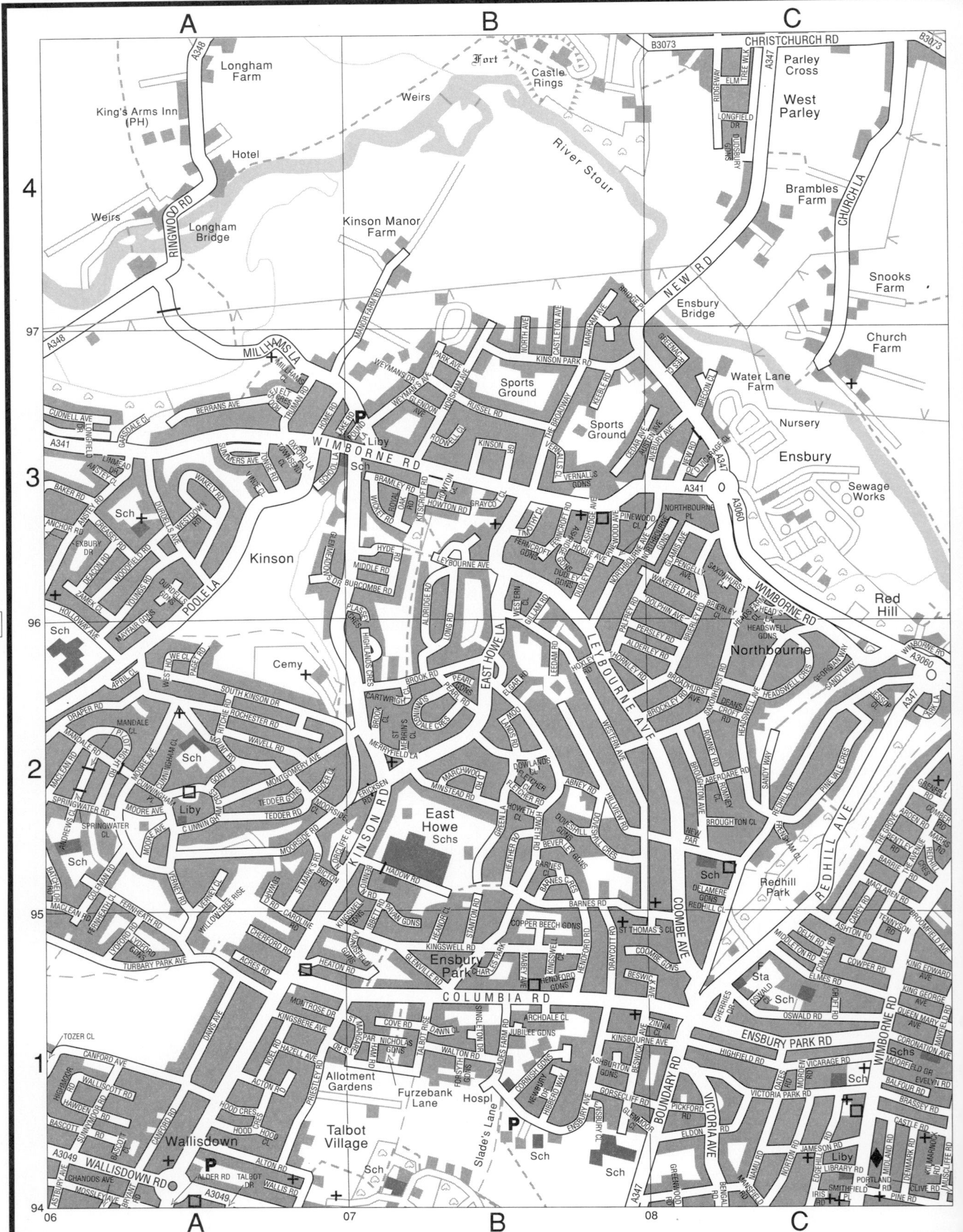
A
B
C
4
3
2
1
97
96
95
94
06
07
08
Longham Farm
King's Arms Inn (PH)
Hotel
Weirs
Longham Bridge
RINGWOOD RD
A348
Fort
Castle Rings
River Stour
Kinson Manor Farm
MANOR FARM RD
B3073
CHRISTCHURCH RD
Parley Cross
West Parley
Brambles Farm
CHURCH LA
Snooks Farm
NEW RD
Ensbury Bridge
Church Farm
Water Lane Farm
Nursery
Ensbury
Sewage Works
Red Hill
A341
A347
A3060
MILLHAMS LA
Sports Ground
KINSON PARK RD
WIMBORNE RD
Liby
Sch
Kinson
POOLE LA
Cemy
EAST HOWE LA
LEYBOURNE AVE
Northbourne
WIMBORNE RD
SOUTH KINSON DR
KINSON RD
East Howe Schs
REDHILL AVE
Redhill Park
COOMBE AVE
TURBARY PARK AVE
Ensbury Park
COLUMBIA RD
ENSBURY PARK RD
BOUNDARY RD
VICTORIA AVE
Allotment Gardens
Furzebank Lane
Hospl
Slade's Lane
Talbot Village
Wallisdown
WALLISDOWN RD
A3049
F Sta
Schs
WIMBORNE RD

206

166

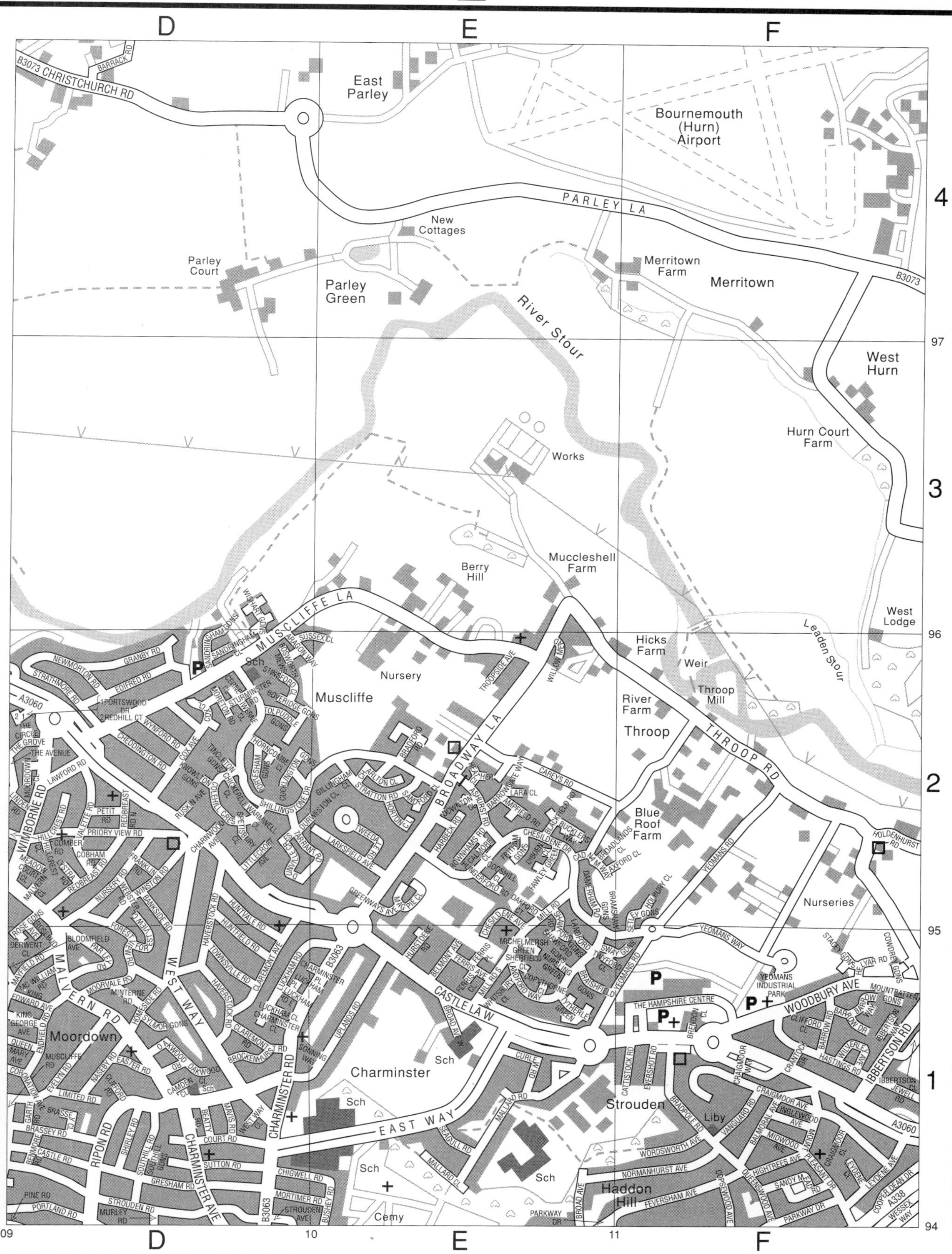
D
E
F
4
3
2
1
97
96
95
94
09
10
11
B3073 CHRISTCHURCH RD
BARRACK RD
East Parley
Bournemouth (Hurn) Airport
PARLEY LA
B3073
New Cottages
Parley Court
Parley Green
Merritown Farm
Merritown
River Stour
West Hurn
Hurn Court Farm
Works
Berry Hill
Muccleshell Farm
West Lodge
Leaden Stour
Hicks Farm
Weir
Throop Mill
River Farm
Throop
THROOP RD
MUSCLIFFE LA
Muscliffe
Nursery
Sch
BROADWAY LA
Blue Roof Farm
HOLDENHURST RD
Nurseries
YEOMANS WAY
YEOMANS INDUSTRIAL PARK
WOODBURY AVE
THE HAMPSHIRE CENTRE
CASTLE LA W
A3060
WIMBORNE RD
MALVERN RD
WEST WAY
Moordown
Charminster
Strouden
Liby
EAST WAY
CHARMINSTER RD
CHARMINSTER AVE
RIPON RD
B3063
Haddon Hill
Cemy
A338
NORMANHURST AVE
WORDSWORTH AVE
IBBERTSON RD

192

207

167

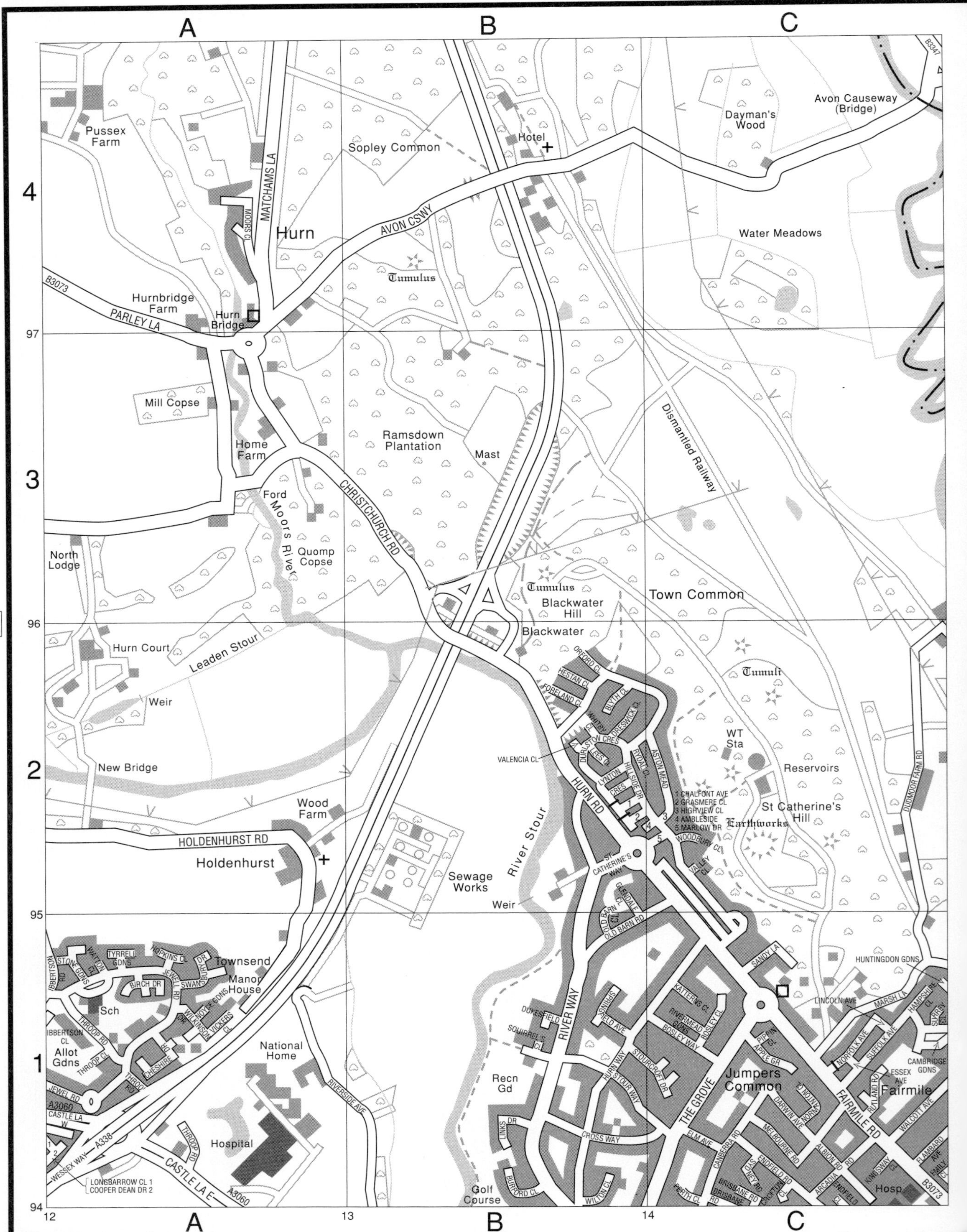
A
B
C
4
3
2
1
97
96
95
94
12
13
14
Pussex Farm
Sopley Common
Hotel
Dayman's Wood
Avon Causeway (Bridge)
B3347
MATCHAMS LA
MOORS CL
Hurn
AVON CSWY
Water Meadows
Tumulus
B3073
PARLEY LA
Hurnbridge Farm
Hurn Bridge
Mill Copse
Ramsdown Plantation
Mast
Dismantled Railway
Home Farm
CHRISTCHURCH RD
Ford
Moors River
Quomp Copse
North Lodge
Tumulus
Blackwater Hill
Town Common
Blackwater
Hurn Court
Leaden Stour
Weir
ORFORD CL
HESTAN CL
FORELAND CL
BLYTH CL
WHITBY CL
DRESWICK CL
DURLSTON CRES
VALENCIA CL
RYDAL CL
ASTON MEAD
HILLSIDE DR
LYNTON CRES
HURN RD
Tumuli
WT Sta
Reservoirs
New Bridge
1 CHALFONT AVE
2 GRASMERE CL
3 HIGHVIEW CL
4 AMBLESIDE
5 MARLOW DR
St Catherine's Hill
Earthworks
WOODBURY CL
VALLEY CL
ST CATHERINE'S WAY
Wood Farm
HOLDENHURST RD
Holdenhurst
Sewage Works
River Stour
Weir
GLENDALE CL
OLD BARN CL
OLD BARN RD
DUDMOOR FARM RD
Townsend
TYRRELL GDNS
HOPKINS CL
STONE GDNS
WATTON CL
JEWELL RD
BIRCH DR
SWANBURY DR
Manor House
Sch
KNOLE GDNS
WILKINSON DR
VICKERS CL
THROOP RD
THROOP CL
IBBERTSON CL
Allot Gdns
CHESHIRE DR
JEWEL RD
A3060
CASTLE LA W
WESSEX WAY
A338
LONGBARROW CL 1
COOPER DEAN DR 2
CASTLE LA E
A3060
THROOP RD
Hospital
National Home
RIVERSIDE AVE
SANDY LA
HUNTINGDON GDNS
DUKESFIELD
SQUIRRELS CL
RIVER WAY
SPRINGFIELD AVE
KATTERNS CL
RIVERMEAD GDNS
BOSLEY WAY
BOSLEY CL
LINCOLN AVE
MARSH LA
HAMPSHIRE CL
SURREY
NORFOLK AVE
SUFFOLK AVE
PIPPIN CL
APPLE GR
STOURCROFT DR
HURN WAY
STOUR WAY
Recn Gd
Jumpers Common
THE GROVE
DARWIN AVE
NORTON
ESSEX AVE
CAMBRIDGE GDNS
RUTLAND RD
Fairmile
FAIRMILE RD
WALCOTT AVE
LINKS DR
CROSS WAY
ELM AVE
CANBERRA RD
MELBOURNE RD
ALBION RD
KINGSWAY CL
FLAMBARD AVE
BURFORD CL
WILTON CL
PERTH CL
BRISBANE RD
ENDFIELD RD
CROYDON
ARCADIA RD
ENDFIELD CL
Hosp
B3073
Golf Course
A
B
C

191

208

168

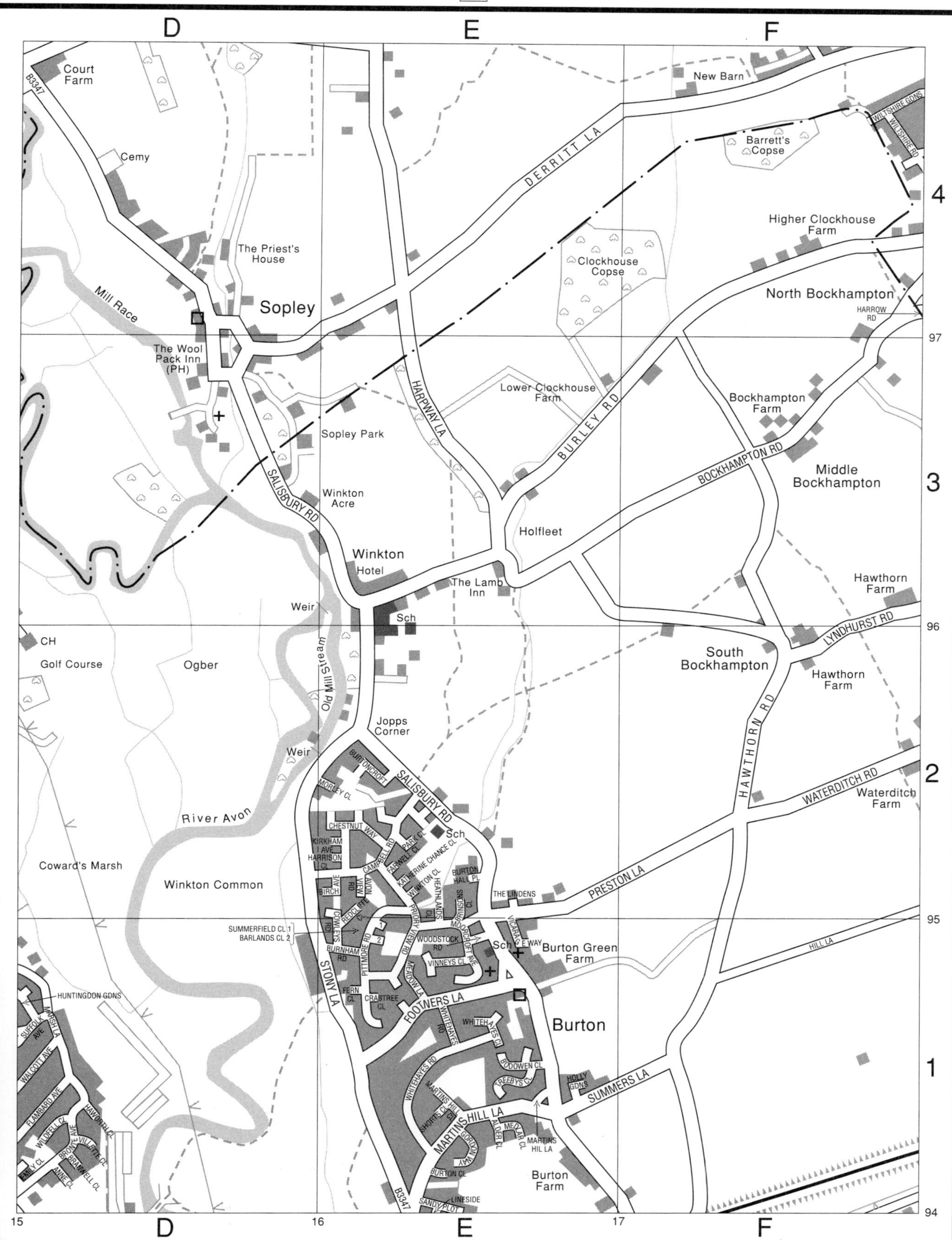
D
E
F
Court Farm
B3347
Cemy
New Barn
DERRITT LA
Barrett's Copse
WILTSHIRE GDNS
WILTSHIRE RD
4
Higher Clockhouse Farm
The Priest's House
Clockhouse Copse
North Bockhampton
HARROW RD
Mill Race
Sopley
97
The Wool Pack Inn (PH)
Lower Clockhouse Farm
HARPWAY LA
BURLEY RD
Bockhampton Farm
Sopley Park
BOCKHAMPTON RD
Middle Bockhampton
3
Winkton Acre
SALISBURY RD
Holfleet
Winkton
Hotel
The Lamb Inn
Hawthorn Farm
Weir
Sch
96
LYNDHURST RD
CH
Golf Course
Ogber
Old Mill Stream
South Bockhampton
Hawthorn Farm
Jopps Corner
HAWTHORN RD
Weir
BURTONCROFT
SALISBURY RD
2
MORLEY CL
WATERDITCH RD
Waterditch Farm
River Avon
CHESTNUT WAY
Sch
KIRKHAM AVE
HARRISON CL
CAMPBELL RD
PARK CL
FARWELL CL
KATHERINE CHANCE CL
Coward's Marsh
BIRCH
AVE
VIEW
AVON
REDCLIFFE
WINTON CL
HEATHLANDS
BURTON HALL PL
Winkton Common
PRESTON LA
THE LINDENS
COWLERS RD
PRIORY VIEW RD
SUMMERFIELD CL 1
BARLANDS CL 2
95
BURNHAM RD
PITTMORE RD
WOODSTOCK RD
VICARAGE WAY
Sch
Burton Green Farm
HILL LA
STONY LA
VINNEYS CL
MEADOW LA
HUNTINGDON GDNS
FERN CL
CRABTREE CL
FOOTNERS LA
WHITEHAYES RD
Burton
SUFFOLK AVE
WHITEHAYES CL
WALCOTT AVE
BODOWEN CL
1
WHITEHAYES RD
FREEBYS CL
HOLLY GDNS
SUMMERS LA
FLAMBARD AVE
HAWORTH CL
MARTINS HILL CL
MARTINS HILL LA
WILDFELL CL
BRONTE AVE
VILLETTE CL
ALDER CL
MEDLAR CL
MARTINS HILL LA
EMILY CL
BRAMWELL CL
ANNE CL
GORDON WAY
BURTON CL
Burton Farm
B3347
LINESIDE
SANDY PLOT
94
15
16
17
D
E
F

194

209

169

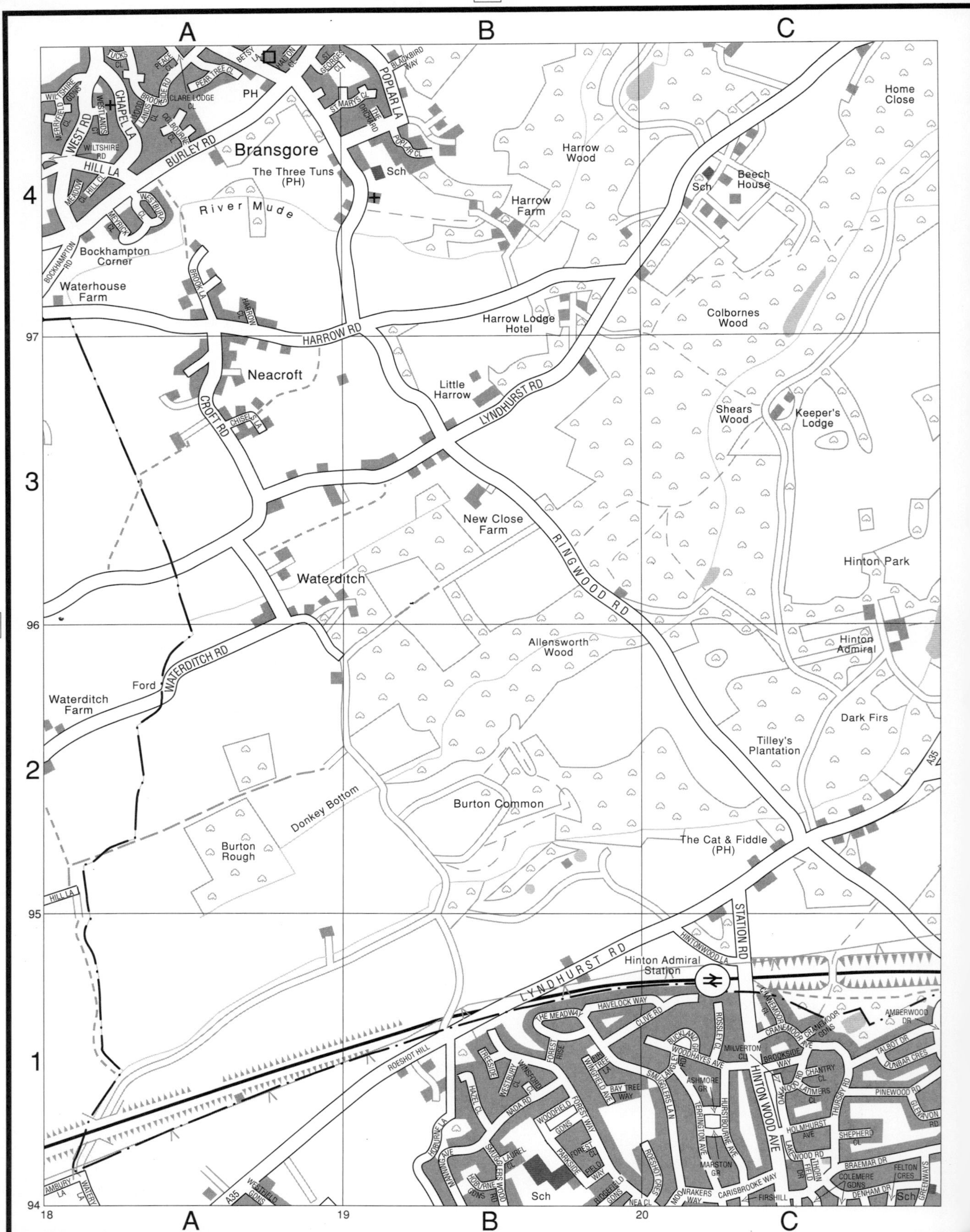

A
B
C
4
3
2
1
97
96
95
94
18
19
20
Bransgore
BURLEY RD
HILL LA
WEST RD
CHAPEL LA
WILTSHIRE RD
WESTLANDS CL
PEACE CL
PEAR TREE CL
CLARE LODGE CL
BETSY LA
HALTON CL
ST GEORGES CL
ST MARYS CL
THE ORCHARD
POPLAR LA
POPLAR CL
BLACKBIRD WAY
PH
The Three Tuns (PH)
Sch
River Mude
Harrow Wood
Harrow Farm
Home Close
Beech House
Bockhampton Corner
BOCKHAMPTON RD
Waterhouse Farm
BROOK LA
HARROW CL
HARROW RD
Harrow Lodge Hotel
Colbornes Wood
Neacroft
CROFT RD
CHISELS LA
Little Harrow
LYNDHURST RD
Shears Wood
Keeper's Lodge
New Close Farm
RINGWOOD RD
Hinton Park
Waterditch
WATERDITCH RD
Ford
Waterditch Farm
Allensworth Wood
Hinton Admiral
Dark Firs
Tilley's Plantation
A35
Burton Common
Donkey Bottom
Burton Rough
The Cat & Fiddle (PH)
HILL LA
STATION RD
HINTONWOOD LA
Hinton Admiral Station
LYNDHURST RD
THE MEADWAY
HAVELOCK WAY
CLIVE RD
ROSSLEY CL
MILVERTON CL
BROOKSIDE WAY
CHANTRY CL
AMBERWOOD DR
TALBOT DR
DUNBAR CRES
ROESHOT HILL
TREESIDE
WESTBURY CL
HAZEL CL
NADA RD
FOREST RISE
BAY TREE WAY
WOODFIELD GDNS
FOREST WAY
SMUGGLERS LA N
ASHMORE GR
HURSTBOURNE AVE
HINTON WOOD AVE
LATIMERS CL
THURSBY RD
PINEWOOD RD
GLENAVON RD
HOLMHURST AVE
SHEPHERD CL
HOBURNE LA
MANNING AVE
PARKSIDE
MARSTON GR
CARISBROOKE WAY
LAKEWOOD RD
BRAEMAR DR
FELTON CRES
COLEMERE GDNS
DENHAM DR
GREENWAYS
MOONRAKERS WAY
FIRSHILL
RIDGEFIELD GDNS
ROESHOT CRES
Sch
AMBURY LA
WATERY LA
WESTFIELD GDNS
A35

193

210

170

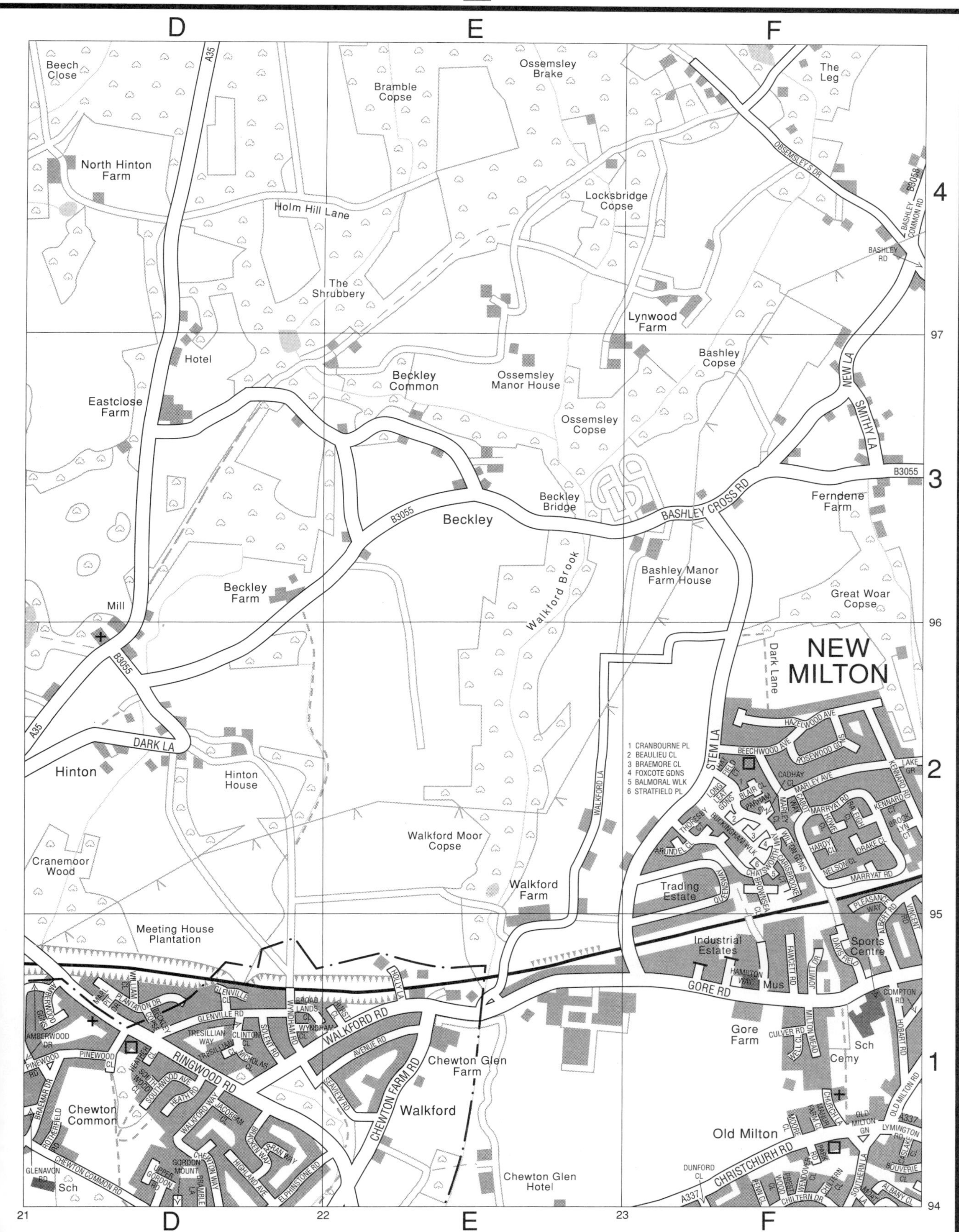
D
E
F
Beech Close
North Hinton Farm
A35
Bramble Copse
Ossemsley Brake
The Leg
Holm Hill Lane
Locksbridge Copse
OBSEMSLEY S DR
B3058
BASHLEY COMMON RD
BASHLEY RD
4
The Shrubbery
Lynwood Farm
97
Hotel
Beckley Common
Ossemsley Manor House
Bashley Copse
NEW LA
Eastclose Farm
Ossemsley Copse
SMITHY LA
B3055
3
Beckley Bridge
BASHLEY CROSS RD
Ferndene Farm
Beckley
Bashley Manor Farm House
Beckley Farm
Mill
Walkford Brook
Great Woar Copse
96
Dark Lane
NEW MILTON
A35
DARK LA
Hinton
Hinton House
STEM LA
HAZELWOOD AVE
BEECHWOOD AVE
ROSEWOOD GDNS
1 CRANBOURNE PL
2 BEAULIEU CL
3 BRAEMORE CL
4 FOXCOTE GDNS
5 BALMORAL WLK
6 STRATFIELD PL
LAKE GR
KENNARD RD
CADHAY CL
MARLEY AVE
2
WALKFORD LA
Walkford Moor Copse
Cranemoor Wood
ARUNDEL CL
MARRYAT RD
NELSON CL
DRAKE CL
HARDY CL
Walkford Farm
Trading Estate
95
Meeting House Plantation
Industrial Estates
PLEASANCE WAY
Sports Centre
GORE RD
HAMILTON WAY
Mus
FAWCETT RD
JOWITT DR
COMPTON RD
WALKFORD RD
RINGWOOD RD
Gore Farm
CULVER RD
MILTON MEAD
Sch
Cemy
HOBART RD
Chewton Glen Farm
CHEWTON FARM RD
1
Chewton Common
Walkford
OLD MILTON RD
A337
Old Milton
LYMINGTON RD
CHRISTCHURCH RD
DUNFORD CL
GLENAVON RD
Sch
CHEWTON COMMON RD
Chewton Glen Hotel
A337
CHILTERN DR
ALBANY CL
SOUTHERN LA
94
21
22
23
D
E
F

196

211

171

195

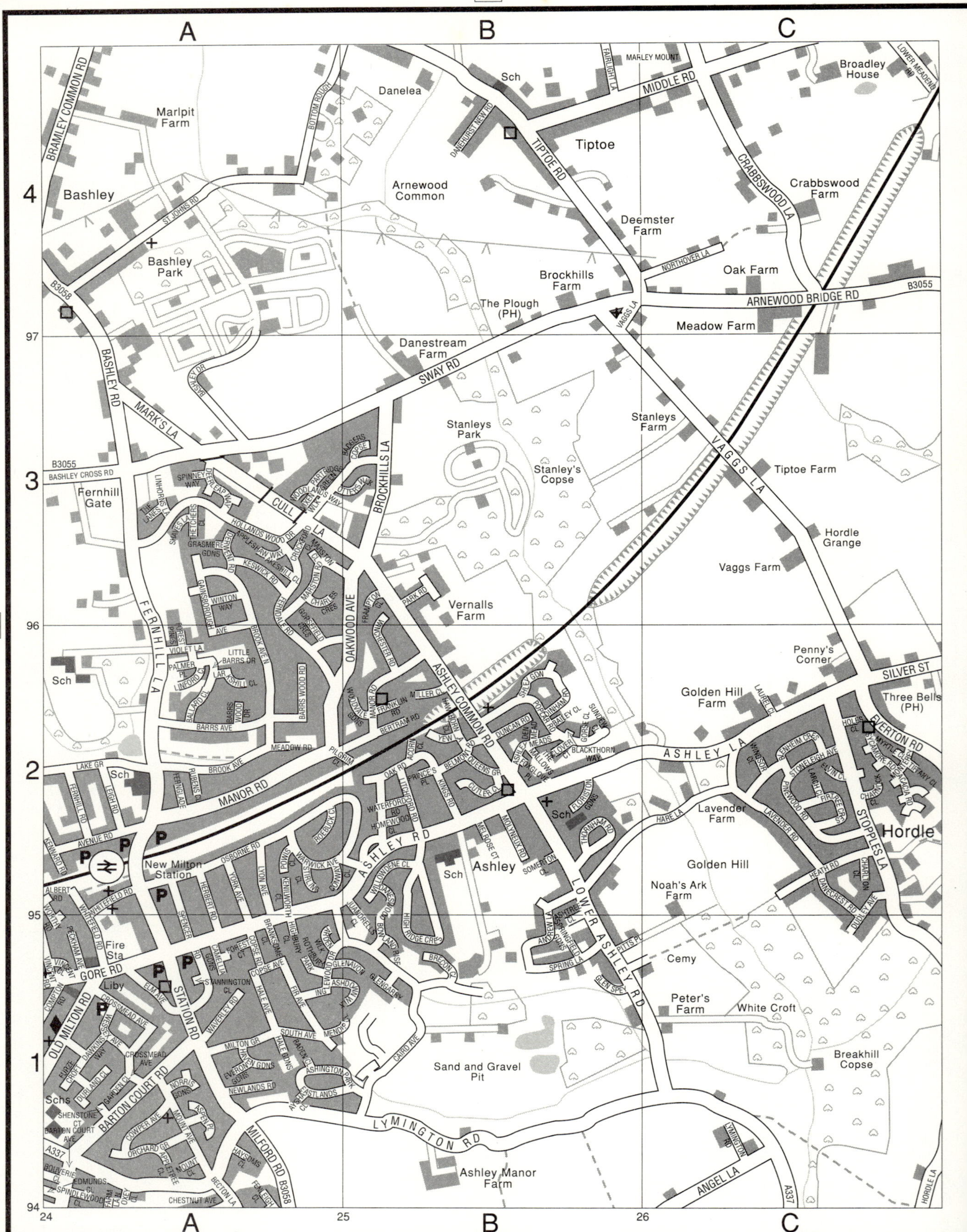
A
B
C
1
2
3
4
24
25
26
94
95
96
97
Marlpit Farm
Danelea
Sch
MARLEY MOUNT
MIDDLE RD
Broadley House
LOWER MEADENS RD
BRAMLEY COMMON RD
BOTTOM ROUGH
DANEHURST NEW RD
FAIRLIGHT LA
Tiptoe
TIPTOE RD
Arnewood Common
Bashley
ST JOHNS RD
Bashley Park
Deemster Farm
CRABBSWOOD LA
Crabbswood Farm
NORTHOVER LA
Oak Farm
Brockhills Farm
B3058
The Plough (PH)
VAGGS LA
ARNEWOOD BRIDGE RD
B3055
Meadow Farm
Danestream Farm
BASHLEY RD
BASHLEY DR
SWAY RD
MARK'S LA
Stanleys Park
Stanleys Farm
B3055
BASHLEY CROSS RD
Stanley's Copse
Tiptoe Farm
Fernhill Gate
CULL LA
BROCKHILLS LA
HOLLANDS WOOD DR
Hordle Grange
Vaggs Farm
OAKWOOD AVE
Vernalls Farm
FERNHILL LA
PARK RD
Penny's Corner
Sch
SILVER ST
Golden Hill Farm
Three Bells (PH)
ASHLEY COMMON RD
EVERTON RD
BARRS AVE
MEADOW RD
PILGRIM CL
ASHLEY LA
BLACKTHORN WAY
LAKE GR
Sch
MANOR RD
BROOK AVE
Lavender Farm
HARE LA
Sch
Hordle
STOPPLES LA
AVENUE RD
ASHLEY RD
New Milton Station
Ashley
Sch
Golden Hill
Noah's Ark Farm
LOWER ASHLEY RD
Fire Sta
GORE RD
Liby
STATION RD
Cemy
OLD MILTON RD
Peter's Farm
White Croft
BARTON COURT RD
Sand and Gravel Pit
Breakhill Copse
Schs
MILFORD RD B3058
LYMINGTON RD
LYMINGTON RD
Ashley Manor Farm
A337
ANGEL LA
A337
HORDLE LA
CHESTNUT AVE
BECTON LA

212

172

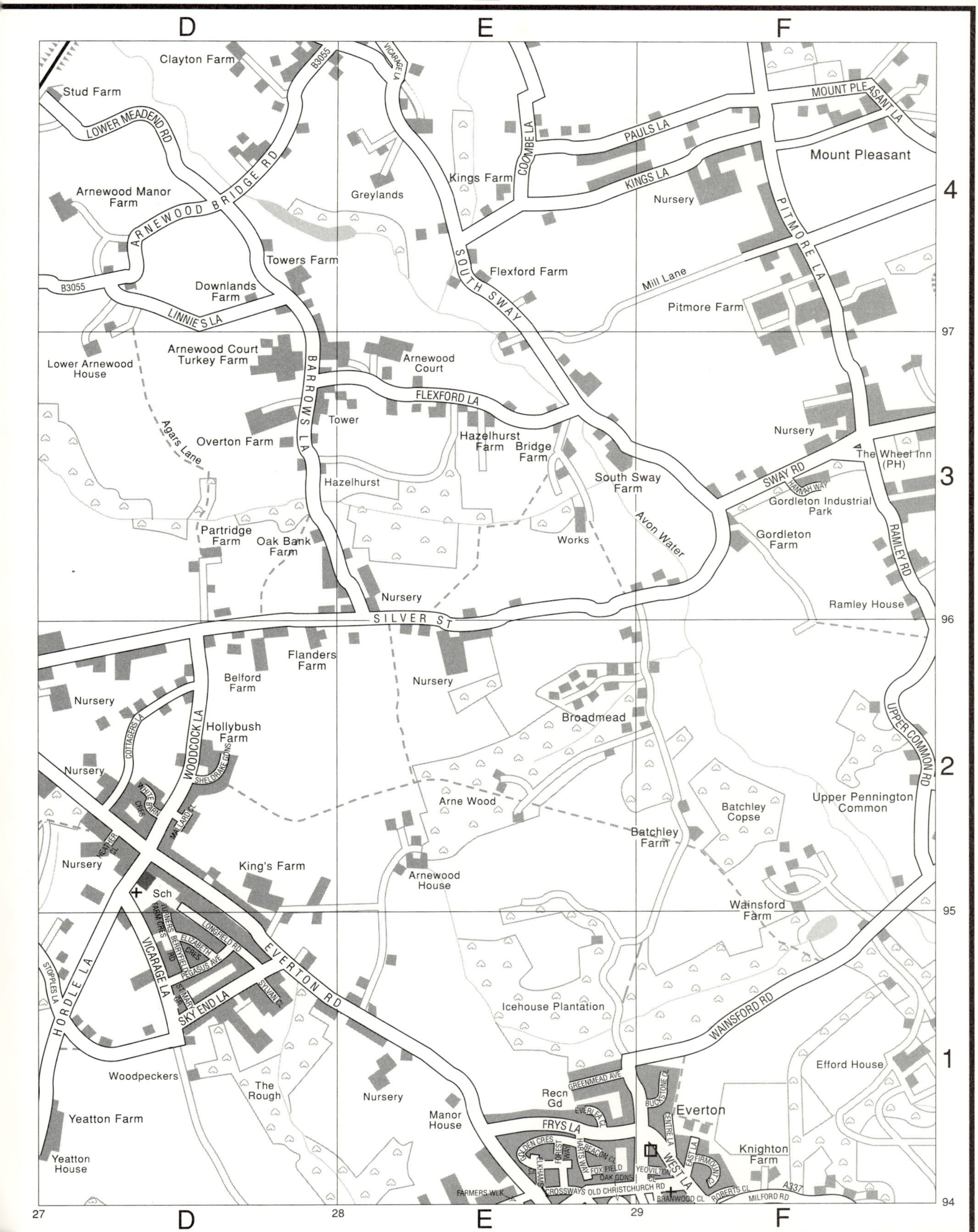
D
E
F
Clayton Farm
Stud Farm
LOWER MEADEND RD
B3055
VICARAGE LA
COOMBE LA
PAULS LA
MOUNT PLEASANT LA
Mount Pleasant
KINGS LA
Kings Farm
Greylands
Arnewood Manor Farm
ARNEWOOD BRIDGE RD
Nursery
PITMORE LA
4
SOUTH SWAY
Towers Farm
Flexford Farm
Mill Lane
Downlands Farm
LINNIES LA
Pitmore Farm
97
Arnewood Court Turkey Farm
Lower Arnewood House
Arnewood Court
BARROWS LA
FLEXFORD LA
Tower
Agars Lane
Overton Farm
Hazelhurst Farm
Bridge Farm
Nursery
The Wheel Inn (PH)
South Sway Farm
SWAY RD
HANNAH WAY
3
Hazelhurst
Gordleton Industrial Park
Avon Water
Gordleton Farm
Partridge Farm
Oak Bank Farm
Works
RAMLEY RD
Nursery
Ramley House
SILVER ST
96
Flanders Farm
Belford Farm
Nursery
Nursery
Broadmead
COTTAGERS LA
WOODCOCK LA
Hollybush Farm
UPPER COMMON RD
SHELDRAKE GDNS
Nursery
2
WHITE BARN CRES
MALLARD CL
Arne Wood
Batchley Copse
Upper Pennington Common
Batchley Farm
HEATHER CL
Nursery
King's Farm
Arnewood House
Sch
Wainsford Farm
95
TURNERS FARM CRES
BERRYFIELD RD
ELIZABETH CRES
LONGFIELD RD
PEGASUS AVE
EVERTON RD
STOPPLES LA
HORDLE LA
VICARAGE LA
ST MARY'S GR
SKY END LA
SYLVAN CL
Icehouse Plantation
WAINSFORD RD
1
Efford House
Woodpeckers
The Rough
Nursery
GREENMEAD AVE
Recn Gd
BUCKSTONE CL
Everton
Yeatton Farm
Manor House
EVERLEA CL
FRYS LA
CENTRE LA
Knighton Farm
Yeatton House
GOLDEN CRES
FOREST WAY
HARTS WAY
BEACON CL
FOX FIELD
YEOVILTON CL
WEST LA
EAST LA
FIRMOUNT CL
ELKHAMS CL
OAK GDNS
OLD CHRISTCHURCH RD
FARMERS WLK
CROSSWAYS
BRANWOOD CL
ROBERTS CL
A337
MILFORD RD
94
27
28
29
D
E
F

198

213

173

197

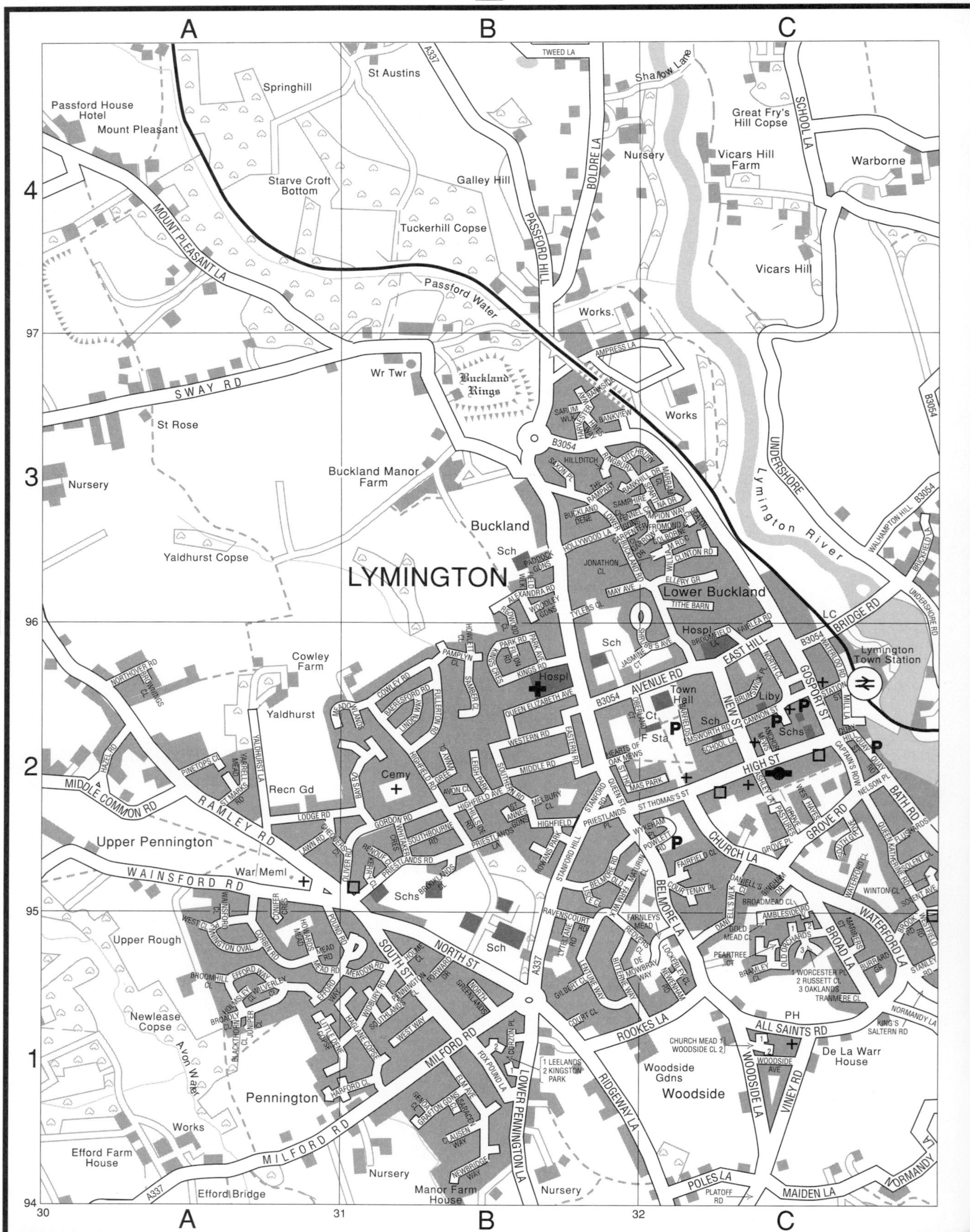
A
B
C
4
3
2
1
97
96
95
94
30
31
32
TWEED LA
St Austins
Springhill
Passford House Hotel
Mount Pleasant
Shallow Lane
SCHOOL LA
Great Fry's Hill Copse
Nursery
Vicars Hill Farm
Warborne
Starve Croft Bottom
Galley Hill
BOLDRE LA
PASSFORD HILL
MOUNT PLEASANT LA
Tuckerhill Copse
Vicars Hill
A337
Passford Water
Works.
AMPRESS LA
SWAY RD
Wr Twr
Buckland Rings
Works
B3054
St Rose
UNDERSHORE
Lymington River
Nursery
Buckland Manor Farm
Buckland
Yaldhurst Copse
Sch
LYMINGTON
Lower Buckland
TITHE BARN
LC
BRIDGE RD
Lymington Town Station
Hospl
Cowley Farm
Yaldhurst
AVENUE RD
Town Hall
Ct
F Sta
Sch
Liby
Schs
NEW ST
GOSPORT ST
EAST HILL
HIGH ST
MIDDLE COMMON RD
RAMLEY RD
Recn Gd
Cemy
Upper Pennington
WAINSFORD RD
War Meml
Schs
CHURCH LA
Upper Rough
NORTH ST
SOUTH ST
Sch
Newlease Copse
Avon Water
MILFORD RD
LOWER PENNINGTON LA
RIDGEWAY LA
ROOKES LA
ALL SAINTS RD
PH
De La Warr House
Woodside Gdns
Woodside
WOODSIDE LA
VINEY RD
Pennington
Works
Efford Farm House
Nursery
Manor Farm House
Nursery
Efford Bridge
POLES LA
MAIDEN LA
NORMANDY
WATERFORD LA
BROAD LA
BELMORE LA
STANFORD HILL
1 WORCESTER PL
2 RUSSETT CL
3 OAKLANDS
CHURCH MEAD 1
WOODSIDE CL 2
1 LEELANDS
2 KINGSTON PARK

214

174

200

not continued, see key diagram

175

199

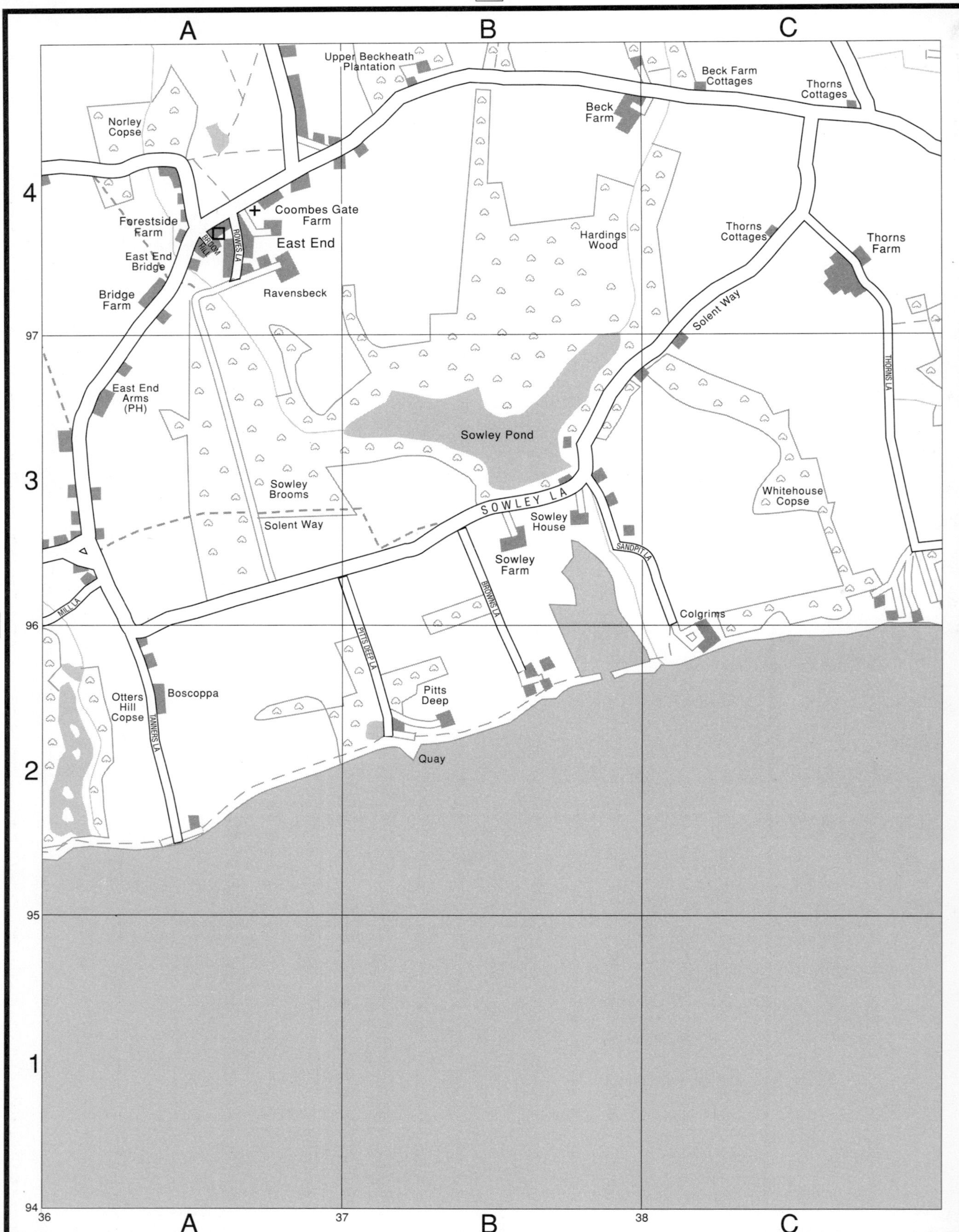

A
B
C
4
3
2
1
97
96
95
94
36
37
38
Upper Beckheath Plantation
Beck Farm Cottages
Thorns Cottages
Beck Farm
Norley Copse
Coombes Gate Farm
East End
Forestside Farm
East End Bridge
BROOM HILL
ROWES LA
Bridge Farm
Ravensbeck
Hardings Wood
Thorns Cottages
Thorns Farm
Solent Way
THORNS LA
East End Arms (PH)
Sowley Pond
Sowley Brooms
Solent Way
SOWLEY LA
Sowley House
Sowley Farm
Whitehouse Copse
SANDPIT LA
BROWNS LA
MILL LA
PITTS DEEP LA
Colgrims
Otters Hill Copse
Boscoppa
TANNERS LA
Pitts Deep
Quay

176

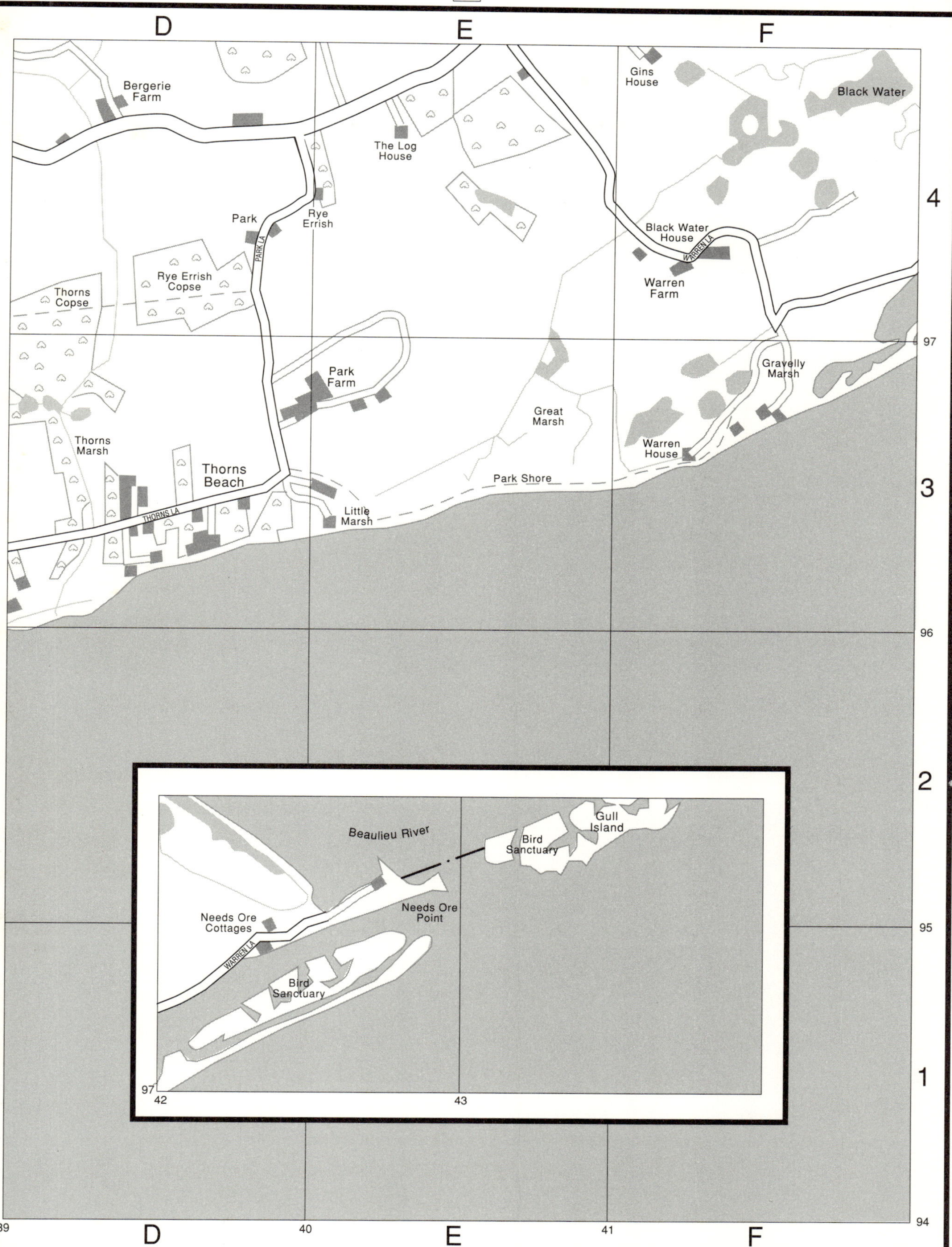

not continued, see key diagram

181

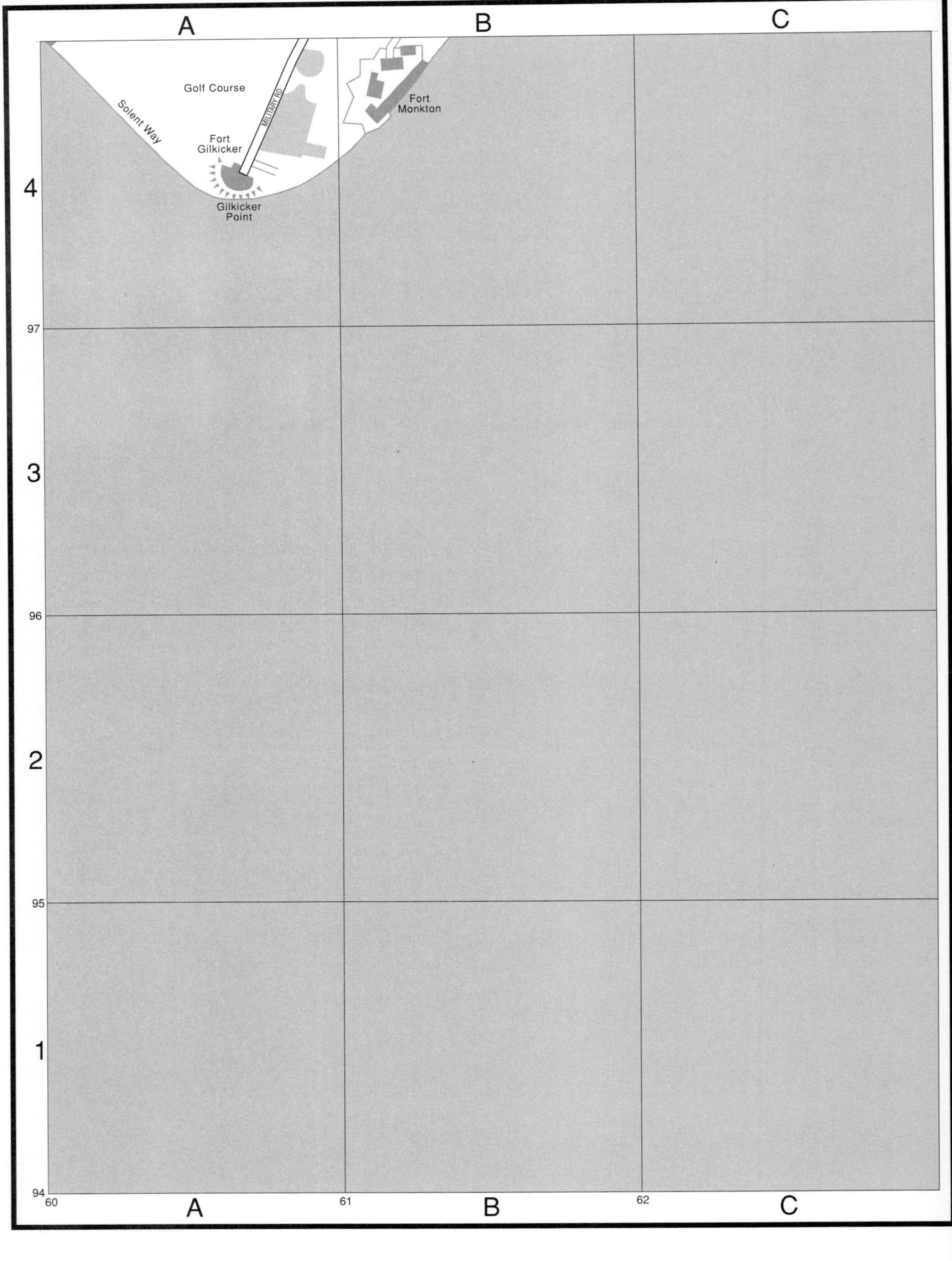
A
B
C
4
3
2
1
97
96
95
94
60
61
62
Golf Course
Solent Way
MILITARY RD
Fort Gilkicker
Gilkicker Point
Fort Monkton

187

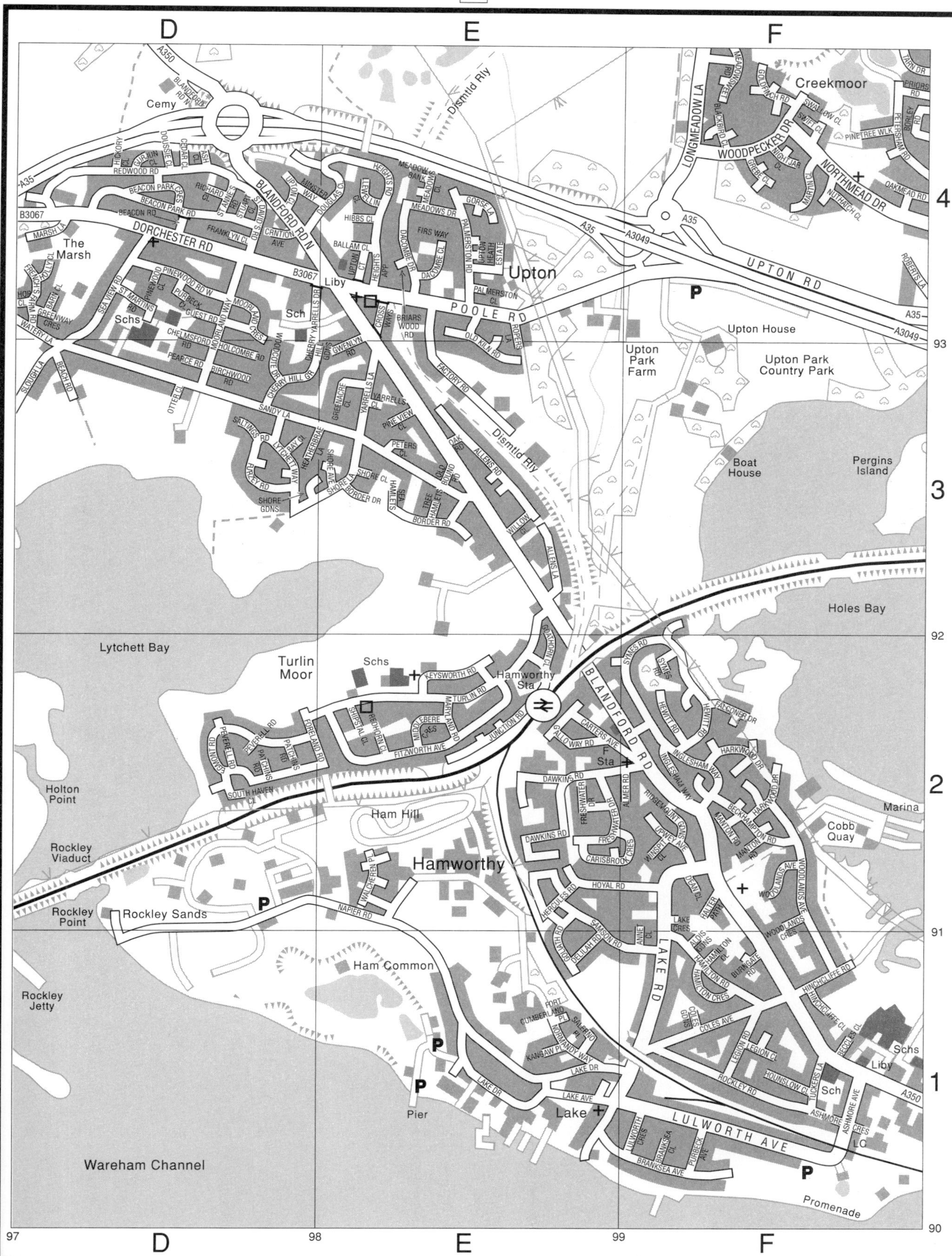
D
E
F
Cemy
The Marsh
Upton
Creekmoor
Upton House
Upton Park Farm
Upton Park Country Park
Boat House
Pergins Island
Holes Bay
Lytchett Bay
Turlin Moor
Schs
Sch
Liby
Hamworthy Sta
Holton Point
Rockley Viaduct
Rockley Point
Rockley Sands
Rockley Jetty
Ham Hill
Hamworthy
Ham Common
Pier
Lake
Marina
Cobb Quay
Wareham Channel
Promenade
LC
F Sta
Dismtld Rly
A350
A35
A3049
B3067
DORCHESTER RD
POOLE RD
UPTON RD
BLANDFORD RD N
BLANDFORD RD
LAKE RD
LULWORTH AVE
LONGMEADOW LA
WOODPECKER DR
NORTHMEAD DR
SANDY LA
FITZWORTH AVE
NAPIER RD
HOYAL RD
HINCHCLIFFE RD
ROCKLEY RD
BRANKSEA AVE
FACTORY RD
ALLENS LA
P
1
2
3
4
90
91
92
93
97
98
99

204

188

203

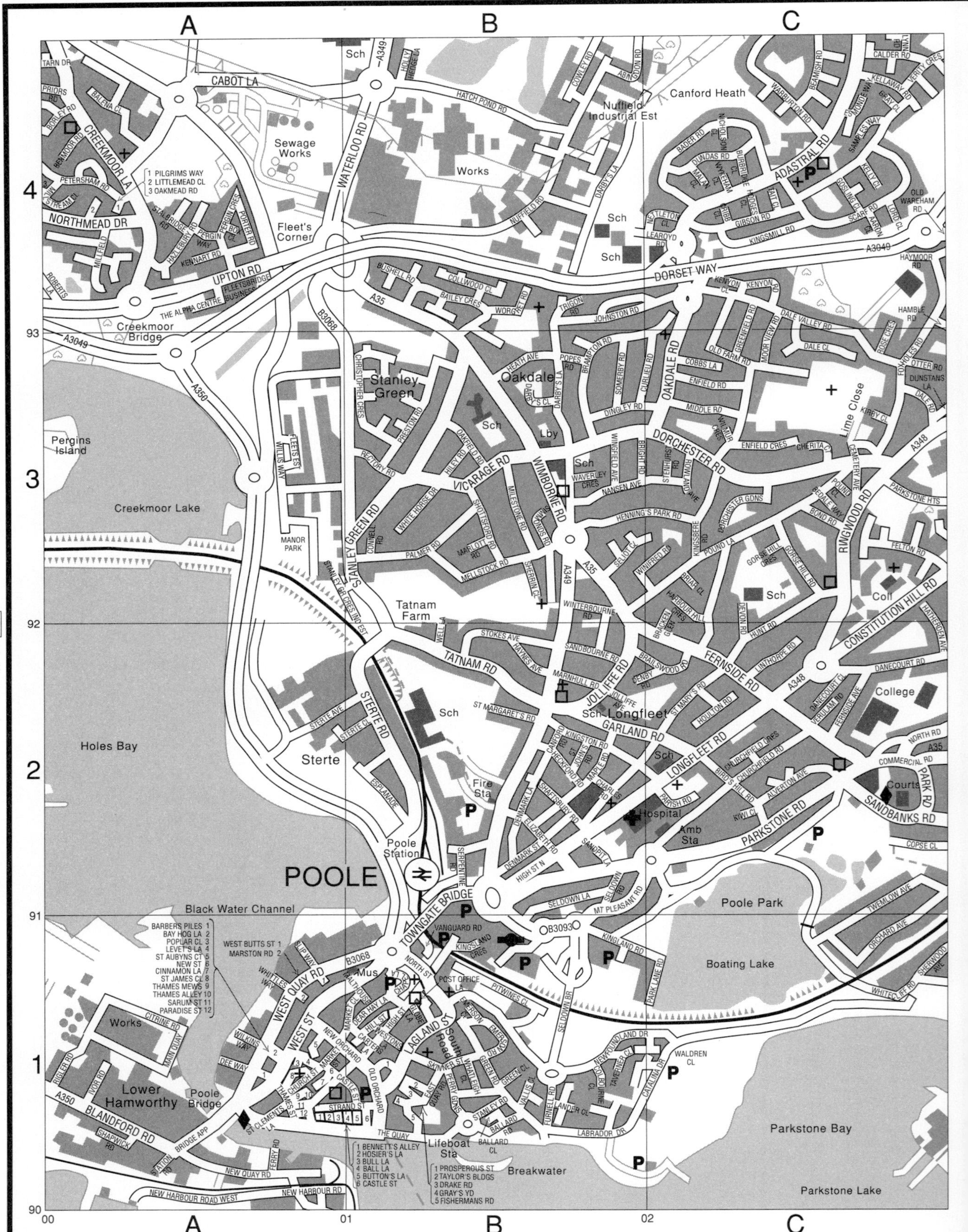
A
B
C
4
3
2
1
93
92
91
90
00
01
02
CABOT LA
HATCH POND RD
Sch
Sewage Works
Works
Canford Heath
Nuffield Industrial Est
CREEKMOOR LA
1 PILGRIMS WAY
2 LITTLEMEAD CL
3 OAKMEAD RD
NORTHMEAD DR
WATERLOO RD
Fleet's Corner
NUFFIELD RD
DARBY'S LA
ADASTRAL RD
KINGSMILL RD
GIBSON RD
OLD WAREHAM RD
A3049
UPTON RD
DORSET WAY
BUSHELL RD
COLLWOOD CL
BAILEY CRES
A35
Creekmoor Bridge
A3049
THE ALPHA CENTRE
FLEETSBRIDGE BUSINESS
B3068
A350
Stanley Green
Oakdale
DALE VALLEY RD
OAKDALE RD
Lime Close
Pergins Island
Creekmoor Lake
VICARAGE RD
WIMBORNE RD
DORCHESTER RD
Lby
Sch
STANLEY GREEN RD
MANOR PARK
A349
A35
RINGWOOD RD
CONSTITUTION HILL RD
Coll
Tatnam Farm
TATNAM RD
FERNSIDE RD
A348
College
Holes Bay
STERTE RD
Sterte
Sch
JOLLIFFE RD
Longfleet
GARLAND RD
LONGFLEET RD
Fire Sta
Hospital
Amb Sta
PARKSTONE RD
SANDBANKS RD
Courts
PARK RD
Poole Station
POOLE
TOWNGATE BRIDGE
Black Water Channel
Poole Park
Boating Lake
BARBERS PILES 1
BAY HOG LA 2
POPLAR CL 3
LEVET'S LA 4
ST AUBYNS CT 5
NEW ST 6
CINNAMON LA 7
ST JAMES CL 8
THAMES MEWS 9
THAMES ALLEY 10
SARUM ST 11
PARADISE ST 12
WEST BUTTS ST 1
MARSTON RD 2
WEST QUAY RD
Mus
WEST ST
B3093
SELDOWN BR
Works
Lower Hamworthy
Poole Bridge
A350
BLANDFORD RD
THE QUAY
Lifeboat Sta
Breakwater
1 BENNETT'S ALLEY
2 HOSIER'S LA
3 BULL LA
4 BALL LA
5 BUTTON'S LA
6 CASTLE ST
1 PROSPEROUS ST
2 TAYLOR'S BLDGS
3 DRAKE RD
4 GRAY'S YD
5 FISHERMANS RD
NEW QUAY RD
NEW HARBOUR ROAD WEST
NEW HARBOUR RD
Parkstone Bay
Parkstone Lake

215

189

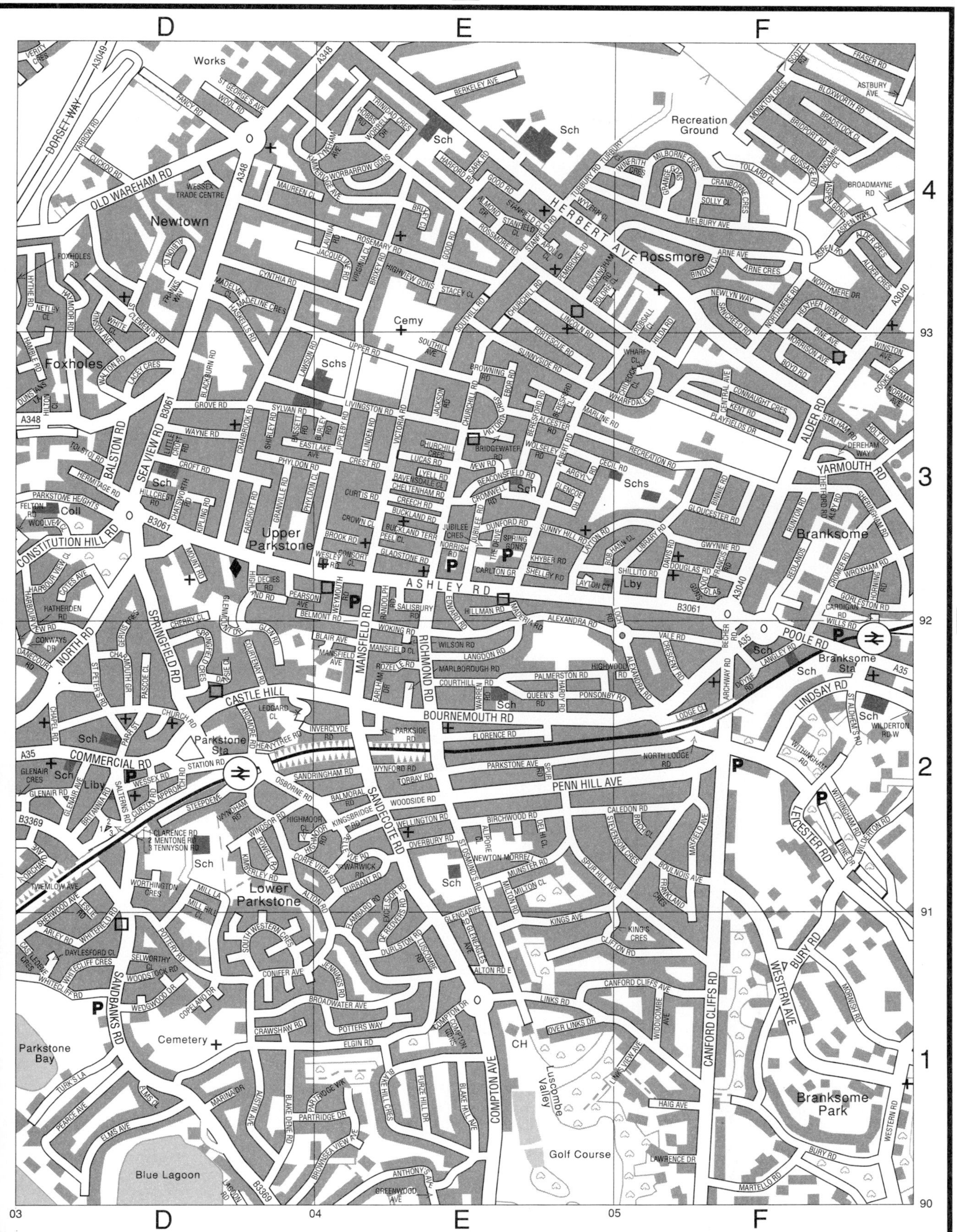
D
E
F
4
3
2
1
93
92
91
90
03
04
05
Works
Recreation Ground
Sch
Newtown
WESSEX TRADE CENTRE
OLD WAREHAM RD
DORSET WAY
HERBERT AVE
Rossmore
Cemy
Schs
Foxholes
Upper Parkstone
ASHLEY RD
Branksome
YARMOUTH RD
POOLE RD
Branksome Sta
Lby
Coll
CONSTITUTION HILL RD
CASTLE HILL
BOURNEMOUTH RD
COMMERCIAL RD
Parkstone Sta
Liby
PARKSTONE AVE
PENN HILL AVE
Lower Parkstone
Cemetery
Parkstone Bay
Blue Lagoon
SANDBANKS RD
COMPTON AVE
CANFORD CLIFFS RD
Luscombe Valley
Golf Course
CH
Branksome Park
WESTERN AVE
LINDSAY RD
LEICESTER RD
ALDER RD
ASHLEY RD
RICHMOND RD
MANSFIELD RD
SANDECOTE RD
SPRINGFIELD RD
SEA VIEW RD
BALSTON RD
NORTH RD

206

216

190

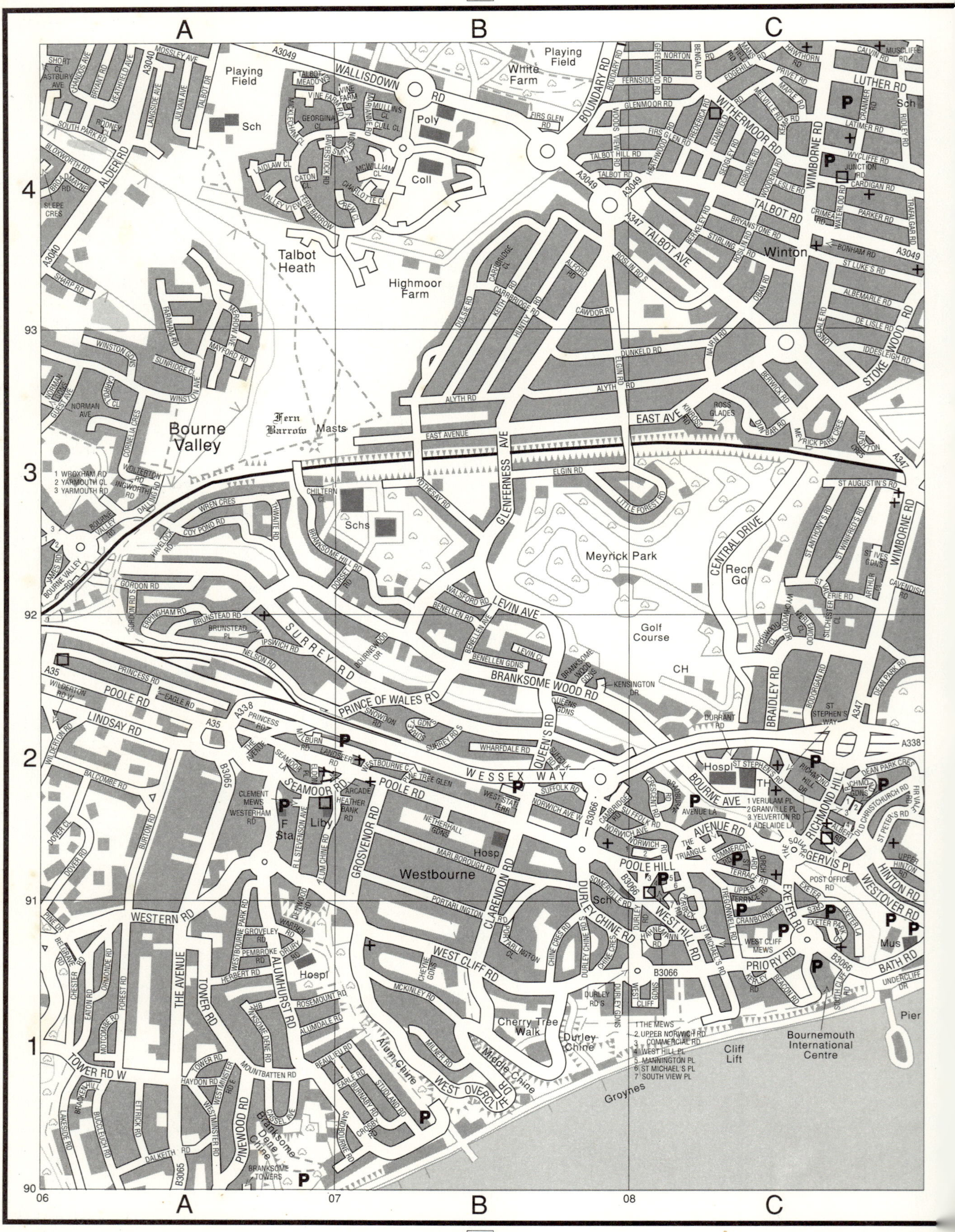

A
B
C
Playing Field
White Farm
Playing Field
WALLISDOWN RD
A3049
Sch
Poly
Coll
Talbot Heath
Highmoor Farm
Winton
WITHERMOOR RD
WIMBORNE RD
LUTHER RD
TALBOT RD
TALBOT AVE
BOUNDARY RD
ALDER RD
A3040
Bourne Valley
Fern Barrow
Masts
EAST AVE
EAST AVENUE
ALYTH RD
DUNKELD RD
CAWDOR RD
ELGIN RD
STOKEWOOD RD
A347
Schs
Meyrick Park
Golf Course
Recn Gd
CENTRAL DRIVE
CH
GLENFERNESS AVE
LEVIN AVE
BRANKSOME WOOD RD
SURREY RD
PRINCE OF WALES RD
POOLE RD
LINDSAY RD
A35
A338
WESSEX WAY
QUEEN'S RD
BOURNE AVE
Hospl
TH
RICHMOND HILL
GERVIS PL
A338
SEAMOOR RD
F Sta
Liby
GROSVENOR RD
Westbourne
Hosp
CLARENDON RD
DURLEY CHINE RD
WEST HILL RD
POOLE HILL
WEST CLIFF RD
EXETER RD
PRIORY RD
BATH RD
WESTOVER RD
Mus
WESTERN RD
THE AVENUE
TOWER RD
ALUMHURST RD
Hospl
Alum Chine
WEST OVERCLIFF DR
Middle Chine
Cherry Tree Walk
Durley Chine
Groynes
Cliff Lift
Bournemouth International Centre
Pier
TOWER RD W
PINEWOOD RD
Branksome Dene Chine
BRANKSOME TOWERS
B3065
B3066
1 WROXHAM RD
2 YARMOUTH CL
3 YARMOUTH RD
1 VERULAM PL
2 GRANVILLE PL
3 YELVERTON RD
4 ADELAIDE LA
1 THE MEWS
2 UPPER NORWICH RD
3 COMMERCIAL RD
4 WEST HILL PL
5 MANNINGTON PL
6 ST MICHAEL'S PL
7 SOUTH VIEW PL
4
93
3
92
2
91
1
90
06
07
08

205

217

191

D
E
F
Cemy
Queen's Park
Golf Course
CH
QUEEN'S PARK AVE
QUEEN'S PARK W DR
QUEEN'S PARK S DR
1 SHELBOURNE CL
2 CAPSTONE PL
3 AVON CL
4 RICHMOND PARK CL
5 EGERTON GDNS
6 ST LEDGER'S PL
LITTLEDOWN AVE
King's Park
Football Ground
Hospl
Schs
RICHMOND PARK ROAD
CHARMINSTER RD
RICHMOND PARK AVE
RICHMOND WOOD RD
ST ALBAN'S AVE
Recn Gd
ALMA RD
HERON COURT RD
ABBOTT RD
GREEN RD
RIPON RD
Mast
Cemy
CAPSTONE RD
BENNETT RD
LOWTHER RD
BEECHEY RD
WESSEX WAY
HOLDENHURST RD
CLEVELAND RD
Springbourne
ST CLEMENT'S RD
Schs
ASHLEY RD
Amb Sta
LANSDOWNE RD
Cricket Ground
Bournemouth Sta
ST PAUL'S RD
SOUTHCOTE RD
KNYVETON RD
VALE RD
DRUMMOND RD
CHRISTCHURCH RD
OLD CHRISTCHURCH RD
Cts
Coll
Fire Sta
Liby
THE LANSDOWNE
GERVIS RD
MANOR RD
BATH RD
EAST OVERCLIFF DR
UNDERCLIFF DR
RUSSELL COTES RD
Mus
Cliff Lift
Groynes
Pier
Boscombe
Hospl
OWLS RD
SEA RD
THE MARINA
BOSCOMBE CLIFF RD
Promenade
CHESSEL AVE
PERCY RD
Coll
A338
A35
A3049
B3063
B3064
B3066
4
3
2
1
93
92
91
90
09
10
11

208

192

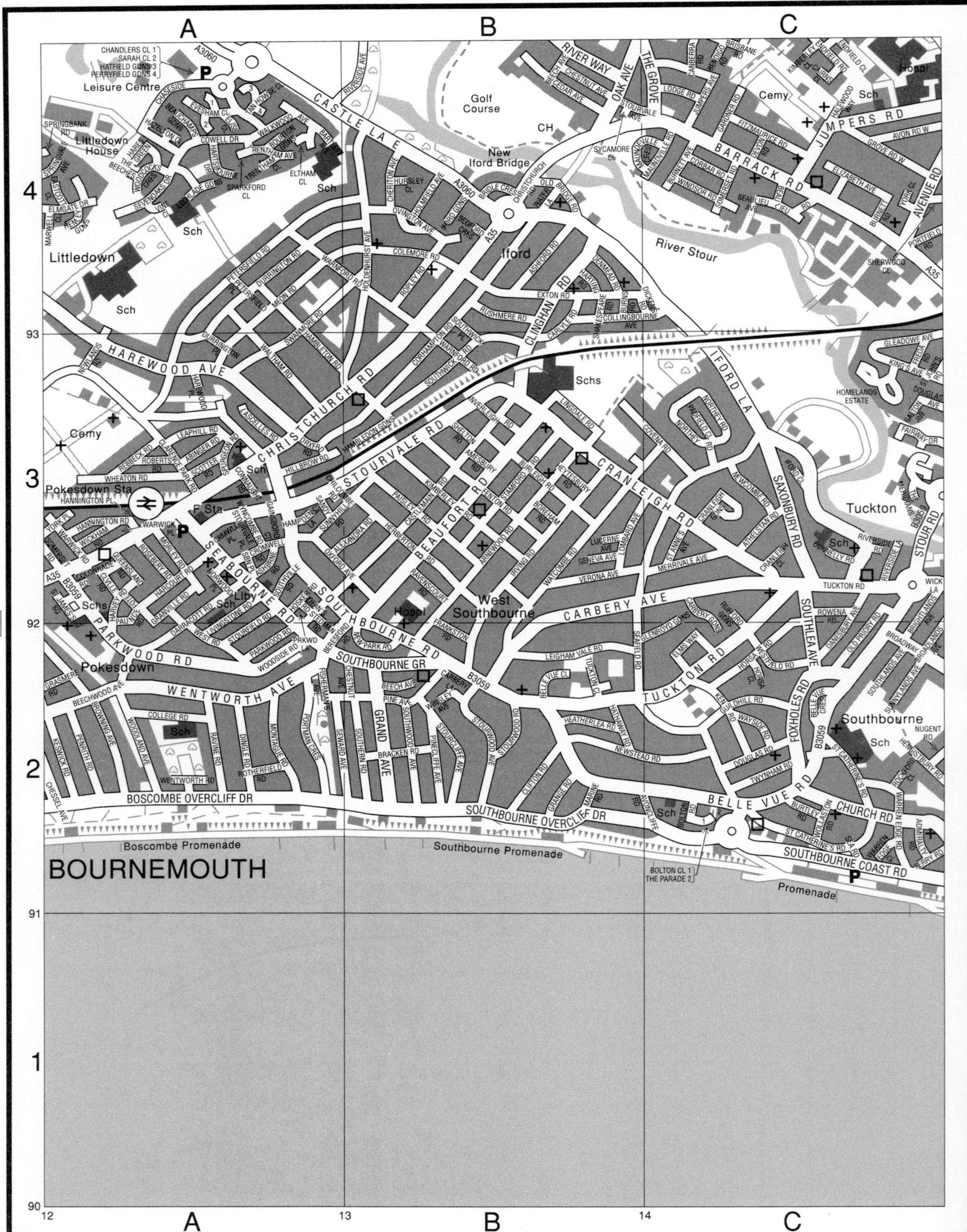
A
B
C
A
B
C
4
3
2
1
93
92
91
90
12
13
14
Golf Course
CH
New Iford Bridge
River Stour
Iford
Littledown House
Littledown
Leisure Centre
Sch
Schs
Cemy
Hospl
Pokesdown Sta
F Sta
Liby
West Southbourne
Pokesdown
Tuckton
Southbourne
HOMELANDS ESTATE
BOURNEMOUTH
Boscombe Promenade
Southbourne Promenade
Promenade
CHANDLERS CL 1
SARAH CL 2
HATFIELD GDNS 3
PERRYFIELD GDNS 4
BOLTON CL 1
THE PARADE 2
CASTLE LANE
A3060
A35
B3059
RIVER WAY
OAK AVE
THE GROVE
JUMPERS RD
BARRACK RD
HAREWOOD AVE
CHRISTCHURCH RD
STOURVALE RD
CRANLEIGH RD
IFORD LA
SAXONBURY RD
CARBERY AVE
SOUTHBOURNE RD
SEABOURNE RD
BEAUFORT RD
PARKWOOD RD
WENTWORTH AVE
TUCKTON RD
BELLE VUE RD
CHURCH RD
FOXHOLES RD
SOUTHLEA AVE
BOSCOMBE OVERCLIFF DR
SOUTHBOURNE OVERCLIFF DR
SOUTHBOURNE COAST RD
STOUR RD
AVENUE RD
CLINGHAN RD
GRAND AVE
SOUTHBOURNE GR
TUCKTON RD
WHEATON RD
HANNINGTON RD
COLLEGE RD
STOURWOOD RD
NEWSTEAD RD
DOUGLAS RD
TWYNHAM RD
GUILDHILL RD
WAYSIDE RD
LEIGHAM VALE RD
VERONA AVE
GENEVA AVE
LUCERNE AVE
MERRIVALE AVE
RUSHMERE RD
COLLINGBOURNE AVE
EXTON RD
COLEMORE RD
DURRINGTON RD
PETERSFIELD RD
WALTHAM RD
SWANMORE RD
HAMBLETON RD
WARNFORD RD
SOUTHWICK RD
CORHAMPTON RD
ROPLEY RD
HOLDENHURST AVE
CHERITON AVE
OVINGTON AVE
HOLMFIELD AVE
HURSLEY CL
BEDFORD CRES
ASHFORD RD
DENMEAD RD
HARTING RD
CARLYLE RD
SHAKESPEARE RD
BURNS RD
INVERLEIGH RD
LINGDALE RD
SHELTON RD
AMESBURY RD
STAMFORD RD
HEYTESBURY RD
BOREHAM RD
FENTON RD
ARNEWOOD RD
IRVING RD
WATCOMBE RD
KIMBERLEY RD
PAISLEY RD
CASTLEMAIN AVE
HERBERTON RD
ALEXANDRA RD
OXFORD AVE
RAVENSCOURT RD
FRANKSTON RD
LOMBARD AVE
COVENA RD
NORTHEY RD
PADFIELD CL
NEWCOMBE RD
CRANLEIGH GDNS
ATHELSTAN RD
ST ANNE'S AVE
SEAFIELD RD
GLENROYD GDNS
CARBERY GDNS
RUFFORD GDNS
ELMS WAY
HORSA RD
WESTFIELD RD
DANESBURY AVE
OLD PRIORY RD
ROWENA RD
TUCKTON RD
RIVERSIDE AVE
DONNELLY RD
BROADWAY
SOUTHLANDS AVE
CLIFTON RD
GRANGE RD
MARINE RD
AVONCLIFFE RD
HATHAWAY RD
HEATHERLEA RD
BELLE VUE CL
TUCKTON CL
STOURCLIFFE AVE
PINECLIFFE AVE
SOUTHWOOD AVE
BRACKEN RD
WINSLEY AVE
CARBERY LA
BEECH AVE
PINE AVE
SOUTHERN RD
SEWARD AVE
CHESTNUT AVE
FISHERMANS AVE
PORTMAN CRES
MONTAGUE RD
DINGLE RD
ROTHERFIELD RD
RAVINE RD
WOODLAND AVE
BROWNING AVE
PENRITH RD
KESWICK RD
CHESSEL AVE
GRASMERE RD
BEECHWOOD AVE
WOODSIDE RD
PARKWOOD RD
WEST RD
DARRACOTT RD
LIVINGSTONE RD
STOURFIELD RD
GRANVILLE RD
HARCOURT RD
ROSEBERY RD
MORLEY RD
SOUTHVILLE RD
CROMWELL RD
GAINSBOROUGH RD
HAMPDEN LA
SUNNYHILL RD
CHILCOMBE RD
HILLBROW RD
DRAYCOTT RD
HAMBLEDON GDNS
LASCELLES RD
LEAPHILL RD
CLARENDON PARK RD
ABINGER RD
ROBERTS RD
SCOTTER RD
REBBECK RD
SPURGEON RD
CONNAUGHT RD
NEWLANDS RD
HAREWOOD PL
DURRINGTON PL
PETERSFIELD PL
MEON RD
SPRINGBANK RD
SPRINGVALE AVE
EASTCOTT CL
ELMGATE DR
KENLEY GDNS
MARWELL CL
SEVENOAKS DR
WOODCOCKS CRES
HAREFIELD
THE BEECHES
HAZELTON CL
BEAUCHAMPS GDNS
CHASESIDE
EVESHAM CL
COWELL DR
HARTSBOURNE DR
TRENTHAM AVE
RENTHAM
WALKWOOD AVE
BOURTON GDNS
ELTHAM CL
SPARKFORD CL
LECHLADE GDNS
VINE CL
BARTLETT
RIVERSIDE AVE
CHESTNUT AVE
CEDAR AVE
BEECH AVE
STOURVALE AVE
SYCAMORE CL
MAUNDEVILLE CRES
MAUNDEVILLE RD
OLD BRIDGE RD
WATERMAN LA
BRIDLE CRES
CHRISTCHURCH RD
LODGE RD
CANBERRA RD
BRISBANE RD
BENDIGO RD
JUMPERS AVE
GARDINER RD
FITZMAURICE RD
CORBAR RD
WINDSOR RD
BURNETT AVE
SOMERSET RD
DEVON RD
BEAULIEU AVE
ELIZABETH AVE
GROVE RD W
AVON RD W
HALEWOOD WAY
KIMBERLEY CL
ENFIELD RD
ENFIELD CL
CAIRNS CL
YORK CL
PORTFIELD CL
SHERWOOD CL
GLEADOWE AVE
KING'S AVE
DOUGLAS AVE
FAIRWAY DR
GALTON AVE
THE MERIDIANS
WICK LA
BRIGHTLANDS AVE
BROADLANDS AVE
SUNNYLANDS AVE
NUGENT RD
HENGISTBURY RD
ROCKFORD CL
WARREN EDGE RD
ADMIRALTY RD
PERRY RD
ST CATHERINE'S RD
SEA RD
WOLLASTON RD
BURTLEY RD
BOLTON RD
IFORD CL
CRANLEIGH CL
KENT RD
WARWICK PL
WARWICK RD
WICKHAM RD
YORK PL
SOMERSET RD
COLONNADE RD
QUEENSLAND RD
CLIVE RD
HARVEY RD
ST JAMES'S RD
PRKWD LA
BERESFORD RD
NEW PARK RD
HOSKER RD
STEDMAN RD
ASHBURNE RD
NORWOOD PL
MORTIMER RD
ST KATHARINE'S

207

193

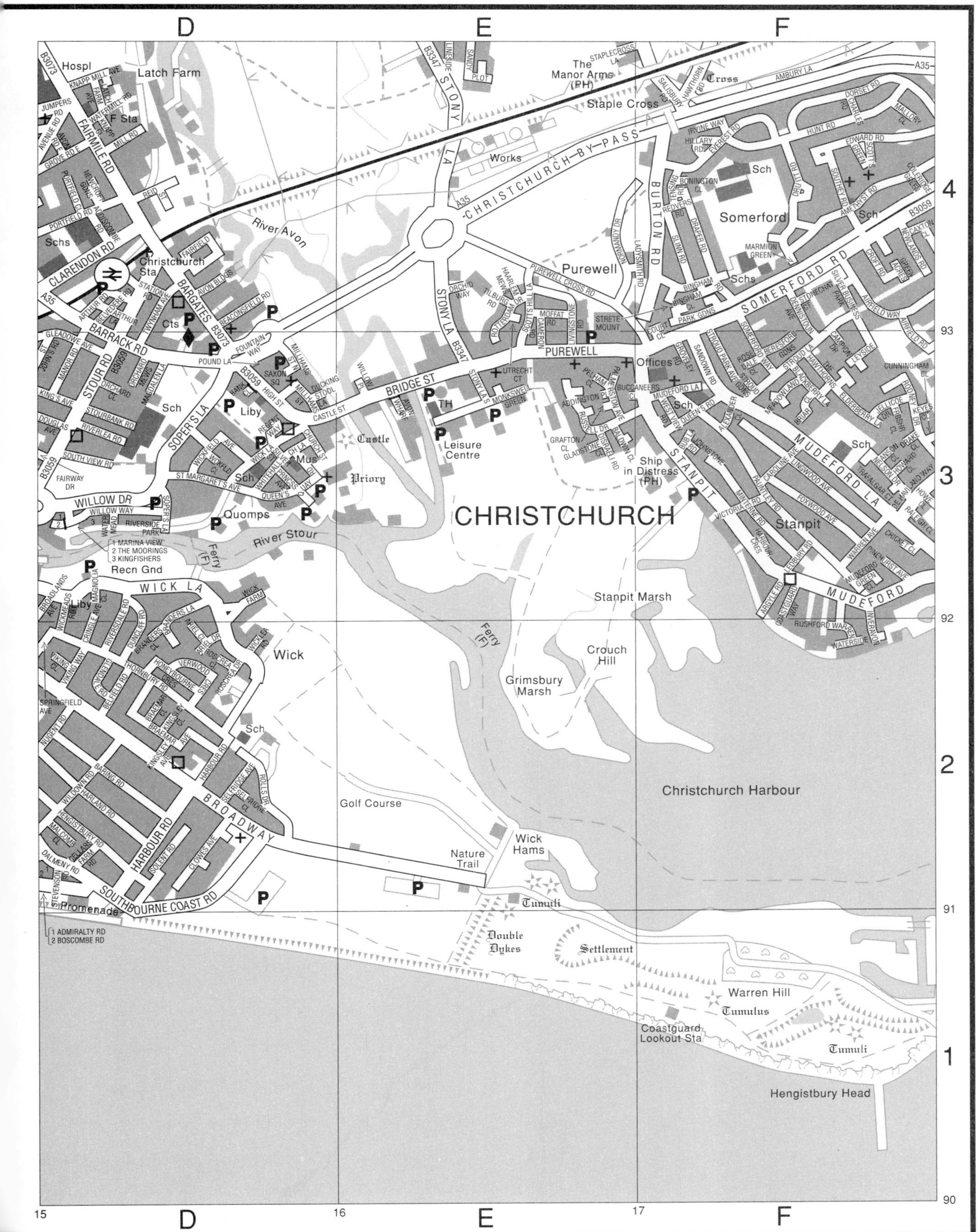
D
E
F
4
3
2
1
93
92
91
90
15
16
17
CHRISTCHURCH
Hospl
Latch Farm
F Sta
FAIRMILE RD
Schs
CLARENDON RD
Christchurch Sta
BARGATES
Cts
BARRACK RD
STOUR RD
Sch
Liby
SOPER'S LA
Mus
Castle
Priory
Quomps
WILLOW DR
River Stour
Ferry (F)
Recn Gnd
1 MARINA VIEW
2 THE MOORINGS
3 KINGFISHERS
WICK LA
Wick
Sch
BROADWAY
HARBOUR RD
SOUTHBOURNE COAST RD
Promenade
1 ADMIRALTY RD
2 BOSCOMBE RD
Golf Course
Nature Trail
Wick Hams
Tumuli
Double Dykes
Settlement
Warren Hill
Tumulus
Coastguard Lookout Sta
Hengistbury Head
Christchurch Harbour
Grimsbury Marsh
Crouch Hill
Stanpit Marsh
Stanpit
MUDEFORD
MUDEFORD LA
STANPIT
Ship in Distress (PH)
Offices
Sch
PUREWELL
Purewell
BRIDGE ST
CASTLE ST
HIGH ST
TH
Leisure Centre
River Avon
CHRISTCHURCH BY-PASS
A35
Works
STONY LA
The Manor Arms (PH)
Staple Cross
Cross
AMBURY LA
BURTON RD
Somerford
SOMERFORD RD
Sch
Schs
B3059
B3073
B3347

210

194

209

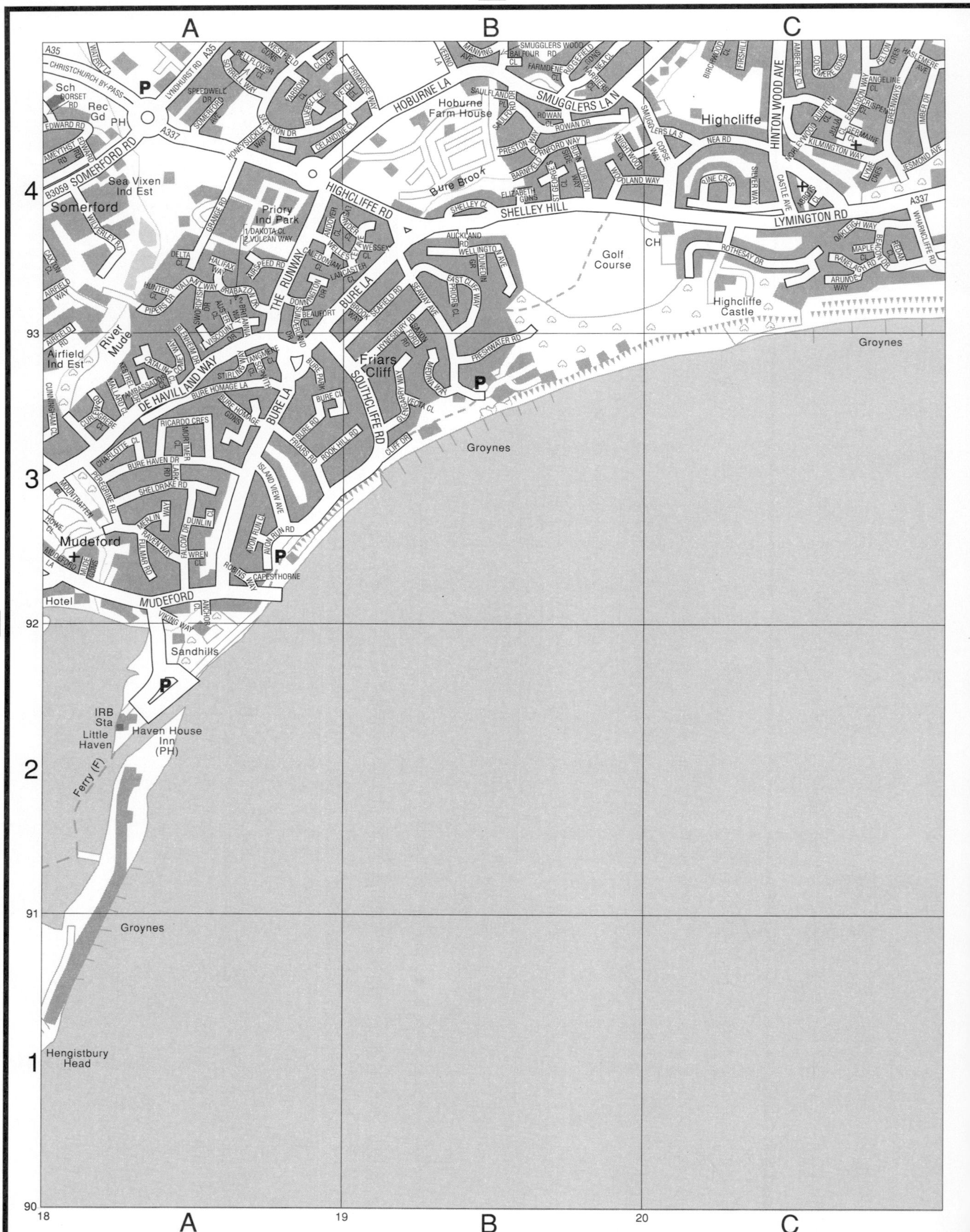
A
B
C
A35
CHRISTCHURCH BY-PASS
Sch
Rec Gd
PH
P
A337
B3059 SOMERFORD RD
Sea Vixen Ind Est
Somerford
Priory Ind Park
1 DAKOTA CL
2 VULCAN WAY
HOBURNE LA
Hoburne Farm House
SMUGGLERS LA N
Highcliffe
HINTON WOOD AVE
NEA RD
Bure Brook
SHELLEY HILL
HIGHCLIFFE RD
LYMINGTON RD
A337
CH
Golf Course
Highcliffe Castle
Groynes
THE RUNWAY
BURE LA
SOUTHCLIFFE RD
Friars Cliff
DE HAVILLAND WAY
River Mude
Airfield Ind Est
BURE HOMAGE LA
RICARDO CRES
BURE HAVEN DR
SHELDRAKE RD
ISLAND VIEW AVE
Mudeford
MUDEFORD
Hotel
Sandhills
IRB Sta
Little Haven
Haven House Inn (PH)
Ferry (F)
Groynes
Hengistbury Head
4
3
2
1
93
92
91
90
18
19
20

195

D E F

4
3
2
1

93
92
91
90

21 22 23

D E F

212

196

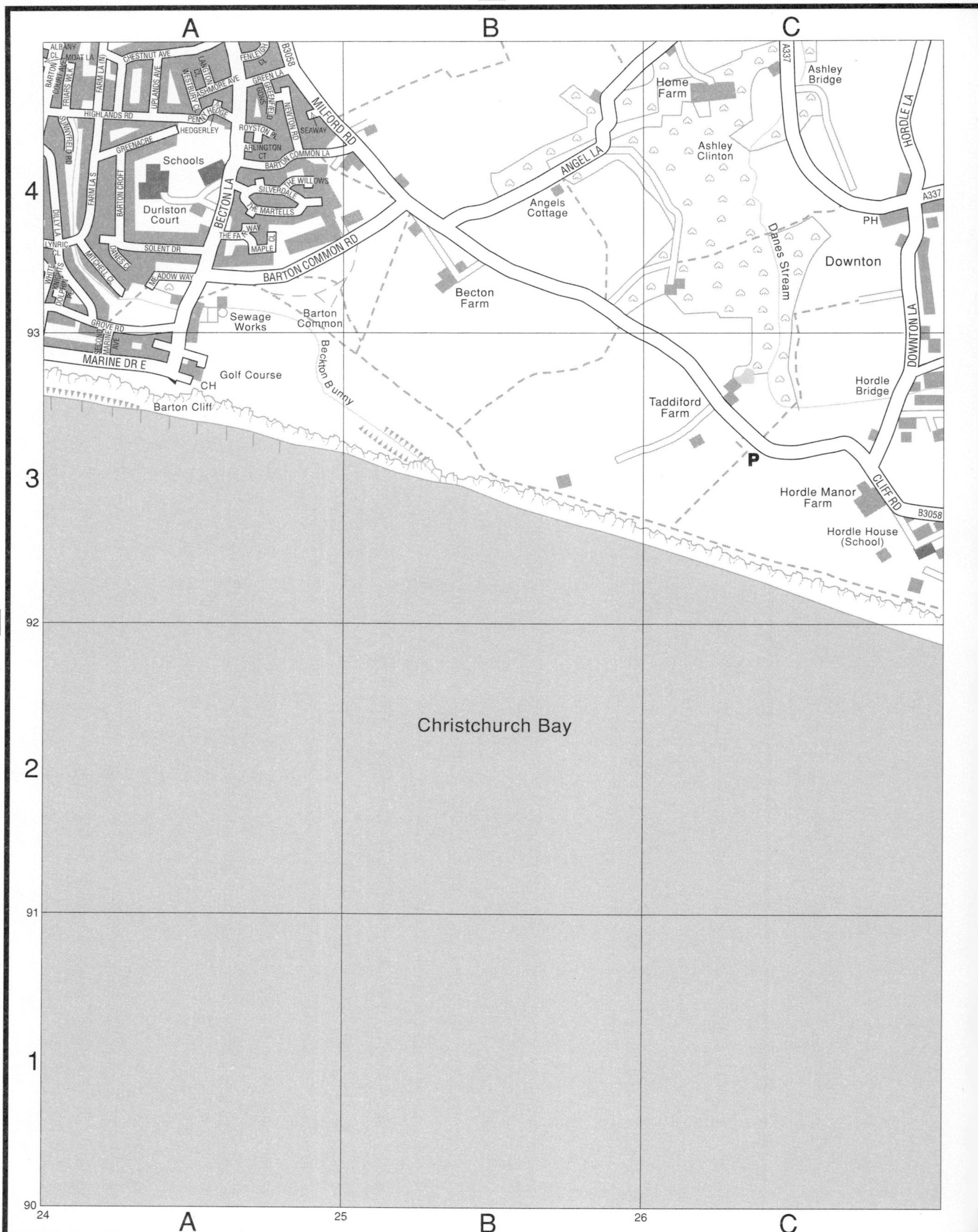
A
B
C
4
3
2
1
93
92
91
90
24
25
26
MILFORD RD
BARTON COMMON RD
ANGEL LA
BECTON LA
Schools
Durlston Court
Sewage Works
Barton Common
Golf Course
CH
Barton Cliff
Beckton Bunny
MARINE DR E
GROVE RD
Becton Farm
Angels Cottage
Home Farm
Ashley Clinton
Ashley Bridge
HORDLE LA
A337
PH
Downton
Danes Stream
DOWNTON LA
Hordle Bridge
Taddiford Farm
P
Hordle Manor Farm
CLIFF RD
B3058
Hordle House (School)
Christchurch Bay

211

197

D
E
F
Leagreen
Leagreen Farm
Downton Manor Farm
Newlands Manor Farm
Newlands Manor
Buona Vista Farm
Everton Grange
Cox's Bridge
Barnes Farm
Lymore
Blackbush Copse
Nursery
School
Lymore Farm
Knold
Danes Stream
Studland Common
Recn Gd
The Vicarage
Hordle Cliff
Rook Cliff
Milford on Sea
Sturt Pond
Solent Way
Hospl
A337
CHRISTCHURCH RD
MILFORD RD A337
B3058
LYMINGTON RD
BARNES LA
MANOR RD
SCHOOL LA
LYMORE LA
NEW LA
CLIFF RD
WHITBY RD
KIVERNELL RD
PARK LA
HIGH ST
KEYHAVEN RD
HURST RD
SEA RD
WESTOVER RD
MILFORD CRES
NEW VALLEY RD
VICTORIA RD
CHERRY TREE CL
CYPRESS GR
4
3
2
1
93
92
91
90
27
28
29

214

198

213

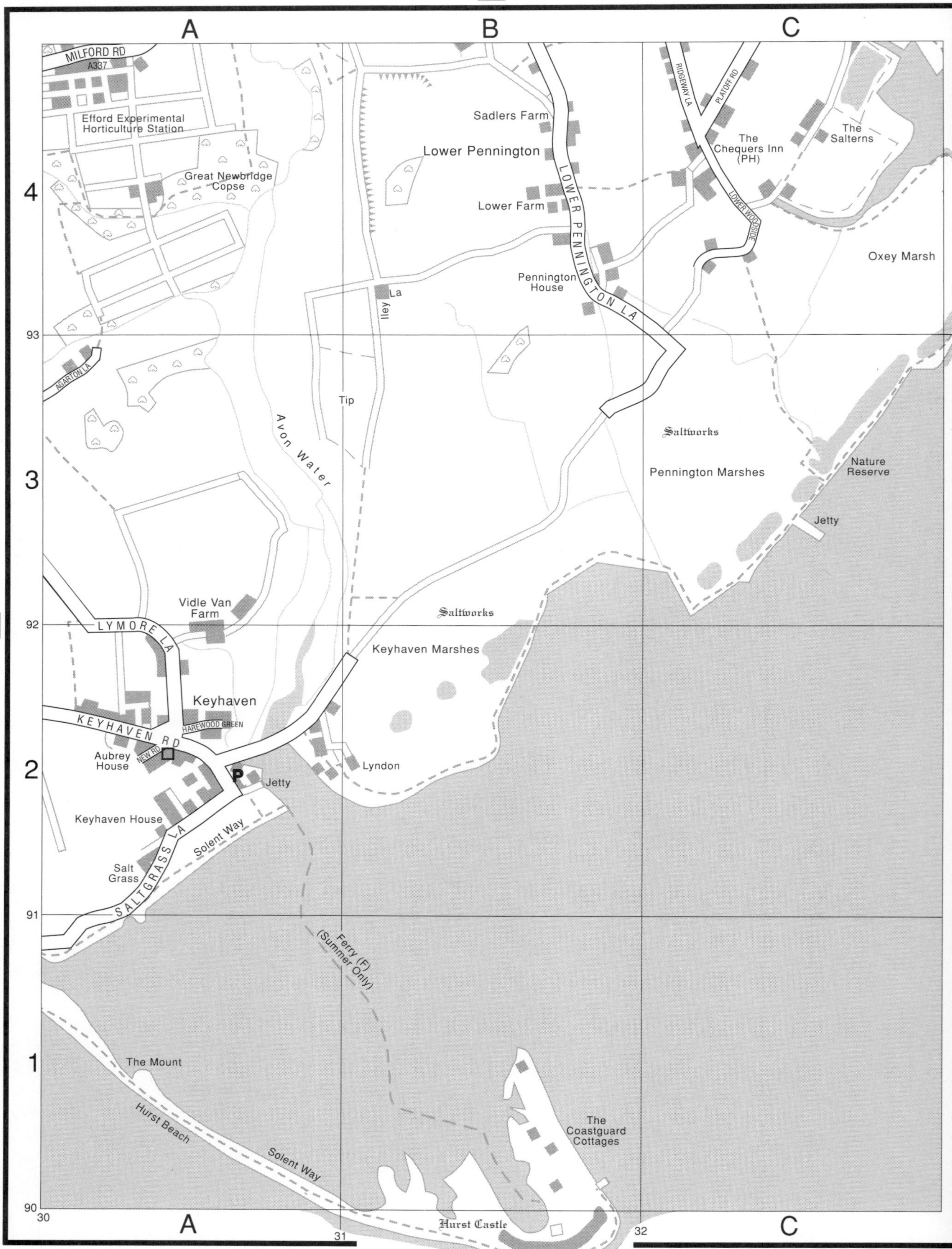
A
B
C
A
C
4
3
2
1
93
92
91
90
30
31
32
MILFORD RD
A337
Efford Experimental
Horticulture Station
Great Newbridge
Copse
Sadlers Farm
Lower Pennington
Lower Farm
LOWER PENNINGTON LA
Pennington
House
Iley La
RIDGEWAY LA
PLATOFF RD
The
Chequers Inn
(PH)
The
Salterns
LOWER WOODSIDE
Oxey Marsh
AGARTON LA
Tip
Avon Water
Saltworks
Pennington Marshes
Nature
Reserve
Jetty
Saltworks
Vidle Van
Farm
LYMORE LA
Keyhaven Marshes
Keyhaven
KEYHAVEN RD
HAREWOOD GREEN
NEW RD
Aubrey
House
P
Jetty
Lyndon
Keyhaven House
Solent Way
SALTGRASS LA
Salt
Grass
Ferry (F)
(Summer Only)
The Mount
Hurst Beach
Solent Way
The
Coastguard
Cottages
Hurst Castle

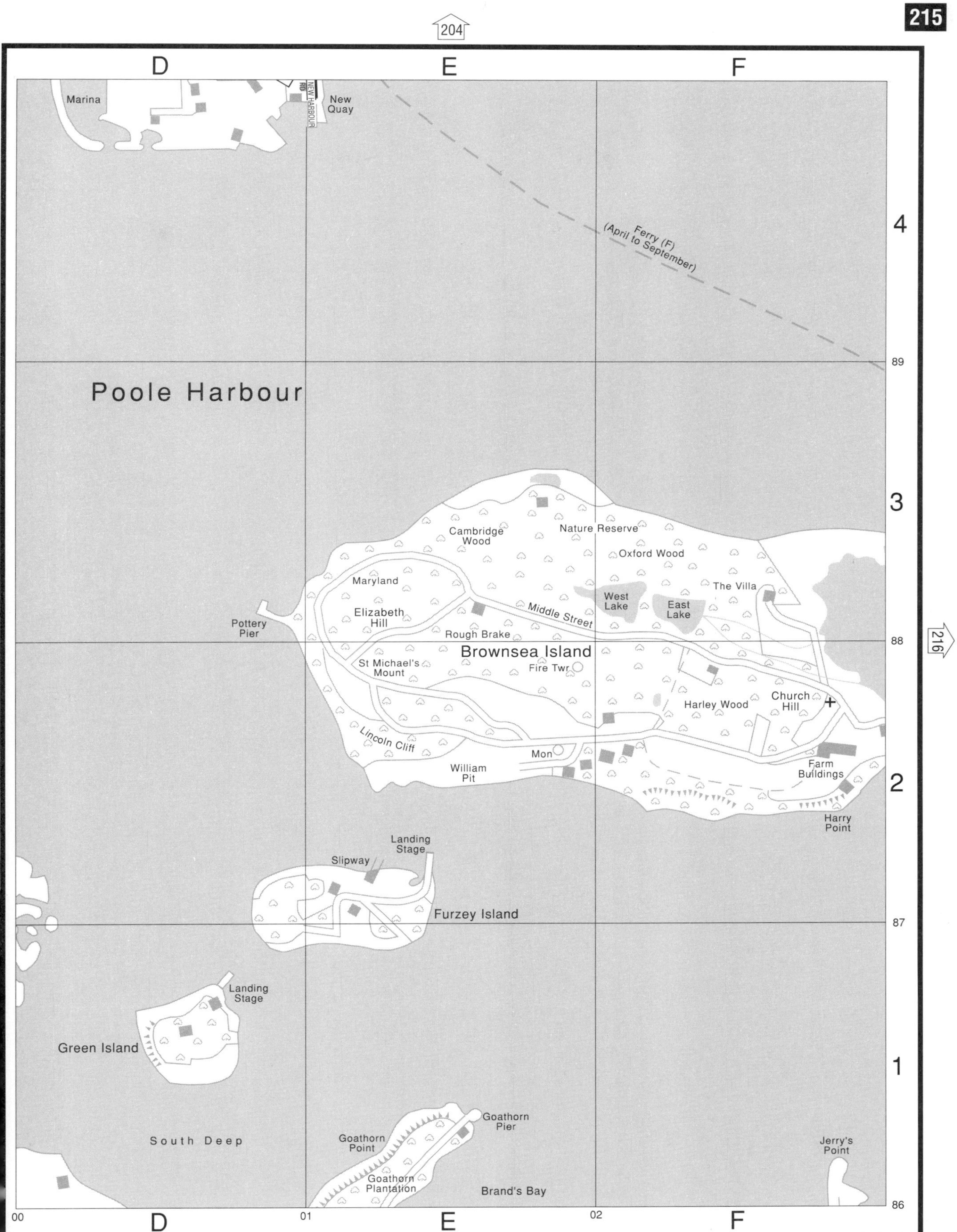

not continued, see key diagram

205

215

not continued, see key diagram

206

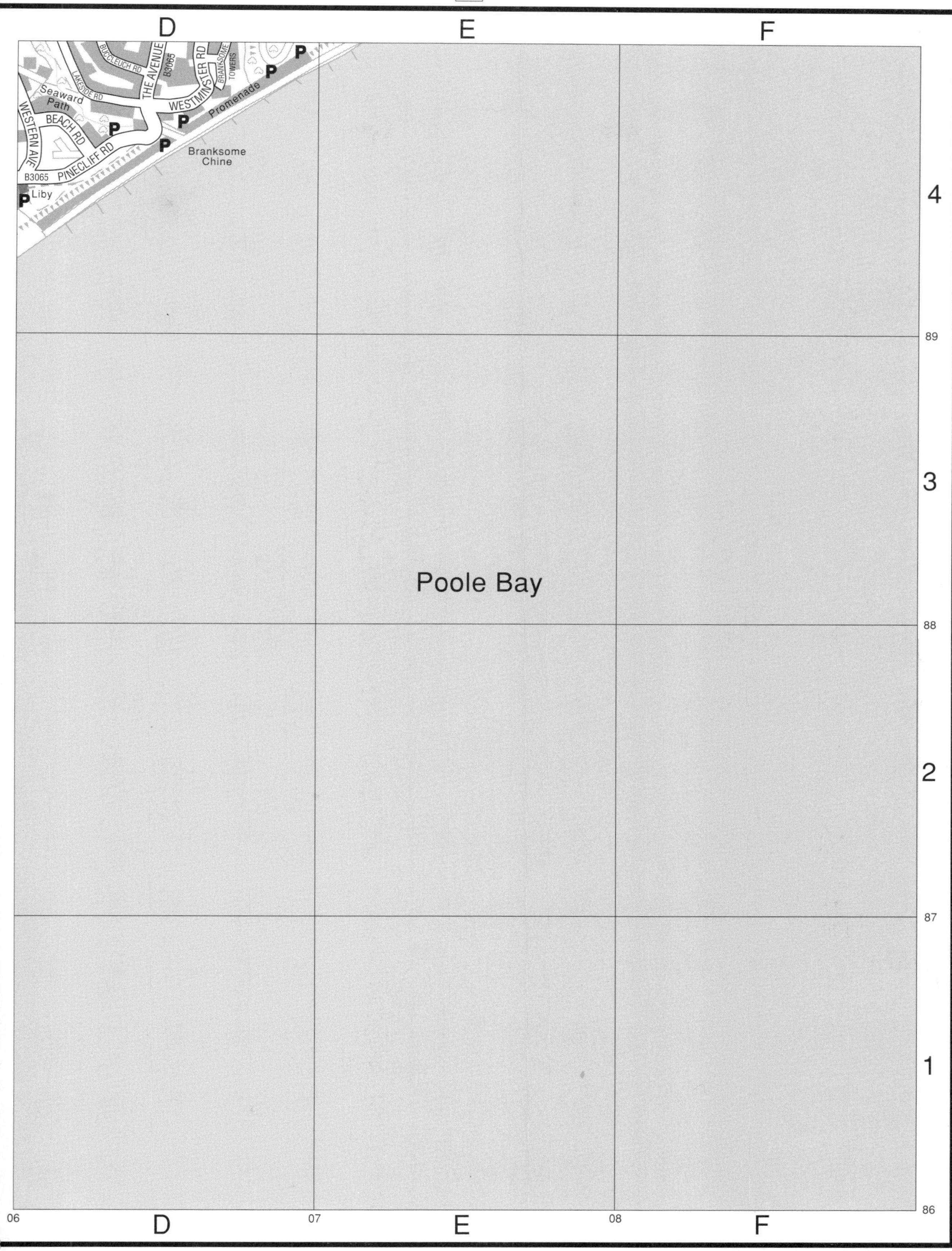
D
E
F
Seaward Path
LAKESIDE RD
BUCCLEUCH RD
THE AVENUE
B3065
WESTMINSTER RD
BRANKSOME TOWERS
WESTERN AVE
BEACH RD
PINECLIFF RD
B3065
Liby
Promenade
Branksome Chine
P
4
89
3
Poole Bay
88
2
87
1
86
06
07
08
D
E
F

USER'S NOTES

EXPLANATION OF THE STREET INDEX REFERENCE SYSTEM

Street names are listed alphabetically and show the locality, the page number and a reference to the square in which the name falls on the map page.

Example:	Abney Rd. Bour..190 B2
Abney Rd	This is the full street name, which may have been abbreviated on the map.
Bour	This is the abbreviation for the town, village or locality in which the street falls.
190	This is the page number of the map on which the street name appears.
B2	The letter and figure indicate the square on the map in which the centre of the street falls. The square can be found at the junction of the vertical column carrying the appropriate letter and the horizontal row carrying the appropriate figure.

ABBREVIATIONS USED IN THE INDEX

Road Names

Approach....................................App
Avenue.......................................Ave
Broadway...................................Bwy
By-Pass...................................By-Ps
Causeway...............................Cswy
Common...............................Comm
Corner..Cnr
Cottages..................................Cotts
Court..Ct
Crescent..................................Cres
Drive...Dr
Drove..Dro
East...E
Gardens..................................Gdns
Grove...Gr
Heights.......................................Hts
Lane...La
North...N
Orchard.....................................Orch
Parade..Par
Passage......................................Pas
Place..Pl
Pleasant....................................Plea
Precinct.....................................Prec
Promenade...............................Prom
Road...Rd
South..S
Square...Sq
Street,Saint..................................St
Terrace......................................Terr
Walk...Wlk
West..W
Yard...Yd

Towns, Villages and Rural Localities

Abbotswood	Abb	28	A2
Alderholt	Alderh	92	C3
Ampfield	Ampf	29	E2
Ashurst	Ashu	100	A2
Awbridge	Awb	26	C2
Barton on Sea	B on S	211	F3
Beaulieu	Beaul	148	C1
Beauworth	Beau	35	D4
Bishop's Waltham	Bi Wa	83	E4
Bishopstoke	Bish	56	C2
Blackfield	Black	177	F4
Boldre	Bold	173	E1
Botley	Botl	105	F3
Bournemouth	Bour	208	A2
Braishfield	Brai	28	B4
Bramdean	Bramd	15	E2
Bramshaw	Bramsh	73	F2
Bransgore	Bran	194	A4
Breamore	Brea	70	A4
Broadstone	Broa	188	A2
Brockenhurst	Brock	146	A1
Brook	Bro	74	A1
Buriton	Buri	65	F3
Burley	Bur	143	D2
Bursledon	Burs	128	A4
Burton	Burt	193	E1
Cadnam	Cadn	98	C4
Chandler's Ford	Ch Fo	55	E4
Cheriton	Cher	14	B3
Chilcomb	Chilc	12	A3
Chilworth	Chilw	54	B1
Christchurch	Christ	209	E3
Clanfield	Clanf	88	A3
Colden Common	Co Com	32	A1
Compton (Winchester)	Comp	31	E4
Compton	Compt	90	C1
Coombe Bisset	Co Bi	23	F4
Cosham	Cos	158	A3
Cranborne	Cranb	91	D4
Croucheston	Crouch	22	A4
Curdridge	Curd	106	C4
Damerham	Dame	68	B3
Denmead	Den	111	D3
Downton	Down	47	D4
Droxford	Drox	61	D1
Durley	Durl	82	A3
East Boldre	E Bol	175	E3
East Dean	E Dean	4	A1
East Meon	E Meo	38	B1
East Tytherley	E Tyth	4	C4
Eastleigh	Eastl	55	F2
Edmondsham	Edmo	91	D2
Emsworth	Ems	136	C1
Exbury	Exb	177	D3
Fair Oak	Fa Oa	57	E1
Fareham	Fare	131	D1
Fawley	Faw	151	D2
Ferndown	Fern	165	E3
Finchdean	Finc	113	E3
Fordingbridge	Fordi	69	F1
Fritham	Fri	72	C1
Froxfield Green	Frox G	39	E4
Gosport	Gos	181	E4
Hamble	Hamble	128	A2
Hambledon	Hambl	86	B1
Hamworthy	Hamw	203	E2
Havant	Hav	135	F2
Hawkley	Hawk	19	F4
Hedge End	He En	105	E3
Hermitage	Herm	137	D4
Hill Brow	Hill B	21	D1
Holbury	Holb	150	B2
Holt Heath	Holt	138	A3
Hordle	Hord	196	C2
Horndean	Horn	112	B4
Hurn	Hurn	192	A4
Hursley	Hurs	30	A4
Hythe	Hyt	126	A3
Ibsley	Ibs	117	D4
Kilmeston	Kilm	14	B1
Kings Worthy	Ki Wo	2	B3
Landford	Lan	49	E2
Langrish	Langr	39	E2
Lee-on-the-Solent	L on S	179	E3
Liss	Liss	21	D2
Littleton	Litt	1	A3
Lockerley	Locke	4	C1
Locks Heath	Lo He	129	E2
Lymington	Lym	198	B3
Lyndhurst	Lyn	121	F3
Marchwood	March	101	F1
Martin	Mar	43	D2
Meonstoke	Meons	61	E3
Michelmersh	Miche	6	B1
Milford on Sea	M on S	213	E2
Minstead	Min	98	A2
Mottisfont	Mott	5	F1
Netley	Net	127	D3
Netley Marsh	Ne Ma	100	A3
New Milton	New M	195	F2
North Baddesley	N Bad	53	F3
North Hayling	N Hay	160	B2
Nursling	Nur	77	E3
Oakley	Oakl	163	F1
Otterbourne	Ott	31	E2
Ower	Ower	75	F3
Owslebury	Ows	33	D2
Pamphill	Pamp	162	C3
Pentridge	Pent	42	A1
Petersfield	Pet	40	B2
Plaitford	Plai	50	A2
Poole	Poole	204	A2
Portchester	Portc	156	B4
Portsmouth	Ports	157	E2
Rake	Ra	21	F2
Redlynch	Red	47	F3
Ringwood	Rin	141	E4
Rockbourne	Rockb	44	C1
Rogate	Roga	41	F3
Romsey	Rom	52	C3
Rowland's Castle	Ro Ca	113	E1
Rownhams	Rown	77	F4
Shedfield	Shed	107	E4
Sherfield English	Sh En	25	E1
Soberton	Sob	85	E3
Sopley	Sop	193	D4
South Harting	S Har	66	C2
South Hayling	S Hay	184	C1
Southampton	Southa	102	B2
Southbourne	Southb	161	F4
Southwick	Southw	132	C3
St Leonards	St Le	139	E2
Steep	Steep	40	B4
Stubbington	Stubb	154	B2
Swanmore	Swan	84	B3
Swanwick	Swanw	129	D4
Sway	Sway	172	A1
Thorney Island	Th Is	161	D2
Totton	Tot	100	C4
Twyford	Twyf	32	A3
Upham	Uph	58	C3
Upton	Upt	203	E4
Verwood	Ver	114	C3
Walderton	Wal	137	F4
Warnford	Warnf	36	C2
Waterlooville	Wat	134	C4
West Dean	W Dean	3	E2
West End	W End	80	C1
West Meon	W Meo	37	D2
West Moors	W Moo	138	C2
West Tisted	W Tis	16	B4
West Wellow	W Wel	50	C2
West Wittering	W Wit	186	C1
Westbourne	Westb	137	D2
Whiteparish	Whit	24	A2
Whitsbury	Whits	45	D2
Wickham	Wickh	108	A2
Wimborne Minster	Wi Mi	163	E3

Aaron Cl. Poole 204 C4
Aaron Ct. March 101 F1
Abbas Green. Hav 135 E4
Abbey Cl. Hyt 126 A2
Abbey Hill Cl. Winch 2 A1
Abbey Hill Rd. Winch 1 C1
Abbey Hill. Net 127 D4
Abbey Pas. Winch 11 D4
Abbey Rd. Fare 130 B1
Abbey Rd. W Moo 166 A4
Abbey The. Rom 52 C4
Abbey Water. Rom 52 C4
Abbeyfield Dr. Fare 130 B1
Abbeyfields Cl. Net 127 E3
Abbots Cl. Christ 210 C4
Abbots Cl. Wat 134 B2
Abbots Way. Fare 130 B1
Abbots Well Rd. Fordi 94 C4
Abbotsbury Rd. Bish 56 C1
Abbotsbury Rd. Broa 187 F3
Abbotsfield Cl. Southa 78 B3
Abbotsfield. Cadn 99 D3
Abbotsfield. Tot 100 C4
Abbotstone Ave. Hav 136 A2
Abbotswood Cl. Rom 28 B1
Abbott Rd. Bour 207 D4
Abbott St. Pamp 162 B3
Abbotts Ann Rd. Winch 1 B2
Abbotts Cl. Winch 2 A1
Abbotts Dro. W Wel 50 C1
Abbotts Rd. Eastl 55 F1
Abbotts Rd. Winch 2 A1
Abbotts Way. Southa 79 D1
Abercrombie Gdns. Southa 78 A2
Aberdare Ave. Cos 158 A4
Aberdare Rd. Bour 190 C2
Aberdeen Cl. Fare 130 C2
Aberdeen Rd. Southa 79 E1
Aberdour Cl. Southa 104 A4
Abingdon Cl. Gos 181 D2
Abingdon Dr. Christ 211 E4
Abingdon Gdns. Southa 78 C2
Abingdon Rd. Poole 204 B4
Abinger Rd. Bour 208 A3
Abney Rd. Bour 190 B2
Above Bar St. Southa 102 C3
Abraham Cl. He En 105 E3
Abshot Cl. Lo He 129 D1
Abshot Rd. Lo He 129 E1
Acacia Ave. Ver 115 E3
Acacia Gdns. Wat 112 A3
Acacia Rd. Hord 196 C2
Acacia Rd. Southa 103 F3
Ackworth Rd. Ports 158 A3
Acland Rd. Bour 207 D4
Acorn Business Centre. Cos 157 E4
Acorn Cl. Cos 158 B4
Acorn Cl. Gos 155 E1
Acorn Cl. March 102 A1
Acorn Cl. New M 196 B2
Acorn Cl. St Le 139 F2
Acre La. Wat 112 B1
Acres Rd. Bour 190 A1
Acton Rd. Bour 190 A1
Adair Rd. Ports 183 D1
Adames Rd. Ports 182 C3
Adams Rd. Hyt 126 A1
Adams Wood Dr. March 101 F1
Adamsfield Gdns. Bour 190 B1
Adamson Cl. Ch Fo 55 E4
Adastral Rd. Poole 204 C4
Adderbury Ave. Ems 136 C2
Addington Pl. Christ 209 E3
Addiscombe Rd. Christ 209 D4
Addison Cl. Rom 28 A1
Addison Cl. Winch 10 B3
Addison Rd. Brock 172 C4
Addison Rd. Eastl 56 A3
Addison Rd. Lo He 128 C3
Addison Rd. Ports 182 C2
Addison Sq. Rin 141 D4
Adelaide La. Bour 206 C2
Adelaide Rd. Southa 103 E4
Adeline Rd. Bour 207 F2
Adlam's La. Sway 172 A1
Admiral Park The. Ports 158 A2
Admirals Cl. Faw 151 D2
Admirals Rd. Lo He 129 D2
Admirals Way. Hyt 126 A3
Admirals Wlk. Gos 180 C2
Admiralty Rd. Bour 208 C2
Admiralty Rd. Ports 182 A3
Adsdean Cl. Hav 135 F2
Adstone La. Ports 158 B2
Adur Cl. W End 80 A1
Aerodrome Rd. Gos 155 F2
Africa Dr. March 124 C4
Agarton La. M on S 213 F3
Aggis Farm Rd. Ver 114 C3
Agincourt Rd. Ports 182 B4
Agnew Rd. Gos 155 E2
Aikman La. Tot 100 A4
Ailsa La. Southa 103 E2
Ainsdale Rd. Cos 134 B1
Ainsley Gdns. Eastl 56 A3
Aintree Dr. Wat 112 A1
Aintree Rd. Tot 76 B1
Airfield Rd. Christ 209 F3
Airfield Way. Christ 209 F4
Airlie Rd. Winch 10 C3
Airport Service Rd. Ports 158 A2
Airspeed Rd. Ports 158 B1
Ajax Cl. Stubb 154 B1
Akeshill Cl. New M 196 A3
Alameda Rd. Wat 134 B2
Alameda Way. Wat 134 B2
Alan Drayton Way. Bish 56 C1
Alan Gr. Fare 130 C1
Albany Cl. B on S 195 F1
Albany Ct. Bi Wa 83 D4
Albany Dr. Bi Wa 83 D4
Albany Dr. W Moo 114 C1
Albany Rd. Bi Wa 83 D4
Albany Rd. Holb 150 B2
Albany Rd. Ports 182 B2
Albany Rd. Rom 52 C4
Albany Rd. Southa 102 B3
Albatross Wlk. Gos 155 D1
Albemarle Ave. Gosp 181 D4
Albemarle Rd. Bour 206 C4
Albert Cl. Net 127 E3
Albert Gr. Ports 182 B2
Albert Rd N. Southa 103 D2
Albert Rd S. Southa 103 D2
Albert Rd. Bi Wa 83 D4
Albert Rd. Bour 206 C2
Albert Rd. Broa 187 E3
Albert Rd. Cos 157 F4
Albert Rd. Eastl 56 A3
Albert Rd. Fern 165 E3
Albert Rd. He En 105 D3
Albert Rd. New M 195 F1
Albert Rd. Poole 205 E3
Albert Rd. Ports 182 C1
Albert Rd. Stubb 155 D1
Albert St. Gos 181 E3
Albion Cl. Poole 205 D4
Albion Cl. Portc 156 A3
Albion Pl. Southa 102 C2
Albion Rd. Christ 192 C1
Albion Rd. Fordi 69 F1
Albretia Ave. Wat 111 F2
Albury Pl. Ch Fo 30 A1
Alby Rd. Poole 205 F3
Alcantara Cres. Southa 103 D2
Alcester Rd. Poole 205 E3
Alchorne Pl. Ports 158 A2
Alder Cl. Burt 193 E1
Alder Cl. Hyt 125 E2
Alder Cl. March 101 F1
Alder Cl. Rom 53 E3
Alder Cres. Poole 205 F4
Alder Dr. Alderh 92 C3
Alder Rd. Poole 205 F3
Alder Rd. Southa 78 A2
Alderfield. Pet 40 C2
Alderhill Dr. Tot 100 A4
Alderholt Rd. Fordi 69 D1
Alderley Rd. Bour 190 C2
Aldermoor Ave. Southa 78 A2
Aldermoor Cl. Southa 78 B2
Aldermoor Rd E. Wat 134 B3
Aldermoor Rd. Gos 180 B4
Aldermoor Rd. Southa 78 A2
Aldermoor Rd. Wat 134 B2
Alderney Ave. Poole 189 E1
Alderney Cl. Southa 77 F2
Alders Rd. Fare 155 D4
Alderwood Ave. N Bad 55 D3
Alderwood Cl. Hav 135 D2
Aldis Gdns. Hamw 203 F1
Aldridge Cl. Clanf 88 B3
Aldridge Rd. Bour 190 B3
Aldridge Rd. Fern 165 F2
Aldroke St. Cos 157 F4
Aldsworth Cl. Cos 158 B4
Aldsworth Gdns. Cos 158 B4
Aldwell St. Ports 182 B2
Alec Rose La. Ports 182 B3
Alecto Rd. Gos 181 D2
Alencon Cl. Gosp 181 E4
Alexander Cl. Christ 209 F3
Alexander Cl. Tot 100 B4
Alexander Cl. Wat 134 B3
Alexander Gr. Fare 155 D4
Alexander Rd. Ch Fo 55 F4
Alexandra Ave. S Hay 184 C1
Alexandra Cl. Hyt 126 A2
Alexandra Rd. Bour 208 B3
Alexandra Rd. Fordi 69 F1
Alexandra Rd. He En 105 D3
Alexandra Rd. Hyt 126 A2
Alexandra Rd. Lym 198 B3
Alexandra Rd. Poole 205 E3
Alexandra Rd. Poole 205 F2
Alexandra Rd. Ports 182 B3
Alexandra Rd. Southa 102 C3
Alexandra St. Gos 181 D3
Alexandra Terr. Winch 10 C4
Alexandra Way. Botl 106 A4
Alford Rd. Bour 206 B4
Alfred Cl. Tot 100 B4
Alfred Rd. Ports 182 A3
Alfred Rd. Stubb 154 B2
Alfred Rose Ct. Southa 79 F2
Alfred St. Southa 103 D3
Alfriston Gdns. Southa 104 A2
Algiers Rd. Ports 183 D4
Alhambra Rd. Ports 182 C1
Alington Rd. Bour 207 D3
Alipore Cl. Poole 205 E2
All Saints Rd. Lym 198 C1
All Saints' Rd. Ports 182 B4
All Saints' St. Ports 182 B3
Allan Gr. Rom 53 D4
Allaway Ave. Cos 157 D4
Allaway Ave. Portc 157 D4
Allbrook Ct. Hav 135 E3
Allbrook Hill. Eastl 56 A4
Allbrook Hill. Ott 56 A4
Allbrook Knoll. Eastl 56 A4
Allcot Rd. Ports 158 A1
Allen Ct. Wi Mi 163 E3
Allen Rd. He En 105 E4
Allen Rd. Wi Mi 163 E2
Allen Water Dr. Fordi 69 F1
Allen's Rd. Ports 182 C1
Allenby Cl. Broa 188 A1
Allenby Gr. Portc 156 B4
Allenby Rd. Broa 188 A1
Allenby Rd. Gos 180 C3
Allendale Ave. Ems 136 C2
Allens La. Meons 61 E3
Allens La. Upt 203 E3
Allens Rd. Upt 203 E3
Allenview Rd. Wi Mi 163 E3
Allerton Cl. Tot 76 B1
Alliance Cl. Gos 180 B4
Allington La. W End 80 C3
Allington Rd. Poole 211 E4
Allington Rd. Southa 101 E4
Allmara Dr. Wat 134 C2
Allotment Rd. He En 105 D3
Allotment Rd. Lo He 128 C3
Alma La. Uph 58 A1
Alma Rd. Bour 207 D4
Alma Rd. Rom 52 C4
Alma Rd. Southa 103 D4
Alma St. Gos 181 D3
Alma Terr. Ports 183 D2
Almatade Rd. Southa 104 A4
Almer Rd. Hamw 203 F2
Almond Cl. Cos 158 B4
Almond Cl. Wat 112 B2
Almond Ct. Southa 102 B3
Almond Gr. Poole 205 E4
Almond Rd. Southa 102 B3
Almondsbury Rd. Cos 132 C1
Almondside. Gos 155 F1
Alpha Centre The. Broa 204 A4
Alphage Rd. Gos 155 F1
Alpine Cl. Southa 104 A4
Alpine Rd. Ashu 99 F2
Alresford Rd. Chilc 12 B4
Alresford Rd. Hav 135 F2
Alresford Rd. It Ab 12 B4
Alresford Rd. Ovin 12 B4
Alresford Rd. Tich 12 B4
Alresford Rd. Winch 11 E4
Alresford Rd. Winch 12 B4
Alsford Rd. Wat 134 B3
Alten Rd. Wat 111 E1
Althorpe Dr. Ports 158 B2
Alton Cl. Fa Oa 57 D1
Alton Gr. Portc 156 B3
Alton Rd E. Poole 205 E1
Alton Rd. Bour 190 A1
Alum Chine Rd. Bour 206 A2
Alum Cl. Holb 150 B2
Alum Way. Portc 131 F1
Alum Way. Southa 104 A4
Alumdale Rd. Bour 206 A1
Alumhurst Rd. Bour 206 A1
Alvara Rd. Gos 181 D1
Alver Rd. Gos 181 D2
Alver Rd. Ports 182 C3
Alvercliffe Dr. Gos 180 C1
Alverstone Rd. Ports 183 D3
Alverton Ave. Poole 204 C2
Alveston Ave. Fare 154 B4
Alyth Rd. Bour 206 B3
Ambassador Cl. Christ 210 A3
Amber Rd. Broa 187 E2
Amberley Cl. Botl 106 A4
Amberley Cl. Christ 210 C4
Amberley Cl. N Bad 53 F3
Amberley Rd. Gosp 181 D4
Amberley Rd. Ports 157 F2
Amberslade Wlk. Hyt 125 F1
Amberwood Cl. Tot 76 B1
Amberwood Dr. Christ 194 C1
Amberwood Gdns. Christ 195 D1
Ambledale. Lo He 128 C2
Ambleside Gdns. Southa 104 A2
Ambleside Rd. Lym 198 C2
Ambleside. Christ 192 C2
Ambleside. He En 105 E3
Ambury La. Burt 209 F4
Amersham Cl. Gos 180 C2
Amesbury Rd. Bour 208 B3
Amethyst Gr. Wat 135 D4
Amethyst Rd. Christ 209 F4
Amey Ind Est. Pet 40 C2
Ameys La. Fern 165 F4
Ameysford Rd. Fern 138 A1
Ameysford Rd. Fern 165 E4
Amoy St. Southa 102 C3
Ampfield Cl. Hav 135 D2
Ampfield Rd. Bour 191 E2
Amport Cl. Winch 1 B2
Amport Ct. Hav 135 E3
Ampress La. Bold 198 B3
Ampthill Rd. Southa 102 A4
Amyas Ct. Ports 183 E2
Ancasta Rd. Southa 103 D4
Anchor Cl. Bour 189 F3
Anchor Cl. Christ 210 A3
Anchor Mews. Lym 198 C2
Anchor Rd. Bour 189 F3
Anchorage Rd. Ports 158 A2
Anchorage The. Gos 181 E2
Anderby Rd. Southa 77 E1
Anderson Cl. Rom 28 B1
Anderson's Rd. Southa 103 D2
Anderwood Dr. Sway 172 A1
Andes Cl. Southa 103 E2
Andes Rd. Nur 77 D2
Andlers Ash Rd. Liss 20 C2
Andover Cl. Christ 210 A4
Andover Rd N. Winch 1 C2
Andover Rd. Ports 182 C1
Andover Rd. Southa 102 B3
Andover Rd. Winch 1 C1
Andrew Bell St. Ports 182 B3
Andrew Cl. Hyt 126 A1
Andrew Cl. Tot 100 B4
Andrew Cres. Wat 111 E1
Andrew La. New M 196 B1
Andrew Pl. Stubb 154 A1
Andrewes Cl. Bi Wa 83 E4
Andrews Cl. Bour 190 A2
Andromeda Rd. Southa 77 F2
Anfield Cl. Fa Oa 57 E1
Angel Cres. Southa 104 A3
Angel La. B on S 212 B4
Angel La. Fern 165 D2
Angelica Ct. Wat 135 D3
Angelica Gdns. Fa Oa 81 E4
Angeline Cl. Christ 210 C4
Angelo Cl. Wat 135 D4
Angelus Cl. Stubb 154 B1
Angerstein Rd. Ports 157 E1
Anglesea Rd. Lon S 180 A2
Anglesea Rd. Ports 182 A3
Anglesea Rd. Southa 78 A1
Anglesea Terr. Southa 103 D2
Anglesey Arms Rd. Gos 181 D1
Anglesey Rd. Gos 181 D1
Angus Cl. Fare 130 C2
Anjou Cres. Fare 130 B1
Anker La. Stubb 154 B2
Ankerwyke. Gos 155 D1
Anmore Cl. Hav 135 E2
Anmore Dr. Wat 111 E1
Anmore La. Horn 111 E3
Anmore Rd. Den 111 D2
Ann's Hill Rd. Gos 181 D3
Anna La. Sop 168 A2
Anne Cl. Christ 193 D1
Anne Cres. Wat 134 C3
Annerley Rd. Bour 207 E2
Annet Cl. Hamw 203 F1
Anson Cl. Christ 209 F3
Anson Cl. Gos 180 B3
Anson Cl. Rin 141 E4
Anson Dr. Southa 104 B3
Anson Gr. Portc 132 C1
Anson Rd. Ports 183 D3
Anstey Cl. Bour 190 A3
Anstey Rd. Bour 190 D3
Anstey Rd. Rom 28 A1
Antell's Way. Alderh 93 D3
Anthill Cl. Den 110 B3
Anthony Gr. Gos 156 A1
Anthony Way. Ems 136 C2
Anthony's Ave. Poole 205 E1
Anton Cl. Rom 53 E4
Anvil Cl. Wat 112 B1
Anvil Cres. Broa 187 F3
Anzac Cl. Stubb 154 B2
Apless La. Den 110 A2
Apollo Cl. Poole 205 E4
Apollo Dr. Wat 134 C2
Apollo Rd. Ch Fo 55 F4
Apple Gr. Christ 192 C1
Apple Ind Est. Lo He 129 E3
Apple Tree Cl. Red 47 E4
Apple Tree Gr. Fern 165 F3
Apple Tree Rd. Alderh 92 C3
Appleshaw Cl. Winch 1 B2
Appleshaw Green. Hav 135 E2
Appleshaw Way. New M 196 A3
Appleton Rd. Fare 130 B1
Appleton Rd. Southa 79 F1
Appletree Cl. New M 196 A1
Appletree Cl. Tot 76 B1
Appletree Ct. Botl 106 A4
Appletree Rd. Red 47 E4
Applewood Gr. Wat 134 B2
Applewood Pl. Tot 100 B3
Approach Rd. Poole 205 D2
April Cl. Bour 190 A2
April Cl. Southa 104 A4
April Gr. Lo He 128 C2
Apsley Cres. Broa 188 B1
Apsley Pl. Ch Fo 30 A1
Apsley Rd. Ports 183 D2
Aquila Way. Hamble 127 F1
Aragon Way. Bour 191 D2
Arcade. Bour 206 A2
Arcadia Ave. Bour 207 D4
Arcadia Cl. Southa 78 B2
Arcadia Rd. Christ 192 C1
Archdale Cl. Bour 190 B1
Archers Cl. Tot 76 B1
Archers Rd. Eastl 56 A2
Archers Rd. Southa 102 C4
Archery Gdns. Southa 103 F1
Archery Gr. Southa 103 F1
Archery La. Fare 131 E1
Archery Rd. Southa 103 F1
Archway Rd. Poole 205 F2
Arden Cl. Gos 180 C2
Arden Cl. Southa 80 A1
Arden Rd. Bour 190 C2
Arden Wlk. New M 196 A1
Ardington Rise. Wat 134 C2
Ardmore Rd. Poole 205 D2
Ardnave Cres. Southa 78 C3
Argyle Cres. Fare 130 C1
Argyle Rd. Christ 209 F3
Argyle Rd. Southa 103 D3
Argyll Rd. Bour 207 F2
Argyll Rd. Poole 205 E3
Ariel Cl. Bour 209 D2
Ariel Dr. Bour 209 D2
Ariel Rd. Ports 182 C3
Arle Cl. Clanf 88 B2
Arley Rd. Poole 205 D1
Arlington Ct. B on S 212 A4
Arliss Rd. Southa 78 A1
Armada Cl. Rown 77 F4
Armada Dr. Hyt 125 F1
Arminers Cl. Gos 181 D1
Armitage Ave. Hyt 125 F1
Armory La. Ports 182 A2
Armstrong Cl. Brock 145 F1
Armstrong Cl. Wat 111 E1
Armstrong Ct. Southa 77 F3
Armstrong La. Brock 145 F1
Armstrong Rd. Brock 145 F1
Armsworth La. Sob 85 F1
Arnaud Cl. Ports 182 B4
Arne Ave. Poole 205 F4
Arne Cres. Poole 205 F4
Arnewood Bridge Rd. Sway 197 D4
Arnewood Rd. Bour 208 B3
Arnheim Cl. Southa 78 B2
Arnheim Rd. Southa 78 B2
Arnold Cl. W Moo 138 C2
Arnold Rd. Eastl 80 A4
Arnold Rd. Southa 79 E1
Arnold Rd. W Moo 138 C2
Arnolds Cl. B on S 211 F4
Arnside Rd. Wat 134 C4
Arnwood Ave. Hyt 149 F4
Arragon Ct. Wat 135 D4
Arran Cl. Cos 133 F1
Arran Way. Christ 195 D1
Arreton. Net 127 E3
Arrow Cl. Eastl 56 A2
Arrowsmith La. Oakl 188 C4
Arrowsmith Rd. Oakl 188 C4
Arters Lawn. Ashu 124 B3
Arthur Cl. Bour 206 C3
Arthur La. Christ 209 D4
Arthur Rd. Christ 209 D4
Arthur Rd. Eastl 56 A2
Arthur Rd. Southa 102 B3
Arthur Rd. Winch 2 A1
Arthur St. Ports 182 C4
Artillery Cl. Cos 157 E4
Arun Rd. W End 80 A1
Arun Way. W Wel 50 B2
Arundel Cl. New M 195 F2
Arundel Dr. Fare 131 D1
Arundel Pl. Ports 182 B3
Arundel Rd. Eastl 56 A3
Arundel Rd. Gos 180 C3
Arundel Rd. Tot 101 D4
Arundel St. Ports 182 B3
Arundel Way. Christ 210 C4
Ascham Rd. Bour 207 D3
Ascot Cl. Lo He 129 E1
Ascot Rd. Broa 188 A2
Ascot Rd. Ports 183 D4
Ascupart St. Southa 103 D2
Asford Gr. Bish 56 B2
Ash Cl. Alderh 93 D3
Ash Cl. Fare 154 C4
Ash Cl. Gos 181 D2
Ash Cl. Hyt 150 A4
Ash Cl. N Bad 53 F3
Ash Cl. Rom 53 E3
Ash Cl. Southa 104 B3
Ash Cl. Upt 203 D4
Ash Cl. Wat 111 F1
Ash Gr. Ashu 100 B2
Ash Gr. Hord 213 E4
Ash Gr. Rin 141 E4
Ash Rd. Ashu 100 A1
Ash Tree Rd. Southa 79 F1
Ashbarn Cres. Winch 10 C3
Ashbourne Rd. Bour 208 A3
Ashbridge Rise. Ch Fo 30 A1

Ashburn Garth. Rin 141 E3
Ashburnham Cl. Southa 103 E3
Ashburton Gdns. Bour 190 B1
Ashburton Rd. Gos 180 C1
Ashburton Rd. Ports 182 B1
Ashby Cres. Tot 100 B4
Ashby Pl. Ports 182 B1
Ashby Rd. Southa 104 A2
Ashby Rd. Tot 100 B4
Ashcroft La. Finc 113 E3
Ashdene Cl. Wi Mi 163 E3
Ashdene Rd. Ashu 100 B2
Ashdown Cl. Ch Fo 30 B1
Ashdown Dr. Ch Fo 30 B1
Ashdown Rd. Black 150 C1
Ashdown Rd. Ch Fo 30 B1
Ashdown Way. Rom 53 D4
Ashdown Wlk. New M 196 B1
Ashdown. Faw 150 C2
Ashdown. Gos 155 E1
Ashe Rd. Hav 136 A3
Ashford Cl. Fordi 69 E1
Ashford Cres. Hyt 126 A2
Ashford Rd. Bour 208 B4
Ashford Rd. Fordi 93 E4
Ashington La. Oakl 163 D1
Ashington Park. New M 196 B1
Ashlea Cl. Fa Oa 57 E1
Ashleigh Cl. Hyt 150 A4
Ashlett Cl. Faw 151 E2
Ashlett Lawn. Hav 135 E3
Ashlett Mews. Faw 151 D2
Ashlett Rd. Faw 151 E2
Ashley Cl. Hav 135 E2
Ashley Cl. Horn 111 F3
Ashley Cl. Swanw 129 D4
Ashley Cl. Winch 1 B2
Ashley Common Rd. New M 196 B2
Ashley Cres. Southa 104 B1
Ashley Ct. Burs 105 D1
Ashley Drive N. St Le 139 F3
Ashley Drive S. St Le 139 F3
Ashley Drive W. St Le 139 F3
Ashley Gdns. Ch Fo 55 F3
Ashley Gdns. New M 196 B2
Ashley Gdns. Shed 83 F2
Ashley La. Hord 196 C2
Ashley La. Lym 198 C2
Ashley La. New M 196 C2
Ashley Meadows. Rom 53 D4
Ashley Meads. New M 196 B2
Ashley Park. St Le 140 A3
Ashley Rd. Bour 207 E3
Ashley Rd. New M 196 B2
Ashley Rd. Poole 205 E3
Ashleycross Cl. Holb 150 B2
Ashling Cl. Bour 207 E4
Ashling Cl. Den 110 C2
Ashling Cres. Bour 207 D4
Ashling Gdns. Den 110 C2
Ashling La. Ports 157 E1
Ashling Park Rd. Den 110 C2
Ashlyn Cl. Fare 130 B1
Ashmead Rd. Southa 77 F2
Ashmeads Cl. Wi Mi 164 A3
Ashmeads Way. Wi Mi 164 A3
Ashmore Ave. B on S 212 A4
Ashmore Ave. Hamw 203 F1
Ashmore Cl. Whit 24 A2
Ashmore Cres. Hamw 203 F1
Ashmore Gr. Christ 194 C1
Ashmore La. W Dean 24 A3
Ashmore La. Whit 24 A3
Ashmore Rd. Winch 1 B1
Ashmore. Wi Mi 163 E2
Ashridge Ave. Bour 190 B3
Ashridge Cl. Southa 102 C4
Ashridge Gdns. Bour 190 B3
Ashtead Cl. Portc 156 A4
Ashton Cl. Bi Wa 59 D1
Ashton Cross. W Wel 51 D1
Ashton La. Bi Wa 59 D1
Ashton Rd. Bour 190 C1
Ashton Way. Stubb 179 E4
Ashtree Cl. New M 196 B1
Ashurst Bridge Rd. Ne Ma 100 B3
Ashurst Bridge Rd. Tot 100 B3
Ashurst Cl. Ashu 100 A1
Ashurst Cl. Winch 1 B2
Ashurst Rd. Bour 191 E2
Ashurst Rd. Cos 157 F4
Ashurst Rd. W Moo 138 C2
Ashwood Cl. Hav 135 D2
Ashwood Cl. S Hay 185 D2
Ashwood Dr. Broa 188 B2
Ashwood Gdns. Tot 100 B4
Aspen Ave. Lo He 152 B4
Aspen Cl. He En 105 E4
Aspen Dr. Ver 115 D3
Aspen Gdns. Poole 205 F4
Aspen Holt. Southa 79 D3
Aspen Pl. New M 196 A1
Aspen Rd. Poole 205 F4
Aspen Way. Poole 205 F4
Aspen Way. Wat 112 A3
Aspengrove. Gos 155 F1
Assheton Ct. Portc 156 B4
Astbury Ave. Poole 190 A1
Aster Rd. Southa 79 E2
Astley St. Ports 182 B2
Aston Mead. Christ 192 C2
Aston Rd. Ports 182 C2
Aston Rd. Wat 134 B4
Astra Ct. Hyt 126 A3
Astra Wlk. Gos 181 E2
Astrid Cl. S Hay 185 E2
Asylum Rd. Southa 103 D3
Atalanta Cl. Ports 183 E3
Atheling Rd. Hyt 126 A2
Athelstan Rd. Bour 208 C3
Athelstan Rd. Southa 103 F3
Athena Ave. Wat 134 C2
Athena Cl. Fa Oa 57 D2
Atherfield Rd. Southa 77 F2
Atherley Rd. S Hay 184 C3
Atherley Rd. Southa 102 B3
Atkins Pl. Fare 130 B2
Atkinson Cl. Gos 181 D1
Atlantis Ave. Wat 134 C1
Attwood Cl. Alderh 92 C3
Attwoods Dro. Comp 31 E4
Aubrey Cl. M on S 213 F2
Auckland Ave. Brock 146 A1
Auckland Pl. Brock 146 A1
Auckland Rd E. Ports 182 B1
Auckland Rd W. Ports 182 B1
Auckland Rd. Christ 210 B4
Auckland Rd. Southa 101 F4
Audemer Ct. Rin 141 E4
Augustine Rd. Cos 158 B4
Augustine Rd. Southa 103 D3
Augustus Cl. Ch Fo 55 F4
Augustus Way. Ch Fo 55 F4
Auriol Dr. Hav 159 D4
Aust Rd. Fare 154 B4
Austen Ave. Bour 190 C3
Austen Ave. Winch 10 B2
Austen Cl. Tot 100 B3
Austen Cl. Winch 2 A1
Auster Cl. Christ 210 A4
Austerberry Way. Gos 180 C4
Austin Ave. Poole 205 D1
Austin Cl. Bour 207 E3
Austin Ct. Cos 133 D1
Australia Cl. Ports 182 B3
Autumn Cl. Fern 165 D4
Autumn Rd. March 102 A1
Avalon. Poole 211 E4
Avebury Ave. Bour 190 C3
Avebury Gdns. Ch Fo 30 A1
Avenger Cl. Ch Fo 55 D3
Avenue Ct. Gos 181 D1
Avenue La. Bour 206 C2
Avenue Rd. Bour 206 C2
Avenue Rd. Brock 172 C4
Avenue Rd. Christ 195 E1
Avenue Rd. Christ 208 C4
Avenue Rd. Fare 130 C1
Avenue Rd. Gos 181 E2
Avenue Rd. Lym 198 C2
Avenue Rd. N Hay 160 A2
Avenue Rd. New M 196 A2
Avenue Rd. Southa 103 D4
Avenue Rd. Wi Mi 163 E2
Avenue The. Bi Wa 83 D4
Avenue The. Bour 190 C2
Avenue The. Fare 130 B1
Avenue The. Pet 40 C2
Avenue The. Poole 206 A1
Avenue The. Southa 102 C4
Avenue The. Southa 102 C4
Avenue The. Twyf 58 A3
Avenue The. W Moo 138 C2
Avery La. Gosp 181 D4
Avington Cl. Bish 56 B3
Avington Cl. Southa 78 C2
Avington Green. Hav 136 A3
Avocet Quay. Herm 161 D4
Avocet Wlk. Gos 155 D1
Avon Ave. St Le 140 B2
Avon Bldgs. Christ 209 D4
Avon Castle Dr. St Le 140 B2
Avon Cl. Bour 207 E3
Avon Cl. L on S 179 F3
Avon Cl. Lym 198 B2
Avon Cres. Rom 53 E4
Avon Cswy. Hurn 192 B4
Avon Gdns. Bran 169 D1
Avon Green. Ch Fo 55 E3
Avon Meade. Fordi 69 F1
Avon Meadow. Down 46 C4
Avon Park. St Le 140 B3
Avon Rd E. Christ 209 D4
Avon Rd W. Christ 208 C4
Avon Rd. Bour 207 E3
Avon Rd. Southa 79 F1
Avon Rd. W Moo 138 C1
Avon Run Cl. Christ 210 A3
Avon Run Rd. Christ 210 A3
Avon View Rd. Burt 193 E2
Avon Way. W End 80 C1
Avon Wharf. Christ 209 E3
Avon Wlk. Portc 156 A4
Avonborne Way. Ch Fo 55 D4
Avoncliffe Rd. Bour 208 C3
Avondale Rd. Ports 182 C4
Avondale Rd. Wat 134 C4
Award Rd. Fern 164 C3
Awbridge Rd. Hav 135 E2
Axford Cl. Bour 191 E2
Aylen Rd. Ports 158 A1
Aylesbury Rd. Bour 207 F2
Aylesbury Rd. Ports 182 C4
Ayling Cl. Gos 180 B4
Aylward St. Ports 182 A3
Aysgarth Rd. Wat 134 C4
Aysha Cl. New M 196 A1
Azalea Cl. St Le 140 A3
Azura Cl. W Moo 139 D3
Back La. Mott 5 F3
Back La. Southw 132 C3
Back La. Sway 172 B1
Back Of The Walls. Southa 103 D2
Back St. Winch 10 C2
Bacon Cl. Southa 103 F1
Bacon La. S Hay 184 C2
Badbury Cl. Broa 188 B2
Badbury View Rd. Broa 187 E4
Badbury View. Wi Mi 163 E3
Baddesley Cl. N Bad 53 F3
Baddesley Gdns. Hav 135 E4
Baddesley Rd. Ch Fo 30 A1
Baden Cl. New M 196 A1
Baden Powell Way. Rom 52 C4
Bader Cl. He En 105 E4
Bader Rd. Poole 204 C4
Badger Brow. Wat 135 D3
Badger Cl. Bish 56 C1
Badger Cl. Fare 130 B1
Badger Farm Rd. Winch 10 B2
Badger Way. Ver 114 C3
Badgers Cl. St Le 139 F3
Badgers Copse. New M 196 B3
Badgers The. Net 127 E3
Badgers Wlk. Hyt 125 F1
Badminston Drove. Faw 178 B4
Badminston La. Faw 151 E1
Badnam Cl. Burs 127 F4
Badshear La. Cher 14 C4
Baeresford Rd. Lym 198 B2
Baffins Rd. Ports 183 D4
Bagber Rd. Tot 100 C4
Baigent Cl. Winch 11 E4
Baigent Rd. Winch 11 E4
Bailey Cl. Botl 106 A3
Bailey Cl. New M 196 B2
Bailey Cl. Winch 10 B3
Bailey Cres. Poole 204 B4
Bailey's Rd. Ports 182 B2
Baker Rd. Bour 190 D3
Baker St. Ports 182 B4
Bakers Dro. Rown 77 F3
Bakers Farm Rd. Ver 114 C4
Balaclava Rd. Southa 104 A4
Balcombe Rd. Poole 206 A2
Balderton Cl. Ports 157 F2
Baldwin Cl. Christ 209 E3
Balena Cl. Broa 204 A4
Balfour Cl. Christ 210 B4
Balfour Rd. Bour 190 C1
Balfour Rd. Ports 157 F1
Balfour Rd. Southa 104 B3
Ball La. Poole 204 B1
Ballam Cl. Upt 203 E4
Ballard Cl. New M 196 A2
Ballard Cl. Poole 204 B1
Ballard Cl. Southa 77 E1
Ballard Rd. Poole 204 B1
Balliol Cl. Lo He 129 E1
Balliol Rd. Ports 182 C4
Balmer Lawn Rd. Brock 146 A2
Balmoral Ave. Bour 191 F1
Balmoral Cl. Ch Fo 55 D4
Balmoral Cl. Gos 155 E1
Balmoral Cl. Southa 78 B3
Balmoral Dr. Wat 134 B2
Balmoral Rd. Fare 130 C2
Balmoral Rd. Poole 205 E2
Balmoral Way. Pet 40 C2
Balmoral Way. Rown 77 F3
Balmoral Wlk. New M 195 F2
Balston Rd. Poole 205 D3
Baltic Rd. W End 80 C1
Banbury Ave. Southa 104 B2
Banfurly Gdns. Hyt 125 F1
Bangor Rd. Southa 102 A3
Banister Gdns. Southa 102 C4
Banister Mews. Southa 102 C4
Banister Rd. Southa 102 C4
Bank Cl. Christ 209 D3
Bank Side. Southa 79 E2
Bank St. Bi Wa 83 E4
Bankhill Dr. Lym 198 B3
Banks The. Locke 26 A3
Bankside Rd. Bour 191 D2
Bankside. Lym 198 B3
Bankview. Lym 198 B3
Bannerman Rd. Pet 40 C2
Banning St. Rom 52 C3
Banstead Rd. Broa 188 A3
Bapaume Rd. Ports 157 F3
Bar End Rd. Winch 11 D3
Barbe Baker Ave. W End 80 B1
Barberry Way. Ver 115 E3
Barbers Piles. Poole 204 A1
Bardon Way. Fare 154 B4
Barfield Cl. Winch 11 D3
Barfields. Lym 198 C2
Barfleur Cl. Fare 130 B1
Barford Cl. Ch Fo 55 D4
Barford La. Down 47 D4
Bargate St. Southa 102 C2
Bargates. Christ 209 D4
Barham Cl. Gos 181 D3
Barham Rd. Pet 40 C2
Baring Rd. Bour 209 D2
Baring Rd. Winch 11 D4
Barlands Cl. Burt 193 E1
Barle Cl. W End 80 A1
Barley Down Dr. Winch 10 B2
Barleycorn Wlk. Cadn 98 C4
Barlow Cl. Stubb 154 A1
Barn Cl. Ems 160 B4
Barn Cl. Upt 203 D4
Barn Fold. Wat 112 B1
Barn Rd. Broa 188 B2
Barnbrook Rd. Lo He 128 C2
Barncroft Way. Hav 135 E2
Barnes Cl. Bour 190 B2
Barnes Cl. Lo He 128 B2
Barnes Cl. Southa 104 B3
Barnes Cl. W Wel 50 C2
Barnes Cl. Winch 10 C3
Barnes Cres. Bour 190 B2
Barnes Cres. Wi Mi 163 F2
Barnes La. Lo He 128 C3
Barnes La. M on S 213 E3
Barnes Rd. Bour 190 B2
Barnes Rd. Ports 182 C3
Barnes Rd. Southa 104 B3
Barnes Wallis Rd. Lo He 129 E2
Barnes Way. Hav 135 E2
Barnet Side La. Frox G 18 B3
Barney Evans Cres. Wat 111 E2
Barney Hayes La. Cadn 99 D4
Barnfield Cl. Southa 103 F1
Barnfield Cl. Southb 137 F1
Barnfield Ct. Southa 103 F1
Barnfield Rd. Pet 41 E2
Barnfield Rd. Southa 103 F1
Barnfield Way. Southa 103 F1
Barnfield. Christ 210 B4
Barns Rd. Fern 166 A3
Barnsfield Cres. Tot 100 B4
Barnside Way. Liss 20 C2
Barnsland. W End 80 B2
Barnwood Rd. Fare 130 B1
Barons Rd. Bour 189 E3
Barrack Rd. Christ 208 C4
Barrack Rd. Fern 166 A1
Barratt Ind Est. Lo He 129 E3
Barrie Rd. Bour 190 C2
Barrington Cl. Eastl 55 F3
Barrow Dr. Bour 191 F1
Barrow Hill Rd. Cadn 75 E2
Barrow Rd. Bour 191 F1
Barrow Way. Bour 191 F1
Barrowgate Way. Bour 191 E2
Barrows La. Lan 49 E3
Barrows La. Sway 197 D3
Barrs Ave. New M 196 A2
Barrs Wood Dr. New M 196 A2
Barrs Wood Rd. New M 196 A2
Barry Gdns. Broa 187 F3
Barry Rd. Southa 104 A3
Barters La. Broa 187 F2
Bartlett Ave. Bour 208 A4
Bartlett Cl. Fare 130 C2
Bartley Ave. Tot 100 C3
Bartley Rd. Ne Ma 99 E2
Barton Cl. Ports 158 A2
Barton Cl. Rom 53 D4
Barton Common La. B on S 212 A4
Barton Common Rd. B on S 212 A4
Barton Court Ave. B on S 212 A4
Barton Court Rd. New M 196 A1
Barton Cres. Southa 79 F1
Barton Croft. B on S 212 A4
Barton Dr. B on S 211 F4
Barton Dr. Hamble 127 F2
Barton Dr. He En 105 E4
Barton La. B on S 211 F4
Barton Park Ind Est. Eastl 56 B1
Barton Rd. Bish 56 B2
Barton Way. B on S 211 F4
Barton Wood Rd. B on S 211 F4
Bartons Rd. Fordi 69 F1
Bartons Rd. Hav 136 A2
Bartons The. Fordi 69 F1
Bartons The. He En 105 D3
Bartonside Rd. B on S 211 E4
Bartram Rd. Tot 101 D3
Barwell Gr. Ems 136 C2
Bascott Cl. Bour 190 A1
Bascott Rd. Bour 190 A1
Bashley Cross Rd. New M 195 F3
Bashley Dr. New M 196 A3
Bashley Rd. New M 196 A3
Basin St. Ports 182 B4
Basing Dean. Frox G 17 F2
Basing Rd. Hav 135 F3
Basing Way. Ch Fo 55 D2
Basingstoke Rd. Ki Wo 2 B4
Basingwell St. Bi Wa 83 E4
Bassett Ave. Southa 78 C3
Bassett Cl. Southa 78 C2
Bassett Cres E. Southa 78 C2
Bassett Cres W. Southa 78 C2
Bassett Ct. Southa 78 C2
Bassett Dale. Southa 78 C3
Bassett Gdns. Southa 78 C2
Bassett Green Cl. Southa 79 D3
Bassett Green Dr. Southa 79 D3
Bassett Green Rd. Southa 79 D3
Bassett Green. Southa 79 D3
Bassett Heath Ave. Southa 78 C3
Bassett Meadow. Southa 78 C2
Bassett Rd. Poole 205 D3
Bassett Row. Southa 78 C3
Bassett Wlk. Hav 135 E3
Bassett Wood Dr. Southa 79 D3
Bassett Wood Rd. Southa 79 D3
Batchelor Green. Burs 128 A4
Batchelor Rd. Bour 189 F2
Batcombe Cl. Bour 189 F2
Bath Cl. Southa 104 A3
Bath La (Lower). Fare 131 E1
Bath La. Fare 131 E1
Bath Rd. Bour 207 D2
Bath Rd. Ems 160 C4
Bath Rd. Lym 198 C2
Bath Rd. Lym 199 D2
Bath Rd. Ports 182 C2
Bath Rd. Southa 104 A3
Bath Sq. Ports 181 F2
Bath St. Southa 103 D4
Bathing La. Ports 181 F2
Batten Rd. Down 46 C4
Battenburg Ave. Ports 157 F1
Battenburg Rd. Gos 181 E3
Battens Way. Hav 135 F2
Batterley Dro. Alderh 91 F2
Battery Cl. Gos 180 C4
Battery Hill. Bi Wa 83 D4
Battery Hill. Winch 10 B3
Battery Row. Ports 182 A2
Baverstock Rd. Poole 206 A4
Baxter Rd. Southa 104 C3
Bay Cl. Southa 104 A2
Bay Cl. Upt 203 D3
Bay Cl. W Moo 138 C4
Bay Hog La. Poole 204 A1
Bay Rd. Gos 180 C2
Bay Rd. Southa 104 A2
Bay Tree Way. Christ 194 B1
Baybridge La. Ows 33 E2
Baybridge Rd. Hav 136 A3
Bayly Ave. Portc 156 B3
Bays Rd. Lym 198 B2
Baythorn Cl. Ports 182 B4
Beach Ave. B on S 211 F4
Beach La. Net 127 D3
Beach Rd. Ems 160 C4
Beach Rd. L on S 179 F3
Beach Rd. Ports 182 B1
Beach Rd. S Hay 184 C2
Beach Rd. Upt 203 D3
Beachway. Portc 156 B3
Beacon Bottom. Lo He 129 D3
Beacon Cl. Hord 197 E1
Beacon Cl. Lo He 129 D3
Beacon Cl. Rown 77 E3
Beacon Ct. Fordi 69 F2
Beacon Dr. Christ 210 C4
Beacon Gdns. Broa 187 F2
Beacon Hill La. Meons 61 E3
Beacon Mews. W End 104 B4
Beacon Mount. Lo He 129 D3
Beacon Park Cres. Upt 203 D4
Beacon Park Rd. Upt 203 D4
Beacon Rd. Bour 206 C1
Beacon Rd. Broa 187 F2
Beacon Rd. Upt 203 D4
Beacon Rd. W End 104 B4
Beacon Sq. Ems 160 C4
Beacon Way. Broa 187 F2
Beacon Way. Lo He 129 D3
Beaconsfield Ave. Cos 158 A4
Beaconsfield Rd. Christ 209 D4
Beaconsfield Rd. Fare 155 D4
Beaconsfield Rd. Poole 205 E3
Beaconsfield Rd. Wat 134 C4
Bealing Cl. Southa 79 D2
Beamish Rd. Poole 204 C4
Bear Cross Ave. Bour 189 F3
Bearslane Cl. Tot 76 B1
Beatrice Rd. Ports 182 C1
Beatrice Rd. Southa 102 B4
Beattie Rise. He En 81 E1
Beatty Cl. Lo He 129 D2
Beatty Cl. Rin 141 E4
Beatty Dr. Gos 180 C2
Beatty Rd. Bour 191 D1
Beaty Ct. Southa 104 B3
Beauchamp Ave. Gos 155 E1
Beauchamps Gdns. Bour 208 A4
Beaucroft La. Wi Mi 163 F3
Beaucroft Rd. Shed 83 F2
Beaucroft Rd. Wi Mi 163 F3
Beaufort Ave. Fare 130 C1
Beaufort Cl. Christ 210 A4
Beaufort Dr. Bi Wa 83 E4
Beaufort Rd. Bour 208 B3
Beaufort Rd. Hav 135 E1

Beaufort Rd. Ports 182 B1
Beaufort Rd. Winch 10 C3
Beaufoys Ave. Fern 165 E4
Beaufoys Cl. Fern 165 E4
Beaulieu Ave. Christ 208 C4
Beaulieu Ave. Hav 135 E3
Beaulieu Ave. Portc 156 A4
Beaulieu Cl. New M 195 F2
Beaulieu Cl. Southa 78 A3
Beaulieu Cl. Winch 1 B2
Beaulieu Pl. Gos 155 D1
Beaulieu Rd. Beaul 122 B2
Beaulieu Rd. Beaul 149 E3
Beaulieu Rd. Bour 206 B1
Beaulieu Rd. Christ 208 C4
Beaulieu Rd. Eastl 56 A2
Beaulieu Rd. Hamble 127 F2
Beaulieu Rd. Hyt 149 F4
Beaulieu Rd. Lyn 122 B2
Beaulieu Rd. March 124 C3
Beaulieu Rd. Ports 157 F1
Beaumaris Cl. Ch Fo 55 D2
Beaumont Cl. Fare 130 B2
Beaumont Cl. Southa 78 C2
Beaumont Ct. Gosp 181 D4
Beaumont Rd. Poole 211 F4
Beaumont Rd. Tot 101 D4
Beaumont Rise. Fare 130 B2
Beauworth Ave. Southa 104 B4
Beaver Dr. Bish 57 D1
Beccles Cl. Hamw 203 F1
Becher Rd. Poole 205 F2
Beck Cl. Lo He 128 C2
Beck St. Ports 182 A3
Beckford La. Southw 109 F1
Beckham La. Pet 40 B2
Beckhampton Rd. Hamw 203 F2
Beckley Copse. Christ 195 D1
Becton La. B on S 212 A4
Bedale Way. Poole 204 C3
Bedenham La. Gos 155 F2
Bedfield La. Ki Wo 2 A3
Bedford Ave. Southa 103 F1
Bedford Cl. Fordi 69 F2
Bedford Cl. Hav 160 A4
Bedford Cl. He En 105 E3
Bedford Cres. Bour 208 B4
Bedford Pl. Southa 102 C3
Bedford Rd N. Poole 189 E1
Bedford Rd S. Poole 189 E1
Bedford Rd. Pet 40 C2
Bedford St. Gos 181 D3
Bedford St. Ports 182 B2
Bedhampton Hill Rd. Hav 135 D1
Bedhampton Rd. Hav 135 E1
Bedhampton Rd. Ports 182 C4
Bedhampton Way. Hav 135 F2
Bedwell Cl. Rown 77 F3
Beech Ave. Bour 208 B2
Beech Ave. Christ 208 B4
Beech Ave. Southa 103 F4
Beech Cl. Alderh 93 D3
Beech Cl. Broa 187 F2
Beech Cl. Ch Fo 30 B1
Beech Cl. Hamble 127 F1
Beech Cl. Hord 213 E4
Beech Cl. Rom 53 E3
Beech Cl. Ver 114 C3
Beech Cl. Wat 111 F1
Beech Cl. Winch 10 A2
Beech Copse. Winch 1 A1
Beech Cres. Hyt 150 A4
Beech Gdns. Hamble 127 F1
Beech Gr. Gos 181 D2
Beech Gr. Ows 33 D2
Beech Gr. S Hay 185 D2
Beech Grange. Lan 49 E1
Beech La. St Le 139 F1
Beech Rd. Ashu 100 A1
Beech Rd. Ch Fo 55 E4
Beech Rd. Clanf 88 B3
Beech Rd. Fare 130 C1
Beech Rd. He En 105 E4
Beech Rd. Southa 102 A3
Beech Way. Wat 112 A3
Beech Wood Cl. Broa 188 A2
Beecham Rd. Ports 182 C4
Beechbank Ave. Broa 187 F1
Beechcroft Cl. Ch Fo 55 E3
Beechcroft Cl. Fare 130 B1
Beechcroft La. Rin 141 D4
Beechcroft Rd. Gos 181 D2
Beechcroft Way. Ch Fo 55 E3
Beechdale Cl. Tot 76 B1
Beechen La. Lyn 122 A2
Beeches Hill. Bi Wa 59 E1
Beeches The. Bour 208 A4
Beeches The. Fa Oa 57 E1
Beeches The. W Wel 50 B2
Beechey Rd. Bour 207 D3
Beechfield Ct. Southa 102 A4
Beechmount Rd. Southa 78 C3
Beechwood Ave. Bour 207 F2
Beechwood Ave. New M 195 F2
Beechwood Ave. Wat 134 C3
Beechwood Cl. Ch Fo 30 A1
Beechwood Cl. Lo He 152 B4
Beechwood Cres. Ch Fo 30 A1
Beechwood Gdns. Southa 103 F4
Beechwood La. Bur 143 D2
Beechwood Rd. Cadn 99 D3
Beechwood Rd. Holb 150 B2
Beechwood Rd. Ports 157 F2
Beechwood Rd. W Moo 138 C1
Beechwood Rise. W End 80 B1
Beechwood Way. Hyt 125 E1
Beechwood. Fordi 69 E1
Beechworth Rd. Hav 136 A1
Beehive Wlk. Ports 182 A2
Beggar's La. Winch 11 D4
Begonia Rd. Southa 79 D2
Behrendt Cl. Gosp 181 D3
Belben Rd. Poole 189 E1
Belbins. Abb 27 F2
Belfield Rd. Bour 209 D2
Belfry Wlk. Lo He 129 E2
Belgrave Rd. Poole 206 A1
Belgrave Rd. Southa 79 E1
Belgravia Rd. Ports 157 F1
Bell Cres. Wat 134 C3
Bell Davies Rd. Stubb 154 A1
Bell Hill Ridge. Pet 40 C3
Bell Hill. Pet 40 C3
Bell Rd. Cos 157 E4
Bell St. Rom 52 C4
Bell St. Southa 103 D2
Bellair Rd. Hav 136 A1
Belle Vue Cl. Bour 208 B2
Belle Vue Cres. Bour 208 C2
Belle Vue Gr. W Moo 138 C1
Belle Vue Rd. Bour 208 C2
Belle Vue Rd. Poole 205 E2
Belle Vue Wlk. Fern 165 F1
Bellemoor Rd. Southa 78 B1
Bellevue La. Ems 136 C1
Bellevue Rd. Eastl 56 A2
Bellevue Rd. Southa 103 D3
Bellfield. Lo He 153 F4
Bellflower Cl. Christ 210 A4
Bells La. Stubb 154 B1
Bellview Terr. Ports 182 A2
Belmont Ave. Bour 191 E1
Belmont Cl. Horn 88 B2
Belmont Cl. Hyt 126 A1
Belmont Cl. Stubb 154 B2
Belmont Cl. Ver 115 D3
Belmont Gr. Hav 135 E1
Belmont Pl. Ports 182 B2
Belmont Rd. Ch Fo 55 E2
Belmont Rd. New M 196 B2
Belmont Rd. Poole 205 E3
Belmont Rd. Southa 103 D4
Belmont St. Ports 182 B2
Belmore La. Lym 198 C2
Belmore La. Ows 33 F2
Belmore La. Uph 34 A2
Belmore Rd. Lym 198 B2
Belstone Rd. Tot 100 C4
Belton Rd. Southa 104 A2
Belvedere Pl. Pet 40 C2
Belvedere Rd. Bour 207 D3
Belvedere Rd. Christ 209 D4
Belvedere Rd. Hyt 126 A1
Belvidere Rd. Southa 103 E3
Belvidere Terr. Southa 103 E3
Belvoir Cl. Fare 155 D4
Bembridge Cl. Southa 79 E3
Bembridge Cres. Ports 182 C1
Bembridge Ct. S Hay 185 E1
Bembridge Dr. S Hay 185 E1
Bembridge. Net 127 E3
Bemister Rd. Bour 207 D4
Bemister's La. Gos 181 F2
Benbow Cl. Horn 112 B4
Benbow Cres. Poole 189 F1
Benbow Gdns. Tot 76 B1
Benbow Pl. Ports 182 A3
Benbridge Ave. Bour 189 F3
Bendigo Rd. Christ 208 C4
Benedict Cl. Rom 53 E4
Benedict Way. Portc 132 C1
Beneficial St. Ports 182 A3
Benellen Ave. Bour 206 B2
Benellen Gdns. Bour 206 B2
Benellen Rd. Bour 206 B3
Bengal Rd. Bour 206 C4
Benger's La. Mott 5 E1
Benham Dr. Ports 157 F2
Benham Gr. Portc 156 B3
Benhams Rd. Southa 80 A1
Benmoor Rd. Broa 204 A4
Benmore Gdns. Ch Fo 55 D4
Benmore Rd. Bour 191 D1
Bennett Rd. Bour 207 E3
Bennett's Alley. Poole 204 A1
Bennetts La. Bur 143 E1
Bennion Rd. Bour 190 B2
Benridge Cl. Broa 188 A2
Benson Cl. Bran 169 D1
Bentham Rd. Gos 181 D2
Bentham Way. Swanw 128 B4
Bentley Cl. Horn 112 B4
Bentley Cl. Ki Wo 2 A3
Bentley Cres. Fare 130 C1
Bentley Green. Southa 104 B4
Bentley Rd. Bour 190 C2
Bentworth Cl. Hav 135 E2
Bepton Down. Pet 41 D2
Bercote Cl. Litt 1 A3
Bere Cl. Broa 188 B1
Bere Cl. N Bad 55 D4
Bere Cl. Winch 1 B1
Bere Farm La. Southw 131 F4
Bere Rd. Den 110 C2
Beresford Cl. Ch Fo 55 F3
Beresford Cl. Poole 205 E3
Beresford Cl. Wat 134 C3
Beresford Gdns. Ch Fo 55 F3
Beresford Gdns. Christ 209 F3
Beresford Rd. Bour 208 A2
Beresford Rd. Ch Fo 55 F3
Beresford Rd. Poole 205 E3
Beresford Rd. Ports 157 F1
Beresford Rd. Stubb 154 B2
Bereweeke Ave. Winch 1 C1
Bereweeke Cl. Winch 1 C1
Bereweeke Rd. Winch 1 C1
Bereweeke Way. Winch 1 C1
Bergen Cres. He En 105 E3
Berkeley Ave. Poole 205 E4
Berkeley Cl. Southa 102 C4
Berkeley Cl. Stubb 154 A1
Berkeley Cl. Ver 114 C4
Berkeley Gdns. He En 105 E3
Berkeley Rd. Bour 206 C4
Berkeley Rd. Southa 102 C3
Berkeley Sq. Hav 136 A1
Berkley Ave. Fern 165 E1
Berkshire Cl. Ports 182 C3
Bernard Ave. Cos 158 A4
Bernard St. Southa 103 D2
Berney Rd. Ports 183 E2
Bernina Ave. Wat 111 E1
Bernina Cl. Wat 111 E1
Bernwood Gr. Black 177 F4
Berrans Ave. Bour 190 D3
Berry Cl. He En 105 E3
Berry La. Stubb 154 A1
Berry La. Twyf 32 A4
Berrybarn La. W Wit 186 C1
Berrydown Rd. Hav 135 E4
Berryfield Rd. Hord 197 D1
Berrylands. Liss 21 D4
Berrywood Gdns. He En 105 D4
Bertie Rd. Ports 183 D2
Bertram Rd. New M 196 B2
Berwick Rd. Bour 206 C3
Berwyn Wlk. Fare 154 C4
Beryl Ave. Gos 180 C4
Beryton Cl. Gosp 181 D3
Beryton Rd. Gosp 181 D3
Besomer Dro. Red 47 F3
Bessborough Rd. Poole 211 F4
Bessemer Cl. Ver 115 E2
Beswick Ave. Bour 190 B1
Bethia Cl. Bour 207 E3
Bethia Rd. Bour 207 E3
Betsy Cl. Bran 169 D1
Betsy La. Bran 169 D1
Bettesworth Rd. Ports 182 C4
Bettiscombe Cl. Broa 188 C1
Betula Cl. Wat 135 D3
Beulah Rd. Southa 78 A1
Bevan Rd. Wat 112 A3
Beverley Cl. Lo He 129 E2
Beverley Gdns. Bour 190 B2
Beverley Gdns. Burs 104 C1
Beverley Gdns. Rom 28 B1
Beverley Gdns. Swan 84 A3
Beverley Gr. Cos 134 C1
Beverley Hts. Southa 79 F2
Beverley Rd. Hyt 149 F4
Beverley Rd. Stubb 154 B1
Beverly Cl. Gos 155 E1
Beverston Rd. Cos 133 D1
Bevis Cl. Lo He 152 B4
Bevis Rd North. Ports 157 E1
Bevis Rd. Gos 181 D3
Bevis Rd. Ports 157 E1
Bevois Hill. Southa 103 D4
Bevois St. Southa 103 D2
Bevois Valley Rd. Southa 103 D4
Bexington Cl. Bour 189 F2
Beyne Rd. Winch 10 A2
Bickerley Gdns. Rin 140 C3
Bickerley Rd. Rin 140 C3
Bickton Wlk. Hav 135 E3
Bicton Rd. Bour 190 A2
Bidbury La. Hav 135 E1
Biddenfield La. Shed 107 E3
Biddenfield La. Wickh 107 E3
Biddlecombe Cl. Gos 180 B4
Bideford Cl. Southa 77 F1
Big Tree Cotts. Sob 85 E3
Biggin Wlk. Fare 154 C4
Bilberry Cl. Lo He 128 F1
Bilberry Dr. March 101 F1
Billett Ave. Wat 134 C4
Billington Gdns. He En 81 E1
Billy Lawn Ave. Hav 135 F3
Bindon Cl. Poole 205 F4
Bindon Cl. Southa 78 A1
Bindon Rd. Southa 78 A1
Bingham Ave. Poole 211 E4
Bingham Cl. Christ 209 F4
Bingham Cl. Ver 115 D2
Bingham Dr. Lym 198 C2
Bingham Rd. Bour 207 D4
Bingham Rd. Christ 209 F4
Bingham Rd. Ver 115 D2
Binness Way. Cos 158 C4
Binnie Rd. Poole 205 F3
Binstead Cl. Southa 79 E3
Binsteed Rd. Ports 182 C4
Birch Ave. Burt 193 E2
Birch Ave. Fern 165 F1
Birch Cl. Broa 187 E3
Birch Cl. Liss 21 D2
Birch Cl. Poole 205 F2
Birch Cl. Rom 53 E3
Birch Cl. Southa 78 A1
Birch Cl. St Le 139 E2
Birch Cl. Wat 111 F2
Birch Dale. Hyt 126 A1
Birch Dr. Bour 192 A1
Birch Dr. Gos 155 E2
Birch Gr. Eastl 56 A3
Birch Gr. W Moo 138 B1
Birch Rd. Chilw 79 D4
Birch Rd. He En 105 E4
Birch Rd. Southa 78 A2
Birch Tree Cl. Ems 136 C2
Birch Tree Dr. Ems 136 C2
Birch Wood. Southa 104 C3
Birchdale Cl. Lo He 152 B4
Birchdale Rd. Wi Mi 163 E3
Birchen Cl. Lo He 129 E2
Birchen Rd. Lo He 129 E2
Birches Cl The. N Bad 53 F3
Birches The. Southa 104 A4
Birchglade. Tot 76 B1
Birchlands. Tot 100 B3
Birchmore Cl. Gos 155 E1
Birchwood Cl. Christ 210 C4
Birchwood Dr. Alderh 93 D3
Birchwood Rd. Poole 205 E2
Birchwood Rd. Upt 203 D3
Birchy Hill. Sway 172 B1
Bird's Hill Rd. Poole 204 C2
Birdham Rd. S Hay 185 F1
Birdlip Cl. Wat 112 A3
Birdlip Rd. Cos 133 D1
Birdwood Gr. Portc 155 F4
Birinus Rd. Winch 2 A1
Birkdale Ave. Cos 134 B1
Birkdale Ct. Broa 188 A3
Birkdale Rd. Broa 188 A3
Biscay Cl. Stubb 154 A2
Bishearne Gdns. Liss 20 C3
Bishop Rd. Bour 207 D4
Bishop St. Ports 182 A3
Bishop's La. Bi Wa 83 E4
Bishop's Wood Rd. Shed 84 B1
Bishops Cl. Bour 207 F4
Bishops Cl. Tot 100 C4
Bishops Cres. Southa 103 F2
Bishops Ct. Bish 56 B3
Bishops Gate. Lo He 129 E2
Bishops La. Shed 84 A1
Bishops Rd. Southa 103 F2
Bishopsfield Rd. Fare 154 C4
Bishopstoke Rd. Bish 56 B2
Bishopstoke Rd. Co Com 56 C4
Bishopstoke Rd. Hav 135 F3
Bisley Ct. Southa 104 A2
Bisterne Cl. Bur 143 E2
Bittern Cl. Gosp 181 D4
Bitterne Cl. Hav 135 F3
Bitterne Cres. Southa 104 A3
Bitterne Rd E. Southa 104 B4
Bitterne Rd W. Southa 103 F4
Bitterne Way. Lym 198 B1
Bitterne Way. Southa 103 F3
Bitterne Way. Ver 115 D3
Black Hill. Ver 115 D3
Black La. Red 48 A2
Black Moor Rd. Ver 115 E2
Blackberry La. Christ 209 F3
Blackberry Terr. Southa 103 D4
Blackbird Cl. Broa 203 F4
Blackbird Cl. Wat 111 F2
Blackbird Rd. Eastl 55 E1
Blackbird Way. Bran 194 B4
Blackbird Way. L on S 179 F4
Blackbrook Park Ave. Fare 130 C1
Blackburn Rd. Poole 205 D3
Blackbush Rd. M on S 213 D3
Blackbushe Cl. Southa 77 F3
Blackcap Cl. Ro Ca 113 D1
Blackdown Cl. Hyt 125 E2
Blackdown Cres. Hav 135 F2
Blackfield Rd. Black 150 C1
Blackfield Rd. Bour 191 E2
Blackfriars Cl. Ports 182 B2
Blackfriars Rd. Ports 182 B3
Blackhill Rd. Ower 74 C4
Blackhorse La. Shed 83 F1
Blackmoor Wlk. Hav 136 A3
Blackmore La. Frox G 18 C2
Blacksmith Cl. Broa 187 E3
Blackthorn Cl. Lym 198 A1
Blackthorn Cl. Southa 103 F3
Blackthorn Dr. Gos 156 A1
Blackthorn Dr. S Hay 185 E2
Blackthorn Rd. S Hay 185 E1
Blackthorn Rd. Southa 103 F3
Blackthorn Way. New M 196 B2
Blackthorn Way. Ver 115 D3
Blackwater Cl. Cos 157 E4
Blackwater Dr. Oakl 188 B4
Blackwater Dr. Tot 76 B1
Blackwater Gr. Alderh 92 C3
Bladon Cl. Hav 136 B2
Bladon Rd. Southa 78 B1
Blair Ave. Poole 205 E2
Blair Cl. New M 195 F2
Blake Dene Rd. Poole 205 D1
Blake Hill Ave. Poole 205 E1
Blake Hill Cres. Poole 205 E1
Blake Rd. Cos 134 B1
Blake Rd. Gos 181 E3
Blakemere Cres. Cos 133 E1
Blakeney Rd. Southa 77 E1
Blanchard Rd. Bi Wa 83 D4
Blandford Rd N. Upt 203 D4
Blandford Rd. Broa 187 E4
Blandford Rd. Co Bi 23 E4
Blandford Rd. Hamw 203 E2
Blandford Rd. Pamp 162 B4
Blandford Rd. Upt 203 E2
Blaney Way. Broa 187 E3
Blankney Cl. Stubb 154 A1
Blaven Wlk. Fare 154 C4
Bleaklow Cl. Southa 101 F4
Blechynden Terr. Southa 102 C3
Blendworth Cres. Hav 135 F2
Blendworth La. Horn 112 C4
Blendworth La. Southa 104 B4
Blendworth Rd. Ports 183 D3
Blenheim Ave. Southa 79 D1
Blenheim Cl. Tot 100 C3
Blenheim Cres. Hord 196 C2
Blenheim Dr. Christ 210 A3
Blenheim Gdns. Gosp 181 D4
Blenheim Gdns. Hav 136 B1
Blenheim Gdns. Hyt 125 E2
Blenheim Gdns. Southa 79 D1
Blenheim Rd. Eastl 56 A1
Blenheim Rd. Wat 112 A3
Blighmont Ave. Southa 102 A3
Blighmont Cres. Southa 102 A3
Blind La. Fa Oa 81 E3
Blind La. W End 81 E3
Blind La. Wi Mi 163 D3
Blind La. Wickh 107 F3
Bliss Cl. Wat 134 C3
Blissford Cl. Hav 136 A3
Blissford Hill. Fordi 94 C4
Blissford Rd. Fordi 94 C4
Bloomsbury Wlk. Southa 103 F1
Blossom Cl. He En 105 F3
Blount Rd. Ports 182 A2
Bloxworth Rd. Poole 205 F4
Blue Anchor La. Southa 102 C2
Blue Ball Hill. Winch 11 D4
Bluebell Cl. Christ 210 A4
Bluebell Cl. Wat 135 D3
Bluebell Copse. Lo He 128 C1
Bluebell La. Broa 187 F1
Bluebell Rd. Southa 79 E2
Blundell La. Burs 105 E1
Blyth Cl. Christ 192 B2
Blyth Cl. Southa 77 E1
Blythe Rd. Broa 187 E3
Blythswood Ct. B on S 211 F4
Boarhunt Cl. Ports 182 B3
Boarhunt Rd. Fare 131 F2
Boatyard Ind Est The. Fare 155 D4
Bob Hann Cl. Poole 205 F3
Bockhampton Rd. Bran 193 F3
Bockhampton Rd. Burt 193 F3
Bodley Rd. Poole 211 F4
Bodmin Rd. Bish 56 C1
Bodmin Rd. Portc 157 D4
Bodorgan Rd. Bour 206 C2
Bodowen Cl. Burt 193 E1
Bodycoats Rd. Ch Fo 55 E3
Bognor Rd. Broa 187 F2
Bohemia La. Red 47 F2
Bolde Cl. Ports 158 A2
Boldens Rd. Gos 181 D1
Bolderwood Cl. Bish 56 C1
Boldre Cl. Hav 135 E2
Boldre Cl. Poole 205 E4
Boldre La. Bold 198 B4
Boldrewood Rd. Southa 78 C2
Bolhinton Ave. March 101 E1
Bolton Cl. Bour 208 C2
Bolton Cres. Fern 166 A3
Bolton Rd. Bour 208 C2
Boltons The. M on S 213 E2
Boltons The. Wat 134 C2
Bonchurch Cl. Southa 79 E3
Bonchurch Rd. Ports 183 D3
Bond Ave. W Moo 138 B2
Bond Cl. Sway 172 A2
Bond Rd. Poole 204 C3
Bond Rd. Southa 79 F1
Bond St. Southa 103 E3
Bondfields Cres. Hav 135 F3
Bones La. Buri 65 E3
Bonfire Cnr. Ports 182 A3
Bonham Rd. Bour 206 C4
Boniface Cl. Tot 100 B4
Boniface Cres. Southa 77 F2

Bonington Cl. Christ 209 F4
Bookdale Cl. Broa 188 A2
Border Dr. Upt 203 E3
Border Rd. Upt 203 E3
Bordon Rd. Hav 135 F3
Boredean La. Frox G 39 E3
Boredean La. Langr 39 E3
Boreham Rd. Bour 208 B3
Borley Rd. Broa 204 A4
Borough Gr. Pet 40 C1
Borough Hill. Pet 40 C2
Borough Rd. Pet 40 B1
Borough The. Down 46 C4
Borrowdale Rd. Southa 77 F1
Borthwick Rd. Bour 207 E3
Boscobel Rd. Winch 1 C1
Boscombe Cliff Rd. Bour 207 F2
Boscombe Gr Rd. Bour 207 E3
Boscombe Overcliff Dr. Exb 208 A2
Boscombe Rd. Bour 209 D2
Boscombe Spa Rd. Bour 207 E2
Bosham Rd. Ports 182 C4
Bosham Wlk. Gos 155 D1
Bosley Cl. Christ 192 C1
Bosley Way. Christ 192 C1
Bosmere Gdns. Ems 136 C1
Bosmere Rd. S Hay 185 F1
Bossington Cl. Rown 77 F3
Boston Rd. Cos 133 F1
Bosville. Eastl 56 A3
Boswell Cl. Botl 106 A3
Boswell Cl. Southa 104 B3
Bosworth Mews. Bour 191 D2
Botany Bay Rd. Southa 104 A2
Botley Dr. Hav 135 E3
Botley Gdns. Southa 104 C2
Botley Rd. Bi Wa 82 C1
Botley Rd. Chilw 53 E3
Botley Rd. Curd 82 C1
Botley Rd. Fa Oa 81 E4
Botley Rd. He En 81 D1
Botley Rd. Lo He 129 D4
Botley Rd. N Bad 53 E3
Botley Rd. Rom 53 E3
Botley Rd. Southa 104 B2
Botley Rd. Swanw 106 A1
Botley Rd. Swanw 129 D4
Botley Rd. W End 81 D1
Bottom La. W Wel 50 C2
Boulnois Ave. Poole 205 F2
Boulter La. Southw 133 D4
Boulton Rd. Ports 182 C2
Bound La. S Hay 185 D1
Boundary Cl. Southa 101 F4
Boundary Dr. Wi Mi 163 E3
Boundary La. St Le 139 F1
Boundary Rd. Bour 190 C1
Boundary Rd. Burs 127 F4
Boundary Way. Hav 135 F1
Boundary Way. Wat 134 A1
Boundstone. Hyt 125 F2
Boundway. Sway 171 F1
Bourne Ave. Bour 206 C2
Bourne Ave. Southa 78 B1
Bourne Cl. Horn 112 A3
Bourne Cl. Ott 31 E2
Bourne Cl. W Wel 50 B2
Bourne Ct. Wi Mi 163 E3
Bourne La. Ne Ma 99 E3
Bourne La. Twyf 58 A3
Bourne Rd. Cos 157 D4
Bourne Rd. Ne Ma 99 E3
Bourne Rd. Southa 102 B3
Bourne Valley Rd. Poole 206 A3
Bourne View. Southb 137 E1
Bournefields. Twyf 32 A4
Bournemouth Ave. Gosp 181 D4
Bournemouth Rd. Ch Fo 55 E2
Bournemouth Rd. Chilw 55 E2
Bournemouth Rd. Lyn 121 F3
Bournemouth Rd. Poole 205 E2
Bournewood Dr. Bour 206 B2
Bourton Gdns. Bour 208 A4
Boveridge Gdns. Bour 191 D2
Bovington Cl. Poole 188 C1
Bowater Cl. Tot 76 B1
Bowater Way. Tot 76 B1
Bowden La. Southa 79 E1
Bowden Rd. Poole 189 E1
Bower Cl. Holb 150 B2
Bower Cl. Southa 103 F1
Bower Rd. Bour 207 E4
Bowers Cl. Wat 112 A2
Bowers Hill. Red 47 F4
Bowerwood Rd. Fordi 93 E4
Bowes Hill. Ro Ca 113 E2
Bowland Rise. N Bad 55 D4
Bowland Rise. New M 196 B1
Bowland Way. Black 177 F4
Bowler Ave. Ports 182 C3
Bowler Ct. Ports 182 C3
Bowman Ct. Southa 104 A2
Box Cl. Broa 204 A4
Boxwood Cl. Portc 132 A1
Boxwood Cl. Wat 134 C3
Boyatt La. Eastl 56 A4
Boyatt La. Ott 56 A4
Boyd Cl. Stubb 154 A1
Boyd Rd. Gos 155 D2
Boyd Rd. Poole 205 F3
Boyes La. Co Com 58 A1
Boyle Cres. Wat 134 B3
Boyne Mead Rd. Ki Wo 2 B4
Boyne Rise. Ki Wo 2 A4
Boynton Cl. Ch Fo 55 D4
Brabazon Dr. Christ 210 A4
Brabazon Rd. Oakl 163 F1
Brabourne Ave. Fern 165 E2
Bracken Cl. N Bad 54 A2
Bracken Cl. Pet 41 E1
Bracken Cl. St Le 139 E2
Bracken Cres. Bish 56 C1
Bracken Glen. Poole 204 C3
Bracken La. Southa 78 A1
Bracken Pl. Chilw 79 D4
Bracken Rd. Bour 208 B4
Bracken Rd. Fern 165 D4
Bracken Rd. N Bad 54 A2
Bracken Way. Christ 195 D1
Brackendale Ct. W Moo 138 C4
Brackendale Rd. Bour 207 E4
Brackenhill Rd. Wi Mi 164 A4
Brackenhill. Poole 206 A1
Brackens The. Hyt 125 E2
Brackens The. Lo He 129 D1
Brackenway Rd. Ch Fo 55 E4
Bracklesham Cl. Southa 103 F2
Bracklesham Rd. Gos 180 B4
Bracklesham Rd. S Hay 185 F1
Brackley Ave. Fa Oa 57 D2
Brackley Way. Tot 100 B4
Bradbourne Rd. Bour 206 C2
Bradford Rd. Bour 191 E2
Bradford Rd. Ports 182 B2
Brading Ave. Gos 155 E1
Brading Ave. Ports 183 D1
Brading Cl. Southa 79 E3
Bradley Grn. Southa 78 A2
Bradley Peak. Winch 1 B1
Bradley Rd. Winch 1 B2
Bradly Rd. Fare 130 B1
Bradpole Rd. Bour 191 F1
Bradshaw Cl. Fa Oa 57 F1
Bradstock Cl. Poole 205 F4
Braehead. Hyt 125 F1
Braemar Ave. Bour 209 D2
Braemar Ave. Cos 158 A4
Braemar Cl. Bour 209 D2
Braemar Cl. Fare 130 C2
Braemar Cl. Gos 155 E1
Braemar Dr. Christ 194 C1
Braemar Rd. Gos 155 E1
Braemore Cl. New M 195 F2
Braeside Cl. Southa 103 F3
Braeside Cl. Winch 10 A2
Braeside Cres. Southa 103 F3
Braeside Rd. Southa 103 F3
Braeside Rd. St Le 139 F2
Braeside Rd. W Moo 138 C2
Braidley Rd. Bour 206 C2
Brailswood Rd. Poole 204 C2
Braintree Rd. Cos 133 E1
Braishfield Cl. Southa 77 F1
Braishfield Gdns. Bour 191 E1
Braishfield Rd. Abb 28 B2
Braishfield Rd. Brai 7 E1
Braishfield Rd. Brai 28 B2
Braishfield Rd. Hav 136 A2
Braishfield Rd. Rom 28 B2
Bramber Rd. Gosp 181 D4
Bramble Cl. Alderh 93 D3
Bramble Cl. Hav 136 B2
Bramble Cl. Holb 150 B2
Bramble Cl. Stubb 154 A1
Bramble Dr. Rom 28 B1
Bramble La. Christ 195 D1
Bramble La. Clanf 88 A4
Bramble La. Lo He 128 C3
Bramble Mews. Southa 104 A4
Bramble Rd. Pet 41 E2
Bramble Rd. Ports 182 C2
Bramble Way. Bran 169 D1
Bramble Way. Gos 155 D1
Brambles Cl. Co Com 57 D4
Brambling Cl. Southa 78 A3
Brambling Rd. Ro Ca 113 D1
Bramblings The. Tot 100 B4
Brambridge Rd. Co Com 31 F1
Brambridge Rd. Twyf 31 F1
Brambridge. Co Com 56 C4
Bramdean Dr. Hav 135 F3
Bramdean Rd. Southa 104 B4
Bramham Moor. Stubb 154 A1
Bramley Cl. Lym 198 C1
Bramley Cl. Wat 134 C4
Bramley Comm Rd. New M 196 A4
Bramley Cres. Southa 104 A1
Bramley Gdns. Gos 181 D1
Bramley Rd. Bour 190 B3
Bramley Rd. Fern 165 E3
Brampton La. Ports 158 B2
Brampton Rd. Poole 204 B3
Bramshaw Cl. Winch 1 B2
Bramshaw Gdns. Bour 191 E2
Bramshott Rd. Ports 182 C2
Bramshott Rd. Southa 126 C4
Bramston Rd. Southa 102 B4
Bramwell Ct. Southa 104 A3
Branches La. Sh En 25 F2
Branders Cl. Bour 209 D2
Branders La. Bour 209 D3
Brandon Rd. Ports 182 B1
Branksea Ave. Hamw 203 F1
Branksea Cl. Hamw 203 F1
Branksome Ave. Southa 78 B1
Branksome Cl. New M 196 A1
Branksome Cl. Winch 10 A3
Branksome Dene Rd. Bour 206 A1
Branksome Hill Rd. Bour 206 A3
Branksome Towers. Poole 211 D4
Branksome Wood Gns. Bour 206 B2
Branksome Wood Rd. Bour 206 B2
Branksome Wood Rd. Poole 206 B2
Bransbury Cl. Southa 78 B2
Bransbury Rd. Ports 183 D2
Bransgore Ave. Hav 135 E2
Bransgore Gdns. Bran 169 E1
Bransley Cl. Rom 28 A1
Branwell Cl. Christ 193 D1
Branwood Cl. Hord 197 F1
Brasenose Cl. Lo He 129 E1
Brasher Cl. Fa Oa 57 D1
Brassey Cl. Bour 191 D1
Brassey Rd. Bour 191 D1
Brassey Rd. Winch 1 C1
Braunston Cl. Cos 133 D1
Brazil Rd. Southa 103 D1
Breach Ave. Southb 137 F1
Breach La. Rin 141 F4
Breamore Cl. Eastl 56 A3
Breamore Rd. Southa 104 B4
Brean Cl. Southa 77 F1
Brecon Ave. Cos 158 A4
Brecon Cl. Bour 190 C3
Brecon Cl. Ch Fo 55 D2
Brecon Cl. Fare 154 C4
Brecon Cl. New M 196 B1
Brecon Rd. Southa 104 B3
Bredenbury Cres. Cos 133 E1
Bredon Wlk. Fare 154 C4
Bremble Cl. Poole 189 E1
Brenchley Cl. Portc 156 A4
Brendon Cl. Bour 191 F1
Brendon Cl. Hyt 125 E2
Brendon Green. Southa 101 F4
Brendon Rd. Fare 154 B4
Brent Ct. Ems 160 C4
Brentwood Cres. Southa 80 A1
Brewells La. Ra 21 F2
Brewer Cl. Lo He 129 D2
Brewer St. Ports 182 B3
Brewers La. Gos 155 E1
Brewers La. W Tis 17 E4
Brewster Cl. Wat 112 A2
Briar Cl. Christ 209 F3
Briar Cl. Gos 180 C2
Briar Cl. Poole 204 C3
Briar Cl. Wat 112 A3
Briar Way. Rom 28 B1
Briar Way. Wi Mi 164 A3
Briar Wood. Liss 21 D4
Briar's The. Wat 111 E1
Briardene Ct. Tot 100 C4
Briarfield Gdns. Wat 112 A3
Briarswood Rd. Upt 203 E4
Briarswood. Southa 78 A1
Briarwood Cl. Fare 155 D4
Briarwood Gdns. S Hay 184 C2
Briarwood Rd. Tot 100 B3
Brick Kiln La. W Tis 17 D4
Brick La. Bran 169 F2
Brickfield La. Ch Fo 55 E3
Brickfield La. Lym 198 C3
Brickfield Rd. Southa 79 E1
Brickmakers Rd. Co Comm 56 C4
Brickworth Rd. Whit 24 A2
Brickyard La. Broa 162 A1
Brickyard La. Fern 165 D3
Brickyard Rd. Swan 84 A2
Bridefield Cl. Wat 111 E2
Bridefield Cres. Wat 111 E2
Bridge App. Hamw 204 A1
Bridge Cl. Burs 105 D1
Bridge Meadows. Liss 20 C2
Bridge Pl. Fern 190 B4
Bridge Rd. Burs 128 B4
Bridge Rd. Ems 136 C1
Bridge Rd. Lo He 128 B4
Bridge Rd. Lym 198 C3
Bridge Rd. Rom 53 D4
Bridge Rd. Southa 103 E2
Bridge Rd. Swanw 128 B4
Bridge St. Christ 209 E3
Bridge St. Fordi 69 F1
Bridge St. Lo He 154 A4
Bridge St. Southw 132 C3
Bridge St. Wickh 108 A2
Bridge St. Winch 11 D4
Bridgefoot Dr. Fare 131 E1
Bridgefoot Hill. Fare 131 E1
Bridgefoot Path. Ems 160 C4
Bridgemary Ave. Gos 155 E2
Bridgemary Gr. Gos 155 E3
Bridgemary Rd. Gos 155 E2
Bridgemary Way. Gos 155 E3
Bridgers Cl. Rown 77 F3
Bridges Ave. Portc 132 C1
Bridges Cl. Eastl 55 F2
Bridges The. Rin 140 C4
Bridgeside Cl. Ports 182 B3
Bridget Cl. Horn 112 B4
Bridgewater Rd. Poole 205 E3
Bridgwater Ct. Southa 102 B3
Bridle Cres. Bour 208 B4
Bridle Way. Wi Mi 164 B3
Bridlington Ave. Southa 102 B4
Bridport Rd. Poole 205 F4
Bridport Rd. Ver 114 C3
Bridport St. Ports 182 B3
Brierley Ave. Fern 165 F1
Brierley Cl. Bour 190 C3
Brierley Rd. Bour 190 C2
Brigantine Rd. Lo He 128 C1
Bright Rd. Poole 204 C3
Brightlands Ave. Bour 208 C3
Brighton Ave. Gos 180 C4
Brighton Rd. Southa 102 C4
Brighton Rd. Sway 172 A1
Brights La. S Hay 184 C3
Brightside Rd. Southa 77 F1
Brightside. Wat 134 B3
Brightstone Cl. Southa 79 E3
Brightstone Rd. Cos 157 F4
Brindle Cl. Southa 79 D3
Brinsons Cl. Burt 193 E2
Brinton La. Hyt 126 A3
Brinton's Rd. Southa 103 D3
Brinton's Terr. Southa 103 D3
Brisbane Rd. Christ 192 C1
Bristol Rd. Ports 182 C1
Britain St. Ports 182 A3
Britannia Rd N. Ports 182 B2
Britannia Rd. Poole 205 D2
Britannia Rd. Ports 182 B2
Britannia Rd. Southa 103 D3
Britannia Way. Christ 210 A4
Briton St. Southa 103 D2
Britten Rd. L on S 179 F3
Britten Way. Wat 134 C2
Brixey Cl. Poole 205 E4
Brixey Rd. Poole 205 E4
Brixworth Cl. Cos 133 D1
Broad Ave W. Bour 191 E1
Broad Ave. Bour 207 E4
Broad Chalke Down. Winch 10 B2
Broad Croft. Ro Ca 113 E2
Broad Gdns. Cos 158 C4
Broad Green. Southa 103 D2
Broad La. Den 110 A3
Broad La. Lym 198 C1
Broad La. N Bad 53 F3
Broad La. Southa 102 C2
Broad La. Swan 84 A3
Broad Mead Rd. W Moo 114 C1
Broad Oak. Botl 105 F4
Broad St. Ports 181 F2
Broad View La. Winch 10 A2
Broad Way. Frox G 39 F4
Broad Way. Hamble 127 F3
Broad Woods La. W Wel 51 D3
Broadcut. Fare 131 E1
Broadfields Cl. M on S 213 E3
Broadhill La. Fordi 94 B4
Broadhurst Ave. Bour 190 C2
Broadlands Ave. Bour 208 C2
Broadlands Ave. Eastl 56 A3
Broadlands Ave. Wat 134 C4
Broadlands Cl. Bour 191 E2
Broadlands Cl. Christ 195 D1
Broadlands Rd. Brock 145 F1
Broadlands Rd. Southa 79 D2
Broadlaw Wlk. Fare 154 C4
Broadley Cl. Holb 150 B2
Broadly Cl. Lym 198 A1
Broadmayne Rd. Poole 206 A4
Broadmead Cl. Lym 198 C2
Broadmead Rd. Nur 77 E3
Broadmeadow Cl. Tot 100 C4
Broadmeadows La. Wat 135 D4
Broadmere Ave. Hav 135 F3
Broadmoor Rd. Broa 187 E4
Broadoak Cl. Holb 150 B2
Broads The. Pamp 163 D3
Broadsands Dr. Gos 180 B2
Broadsands Wlk. Gos 180 C2
Broadshard La. Rin 141 D4
Broadwater Ave. Poole 205 E1
Broadwater Rd. Rom 52 C3
Broadwater Rd. Southa 79 F2
Broadway Gdns. Wi Mi 163 E2
Broadway La. Bour 191 E2
Broadway La. Horn 111 E4
Broadway The. Bour 190 B3
Broadway The. Southa 79 D1
Broadway The. Winch 11 D4
Broadway. Bour 209 D2
Brockenhurst Ave. Hav 135 E3
Brockenhurst Rd. Bour 191 D1
Brockhampton La. Hav 135 F1
Brockhampton Rd. Hav 135 E1
Brockhills La. New M 196 B3
Brockhurst Rd. Gos 180 C4
Brockishill Rd. Cadn 99 D3
Brocklands. Hav 135 E1
Brockley Rd. Bour 190 C2
Brockmeadow. Fare 130 C1
Brockwood Bottom. Bramd 36 C4
Brodrick Ave. Gos 181 D2
Brog St. Brea 162 B1
Brokenford Ave. Tot 100 C4
Brokenford La. Tot 100 C4
Bromley Rd. Southa 79 F1
Brompton Rd. Ports 182 C2
Bromyard Cres. Cos 133 E1
Bronte Ave. Christ 193 D1
Bronte Cl. Tot 100 B3
Bronte Way. Southa 103 F3
Brook Ave N. New M 196 A2
Brook Ave. Lo He 128 B2
Brook Ave. New M 196 A2
Brook Cl. Bour 190 B2
Brook Cl. Lo He 128 C2
Brook Cl. N Bad 54 A2
Brook Cnr. Bro 74 A1
Brook Dr. Ver 115 D2
Brook Gdns. Ems 160 B4
Brook La. Botl 105 F3
Brook La. Bran 194 A4
Brook La. Broa 187 E3
Brook La. Hambl 86 B3
Brook La. Lo He 128 B2
Brook La. Woodg 70 C4
Brook Rd. Bour 190 B2
Brook Rd. Fa Oa 57 E1
Brook Rd. Lym 198 C1
Brook Rd. Poole 205 E3
Brook Rd. Southa 104 A4
Brook Rd. Wi Mi 163 F2
Brook St. Bi Wa 83 E4
Brook Terr. Fordi 93 F4
Brook Valley. Southa 78 A1
Brook Way. Christ 210 B4
Brook Way. Rom 28 A1
Brook Wlk. Tot 76 B1
Brookdale Cl. Wat 134 C4
Brooke Cl. Ki Wo 2 A4
Brookers La. Gos 155 D2
Brookfield Cl. Hav 135 F1
Brookfield Gdns. Lo He 128 C2
Brookfield Rd. Fa Oa 57 E1
Brookfield Rd. Ports 182 C3
Brookfields. W Wel 50 B2
Brooklands Cl. Lym 198 B2
Brooklands Rd. Bi Wa 83 E4
Brooklands Rd. Hav 135 D1
Brookley Rd. Brock 146 A1
Brooklyn Cl. Ott 31 E2
Brooklyn Ct. New M 195 F2
Brooklyn Dr. Wat 134 C4
Brooklynn Cl. Shed 83 F1
Brookmead Way. Hav 159 F4
Brooks Cl. Rin 141 D3
Brookside Ave. Southa 101 F4
Brookside Cl. Bran 169 D1
Brookside Cl. Den 110 C2
Brookside Rd. Bran 194 A4
Brookside Rd. Brock 145 F1
Brookside Rd. Hav 135 E1
Brookside Rd. Hav 159 F4
Brookside Rd. Wi Mi 163 F2
Brookside Way. Christ 194 C1
Brookside Way. Southa 79 F2
Brookside Way. W End 80 C2
Brookside. Gos 155 D3
Brookside. Ibs 55 B1
Brookside. Lan 49 E2
Brookside. Tot 100 C3
Brookvale Rd. Southa 79 D1
Brookwood Ave. Eastl 55 F2
Brookwood Rd. Southa 101 E4
Broom Cl. Ports 183 E2
Broom Cl. Wat 135 D3
Broom Hill Way. Eastl 56 A4
Broom Hill. E Bol 200 A4
Broom Rd. Pet 41 E1
Broom Rd. Poole 189 E1
Broom Sq. Ports 183 E2
Broom Way. L on S 179 F4
Broom Way. Stubb 179 F4
Broomfield Ave. Bour 190 C1
Broomfield Cres. Gos 180 A4
Broomfield Dr. Alderh 93 D3
Broomfield La. Lym 198 C2
Broomhill Cl. Lym 198 A1
Broomhill. Lan 49 E1
Brooms Gr. Southa 104 B2
Broomy Cl. Hyt 125 E2
Brougham La. Gos 181 D3
Brougham Rd. Ports 182 B2
Brougham St. Gos 181 D3
Broughton Ave. Bour 190 C2
Broughton Cl. Bour 190 C2
Broughton Cl. Southa 78 A1
Broughton Rd. Lyn 121 F3
Brow The. Wat 134 B1
Browndown Rd. Gos 180 B2
Brownen Rd. Bour 207 D4
Brownhill Cl. Ch Fo 55 E4
Brownhill Ct. Southa 77 F2
Brownhill Gdns. Ch Fo 55 E4
Brownhill Rd. Brock 170 C2
Brownhill Rd. Ch Fo 55 E4
Brownhill Rd. N Bad 54 A2
Brownhill Way. Nur 77 E2
Brownhill Way. Southa 77 E2

Browning Ave. Bour 208 A2
Browning Ave. Portc 132 C1
Browning Ave. Southa 104 B3
Browning Cl. Eastl 55 F2
Browning Cl. Tot 100 B4
Browning Dr. Winch 10 B4
Browning Rd. Poole 205 E3
Brownings Cl. Lym 198 A2
Brownlow Ave. Southa 104 A3
Brownlow Cl. Ports 182 B4
Brownlow Gdns. Southa 104 A3
Browns La. Beaul 200 B3
Browns La. Dame 68 A3
Brownsea Ave. Broa 187 E3
Brownsea Cl. New M 195 F2
Brownsea Rd. Poole 211 D2
Brownsea View Ave. Poole 205 E1
Brownsholme Cl. Eastl 56 A3
Brownwich La. Lo He 153 E3
Broxburn Cl. Ch Fo 30 C1
Broxhead Rd. Hav 136 A3
Bruce Cl. Fare 88 A2
Bruce Rd. Ports 182 C1
Brudenell Ave. Poole 211 E4
Brue Cl. N Bad 55 D4
Brune La. Stubb 155 D1
Brune Way. Fern 165 E2
Brunel Cl. Ver 115 E2
Brunel Rd. Ports 157 F2
Brunel Rd. Southa 101 E4
Brunel Rd. Tot 76 B2
Brunel Way. Lo He 129 E2
Brunell Rd. Poole 211 E3
Brunstead Pl. Poole 206 A2
Brunstead Rd. Poole 206 A2
Brunswick Cl. Fa Oa 57 D2
Brunswick Gdns. Hav 135 E1
Brunswick Pl. Lym 198 C2
Brunswick Pl. Southa 103 D3
Brunswick Rd. Fa Oa 57 D2
Brunswick Sq. Southa 103 D2
Brunswick St. Ports 182 B2
Bruyn Rd. Fordi 70 A1
Bryanston Rd. Southa 103 F3
Bryanstone Rd. Bour 206 C4
Bryant Rd. Poole 206 A4
Brympton Cl. Fordi 69 E1
Bryony Cl. Lo He 128 C1
Bryony Way. Wat 135 D4
Bryson Rd. Cos 157 E4
Bub La. Christ 209 F3
Bubbs La. W End 81 E2
Buccaneers Cl. Christ 209 F3
Buccleuch Rd. Poole 206 A1
Bucehayes Cl. Christ 211 D4
Buchanan Ave. Bour 207 F3
Buchanan Rd. Southa 77 F3
Buckingham Rd. Pet 40 B2
Buckingham Rd. Poole 205 E4
Buckingham St. Ports 182 B3
Buckingham Wlk. New M 195 F2
Buckland Cl. Eastl 56 A3
Buckland Cl. Wat 111 E1
Buckland Dene. Lym 198 B3
Buckland Gdns. Tot 76 B1
Buckland Gr. Christ 194 C1
Buckland Path. Ports 182 B4
Buckland Rd. Poole 205 E3
Buckland St. Ports 182 C4
Buckland Terr. Poole 205 E3
Bucklers Ct. Hav 135 E4
Bucklers Ct. Ports 157 E1
Bucklers Rd. Gosp 181 E4
Bucklers The. M on S 213 D3
Bucklers Way. Bour 191 E2
Buckley Ct. Southa 78 A1
Buckmore Ave. Pet 40 B2
Bucks Head Hill. Meons 61 E3
Bucksey Rd. Gos 180 B4
Buckstone Cl. Hord 197 F1
Buckthorn Cl. Broa 187 F1
Budden's La. Sob 108 C4
Buddens Rd. Wickh 108 A2
Buddle Hill. Fordi 94 B2
Budds La. Rom 27 F1
Bude Cl. Portc 132 C1
Bugle St. Southa 102 C2
Bulbarrow Wlk. Fare 154 C4
Buldowne Wlk. Sway 172 A2
Bull Drove. Winch 11 D3
Bull Hill. Bold 174 A1
Bull La. Min 98 B2
Bull La. Poole 204 B1
Bull La. Shed 83 E2
Bullar Rd. Southa 103 F4
Bullar St. Southa 103 D3
Bullfinch Cl. Broa 187 F1
Bullfinch Cl. Tot 100 B4
Bullfinch Ct. L on S 179 F4
Bullrush Cl. Hyt 125 F1
Bulls Copse La. Wat 112 A3
Bulls Drove. W Tyth 4 A3
Bunkers Hill. Den 110 B2
Bunns La. Hambl 109 F3
Bunny La. Mich 27 F3
Bunny La. Sh En 25 D2
Bunstead La. Hurs 30 B4
Bunting Gdns. Wat 111 F2
Bunting Rd. Fern 165 D4
Burbidge Gr. Ports 183 D1
Burbush Cl. Holb 150 B2
Burcombe Rd. Bour 190 B3
Burcote Dr. Ports 158 A2
Burdale Dr. S Hay 185 E2
Bure Cl. Christ 210 A3
Bure Haven Dr. Christ 210 A3
Bure Homage Gdns. Christ 210 A3
Bure Homage La. Christ 210 A3
Bure La. Christ 210 A3
Bure Park. Christ 210 A3
Bure Rd. Christ 210 A3
Burford Cl. Christ 192 B1
Burford La. Brock 146 A1
Burgate Cl. Hav 135 E2
Burgate Fields. Fordi 70 A2
Burgess Cl. S Hay 185 E1
Burgess Gdns. Southa 78 C2
Burgess Rd. Southa 79 D2
Burghclere Rd. Hav 136 A3
Burghclere Rd. Southa 126 C4
Burgoyne Rd. Ports 182 B1
Burgoyne Rd. Southa 104 C2
Burgundy Cl. Lo He 128 C1
Burion Cl. St Le 139 F3
Buriton Cl. Portc 132 B1
Buriton Rd. Winch 1 B2
Buriton St. Ports 182 B3
Burke Dr. Southa 104 B3
Burleigh Rd. Bour 208 B3
Burleigh Rd. Ports 182 C4
Burley Cl. Ch Fo 55 D2
Burley Cl. Hav 136 A3
Burley Cl. Ver 114 C3
Burley Down. Ch Fo 55 D2
Burley Lawn. Bur 143 D2
Burley Rd. Bran 194 A4
Burley Rd. Brock 172 C4
Burley Rd. Burt 193 E3
Burley Rd. Poole 205 E3
Burley Rd. Winch 1 B2
Burlington Rd. Ports 157 F1
Burlington Rd. Southa 102 C3
Burn Cl. Ver 115 D2
Burnaby Rd. Bour 206 B1
Burnaby Rd. Ports 182 A2
Burnbake Rd. Ver 115 D3
Burnbank Gdns. Tot 100 C4
Burnbrae Rd. Fern 165 E1
Burnett Ave. Christ 208 C4
Burnett Cl. Southa 79 F1
Burnett Cl. Winch 1 B1
Burnett Rd. Christ 208 C4
Burnett Rd. Gos 180 C3
Burnetts Flds. Fa Oa 81 E4
Burnetts Gdns. Fa Oa 81 E4
Burnetts La. Fa Oa 81 E3
Burnetts La. W End 81 E3
Burney Rd. Gos 180 C2
Burngate Rd. Hamw 203 F1
Burnham Beeches. N Bad 55 D3
Burnham Chase. Southa 104 B4
Burnham Dr. Bour 207 E4
Burnham Rd. Burt 193 E1
Burnham Rd. Cos 134 B1
Burnham Rd. Fordi 69 F2
Burnham Wood. Fare 88 A2
Burns Cl. Eastl 55 F1
Burns Rd. Bour 208 B4
Burns Rd. Eastl 55 F1
Burns Rd. Southa 104 B3
Burnside. Christ 210 B4
Burnside. Gos 155 D3
Burnside. Wat 112 A1
Burnt House La. Bold 174 A1
Burnt House La. Bran 169 D1
Burnt House La. Stubb 154 B2
Burr Cl. Co Com 56 C4
Burrard Gr. Lym 198 C1
Burrfields Rd. Ports 158 A1
Burridge Rd. Swanw 106 A1
Burrill Ave. Cos 158 A4
Burrows La. Ver 114 C4
Bursledon Hts. Burs 105 D1
Bursledon Pl. Wat 134 B3
Bursledon Rd. He En 105 D3
Bursledon Rd. Southa 104 B3
Bursledon Rd. Wat 134 B3
Burt's La. Holt 138 A4
Burt's La. Ver 138 A4
Burtley Rd. Bour 208 C2
Burton Cl. Burt 193 E1
Burton Hall Pl. Burt 193 E2
Burton Rd. Christ 209 F4
Burton Rd. Poole 206 A2
Burton Rd. Southa 102 C3
Burtoncroft. Burt 193 E2
Burts Hill. Wi Mi 163 E3
Burwood Gr. S Hay 185 D2
Bury Cl. Gos 181 D2
Bury Cres. Gos 181 D2
Bury Hall La. Gos 180 C2
Bury La. Tot 101 D3
Bury Rd. Gos 181 D2
Bury Rd. March 101 F2
Bury Rd. Poole 205 F1
Bush St E. Ports 182 B2
Bush St W. Ports 182 B2
Bushell Rd. Poole 204 B4
Bushey Rd. Bour 191 E1
Bushmead Dr. St Le 139 F3
Bushy Mead. Wat 134 B2
Busket La. Winch 11 D4
Busketts Way. Ashu 100 A1
Butcher St. Ports 182 A3
Bute Dr. Christ 211 D4
Butlers Cl. Locke 4 C1
Butlers La. Rin 117 E1
Butser Wlk. Fare 154 C4
Butser Wlk. Pet 41 D2
Butt's Cl. Southa 104 B2
Butt's Cres. Southa 104 B2
Butt's Rd. Southa 104 B2
Butt's Sq. Southa 104 B2
Buttercup Way. Lo He 128 C2
Butterfield Rd. Southa 78 C2
Buttermere Cl. Southa 77 F1
Button's La. Poole 204 B1
Button's La. W Wel 50 C2
Butts Ash Gdns. Hyt 126 A1
Butts Ash La. Hyt 149 F4
Butts Bridge Hill. Hyt 126 A1
Butts The. Meons 61 E3
Buttsash Ave. Hyt 150 A4
Buttsbridge Rd. Hyt 126 A1
By Pass Rd. Rom 52 C3
By The Wood. Tot 76 B1
Bye Rd. Swanw 128 B4
Byerley Cl. Westb 137 D3
Byerley Rd. Ports 182 C3
Byers The. Stubb 154 B2
Byeways. Hyt 125 F1
Byrd Cl. Wat 134 C3
Byron Ave. Winch 10 B4
Byron Cl. Bi Wa 83 F4
Byron Cl. Fare 88 A1
Byron Rd. B on S 211 F4
Byron Rd. Bour 207 F2
Byron Rd. Eastl 56 A2
Byron Rd. Ports 182 C4
Byron Rd. Southa 104 B3
Byron Rd. Wi Mi 163 E3
Cable St. Southa 103 E3
Cabot Dr. Hyt 125 E2
Cabot La. Broa 204 A4
Cabot Way. New M 195 F2
Cadhay Cl. New M 195 F2
Cadland Ct. Southa 103 E1
Cadland Rd. Faw 150 B4
Cadlands Park Estate. Faw 150 B3
Cadnam La. Cadn 74 C1
Cadnam Lawn. Hav 135 E4
Cadnam Rd. Ports 183 D2
Cadnam Way. Bour 191 E2
Cadogan Rd. Rin 141 D4
Cador Dr. Portc 156 A3
Caerleon Ave. Southa 104 B3
Caerleon Dr. Southa 104 B3
Caernarvon Gdns. Ch Fo 55 D2
Caesar's Way. Broa 187 F2
Cains Cl. Stubb 154 B2
Caird Ave. New M 196 B1
Cairns Cl. Christ 208 C4
Cairo Terr. Ports 182 B4
Caister Cl. Fern 165 E3
Caistor Cl. Southa 78 A2
Cakeham Rd. W Wit 186 C1
Calbourne. Net 127 E4
Calcott Hill. Curd 82 C2
Calder Cl. Southa 101 F4
Calder Rd. Poole 204 C4
Calderwood Dr. Southa 104 A2
Caledon Rd. Poole 205 F2
Caledonia Dr. Hyt 125 E2
Caledonian Cl. Christ 210 A4
Callow End. Curd 82 C1
Calmore Cl. Bour 191 E2
Calmore Cres. Tot 76 A1
Calmore Dr. Tot 76 B1
Calmore Gdns. Tot 100 B4
Calmore Rd. Tot 100 B4
Calpe Ave. Lyn 121 F3
Calshot Cl. Faw 178 C4
Calshot Dr. Ch Fo 55 D2
Calshot Rd. Faw 151 D1
Calshot Rd. Hav 135 E4
Calshot Way. Gos 155 D1
Calvin Rd. Bour 206 C4
Camber Pl. Ports 182 A2
Cambria Dr. Hyt 125 E2
Cambrian Cl. Burs 105 D1
Cambrian Wlk. Fare 154 C4
Cambridge Dr. Ch Fo 55 E2
Cambridge Gdns. Christ 192 C1
Cambridge Green. Ch Fo 55 E1
Cambridge Green. Lo He 129 E1
Cambridge Rd. Bour 206 B2
Cambridge Rd. Gos 180 C3
Cambridge Rd. L on S 179 F3
Cambridge Rd. Ports 182 A2
Cambridge Rd. Southa 103 D4
Camcross Cl. Cos 133 D1
Camden Cl. Bour 191 D1
Camden St. Gos 181 D3
Camel Green Rd. Alderh 93 D3
Camelia Gdns. Southa 80 A1
Camelia Gr. Fa Oa 57 F1
Camellia Cl. W Moo 114 C1
Camellia Gdns. New M 196 A1
Camelot Cres. Portc 132 A1
Cameron Cl. Gos 155 E2
Cameron Rd. Christ 209 E4
Camley Cl. Southa 103 F1
Cammel Rd. Fern 165 E1
Camp Rd. Gos 155 E2
Campbell Cres. Wat 134 B3
Campbell Rd. Bour 207 E3
Campbell Rd. Burt 193 E2
Campbell Rd. Eastl 56 A1
Campbell Rd. Ports 182 C2
Campbell St. Southa 103 E3
Campbell Way. Fa Oa 57 E1
Campion Cl. Fa Oa 81 E3
Campion Cl. Lo He 128 C1
Campion Cl. Wat 135 D3
Campion Dr. Christ 209 F3
Campion Rd. Southa 104 B3
Campion Way. Ki Wo 2 B4
Campion Way. Lym 198 C3
Cams Bay Cl. Portc 131 F1
Cams Hill. Hambl 86 A1
Canada Rd. Southa 103 F1
Canada Rd. W Wel 50 B1
Canal Cl. Rom 28 A1
Canal Wlk. Ports 182 B3
Canal Wlk. Southa 103 D2
Canberra Rd. Christ 192 C1
Canberra Rd. Nur 77 D2
Canberra Rd. Th Is 161 D2
Cande Cl. Lo He 128 C1
Candover Ct. Southa 127 D4
Candy La. Southa 104 C3
Candys Cl. Broa 162 C1
Candys La. Broa 162 C1
Canford Ave. Bour 190 A1
Canford Bottom. Wi Mi 164 B3
Canford Cl. Shed 107 F4
Canford Cl. Southa 77 E1
Canford Cliffs Ave. Poole 205 F1
Canford Cres. Poole 211 F4
Canford Heath Rd. Broa 188 C1
Canford Heath Rd. Poole 188 C1
Canford Magna. Oakl 164 A1
Canford Rd. Bour 190 A1
Canford Rd. Poole 204 B2
Canford View Dr. Wi Mi 164 A3
Canhouse La. Ra 21 F2
Cannock Wlk. Fare 154 C4
Cannon Cl. Broa 188 A1
Cannon Ct. Fa Oa 57 E1
Cannon Hill Gdns. Wi Mi 164 A4
Cannon Hill Rd. Wi Mi 164 A4
Cannon St. Lym 198 C2
Cannon St. Southa 102 B4
Cannon's Barn Cl. Portc 132 B1
Canon St. Winch 10 C4
Canterbury Ave. Southa 104 B2
Canterbury Cl. L on S 180 A2
Canterbury Cl. W Moo 138 C1
Canterbury Dr. Hyt 125 E2
Canterbury Rd. Ports 182 C2
Canterbury Rd. Stubb 154 B2
Canterton La. Bro 98 A4
Canton St. Southa 102 C3
Canute Dr. Bran 169 D1
Canute Rd. Southa 103 D2
Canute Rd. Winch 11 D3
Capel Ley. Wat 134 C2
Capella Gdns. Hyt 125 E2
Capesthorne. Christ 210 A3
Capon Cl. Southa 79 F2
Capstone Pl. Bour 207 E3
Capstone Rd. Bour 207 D3
Captain's Pl. Southa 103 D2
Captain's Row. Lym 198 C2
Captains Row. Ports 182 A2
Carberry Dr. Portc 156 B4
Carbery Ave. Bour 208 B3
Carbery Ct. Hav 135 E4
Carbery Gdns. Bour 208 C3
Carbery La. Bour 208 B2
Carbis Cl. Ports 157 D4
Cardew Rd. Liss 21 D2
Cardiff Rd. Ports 157 E1
Cardigan Rd. Bour 206 C4
Cardinal Dr. Wat 112 A1
Cardinal Way. Lo He 129 D1
Carey Rd. Bour 190 C2
Carey Rd. Southa 104 B3
Careys Cotts. Brock 145 F1
Careys Rd. Bour 191 E2
Carisbrook Cres. Hamw 203 E2
Carisbrooke Ave. Stubb 154 A1
Carisbrooke Cres. Ch Fo 55 F3
Carisbrooke Ct. New M 195 F2
Carisbrooke Ct. Rom 28 A1
Carisbrooke Dr. Southa 103 F3
Carisbrooke Rd. Gos 155 D1
Carisbrooke Rd. Ports 183 D2
Carisbrooke Way. Christ 194 C1
Carisbrooke. Net 127 E4
Carless Cl. Gos 180 B4
Carlisle Rd. Ports 182 B3
Carlisle Rd. Southa 102 A4
Carlton Ave. B on S 211 F4
Carlton Cres. Southa 102 C3
Carlton Gr. Poole 205 E3
Carlton Pl. Southa 102 C3
Carlton Rd. Bour 207 E2
Carlton Rd. Gos 181 E3
Carlton Rd. Portc 132 C1
Carlton Rd. Southa 102 C4
Carlton Way. Gos 181 E3
Carlyle Rd. Bour 208 B3
Carlyle Rd. Gos 181 D3
Carlyn Dr. Ch Fo 55 E4
Carmans La. Comp 31 E4
Carmarthen Ave. Cos 158 A4
Carnarvon Rd. Bour 207 F2
Carnarvon Rd. Gos 181 D2
Carnarvon Rd. Ports 182 C4
Carnation Rd. Southa 79 E2
Carne Cl. Ch Fo 55 E4
Carne Pl. Ports 157 D4
Caroline Ave. Christ 209 F3
Caroline Gdns. Fare 130 B1
Caroline Rd. Bour 190 A2
Carolyn Cl. Southa 103 F1
Carpenter Cl. Hyt 126 A2
Carpenter Cl. Lym 198 B3
Carran Wlk. Fare 154 C4
Carrbridge Cl. Bour 206 B4
Carrbridge Rd. Bour 206 B4
Carrington Cl. M on S 213 F3
Carrington La. M on S 213 F2
Carrol Cl. Fa Oa 57 E1
Carroll Ave. Fern 165 F3
Carroll Cl. Poole 206 A3
Carronade Wlk. Ports 157 F3
Carshalton Ave. Cos 158 A4
Carsworth Way. Poole 189 D1
Carter's Clay Rd. Locke 26 A3
Carters Ave. Hamw 203 E2
Carters Cl. Woodg 47 E2
Carters La. Poole 204 B1
Carthage Cl. Ch Fo 55 F4
Cartref Cl. Ver 114 C3
Cartwright Cl. Bour 190 B2
Carvers La. Rin 141 D4
Carysfort Rd. Bour 207 E2
Cask St. Ports 182 B3
Caslake Cl. B on S 195 F1
Caspar John Cl. Stubb 154 A1
Cassel Ave. Bour 206 A1
Castle Ave. Christ 210 C4
Castle Ave. Hav 136 A1
Castle Ave. Ports 182 B1
Castle Ave. Winch 10 C4
Castle Cl. M on S 213 F2
Castle Cl. Ports 182 B2
Castle Farm La. Wickh 108 A1
Castle Gdn. Pet 40 C2
Castle Gr. Portc 156 B4
Castle Hill La. Bur 142 C2
Castle Hill. Poole 205 D2
Castle Hill. Winch 10 C4
Castle La E. Bour 208 B4
Castle La W. Bour 191 E1
Castle La. Ch Fo 55 D2
Castle La. Faw 178 C4
Castle La. N Bad 54 B2
Castle La. Southa 102 C2
Castle Meadow. Down 46 C4
Castle Rd. Bour 191 D1
Castle Rd. Net 127 D3
Castle Rd. Ports 182 B2
Castle Rd. Ro Ca 113 D1
Castle Rd. Southa 79 F1
Castle Rd. Southw 132 C3
Castle Sq. Southa 102 C2
Castle St. Christ 209 E3
Castle St. Lo He 154 A4
Castle St. Poole 204 B1
Castle St. Portc 156 B4
Castle St. Southa 103 D4
Castle Trading Est. Portc 156 C4
Castle View Rd. Portc 156 C3
Castle Way. Hav 136 A1
Castle Way. Southa 102 C2
Castledene Cres. Poole 205 D1
Castlemain Rd. Bour 208 B3
Castleman Way. Rin 141 D3
Castlemans La. N Hay 160 A1
Castleshaw Cl. Southa 101 F4
Castleton Ave. Bour 190 B3
Catalina Cl. Christ 210 A3
Catalina Dr. Poole 204 C1
Catamaran Cl. Lo He 128 C1
Cateran Cl. Southa 101 F4
Cathay Gdns. Hyt 125 E2
Cathedral View. Winch 11 D3
Catherine Cl. W End 80 C1
Catherine Cres. Down 46 B4
Catherine Gdns. W End 80 C1
Catherington Hill. Horn 88 A1
Catherington La. Horn 112 A4
Catherington La. Wat 112 A4
Catherington Way. Hav 135 F2
Catisfield La. Fare 130 A1
Catisfield Rd. Fare 130 B1
Catisfield Rd. Ports 183 D2
Caton Cl. Poole 206 A4
Cattistock Rd. Bour 191 F1
Causeway Cres. Tot 101 D4
Causeway Farm. Wat 112 A3

Causeway The. Pet 40 C1
Causeway The. Portc 131 F1
Causeway. Rom 52 B3
Cavalier Cl. Hyt 125 E2
Cavan Cres. Broa 188 A1
Cavanna Cl. Gos 155 D1
Cavell Dr. Cos 133 F1
Cavendish Cl. Rom 28 A1
Cavendish Cl. Wat 134 C4
Cavendish Dr. Wat 134 C4
Cavendish Gr. Southa 102 C4
Cavendish Gr. Winch 2 A2
Cavendish Mews. Southa 102 C4
Cavendish Pl. Bour 207 D3
Cavendish Rd. Bour 207 D3
Cavendish Rd. Ports 182 B2
Caversham Cl. Southa 104 A2
Caversham Cl. W End 80 B1
Cawdor Rd. Bour 206 B4
Cawte Rd. Southa 102 B3
Cawte's Place. Fare 88 B1
Caxton Ave. Southa 104 A3
Caxton Cl. Christ 210 A4
Cecil Ave. Ashu 100 B1
Cecil Ave. Bour 207 E4
Cecil Ave. Southa 78 A1
Cecil Cl. Broa 187 F3
Cecil Gr. Ports 182 A2
Cecil Hill. Bour 207 D4
Cecil Pl. Ports 182 A2
Cecil Rd. Bour 207 F2
Cecil Rd. Poole 205 E3
Cecil Rd. Southa 103 F2
Cedar Ave. Bour 190 B3
Cedar Ave. Christ 208 B4
Cedar Ave. Southa 102 B4
Cedar Ave. St Le 139 F2
Cedar Cl. Gos 156 A1
Cedar Cl. He En 105 E4
Cedar Cl. Ki Wo 2 A4
Cedar Cl. Upt 203 D4
Cedar Cl. Wat 134 C3
Cedar Cres. N Bad 53 F3
Cedar Cres. Wat 112 B3
Cedar Dr. Hord 213 E4
Cedar Dr. Wi Mi 164 A3
Cedar Gdns. Southa 103 D4
Cedar Gr. Ports 183 D4
Cedar Lawn. Rom 28 B1
Cedar Pl. Bran 169 D1
Cedar Rd. Eastl 55 F1
Cedar Rd. Hyt 150 A4
Cedar Rd. Southa 103 D4
Cedar Way. Fare 154 C4
Cedar Way. Fern 165 E4
Cedar Wood Cl. Fa Oa 57 F1
Cedar Wood Cl. Tot 100 B4
Cedarmount. Lyn 121 F2
Cedric Cl. Black 177 F4
Cedric Mews. Hamble 128 A2
Celandine Ave. Lo He 128 C1
Celandine Cl. Christ 210 A4
Celia Cl. Wat 135 D4
Cellars Farm Rd. Bour 209 D2
Cement Terr. Southa 102 C2
Cemetery Ave. Poole 204 C3
Cemetery La. Den 110 C3
Cemetery La. Westb 137 E2
Cemetery Rd. Southa 102 C4
Cemetery Rd. Wi Mi 163 D3
Centaur St. Ports 182 B4
Central Ave. Broa 187 E4
Central Ave. Poole 205 F3
Central Bridge. Southa 103 D2
Central Drive. Bour 206 C3
Central Rd. Cos 158 B4
Central Rd. Portc 156 A4
Central Rd. Southa 103 D1
Central St. Ports 182 B3
Central Sta Bridge. Southa 102 C3
Centre La. Hord 197 F1
Centre Way. Lo He 129 D2
Cerne Cl. Bour 191 D2
Cerne Cl. N Bad 53 F2
Cerne Cl. W End 80 A1
Chadderton Gdns. Ports 182 A2
Chaddesley Glen. Poole 211 F3
Chaddesley Wood Rd. Poole 211 F3
Chadwell Ave. Southa 104 A2
Chadwick Rd. Eastl 55 F1
Chafen Rd. Southa 103 E4
Chaffey Cl. Rin 141 E4
Chaffinch Cl. Broa 187 F1
Chaffinch Cl. Tot 100 B4
Chaffinch Green. Wat 111 F2
Chaffinch Way. L on S 179 F4
Chaffinch Way. Portc 155 F4
Chalbury Cl. Poole 189 D1
Chaldon Rd. Poole 188 C1
Chale Cl. Gos 155 E1
Chalewood Rd. Black 177 F4
Chalfont Ave. Christ 192 B2
Chalfont Ct. Southa 78 A1
Chalk Cl. Red 47 E4
Chalk Hill Rd. Horn 112 B4
Chalk Hill. Sob 85 E3
Chalk Hill. W End 80 B1
Chalk La. Fare 131 D4
Chalk Ridge. Horn 88 B2
Chalkpit Rd. Cos 133 D1
Chalkridge Rd. Cos 134 A1
Challenger Way. Hyt 125 E1
Challis Ct. Southa 103 D2
Chalmers Way. Hamble 127 F2
Chaloner Cres. Hyt 126 A1
Chalton Cres. Hav 135 E2
Chalton La. Clanf 88 B3
Chalvington Rd. Ch Fo 55 E2
Chalybeate Cl. Southa 78 A1
Chamberlain Gr. Fare 155 D4
Chamberlain Rd. Southa 79 D2
Chamberlayne Rd. Burs 127 F4
Chamberlayne Rd. Eastl 56 A1
Chamberlayne Rd. Net 127 D3
Chambers Ave. Rom 53 D4
Chancel Rd. Lo He 129 D2
Chander Cl. Fern 165 F2
Chandlers Cl. Bour 208 A4
Chandlers Cl. S Hay 185 E1
Chandos Ave. Poole 206 A4
Chandos St. Southa 103 D2
Channel Way. Southa 103 E2
Channels Farm Rd. Southa 79 E3
Chantrell Wlk. Fare 130 B2
Chantry Cl. Christ 194 C1
Chantry Rd. Gosp 181 D4
Chantry Rd. Horn 112 A4
Chantry Rd. Southa 103 D2
Chantry The. Lo He 129 E2
Chapel Cl. Broa 187 E3
Chapel Cres. Southa 104 A2
Chapel Dro. Fa Oa 81 E4
Chapel Dro. He En 105 D3
Chapel La. Black 151 D1
Chapel La. Black 177 F4
Chapel La. Bran 194 A4
Chapel La. Broa 187 E3
Chapel La. Bur 143 D2
Chapel La. Curd 106 C4
Chapel La. E Bol 175 E3
Chapel La. Locke 26 A3
Chapel La. Lyn 121 F3
Chapel La. Mich 27 E4
Chapel La. Ott 31 D1
Chapel La. Poole 204 B1
Chapel La. Red 47 F3
Chapel La. Red 73 E4
Chapel La. Sway 172 B1
Chapel La. Tot 100 C3
Chapel La. Wat 134 C4
Chapel La. Wi Mi 163 D3
Chapel Rd. Lo He 128 C3
Chapel Rd. Poole 205 D2
Chapel Rd. Sob 85 D1
Chapel Rd. Southa 103 D2
Chapel Rd. Swan 84 A3
Chapel Rd. W End 80 C1
Chapel Rise. St Le 140 B1
Chapel St. E Meo 38 B1
Chapel St. Gosp 181 D4
Chapel St. Ports 182 A2
Chapel St. Ports 182 C4
Chapel St. Southa 103 D2
Chapelside. Lo He 154 A4
Chaplains Ave. Wat 111 E2
Chaplains Cl. Wat 111 E2
Charborough Rd. Broa 188 A2
Charden Rd. Bish 57 D1
Charden Rd. Gos 180 B4
Charfield Cl. Fare 154 B4
Charfield Cl. Winch 10 C3
Chark La. L on S 179 F4
Charlcot Lawn. Hav 135 E3
Charlecote Dr. Ch Fo 55 D4
Charlemont Dr. Portc 131 F1
Charles Cl. Wat 134 B3
Charles Cl. Winch 2 A1
Charles Cres. New M 196 A3
Charles Dickens St. Ports 182 B3
Charles Keightley Ct. Wi Mi 163 E2
Charles Knott Gdns. Southa 102 C4
Charles Park. Bour 190 B1
Charles Rd. Christ 209 F4
Charles Rd. Poole 204 B2
Charles St. Pet 40 C2
Charles St. Ports 182 B3
Charles St. Southa 103 D2
Charles Watts Way. He En 105 D4
Charlesbury Ave. Gos 180 C2
Charleston Cl. S Hay 184 C2
Charleston Rd. Faw 150 B4
Charlesworth Dr. Wat 111 E1
Charlesworth Gdns. Wat 111 E1
Charlotte Cl. Christ 210 A3
Charlotte Cl. Poole 206 B4
Charlotte Pl. Southa 103 D3
Charlotte St. Ports 182 B3
Charlton Cl. Bour 191 E2
Charlton Cl. Hord 196 C2
Charlton Rd. Southa 102 B4
Charminster Ave. Bour 191 D1
Charminster Cl. Bour 191 D1
Charminster Cl. Wat 134 C4
Charminster Pl. Bour 191 E1
Charminster Rd. Bour 207 D4
Charmouth Gr. Poole 205 D2
Charmouth Terr. Southa 78 A1
Charmus Rd. Tot 76 A1
Charmwen Cres. W End 80 B1
Charnock Cl. Hord 196 C2
Charnwood Ave. Bour 191 D2
Charnwood Cl. Ch Fo 30 B1
Charnwood Cl. Tot 76 B1
Charnwood Cl. W Moo 138 C1
Charnwood Cres. Ch Fo 30 B1
Charnwood Dr. Fordi 69 F2
Charnwood Gdns. Ch Fo 30 B1
Charnwood Way. Black 177 F4
Charnwood. Gos 155 F1
Charter Rd. Bour 189 E3
Chartwell Cl. Eastl 56 A3
Chartwell Cl. Lo He 129 E1
Chartwell Dr. Hav 136 B2
Chase Cl. Liss 21 D2
Chase Farm Cl. Shed 83 F2
Chase Gr. Shed 83 F2
Chase Rd. Liss 21 D2
Chase The. Gos 180 C2
Chase The. Lo He 129 E1
Chase The. St Le 140 B3
Chase The. Ver 115 E3
Chaseside. Bour 208 A4
Chasewater Ave. Ports 183 D4
Chatburn Ave. Wat 111 F2
Chatfield Rd. Gos 155 E2
Chatham Dr. Ports 182 A2
Chatham Rd. Winch 10 B3
Chatsworth Ave. Cos 158 A3
Chatsworth Cl. Fare 130 B1
Chatsworth Rd. Bour 207 E3
Chatsworth Rd. Eastl 56 A3
Chatsworth Rd. Poole 205 D3
Chatsworth Rd. Southa 104 A3
Chatsworth Way. New M 195 F2
Chaucer Ave. Portc 132 C1
Chaucer Cl. Fare 130 C1
Chaucer Cl. Wat 111 F1
Chaucer Cl. Wi Mi 163 E3
Chaucer Dr. M on S 213 E3
Chaucer Rd. Poole 211 F4
Chaucer Rd. Southa 104 B3
Chaundler Rd. Winch 2 A1
Chaveney Cl. Hyt 125 F1
Chawton Cl. Southa 104 B4
Chawton Cl. Winch 1 B2
Cheam Rd. Broa 187 F2
Cheam Way. Tot 76 B1
Cheater's La. Alderh 92 B4
Cheddar Cl. Southa 103 F2
Cheddington Rd. Bour 191 D2
Chedington Cl. Broa 188 C1
Chedworth Cres. Cos 133 D1
Chelmsford Rd. Ports 157 F1
Chelmsford Rd. Upt 203 D3
Chelsea Rd. Ports 182 B2
Cheltenham Cres. L on S 179 F4
Cheltenham Rd. Cos 157 D4
Cheltenham Rd. Poole 205 E3
Chene Rd. Wi Mi 163 E2
Cheping Gdns. Botl 106 A3
Chepstow Cl. N Bad 55 D3
Chepstow Cl. Tot 100 B4
Chepstow Court. Wat 112 A1
Chequers Cl. Lym 198 B2
Cherbourg Rd. Eastl 56 A1
Cherford Rd. Bour 190 A1
Cherita Ct. Poole 204 C3
Cheriton Ave. Bour 208 B4
Cheriton Ave. Southa 104 B4
Cheriton Cl. Hav 135 E2
Cheriton Cl. Horn 112 A4
Cheriton Cl. Winch 1 B1
Cheriton Rd. Eastl 55 F1
Cheriton Rd. Gos 180 C2
Cheriton Rd. Winch 10 C4
Cheriton Way. Wi Mi 163 E3
Cherque La. Stubb 180 A4
Cherries Dr. Bour 190 C1
Cherry Cl. Lon S 180 A3
Cherry Cl. Poole 205 D2
Cherry Drove. Fa Oa 81 E3
Cherry Gr. Fern 165 E3
Cherry Hill Gdns. Upt 203 E3
Cherry Hill Gr. Upt 203 D3
Cherry Tree Ave. Fare 154 B4
Cherry Tree Ave. Wat 112 A1
Cherry Tree Cl. Hord 213 E4
Cherry Tree Cl. St Le 139 E2
Cherry Wlk. Southa 102 B4
Cherrygarth Rd. Fare 130 B1
Cherryton Gdns. Holb 150 A2
Cherrywood Gdns. S Hay 185 D2
Cherrywood Gdns. Tot 100 B4
Chervil Cl. Horn 88 B1
Cherville St. Rom 52 C4
Cherwell Cres. Southa 101 F4
Cherwell Gdns. Ch Fo 55 E3
Cheshire Dr. Bour 192 A1
Cheshire Way. Southb 137 F1
Chesil St. Winch 11 D4
Chesildene Ave. Bour 191 E2
Chesildene Dr. Bour 191 E2
Cheslyn Rd. Ports 183 D3
Chessel Ave. Bour 207 F2
Chessel Ave. Southa 103 F3
Chessel Cres. Southa 103 F4
Chester Cres. Lon S 180 A2
Chester Pl. Ports 182 B1
Chester Rd. Poole 206 A1
Chester Rd. Southa 80 A1
Chester Rd. Winch 11 D4
Chesterfield Cl. Poole 211 F4
Chesterfield Rd. Ports 183 D4
Chesterton Gdns. Wat 111 F2
Chestnut Ave. Ashu 100 B2
Chestnut Ave. B on S 212 A4
Chestnut Ave. Bour 208 B2
Chestnut Ave. Ch Fo 55 E1
Chestnut Ave. Christ 208 B4
Chestnut Ave. Eastl 55 E1
Chestnut Ave. Hav 135 D2
Chestnut Ave. Litt 1 A2
Chestnut Ave. Ports 182 C2
Chestnut Ave. Wat 112 B3
Chestnut Cl. Ch Fo 55 E2
Chestnut Cl. Den 110 C2
Chestnut Cl. Rom 53 E3
Chestnut Gr. Fern 164 C3
Chestnut Rd. Brock 146 A1
Chestnut Rd. Southa 78 A1
Chestnut Rise. Drox 61 D1
Chestnut Rise. Eastl 55 E1
Chestnut Way. Burt 193 E2
Chestnut Way. Lo He 129 E1
Chestnut Wlk. Botl 105 F4
Chestnut Wlk. Gos 156 A1
Chetnole Cl. Poole 189 D1
Chettle Rd. Southa 104 C3
Chetwode Way. Broa 188 A1
Chetwynd Dr. Southa 78 C2
Chetwynd Rd. Ports 182 C2
Chetwynd Rd. Southa 78 C3
Cheviot Cres. Southa 101 F4
Cheviot Dr. Hyt 125 E2
Cheviot Rd. Southa 101 F4
Cheviot Way. Ver 114 C3
Cheviot Wlk. Fare 154 C4
Chewton Comm Rd. Christ 211 D4
Chewton Farm Rd. Christ 195 E1
Chewton Lodge. Christ 211 D4
Chewton Way. Christ 195 D1
Cheyne Gdns. Bour 206 B1
Cheyne Way. L on S 179 F3
Chichester Ave. S Hay 185 D2
Chichester Cl. Gos 155 D1
Chichester Cl. He En 81 E1
Chichester Cl. Lo He 128 C2
Chichester Cl. W Wel 51 D1
Chichester Rd. N Hay 160 B1
Chichester Rd. Ports 182 C4
Chichester Rd. Rin 117 E1
Chichester Rd. Southa 104 A4
Chichester Wlk. Oakl 163 F1
Chicken Hall La. Eastl 56 B1
Chickerell Cl. Bour 191 D2
Chidden Cl. E Meo 38 B1
Chidden Holt. N Bad 55 D3
Chideock Cl. Poole 205 F3
Chidham Cl. Hav 135 F1
Chidham Dr. Hav 135 F1
Chidham Rd. Cos 134 A1
Chidham Sq. Hav 135 F1
Chigwell Rd. Bour 191 D1
Chilbolton Ave. Winch 10 B4
Chilcomb Cl. L on S 179 F3
Chilcomb La. Chilc 11 F3
Chilcomb La. Winch 11 E3
Chilcomb Rd. Southa 104 B4
Chilcombe Cl. Hav 135 F2
Chilcombe Rd. Bour 208 A3
Chilcote Rd. Ports 183 D4
Childe Sq. Ports 157 E1
Chilgrove Rd. Cos 158 B4
Chilham Cl. Eastl 56 A4
Chillenden Ct. Tot 100 B3
Chillerton. Net 127 E4
Chillington Gdns. Ch Fo 30 A1
Chilsdown Way. Wat 134 C2
Chiltern Cl. B on S 195 F1
Chiltern Cl. Poole 206 A3
Chiltern Cl. Tot 100 B3
Chiltern Dr. B on S 211 F4
Chiltern Dr. Ver 114 C3
Chiltern Green. Southa 101 F4
Chiltern Wlk. Fare 154 C4
Chilworth Cl. Chilw 54 B1
Chilworth Gr. Gos 181 D3
Chilworth Rd. Chilw 54 C1
Chine Ave. Southa 103 F3
Chine Cl. Lo He 129 D2
Chine Cres Rd. Bour 206 B1
Chine Cres. Bour 206 B1
Chine The. Gos 155 F1
Chine Wlk. Fern 165 F1
Chinham Rd. Ne Ma 99 E3
Chipstead Rd. Cos 157 F4
Chisels La. Bran 194 A3
Chisholm Cl. Southa 77 F3
Chitty Rd. Ports 183 D1
Chivers Cl. Ports 182 B2
Christchurch Bay Rd. B on S 211 F4
Christchurch By Pass. Christ 209 E4
Christchurch Gdns. Wat 134 A1
Christchurch Gdns. Winch 10 C3
Christchurch Rd. B on S 211 E4
Christchurch Rd. Bour 207 E2
Christchurch Rd. Fern 165 E1
Christchurch Rd. Hord 213 E4
Christchurch Rd. Hurn 192 A3
Christchurch Rd. Rin 141 D2
Christchurch Rd. Winch 10 C3
Christopher Cres. Poole 204 B3
Christopher Way. Ems 136 C1
Church Cl. Bish 56 B2
Church Cl. Clanf 88 A3
Church Cl. Lo He 129 D2
Church Cl. N Bad 54 A2
Church End. Southa 102 B4
Church Farm Cl. Hyt 125 D3
Church Hatch. Down 47 D4
Church Hill. M on S 213 F2
Church Hill. Red 47 F3
Church Hill. Ver 114 C3
Church Hill. W End 80 B1
Church La. Awb 26 B2
Church La. Bold 173 F1
Church La. Botl 106 A3
Church La. Brai 28 B4
Church La. Bramd 15 E2
Church La. Brock 173 D4
Church La. Bur 143 D2
Church La. Burs 128 A4
Church La. Christ 209 D3
Church La. Co Com 56 C4
Church La. Dame 68 B2
Church La. Durl 81 E3
Church La. E Bol 175 E3
Church La. Faw 151 D2
Church La. Fern 190 C4
Church La. Frox G 17 E2
Church La. Hambl 86 B2
Church La. Hav 160 A4
Church La. He En 105 D3
Church La. It Ab 2 C3
Church La. Ki Wo 2 B3
Church La. Litt 1 A3
Church La. Lym 198 C2
Church La. N Hay 160 B2
Church La. New M 195 F1
Church La. Nur 76 C3
Church La. Plai 50 A3
Church La. Rom 52 C4
Church La. Rom 54 D4
Church La. Sh En 25 E2
Church La. Southa 79 D1
Church La. Southa 102 C2
Church La. Swan 84 B3
Church La. Sway 172 A1
Church La. Twyf 32 A4
Church La. W Meo 37 E3
Church Mead. Lym 198 C1
Church Path N. Ports 182 B3
Church Path. Ems 160 C4
Church Path. Fare 131 E1
Church Path. Gos 181 E2
Church Path. Horn 112 B3
Church Path. Lo He 154 A4
Church Pl. Rom 52 C4
Church Rd. Bish 56 B3
Church Rd. Bour 208 C2
Church Rd. Fern 165 E3
Church Rd. Gos 181 D1
Church Rd. Liss 20 C3
Church Rd. Lo He 129 D2
Church Rd. Miche 6 B1
Church Rd. Poole 205 D2
Church Rd. Ports 182 B3
Church Rd. Rom 52 C4
Church Rd. S Hay 185 D3
Church Rd. Shed 107 F4
Church Rd. Sob 109 E3
Church Rd. Southa 103 E1
Church Rd. Southb 161 F4
Church Rd. Steep 40 C4
Church Rd. Swan 84 A3
Church Rd. Th Is 161 E1
Church Rd. W Moo 114 C1
Church Rd. Westb 137 D2
Church St. Christ 209 D3
Church St. E Meo 38 C1
Church St. Fordi 93 F4
Church St. Lo He 154 A4
Church St. Poole 204 A1
Church St. Ports 182 B3
Church St. Rom 52 C4
Church St. Southa 78 B1
Church St. Uph 58 C3
Church View Cl. Southa 104 A2
Church View. Ports 183 D3
Church View. Shed 107 F4
Church View. Westb 137 D2
Church Wlk. Red 48 A3
Churcher Cl. Gos 180 B2
Churcher Rd. Westb 137 D2
Churcher Wlk. Gos 180 B2
Churchfield Cres. Poole 204 C2
Churchfield La. Ibs 93 F1
Churchfield Rd. Pet 41 D2
Churchfield Rd. Poole 204 C2
Churchfield. Ver 114 C3
Churchfields Rd. Twyf 58 A3
Churchfields. Faw 151 D2
Churchill Ave. Bi Wa 59 D1
Churchill Cl. Alderh 92 C3
Churchill Cl. Lo He 129 E1

Cottesway E. Stubb 154 A1
Cotton Cl. Bish 56 C2
Cotton Cl. Broa 187 F3
Cotton Dr. Ems 136 C2
Cotwell Ave. Wat 112 A2
Coulmere Rd. Gosp 181 D3
Coulsdon Rd. He En 105 E3
Coultas Rd. Ch Fo 30 C1
Countess Cl. Oakl 188 C4
Countess Gdns. Bour 207 F4
Country View. Stubb 154 A2
Country View. W Wel 50 C2
Course Park Cres. Lo He 129 E1
Court Barn Cl. L on S 179 F4
Court Barn La. L on S 179 F4
Court Cl. Christ 209 F4
Court Cl. Cos 158 A4
Court Cl. Lym 198 B1
Court Cl. Southa 104 A3
Court Cl. Tot 76 B1
Court Hill. Dame 68 C3
Court La. Cos 158 A4
Court Mead. Cos 158 A4
Court Rd. Bour 191 D1
Court Rd. Ki Wo 2 B3
Court Rd. L on S 179 F4
Court Rd. Southa 102 C4
Court Royal Mews. Southa 102 C4
Courtenay Dr. Wi Mi 163 E3
Courtenay Pl. Lym 198 C2
Courtenay Rd. Poole 205 D2
Courtenay Rd. Winch 2 A2
Courthill Rd. Poole 205 E2
Courtier Cl. Hyt 125 E2
Courtland Gdns. Southa 79 D3
Courtmount Gr. Cos 158 A4
Cousins Gr. Ports 183 D1
Cove Rd. Bour 190 B1
Covena Rd. Bour 208 C3
Coventry Cl. Broa 187 E2
Coventry Cres. Broa 188 A1
Coventry Rd. Southa 102 C3
Covert Gr. Wat 135 D3
Covert The. Rom 53 D3
Covington Rd. Westb 137 D3
Cow La. Cos 157 E4
Cow La. Portc 156 B4
Cowan Rd. Wat 134 B3
Coward Rd. Gos 181 D1
Cowdray Cl. Bish 56 C1
Cowdray Cl. Southa 78 A2
Cowdray Park. Stubb 154 A1
Cowdrey Gdns. Bour 191 F1
Cowell Dr. Bour 208 A4
Cowes La. Lo He 152 B3
Cowgrove Rd. Pamp 162 C3
Cowleas Cotts. Awb 26 C3
Cowley Cl. Southa 77 F1
Cowley Rd. Lym 198 B2
Cowley Rd. Poole 204 B4
Cowleys Rd. Burt 193 E1
Cowper Ave. New M 196 A1
Cowper Rd. Bour 190 C1
Cowper Rd. Ports 182 C4
Cowper Rd. Southa 104 B3
Cowpitts La. Rin 117 E1
Cowslip Cl. Gos 155 E1
Cowslip Rd. Broa 187 F1
Cox Ave. Bour 191 D2
Cox Cl. Bour 191 D2
Cox Dale. Lo He 129 E1
Cox Row. Ch Fo 55 E2
Cox's Dr. Southa 104 A1
Cox's La. Southa 103 E2
Coxes Meadows. Pet 40 C3
Coxford Cl. Southa 78 A1
Coxford Dro. Southa 78 A2
Coxs Hill. Twyf 32 A4
Coxstone La. Rin 141 D3
Coy Pond Rd. Poole 206 A3
Crab Orchard Way. W Moo 114 C1
Crabapple Cl. Tot 100 B4
Crabbs Way. Tot 100 A4
Crabbswood La. Sway 196 C4
Crabden La. Horn 88 C1
Crableck La. Lo He 128 B3
Crabthorne Farm La. Stubb 154 A2
Crabton Close Rd. Bour 207 F2
Crabtree Cl. Burt 193 E1
Crabtree. Southa 77 F1
Crabwood Cl. Southa 77 F1
Crabwood Ct. Hav 135 E4
Crabwood Dr. W End 80 C1
Crabwood Rd. Southa 77 F1
Cracknore Hard. March 102 A1
Cracknore Rd. Southa 102 B3
Craigmoor Ave. Bour 191 F1
Craigmoor Cl. Bour 191 F1
Craigmoor Way. Bour 191 F1
Craigside Rd. St Le 139 E2
Craigwell Rd. Wat 134 B2
Craigwood Dr. Fern 165 F2
Crampmoor La. N Bad 28 C1
Cranberry Cl. March 101 F1
Cranborne Cres. Poole 205 F4
Cranborne Gdns. Ch Fo 30 A1
Cranborne Rd. Alderh 92 A3
Cranborne Rd. Bour 206 C1
Cranborne Rd. Cos 134 A1
Cranborne Rd. Wi Mi 163 E4
Cranborne Wlk. Fare 154 C4
Cranbourne Cl. Southa 78 B1
Cranbourne Dr. Ott 31 D2
Cranbourne Park. He En 105 E2
Cranbourne Pl. New M 195 F2
Cranbourne Rd. Gos 181 E2
Cranbrook Rd. Poole 205 D3
Cranbury Ave. Southa 103 D3
Cranbury Cl. Down 46 C3
Cranbury Cl. Ott 31 D2
Cranbury Ct. Eastl 56 A1
Cranbury Gdns. Burs 104 C1
Cranbury Pl. Southa 103 D3
Cranbury Rd. Eastl 56 A1
Cranbury Rd. Southa 103 F2
Cranbury Terr. Southa 103 D3
Crane Dr. Ver 114 C4
Cranemoor Ave. Christ 194 C1
Cranemoor Cl. Christ 194 C1
Cranemoor Gdns. Christ 194 C1
Craneswater Ave. Ports 182 C1
Craneswater Gate. Ports 182 C1
Craneswater Park. Ports 182 C1
Cranfield Ave. Wi Mi 163 E3
Cranford Gdns. Ch Fo 55 D4
Cranford Rd. Pet 40 C1
Cranford Way. Southa 79 D1
Cranleigh Ave. Ports 182 C3
Cranleigh Cl. Bour 208 C3
Cranleigh Gdns. Bour 208 C3
Cranleigh Rd. Bour 208 C3
Cranleigh Rd. He En 105 E3
Cranleigh Rd. Portc 156 A4
Cranleigh Rd. Ports 182 C3
Cranmer Rd. Bour 206 C4
Cranmore. Net 127 E4
Crantock Gr. Bour 191 F1
Cranwell Cl. Bour 189 F2
Cranwell Cl. Bran 169 D1
Cranworth Rd. Winch 1 C1
Crasswell St. Ports 182 B3
Craven Ct. Fare 130 C2
Craven Rd. Ch Fo 55 E3
Craven St. Southa 103 D3
Craven Wlk. Southa 103 D3
Crawford Cl. Nur 77 E3
Crawford Dr. Fare 130 C2
Crawley Ave. Hav 136 A3
Crawley Hill. W Wel 50 C1
Crawshaw Rd. Poole 205 D1
Crawte Ave. Holb 150 B1
Creasey Rd. Bour 190 D3
Credenhill Rd. Cos 133 E1
Creedy Gdns. W End 80 A2
Creek End. Ems 160 C4
Creek Rd. S Hay 185 E1
Creekmoor La. Broa 204 A4
Creighton Rd. Southa 101 F3
Cremyll Cl. Stubb 154 B1
Crescent Cl. Winch 10 A2
Crescent Dr. B on S 211 F4
Crescent Rd. Fare 88 A1
Crescent Rd. Gos 181 D1
Crescent Rd. Lo He 128 C1
Crescent Rd. N Bad 53 F3
Crescent Rd. Poole 205 F2
Crescent Rd. Ver 115 D3
Crescent Rd. Wi Mi 163 E2
Crescent The. B on S 211 E4
Crescent The. Bour 207 F2
Crescent The. Eastl 56 A2
Crescent The. March 101 F1
Crescent The. Ne Ma 99 F2
Crescent The. Net 127 E3
Crescent The. Rom 53 D4
Crescent The. Southa 104 A1
Crescent The. Southb 161 E4
Crescent The. Twyf 58 A3
Crescent The. Wat 134 B2
Crescent Wlk. Fern 165 F1
Cressey Rd. Rom 52 C4
Cressy Rd. Ports 182 B4
Crest Cl. Portc 131 E1
Crest Rd. Poole 205 E3
Crest The. Wat 134 B1
Crest Way. Southa 104 B2
Cresta Gdns. Fern 165 F1
Crestland Cl. Wat 112 A2
Crete Cotts. Hyt 125 F1
Crete La. Hyt 125 F1
Crete Rd. Hyt 125 F1
Cribb Cl. Poole 204 C4
Crichel Mount Rd. Poole 211 E4
Crichel Rd. Bour 207 D4
Cricket Cl. Christ 209 F3
Cricket Dr. Wat 112 A3
Cricklemead. Bi Wa 83 E4
Crigdon Cl. Southa 101 F4
Crimea Rd. Bour 206 C4
Cringle Ave. Bour 209 D2
Cripple Gate La. Beaul 175 E3
Cripple Gate La. E Bol 175 E3
Cripstead La. Winch 10 C3
Crispen Cl. Christ 210 C4
Crispin Cl. Lo He 129 D2
Crisspyn Cl. Horn 112 A3
Crittall Cl. Sway 172 B1
Crockford Cl. New M 196 A3
Crockford Rd. Westb 137 D2
Croft Cl. Broa 187 E4
Croft Hts. Whit 24 A2
Croft La. N Hay 159 F1
Croft Rd. Bour 190 C1
Croft Rd. Bran 194 A3
Croft Rd. Christ 209 F4
Croft Rd. Poole 205 D3
Croft Rd. Ports 157 E1
Croft Rd. Rin 117 E1
Croft The. Ch Fo 55 E2
Croft The. Crouch 22 B4
Croft The. Stubb 154 B2
Croft The. Tot 76 B1
Croftlands Ave. Stubb 154 B2
Crofton Ave. Stubb 179 E4
Crofton Cl. Christ 192 C1
Crofton Cl. Wat 134 B3
Crofton La. Stubb 154 A1
Crofton Rd. Ports 157 F1
Crofton Rd. Ports 183 D3
Crofton Way. Lo He 128 B1
Crofton Way. Swan 84 A3
Cromarty Ave. Ports 183 D2
Cromarty Cl. Stubb 154 A2
Cromarty Rd. Southa 77 F3
Crombie Cl. Wat 111 F2
Cromer Rd. Bour 207 E4
Cromer Rd. Cos 133 F1
Cromer Rd. Poole 205 F3
Cromer Rd. Southa 77 E1
Cromhall Cl. Fare 154 B4
Crompton Way. Lo He 129 E3
Cromwell Pl. Bour 208 A3
Cromwell Rd. Bour 208 A3
Cromwell Rd. Poole 205 E3
Cromwell Rd. Ports 183 D1
Cromwell Rd. Southa 102 C4
Cromwell Rd. Wi Mi 163 E2
Cromwell Rd. Winch 10 C3
Crondall Ave. Hav 135 F3
Crooked Hays Cl. March 55 F1
Crooked Walk La. Southw 132 C2
Crookham Cl. Hav 135 E2
Crookham Rd. Southa 126 C4
Crookhorn La. Sob 85 E4
Crookhorn La. Wat 134 C2
Crosby Rd. Bour 206 B1
Crosfield Cl. W Wel 51 D1
Cross La. Bi Wa 59 D1
Cross Rd. Lon S 180 A2
Cross Rd. Southa 103 F4
Cross St. Bi Wa 83 E4
Cross St. Ports 182 A3
Cross St. Ports 182 B2
Cross St. Winch 10 C4
Cross The. Bur 143 D2
Cross The. E Meo 38 B1
Cross Way. Christ 192 B1
Cross Way. Comp 31 E3
Cross Way. Hav 135 F1
Crossfell Wlk. Fare 154 C4
Crosshouse Rd. Southa 103 E2
Crossland Cl. Gos 181 E2
Crossland Dr. Hav 136 A2
Crossmead Ave. New M 196 A1
Crossways Cl. Down 46 C4
Crossways The. Gos 181 D3
Crossways. Hord 197 E1
Crossways. Upt 203 E4
Crosswell Cl. Southa 104 B3
Crouch La. Horn 112 A4
Croucher's Croft. Winch 1 B1
Crow Arch La. Rin 141 D3
Crowder Terr. Winch 10 C4
Crowders Green. Co Com 56 C4
Crown Cl. Poole 205 E3
Crown Cl. Wat 134 C2
Crown Mead. Wi Mi 163 E3
Crown St. Ports 182 B3
Crown St. Southa 102 A4
Crows Nest La. Botl 81 F1
Crowsbury Cl. Ems 136 C2
Crowsport. Hamble 128 A2
Crowther Cl. Southa 104 B2
Croydon Cl. Southa 78 A2
Crummock Rd. N Bad 55 D4
Crusader Rd. Bour 189 E2
Crusader Rd. He En 105 E3
Cruse Cl. Sway 172 A1
Crystal Way. Wat 135 D4
Cucklington Gdns. Bour 191 D2
Cuckmere La. Southa 101 E4
Cuckoo Bushes La. Ch Fo 55 E4
Cuckoo Hill Way. Bran 169 E1
Cuckoo La. Southa 102 C2
Cuckoo La. Stubb 154 A2
Cudnell Ave. Bour 190 A3
Cudworth Mead. He En 81 E1
Cuffnells Cl. Ibs 117 D4
Cul-de-sac. B on S 211 E4
Culford Ave. Tot 100 C3
Culford Way. Tot 100 C3
Cull Cl. Poole 206 B4
Cull La. New M 196 A3
Culliford Cres. Broa 188 C1
Culloden Cl. Fare 130 C1
Culver Cl. Southa 77 E1
Culver Dr. S Hay 185 E1
Culver Rd. New M 195 F1
Culver Rd. Ports 183 D1
Culver. Net 127 E4
Culverhayes Rd. Wi Mi 163 D3
Culverwell Gdns. Winch 10 C4
Culvery Gdns. W End 80 A1
Cumber Rd. Lo He 128 C2
Cumberland Ave. Ch Fo 55 F3
Cumberland Ave. Ems 136 C2
Cumberland Cl. Ch Fo 55 F3
Cumberland Pl. Southa 102 C3
Cumberland Rd. Ports 182 C3
Cumberland St. Ports 182 A3
Cumberland St. Southa 103 D2
Cumberland Way. Hyt 125 E2
Cumbrian Way. Southa 101 F4
Cummins Green. Burs 105 D1
Cumnor Rd. Bour 207 D2
Cunard Ave. Southa 102 B4
Cunard Rd. Southa 103 D1
Cundellway. Ki Wo 2 A4
Cunningham Ave. Bi Wa 83 D4
Cunningham Cl. Bour 190 A2
Cunningham Cl. Christ 210 A3
Cunningham Cl. Rin 141 E4
Cunningham Cres. Bour 190 A2
Cunningham Cres. Southa 104 A2
Cunningham Dr. Gos 155 E2
Cunningham Dr. Lo He 129 D2
Cunningham Pl. Bour 190 A2
Cunningham Rd. Horn 112 B4
Cunningham Rd. Wat 134 B3
Cupernham Cl. Rom 28 A1
Cupernham La. Abb 28 A1
Cupernham La. Rom 28 A1
Curdridge Cl. Hav 136 A3
Curdridge La. Curd 83 E2
Curdridge La. Shed 83 E2
Curlew Cl. Fern 165 D4
Curlew Cl. Hyt 126 B1
Curlew Cl. Southa 78 A3
Curlew Dr. Hyt 126 A1
Curlew Dr. Portc 155 F4
Curlew Gdns. Wat 111 F2
Curlew Path. Ports 183 D3
Curlew Rd. Bour 191 E1
Curlew Rd. Christ 210 A3
Curlew Sq. Eastl 55 F1
Curlew Wlk. Gos 155 D2
Curlew Wlk. Hyt 126 A1
Curlews The. Ver 115 D3
Curlieu Rd. Poole 204 B3
Curtis Mead. Ports 157 F2
Curtis Rd. Poole 205 E3
Curtiss Gdns. Gos 180 C2
Curve The. Gos 155 D1
Curve The. Horn 111 F3
Curzon Ct. Southa 78 B2
Curzon Howe Rd. Ports 182 A3
Curzon Pl. Lym 198 B1
Curzon Rd. Bour 207 E3
Curzon Rd. Poole 205 D2
Curzon Rd. Wat 134 C4
Curzon Way. Christ 210 B4
Custards Rd. Lyn 122 A3
Custards The. Lyn 121 F3
Cut Throat La. Drox 61 D1
Cut Throat La. Swan 84 B3
Cutbush La. Southa 80 A2
Cutbush La. Southa 104 A4
Cutbush La. W End 80 A2
Cuthbert Rd. Ports 182 C3
Cuthburga Rd. Wi Mi 163 E2
Cuthbury Cl. Wi Mi 163 D2
Cuthbury Gdns. Wi Mi 163 D3
Cutler Cl. New M 196 B2
Cutlers La. Stubb 154 B2
Cutlers Pl. Wi Mi 164 A3
Cutter Ave. Lo He 128 C1
Cutts Arch. Drox 85 D3
Cutts Arch. Sob 85 D3
Cygnet Ct. Portc 155 F4
Cygnet Rd. Cos 158 C4
Cygnus Gdns. Hyt 125 D2
Cynthia Rd. Poole 205 D4
Cypress Ave. Southa 103 F3
Cypress Cres. Wat 112 A3
Cypress Gdns. Botl 106 A4
Cypress Gdns. Tot 100 B4
Cypress Gr. Hord 213 E4
Cyprus Rd. Lo He 129 E1
Cyprus Rd. Ports 182 C4
Cyril Rd. Bour 207 E3

Dacombe Cl. Upt 203 E4
Dacombe Dr. Upt 203 E4
Daffodil Rd. Southa 79 E2
Daggons Rd. Alderh 92 B3
Dahlia Rd. Southa 79 D2
Daintree Cl. Southa 104 B2
Dairy La. Nur 77 D3
Dairymoor. Wickh 108 A2
Daisy La. Gos 181 D2
Daisy La. Lo He 129 E2
Daisy Mead. Wat 135 D4
Daisy Rd. Southa 79 D2
Dakota Cl. Christ 210 A4
Dale Cl. Litt 1 A3
Dale Cl. Poole 204 C3
Dale Dr. Gos 155 D3
Dale Rd. Hyt 125 F2
Dale Rd. Poole 204 C3
Dale Rd. Southa 78 B1
Dale Rd. Stubb 154 B2
Dale The. Wat 134 B1
Dale Valley Cl. Southa 78 B1
Dale Valley Gdns. Southa 78 B1
Dale Valley Rd. Poole 204 C4
Dale Valley Rd. Southa 78 B2
Dales Cl. Wi Mi 164 B3
Dales Dr. Wi Mi 164 A3
Dales Way. Tot 100 A4
Dalewood Ave. Bour 189 F3
Dalewood Rd. Fare 130 B1
Dalkeith Rd. Broa 187 E2
Dalkeith Rd. Poole 206 A1
Dalling Rd. Poole 206 A3
Dallington Cl. Stubb 154 B1
Dalmeny Rd. Bour 209 D2
Damask Gdns. Wat 112 A1
Damen Cl. He En 105 D3
Damerham Rd. Bour 191 E2
Dampier Cl. Gos 180 B4
Damson Hill. Bi Wa 60 A1
Damson Hill. Swan 60 A1
Danbury Ct. Ems 137 D1
Dances Way. S Hay 184 C2
Dandelion Cl. Gos 155 D1
Dando Rd. Den 111 D2
Dandy's Ford La. Sh En 25 F1
Dane Cl. Black 150 C1
Dane Dr. Fern 165 F2
Danebury Cl. Hav 135 F3
Danebury Gdns. Ch Fo 55 D2
Danebury Way. Nur 77 E2
Danecourt Cl. Poole 204 C2
Danecourt Rd. Poole 204 C2
Danecrest Rd. Hord 196 C2
Danehurst New Rd. New M 196 B4
Danes Cl. B on S 212 A4
Danes Rd. Awb 26 B2
Danes Rd. Portc 132 A1
Danes Rd. Winch 2 A1
Danesbrook La. Wat 135 D4
Danesbury Ave. Bour 208 C2
Danestream Cl. M on S 213 E2
Daneswood Rd. New M 196 B2
Daniell's Cl. Lym 198 C2
Daniell's Wlk. Lym 198 C2
Dansie Cl. Poole 205 D2
Dapple Pl. March 102 A1
Darby's Cl. Poole 204 B3
Darby's La. Poole 204 B3
Darby's La. Poole 204 B4
Dark La. Black 150 C1
Dark La. Bran 195 D2
Darley Rd. Fern 165 E2
Darlington Gdns. Southa 78 B1
Darlington Rd. Ports 182 C2
Darracott Rd. Bour 208 A3
Darren Cl. Stubb 154 B2
Dart Rd. W End 80 A2
Dartington Rd. Bish 56 B3
Dartmouth Mews. Ports 182 A2
Dartmouth Rd. Ports 158 A1
Darwin Ave. Christ 192 C1
Darwin Rd. Eastl 56 A2
Darwin Rd. Southa 102 C4
Daubney Gdns. Hav 135 E3
Daulston Rd. Ports 182 C4
Daventry La. Ports 158 B2
David Ct. Rom 53 D3
David's La. St Le 140 B3
Davidia Ct. Wat 135 D3
Davis Cl. Gos 180 B4
Davis Field. New M 195 F1
Davis Rd. Poole 205 F3
Daw La. N Hay 184 C4
Dawkins Rd. Hamw 203 E2
Dawkins Way. New M 196 A1
Dawlish Ave. Southa 102 B4
Dawn Cl. Bour 190 B1
Dawn Gdns. Winch 10 B3
Dawnay Cl. Southa 79 E3
Daws Ave. Bour 190 A1
Dawson Rd. Southa 104 B1
Day La. Horn 111 F4
Day's Ct. Wi Mi 163 E2
Daylesford Cl. Poole 205 D1
Dayrell Cl. Tot 76 A1
Dayshes Cl. Gos 155 D2
Dayslondon Rd. Wat 134 B3
De Courtenai Cl. Bour 189 F3
De Haviland Cl. Oakl 163 F1
De Havilland Way. Christ 210 A3
De La Warr Rd. M on S 213 E2
De Lisle Cl. Ports 157 F2
De Lisle Rd. Bour 206 C4
De Maulley Rd. Poole 211 F4
De Montfort Rd. Oakl 163 E1
De Mowbray Way. Lym 198 B1
De Redvers Rd. Poole 205 E1
Deacon Cl. Southa 104 A3
Deacon Cres. Southa 104 A3
Deacon Rd. Bour 190 D3
Deacon Rd. Lo He 129 D1
Deacon Rd. Southa 104 A3
Deadman Hill. Fordi 71 E3

Deal Cl. Stubb 154 B2
Deal Rd. Cos 133 F1
Dean Cl. Hamw 203 F2
Dean Cl. Winch 1 B1
Dean Ct. He En 105 E4
Dean La. Bi Wa 59 F2
Dean La. Ro Ca 113 E3
Dean La. Spar 1 A1
Dean La. Whit 24 A2
Dean La. Winch 1 A1
Dean Park Cres. Bour 206 C2
Dean Park Rd. Bour 206 C2
Dean Rd. Cos 157 F4
Dean Rd. Fa Oa 57 E1
Dean Rd. Southa 104 A4
Dean Rd. W Dean 3 D1
Dean Rd. W Tyth 3 F3
Dean St. Ports 182 A3
Dean Swift Cres. Poole 211 E4
Dean Villas. Wickh 130 C4
Dean's Rd. Bour 208 A3
Deane Cl. Lo He 128 C2
Deane Down Dro. Litt 1 A2
Deane Gdns. L on S 179 F3
Deane's Park Rd. Fare 131 E1
Deanery The. Ch Fo 55 D4
Deanfield Cl. Hamble 127 F1
Deans Court La. Wi Mi 163 E2
Deans Ct. M on S 213 E3
Deans Gate. Stubb 154 B1
Deans Gr. Wi Mi 163 E4
Deanscroft Rd. Bour 190 C2
Deanswood Dr. Wat 111 F1
Dear Hay La. Poole 204 B1
Decies Rd. Poole 205 D3
Dee Cl. N Bad 55 D3
Dee Way. Poole 204 A1
Deep Dell. Wat 112 A3
Deepdene La. Bour 189 F3
Deeping Cl. Southa 103 F1
Deeping Gate. Wat 135 D4
Deerhurst Cl. Tot 100 B3
Deerhurst Cres. Cos 133 D1
Deerleap Cl. Hyt 126 A2
Deerleap La. Ashu 100 B1
Deerleap Way. Hyt 126 A2
Deerleap Way. New M 196 A3
Defender Rd. Southa 103 E2
Delamere Gdns. Bour 190 C2
Delamere Rd. Ports 182 C2
Delft Cl. Lo He 128 C2
Delft Gdns. Wat 111 E1
Delhi Cl. Poole 205 E2
Delhi Rd. Bour 190 C1
Delilah Rd. Hamw 203 E1
Delius Ave. Southa 104 B2
Delius Wlk. Wat 134 C3
Dell Cl. Broa 187 F2
Dell Cl. Fa Oa 57 E1
Dell Cl. Wat 134 A1
Dell Piece East. Horn 112 B3
Dell Piece West. Horn 112 B3
Dell Quay Cl. Gos 155 D1
Dell Rd. Southa 79 F1
Dell Rd. Winch 11 E3
Dell The. B on S 211 E4
Dell The. Hav 135 D1
Dell The. Portc 131 F1
Dell Wharf. Southa 103 E4
Dellfield. Frox G 18 C1
Delme Dr. Fare 131 E1
Delph Rd. Oakl 188 B4
Delphi Way. Wat 134 C1
Delta Cl. Christ 210 A4
Dempsey Cl. Southa 104 A2
Denbigh Cl. Eastl 55 F3
Denbigh Cl. Tot 100 B3
Denbigh Dr. Fare 130 C1
Denbigh Gdns. Southa 78 C2
Denby Rd. Poole 204 C2
Dene Cl. Rin 117 E1
Dene Cl. Rown 78 C4
Dene Hollow. Cos 158 B4
Dene Rd. Ashu 100 B1
Dene Way. Ashu 100 B2
Dene Wlk. Fern 165 F1
Deneve Ave. Broa 188 B1
Denewood Copse. W Moo 138 B2
Denewood Rd. W Moo 138 B2
Denewulf Cl. Bi Wa 83 E4
Denham Cl. Broa 188 C2
Denham Cl. Stubb 154 A1
Denham Cl. Winch 1 C1
Denham Ct. Winch 2 A1
Denham Dr. Christ 194 C1
Denham Gdns. Net 127 D3
Denhill Cl. S Hay 184 C3
Denholm Cl. Rin 117 E1
Denison Rd. Broa 188 B1
Denmark La. Poole 204 B2
Denmark Rd. Bour 190 C1
Denmark St. Poole 204 B2
Denmead Rd. Bour 208 B4
Denmead Rd. Southa 104 B4
Denmead. New M 196 B2
Denning Mews. Ports 182 B3
Dennis Rd. Broa 187 E3
Dennis Way. Liss 21 D2
Dennistoun Ave. Christ 209 F4
Denny Cl. Faw 151 D2
Denville Ave. Portc 156 B3
Denville Cl. Cos 158 C4
Denvilles Cl. Hav 136 A1
Denwood Rd. Bour 206 A2
Denzil Ave. Net 127 E3
Denzil Ave. Southa 103 D3
Depedene Cl. Holb 150 B2
Derby Rd. Bour 207 E2
Derby Rd. Eastl 55 F1
Derby Rd. Eastl 56 A1
Derby Rd. Ports 157 E1
Derby Rd. Southa 103 D3
Dereham Way. Poole 205 F3
Deridene Ct. Tot 100 B3
Derlyn Rd. Fare 88 A1
Derritt La. Bran 193 E4
Derritt La. Sop 193 E4
Derwent Cl. Bour 191 D1
Derwent Cl. Fern 166 A3
Derwent Cl. Horn 88 B1
Derwent Cl. Stubb 154 B2
Derwent Cl. W End 80 A1
Derwent Rd. L on S 179 F3
Derwent Rd. New M 196 A3
Derwent Rd. Southa 77 F1
Derwentwater Rd. Oakl 163 E1
Desborough Cl. Cos 133 D1
Desborough Cl. Eastl 56 A1
Desborough Rd. Eastl 56 A1
Devenish Rd. Winch 1 B2
Deverall Pl. Wat 134 B2
Devine Gdns. Bish 56 C1
Devon Cl. Ch Fo 55 E2
Devon Dr. Ch Fo 55 E2
Devon Rd. Christ 208 C4
Devon Rd. Poole 204 C3
Devon Rd. Ports 158 A2
Devonshire Ave. Ports 183 D2
Devonshire Gdns. Burs 105 D1
Devonshire Gdns. Hyt 150 A4
Devonshire Rd. Southa 102 C3
Devonshire Sq. Ports 182 C2
Devonshire Way. Fare 154 B4
Dew La. Eastl 55 F2
Dewar Cl. Lo He 129 E3
Dewlands Rd. Ver 114 B3
Dewlands Way. Ver 114 C3
Dial Cl. Bran 169 E1
Diamond Cl. Fordi 93 F4
Diamond St. Ports 182 A2
Diana Cl. Gos 180 C2
Diana Way. Broa 187 F4
Dibben Wlk. Rom 28 B1
Dibble Dr. N Bad 53 F2
Dibden Cl. Bour 191 E2
Dibden Cl. Hav 135 E2
Dibden Lodge Cl. Hyt 125 F3
Dibles Rd. Lo He 128 C1
Dickens Cl. Ports 182 B4
Dickens Dell. Tot 100 A4
Dickens Rd. Bour 208 C4
Dickson Park. Wickh 108 A2
Didcot Rd. Southa 78 B1
Dieppe Cres. Ports 157 F2
Dieppe Gdns. Gos 180 C2
Diligence Cl. Burs 105 D1
Dilly La. B on S 212 A4
Dimond Cl. Southa 79 F1
Dimond Hill. Southa 79 F1
Dimond Rd. Southa 79 F1
Dingle Rd. Bour 208 A2
Dingle Way. Lo He 129 D2
Dingley Rd. Poole 204 B3
Dinham Rd. New M 196 B2
Dinsey Cl. Southa 101 F4
Diprose Rd. Broa 187 F4
Discovery Cl. Stubb 154 B3
Disraeli Rd. Christ 209 E3
Ditcham Cres. Hav 135 F2
Ditchbury. Lym 198 B3
Ditton Cl. Stubb 154 B2
Dock La. Beaul 149 D1
Dock Rd. Gos 181 E2
Dockenfield Cl. Hav 135 E2
Doctor's Hill. Sh En 26 A2
Doctors La. W Meo 37 E3
Dodds La. Swan 84 B3
Dodwell La. Burs 105 D2
Dogdean. Wi Mi 163 E4
Dogkennel La. Hambl 86 C2
Dogwood Dell. Wat 134 C3
Dolbery Rd N. Poole 189 E1
Dolbery Rd S. Poole 189 E1
Dolman Rd. Gos 181 E2
Dolphin Ave. Bour 190 C3
Dolphin Cl. Bish 56 C1
Dolphin Cres. Gos 181 E2
Dolphin Ct. Stubb 154 A2
Dolphin Hill. Twyf 58 A3
Dolphin Pl. B on S 212 A4
Dolphin Way. Gos 181 E1
Dolton Rd. Southa 77 F2
Dome Al. Winch 11 D4
Dominie Wlk. L on S 179 F3
Dominion Rd. Bour 189 F2
Domum Rd. Ports 157 F1
Domum Rd. Winch 11 D3
Donaldson Rd. Cos 157 F3
Doncaster Dr. Eastl 79 F4
Doncaster Rd. Eastl 80 A4
Donigers Cl. Swan 84 A3
Donigers Dell. Swan 84 A3
Donnelly Rd. Bour 208 C3
Donnelly St. Gos 181 D3
Donnington Dr. Ch Fo 55 D2
Donnington Dr. Christ 210 A4
Donnington Gr. Southa 79 E1
Donoughmore Rd. Bour 207 F2
Dorcas Cl. Wat 112 A1
Dorchester Gdns. Poole 204 C3
Dorchester Rd. Poole 204 C3
Dorchester Rd. Upt 203 D4
Dore Ave. Portc 132 B1
Dores La. Brai 29 D4
Dores La. Hurs 29 D4
Doric Cl. Ch Fo 55 F4
Dorking Cres. Cos 157 F4
Dorland Gdns. Tot 100 B3
Dorlands Rd. Horn 112 B4
Dormington Rd. Cos 133 E1
Dormy Cl. Lo He 128 B2
Dormy Way. Gos 155 D1
Dornie Rd. Poole 211 F4
Dornmere La. Wat 135 D4
Dorothy Dymond St. Ports 182 B3
Dorrien Rd. Gosp 181 D4
Dorrita Ave. Wat 112 A2
Dorrita Cl. Ports 182 C1
Dorrits The. Tot 100 A4
Dorset Ave. Fern 165 E2
Dorset Cl. Horn 112 A3
Dorset Lake Ave. Poole 211 D4
Dorset Rd. Bour 206 B3
Dorset Rd. Ch Fo 55 E2
Dorset Rd. Christ 209 F4
Dorset St. Southa 103 D3
Dorstone Rd. Cos 133 E1
Douglas Ave. Christ 209 D3
Douglas Cl. Upt 203 E4
Douglas Cres. Southa 104 B3
Douglas Gdns. Poole 205 F3
Douglas Rd. Bour 208 C2
Douglas Rd. Poole 205 F3
Douglas Way. Hyt 125 F2
Doussie Cl. Upt 203 D4
Dove Cl. Wat 111 F2
Dove Dale. Eastl 55 E1
Dove Gdn. Lo He 129 D3
Dove La. Hurs 29 D4
Dover Cl. Poole 206 A2
Dover Cl. Stubb 154 A2
Dover Ct. S Hay 184 C3
Dover Rd. Poole 206 A2
Dover Rd. Ports 183 D4
Dover St. Southa 103 D4
Dovercourt Rd. Cos 158 A3
Doveshill Cres. Bour 190 B2
Doveshill Gdns. Bour 190 B2
Dowds Cl. He En 105 D4
Dowlands Cl. Bour 190 B2
Dowlands Rd. Bour 190 B2
Down End Rd. Cos 134 B1
Down End. Cos 134 B1
Down Farm La. Ki Wo 1 C4
Down Lodge Cl. Alderh 93 D3
Down Rd. Horn 88 A1
Down's Park Ave. Tot 101 D3
Down's Park Cres. Tot 101 D3
Down's Park Rd. Tot 101 D3
Downend Rd. Portc 131 F1
Downey Cl. Bour 189 F1
Downham Cl. Wat 111 F2
Downhouse Rd. Horn 88 A2
Downland Cl. Botl 105 F4
Downland Cl. Lo He 129 D2
Downland Pl. He En 105 D3
Downlands Cl. Bour 190 B2
Downlands Cl. Down 46 C3
Downlands Rd. Bour 190 B2
Downlands Rd. Winch 10 A2
Downley Rd. Hav 136 A2
Downscroft Gdns. He En 105 D4
Downside Ave. Southa 104 A3
Downside Rd. Wat 134 B2
Downside Rd. Winch 1 A1
Downside. Gos 155 E1
Downsway The. Portc 156 B4
Downton Cl. Bour 191 E2
Downton Hill. Red 47 E4
Downton La. M on S 212 C4
Downton Rd. Southa 79 F1
Downview Rd. Mar 43 D2
Downwood Cl. Fordi 69 E1
Downwood Way. Horn 88 B1
Doyle Ave. Ports 157 F2
Doyle Cl. Ports 157 F2
Doyle Ct. Southa 103 F1
Doyne Rd. Poole 205 F2
Dradfield La. Sob 109 E4
Dragon La. Rin 168 A4
Dragon St. Pet 40 C2
Dragoon Cl. Southa 104 B2
Drake Cl. Christ 209 F3
Drake Cl. Lo He 129 D3
Drake Cl. March 102 A1
Drake Cl. New M 195 F2
Drake Cl. Rin 117 E1
Drake Rd. Bish 56 C2
Drake Rd. L on S 179 E4
Drakes Cl. Hyt 125 F1
Draper Rd. Bour 190 A2
Draper Rd. Christ 209 F4
Draycote Rd. Horn 88 B2
Draycott Rd. Bour 190 B1
Drayton Cl. Southa 126 C4
Drayton Cl. Southa 127 D4
Drayton La. Cos 134 A1
Drayton Pl. Tot 100 B4
Drayton Rd. Ports 157 F1
Drayton St. Winch 10 B3
Dresden Dr. Wat 111 E2
Dreswick Cl. Christ 192 B2
Drew Cl. Poole 206 B4
Drift Rd. Clanf 88 B2
Drift Rd. Fare 131 E1
Drift The. Ro Ca 113 D1
Driftwood Gdns. Ports 183 E1
Driftwood Gdns. Tot 100 B3
Drinkwater Cl. Eastl 55 F2
Drive The. Fare 88 A1
Drive The. Gos 155 D1
Drive The. Hav 135 F2
Drive The. Plai 25 D1
Drive The. Poole 205 E3
Drive The. Sh En 25 D1
Drive The. Southb 161 E4
Drive The. Tot 100 C3
Drive The. W End 80 A2
Drive The. W Wel 51 D1
Drove Cl. Twyf 31 F3
Drove Rd. Southa 104 A2
Drove Rd. Southw 133 D2
Drove The. Black 150 C1
Drove The. Durl 82 B4
Drove The. Fa Oa 81 E3
Drove The. Southa 104 A4
Drove The. Swan 84 A3
Drove The. Tot 76 A1
Drove The. Twyf 31 F3
Drove The. W End 80 C2
Drove The. W Wel 50 C2
Droxford Rd. Bour 208 A3
Droxford Rd. Swan 84 B3
Druids Cl. Fern 165 E1
Druitt Rd. Christ 209 F4
Drum La. Pet 40 C2
Drum Mead. Pet 40 C2
Drummond Cl. Winch 10 C3
Drummond Ct. Southa 103 F2
Drummond Rd. Bour 207 E2
Drummond Rd. He En 81 E1
Drummond Rd. Hyt 126 A2
Drummond Rd. Ports 182 B3
Drummond Way. Ch Fo 55 D4
Drury Rd. Bour 206 A1
Dryden Ave. Portc 132 C1
Dryden Cl. St Le 139 F3
Dryden Cl. Wat 111 F1
Dryden Pl. M on S 213 E3
Dryden Rd. Southa 104 C3
Duck Island La. Rin 141 D3
Duck La. Bour 189 F2
Ducking Stool La. Christ 209 D3
Duckmead La. Liss 21 D3
Duddon Cl. W End 80 A1
Dudleston Heath Dr. Wat 112 A1
Dudley Ave. Fordi 69 F2
Dudley Ave. Hord 196 C2
Dudley Gdns. Bour 190 B3
Dudley Rd. Bour 190 B3
Dudley Rd. Ports 183 D4
Dudmoor Farm Rd. Christ 192 C2
Dudsbury Ave. Fern 165 E2
Dudsbury Cres. Fern 165 F2
Dudsbury Gdns. Fern 190 C4
Dudsbury Rd. Fern 165 E1
Duffield La. Westb 137 F2
Dugald Drummond St. Ports 182 B3
Dugdell Cl. Fern 165 F3
Duisburg Way. Ports 182 A1
Duke Cres. Ports 182 B4
Duke Rd. He En 105 E3
Duke St. Southa 103 D2
Dukes Cl. Pet 40 B2
Dukes Dr. Bour 189 F3
Dukes Rd. Gosp 181 D3
Dukes Rd. Southa 103 E4
Dukes Wood Dr. Hyt 126 A1
Dukesfield. Christ 192 B1
Dulsie Rd. Bour 206 B4
Dumbarton Cl. Ports 182 B4
Dummer Ct. Hav 135 E3
Dummer Rd. Brai 28 B4
Dumpers Drove. Fa Oa 81 E4
Dunbar Cl. Southa 77 F3
Dunbar Cres. Christ 194 C1
Dunbar Rd. Bour 206 C3
Dunbar Rd. Ports 183 D2
Dunbridge La. Awb 26 C3
Dunbridge La. Mott 5 E1
Dunbridge La. Mott 26 C4
Duncan Cl. Southa 126 C4
Duncan Ct. Southa 104 B3
Duncan Rd. Lo He 129 D3
Duncan Rd. New M 196 B2
Duncan Rd. Ports 182 B1
Duncans Dr. Fare 154 A4
Duncliff Rd. Bour 209 D2
Duncombe Rd. E Meon 63 E4
Dundas Cl. Ports 158 A1
Dundas La. Ports 158 A1
Dundas Rd. Poole 204 C4
Dundas Spur. Ports 158 A1
Dundee Cl. Fare 130 C2
Dundee Rd. Southa 79 E1
Dundonald Cl. S Hay 185 D3
Dundridge La. Drox 60 B1
Dundry Way. He En 105 E4
Dunedin Cl. Fern 165 D2
Dunedin Dr. Fern 165 D2
Dunedin Gr. Christ 210 B4
Dunfield Way. Black 150 C1
Dunford Cl. B on S 211 F4
Dunford Cl. New M 195 F1
Dunford Rd. Poole 205 E3
Dunhurst Cl. Hav 136 A2
Dunkeld Rd. Bour 206 C3
Dunkeld Rd. Gosp 181 D4
Dunkirk Cl. Southa 78 B2
Dunkirk Rd. Southa 78 B2
Dunlin Cl. Christ 210 A3
Dunlin Cl. Ports 183 E3
Dunnings La. N Bad 53 F3
Dunnock Cl. Fern 165 D4
Dunnock Cl. Ro Ca 113 D1
Dunsbury Way. Hav 135 F3
Dunsmore Cl. Ports 182 B2
Dunstable Wlk. Fare 154 B4
Dunstans La. Poole 205 D3
Dunster Cl. Southa 78 B3
Dunvegan Dr. Southa 78 B3
Dunville Cres. Bour 191 D2
Dunyeats Rd. Broa 188 A2
Durban Cl. Rom 28 A1
Durban Rd. Ports 182 C4
Durdells Ave. Bour 190 D3
Durdells Gdns. Bour 190 D3
Durford Ct. Hav 135 E3
Durford Rd. Pet 41 E2
Durham Gdns. Wat 134 C3
Durham St. Gos 181 D3
Durham St. Ports 182 B3
Durland Cl. New M 196 A1
Durley Ave. Wat 111 F2
Durley Chine Rd S. Bour 206 B1
Durley Chine Rd. Bour 206 B1
Durley Cres. Tot 100 B3
Durley Gdns. Bour 206 B1
Durley Hall Rd. Durl 58 B1
Durley La. Durl 82 B4
Durley Rd S. Bour 206 B1
Durley Rd. Bour 206 C1
Durley Rd. Durl 81 F4
Durley Rd. Fa Oa 81 F4
Durley Rd. Gosp 181 D3
Durlston Cres. Christ 192 B2
Durlston Rd. Poole 205 E1
Durlston Rd. Southa 77 E1
Durnford Rd. Southa 103 D3
Durngate Pl. Winch 11 D4
Durngate Terr. Winch 11 D4
Durnstown. Sway 172 B1
Durrant Rd. Bour 206 C2
Durrant Rd. Poole 205 E2
Durrant Way. Sway 172 A1
Durrants Gdns. Ro Ca 136 A4
Durrants Rd. Ro Ca 136 A4
Durrington Pl. Bour 208 A3
Durrington Rd. Bour 208 A4
Dursley Cres. Cos 157 E4
Durweston Cl. Bour 191 D2
Dutton La. Eastl 56 A2
Dutton's Rd. Rom 52 C4
Dyer Rd. Southa 102 B4
Dymoke St. Ems 136 C2
Dymott Cl. Southa 102 B3
Dyneley Gr. Southa 80 A1
Dyram Cl. Eastl 55 F3
Dysart Ave. Cos 158 A4
Dyserth Cl. Southa 104 A1
Dyson Dr. Winch 2 A1

Eadens La. Ne Ma 99 E4
Eagle Ave. Wat 111 F2
Eagle Cl. Ch Fo 55 D2
Eagle Cl. Portc 155 F4
Eagle Rd. Poole 206 A2
Eames La. Hawk 19 F4
Earl's Rd. Southa 103 D4
Earle Rd. Bour 206 B1
Earlham Dr. Poole 205 E2
Earls Cl. Bish 57 D1
Earls Rd. Fare 155 D4
Earlsdon St. Ports 182 B2
Earlsdon Way. Christ 210 C4
Earlswood Dr. Alderh 92 C3
Earnley Rd. S Hay 185 F1
East Ave. B on S 211 E4
East Avenue. Bour 206 C3
East Bank Rd. Brock 173 D4
East Bargate. Southa 103 D2
East Borough. Wi Mi 163 D3
East Cams Cl. Portc 131 F1
East Cl. B on S 211 E4
East Cliff Way. Christ 210 B4

East Cosham Rd. Cos 158 A4
East Ct. Cos 158 A4
East Ct. Ports 182 C4
East Dean Rd. Locke 4 C1
East Dr. Bish 56 C2
East Field Cl. Southb 137 F1
East Hill Cl. Fare 131 E1
East Hill Dr. Liss 21 D2
East Hill. Lym 198 C2
East Hoe Rd. Sob 86 A2
East House Ave. Stubb 154 B1
East Howe Gdns. Bour 190 B2
East La. Hord 197 F1
East Leigh Rd. Hav 136 B2
East Lodge Park. Cos 158 B4
East Lodge. Fare 130 B1
East Lodge. Fare 130 B1
East Overcliff Dr. Bour 207 E2
East Park Terr. Southa 103 D3
East Quay Rd. Poole 204 B1
East St. Fare 131 E1
East St. Hambl 86 B2
East St. Hav 135 F1
East St. Lo He 154 A4
East St. Portc 156 C4
East St. Ports 182 A2
East St. Southa 103 D2
East St. Westb 137 D2
East St. Wi Mi 163 E2
East Surrey St. Ports 182 B3
East View Rd. Rin 141 D4
East Way. Bour 191 E1
East Way. Broa 187 E3
East Woodhay Rd. Winch 1 B2
Eastbourne Ave. Gos 180 C4
Eastbourne Ave. Southa 102 B4
Eastbourne Rd. Ports 183 D4
Eastbrook Cl. Gos 180 C4
Eastbrook Cl. Lo He 129 D3
Eastbrook Row. Wi Mi 163 E2
Eastchurch Cl. Southa 77 F2
Eastcliff Cl. L on S 179 F4
Eastcot Cl. Holb 150 B2
Eastcott Cl. Bour 208 A4
Easter Rd. Bour 191 D1
Eastern Ave. Ports 183 D3
Eastern Par. Fare 155 D4
Eastern Par. Ports 182 C1
Eastern Rd. Cos 158 B2
Eastern Rd. Hav 136 A1
Eastern Rd. Lym 198 B2
Eastern Rd. Ports 158 B2
Eastern Villas Rd. Ports 182 C1
Eastern Way. Fare 131 E1
Eastern Way. M on S 213 F2
Eastfield Ave. Fare 154 C4
Eastfield Ct. Rin 141 E4
Eastfield La. Rin 141 E4
Eastfield Rd. Ports 183 D2
Eastfield Rd. Southa 103 E4
Eastgate St. Southa 103 D2
Eastgate St. Winch 11 D4
Eastlake Ave. Poole 205 E3
Eastlake Cl. Pet 41 E2
Eastlake Hts. Ports 183 E2
Eastlands. New M 196 A1
Eastleigh Rd. Fa Oa 57 E1
Eastmeare Ct. Tot 100 B3
Eastney Farm Rd. Ports 183 E2
Eastney Rd. Ports 183 D2
Eastney St. Ports 183 D1
Eastoke Ave. S Hay 185 E1
Easton La. It Ab 2 C2
Eastover Ct. Hav 135 E3
Eastville Rd. Fa Oa 57 E1
Eastways. Bi Wa 83 E4
Eastwood Ave. Fern 165 F3
Eastwood Cl. S Hay 185 D3
Eastwood Rd. Ports 157 F2
Eastworth Rd. Ver 114 C4
Eaton Rd. Poole 206 A1
Ebden Rd. Winch 11 D4
Ebery Gr. Ports 183 E4
Ebor Cl. Fern 165 F1
Ebor Rd. Poole 205 E3
Ecton La. Ports 158 B2
Eddystone Rd. Tot 76 B1
Edelvale Rd. Southa 80 A1
Eden Gr. Wi Mi 163 E2
Eden Rd. W End 80 A1
Eden Rise. Fare 155 D4
Eden St. Ports 182 B3
Eden Wlk. N Bad 55 D3
Edgar Cres. Portc 156 B3
Edgar Rd. Winch 10 C4
Edgarton Rd. Broa 188 B2
Edgecombe Cres. Gos 180 B4
Edgehill Rd. Bour 190 C1
Edgehill Rd. Southa 79 F1
Edgell Rd. Westb 137 D2
Edgemoor Rd. W Moo 139 D1
Edgerly Gdns. Cos 157 F3
Edgeware Rd. Ports 183 D3
Edifred Rd. Bour 191 D2
Edinburgh Rd. Ports 182 B3
Edington Cl. Bi Wa 83 D4
Edington Rd. Winch 2 A1
Edmund Rd. Ports 182 C2
Edmunds Cl. He En 105 E3
Edneys La. Den 111 D3
Edward Ave. Bish 56 B2
Edward Cl. Black 150 C1
Edward Gdns. Hav 135 E1
Edward Gr. Portc 132 C1
Edward Rd. Bour 190 A2
Edward Rd. Christ 209 F4
Edward Rd. Hyt 126 A2
Edward Rd. Poole 205 E3
Edward Rd. Southa 102 B4
Edward Rd. Winch 10 C3
Edward St. Southa 103 D2
Edwards Cl. Wat 111 F2
Edwina Cl. N Bad 54 A2
Edwina Cl. Rin 117 E1
Edwina Cl. Southa 104 A3
Edwina Dr. Broa 188 A1
Effingham Gdns. Southa 104 B2
Efford Way. Lym 198 A1
Egan Cl. Ports 157 F2
Egbert Rd. Winch 2 A1
Egdon Dr. Oakl 188 C4
Egerton Gdns. Bour 207 E3
Egerton Rd. Bour 207 E3
Eglantine Cl. Wat 112 A2
Eglantine Walk. Wat 112 B2
Egmont Cl. St Le 140 B1
Egmont Dr. St Le 140 B1
Egmont Rd. Hamw 203 D2
Eight Acres. Rom 53 D4
Elaine Gdns. Wat 112 A3
Elan Cl. W End 80 A1
Elcombes Cl. Lyn 121 F3
Elder Cl. March 102 A1
Elder Cl. Winch 10 B2
Elder Rd. Hav 136 A2
Elderberry Cl. Clanf 88 B2
Elderberry La. Christ 209 F3
Elderberry Way. Wat 112 B2
Elderfield Cl. Ems 137 D2
Elderfield Rd. Hav 135 E4
Eldon Ave. B on S 211 F4
Eldon Cl. B on S 211 F4
Eldon Pl. Bour 206 A2
Eldon Rd. Bour 190 C1
Eldon Rd. Brai 7 D3
Eldon Rd. Brai 28 A4
Eldon Rd. Ki So 7 D3
Eldon St. Ports 182 B2
Eleanor Dr. Bour 189 E3
Electron Way. Ch Fo 55 E3
Elettra Ave. Wat 134 B4
Elfin Dr. Fern 165 E4
Elgar Cl. Gos 181 D1
Elgar Cl. Southa 104 B2
Elgar Rd. Bour 190 B2
Elgar Rd. Southa 104 B2
Elgar Wlk. Wat 134 C3
Elgin Cl. Fare 130 C1
Elgin Cl. Hyt 126 A2
Elgin Rd. Bour 206 B3
Elgin Rd. Cos 157 F3
Elgin Rd. Poole 205 E1
Elgin Rd. Southa 102 B3
Eling Cl. Winch 1 B2
Eling Hill. Tot 101 D3
Eling La. Tot 101 D3
Eling View. Southa 101 E4
Elise Cl. Bour 208 A4
Elizabeth Ave. Christ 208 C4
Elizabeth Cl. Down 46 B4
Elizabeth Cl. W End 80 B1
Elizabeth Cl. Wickh 107 F2
Elizabeth Cres. Hord 197 D1
Elizabeth Ct. Fare 154 C4
Elizabeth Gdns. Christ 210 B4
Elizabeth Gdns. Hyt 126 A1
Elizabeth Gdns. Ports 182 C1
Elizabeth Rd. Poole 204 B2
Elizabeth Rd. Stubb 154 B1
Elizabeth Rd. Wat 134 C3
Elizabeth Rd. Wi Mi 163 E3
Elizabeth Rd. Wickh 108 A2
Elizabeth Way. Eastl 56 A3
Elkhams Cl. Hord 197 E1
Elkstone Rd. Cos 133 D1
Ella Nore La. W Wit 186 C1
Ellachie Gdns. Gos 181 D1
Ellachie Mews. Gos 181 D1
Ellachie Rd. Gos 181 D1
Elland Cl. Fa Oa 57 E1
Elldene Ct. Tot 100 C3
Ellen Gdns. N Bad 55 D3
Ellerslie Cl. Stubb 154 A1
Ellery Gr. Lym 198 C3
Ellesfield Dr. Fern 165 E1
Ellesmere Orch. Westb 137 D3
Ellingham Dro. Rin 117 D3
Elliot Cl. Tot 100 B4
Elliot Rd. Bour 189 F2
Elliot Rise. He En 81 E1
Ellis Rd. Southa 104 C3
Ellisfield Rd. Hav 135 F2
Ellwood Ave. Southa 104 C3
Ellwood Cl. Southa 104 C3
Elm La. Hav 135 F1
Elm Ave. Christ 192 C1
Elm Ave. Lym 198 B1
Elm Ave. New M 196 A1
Elm Cl. Southa 78 C2
Elm Close Estate. S Hay 184 C2
Elm Cres. Hyt 150 A4
Elm Cres. Uph 58 C3
Elm Gr. Eastl 55 F1
Elm Gr. Gos 181 D3
Elm Gr. Ports 182 B2
Elm Gr. S Hay 185 D2
Elm Park Rd. Hav 135 F1
Elm Rd. Bi Wa 83 F4
Elm Rd. Hav 160 A4
Elm Rd. Winch 10 C4
Elm St. Ports 182 A2
Elm St. Southa 103 D2
Elm Terr. Southa 103 D2
Elm Tree Cl. Ashu 100 A1
Elm Tree Wlk. Fern 190 C4
Elmdale Gr. W Wel 51 D1
Elmers Way. Bran 169 D1
Elmes Dr. Southa 101 F4
Elmes Rd. Bour 190 C1
Elmeswelle Rd. Wat 112 A3
Elmfield La. Faw 178 C4
Elmgate Dr. Bour 208 A4
Elmhurst Rd. Fare 155 D4
Elmhurst Rd. Gos 181 E2
Elmhurst Rd. W Moo 138 C1
Elmhurst Way. W Moo 138 C1
Elmleigh Rd. Hav 135 F1
Elmore Ave. Lon S 180 A3
Elmore Cl. L on S 179 F3
Elmore Dr. St Le 139 F3
Elmore Rd. L on S 179 F3
Elms Ave. Poole 205 D1
Elms Cl. Fordi 69 D1
Elms Cl. Poole 205 D1
Elms Rd. Fare 155 D4
Elms Way. Bour 208 C2
Elmsleigh Ct. Southa 79 D2
Elmsleigh Gdns. Southa 79 D2
Elmslie Gdns. Burs 104 C1
Elmstead Rd. Poole 211 F4
Elmtree Gdns. Rom 53 E3
Elmtree Rd. Cos 158 B4
Elmwood Ave. Fordi 69 E1
Elmwood Ave. Wat 134 C3
Elmwood Rd. Ports 157 F2
Elmwood Way. Christ 211 D4
Elphinstone Rd. Christ 195 D1
Elphinstone Rd. Ports 182 B1
Elsfred Rd. Stubb 154 A1
Elson La. Gosp 181 D4
Elson Rd. Gos 180 C4
Elson Rd. Gosp 181 D4
Elstead Gdns. Wat 134 B2
Elstree Rd. Southa 103 F3
Eltham Cl. Bour 208 A4
Elvin Cl. Hord 196 C2
Elwell Gn. S Hay 184 C2
Elwyn Rd. Bour 207 E3
Emanuel St. Ports 182 B4
Emberly Cl. Fern 166 A4
Embley Cl. Tot 76 B1
Embley La. W Wel 51 F4
Embley Park Ind Est. W Wel ... 51 F4
Embsay Rd. Swanw 128 B4
Emerald Cl. Southa 104 A3
Emerald Cl. Wat 135 D4
Emerson Cl. Poole 204 B1
Emerson Rd. Poole 204 B1
Emily Cl. Christ 193 D1
Emmanuel Cl. Lo He 129 E1
Emmett Rd. Southa 77 F3
Emmons Cl. Hamble 128 A1
Empress Rd. Lyn 121 F3
Empress Rd. Southa 103 D1
Empress Rd. Southa 103 D4
Empshott Rd. Ports 182 C2
Empson Wlk. L on S 179 F4
Emsbrook Dr. Ems 136 C1
Emsworth Common Rd. Ems 136 B3
Emsworth House Cl. Ems 136 C1
Emsworth Rd. Hav 136 A1
Emsworth Rd. Lym 198 C2
Emsworth Rd. Ports 157 F1
Emsworth Rd. Southa 102 A4
Emsworth Rd. Th Is 161 E2
Encombe Cl. Poole 205 F4
Endeavour Cl. Southa 102 A4
Endeavour Rd. Gos 181 E2
Endeavour Way. Hyt 126 A3
Enderwood Cl. Tot 100 A4
Endfield Cl. Christ 192 C1
Endfield Rd. Bour 191 D1
Endfield Rd. Christ 192 C1
Endle St. Southa 103 E2
Endofield Cl. Gos 154 C3
Enfield Cres. Poole 204 C3
Enfield Gr. Southa 103 F2
Enfield Rd. Poole 204 C3
Englands Way. Bour 189 E2
Englefield Rd. Southa 103 E4
English Rd. Southa 102 A4
Enmill La. Hurs 9 F3
Ennerdale Cl. Horn 88 B1
Ennerdale Gdns. W End 80 A1
Ennerdale Rd. Southa 77 F1
Ennerdale Rd. Stubb 154 B2
Ensbury Ave. Bour 190 B1
Ensbury Cl. Bour 190 B1
Ensbury Park Rd. Bour 190 C1
Ensign Park. Hamble 127 F1
Enterprise Rd. Horn 112 B4
Enterprise Way. Southa 103 D1
Eperston Rd. Wat 112 A3
Epping Cl. Southa 80 A1
Epworth Rd. Ports 157 F1
Eric Rd. Stubb 154 B1
Erica Cl. Lo He 128 C2
Erica Cl. Wat 112 A2
Erica Dr. Broa 187 E3
Erica Way. Wat 112 A2
Ericksen Rd. Bour 190 B2
Ernest Cl. Ems 136 C1
Ernest Rd. Hav 135 E2
Ernest Rd. Ports 182 C4
Erpingham Rd. Poole 206 A3
Erskine Rd. Winch 10 C4
Escombe Rd. Bish 56 B2
Escur Cl. Ports 157 F2
Esdaile La. Bur 142 C2
Esher Gr. Wat 111 E1
Eskdale Cl. Horn 88 B1
Esmond Cl. Ems 160 C4
Esmonde Cl. L on S 179 F3
Esmonde Way. Poole 204 C4
Esplanade Gdns. Ports 183 E1
Esplanade The. Gos 181 F2
Esplanade. B on S 211 F4
Esplanade. Poole 204 B2
Esplanade. Ports 183 D1
Essex Ave. Christ 192 C1
Essex Green. Ch Fo 55 E1
Essex Rd. Ports 183 D2
Esslemont Rd. Ports 182 C2
Estella Rd. Ports 182 B4
Estridge Cl. Burs 105 D1
Ethel Rd. Ports 182 C3
Ethelbert Rd. Wi Mi 163 E2
Ethelburt Ave. Southa 79 E3
Ethelred Gdns. Tot 100 B3
Eton Rd. Ports 182 C2
Ettrick Rd. Poole 206 A1
Euston Rd. Ports 183 D3
Evans Cl. Bour 189 F1
Evans Rd. Ports 183 D2
Evans St. Southa 103 D2
Evelegh Rd. Cos 158 B4
Evelyn Cl. Shed 83 F2
Evelyn Cres. Southa 102 B4
Evelyn Rd. Bour 191 D1
Evening Glade. Fern 165 F2
Evenlode Rd. Southa 77 F1
Everdon La. Ports 158 B2
Everest Rd. Christ 209 F4
Everglade Ave. Wat 111 F2
Everglades Cl. Fern 165 E4
Evergreen Cl. March 101 F1
Evergreen Cl. W Moo 138 C4
Evergreen Cl. Wat 134 B4
Evering Ave. Poole 189 E1
Evering Gdns. Poole 189 E1
Everlea Cl. Hord 197 E1
Everon Gdns. New M 196 A1
Evershot Rd. Bour 191 F1
Eversley Cres. Hav 135 F2
Eversley Pl. Winch 10 B3
Everton Rd. Hord 197 D1
Evesham Cl. Bour 208 A4
Evesham Cl. Southa 79 D3
Ewart Ct. Hyt 126 A3
Ewart Rd. Ports 182 C4
Ewell Way. Tot 76 B1
Ewhurst Cl. Hav 135 E2
Exbury Cl. Bish 56 C1
Exbury Dr. Bour 189 F3
Exbury Rd. Black 150 C1
Exbury Rd. Hav 136 A3
Excelsior Rd. Poole 205 E2
Exchange Rd. Ports 182 A3
Exeter Cl. Eastl 55 F3
Exeter Cl. Ems 136 C2
Exeter Cl. Lo He 128 C2
Exeter Cl. Southa 80 A1
Exeter Cres. Bour 206 A1
Exeter La. Bour 206 C1
Exeter Park Rd. Bour 206 C1
Exeter Rd. Bour 206 C1
Exeter Rd. Ports 182 C1
Exeter Rd. Southa 104 A4
Exford Ave. Southa 104 B4
Exford Dr. Southa 104 B4
Exleigh Cl. Southa 104 A3
Exmoor Cl. Tot 100 A4
Exmoor Rd. Southa 103 D3
Exmouth Rd. Gosp 181 D4
Exmouth Rd. Ports 182 B1
Exmouth St. Southa 103 D3
Exton Gdns. Portc 132 B1
Exton Rd. Bour 208 B4
Exton Rd. Hav 136 A3
Eyeworth Wlk. Hyt 125 E2
Eynham Ave. Southa 104 B3
Eynham Cl. Southa 104 B3
Eyre Cl. Tot 100 B3
Fabian Cl. Wat 135 D4
Factory Rd. Eastl 56 A1
Factory Rd. Upt 203 E3
Fair Field. Rom 28 A1
Fair Green. Southa 104 A3
Fair Isle Cl. Stubb 154 A2
Fair Oak Ct. Fa Oa 57 E1
Fair Oak Dr. Hav 135 F2
Fairacre Rise. Fare 154 A4
Fairbourne Cl. Wat 111 F1
Fairclose Dr. Litt 1 A3
Fairdown Cl. Winch 11 E4
Fairfax Ct. Southa 104 C3
Fairfax Mews. Southa 104 C3
Fairfield Ave. Fare 154 C4
Fairfield Cl. Ems 136 C1
Fairfield Cl. Hyt 126 A2
Fairfield Cl. Lym 198 C2
Fairfield Cl. Wi Mi 163 F3
Fairfield Rd. Comp 31 E3
Fairfield Rd. Hav 135 F1
Fairfield Rd. Wi Mi 163 E2
Fairfield Rd. Winch 1 C1
Fairfield Sq. Cos 157 F4
Fairfield. Christ 209 D4
Fairhome Cl. Gosp 181 D4
Fairisle Rd. Southa 77 F2
Fairlawn Cl. Rown 77 F3
Fairlea Rd. Ems 136 C2
Fairlea Rd. Lym 198 C3
Fairlie Park. Rin 117 D1
Fairlie. Rin 117 E1
Fairlight La. Sway 196 B4
Fairmead Walk. Wat 112 A2
Fairmead Way. Tot 100 C3
Fairmile Rd. Christ 192 C1
Fairoak Rd. Bish 57 D1
Fairoak Rd. Fa Oa 57 D1
Fairthorne Gdns. Gos 181 D2
Fairview Cl. Hyt 126 A2
Fairview Cl. Rom 28 A1
Fairview Cres. Broa 188 A3
Fairview Dr. Broa 188 A3
Fairview Dr. Hyt 126 A2
Fairview Dr. Rom 28 A1
Fairview Par. Hyt 126 A1
Fairview Rd. Broa 188 A3
Fairwater Cl. Gos 155 D1
Fairway Ave. Poole 211 E4
Fairway Bus Pk. Ports 158 B1
Fairway Dr. Christ 208 C3
Fairway Gdns. Rown 77 F3
Fairway Rd. Hyt 125 F2
Fairway The. B on S 212 A4
Fairway The. Gos 155 E1
Fairway The. Portc 156 B4
Fairway The. Ro Ca 113 E1
Fairways. Fern 165 F3
Fairwood Rd. Ver 115 E3
Fairy Cross Way. Wat 112 A1
Falaise Rd. Southa 78 B2
Falcon Cl. Portc 155 F4
Falcon Dr. Christ 210 A3
Falcon Fields. Faw 151 D2
Falcon Green. Cos 158 C4
Falcon Sq. Eastl 55 F1
Falcon View. Winch 10 B2
Falcon Way. Botl 81 F1
Falconer Ct. Faw 150 B3
Falconer Dr. Hamw 203 F2
Falkland Rd. Ch Fo 55 E2
Falkland Rd. Southa 102 A4
Fallow Field. Winch 10 B2
Fancy Rd. Poole 205 D4
Fanshawe St. Southa 103 D3
Far Meadow Way. Ems 160 B4
Farcroft Rd. Poole 205 D3
Farcross Rd. Holb 150 B2
Fareham Park Rd. Fare 130 B2
Fareham Rd. Gos 155 E2
Fareham Rd. Southw 132 C3
Fareham Rd. Wickh 108 A2
Faringdon Rd. Southa 104 B4
Farleigh Cl. Hav 135 E3
Farley Cl. Fa Oa 57 E1
Farley Cl. Winch 10 A2
Farley Ct. Southa 78 B1
Farley La. Brai 7 F1
Farley La. Hurs 7 F1
Farley Mount Rd. Hurs 9 D2
Farlington Ave. Cos 134 B1
Farlington Rd. Ports 157 F1
Farm Cl. Rin 141 D4
Farm Edge Rd. Stubb 154 B1
Farm La (N). B on S 212 A4
Farm La S. B on S 212 A4
Farm La. Southb 161 F4
Farm Rd. Lo He 129 F1
Farm Rd. W Moo 138 B1
Farm View Ave. Clanf 88 A3
Farm View. Ems 136 C2
Farmdene Cl. Christ 210 B4
Farmers Wlk. Hord 213 E4
Farmery Cl. Southa 79 E2
Farmhouse Way. Wat 112 A3
Farmlea Rd. Portc 157 D4
Farmside Gdns. Ports 157 F2
Farnham Rd. Liss 20 B2
Farnham Rd. Poole 206 A4
Farnham Rd. Steep 20 B2
Farnleys Mead. Lym 198 C1

Faroes Cl. Stubb 154 A2
Farrier Way. Fare 155 D3
Farriers Cl. Wi Mi 164 A3
Farriers Way. Wat 112 B1
Farriers Wlk. Gos 181 E3
Farringdon Rd. Hav 136 A2
Farringford Rd. Southa 104 B3
Farthing La. Ports 182 A2
Farthings Gate. Wat 134 C2
Farwell Cl. Burt 193 E2
Farwell Rd. Poole 189 E1
Fastnet Cl. Southa 77 F3
Fastnet Way. Stubb 154 A2
Fathersfield. Brock 145 F1
Fathoms Reach. S Hay 184 C2
Fawcett Rd. New M 195 F1
Fawcett Rd. Ports 182 C2
Fawley By Pass. Faw 151 D2
Fawley Green. Bour 191 E2
Fawley La. Frox G 17 D2
Fawley La. Ows 33 D4
Fawley Rd. Faw 150 C2
Fawley Rd. Hyt 150 A4
Fawley Rd. Ports 157 F3
Fawley Rd. Southa 102 A3
Fay Cl. Stubb 154 B1
Fayre La. Fare 155 D4
Fearon Rd. Ports 157 F1
Felix Rd. Gosp 181 D4
Fell Cl. Lo He 129 D2
Fell Dr. L on S 179 F4
Felmer Dr. Ki Wo 2 B4
Feltham Cl. Rom 53 E4
Felton Cres. Christ 210 C4
Felton Rd. Poole 204 C3
Feltons Pl. Ports 157 F3
Fenleigh Cl. B on S 196 A1
Fennel Gdns. Lym 198 C3
Fennell Cl. Wat 111 E1
Fenton Rd. Bour 208 B3
Fern Barrow. Poole 206 A4
Fern Cl. Alderh 93 D3
Fern Cl. Burt 193 E1
Fern Cl. Pet 41 E2
Fern Rd. Hyt 125 F2
Fern Rd. Southa 103 F1
Fern Way. Lo He 129 E2
Ferncroft Cl. Stubb 154 B1
Ferncroft Gdns. Bour 190 B3
Ferncroft Rd. Bour 190 B3
Ferndale Mews. Gos 155 D2
Ferndale Rd. March 101 F1
Ferndale Rd. New M 196 A3
Ferndale. He En 105 E3
Ferndale. Wat 135 D4
Ferndene Way. Southa 103 F4
Ferneham Rd. Fare 130 B1
Fernglade. New M 196 A2
Fernheath Cl. Bour 190 A2
Fernheath Rd. Bour 190 A2
Fernhill Cl. Poole 189 D1
Fernhill La. New M 196 A2
Fernhill Rd. New M 196 A2
Fernhills Rd. Hyt 126 A1
Fernhurst Cl. S Hay 184 B2
Fernhurst Rd. Ports 182 C2
Fernie Cl. Stubb 154 A1
Fernlea Ave. Fern 165 E2
Fernlea Cl. Fern 165 E2
Fernlea Cl. St Le 139 F2
Fernlea Gdns. Fern 165 E2
Fernlea Gdns. Southa 78 C2
Fernside Ave. Poole 204 C2
Fernside Cl. Holb 150 B2
Fernside Cl. Southa 101 F4
Fernside Rd. Bour 206 C4
Fernside Rd. Poole 204 C2
Fernside Rd. W Moo 138 C1
Fernside Way. Fa Oa 57 F1
Fernwood Cl. St Le 140 A3
Fernwood Cres. Southa 103 F4
Fernyhurst Ave. Rown 77 F3
Ferris Ave. Bour 191 E1
Ferris Cl. Bour 191 E1
Ferris Pl. Bour 191 E1
Ferrol Rd. Gos 181 E3
Ferry Rd. Bour 208 C2
Ferry Rd. Br Is 211 D1
Ferry Rd. Hamw 204 A1
Ferry Rd. Hyt 125 F2
Ferry Rd. Ports 183 E2
Ferry Rd. S Hay 184 A2
Ferry Way. Poole 211 D2
Ferrybridge Green. He En 105 E3
Festing Gr. Ports 183 D1
Festing Rd. Ports 182 C1
Feversham Ave. Bour 191 F1
Fey Rd. Gos 181 E3
Fibbards Rd. Brock 145 F1
Field Cl. Comp 31 E3
Field Cl. Gos 155 D3
Field Cl. Lo He 129 D1
Field Cl. Rom 53 D4
Field Cl. Southa 79 E3
Field End. Ki Wo 2 B4
Field Way. Christ 194 B1
Field Way. Comp 31 E3
Field Way. Den 110 C2
Field Wlk. Lym 198 B3
Fielden Cl. N Bad 53 F2
Fielders' Way. W Wel 51 D1
Fieldfare Cl. Clanf 88 B2
Fieldfare Ct. Tot 100 B4
Fieldmore Rd. Gosp 181 D4
Fields Cl. Black 150 C1
Fieldway. Rin 141 D4
Fifth Ave. Cos 157 F4
Fifth Ave. Hav 136 A1
Fifth St. Ports 182 C3
Filmer Cl. Gos 180 B4
Filmorehill La. Frox G 17 D2
Filton Cl. Tot 76 B1
Filton Rd. Lym 198 B2
Finch Rd. Ports 183 E2
Finch's La. Twyf 32 A3
Finchdean Rd. Hav 135 E2
Finchdean Rd. Ro Ca 113 E2
Finchfield Ave. Bour 189 F3
Finchmead La. Pet 40 A2
Findon Rd. Gosp 181 D4
Finisterre Cl. Stubb 154 A2
Finlay Cl. Southa 104 B2
Fiona Cl. Winch 11 E4
Fir Ave. New M 196 A1
Fir Cl. Lyn 121 F2
Fir Cl. W Moo 138 C2
Fir Copse Rd. Wat 134 B2
Fir Croft Dr. Ch Fo 55 E3
Fir Rd. Ashu 100 A1
Fir Tree Cl. Fa Oa 81 E4
Fir Tree Cl. St Le 139 E1
Fir Tree Gdns. Wat 112 B3
Fir Tree Hill. Alderh 93 D3
Fir Tree La. Christ 194 B1
Fir Tree Rd. Cadn 99 D4
Fir Tree Rd. S Hay 185 D2
Fir Vale Rd. Bour 206 C2
Firbank Rd. Bour 207 D4
Firecrest Cl. Southa 78 A3
Firgrove Cl. N Bad 53 F2
Firgrove Cres. Ports 157 F3
Firgrove La. Southw 108 C1
Firgrove Rd. N Bad 54 A3
Firgrove Rd. Southa 102 B4
Firlands Rise. Cos 135 D1
Firmain Rd. Poole 189 E1
Firmount Cl. Hord 197 F1
Firs Ave. Wat 111 F1
Firs Cres. Ki Wo 2 A4
Firs Dr. He En 105 D3
Firs Glen Rd. Bour 206 C4
Firs Glen Rd. Ver 115 D2
Firs Glen Rd. W Moo 138 C1
Firs La. Poole 211 D4
Firs The. Gos 155 E1
Firs The. Southa 78 C2
Firs Way. Upt 203 E4
Firshill. Christ 210 C4
Firside Rd. Broa 187 E2
First Ave. Cos 157 F4
First Ave. Cos 158 C4
First Ave. Hav 136 A1
First Ave. Horn 88 B2
First Ave. Southa 101 E4
First Ave. Southb 161 E4
First Marine Ave. B on S 211 F4
Firtree Cres. Hord 196 C2
Firtree La. Fa Oa 81 D4
Firtree Way. Southa 104 A3
Fisgard Rd. Gosp 181 D4
Fisher Cl. Stubb 154 A2
Fisher Rd. Gos 155 E2
Fisher's Rd. Tot 101 D3
Fisherman's Ave. Bour 208 A2
Fishermans Rd. Poole 204 B1
Fishermans The. Ems 161 D4
Fishermans Wlk. S Hay 185 F1
Fishers Gr. Cos 158 C4
Fishers Hill. Fare 130 A1
Fishery La. S Hay 185 E1
Fishlake Meadows. Rom 28 A1
Fitzharris Ave. Bour 207 D4
Fitzherbert Rd. Cos 158 C4
Fitzherbert Spur. Cos 158 C4
Fitzherbert St. Ports 182 B3
Fitzhugh Pl. Southa 102 C4
Fitzmaurice Rd. Christ 208 C4
Fitzpain Cl. Fern 165 E1
Fitzpain Rd. Fern 165 E1
Fitzpatrick Ct. Cos 133 E1
Fitzroy Cl. Rown 78 C4
Fitzwilliam Ave. Stubb 154 A1
Fitzwilliam Cl. Bour 189 F3
Fitzworth Ave. Hamw 203 E2
Fitzwygram Cres. Hav 135 F2
Five Elms Dr. Rom 53 E3
Five Heads Rd. Horn 112 A4
Five Post La. Gos 181 D3
Fivefields Cl. Winch 11 E4
Fivefields Rd. Winch 11 E4
Flag Wlk. Wat 111 F2
Flaghead Chine Rd. Poole 211 F3
Flambard Ave. Christ 193 D1
Flambard Rd. Poole 205 E2
Flamborough Cl. Southa 77 E2
Flamingo Ct. Portc 155 F4
Flamston St. Crouch 22 A4
Flanders Rd. He En 105 D4
Flathouse Rd. Ports 182 B4
Fleet Cl. Gos 155 E1
Fleet End Bottom. Lo He 152 C4
Fleet End Rd. Lo He 152 C4
Fleetend Cl. Hav 135 F3
Fleets Est. Poole 204 A3
Fleetsbridge Bus Ctre. Broa 204 A4
Fleming Ave. N Bad 54 A2
Fleming Cl. Lo He 129 E2
Fleming Ct. N Bad 54 A2
Fleming Pl. Co Com 31 F1
Fletcher Cl. Bour 190 B2
Fletcher Rd. Bour 190 B2
Fletchwood La. Ashu 99 F1
Fletchwood Rd. Tot 100 A3
Fleuret Cl. Hyt 126 A1
Flexford Cl. Ch Fo 30 A1
Flexford Gdns. Hav 136 A2
Flexford La. Sway 197 E3
Flexford Rd. N Bad 54 C4
Flint St. Ports 182 A2
Floating Bridge Rd. Southa 103 E2
Floral Farm. Oakl 164 A1
Florence Cl. W Wel 51 D1
Florence Rd. Bour 207 F2
Florence Rd. Poole 205 E2
Florence Rd. Ports 182 B1
Florence Rd. Southa 103 E1
Florentine Way. Wat 135 D4
Florins The. Wat 134 C2
Floriston Gdns. New M 196 B2
Flowerdown Cl. Tot 100 B4
Flowers Cl. Hamble 127 F2
Flowers La. Plai 50 B3
Flushards. Lym 198 C2
Flying Bull Cl. Ports 182 B4
Flying Bull La. Ports 182 B4
Foldsgate Cl. Lyn 121 F3
Folkestone Rd. Ports 183 D4
Folly Farm La. St Le 140 B3
Folly Field. Bi Wa 83 E4
Folly La. Pet 40 C2
Font Cl. Lo He 129 E2
Fontley Rd. Swanw 130 A3
Fontmell Rd. Broa 188 B2
Fontwell Cl. Tot 76 B1
Fontwell Mews. Wat 112 A1
Fontwell Rd. Ports 182 B1
Foord Rd. He En 105 D2
Football Green. Min 98 B2
Footner Cl. Rom 28 B1
Footners La. Burt 193 E1
Forbes Cl. Southa 77 F3
Forbes Rd. Ki Wo 2 A4
Forbury Rd. Ports 182 B2
Ford Ave. Ch Fo 55 E2
Ford Cl. Fern 165 F4
Ford La. Fern 166 A4
Ford Rd. Gos 180 C3
Fordingbridge Rd. Alderh 93 D4
Fordingbridge Rd. Fordi 93 D4
Fordingbridge Rd. Ports 183 D2
Fordington Ave. Winch 10 C4
Fordington Rd. Winch 1 C1
Foreland Cl. Christ 192 B2
Foreland Ct. S Hay 185 E1
Foreland Rd. Hamw 203 E2
Forest Ave. Wat 112 A2
Forest Cl. Ch Fo 55 E4
Forest Cl. Christ 194 B1
Forest Cl. N Bad 53 F3
Forest Cl. Shed 83 F2
Forest Cl. Ver 115 E2
Forest Cl. Wat 111 F2
Forest Cnr. Liss 21 D4
Forest Ct. New M 196 A1
Forest Edge Cl. St Le 139 E3
Forest Edge Dr. St Le 139 E3
Forest Edge Rd. Rin 141 F3
Forest Edge. Fawl 151 D2
Forest End. Wat 134 B4
Forest Front. Hyt 150 A4
Forest Gate. Black 177 F4
Forest Gdns. Lyn 121 F3
Forest Gdns. Shed 83 F2
Forest Glade Cl. Brock 145 E1
Forest Hall. Brock 146 A1
Forest Hill Way. Hyt 125 F1
Forest Hills Dr. Southa 79 F2
Forest La. Fare 131 D4
Forest La. Holb 150 A3
Forest La. Rin 141 F3
Forest Mead. Den 110 C2
Forest Meadow. Hyt 150 A4
Forest Park Rd. Brock 145 F1
Forest Pines. New M 196 A2
Forest Rd. Bran 169 F2
Forest Rd. Bur 143 D3
Forest Rd. Ch Fo 55 E4
Forest Rd. Den 110 B2
Forest Rd. Greath 20 C4
Forest Rd. Liss 21 D3
Forest Rd. Poole 206 A1
Forest Rd. Red 47 F2
Forest Rd. Shed 83 F2
Forest Rd. Swan 83 F2
Forest Rd. W Moo 138 C2
Forest Rd. Woodg 47 F2
Forest Rise. Christ 194 B1
Forest Rise. Liss 21 D3
Forest View Cl. Bour 191 D1
Forest View Dr. Fern 165 D3
Forest View Rd. Bour 191 D1
Forest View. Southa 102 C2
Forest Way. Christ 194 B1
Forest Way. Fern 165 D3
Forest Way. Gos 155 F1
Forest Way. Hord 197 E1
Forester Rd. Sob 85 D1
Foresters Gate. Black 177 E4
Foresters Rd. Black 150 C1
Forestside Ave. Hav 136 A3
Forestside Gdns. Rin 117 E1
Forge Cl. Burs 105 D1
Forge Rd. Black 177 F4
Forneth Gdns. Fare 154 A4
Forster Rd. Southa 103 D4
Forsyth Gdns. Bour 190 B1
Forsythia Cl. He En 105 D4
Fort Cumberland Pl. Hamw 203 E1
Fort Cumberland Rd. Ports 183 E2
Fort Fareham Rd. Fare 154 C3
Fort Rd. Gos 181 D1
Fort Rd. Southa 103 F2
Fortescue Rd. Bour 207 D3
Fortescue Rd. Poole 205 E4
Forth Cl. N Bad 55 D3
Forth Cl. Stubb 154 A2
Forties Cl. Stubb 154 A2
Forton Rd. Gos 181 D3
Forton Rd. Ports 182 C3
Fortunes Way. Cos 134 C1
Forward Dr. Lym 198 B1
Foster Cl. Stubb 154 B2
Foster Rd. Gos 181 D2
Foster Rd. Ports 182 B3
Founders Way. Gos 155 E1
Foundry Cres. Burs 127 F4
Foundry La. Southa 102 A4
Foundry Rd. Red 47 E4
Fountain Ct. He En 105 D3
Fountain St. Ports 182 B3
Fountain Way. Christ 209 D3
Four Acre. Botl 106 A3
Four Marks Green. Hav 136 A3
Four Wells Rd. Wi Mi 164 A4
Fourpost Hill. Southa 102 C3
Fourshells Cl. Black 150 C1
Fourth Ave. Cos 157 F4
Fourth Ave. Hav 136 A1
Fourth St. Ports 182 C3
Fowey Cl. N Bad 55 D3
Fowey The. Black 150 C1
Fowlers Rd. He En 105 D4
Fowlers Wlk. Chilw 54 B1
Fox Cl. Bish 56 C1
Fox Field. Hord 197 E1
Fox La. Fern 164 B3
Fox La. Winch 10 B3
Fox Pound La. Lym 198 B1
Fox's Paddock. Black 177 F4
Foxbury Cl. Hyt 126 A1
Foxbury Gr. Portc 156 A4
Foxbury La. Gos 155 E2
Foxbury La. Westb 137 E2
Foxbury Rd. St Le 166 C4
Foxcote Gdns. New M 195 F2
Foxcott Cl. Southa 126 C4
Foxcott Gr. Hav 135 F3
Foxcroft Dr. Holb 150 A2
Foxcroft Dr. Wi Mi 164 A3
Foxes Cl. Ver 114 C3
Foxes Cl. Wat 134 C3
Foxes La. Nur 77 D2
Foxes La. Plai 50 C3
Foxglove Pl. New M 196 B2
Foxgloves. Fare 88 B2
Foxhayes La. Black 177 F4
Foxhills Cl. Ashu 100 B2
Foxhills. Ashu 100 B2
Foxhills. Ver 115 D3
Foxholes Rd. Bour 208 C2
Foxholes Rd. Poole 204 C3
Foxlands. Black 177 F4
Foxlea Gdns. Gosp 181 D4
Foxley Dr. Ports 158 A2
Foxtail Dr. Hyt 125 F1
Foxwood Ave. Christ 209 F3
Foy Gdns. Lo He 128 B1
Foyle Rd. N Bad 55 D3
Frampton Cl. Co Com 31 F1
Frampton Cl. New M 196 B3
Frampton Rd. Bour 207 D4
Frampton Way. Ki Wo 2 B4
Frampton Way. Tot 100 C3
Frances Rd. Bour 207 E2
Frances Rd. Wat 134 B2
Francis Ave. Bour 189 E2
Francis Ave. Ports 182 C2
Francis Cl. Lon S 180 A3
Francis Gdns. Winch 2 A2
Francis Pl. Stubb 154 B1
Francis Rd. Horn 88 B2
Francis Rd. Poole 205 F3
Frankland Cres. Poole 205 F2
Franklin Rd. Bour 191 D2
Franklin Rd. Gos 180 B4
Franklin Rd. New M 196 B2
Franklin Rd. Twyf 32 A4
Franklyn Ave. Southa 104 A2
Franklyn Cl. Upt 203 D4
Franks Way. Poole 205 D4
Frankston Rd. Bour 208 B2
Fraydene. Southb 161 E4
Fraser Cl. Southa 77 F3
Fraser Gdns. Southb 137 F1
Fraser Rd. Gos 155 E2
Fraser Rd. Hav 135 E1
Fraser Rd. Ki Wo 2 B4
Fraser Rd. Poole 205 F4
Fraser Rd. Ports 182 B2
Frater La. Gos 156 A1
Fratton Rd. Ports 182 C3
Fratton Way. Fa Oa 57 E1
Frayslea. Hyt 126 A1
Freda Rd. Christ 208 C3
Freda Routh Gdns. Fa Oa 57 E1
Frederica Rd. Bour 206 C4
Frederick St. Ports 182 B3
Frederick St. Southa 103 D3
Free St. Bi Wa 83 E4
Freefolk Green. Hav 136 A3
Freegrounds Ave. He En 105 E3
Freegrounds Cl. He En 105 E3
Freegrounds Rd. He En 105 E3
Freemans La. Wi Mi 164 A3
Freemantle Cl. Southa 103 F3
Freemantle Com Rd. Southa 103 F3
Freemantle Rd. Gosp 181 D4
Freestone Rd. Ports 182 B1
French Rd. Broa 188 A1
French St. Ports 182 A2
French St. Southa 102 C2
French's Farm Rd. Upt 203 D4
Frenches La. W Wel 51 E4
Frenchmans Rd. Pet 40 C2
Frenchmoor La. E Dean 3 F2
Frenchmoor La. W Tyth 3 F2
Frendstaple Rd. Wat 135 D3
Frensham Cl. Bour 190 C2
Frensham Cl. He En 105 E3
Frensham Ct. He En 105 E3
Frensham Rd. Ports 182 C2
Freshfield Gdns. Wat 134 C4
Freshfield Rd. Southa 102 A4
Freshfield Sq. Southa 102 A4
Freshwater Dr. Hamw 203 E2
Freshwater Rd. Christ 210 B3
Freshwater Rd. Cos 157 F4
Friars Croft. Tot 76 B1
Friars Pond Rd. Fare 130 B1
Friars Rd. Christ 210 A3
Friars Rd. Eastl 55 F1
Friars Way. Southa 79 E2
Friars Wlk. B on S 212 A4
Friarscroft. Net 127 D4
Friarsgate. Winch 11 D4
Friary Cl. Ports 182 B1
Frith La. Wickh 108 A4
Fritham Cl. Tot 100 B4
Fritham Gdns. Bour 191 E2
Fritham Rd. Southa 104 B4
Frobisher Ave. Poole 189 F1
Frobisher Cl. Christ 209 F3
Frobisher Cl. Gos 180 B3
Frobisher Cl. Rin 117 E1
Frobisher Gdns. Southa 104 B2
Frobisher Gr. Portc 156 B4
Froddington Rd. Ports 182 B2
Froghall. Hyt 126 A1
Frogham Green. Hav 135 E3
Frogham Hill. Fordi 94 B3
Frogmore La. Horn 112 A3
Frogmore La. Nur 77 E2
Frogmore La. Wat 112 A3
Frogmore Rd. Ports 183 D3
Frogmore. Fare 154 B4
Frome Cl. March 102 A1
Fromond Cl. Lym 198 C3
Fromond Rd. Winch 1 B2
Frost La. Hyt 126 A1
Frost Rd. Bour 189 F2
Frosthole Cl. Fare 130 C2
Frosthole Cres. Fare 130 C2
Froxfield Cl. Winch 1 B2
Froxfield Gdns. Portc 132 B1
Fry Cl. Hamble 128 A2
Fry's La. Meons 61 E2
Fryern Cl. Ch Fo 55 F3
Fryern Court Rd. Fordi 69 F3
Fryers Copse. Wi Mi 164 B3
Fryers Rd. W Moo 138 B4
Frys La. Hord 197 E1
Fuchsia Gdns. Southa 78 B1
Fulflood Rd. Hav 135 F3
Fullerton Cl. Hav 136 A3
Fullerton Cl. Southa 126 C4
Fullerton Rd. Lym 198 B2
Fulmar Cl. Southa 78 A3
Fulmar Rd. Christ 210 A3
Fulmar Wlk. Gos 155 D2
Fulmer Wlk. Wat 111 F2
Fulwood Ave. Bour 189 F3
Funtington Rd. Ports 182 C4
Funtley Hill. Fare 130 C2
Funtley La. Fare 130 C3
Funtley Rd. Fare 130 C3

Furley Cl. Winch 11 D4
Furneaux Gdns. Fare 88 A2
Furnell Rd. Poole 204 B1
Furness Rd. Ports 182 B1
Furnston Gr. Southb 137 F1
Fury Way. Stubb 154 A2
Furze Cl. Southa 104 A3
Furze Croft. New M 196 A1
Furze Hill Dr. Poole 205 E1
Furze La. Ports 183 E2
Furze Rd. Southa 104 A3
Furze Way. Wat 112 A2
Furzebrook Cl. Broa 188 C2
Furzedale Gdns. Hyt 126 A1
Furzedale Park. Hyt 126 A1
Furzedown Cres. Hav 136 A3
Furzedown Mews. Hyt 126 A1
Furzedown Rd. Ki So 7 D4
Furzedown Rd. Southa 79 D1
Furzehall Ave. Fare 88 A2
Furzehill. Wi Mi 163 E4
Furzelands Rd. W Moo 138 C4
Furzeley Rd. Den 110 C1
Furzey Ave. Hyt 126 A1
Furzey Cl. Black 150 C1
Furzey La. E Bol 148 A1
Furzey Rd. Upt 203 D3
Furzley Ct. Hav 135 E3
Furzley La. Bramsh 74 B3
Furzley Rd. Cadn 74 B2
Furzy Whistlers Cl. Bran 169 D1
Fyeford Cl. Rown 77 F3
Fyning St. Ports 182 B3

Gage Cl. March 102 A1
Gain's Rd. Ports 182 C1
Gainsborough Ave. New M 196 A3
Gainsborough Cl. Southa 104 B1
Gainsborough Ct. Bour 208 A3
Gainsborough Rd. Bour 207 F4
Gainsborough Rd. St Le 139 F3
Gainsford Rd. Southa 103 F3
Galaxie Rd. Wat 112 A2
Gale Moor Ave. Gos 180 B2
Gallops The. Lo He 129 E1
Galloway Rd. Hamw 203 E2
Gallows Dr. Fern 165 F1
Galsworthy Rd. Tot 100 B4
Galt Rd. Cos 158 C4
Galton Ave. Christ 208 C3
Gamble Cl. Southa 103 F2
Gamble Rd. Ports 182 B4
Gamblins La. Shed 107 F4
Ganger Farm La. Rom 28 B1
Ganger Rd. Rom 28 B1
Gannet Cl. Hyt 126 A1
Gannet Cl. Southa 78 A3
Gannets The. Stubb 154 A2
Garbett Rd. Winch 11 E4
Garden City. Hyt 125 D3
Garden Cl. Lyn 121 F3
Garden Cl. New M 196 A1
Garden Cl. S Hay 184 C2
Garden Ct. Portc 156 B4
Garden La. Ports 182 B2
Garden La. St Le 139 F2
Garden La. Winch 11 D4
Garden Mews. Lo He 128 B1
Garden Rd. Bur 142 C2
Garden Wlk. Fern 165 F4
Gardeners La. Awb 52 A2
Gardeners La. Rom 52 A2
Gardens Cres. Poole 211 D4
Gardens Rd. Poole 211 D4
Gardens The. Hambl 86 B2
Gardens The. Hav 136 A1
Gardiner Cl. March 102 A1
Gardner Rd. Christ 208 C4
Gardner Rd. Lo He 153 F4
Gardner Rd. Rin 141 D3
Garendon Ct. Fordi 69 F1
Garfield Ave. Bour 207 E3
Garfield Cl. Bi Wa 83 E4
Garfield Rd. Bi Wa 83 E4
Garfield Rd. Net 127 D3
Garfield Rd. Ports 182 B4
Garfield Rd. Southa 103 F4
Garland Av. Ems 136 C2
Garland Rd. Poole 204 B2
Garnett Cl. Stubb 154 B2
Garnier Park. Wickh 108 A2
Garnier Rd. Winch 11 D3
Garnier St. Ports 182 C3
Garnock Rd. Southa 103 E1
Garrick Gdns. Southa 104 A1
Garrison Hill. Drox 61 D1
Garrow Dr. Lym 198 C3
Garsdale Cl. Bour 190 A3
Garsons Rd. Southb 161 E4
Garston Cl. E Meon 63 E4
Garstons Cl. Lo He 153 F4
Garstons Rd. Lo He 153 F4
Garth Cl. St Le 139 E2
Garth Rd. Bour 191 D1
Garton Rd. Southa 103 E2
Gashouse Hill. Net 127 E3
Gatcombe Ave. Ports 158 A1
Gatcombe Dr. Ports 157 F2
Gatcombe Gdns. Fare 154 A4
Gatcombe Gdns. W End 80 A1
Gatcombe. Net 127 E4
Gate House Rd. Portc 156 A4
Gatwick Cl. Southa 78 A2
Gaydon Rise. Bour 189 F2
Gaylyn Way. Fare 154 A4
Gaza Ave. E Bol 175 E3
Gazing La. W Wel 50 C2
Geddes Way. Pet 41 E2
Gemini Cl. Southa 77 F2
Geneva Ave. Bour 208 B3
Genoa Cl. Lym 198 B1
Gento Cl. He En 105 F3
Geoffrey Ave. Wat 134 A1
Geoffrey Cres. Fare 155 D3
George Byng Way. Ports 182 B4
George Eyston Dr. Winch 10 B3
George Rd. M on S 213 E3
George St. Eastl 56 A2
George St. Gos 181 E3
George St. Ports 182 C4
Georges Mews. Broa 187 E4
Georgian Cl. Rin 141 D4
Georgian Way. Bour 190 C2
Georgina Cl. Poole 206 B4
Gerald Rd. Bour 207 D3
Gerard Cres. Southa 104 B3
Germaine Cl. Christ 210 C4
Gervis Cres. Poole 205 D2
Gervis Pl. Bour 206 C2
Gervis Rd. Bour 207 D2
Gibbs Rd. Southa 102 C3
Gibraltar Cl. Fare 130 B1
Gibraltar Rd. Ports 183 E2
Gibson Cl. L on S 179 F4
Gibson Rd. Poole 204 C4
Giddylake. Wi Mi 163 E3
Gifford Cl. Fare 130 C2
Gilbert Cl. Alderh 93 D3
Gilbert Cl. Gos 180 B4
Gilbert Cl. Lym 198 B1
Gilbert Mead. S Hay 184 C2
Gilbert Rd. Bour 207 E3
Gilbert Way. Wat 134 C3
Gilbury Cl. Southa 79 F2
Giles Cl. Fare 88 A2
Giles Cl. Gos 181 D3
Giles Cl. He En 81 E1
Giles Hill. Winch 11 D4
Giles La. Lan 50 A2
Gilkicker Rd. Gos 181 E1
Gillam Rd. Bour 190 B3
Gillcrest. Lo He 129 E2
Gillies The. Fare 131 D1
Gillingham Cl. Bour 191 E2
Gillingham Cl. Ki Wo 2 B4
Gillingham Rd. M on S 213 E2
Gillman Rd. Cos 134 C1
Gilpin Cl. Bold 173 F1
Gilpin Cl. Southa 104 C3
Gilpin Hill. Sway 172 A1
Girton Cl. Lo He 129 E1
Gitsham Gdns. Wat 134 B2
Gladdis Rd. Bour 189 F2
Glade The. Black 177 F4
Glade The. Ch Fo 30 C1
Glade The. Fare 130 B2
Glade The. S Hay 185 E1
Glade The. St Le 139 F3
Glade The. Wat 135 D4
Gladelands Way. Broa 187 F2
Glades The. Lo He 129 D2
Gladstone Cl. Christ 209 E3
Gladstone Gdns. Portc 156 B4
Gladstone Pl. Ports 182 B4
Gladstone Rd E. Bour 207 F3
Gladstone Rd W. Bour 207 E3
Gladstone Rd. Bour 207 F3
Gladstone Rd. Gos 181 D4
Gladstone Rd. Poole 205 E3
Gladstone Rd. Southa 104 A3
Gladys Ave. Ports 157 E1
Gladys Ave. Wat 112 A2
Glamis Ave. Bour 190 C3
Glamis Cl. Wat 135 D4
Glamorgan Rd. Horn 88 A2
Glasgow Rd. Ports 183 D2
Glasslaw Rd. Southa 104 A4
Glasspool. Den 110 C3
Gleadowe Ave. Christ 208 C3
Glebe Cl. S Hay 184 C3
Glebe Cnr. Wickh 108 A2
Glebe Ct. Botl 106 A4
Glebe Ct. Fa Oa 57 E1
Glebe Ct. Southa 79 D1
Glebe Dr. Gos 155 E1
Glebe Meadow. E Dean 4 A1
Glebe Park Ave. Cos 135 D1
Glebe Rd. Buri 65 E3
Glebe Rd. Southa 103 D2
Glebe The. Stubb 154 B1
Glebefields. M on S 213 E3
Glen Cl. B on S 211 E4
Glen Dale. Ro Ca 113 E1
Glen Eyre Dr. Southa 79 D3
Glen Eyre Rd. Southa 78 C3
Glen Eyre Way. Southa 79 D2
Glen Fern Rd. Bour 207 D2
Glen Rd. Bour 207 F2
Glen Rd. Lo He 128 C4
Glen Rd. Poole 205 D2
Glen Rd. Southa 103 E1
Glen Rd. Swanw 128 C4
Glen Spey. New M 196 B1
Glen The. Gos 155 F1
Glenair Ave. Poole 205 D2
Glenair Cres. Poole 205 D2
Glenair Rd. Poole 205 D2
Glenavon Rd. Christ 194 C1
Glenavon. New M 196 B1
Glenbrook Wlk. Fare 154 B4
Glencarron Way. Southa 78 C2
Glencoe Rd. Bour 207 F4
Glencoe Rd. Poole 205 E3
Glencoe Rd. Ports 182 C4
Glencoyne Gdns. Southa 77 F1
Glenda Cl. Lo He 152 B4
Glendale Ave. Fern 165 F3
Glendale Cl. Christ 192 B2
Glendale Cl. Wi Mi 163 E3
Glendale Rd. Bour 209 D2
Glendale. Lo He 129 D1
Glendale. Swan 84 A2
Glendon Ave. Bour 190 B3
Glendowan Rd. N Bad 55 D4
Glendrive. B on S 211 E4
Gleneagles Ave. Poole 205 E1
Gleneagles Cl. Fern 165 F3
Gleneagles Dr. Wat 112 A1
Glenelg. Fare 130 C1
Glenesha Gdns. Fare 130 C1
Glenferness Ave. Bour 206 B3
Glenfield Ave. Southa 103 F4
Glenfield Cres. Southa 103 F4
Glenfield Way. Southa 103 F4
Glengariff Rd. Poole 205 E2
Glengarry Way. Christ 210 B3
Glengarry. New M 196 B1
Glenives Cl. St Le 140 A2
Glenlea Cl. W End 80 B1
Glenlea Dr. W End 80 B1
Glenleigh Ave. Cos 157 F4
Glenleigh Park. Hav 136 A1
Glenmeadows Dr. Bour 190 D3
Glenmoor Cl. Bour 190 B1
Glenmoor Rd. Bour 206 C4
Glenmoor Rd. Fern 165 E2
Glenmount Dr. Poole 205 D2
Glenn Rd. W End 80 B1
Glenroyd Gdns. Bour 208 C2
Glenside Ave. Southa 104 B2
Glenside. Christ 211 D4
Glenside. Hyt 125 F2
Glenthorne Cl. Stubb 154 B1
Glenthorne Meadow. E Meo 38 C1
Glenthorne Rd. Ports 158 A1
Glenville Cl. Christ 195 D1
Glenville Rd. Bour 190 B1
Glenville Rd. Christ 195 D1
Glenwood Ave. Southa 79 D3
Glenwood Cl. W Moo 138 C1
Glenwood Ct. Fa Oa 57 F1
Glenwood Gdns. Wat 111 F2
Glenwood La. W Moo 138 C1
Glenwood Rd. Southb 137 F1
Glenwood Rd. Ver 114 C3
Glenwood Rd. W Moo 138 C1
Glenwood Way. W Moo 138 C1
Glidden Cl. Ports 182 B3
Glidden La. Hambl 86 C2
Glissons. Fern 165 D1
Globe La. Poole 204 B1
Gloster Ct. Lo He 129 E3
Gloucester Cl. Pet 40 B2
Gloucester Pl. Ports 182 B2
Gloucester Rd. Bour 207 F3
Gloucester Rd. Poole 205 F3
Gloucester Rd. Wat 134 C3
Gloucester Terr. Ports 182 B2
Gloucester View. Ports 182 B2
Glyn Dr. Stubb 154 B1
Glyn Way. Stubb 154 B1
Glynville Cl. Wi Mi 164 A4
Glynville Rd. Wi Mi 164 A4
Goathorn Cl. Hamw 203 E2
Goddard Cl. W Wel 50 C2
Godiva Lawn. Ports 183 E2
Godmanston Cl. Poole 189 D1
Godshill Cl. Bour 191 E2
Godwin Cl. Ems 136 C2
Godwin Cl. Winch 1 B1
Godwit Cl. Gos 181 D4
Godwit Rd. Ports 183 E3
Gofton Ave. Cos 158 A4
Goggs La. Red 47 F3
Gold Mead Cl. Lym 198 C1
Gold St. Ports 182 A2
Goldcrest Gdns. Southa 78 A3
Goldcrest La. Tot 100 B4
Golden Cres. Hord 197 E1
Golden Ct. W End 80 C2
Golden Gr. Southa 103 D3
Golden Hind Park. Hyt 125 F1
Goldfinch La. L on S 179 F4
Goldfinch Rd. Broa 203 F4
Goldring Cl. S Hay 185 D2
Goldsmith Ave. Ports 182 C2
Goldsmith Cl. Tot 100 B4
Goldsmith Rd. Eastl 55 F1
Golf Course Rd. Southa 78 C3
Golf Links Rd. Broa 188 A3
Golf Links Rd. Fern 165 F2
Goliath Rd. Hamw 203 E1
Gomer La. Gos 180 C2
Good Rd. Poole 205 E4
Good Rd. Poole 205 E4
Goodens The. Cher 14 B3
Goodison Cl. Fa Oa 57 D1
Goodlands Vale. He En 105 D4
Goodsell Cl. Stubb 154 A1
Goodwin Cl. Southa 77 E1
Goodwood Cl. Gos 181 D4
Goodwood Cl. Lo He 129 E1
Goodwood Cl. Wat 112 A1
Goodwood Ct. Southb 161 F4
Goodwood Gdns. Tot 100 B4
Goodwood Rd. Eastl 55 F2
Goodwood Rd. Gos 181 D4
Goodwood Rd. Ports 182 C2
Gordon Ave. Southa 103 D4
Gordon Ave. Winch 11 E3
Gordon Mount. Christ 211 D4
Gordon Rd S. Poole 206 A3
Gordon Rd. Bour 207 E2
Gordon Rd. Ch Fo 30 B1
Gordon Rd. Christ 211 D4
Gordon Rd. Curd 83 D1
Gordon Rd. Fare 88 A1
Gordon Rd. Gos 181 D2
Gordon Rd. Herm 161 D4
Gordon Rd. Lym 198 B2
Gordon Rd. Poole 206 A3
Gordon Rd. Ports 182 A2
Gordon Rd. Wat 134 B3
Gordon Rd. Wi Mi 163 F2
Gordon Rd. Winch 11 D4
Gordon Terr. Southa 104 A1
Gordon Way. Burt 193 E1
Gore Rd. New M 195 F1
Gorey Ave. Poole 189 E1
Goring Ave. Clanf 88 B2
Goring Field. Winch 1 B1
Gorleston Rd. Poole 205 F3
Gorley Ct. Hav 135 E3
Gorley Lynch. Fordi 94 B2
Gorley Rd. Rin 117 E1
Gorran Ave. Gos 155 E1
Gorse Cl. Lo He 128 C1
Gorse Cl. New M 196 B2
Gorse Cl. St Le 139 E2
Gorse Hill Cres. Poole 204 C3
Gorse Hill Rd. Poole 204 C3
Gorse La. Upt 203 E4
Gorse Rd. Broa 187 E3
Gorse Rd. Pet 41 E2
Gorsecliff Rd. Bour 190 B1
Gorsefield Cres. New M 196 A2
Gorseland Ct. Fern 165 F2
Gorselands Rd. Southa 80 A1
Gorselands Way. Gos 180 B4
Gort Cres. Southa 104 A2
Gort Rd. Bour 190 A2
Gort Rd. Broa 188 A1
Gosling Cl. Poole 204 C4
Gosport La. Lyn 122 A2
Gosport Rd. Fare 155 D4
Gosport Rd. L on S 179 F3
Gosport Rd. Stubb 154 C1
Gosport St. Lym 198 C2
Gough Cres. Broa 188 A1
Gould Cl. Gos 180 B3
Gover Rd. Southa 101 E4
Grace Dieu Gdns. Burs 104 C1
Grace La. Woodg 70 C4
Graddidge Way. Tot 100 B3
Graemar La. Sh En 25 E1
Grafton Cl. Christ 209 E3
Grafton Gdns. Lym 198 B1
Grafton Gdns. Southa 78 B3
Grafton Rd. Bour 207 D3
Grafton Rd. Winch 10 C3
Graham Rd. Gos 181 D4
Graham Rd. Ports 182 C2
Graham Rd. Southa 103 D3
Graham St. Southa 103 E3
Grainger Gdns. Southa 104 B2
Grammar School La. Wi Mi 163 D2
Granada Cl. Wat 112 A2
Granada Rd. He En 105 D3
Granada Rd. Ports 182 C1
Granby Gr. Southa 79 D2
Granby Rd. Bour 191 D2
Grand Ave. Bour 208 B2
Grand Par. Ports 182 A2
Grand Par. S Hay 185 D1
Grange Cl. Gos 180 C3
Grange Cl. Hav 136 A1
Grange Cl. Hord 213 F4
Grange Cl. Southa 79 F2
Grange Cl. Winch 10 C2
Grange Cres. Gos 180 C3
Grange Ct. Net 127 D4
Grange Gr. Gos 155 E1
Grange La. Gos 180 B4
Grange Rd. Bour 208 B2
Grange Rd. Broa 188 A2
Grange Rd. Christ 210 A4
Grange Rd. Gos 180 B3
Grange Rd. He En 105 E4
Grange Rd. Net 127 E4
Grange Rd. Pet 40 C1
Grange Rd. Ports 157 E1
Grange Rd. Southa 78 A1
Grange Rd. St Le 139 F1
Grange Rd. Winch 10 C2
Grange The. Hord 213 F4
Grangewood Gdns. Fa Oa 57 D1
Grant Rd. Cos 158 B4
Grant's Ave. Bour 207 E3
Grantham Ave. Hamble 127 F2
Grantham Ct. Eastl 56 A1
Grantham Rd. Bour 207 E3
Grantham Rd. Eastl 56 A1
Grantham Rd. Southa 103 F3
Grantley Rd. Bour 207 F2
Grants Cl. Bour 207 F3
Granville Cl. Hav 136 A1
Granville Pl. Bour 206 C2
Granville Pl. Winch 11 D3
Granville Rd. Bour 208 A3
Granville Rd. Poole 205 D3
Granville St. Southa 103 D2
Grasdean Cl. Southa 80 A1
Grasmere Cl. Christ 192 B2
Grasmere Cl. W End 80 A1
Grasmere Gdns. New M 196 A3
Grasmere Rd. Bour 208 A2
Grasmere Rd. Poole 211 D2
Grasmere Way. Stubb 154 B2
Grasmere. Eastl 55 F1
Grassmere Way. Wat 112 B1
Grassymead. Lo He 129 E2
Grateley Cl. Southa 126 C4
Grateley Cres. Hav 135 E2
Gravel Cl. Down 46 C4
Gravel Hill. Broa 188 B3
Gravel Hill. Oakl 188 B3
Gravel Hill. Shed 84 A2
Gravel Hill. Swan 84 A2
Gravel La. Rin 140 C4
Gray Cl. Lo He 128 C1
Gray Cl. Poole 204 C4
Gray's Yd. Poole 204 B1
Graycot Cl. Bour 190 B3
Grayland Cl. S Hay 184 C2
Grays Ave. Hyt 126 A2
Grays Cl. Co Com 56 C4
Grays Cl. Gos 180 C2
Grays Cl. Rom 53 D4
Grays Ct. Ports 182 A2
Grayshott Cl. Winch 1 B2
Grayshott Rd. Gos 180 C2
Grayshott Rd. Ports 182 C2
Great Copse Dr. Hav 135 F3
Great Elms Cl. Holb 150 A2
Great Field Rd. Winch 1 B2
Great Gays. Stubb 154 A1
Great Mead. Den 111 D2
Great Mead. Lyn 121 F2
Great Minster St. Winch 11 D4
Great Southsea St. Ports 182 B2
Great Well Dr. Rom 53 D4
Greatbridge Rd. Awb 27 F1
Greatbridge Rd. Rom 27 F1
Greatfield Way. Ro Ca 113 D2
Greatwood Cl. Hyt 126 A1
Grebe Cl. Broa 203 F4
Grebe Cl. Christ 210 A3
Grebe Cl. M on S 213 F2
Grebe Cl. Portc 155 F4
Grebe Cl. Wat 111 F2
Green Acres Cl. St Le 140 B3
Green Acres. Christ 209 F4
Green Bottom. Wi Mi 164 A4
Green Cl. Hyt 126 A2
Green Cl. Ne Ma 99 F2
Green Cl. Poole 204 B1
Green Cl. Whit 24 A2
Green Cres. Gos 155 E1
Green Dr. Alderh 93 D3
Green Farm Gdns. Ports 157 F2
Green Hollow Cl. Fare 130 C2
Green Jacket Cl. Winch 10 C3
Green La. Ampf 29 D1
Green La. B on S 212 A4
Green La. Bi Wa 83 E4
Green La. Black 177 F4
Green La. Bour 190 B2
Green La. Burs 104 C1
Green La. Chilw 54 C1
Green La. Clanf 88 B3
Green La. Den 110 C2
Green La. Fern 165 D1
Green La. Fordi 69 F1
Green La. Frox G 18 C3
Green La. Gos 181 E4
Green La. Hamble 128 A1
Green La. Lo He 128 C1
Green La. Ports 158 A2
Green La. Rin 141 D4
Green La. Rin 141 E2
Green La. Rockb 69 E4
Green La. S Hay 184 C2
Green La. Sob 86 A3
Green La. Southa 77 F1
Green La. Swanw 106 A1

Green La. Swanw 128 B4
Green Park Cl. Winch 2 A1
Green Park Rd. Southa 101 F4
Green Pond La. Ampf 29 E2
Green Rd. Bour 207 D4
Green Rd. Gos 181 D1
Green Rd. Poole 204 B1
Green Rd. Ports 182 B2
Green Rd. Stubb 154 B2
Green The. Liss 20 C3
Green The. Lo He 128 C3
Green The. Ro Ca 113 E1
Green The. Rom 28 B1
Green The. Whit 24 A2
Green Ways. Swan 84 A3
Green Wlk. Fare 130 C2
Green's Cl. Bish 57 D1
Greenacre Cl. Upt 203 E3
Greenacre Gdns. Wat 134 B2
Greenacre. B on S 212 A4
Greenacres Cl. Bour 190 C3
Greenacres Dr. Ott 31 E2
Greenacres. Down 46 B4
Greenaway La. Lo He 128 B1
Greenbank Cres. Southa 78 C3
Greenbanks Cl. M on S 213 E2
Greenbanks Gdns. Fare 131 E1
Greenclose La. Wi Mi 163 E2
Greendale Cl. Ch Fo 55 F3
Greendale The. Fare 130 B2
Greenfield Gdns. B on S 212 A4
Greenfield Rd. Poole 204 C4
Greenfield Rise. Wat 112 A2
Greenfields Ave. Tot 76 C1
Greenfields Cl. Tot 76 C1
Greenfields. Liss 21 D2
Greenfinch Cl. Broa 187 F1
Greenfinch Cl. Eastl 55 E1
Greenhayes. Broa 188 B1
Greenhays Rise. Wi Mi 163 E3
Greenhill Cl. Wi Mi 163 E3
Greenhill Cl. Winch 10 C4
Greenhill La. Rown 77 F4
Greenhill La. Wi Mi 163 E3
Greenhill Rd. Wi Mi 163 E3
Greenhill Rd. Winch 10 B4
Greenhill Terr. Winch 10 C4
Greenlea Cl. Wat 134 A1
Greenlea Cres. Southa 79 E3
Greenlea Rd. Gos 180 C4
Greenmead Ave. Hord 197 E1
Greens Cl. Bi Wa 83 D4
Greens Meade. Red 47 E3
Greensleeves Ave. Broa 188 A3
Greensome Dr. Fern 165 F3
Greenway Cl. Lym 198 B2
Greenway Cres. Upt 203 D4
Greenway La. Buri 65 E3
Greenway Rd. Gos 181 D3
Greenway. E Meo 38 C1
Greenways Ave. Bour 191 E2
Greenways Rd. Brock 146 A1
Greenways. Ch Fo 55 F3
Greenways. Christ 210 C4
Greenways. M on S 213 E3
Greenways. Southa 79 E3
Greenwich The. Black 150 C1
Greenwood Ave. Cos 157 E4
Greenwood Ave. Fern 165 F3
Greenwood Ave. Poole 216 E4
Greenwood Ave. Rown 77 E3
Greenwood Cl. Eastl 55 F1
Greenwood Cl. Fare 88 A2
Greenwood Cl. Rom 53 D4
Greenwood Cl. St Le 140 A2
Greenwood La. Durl 82 F4
Greenwood Rd. Bour 206 C4
Greenwood Way. St Le 140 A2
Greetham St. Ports 182 B3
Gregory Gdns. Tot 76 B1
Gregory La. Durl 82 B3
Gregson Ave. Gos 155 E2
Gregson Cl. Gos 155 E2
Grenadier Cl. Lo He 129 D1
Grendon Cl. Southa 79 D3
Grenehurst Way. Pet 40 C2
Grenfell Rd. Bour 190 C2
Grenville Cl. Rin 117 E1
Grenville Ct. Southa 102 C4
Grenville Gdns. Hyt 126 A1
Grenville Rd. Ports 182 C2
Grenville Rd. Wi Mi 163 E2
Gresham Rd. Bour 191 D1
Greville Green. Ems 136 C2
Greville Rd. Southa 102 B4
Greyfriars Rd. Fare 130 B1
Greyshott Ave. Fare 154 B4
Greystoke Ave. Bour 189 F3
Greystones. Christ 211 D4
Greywell Ave. Southa 78 B2
Greywell Rd. Hav 135 F2
Griffin Ct. Southa 103 E4
Griffon Cl. Burs 105 D1
Grigg La. Brock 146 A1
Grindle Cl. Portc 132 B1
Gritanwood Rd. Ports 183 D2
Grosvenor Cl. Southa 79 E1
Grosvenor Cl. St Le 139 E3
Grosvenor Dr. Winch 2 A1
Grosvenor Gdns. Bour 207 F2
Grosvenor Gdns. Southa 79 E1
Grosvenor Gdns. W End 104 B4
Grosvenor Rd. Bour 206 B2
Grosvenor Rd. Ch Fo 30 C1
Grosvenor Rd. Southa 79 E1
Grosvenor Sq. Southa 102 C3
Grosvenor St. Ports 182 B2
Grove Ave. Gos 181 E3
Grove Ave. Portc 156 B3
Grove Gdns. Southa 104 A1
Grove La. Red 47 F4
Grove Pastures. Lym 198 C2
Grove Pl. Lym 198 C2
Grove Pl. Southa 104 A1
Grove Rd E. Christ 209 D4
Grove Rd N. Ports 182 B2
Grove Rd S. Ports 182 B2
Grove Rd W. Christ 208 C4
Grove Rd. B on S 212 A4
Grove Rd. Bour 207 D2
Grove Rd. Comp 31 E3
Grove Rd. Cos 158 B4
Grove Rd. Fare 88 A1
Grove Rd. Gos 181 D4
Grove Rd. Hav 135 F1
Grove Rd. L on S 179 F3
Grove Rd. Lym 198 C2
Grove Rd. Poole 205 D3
Grove Rd. Southa 102 B4
Grove Rd. Twyf 31 F3
Grove Rd. Wi Mi 163 E2
Grove St. Southa 103 D2
Grove The. Bour 190 C2
Grove The. Burs 105 D1
Grove The. Christ 192 C1
Grove The. Fern 165 E2
Grove The. Net 127 E4
Grove The. Southa 104 A1
Grove The. Stubb 154 A1
Grove The. Ver 115 D3
Grove The. Westb 137 D2
Grovelands Rd. Winch 1 A1
Groveley Rd. Bour 206 A1
Groveley Rd. Christ 209 F3
Grovely Way. N Bad 28 C1
Grovely Ave. Bour 207 F2
Groves Down. W Wel 50 C2
Grundles. Pet 41 D2
Gruneisen Rd. Ports 157 E1
Gudge Heath La. Fare 130 C1
Guelders The. Wat 134 C2
Guernsey Cl. Southa 77 F2
Guernsey Rd. Poole 189 E1
Guest Ave. Poole 206 A3
Guest Rd. Bish 56 B2
Guest Rd. Upt 203 D4
Guildford Dr. Ch Fo 55 D2
Guildford Rd. Ports 182 C3
Guildford St. Southa 103 D3
Guildhall Sq. Ports 182 B3
Guildhall Wlk. Ports 182 B3
Guildhill Rd. Bour 208 C2
Guilford Cl. Southb 137 F1
Guillemot Cl. Hyt 126 A1
Guillemot Gdns. Gos 155 D2
Gull Cl. Gos 155 D1
Gulliver Cl. Poole 211 E4
Gullycroft Mead. He En 105 D4
Gunners Way. Gos 155 F1
Gunstore Rd. Ports 158 A2
Gunwharf Rd. Ports 182 A2
Gurjun Cl. Upt 203 D4
Gurnard Rd. Cos 157 F4
Gurnays Mead. W Wel 50 C2
Gurney Rd. Broa 187 F3
Gurney Rd. Ports 183 D2
Gurney Rd. Southa 102 B4
Gussage Rd. Poole 205 F4
Gutner La. N Hay 160 B1
Gwatkin Cl. Hav 135 E2
Gwenlyn Rd. Upt 203 E3
Gwynne Rd. Poole 205 F3
Gypsy La. Rin 141 D4

Haarlem Mews. Christ 209 E4
Hack Dr. Co Com 57 D4
Hacketts La. Drox 60 C1
Hackleys La. W Wel 51 D3
Hackupps La. Miche 6 B1
Hadden Rd. Bour 207 E4
Haddon Cl. Fare 130 C1
Haddon Dr. Eastl 56 A3
Haddons Dr. W Moo 138 B4
Hadleigh Gdns. Eastl 56 A3
Hadleigh Rd. Cos 157 E4
Hadley Field. Holb 150 A3
Hadley Way. Broa 187 F2
Hadow Rd. Bour 190 B2
Hadrian Cl. Fern 165 E1
Hadrian Way. Rown 78 C4
Hadrians Cl. Ch Fo 55 F4
Haglane Copse. Lym 198 B1
Hahnemann Rd. Bour 206 C1
Haig Ave. Poole 205 F1
Haig Rd. Bish 57 D1
Halden Cl. Rom 28 A1
Hale Ave. New M 196 A1
Hale Gdns. New M 196 A1
Hale La. Woodg 47 D2
Hale St N. Ports 182 B3
Hale St S. Ports 182 B3
Hales Dr. He En 105 D3
Halewood Way. Christ 208 C4
Half Moon St. Ports 182 A3
Halfpenny Dell. Wat 134 C2
Halfpenny La. Ports 182 A2
Halifax Rise. Wat 134 C4
Halifax Way. Christ 210 A4
Hall Cl. Bi Wa 83 E4
Hall Lands La. Fa Oa 57 E1
Hall Rd. Bour 189 F2
Hall Way The. Litt 1 A3
Hallet Cl. Southa 80 A1
Hallett Rd. Hav 136 A1
Halletts Cl. Stubb 154 B2
Halliday Cl. Gos 181 D3
Halliday Cres. Ports 183 E2
Halsey Cl. Gos 180 C2
Halstead Rd. Cos 157 E4
Halstead Rd. Southa 79 F1
Halstock Cres. Broa 188 B1
Halter Path. Hamw 203 F2
Halter Rise. Wi Mi 164 B3
Halterworth Cl. Rom 53 D4
Halterworth La. Rom 53 E4
Halton Cl. Bran 194 A4
Haltons Cl. Tot 76 B1
Ham La. Fern 164 C2
Ham La. Gos 156 A1
Ham La. Horn 112 A4
Ham La. Southb 161 E4
Ham La. Wi Mi 164 C2
Hambert Way. Tot 100 C3
Hamble Cl. Lo He 128 B1
Hamble Ct. Ch Fo 55 E3
Hamble House Gns. Hamble 128 A1
Hamble La. Burs 127 F4
Hamble La. Hamble 127 F4
Hamble La. Wat 134 C3
Hamble Rd. Poole 205 D3
Hambledon Cl. Winch 1 B2
Hambledon Gdns. Bour 208 B3
Hambledon La. Sob 85 F2
Hambledon Par. Wat 111 E1
Hambledon Rd. Clanf 88 A3
Hambledon Rd. Den 111 D2
Hambledon Rd. Hambl 110 B4
Hambledon Rd. Wat 111 D2
Hambleton Rd. Bour 208 A3
Hamblewood. Botl 106 A3
Hambrook Rd. Gos 181 D3
Hambrook St. Ports 182 A2
Hamdown Cres. W Wel 51 D1
Hameldon Cl. Southa 101 F4
Hamilton Cl. Bour 207 E3
Hamilton Cl. Hamw 203 F1
Hamilton Cl. Hav 159 F4
Hamilton Cres. Hamw 203 F1
Hamilton Ct. M on S 213 E2
Hamilton Gr. Gos 155 D1
Hamilton Rd. Bish 56 B2
Hamilton Rd. Bour 207 E2
Hamilton Rd. Broa 187 F3
Hamilton Rd. Hamw 203 F1
Hamilton Rd. Hyt 150 A4
Hamilton Rd. Portc 156 C4
Hamilton Rd. Ports 182 B1
Hamilton Way. New M 195 F1
Hamlet Way. Gos 156 A1
Hammond's Green. Tot 100 B4
Hammonds Cl. Tot 100 C4
Hammonds La. Tot 100 C4
Hammonds Way. Tot 100 C4
Hampage Green. Hav 135 E4
Hampden La. Bour 208 A3
Hampshire Centre The. Bour 191 F1
Hampshire Cl. Christ 192 C1
Hampshire Hatches La. Rin 141 D2
Hampshire St. Ports 182 C4
Hampshire Terr. Ports 182 A2
Hampton Cl. Black 177 F4
Hampton Cl. Wat 135 D4
Hampton Dr. Rin 117 D1
Hampton Gdns. Black 177 F4
Hampton Gr. Fare 130 A1
Hampton Hill. Swan 84 A3
Hampton La. Black 150 C1
Hampton La. Winch 1 B1
Hamptworth Rd. Red 48 B2
Hamtun Cres. Tot 76 C1
Hamtun Gdns. Tot 76 C1
Hamtun Rd. Southa 104 B2
Hamtun St. Southa 102 C2
Hanbidge Cres. Gos 155 E2
Hanbidge Wlk. Gos 155 E2
Handel Rd. Southa 102 C3
Handel Terr. Southa 102 C3
Handford Pl. Southa 102 C3
Handley Rd. Gos 180 C3
Hangers The. Bi Wa 59 F1
Hanham Rd. Broa 187 E3
Hanham Rd. Wi Mi 163 E3
Hankinson Rd. Bour 207 D4
Hanley Rd. Southa 102 B4
Hannah Gdns. Wat 134 C4
Hannah Way. Hord 197 F3
Hannay Rise. Southa 104 B3
Hannington Pl. Bour 208 A3
Hannington Rd. Bour 208 A3
Hannington Rd. Hav 135 E4
Hanover Bldgs. Southa 103 D2
Hanover Gdns. Fare 88 A2
Hanover St. Ports 182 A3
Hants Corporate Pk. Chilw 55 D1
Hanway Rd. Ports 182 C4
Harbeck Rd. Bour 191 E2
Harborough Rd. Southa 102 C3
Harbour Cl. Poole 211 E3
Harbour Cres. Christ 209 F3
Harbour Hill Cres. Poole 204 C3
Harbour Rd. Bour 209 D2
Harbour Rd. Gos 181 F3
Harbour Rd. S Hay 184 B2
Harbour View Cl. Poole 205 D3
Harbour View Rd. Poole 205 D2
Harbour View. Portc 156 B3
Harbour Way. Ems 161 D4
Harbour Way. Ports 157 E1
Harbour Wlk. Ports 182 A2
Harbourne Gdns. W End 80 A1
Harbourside. Hav 159 F3
Harbridge Ct. Hav 135 E4
Harbridge Dro. Ibs 93 E2
Harcombe Cl. Broa 188 C2
Harcourt Cl. Wat 112 A2
Harcourt Rd. Bour 208 A3
Harcourt Rd. Fare 154 A4
Harcourt Rd. Gos 181 D3
Harcourt Rd. Ports 182 C4
Harcourt Rd. Southa 103 F4
Hard The. Ports 182 A3
Harding La. Fa Oa 57 D2
Harding Rd. Gos 180 C3
Hardley La. Hyt 150 A4
Hardwick Rd. Ch Fo 55 E3
Hardwicke Cl. Southa 77 F1
Hardwicke Way. Hamble 127 F2
Hardy Cl. Lo He 129 D2
Hardy Cl. New M 195 F2
Hardy Cl. W Moo 138 C1
Hardy Cres. Wi Mi 163 E2
Hardy Dr. Hyt 126 A1
Hardy Rd. Cos 158 C4
Hardy Rd. Eastl 56 A1
Hardy Rd. Poole 205 E2
Hardy Rd. W Moo 138 C1
Hare La. Alderh 91 F3
Hare La. Hord 196 C2
Hare La. New M 196 C2
Harebell Cl. Fare 88 B2
Harefield Ct. Rom 53 D4
Harefield Rd. Southa 79 E2
Hares Green. Bour 208 A4
Harestock Cl. Litt 1 B3
Harestock Rd. Hav 135 E2
Harestock Rd. Winch 1 B2
Harewood Ave. Bour 208 A3
Harewood Cl. Eastl 56 A3
Harewood Cres. Bour 207 F4
Harewood Gdns. Bour 207 F4
Harewood Green. M on S 214 A2
Harewood Pl. Bour 208 A3
Harford Cl. Lym 198 B1
Harford Rd. Poole 205 E4
Harkness Dr. Wat 135 D4
Harkwood Dr. Hamw 203 F2
Harland Cres. Southa 78 B1
Harland Rd. Bour 209 D2
Harlech Dr. Ch Fo 55 D2
Harleston Rd. Cos 133 E1
Harleston Villas. Wi Mi 163 E2
Harlyn Rd. Southa 77 F1
Harness Cl. Wi Mi 164 A3
Harold Cl. Tot 100 B3
Harold Rd. Ports 182 C2
Harold Rd. S Hay 185 D1
Harold Rd. Southa 102 B4
Harold Rd. Stubb 154 B2
Harold Rd. Westb 137 D2
Harpway La. Burt 193 E3
Harpway La. Sop 193 E3
Harrage The. Rom 52 C4
Harrier Cl. L on S 179 F3
Harrier Cl. Southa 78 A3
Harrier Dr. Oakl 163 E1
Harrier Way. Pet 41 E1
Harriers Cl. Christ 210 B4
Harriet Cl. Stubb 154 A1
Harris Ave. He En 105 E4
Harris Rd. Gos 155 E2
Harrison Ave. Bour 207 E3
Harrison Cl. Burt 193 E2
Harrison Rd. Fare 88 A1
Harrison Rd. Southa 79 E2
Harrison's Cut. Southa 103 D2
Harrow Cl. Bran 194 A4
Harrow Down. Winch 10 B2
Harrow La. Pet 40 C3
Harrow Rd. Bran 194 A4
Harrow Rd. Ports 182 C2
Harry Barrow Cl. Rin 141 D3
Hart Hill. Hyt 126 B1
Hart Plain Ave. Wat 111 F2
Hart's Farm Way. Hav 159 E4
Harthill Dro. Red 47 F3
Harting Down. Pet 41 D2
Harting Gdns. Portc 132 B1
Harting Rd. Bour 208 B4
Hartington Rd. Gos 180 C3
Hartington Rd. Southa 103 D3
Hartland Ct. Southb 137 E1
Hartland's Rd. Fare 88 A1
Hartley Ave. Southa 79 D2
Hartley Cl. Bish 57 D1
Hartley Cl. Hyt 126 A1
Hartley Rd. Bish 57 D1
Hartley Rd. Ports 157 F2
Hartley Wlk. Hyt 126 A1
Harts Way. Hord 197 E1
Hartsbourne Dr. Bour 208 A4
Hartsgrove Ave. Black 150 C1
Hartsgrove Cl. Black 150 C1
Hartwell Rd. Ports 158 A2
Harvest Cl. Winch 10 B2
Harvest Rd. Den 110 C2
Harvester Way. Lym 198 B3
Harvestgate Wlk. Hav 135 E3
Harvesting La. E Meo 64 B3
Harvey Cres. Lo He 128 C1
Harvey Ct. Black 150 C1
Harvey Rd. Bish 56 C1
Harvey Rd. Bour 208 A3
Harvey Rd. Oakl 188 C4
Harwich Rd. Cos 133 E1
Harwood Cl. Gos 155 E2
Harwood Cl. Tot 100 B4
Harwood Pl. Ki Wo 2 B4
Harwood Rd. Gos 155 E2
Haselbury Rd. Tot 100 C4
Haselworth Dr. Gos 181 D1
Haskells Cl. Lyn 121 F2
Haskells Rd. Poole 205 D4
Haslar Cres. Wat 111 E1
Haslar Rd. Gos 181 E1
Haslemere Ave. Christ 211 D4
Haslemere Gdns. S Hay 185 F1
Haslemere Pl. Christ 211 D4
Haslemere Rd. Ports 182 C2
Haslemere Rd. Southb 137 E1
Hasler Rd. Broa 188 B1
Haslop Rd. Wi Mi 164 A4
Hassocks The. Wat 135 D4
Hastings Ave. Gos 180 C4
Hastings Rd. Bour 191 F1
Hastings Rd. Broa 188 A1
Hatch Ct. Hav 135 E4
Hatch La. Liss 21 E2
Hatch Pond Rd. Poole 204 B4
Hatchers La. Ows 33 D3
Hatchet Cl. Woodg 47 E2
Hatchet La. E Bol 175 E4
Hatchley La. Ows 58 A3
Hatfield Ct. New M 195 F2
Hatfield Gdns. Bour 208 A4
Hatfield Rd. Ports 183 D2
Hathaway Cl. Eastl 56 A2
Hathaway Gdns. Wat 112 A1
Hathaway Rd. Bour 208 B2
Hatherden Ave. Poole 204 C3
Hatherley Cres. Portc 156 A4
Hatherley Dr. Portc 156 A4
Hatherley Rd. Cos 133 D1
Hatherley Rd. Winch 1 C1
Hatley Rd. Southa 104 A4
Hatt La. Mott 5 F1
Havant Farm Cl. Hav 135 F2
Havant Rd. Cos 158 B4
Havant Rd. Ems 160 C4
Havant Rd. Horn 112 B3
Havant Rd. N Hay 159 F1
Havant Rd. Ports 182 C4
Havant St. Ports 182 A3
Havant-by-pass. Hav 160 A4
Havelock Rd. Lo He 128 B1
Havelock Rd. Poole 206 A3
Havelock Rd. Ports 182 B2
Havelock Rd. Southa 102 C3
Havelock Way. Christ 194 B1
Haven Cres. Stubb 153 F1
Haven Gdns. New M 196 A1
Haven Rd. Broa 187 E3
Haven Rd. Poole 211 F4
Haven Rd. S Hay 185 F1
Haven The. Eastl 56 A3
Haven The. Gos 181 D1
Haven The. Ports 183 D3
Havendale. He En 105 E3
Haverstock Rd. Bour 191 D2
Haverstone Way. Southa 79 E2
Haviland Mews. Bour 207 F3
Haviland Rd E. Bour 207 F3
Haviland Rd W. Bour 207 F2
Haviland Rd. Bour 207 F3
Haviland Rd. Fern 165 D4
Havisham Rd. Ports 182 B4
Hawden Rd. Bour 190 A1
Hawfinch Cl. Southa 78 A3
Hawk Cl. Stubb 154 A1
Hawk Cl. Wi Mi 164 A4
Hawkchurch Gdns. Broa 188 C1
Hawke St. Ports 182 A3
Hawker Cl. Oakl 163 F1
Hawkeswood Rd. Southa 103 E4
Hawkewood Ave. Wat 111 E1
Hawkhill. Hyt 125 E2

Hawkhurst Cl. Southa 104 A1
Hawkins Cl. Rin 117 E1
Hawkins Rd. Gos 155 E1
Hawkins Rd. Poole 189 F1
Hawkley Green. Southa 126 C4
Hawkley Rd. Hawk 20 B3
Hawkley Rd. Liss 20 B3
Hawkwell. Portc 155 F4
Hawkwood Rd. Bour 207 F2
Hawley Cl. Hav 135 F3
Haworth Cl. Christ 193 D1
Hawstead Green. Hav 135 E3
Hawthorn Cl. Fa Oa 57 E1
Hawthorn Cl. He En 105 E3
Hawthorn Cl. New M 196 B2
Hawthorn Cres. Cos 158 A3
Hawthorn Dr. Broa 187 F1
Hawthorn Dr. Sway 172 A1
Hawthorn La. Lo He 128 C3
Hawthorn Rd. Bour 206 C4
Hawthorn Rd. Burt 193 F2
Hawthorn Rd. Den 110 C2
Hawthorn Rd. Horn 88 B1
Hawthorn Rd. Hyt 125 F2
Hawthorn Rd. Southa 79 D1
Hawthorn Wlk. L on S 179 F3
Hawthorne Gr. S Hay 185 D2
Hawthorne Rd. Tot 100 B4
Hawthorns The. Christ 209 F3
Hawthorns The. March 102 A1
Hay St. Ports 182 A3
Hayburn Rd. Southa 77 E1
Haydn Cl. Ki Wo 2 A4
Haydock Cl. Tot 100 B4
Haydock Mews. Wat 112 A1
Haydon Rd. Poole 206 A1
Hayes Ave. Bour 207 F3
Hayes Cl. Fare 130 B2
Hayes Cl. Wi Mi 164 A2
Hayes La. Wi Mi 164 A3
Hayes Mead. Holb 150 A3
Hayes Terr. Gos 181 D3
Hayeswood Rd. Wi Mi 164 A3
Hayle Rd. W End 80 A1
Hayley Cl. Hyt 149 F4
Hayling Ave. Ports 183 D4
Hayling Cl. Fare 154 B4
Haymoor Rd. Poole 205 D4
Haynes Ave. Poole 204 B2
Hays Cotts. Steep 40 B4
Haysoms Cl. B on S 196 A1
Hayter Gdns. Rom 53 D4
Hayters Way. Alderh 93 D3
Hayward Cl. Tot 100 B4
Hayward Cres. Ver 114 C3
Hayward Ct. Holb 150 B2
Hayward Way. Ver 114 C3
Haywards Farm Cl. Ver 114 C3
Haywards La. Broa 187 E4
Hazel Cl. Alderh 93 D3
Hazel Cl. Ch Fo 30 B1
Hazel Cl. Christ 194 B1
Hazel Dr. Fern 165 E4
Hazel Farm Rd. Tot 100 B4
Hazel Gr. Ashu 99 F2
Hazel Gr. Clanf 88 B3
Hazel Gr. Lo He 129 D1
Hazel Gr. Winch 10 B3
Hazel Rd. Clanf 88 B3
Hazel Rd. Lym 198 A2
Hazel Rd. Southa 103 E2
Hazelbank Cl. Pet 41 D2
Hazeldean Dr. Ro Ca 113 D1
Hazeldown Rd. Rown 77 F3
Hazeleigh Ave. Southa 103 F1
Hazeley Green. Hav 136 A3
Hazeley Rd. Twyf 58 B4
Hazelholt Dr. Hav 135 E2
Hazell Ave. Bour 190 A1
Hazelton Cl. Bour 208 A4
Hazelwood Ave. Hav 135 D2
Hazelwood Ave. New M 195 F2
Hazelwood Rd. Southa 80 A1
Hazelwood. Stubb 154 A3
Hazlebury Rd. Broa 204 A4
Hazlemere Dr. St Le 139 F2
Hazleton Way. Wat 112 A3
Head Down. Pet 41 D2
Head's La. Bour 190 C3
Headland Dr. Lo He 129 D2
Headlands The. Down 46 C4
Headley Cl. L on S 179 F3
Headon View. W Meo 37 E3
Heads Farm Cl. Bour 190 C3
Headswell Ave. Bour 190 C2
Headswell Cres. Bour 190 C2
Headswell Gdns. Bour 190 C2
Heanor Cl. Bour 190 B1
Hearne Gdns. Shed 84 A1
Hearts Of Oak Mews. Lym 198 B2
Heath Ave. Poole 204 B3
Heath Cl. Fa Oa 57 E1
Heath Cl. Horn 112 A4
Heath Cl. Wi Mi 164 A4
Heath Farm Cl. Fern 165 E2
Heath Farm Rd. Fern 165 E2
Heath Farm Way. Fern 165 E2
Heath Gdns. Net 127 E4
Heath House Cl. He En 105 D2
Heath Lawns. Fare 130 B1
Heath Rd E. Pet 41 D1
Heath Rd N. Lo He 128 C2
Heath Rd S. Lo He 128 C2
Heath Rd W. Pet 41 D1
Heath Rd. Christ 195 D1
Heath Rd. Hord 196 C2
Heath Rd. Lo He 129 D2
Heath Rd. N Bad 54 A2
Heath Rd. Pet 41 D2
Heath Rd. Sob 85 D1
Heath Rd. Southa 104 A3
Heath Rd. St Le 139 E2
Heath The. Den 111 D2
Heathcote Pl. Hurs 30 A4
Heathcote Rd. Bour 207 F2
Heathcote Rd. Ch Fo 55 E3
Heathcote Rd. Ports 157 F1
Heathen La. Durl 82 A2
Heather Chase. Bish 57 D1
Heather Cl. Broa 187 F3
Heather Cl. Christ 195 D1
Heather Cl. Gos 155 D1
Heather Cl. Hord 197 D2
Heather Cl. St Le 139 F2
Heather Cl. Tot 100 C4
Heather Cl. Wat 134 C3
Heather Ct. Southa 104 B4
Heather Dr. Fern 165 E4
Heather Gdns. Fare 130 B2
Heather Rd. Black 150 C1
Heather Rd. Bour 190 B2
Heather Rd. Pet 41 E2
Heather View Rd. Poole 205 F4
Heather Way. Fern 165 E4
Heatherbank Rd. Bour 206 B2
Heatherbrae Gdns. N Bad 53 F2
Heatherbrae La. Upt 203 E3
Heatherdeane Rd. Southa 79 D1
Heatherdene Rd. Ch Fo 30 C1
Heatherdown Rd. W Moo 139 D1
Heatherdown Way. W Moo 139 D1
Heatherfield. Buri 65 E3
Heatherlands Rd. Rown 78 C4
Heatherlea Rd. Bour 208 B2
Heatherstone Ave. Hyt 125 F1
Heatherton Mews. Ems 136 C1
Heatherview Cl. N Bad 53 F3
Heathfield Ave. Fare 130 B1
Heathfield Ave. Poole 206 A4
Heathfield Cl. Ch Fo 30 B1
Heathfield Cl. Southa 104 A2
Heathfield Rd. Ch Fo 30 B1
Heathfield Rd. Pet 41 E2
Heathfield Rd. Ports 157 E1
Heathfield Rd. Southa 104 B2
Heathfield Rd. W Moo 139 D1
Heathfield Way. W Moo 138 C1
Heathfield. Hyt 125 F1
Heathhouse La. He En 105 E2
Heathlands Ave. Fern 165 E1
Heathlands Cl. Burt 193 E2
Heathlands Cl. Ch Fo 55 E4
Heathlands Rd. Ch Fo 55 E4
Heathwood Ave. B on S 211 F4
Heathwood Rd. Bour 206 C4
Heathy Cl. B on S 211 F4
Heaton Rd. Bour 190 A1
Heaton Rd. Gos 181 D4
Heavytree Rd. Poole 205 D2
Hebrides Cl. Stubb 154 A2
Heckfield Cl. Hav 136 A3
Heckford Rd. Broa 187 E3
Heckford Rd. Poole 204 B2
Hector Cl. Wat 134 C1
Hedera Rd. Lo He 128 C2
Hedge End Bus Ctre. He En 81 D1
Hedge End Wlk. Hav 136 A3
Hedgerley. B on S 212 A4
Hedgerow Drive. Southa 80 A1
Hedgerow Gdns. Ems 136 C2
Heidelberg Rd. Ports 182 C2
Heights App. Upt 203 E4
Heights Rd. Upt 203 E4
Heights The. Fare 88 B1
Helena Rd. Ports 182 C1
Helford Gdns. W End 80 A1
Hellyer Rd. Ports 183 D2
Helsby Cl. Fare 154 C4
Helsted Cl. Gos 180 C2
Helston Dr. Ems 136 C2
Helston Rd. Portc 132 C1
Helvellyn Rd. Southa 101 F4
Helyar Rd. Bour 191 F1
Hemdean Gdns. W End 80 B1
Hemlock Rd. Wat 111 F2
Hemming Cl. Tot 100 C3
Hempsted Rd. Cos 133 D1
Hemsley Wk. Wat 112 A2
Henbury Cl. Broa 187 E3
Henbury Cl. Poole 189 D1
Henbury Rise. Broa 187 E3
Henbury View Rd. Broa 187 E3
Henderson Rd. Ports 183 E2
Hendford Gdns. Bour 190 B1
Hendford Rd. Bour 190 B1
Hengist Rd. Bour 207 E2
Hengistbury Rd. B on S 211 F4
Hengistbury Rd. Bour 209 D2
Henley Gdns. Bour 208 A4
Henley Gdns. Fare 130 B2
Henley Rd. Ports 182 C2
Henning's Park Rd. Poole 204 C3
Henry Cl. Holb 150 A3
Henry Rd. Bish 56 B2
Henry Rd. Southa 102 B4
Henry St. Gos 181 E2
Henry St. Southa 102 C3
Henstead Rd. Southa 102 C3
Hensting La. Co Com 57 E4
Hensting La. Ows 58 C1
Henty Rd. Southa 102 A4
Henville Cl. Gos 180 B4
Henville Rd. Bour 207 E3
Henwood Down. Pet 41 D2
Hepworth Cl. Southa 104 B1
Herald Rd. He En 81 D1
Herbert Ave. Poole 205 E4
Herbert Rd. Bour 206 A1
Herbert Rd. Gos 180 C3
Herbert Rd. New M 196 A2
Herbert Rd. Ports 182 C1
Herbert Rd. Red 47 E3
Herbert St. Ports 182 B4
Herbert Walker Ave. Southa 102 B2
Herberton Rd. Bour 208 B3
Hercules Rd. Hamw 203 E2
Hercules St. Ports 182 B4
Hereward Cl. Rom 53 D4
Herm Rd. Poole 189 E1
Hermitage Cl. Bi Wa 83 D4
Hermitage Gdns. Wat 134 C4
Hermitage Rd. Poole 205 D3
Hern La. Fordi 94 A3
Herne Rd. Cos 157 F4
Herne Rd. Pet 41 D2
Heron Cl. Ports 183 D3
Heron Cl. Sway 172 A1
Heron Court Rd. Bour 207 D4
Heron Dr. Wi Mi 164 A4
Heron Quay. Herm 161 D4
Heron Sq. Eastl 55 F1
Heron Way. Gos 155 D2
Herons Cl. Stubb 154 B2
Heronswood. Tot 76 B1
Herrick Cl. Southa 104 B2
Herriot Cl. Wat 112 A3
Herstone Cl. Poole 188 C1
Hertford Cl. Fordi 69 F2
Hertford Pl. Ports 182 B4
Hertsfield. Lo He 129 E2
Hesketh Cl. St Le 140 A3
Hestan Cl. Christ 192 B2
Hester Rd. Ports 183 D2
Hestia Cl. Rom 53 E4
Heston Way. W Moo 138 B2
Heston Wlk. Gos 180 C2
Hewett Cl. Lo He 153 F4
Hewett Rd. Lo He 153 F4
Hewett Rd. Ports 157 F1
Hewetts Rise. Lo He 152 B4
Hewitt Cl. Gos 181 D4
Hewitt Rd. Hamw 203 F2
Hewitt's Rd. Southa 102 B3
Heyes Dr. Southa 104 B2
Heysham Rd. Broa 188 A2
Heysham Rd. Southa 102 A4
Heyshott Rd. Ports 182 C2
Heytesbury Rd. Bour 208 B3
Heyward Rd. Ports 182 C2
Heywood Gdns. Hav 135 E3
Heywood Green. Southa 104 C3
Hibberd Way. Bour 190 B1
Hibbs Cl. Upt 203 E4
Hickory Cl. Upt 203 D4
Hickory Dr. Winch 1 B2
High Cross La. Frox G 18 B1
High Cross. Frox G 18 C1
High Dr. Gos 155 E1
High Firs Gdns. Rom 53 E4
High Firs Rd. Rom 53 E4
High Firs Rd. Southa 104 B3
High Howe Cl. Bour 189 F2
High Howe La. Bour 189 F2
High Lawn Way. Hav 135 F3
High Mead La. Fern 165 D1
High Mead. Fare 130 C2
High Mead. Fern 165 D1
High Meadow. Southa 104 B3
High Oaks Cl. Lo He 129 D2
High Park Rd. Broa 187 F2
High Rd. Southa 79 E2
High Ridge Cres. New M 196 B2
High St N. Poole 204 B2
High St. Beaul 148 C1
High St. Bi Wa 83 E4
High St. Botl 106 A4
High St. Buri 65 E3
High St. Burs 128 A4
High St. Christ 209 D3
High St. Cos 157 F4
High St. Dame 68 B3
High St. Down 47 D4
High St. Drox 61 D1
High St. E Meo 38 C1
High St. Eastl 56 A1
High St. Ems 160 C4
High St. Fare 131 E1
High St. Fordi 69 F1
High St. Gos 181 E2
High St. Hambl 86 B2
High St. Hamble 128 A1
High St. Hyt 126 A3
High St. L on S 179 F3
High St. Lo He 153 F4
High St. Lym 198 C2
High St. Lyn 121 F3
High St. M on S 213 E2
High St. Meons 61 E2
High St. Pet 40 C2
High St. Poole 204 B1
High St. Ports 182 A2
High St. Rin 140 C4
High St. Shed 107 F4
High St. Sob 85 D2
High St. Southa 103 D2
High St. Southw 132 C3
High St. St Le 139 F3
High St. Tot 101 D4
High St. Twyf 58 A3
High St. W End 80 B1
High St. Wi Mi 163 D2
High St. Winch 10 C4
High St. Woodg 70 C4
High Town Hill. Rin 141 F4
High Trees Dr. Winch 1 C1
High Trees Wlk. Fern 165 E4
High Trees. Wat 134 C4
High View Way. Southa 103 F4
High Way. Broa 187 F2
High Wlk. Fare 130 C2
Highbank Ave. Wat 134 B2
Highbury Cl. Fa Oa 57 E1
Highbury Cl. New M 196 A2
Highbury Gr. Cos 158 A3
Highbury St. Ports 182 A2
Highclere Ave. Hav 135 F2
Highclere Rd. Southa 78 B2
Highclere Way. Ch Fo 55 D2
Highcliff Ave. Southa 103 D4
Highcliffe Dr. Eastl 56 A4
Highcliffe Rd. Christ 210 B4
Highcliffe Rd. Gos 180 C2
Highcliffe Rd. Winch 11 D3
Highcroft La. Horn 112 B4
Highcrown Mews. Southa 79 D1
Highcrown St. Southa 79 D1
Higher Blandford Rd. Broa 187 F3
Higher Merley La. Broa 187 F4
Highfield Ave. Fare 154 C4
Highfield Ave. Lym 198 B2
Highfield Ave. Rin 141 D4
Highfield Ave. Twyf 58 A3
Highfield Ave. Wat 111 F1
Highfield Cl. Broa 187 F3
Highfield Cl. Ch Fo 55 F3
Highfield Cl. Southa 79 D1
Highfield Cl. Sway 172 A1
Highfield Cl. Wat 111 F1
Highfield Cres. Southa 79 D1
Highfield Dr. Rin 141 D4
Highfield Gdns. Liss 21 D2
Highfield Gdns. Sway 172 A1
Highfield La. Red 47 E3
Highfield La. Southa 79 D1
Highfield Rd. Bour 190 C1
Highfield Rd. Broa 187 F3
Highfield Rd. Ch Fo 55 F3
Highfield Rd. Gos 180 C3
Highfield Rd. Lym 198 B2
Highfield Rd. Pet 40 C2
Highfield Rd. Ports 182 B3
Highfield Rd. Rin 141 D4
Highfield Rd. Southa 79 D1
Highfield Rd. W Moo 138 C2
Highfield. Lym 198 B2
Highfield. Twyf 58 A3
Highfields. Lo He 128 C1
Highgate Rd. Ports 158 A1
Highgrove Cl. Tot 100 B3
Highgrove Rd. Ports 183 D4
Highland Ave. Christ 195 D1
Highland Cres. Bour 190 B2
Highland Rd. Ems 136 C1
Highland Rd. Poole 205 D3
Highland Rd. Ports 183 D1
Highland Rd. Wi Mi 163 E3
Highland St. Ports 183 D1
Highland View Cl. Wi Mi 163 E3
Highlands Cl. Hyt 126 A1
Highlands Cl. N Bad 53 F3
Highlands Cres. Bour 190 B2
Highlands Rd. B on S 212 A4
Highlands Rd. Cos 158 B4
Highlands Rd. Fare 130 B2
Highlands Way. Hyt 125 F1
Highlands Way. Whit 24 A2
Highmoor Cl. Broa 187 E3
Highmoor Cl. Poole 205 E2
Highmoor Rd. Bour 190 A1
Highmoor Rd. Broa 187 E3
Highmoor Rd. Poole 205 E2
Highmount Cl. Winch 11 E4
Highnam Gdns. Lo He 128 C2
Hightown Gdns. Rin 141 E3
Hightown Rd. Rin 141 D3
Hightrees Ave. Bour 191 F1
Highview Cl. Christ 192 C2
Highview Gdns. Poole 205 E4
Highways Rd. Comp 31 E3
Highwood Cl. Alderh 92 B3
Highwood La. N Bad 53 E4
Highwood Lawn. Hav 135 E4
Highwood Rd. Brock 172 C4
Highwood Rd. Gos 180 B4
Highwood Rd. Poole 205 F2
Higworth La. S Hay 184 C3
Hilary Ave. Cos 158 A4
Hilary Cl. Lyn 122 A2
Hilary Rd. Broa 188 B1
Hilda Gdns. Den 111 D2
Hilda Rd. Poole 205 F4
Hilden Way. Litt 1 A3
Hiley Rd. Poole 204 B3
Hilier Wlk. L on S 179 F3
Hill Brow Rd. Hill B 21 D1
Hill Brow Rd. Liss 21 D1
Hill Cl. Bran 194 A4
Hill Cl. Fa Oa 57 E3
Hill Coppice Rd. Lo He 129 E3
Hill Dr. Fare 130 B2
Hill Farm Rd. Southa 102 C3
Hill Head Rd. Stubb 154 A1
Hill Houses La. Cher 14 A3
Hill La. Bran 194 A4
Hill La. Co Com 31 F1
Hill La. Southa 78 C1
Hill Park Rd. Fare 130 B2
Hill Park Rd. Gos 180 C3
Hill Pl. Burs 128 A4
Hill Rd. Portc 132 B1
Hill Rise. Twyf 58 A3
Hill St. Ower 76 B3
Hill St. Poole 204 B1
Hill Top Gdns. Horn 88 B2
Hill View Rd. Brai 28 B3
Hill View Rd. Fern 165 E3
Hill View Rd. Mich 27 E4
Hill View Rd. Portc 132 B1
Hill View. E Meo 38 B1
Hill Wlk. Fare 130 B2
Hillary Cl. Fare 130 C1
Hillary Rd. Christ 209 F4
Hillborough Cres. Ports 182 B2
Hillbourne Rd. Broa 188 A1
Hillbrow Cl. Fare 130 B2
Hillbrow Cl. Ro Ca 113 D1
Hillbrow Rd. Bour 208 A3
Hillbury Rd. Alderh 93 D3
Hillcrest Ave. Ch Fo 55 F3
Hillcrest Ave. Fern 165 E4
Hillcrest Cl. Bour 191 D2
Hillcrest Cl. N Bad 53 F3
Hillcrest Dr. Ch Fo 55 E3
Hillcrest Gdns. Shed 83 E2
Hillcrest Rd. Bour 191 D2
Hillcrest Rd. Broa 187 E3
Hilldene Way. W End 80 C1
Hillditch. Lym 198 B3
Hilldown Rd. Southa 79 D1
Hilldowns Ave. Ports 157 E1
Hillgrove Rd. Southa 79 F2
Hillier Way. Winch 2 A1
Hillman Rd. Poole 205 E3
Hillmead Gdns. Hav 135 D1
Hillside Ave. Rom 53 D4
Hillside Ave. Southa 79 F1
Hillside Ave. Wat 134 A1
Hillside Cl. Ch Fo 55 E3
Hillside Cl. Horn 88 B2
Hillside Cl. W Dean 3 E1
Hillside Cl. Winch 1 B1
Hillside Cres. Portc 132 C1
Hillside Dr. Christ 192 B2
Hillside Gdns. Broa 187 E2
Hillside Ind Est. Horn 112 B4
Hillside Mews. Broa 187 E2
Hillside Rd. Broa 187 E3
Hillside Rd. Lym 198 B2
Hillside Rd. Poole 189 F1
Hillside Rd. Ver 114 C4
Hillside Rd. Winch 1 B1
Hillside Rd. Woodl 114 A3
Hillsley Rd. Cos 132 C1
Hillson Dr. Fare 130 B2
Hillsons Rd. Botl 106 B4
Hilltop Cl. Fern 165 D4
Hilltop Cres. Wat 134 B1
Hilltop Ct. Southa 102 A3
Hilltop Dr. Southa 104 B2
Hilltop Rd. Broa 187 F3
Hilltop Rd. Fern 165 D4
Hillview Rd. Bour 190 B2
Hillview Rd. Hyt 125 F2
Hillview. Wat 112 B3
Hillway The. Ch Fo 55 E4
Hillway The. Portc 156 B4
Hillway. St Le 139 F3
Hilly Cl. Ows 33 D2
Hillyfields. Nur 77 E2
Hilsea Cres. Ports 157 F3
Hiltingbury Ave. Hav 136 A3
Hiltingbury Cl. Ch Fo 30 B1
Hiltingbury Rd. Ch Fo 30 B1
Hiltom Rd. Rin 141 D4
Hilton Cl. Poole 205 D3

Hilton Rd. Gos 181 E2
Hilton Rd. He En 105 E4
Hinchcliffe Cl. Hamw 203 F1
Hinchcliffe Rd. Hamw 203 F1
Hinkler Rd. Southa 104 C3
Hinton Cl. Hav 135 E2
Hinton Cres. Southa 104 C2
Hinton Hill. Cher 14 C2
Hinton Rd. Bour 206 C2
Hinton Wood Ave. Christ 194 C1
Hintonwood La. Christ 194 C1
Hipley Rd. Hav 136 A2
Hirst Rd. Hyt 126 A2
Hive Gdns. Poole 211 E3
Hives Way. Lym 198 B3
Hoad's Hill. Wickh 108 A1
Hoadlands. Pet 41 D2
Hobart Dr. Hyt 126 A2
Hobart Rd. New M 195 F1
Hobb La. He En 105 E3
Hobbs Pass. Gos 181 F2
Hobbs Rd. Poole 205 E4
Hobby Cl. Ports 158 A2
Hobson Way. Holb 150 B2
Hoburne Gdns. Christ 194 B1
Hoburne La. Christ 194 B1
Hockham Ct. Hav 135 E4
Hockley Cl. Cos 157 E4
Hocombe Dr. Ch Fo 30 A1
Hocombe Park Cl. Ch Fo 30 A1
Hocombe Rd. Ch Fo 30 B1
Hocombe Wood Rd. Ch Fo 30 A1
Hodder Cl. N Bad 55 D3
Hodges Cl. Poole 204 C4
Hoe La. N Bad 53 E2
Hoe Rd. Bi Wa 83 F4
Hoe St. Sob 109 F4
Hoe The. Gos 155 F1
Hoeford Cl. Fare 155 D3
Hogarth Cl. Rom 28 A1
Hogarth Cl. Southa 104 B1
Hogue Ave. Bour 190 B3
Holbrook Rd. Fare 155 D4
Holbrook Rd. Ports 182 B3
Holbury Cl. Bour 191 F2
Holbury Dro. Holb 150 B2
Holbury La. E Tyth 4 B2
Holbury La. Locke 4 B2
Holcombe Rd. Upt 203 D3
Holcot la. Ports 158 B2
Holcroft Rd. Southa 104 C3
Holdaway Cl. Ki Wo 2 B4
Holden La. Meons 34 C4
Holdenhurst Ave. Bour 208 B4
Holdenhurst Cl. Horn 88 B1
Holdenhurst Rd. Bour 192 A2
Holdenhurst Rd. Bour 207 E3
Hole La. Curd 83 D1
Hole La. Sob 110 A4
Holes Cl. Hord 196 C2
Holkham Cl. Southa 77 F2
Hollam Cl. Fare 154 A4
Hollam Cres. Fare 154 A4
Hollam Dr. Fare 154 A4
Hollam Rd. Ports 183 D2
Holland Cl. Ch Fo 55 D2
Holland Pl. Gos 155 E1
Holland Pl. Southa 78 A1
Holland Rd. Ports 182 C2
Holland Rd. Southa 103 E1
Holland Rd. Tot 100 B4
Holland Way. Broa 187 F3
Hollands Cl. Litt 1 A3
Hollands Wood Dr. New M 196 A3
Hollies Cl. Sway 172 A1
Hollingbourne Cl. Southa 103 E4
Hollman Dr. Rom 52 B4
Hollow La. S Hay 184 C2
Holloway Ave. Bour 189 F3
Holly Cl. Hyt 150 A4
Holly Cl. Lo He 128 C2
Holly Cl. St Le 139 E2
Holly Cl. Upt 203 D4
Holly Dell. Southa 78 C3
Holly Dr. Ver 114 C3
Holly Dr. Wat 135 D3
Holly Gdns. Burt 193 E1
Holly Gdns. M on S 213 E3
Holly Gr. Fare 130 C2
Holly Green Rise. Bour 189 F2
Holly Hatch Rd. Tot 100 C3
Holly Hedge La. Broa 204 B4
Holly Hill Cl. Southa 78 C3
Holly Hill La. Lo He 128 B3
Holly Hill. Southa 78 C3
Holly La. Bold 174 A1
Holly La. Christ 195 E1
Holly Oak Rd. Southa 78 A2
Holly Rd. Ashu 100 A1
Holly Rd. Black 177 F4
Holly St. Gos 181 E2
Hollybank Cl. Hyt 126 A2
Hollybank Cl. Wat 112 B3
Hollybank Cres. Hyt 125 F2
Hollybank La. Ems 136 C2
Hollybank Rd. Hyt 125 F2
Hollybank. L on S 179 F3
Hollybrook Ave. Southa 78 B2
Hollybrook Cl. Southa 78 A1
Hollybrook Gdns. Lo He 129 D3
Hollybrook Rd. Southa 78 B1
Hollywood Cl. N Bad 53 F2
Hollywood La. Lym 198 B3
Holm Cl. Rin 117 E1
Holman Cl. Wat 112 A1
Holmdale Rd. Gos 180 C4
Holme Cl. Lym 198 B1
Holme Rd. Christ 211 D4
Holmefield Ave. Fare 154 C4
Holmes Cl. Net 127 D3
Holmesland Dr. Botl 105 F4
Holmesland La. Botl 105 F4
Holmesland Wlk. Botl 105 F4
Holmfield Ave. Bour 208 B4
Holmgrove. Lo He 129 E2
Holmhurst Ave. Christ 194 C1
Holmsley Cl. Lym 198 A1
Holmsley Cl. Southa 104 B4
Holmsley Rd. Brock 170 C1
Holmsley Rd. New M 170 C1
Holmwood Garth. Rin 141 E3
Holne Ct. Ports 183 E2
Holnest Rd. Broa 188 B1
Holst Way. Wat 134 C3
Holt Cl. Wickh 107 F2
Holt Ct. Southa 126 C4
Holt Down. Pet 41 D2
Holt Gdns. Ro Ca 113 D2
Holt Rd. Poole 205 F3
Holt Rd. Southa 102 C3
Holt Rd. Ver 138 B4
Holworth Cl. Bour 189 F2
Holy Rood Pl. Southa 103 D2
Holyborne Rd. Rom 53 D4
Holybourne Rd. Hav 135 F2
Holyrood Ave. Southa 79 D1
Holyrood Cl. Wat 135 D4
Holywell Cl. Broa 188 B2
Holywell Rd. Shed 84 B1
Home Farm Cl. Hyt 126 A2
Home Farm Way. Ver 114 C3
Home Mead. Den 110 C2
Home Rd. Bour 190 D3
Home Rule Rd. Lo He 129 D2
Homefield Rd. Cos 158 B4
Homefield Rd. Westb 137 D2
Homefield Way. Clanf 88 A3
Homefield. Rom 28 A1
Homelands Estate. Christ 208 C3
Homer Cl. Gos 180 A4
Homer Cl. Wat 111 F1
Homeside Rd. Bour 191 D1
Homewell. Hav 135 F1
Homewood Cl. New M 196 B2
Honey La. Bur 142 C1
Honey La. Fare 130 B3
Honeybourne Cres. Bour 209 D2
Honeycritch La. Frox G 19 E2
Honeysuckle Cl. Gos 155 D2
Honeysuckle Cl. Lo He 129 D3
Honeysuckle Cl. Winch 10 C2
Honeysuckle Ct. Wat 135 D3
Honeysuckle La. Broa 187 F1
Honeysuckle Rd. Southa 79 E2
Honeysuckle Way. Christ 210 A4
Honeywood Cl. Ports 157 F2
Honeywood Cl. Tot 76 B1
Honister Cl. Southa 101 F4
Hood Cl. Bour 190 A1
Hood Cl. Lo He 129 D2
Hood Cres. Bour 190 A1
Hood Rd. Southa 104 C4
Hook Cl. Ch Fo 30 A1
Hook Cres. Ch Fo 30 A1
Hook La. Lo He 153 D4
Hook Park Rd. Lo He 152 C3
Hook Rd. Ampf 29 F1
Hook Rd. Ch Fo 29 F1
Hook Water Cl. Ch Fo 30 A1
Hook Water Rd. Ch Fo 30 A1
Hook's Farm Way. Hav 135 E2
Hook's La. Hav 135 E2
Hooke Cl. Poole 189 D1
Hookpit Farm La. Ki Wo 2 A4
Hookwood La. Ampf 29 F1
Hop Cl. Upt 203 D4
Hope Rd. W End 80 C1
Hope St. Ports 182 B3
Hopfield Cl. Wat 134 C4
Hopfield Mews. Wat 134 C4
Hopkins Cl. Bour 192 A1
Horace Rd. Bour 207 F2
Hordle La. Hord 197 D1
Hordle Rd. Hav 135 E2
Horlock Rd. Brock 146 A1
Hornbeam Cl. He En 105 E3
Hornbeam Rd. Hav 136 A2
Hornbeam Way. Wi Mi 163 F3
Hornby Cl. Lo He 152 B4
Horndean Rd. Ems 136 C2
Hornet Cl. Fare 130 B1
Hornet Cl. Gos 181 E2
Hornet Rd. Th Is 161 D2
Horning Rd. Poole 205 F3
Horns Drove. Rown 77 F3
Horns Hill. Sob 85 D1
Horsa Cl. Bour 208 C2
Horsa Rd. Bour 208 C2
Horsea La. Ports 157 F2
Horsebridge Rd. Hav 136 A2
Horsebridge Way. Rown 77 F3
Horsecroft. Rom 52 C4
Horsefair Ct. Rom 52 C4
Horsefair The. Rom 52 C4
Horseshoe Cl. Lo He 129 E1
Horseshoe Cl. Wi Mi 164 A3
Horseshoe Dr. Rom 28 A1
Horseshoe Lodge. Lo He 128 C1
Horseshoe The. Poole 211 E2
Horsham Ave. Bour 190 B3
Horton Cl. Bour 191 E2
Horton Rd. Gos 155 E2
Horton Rd. St Le 139 F3
Horton Rd. Ver 114 A1
Horton Way. Bish 56 C1
Horton Way. Ver 114 B3
Hosier's La. Poole 204 A1
Hosker Rd. Bour 208 A3
Hospital La. Portc 156 C3
Hospital Rd. Shed 108 A4
Hotspur Cl. Hyt 125 F3
Houchin St. Bi Wa 83 E4
Houghton Cl. Hav 136 A3
Houlton Rd. Poole 204 C2
Hound Cl. Net 127 E3
Hound Rd. Net 127 E3
Hound Road Gdns. Net 127 E3
Hound Way. Net 127 E3
Hounds Way. Wi Mi 164 A3
Houndwell Pl. Southa 103 D2
Hounsdown Ave. Tot 100 C3
Hounsdown Cl. Tot 100 C3
Hounslow Cl. Hamw 203 F1
House Farm Rd. Gos 180 C2
Hoveton Gr. Ch Fo 55 D4
Howard Cl. Bur 143 D2
Howard Cl. Ch Fo 55 E2
Howard Cl. Christ 209 F3
Howard Cl. Fa Oa 57 E1
Howard Cl. Southa 79 F2
Howard Rd. Bour 207 E4
Howard Rd. Ports 157 F2
Howard Rd. Southa 102 B3
Howard Rd. Ver 114 C3
Howard's Gr. Southa 102 B4
Howards Mead. Lym 198 A1
Howe Cl. Christ 209 F3
Howe Cl. New M 195 F2
Howe La. Ver 114 C3
Howe Rd. Gos 180 B3
Howerts Cl. Lo He 152 B4
Howeth Cl. Bour 190 B2
Howeth Rd. Bour 190 B2
Howlett Cl. Lym 198 B2
Howton Cl. Bour 190 B3
Howton Rd. Bour 190 B3
Hoxley Rd. Bour 190 B2
Hoyal Rd. Hamw 203 E2
Hoylake Cl. Gos 155 E1
Hoylake Rd. Cos 134 B1
Hoylecroft Cl. Fare 130 C2
Hubert Rd. Winch 10 C2
Hudson Cl. Poole 189 E1
Hudson Cl. Rin 141 E4
Hudson Ct. Tot 100 B3
Hudson Rd. Ports 182 B2
Hugh's Cl. Black 150 C1
Hulbert Rd. Hav 135 D2
Hulbert Rd. Wat 134 C4
Hull Cres. Bour 189 F2
Hull Rd. Bour 189 F2
Hull Way. Bour 189 F2
Hulles Way. N Bad 53 F2
Hulse Rd. Southa 102 C4
Humber Cl. Stubb 154 A2
Humber Gdns. Burs 105 D1
Humber Rd. Fern 166 A3
Hundred Acres Rd. Sob 108 C3
Hundred Acres Rd. Wickh 108 C3
Hundred La. Bold 199 D4
Hundred The. Rom 52 C4
Hundred The. Wat 111 E1
Hungerfield Cl. Bran 169 D1
Hungerford Hill. Fordi 94 B3
Hungerford Rd. Bour 191 E2
Hungerford. Burs 128 A4
Hunt Ave. Net 127 E3
Hunt Rd. Christ 209 F4
Hunt Rd. Poole 204 C3
Hunter Cl. Christ 210 A4
Hunter Cl. Gos 180 B4
Hunter Cl. Holb 150 A3
Hunter Rd. Ports 183 D2
Hunter Rd. Th Is 161 D2
Hunters Cl. Ver 115 E3
Hunters Cres. Rom 28 B1
Hunters Cres. Tot 100 A3
Hunters Hill. Ashu 100 B2
Hunters Lodge. Fare 130 A1
Hunters Ride. Wat 134 C3
Hunters Way. Bish 57 D1
Huntfield Rd. Bour 191 D1
Huntingdon Cl. Lo He 129 E1
Huntingdon Cl. Tot 76 C1
Huntingdon Dr. Oakl 163 F1
Huntingdon Gdns. Christ 193 D1
Huntley Cl. Cos 133 D1
Huntly Rd. Bour 206 B4
Huntly Way. Southa 103 F4
Hunton Cl. Southa 78 B2
Hunts Pond Rd. Lo He 129 E2
Huntsbottom La. Liss 21 D2
Huntvale Rd. Bour 191 D2
Hurdle Way. Comp 31 E4
Hurdles The. Lo He 129 E1
Hurlingham Gdns. Southa 79 D3
Hurn Cl. St Le 140 B3
Hurn La. St Le 140 B3
Hurn Rd. Christ 192 B2
Hurn Rd. Hurn 192 B2
Hurn Rd. St Le 140 B2
Hurn Way. Christ 192 B1
Hursley Cl. Bour 208 B4
Hursley Dr. Black 177 F4
Hursley Rd. Ch Fo 55 E4
Hursley Rd. Hav 135 E3
Hurst Cl. Ch Fo 55 D2
Hurst Cl. Christ 195 E1
Hurst Cl. Stubb 154 A1
Hurst Cl. Tot 100 C4
Hurst Green Cl. Wat 112 A1
Hurst Green. Gos 155 D1
Hurst Hill. Poole 211 E4
Hurst La. Co Com 58 A4
Hurst La. Frox G 18 A2
Hurst Rd. M on S 213 F2
Hurst Rd. Rin 117 D1
Hurstbourne Ave. Christ 194 C1
Hurstbourne Cl. Hav 135 E3
Hurstdene Rd. Bour 191 E1
Hurstville Dr. Wat 134 C4
Hurstwood Ave. Southb 137 F1
Hussar Ct. Wat 111 E1
Hussey Cl. Winch 2 A1
Huxley Cl. Lo He 129 D1
Hyacinth Cl. Broa 187 F1
Hyde Abbey Rd. Winch 11 D4
Hyde Church La. Winch 2 A1
Hyde Church Path. Winch 2 A1
Hyde Cl. Southa 78 B1
Hyde Cl. Sway 172 A1
Hyde Cl. Tot 100 A4
Hyde Cl. Winch 1 C1
Hyde Gate. Winch 2 A1
Hyde La. Down 46 B4
Hyde La. Fordi 94 B3
Hyde Park Rd. Ports 182 B3
Hyde Rd. Bour 190 B3
Hyde St. Ports 182 B2
Hyde St. Winch 2 A1
Hyden Farm La. Hambl 87 E4
Hylton Rd. Pet 40 C2
Hyman Way. Tot 100 C4
Hynesbury Rd. Christ 210 B4
Hythe By Pass. Hyt 149 F4
Hythe Rd. Cos 157 F4
Hythe Rd. March 124 C4
Hythe Rd. Poole 205 D4

Ibbertson Cl. Bour 191 F1
Ibbertson Rd. Bour 191 F1
Ibbertson Way. Bour 191 F1
Ibbett Rd. Bour 190 B2
Ibbotson Way. Tot 100 B3
Ibsley Cl. Bour 207 E3
Ibsley Dro. Ibs 94 A1
Ibsley Gr. Hav 135 E2
Icarus Pl. Wat 134 C1
Iddesleigh Rd. Bour 207 D3
Idsworth Rd. Ports 183 D4
Idsworth Rd. Wat 112 A1
Iford Cl. Bour 208 C3
Iford Gdns. Bour 208 B4
Iford La. Bour 208 C3
Ilex Cres. Lo He 128 C2
Ilex Wlk. S Hay 185 E1
Imber Dr. Christ 210 C4
Imber Rd. Winch 11 E4
Imber Way. Southa 104 B2
Imperial Ave. Southa 102 A4
Imperial Rd. Southa 103 D4
Ingle Glen. Hyt 126 A1
Ingle Green. Tot 76 A1
Ingledene Cl. Gos 181 D2
Ingledene Cl. Hav 135 E1
Inglesham Way. Hamw 203 F2
Ingleside Cl. Fare 154 A4
Ingleside. Net 127 C4
Ingleton Rd. Southa 77 E1
Inglewood Dr. New M 196 A1
Inglis Rd. Ports 182 C2
Ingoldfield La. Sob 109 E4
Ingram Ct. Southa 103 E4
Ingworth Rd. Poole 206 A3
Inhams La. Den 110 B3
Inhurst Ave. Wat 135 D4
Inhurst Rd. Ports 157 F1
Inkerman Rd. Southa 103 E2
Inkpen Wlk. Hav 135 E4
Inlands Rd. Southb 161 F4
Inmans La. Pet 41 D3
Insley Cres. Broa 187 F3
International Way. Southa 126 C4
Inveravon. Christ 209 F2
Inverclyde Rd. Poole 205 E2
Invergordon Ave. Cos 158 A4
Inverkip Cl. L on S 179 F4
Inverleigh Rd. Bour 208 B3
Inverness Ave. Fare 130 C2
Inverness Rd. Gos 181 D3
Inverness Rd. Poole 211 F4
Inverness Rd. Ports 182 C4
Inwood Rd. Liss 21 D2
Ionic Cl. Ch Fo 55 F4
Iping Ave. Hav 135 F2
Ipley Way. Hyt 126 A1
Ipswich Rd. Bour 206 A2
Ireland Way. Wat 134 C3
Iris Rd. Bour 190 C1
Iris Rd. Southa 79 D2
Iron Mill Cl. Fare 130 B2
Ironbridge La. Ports 183 E2
Ironmill La. Swanw 130 A3
Irvine Cl. Fare 88 A2
Irvine Way. Christ 209 F4
Irving Rd. Bour 208 B3
Irving Rd. Southa 77 F1
Irwell Cl. N Bad 55 D3
Isambard Brunel Rd. Ports 182 B3
Isis Cl. Southa 101 F4
Island Cl. N Hay 160 A2
Island View Ave. Christ 210 A3
Island View Cl. M on S 213 F2
Island View Rd. B on S 211 E4
Island View Terr. Ports 157 E1
Island View Wlk. Portc 132 B1
Islay Gdns. Cos 133 F1
Itchen Ave. Bish 56 C1
Itchen Cl. W Wel 50 B2
Itchen Rd. Hav 136 A3
Itchen Rd. Southa 103 D1
Itchen View. Southa 79 F2
Itchenor Rd. S Hay 185 F1
Itchenside Cl. Southa 79 F2
Itchin Cl. Tot 100 B3
Ithlca Cl. S Hay 185 D2
Ivamy Pl. Bour 189 F1
Ivanhoe Rd. Southa 78 B1
Ivor Cl. Holb 150 B2
Ivor Rd. Broa 187 E2
Ivor Rd. Poole 204 A1
Ivy Cl. St Le 139 E2
Ivy Ct. Wat 134 B2
Ivy La. Rin 117 D2
Ivy La. W End 80 B1
Ivy Orch. Clanf 88 A3
Ivy Rd. Oakl 188 B4
Ivy Rd. Southa 103 E4
Ivyhouse La. Frox G 18 C2
Iwerne Cl. Bour 191 D2

Jackdaw Rise. Eastl 55 E1
Jackman's Hill. Ows 33 D3
Jackson Cl. Cos 158 B3
Jackson Rd. Poole 205 E3
Jacob's Gutter La. Tot 101 D2
Jacob's St. Ports 182 B3
Jacobean Cl. Christ 195 D1
Jacobs Cl. Clanf 88 B3
Jacobs Cl. Rom 53 D4
Jacobs Wlk. Tot 100 C3
Jacomb Pl. Gos 155 E1
Jacqueline Ave. Wat 134 B2
Jacqueline Rd. Poole 205 E4
Jamaica Pl. Gos 181 E2
James Cl. Gos 155 E2
James Cl. S Hay 184 C2
James Copse Rd. Horn 111 F3
James Ct. Rom 53 D3
James Grieve Ave. Lo He 129 D1
James Rd. Gos 155 E2
James Rd. Hav 135 F1
James Rd. Poole 206 A3
James St. Southa 103 D2
Jameson Rd. Bour 190 C1
Jameson Rd. Southa 103 F2
Janaway Gdns. Southa 103 E4
Janes Cl. Black 177 F4
Janson Rd. Southa 102 B4
Jarndyce Wlk. Ports 182 B4
Jarvis Fields. Burs 128 A4
Jasmine Ct. Lym 198 C2
Jasmine Gr. Wat 135 D3
Jasmine Rd. He En 105 D4
Jasmine Wlk. Fare 154 C4
Jasmond Rd. Cos 157 F3
Jason Pl. Wat 134 C1
Jason Way. Gos 180 C4
Java Rd. Southa 103 D1
Javelin Rd. Th Is 161 D2
Jay's Ct. Christ 211 D4
Jealous La. Sway 173 D1
Jefferson Ave. Bour 207 E3
Jeffries Cl. Rown 77 F3
Jellicoe Ave. Gos 180 C2
Jellicoe Dr. Christ 209 F3
Jenkins Gr. Ports 183 D4
Jenner Way. Rom 53 E4
Jennings Rd. Poole 205 E1
Jennings Rd. Tot 101 D4
Jephcote Rd. Bour 189 F2
Jermyns La. Abb 28 B2
Jermyns La. Ampf 28 B2
Jerome Ct. Southa 104 B3
Jerram Cl. Gos 180 C2

Jerrett's La. Nur 77 E2
Jersey Cl. Poole 189 E1
Jersey Cl. Southa 77 F2
Jersey Cl. Stubb 154 B1
Jersey Rd. Poole 189 E1
Jersey Rd. Ports 182 C4
Jervis Court La. Bi Wa 84 A4
Jervis Court La. Swan 84 A4
Jervis Dr. Gos 181 D3
Jervis Rd. Ports 157 E1
Jesmond Ave. Christ 210 C4
Jesmond Gr. Lo He 129 D1
Jessamine Rd. Southa 78 A1
Jessica Ave. Ver 114 B4
Jessica Cl. Wat 112 A1
Jessie Rd. Gos 181 D2
Jessie Rd. Hav 135 E2
Jessie Rd. Ports 182 C2
Jessop Cl. Bour 190 C2
Jessop Cl. Hyt 125 F3
Jessop Rd. Wi Mi 164 A3
Jessop Wlk. Hyt 125 F3
Jewell Rd. Bour 192 A1
Jewry St. Winch 11 D4
Jinny La. Mich 27 F3
Joanna Cl. Down 46 B4
Jockey La. Bish 56 C3
Jodrell Cl. Horn 112 B4
John St. Southa 103 D2
John's Rd. Southa 103 E2
Johns Rd. Fare 155 D4
Johnson St. Southa 103 D2
Johnston Rd. Poole 204 B4
Johnstone Rd. Christ 209 F3
Jolliffe Ave. Poole 204 B2
Jolliffe Rd. Poole 204 B2
Jonathan Rd. Fare 130 C1
Jonathon Cl. Lym 198 C3
Jones La. Hyt 126 A3
Jordans La. Bold 199 D4
Jordans La. Sway 172 B1
Joseph St. Gos 181 E2
Josian Wlk. Southa 103 D3
Jowitt Dr. New M 195 F1
Joyce Dickson Cl. Rin 141 D3
Joys La. Bold 199 F4
Joys Rd. W Moo 138 C4
Juandrells Cl. New M 196 B2
Jubilee Rd. Poole 205 E3
Jubilee Ave. Portc 132 C1
Jubilee Cl. Eastl 55 F1
Jubilee Cl. Fordi 69 E1
Jubilee Cl. Rin 141 E4
Jubilee Cres. Poole 205 E3
Jubilee Ct. Fare 155 D4
Jubilee Gdns. Bour 190 B1
Jubilee Gdns. Southa 104 A4
Jubilee Rd. Broa 187 F4
Jubilee Rd. Fordi 69 E1
Jubilee Rd. Gos 181 D3
Jubilee Rd. Portc 156 B4
Jubilee Rd. Ports 182 C2
Jubilee Rd. Rom 52 C4
Jubilee Rd. Wat 111 F1
Jubilee Terr. Ports 182 A2
Julia Cl. Christ 210 C4
Julian Cl. Southa 78 C3
Julian Rd. Southa 104 A2
Julian's Rd. Pamp 163 D2
Julian's Rd. Wi Mi 163 D2
Julie Ave. Fare 130 C1
Juliet Ct. Wat 135 D4
Julius Cl. Ch Fo 55 F3
Julyan Ave. Poole 206 A4
Jumar Cl. Lo He 152 B4
Jumpers Ave. Christ 208 C4
Jumpers Rd. Christ 208 C4
Junction Rd. Bour 206 C4
Junction Rd. Hamw 203 E2
Junction Rd. Tot 101 D4
Juniper Cl. Fern 165 E4
Juniper Cl. Lym 198 A1
Juniper Cl. N Bad 53 F3
Juniper Cl. W Moo 138 C4
Juniper Cl. Winch 10 B3
Juniper Rd. Horn 88 B1
Juniper Rd. Southa 103 F4
Juniper Sq. Hav 159 F4
Jupiter Cl. Southa 77 F2
Jupiter Way. Broa 187 F4
Jurd Way. Burs 104 C1
Justin Cl. Fare 154 C4
Justinian Cl. Ch Fo 55 F4
Jute Cl. Portc 132 A1

Kanes Hill. Southa 104 C3
Kangaw Pl. Hamw 203 E1
Karen Ave. Cos 158 B3
Kassassin St. Ports 183 D1
Kassel Cl. Wat 135 D4
Katherine Chance Cl. Burt 193 E2
Kathleen Rd. Southa 104 A2
Katrina Gdns. S Hay 185 D3
Katrine Cres. N Bad 55 D4
Katterns Cl. Christ 192 C1
Kayleigh Cl. Tot 100 B3
Kealy Rd. Gosp 181 D3
Kearsney Ave. Ports 157 F1
Keast Wlk. Gos 155 E2
Keats Ave. M on S 213 E3
Keats Ave. Portc 132 C1
Keats Cl. Wat 111 F2
Keats Cl. Winch 10 B2
Keats Rd. Southa 104 B3
Keble Cl. Ch Fo 55 E2
Keble Rd. Ch Fo 55 E2
Keble St. Winch 10 B3
Keeble Rd. Bour 190 B3
Keep The. Portc 156 B4
Keepers La. Fern 164 C3
Keepers La. Mott 5 E1
Keepers Way. N Bad 55 D3
Kefford Cl. Horn 112 A3
Keighley Ave. Broa 187 F1
Keith Cl. Gos 181 D3
Keith Rd. Bour 206 B4
Kelburn Cl. Ch Fo 55 D4
Kellaway Rd. Poole 204 C4
Kellett Rd. Southa 102 C4
Kelly Cl. Poole 204 C4
Kelly Rd. Wat 134 C3
Kelmscott Gdns. Ch Fo 30 A1
Kelsey Ave. Southb 137 F1
Kelsey Cl. Liss 21 D3
Kelsey Cl. Lo He 129 D1
Kelsey Head. Ports 157 D4
Kelvin Cl. Hyt 126 A2
Kelvin Gr. Net 127 E3
Kelvin Gr. Portc 156 B4
Kelvin Rd. Eastl 55 F1
Kemp Rd. Bour 206 C4
Kempland La. Frox G 17 E2
Kempton Pk. Wat 112 A1
Kemshott Ct. Hav 135 E3
Ken Berry Ct. Hav 136 A3
Ken Rd. Bour 208 C2
Kench The. S Hay 183 F3
Kendal Ave. Ports 158 A1
Kendal Ave. Southa 101 E4
Kendal Cl. Ch Fo 55 F4
Kendal Cl. Wat 112 A2
Kenilworth Cl. L on S 179 F4
Kenilworth Cl. New M 196 A2
Kenilworth Dr. Eastl 56 A3
Kenilworth Gdns. W End 80 C1
Kenilworth Rd. Ports 182 B1
Kenilworth Rd. Southa 102 C3
Kenmore Cl. Tot 100 C3
Kennard Ct. New M 195 F2
Kennard Rd. New M 195 F2
Kennart Rd. Broa 204 A4
Kennedy Ave. Fare 130 B2
Kennedy Cl. Wat 134 C2
Kennedy Cres. Gos 180 C1
Kennedy Rd. Southa 77 F2
Kennel La. Litt 1 B2
Kennet Cl. Gos 181 D1
Kennet Cl. Rom 53 E4
Kennet Cl. W End 80 A2
Kennet Rd. Rom 53 E4
Kennington Rd. Cadn 99 D4
Kensington Park. M on S 213 E2
Kensington Cl. Bish 56 B3
Kensington Dr. Bour 206 B2
Kensington Flds. Hyt 125 E2
Kensington Rd. Gos 181 E2
Kensington Rd. Ports 157 F1
Kenson Gdns. Southa 104 A2
Kent Gr. Portc 156 B3
Kent La. Ibs 93 E1
Kent Rd. Ch Fo 55 E2
Kent Rd. Gos 155 D2
Kent Rd. Poole 205 F3
Kent Rd. Ports 182 B2
Kent Rd. Southa 79 E1
Kent St. Ports 182 A3
Kent St. Southa 103 E3
Kentidge Rd. Wat 134 B3
Kentish Rd. Southa 102 B4
Kenwood Rd. Portc 156 B3
Kenwyn Cl. W End 80 A1
Kenya Rd. Portc 156 A4
Kenyon Cl. Poole 204 C4
Kenyon Rd. Poole 204 C4
Kenyon Rd. Ports 157 F1
Kepple Cl. Rin 141 D4
Kerley Rd. Bour 206 C1
Kerrfield Mews. Winch 10 B4
Kerrfield. Winch 10 B4
Kerry Cl. Ch Fo 55 E3
Kerry Cl. Lym 198 B2
Kesteven Way. Southa 104 A4
Kestrel Cl. Bi Wa 83 D4
Kestrel Cl. Botl 81 F1
Kestrel Cl. Clanf 88 B2
Kestrel Cl. Fern 165 D4
Kestrel Cl. March 101 F1
Kestrel Cl. Southa 78 A3
Kestrel Cl. Stubb 154 A2
Kestrel Cl. Winch 10 B2
Kestrel Dr. Christ 210 A3
Kestrel Pl. Cos 158 C4
Kestrel Rd. Eastl 55 F1
Kestrel Way. Alderh 93 D3
Keswick Ave. Ports 183 D4
Keswick Rd. Bour 208 A2
Keswick Rd. New M 196 A3
Keswick Rd. Southa 103 E1
Keswick Way. Ver 114 C3
Kettering Terr. Ports 182 B4
Kevlyn Cres. Burs 104 C1
Kew La. Burs 128 A4
Kewlake La. Cadn 74 B1
Keydell Ave. Wat 112 A3
Keydell Cl. Wat 112 A3
Keyes Cl. Christ 209 F3
Keyes Cl. Gos 155 E2
Keyes Cl. Poole 189 F1
Keyes Rd. Gos 155 E2
Keyhaven Cl. Gos 155 D1
Keyhaven Dr. Hav 135 E3
Keyhaven Rd. M on S 213 F2
Keynsham Rd. Southa 104 A3
Keysworth Ave. B on S 211 F4
Keysworth Rd. Hamw 203 E2
Khartoum Rd. Southa 79 D1
Khyber Rd. Poole 205 E3
Kidmore La. Den 110 C3
Kielder Cl. N Bad 55 D4
Kielder Gr. Gos 155 E1
Kilham La. Winch 10 A3
Killarney Cl. Southa 104 C2
Kilmarnock Rd. Bour 190 C1
Kilmeston Cl. Hav 135 F3
Kilmeston Rd. Cher 14 B2
Kilmeston Rd. Kilm 14 B1
Kilmington Way. Christ 210 C4
Kilmiston Dr. Portc 132 B1
Kilmiston Rd. Ports 182 C4
Kiln Acre. Fare 88 A2
Kiln Cl. Broa 187 E2
Kiln Cl. Hyt 125 F2
Kiln Hill. Sob 109 D4
Kiln La. Brai 28 B3
Kiln La. Buri 65 E3
Kiln La. Co Com 31 E1
Kiln La. Ott 31 E1
Kiln La. Red 47 F4
Kiln Rd. Fare 88 A2
Kiln Rd. Ports 158 A1
Kilnside. Den 110 C2
Kilnyard Cl. Tot 76 B1
Kilpatrick Cl. Ports 182 B4
Kilwich Way. Portc 156 A3
Kimber Rd. Bour 189 F2
Kimberley Cl. Christ 208 C4
Kimberley Cl. Fa Oa 57 E1
Kimberley Rd. Bour 208 B3
Kimberley Rd. Poole 205 D2
Kimberley Rd. Ports 183 D1
Kimbers. Pet 40 C2
Kimbolton Rd. Ports 183 D3
Kimbridge Cres. Hav 136 A3
Kimbridge La. Mich 27 D4
Kimmeridge Ave. Poole 205 E4
Kimpton Cl. L on S 179 F3
Kineton Rd. Southa 78 C1
King Albert St. Ports 182 B3
King Alfred Pl. Winch 2 A1
King Alfred Terr. Winch 2 A1
King Arthur's Ct. Cos 158 B4
King Charles St. Ports 182 A2
King Cl. St Le 139 F2
King Cup Ave. Lo He 128 C2
King Edward Ave. Bour 191 D1
King Edward Ave. Southa 102 A4
King Edward Ct. Ports 182 A2
King Edward's Cres. Ports 157 E1
King George Ave. Bour 190 C1
King George Ave. Pet 40 C2
King George Rd. Portc 156 B4
King George's Ave. Southa 101 F4
King Henry 1 St. Ports 182 A3
King John Ave. Bour 189 E3
King John Ave. Portc 156 A4
King La. Frox G 39 F4
King Richard 1 Rd. Ports 182 A2
King Richard Dr. Bour 189 E3
King St. Ems 161 D4
King St. Gos 181 E3
King St. Ports 182 B2
King St. Southa 103 D2
King St. Westb 137 D2
King St. Wi Mi 163 D2
King William St. Ports 182 A3
King's Arms La. Rin 140 C4
King's Arms Row. Rin 140 C4
King's Ave. Christ 208 C3
King's Cl. Ch Fo 55 E4
King's Copse Rd. Black 177 E4
King's Croft La. Hav 135 E1
King's La. Frox G 18 B2
King's Park Dr. Bour 207 F3
King's Park Rd. Bour 207 F3
King's Park Rd. Southa 103 D3
King's Rd. Bour 207 D4
King's Rd. Ems 160 C4
King's Rd. Fare 88 A1
King's Rd. L on S 179 F4
King's Rd. Ports 182 A2
King's Saltern Rd. Lym 199 D1
King's Terr. Ems 160 C4
Kingdom Cl. Lo He 129 E3
Kingfisher Cl. Hamble 128 A2
Kingfisher Cl. Ro Ca 113 D1
Kingfisher Cl. W Moo 138 C1
Kingfisher Copse. Lo He 129 D2
Kingfisher Park. W Moo 138 C3
Kingfisher Rd. Eastl 55 F1
Kingfisher Way. March 101 F1
Kingfisher Way. Rin 117 D1
Kingfishers The. Ver 115 D3
Kingfishers. Christ 209 D3
Kingfishers. Portc 155 F4
Kings Ave. Hamble 127 F2
Kings Ave. Poole 205 E2
Kings Ave. Winch 10 C3
Kings Cl. Lyn 121 F3
Kings Cl. Ro Ca 113 D1
Kings Cl. Twyf 32 A4
Kings Cl. W Moo 138 C1
Kings Copse Rd. He En 105 E3
Kings Cres. Lym 198 B2
Kings Field Gdns. Burs 105 D1
Kings Field. Burs 105 D1
Kings Head Yd. Winch 11 D4
Kings La. Chilc 11 F3
Kings La. Sway 197 F4
Kings Mede. Wat 112 A3
Kings Rd. Ch Fo 55 E3
Kings Rd. Gos 181 D3
Kings Rd. Lym 198 B2
Kings Rd. New M 196 B2
Kings Rd. Pet 40 B2
Kings Rd. S Hay 185 D3
Kings Ride. Black 177 F4
Kings Somborne Rd. Brai 7 E1
Kingsbere Ave. Bour 190 A1
Kingsbere Rd. Poole 204 C3
Kingsbridge Rd. Poole 205 E2
Kingsbury Rd. Southa 103 D4
Kingsbury's La. Rin 140 C4
Kingsclere Ave. Hav 135 E3
Kingsclere Ave. Southa 126 C4
Kingscote Rd. Cos 132 C1
Kingscote Rd. Wat 111 E2
Kingscroft Ct. Hav 135 E1
Kingsdown Rd. Wat 111 E1
Kingsdown Way. Southa 80 A1
Kingsey Ave. Ems 160 C4
Kingsfernsden La. Pet 41 D3
Kingsfield. Lym 199 D1
Kingsfield. Rin 141 D4
Kingsfold Ave. Southa 79 F2
Kingsford Cl. Red 47 E3
Kingsgate Rd. Winch 10 C3
Kingsgate St. Winch 11 D3
Kingsland Cl. Cos 133 E1
Kingsland Cres. Poole 204 B1
Kingsland Sq. Southa 103 D2
Kingsley Ave. Bour 209 D2
Kingsley Cl. Bour 209 D2
Kingsley Gdns. Tot 100 A4
Kingsley Green. Hav 135 F3
Kingsley Pl. Winch 10 C3
Kingsley Rd. Gos 180 C4
Kingsley Rd. Ports 183 E2
Kingsley Rd. Southa 102 A4
Kingsmead Ave. Stubb 154 B1
Kingsmead. Sob 108 B4
Kingsmill Cl. Gos 180 C2
Kingsmill Rd. Poole 204 C4
Kingston Cres. Ports 182 B4
Kingston Gdns. Fare 130 B2
Kingston Park. Lym 198 B1
Kingston Rd. Gos 180 C3
Kingston Rd. Poole 204 B2
Kingston Rd. Ports 182 C4
Kingston Rd. Southa 102 B3
Kingston. Net 127 E4
Kingsway Cl. Christ 192 C1
Kingsway Gdns. Ch Fo 55 F4
Kingsway The. Portc 156 B4
Kingsway. Ch Fo 55 F4
Kingsway. Fern 165 D4
Kingsway. N Hay 160 A2
Kingsway. Southa 103 D3
Kingswell Cl. Bour 190 B1
Kingswell Gdns. Bour 190 A1
Kingswell Rd. Bour 190 B1
Kingswell St. Ports 182 B3
Kingswood. March 102 A1
Kingsworthy Rd. Hav 135 F2
Kinnell Cl. Ems 160 C4
Kinross Cres. Cos 158 A4
Kinross Rd. Bour 206 C3
Kinross Rd. Tot 100 C3
Kinsbourne Ave. Bour 190 B1
Kinsbourne Cl. Southa 104 C3
Kinsbourne Way. Southa 104 C3
Kinson Gr. Bour 190 B3
Kinson Park Rd. Bour 190 B3
Kinson Rd. Bour 190 B2
Kintyre Rd. Cos 133 F1
Kinver Cl. Rom 28 A1
Kipling Rd. Eastl 55 F2
Kipling Rd. Poole 205 D3
Kipling Rd. Ports 157 F2
Kirby Cl. Poole 204 C3
Kirby Rd. Ports 157 F1
Kirkham Ave. Burt 193 E2
Kirkstall Rd. Ports 182 C1
Kirkway. Broa 188 A2
Kirtley Cl. Cos 158 B3
Kirton Rd. Cos 158 B4
Kitchener Cres. Broa 188 A1
Kitchener Rd. Southa 79 E1
Kitchers Cl. Sway 172 A1
Kite Cl. Wat 111 F2
Kites Croft Cl. Lo He 129 E1
Kitnocks Hill. Curd 106 C4
Kitscroft Rd. Bour 190 B3
Kitt's La. W Meo 16 B1
Kittiwake Cl. Gos 155 D1
Kitwalls La. M on S 213 E3
Kivernell Rd. M on S 213 E2
Kiwi Cl. Poole 204 C2
Knapp Cl. Christ 209 D4
Knapp La. Ampf 29 E2
Knapp Mill Ave. Christ 209 D4
Knapps Hard. W Meo 37 D3
Knatchbull Cl. Rom 52 C4
Knellers La. Ashu 100 B2
Knight Cl. Winch 2 A1
Knighton Heath Cl. Bour 189 F2
Knighton Heath Rd. Bour 189 F2
Knighton La. Oakl 189 E4
Knighton Park. B on S 211 F4
Knighton Rd. Southa 103 F2
Knights Bank Rd. Stubb 153 F1
Knights Rd. Bour 189 E3
Knightstone Grange. Hyt 126 A1
Knightwood Ave. Hav 136 A3
Knightwood Ave. Lyn 121 F3
Knightwood Cl. Ashu 100 A1
Knightwood Cl. Christ 210 B4
Knightwood Cl. Lyn 121 F3
Knightwood Rd. Ch Fo 55 D3
Knightwood Rd. Hyt 126 A2
Knightwood Rd. N Bad 55 D3
Knobcrook Rd. Wi Mi 163 D3
Knole Gdns. Bour 207 E2
Knole Rd. Bour 207 E2
Knoll Gdns. St Le 139 F2
Knoll La. Broa 187 D4
Knowland Dr. M on S 213 E3
Knowle Hill. Eastl 56 A4
Knowle La. Fa Oa 57 F1
Knowle Rd. Brock 145 F1
Knowles Meadow. Hill B 21 D1
Knowlton Gdns. Bour 191 D2
Knowlton Rd. Broa 188 C1
Knowsley Cres. Cos 158 A4
Knowsley Rd. Cos 157 F4
Knox Rd. Hav 135 E1
Knox Rd. Ports 157 E1
Knyght Cl. Rom 53 D3
Knyveton Rd. Bour 207 E2
Kootenay Ave. Southa 104 C4
Kooyong Cl. W Wel 51 D1
Kynegils Rd. Winch 1 C1
Kynon Cl. Gos 181 E4
Kyrchil La. Wi Mi 163 F3
Kyrchil Way. Wi Mi 163 F4
Kytes La. Durl 82 B3

Labrador Dr. Poole 204 B1
Laburnam Cl. N Bad 54 A3
Laburnum Ave. Cos 158 B4
Laburnum Cl. Fern 165 D3
Laburnum Cl. N Bad 54 A3
Laburnum Cl. Ver 115 E3
Laburnum Cres. Hyt 150 A4
Laburnum Dr. Hord 213 F4
Laburnum Gr. Eastl 56 A2
Laburnum Gr. Ports 157 F1
Laburnum Gr. S Hay 185 D2
Laburnum Rd. Fare 155 D3
Laburnum Rd. He En 105 E3
Laburnum Rd. Southa 79 E2
Laburnum Rd. Wat 134 B3
Lacey Cres. Poole 205 D3
Lackford Ave. Tot 100 C3
Lacon Cl. Southa 103 F4
Lacy Cl. Wi Mi 163 E3
Lacy Dr. Wi Mi 163 E3
Ladram Rd. Gos 180 C2
Lady Betty's Dr. Lo He 129 F3
Ladybridge Rd. Wat 134 B2
Ladycross Rd. Hyt 126 A1
Ladysmith Rd. Christ 209 F4
Ladywood. Eastl 55 F3
Lagado Cl. Poole 211 E4
Lagland St. Poole 204 B1
Lagoon Rd. Poole 211 D4
Laidlaw Cl. Poole 206 A4
Lake Ave. Hamw 203 E1
Lake Cres. Hamw 203 F2
Lake Dr. Hamw 203 E1
Lake Farm Cl. He En 105 E4
Lake Gr. New M 196 A2
Lake Rd. Bour 190 B3
Lake Rd. Ch Fo 55 F4
Lake Rd. Curd 106 C4
Lake Rd. Hamw 203 F1
Lake Rd. Ports 182 B3
Lake Rd. Southa 103 E1
Lake Rd. Ver 115 D3
Lakeland Gdns. March 101 F1
Lakelands Dr. Southa 102 A3
Lakeside Ave. Ports 183 D4
Lakeside Ave. Rown 77 F3
Lakeside Rd. Poole 206 A1
Lakeside. Fare 130 C3
Lakeside. L on S 179 F2

Lakeside. Rin 141 E3
Lakesmere Rd. Horn 112 B3
Lakeview Dr. Rin 141 E3
Lakewood Cl. Ch Fo 55 E4
Lakewood Rd. Ashu 100 B2
Lakewood Rd. Ch Fo 30 C1
Lakewood Rd. Christ 194 C1
Lamb Cl. Broa 188 B1
Lambert Cl. Wat 134 C3
Lambourn Cl. Fare 154 B4
Lambourne Cl. Hyt 125 F1
Lambourne Dr. Lo He 129 D2
Lambourne Rd. W End 80 A1
Lambsgreen La. Broa 162 C1
Lammas Rd. Hyt 126 A1
Lampeter Ave. Cos 158 A4
Lancaster Cl. Broa 187 F3
Lancaster Cl. Burs 105 D1
Lancaster Cl. Christ 210 B4
Lancaster Cl. L on S 180 A2
Lancaster Cl. Portc 132 A1
Lancaster Dr. Broa 187 F3
Lancaster Dr. Ver 114 C3
Lancaster Rd. Southa 77 F2
Lancaster Way. Wat 134 C3
Lander Cl. Poole 204 B1
Landford Gdns. Bour 191 E1
Landford Way. Bour 191 E1
Landguard Rd. Ports 183 D2
Landguard Rd. Southa 102 B3
Landon Rd. Gos 180 B4
Landport St. Ports 182 A2
Landport St. Ports 182 B3
Landport Terr. Ports 182 A2
Landport View. Ports 182 B3
Lands End Rd. Burs 128 B4
Landsdowne St. Ports 182 A2
Landseer Rd. Bour 206 B2
Landseer Rd. Southa 104 B2
Lane End Rd. Ems 160 C4
Lane The. Faw 151 D2
Lane The. Gos 181 D1
Lane The. Ports 182 C1
Lanes End. Stubb 154 B1
Lanes The. New M 196 A3
Lanesbridge Cl. Ne Ma 99 F3
Langbar Cl. Southa 103 F3
Langbrook Cl. Hav 159 F4
Langdale Ave. Cos 158 A4
Langdale Cl. Southa 101 F4
Langdon Rd. Poole 205 E2
Langdown Lawn Cl. Hyt 126 A1
Langdown Lawn. Hyt 126 A2
Langdown Rd. Hyt 126 A2
Langford La. Red 47 F4
Langford Rd. Ports 182 C4
Langham Cl. N Bad 53 F2
Langhorn Rd. Southa 79 E2
Langley Gdn. Fordi 70 A2
Langley Green. Fordi 70 A2
Langley Lodge Gdns. Black 177 F4
Langley Rd. Christ 194 C1
Langley Rd. Poole 205 F2
Langley Rd. Ports 182 C4
Langley Rd. Southa 102 A3
Langrish Cl. Hav 136 A3
Langrish Rd. Southa 78 A2
Langside Ave. Poole 206 A4
Langstone Ave. Hav 159 F4
Langstone High St. Hav 159 F3
Langstone Rd. Hav 159 F4
Langstone Rd. Ports 183 D3
Langstone Wlk. Gos 155 D1
Langton Cl. B on S 212 A4
Langton Cl. Winch 1 C1
Langton Farm Gdns. Ports 182 C4
Langton Rd. Bi Wa 83 E4
Langton Rd. Bour 207 F3
Lanham La. Spar 9 F4
Lanham La. Winch 1 A1
Lankhills Rd. Winch 2 A1
Lansdown Ave. Portc 156 B3
Lansdowne Ave. Wat 134 A1
Lansdowne Ave. Winch 10 C3
Lansdowne Cl. Rom 52 C4
Lansdowne Cres. Bour 207 D2
Lansdowne Gdns. Bour 207 D2
Lansdowne Gdns. Rom 52 C4
Lansdowne Hill. Southa 102 C2
Lansdowne Rd. Bour 207 D3
Lansdowne Rd. Southa 102 A4
Lansdowne The. Bour 207 D2
Lantana Cl. Wat 134 C3
Lapthorn Cl. Gos 155 D2
Lapwing Cl. Gos 181 D4
Lapwing Dr. Tot 100 B4
Lapwing Gr. Portc 155 F4
Lapwing Rd. Wi Mi 164 A4
Lara Cl. Bour 191 E2
Larch Ave. Holb 150 B3
Larch Cl. Broa 187 F1
Larch Cl. Hord 196 C2
Larch Cl. L on S 180 A3
Larch Cl. St Le 140 A2
Larch Rd. Southa 78 A2
Larch Way. Fern 165 E4
Larchdale Cl. Lo He 152 B4
Larches Gdns. Fare 130 B1
Larchfield Way. Wat 112 B3
Larchwood Ave. Hav 135 D2
Larchwood Rd. Tot 100 B3
Larcombe Rd. Pet 40 B1
Larg Dr. Winch 1 B2
Lark Hill Rise. Winch 10 B2
Lark Rd. Christ 210 A3
Larkhill Rd. Ports 157 F2
Larks Cl. Fern 165 D4
Larks Rise. Fern 165 D4
Larksfield Ave. Bour 191 E2
Larkshill Cl. New M 196 A2
Larkspur Chase. Southa 104 C3
Larkspur Cl. Lo He 128 C1
Larkspur Gdns. He En 105 E3
Larkspur Gdns. Holb 150 A2
Larkwhistle Wlk. Hav 135 E4
Lascelles Rd. Bour 208 A3
Laser Cl. Lo He 128 C1
Lasham Green. Hav 136 A3
Lasham Wlk. Fare 154 B4
Latch Farm Ave. Christ 209 D4
Latchmore Dr. Hyt 125 E2
Latchmore Forest Gr. Wat 112 A2
Latchmore Gdns. Wat 111 F2
Latelie Cl. Net 127 E3
Latham Cl. Fa Oa 57 D1
Latham Ct. Southa 102 A4
Latham Rd. Fa Oa 57 D1
Latham Rd. Rom 53 D4
Latimer Rd. Bour 206 C4
Latimer St. Rom 52 C4
Latimer St. Southa 103 D2
Latimers Cl. Christ 194 C1
Lauder Cl. Southb 137 F1
Launcelyn Cl. N Bad 53 F2
Launceston Dr. Eastl 55 F3
Laundry La. M on S 213 F2
Laundry Rd. Southa 78 A1
Laurel Cl. Broa 187 E3
Laurel Cl. Christ 194 B1
Laurel Cl. Hord 196 C2
Laurel Cl. Hyt 125 F2
Laurel Cl. Lo He 129 D2
Laurel Cl. Southa 103 E2
Laurel Cl. St Le 139 F2
Laurel Dr. Broa 188 B2
Laurel Gdns. Lo He 129 D2
Laurel La. St Le 139 F2
Laurel Rd. Lo He 129 D2
Laurel Rd. Wat 112 B2
Laurels The. Fern 165 E4
Lauriston Dr. Ch Fo 30 A1
Laurus Cl. Wat 135 D3
Laurus Wlk. L on S 179 F3
Lavant Cl. Wat 112 A1
Lavant St. Pet 40 C2
Lavender Rd. Hord 196 C2
Lavender Rd. Wat 135 D3
Lavender Way. Broa 187 E2
Laverock Lea. Portc 132 B1
Laverstoke Cl. Rown 77 F3
Lavey's La. Swanw 130 A3
Lavington Gdns. N Bad 53 F2
Lavinia Rd. Gos 181 D3
Lavinia Rd. Poole 205 E4
Lawford Rd. Bour 191 D2
Lawn Cl. Gos 180 B4
Lawn Dr. Lo He 129 D1
Lawn Rd. Eastl 56 A3
Lawn Rd. Lym 198 A2
Lawn Rd. M on S 213 F2
Lawn Rd. Southa 103 D4
Lawn St. Winch 11 D4
Lawns Cl. Wi Mi 164 B3
Lawns Rd. Wi Mi 164 A3
Lawns The. Christ 211 D4
Lawnside Rd. Southa 102 A4
Lawnswood Cl. Wat 111 F1
Lawrence Ave. Wat 111 F1
Lawrence Dr. Poole 205 F1
Lawrence Gr. Southa 103 F1
Lawrence La. Fordi 94 A2
Lawrence Rd. Fare 130 C1
Lawrence Rd. Ports 182 C2
Lawrence Rd. Rin 117 E1
Lawson Cl. Swanw 128 B4
Lawson Rd. Poole 205 D3
Lawson Rd. Ports 182 C2
Laxton Cl. Lo He 129 D2
Laxton Cl. Southa 104 A1
Layard Dr. Wi Mi 163 E1
Laymoor La. Fern 164 B3
Layton Ct. Poole 205 E3
Layton Rd. Gos 155 E2
Layton Rd. Poole 205 E3
Lazy Acre. Southb 161 E4
Lea Rd. Black 177 F4
Lea The. Ver 115 D3
Lea Way. Bour 189 F3
Leacock Cl. Swan 84 A3
Leafy La. Lo He 129 F3
Lealand Gr. Cos 158 B4
Lealand Rd. Cos 158 B4
Leamington Cres. L on S 179 F3
Leamington Rd. Bour 207 D4
Leander Cl. Eastl 56 A3
Leaphill Rd. Bour 208 A3
Lear Rd. Gos 181 D3
Learoyd Rd. Poole 204 C4
Leaside Way. Southa 79 E3
Leaway The. Portc 156 B4
Lebanon Rd. Southa 101 E4
Lechlade Gdns. Bour 208 A4
Lechlade Gdns. Fare 130 C2
Leckford Cl. Portc 132 B1
Leckford Cl. Southa 104 B4
Leckford Rd. Hav 136 A3
Ledbury Rd. Christ 209 F3
Ledbury Rd. Cos 133 E1
Lederle La. Gos 155 E3
Ledgard Cl. Poole 205 D2
Lee Church La. Rom 76 C4
Lee Dro. Rom 53 D1
Lee La. Nur 77 D4
Lee Rd. Gos 181 D3
Leedam Rd. Bour 190 B2
Leelands. Lym 198 B1
Leep La. Gos 181 D1
Lees Cl. Christ 192 B2
Lees La N. Gos 181 D3
Lees La. Gos 181 D3
Leesland Rd. Gos 181 D3
Leeson Dr. Fern 165 D4
Leeson Rd. Bour 207 F4
Legg La. Wi Mi 163 E2
Legion Cl. Hamw 203 F1
Legion La. Ki Wo 2 B4
Legion Rd. Hamw 203 F1
Legion Rd. S Hay 185 D2
Leicester Rd. Poole 205 F2
Leicester Rd. Southa 78 B1
Leicester Way. Winch 2 B1
Leigh Gdns. Wi Mi 163 E2
Leigh La. Wi Mi 163 F3
Leigh Park. Lym 198 B2
Leigh Rd. Ch Fo 55 F2
Leigh Rd. Eastl 55 F2
Leigh Rd. Fern 88 A1
Leigh Rd. Hav 135 F1
Leigh Rd. New M 196 A2
Leigh Rd. Southa 79 D1
Leigh Rd. Wi Mi 163 F2
Leigham Vale Rd. Bour 208 B2
Leighton Rd. Southa 103 F2
Leith Ave. Portc 132 B1
Lemon Rd. Southa 102 A4
Lendorber Ave. Cos 158 A4
Lennox Cl. Ch Fo 55 F4
Lennox Cl. Gos 181 E1
Lennox Cl. Southa 77 F3
Lennox Rd N. Ports 182 B1
Lennox Rd S. Ports 182 B1
Lensyd Gdns. Wat 111 F3
Lentune Way. Lym 198 B1
Leofric Ct. Ports 183 E2
Leominster Rd. Cos 133 D1
Leonard Rd. Gos 181 E3
Leopold Dr. Bi Wa 83 D4
Leopold St. Ports 182 C1
Lepe Rd. Black 178 A2
Lepe Rd. Exb 179 A1
Lerryn Rd. Gos 155 E1
Leslie Rd. Bour 206 C4
Leslie Rd. Poole 205 D2
Lester Ave. Hav 135 E1
Lester Rd. Gos 180 C3
Leven Ave. Bour 206 B3
Leven Cl. Bour 206 B2
Leven Cl. N Bad 55 D4
Leventhorpe Ct. Gos 181 E2
Leveson Cl. Gos 180 C2
Levet's La. Poole 204 A1
Leviathan Cl. Stubb 154 B1
Lewens Cl. Wi Mi 163 E2
Lewens La. Wi Mi 163 E2
Lewesdon Dr. Broa 187 F2
Lewin Cl. Co Com 56 C4
Lewis Cl. Eastl 56 A3
Lewis Rd. Ems 137 D2
Lewis Silkin Way. Southa 78 A2
Lewry Cl. He En 105 E4
Lexby Rd. Tot 101 D3
Lexden Gdns. S Hay 184 C2
Leybourne Ave. Bour 190 B2
Leybourne Ave. Bour 190 B3
Leybourne Ave. Southa 104 A4
Leydene Ave. Bour 191 F1
Leydene Cl. Bour 191 F1
Leyland Rd. Poole 189 F1
Leyside. Christ 209 F3
Leyton Rd. Southa 103 E3
Liberty Cl. W Moo 139 D3
Liberty Rd. Sob 109 D4
Library Rd. Bour 190 C1
Library Rd. Fern 165 E3
Library Rd. Poole 205 F3
Library Rd. Tot 101 D4
Lichen Way. March 101 F1
Lichfield Rd. Lo He 129 E2
Lichfield Rd. Ports 183 D3
Liddel Way. N Bad 55 D3
Liddiard Gdns. Ports 183 D1
Liddiards Way. Wat 134 C2
Lightfoot Lawn. Ports 183 E2
Lilac Cl. Rin 141 D4
Lilac Rd. Southa 79 D2
Lilliput Rd. Poole 211 E4
Lily Ave. Wat 134 A1
Limberline Rd. Ports 158 A2
Limberline Spur. Ports 158 A3
Lime Ave. Southa 104 A3
Lime Cl. Hyt 125 F1
Lime Cl. Southa 104 A3
Lime Gr. Cos 133 D1
Lime Gr. Hord 213 E4
Lime Gr. S Hay 184 B2
Lime Kiln La. Holb 150 A3
Lime St. Southa 103 D2
Lime Wlk. Botl 105 F4
Lime Wlk. Hyt 125 F1
Limekiln La. Bi Wa 59 F2
Limes Cl. Liss 20 C2
Limes The. Gos 155 E1
Limes The. Hav 159 F4
Limes The. March 102 A1
Limited Rd. Bour 191 D1
Lin Brook Dr. Rin 117 E1
Linacre Cres. Southa 104 B3
Lince Gr. Burs 127 F4
Lincoln Ave. Bour 207 E3
Lincoln Ave. Christ 192 C1
Lincoln Cl. Lo He 129 E2
Lincoln Ct. Southa 78 C1
Lincoln Rd. Poole 205 E4
Lincoln Rd. Ports 182 C3
Lincoln Rise. Wat 112 A2
Lind Rd. Gos 181 E1
Linda Gr. Wat 111 F2
Linda Rd. Faw 151 D2
Linden Cl. Fern 165 E1
Linden Cl. Shed 83 F2
Linden Dr. Liss 20 C2
Linden Gdns. He En 105 E3
Linden Gdns. Rin 140 C4
Linden Gr. Ch Fo 55 E4
Linden Gr. Gos 181 D2
Linden Gr. S Hay 185 D2
Linden Lea. Portc 132 B1
Linden Rd. Bour 191 D2
Linden Rd. Fern 165 E1
Linden Rd. Poole 205 E3
Linden Rd. Rom 52 C4
Linden Rd. Southa 78 A2
Linden Way. Hav 135 F2
Linden Way. Lym 198 B2
Linden Way. Wat 112 B3
Linden Wlk. N Bad 53 F3
Lindens Cl. Ems 136 C1
Lindens The. Burt 193 E2
Lindisfarne Cl. Cos 158 A4
Lindley Ave. Ports 183 D1
Lindsay Rd. Poole 206 A2
Lindsay Rd. Southa 104 B3
Lindway. Lo He 129 D3
Lineside. Burt 209 E4
Linford Cl. New M 196 A2
Linford Cres. Southa 78 B2
Linford Ct. Hav 135 E4
Linford Rd. Rin 117 E1
Ling Dale. Rown 78 C4
Lingdale Rd. Bour 208 B3
Lingwood Ave. Christ 209 F3
Lingwood Cl. Rown 78 C4
Lingwood Wlk. Rown 78 C4
Linhorns La. New M 196 A3
Link Rd. Rin 141 E4
Link Rd. Southa 77 F2
Link Rise. Broa 187 F3
Link The. Wat 112 A1
Link Way. Stubb 154 B1
Linkenholt Way. Hav 135 E2
Links Cl. Ro Ca 113 D1
Links Dr. Christ 192 B1
Links La. Ro Ca 113 D1
Links Rd. Poole 205 E1
Links Rd. Winch 1 B1
Links The. Gos 155 E1
Links View Ave. Poole 205 F1
Linkside Ave. Bour 207 F4
Linmead Dr. Bour 190 A3
Linnet Cl. Pet 41 E1
Linnet Cl. Rin 141 E3
Linnet Cl. Wat 111 F2
Linnet Ct. Gos 180 C3
Linnet Sq. Eastl 55 E1
Linnets The. Portc 155 F4
Linnets The. Tot 100 B4
Linnies La. Sway 197 D4
Linthorpe Rd. Poole 204 C2
Linwood Cl. Hyt 126 A1
Linwood Rd. Bour 207 D4
Lion St. Ports 182 A3
Lion Terr. Ports 182 A3
Lionheart Cl. Bour 189 E3
Lionheart Way. Burs 105 D1
Lions La. St Le 139 E3
Lions Wood. St Le 139 F2
Lisbon Rd. Southa 102 B3
Lisle Cl. Lym 198 B2
Lisle Cl. Winch 10 A2
Lisle Court Rd. Bold 199 E2
Lisle Way. Ems 136 C2
Liss Rd. Ports 182 C2
Litchfield Cres. Southa 79 F1
Litchfield Rd. Southa 79 F1
Litchfield Rd. Winch 1 B2
Litchford Rd. New M 196 B2
Little Abshot Rd. Lo He 153 D4
Little Anglesey Rd. Gos 181 D1
Little Arthur St. Ports 182 C4
Little Ashton La. Bi Wa 59 F2
Little Barrs Dr. New M 196 A2
Little Bull La. Shed 83 E1
Little Burn. Sway 172 A1
Little Coburg St. Ports 182 B3
Little Corner. Den 111 D2
Little Croft Rd. Poole 205 D3
Little Dene Copse. Lym 198 A1
Little Dewlands. Ver 114 B3
Little Forest Rd. Bour 206 C3
Little Gays. Stubb 154 A1
Little George St. Ports 182 C4
Little Green Orch. Gos 181 D1
Little Green. Gos 181 D1
Little Hambrook St. Ports 182 A2
Little Kimble Wlk. He En 105 E3
Little La. Gos 181 D1
Little Lance's Hill. Southa 103 F3
Little Lonnen. Wi Mi 163 F4
Little Mead. Den 111 D2
Little Minster St. Winch 11 D4
Little Oak Rd. Southa 78 C2
Little Park Cl. He En 105 D3
Little Park Farm Rd. Lo He 129 E3
Little Quob La. W End 80 C1
Little Shore La. Bi Wa 83 E4
Little Southsea St. Ports 182 A2
Little Woodfalls Dr. Red 47 E2
Littlecroft Ave. Bour 191 D2
Littledown Ave. Bour 207 F4
Littledown Dr. Bour 207 F4
Littlegreen Ave. Hav 136 A2
Littlemead Cl. Broa 204 A4
Littlemeads. Rom 52 B4
Littlemill La. Dame 68 B3
Littlemoor Ave. Bour 189 E2
Littlepark Ave. Hav 135 D2
Littleton Gr. Hav 135 F2
Littleton La. Litt 1 A3
Littleton Rd. Litt 1 A2
Littlewood Gdns. Lo He 128 C2
Littlewood Gdns. W End 80 B1
Liverpool Rd. Ports 182 C3
Liverpool St. Southa 103 D4
Livingston Rd. Poole 205 E3
Livingstone Rd. Bour 208 A3
Livingstone Rd. Christ 209 E4
Livingstone Rd. Ports 182 B2
Livingstone Rd. Southa 103 D4
Livingstone Rd. Wi Mi 163 F2
Llewellin Cl. Upt 203 E4
Lloyd Ave. March 101 F1
Loane Rd. Southa 103 F2
Lobelia Ct. Wat 135 D3
Lobelia Rd. Southa 79 E3
Locarno Rd. Ports 158 A1
Loch Rd. Poole 205 F3
Lock App. Ports 157 D4
Lock View. Ports 157 D4
Locke Rd. He En 105 E4
Lockerley Cl. Lym 198 C1
Lockerley Cres. Southa 77 F1
Lockerley Rd. Hav 136 A2
Lockhams Rd. Curd 106 C4
Locks Rd. Lo He 129 D2
Locksheath Park Rd. Lo He 129 D1
Locksheath Cl. Hav 135 E3
Locksley Dr. Fern 165 E2
Locksley Rd. Eastl 55 F1
Locksway Rd. Ports 183 E2
Lockswood Rd. Lo He 128 C2
Lockyers Dr. Fern 165 F3
Lode Hill. Down 47 D4
Lodge Ave. Cos 158 A4
Lodge Cl. Poole 205 F2
Lodge Dr. Hyt 126 A1
Lodge Dro. Red 47 E2
Lodge Gdns. Gos 181 D2
Lodge Rd. Christ 208 C4
Lodge Rd. Hav 135 D1
Lodge Rd. Lo He 129 D2
Lodge Rd. Lym 198 A2
Lodge Rd. Southa 103 D4
Lodge Vale. W Wel 51 D1
Lodgebury Cl. Southb 161 F4
Loewy Cres. Poole 189 E1
Logan Cl. Southa 77 F3
Lombard Ave. Bour 208 B3
Lombard St. Ports 182 A2
Lombardy Cl. Gos 155 F1
Lombardy Cl. Ver 115 D3
Lombardy Rise. Wat 134 C3
Lomer La. Ibs 93 E2
Lomond Cl. Ports 182 B4
Londesborough Rd. Ports 182 C2
London Ave. Ports 157 E1
London La. Sop 166 C1
London Rd. Clanf 88 B2
London Rd. Cos 134 B2
London Rd. Hill B 21 D1
London Rd. Horn 88 B2
London Rd. Ki Wo 2 A3
London Rd. Pet 41 D3
London Rd. Ports 157 F2
London Rd. Southa 103 D3
London Rd. Steep 41 E3

London Rd. Wat 134 B2
Lone Pine Dr. Fern 165 F2
Lone Pine Way. Fern 165 F1
Lone Valley. Wat 134 B2
Long Beech Dr. Tot 100 B3
Long Cl. Down 46 C4
Long Copse La. Ems 137 D2
Long Copse. Holb 150 C2
Long Curtain Rd. Ports 182 A1
Long Down. Pet 41 D2
Long Dr. Gos 155 E1
Long Dr. W End 80 C1
Long La. Burs 105 D1
Long La. Holb 150 B3
Long La. March 101 E1
Long La. Rin 141 D2
Long La. Wi Mi 163 F4
Long Lane Cl. Holb 150 B2
Long Priors. W Meo 37 D3
Long Rd. Bour 190 B3
Long Rd. Sob 85 E3
Long Water Dr. Gos 181 E1
Long Wlk. It Ab 2 C2
Longacre Dr. Fern 165 E2
Longacre. Liss 21 D2
Longacres. Lo He 129 E2
Longbarrow Cl. Bour 192 A1
Longbridge Cl. Tot 76 B1
Longbridge Ct. Tot 76 B1
Longbridge Park. Southa 103 E2
Longclose Rd. He En 105 E4
Longdean Cl. Cos 133 D1
Longespee Rd. Oakl 188 C4
Longfield Ave. Fare 154 C4
Longfield Dr. Bour 190 A3
Longfield Dr. Fern 190 C4
Longfield Rd. Ems 136 C2
Longfield Rd. Fa Oa 57 E1
Longfield Rd. Hord 197 D1
Longfield Rd. Winch 11 E4
Longfleet Rd. Poole 204 C2
Longlands Rd. Southb 161 E4
Longleat Gdns. New M 195 F2
Longleat Gdns. Southa 78 A2
Longmead Ave. Bish 56 B2
Longmead Gdns. Hav 159 F4
Longmead Rd. Bur 142 C2
Longmead Rd. Southa 80 A1
Longmead. Liss 20 C2
Longmeadow Gdns. Hyt 126 A2
Longmeadow La. Broa 203 F4
Longmore Ave. Southa 103 E1
Longmore Cres. Southa 103 E1
Longmynd Dr. Fare 154 B4
Longridge Rd. He En 105 E3
Longs La. Stubb 154 B2
Longshore Way. Ports 183 E2
Longstaff Gdns. Fare 130 C2
Longstock Cl. Southa 127 D4
Longstock Cres. Tot 100 C4
Longstock Rd. Hav 136 A3
Longwood Ave. Wat 112 A2
Longwood Dean La. Cher 34 A3
Lonnen Rd. Wi Mi 164 A4
Lonsdale Ave. Cos 158 A4
Lonsdale Ave. Portc 156 B3
Lonsdale Rd. Bour 206 C3
Loperwood La. Ne Ma 76 A2
Loperwood La. Ower 76 A2
Loperwood La. Tot 76 A2
Loperwood. Ne Ma 76 A1
Loraine Ave. Christ 211 E4
Lord Cl. Poole 204 C4
Lord Montgomery Wy. Ports 182 C4
Lord Mountbatten Cl. Southa 79 F2
Lord's Hill Centre E. Southa 77 F2
Lord's Hill Centre W. Southa 77 F2
Lord's Hill Way. Southa 78 A3
Lordington Cl. Cos 158 A4
Lords St. Ports 182 B3
Lordswood Cl. Southa 78 B2
Lordswood Gdns. Southa 78 B2
Lordswood Rd. Southa 78 B2
Lordswood. Co Com 56 C4
Lorne Park Rd. Bour 207 D2
Lorne Rd. Ports 182 C2
Loughwood Cl. Eastl 56 A3
Lovage Gdns. Tot 100 B4
Lovage Way. Horn 88 B1
Love La. Pet 41 D2
Love La. Rom 52 C4
Love La. Twyf 58 A3
Love La. Woodg 70 C4
Lovedean La. Horn 111 F3
Lovedean La. Wat 111 F3
Lovedon La. Ki Wo 2 B4
Lovett Rd. Ports 158 A2
Lovett Wlk. Winch 1 B2
Lowcay Rd. Ports 182 C1
Lowden Cl. Winch 10 B2
Lower Alfred St. Southa 103 D3
Lower Ashley Rd. New M 196 B1
Lower Banister St. Southa 102 C3
Lower Bartons. Fordi 69 F1
Lower Baybridge La. Ows 33 E1
Lower Bellfield. Lo He 153 F4
Lower Bere Wood. Wat 134 C4
Lower Blandford Rd. Broa 188 A2
Lower Brook St. Winch 11 D4
Lower Brookfield Rd. Ports 182 C3
Lower Brownhill Rd. Southa 77 E2
Lower Buckland Rd. Lym 198 B3
Lower Canal Wlk. Southa 103 D2
Lower Chase Rd. Shed 83 F2
Lower Chase Rd. Swan 83 F2
Lower Church Path. Ports 182 B3
Lower Church Rd. Lo He 129 E2
Lower Common La. W Moo 139 D4
Lower Common Rd. W Wel 50 C2
Lower Crabbick La. Den 110 A3
Lower Densome Wd. Woodg 70 C4
Lower Derby Rd. Ports 157 E1
Lower Drayton La. Cos 158 A4
Lower Duncan Rd. Lo He 129 D3
Lower Farlington Rd. Cos 158 C4
Lower Forbury Rd. Ports 182 B2
Lower Golf Links Rd. Broa 188 A3
Lower Gr. Whits 45 D1
Lower Grove Rd. Hav 160 A4
Lower Heyshott. Pet 41 D2
Lower La. Bi Wa 83 E4
Lower Lamborough La. Cher 14 B3
Lower Mead. Pet 41 D2
Lower Meadend Rd. Sway 197 D4
Lower Moors Rd. Co Com 31 F1
Lower Mortimer Rd. Southa 103 E2
Lower Mullin's La. Hyt 125 F2
Lower New Rd. W End 80 B1
Lower Northam Rd. He En 105 E4
Lower Pennington La. Lym 214 B4
Lower Quay Cl. Fare 155 D4
Lower Quay Rd. Fare 155 D4
Lower Quay. Fare 155 D4
Lower Rd. Hav 135 E1
Lower Sandy Down La. Bold 173 E2
Lower Spinney. Lo He 152 B4
Lower St Helens Rd. He En 105 E3
Lower St. Brai 28 A4
Lower Stanmore La. Winch 10 C3
Lower Swanwick Rd. Swanw 128 B4
Lower Vicarage Rd. Southa 103 E2
Lower Wardown. Pet 41 D2
Lower William St. Southa 103 E3
Lower Wingfield St. Ports 182 B3
Lower Woodside. Lym 214 C4
Lower York St. Southa 103 E3
Lowestoft Rd. Cos 133 E1
Lowford Hill. Burs 104 C1
Lowry Gdns. Southa 104 B1
Lowther Gdns. Bour 207 E3
Lowther Rd. Bour 207 D3
Loxwood Rd. Horn 111 F3
Luard Ct. Hav 136 A1
Lucas Cl. Southa 77 F3
Lucas Rd. Poole 205 E3
Luccombe Pl. Southa 78 B1
Luccombe Rd. Southa 78 B1
Lucerne Ave. Bour 208 B3
Lucerne Ave. Wat 111 E1
Lucerne Gdns. He En 105 D3
Lucerne Rd. M on S 213 E2
Luckham Cl. Bour 191 D1
Luckham Pl. Bour 191 D1
Luckham Rd E. Bour 191 D1
Luckham Rd. Bour 191 D1
Lucknow St. Ports 182 C3
Lucky La. Bold 174 A1
Ludlow Rd. Cos 133 E1
Ludlow Rd. Southa 103 F2
Ludwell's La. Swan 83 F2
Lugano Cl. Wat 111 E1
Lulworth Ave. Hamw 203 F1
Lulworth Cl. Ch Fo 55 D2
Lulworth Cl. S Hay 185 D3
Lulworth Cl. Southa 77 F1
Lulworth Cres. Hamw 203 F1
Lulworth Green. Southa 77 F1
Lulworth Rd. L on S 179 F3
Lumby Dr. Rin 141 D4
Lumley Rd. Herm 137 D1
Lumsden Ave. Southa 102 B4
Lumsden Rd. Ports 183 E2
Lundy Cl. Southa 77 F3
Lundy Wlk. Stubb 154 A2
Lunedale Rd. Hyt 149 F4
Lupin Rd. Southa 79 E3
Luther Rd. Bour 206 C4
Lutman St. Ems 136 C2
Luton Rd. Southa 104 A2
Luzborough La. Rom 53 E3
Lyburn Rd. Red 48 C1
Lychgate Dr. Horn 112 A4
Lychgate Green. Stubb 154 B3
Lydford Gdns. Bour 190 A1
Lydford Rd. Bour 190 A1
Lydgate Cl. Southa 104 B2
Lydgate Green. Southa 104 B2
Lydgate Rd. Southa 104 B2
Lydgate The. M on S 213 D3
Lydgate. Tot 100 B4
Lydiard Cl. Eastl 56 A3
Lydlinch Cl. Fern 165 E1
Lydlynch Rd. Tot 100 C4
Lydney Cl. Cos 157 D4
Lydney Rd. Lo He 128 C2
Lydwell Cl. Bour 189 F3
Lyell Rd. Poole 205 E3
Lymbourn Rd. Hav 136 A1
Lyme Cl. Eastl 55 F3
Lyme Cres. Christ 210 C4
Lymefields. M on S 213 F3
Lymer La. Nur 77 E3
Lymington Rd. B on S 196 A1
Lymington Rd. Brock 146 A1
Lymington Rd. Christ 210 C4
Lymington Rd. M on S 213 F3
Lymore La. M on S 213 F3
Lymore La. M on S 214 A2
Lymore Valley. M on S 213 F3
Lynch Cl. Winch 1 C1
Lyndale Cl. M on S 213 F3
Lyndale Rd. Lo He 129 E2
Lynden Cl. Fare 154 A4
Lyndhurst Cl. S Hay 185 D2
Lyndhurst Cl. Winch 1 B2
Lyndhurst Rd. Ashu 100 A1
Lyndhurst Rd. Bran 194 B1
Lyndhurst Rd. Bran 194 B3
Lyndhurst Rd. Brock 146 A1
Lyndhurst Rd. Bur 143 E3
Lyndhurst Rd. Burt 194 B3
Lyndhurst Rd. Cadn 98 C4
Lyndhurst Rd. Christ 194 B1
Lyndhurst Rd. Gos 181 D2
Lyndhurst Rd. Lan 49 E2
Lyndhurst Rd. Ports 157 F1
Lyndock Cl. Southa 103 F1
Lyndock Pl. Southa 103 F1
Lyndum Cl. Pet 40 C2
Lyne Pl. Wat 112 A3
Lyne's La. Rin 140 C4
Lynford Ave. Winch 1 C1
Lynford Way. Winch 1 C1
Lynn Cl. W End 80 A2
Lynn Rd. Ports 182 C4
Lynric Cl. B on S 212 A4
Lynton Cres. Christ 192 B2
Lynton Gdns. Fare 130 C2
Lynton Gr. Ports 183 D4
Lynton Rd. He En 105 E4
Lynton Rd. Pet 40 C2
Lynwood Ave. Wat 111 E2
Lynwood Cl. Fern 165 E4
Lynwood Dr. Oakl 188 C4
Lynx Cl. Bish 56 C1
Lyon Ave. New M 196 A2
Lyon Rd. Poole 189 F1
Lyon St. Southa 103 D3
Lysander Cl. Christ 210 B4
Lysander Way. Wat 135 D4
Lysses Ct. Fare 131 E1
Lyster Rd. Fordi 70 A1
Lystra Rd. Bour 191 D2
Lytchett Dr. Broa 188 A2
Lytchett Way. Upt 203 D3
Lyteltane Rd. Lym 198 B1
Lytham Rd. Broa 188 A2
Lytham Rd. Southa 80 A1
Lythe La. Steep 40 A3
Lytton Rd. Bour 207 E3
Lytton Rd. Hyt 126 A1

Mabey Ave. Bour 190 B1
Mabey Cl. Gos 181 E1
Mablethorpe Rd. Cos 133 F1
Macandrew Rd. Poole 211 F4
Macarthur Cres. Southa 104 A4
Macaulay Ave. Portc 132 C1
Macaulay Rd. Broa 188 A2
Maclaren Rd. Bour 190 C2
Maclean Rd. Bour 189 F2
MacNacnaghten Rd. Southa 103 E4
Madden Cl. Gos 180 C2
Maddison St. Southa 102 C2
Maddoxford La. Botl 82 A1
Maddoxford Way. Botl 81 F1
Madeira Rd. Bour 207 D2
Madeira Rd. Ports 157 F2
Madeline Cl. Poole 205 D4
Madeline Cres. Poole 205 D4
Madeline Rd. Pet 40 C2
Maderia Rd. Poole 205 E3
Madison Ave. Bour 207 E3
Mafeking Rd. Ports 182 C2
Mag's Barrow. Fern 165 F1
Magazine La. March 102 A2
Magdala Rd. Cos 157 F4
Magdala Rd. S Hay 184 C2
Magdalen Hill. Winch 11 D4
Magdalen La. Christ 209 D3
Magdalen Rd. Ports 157 F2
Magdalene Way. Lo He 129 E1
Magennis Cl. Gos 180 B4
Magna Cl. Bour 189 F3
Magna Gdns. Bour 189 F3
Magna Rd. Bour 189 E4
Magna Rd. Oakl 189 E4
Magnolia Cl. Bour 209 D3
Magnolia Cl. Fare 154 C4
Magnolia Gr. Fa Oa 57 F1
Magnolia Rd. Southa 103 F3
Magnolia Way. Wat 112 B2
Magpie Cl. Bour 191 E2
Magpie Dr. Tot 100 B4
Magpie Gdns. Southa 104 B2
Magpie La. Eastl 55 F1
Magpie La. L on S 179 F4
Magpie Rd. Ro Ca 113 E3
Magpie Wlk. Wat 111 E2
Maiden La. Lym 198 C1
Maidford Gr. Ports 158 B2
Maidment Cl. Bour 189 F2
Maidstone Cres. Cos 133 F1
Main Quay. Hamw 204 A1
Main Rd. Co Com 32 A1
Main Rd. Herm 161 E4
Main Rd. Hyt 125 E3
Main Rd. Litt 1 A3
Main Rd. March 101 F1
Main Rd. Ows 33 D2
Main Rd. Southb 161 E4
Main Rd. Tot 100 C2
Mainstone. Rom 52 B3
Mainstream Ct. Bish 56 B2
Maisemore Gdns. Ems 160 B4
Maitland St. Ports 182 B4
Maizemore Wlk. L on S 179 F3
Majestic Rd. Nur 77 D2
Malan Cl. Poole 204 C4
Malcolm Cl. Ch Fo 30 C1
Malcolm Cl. Lo He 129 D2
Malcolm Rd. Ch Fo 30 C1
Malcomb Cl. Bour 209 D2
Malcroft Mews. March 102 A1
Maldon Cl. Bish 56 B2
Maldon Rd. Cos 157 E4
Maldon Rd. Southa 103 F2
Malibres Rd. Ch Fo 55 F4
Malin Cl. Southa 77 F2
Malin Cl. Stubb 154 A2
Malins Rd. Ports 182 B4
Mall The. Bur 143 D2
Mall The. Ports 157 E1
Mallard Cl. Bi Wa 83 D4
Mallard Cl. Bour 191 E1
Mallard Cl. Christ 210 A3
Mallard Cl. Hord 197 D2
Mallard Cl. Rom 52 C4
Mallard Gdns. Gos 155 D1
Mallard Rd. Bour 191 E1
Mallard Rd. Ports 183 D3
Mallard Rd. Ro Ca 113 D1
Mallard Rd. Wi Mi 164 A4
Mallards Rd. Burs 127 F4
Mallards The. Hav 159 F4
Mallory Cl. Christ 209 F4
Mallory Cres. Fare 88 A2
Mallow Cl. Lo He 128 C1
Mallow Cl. Wat 134 C3
Mallow Rd. He En 105 D3
Mallows The. New M 196 B2
Malmesbury Cl. Fa Oa 57 E1
Malmesbury Gdns. Winch 1 B1
Malmesbury Park Pl. Bour 207 E3
Malmesbury Park Rd. Bour 207 D3
Malmesbury Pl. Southa 102 B4
Malmesbury Rd. Rom 52 C4
Malmesbury Rd. Southa 102 B4
Malmesbury Rd. St Le 139 F2
Maloren Way. W Moo 139 D1
Malory Cl. Southa 104 B3
Malt La. Bi Wa 83 E4
Malta Rd. Ports 182 C4
Malthouse Cl. It Ab 2 C2
Malthouse Cl. Rom 52 C4
Malthouse Gdns. March 101 F1
Malthouse La. Fare 88 A1
Malthouse Rd. Ports 182 B4
Malthouse. Poole 204 B1
Maltings The. Fare 88 B1
Malvern Ave. Fare 154 C4
Malvern Cl. Bi Wa 83 E4
Malvern Cl. Bour 191 D2
Malvern Dr. Hyt 125 E2
Malvern Rd. Bour 191 D1
Malvern Rd. Gos 180 C3
Malvern Rd. Hill B 21 D1
Malvern Rd. Ports 182 B1
Malvern Rd. Southa 78 B1
Malwood Ave. Southa 78 B2
Malwood Cl. Hav 136 A3
Malwood Gdns. Tot 100 B4
Malwood Rd W. Hyt 125 F2
Malwood Rd. Hyt 126 A2
Manchester Rd. Net 127 D3
Manchester Rd. Ports 182 C3
Manchester Rd. Sway 172 A2
Mancroft Ave. Stubb 154 B1
Mandale Cl. Bour 190 A2
Mandale Rd. Bour 189 F2
Mandela Way. Southa 102 C3
Manderley. M on S 213 F2
Manley Rd. Burs 104 C1
Manners Rd. Ports 182 C2
Manning Ave. Christ 194 B1
Manning's Heath Rd. Poole 189 D1
Manningford Cl. Winch 2 A2
Mannington Pl. Bour 206 C2
Mannington Way. W Moo 138 B1
Manns Cl. W End 80 B1
Mannyngham Way. Mich 27 E4
Manor Ave. Poole 189 E1
Manor Cl. Burs 104 C1
Manor Cl. Fern 165 F3
Manor Cl. Fordi 69 F1
Manor Cl. Hav 135 F1
Manor Cl. M on S 213 E3
Manor Cl. Tot 100 C3
Manor Cl. Wickh 108 A2
Manor Cl. Winch 11 D4
Manor Cres. Burs 104 C1
Manor Cres. Cos 158 A4
Manor Ct. Lo He 129 E2
Manor Ct. Rin 140 C4
Manor Farm Cl. Bish 56 C1
Manor Farm Cl. New M 195 F1
Manor Farm Gr. Bish 56 C1
Manor Farm La. Miche 6 C1
Manor Farm Rd. Bour 190 B4
Manor Farm Rd. Fordi 69 E1
Manor Farm Rd. Southa 79 E1
Manor Gdns. Rin 140 C4
Manor Gdns. Southb 137 E1
Manor House Ave. Southa 101 F3
Manor La. Ver 114 C3
Manor Lodge Rd. Ro Ca 113 D1
Manor Mews. Cos 158 B4
Manor Park Ave. Ports 183 D4
Manor Park. Poole 204 A3
Manor Rd N. Southa 103 F2
Manor Rd S. Southa 103 F2
Manor Rd. Bish 56 C1
Manor Rd. Bour 207 E2
Manor Rd. Chilw 54 B1
Manor Rd. Christ 209 D3
Manor Rd. Durl 82 B4
Manor Rd. Holb 150 B2
Manor Rd. Hyt 125 D2
Manor Rd. M on S 213 E3
Manor Rd. N Hay 184 C3
Manor Rd. New M 196 A2
Manor Rd. Ports 182 C4
Manor Rd. Rin 141 D4
Manor Rd. S Hay 184 C3
Manor Rd. Southb 137 E1
Manor Rd. Twyf 31 F3
Manor Rd. Ver 114 C3
Manor Terr. Burs 104 C1
Manor Way. L on S 179 F3
Manor Way. S Hay 185 D1
Manor Way. Southb 137 E1
Manor Way. Ver 114 C4
Mansbridge Rd. Eastl 56 A1
Mansbridge Rd. Southa 79 F2
Mansel Ct. Southa 77 F1
Mansel Rd E. Southa 77 F1
Mansel Rd W. Southa 77 E1
Mansell Cl. Hyt 125 F1
Mansfield Ave. Poole 205 E2
Mansfield Cl. Fern 165 E1
Mansfield Cl. Poole 205 E2
Mansfield Rd. Bour 190 C1
Mansfield Rd. Gos 180 B4
Mansfield Rd. Poole 205 E2
Mansion Rd. Ports 182 C1
Mansion Rd. Southa 102 B3
Mansvid Ave. Cos 158 A4
Mantle Cl. Gos 180 B4
Manton Rd. Hamw 203 F2
Maple Cl. B on S 212 A4
Maple Cl. Christ 210 C4
Maple Cl. Ems 136 C1
Maple Cl. L on S 179 F3
Maple Cl. Rom 53 E3
Maple Cres. Clanf 88 B3
Maple Dr. Den 111 D2
Maple Dr. Fern 165 E4
Maple Dr. Ki Wo 2 A4
Maple Gdns. Tot 100 B3
Maple Rd. Bour 206 C4
Maple Rd. Hyt 150 A4
Maple Rd. Poole 204 B2
Maple Rd. Ports 182 B1
Maple Rd. Southa 103 F4
Maple Sq. Eastl 55 F1
Mapleton Rd. He En 105 E3
Mapletree Ave. Wat 112 B2
Maplewood Cl. Tot 100 B3
Maplin Rd. Southa 77 E1
Mapperton Cl. Poole 189 D1
Maralyn Ave. Wat 134 C3
Marathon Cl. Fa Oa 57 D1
Marbream Cl. Fordi 69 E1
Marchwood By Pass. Hyt 124 C4
Marchwood By Pass. March 124 C4
Marchwood By Pass. Tot 101 D2
Marchwood Rd. Bour 190 B2
Marchwood Rd. Hav 135 F3
Marchwood Rd. Southa 102 A3
Marchwood Rd. Tot 101 E2
Marcus Cl. Fa Oa 57 D1
Mardale Rd. Southa 101 E4
Mardale Wlk. Southa 101 E4
Marden Way. Pet 41 D2
Mardon Cl. Southa 79 F3
Mare La. Twyf 58 C3
Margam Ave. Southa 103 F3
Margards La. Ver 114 C3
Margaret Cl. Wat 111 E1
Margarita Rd. Fare 130 C1
Margate Rd. Ports 182 B2
Margery's Ct. Ports 182 A3
Marian Cl. Broa 187 E2
Marian Rd. Broa 187 E2
Marianne Cl. Southa 101 F3

Marianne Rd. Poole 206 B4
Marianne Rd. Wi Mi 164 A4
Marie Ave. Down 46 B4
Marie Rd. Southa 104 B2
Marigold Cl. Fare 130 C1
Marina Cl. Bour 207 F2
Marina Cl. Ems 161 D4
Marina Dr. Poole 205 D1
Marina Gr. Portc 156 B3
Marina Gr. Ports 183 D4
Marina Keep. Ports 157 D3
Marina The. Bour 207 F2
Marina View. Christ 209 D3
Marine Ct. Ports 183 D1
Marine Dr E. B on S 212 A3
Marine Dr W. B on S 211 F4
Marine Dr. B on S 211 F4
Marine Par. Southa 103 D2
Marine Parade E. L on S 179 F3
Marine Parade W. L on S 179 E3
Marine Rd. Bour 208 B2
Marine Wlk. S Hay 185 E2
Mariner's Cl. Hamble 128 A2
Mariners Ct. Lym 198 C1
Mariners Mews. Hyt 126 A2
Mariners Way. Gos 181 E2
Mariners Way. Lo He 128 B1
Mariners Wlk. Ports 183 D3
Marion Rd. Ports 182 C1
Maritime Way. Southa 103 D1
Marjoram Cres. Wat 112 A2
Mark Cl. Ports 157 F2
Mark Cl. Southa 102 A4
Mark Ct. Wat 134 C4
Mark's La. New M 196 A3
Mark's Rd. Stubb 154 C1
Markall Cl. Cher 14 B3
Market Cl. Poole 204 B1
Market La. Winch 11 D4
Market Par. Hav 135 F1
Market Pl. Fordi 69 F1
Market Pl. Rin 140 C4
Market Pl. Rom 52 C4
Market St. Eastl 56 A1
Market St. Poole 204 A1
Market St. Winch 11 D4
Market Way. Wi Mi 163 E2
Marketway. Ports 182 B3
Markham Ave. Bour 190 B4
Markham Rd. Bour 207 D4
Marks Rd. Bour 190 C2
Marks Tey Rd. Stubb 154 B3
Markway Cl. Ems 136 B1
Marlaxton Cl. Eastl 55 F3
Marlborough Cl. Wat 134 B3
Marlborough Ct. Hyt 125 F1
Marlborough Gr. Portc 156 B4
Marlborough Park. Hav 136 B2
Marlborough Pl. Wi Mi 163 E3
Marlborough Rd. Bour 206 B2
Marlborough Rd. Ch Fo 30 C1
Marlborough Rd. Gos 180 C3
Marlborough Rd. Poole 205 E2
Marlborough Rd. Southa 102 A4
Marldell Cl. Hav 136 A3
Marles Cl. Gos 180 B4
Marley Ave. New M 195 F2
Marley Cl. New M 195 F2
Marley Mount. Sway 171 F1
Marlhill Cl. Southa 79 F1
Marline Rd. Poole 205 E3
Marlott Rd. Poole 204 B3
Marlow Cl. Fare 130 C2
Marlow Dr. Christ 192 C2
Marlow Rd. Bi Wa 83 D4
Marlpit Dr. Christ 195 D1
Marls Rd. He En 105 F3
Marmion Ave. Ports 182 B1
Marmion Green. Christ 209 F4
Marmion Rd. Ports 182 B1
Marne Rd. Southa 104 A4
Marnhull Rd. Poole 204 B2
Marpet Cl. Bour 189 F3
Marples Way. Hav 135 E1
Marquis Way. Bour 189 E3
Marram Cl. Lym 198 C3
Marryat Ct. Christ 211 D4
Marryat Rd. New M 195 F2
Marsden Rd. Cos 157 D4
Marsh Cl. Cos 158 B3
Marsh La. Brea 70 A4
Marsh La. Christ 192 C1
Marsh La. Faw 151 D2
Marsh La. Southa 103 D2
Marsh La. Upt 203 D4
Marsh Par. Hyt 126 A2
Marsh The. Hyt 126 A2
Marshal Rd. Broa 188 A1
Marshall Rd. S Hay 185 E1
Marshfield. Wi Mi 163 F4
Marshlands Rd. Cos 158 B4
Marshwood Ave. Broa 188 C1
Marshwood Ave. Wat 135 D4
Marston Cl. New M 196 A3
Marston Gr. Christ 194 C1
Marston La. Ports 158 A2
Marston Rd. New M 196 A3
Marston Rd. Southa 104 C3
Martello Cl. Gos 180 B2
Martello Park. Poole 211 F4
Martello Rd S. Poole 211 F4
Martells Ct. Ports 182 A2
Martells The. B on S 212 A4
Martha St. Ports 182 B3
Martin Ave. Den 111 D2
Martin Ave. Stubb 154 B1
Martin Cl. Broa 203 F4
Martin Cl. L on S 179 F4
Martin Rd. Hav 136 A3
Martin Rd. Ports 183 D4
Martin Rd. Stubb 154 B1
Martin St. Bi Wa 83 D4
Martin's Rd. Brock 146 A1
Martindale Ave. Wi Mi 164 A3
Martins Cl. Fern 165 F4
Martins Dr. Fern 165 F4
Martins Fields. Comp 10 B1
Martins Hill Cl. Burt 193 E1
Martins Hill La. Burt 193 E1
Martins The. Fa Oa 57 E1
Martins Way. Fern 165 F4
Marvic Ct. Hav 135 F3
Marvin Cl. He En 105 F4
Marvin Way. He En 105 E4
Marvin Way. Southa 104 B3
Marwell Cl. Bour 208 A4
Mary Rose Cl. Fare 130 C2
Mary Rose St The. Ports 182 B3
Marybridge Cl. Tot 100 C3
Maryfield. Southa 103 D2
Maryland Cl. Southa 79 F2
Maryland Gdns. M on S 213 D2
Maryland Rd. Hamw 203 E2
Masefield Ave. Portc 132 C1
Masefield Cl. Eastl 55 F2
Masefield Cres. Wat 111 F2
Masefield Green. Southa 104 B3
Masseys La. E Bol 175 E4
Masten Cres. Gos 180 B4
Matapan Rd. Ports 157 F2
Matchams La. Hurn 166 A2
Matchams La. St Le 166 A2
Matheson Rd. Southa 78 A3
Matley Gdns. Tot 100 A4
Matlock Rd. Fern 165 E2
Matthews Cl. Hav 135 E2
Matthews La. E Bol 175 E3
Maturin Cl. Lym 198 B2
Maundeville Cres. Christ 208 C4
Maundville Rd. Christ 208 C4
Maunsell Way. He En 81 E1
Maureen Cl. Poole 205 D4
Mauretania Rd. Nur 77 D2
Maurice Rd. Bour 207 E4
Maurice Rd. Ports 183 E2
Maury's La. W Wel 50 B2
Mavis Cres. Hav 135 F1
Mavis Rd. Bour 191 D1
Maxstoke Cl. Ports 182 B3
Maxwell Rd. Bour 207 D4
Maxwell Rd. Broa 187 F2
Maxwell Rd. Poole 211 F4
Maxwell Rd. Ports 183 D2
Maxwell Rd. Southa 104 A2
May Ave. Lym 198 B3
May Bush La. Sob 85 D1
May Cl. Holb 150 B2
May Copse. Holb 150 B2
May Cres. Holb 150 B2
May La. Bold 174 A1
May Rd. Southa 102 B4
May Tree Cl. Winch 10 B2
May's La. Stubb 154 B2
Maybray-King Way. Southa 104 A4
Maybush Ct. Southa 78 A1
Maybush Rd. Southa 77 F1
Mayfair Ct. Botl 106 A4
Mayfair Gdns. Bour 190 A2
Mayfair Gdns. Southa 102 C4
Mayfield Ave. Poole 205 F2
Mayfield Ave. Tot 100 C4
Mayfield Cl. Fern 165 E3
Mayfield Cl. Stubb 154 B2
Mayfield Dr. Fern 165 E3
Mayfield Rd. Bour 191 D1
Mayfield Rd. Fordi 69 E1
Mayfield Rd. Gos 181 E2
Mayfield Rd. Ports 157 F1
Mayfield Rd. Southa 79 E2
Mayfield Way. Fern 165 E3
Mayfield. L on S 179 F3
Mayflower Cl. Ch Fo 55 D3
Mayflower Cl. Lym 199 D1
Mayflower Cl. Stubb 154 B1
Mayflower Dr. Ports 183 E3
Mayflower Rd. Southa 102 A4
Mayflowers The. Southa 79 D2
Mayfly Cl. Fordi 69 F1
Mayford Rd. Poole 206 A3
Mayhall Rd. Ports 158 A1
Mayhill La. Drox 84 C4
Mayhill La. Swan 84 C4
Maylands Ave. Ports 183 D3
Maylands Rd. Hav 135 D1
Mayles Cl. Wickh 108 A2
Mayles La. Wickh 107 F1
Mayles Rd. Ports 183 D3
Maylings Farm Rd. Fare 130 C2
Maylings Farm Rd. Fare 130 C2
Maylyn Rd. Upt 187 D1
Maynard Cl. Gos 155 E2
Maynard Pl. Horn 112 A4
Maynard Rd. Tot 100 C4
Mayo Cl. Ports 182 B4
Maypole Villas. Ott 56 A4
Mayridge. Lo He 129 E2
Mays Firs. Woodg 47 F1
Mays Gdns. Bour 189 F2
Maytree Cl. Fa Oa 57 E1
Maytree Cl. Lo He 129 D2
Maytree Gdns. Wat 111 F2
Maytree Rd. Ch Fo 30 B1
Maytree Rd. Fare 88 A1
Mayvale Cl. March 101 F1
Mc William Rd. Bour 191 D1
Mckinley Rd. Bour 206 B1
Mcwilliam Cl. Poole 206 B4
Mead Cl. Broa 188 A1
Mead Cl. Rom 53 D4
Mead Cres. Southa 79 E2
Mead End Rd. Den 111 D2
Mead End Rd. Sway 171 F1
Mead Rd. Ch Fo 55 E3
Mead Rd. Lym 198 A1
Mead Rd. Winch 10 C2
Mead The. Gos 155 D2
Mead The. Hyt 125 F2
Mead The. Liss 20 C2
Meadbrook Gdns. Ch Fo 55 E3
Meadcroft Cl. Lo He 152 B4
Meadend Cl. Hav 136 A3
Meadow Ave. Fordi 69 F1
Meadow Ave. Lo He 129 D2
Meadow Cl. Bran 194 A4
Meadow Cl. Bur 142 C1
Meadow Cl. Fern 165 E1
Meadow Cl. Fordi 69 F1
Meadow Cl. N Bad 54 A2
Meadow Cl. Rin 141 D4
Meadow Cl. Shed 83 F2
Meadow Cl. Tot 100 C3
Meadow Cl. W End 80 C1
Meadow Court Cl. Bour 191 D2
Meadow Ct. Fordi 69 F1
Meadow Ct. Whit 24 B2
Meadow Edge. Wat 134 A1
Meadow Gdns. Shed 83 F2
Meadow Gr. Ch Fo 55 E2
Meadow Gr. Ver 115 D3
Meadow La. Burt 193 E1
Meadow La. Hamble 128 A1
Meadow Rd. Lym 198 B1
Meadow Rd. New M 196 A2
Meadow Rd. Rin 141 D4
Meadow Rise. Broa 187 F3
Meadow Rise. Wat 112 A2
Meadow St. Ports 182 A2
Meadow The. Den 110 C2
Meadow View Rd. Bour 189 F2
Meadow Way. B on S 212 A4
Meadow Way. Faw 151 D2
Meadow Way. Rin 141 D4
Meadow Way. Ver 115 D3
Meadow Way. Winch 10 B2
Meadow Wlk. Gos 155 D3
Meadow Wlk. Liss 20 C2
Meadowbank Rd. Fare 130 B1
Meadowbank. Upt 203 E4
Meadowcroft Cl. Ott 31 E2
Meadowhead Rd. Southa 78 C2
Meadowland. Christ 209 F3
Meadowland. Ki Wo 2 A4
Meadowlands. Hav 136 A1
Meadowlands. Lym 198 B2
Meadowlands. Ro Ca 113 E2
Meadowmead Ave. Southa 102 A4
Meadows Cl. Upt 203 E4
Meadows Dr. Upt 203 E4
Meadows The. Fare 88 B2
Meadows The. Lyn 121 F2
Meadows The. Lyn 122 A2
Meadows The. Rom 28 A1
Meadows The. Wat 134 B4
Meadowside Cl. Southa 79 F2
Meadowsweet Rd. Broa 203 F4
Meadowsweet Way. Fa Oa 81 E3
Meadowsweet. Wat 112 A1
Meads The. N Bad 55 D3
Meads The. Rom 52 B4
Meadway The. Christ 194 B1
Mears Rd. Fa Oa 57 E1
Meath Cl. S Hay 185 E1
Medina Cl. Ch Fo 55 F3
Medina Rd. Cos 157 F4
Medina Rd. Southa 78 A1
Medina Way. Christ 210 B3
Medlar Cl. Burt 193 E1
Medlar Cl. He En 105 E3
Medstead Rd. Hav 135 F2
Medwall Green. Southa 104 B3
Medway Dr. N Bad 55 D4
Medway Rd. Fern 166 A3
Meerut Rd. Brock 145 F1
Meeting House La. Rin 140 C4
Megan Rd. W End 80 B1
Megana Way. Brai 28 B3
Meggeson Ave. Southa 80 A1
Melboure Rd. Christ 192 C1
Melbourne Gdns. He En 105 E3
Melbourne Pl. Ports 182 B2
Melbourne Rd. Bour 207 E3
Melbourne Rd. Christ 192 C1
Melbourne Rd. He En 105 E3
Melbourne St. Southa 103 D2
Melbury Ave. Poole 205 F4
Melbury Cl. Fern 165 E2
Melbury Cl. Lym 198 B2
Melchet Cl. Plai 25 D1
Melchet Rd. Southa 104 B4
Melick Cl. March 101 F1
Mellstock Rd. Poole 204 B3
Melrose Cl. Ports 183 D2
Melrose Ct. New M 196 B2
Melrose Ct. Tot 76 B1
Melrose Gdns. Gos 180 C4
Melrose Rd. Southa 78 B1
Melverley Gdns. Wi Mi 163 E3
Melville Cl. Southa 78 B3
Melville Rd. Bour 206 C4
Melville Rd. Gosp 181 D4
Melville Rd. Ports 183 E2
Mendip Cl. New M 196 B1
Mendip Cl. Ver 114 C3
Mendip Gdns. Hyt 125 E2
Mendip Rd. Southa 101 F4
Mendip Rd. Ver 114 C3
Mendips Rd. Fare 154 C4
Mengham Ave. S Hay 185 D1
Mengham La. S Hay 185 D2
Mengham Rd. S Hay 185 D2
Menslands La. Sob 109 F4
Mentone Rd. Poole 205 D2
Menzies Cl. Southa 77 F3
Meon Cl. Clanf 88 B2
Meon Cl. Gos 155 D1
Meon Cl. Pet 40 C2
Meon Cl. Rom 53 E4
Meon Cres. Ch Fo 55 E3
Meon Ct. Southa 104 B4
Meon Rd. Bour 208 A4
Meon Rd. Ports 183 D3
Meon Rd. Rom 53 E4
Meonwara Cres. W Meo 37 E3
Mercer Way. Rom 53 D4
Merchants Wlk. Southa 102 C2
Merchistoun Rd. Horn 112 A4
Mercury Cl. Southa 77 F2
Mercury Gdns. Hamble 128 A2
Mercury Pl. Wat 134 C1
Merdon Ave. Ch Fo 55 E4
Merdon Cl. Ch Fo 55 E4
Meredith Gdns. Tot 100 B3
Meredith Rd. Ports 157 F2
Meredun Cl. Hurs 30 A4
Merepond La. E Meo 17 D1
Merepond La. Frox G 17 F2
Merganser Cl. Gos 181 D4
Meriden Cl. Poole 211 F4
Meriden Rd. Ports 182 A2
Meridians The. Christ 208 C3
Merino Way. W Moo 138 C1
Merlewood Cl. Bour 206 C2
Merley Dr. Christ 211 D4
Merley La. Oakl 163 F1
Merley Park Rd. Broa 187 F4
Merley Park Rd. Oakl 163 E1
Merley Ways. Oakl 163 E1
Merlin Cl. Bi Wa 83 D4
Merlin Cl. He En 105 D4
Merlin Cl. Rin 141 E3
Merlin Dr. Ports 158 A2
Merlin Gdns. Portc 132 A1
Merlin Way. Christ 210 A3
Mermaid Way. Southa 103 D1
Merrick Way. N Bad 55 D4
Merridale Rd. Southa 103 F3
Merriefield Cl. Broa 188 A3
Merriefield Dr. Broa 188 A3
Merrieleas Cl. Ch Fo 55 E4
Merrieleas Dr. Ch Fo 55 E4
Merriemeade Cl. Hyt 125 F1
Merriemeade Par. Hyt 125 F1
Merrifield. Wi Mi 163 F4
Merrivale Ave. Bour 208 C3
Merrivale Cl. Hyt 125 F2
Merrivale Ct. Southb 137 E1
Merrivale Rd. Ports 157 F2
Merrow Ave. Poole 206 A4
Merrow Cl. Portc 156 A4
Merry Gdns. N Bad 54 A3
Merryfield Ave. Hav 135 E3
Merryfield Cl. Bran 194 A4
Merryfield La. Bour 190 B2
Merryfield Rd. Pet 41 D2
Merryfield. Lo He 129 E2
Merryoak Green. Southa 103 F3
Merryoak Rd. Southa 103 F3
Merrytree Cl. W Wel 50 C2
Merryweather Estate. Rin 141 E4
Mersea Gdns. Southa 104 A2
Mersham Gdns. Southa 104 A4
Merstone Rd. Gos 155 E1
Merthyr Ave. Cos 158 A4
Merton Ave. Portc 156 B3
Merton Cl. Fordi 69 F2
Merton Cres. Portc 156 B3
Merton Gr. Rin 140 C4
Merton Rd. Ports 182 B1
Merton Rd. Southa 79 D2
Meryl Rd. Ports 183 E2
Mesh Pond. Down 46 B4
Mesh Rd. Miche 6 A1
Meteor Rd. Th Is 161 D2
Methuen Cl. Bour 207 E3
Methuen Rd. Bour 207 D3
Methuen Rd. Broa 188 A1
Methuen Rd. Ports 183 D2
Methuen St. Southa 103 D4
Metuchen Way. He En 105 E2
Mews Ct. Ott 31 D2
Mews La. Winch 10 C4
Mews The. Black 177 F4
Mews The. Bour 207 E3
Mews The. Rown 77 F3
Mewsey Ct. Hav 135 E4
Mey Cl. Wat 135 D4
Meynell Cl. Eastl 55 F2
Meyrick Cl. Bran 194 A4
Meyrick Park Cres. Bour 206 C3
Meyrick Rd. Bour 207 D2
Meyrick Rd. Hav 135 E1
Meyrick Rd. Ports 157 E1
Michael's Way. Hyt 125 F2
Michaels Way. Fa Oa 57 E1
Michelgrove Rd. Bour 207 F2
Michelmersh Cl. Rown 77 F3
Michelmersh Green. Bour 191 E1
Michigan Way. Tot 100 B4
Mickleham Cl. Poole 206 A4
Midanbury Cres. Southa 79 F1
Midanbury La. Southa 103 F4
Midanbury Wlk. Southa 103 F4
Midas Cl. Wat 134 C2
Middle Brook St. Winch 11 D4
Middle Common Rd. Lym 198 A2
Middle Ct. Ports 182 C4
Middle La. Rin 141 D4
Middle Mead. Fare 154 A4
Middle Meadow. Liss 21 D2
Middle Park Way. Hav 135 E3
Middle Rd. Bour 190 B3
Middle Rd. Lo He 129 D3
Middle Rd. Lym 198 B2
Middle Rd. N Bad 54 A2
Middle Rd. Poole 204 C3
Middle Rd. Southa 104 A2
Middle Rd. Sway 172 A1
Middle Rd. Winch 10 C4
Middle St. Ports 182 B2
Middle St. Southa 103 D4
Middlebere Cres. Hamw 203 E2
Middlebridge St. Rom 52 C3
Middlebrook. Bi Wa 83 E4
Middlecroft La. Gos 180 C3
Middlefield. W Wit 186 C1
Middlehill Dr. Wi Mi 164 A3
Middlehill Rd. Wi Mi 164 A3
Middlesex Rd. Ports 183 D2
Middleton Cl. Fare 154 C4
Middleton Cl. Southa 80 A1
Middleton Rd. Bour 190 C1
Middleton Rd. Rin 141 D4
Middleton Wlk. Fare 154 C4
Midfield Cl. Fare 154 C4
Midland Rd. Bour 190 C1
Midlands Estate. W End 80 B1
Midlington Hill. Drox 85 D4
Midlington Rd. Drox 85 D4
Midway Path. Poole 211 E2
Midway Rd. Ports 157 F3
Midway. Hyt 125 F2
Midways. Stubb 154 B1
Midwood Ave. Bour 191 F1
Milbeck Cl. Wat 112 A2
Milborne Cres. Poole 205 F4
Milbourne Rd. Fern 165 E3
Milburn Rd. Bour 206 A2
Milbury Cres. Southa 104 A3
Mildmay St. Winch 10 B3
Miles La. Whit 24 B3
Milestone Rd. Poole 204 B3
Milford Cl. Hav 135 E2
Milford Cl. W Moo 138 C1
Milford Cres. M on S 213 F2
Milford Ct. Gos 180 B2
Milford Ct. M on S 213 F2
Milford Ct. Ports 183 D2
Milford Dr. Bour 189 F3
Milford Gdns. Ch Fo 55 F3
Milford Rd. B on S 212 A4
Milford Rd. Lym 198 A1
Milford Rd. Ports 182 B3
Military Rd. Cos 134 B1
Military Rd. Fare 131 E1
Military Rd. Gos 181 E1
Military Rd. Gos 202 A4
Military Rd. Ports 157 F3
Milkwood Ct. Tot 100 B4
Mill Cl. Den 111 D2
Mill Cl. Nur 77 E3
Mill Ct. Fordi 69 F1
Mill End. Dame 68 B2
Mill End. Herm 161 D4
Mill Hill Cl. Poole 205 D2
Mill Hill. Botl 106 A3

Mill La. Bold 199 F3
Mill La. Brock 146 A1
Mill La. Bur 143 E2
Mill La. Burt 193 F1
Mill La. Christ 211 D4
Mill La. Crouch 22 B4
Mill La. Drox 61 E1
Mill La. Durl 82 B2
Mill La. Gos 181 D3
Mill La. Hav 135 E1
Mill La. Hav 159 F3
Mill La. Herm 137 D1
Mill La. Ki Wo 2 B3
Mill La. Lym 198 C2
Mill La. Min 98 C1
Mill La. Nur 76 C2
Mill La. Pet 41 D3
Mill La. Poole 205 D2
Mill La. Ports 182 B4
Mill La. Rom 52 B4
Mill La. Sh En 25 F1
Mill La. Southw 133 F2
Mill La. Steep 40 C4
Mill La. Westb 137 D1
Mill La. Wi Mi 163 E3
Mill La. Wickh 108 A3
Mill Pond Rd. Gos 181 D3
Mill Pond The. Holb 150 A3
Mill Quay. Herm 161 D4
Mill Rd S. Bour 191 E1
Mill Rd. Bour 191 E2
Mill Rd. Christ 209 D4
Mill Rd. Den 111 D2
Mill Rd. Fare 155 D4
Mill Rd. Gos 181 D3
Mill Rd. Liss 21 D3
Mill Rd. Ports 157 E1
Mill Rd. Southa 102 A4
Mill Rd. Tot 101 D4
Mill Rd. Wat 134 C3
Mill Rd. Westb 137 D2
Mill Rise. Mott 5 E1
Mill Rythe La. N Hay 185 D4
Mill St. Broa 162 A1
Mill St. Eastl 56 A2
Mill St. Lo He 154 A4
Mill Way. Tot 100 C3
Millais Rd. Southa 103 F2
Milland Rd. Winch 11 D3
Millbank St. Southa 103 E3
Millbrook Cl. Ch Fo 55 D3
Millbrook Cl. Liss 21 D2
Millbrook Dr. Hav 136 A3
Millbrook Point Rd. Southa 102 A3
Millbrook Rd E. Southa 102 B3
Millbrook Rd W. Southa 102 A3
Miller Cl. New M 196 B2
Miller Dr. Fare 88 A1
Miller Dr. Fare 130 C1
Millers La. Hurs 9 F2
Millers La. Winch 10 A2
Millers Way. Hyt 125 F1
Millfield. Broa 204 A4
Millhams Cl. Bour 190 A3
Millhams La. Bour 190 A3
Millhams St N. Christ 209 D3
Millhams St. Christ 209 D3
Millstream Cl. Broa 204 A4
Millstream Cl. Wi Mi 163 E2
Millstream Rise. Rom 52 B4
Millstream Trading Est. Rin 141 D3
Milne Cl. Hyt 125 E1
Milne Rd. Broa 188 A1
Milner Ct. Southa 102 B4
Milner Pl. Winch 10 C3
Milner Rd. Bour 206 B1
Milnthorpe La. Winch 10 C4
Milton Cl. Poole 205 E2
Milton Gr. Lo He 129 D1
Milton Gr. New M 196 A1
Milton Mead. New M 195 F1
Milton Par. Wat 111 F1
Milton Park Ave. Ports 183 D2
Milton Rd. Bour 207 D3
Milton Rd. Eastl 56 A3
Milton Rd. Poole 205 E2
Milton Rd. Ports 183 D3
Milton Rd. Southa 102 C3
Milton Rd. Wat 111 F1
Milton Rd. Wi Mi 163 E3
Milverton Cl. Christ 194 C1
Milverton Cl. Tot 101 D3
Milverton Rd. Tot 101 D3
Milverton Rd. Winch 10 C4
Milvil Rd. L on S 179 F3
Mimosa Ave. Oakl 188 C4
Mimosa Dr. Fa Oa 57 F1
Mincingfield La. Durl 82 B3
Minden Way. Winch 10 B3
Minerva Cl. Wat 134 C1
Minstead Ave. Southa 104 B4
Minstead Cl. Winch 1 B2
Minstead Rd. Bour 190 B2
Minstead Rd. Ports 183 D2
Minster La. Winch 11 D4
Minster View. Wi Mi 163 E3
Minster Way. Upt 203 D4
Mint Rd. Liss 21 D3
Minter's Lepe. Wat 134 C2
Mintern Cl. Bish 56 B3
Minterne Rd. Bour 191 D1
Minterne Rd. Christ 209 F3
Minterne Rd. Poole 211 E4
Mirror Cl. Lo He 128 C1
Mislingford Rd. Swan 84 B2
Missenden Acres. He En 105 E4
Mission La. Wat 112 A2
Mission Rd. Broa 188 A1
Misslebrook La. Chilw 54 B2
Mitchell Cl. B on S 212 A4
Mitchell Cl. Lo He 129 E3
Mitchell Dr. Fa Oa 57 E2
Mitchell Point. Hamble 127 F1
Mitchell Rd. Hav 135 D2
Mitchell Way. Ports 158 A2
Mitchells Cl. Red 47 E3
Mitchells Cl. Rom 52 C4
Mitre Copse. Bish 56 C1
Moat Cl. Holb 150 A2
Moat Dr. Gos 180 B2
Moat Hill. Southa 79 F2
Moat La. B on S 211 F4
Moat Wlk. Gos 180 B2
Mockbeggar La. Ibs 117 D4
Moffat Rd. Christ 209 E4
Moggs Mead. Pet 41 D2
Mole Hill. Wat 134 C3
Molesworth Rd. Gos 181 E2
Molyneux Rd. New M 196 B2
Momford Rd. Winch 10 A2
Mon Cres. Southa 104 B4
Monarch Cl. Lo He 129 D1
Monarch Cl. Wat 135 D4
Monarch Way. W End 80 C1
Monastery Rd. Southa 103 F4
Monckton Rd. Gos 181 D1
Monckton Rd. Ports 158 A1
Moneyfield Ave. Ports 158 A1
Moneyfly Rd. Ver 115 D3
Monk's Hill. Westb 137 D3
Monks Brook Cl. Eastl 55 F1
Monks Cl. W Moo 166 A4
Monks Orch. Pet 40 C3
Monks Pl. Tot 100 B3
Monks Rd. Net 127 D3
Monks Rd. Winch 2 A1
Monks Way. Bour 189 E3
Monks Way. Eastl 55 F1
Monks Way. Southa 79 F2
Monks Way. Stubb 179 D4
Monks Wlk. Hyt 149 F4
Monks Wood Cl. Southa 79 D3
Monks Wood. Pet 40 C3
Monkswell Green. Christ 209 E3
Monkton Cl. Fern 165 E3
Monkton Cres. Poole 205 F4
Monkton La. Tot 100 B3
Monkwood Cl. Hav 135 E3
Monkworthy Dr. St Le 139 F3
Monmouth Cl. N Bad 55 D3
Monmouth Cl. Ver 115 D2
Monmouth Ct. Rin 140 C4
Monmouth Dr. Ver 115 D2
Monmouth Rd. Ports 157 E1
Monmouth Sq. Winch 10 A3
Monnow Gdns. W End 80 A1
Monroe Cl. Gos 180 C2
Monsal Ave. Fern 165 E2
Montacute Way. Oakl 188 C4
Montagu Rd. Christ 211 D4
Montague Ave. Southa 104 B2
Montague Cl. Southa 104 B2
Montague Gdns. Pet 41 E2
Montague Rd. Bish 56 B2
Montague Rd. Bour 208 A2
Montague Rd. Ports 157 F1
Montana Ct. Wat 135 D3
Monterey Dr. Hord 196 C2
Montfort Cl. Rom 53 E4
Montfort Rd. Rom 53 E3
Montgomerie Rd. Ports 182 B2
Montgomery Ave. Bour 190 A2
Montgomery Ave. Tot 100 B4
Montgomery Rd. Gos 155 E2
Montgomery Rd. Hav 136 A1
Montgomery Rd. Southa 104 A4
Montgomery Way. Ch Fo 55 D2
Montgomery Wlk. Wat 134 B3
Montrose Ave. Portc 132 C1
Montrose Dr. Bour 190 A1
Montserrat Rd. L on S 179 F3
Monument La. Bold 199 D3
Monument La. Southw 132 B2
Monument La. Wal 137 F4
Moody Rd. Stubb 154 B1
Moody's Hill. W Dean 3 E1
Mooncross Ave. Tot 100 C2
Moonhills La. Beaul 149 D1
Moonrakers Way. Christ 194 C1
Moor La. Whit 48 B4
Moor Park. Wat 112 A1
Moor Rd. Broa 188 A3
Moor View Rd. Poole 204 C4
Moorcroft Ave. Burt 193 E1
Moordown Cl. Bour 191 D2
Moore Ave. Bour 190 A2
Moore Cl. New M 195 F1
Moore Cres. Net 127 E4
Moore Gdns. Gos 180 C2
Moorfield Gr. Bour 190 C1
Moorfields Rd. Poole 211 F4
Moorgreen Rd. Hav 136 A3
Moorgreen Rd. W End 80 C1
Moorhead Ct. Southa 103 E1
Moorhill Gdns. W End 104 C4
Moorhill Rd. W End 104 B4
Moorings The. Christ 209 D3
Moorings Way. Ports 183 E3
Moorland Ave. B on S 211 F4
Moorland Cres. Upt 203 D4
Moorland Gate. Rin 141 D3
Moorland Rd. Bour 207 E2
Moorland Rd. Ports 182 C3
Moorland Way. Upt 203 D4
Moorlands Cres. Southa 104 A4
Moorlands Rd. Brock 145 E1
Moorlands Rd. Swan 84 A4
Moorlands Rd. Ver 114 C4
Moorlands Rd. W Moo 138 C2
Moorlands Rise. W Moo 138 C2
Moors Cl. Co Com 31 F1
Moors Cl. Hurn 192 A4
Moorside Cl. Bour 190 A2
Moorside Rd. Bour 190 A2
Moorside Rd. Broa 187 E3
Moorside Rd. W Moo 138 C1
Moorside Rd. Winch 2 B1
Moortown Ave. Cos 134 B1
Moortown La. Rin 141 E2
Moorvale Rd. Bour 191 D1
Moot Cl. Down 47 D4
Moot Gdns. Down 46 C3
Moot La. Down 46 C3
Moot La. Red 46 C3
Mopley Cl. Black 177 F4
Mopley. Black 177 F4
Morant Rd. Rin 117 D1
Moraunt Cl. Gosp 181 E4
Moraunt Dr. Portc 156 A3
Mordaunt Rd. Southa 103 D4
Morden Ave. Fern 165 E2
Morden Rd. Bour 190 C1
Moreland Rd. Gos 181 D3
Morelands Ct. Wat 134 C2
Morelands Rd. Wat 134 C2
Morestead Rd. Chilc 11 F2
Morestead Rd. Ows 11 F1
Morestead Rd. Ows 58 C4
Morestead Rd. Winch 11 E2
Moreton Rd. Bour 191 D2
Morgan Rd. He En 105 E3
Morgan Rd. Ports 183 E2
Morgan's La. Pent 42 A1
Morgans Dr. Stubb 154 B3
Morgans Rise Rd. Red 47 E4
Morgans Vale Rd. Red 47 E3
Morland Rd. Southa 78 B1
Morley Cl. Burt 193 E2
Morley Cl. Southa 103 F3
Morley Cres. Wat 112 A2
Morley Dr. Bi Wa 83 E4
Morley Rd. Bour 208 A3
Morley Rd. Ports 183 D1
Morningside Ave. Portc 132 C1
Mornington Dr. Winch 1 B1
Mornish Rd. Poole 205 F1
Morpeth Ave. Tot 100 C4
Morris Cl. Gos 155 E2
Morris Rd. Southa 102 C3
Morrison Ave. Poole 205 F3
Morshead Cres. Fare 88 A2
Mortimer Cl. Christ 210 A3
Mortimer Cl. Ki Wo 2 A3
Mortimer Cl. Net 127 D3
Mortimer Cl. Tot 76 B1
Mortimer Rd. Botl 106 A3
Mortimer Rd. Bour 191 D1
Mortimer Rd. Cos 133 E1
Mortimer Rd. Southa 103 F2
Mortimer Way. N Bad 53 F2
Mortimer's Indl Units. Ower 75 F3
Mortimers Dr. Fa Oa 57 E1
Mortimers La. Fa Oa 58 A2
Mortimers Lawn. Hav 135 E4
Mortimore Rd. Gos 180 C3
Mosdell Rd. Southb 161 F4
Moss Cl. Liss 21 D2
Moss Dr. March 101 F1
Moss Rd. Winch 11 D4
Mossleigh Ave. Southa 77 F3
Mossley Ave. Poole 190 A1
Motcombe Rd. Poole 206 A1
Mottisfont Cl. Southa 102 A3
Mottisfont Rd. Eastl 56 A2
Moulin Ave. Ports 182 C1
Mound Cl. Gos 181 D2
Mount Ave. New M 196 A1
Mount Cl. New M 196 A1
Mount Cl. Winch 1 C2
Mount Dr. Ch Fo 55 F2
Mount Dr. Fare 154 A4
Mount Grace Dr. Poole 211 E4
Mount House Cl. Hyt 126 A3
Mount La. Locke 25 F4
Mount Pleasant Dr. Bour 191 F1
Mount Pleasant La. Lym 198 A4
Mount Pleasant La. Rin 141 D4
Mount Pleasant La. Sway 198 A4
Mount Pleasant Rd. Gos 181 D2
Mount Pleasant Rd. Southa 103 D3
Mount Pleasant. Ki Wo 2 B3
Mount Rd. Bour 190 A2
Mount Rd. Poole 205 D3
Mount Temple. Rom 53 D4
Mount The. Gos 155 F1
Mount The. Rin 141 E4
Mount The. Southa 78 C2
Mount View Rd. Winch 10 A2
Mount View. Eastl 56 A2
Mountain Ash Cl. Southa 104 B4
Mountbatten Cl. Christ 210 A3
Mountbatten Cl. Gos 155 E2
Mountbatten Ct. Winch 1 C2
Mountbatten Dr. Fern 165 E3
Mountbatten Dr. Wat 134 B3
Mountbatten Gdns. Bour 191 F1
Mountbatten Pl. Ki Wo 2 B4
Mountbatten Rd. Bour 206 A1
Mountbatten Rd. Eastl 56 A3
Mountbatten Rd. Tot 100 B4
Mountbatten Way. Rom 52 C4
Mountbatten Way. Southa 102 B3
Mountfield. Hyt 125 F2
Mountjoy Cl. Oakl 163 F1
Mountwood Rd. Southb 137 E1
Mousehole La. Hyt 126 A2
Mousehole La. Southa 103 F4
Mousehole Rd. Portc 132 C1
Mowbray Rd. Southa 104 A2
Moxhams. Fordi 69 F1
Mt Pleasant Dr. Bran 169 E1
Mt Pleasant Rd. Poole 204 B2
Muccleshell Cl. Hav 136 A2
Muddyford Rd. Red 47 E4
Mude Gdns. Christ 210 A3
Mudeford Green Cl. Christ 209 F3
Mudeford La. Christ 209 F3
Mudeford. Christ 210 A3
Mulberry Ave. Cos 158 A4
Mulberry Ave. Stubb 154 B1
Mulberry Cl. Gos 181 D2
Mulberry Gdns. Fordi 93 F4
Mulberry Gr. Hord 213 E4
Mulberry La. Cos 158 A4
Mulberry Rd. March 101 F1
Mulberry Wlk. Southa 102 B4
Mullen Cl. Southa 103 F2
Mullins Cl. Poole 206 B4
Mumby Rd. Gos 181 E3
Mundays Row. Horn 88 B1
Munro Cres. Southa 101 F4
Munster Rd. Poole 205 E2
Munster Rd. Ports 157 E1
Murefield Rd. Ports 182 B3
Muriel Rd. Wat 134 C4
Murley Rd. Bour 207 D4
Murray Cl. Fare 130 C1
Murray Cl. Southa 104 C3
Murray Rd. Horn 112 A3
Murrills Estate. Portc 156 C4
Muscliffe La. Bour 191 D2
Muscliffe Rd. Bour 190 C1
Museum Rd. Ports 182 A2
My Lords La. S Hay 185 D2
Myers Cl. Swan 84 A3
Myrtle Ave. Portc 156 B4
Myrtle Ave. Tot 100 B3
Myrtle Cl. Gos 155 D2
Myrtle Cl. Hord 196 C2
Myrtle Gr. Ports 183 D4
Myrtle Rd. Bour 207 E3
Myrtle Rd. Southa 78 A2
Myvern Cl. Holb 150 B2

Nada Rd. Christ 194 B1
Nailsworth Rd. Cos 133 D1
Nairn Rd. Bour 206 C3
Nairn Rd. Poole 211 F4
Naish Ct. Hav 135 E4
Naish Dr. Gos 156 A1
Naish Rd. B on S 211 F4
Namu Rd. Bour 190 C1
Nancy Rd. Ports 182 C3
Nansen Ave. Poole 204 B3
Napier Cres. Fare 130 B1
Napier Rd. Hamw 203 E2
Napier Rd. Horn 112 B3
Napier Rd. Ports 182 B1
Napier Rd. Southa 104 C3
Narrow La. Rom 52 C4
Narvik Rd. Ports 157 E2
Naseby Cl. Cos 133 D1
Naseby Rd. Bour 191 D1
Nash Cl. Hyt 125 E1
Nash Rd. Hyt 125 E1
Nashe Cl. Fare 130 B2
Nashe Way. Fare 130 B2
Nasmith Cl. Gos 180 B2
Nations Hill. Ki Wo 2 B3
Navigator's Way. He En 105 E4
Nea Cl. Christ 210 B4
Nea Rd. Christ 210 C4
Neath Way. N Bad 55 D3
Needles Point. M on S 213 E2
Neelands Gr. Portc 156 C4
Neilson Cl. Ch Fo 55 E4
Nelson Ave. Portc 156 A4
Nelson Ave. Ports 157 E1
Nelson Cl. Holb 150 B2
Nelson Cl. New M 195 F2
Nelson Cl. Rom 52 C4
Nelson Cres. Horn 112 B4
Nelson Ct. Fare 154 C3
Nelson Ct. Hyt 126 A1
Nelson Dr. Christ 209 F3
Nelson La. Portc 132 B1
Nelson Pl. Lym 198 C2
Nelson Rd. Bish 56 B2
Nelson Rd. Bour 206 A2
Nelson Rd. Gos 181 D2
Nelson Rd. Poole 206 A2
Nelson Rd. Ports 182 B4
Nelson Rd. Southa 102 B3
Nelson Rd. Winch 11 E3
Nepean Cl. Gos 181 D1
Neptune Ct. Southa 77 F2
Neptune Rd. Fare 130 B1
Neptune Way. Southa 103 D1
Nerissa Cl. Wat 135 D4
Nerquis Cl. Rom 53 D4
Nesbitt Cl. Gos 155 D2
Nessus St. Ports 182 B4
Netherfield Cl. Hav 136 A1
Netherhall Gdns. Bour 206 B2
Netherton Rd. Gos 180 C4
Netherwood Pl. Wi Mi 163 D3
Netley Cl. Ch Fo 55 D2
Netley Cl. Poole 205 D4
Netley Firs Rd. He En 104 C3
Netley Firs Rd. He En 105 D3
Netley Hill Estate. He En 104 C2
Netley Lodge Cl. Net 127 E3
Netley Rd. Lo He 129 E1
Netley Rd. Ports 182 B1
Netley Terr. Ports 182 B1
Nettlecombe Ave. Ports 182 C1
Nettlestone Rd. Ports 183 D1
Nettlestone. Net 127 E4
Nettleton Cl. Poole 204 C4
Netton Cl. Crouch 22 A4
Netton St. Crouch 22 B4
Neva Rd. Southa 103 F4
Neville Ave. Portc 156 B3
Neville Gdns. Ems 136 C2
Neville Rd. Ports 183 D4
Neville Shute Rd. Ports 158 A2
New Borough Rd. Wi Mi 163 E2
New Brighton Rd. Ems 136 C1
New Cotts. Nur 77 E1
New Cut. N Hay 159 F2
New Down La. Cos 134 A1
New Down La. Southw 134 A1
New Forest Dr. Brock 145 E1
New Harbour Rd. Hamw 204 A1
New Harbour Rd W. Hamw 204 A1
New Inn La. Cadn 99 D3
New Inn Rd. Cadn 99 D4
New La. Hav 136 A2
New La. M on S 213 F2
New La. New M 195 F3
New Orchard. Poole 204 A1
New Par. Bour 190 C2
New Par. Portc 156 B4
New Park Rd. Bour 208 B2
New Quay Rd. Hamw 204 A1
New Rd E. Ports 182 C4
New Rd. Ashu 100 B1
New Rd. Black 150 C1
New Rd. Bour 190 C3
New Rd. Clanf 88 B3
New Rd. Co Com 31 F1
New Rd. Fa Oa 57 D1
New Rd. Fare 88 A1
New Rd. Faw 150 B4
New Rd. Fern 165 F2
New Rd. Hav 135 F1
New Rd. Horn 111 F3
New Rd. Hyt 150 B4
New Rd. Ibs 117 D4
New Rd. Lan 49 F1
New Rd. Litt 1 A3
New Rd. Lo He 152 C4
New Rd. M on S 214 A2
New Rd. Meons 61 E2
New Rd. Mich 27 E4
New Rd. Net 127 D3
New Rd. Poole 205 E3
New Rd. Ports 182 C4
New Rd. Rin 141 D2
New Rd. Rockb 44 C1
New Rd. Rom 53 D4
New Rd. Southa 103 D3
New Rd. Southb 161 F4
New Rd. Swan 84 A3
New Rd. Swanw 128 C4
New Rd. Westb 137 D2
New Rd. Woodl 114 A3
New St. Lym 198 C2
New St. Poole 204 A1
New St. Rin 141 D3
New Town. Portc 156 B4
New Valley Rd. M on S 213 E3
Newbarn La. Wal 137 F4
Newbarn Rd. Hav 135 E2
Newbolt Cl. Wat 111 F2

Newbolt Rd. Portc 132 C1
Newbridge Rd. Cadn 75 D1
Newbridge Way. Lym 198 B1
Newbridge. Net 127 E3
Newbroke Rd. Gos 180 C4
Newburgh St. Winch 10 C4
Newbury Cl. Fa Oa 57 D1
Newbury Dr. Bour 190 B1
Newbury Rd. Southa 78 B1
Newcliffe Gdns. He En 105 D3
Newcombe Rd. Bour 208 C3
Newcombe Rd. Southa 102 C3
Newcombe Rd. W Moo 138 B2
Newcome Rd. Ports 182 C3
Newcomen Rd. Ports 157 E1
Newcroft Gdns. Christ 209 D4
Newenham Rd. Lym 198 C1
Newfield Rd. Liss 21 D3
Newfoundland Dr. Poole 204 B1
Newgate La. Fare 155 D2
Newgate La. Gos 155 E3
Newgate La. Stubb 155 D2
Newland Ave. Gos 181 D2
Newlands Ave. Southa 102 B4
Newlands Cl. Black 150 C1
Newlands Copse. Black 150 C1
Newlands La. Den 134 A4
Newlands La. Southw 134 A4
Newlands Rd. Bour 208 A3
Newlands Rd. Christ 209 F4
Newlands Rd. Faw 150 C1
Newlands Rd. New M 196 A1
Newlands Rd. Wat 134 B3
Newlands Way. Broa 187 E2
Newlease Rd. Wat 134 C3
Newlyn Way. Poole 205 F4
Newlyn Way. Ports 157 D4
Newlyn Wlk. Rom 28 A1
Newman St. Southa 102 A4
Newman's La. W Moo 138 B2
Newmans Cl. W Moo 138 C3
Newmans Hill. Shed 84 B1
Newmans Hill. Swan 84 B1
Newmer Ct. Hav 135 E3
Newmorton Rd. Bour 191 D2
Newney Cl. Ports 157 F2
Newport La. Brai 28 B4
Newport Rd. Gos 180 C3
Newstead Rd. Bour 208 C2
Newton Cl. Stubb 154 B3
Newton Cl. Whit 24 A2
Newton La. Rom 52 C4
Newton La. Whit 24 A2
Newton Morrell. Poole 205 E2
Newton Pl. L on S 179 F4
Newton Rd. B on S 212 A4
Newton Rd. Poole 211 F4
Newton Rd. Southa 79 F1
Newton Rd. Twyf 32 A4
Newtown La. Broa 187 E4
Newtown La. S Hay 184 C2
Newtown La. Ver 115 D3
Newtown Rd. Eastl 56 A2
Newtown Rd. Lo He 152 B4
Newtown Rd. Sh En 26 A2
Newtown Rd. Southa 104 A1
Newtown Rd. Ver 115 D3
Nichol Rd. Ch Fo 30 B1
Nicholas Cl. Christ 195 D1
Nicholas Cres. Fare 130 C1
Nicholas Gdns. Bour 190 B1
Nicholas Rd. Black 177 F4
Nicholl Pl. Gos 155 E1
Nichols Rd. Southa 103 D3
Nicholson Cl. Poole 204 C4
Nicholson Way. Hav 135 F2
Nickel Cl. Winch 11 D4
Nickel St. Ports 182 A2
Nickleby Gdns. Tot 100 A4
Nickleby Rd. Clanf 88 A3
Nightingale Ave. Eastl 55 E1
Nightingale Cl. Gos 180 C3
Nightingale Cl. Ro Ca 113 D1
Nightingale Cl. Rom 53 D4
Nightingale Cl. Ver 115 D3
Nightingale Cl. W Wel 50 B2
Nightingale Cres. Shed 107 F4
Nightingale Dr. Tot 100 B4
Nightingale Gr. Southa 102 B4
Nightingale Mews. Net 127 E3
Nightingale Park. Hav 136 A1
Nightingale Rd. Burs 127 F4
Nightingale Rd. Pet 40 C1
Nightingale Rd. Ports 182 A1
Nightingale Rd. Southa 102 B4
Nightingale Wlk. Net 127 E3
Nightjar Cl. Broa 203 F4
Nile Rd. Southa 79 D1
Nile St. Ems 160 C4
Nimrod Dr. Gos 180 B3
Nine Elms La. Fare 131 F2
Ninian Cl. Fa Oa 57 E1
Ninian Park Rd. Ports 158 A1
Niton Cl. Gos 155 E1
Noads Cl. Hyt 125 F1
Noads Way. Hyt 125 F1
Nobbs La. Ports 182 A2
Nobes Ave. Gos 155 E2
Nobes Cl. Gos 155 E1
Noble Cl. Bour 189 F1
Noble Rd. He En 105 E3
Noel Cl. Brock 146 A1
Noel Rd. Bour 190 A1
Nook The. Eastl 56 A3
Nook The. Gos 155 F1
Noon Gdns. Ver 115 D3
Noon Hill Dr. Ver 115 D3
Noon Hill Rd. Ver 115 D3
Norbury Cl. Ch Fo 55 D4
Norbury Gdns. Hamble 127 F1
Norcliffe Cl. Bour 190 A2
Norcliffe Rd. Southa 103 D4
Norcroft Ct. Southa 78 B1
Nordik Gdns. He En 105 E3
Nore Farm Ave. Ems 136 B1
Noreuil Rd. Pet 40 B2
Norfolk Ave. Christ 192 C1
Norfolk Rd. Gos 180 C4
Norfolk Rd. Southa 102 B4
Norfolk St. Ports 182 B2
Norgett Way. Portc 156 A4
Norham Ave. Southa 78 B1
Norham Cl. Southa 78 B1
Norland Rd. Ports 182 C2
Norlands Dr. Ott 31 E2
Norley Cl. Hav 135 F3
Norleywood Rd. Bold 199 F4
Norleywood. Christ 210 C4
Norman Ave. Poole 206 A3
Norman Cl. Portc 156 B3
Norman Gdns. He En 105 D3
Norman Gdns. Poole 206 A3
Norman Rd. Black 177 F4
Norman Rd. Gos 181 D3
Norman Rd. Ports 182 C2
Norman Rd. S Hay 185 D1
Norman Rd. Southa 102 B3
Norman Rd. Winch 10 C3
Norman Way. Hav 135 E1
Normandy Cl. Sway 172 A1
Normandy Dr. Christ 209 E4
Normandy Gdns. Gos 180 C2
Normandy La. Lym 198 C1
Normandy Rd. Ports 157 F2
Normandy Way. Fordi 69 F1
Normandy Way. Hamw 203 E1
Normandy Way. March 102 A1
Normanhurst Ave. Bour 191 F1
Normanton Cl. Christ 192 C1
Norris Cl. Rom 28 B1
Norris Cl. St Le 139 F2
Norris Gdns. Hav 160 A4
Norris Gdns. New M 196 A1
Norris Hill. Southa 79 F1
Norrish Rd. Poole 205 E3
Norset Rd. Fare 130 B1
North Ave. Bour 190 B3
North Ave. Ports 157 F3
North Bay. Th Is 161 D2
North Cl. Gos 180 C2
North Cl. Hav 160 A4
North Cl. Lym 198 C2
North Cl. Rom 28 B1
North Common La. Lan 49 D3
North Cres. S Hay 185 D2
North Cross St. Gos 181 E2
North Cross St. Ports 182 B4
North Ct. Ports 182 C4
North Dr. Litt 1 A3
North East Cl. Southa 104 B3
North East Rd. Southa 104 A2
North End Ave. Ports 157 E1
North End Cl. Ch Fo 55 E2
North End Gr. Ports 157 E1
North End La. Ibs 93 E2
North Front. Southa 103 D3
North Greenlands. Lym 198 B1
North Hill Cl. Winch 1 C1
North Hill. Fare 88 A2
North La. Beaul 148 C3
North La. Buri 65 F3
North La. Clanf 88 B4
North La. E Meo 64 B1
North La. Red 73 E4
North La. W Tyth 4 A4
North Lodge Rd. Poole 205 F2
North Mead. M on S 213 D3
North Millers Dale. Ch Fo 55 D4
North Path. Gos 180 B3
North Poulner Rd. Rin 117 D1
North Rd. Bour 207 F3
North Rd. Brock 146 A1
North Rd. Horn 88 B1
North Rd. Hyt 125 F1
North Rd. Ki Wo 2 A4
North Rd. Pet 40 C2
North Rd. Poole 205 D2
North Rd. Southa 103 E4
North Shore Rd. S Hay 184 B2
North St. Ems 136 C1
North St. Gos 181 E2
North St. Hav 135 E1
North St. Lym 198 B1
North St. Poole 204 B1
North St. Ports 182 B3
North St. Westb 137 D2
North Town. Twyf 32 A4
North Wallington. Fare 131 E1
North Walls. Winch 11 D4
North Way. Gos 155 E2
North Way. Hav 135 F1
North Way. Lo He 129 F2
North Weirs. Brock 145 E1
Northam Rd. Southa 103 D3
Northam St. Ports 182 B3
Northampton La. Black 177 F4
Northarbour Rd. Cos 157 E4
Northarbour Spur. Cos 157 E4
Northbourne Ave. Bour 190 B3
Northbourne Cl. Hyt 126 A1
Northbourne Gdns. Bour 190 C3
Northbourne Pl. Bour 190 B3
Northbrook Ave. Winch 11 E4
Northbrook Cl. Ports 182 B4
Northbrook Cl. Winch 11 E4
Northbrook Rd. Broa 188 A1
Northbrook Rd. Southa 103 D3
Northcote Rd. Bour 207 D2
Northcote Rd. Ports 182 C2
Northcote Rd. Southa 79 E1
Northcroft Rd. Gos 180 C3
Northdene Rd. Ch Fo 55 E3
Northend La. Drox 61 D1
Northern Access Rd. Faw 151 E1
Northern Anchorage. Southa 103 E2
Northern Par. Ports 157 F2
Northern Rd. Cos 157 F4
Northerwood Ave. Lyn 121 F3
Northerwood Cl. N Bad 53 F2
Northey Rd. Bour 208 C3
Northfield Ave. Fare 154 C4
Northfield Cl. Bi Wa 59 D1
Northfield Cl. Horn 88 B1
Northfield Park. Portc 132 A1
Northfield Rd. M on S 213 F2
Northfield Rd. Rin 117 D1
Northfield Rd. Southa 79 F2
Northfields Farm La. Wickh 108 A3
Northgate Ave. Ports 182 C4
Northlands Cl. Tot 100 B4
Northlands Dr. Winch 2 A1
Northlands Gdns. Southa 102 C4
Northlands Rd. Eastl 56 A2
Northlands Rd. Rom 53 E3
Northlands Rd. Southa 102 C4
Northlands Rd. Tot 100 C4
Northleigh Cnr. Southa 79 F3
Northleigh La. Wi Mi 163 F3
Northmead Dr. Broa 203 F4
Northmere Dr. Poole 205 F4
Northmere Rd. Poole 205 F4
Northmore Cl. Lo He 129 D3
Northmore Rd. Lo He 129 D3
Northney La. N Hay 160 B2
Northney Rd. N Hay 160 A2
Northolt Gdns. Southa 78 A3
Northover La. Sway 196 C4
Northover Rd. Lym 198 A2
Northover Rd. Ports 183 D4
Northumberland Rd. Ports 182 C3
Northumberland Rd. Southa 103 D3
Northways. Stubb 154 B1
Northwood Cl. Southa 79 D3
Northwood La. N Hay 160 A1
Northwood Rd. Ports 157 F3
Northwood Sq. Fare 88 A1
Nortoft Rd. Bour 207 D3
Norton Cl. Southa 103 F2
Norton Cl. Southw 132 C3
Norton Cl. Wat 134 B4
Norton Dr. Fare 88 A2
Norton Rd. Bour 206 C4
Norton Rd. Southw 132 C3
Norton Welch Cl. N Bad 54 A2
Norway Rd. Ports 158 A2
Norwich Ave W. Bour 206 B2
Norwich Ave. Bour 206 B2
Norwich Cl. Lo He 128 C2
Norwich Pl. L on S 179 F4
Norwich Rd. Bour 206 C2
Norwich Rd. Cos 133 E1
Norwich Rd. Southa 79 F1
Norwood Pl. Bour 208 A3
Nottingham Pl. L on S 179 F4
Nouale La. Rin 141 E4
Novello Gdns. Wat 134 C3
Noyce Dr. Fa Oa 57 E1
Noyce Gdns. Bour 192 A1
Nuffield Rd. Poole 204 B4
Nugent Rd. Bour 209 D2
Nunns Park. Whit 24 A2
Nuns Rd. Winch 2 A1
Nurse's Path. Twyf 58 A3
Nursery Cl. Ems 136 C2
Nursery Cl. Gos 155 D2
Nursery Gdns. Ch Fo 55 E2
Nursery Gdns. Rom 53 D4
Nursery Gdns. Southa 104 A3
Nursery Gdns. Wat 112 A3
Nursery Gdns. Winch 10 B4
Nursery Gr. He En 105 E3
Nursery La. Stubb 154 B1
Nursery Rd. Bour 191 D2
Nursery Rd. Rin 141 D3
Nursery Rd. Southa 79 E1
Nursling Green. Bour 191 E1
Nursling St. Nur 77 E3
Nutash. Lo He 129 E2
Nutbeem Rd. Eastl 56 A1
Nutbourne Rd. Cos 158 B4
Nutbourne Rd. S Hay 185 F1
Nutfield Ct. Southa 77 F2
Nutfield Pl. Ports 182 B3
Nutfield Rd. Rown 77 E3
Nuthatch Cl. Broa 203 F4
Nuthatch Cl. Fern 165 D4
Nuthatch Cl. Ro Ca 113 D1
Nutley Cl. Bour 189 F2
Nutley Rd. Hav 135 E3
Nutley Way. Bour 189 F2
Nutsey Ave. Tot 76 B1
Nutsey La. Tot 76 C1
Nutshalling Ave. Rown 77 F3
Nutshalling Cl. Tot 76 B1
Nutwick Rd. Hav 136 A2
Nutwood Rd. Chilw 79 D4
Nyewood Ave. Portc 132 B1
Nyria Way. Gos 181 E2

O'connell Rd. Eastl 55 F1
Oak Ave. Christ 208 B4
Oak Cl. Fern 165 F1
Oak Cl. Hyt 125 F1
Oak Cl. Lyn 121 F2
Oak Cl. Southa 101 E4
Oak Cl. Uph 58 C3
Oak Cl. Wat 111 F1
Oak Coppice Cl. Fa Oa 57 D1
Oak Dr. Fa Oa 57 E1
Oak Gdns. Hord 213 E4
Oak Green Way. Southa 104 A4
Oak La. Rin 141 D4
Oak Rd. Alderh 92 C3
Oak Rd. Bi Wa 83 F4
Oak Rd. Bour 207 E3
Oak Rd. Burs 127 F4
Oak Rd. Clanf 88 B3
Oak Rd. Fare 130 B1
Oak Rd. Hyt 125 F1
Oak Rd. New M 196 B2
Oak Rd. Southa 103 F1
Oak Rd. Upt 203 E3
Oak St. Gos 181 E2
Oak Tree Cl. Co Comm 56 C4
Oak Tree Dr. Ems 136 C2
Oak Tree Dr. Liss 21 D2
Oak Tree Gdns. He En 105 D3
Oak Tree Rd. Southa 79 F1
Oak Tree Way. Eastl 56 A3
Oak Wlk. Fa Oa 57 E1
Oakapple Gdns. Cos 158 B4
Oakbank Rd. Southa 103 E2
Oakcroft La. Stubb 154 B3
Oakdale Rd. Poole 204 C3
Oakdene Cl. Wi Mi 163 E3
Oakdene. Gos 155 E1
Oakdene. Tot 100 B4
Oakdown Rd. Stubb 154 B2
Oakenbrow. Hyt 125 E2
Oakes The. Stubb 154 A2
Oakfield Ct. Hav 136 A3
Oakfield Rd. Cadn 99 D4
Oakfield Rd. Poole 204 B3
Oakfield Rd. Tot 100 C4
Oakfields. Eastl 56 A4
Oakford Ct. Bour 191 E2
Oakgrove Gdns. Bish 56 C1
Oakgrove Rd. Bish 56 C1
Oakhill Cl. Burs 105 D1
Oakhill Cl. Ch Fo 55 F3
Oakhill. Burs 105 D1
Oakhurst Cl. Net 127 E3
Oakhurst Cl. W Moo 138 C1
Oakhurst Dr. Wat 135 D4
Oakhurst Gdns. Wat 134 A1
Oakhurst La. W Moo 138 C1
Oakhurst Rd. Southa 79 D2
Oakhurst Rd. W Moo 138 C1
Oakhurst Way. Net 127 E3
Oakland Dr. March 101 F1
Oakland Wlk. Fern 165 F1
Oaklands Ave. Tot 100 C4
Oaklands Cl. Fordi 69 F1
Oaklands Cl. Ver 114 C3
Oaklands Gdns. Lo He 129 E1
Oaklands Gr. Wat 111 F2
Oaklands Rd. Hav 136 A1
Oaklands Rd. Pet 40 C2
Oaklands The. Ch Fo 55 E2
Oaklands Way. Hyt 125 E2
Oaklands Way. Lo He 129 E1
Oaklands Way. Southa 78 C2
Oaklands. Lym 198 C1
Oaklea Cl. Wat 134 A1
Oakleigh Cres. Tot 100 C3
Oakleigh Dr. Red 73 E4
Oakleigh Gdns. Rom 53 D4
Oakleigh Way. Christ 210 C4
Oakley Cl. Holb 150 B2
Oakley Hill. Oakl 163 E1
Oakley La. Oakl 163 F1
Oakley Rd. Hav 135 E3
Oakley Rd. Mott 5 F2
Oakley Rd. Oakl 163 E1
Oakley Rd. Southa 102 A4
Oakley Straight. Oakl 163 F1
Oakmead Rd. Broa 203 F4
Oakmeadow Cl. Ems 137 D2
Oakmount Ave. Ch Fo 55 E2
Oakmount Ave. Southa 79 D1
Oakmount Ave. Tot 100 C4
Oakmount Dr. Wat 111 F1
Oakmount Rd. Ch Fo 55 F3
Oakridge Rd. Southa 101 E4
Oaks Coppice. Wat 112 A3
Oaks Dr. St Le 139 E2
Oaks The. Southa 103 F3
Oaks The. Ver 114 C4
Oakshott Dr. Hav 136 A3
Oaktree Ct. M on S 213 E2
Oakwood Ave. Hav 135 D2
Oakwood Ave. New M 196 B2
Oakwood Ave. Ott 31 E2
Oakwood Cl. Bour 191 D1
Oakwood Cl. Ch Fo 30 B1
Oakwood Cl. Lo He 152 B4
Oakwood Cl. Ott 31 E2
Oakwood Cl. Rom 28 B1
Oakwood Dr. Southa 78 B3
Oakwood Rd. Bour 191 D1
Oakwood Rd. Ch Fo 55 E4
Oakwood Rd. Christ 194 C1
Oakwood Rd. Ports 157 F2
Oakwood Rd. S Hay 184 C2
Oakwood Way. Hamble 128 A2
Oates Rd. Bour 190 C1
Oatfield Gdns. Tot 76 B1
Oatlands Cl. Botl 81 F1
Oatlands Rd. Botl 81 F1
Oatlands. Rom 52 C4
Oban Rd. Bour 206 C4
Obelisk Rd. Southa 103 F1
Ober Rd. Brock 145 F1
Oberfield Rd. Brock 145 E1
Oberland Ct. Lym 198 B2
Oberon Cl. Wat 135 D4
Obsemsley S Dr. New M 195 F4
Occupation La. Lo He 153 F4
Ocean Cl. Fare 130 B1
Ocean Rd. Southa 103 D1
Ocean Way. Southa 103 D1
Ockendon Cres. Ports 182 B2
Ocknell Gr. Hyt 125 E2
Octavia Hill. Winch 10 B3
Octavia Rd. Southa 79 F2
Octavius Ct. Wat 112 A1
Odell Cl. Fare 130 C2
Odiham Cl. Ch Fo 55 D2
Odiham Cl. Southa 77 F2
Oelander Cl. Lo He 129 D3
Oglander Rd. Winch 2 A1
Ogle Rd. Southa 102 C2
Okeford Rd. Broa 188 B1
Okement Cl. W End 80 A1
Old Barn Cl. Christ 192 B1
Old Barn Cl. Rin 141 E4
Old Barn Cres. Hambl 86 B1
Old Barn Farm Rd. W Moo 139 D3
Old Barn Rd. Christ 192 B1
Old Bound Rd. Upt 203 E3
Old Brickyard Rd. Fordi 69 D1
Old Bridge Cl. Burs 128 A4
Old Bridge House Rd. Burs 128 A4
Old Bridge Rd. Bour 208 B4
Old Bridge Rd. Ports 182 C1
Old Canal. Ports 183 D2
Old Christchurch Rd. Hord 197 E1
Old Coastguard Rd. Poole 211 D2
Old Commercial Rd. Ports 182 B4
Old Common. Lo He 129 D2
Old Cottage Cl. W Wel 50 C2
Old Cracknore Cl. March 102 A1
Old Farm Cl. Rin 117 E1
Old Farm Copse. W Wel 50 C2
Old Farm Dr. Southa 79 F2
Old Farm La. Stubb 154 B1
Old Farm La. Westb 137 E2
Old Farm Rd. Poole 204 C3
Old Farm Way. Cos 158 C4
Old Farm Wlk. Lym 198 B2
Old Forge Cl. Alderh 92 C3
Old Forge Rd. Fern 164 C3
Old Garden Cl. Lo He 129 E1
Old Gardens. Winch 1 C1
Old Gosport Rd. Fare 155 D4
Old Hillside Rd. Winch 1 B1
Old Kennels Cl. Winch 10 A2
Old Kennels La. Winch 10 A2
Old Kiln Rd. Upt 203 E4
Old London Rd. Ports 157 F2
Old Lyndhurst Rd. Cadn 98 C4
Old Magazine Cl. March 101 F1
Old Manor Way. Cos 158 A4
Old Market Rd. Broa 187 D4
Old Mill La. Hambl 87 E2
Old Mill La. Steep 41 D3
Old Mill Way. Southa 78 A1
Old Milton Gn. B on S 195 F1
Old Milton Rd. New M 196 A1
Old Orchard. Poole 204 B1
Old Orchards. Lym 198 C1
Old Parsonage Ct. Ott 31 E2
Old Pines Cl. Fern 165 F2
Old Priory Cl. Hamble 128 A1
Old Priory Rd. Bour 208 C2

Old Rd. Gos 181 E2
Old Rd. Rom 53 D4
Old Rd. Southa 103 D1
Old Rd. Wi Mi 163 D3
Old Rectory Cl. Westb 137 D2
Old Rectory Gdns. Ki Wo 2 B3
Old Rectory Rd. Cos 158 B4
Old Redbridge Rd. Southa 101 E4
Old Reservoir Rd. Cos 158 B4
Old River. Den 110 C2
Old Road The. Cos 157 F3
Old Romsey Rd. Cadn 98 C4
Old Salisbury La. Awb 27 D1
Old School Cl. Net 127 E3
Old School Gdns. W End 80 C1
Old St. Stubb 154 A2
Old Stacks Gdns. Rin 141 E3
Old Star Pl. Ports 182 A3
Old Station App. Winch 11 D4
Old Swanwick La. Swanw 128 B4
Old Timbers. S Hay 184 C2
Old Turnpike. Fare 88 A2
Old Van Diemans Rd. Wat 134 B3
Old Vicarage Cl. Bour 190 C3
Old Vineries The. Fordi 69 E1
Old Wareham Rd. Poole 205 D4
Old Winchester Hill La. Plai 37 E1
Old Wymering La. Cos 157 F4
Oldbarn Cl. Tot 76 B1
Oldbury Ct. Southa 77 E1
Oldbury Way. Fare 154 B4
Oldgate Gdns. Ports 157 F2
Olinda St. Ports 182 C3
Olive Cres. Portc 156 B3
Olive Rd. Southa 78 A2
Oliver Rd. Lym 198 B2
Oliver Rd. Ports 183 D2
Oliver Rd. Southa 79 E2
Oliver's Battery Cres. Winch 10 A2
Oliver's Battery Gdns. Winch 10 A2
Oliver's Battery Rd N. Winch 10 A3
Oliver's Battery Rd S. Winch 10 A2
Olivers Cl. Tot 100 A4
Olivers Rd. Wi Mi 164 A3
Olivers Way. Wi Mi 164 A3
Olivia Cl. Wat 112 A1
Olympic Way. Fa Oa 57 D1
Omdurman Rd. Southa 79 D1
Omega St. Ports 182 B3
Onibury Cl. Southa 80 A1
Onslow Gdns. Wi Mi 163 E3
Onslow Rd. Ports 182 B1
Onslow Rd. Southa 103 D3
Ophir Gdns. Bour 207 E3
Ophir Rd. Bour 207 D3
Ophir Rd. Ports 157 F2
Oracle Dr. Wat 134 C2
Oratory Gdns. Poole 211 F4
Orchard Ave. Bish 56 C1
Orchard Ave. Poole 204 C1
Orchard Ave. Poole 205 D2
Orchard Cl. Broa 187 E4
Orchard Cl. Christ 209 D3
Orchard Cl. Co Com 31 F1
Orchard Cl. Faw 151 D2
Orchard Cl. Fern 165 F3
Orchard Cl. Fordi 69 F1
Orchard Cl. Gos 156 A1
Orchard Cl. Horn 112 B3
Orchard Cl. N Bad 53 F3
Orchard Cl. Rin 141 D4
Orchard Cl. Tot 100 C3
Orchard Ct. He En 105 F4
Orchard Gdns. Fordi 69 F1
Orchard Gr. New M 196 A1
Orchard Gr. Portc 156 A4
Orchard Gr. Wat 111 F2
Orchard La. Broa 187 E4
Orchard La. Herm 161 D4
Orchard La. Rom 52 C4
Orchard La. Southa 103 D2
Orchard Mews. Christ 209 D3
Orchard Pl. Southa 103 D2
Orchard Rd. Fa Oa 57 E1
Orchard Rd. Hav 159 F4
Orchard Rd. Lo He 128 C1
Orchard Rd. Ports 182 C2
Orchard Rd. Red 47 F4
Orchard Rd. S Hay 185 D1
Orchard St. Bour 206 C2
Orchard The. Bran 194 B4
Orchard The. Chilw 54 C1
Orchard The. Cos 157 F4
Orchard The. Den 110 C2
Orchard The. M on S 213 E2
Orchard Way. Hyt 125 F1
Orchardlea. Swan 84 B2
Orchards Way. Southa 79 D1
Orchards Way. W End 80 B1
Orcheston Rd. Bour 207 E3
Orchid Way. Christ 209 E4
Ordnance Rd. Gos 181 E2
Ordnance Rd. Southa 103 D3
Ordnance Row. Ports 182 A3
Oregon Cl. Southa 104 A2
Orford Cl. Christ 192 B2
Oriana Way. Nur 77 D2
Oriel Dr. Lo He 129 D1
Oriel Rd. Ports 157 E1
Orient Dr. Winch 1 B2
Oriental Terr. Southa 103 D2
Orion Cl. Southa 77 F2
Orion Cl. Stubb 154 B1
Orkney Cl. Southa 77 F2
Orkney Rd. Cos 133 F1
Ormesby Dr. Ch Fo 30 A1
Ormond Cl. Fa Oa 57 D1
Ormonde Rd. Poole 206 A1
Ormsby Rd. Ports 182 B2
Orpen Rd. Southa 104 B2
Orwell Cres. Lo He 129 E1
Orwell Rd. Southa 77 F1
Osborn Cres. Gos 155 D2
Osborn Rd. Fare 88 A1
Osborne Cl. Net 127 E3
Osborne Cl. Wat 135 D4
Osborne Dr. Ch Fo 55 F3
Osborne Gdns. Fa Oa 57 F1
Osborne Gdns. Southa 79 E1
Osborne Rd S. Fare 88 B1
Osborne Rd. Bour 206 C4
Osborne Rd. L on S 179 F3
Osborne Rd. Lo He 152 B4
Osborne Rd. New M 196 A2
Osborne Rd. Pet 40 C2
Osborne Rd. Poole 205 D2
Osborne Rd. Ports 182 B1
Osborne Rd. Southa 103 E4
Osborne Rd. Tot 101 D4
Osborne Rd. Wi Mi 163 E2
Osborne View Rd. Stubb 154 A1
Osier Cl. Ports 157 E2
Oslands La. Swanw 128 B4
Osprey Cl. Cos 158 C4
Osprey Cl. March 101 F1
Osprey Cl. Southa 78 A3
Osprey Dr. S Hay 185 D2
Osprey Gdns. L on S 179 F3
Osprey Quay. Herm 161 D4
Osterley Cl. He En 105 F3
Osterly Rd. Southa 103 F3
Oswald Cl. Bour 190 C1
Oswald Rd. Bour 190 C1
Othello Dr. Wat 135 D4
Otter Cl. Bish 57 D1
Otter Cl. Upt 203 D3
Otter Cl. Ver 115 D3
Otterbourne Cres. Hav 135 E3
Otters Wlk. New M 196 B3
Ouse Cl. N Bad 55 D4
Outer Circle. Southa 78 A2
Outlands La. Curd 106 B4
Outram Rd. Ports 182 B2
Oval Gdns. Gos 180 C2
Oval Rd. Locke 4 F1
Oval The. Liss 20 C2
Over Links Dr. Poole 205 E1
Overbrook Way. N Bad 53 F3
Overbrook. Hyt 125 F2
Overbury Rd. Poole 205 E2
Overcliff Rise. Southa 78 C2
Overcombe Cl. Broa 188 C1
Overstrand Cres. M on S 213 E2
Overton Cres. Hav 135 E3
Overton Rd. Southb 137 F1
Oviat Cl. Tot 100 A4
Ovington Ave. Bour 208 B4
Ovington Rd. Eastl 56 A1
Owen Cl. Gos 180 B4
Owen Rd. Eastl 55 F1
Owen St. Ports 183 D1
Owen's Rd. Winch 1 C1
Owls Rd. Bour 207 F2
Owls Rd. Ver 115 D3
Owslebury Bottom. Ows 33 D3
Owslebury Gr. Hav 135 F3
Oxburgh Cl. Eastl 55 F3
Oxenwood Green. Hav 135 E3
Oxey Cl. B on S 196 A1
Oxford Ave. Bour 208 B3
Oxford Ave. Southa 103 D3
Oxford Cl. Fare 88 A1
Oxford La. Bour 190 D3
Oxford Rd. Bour 207 D2
Oxford Rd. Gos 180 C3
Oxford Rd. Ports 182 C2
Oxford Rd. Southa 103 D4
Oxford St. Southa 103 D2
Oxleys Cl. Fare 154 A4
Oyster Mews. Ports 182 A2
Oyster Quay. Ports 157 D4
Oyster St. Ports 182 A2
Packridge La. Rown 53 F1
Pacton Rd. Ems 136 C2
Padbury Cl. Ports 157 F2
Paddington Gr. Bour 189 E2
Paddington Rd. Ports 157 F1
Paddock Cl. Fern 165 D3
Paddock Cl. St Le 139 F2
Paddock End. Den 110 C2
Paddock Gdns. Lym 198 B3
Paddock Gr. Ver 115 D3
Paddock The. Eastl 56 A3
Paddock The. Fordi 94 C3
Paddock The. Gos 181 D2
Paddock The. Ki Wo 2 B3
Paddock The. Stubb 154 B2
Paddock The. Tot 76 B1
Paddock Wlk. Portc 157 D4
Paddocks The. Brock 145 F1
Paddocks The. Faw 151 D2
Padfield Cl. Bour 208 C3
Padget Rd. Rin 117 E1
Padnell Ave. Wat 112 A1
Padnell Pl. Wat 112 A1
Padnell Rd. Wat 112 A2
Padstow Pl. Fordi 93 F4
Padwell Rd. Southa 103 D4
Padwick Ave. Cos 158 A4
Paffard Cl. Gos 180 B4
Pages La. E Bol 175 E3
Paget Cl. Wi Mi 164 A4
Paget Rd. Bour 190 A2
Paget Rd. Gos 181 D1
Paget St. Southa 103 D2
Pagham Cl. Herm 161 D4
Pagham Gdns. S Hay 185 F1
Paignton Ave. Ports 183 D4
Paignton Rd. Southa 77 F1
Pain's Rd. Ports 182 B2
Painswick Cl. Cos 157 E4
Painswick Cl. Lo He 128 C3
Paisley Rd. Bour 208 B3
Palace La. Beaul 149 D1
Palfrey Rd. Bour 190 B3
Palk Rd. Hav 135 E1
Pallant Gdns. Fare 131 E1
Pallant The. Hav 135 F1
Pallet Cl. Co Comm 56 C4
Pallot Cl. Burs 104 C1
Palm Hall Cl. Winch 11 E4
Palm Rd. Southa 78 A2
Palmer Pl. New M 196 A2
Palmer Rd. Poole 204 B3
Palmer's Rd. Ems 136 C1
Palmers Cl. Fa Oa 57 E1
Palmerston Ave. Christ 209 E3
Palmerston Ave. Fare 88 A1
Palmerston Cl. Upt 203 E4
Palmerston Dr. Fare 155 D4
Palmerston Rd. Bour 207 E3
Palmerston Rd. Poole 205 E2
Palmerston Rd. Ports 182 B1
Palmerston Rd. S Hay 185 D2
Palmerston Rd. Southa 103 D2
Palmerston Rd. Upt 203 E4
Palmerston St. Rom 52 C4
Palmerston Way. Gos 180 C1
Palmyra Rd. Gos 181 D4
Pamplyn Cl. Lym 198 B2
Pan St. Ports 182 B3
Pangbourne Ave. Cos 158 A4
Pangbourne Cl. Southa 104 A2
Pannall Rd. Gosp 181 D4
Panorama Rd. Poole 211 D2
Pansy Rd. Southa 79 D2
Pantheon Rd. Ch Fo 55 F4
Pantiles The. Fordi 69 E1
Panton Cl. Ems 136 C2
Panwell Rd. Southa 104 A4
Parade Ct. Ports 157 F3
Parade The. Bour 208 C2
Parade The. Broa 188 A1
Paradise La. Bi Wa 83 F3
Paradise La. Ne Ma 99 E3
Paradise La. Portc 131 F1
Paradise La. Westb 137 D2
Paradise St. Poole 204 A1
Paradise St. Ports 182 B3
Parchment St. Winch 11 D4
Parchment The. Hav 135 F1
Pardoe Cl. He En 105 E3
Pardys Hill. Broa 187 E4
Parham Cl. New M 195 F2
Parham Dr. Eastl 55 F2
Parham Rd. Bour 190 B1
Parham Rd. Gos 181 E3
Parish Rd. Poole 204 C2
Park View. Botl 106 A4
Park Ave. Bour 190 B3
Park Ave. Lym 198 B2
Park Ave. Wat 134 B2
Park Ave. Winch 11 D4
Park Cl. Brock 146 A1
Park Cl. Burt 193 E2
Park Cl. Gos 180 C3
Park Cl. Hyt 126 A2
Park Cl. M on S 213 F2
Park Cl. Winch 2 A1
Park Cres. Ems 136 B1
Park Ct. N Bad 53 E3
Park Dr. Ver 114 C4
Park Farm Ave. Fare 130 B2
Park Farm Cl. Fare 130 B2
Park Farm Rd. Wat 134 B2
Park Gdns. Christ 209 F4
Park Glen. Lo He 129 E2
Park Gr. Cos 157 F4
Park Hill Cl. Holb 150 B2
Park Homer Rd. Wi Mi 163 F3
Park House Farm Way. Hav 135 E3
Park La. Alderh 92 C3
Park La. Bour 200 A4
Park La. Bour 190 C2
Park La. Cos 158 A4
Park La. Drox 61 D1
Park La. Fare 88 A1
Park La. Hav 135 E2
Park La. Hav 135 E4
Park La. Holb 150 A2
Park La. Ki Wo 2 B3
Park La. M on S 213 E2
Park La. March 101 E1
Park La. Ott 31 D1
Park La. Ro Ca 137 E4
Park La. Stubb 154 B2
Park La. Swan 60 B1
Park La. Twyf 58 A3
Park La. Wi Mi 163 E2
Park Lane Rd. Poole 204 C1
Park Par. Hav 135 F2
Park Rd N. Hav 135 F1
Park Rd S. Hav 135 F1
Park Rd. B on S 195 F1
Park Rd. Bi Wa 83 D4
Park Rd. Bour 207 D3
Park Rd. Ch Fo 55 E4
Park Rd. Den 110 C3
Park Rd. Fordi 69 F1
Park Rd. Gos 181 D2
Park Rd. Lym 198 B2
Park Rd. M on S 213 F2
Park Rd. New M 196 B3
Park Rd. Poole 204 C2
Park Rd. Ports 182 A3
Park Rd. S Hay 184 B2
Park Rd. Southa 102 B3
Park Rd. Southb 137 E1
Park Rd. Wat 134 B2
Park Rd. Winch 1 C1
Park St. Gos 181 D3
Park St. Ports 182 A2
Park St. Southa 102 A4
Park The. B on S 211 E4
Park The. Drox 61 D1
Park View. He En 105 D4
Park Way. Fa Oa 57 F1
Park Way. Hav 135 F1
Park Way. W Moo 138 C1
Park Wlk. Fare 130 B2
Park Wlk. Southa 103 D3
Parker Cl. Gos 156 A1
Parker Rd. Bour 206 C4
Parkland Cl. Ver 115 E2
Parkland Dr. B on S 211 F4
Parklands Ave. Wat 112 A3
Parklands Cl. Ch Fo 55 E4
Parklands Cl. Gos 181 D3
Parklands. Lo He 129 D2
Parklands. Southa 79 F1
Parkside Ave. Southa 101 E4
Parkside Rd. Poole 205 E2
Parkside. Christ 194 B1
Parkside. Hav 135 E1
Parkside. Rin 141 D3
Parkside. Tot 100 C3
Parkstone Ave. Poole 205 E2
Parkstone Ave. Ports 182 C1
Parkstone Hts. Poole 205 D3
Parkstone Rd. Poole 204 C2
Parkville Rd. Southa 79 E2
Parkwater Rd. Whit 25 B1
Parkway Dr. Bour 207 F4
Parkway Gdns. Ch Fo 55 E4
Parkway The. Gos 155 D1
Parkway The. Southa 79 D3
Parkway. Swanw 129 F4
Parkwood Cl. He En 105 E4
Parkwood La. Bour 208 A3
Parkwood Rd. Bour 208 A2
Parkwood Rd. Wi Mi 163 E2
Parley Cl. Fern 165 F1
Parley La. Fern 191 E4
Parley Rd. Bour 191 D1
Parliament Pl. Winch 10 B2
Parmiter Dr. Wi Mi 163 F2
Parmiter Rd. Wi Mi 163 F2
Parmiter Way. Wi Mi 163 F2
Parnell Rd. Eastl 55 F1
Parr Rd. Cos 157 E4
Parr St. Poole 205 D2
Parry Rd. Southa 104 B2
Parsonage Barn La. Rin 141 D4
Parsonage Cl. Fordi 69 F1
Parsonage La. Durl 82 A3
Parsonage Park Dr. Fordi 69 F1
Parsonage Rd. Bour 207 D2
Parsonage Rd. Southa 103 E3
Parsons Cl. Ports 157 F2
Partridge Dr. Poole 205 E1
Partridge Down. Winch 10 A2
Partridge Dr. Poole 205 D1
Partridge Gdns. Wat 111 E2
Partridge Green. New M 196 A3
Partridge Rd. Brock 172 C4
Partridge Rd. Hyt 125 F1
Partry Cl. N Bad 55 D4
Pascoe Cl. Poole 205 D2
Passage La. Lo He 128 A1
Passfield Ave. Eastl 55 F1
Passfield Cl. Eastl 55 F1
Passfield Wlk. Hav 136 A3
Passford Hill. Bold 198 B4
Passingham Walk. Wat 112 A2
Pastures The. Cher 14 B3
Pastures The. Den 110 C2
Pastures The. Lo He 129 E2
Patchins Rd. Hamw 203 D2
Patchway Dr. Fare 154 B4
Patricia Cl. W End 80 B1
Patricia Dr. He En 105 E4
Patrick's Cl. Liss 21 D2
Patrick's Copse Rd. Liss 21 D2
Paulet Cl. Southa 80 A1
Paulet Pl. Winch 10 C3
Pauletts La. Ower 76 A2
Pauletts La. Tot 76 A2
Pauls La. Sway 197 F4
Paulsgrove Rd. Ports 182 C4
Paulson Cl. Ch Fo 55 E4
Pauncefoot Hill. Rom 52 B3
Pauncefote Rd. Bour 208 A3
Pauntley Rd. Christ 209 F3
Pavan Gdns. Bour 190 B1
Paxton Cl. He En 105 E3
Paxton Rd. Fare 155 D4
Payne Cl. W Moo 138 C3
Payne's La. Fa Oa 57 E2
Payne's Rd. Southa 102 B3
Paynes Hay Rd. Brai 28 B4
Peace Cl. Bran 194 A4
Peach Rd. Southa 78 A2
Peacock La. Ports 182 A2
Peak Cl. Southa 101 F4
Peak Dr. Fare 154 B4
Peak La. Bi Wa 59 D2
Peak La. Fare 154 B4
Peak Rd. Clanf 88 A3
Peak The. Ro Ca 113 E1
Peake New Rd. Warnf 61 F4
Pealsham Gdns. Fordi 69 F1
Pear Tree Cl. Alderh 92 C3
Pear Tree Cl. Botl 81 F1
Pear Tree Cl. Bran 194 A4
Pear Tree Dr. Red 73 E4
Pearce Ave. Poole 205 D1
Pearce Ct. Gos 181 E3
Pearce Rd. Upt 203 D3
Pearl Gdns. Bour 190 B2
Pearl Rd. Bour 190 B2
Pearson Ave. Poole 205 D3
Peartree Ave. Southa 103 F3
Peartree Cl. Southa 103 E2
Peartree Cl. Stubb 154 B2
Peartree Cl. W Wel 50 B2
Peartree Ct. Lym 198 C1
Peartree Rd. Hyt 125 F1
Peartree Rd. Southa 103 E2
Pebble Ct. March 101 F1
Pebmarsh Rd. Cos 157 E4
Peckham Ave. New M 196 A1
Pedula Way. Bish 56 C3
Peel Cl. Poole 205 E3
Peel Cl. Rom 28 B1
Peel Rd. Gos 181 E2
Peel St. Southa 103 E3
Peewit Hill Cl. Burs 105 D2
Peewit Hill. Burs 105 D2
Pegasus Ave. Hord 197 D1
Pegasus Cl. Hamble 127 F1
Pegasus Cl. Southa 77 F2
Pelham Cl. Christ 209 E3
Pelham Rd. Gos 181 D3
Pelham Rd. Ports 182 B2
Pelican Cl. Fare 130 B1
Pelican Ct. Hurs 30 A4
Pelican Mead. Rin 141 E3
Pembers Cl. Fa Oa 57 E1
Pemberton Rd. Lyn 122 A3
Pembrey Cl. Southa 78 A3
Pembridge Rd. Fordi 70 A1
Pembroke Cl. Eastl 55 F3
Pembroke Cl. Ports 182 A2
Pembroke Cl. Rom 52 C4
Pembroke Cl. Tot 101 D4
Pembroke Cres. Stubb 154 A1
Pembroke Rd. Bour 206 A1
Pembroke Rd. Poole 205 E4
Pembroke Rd. Ports 182 A2
Pembroke Rd. Southa 104 A2
Pembury Rd. Hav 160 A4
Pembury Rd. Stubb 154 B2
Pemerton Rd. Winch 1 B2
Penarth Ave. Cos 158 A4
Pendennis Rd. Portc 132 C1
Pendle Cl. Southa 101 F4
Pendle Green. Locke 4 C1
Penelope Gdns. Burs 104 C1
Penfords Paddock. Bi Wa 83 E4
Pengelly Ave. Bour 190 C3
Penhale Gdns. Lo He 129 D1
Penhale Rd. Ports 182 C3
Penhale Way. Tot 100 C3
Penhurst Rd. Hav 135 D1
Peninsula Rd. Winch 10 C4
Penistone Cl. Southa 104 A1
Penjar Ave. Wat 134 B2
Penk Ridge. Cos 158 B4
Penn Cl. B on S 195 F1
Penn Ct. W Moo 138 B1
Penn Hill Ave. Poole 205 F2
Penn Way. Gos 180 C2
Pennant Hills. Hav 135 D1
Pennard Way. Ch Fo 55 D2

Pennerley Ct. Hav 135 E4
Pennine Gdns. Hyt 125 E2
Pennine Rd. Southa 101 F4
Pennine Way. Ch Fo 55 E2
Pennine Way. L on S 180 A2
Pennine Way. Ver 114 C3
Pennine Wlk. Fare 154 C4
Pennington Cl. Co Comm 56 C4
Pennington Cl. Lym 198 B1
Pennington Cl. W Moo 138 B1
Pennington Cres. W Moo 138 B1
Pennington Oval. Lym 198 A1
Pennington Rd. W Moo 138 B1
Pennington Way. Fare 130 B2
Penns Rd. Pet 40 C2
Penny Hedge. B on S 212 A4
Penny La. Herm 161 D4
Penny Pl. Wat 134 C2
Penny St. Ports 182 A2
Penny's Cl. Fordi 69 F2
Penny's Cres. Fordi 69 F2
Penny's La. Fordi 69 F2
Penny's Wlk. Fern 165 E3
Penny-cress. Lo He 128 C1
Penrhyn Ave. Cos 158 A4
Penrhyn Cl. Eastl 55 F3
Penrith Cl. Ver 114 C3
Penrith Rd. Bour 208 A2
Penrose Cl. Ports 157 E1
Penrose Rd. Fern 165 E3
Penshurst Way. Eastl 56 A3
Pentire Ave. Southa 78 B1
Pentire Way. Southa 78 B1
Pentland Cl. Hyt 125 E2
Pentland Rise. Portc 132 B1
Penton Rd. Twyf 32 A4
Pentons Hill. Fordi 94 B3
Pentridge Way. Tot 100 C3
Penwood Green. Hav 136 A3
Peper Harow. Wat 112 A3
Peppard Cl. Southa 104 A4
Pepys Ave. Southa 104 B3
Pepys Cl. Gos 181 D1
Pepys Cl. Ports 182 C2
Percival Rd. Ports 182 C4
Percy Cl. Hyt 125 F3
Percy Rd. Bour 207 F2
Percy Rd. Gos 181 E2
Percy Rd. Ports 182 C2
Percy Rd. Southa 102 A4
Peregrine Cl. Tot 100 B3
Peregrine Rd. Christ 210 A3
Peregrines The. Portc 155 F4
Pergin Cres. Broa 204 A4
Pergin Way. Broa 204 A4
Pern Dr. Botl 106 A4
Peronne Cl. Ports 157 F3
Peronne Rd. Ports 157 F3
Perran Rd. Southa 77 E1
Perry Gdns. Poole 204 B1
Perryfield Gdns. Bour 208 A4
Perrywood Cl. Holb 150 B2
Perrywood Gdns. Tot 100 A4
Perseus Pl. Wat 134 C2
Pershore Cl. Lo He 129 D2
Persley Rd. Bour 190 C2
Perth Cl. Christ 192 C1
Perth Rd. Gos 155 E2
Perth Rd. Ports 183 D2
Pervin Rd. Cos 157 F4
Peststead La. Sob 85 E2
Peterborough Rd. Cos 133 F1
Peterborough Rd. Southa 103 D4
Peterfields Rd. Chilc 12 A3
Peters Cl. Lo He 128 C2
Peters Cl. Upt 203 E3
Peters Rd. Lo He 128 C2
Peterscroft Ave. Ashu 100 A1
Petersfield La. Clanf 88 B4
Petersfield Pl. Bour 208 A4
Petersfield Rd. Bour 208 A4
Petersfield Rd. Buri 65 E3
Petersfield Rd. Cher 14 B2
Petersfield Rd. Hav 135 F2
Petersfield Rd. Hav 136 C4
Petersfield Rd. Winch 11 E4
Petersham Rd. Broa 204 A4
Petit Rd. Bour 191 D2
Petrel Wlk. Gos 155 D1
Petrie Rd. L on S 179 F3
Petticoat La. Red 47 F4
Pettinger Gdns. Southa 103 E4
Petty Cl. Rom 53 D3
Pettycot Cres. Gos 155 D2
Petworth Gdns. Eastl 56 A3
Petworth Rd. Ports 183 D3
Petwyn Cl. Fern 166 A3
Pevensey Cl. Southa 77 E1
Peverell Rd. Hamw 203 D2
Peverells Rd. Ch Fo 55 F4
Peverells Wood Ave. Ch Fo 55 F4
Peverells Wood Cl. Ch Fo 55 F3
Peveril Cl. St Le 139 F3
Peveril Rd. Southa 103 F2
Pewsey Pl. Southa 78 B1
Phelipps Rd. Broa 187 F3
Philip Rd. Wat 134 C3
Phillimore Rd. Southa 79 E2
Philpott Dr. March 101 F1
Phoenix Cl. Burs 105 D1
Phoenix Sq. Ports 157 F2
Pickard Rd. Fern 165 F4
Pickering Cl. Broa 188 A1
Picket Cl. Fordi 69 F1
Pickford Rd. Bour 190 C1
Pier Rd. Ports 182 A2
Pier St. L on S 179 F3
Pigeon House La. Southw 133 E2
Pikes Hill Ave. Lyn 121 F3
Pikes Hill. Lyn 121 F3
Pilands Wood Rd. Burs 127 F4
Pilchards Ave. Fa Oa 57 D2
Pilford Heath Rd. Wi Mi 164 A4
Pilgrim Cl. New M 196 B2
Pilgrim Pl. Southa 79 F2
Pilgrims Cl. Ch Fo 55 D3
Pilgrims Cl. N Bad 55 D3
Pilgrims Gate. Winch 1 C1
Pilgrims Way. Broa 204 A4
Pilgrims Way. Stubb 154 A1
Pill Hill. Whit 24 A2
Pilley Bailey. Bold 174 A1
Pilley Hill. Bold 173 F1
Pilley St. Bold 174 A1
Pilning Cl. Fare 154 B4
Pilot Hight Rd. Bour 190 A2
Pilsdon Dr. Broa 188 C2
Pimpern Cl. Broa 188 C1
Pimpernel Cl. Lo He 128 C1
Pine Ave. Bour 208 B2
Pine Ave. Poole 205 F4
Pine Cl. Ashu 100 B2
Pine Cl. B on S 211 F4
Pine Cl. Fern 165 E4
Pine Cl. Hyt 125 F1
Pine Cl. Lan 49 E1
Pine Cl. N Bad 53 F3
Pine Cl. Winch 10 A2
Pine Cres. Christ 210 C4
Pine Ct. Ems 136 C2
Pine Dr E. Southa 104 C4
Pine Dr. Clanf 88 B3
Pine Dr. Poole 205 F2
Pine Dr. Southa 104 B4
Pine Dr. St Le 139 F2
Pine Glen Ave. Fern 165 E4
Pine Gr. Hav 136 A1
Pine Manor Rd. St Le 139 E3
Pine Rd. Alderh 92 C3
Pine Rd. Bi Wa 83 E4
Pine Rd. Bour 207 D4
Pine Rd. Broa 162 C1
Pine Rd. Ch Fo 55 E4
Pine Rd. Rom 53 E3
Pine Tree Gdns. Wat 112 A1
Pine Tree Glen. Bour 206 B2
Pine Trees Cl. Fare 154 B4
Pine View Cl. Red 47 E2
Pine View Cl. Upt 203 E3
Pine View Cl. Ver 114 B4
Pine View Rd. Ver 114 B4
Pine Way. Rown 78 C4
Pine Wlk. Liss 21 D3
Pine Wlk. Lo He 129 D3
Pine Wlk. Rown 78 C4
Pine Wlk. Ver 115 D3
Pinecliff Rd. Poole 211 D4
Pinecliffe Ave. Bour 208 B2
Pinecliffe Rd. B on S 211 E4
Pinefield Rd. Southa 79 F1
Pinegrove Rd. Southa 103 F2
Pineholt Cl. St Le 140 A3
Pinehurst Ave. Christ 209 F3
Pinehurst Rd. Rown 78 C4
Pinehurst Rd. W Moo 138 C1
Pinelands Rd. Rown 78 C4
Pines The. Portc 132 A1
Pinesprings Dr. Broa 187 F1
Pinetops Cl. Lym 198 A2
Pinetree Wlk. Broa 203 F4
Pineview Cl. Burs 105 D1
Pinewood Ave. Bour 190 B3
Pinewood Ave. Hav 135 D2
Pinewood Cl. Bour 190 B3
Pinewood Cl. Christ 195 D1
Pinewood Cl. Rom 28 B1
Pinewood Cl. Stubb 154 B2
Pinewood Cl. Upt 203 D4
Pinewood Cres. Hyt 126 A1
Pinewood Dr. Hyt 126 A1
Pinewood Gdns. Fern 165 E4
Pinewood Park. Southa 104 C3
Pinewood Rd W. Upt 203 D4
Pinewood Rd. Christ 194 C1
Pinewood Rd. Fern 165 E4
Pinewood Rd. Hord 196 C2
Pinewood Rd. Poole 206 A1
Pinewood Rd. St Le 139 F2
Pinewood. Gos 155 F1
Pinewood. Southa 78 C3
Pink Rd. Ports 182 C4
Pinks Hill. Fare 88 B1
Pipers Ash. Rin 141 E4
Pipers Cl. Tot 100 B3
Pipers Dr. Christ 210 A4
Pipers Mead. Clanf 88 A3
Pipers Wood Ind Park. Wat 134 B4
Piping Cl. Co Com 56 C4
Piping Green. Co Com 56 C4
Piping Rd. Co Com 56 C4
Pipit Cl. Gos 181 D4
Pippin Cl. Christ 192 C1
Pirrie Cl. Southa 78 B1
Pit Hill La. Hambl 86 C1
Pitchponds Rd. Lo He 152 B4
Pitcroft La. Buri 65 F3
Pitcroft Rd. Ports 157 E1
Pitmore Cl. Ott 56 A4
Pitmore La. Sway 172 B1
Pitmore Rd. Ott 56 A4
Pitreavie Rd. Cos 157 F3
Pitt Rd. Southa 102 B3
Pittmore Rd. Burt 193 E1
Pitts Deep La. Bold 200 B2
Pitts Pl. New M 196 B1
Pitwines Cl. Poole 204 B1
Pitymoor La. Southw 133 D2
Place Cres. Wat 134 C3
Place House Cl. Fare 130 B1
Place La. Comp 31 F4
Plaitford Gr. Hav 135 E3
Plaitford Wlk. Southa 77 F1
Plantaganet Cres. Bour 189 E3
Plantation Dr. Christ 195 D1
Plantation Dr. March 101 F1
Plantation Rd. Broa 188 B1
Plantation Rd. Hill B 21 D1
Plantation Rd. W Wel 74 E4
Plantation. Hord 213 F4
Plants Cl. W Wel 51 D1
Plassey Cres. Bour 190 B3
Platform Rd. Southa 103 D1
Platoff Rd. Lym 214 C4
Player Ct. Fordi 69 F2
Players Cres. Tot 100 C3
Playfair Rd. Ports 182 B2
Playfields Dr. Poole 205 F3
Pleasance Way. New M 195 F2
Pleasant La. Th Is 161 E1
Pleasant Rd. Ports 183 D2
Plecy Cl. Fern 165 E1
Plemont Cl. Poole 189 F1
Pless Rd. M on S 213 D3
Plough La. Sob 85 E1
Plough Way. Winch 10 B2
Plover Cl. Southa 78 A3
Plover Cl. Stubb 154 A1
Plover Dr. M on S 213 F2
Plover Rd. Tot 100 B4
Plover Reach. Ports 183 D3
Plovers Down. Winch 10 A2
Plumer Rd. Broa 188 A1
Plumley Wlk. Hav 135 E4
Plumpton Gdns. Ports 158 A2
Plumpton Gr. Wat 112 A1
Plymouth Dr. Stubb 154 A2
Plymouth St. Ports 182 B2
Pococks La. Hawk 19 F4
Poets Way. Winch 10 B4
Pointout Cl. Southa 78 C2
Pointout Rd. Southa 78 C2
Poles La. Hurs 30 B3
Poles La. Lym 198 C1
Poles La. Ott 31 D2
Police Station La. Drox 61 D1
Pollards Moor Rd. Cadn 75 D1
Pollesden Cl. Ch Fo 55 D4
Polygon The. Southa 102 C3
Pomona Cl. Fern 165 E3
Pond Cl. March 101 F1
Pond La. Clanf 88 A3
Pond Piece. Den 110 C2
Pond Rd. Lo He 128 C3
Pondhead Cl. Holb 150 B2
Pondside La. Bi Wa 83 D4
Ponsonby Rd. Poole 205 F2
Pook La. Fare 88 B2
Pook La. Hav 160 A4
Pooksgreen. March 101 E1
Poole Hill. Bour 206 C2
Poole La. Bour 190 A2
Poole Rd. Bour 206 B2
Poole Rd. Poole 206 B2
Poole Rd. Southa 103 F2
Poole Rd. Upt 203 E4
Poole Rd. Wi Mi 163 E2
Popes La. Tot 100 C4
Popes La. Uph 58 B2
Popes Rd. Poole 204 B3
Popham Ct. Hav 135 E3
Poplar Cl. Christ 211 D4
Poplar Cl. Poole 204 A1
Poplar Cl. Wi Mi 163 E3
Poplar Cres. Rin 141 D4
Poplar Dr. Fare 154 C4
Poplar Dr. March 101 E1
Poplar Gr. S Hay 185 D2
Poplar La. Bran 194 B4
Poplar Rd. New M 196 B2
Poplar Rd. Southa 103 F3
Poplar Way. He En 105 E3
Poplar Way. N Bad 53 F3
Poplar Way. Rin 141 D4
Poplars The. Shed 83 F2
Poppy Cl. Lo He 128 C1
Poppy Rd. Southa 79 E3
Porchester Pl. Bour 207 D3
Porchester Rd. Bour 207 D3
Porchester Rd. Southa 103 F2
Porlock Rd. Southa 77 E1
Port La. Hurs 30 B4
Port La. Winch 10 A1
Port Royal Rd. Ports 182 B3
Port Way. Ports 157 D4
Portal Rd. Bish 56 B2
Portal Rd. Gos 155 E2
Portal Rd. Southa 104 A2
Portal Rd. Tot 100 B4
Portal Rd. Winch 11 D3
Portarlington Cl. Bour 206 B1
Portarlington Rd. Bour 206 B1
Portchester La. Southw 132 B2
Portchester Rd. Portc 156 A4
Portchester Rd. Ports 182 C4
Portchester Rise. Eastl 56 A4
Portelet Cl. Poole 189 E1
Porteous Pl. He En 105 E3
Porter Rd. Broa 204 A4
Porter's La. March 102 C2
Porters La. Wi Mi 164 B3
Portersbridge St. Rom 52 C4
Portesham Gdns. Bour 191 D2
Portesham Way. Broa 188 C2
Porteus Cres. Ch Fo 55 F3
Portfield Cl. Christ 209 D4
Portfield Rd. Christ 209 D4
Portfield Rd. Ports 158 A2
Portland Dr. Gos 180 B2
Portland Rd. Bour 207 D4
Portland Rd. Ports 182 B1
Portland Rd. Wat 134 C4
Portland Sq. Liss 20 C2
Portland St. Fare 88 A1
Portland St. Ports 182 A3
Portland St. Southa 102 C2
Portland Terr. Southa 102 C2
Portman Cres. Bour 208 A2
Portman Rd. Bour 207 F3
Portobello Gr. Portc 132 C1
Portsdown Ave. Cos 158 B4
Portsdown Hill Rd. Cos 133 D1
Portsdown Hill Rd. Hav 135 D1
Portsdown Hill Rd. Portc 132 B1
Portsdown Rd. Portc 156 C4
Portsmouth Rd. Burs 105 D1
Portsmouth Rd. Co Com 57 E3
Portsmouth Rd. Cos 157 F4
Portsmouth Rd. Horn 112 A3
Portsmouth Rd. L on S 180 A2
Portsmouth Rd. Southa 104 B1
Portsmouth Rd. Wat 112 A3
Portsview Ave. Portc 132 C1
Portsview Gdns. Portc 132 B1
Portswood Ave. Southa 103 D4
Portswood Dr. Bour 191 D2
Portswood Park. Southa 103 D4
Portswood Rd. Hav 135 E3
Portswood Rd. Ports 157 F3
Portswood Rd. Southa 79 E1
Portview Rd. Southa 79 F1
Portway Cl. Southa 104 A4
Posbrook La. Lo He 153 F3
Posbrooke Rd. Ports 183 D2
Post Office La. Poole 204 B1
Post Office La. St Le 140 A3
Post Office Rd. Bour 206 C2
Post Office Rd. Wat 134 B3
Postern Cl. Portc 156 B4
Potteries The. Fare 88 A2
Potterne Way. Ver 115 D2
Potters Ave. Fare 88 A2
Potters Heron Cl. Ampf 29 F2
Potters Heron La. Ampf 29 F2
Potters Way. Poole 205 E1
Pottery Rd. Poole 205 D1
Poulner Cl. Southa 104 A1
Poulner Ct. Hav 135 E3
Poulner Hill. Rin 141 F4
Poulner Park. Rin 117 E1
Pound Cl. Gos 180 B4
Pound Cl. Poole 204 C3
Pound Cl. Rin 141 D4
Pound Cotts. Meons 61 E3
Pound Gate Dr. Lo He 153 E4
Pound La. Ampf 29 D1
Pound La. Ashu 100 C2
Pound La. Bour 190 B3
Pound La. Bur 142 C1
Pound La. Cadn 75 E1
Pound La. Christ 209 D3
Pound La. Dame 68 A3
Pound La. Meons 61 E3
Pound La. N Bad 29 D1
Pound La. Plai 50 B3
Pound La. Poole 204 C3
Pound La. Sh En 25 F1
Pound Lea. S Hay 185 D3
Pound Rd. Burs 104 C1
Pound Rd. Ki Wo 2 B4
Pound Rd. Lym 198 A1
Pound Rd. W Wit 186 C1
Pound St. Southa 104 A4
Pound Tree Rd. Southa 103 D2
Pounds Terr. Ports 182 A3
Powell Cres. Tot 100 C3
Powell Rd. Poole 205 D2
Power Rd. Ports 182 C3
Powerscourt Rd. B on S 211 F4
Powerscourt Rd. Ports 182 C4
Powis Cl. New M 196 A2
Powlett Rd. Lym 198 C2
Poynings Pl. Ports 182 A2
Precinct The. Wat 134 C4
Precosa Rd. He En 105 F3
Prelate Way. Lo He 129 E1
Premier Centre The. N Bad 53 E3
Preshaw Cl. Southa 78 B2
Preston La. Burt 193 E2
Preston Rd. Poole 204 B3
Preston Rd. Ports 182 C4
Preston Way. Christ 210 B4
Prestwood Cl. B on S 195 F1
Prestwood Rd. He En 105 E3
Pretoria Rd. He En 105 D3
Pretoria Rd. Ports 182 C2
Prickett Hill. Shed 107 F4
Pricketts Hill. Wickh 108 A3
Prideaux - Brune Ave. Gos 155 E2
Priest Croft Dr. Black 150 C1
Priestlands Cl. Ne Ma 100 A3
Priestlands La. Lym 198 B2
Priestlands Pl. Lym 198 B2
Priestlands Rd. Lym 198 B2
Priestlands. Rom 52 C4
Priestley Cl. Tot 100 B4
Priestley Rd. Bour 190 A1
Priestwood Cl. Southa 104 B4
Primate Rd. Lo He 129 E1
Primrose Cl. Gos 155 D3
Primrose Cl. He En 105 E3
Primrose Ct. Wat 135 D3
Primrose La. Ra 21 E2
Primrose La. Red 47 E3
Primrose Rd. Southa 79 D2
Primrose Way. Broa 187 F4
Primrose Way. Christ 210 B4
Primrose Way. Lo He 128 C1
Primrose Way. Rom 28 B1
Prince Albert Rd. Ports 183 D2
Prince Albert St. Ports 183 D2
Prince Alfred St. Gos 181 D2
Prince George St. Ports 182 A3
Prince George's St. Hav 135 F1
Prince Of Wales Av. Southa 102 A4
Prince Of Wales Cl. Wat 135 D4
Prince Of Wales Rd. Bour 206 B2
Prince Of Wales Rd. Gos 181 E2
Prince William Ct. Bish 56 C1
Prince's Ct. Southa 103 E3
Prince's Pl. New M 196 B2
Prince's Pl. Ports 182 B4
Prince's Rd. Rom 52 C4
Prince's St. Ports 182 B4
Prince's St. Southa 103 E3
Princes Cl. Bi Wa 83 D4
Princes Cl. Red 47 F4
Princes Cres. Lyn 122 A3
Princes Dr. Wat 112 A1
Princes Hill. Red 47 F4
Princes Pl. Winch 10 C3
Princes Rd. Fern 165 E3
Princes Rd. Pet 40 B2
Princes Rd. Southa 102 B3
Princess Ave. Christ 209 D3
Princess Cl. W End 80 C1
Princess Gdns. Horn 112 B4
Princess Rd. Ashu 100 A1
Princess Rd. Bour 206 A2
Princess Rd. Poole 206 A2
Pringles Cl. Fern 165 F3
Pringles Dr. Fern 165 F3
Prinstead Cl. Winch 11 D3
Prinstead La. Southb 161 E4
Prinsted Cres. Cos 158 B4
Priors Barton. Winch 10 C3
Priors Cl. Christ 210 B4
Priors Cl. Southb 137 F1
Priors Dean Rd. Winch 1 B2
Priors Hill La. Net 127 F4
Priors Leaze La. Southb 137 F1
Priors Rd. Broa 204 A4
Priors Way. Winch 10 A2
Priors Wlk. Wi Mi 163 D3
Priorsdean Ave. Ports 183 D3
Priorsdean Cres. Hav 135 E2
Priory Ave. Southa 79 E1
Priory Cl. Bi Wa 83 D4
Priory Cl. Southa 79 E1
Priory Cres. Ports 183 D2
Priory Gdns. Portc 156 B4
Priory Gdns. Wat 111 F1
Priory Rd. Bour 206 C1
Priory Rd. Eastl 55 F1
Priory Rd. Fare 130 B1
Priory Rd. Gosp 181 D4
Priory Rd. Net 127 D3
Priory Rd. Ports 183 D1
Priory Rd. Southa 103 E4
Priory Rd. W Moo 166 A4
Priory View Rd. Bour 191 D2
Priory View Rd. Burt 193 E1
Privet Rd. Bour 206 C4
Privett Pl. Gos 180 C2
Privett Rd. Fare 130 B1
Privett Rd. Frox G 18 C1

Privett Rd. Gos 180 C2
Privett Rd. Wat 134 B2
Prochurch Rd. Wat 112 A2
Proctor Cl. Southa 104 B3
Proctor Dr. N Bad 53 F2
Proctor La. Ports 182 C3
Promenade The. Ems 160 C4
Promenade The. Hyt 126 A3
Prospect La. Hav 136 A3
Prospect Pl. Ch Fo 55 E3
Prospect Pl. Hyt 126 A3
Prospect Rd. Ports 182 B4
Prosperous St. Poole 204 B1
Provene Cl. Shed 83 F2
Provene Gdns. Shed 83 F2
Providence Hill. Burs 105 D1
Provost St. Fordi 69 F1
Pruetts La. Liss 20 C1
Prunus Cl. Fern 165 D4
Prunus Cl. Southa 78 B3
Prunus Dr. Fern 165 D4
Pudbrooke Gdns. He En 105 D4
Pudding La. Ki Wo 2 A3
Puddletown Cres. Poole 188 C1
Puffin Cres. Stubb 154 A2
Puffin Gdns. Gos 155 D2
Puffin Wlk. Wat 111 E2
Pug's Hole. W Tyth 4 A3
Pulens La. Pet 41 D2
Pump La. Gos 155 E1
Pundle Green Estate. Cadn 99 D3
Punsholt La. W Meo 16 C3
Punsholt La. W Tis 16 C3
Purbeck Ave. Hamw 203 F1
Purbeck Cl. Upt 203 D4
Purbeck Dr. Fare 154 B4
Purbeck Dr. Ver 114 C3
Purbeck Rd. B on S 211 E4
Purbeck Rd. Bour 206 C1
Purbeck St. Ports 182 A3
Purbeck Wlk. Fare 154 B4
Purbrook Cl. Southa 78 B2
Purbrook Gdns. Wat 134 B3
Purbrook Heath Rd. Southw 134 A3
Purbrook Rd. Ports 182 C3
Purbrook Way. Hav 135 E2
Purcell Cl. Wat 134 C3
Purcell Rd. Southa 104 B2
Purewell Cross Rd. Christ 209 E4
Purewell. Christ 209 E3
Purkess Cl. Ch Fo 55 E4
Purkiss Cl. Ne Ma 99 E3
Purley Way. Plai 50 A2
Purrocks The. Pet 40 C3
Putmans La. S Har 66 C4
Pycroft Cl. N Hay 160 B2
Pycroft Cl. Southa 104 A3
Pye Cl. Broa 187 F4
Pye Cnr. Wi Mi 163 D2
Pye St. Ports 182 B3
Pylands La. Burs 105 D2
Pyle Cl. Wat 112 A2
Pylewell Rd. Hyt 126 A2
Pyrford Cl. Gos 180 C2
Pyrford Cl. Wat 111 F1
Pytchley Cl. Stubb 154 A1

Quadrangle The. Eastl 56 A2
Quantock Rd. Southa 101 F4
Quantocks The. Hyt 125 E2
Quarely Rd. Hav 135 E3
Quarry Cl. Wi Mi 164 A4
Quarry Dr. Wi Mi 164 A4
Quarry Rd. Wi Mi 164 A4
Quarry Rd. Winch 11 E4
Quartremaine Rd. Ports 158 A2
Quavey Rd. Red 47 F3
Quay Haven. Swanw 128 B4
Quay Hill. Lym 198 C2
Quay La. Gos 156 A1
Quay Rd. Christ 209 D3
Quay Rd. Lym 198 C2
Quay St. Fare 131 E1
Quay St. Lym 198 C2
Quay The. Hamble 128 A1
Quay The. Poole 204 B1
Quayle Dr. Bour 189 F3
Quayside Rd. Southa 103 E4
Quebec Gdns. Burs 104 C1
Queen Anne Dr. Oakl 188 C4
Queen Anne's Dr. Hav 135 E1
Queen Elizabeth Ave. Lym 198 B2
Queen Katherine Rd. Lym 198 C2
Queen Mary Ave. Bour 190 C1
Queen Mary Rd. Portc 156 B4
Queen St. Ems 161 D4
Queen St. Lym 198 B2
Queen St. Ports 182 A3
Queen St. Twyf 31 F3
Queen St. Woodg 47 D1
Queen's Ave. Christ 209 D3
Queen's Cl. Rom 53 D4
Queen's Cres. Ports 182 B2
Queen's Gr. Ports 182 B2
Queen's Par. Lyn 121 F3
Queen's Park Ave. Bour 207 E4
Queen's Park Gdns. Bour 207 E4
Queen's Park Rd. Bour 207 E4
Queen's Park S Dr. Bour 207 E4
Queen's Park W Dr. Bour 207 E4
Queen's Pl. Ports 182 B2
Queen's Rd. Bour 206 B2
Queen's Rd. Broa 187 E3
Queen's Rd. Ch Fo 30 B1
Queen's Rd. Christ 209 F3
Queen's Rd. Fare 88 A1
Queen's Rd. Gos 181 E2
Queen's Rd. Lo He 152 B4
Queen's Rd. Poole 205 E2
Queen's Rd. Ports 182 C4
Queen's Rd. Southa 78 B1
Queen's Rd. Wat 111 F1
Queen's Rd. Winch 10 B4
Queen's Terr. Southa 103 D2
Queen's Way. Ports 182 B2
Queen's Way. Southa 103 D2
Queens Cl. Hyt 126 A2
Queens Cl. L on S 179 F3
Queens Cl. W Moo 138 B1
Queens Cres. Horn 112 B4
Queens Cres. Stubb 154 B2
Queens Gdns. Bour 206 B2
Queens Gdns. Fordi 69 F1
Queens Gr. New M 196 B2
Queens Gr. Wat 134 B3
Queens Rd. Fern 165 E4
Queens Rd. L on S 179 F2
Queens Rd. Lyn 122 A3
Queens Rd. Pet 40 B2
Queens View. Net 127 D3
Queens Way. Rin 141 D4
Queensland Rd. Bour 208 A3
Queenstown Rd. Southa 102 B3
Queensway The. Portc 156 A4
Queensway. N Hay 160 A2
Queensway. New M 195 F2
Queenswood Ave. Bour 191 F1
Queenswood Dr. Fern 165 E4
Quilter Cl. Southa 104 B2
Quince La. Wi Mi 163 E3
Quinton Cl. Christ 210 C4
Quinton Cl. Ports 182 B2
Quintrell Ave. Portc 156 A4
Quob La. Eastl 80 C2
Quomp. Rin 141 D4

R L Stevenson Ave. Bour 206 A2
Racecourse View. Lyn 121 F3
Rachel Cl. Fa Oa 57 D1
Racton Ave. Cos 158 A4
Radcliffe Rd. Southa 103 D3
Radclyffe Rd. Fare 131 E1
Radipole Rd. Poole 189 D1
Radnor St. Ports 182 B2
Radstock Rd. Southa 103 F2
Radway Cres. Southa 102 B4
Radway Rd. Southa 78 C1
Raebarn Cl. Cher 14 B3
Raeburn Dr. He En 105 E4
Raglan Cl. Ch Fo 55 D2
Raglan St. Ports 182 B3
Ragmore La. Frox G 18 C3
Rails La. S Hay 185 E1
Railway View Rd. Southa 103 E4
Railway View. Ports 182 B3
Rake Rd. Liss 21 D2
Raleigh Cl. Christ 209 F3
Raleigh Cl. New M 195 F2
Raleigh Cl. Rin 141 E4
Raleigh Rd. Poole 189 F1
Raley Rd. Lo He 129 D1
Ralph La. Rom 28 A1
Ralph Rd. Broa 187 F4
Ramalley La. Ch Fo 55 D4
Ramblers Way. Wat 112 B1
Ramley Rd. Lym 198 A2
Rampart Gdns. Ports 157 F3
Rampart Rd. Southa 103 E4
Rampart The. Lym 198 B3
Ramsay Pl. Gos 155 E1
Ramsay Rd. Ki Wo 2 B4
Ramsay Rd. S Hay 185 D2
Ramsdale Ave. Hav 135 E3
Ramsdean Rd. Langr 39 F1
Ramshill. Pet 41 D2
Rances Way. Winch 10 C3
Randall Cl. Tot 76 B1
Randall Rd. Ch Fo 30 B1
Randall's La. Bur 142 C3
Randalls Hill. Upt 187 D1
Randolph Rd. Bour 207 F2
Randolph Rd. Poole 205 E3
Randolph St. Southa 102 B4
Ranelagh Gdns. Southa 102 C4
Ranelagh Rd. Christ 210 C4
Ranelagh Rd. Hav 135 E1
Ranelagh Rd. Ports 157 E1
Range Gdns. Southa 104 A2
Range Gn. Ports 157 E2
Rannoch Cl. Fare 130 C2
Ransome Cl. Lo He 153 F4
Ranvilles La. Fare 154 A4
Rapson Cl. Cos 133 E1
Rareridge La. Bi Wa 83 F4
Ratcliffe Rd. He En 105 E4
Ratcliffe Rd. Hyt 125 F1
Ratley La. Awb 26 C2
Raven Rd. Southa 103 D3
Raven Sq. Eastl 55 E1
Raven Way. Christ 210 A3
Ravens Cl. Stubb 154 B1
Ravens Way. M on S 213 E2
Ravenscourt Rd. Bour 208 B3
Ravenscourt Rd. Lym 198 B1
Ravenscroft Cl. Burs 104 C1
Ravenscroft Way. Botl 81 F1
Ravenswood. Lo He 129 E2
Ravine Rd. Bour 208 A2
Ravine Rd. Poole 211 F4
Raymond Cl. Holb 150 B2
Raymond Cl. Ver 115 D3
Raymond Cl. W End 80 C2
Raymond Rd. Portc 132 C1
Raymond Rd. Southa 102 B4
Rayners Gdns. Southa 79 E2
Raynes Rd. Lon S 180 A2
Reading Room La. Curd 106 B4
Readon Cl. Pet 41 D2
Rebbeck Rd. Bour 208 A3
Recess The. Eastl 56 A3
Record Rd. Ems 136 C1
Recreation Rd. Poole 205 F3
Rectory Ave. Broa 162 B1
Rectory Cl. Gos 181 D1
Rectory Cl. Stubb 154 B2
Rectory Ct. Botl 105 F4
Rectory Hill. W Dean 3 E2
Rectory La. Brea 46 A1
Rectory La. Meons 61 E3
Rectory La. Mott 5 F1
Rectory La. Twyf 58 A3
Rectory Rd. Hav 159 F4
Rectory Rd. Poole 204 B3
Red Barn Ave. Portc 132 B1
Red Barn La. Fare 130 C2
Red Hill Cres. Southa 78 C2
Red Hill Way. Southa 78 C2
Red La. Broa 187 D4
Red La. Ows 58 A3
Red La. W Tyth 4 A4
Red Leaves. Shed 83 F1
Red Lodge. Ch Fo 55 D2
Red Oaks Cl. Fern 165 D4
Redan Cl. Christ 210 C4
Redan The. Gos 181 E1
Redbreast Rd N. Bour 191 D2
Redbreast Rd. Bour 191 D2
Redbridge Causeway. Tot 101 D4
Redbridge Gr. Hav 135 E2
Redbridge Hill. Southa 77 F1
Redbridge La. Nur 77 E2
Redbridge Rd. Southa 101 E4
Redcar Ave. Ports 158 A1
Redcar St. Southa 102 A4
Redcliffe Cl. Burt 193 E2
Redcote Cl. Southa 104 A4
Redcotts La. Wi Mi 163 D3
Redcotts Rd. Wi Mi 163 D3
Redcroft La. Burs 105 D1
Redfords The. Tot 76 C1
Redhill Ave. Bour 190 C2
Redhill Cl. Bour 190 C2
Redhill Cl. Southa 78 C2
Redhill Cres. Bour 190 C2
Redhill Ct. Bour 191 D2
Redhill Dr. Bour 190 C2
Redhill Rd. Ro Ca 61 D1
Redhill Rd. Ro Ca 136 A4
Redhill. Southa 78 C2
Redhoave Rd. Broa 188 C1
Redhorn Cl. Hamw 203 E2
Redlands Dr. Southa 103 F3
Redlands Gr. Ports 183 E2
Redlands La. Ems 136 C2
Redlands La. Fare 154 C4
Redlands. Poole 205 F3
Redlynch Cl. Hav 136 A2
Redmans View. Ver 114 C3
Redmoor Cl. Southa 103 F3
Redrise Cl. Holb 150 B2
Redshank Cl. Broa 187 F1
Redvers Cl. Lym 198 B1
Redvers Rd. Christ 209 F4
Redward Rd. Southa 77 F3
Redwing Ct. Ports 183 E3
Redwing Gdns. Tot 100 B4
Redwing Rd. Clanf 88 B2
Redwood Cl. Hyt 125 E2
Redwood Cl. Lym 198 B3
Redwood Cl. Rin 141 D4
Redwood Dr. Fern 165 E4
Redwood Dr. Portc 156 A4
Redwood Gdns. Tot 100 B4
Redwood Rd. Upt 203 D4
Redwood Way. Southa 79 D3
Reed Dr. March 101 F1
Reedmace Cl. Wat 135 D3
Reeds La. Liss 21 E3
Reeds La. Ra 21 E3
Reeds Pl. Gos 181 D3
Reeds Rd. Gosp 181 D4
Reeves Cl. W Wel 50 C2
Reeves Way. Burs 104 C1
Regal Cl. Cos 157 F4
Regency Ct. Hav 159 F4
Regency Gdns. Wat 134 B3
Regent Cl. Ott 31 E2
Regent Dr. Bour 207 F4
Regent Pl. Ports 182 A2
Regent Rd. Ch Fo 55 E3
Regent St. Ports 182 B4
Regent St. Southa 102 C2
Regent Way. Christ 209 D3
Regent's Gr. Southa 102 A4
Regent's Park Gdns. Southa 102 A4
Regent's Park Rd. Southa 102 A4
Reginald Rd. Ports 183 D2
Reid St. Christ 209 D4
Relay Rd. Wat 134 B4
Reliant Cl. Ch Fo 55 D3
Rempstone Rd. Oakl 188 B4
Renault Dr. Broa 188 A1
Renda Rd. Holb 150 B2
Renny Rd. Ports 182 C3
Renouf Cl. Lym 198 B2
Renown Cl. Ch Fo 55 D3
Renown Gdns. Wat 111 F3
Repton Cl. Gos 180 C2
Repton Gdns. He En 81 E1
Reservoir La. He En 105 D3
Reservoir La. Pet 40 C3
Rest-a-wyle Ave. S Hay 185 D3
Retreat Rd. Wi Mi 163 E2
Retreat The. Eastl 56 A2
Retreat The. Ports 182 B2
Retreat The. Tot 101 D3
Revenge Cl. Ports 183 E3
Rewlands Dr. Winch 1 B2
Reynolds Ct. Rom 53 D3
Reynolds Dale. Tot 100 B3
Reynolds Rd. Fa Oa 57 E1
Reynolds Rd. Southa 102 B4
Rhinefield Cl. Bish 56 C1
Rhinefield Cl. Brock 145 F1
Rhinefield Cl. Hav 135 E2
Rhinefield Rd. Brock 145 D1
Rhinefield Rd. Brock 170 C1
Rhiners Cl. Sway 172 A1
Rhyme Hall Mews. Faw 151 D2
Ribble Cl. Broa 188 A1
Ribble Cl. Ch Fo 55 E3
Ribble Ct. Southa 77 F1
Ricardo Cres. Christ 210 A3
Richard Cl. Upt 203 D4
Richard Gr. Gos 156 A1
Richards Cl. Lo He 129 D2
Richlans Rd. He En 105 E3
Richmond Cl. Ch Fo 30 B1
Richmond Cl. S Hay 184 C2
Richmond Cl. Tot 76 A1
Richmond Dr. S Hay 184 C2
Richmond Gdns. Bour 206 C2
Richmond Hill Dr. Bour 206 C2
Richmond Hill. Bour 206 C2
Richmond La. Rom 28 A1
Richmond Park Ave. Bour 207 E4
Richmond Park Cl. Bour 207 E3
Richmond Park Cres. Bour 207 E4
Richmond Park Rd. Bour 207 E4
Richmond Pl. Ports 182 A3
Richmond Rd. Gos 181 D2
Richmond Rd. L on S 179 F3
Richmond Rd. Poole 205 E2
Richmond Rd. Ports 182 B1
Richmond Rd. Southa 102 B3
Richmond Rd. Wi Mi 163 E2
Richmond Rise. Portc 132 B1
Richmond St. Southa 103 D2
Richmond Wood Rd. Bour 207 E4
Richville Rd. Southa 102 A4
Ridding Cl. Southa 78 B1
Riders La. Hav 135 F2
Ridge Cl. Clanf 88 B2
Ridge La. Rom 76 B4
Ridge La. Swanw 106 B2
Ridge The. Red 47 E3
Ridge Top La. Frox G 39 F3
Ridgefield Gdns. Christ 210 B4
Ridgemount Ave. Southa 78 C3
Ridgemount Gdns. Hamw 203 F2
Ridgeway Cl. Ch Fo 55 F3
Ridgeway Cl. Cos 132 C1
Ridgeway Cl. Fa Oa 57 E2
Ridgeway La. Lym 198 B1
Ridgeway The. Portc 131 F1
Ridgeway Wlk. Ch Fo 55 F3
Ridgeway. Broa 187 E4
Ridgeway. Broa 188 A2
Ridgeway. Fern 190 C4
Ridgeway. Winch 10 B3
Ridgewood Cl. Hyt 125 E2
Ridings The. Fa Oa 57 D1
Ridings The. Liss 21 D2
Ridings The. Ports 157 F2
Ridings The. Shed 83 F2
Ridley Cl. Holb 150 B2
Ridley Rd. Bour 206 C4
Rigby Rd. Southa 103 D4
Riggs Gdns. Bour 189 F1
Rigler Rd. Hamw 204 A1
Rimington Gdns. Rom 28 A1
Rimington Rd. Wat 111 F2
Rimmer's Ct. Ports 181 F2
Ring The. Rown 78 C4
Ringbury. Lym 198 B3
Ringwood Dr. N Bad 53 F3
Ringwood Rd. Alderh 93 D3
Ringwood Rd. Bour 189 F2
Ringwood Rd. Bran 194 B3
Ringwood Rd. Bur 142 C3
Ringwood Rd. Christ 195 D1
Ringwood Rd. Fern 165 E2
Ringwood Rd. Fordi 94 B2
Ringwood Rd. Ne Ma 100 B4
Ringwood Rd. Poole 204 C3
Ringwood Rd. Ports 183 D2
Ringwood Rd. St Le 139 E1
Ringwood Rd. Tot 100 B4
Ringwood Rd. Ver 115 D3
Ringwood Rd. W Moo 138 C4
Ripley Gr. Ports 183 D4
Ripon Rd. Bour 191 D1
Ripplewood. March 102 A1
Ripstone Gdns. Southa 79 D2
Rise The. Brock 145 F1
Rise The. Wat 134 B1
Ritchie Ct. Southa 104 A2
Ritchie Pl. W Moo 138 B2
Ritchie Rd. Bour 190 A2
Rival Moor Rd. Pet 41 E1
River Cl. Wi Mi 163 E3
River Gdns. M on S 213 F2
River Green. Hamble 128 A1
River La. Fare 130 B3
River Mews. Bish 56 B2
River St. Ports 182 B2
River St. Westb 137 D2
River View Rd. Southa 79 E1
River Way. Christ 192 B1
River Wlk. Southa 79 F2
Riverdale Ave. Wat 135 D4
Riverdale Cl. Fordi 69 F1
Riverlea Rd. Christ 209 D3
Rivermead Cl. Rom 52 B4
Rivermead Gdns. Christ 192 C1
Riversdale Cl. Southa 126 C4
Riversdale Rd. Bour 209 D2
Riverside Ave. Bour 192 B1
Riverside Ave. Fare 88 B1
Riverside Cl. Cadn 99 E3
Riverside Cl. Liss 20 C2
Riverside Ct. Southa 103 E4
Riverside Gdns. Rom 52 C3
Riverside La. Bour 208 C3
Riverside Park. Christ 209 D3
Riverside Rd. Bour 208 C3
Riverside Rd. W Moo 138 B1
Riverside Terr. Fare 131 E1
Riverside. Bish 56 B2
Riverside. Rin 140 C3
Riverview Terr. Swanw 128 B4
Riverview. Tot 100 C3
Road View. Ports 182 B4
Roads Hill. Horn 88 A1
Robert Cecil Ave. Southa 79 F2
Robert Whitworth Dr. Rom 52 C4
Roberts Cl. Hord 197 F1
Roberts Cl. Wickh 108 A2
Roberts La. Broa 204 A4
Roberts Rd. Bour 208 A3
Roberts Rd. Broa 188 A1
Roberts Rd. Gos 180 C3
Roberts Rd. Hyt 125 F2
Roberts Rd. Southa 102 C3
Roberts Rd. Tot 100 C3
Robin Gdns. Tot 100 B4
Robin Gdns. Wat 111 E2
Robin Sq. Eastl 55 E1
Robina Cl. Wat 135 D4
Robina Grn. Southa 78 B3
Robins Cl. Stubb 154 B2
Robins Meadow. Lo He 129 E1
Robins Way. Christ 210 A3
Robinson Ct. Portc 132 B1
Robinson Rd. Stubb 154 A1
Robinson Way. Ports 158 B2
Robinswood Dr. Fern 165 E4
Rochester Rd. Bour 190 A2
Rochester Rd. Ports 182 C2
Rochester St. Southa 103 E3
Rochford Rd. Cos 157 E4
Rockall Cl. Southa 77 F3
Rockbourne Cl. Hav 135 E2
Rockbourne La. Dame 68 B4
Rockbourne La. Rockb 68 B4
Rockbourne Rd. Winch 1 B2
Rockford Cl. Bour 208 C2
Rockingham Way. Portc 156 A4
Rockleigh Dr. Tot 100 B3
Rockleigh Rd. Southa 78 B2
Rockley Rd. Hamw 203 F1
Rockram Gdns. Hyt 125 E2
Rockstone La. Southa 103 D4
Rockstone Pl. Southa 102 C3
Rockville Dr. Wat 134 C4
Rodbourne Cl. Hord 213 E4
Rodfield La. Ovin 13 E3
Rodney Cl. Gos 180 B3
Rodney Cl. Poole 206 A4
Rodney Ct. Southa 104 B2
Rodney Dr. Christ 209 F3
Rodney Rd. Ports 183 D3
Rodney Way. Horn 112 A3
Rodwell Cl. Bour 190 B3
Roebuck Cl. Cos 157 F4

Roebuck Cl. New M 196 A2
Roeshot Cres. Christ 194 C1
Roeshot Hill. Christ 194 B1
Roewood Cl. Holb 150 B2
Roewood Rd. Holb 150 B2
Rogate Gdns. Portc 132 B1
Rogers Cl. Bish 56 C2
Rogers Cl. Gos 181 D3
Rogers Mead. N Hay 159 F2
Rogers Rd. Bish 56 C2
Roland Cl. Horn 112 A3
Rollestone Rd. Holb 150 B1
Rolls Dr. Bour 209 D2
Roman Cl. Ch Fo 55 F4
Roman Dr. Rown 78 C4
Roman Gdns. Hyt 125 E1
Roman Gr. Portc 156 B3
Roman Hts. Broa 187 F4
Roman Meadow. Down 46 C4
Roman Rd. Broa 187 F3
Roman Rd. Hav 136 B1
Roman Rd. Holb 150 A3
Roman Rd. Hyt 125 E1
Roman Rd. Hyt 149 F4
Roman Rd. Rown 78 C4
Roman Rd. Twyf 58 A3
Roman Way. Hav 135 E1
Roman Way. Hyt 125 E1
Roman Way. Pamp 162 B3
Roman's Rd. Winch 11 D3
Romford Rd. Lo He 152 B4
Romill Cl. W End 80 A2
Romney Cl. Bour 190 C2
Romney Rd. Bour 190 C2
Romsey Ave. Portc 156 A4
Romsey Ave. Ports 183 D3
Romsey Cl. Eastl 56 A2
Romsey Ind Est. Rom 52 C4
Romsey Rd. Cadn 75 E2
Romsey Rd. Eastl 56 A2
Romsey Rd. Horn 88 B1
Romsey Rd. Lyn 121 F3
Romsey Rd. Ower 75 E2
Romsey Rd. Rown 77 F2
Romsey Rd. Southa 77 F2
Romsey Rd. W Wel 51 D2
Romsey Rd. Whit 24 C2
Romsey Rd. Winch 10 B4
Rook Hill Rd. Christ 210 B3
Rookcliff Way. M on S 213 E2
Rookery Ave. Swanw 129 E4
Rookery La. Brea 45 F1
Rookery The. Herm 137 D1
Rookes Cl. Horn 112 A3
Rookes La. Lym 198 B1
Rookley. Net 127 E4
Rooks Down Rd. Winch 10 B3
Rooksbridge. Hyt 125 E2
Rooksbury Croft. Hav 136 A3
Rooksway Gr. Portc 155 F4
Rookwood Cl. Eastl 56 A3
Rookwood View. Den 110 C3
Roosevelt Cres. Bour 190 D3
Rope Hill. Bold 173 E1
Rope Wlk. Hamble 128 A1
Ropers La. Upt 203 E4
Ropley Cl. Southa 127 D4
Ropley Rd. Bour 208 B4
Ropley Rd. Hav 136 A3
Rosamund Ave. Oakl 163 F1
Roscrea Cl. Bour 209 D2
Roscrea Dr. Bour 209 D2
Rose Cl. He En 105 E4
Rose Cl. Hyt 126 A1
Rose Cres. Poole 204 C3
Rose Gdns. Bour 191 D2
Rose Hill. Wat 112 A3
Rose Rd. Southa 103 D4
Rose Rd. Tot 101 D3
Rosebank Cl. Rown 77 F3
Rosebay Ct. Wat 134 C3
Rosebay. Fa Oa 81 E3
Rosebery Ave. Cos 158 A4
Rosebery Ave. Hyt 126 A1
Rosebery Cres. Eastl 56 A3
Rosebery Rd. Bour 208 A3
Rosebud Ave. Bour 191 D1
Rosedale Ave. Rom 53 D4
Rosedale Cl. Christ 209 F3
Rosedale Cl. Lo He 153 F4
Rosehill Cl. Bran 169 D1
Rosehill Dr. Bran 169 D1
Roselands Cl. Fa Oa 57 D2
Roselands Gdns. Southa 79 D1
Roselands. W End 104 B4
Roselands. Wat 112 A3
Roseleigh Dr. Tot 100 C3
Rosemary Gdns. He En 105 E3
Rosemary La. Ports 182 A3
Rosemary Rd. Poole 205 E4
Rosemary Way. Wat 112 A3
Rosemary Wlk. L on S 179 F3
Rosemoor Gr. Ch Fo 30 A1
Rosemount Rd. Bour 206 A1
Rosendale Rd. Ch Fo 55 E2
Rosery The. Gos 181 D1
Rosetta Rd. Ports 183 D2
Rosewall Rd. Southa 77 F2
Rosewarne Ct. Winch 2 A1
Rosewood Gdns. Clanf 88 B3
Rosewood Gdns. March 102 A1
Rosewood Gdns. New M 195 F2
Rosewood. Gos 155 F1
Rosina Cl. Wat 135 D4
Roslin Rd S. Bour 206 C4
Roslin Rd. Bour 206 C4
Rosoman Rd. Southa 103 F2
Ross Gdns. Bour 189 E3
Ross Gdns. Southa 78 A1
Ross Glades. Bour 206 C3
Ross Rd. Rin 117 E1
Ross Way. L on S 179 F4
Rossan Ave. Lo He 152 B4
Rossington Ave. Southa 103 F4
Rossington Way. Southa 103 F4
Rossiters La. Ne Ma 99 F3
Rossley Cl. Christ 194 C1
Rosslyn Cl. N Bad 54 A2
Rossmore Rd. Poole 205 E4
Rossmore Rd. Poole 205 E4
Rostrevor La. Ports 182 C1
Rosyth Rd. Southa 103 F4
Rotary Cl. Wi Mi 163 F4
Rotary Ct. Net 127 D3
Rothbury Cl. Southa 104 A2
Rothbury Cl. Tot 76 B1
Rothbury Park. New M 196 A1
Rother Cl. Pet 41 E2
Rother Cl. W End 80 A1
Rother Dale. Southa 104 C2
Rotherbank Farm La. Liss 21 D3
Rothercombe La. Pet 40 A2
Rotherfield Rd. Bour 208 A2
Rotherfield Rd. Christ 195 D1
Rotherwick Cl. Hav 136 A3
Rothesay Dr. Christ 210 C4
Rothesay Rd. Bour 206 B3
Rothesay Rd. Gosp 181 D4
Rothsbury Dr. N Bad 55 D3
Rothville Pl. Ch Fo 30 A1
Rothwell Cl. Cos 133 D1
Rotterdam Dr. Christ 209 E4
Roughdown La. Holb 150 B1
Roumelia La. Bour 207 F2
Round Hill. Fordi 69 F1
Roundabouts The. Liss 21 D3
Roundcopse. Hyt 125 E2
Roundhaye Rd. Bour 189 F3
Roundhill Cl. Southa 80 A1
Roundhouse Dr. Tot 100 A3
Roundhouse Meadow. Herm 161 D4
Roundway. Wat 134 C4
Roundways. Bour 189 F2
Routs Way. Rown 77 F4
Row The. Red 47 E4
Row Wood La. Gos 155 D1
Rowallan Ave. Gos 180 B4
Rowan Ave. Wat 112 A1
Rowan Cl. Christ 210 B4
Rowan Cl. L on S 179 F3
Rowan Cl. Rom 53 E3
Rowan Cl. Southa 78 A2
Rowan Cl. St Le 139 E2
Rowan Cl. Swan 84 A2
Rowan Cl. Sway 172 A1
Rowan Dr. Broa 187 F1
Rowan Dr. Christ 210 B4
Rowan Dr. Ver 115 D2
Rowan Gdns. He En 105 E3
Rowan Rd. Hav 136 A2
Rowan Tree Cl. Liss 21 D2
Rowan Way. Fare 154 B4
Rowans Park. Lym 198 B2
Rowans The. March 101 F1
Rowbarrow Cl. Broa 188 C1
Rowborough Rd. Southa 103 F4
Rowbury Rd. Hav 135 E3
Rowdell Cl. Bour 190 B3
Rowden Cl. W Wel 50 C1
Rowe Asheway. Lo He 128 C2
Rowena Rd. Bour 208 C3
Rowes Alley. Ports 181 F2
Rowes La. E Bol 200 A4
Rowhay La. Ows 58 B3
Rowhill Dr. Hyt 125 E2
Rowin Cl. S Hay 185 E1
Rowland Ave. Poole 204 C3
Rowland Ct. Fare 130 C1
Rowland Rd. Portc 132 C1
Rowlands Castle Rd. Horn 112 C3
Rowlands Cl. Ch Fo 55 D2
Rowlands Hill. Wi Mi 163 E3
Rowlands Wlk. Southa 80 A1
Rowley Cl. Botl 105 F4
Rowley Dr. Botl 105 F4
Rowlings Rd. Winch 1 B2
Rowner Cl. Gos 155 E1
Rowner La. Gos 155 E1
Rowner Rd. Gos 155 D1
Rowner Rd. Stubb 155 D1
Rownhams Cl. Rown 77 F3
Rownhams Ct. Southa 77 F2
Rownhams La. Rown 53 F1
Rownhams Rd N. Southa 77 F3
Rownhams Rd. Bour 191 E2
Rownhams Rd. Hav 135 E3
Rownhams Rd. N Bad 54 A2
Rownhams Rd. Southa 77 F2
Rownhams Way. Rown 77 F3
Royal Crescent Rd. Southa 103 D2
Royal Gdns. Ro Ca 113 D1
Royal Oak Rd. Bour 190 B3
Royal Way. Wat 135 D4
Royden La. Bold 173 E1
Roydon Cl. Winch 10 C3
Royston Ave. Eastl 56 A3
Royston Cl. Southa 79 D1
Royston Dr. Wi Mi 163 E3
Royston Pl. B on S 212 A4
Rozel Ct. Southa 77 F2
Rozelle Cl. Litt 1 A3
Rozelle Rd. Poole 205 E2
Rubens Cl. New M 196 A2
Ruby Rd. Southa 104 A3
Rudgswick Cl. Portc 156 A4
Rudmore Rd. Ports 182 B4
Rudmore Sq. Ports 182 B4
Ruffield Cl. Winch 1 B1
Rufford Cl. Eastl 56 A3
Rufford Gdns. Bour 208 C3
Rufus Cl. Ch Fo 55 F4
Rufus Gdns. Tot 100 B4
Rugby Rd. Broa 188 A1
Rugby Rd. Ports 182 C2
Rumbridge Gdns. Tot 101 D4
Rumbridge St. Tot 101 D3
Runnymede Ave. Bour 189 F3
Runnymede. Fare 130 B2
Runnymede. W End 80 B1
Runton Rd. Poole 205 F3
Runway The. Christ 210 A4
Rushall La. Broa 187 D3
Rushcombe Way. Broa 187 F3
Rushes Rd. Pet 40 C2
Rushes The. March 101 F1
Rushford Warren. Christ 209 F2
Rushington Ave. Tot 100 C3
Rushington La. Tot 100 C3
Rushmere La. Hambl 110 C4
Rushmere Rd. Bour 208 B4
Rushmere Wlk. Hav 135 E3
Rushpole Ct. Hyt 125 E2
Rushton Cres. Bour 206 C3
Ruskin Ave. Bour 191 D2
Ruskin Rd. Eastl 56 A3
Ruskin Rd. Ports 183 D3
Ruskin Way. Wat 111 F2
Rusland Cl. Ch Fo 55 D4
Russel Rd. Bour 190 B3
Russell Cl. L on S 179 F3
Russell Cotes Rd. Bour 207 D1
Russell Dr. Christ 209 E3
Russell Gdns. St Le 140 A3
Russell Pl. Southa 79 D1
Russell Rd. Hav 135 F2
Russell Rd. L on S 179 F3
Russell Rd. Winch 2 A1
Russell St. Gos 181 D3
Russell St. Southa 103 D2
Russell Way. Pet 41 D1
Russet Cl. Fern 165 E3
Russett Cl. Lym 198 C1
Russett Cl. Swan 84 A2
Rustan Cl. Fa Oa 57 E1
Rustan Cl. He En 105 D3
Rutland Rd. Bour 207 D4
Rutland Rd. Christ 192 C1
Rutland Way. W End 80 A1
Ruxley Cl. Holb 150 B2
Ryan Cl. Fern 165 E4
Ryan Gdns. Fern 165 E4
Rydal Cl. Christ 192 B2
Rydal Rd. Gos 181 D4
Ryde Pl. L on S 180 A2
Ryde Terr. Southa 103 D2
Rye Dale. Ashu 100 B2
Rye Paddock La. Faw 151 D2
Ryecroft Ave. Bour 189 F3
Ryecroft. Lo He 129 E1
Ryedown La. W Wel 51 F2
Ryefield Cl. Pet 41 E2
Rylandes Ct. Southa 77 F2

Sabre Rd. Th Is 161 D2
Sackville St. Ports 182 B2
Saddle Cl. Wi Mi 164 B3
Saddlers Cl. Eastl 56 A3
Sadlers La. Hyt 126 A1
Saffron Dr. Christ 210 A4
Sage Cl. Wat 135 D3
Sages La. Frox G 17 E3
St Agatha's Rd. Hamble 128 A2
St Alban's Ave. Bour 207 E4
St Alban's Cres. Bour 207 D4
St Alban's Rd. Bour 207 D4
St Alban's Rd. Hav 136 A2
St Alban's Rd. Ports 182 C2
St Alban's Rd. Southa 103 D3
St Aldhem's Rd. Poole 205 F2
St Andrew Cl. Horn 88 B1
St Andrew's Rd. Cos 158 C4
St Andrew's Rd. Gos 181 D2
St Andrew's Rd. Ports 182 B2
St Andrew's Rd. S Hay 185 D1
St Andrews Cl. Mich 27 E3
St Andrews Cl. N Bad 53 F3
St Andrews Green. Meons 61 E3
St Andrews Park. Fa Oa 81 E3
St Andrews Rd. Broa 188 A3
St Andrews Rd. Southa 103 D3
St Ann's Cres. Gos 181 D3
St Ann's Rd. Horn 112 B4
St Anne's Ave. Bour 208 C3
St Anne's Gdns. Southa 103 F1
St Anne's Gr. Fare 154 C4
St Anne's Rd. Ports 182 C2
St Anne's Rd. Southa 103 F1
St Anne's Rd. Upt 203 D4
St Annes Cl. Winch 10 B2
St Annes Gdns. Lym 198 B2
St Annes La. Shed 107 F4
St Anthony's Rd. Bour 206 C3
St Aubin's Ave. Southa 104 A3
St Aubin's Park. S Hay 184 B2
St Aubyns Ct. Poole 204 A1
St Augustin's Rd. Bour 206 C3
St Augustine Rd. Ports 182 C2
St Austell Cl. Bish 56 C2
St Barbara Way. Ports 157 F2
St Barbe Cl. Rom 53 D3
St Bartholomew's Gns. Ports 182 B2
St Birinus Rd. Red 47 E3
St Blaize Rd. Rom 53 E4
St Brelade Pl. Southa 77 E2
St Brelades Ave. Poole 189 E1
St Catherine St. Ports 182 B1
St Catherine's Rd. Bour 208 C2
St Catherine's Rd. S Hay 184 B2
St Catherine's Rd. Southa 79 F1
St Catherine's Rd. Winch 11 D3
St Catherine's Way. Christ 192 B2
St Catherines Rd. Eastl 56 A3
St Catherines View. He En 105 D3
St Catherines Way. Portc 131 F1
St Catherines. Wi Mi 163 E2
St Chad's Ave. Ports 157 F1
St Christopher Ave. Fare 88 B2
St Christopher's Rd. Hav 135 E2
St Christophers Cl. N Bad 54 A2
St Christophers Gdns. Gos 155 E1
St Clair Rd. Poole 211 F4
St Clares Ave. Hav 135 E4
St Clement St. Winch 11 D4
St Clement's Gdns. Bour 207 E3
St Clement's Rd. Bour 207 E3
St Clements Cl. Rom 52 C4
St Clements La. Poole 204 A1
St Clements Rd. Poole 205 D4
St Colman's Ave. Cos 158 A4
St Cross Rd. Winch 10 C3
St Cuthberts Cl. Lo He 129 D2
St Cuthberts La. Lo He 129 D2
St David's Cl. Tot 76 B1
St David's Rd. Clanf 88 B3
St David's Rd. Ports 182 B2
St David's Rd. Upt 203 D4
St Davids Rd. Lo He 128 C2
St Denys Rd. Southa 79 E1
St Denys Wlk. Hav 135 E3
St Edmund Cl. Lo He 129 D1
St Edmund's Rd. Southa 102 A4
St Edward's Rd. Gos 181 D2
St Edward's Rd. Ports 182 B2
St Edwards Rd. Net 127 D4
St Elizabeth's Ave. Southa 104 A4
St Evox Cl. Southa 77 F3
St Faith's Cl. Gos 181 D3
St Faith's Rd. Ports 182 B3
St Faith's Rd. Winch 10 C3
St Francis Ave. Southa 104 A4
St Francis Cl. Black 177 F4
St Francis Pl. Hav 135 F2
St Francis Rd. Black 177 F4
St Francis Rd. Gos 181 E1
St Gabriel's Rd. Southa 104 A4
St George Cl. Burs 104 C1
St George's Ave. Bour 207 E4
St George's Ave. Hav 136 A1
St George's Ave. Poole 205 D4
St George's Bus Ctr. Ports 182 A3
St George's Cl. Christ 210 B4
St George's Cres. Fordi 69 F1
St George's Dr. Fern 165 E2
St George's Rd. Cos 157 F4
St George's Rd. Ports 182 A2
St George's Rd. Ports 183 D1
St George's Rd. S Hay 184 B2
St George's Sq. Bi Wa 83 E4
St George's St. Southa 103 D2
St George's St. Winch 11 D4
St George's Way. Ports 182 A3
St George's Wlk. Wat 134 C4
St Georges Cl. Bran 194 A4
St Georges Rd. Fordi 69 F1
St Georges Rd. Lo He 128 C2
St Georges Sq. Ports 182 A3
St Giles Way. Horn 88 B1
St Helen's Cl. Ports 182 C1
St Helen's Par. Ports 182 C1
St Helen's Park Cres. Ports 182 C1
St Helen's Rd. Gos 180 C2
St Helen's Rd. S Hay 184 B2
St Helena Gdns. Southa 79 F2
St Helena Way. Portc 156 B4
St Helier Pl. Southa 77 F2
St Helier Rd. Poole 189 E1
St Hellen's Rd. Cos 158 B4
St Hermans Rd. S Hay 185 E1
St Hilda Ave. Horn 88 B1
St Hubert Rd. Horn 88 B1
St Ives End Rd. St Le 140 A2
St Ives Gdns. Bour 206 C3
St Ives Park. St Le 140 A3
St Ives Wood. St Le 140 A3
St James Cl. Clanf 88 B2
St James Cl. Poole 204 A1
St James Rd. Fern 165 D3
St James Rd. W End 80 B1
St James Rd. Sway 172 B1
St James Way. Portc 156 B4
St James' La. Winch 10 C4
St James' Rd. Ems 136 C1
St James' Terr. Winch 10 C4
St James's Cl. Southa 78 B1
St James's Park Rd. Southa 78 B1
St James's Rd. Ports 182 B2
St James's Rd. Southa 102 B4
St James's Sq. Bour 208 A3
St James's St. Ports 182 A3
St John 's Centre. He En 105 E3
St John' S Rd. Southb 137 E1
St John's Ave. Wat 134 C2
St John's Cl. Gos 181 D3
St John's Cl. Wi Mi 163 E2
St John's Hill. Wi Mi 163 E3
St John's Rd. Bour 207 F2
St John's Rd. Christ 209 D3
St John's Rd. Cos 158 A4
St John's Rd. Eastl 56 A2
St John's Rd. Hav 135 E2
St John's Rd. He En 105 D3
St John's Rd. Lo He 129 D1
St John's Rd. Poole 204 B2
St John's Rd. Winch 11 D4
St John's St. Hyt 126 A2
St John's St. Winch 11 D4
St Johns Ct. March 101 F1
St Johns Dr. March 101 F1
St Johns Glebe. Rown 77 F3
St Johns Rd. New M 196 A4
St Johns Sq. Gos 181 D3
St Just Cl. Fern 165 E2
St Lawrence Cl. He En 81 E1
St Lawrence Rd. Eastl 56 A2
St Lawrence Rd. Southa 103 D2
St Ledger's Pl. Bour 207 E3
St Ledger's Rd. Bour 207 E3
St Leonard's Ave. S Hay 185 D2
St Leonard's Rd. Bour 207 D3
St Leonard's Rd. Winch 11 E3
St Leonards Way. St Le 139 E2
St Luke's Rd. Bour 206 C4
St Luke's Rd. Gos 181 D3
St Margaret's Ave. Christ 209 D3
St Margaret's Cl. Southa 104 A4
St Margaret's Rd. Bish 56 B2
St Margaret's Rd. Bour 190 B1
St Margaret's Rd. Poole 204 B2
St Margarets Cl. Wi Mi 163 D3
St Margarets Hill. Wi Mi 163 D3
St Margarets La. Lo He 129 F1
St Margarets Rd. S Hay 185 D2
St Mark's Cl. Gos 181 D1
St Mark's Rd. Bour 190 A2
St Mark's Rd. Gos 181 D1
St Mark's Rd. Ports 157 E1
St Marks Rd. Lym 198 A2
St Martin Cl. Winch 11 D4
St Martin's Cl. Southa 77 F2
St Martins Rd. Upt 203 D4
St Mary Gr. Hord 197 D1
St Mary St. Winch 10 B3
St Mary's Ave. Gos 181 D1
St Mary's Cl. Ki Wo 2 B3
St Mary's Cl. Red 47 F2
St Mary's Pl. Southa 103 D2
St Mary's Rd. Bour 207 E3
St Mary's Rd. Fern 165 E3
St Mary's Rd. Liss 20 C2
St Mary's Rd. Net 127 E3
St Mary's Rd. Poole 204 C2
St Mary's Rd. Ports 182 C3
St Mary's Rd. S Hay 184 C2
St Mary's Rd. Southa 103 D3
St Mary's Rd. Stubb 154 B2
St Mary's St. Southa 103 D2
St Marys Cl. Bran 194 B4
St Matthew's Rd. Cos 157 F4
St Matthews Ct. Gos 181 E3
St Matthews Rd. Winch 1 B1
St Merrin's Cl. Bour 190 B2
St Michael's Gdns. Winch 10 C4
St Michael's Gr. Fare 154 C4
St Michael's Pass. Winch 11 D3
St Michael's Pl. Bour 206 C2
St Michael's Rd. Bour 206 C1
St Michael's Rd. Hav 135 E2
St Michael's Rd. Ports 182 A2
St Michael's Rd. Winch 10 C3
St Michael's Sq. Southa 102 C2
St Michael's St. Southa 102 C2
St Michaels Cl. Ver 114 C3
St Michaels Rd. Lo He 129 D1
St Michaels Rd. Tot 100 C4
St Michaels Rd. Ver 114 C2

St Michaels Way. Horn 88 B1
St Monica Rd. Southa 104 A2
St Nicholas Ave. Gos 180 B4
St Nicholas Rise. Ki Wo 2 A3
St Nicholas St. Ports 182 A2
St Nicholas' Rd. Hav 135 E2
St Osmund's Rd. Poole 205 E2
St Patrick's La. Liss 21 E3
St Patrick's La. Ra 21 E3
St Paul's Hill. Winch 10 C4
St Paul's La. Bour 207 D2
St Paul's Rd. Bour 207 D2
St Paul's Rd. Lo He 128 C3
St Paul's Rd. Ports 182 A2
St Paul's Sq. Ports 182 A2
St Peter St. Winch 11 D4
St Peter's Ave. N Hay 160 B1
St Peter's Gr. Ports 182 B2
St Peter's Rd. Bour 207 D2
St Peter's Rd. Pet 40 C2
St Peter's Rd. Poole 205 D2
St Peter's St. Bi Wa 83 E4
St Peters Cl. Curd 106 B4
St Peters Rd. N Hay 160 B2
St Philip's Way. Southa 104 A4
St Piran's Ave. Ports 183 D4
St Ronan's Ave. Ports 182 C1
St Ronan's Rd. Ports 182 C1
St Simon Cl. Lo He 129 D2
St Simon's Rd. Ports 182 B1
St Stephen's Rd. Bour 206 C2
St Stephen's Rd. Ports 182 C4
St Stephen's Rd. Winch 1 B1
St Stephen's Way. Bour 206 C2
St Stephens La. Ver 115 D4
St Swithun Cl. Bi Wa 83 D4
St Swithun St. Winch 11 D4
St Swithun's Cl. N Bad 28 B1
St Swithun's Rd S. Bour 207 D2
St Swithun's Rd. Bour 207 D2
St Swithun's Rd. Ports 157 F1
St Theresas Cl. Hav 135 E2
St Thomas Ave. S Hay 184 B2
St Thomas Park. Lym 198 B2
St Thomas St. Winch 11 D4
St Thomas's Cl. Bour 190 C1
St Thomas's Rd. Gosp 181 D4
St Thomas's St. Lym 198 C2
St Thomas's St. Ports 182 A2
St Ursula Gr. Ports 182 B2
St Valerie Rd. Bour 206 C3
St Valerie Rd. Gos 181 D2
St Vincent Cres. Horn 112 A3
St Vincent Rd. Gos 181 D3
St Vincent Rd. Ports 182 B1
St Vincent St. Ports 182 A2
St Winifred's Rd. Bour 206 C3
St Winifred's Rd. Southa 78 B1
Salcombe Ave. Ports 158 A1
Salcombe Cl. Ch Fo 55 D2
Salcombe Cres. Tot 100 C3
Salcombe Rd. Southa 102 B4
Salcombe Rd. Tot 100 C3
Salcot Rd. Winch 2 A1
Salem St. Southa 78 B1
Salerno Dr. Gos 180 C2
Salerno Pl. Hamw 203 E1
Salerno Rd. Ports 157 E2
Salerno Rd. Southa 78 B2
Salisbury Cl. Eastl 56 A2
Salisbury Rd. Bour 207 F2
Salisbury Rd. Burt 193 E2
Salisbury Rd. Cos 158 A4
Salisbury Rd. Fordi 70 A1
Salisbury Rd. Ower 76 A2
Salisbury Rd. Poole 205 E3
Salisbury Rd. Ports 182 C1
Salisbury Rd. Rin 140 C4
Salisbury Rd. Sop 193 E2
Salisbury Rd. Southa 79 D2
Salisbury Rd. Tot 76 C1
Salisbury Rd. W Wel 50 B2
Salisbury St. Fordi 69 F1
Salisbury St. Southa 102 C3
Salisbury Terr. L on S 179 F3
Salmon Dr. Bish 56 C1
Salt La. Meons 34 C2
Salter Rd. Poole 211 E2
Salterns Ave. Ports 183 D3
Salterns Cl. S Hay 185 E2
Salterns Estate. Fare 155 D4
Salterns La. Burs 128 A4
Salterns La. Fare 155 D4
Salterns La. Faw 151 D2
Salterns La. S Hay 185 E2
Salterns Rd. Poole 205 D2
Salterns Rd. Stubb 179 D4
Salterns Way. Poole 211 D4
Salters Acres. Winch 1 B2
Salters La. Winch 1 A1
Saltgrass La. M on S 214 A2
Saltings Rd. Upt 203 D3
Saltings The. Cos 158 C4
Saltings The. Hav 159 F3
Saltmarsh La. S Hay 184 C3
Saltmarsh Rd. Southa 103 D2
Salvia Cl. Wat 135 D3
Salwey Rd. He En 105 E3
Salworth La. Sob 85 D2
Samber Cl. Lym 198 B2
Samphire Cl. Lym 198 C3
Samples Way. Poole 204 C4
Samson Cl. Gos 180 B4
Samson Rd. Hamw 203 E1
Samuel Rd. Ports 182 C3
San Diego Rd. Gos 181 D3
Sancreed Rd. Poole 205 F4
Sand Cl. W Wel 50 C2
Sandbanks Rd. Poole 205 D1
Sandbourne Rd. Bour 206 B1
Sandbourne Rd. Poole 204 B2
Sandcroft Cl. Gos 180 C2
Sandecote Rd. Poole 205 E2
Sandell Ct. Southa 79 D3
Sanderling Rd. Ports 183 E3
Sanderlings The. S Hay 185 D1
Sanderlings. Rin 141 E3
Sandford Ave. Gos 180 B2
Sandford Cl. Bour 191 E2
Sandford Way. Broa 187 F1
Sandhills Cl. Broa 188 B1
Sandhurst Rd. Southa 102 C3
Sandilands Way. Hyt 126 A1
Sandisplatt. Fare 154 B4
Sandle Copse. Fordi 69 D1
Sandleford Rd. Hav 135 E4
Sandleheath Ind Est. Fordi 69 D1
Sandleheath Rd. Alderh 92 C4
Sandlewood Cl. Clanf 88 B3
Sandlewood Cl. Tot 100 B4
Sandown Cl. Gos 180 B2
Sandown Rd. Christ 209 F3
Sandown Rd. Cos 157 F4
Sandown Rd. Southa 78 A1
Sandpiper Cl. Broa 187 F1
Sandpiper Cl. March 101 F1
Sandpiper Rd. Southa 78 A3
Sandpipers. Cos 158 C4
Sandpit La. Beaul 200 B3
Sandpit La. Poole 204 B2
Sandport Gr. Portc 156 A4
Sandringham Cl. Bour 191 D2
Sandringham Gdns. Bour 191 D2
Sandringham Rd. Fare 154 B4
Sandringham Rd. Pet 40 C2
Sandringham Rd. Poole 205 E2
Sandringham Rd. Ports 182 C3
Sandringham Rd. Southa 79 F1
Sandy Beach Estate. S Hay 185 F1
Sandy Brow. Wat 134 B2
Sandy Cl. Pet 41 E2
Sandy Cl. Wi Mi 164 A4
Sandy Down. Bold 173 E2
Sandy La. Abb 28 A2
Sandy La. Bish 57 E1
Sandy La. Bour 208 A3
Sandy La. Christ 192 C1
Sandy La. Lo He 153 F4
Sandy La. Lyn 121 F3
Sandy La. N Bad 54 A3
Sandy La. Pamp 162 A3
Sandy La. Ra 21 F2
Sandy La. Red 47 F4
Sandy La. Shed 83 E1
Sandy La. Shed 107 E4
Sandy La. St Le 140 A3
Sandy La. Upt 203 D3
Sandy La. Ver 115 D3
Sandy La. W Moo 114 C1
Sandy La. Wi Mi 164 A4
Sandy Mead Rd. Bour 191 F1
Sandy Plot. Burt 209 E4
Sandy Point Rd. S Hay 185 F1
Sandy Way. Bour 190 C2
Sandycroft. Lo He 152 B4
Sandyfield Cres. Wat 111 F2
Sandyhurst Cl. Broa 188 B1
Sanross Cl. Stubb 154 A1
Sapphire Ridge. Wat 135 D4
Saracen Cl. Lym 198 B1
Saracens Rd. Ch Fo 55 F4
Sarah Cl. Bour 208 A4
Sark Rd. Poole 205 E4
Sarnia Ct. Southa 77 F2
Sarum Ave. W Moo 138 C2
Sarum Rd. Ch Fo 55 F3
Sarum Rd. Hurs 9 F4
Sarum Rd. Winch 10 A4
Sarum St. Poole 204 A1
Sarum Wlk. Lym 198 B3
Satchell La. Hamble 128 A2
Saturn Cl. Southa 77 F2
Saulfland Pl. Christ 210 B4
Saulford Dr. Christ 210 B4
Saunders La. Awb 26 C3
Savage Cl. Gos 180 B3
Savernake Cl. Gos 155 E1
Savernake Cl. Rom 28 A1
Saville Cl. Bish 56 B3
Saville Cl. Gos 180 C2
Saville Gdns. Fare 88 A2
Saville Gdns. Fare 88 A2
Sawyer Cl. Winch 1 A1
Saxholm Cl. Southa 78 C3
Saxholm Dale. Southa 78 C3
Saxholm Way. Southa 78 C3
Saxley Ct. Hav 135 E3
Saxon Cl. Horn 88 B2
Saxon Cl. Lo He 128 C1
Saxon Cl. Portc 132 A1
Saxon Gdns. He En 105 D3
Saxon Meadow. Down 47 D4
Saxon Pl. Lym 198 B3
Saxon Rd. Black 150 C1
Saxon Rd. Southa 102 B3
Saxon Rd. Winch 2 A1
Saxon Sq. Christ 209 D3
Saxon Way. Alderh 93 D3
Saxon Way. Rom 53 D4
Saxonbury Rd. Bour 208 C3
Saxonford Rd. Christ 210 B4
Saxonhurst Cl. Bour 190 C3
Saxonhurst Rd. Bour 190 C2
Saxonhurst. Down 47 D4
Sayers Rd. Bish 56 C2
Scafell Ave. Fare 154 B4
Scallows La. Plai 50 C3
Scantabout Ave. Ch Fo 55 F4
Scarf Rd. Poole 204 C4
Scholars' Wlk. Cos 158 B4
School Cl. Ch Fo 55 D3
School Cl. N Bad 55 D3
School Hill. Sob 85 E3
School La. Bold 198 C4
School La. Bour 190 D3
School La. Ch Fo 55 D3
School La. Compt 90 C1
School La. Den 110 B3
School La. Ems 160 C4
School La. Hamble 128 A1
School La. Ki Wo 2 A3
School La. Lym 198 C2
School La. M on S 213 F3
School La. Pet 41 D3
School La. Red 73 E4
School La. Rin 141 D4
School La. Southb 161 F4
School La. St Le 140 A2
School La. W Moo 138 C4
School La. Westb 137 D3
School La. Wi Mi 163 D3
School Rd. Bran 169 E2
School Rd. Burs 128 A4
School Rd. Faw 151 D2
School Rd. Gos 155 F1
School Rd. Hav 135 F1
School Rd. Hyt 126 A2
School Rd. Red 48 A3
School Rd. Rom 28 B1
School Rd. Tot 101 D3
School Rd. Twyf 31 F3
School Rd. W Wel 50 C1
School Rd. Wickh 108 A2
Schooner Way. Lo He 128 C1
Schooner Way. Ports 183 E3
Scimitars The. Stubb 154 A2
Scivier's La. Uph 58 B1
Scotland Cl. Fa Oa 57 F1
Scott Cl. Poole 189 F1
Scott Cl. Stubb 154 B2
Scott Rd. Eastl 55 F1
Scott Rd. Poole 189 F1
Scott Rd. Ports 158 A3
Scott Rd. Southa 103 F1
Scott's Green. Christ 209 F4
Scotter Rd. Bish 56 B2
Scotter Rd. Bour 208 A3
Scotter Sq. Bish 56 B2
Scotts Cl. Co Com 57 D4
Scotts Hill La. Christ 209 E4
Scratchface La. Hav 135 D1
Scratchface La. Wat 134 C2
Scullards La. Southa 102 C2
Sea Crest Rd. L on S 179 F3
Sea Front Estate. S Hay 185 D1
Sea Front. S Hay 184 C2
Sea Grove Ave. S Hay 185 D1
Sea Hamlets. Upt 203 E3
Sea Kings. Stubb 154 A1
Sea La. Stubb 179 E4
Sea Rd. B on S 211 F4
Sea Rd. Bour 207 F2
Sea Rd. Bour 208 C2
Sea Rd. M on S 213 F2
Sea Rd. Southa 103 E2
Sea View Estate. Net 127 D3
Sea View Rd. Cos 134 B1
Sea View Rd. Poole 205 D3
Sea View Rd. S Hay 185 E2
Sea View Rd. Upt 203 D4
Seabird Way. Fare 155 D4
Seabourne Pl. Bour 208 A3
Seabourne Rd. Bour 208 A3
Seacombe Green. Southa 77 E1
Seacombe Rd. Poole 211 D2
Seacroft Ave. B on S 211 F4
Seafarers Wlk. S Hay 185 F1
Seafield Cl. B on S 211 F4
Seafield Park Rd. Stubb 154 A1
Seafield Rd. B on S 211 F4
Seafield Rd. Bour 208 B2
Seafield Rd. Christ 210 B4
Seafield Rd. Portc 156 A4
Seafield Rd. Ports 158 A1
Seafield Rd. Southa 77 F2
Seafields. Ems 160 C4
Seaford Cl. Burs 104 C1
Seagarth Cl. Southa 78 B2
Seagarth La. Southa 78 B2
Seager's Ct. Ports 181 F2
Seagrove Rd. Ports 157 E1
Seagull Cl. Ports 183 E3
Seagull La. Ems 136 C1
Seagull Rd. Bour 191 E1
Seagulls The. L on S 180 A2
Seahorse Wlk. Gos 181 E3
Seamans La. Min 98 B2
Seamead. Stubb 179 E4
Seamoor La. Bour 206 A2
Seamoor Rd. Bour 206 A2
Searles Hill. Twyf 58 A3
Seaton Ave. Ports 183 D4
Seaton Cl. Christ 211 D4
Seaton Cl. Lym 198 C3
Seaton Cl. Stubb 154 B1
Seaton Cl. W End 80 B1
Seaton Rd. Christ 211 D4
Seatown Cl. Poole 189 D1
Seaview Ave. Portc 132 C1
Seaview Rd. B on S 211 E4
Seaview Rd. Christ 195 E1
Seaward Ave. B on S 211 F4
Seaward Gdns. Southa 103 F2
Seaward Rd. Hyt 126 A2
Seaward Rd. Southa 103 F2
Seaway Ave. Christ 210 B4
Seaway Cres. Ports 183 E2
Seaway Gr. Portc 156 B3
Seaway. B on S 212 A4
Seawinds. M on S 213 D3
Sebastian Gr. Wat 135 D4
Second Ave. Cos 157 F4
Second Ave. Cos 158 C4
Second Ave. Ems 136 A1
Second Ave. Southa 101 E4
Second Ave. Southb 161 E4
Second Marine Ave. B on S 212 A3
Sedbergh Rd. Southa 77 E1
Sedgefield Cl. Portc 156 C4
Sedgefield Cl. Tot 100 B4
Sedgeley Gr. Gos 181 D4
Sedgemead. Net 127 D3
Sedgewick Cl. Gos 180 B4
Sedgewick Rd. Bish 56 B2
Sedgewick Rd. Southa 104 B3
Sedgley Cl. Ports 182 B2
Sedgley Rd. Bour 206 C4
Segars La. Twyf 31 F3
Segensworth Rd. Lo He 129 F2
Selangor Ave. Ems 136 B1
Selborne Ave. Hav 135 E3
Selborne Ave. Southa 104 B4
Selborne Cl. Pet 41 D3
Selborne Rd. Tot 100 B4
Selborne Wlk. Southa 104 B4
Selbourne Dr. Eastl 56 A2
Selbourne Gdns. Gos 180 C2
Selbourne Rd. Hav 135 F1
Selbourne Terr. Ports 182 C3
Selby Cl. Broa 188 A2
Seldon Cl. Winch 10 A2
Seldown Br. Poole 204 B1
Seldown La. Poole 204 B2
Seldown Rd. Poole 204 B2
Selfridge Ave. Bour 209 D2
Selhurst Way. Fa Oa 57 E1
Seliot Cl. Poole 204 B3
Selkirk Cl. Oakl 163 F1
Sellwood Rd. Net 127 E3
Selsdon Ave. Rom 53 D4
Selsey Ave. Gos 181 D4
Selsey Ave. Ports 183 D1
Selsey Cl. S Hay 185 F1
Selsey Cl. Southa 77 F1
Selsmore Ave. S Hay 185 E1
Selsmore Rd. S Hay 185 D2
Selworthy Cl. Poole 205 D1
Selwyn Gdns. Eastl 56 A3
Sengana Cl. He En 105 F3
Senlac Rd. Rom 53 D4
Sennen Pl. Ports 157 D4
Sentinel Cl. Wat 112 A1
Sephton Cl. Gos 180 B3
September Cl. W End 80 B1
Serle Cl. Tot 100 A4
Serle Gdns. Tot 100 B3
Sermon Rd. Winch 1 A1
Serpentine Rd. Fare 88 A1
Serpentine Rd. Poole 204 B2
Serpentine Rd. Ports 182 B1
Serpentine Rd. Wat 134 B2
Service Rd. Cos 157 E4
Set Thorn Rd. Sway 172 B1
Setley Gdns. Bour 191 F2
Setters Cl. Co Comm 56 C4
Settle Cl. Southa 102 A4
Settlers Cl. Ports 182 B3
Sevenoaks Dr. Bour 208 A4
Sevenoaks Rd. Cos 157 F4
Severn Cl. Cos 133 D1
Severn Cl. Portc 156 A4
Severn Rd. Fern 166 A3
Severn Rd. Southa 101 F4
Severn Rd. W End 80 B1
Seward Ave. Bour 208 B2
Seward Rise. Rom 53 E4
Seymour Cl. Ch Fo 55 F3
Seymour Cl. Ports 182 B4
Seymour Cl. Southa 78 B2
Seymour Cl. Tot 76 B1
Seymour La. N Bad 53 F2
Seymour Rd. Lon S 180 A2
Seymour Rd. Rin 117 D1
Seymour Rd. Southa 78 B2
Shackleton Rd. Gos 180 B4
Shackleton Sq. Bran 169 D1
Shadwell Rd. Ports 157 F1
Shaftesbury Ave. Ch Fo 55 E2
Shaftesbury Ave. Southa 79 D1
Shaftesbury Ave. Wat 134 C2
Shaftesbury Cl. W Moo 138 C1
Shaftesbury Rd. Gos 181 E2
Shaftesbury Rd. W Moo 138 C1
Shaftesbury St. Fordi 69 F1
Shaftsbury Rd. Bour 207 E3
Shaftsbury Rd. Poole 204 B2
Shaftsbury Rd. Ports 182 B1
Shaggs Meadow. Lyn 122 A3
Shakespeare Rd. Ports 182 C4
Shakespeare Ave. Southa 103 D4
Shakespeare Dr. Tot 76 B1
Shakespeare Gdns. Wat 111 F2
Shakespeare Rd. Bour 208 B4
Shakespeare Rd. Eastl 56 A2
Shakespeare Rd. Wi Mi 163 E3
Shalbourne Rd. Gos 181 D4
Shalcombe. Net 127 E4
Shalden Cl. Southa 78 B2
Shales Rd. Southa 104 A4
Shallows The. Brea 70 B4
Shamblehurst La. He En 81 E2
Shamblehurst La. W End 81 E2
Shamrock Cl. Gos 181 E2
Shamrock Rd. Southa 103 E2
Shamrock Way. Hyt 126 A3
Shanklin Cres. Southa 78 B1
Shanklin Rd. Ports 182 C2
Shanklin Rd. Southa 78 B1
Shannon Cl. Fare 130 B1
Shannon Rd. Stubb 154 A2
Shannon Way. N Bad 55 D3
Shapland Ave. Bour 189 F3
Shappen Hill La. Bur 142 C1
Shapwick Rd. Hamw 204 A1
Shard Cl. Ver 115 D3
Sharon Rd. W End 80 B1
Sharp Rd. Poole 206 A4
Sharp's Rd. Hav 136 A3
Sharpley Cl. Fordi 69 F2
Sharpness Cl. Fare 154 B4
Sharvells Rd. M on S 213 E3
Shavard La. Meons 61 E3
Shaves La. New M 196 A3
Shaw Cl. Tot 100 B4
Shaw Rd. Rin 117 E1
Shawfield Rd. Hav 136 A1
Shawford Cl. Southa 78 C2
Shawford Gdns. Bour 191 E1
Shawford Gr. Hav 135 E3
Shawford Rd. Bour 191 E2
Shayer Rd. Southa 78 B1
Shear Hill. Steep 41 D3
Sheardley La. Sob 29 D1
Shearer Rd. Ports 182 C4
Shears Brook Cl. Bran 169 D1
Shears Rd. Bish 56 C2
Shearwater Cl. Gos 155 D1
Shearwater Dr. Cos 158 C4
Sheep Pond La. Drox 61 D2
Sheep St. Pet 40 C2
Sheepwash La. Den 133 F4
Sheffield Cl. Bish 56 B3
Sheffield Rd. Ports 182 C3
Shelbourne Cl. Bour 207 E3
Shelbourne Rd. Bour 207 D3
Sheldrake Gdns. Hord 197 D2
Sheldrake Gdns. Southa 78 A3
Sheldrake Rd. Christ 210 A3
Shelford Rd. Ports 183 D3
Shellcroft. Lo He 152 B4
Shelley Ave. Portc 132 C1
Shelley Cl. Christ 210 B4
Shelley Cl. St Le 139 F3
Shelley Cl. Winch 10 B4
Shelley Gdns. Wat 111 F2
Shelley Hill. Christ 210 B4
Shelley La. Ower 51 F1
Shelley Rd E. Bour 207 F3
Shelley Rd. Bour 207 E3
Shelley Rd. Eastl 55 F1
Shelley Rd. Poole 205 E3
Shelley Rd. Southa 104 C3
Shelley Rd. Tot 76 B1
Shelton Rd. Bour 208 B3
Shenstone Ct. New M 196 A1
Shepards Cl. Fare 154 B4
Shepherd Cl. Christ 194 C1
Shepherds Cl. Cadn 99 D3
Shepherds Cl. Winch 10 A2
Shepherds Hey Rd. Tot 76 A1
Shepherds La. Comp 31 E3
Shepherds Purse Cl. Lo He 128 C1
Shepherds Rd. Cadn 99 E3
Shepherds Rd. Winch 11 E4
Sheppards Field. Wi Mi 163 D3

Sherborn Cres. Poole 189 D1
Sherborne Ct. Eastl 56 A3
Sherborne Dr. Fern 165 E2
Sherborne Way. He En 105 E3
Sherbrooke Cl. Ki Wo 2 B4
Sherfield Ave. Hav 136 A3
Sherfield Cl. Bour 191 E1
Sherfield English La. Plai 50 B3
Sheridan Cl. Southa 104 B3
Sheridan Cl. Winch 10 B3
Sheridan Gdns. Tot 100 B4
Sheringham Rd. Cos 133 E1
Sheringham Rd. Poole 205 F3
Sherley Green. Burs 105 D1
Sherrin Cl. Poole 204 B3
Sherringham Cl. Faw 151 D2
Sherwin Wlk. Gos 181 D2
Sherwood Ave. Fern 165 E2
Sherwood Ave. He En 105 E2
Sherwood Ave. Poole 205 D2
Sherwood Cl. Liss 21 D4
Sherwood Dr. Ver 115 D3
Sherwood Gdns. Lo He 128 C2
Sherwood Rd. Ch Fo 30 C1
Sherwood Rd. Gos 181 D2
Sherwood Way. Black 177 F4
Shetland Cl. Tot 100 A4
Shillinglee. Wat 134 C2
Shillingstone Dr. Bour 191 D2
Shillito Rd. Poole 205 F3
Shingle Bank Dr. M on S 213 E2
Ship Leopard St. Ports 182 A3
Shipcote La. Bi Wa 59 E1
Shipley Rd. Twyf 32 A4
Shipstal Cl. Hamw 203 E2
Shipton Green. Hav 135 E3
Shire Cl. Wat 112 B1
Shires The. He En 105 D3
Shires Wlk. Tot 100 A4
Shirley Ave. Ports 183 E2
Shirley Ave. Southa 102 B4
Shirley Cl. Bran 169 D1
Shirley Cl. W Moo 138 C1
Shirley High St. Southa 102 A4
Shirley Holms. Bold 173 D1
Shirley Holms. Sway 173 D1
Shirley Park Rd. Southa 102 A4
Shirley Rd. Bour 191 D1
Shirley Rd. Poole 205 D3
Shirley Rd. Ports 182 C1
Shirley Rd. Southa 102 B4
Shoblands Way. Hyt 126 A1
Shoe La. Uph 58 C3
Sholing Ct. Hav 135 E3
Sholing Rd. Southa 103 F2
Shoot Hill. Den 109 E2
Shoot Hill. Southw 109 E2
Shoot La. Gos 180 A4
Shoot La. Lon S 180 A4
Shooters Hill Cl. Southa 104 A2
Shop La. Southa 104 C1
Shore Ave. Ports 183 D3
Shore Ave. Upt 203 E3
Shore Cl. M on S 213 E2
Shore Cl. Upt 203 E3
Shore Cres. Bi Wa 83 E4
Shore Gdns. Upt 203 D3
Shore La. Bi Wa 83 E4
Shore La. Upt 203 E3
Shore Rd. Hyt 126 A2
Shore Rd. Lo He 128 B1
Shore Rd. Poole 211 E3
Shorefield Cres. M on S 213 E3
Shorefield Rd. M on S 213 D3
Shorefield Rd. March 101 F1
Shorefield Way. M on S 213 E3
Shorewell. Net 127 E4
Short Cl. Poole 206 A4
Short Hill. Red 73 D4
Short Hill. Rom 28 B1
Short Rd. Stubb 154 A1
Shorts Cl. Burt 193 E1
Shorts Rd. Fa Oa 57 E1
Shotterfield Terr. Liss 20 C2
Shotters Hill Cl. W End 80 B1
Shotts La. Bold 199 E2
Shottsford Rd. Poole 204 B3
Shravenshill Cl. Tot 76 B1
Shrubb's Ave. Lym 198 C2
Shrubbery The. Gos 180 C4
Shrubbs Hill Rd. Lyn 121 F3
Shrubland Cl. Southa 104 A4
Sibland Cl. Fare 154 B4
Sidings The. Down 47 D4
Sidings The. Net 127 E3
Sidlesham Cl. S Hay 185 F1
Sidmouth Ave. Ports 183 D4
Silchester Cl. Bour 206 C3
Silchester Rd. Ports 183 D4
Silkin Gdns. Tot 100 B3
Silkstead Ave. Hav 135 F3
Sillen La. Mar 43 D2
Silver Birch Ave. Fare 154 C4
Silver Birch Cl. Liss 21 D2
Silver Birch Cl. Southa 104 B2
Silver Business Park. Christ 209 F4
Silver Hill. Winch 11 D4
Silver St. Christ 209 D3
Silver St. Hord 197 E3
Silver St. Lyn 121 E3
Silver St. Ports 182 A2
Silver Way. Christ 210 C4
Silverdale Cres. Alderh 93 D3
Silverdale Cl. Broa 187 F2
Silverdale Rd. Southa 102 C4
Silverdale. B on S 212 A4
Silverlock Cl. Ports 182 B4
Silvers End. Hyt 126 A1
Silvers Wood. Tot 76 B1
Silverthorne Way. Wat 134 B4
Silvertrees. Ems 136 C1
Silwood Cl. Winch 1 B1
Simmonds Green. S Hay 185 E2
Simmonds Rd. Poole 204 B3
Simmons Cl. He En 105 E4
Simnel St. Southa 102 C2
Simon Way. Southa 104 C3
Simpson Cl. Portc 156 B4
Simpson Rd. Ports 157 E1
Sinah La. S Hay 184 B2
Sinclair Rd. Southa 78 A3
Singleton Dr. Bour 190 B1
Sir George's Rd. Southa 102 B3
Sirdar Rd. Southa 79 E2
Siskin Cl. Bi Wa 83 D4
Siskin Cl. Fern 165 D4
Siskin Cl. Southa 78 A3
Siskin Gr. Wat 135 D3
Sissinghurst Rd. Portc 156 A4
Siverdale Dr. Wat 111 E2
Six Dials. Southa 103 D3
Six Oaks Rd. N Bad 54 A3
Sixth Ave. Cos 157 F4
Sizer Way. Hyt 125 D2
Skew Rd. Portc 132 B1
Skinner St. Poole 204 B1
Skintle Green. Co Comm 56 C4
Skipper Way. L on S 180 A3
Skipton Cl. Broa 188 A1
Skipton Rd. Ch Fo 55 E2
Sky End La. Hord 197 D1
Slab La. Red 47 E3
Slab La. W Wel 50 C2
Slades Farm Rd. Bour 190 B1
Slades Hill. Black 150 C1
Sleepbrook Cl. Ver 114 C3
Sleepers Delle Gdns. Winch 10 C3
Sleepers Hill Gdns. Winch 10 B3
Sleepers' Hill Rd. Winch 10 B3
Sleight La. Broa 187 E4
Slindon Gdns. Hav 135 F1
Slindon St. Ports 182 B3
Slingsby Cl. Ports 182 A2
Slinn Rd. Christ 209 F4
Slip Way. Poole 204 A1
Slipper Rd. Herm 161 D4
Slipway The. Ports 157 D4
Sloane Ave. Holb 150 B2
Sloane Park. Shed 107 E4
Sloe Tree Cl. Lo He 129 E1
Slough La. Upt 203 D3
Smallcuts Ave. Southb 137 E1
Smeaton St. Ports 157 E1
Smeeton Rd. L on S 179 F3
Smith Gr. He En 105 E3
Smith La. Th Is 161 E1
Smith St. Gos 181 D3
Smith's Field. Rom 28 A1
Smithfield Pl. Bour 190 C1
Smiths La. Shed 107 F4
Smithson Cl. Poole 206 B4
Smithy La. New M 195 F3
Smugglers La N. Christ 194 C1
Smugglers La S. Christ 210 C4
Smugglers La. Wi Mi 163 F4
Smugglers Wood Rd. Christ 194 B1
Smythe Rd. Southa 104 B2
Snailing La. Hawk 20 B4
Snails La. Rin 117 D2
Snakemoor La. Durl 81 F3
Snakemoor La. Fa Oa 81 F3
Snape Cl. Gos 180 B4
Snapgragon Cl. Lo He 128 C1
Snellgrove Cl. Tot 76 B1
Snooks La. Bold 199 D3
Snowdon Dr. Fare 154 C4
Snowdon Rd. Bour 206 B2
Soake Rd. Den 111 D2
Soalwood La. Frox G 39 F4
Soberton Rd. Bour 207 E3
Soberton Rd. Hav 135 F2
Soldridge Cl. Hav 136 A3
Solent Ave. Lym 199 D2
Solent Ave. Southa 104 C3
Solent Cl. Ch Fo 55 F3
Solent Cl. Lym 198 C2
Solent Dr. B on S 212 A4
Solent Dr. Hyt 125 F2
Solent Dr. Lo He 152 B3
Solent Ind Est. He En 81 D1
Solent Rd. B on S 211 E4
Solent Rd. Bour 209 D2
Solent Rd. Christ 195 D1
Solent Rd. Cos 158 B4
Solent Rd. Hav 135 F1
Solent Rd. Hyt 149 F4
Solent Rd. Southa 102 C2
Solent Rd. Stubb 154 A1
Solent View. Faw 178 C4
Solent Village. Lo He 129 F3
Solent Way. Gos 180 C2
Solent Way. M on S 213 F2
Solly Cl. Poole 205 F4
Solomons La. Shed 83 F1
Solona Cl. Ch Fo 55 F4
Somborne Dr. Hav 135 F3
Somerby Rd. Poole 204 B3
Somerford Ave. Christ 210 A4
Somerford Cl. Southa 104 A3
Somerford Rd. Christ 209 F4
Somerford Way. Christ 209 F3
Somerley Rd. Bour 207 D4
Somers Cl. Winch 10 B3
Somers Rd N. Ports 182 C3
Somers Rd. Ports 182 B2
Somerset Ave. Southa 104 B4
Somerset Cres. Ch Fo 55 E2
Somerset Rd. Bour 208 A3
Somerset Rd. Christ 208 C4
Somerset Rd. Ports 182 B1
Somerset Rd. Southa 79 E1
Somerset Terr. Southa 102 B3
Somerton Ave. Southa 104 A4
Somerton Cl. New M 196 B2
Somervell Cl. Gos 181 D1
Somervell Dr. Fare 88 A2
Somerville Pl. Ports 157 E1
Somerville Rd. Bour 206 B2
Somerville Rd. Ki Wo 2 B4
Somerville Rd. Rin 141 E4
Sonnet Way. Wat 135 D4
Sonning Way. Bour 191 D1
Soper's La. Christ 209 D3
Sopers La. Broa 188 A1
Sopwith Cl. Christ 210 A3
Sopwith Cres. Oakl 163 F1
Sorrel Cl. Rom 28 B1
Sorrel Cl. Wat 135 D3
Sorrel Gdns. Broa 187 F1
Sorrell Cl. Lo He 128 C1
Sorrell Way. Christ 210 A4
South Ave. New M 196 A1
South Ave. Ports 157 F2
South Baddesley Rd. Bold 199 D2
South Bay. Th Is 161 D2
South Cl. Gos 180 C1
South Cl. Hav 160 A4
South Cl. Rom 28 B1
South Cliff Rd. Bour 206 C1
South Cross St. Gos 181 E2
South Ct. Hamble 127 F1
South Dr. Litt 1 A2
South East Cres. Southa 104 A2
South East Rd. Southa 104 A2
South End Cl. Hurs 30 A4
South Front. Southa 103 D2
South Grove. Lym 198 C2
South Haven Cl. Hamw 203 D2
South Hill. Alderh 93 D3
South Hill. Drox 85 D4
South Kinson Dr. Bour 190 A2
South La. Clanf 88 A3
South La. Clanf 89 D2
South La. Down 46 C4
South La. Horn 89 D2
South La. Ows 65 E2
South La. Red 73 E4
South La. Southb 137 F1
South La. Westb 137 F2
South Lodge. Fare 130 A1
South Mill Rd. Southa 102 A4
South Millers Dale. Ch Fo 55 D4
South Par. Ports 182 B1
South Park Rd. Poole 206 A4
South Path. Gos 180 B3
South Pl. Lon S 180 A2
South Rd. Bour 207 E3
South Rd. Broa 187 F3
South Rd. Cos 158 B4
South Rd. Horn 88 B1
South Rd. Ports 182 C4
South Rd. S Hay 184 C2
South Rd. Southa 103 E4
South St. Eastl 80 A4
South St. Ems 160 C4
South St. Gos 181 E2
South St. Hav 135 F1
South St. Hyt 126 A2
South St. Lo He 153 F4
South St. Lym 198 B1
South St. Ports 182 A2
South Sway. Sway 197 E4
South View Pl. Bour 206 C1
South View Rd. Christ 209 D3
South View Rd. Southa 102 B4
South View Rd. Winch 10 A2
South View. Winch 10 C4
South Way. Lo He 129 F2
South Weirs. Brock 172 B4
South Western Cres. Poole 205 D1
Southampton Hill. Lo He 129 F1
Southampton Rd. Cadn 99 D4
Southampton Rd. Cos 157 E4
Southampton Rd. Eastl 56 A1
Southampton Rd. Fare 88 A1
Southampton Rd. Fare 154 A4
Southampton Rd. Fordi 70 A1
Southampton Rd. Hyt 125 F2
Southampton Rd. Lo He 129 E2
Southampton Rd. Lyn 122 A3
Southampton Rd. N Bad 53 D3
Southampton Rd. Rin 140 C4
Southampton Rd. Rom 53 D3
Southampton St. Southa 102 C3
Southbourne Ave. Cos 158 A4
Southbourne Ave. Herm 161 D4
Southbourne Ave. Holb 150 B2
Southbourne Coast Rd. Bour 208 C2
Southbourne Gr. Bour 208 B2
Southbourne Ovrcliff D. Bour 208 B2
Southbourne Rd. Bour 208 B2
Southbourne Rd. Lym 198 B2
Southbrook Cl. Hav 159 F4
Southbrook Cl. Poole 189 D1
Southbrook Rd. Hav 159 F4
Southbrook Rd. Southa 102 C3
Southcliff Rd. Southa 103 D4
Southcliff. L on S 179 F4
Southcliffe Rd. B on S 211 E4
Southcliffe Rd. Christ 210 B3
Southcote Rd. Bour 207 E2
Southcroft Rd. Gos 180 C3
Southdene Rd. Ch Fo 55 E3
Southdown Rd. Comp 31 E3
Southdown Rd. Cos 158 A4
Southdown Rd. Horn 88 A1
Southdown View. Wat 111 E1
Southdown Way. W Moo 138 C1
Southend La. Sob 109 E4
Southern Ave. W Moo 139 D1
Southern Gdns. Tot 100 C4
Southern La. B on S 211 F4
Southern Rd. Bour 208 B2
Southern Rd. Lym 198 B2
Southern Rd. Southa 102 C2
Southern Rd. W End 80 C1
Southernhay Rd. Ver 115 D3
Southey Rd. Christ 209 F4
Southfield La. Bur 143 E1
Southfield Wlk. Hav 135 E4
Southfield. Rin 141 D3
Southfields Cl. Bi Wa 83 E4
Southgate St. Winch 10 C4
Southill Ave. Poole 205 E3
Southill Gdns. Bour 191 D1
Southill Rd. Bour 191 D1
Southill Rd. Poole 205 E4
Southlands Ave. Bour 208 C2
Southlands Ave. Broa 187 F3
Southlands. Cos 158 A4
Southlands. Lym 198 B1
Southlea Ave. Bour 208 C2
Southleigh Gr. S Hay 184 C2
Southleigh Rd. Hav 136 B2
Southmead Rd. Fare 130 C1
Southmoor La. Hav 159 E4
Southsea Terr. Ports 182 A2
Southville Rd. Bour 208 A3
Southway. Gos 155 E2
Southways. Stubb 154 B1
Southwick Ave. Portc 132 C1
Southwick Cl. Winch 1 B2
Southwick Ct. Fare 155 D3
Southwick Hill Rd. Cos 133 F1
Southwick Pl. Bour 208 B4
Southwick Rd. Bour 208 B3
Southwick Rd. Cos 133 E1
Southwick Rd. Den 110 C2
Southwick Rd. Southw 108 B2
Southwick Rd. Wickh 108 B2
Southwood Ave. Bour 208 B2
Southwood Ave. Christ 195 D1
Southwood Cl. Christ 195 D1
Southwood Cl. Fern 165 E3
Southwood Gdns. Lo He 128 C2
Southwood Rd. Ports 157 F2
Southwood Rd. S Hay 185 E1
Sovereign Cl. Bour 207 F4
Sovereign Cl. Ports 183 E3
Sovereign Dr. He En 105 E3
Sovereign Dr. Ports 183 E3
Sovereign La. Wat 134 C2
Sovereign Way. Eastl 55 F3
Sowden Cl. He En 105 D4
Sowley La. Beaul 200 B3
Spa Rd. Southa 102 C2
Spain The. Pet 40 C2
Spalding Rd. Southa 104 C3
Spaniard's La. N Bad 53 D2
Spaniard's La. Rom 53 D2
Sparkford Cl. Bour 208 A4
Sparkford Cl. Winch 10 C3
Sparkford Rd. Winch 10 C4
Sparrow Cl. Wat 111 F2
Sparrow Ct. L on S 179 F4
Sparrow Gr. Ott 31 E2
Sparrow Sq. Eastl 55 E1
Sparsholt Cl. Wat 135 D3
Sparsholt Rd. Hurs 9 E2
Sparsholt Rd. Southa 126 C4
Spartan Cl. Stubb 154 B3
Spartina Dr. Lym 198 C3
Spear Rd. Southa 103 D4
Specks La. Ports 183 D3
Speedwell Cl. Ch Fo 55 D3
Speedwell Cl. Lo He 128 C1
Speedwell Dr. Christ 210 A4
Speggs Wlk. He En 105 E3
Speltham Hill. Hambl 86 B1
Spencer Cl. S Hay 185 D2
Spencer Ct. Stubb 154 C1
Spencer Dr. L on S 179 F3
Spencer Gdns. Wat 111 F2
Spencer Rd. Bour 207 E2
Spencer Rd. Eastl 55 F1
Spencer Rd. Ems 136 C2
Spencer Rd. New M 196 A1
Spencer Rd. Poole 211 F4
Spencer Rd. Ports 182 C1
Spencer Rd. Southa 104 B3
Spenlow Cl. Ports 182 B4
Spenser Cl. Lo He 152 B4
Spetisbury Cl. Bour 191 D2
Spicer La. Bour 189 F3
Spicer St. Ports 182 B3
Spicer's Hill. Tot 100 C3
Spicer's Way. Tot 100 C3
Spindle Cl. Hav 136 B2
Spindle Warren. Hav 136 B2
Spindlewood Cl. B on S 196 A1
Spindlewood Cl. Southa 79 D3
Spinnaker Cl. S Hay 184 C2
Spinnaker View. Cos 135 D1
Spinners Cl. W Moo 138 C1
Spinney Cl. St Le 139 E2
Spinney Cl. Wat 111 F2
Spinney Dale. Hyt 126 A1
Spinney Gdns. Hyt 126 A1
Spinney The. Comp 31 E3
Spinney The. Den 110 C2
Spinney The. Fa Oa 57 D1
Spinney The. Gos 155 E1
Spinney The. Portc 131 F1
Spinney The. Southa 78 C3
Spinney The. Tot 76 B1
Spinney The. Wat 112 A3
Spinney Way. New M 196 A3
Spinney Wlk. Southa 79 F2
Spinneys La. Fern 165 E3
Spithead Ave. Gos 181 E1
Spittlefields. Rin 141 D4
Spouts La. Plai 50 B3
Spring Cl. Fa Oa 57 E1
Spring Cl. Southa 103 F2
Spring Cres. Southa 103 D4
Spring Garden La. Gos 181 E3
Spring Gdns. Ems 161 D4
Spring Gdns. N Bad 54 A3
Spring Gdns. Poole 205 E3
Spring Gdns. Ports 182 A3
Spring Gr. Burs 105 D1
Spring House Cl. Co Com 58 A1
Spring La. Bish 56 B2
Spring La. Co Com 31 F1
Spring La. New M 196 B1
Spring La. Swan 84 A3
Spring Pl. Rom 52 C4
Spring Rd. Bour 207 E3
Spring Rd. Lo He 128 C3
Spring Rd. Lym 199 D2
Spring Rd. Southa 103 F2
Spring Rd. Wat 112 A2
Spring St. Ports 182 B3
Spring The. Den 110 C2
Spring Vale. Swan 84 A2
Spring Vale. Wat 112 A2
Springbank Rd. Bour 207 F4
Springcroft. Gos 155 D3
Springdale Ave. Broa 187 F3
Springdale Gr. Broa 187 F2
Springdale Rd. Broa 187 F2
Springfield Ave. Bour 209 D2
Springfield Ave. Christ 192 B1
Springfield Ave. Holb 150 B2
Springfield Cl. Co Com 31 F1
Springfield Cl. Hav 135 D1
Springfield Cl. Lym 199 D2
Springfield Cl. Ver 114 C3
Springfield Cres. Poole 205 D2
Springfield Cres. Red 47 E3
Springfield Dr. Tot 100 C3
Springfield Gdns. New M 196 B1
Springfield Gr. Holb 150 B2
Springfield Rd. Poole 205 D2
Springfield Rd. Ver 114 C3
Springfield Way. Stubb 154 B1
Springfields Cl. Co Com 58 A1
Springford Cl. Southa 78 A2
Springford Cres. Southa 78 A2
Springford Gdns. Southa 78 A2
Springford Rd. Southa 78 A2
Springhill Rd. Ch Fo 55 E3
Springvale Ave. Bour 208 A4
Springvale Ave. Ki Wo 2 A3
Springvale Rd. Ki Wo 2 A4
Springwater Cl. Bour 190 A2
Springwater Rd. Bour 190 A2
Springwood Ave. Wat 134 C3
Spruce Ave. Wat 135 D4
Spruce Cl. Broa 187 F1
Spruce Cl. Lo He 152 B4
Spruce Dr. Southa 104 C3
Spruce Wlk. L on S 179 F3
Spur Cl. Wi Mi 164 B3
Spur Hill Ave. Poole 205 F2

Spur Rd. Cos 157 F4
Spur Rd. Poole 205 F4
Spur Rd. Wat 134 C4
Spur The. Gos 180 C1
Spur The. Wickh 108 A2
Spurgeon Rd. Bour 208 A3
Spurlings Rd. Fare 88 B2
Square The. Bour 206 B2
Square The. Faw 151 D2
Square The. Gos 181 E4
Square The. Hamble 128 A1
Square The. Lo He 153 F4
Square The. Pet 40 C2
Square The. Sh En 26 A2
Square The. Southb 161 E4
Square The. Westb 137 D2
Square The. Wi Mi 163 D3
Square The. Wickh 108 A2
Square The. Winch 11 D4
Squarey Cl. Down 46 C3
Squires Wlk. Southa 103 F1
Squirrel Cl. Bish 56 C1
Squirrel Dr. Southa 104 A2
Squirrel's Cl. Christ 192 B1
Squirrels Wlk. Hyt 125 F1
Stable Cl. Lo He 129 E1
Stacey Cl. Poole 205 E4
Stacey Ct. Hav 135 E4
Stacey Gdns. Bour 191 F1
Staff Rd. Mich 27 D4
Staff Rd. Miche 6 A1
Stafford Rd. Bour 207 D2
Stafford Rd. Pet 40 C3
Stafford Rd. Ports 182 B2
Stafford Rd. Southa 102 B3
Stag Cl. Bish 56 C1
Stag Gates. Black 150 C1
Stagbrake Cl. Holb 150 A2
Staghorn Rd. Horn 112 B4
Stags La. Ows 33 D3
Stainer Cl. Southa 104 B2
Stake's La. Uph 59 F4
Stakes Hill Rd. Wat 134 C3
Stakes La. Uph 58 C2
Stakes Rd. Wat 134 B2
Stalbridge Dr. Fern 165 E2
Stalbridge Rd. Broa 204 A4
Stalham Rd. Poole 205 F3
Stamford Ave. S Hay 184 C2
Stamford Rd. Bour 208 B3
Stamford St. Ports 182 C3
Stamford Way. Fa Oa 57 E1
Stamshaw Rd. Ports 157 E1
Stanbridge La. Awb 27 D2
Stanbridge Rd. Hav 136 A2
Standard Way. Fare 131 F1
Standford St. Southa 103 D2
Standing Hill. W Tyth 3 F4
Stanfield Cl. Poole 205 E4
Stanfield Rd. Bour 206 C4
Stanfield Rd. Fern 165 E3
Stanfield Rd. Poole 205 E4
Stanford Cl. Cos 157 E4
Stanford Ct. Southa 104 B2
Stanford Hill. Lym 198 B2
Stanford Rd. Lym 198 B2
Stanford Rise. Sway 172 A1
Stanhope Rd. Ports 182 B3
Stanley Ave. Ports 183 D4
Stanley Cl. Fare 130 C1
Stanley Cl. Gos 156 A1
Stanley Cl. Ver 115 D3
Stanley Gr Crs Ind Est. Poole 204 B3
Stanley Green Rd. Poole 204 B3
Stanley La. Ports 182 B1
Stanley Rd. Bour 207 E3
Stanley Rd. Christ 211 D4
Stanley Rd. Ems 161 D4
Stanley Rd. Holb 150 B2
Stanley Rd. Lym 199 D1
Stanley Rd. Poole 204 B1
Stanley Rd. Ports 157 E1
Stanley Rd. Southa 79 E1
Stanley Rd. Tot 76 B1
Stanley St. Ports 182 B1
Stanmore La. Winch 10 B3
Stannington Cl. New M 196 A1
Stannington Cres. Tot 100 C4
Stannington Way. Tot 100 C4
Stanpit. Christ 209 F3
Stanstead Cl. Ro Ca 113 E1
Stanstead Rd. Eastl 55 F2
Stansted Cres. Hav 136 A3
Stansted Rd. Ports 182 C2
Stanswood Rd. Black 178 B3
Stanswood Rd. Faw 178 C4
Stanswood Rd. Hav 135 E3
Stanton Rd. Bour 190 B1
Stanton Rd. Pet 40 C2
Stanton Rd. Southa 102 A4
Stapehill Cres. Wi Mi 164 B3
Stapehill Rd. Fern 164 C2
Staple Ash La. Frox G 39 E4
Staple Cl. Wat 111 E1
Staple Gdns. Winch 10 C4
Staplecross La. Burt 209 F4
Stapleford Ave. Fern 165 F3
Stapleford Cl. Rom 28 A1
Stapleford La. Durl 81 F3
Staplehurst Cl. Southa 104 A1
Staplers Reach. Gos 155 D1
Stapleton Rd. Ports 183 D4
Staplewood La. Ashu 124 B4
Staplewood La. March 124 B4
Star La. Rin 140 C4
Stares Cl. Gos 180 B4
Starina Gdns. Wat 135 D4
Starling Sq. Eastl 55 E1
Station App. Broa 188 A2
Station App. Ports 182 A3
Station Cl. Wickh 108 A2
Station Hill. Burs 128 A4
Station Hill. Curd 106 B4
Station Hill. Eastl 56 A2
Station Hill. Winch 10 C4
Station La. Ch Fo 55 E3
Station Rd N. Tot 101 D4
Station Rd S. Tot 101 D4
Station Rd. Alderh 92 C3
Station Rd. Bi Wa 83 E4
Station Rd. Bran 194 C1
Station Rd. Bur 170 B4
Station Rd. Burs 128 A4
Station Rd. Christ 209 D4
Station Rd. Cos 158 B4
Station Rd. Fordi 69 E1
Station Rd. Gos 180 C4
Station Rd. Hamw 204 A1
Station Rd. Liss 20 C2
Station Rd. Lo He 129 D3
Station Rd. Net 127 E3
Station Rd. New M 196 A1
Station Rd. Nur 77 D3
Station Rd. Pet 40 C2
Station Rd. Poole 205 D2
Station Rd. Portc 156 B4
Station Rd. Ports 183 D4
Station Rd. Rom 52 C4
Station Rd. S Hay 184 C2
Station Rd. Sob 85 E4
Station Rd. Southa 103 F2
Station Rd. Sway 172 A1
Station Rd. Ver 114 C4
Station Rd. W Meo 37 E2
Station Rd. W Moo 138 B1
Station Rd. Wi Mi 163 E2
Station Rd. Wickh 108 A2
Station St. Lym 198 C2
Station St. Ports 182 B3
Station Terr. Wi Mi 163 E2
Staunton Ave. S Hay 184 B2
Staunton Rd. Hav 135 F1
Staunton St. Ports 182 B3
Stead Cl. S Hay 185 D2
Stedman Rd. Bour 208 A3
Steel St. Ports 182 A2
Steele Cl. Ch Fo 55 E2
Steels Dro. Woodg 70 C4
Steels La. Dame 68 B2
Steep Cl. Portc 132 B1
Steepdene. Poole 205 D2
Steeple Cl. Broa 188 B2
Steeple Way. Lo He 129 E2
Steepleton Rd. Broa 188 B2
Steerforth Cl. Ports 182 B4
Stein Rd. Southb 137 E1
Stem La. New M 195 F2
Stenbury Way. Net 127 E4
Stenhurst Rd. Poole 204 C3
Step Terr. Winch 10 C4
Stephen Cl. Wat 112 A1
Stephen Langton Dr. Bour 189 E3
Stephen Martin Gdns. Fordi 69 F1
Stephen Rd. Fare 130 C1
Stephenson Cl. Gos 181 D1
Stephenson Rd. Tot 76 B1
Steplake La. Sh En 25 E1
Steplake Rd. Plai 50 B4
Sterte Ave. Poole 204 A2
Sterte Cl. Poole 204 B2
Sterte Rd. Poole 204 B2
Steuart Rd. Southa 103 E4
Stevenson Cres. Poole 205 F2
Stevenson Rd. Bour 209 D2
Stevensons Cl. Wi Mi 163 E2
Steventon Rd. Southa 104 B4
Stewart Cl. Bour 207 E3
Stewart Pl. Ports 182 C4
Stewart Rd. Bour 207 D3
Stewarts Green. Hambl 86 B2
Stewarts Way. Fern 165 F4
Stibbs Way. Bran 169 E1
Stillmore Rd. Bour 189 E2
Stinchar Dr. N Bad 55 D3
Stinsford Cl. Bour 191 D2
Stinsford Rd. Broa 188 B1
Stirling Ave. Wat 134 C4
Stirling Cl. New M 196 A2
Stirling Cl. Tot 77 D1
Stirling Cres. He En 81 E1
Stirling Cres. Tot 101 D4
Stirling Ct. Fare 130 C2
Stirling Rd. Bour 206 C4
Stirling St. Ports 182 B4
Stirling Way. Christ 210 A3
Stirling Wlk. Rom 52 C4
Stirrup Cl. Wi Mi 164 B3
Stoborough Dr. Broa 188 A1
Stock La. Lan 49 E3
Stockbridge Cl. Hav 136 A3
Stockbridge Cl. Poole 189 D1
Stockbridge Rd. Winch 1 B2
Stocker Pl. Gos 155 E1
Stockers Ave. Winch 1 B1
Stockheath La. Hav 135 F2
Stockheath Rd. Hav 135 F2
Stockheath Way. Hav 135 F2
Stockholm Dr. He En 105 E3
Stockley Cl. Holb 150 B2
Stockton Cl. He En 105 E4
Stoddart Ave. Southa 103 F3
Stodham La. Liss 20 C1
Stoke Common Rd. Bish 56 C3
Stoke Gdns. Gos 181 E2
Stoke Hts. Fa Oa 57 D2
Stoke Park Rd. Bish 56 B2
Stoke Rd. Gos 181 E2
Stoke Rd. Southa 78 A1
Stoke Rd. Winch 2 A2
Stoke Wood Cl. Fa Oa 57 D1
Stoke Wood Rd. Bour 206 C3
Stokes Ave. Poole 204 B2
Stokes Bay Rd. Gos 180 C1
Stokesay Cl. Hyt 150 A4
Stone Gdns. Bour 192 A1
Stone La. Gos 181 D2
Stone La. Gos 181 D2
Stone La. Wi Mi 163 D3
Stone Sq. Hav 135 F2
Stone St. Ports 182 A2
Stonechat Cl. Fern 165 D4
Stonechat Cl. Pet 41 E1
Stonechat Ct. Christ 209 F4
Stonechat Dr. Tot 100 B4
Stoneham Cemy Rd. Southa 79 F2
Stoneham Cl. Pet 40 B2
Stoneham Cl. Southa 79 E3
Stoneham Gdns. Burs 104 C1
Stoneham La. Chilw 79 E3
Stoneham La. Southa 79 E3
Stoneham Park. Pet 40 B2
Stoneham Way. Southa 79 F3
Stonehills. Faw 151 E2
Stoneleigh Ave. Hord 196 C2
Stoneleigh Cl. Portc 156 A4
Stoners Cl. Gos 155 D2
Stoney La. Winch 1 B1
Stony La S. Christ 209 E3
Stony La. Burt 193 E1
Stonymoor Cl. Holb 150 B2
Stopples La. Hord 196 C2
Stour Cl. Fern 164 B2
Stour Cl. W End 80 A2
Stour Cl. W Wel 50 B2
Stour Rd. Bour 207 E3
Stour Rd. Christ 209 D3
Stour View Gdns. Pamp 162 C1
Stour Way. Christ 192 B1
Stourbank Rd. Christ 209 D3
Stourcliffe Ave. Bour 208 B2
Stourcroft Dr. Christ 192 C1
Stourfield Rd. Bour 208 A2
Stourpaine Rd. Broa 188 B1
Stourvale Ave. Christ 208 B4
Stourvale Gdns. Ch Fo 55 E3
Stourvale Pl. Bour 208 A3
Stourvale Rd. Bour 208 B3
Stourwood Ave. Bour 208 B2
Stourwood Rd. Bour 208 B2
Stouts La. Bran 169 D1
Stowe Rd. Ports 183 D2
Stradbrook. Gos 155 D1
Stragwyne Cl. N Bad 53 F3
Straight Mile The. Ampf 28 C1
Straight Mile The. N Bad 28 C1
Strand St. Poole 204 B1
Strand The. S Hay 185 E1
Strand. Southa 103 D2
Stratfield Dr. Ch Fo 30 A1
Stratfield Park. Wat 134 B4
Stratfield Pl. New M 195 F2
Stratford Pl. Eastl 56 A2
Stratford Rd. Wat 135 D4
Strathmore Dr. Ver 115 D3
Strathmore Rd. Bour 191 D2
Strathmore Rd. Gos 181 E2
Stratton Cl. Cos 157 E4
Stratton Rd. Bour 191 E2
Stratton Rd. Southa 78 B1
Stratton Rd. Winch 11 E4
Strawberry Fields. He En 105 D3
Strawberry Hill. Lo He 128 C2
Streamleaze. Lo He 129 E1
Street End. N Bad 54 A3
Street The. Whit 24 A2
Strete Mount. Christ 209 F4
Stride Ave. Ports 183 D3
Strides La. Rin 140 C4
Strides Way. Tot 100 A4
Strode Gdns. St Le 140 A3
Strode Rd. Ports 157 E1
Stroud Cl. Wi Mi 164 A3
Stroud Gdns. Christ 209 F3
Stroud Green La. Stubb 154 B3
Stroud La. Christ 209 F3
Stroud Park Ave. Christ 209 F3
Strouden Ave. Bour 207 D4
Strouden Ct. Hav 135 E4
Strouden Rd. Bour 191 D1
Stroudley La. Cos 158 B3
Stroudley Way. He En 81 E1
Stroudwood Rd. Fa Oa 58 A2
Stroudwood Rd. Hav 136 A2
Struan Cl. St Le 139 F3
Struan Ct. St Le 140 A3
Struan Dr. St Le 140 A3
Struan Gdns. St Le 139 F3
Stuart Cl. Stubb 154 B1
Stuart Cl. Upt 203 D4
Stuart Cres. Winch 10 C3
Stuart Rd. Christ 211 D4
Stubbington Ave. Ports 157 F1
Stubbington Green. Stubb 154 B2
Stubbington La. Stubb 154 B1
Stubbington Way. Fa Oa 57 E1
Stubbs Dro. He En 105 E4
Stubbs Rd. Southa 104 B1
Stuckton Rd. Fordi 94 A4
Studland Cl. Southa 77 E1
Studland Dr. M on S 213 E3
Studland Rd. Bour 206 B1
Studland Rd. L on S 179 F3
Studland Rd. Southa 77 E1
Studley Ave. Holb 150 B2
Studley Cl. Christ 211 E4
Sturminster Rd. Bour 191 D2
Styles The. Crouch 22 B4
Sudbury Rd. Cos 157 E4
Suetts La. Bi Wa 83 F4
Suffolk Ave. Christ 192 C1
Suffolk Ave. Southa 102 B4
Suffolk Cl. Ch Fo 55 E1
Suffolk Dr. Ch Fo 55 E1
Suffolk Green. Ch Fo 55 E1
Suffolk Rd S. Bour 206 B2
Suffolk Rd. Bour 206 B2
Suffolk Rd. Ports 183 D2
Sullivan Rd. Southa 104 B2
Sullivan Way. Wat 134 C3
Sultan Rd. Ems 136 C1
Sultan Rd. Ports 182 B4
Sumar Cl. Stubb 154 B3
Summer La. Exb 177 D3
Summercroft Way. W Moo 138 C2
Summerfield Cl. Burt 193 E1
Summerfield Gdns. Southa 79 E3
Summerfields. Bour 207 F4
Summerfields. Lo He 129 D1
Summerhill Rd. Wat 112 A2
Summerlands Rd. Fa Oa 57 E1
Summerlands Wlk. Hav 136 A3
Summers Ave. Bour 190 D3
Summers La. Burt 193 F1
Summers St. Southa 103 E3
Summit Way. Southa 79 F1
Sumner Rd. Buri 65 E3
Sun St. Ports 182 A3
Sunbeam Way. Gos 181 D2
Sunbury Ct. Fare 130 C2
Sunderland Dr. Christ 210 A4
Sunderton La. Clanf 88 B3
Sundew Cl. New M 196 B2
Sundew Rd. Broa 187 F1
Sundridge Cl. Cos 157 F4
Sunningdale Cl. Bish 56 C1
Sunningdale Cl. Gos 155 E1
Sunningdale Cres. Bour 190 B2
Sunningdale Gdns. Southa 104 A4
Sunningdale Rd. Portc 156 B4
Sunningdale Rd. Ports 183 D4
Sunningdale. Hyt 125 F2
Sunny Hill Rd. Poole 205 E3
Sunny Way. Tot 100 C4
Sunnybank Dr. Wi Mi 164 A3
Sunnybank Rd. Wi Mi 164 A3
Sunnybank Way. Wi Mi 164 A3
Sunnydown Rd. Winch 10 A2
Sunnyfield Rd. B on S 212 A4
Sunnyheath. Hav 135 F2
Sunnyhill Rd. Bour 208 B3
Sunnylands Ave. Bour 208 C2
Sunnymead Dr. Wat 111 E1
Sunnymoor Rd. Bour 190 A1
Sunnyside Rd. Poole 205 E3
Sunnyside Wlk. Hav 135 E4
Sunridge Cl. Poole 206 A3
Sunset Ave. Tot 100 C4
Sunset Rd. Tot 100 C4
Sunvale Cl. Southa 104 A2
Sunwood Rd. Hav 135 E3
Surrey Cl. Christ 192 C1
Surrey Gdns. Bour 206 B2
Surrey Rd S. Bour 206 B2
Surrey Rd. Bour 206 A2
Surrey Rd. Ch Fo 55 E2
Surrey Rd. Poole 206 A2
Surrey Rd. Southa 103 E1
Surrey St. Ports 182 B3
Sussex Cl. Bour 191 D2
Sussex Gdns. Pet 40 C1
Sussex Pl. Ports 182 B2
Sussex Pl. Ports 182 B3
Sussex Rd. Ch Fo 55 E2
Sussex Rd. Pet 41 D1
Sussex Rd. Ports 182 B2
Sussex Rd. Southa 103 D2
Sussex St. Winch 10 C4
Sussex Terr. Ports 182 B2
Sutherland Ave. Broa 187 F3
Sutherland Cl. Rom 28 A1
Sutherland Ct. Ch Fo 55 E3
Sutherland Rd. Ports 182 C2
Sutherland Rd. Southa 77 F3
Sutherlands Way. Ch Fo 55 D4
Sutton Cl. Poole 189 D1
Sutton Cl. Ports 158 A2
Sutton Cl. Wat 111 E2
Sutton Gdns. Winch 11 D4
Sutton Pl. Brock 146 A1
Sutton Rd. Bour 191 D1
Sutton Rd. Tot 76 C1
Sutton Rd. Wat 111 E2
Swale Dr. N Bad 55 D4
Swallow Cl. Broa 203 F4
Swallow Cl. Hav 136 A1
Swallow Cl. Tot 100 A3
Swallow Ct. L on S 179 F4
Swallow Dr. M on S 213 F2
Swallow Sq. Eastl 55 E1
Swallow Way. Wi Mi 164 A4
Swallow Wood. Fare 88 A2
Swallows The. Clanf 88 A3
Swan Cl. Ems 161 D4
Swan La. Winch 10 C4
Swan Mead. Rin 141 E3
Swan St. Pet 40 C2
Swanage Cl. Southa 103 F2
Swanage Rd. L on S 179 F3
Swancote. Portc 155 F4
Swanley Cl. Eastl 56 A3
Swanmore Ave. Southa 104 B2
Swanmore Cl. Winch 1 B2
Swanmore Rd. Bour 208 A4
Swanmore Rd. Drox 84 C4
Swanmore Rd. Hav 135 E4
Swanmore Rd. Swan 84 A3
Swanmore Rd. Swan 84 C4
Swansbury Dr. Bour 192 A1
Swanton Gdns. Ch Fo 55 D4
Swanwick La. Swanw 128 C4
Swanwick Shore Rd. Swanw 128 B4
Swarraton Rd. Hav 136 A2
Sway Gdns. Bour 191 E1
Sway Rd. Hord 198 A3
Sway Rd. Lym 198 A3
Sway Rd. New M 196 B3
Swaythling Rd. Hav 135 E3
Swaythling Rd. W End 80 B1
Sweetbriar Gdns. Wat 134 C3
Sweyns Lease. E Bol 175 E3
Swift Cl. Broa 203 F4
Swift Cl. Eastl 55 E1
Swift Cl. L on S 179 F4
Swift Cl. Winch 10 B3
Swift Gdns. Southa 103 E1
Swift Hollow. Southa 103 E1
Swift Rd. Southa 103 E1
Swift Rd. Th Is 161 D2
Swinburn Gdns. Wat 111 F2
Swincombe Rise. W End 80 A1
Swiss Rd. Wat 134 C4
Swivelton La. Fare 132 A2
Sword Cl. Gos 180 C1
Sword Sands Rd. Ports 183 E4
Swordfish Dr. Christ 210 A4
Sycamore Ave. Ch Fo 30 B1
Sycamore Cl. Broa 187 F1
Sycamore Cl. Christ 208 B4
Sycamore Cl. Clanf 88 B3
Sycamore Cl. Gos 155 F1
Sycamore Cl. Lo He 129 E1
Sycamore Cl. M on S 213 E3
Sycamore Cl. N Bad 53 F3
Sycamore Cl. Rom 53 E3
Sycamore Cl. Wat 111 F2
Sycamore Dr. Holb 150 A3
Sycamore Dr. Ki Wo 2 A4
Sycamore Dr. S Hay 184 C2
Sycamore Rd. Bi Wa 83 F4
Sycamore Rd. Hord 196 C2
Sycamore Rd. Hyt 125 F2
Sycamore Rd. Southa 78 A1
Sycamore Wlk. Botl 105 F4
Sydenham Terr. Ports 182 C3
Sydling Cl. Poole 189 D1
Sydmanton Cl. Rom 53 D3
Sydmonton Ct. Hav 136 A3
Sydney Ave. Hamble 127 F2
Sydney Rd. Bish 56 B2
Sydney Rd. Broa 188 A2
Sydney Rd. Christ 192 C1
Sydney Rd. Gos 181 D2
Sydney Rd. Southa 78 A1
Syers Cl. Liss 20 C2
Syers Rd. Liss 20 C2
Sylmor Gdns. Bour 191 D1
Sylvan Ave. Southa 104 B3
Sylvan Cl. Hord 197 D1
Sylvan Cl. St Le 139 E2
Sylvan Dr. N Bad 53 F2
Sylvan La. Hamble 128 A1
Sylvan Rd. Poole 205 D3
Sylvan View. Wat 134 C3
Sylvester Rd. Wat 111 F1
Sylvia Cres. Tot 76 C1

Symes Rd. Hamw 203 F2
Symes Rd. Rom 53 D4
Symonds St. Winch 11 D4
Sywell Cres. Ports 158 B2

Tadburn Cl. Ch Fo 55 E3
Tadburn Cl. Rom 53 D4
Tadburn Rd. Rom 53 D3
Tadden Wlk. Broa 187 F1
Tadfield Cres. Rom 53 D4
Tadfield Rd. Rom 53 D4
Tagdell La. Horn 111 F4
Tait Cl. Poole 204 C4
Tait Pl. Gos 155 E1
Talbot Ave. Bour 206 C4
Talbot Cl. Hav 135 E2
Talbot Cl. Southa 78 C2
Talbot Dr. Christ 194 C1
Talbot Dr. Poole 206 A4
Talbot Hill Rd. Bour 206 B4
Talbot Meadows. Poole 206 A4
Talbot Rd. Bour 206 C4
Talbot Rd. Hav 135 E2
Talbot Rd. Hyt 125 F1
Talbot Rd. Ports 182 C2
Talbot Rise. Bour 190 B1
Talland Rd. Lo He 129 D1
Tamar Cl. Fern 166 A3
Tamar Cl. Portc 132 A1
Tamar Down. Wat 135 D4
Tamar Gdns. W End 80 A1
Tamar Gr. Hyt 125 F2
Tamarisk Cl. Stubb 154 B1
Tamarisk Cl. Wat 135 D3
Tamarisk Gdns. Southa 103 F4
Tamarisk Rd. He En 105 D4
Tamella Rd. He En 105 F3
Tammys Turn. Fare 154 A4
Tamorisk Dr. Tot 100 B3
Tamworth Rd. Bour 207 F3
Tamworth Rd. Ports 183 D3
Tan Howse Cl. Bour 208 A4
Tanfield La. Wickh 108 A2
Tanfield Park. Wickh 108 A2
Tangier La. Bi Wa 83 D4
Tangier Rd. Ports 183 D4
Tanglewood. Fare 88 A2
Tanglewood. March 102 A1
Tangley Wlk. Hav 136 A3
Tangmere Cl. Christ 210 A3
Tangmere Dr. Southa 78 A2
Tangyes Cl. Stubb 154 B2
Tanhouse Cl. He En 105 E3
Tanhouse La. He En 105 E3
Tankerdale La. Steep 41 E4
Tankerton Cl. Cos 157 F4
Tankerville Rd. Southa 103 E2
Tanner's Brook Way. Southa 101 F3
Tanner's La. Den 111 D3
Tanner's Ridge. Wat 134 C2
Tanneries Ind Est The. Hav 135 F1
Tanners La. Bold 200 A2
Tanners La. Fare 154 C3
Tanners La. W Wel 51 E4
Tanners Rd. N Bad 54 A2
Tanners The. Lo He 129 E1
Tanslewood Cl. Wat 134 B2
Tansy Cl. Wat 135 D3
Tanyards The. Ch Fo 30 A1
Taplin Dr. He En 105 E4
Taplings Cl. Winch 1 B2
Taplings Rd. Winch 1 B2
Taranto Rd. Southa 78 B2
Tarbery Cres. Horn 112 B4
Target Rd. Ports 157 E1
Tarius Cl. Gos 155 E2
Tarleton Rd. Cos 133 D1
Tarn Dr. Broa 203 F4
Tarn Rise. Horn 88 B1
Tarrant Cl. Broa 188 C1
Tarrant Gdns. Hav 135 E2
Tarrant Rd. Bour 191 D2
Tasman Cl. Southa 103 D1
Taswell Rd. Ports 182 B1
Tatchbury La. Ne Ma 99 F4
Tate Rd. Southa 101 E4
Tates Rd. Hyt 126 A1
Tates Rd. Hyt 126 A2
Tatnam Rd. Poole 204 B2
Tattenham Rd. Brock 172 C4
Tattershall Cres. Portc 156 A4
Tatwin Cl. Southa 104 B3
Tatwin Cres. Southa 104 B3
Taunton Dr. Southa 104 A4
Tavell's La. March 101 F1
Tavells Cl. March 101 F1
Taverner Cl. Poole 204 B1
Taverners Cl. Southa 104 B2
Tavistock Cl. Rom 28 A1
Tavistock Gdns. Hav 136 A1
Tavy Cl. N Bad 55 D3
Taw Dr. N Bad 55 D3
Taylor's Bldgs. Poole 204 B1
Teachers Way. Holb 150 A2
Teal Cl. Portc 155 F4
Teal Cl. S Hay 185 D2
Teal Cl. Tot 100 B4
Teal Wlk. Gos 155 D2
Teasel Way. W Moo 138 C1
Teazle Cl. Pet 41 E1
Tebourba Dr. Gos 181 D2
Tebourba Way. Southa 101 F4
Tedder Cl. Bour 190 A2
Tedder Gdns. Bour 190 A2
Tedder Rd. Bour 190 A2
Tedder Rd. Gos 155 E2
Tedder Rd. Southa 104 A4
Tedder Way. Tot 100 B4
Teddington Rd. Ports 183 D2
Tees Cl. N Bad 55 D4
Tees Farm Rd. Co Comm 56 C4
Tees Green. Co Comm 56 C4
Teg Down Meads. Winch 1 B1
Teg Down. Pet 41 D2
Teglease Green. Hav 135 E4
Teignmouth Rd. Gos 180 C4
Teignmouth Rd. Ports 183 D4
Telegraph Rd. W End 80 C1
Telephone Rd. Ports 182 C2
Telford Rd. Fern 165 D4
Telford Rd. Ports 157 F2
Teme Cres. Southa 101 F4
Teme Rd. Southa 101 F4
Tempest Ave. Wat 135 D4
Templars Mede. Ch Fo 55 D2
Templars Way. Chilw 55 D2
Temple Gdns. Southa 103 F1
Temple La. E Meon 63 E4
Temple Rd. Liss 21 D3
Temple Rd. Southa 103 F1
Temple St. Ports 182 B3
Templecombe Rd. Bish 56 C1
Templemere. Fare 154 A4
Templer Cl. Bour 189 F1
Tenby Cl. Southa 104 A4
Tenby Dr. Ch Fo 55 D2
Tennyson Cl. Bi Wa 83 F4
Tennyson Cl. Holb 150 A3
Tennyson Cres. Wat 111 E1
Tennyson Gdns. Fare 88 A1
Tennyson Rd. Bour 190 C1
Tennyson Rd. Eastl 55 F1
Tennyson Rd. Poole 205 D2
Tennyson Rd. Ports 182 C4
Tennyson Rd. Southa 79 D1
Tennyson Rd. Tot 76 B1
Tennyson Rd. Wi Mi 163 E3
Tensing Rd. Christ 209 F4
Tenterton Ave. Southa 104 A1
Terence Ave. Broa 188 B1
Terence Rd. Broa 187 E3
Terminus Terr. Southa 103 D2
Tern Cl. Hyt 126 A1
Tern Wlk. Gos 155 D2
Terrace Rd. Bour 206 C2
Terrace The. Dame 68 B3
Terriate Cl. Ch Fo 55 E4
Terrington Ave. Christ 194 C1
Test La. Nur 77 D1
Test La. Southa 77 D1
Test Rd. Southa 126 A4
Test Valley Bsns Ctre. Nur 77 E1
Testbourne Ave. Tot 100 B4
Testbourne Cl. Tot 100 B4
Testbourne Rd. Tot 100 B3
Testcombe Rd. Gos 181 D2
Testlands Ave. Nur 77 E3
Testwood Ave. Tot 76 C1
Testwood Cres. Tot 76 B1
Testwood La. Tot 101 D4
Testwood Pl. Tot 101 D4
Testwood Rd. Hav 135 E3
Testwood Rd. Southa 102 A3
Tethering Dro. Woodg 47 F2
Tetney Cl. Southa 77 F2
Teviot Rd. N Bad 55 D3
Tewkesbury Ave. Fare 130 B2
Tewkesbury Ave. Gosp 181 D4
Tewkesbury Cl. Cos 157 E4
Texas Dr. Winch 10 A2
Thackeray Rd. Southa 103 D4
Thacking Green. Co Comm 56 C4
Thames Alley. Poole 204 A1
Thames Cl. Fern 166 A3
Thames Cl. W End 80 A2
Thames Dr. Fare 130 B2
Thames Mews. Poole 204 A1
Thames St. Poole 204 A1
Thamesmead Cl. Gos 180 C4
Thetchers Cl. New M 196 A3
Thetford Gdns. N Bad 55 D4
Thetford Rd. Gos 180 C4
Thetford Rd. Poole 205 F3
Thicket The. Gos 155 F1
Thicket The. Portc 131 F1
Thicket The. Ports 182 B2
Thicket The. Rom 53 E3
Thicket The. Wat 134 B2
Third Ave. Cos 157 F4
Third Ave. Hav 136 A1
Third Ave. Southa 101 F3
Thirlmere Cl. Stubb 154 B2
Thirlmere Rd. Southa 77 F1
Thirlmere. Eastl 55 F1
Thirlstane Firs. Ch Fo 55 D2
Thistlebarrow Rd. Bour 207 F3
Thistledown. Wat 112 A3
Thomas Cl. Tot 100 B3
Thomas Lewis Way. Southa 79 E1
Thomas Rd. N Bad 54 A2
Thomas St. Ports 182 B3
Thompson's La. Co Com 57 F4
Thompsons La. Den 55 B3
Thoresby Ct. New M 195 F2
Thorn Cl. Eastl 56 A3
Thorn Cl. Pet 41 E1
Thorn Rd. Broa 188 B2
Thornbrake Rd. Gos 181 E2
Thornbury Ave. Black 177 F4
Thornbury Ave. Southa 102 C4
Thornbury Cl. Fare 154 B4
Thornbury Hts. Ch Fo 30 C1
Thornbury Rd. Bour 209 D2
Thornbury Wood. Ch Fo 30 C1
Thornby Ct. Ports 158 A2
Thorncliffe Cl. Ports 157 F2
Thorncombe Cl. Bour 191 D2
Thorncombe Cl. Broa 188 C1
Thorncroft Rd. Ports 182 C3
Thorndike Cl. Southa 78 A1
Thorndike Rd. Southa 77 F1
Thorness Cl. Southa 77 E1
Thorney Cl. Fare 154 B4
Thorney Old Park. Th Is 161 E1
Thorney Rd. Herm 161 D3
Thorney Rd. Th Is 161 D3
Thornfield Cl. Horn 88 B1
Thornfield Dr. Christ 194 C1
Thorngate Way. Gos 181 E2
Thornham La. Th Is 161 E3
Thornham Rd. New M 196 B2
Thornhill Ave. Southa 104 B3
Thornhill Cl. Black 150 C1
Thornhill Park Rd. Southa 104 C4
Thornhill Rd. Black 150 C1
Thornhill Rd. Southa 78 C2
Thorni Ave. Fare 130 B2
Thornleigh Rd. Southa 103 F1
Thornley Rd. Bour 190 B2
Thorns La. Beaul 200 C3
Thornton Ave. Lo He 128 B1
Thornton Cl. Wat 134 A1
Thornton Rd. Gos 181 D4
Thornycroft Ave. Southa 103 E1
Thorold Rd. Ch Fo 30 C1
Thorold Rd. Southa 79 F1
Three Acre Dr. B on S 211 F4
Three Acres. Den 111 D2
Three Cross Rd. W Moo 138 C3
Three Horse Shs La. W Meo 16 B1
Three Oaks. Southa 104 C3
Three Tun Cl. Ports 182 A3
Threefield La. Southa 103 D2
Thresher Cl. Wat 112 A1
Throop Cl. Bour 192 A1
Throop Rd. Bour 191 F2
Thrush Rd. Poole 189 E1
Thrush Wlk. Wat 111 F2
Thruxton Ct. Southa 103 F3
Thruxton Rd. Hav 135 E3
Thurbern Rd. Ports 157 F1
Thurmell Cl. He En 105 E2
Thurmell Wlk. He En 105 E2
Thurmond Cres. Winch 10 B3
Thurmond Rd. Winch 10 B3
Thursby Rd. Christ 194 C1
Thurston Cl. Ch Fo 55 E4
Thwaite Rd. Poole 206 A3
Tichborne Rd. Eastl 80 A4
Tichborne Rd. Southa 104 B4
Tichborne Way. Gos 155 E1
Tickleford Dr. Southa 104 A1
Tickner Cl. He En 105 F3
Ticonderoga Gdns. Southa 103 F1
Tidcombe Green. Hav 135 E4
Tides Way. March 101 F1
Tidworth Rd. Hav 135 F2
Tiffany Cl. Hord 196 C2
Tilbrook Rd. Southa 102 A4
Tilburg Rd. Christ 209 E4
Tilden Rd. Comp 31 E3
Tilebarn La. Brock 173 D3
Tilford Rd. Horn 111 F3
Tillingbourn. Lo He 129 E2
Tilmore Gdns. Pet 40 C3
Tilmore Rd. Pet 40 C3
Timberlane. Wat 134 B2
Timberley La. Red 48 A3
Timberly Cl. Holb 150 B2
Timbers The. Fare 130 B1
Timothy Cl. Bour 190 B3
Timpson Rd. Ports 182 C3
Timsbury Cres. Hav 135 F1
Timsbury Dr. Southa 77 F1
Timson Cl. Tot 100 B3
Tincleton Gdns. Bour 191 D2
Tindale Rd. Southa 77 F1
Tinneys Cl. Red 47 E2
Tintagel Cl. Southa 78 B3
Tintern Cl. Cos 133 D1
Tintern Gr. Southa 102 C3
Tintern Rd. Gos 181 D2
Tipner Green. Ports 157 E2
Tipner La. Ports 157 E2
Tipner Rd. Ports 157 E1
Tiptoe Green. Hav 136 A3
Tiptoe Rd. New M 196 B4
Tiptree Cl. Eastl 56 A3
Titchborne Cl. Hav 135 E3
Titchfield Hill. Lo He 154 A4
Titchfield Industries. Lo He 154 A4
Titchfield La. Wickh 107 E2
Titchfield Park Rd. Lo He 129 E2
Titchfield Rd. Fare 154 A3
Tithe The Barn. Lym 198 C3
Tithe The. Den 110 C2
Tithelands La. Bramd 15 F2
Tithewood Cl. Ch Fo 30 A1
Titus Gdns. Wat 135 D4
Tivoli Cl. Ch Fo 55 F4
Toby St. Ports 182 B3
Todber Cl. Bour 189 F2
Tokar St. Ports 183 D1
Tokio Rd. Ports 158 A1
Tollard Cl. Poole 205 F4
Tollbar Way. He En 81 D1
Tollerford Rd. Broa 188 B1
Tollgate Rd. Swanw 128 B4
Tollgate. Ch Fo 55 E1
Tolpuddle Gdns. Bour 191 D2
Tolstoi Rd. Poole 205 D3
Toms La. Rin 118 A4
Tonbridge St. Ports 182 B1
Tonge Rd. Bour 190 D3
Tonnant Cl. Stubb 154 B1
Toogoods Way. Nur 77 E3
Toothill Rd. Rown 53 E1
Top La. Rin 141 D4
Topaz Gr. Wat 135 D4
Tor Cl. Portc 131 F1
Tor Way. Pet 41 D2
Torbay Rd. Poole 205 E2
Torberry Dr. Pet 41 D1
Torch Cl. Fa Oa 57 D1
Torcross Cl. Southa 103 F1
Torfrida Ct. Ports 183 E2
Tormead. Hyt 125 F2
Tornay Gr. N Bad 53 F2
Toronto Pl. Gos 181 D3
Toronto Rd. Ports 182 C4
Torquay Ave. Gos 181 D4
Torquay Ave. Southa 102 B4
Torre Cl. Eastl 56 A3
Torridge Gdns. W End 80 A2
Torrington Cl. Southa 104 A2
Torrington Rd. Ports 157 F2
Tortworth Cl. Fare 154 B4
Torwood Gdns. Bish 56 C1
Tosson Cl. Southa 101 F4
Totland Cl. Southa 101 F4
Totland Rd. Cos 157 F4
Totland Rd. Gos 155 E1
Totmel Rd. Poole 189 D1
Totnes Cl. Eastl 55 F3
Tottehale Cl. N Bad 53 F2
Tottenham Rd. Ports 182 C3
Totton By Pass. Tot 101 D4
Totton Wlk. Hav 135 E3
Tournerbury La. S Hay 185 D2
Tourney Rd. Bour 189 F3
Tovey Pl. Ki Wo 2 B4
Tower Gdns. Southa 78 C2
Tower La. Eastl 56 B1
Tower La. Wi Mi 163 E3
Tower Rd W. Poole 206 A1
Tower Rd. Bour 207 E3
Tower Rd. Poole 206 A1
Tower Rd. Ports 182 C2
Tower Rd. Winch 10 C4
Tower St. Ems 161 D4
Tower St. Ports 181 F2
Tower St. Winch 10 C4
Towers Farm. Broa 187 E4
Towers Gdn. Hav 159 F3
Towers Way. Broa 187 E4
Town Hall Rd. Hav 135 F1
Town La. Pet 41 D3
Town Quay. March 102 C1
Town Quay. Ports 181 F2
Town St. Ports 182 B3
Towngate Bridge. Poole 204 B2
Townhill Way. Southa 80 A1
Townhill Way. W End 80 A1
Townsend Cl. Bour 190 D3
Townsville Rd. Bour 191 D1
Towpath Mead. Ports 183 E2
Toynbee Cl. Eastl 56 A2
Toynbee Rd. Eastl 56 A2
Tozer Cl. Bour 189 F1
Trafalgar Cl. Ch Fo 55 D3
Trafalgar Ct. Christ 209 F3
Trafalgar Ct. Fare 154 C4
Trafalgar Pl. Ports 182 C3
Trafalgar Rd. Bour 206 C4
Trafalgar Rd. Southa 102 B3
Trafalgar Sq. Gos 181 D3
Trafalgar St. Winch 10 C4
Trafalgar Way. Hyt 126 A1
Trafford Rd. Fa Oa 57 E1
Trampers La. Southw 109 D1
Tranby Rd. Southa 103 F2
Tranmere Cl. Lym 198 C1
Tranmere Rd. Ports 183 D2
Treadwheel Rd. Ro Ca 113 D3
Treagore Rd. Tot 76 B1
Trearnan Cl. Southa 101 F4
Treble Cl. Winch 10 A2
Tredegar Rd. Ports 183 D2
Tree Hamlets. Upt 203 E3
Tree Side Way. Wat 111 F1
Treeside Ave. Tot 101 D4
Treeside Rd. Southa 102 B4
Treeside. Christ 194 B1
Trefoil Cl. Wat 135 D4
Tregaron Ave. Cos 158 A4
Tregonwell Rd. Bour 206 C1
Treloar Rd. S Hay 185 F1
Treloyhan Cl. Ch Fo 55 E2
Tremona Ct. Southa 78 A1
Tremona Rd. Southa 78 A1
Trenley Cl. Holb 150 B2
Trent Cl. Southa 79 F1
Trent Rd. Southa 79 F1
Trent Way. Fern 166 A3
Trent Way. L on S 179 F3
Trent Way. W End 80 B1
Trent Wlk. Portc 156 A4
Trentham Ave. Bour 208 A4
Trentham Cl. Bour 208 A4
Tresillian Cl. Christ 195 D1
Tresillian Gdns. W End 80 A1
Tresillian Way. Christ 195 D1
Trevis Rd. Ports 183 E2
Trevone Cl. Tot 100 C3
Trevor Rd. Ports 182 C2
Trevose Cl. Ch Fo 55 E2
Trevose Cl. Gos 155 E1
Trevose Cres. Ch Fo 55 E3
Trevose Way. Lo He 129 D1
Triangle Gdns. Nur 77 E2
Triangle La. Lo He 153 F3
Triangle The. Bour 206 C2
Triangle The. Whit 24 A2
Tribe Rd. Gos 181 D3
Tricketts La. Fern 165 F3
Trigon Rd. Poole 204 B4
Trimm's Dro. Woodg 70 C4
Trinidad Cres. Poole 205 E4
Trinity Cl. Gos 181 F2
Trinity Ct. Tot 76 C1
Trinity Gdns. Fare 131 D1
Trinity Green. Gos 181 F2
Trinity Rd. Bour 207 D2
Trinity Rd. Southa 103 D3
Trinity St. Fare 88 A1
Tristan Cl. Faw 178 C4
Triton Centre The. N Bad 53 E3
Triumph Cl. Fare 130 B1
Trojan Way. Wat 134 C2
Troon Cres. Cos 134 B1
Troon Rd. Broa 188 A3
Troopside Ave. Bour 191 E2
Trosnant Rd. Hav 135 F1
Trotters La. Wi Mi 164 A3
Trotts La. March 101 E1
Trotts La. Tot 101 E2
Trowbridge Cl. Rown 77 F3
Truman Rd. Bour 190 D3
Truro Rd. Portc 132 C1
Truro Rise. Bish 56 C2
Truscott Ave. Bour 207 D4
Trussell Cl. Winch 1 B2
Trussell Cres. Winch 1 B2
Tuckers La. Hamw 203 F1
Tucks Cl. Bran 194 A4
Tuckton Cl. Bour 208 B2
Tuckton Rd. Bour 208 C2
Tudor Ave. Ems 136 C2
Tudor Cl. Alderh 93 D3
Tudor Cl. Gos 180 B4
Tudor Cl. Portc 132 A1
Tudor Cl. Tot 100 B4
Tudor Cres. Ports 157 F3
Tudor Ct. Fare 154 C4
Tudor Gdns. He En 105 D3
Tudor Meadows. He En 105 D3
Tudor Rd. Broa 188 A2
Tudor Way. Ki Wo 2 A4
Tudor Wood Cl. Southa 78 C2
Tukes Ave. Gos 155 D2
Tulip Rd. Southa 79 E2
Tunstall Rd. Southa 104 C2
Tuppenny La. Herm 161 D4
Turbary Park Ave. Bour 190 A1
Turbary Rd. Fern 165 F3
Turbury Cl. Poole 205 E4
Turbury Rd. Poole 205 E4
Turk's La. Poole 205 D1
Turlin Rd. Hamw 203 E2
Turner Ave. Gos 155 E1
Turner Cres. Southa 104 A1
Turner Rd. Ports 182 B4
Turners Farm Cres. Hord 197 D1
Turnpike Way. He En 105 D4
Turnstone Gdns. Southa 78 A3
Turnworth Cl. Broa 188 B2
Turtle Cl. Stubb 154 A2
Tuscan Wlk. Ch Fo 55 F3
Tuscany Way. Wat 135 D4
Tussocks The. March 101 F1
Tutland Rd. N Bad 53 F2
Tutt's La. W Wel 50 C2
Tweed Cl. N Bad 55 D4
Tweed La. Bold 198 B4
Tweedale Rd. Bour 191 E2

Twemlow Ave. Poole 204 C2
Twiggs End Cl. Lo He 128 C2
Twiggs La. March 124 C4
Twiggs Lane End. Ashu 124 B3
Twyford Ave. Ports 157 E1
Twyford Ave. Southa 78 B1
Twyford Cl. Bour 191 E1
Twyford Dr. L on S 179 F3
Twyford Rd. Eastl 56 A3
Twyford Way. Poole 189 D1
Twynham Ave. Christ 209 D4
Twynham Cl. Down 46 C3
Twynham Rd. Bour 208 C2
Twynhams Hill. Shed 108 A4
Tylers Cl. Lym 198 B3
Tyleshades The. Rom 53 D3
Tyne Cl. N Bad 55 D3
Tynedale Cl. Gos 180 C4
Tyneham Ave. Poole 205 E4
Tyrells La. Bur 142 C2
Tyrrel Lawn. Hav 135 E4
Tyrrel Rd. Ch Fo 55 E4
Tyrrell Gdns. Bour 192 A1
Tyrrells Ct. Bran 169 D1
Tyseley Rd. Ports 182 B2
Tytherley Green. Bour 191 E1
Tytherley Green. Hav 136 A3
Tytherley Rd. Southa 104 B4

Uddens Dr. Wi Mi 164 B4
Ullswater Ave. W End 80 A1
Ullswater Rd. Oakl 163 E1
Ullswater Rd. Southa 77 F1
Ullswater. Eastl 56 A1
Undercliff Dr. Bour 207 E1
Undercliff Gdns. Southa 78 C2
Undercliff Rd. Bour 207 F2
Underdown Ave. Wat 134 B1
Undershore Rd. Bold 199 D2
Undershore Rd. Lym 198 C3
Undershore. Lym 198 C3
Underwood Cl. Broa 188 A1
Underwood Cl. Southa 78 C2
Underwood Rd. Bish 56 C2
Underwood Rd. Southa 78 C2
Unicorn Rd. Ports 182 A3
Union La. Drox 61 D1
Union Pl. Ports 182 B3
Union Rd. Hav 135 F1
Union Rd. Southa 103 E3
Union St. Fare 131 E1
Union St. Ports 182 A3
Union St. Winch 11 D4
University Cres. Southa 79 D2
University Parkway. Chilw 54 B1
University Rd. Southa 79 D2
Upham St. Uph 58 B3
Uplands Ave. B on S 212 A4
Uplands Cl. W Moo 166 A4
Uplands Cres. Fare 88 A1
Uplands Rd. Bour 191 E1
Uplands Rd. Cos 158 B4
Uplands Rd. Den 110 B3
Uplands Rd. Ro Ca 113 E1
Uplands Rd. W Moo 139 D1
Uplands Rd. Winch 1 C2
Uplands Way. Southa 79 D1
Upper Arundel St. Ports 182 B3
Upper Banister St. Southa 102 C3
Upper Bere Wood. Wat 134 C4
Upper Brook Dr. Lo He 128 C1
Upper Brook St. Winch 11 D4
Upper Brownhill Rd. Southa 77 F2
Upper Bugle St. Southa 102 C2
Upper Church Rd. Shed 107 F4
Upper Common Rd. Lym 197 F2
Upper Crabbick La. Den 110 B3
Upper Crescent Rd. N Bad 53 F3
Upper Deacon Rd. Southa 104 B3
Upper Golf Links Rd. Broa 188 A3
Upper Gordon Rd. Christ 195 D1
Upper Heyshott. Pet 41 D2
Upper High St. Winch 10 C4
Upper Hinton Rd. Bour 206 C2
Upper House Ct. Wickh 108 A2
Upper Market St. Eastl 56 A2
Upper Mead Cl. Fa Oa 57 E1
Upper Moors Rd. Co Comm 56 C4
Upper Mullins La. Hyt 125 F2
Upper New Rd. W End 80 B1
Upper Northam Cl. He En 105 D3
Upper Northam Rd. He En 104 C3
Upper Northam Rd. He En 105 D3
Upper Norwich Rd. Bour 206 C2
Upper Old St. Stubb 154 A2
Upper Piece. Den 111 D2
Upper Rd. Poole 205 E3
Upper Shaftesbury Ave. Southa 79 D1
Upper Spinney. Lo He 152 B4
Upper St Helens Rd. He En 105 D3
Upper Terrace Rd. Bour 206 C2
Upper Toothill Rd. Rown 77 F4
Upper Wardown. Pet 41 D2
Upper Weston La. Southa 104 A1
Upper Wharf. Fare 155 E4
Uppleby Rd. Poole 205 E3
Upton Cl. Hav 135 E4
Upton Cl. Upt 203 D4
Upton Cres. Rown 77 E4
Upton Ct. Upt 203 E4
Upton Grey Cl. Winch 1 B2
Upton Heath Estate. Upt 203 E4
Upton Rd. Broa 204 A4
Upton Rd. Poole 203 F4
Upton Way. Broa 187 F2
Upwey Ave. Hamw 203 F2
Utrecht Ct. Christ 209 E4

Vaggs La. Hord 196 C3
Vaggs La. New M 196 C3
Vale Dr. Southa 79 F1
Vale Gr. Gos 181 D4
Vale Rd. Bour 207 E2
Vale Rd. Poole 205 F2
Vale Rd. Red 47 E3
Vale Rd. Winch 11 E3
Vale The. Horn 88 B1
Vale The. Hyt 125 F2
Vale The. Ports 182 B1
Valencia Cl. Christ 192 B2
Valentine Ave. Southa 104 B2
Valentine Cl. Fare 130 B1
Valentine Ct. Wat 135 D4
Valerian Cl. Fa Oa 81 E3
Valerian Rd. He En 105 E3
Valetta Park. Ems 160 C4
Valetta Rd. Th Is 161 E1
Valette Rd. Bour 191 D2
Valiant Rd. Th Is 161 E1
Valiant Way. Christ 210 A4
Valley Cl. Black 150 C1
Valley Cl. Christ 192 C2
Valley Cl. Co Com 56 C4
Valley Cl. Red 47 E3
Valley Cl. Wat 134 B2
Valley La. Bran 169 F2
Valley Park Dr. Clanf 88 B2
Valley Rd. Ch Fo 55 E4
Valley Rd. Litt 1 A3
Valley Rd. Tot 100 C3
Valley Rise. Lo He 128 C2
Valley The. Winch 10 B3
Valley View. Poole 206 A4
Valleydene. Hyt 125 F1
Vallis Cl. Poole 204 B1
Valsheba Dr. Stubb 154 A1
Vanburgh Way. Ch Fo 30 A1
Vanguard Rd. Bour 191 F1
Vanguard Rd. Poole 204 B1
Vanguard Rd. Southa 104 A4
Vanstone Rd. Gos 180 B4
Vardy Cl. Southa 104 B2
Varna Rd. Southa 102 B3
Varsity Rd. Th Is 161 E1
Vaudrey Cl. Southa 78 B1
Vaughan Cl. Southa 104 C3
Vauxhall Way. Pet 40 C2
Veal's La. March 125 D4
Vecta Cl. Christ 210 B3
Vectis Rd. B on S 211 E4
Vectis Rd. Gos 180 C2
Vectis Way. Cos 157 F4
Velder Ave. Ports 183 D3
Vellan Ct. Southa 77 E1
Velmore Rd. Ch Fo 55 D2
Velsheda Ct. Hyt 126 A3
Venator Pl. Wi Mi 163 E3
Venice Cl. Wat 135 D4
Venning Ave. Bour 189 F3
Ventnor Ct. Southa 79 E3
Ventnor Rd. Gos 155 D2
Ventnor Rd. Ports 182 C2
Ventnor Way. Portc 131 F1
Venture Rd. Chilw 54 B1
Verbena Cres. Wat 112 A2
Verbena Way. He En 105 E3
Verdon Ave. Hamble 127 F2
Verger Cl. Lo He 129 E2
Verity Cres. Poole 189 D1
Verity Cres. Poole 205 D4
Vermont Cl. Southa 78 C2
Vernalls Cl. Bour 190 B3
Vernalls Gdns. Bour 190 B3
Verne Rd. Ver 115 D3
Verney Cl. Bour 190 A2
Verney Rd. Bour 190 A2
Vernham Rd. Winch 1 C1
Verno La. Christ 210 B4
Vernon Ave. Ports 183 D3
Vernon Cl. Gos 181 D3
Vernon Hill. Bi Wa 59 E1
Vernon Mews. Ports 183 D3
Vernon Rd. Gos 181 D3
Vernon Rd. Ports 158 A1
Vernon Wlk. Southa 102 C3
Verona Ave. Bour 208 B3
Verona Rd. Ch Fo 55 F3
Verulam Pl. Bour 206 C2
Verulam Rd. Poole 204 C2
Verulam Rd. Southa 103 D4
Verwood Cres. Bour 209 D2
Verwood Rd. Hav 136 A3
Verwood Rd. Ver 114 A4
Verwood Rd. W Moo 114 C1
Verwood Rd. Woodl 114 A4
Veryan. Fare 130 C1
Vespasian Rd. Southa 103 E4
Vespasian Way. Ch Fo 55 F4
Vesta Way. Ch Fo 55 F4
Vetch Cl. Christ 210 B4
Vian Cl. Gos 155 E2
Vian Pl. Ki Wo 2 B4
Vian Rd. Wat 134 C3
Vicarage Dr. He En 105 D3
Vicarage La. Cadn 75 D1
Vicarage La. Curd 106 B4
Vicarage La. Hambl 86 B2
Vicarage La. Hord 197 D1
Vicarage La. Stubb 154 B2
Vicarage La. Swan 84 B3
Vicarage La. Sway 197 E4
Vicarage Park. Red 47 E3
Vicarage Rd. Bour 190 C1
Vicarage Rd. March 101 F1
Vicarage Rd. Poole 204 B3
Vicarage Rd. Red 48 A3
Vicarage Rd. Ver 114 C3
Vicarage Way. Burt 193 E1
Vice La. Bramsh 74 A2
Viceroy Rd. Southa 104 A2
Vickers Cl. Bour 192 A1
Victena Rd. Fa Oa 57 E1
Victor Rd. Ports 182 C4
Victor Rd. Th Is 161 E1
Victor St. Southa 78 A1
Victoria Ave. Bour 190 C1
Victoria Ave. S Hay 184 C2
Victoria Ave. Wat 134 A2
Victoria Cl. Broa 187 E3
Victoria Cres. Poole 205 E3
Victoria Gdns. Fern 165 E3
Victoria Gdns. Fordi 69 E1
Victoria Glade. Net 127 E3
Victoria Gr. Ports 182 B2
Victoria Park Rd. Bour 190 C1
Victoria Pl. Bour 207 E3
Victoria Pl. Gos 181 D2
Victoria Pl. Wi Mi 163 D3
Victoria Rd N. Ports 182 B2
Victoria Rd S. Ports 182 B1
Victoria Rd. Bi Wa 83 D4
Victoria Rd. Bour 207 E3
Victoria Rd. Christ 209 F3
Victoria Rd. Eastl 56 A3
Victoria Rd. Ems 136 C1
Victoria Rd. Fern 165 E3
Victoria Rd. Fordi 69 E1
Victoria Rd. M on S 213 E2
Victoria Rd. N Hay 159 F1
Victoria Rd. Net 127 D3
Victoria Rd. Poole 205 E3
Victoria Rd. Southa 103 E1
Victoria Rd. Wat 134 C4
Victoria Rd. Wi Mi 163 D3
Victoria Rd. Winch 1 C1
Victoria Sq. L on S 179 F3
Victoria St. Gos 181 E3
Victoria St. Ports 182 B4
Victoria St. Southa 103 E3
Victory Cl. Ch Fo 55 D3
Victory Cl. W Moo 139 D3
Victory Cres. Southa 102 A3
Victory Gn. Ports 157 E1
Victory Rd. Ports 182 A3
Victory Rd. Southa 102 A3
Victory Rd. Stubb 154 B1
Victory Sq. Southa 102 A3
Victory Way. Rown 77 F4
Viewside Cl. Broa 187 E3
Viking Cl. Black 177 F4
Viking Cl. Bour 209 D2
Viking Cl. Southa 77 F2
Viking Cl. Stubb 154 A2
Viking Way. Bour 209 D2
Viking Way. Christ 210 A3
Viking Way. Horn 88 B2
Vikings The. Rom 53 D4
Villa Gdns. Wat 134 C4
Village Rd. Gos 180 C1
Village St. Pet 41 D3
Villette Cl. Christ 193 D1
Villiers Rd. Hyt 149 F4
Villiers Rd. Ports 182 B1
Villiers Rd. Southa 102 B4
Vimoutiers Ct. Fordi 69 F1
Vince Cl. Bour 190 D3
Vincent Ave. Southa 78 B1
Vincent Cl. New M 196 A1
Vincent Gr. Portc 156 B4
Vincent Rd. New M 196 A1
Vincent St. Southa 102 B4
Vincent's Gr. Southa 102 A4
Vincent's Wlk. Southa 103 D2
Vine Bank. Southa 104 A4
Vine Cl. Bour 208 A4
Vine Cl. Lo He 128 B2
Vine Coppice. Wat 134 C2
Vine Farm Cl. Poole 206 B4
Vine Farm Rd. Poole 206 A4
Vine Gdns. Southa 77 F2
Vine Hill. Pamp 162 C3
Vine Rd. Southa 78 A2
Vinegar Hill. M on S 213 E3
Vineries Cl. Wi Mi 163 F3
Vineries The. Wi Mi 163 F3
Vinery Gdns. Southa 78 B1
Vinery Rd. Southa 78 B1
Vineside. Gos 155 F1
Viney Ave. Rom 53 D4
Viney Rd. Lym 198 C1
Vineyard Cl. Southa 103 E2
Vineyards The. N Bad 54 A2
Vinnells La. W Meo 37 E3
Vinneys Cl. Burt 193 E1
Vinson Rd. Liss 21 D2
Violet Ave. Stubb 154 A1
Violet Farm Cl. Broa 187 E4
Violet La. New M 196 A2
Violet Rd. Southa 79 D2
Virginia Cl. Poole 205 E4
Virginia Park Rd. Gos 180 C3
Viscount Dr. Christ 210 A3
Viscount Wlk. Bour 189 E3
Vita Rd. Ports 157 F2
Vivash Rd. Ports 182 C3
Vixen Cl. Stubb 154 A1
Vixen Wlk. New M 196 A3
Vulcan Cl. Southa 101 F3
Vulcan Rd. Southa 101 F3
Vulcan Rd. Th Is 161 E1
Vulcan Way. Christ 210 A4

Wad The. W Wit 186 C1
Wade Court Rd. Hav 160 A4
Wade La. Hav 160 A4
Wadham Rd. Ports 157 E1
Wadhurst Gdns. Southa 127 D4
Wadhurst Rd. He En 105 E3
Wagtail Way. Portc 155 F4
Wainscot Rd. Ports 183 D1
Wainsford Cl. Lym 198 A1
Wainsford Rd. Hord 197 F1
Wainsford Rd. Hord 213 F4
Wainsford Rd. Lym 197 F1
Wainwright Cl. Cos 158 B3
Wait End Rd. Wat 134 C3
Wake Lawn. Ports 183 E2
Wakefield Ave. Bour 190 C3
Wakefield Ave. Fare 130 C2
Wakefield Ct. Southa 80 A1
Wakefield Rd. Southa 80 A1
Wakely Rd. Bour 190 D3
Wakesford Way. Hav 136 C4
Walberton Ave. Cos 158 A4
Walcheren Pl. Hamw 203 E2
Walcott Ave. Christ 192 C1
Walden Gdns. Horn 112 A4
Walden Rd. Ports 157 E1
Walditch Gdns. Broa 188 C1
Waldren Cl. Poole 204 C1
Wales St. Winch 11 D4
Walford Cl. Wi Mi 163 E3
Walford Rd. Cos 133 E1
Walhampton Hill. Lym 198 C3
Walker Gdns. He En 81 E1
Walker Pl. Gos 155 E1
Walker Rd. Ports 157 E1
Walker's Lane S. Black 177 F4
Walkers Cl. Fa Oa 57 E1
Walkers La N. Black 150 C1
Walkford La. New M 195 E2
Walkford Rd. Christ 195 E1
Walkford Way. Christ 195 D1
Walkwood Ave. Bour 208 A4
Wallace Rd. Broa 188 A2
Wallace Rd. Ports 182 C4
Wallace Rd. Southa 103 F1
Wallington Ct. Fare 154 C3
Wallington Dr. Ch Fo 55 D4
Wallington Hill. Fare 131 E1
Wallington Rd. Ports 157 F1
Wallington Shore Rd. Fare 131 E1
Wallington Way. Fare 131 E1
Wallis Gdns. Wat 111 F1
Wallis Rd. Bour 190 A1
Wallis Rd. Wat 111 F1
Walliscott Rd. Bour 190 A1
Wallisdean Ave. Fare 154 C4
Wallisdean Rd. Ports 183 D4
Wallisdown Rd. Bour 190 A1
Wallisdown Rd. Poole 206 B4
Wallrock Wlk. Ems 136 C2
Walmer Cl. Eastl 56 A4
Walmer Rd. Ports 182 C3
Walnut Ave. Southa 79 F3
Walnut Cl. Ch Fo 30 B1
Walnut Cl. Southa 77 F1
Walnut Dr. Stubb 154 A1
Walnut Gr. Southa 77 F1
Walnut Tree Cl. S Hay 184 C2
Walnut Tree Dr. Westb 137 F2
Walpole Rd. Bour 207 F3
Walpole Rd. Gos 181 E2
Walpole Rd. Winch 10 B3
Walpole Terr. Gos 181 D2
Walsall Rd. Ports 183 D3
Walsford Rd. Bour 206 B3
Walsingham Cl. Cos 133 E1
Walsingham Dene. Bour 207 F4
Walsingham Gdns. Southa 79 F2
Waltham Cl. Drox 61 D1
Waltham Cl. Portc 132 B1
Waltham Cres. Southa 78 B2
Waltham Rd. Bour 208 A3
Waltham St. Ports 182 A2
Walton Cl. Gos 181 D2
Walton Ct. Fare 130 B2
Walton Pl. Winch 10 B3
Walton Rd. Bour 190 B1
Walton Rd. Cos 158 A3
Walton Rd. Gos 181 D2
Walton Rd. Poole 205 D3
Walton Rd. Southa 104 B2
Waltons Ave. Holb 150 B2
Wandesford Pl. Gos 156 A1
Wangfield La. Curd 82 B1
Wansbeck Cl. N Bad 55 D3
Wanstead Cl. Rin 117 D1
Warbler Cl. Southa 78 A3
Warblington Ave. Hav 136 A1
Warblington Cl. Ch Fo 55 D2
Warblington Rd. Ems 160 C4
Warblington St. Ports 182 A2
Warborne La. Bold 199 D4
Warburton Cl. Southa 104 C2
Warburton Rd. Poole 204 C4
Warburton Rd. Southa 104 C2
Ward Cres. Ems 137 D2
Ward Rd. Ports 183 D1
Warden Cl. W End 80 B1
Wardens Cl. S Hay 184 C3
Wardle Rd. Co Com 56 B4
Wareham Rd. Broa 187 E2
Wareham Rd. Upt 187 E2
Warfield Ave. Wat 134 C4
Warfield Cres. Wat 134 C4
Warland Way. Broa 187 F4
Warlock Cl. Southa 104 B2
Warmwell Cl. Bour 191 D2
Warmwell Cl. Poole 188 C1
Warnes La. Bur 142 C1
Warnford Cl. Gos 180 C2
Warnford Cres. Hav 135 E3
Warnford Rd. Bour 208 B4
Warren Ave. Ch Fo 55 F3
Warren Ave. Christ 209 F3
Warren Ave. Ports 183 D3
Warren Ave. Southa 78 A1
Warren Cl. Ch Fo 55 F3
Warren Cl. S Hay 184 B2
Warren Cl. Southa 78 A1
Warren Cl. St Le 140 B3
Warren Cres. Southa 78 A1
Warren Dr. St Le 140 B3
Warren Edge Cl. Bour 208 C2
Warren Edge Rd. Bour 208 C2
Warren Gdns. Rom 28 A1
Warren La. Beaul 200 C4
Warren La. Cole 19 E3
Warren La. Frox G 19 D2
Warren La. Ows 33 F4
Warren La. St Le 140 B3
Warren Pl. Tot 76 B1
Warren Rd. Bour 206 A1
Warren Rd. Liss 21 D4
Warren Rd. Poole 205 E2
Warren Rd. Winch 11 E4
Warren The. Holb 150 A3
Warren Wlk. Fern 165 D4
Warrior Busnss Ctr The. Cos 158 C4
Warrys Cl. Hyt 150 A4
Warsash Cl. Hav 135 F3
Warsash Gr. Gos 155 D1
Warsash Rd. Lo He 129 D1
Warton Cl. E Bol 175 E3
Warwick Ave. New M 196 A2
Warwick Cl. Ch Fo 55 D2
Warwick Cl. Lon S 180 A2
Warwick Cl. Winch 2 A1
Warwick Cres. Burs 127 F4
Warwick Cres. Ports 182 B2
Warwick Pl. Bour 208 A3
Warwick Pl. W Wel 50 C2
Warwick Rd. Bour 208 A3
Warwick Rd. Poole 205 E2
Warwick Rd. Southa 78 B1
Warwick Rd. Tot 100 C4
Wasdale Cl. Horn 88 B1
Washbrook Rd. Cos 133 E1
Washington Ave. Bour 207 E3
Washington Rd. Ems 136 C1
Washington Rd. Ports 182 B4
Watcombe Rd. Bour 208 B3
Water Cl. Winch 11 D4
Water La. Bour 208 B4
Water La. Hyt 125 F1
Water La. Tot 100 C4
Water La. Winch 11 D4
Water Tower Rd. Broa 188 B2
Water's Edge. He En 105 D3
Waterbeech Dr. He En 105 E4
Waterberry Dr. Wat 111 E1
Waterditch Rd. Bran 194 A2
Waterditch Rd. Burt 194 A2
Waterford Cl. Lym 198 C2
Waterford Gdns. Christ 211 D4
Waterford Pl. Christ 211 D4
Waterford Rd. Christ 211 D4
Waterford Rd. New M 196 B2
Waterhouse La. Southa 102 A4
Waterhouse Way. Southa 102 A4
Waterlock Gdns. Ports 183 E2
Waterloo Cl. Wat 111 E2
Waterloo Ind Est. He En 81 D1
Waterloo Rd. Bour 206 C4

Waterloo Rd. Broa 187 D3
Waterloo Rd. Broa 204 B4
Waterloo Rd. Gos 181 E1
Waterloo Rd. Hav 135 F1
Waterloo Rd. Lym 198 C2
Waterloo Rd. Southa 102 B3
Waterloo St. Ports 182 B2
Waterloo Terr. Southa 102 C3
Watermans La. Hyt 125 F1
Watermead Rd. Cos 158 C4
Watermead. Christ 209 D3
Watermill Rd. Christ 209 D4
Waters Green Ct. Brock 146 A1
Waters The. Fare 130 C3
Watersedge Gdns. Ems 160 C4
Watersedge Rd. Portc 157 D4
Waterside Cl. Rin 117 D1
Waterside Gdns. Fare 131 E1
Waterside Rd. Rom 28 A1
Waterside Sq. Hyt 125 F3
Waterside. Christ 209 F2
Waterside. Hyt 126 A3
Waterworks Rd. Cos 158 B4
Waterworks Rd. Ott 31 E2
Waterworks Rd. Pet 41 D3
Watery La. Christ 210 A4
Watery La. Upt 203 D4
Watkin Rd. Bour 207 F2
Watkin Rd. He En 81 E1
Watley La. Twyf 58 A3
Watson Wlk. Tot 100 B4
Watton Cl. Bour 192 A1
Watton La. Meons 61 F1
Watton Rd. Holb 150 B2
Watts Rd. He En 105 E4
Watts Rd. Ports 182 B4
Wavell Ave. Broa 188 A1
Wavell Rd. Bour 190 A2
Wavell Rd. Gos 155 E2
Wavell Rd. Southa 104 A4
Wavell Way. Winch 10 B3
Wavendon Ave. B on S 211 F4
Waveney Green. Southa 77 F1
Waveny Cl. L on S 179 F3
Waverley Ave. Net 127 E3
Waverley Cl. Fordi 69 F2
Waverley Cl. Rom 28 A1
Waverley Cres. Poole 204 B3
Waverley Ct. Net 127 E3
Waverley Gr. Ports 182 C1
Waverley Path. Gos 180 C2
Waverley Rd. Bour 207 D2
Waverley Rd. Cos 158 B4
Waverley Rd. Fordi 69 F2
Waverley Rd. New M 196 A1
Waverley Rd. Ports 182 C1
Waverley Rd. Southa 102 B3
Wayfarer Cl. Lo He 128 C1
Wayfarer Cl. Ports 183 E3
Wayground Rd. Broa 162 C1
Wayman Rd. Broa 187 F3
Wayne Rd. Poole 205 D3
Waynflete Cl. Bi Wa 83 E4
Waynflete Pl. Winch 10 B3
Wayside Cl. M on S 213 E3
Wayside Rd. Bour 208 C2
Wayside Rd. St Le 166 C4
Wayte St. Cos 157 F4
Weald Cl. Lo He 129 D2
Weardale Rd. Ch Fo 55 E2
Weavers Cl. W Moo 138 C1
Weavers Green. Hav 136 B2
Weavers Pl. Ch Fo 55 D4
Weavills Rd. Bish 57 D1
Web Cl. Eastl 56 A2
Webb Cl. S Hay 185 D1
Webb La. S Hay 185 D1
Webb Rd. Portc 156 B3
Webb's Way. Bour 189 F1
Webbs Cl. St Le 139 E3
Webburn Gdns. W End 80 A2
Webster Rd. Bour 191 D2
Webster Rd. Winch 1 A1
Wedgewood Cl. Holb 150 B2
Wedgewood Cl. Stubb 154 B1
Wedgewood Way. Wat 111 F1
Wedgwood Dr. Poole 205 D1
Wedmore Cl. Winch 10 A2
Weeke Manor Cl. Winch 1 B1
Weevil La. Gos 181 E3
Welbeck Ave. Southa 79 D1
Welch Rd. Gos 181 D4
Welch Rd. Ports 182 C1
Welch Way. Southa 77 F3
Welchwood Cl. Wat 111 F3
Weldon Ave. Bour 189 F3
Well Cl. New M 195 F1
Well Copse Cl. Horn 88 B1
Well Hill. Hambl 110 B4
Well House Cl. Whits 45 D2
Well House La. Ki Wo 1 C3
Well La. Hamble 128 A1
Well La. Poole 204 B2
Well La. Swan 84 A4
Well Meadow. Hav 135 F3
Welland Gdns. W End 80 A1
Welland Green. Southa 101 F4
Welland Rd. Wi Mi 163 E2
Wellands Rd. Lyn 122 A3
Wellbrook Gdns. Ch Fo 55 D4
Wellers Cl. Tot 100 A4
Welles Rd. Ch Fo 55 E3
Wellesley Ave. Christ 210 B4
Wellesley Cl. Wat 134 C4
Wellington Ave. Christ 210 B4
Wellington Ave. Southa 104 A4
Wellington Cl. Horn 112 B3
Wellington Gr. Portc 156 B4
Wellington Rd. Bour 207 D3
Wellington Rd. Poole 205 E2
Wellington Rd. Southa 79 F1
Wellington St. Ports 182 B2
Wellington Way. Wat 134 C4
Wellow Cl. Hav 135 E2
Wellow Cl. Southa 104 B4
Wellow Dro. Plai 50 C4
Wellow Gdns. Lo He 129 E1
Wellow Wood Rd. Plai 50 B4
Wellowbrook Cl. N Bad 55 D3
Wells Pl. Eastl 56 A1
Wellsmoor. Lo He 129 E2
Wellswood Gdns. Ro Ca 113 E2
Wellsworth La. Ro Ca 113 E2
Wembley Gr. Cos 158 A3
Wembley Way. Fa Oa 57 E1
Wendover Cl. B on S 195 F1
Wendover Rd. Hav 135 F1
Wentworth Ave. Bour 208 A2
Wentworth Dr. Broa 188 A3
Wentworth Dr. Horn 112 A4
Wentworth Gdns. Holb 150 B2
Wentworth Gdns. Southa 104 A1
Wentworth Gr. Holb 150 B2
Wentworth Rd. Bour 208 A2
Wescott Way. Bour 189 F2
Wesley Cl. Southa 104 B2
Wesley Gr. Ports 158 A2
Wesley Rd. Ki Wo 2 B4
Wesley Rd. Wi Mi 163 F3
Wessex Ave. New M 196 A1
Wessex Cl. Black 177 F4
Wessex Cl. Christ 210 B4
Wessex Dr. Winch 1 C1
Wessex Estate. Rin 141 D4
Wessex Gdns. Portc 156 A4
Wessex Gdns. Rom 53 D4
Wessex La. Southa 79 E2
Wessex Rd. Horn 88 B2
Wessex Rd. Poole 205 D2
Wessex Rd. Rin 141 D4
Wessex Trade Centre. Poole 205 D4
Wessex Way. Bour 207 E3
West Ave. W Moo 138 C4
West Bargate. Southa 102 C2
West Bay Rd. Southa 102 B3
West Borough. Wi Mi 163 D3
West Butts St. Poole 204 A1
West Cl. Lym 198 A1
West Cl. Ver 114 B3
West Cliff Gdns. Bour 206 C1
West Cliff Mews. Bour 206 C1
West Cliff Rd. Bour 206 B1
West Common. Black 177 F3
West Ct. Ports 182 C4
West Dr. Bish 56 B2
West End Cl. Winch 10 C4
West End Rd. He En 104 C2
West Haye Rd. S Hay 185 E1
West Hayes. Lym 198 C2
West Hill Dr. Hyt 125 F3
West Hill Dr. Winch 10 C4
West Hill Park. Winch 10 B4
West Hill Pl. Bour 206 B2
West Hill Rd. Bour 206 C1
West Hoe La. Bi Wa 83 F4
West Horton La. Bish 56 C1
West Howe Cl. Bour 190 A2
West La. Hord 197 F1
West La. N Bad 53 F3
West La. N Hay 184 C3
West La. S Hay 184 C3
West Marlands Rd. Southa 102 C3
West Moors Rd. Fern 165 E4
West Moors Rd. W Moo 138 B3
West Moors Rd. W Moo 138 C4
West Overcliff Dr. Bour 206 B1
West Park La. Dame 68 B3
West Park Rd. Southa 102 C3
West Quay Rd. Poole 204 A1
West Quay Rd. Southa 102 C2
West Rd. Bour 208 A2
West Rd. Bran 194 A4
West Rd. Ems 160 C4
West Rd. He En 104 C3
West Rd. Hyt 125 E1
West Rd. M on S 213 D3
West Rd. Southa 103 D1
West Rd. Southa 103 F1
West Row. Wi Mi 163 D2
West St. Ems 160 C4
West St. Fare 88 A1
West St. Fordi 69 F1
West St. Hambl 86 B1
West St. Hav 135 F1
West St. Hyt 125 F3
West St. Lo He 153 F4
West St. Poole 204 A1
West St. Portc 156 B4
West St. Ports 181 F2
West St. Rin 140 C4
West St. Sob 85 E3
West St. Southa 102 C2
West St. Southw 132 C3
West St. Wi Mi 163 D3
West Station Terr. Bour 206 B2
West View Rd. Christ 209 F3
West Way Cl. Bour 191 D1
West Way. Bour 191 D1
West Way. Broa 188 A2
West Way. Lo He 129 F2
West Way. Lym 198 B1
Westbeams Rd. Sway 172 A1
Westborn Rd. Fare 88 B1
Westbourne Ave. Ems 137 D1
Westbourne Ave. Holb 150 B2
Westbourne Cl. Bour 206 B2
Westbourne Cl. Ems 137 D1
Westbourne Cres. Southa 79 D1
Westbourne Park Rd. Bour 206 A1
Westbourne Rd. Ems 137 A2
Westbourne Rd. Ports 182 C4
Westbourne Rd. Westb 137 D2
Westbrook Cl. Lo He 129 D3
Westbrook Gr. Wat 134 B2
Westbrook Rd. Portc 156 B3
Westbrook Way. Southa 79 E2
Westbrooke Cl. Wat 112 A3
Westbury Cl. B on S 212 A4
Westbury Cl. Bran 194 A4
Westbury Cl. Christ 194 B1
Westbury Cl. Cos 133 D1
Westbury Ct. He En 105 E3
Westbury Rd. Fare 88 B1
Westbury Rd. Rin 141 D4
Westbury Rd. Southa 101 F4
Westby Rd. Bour 207 F2
Westcliff Cl. L on S 179 F4
Westcliff Wlk. Hyt 125 F3
Westcot Rd. Holb 150 A2
Westcroft Park. Broa 188 B2
Westcroft Rd. Gos 180 C3
Westdown Rd. Bour 190 D3
Westerham Cl. Cos 157 F4
Westerham Rd. Bour 206 A2
Westering. Rom 53 E4
Western Ave. B on S 211 E4
Western Ave. Bour 190 B2
Western Ave. Ems 160 B4
Western Ave. Poole 205 F1
Western Ave. Southa 102 A3
Western Cl. Bour 190 B3
Western District Cut. Southa 102 B4
Western Espl. Southa 102 C2
Western Par. Ems 160 C4
Western Par. Ports 182 A1
Western Rd. Ch Fo 30 C1
Western Rd. Cos 157 E4
Western Rd. Fare 88 A1
Western Rd. Hav 135 F1
Western Rd. Liss 20 C2
Western Rd. Lym 198 B2
Western Rd. Poole 206 A1
Western Rd. W End 80 C1
Western Rd. Winch 10 C4
Western Terr. Ports 157 E1
Western Way. Fare 131 D1
Western Way. Gos 180 C1
Westfield Ave. Fare 154 C4
Westfield Ave. S Hay 184 C2
Westfield Cl. Hamble 127 F1
Westfield Cl. Wi Mi 163 D3
Westfield Cnr. Southa 79 F2
Westfield Comm. Hamble 127 F1
Westfield Cres. Ch Fo 55 E2
Westfield Dro. Beau 34 C4
Westfield Gdns. Christ 194 A1
Westfield Rd. Bour 208 C2
Westfield Rd. Ch Fo 55 E2
Westfield Rd. Gos 181 D2
Westfield Rd. Lym 199 D1
Westfield Rd. Ports 183 D2
Westfield Rd. Southa 102 A4
Westfield Rd. Tot 100 C4
Westgate St. Southa 102 C2
Westgate. Stubb 154 B1
Westham Cl. Broa 188 C2
Westheath Rd. Broa 188 A2
Westland Dr. Wat 134 C2
Westland Gdns. Gos 181 D2
Westlands Ct. Bran 194 A4
Westlands Gr. Portc 156 B4
Westley Cl. Winch 1 B1
Westley Gr. Fare 154 C4
Westmead Cl. S Hay 184 C2
Westminster Gate. Winch 10 A3
Westminster Gdns. Lo He 129 E2
Westminster Pl. Ports 182 B4
Westminster Rd E. Poole 206 A1
Westminster Rd. M on S 213 D2
Westminster Rd. Poole 206 A1
Westmorland Way. Ch Fo 55 F3
Weston Ave. Ports 183 D2
Weston Cl. Southa 103 F1
Weston Cres. Southa 104 B4
Weston Dr. Bour 207 D2
Weston Grove Rd. Southa 103 E1
Weston La. Buri 65 E4
Weston La. Nur 77 D2
Weston La. Southa 103 F1
Weston Par. Southa 126 C4
Weston Rd. Eastl 56 A2
Weston Rd. Pet 41 D2
Weston Rd. Wi Mi 163 F4
Westons La. Poole 204 B1
Westover La. St Le 140 B3
Westover Rd. Bour 206 C2
Westover Rd. M on S 213 E2
Westover Rd. Ports 183 D4
Westover Rd. Southa 101 E4
Westridge Rd. Southa 103 D4
Westrow Gdns. Southa 102 C4
Westrow Rd. Southa 102 C4
Westside View. Wat 111 E1
Westview Rd. Spar 1 A1
Westward Rd. He En 105 E4
Westway. Cos 158 C4
Westways. Stubb 154 B1
Westwood Ave. Fern 165 E3
Westwood Cl. Ems 137 D1
Westwood Ct. Tot 76 B1
Westwood Gdns. Ch Fo 55 F4
Westwood Rd. Lyn 121 F3
Westwood Rd. Net 127 D4
Westwood Rd. Ports 157 F2
Westwood Rd. Southa 103 D4
Westwood View. Kilm 14 C1
Wetherby Cl. Broa 188 A1
Wetherby Ct. Tot 100 B4
Wetherby Gdns. Tot 100 B4
Weyhill Cl. Hav 135 E3
Weyhill Cl. Portc 132 B1
Weyman's Ave. Bour 190 B3
Weymans Dr. Bour 190 B3
Weymouth Ave. Gos 180 C4
Weymouth Rd. Poole 205 E3
Weymouth Rd. Ports 157 E1
Whaddon Chase. Stubb 154 A1
Whaddon Ct. Hav 135 E3
Whaddon La. Co Com 58 A4
Whaddon La. Ows 33 D2
Whale Island Way. Ports 157 E1
Whalesmead Cl. Bish 56 C1
Whalesmead Rd. Bish 56 C1
Wharf Cl. Poole 205 F3
Wharf Hill. Winch 11 D3
Wharf Rd. Ports 182 B4
Wharf Rd. Southa 103 E2
Wharfdale Rd. Bour 206 B2
Wharfdale Rd. Poole 205 F3
Wharncliffe Gdns. Christ 211 D4
Wharncliffe Rd. Bour 207 E2
Wharncliffe Rd. Christ 211 D4
Wharncliffe Rd. Southa 103 E2
Whartons Cl. Ashu 100 B2
Whartons La. Ashu 100 B2
Whatleigh Cl. Poole 204 B1
Wheatcroft Dr. Southa 80 A1
Wheatcroft Rd. L on S 179 F3
Wheatear Dr. Pet 41 E1
Wheatears Dr. W Wel 50 C2
Wheatland Cl. Winch 10 B3
Wheatlands Ave. S Hay 185 F1
Wheatlands Cl. S Hay 185 F1
Wheatlands. Lo He 129 E2
Wheatley Green. Hav 135 E3
Wheaton Rd. Bour 208 A3
Wheatsheaf Ct. He En 105 D3
Wheatsheaf Dr. Wat 111 E2
Wheatstone Rd. Ports 182 C2
Wheeler Cl. Gos 181 D3
Wheelers La. Bour 189 E3
Wheelers Wlk. Black 177 F4
Whernside Cl. Southa 101 F4
Whichers Gate Cl. Hav 136 A4
Whichers Gate Cl. Ro Ca 136 A4
Whichers Gate Rd. Ro Ca 136 A4
Whitemoor La. Rom 75 F2
Whimbrel Cl. Ports 183 E3
Whinchat Cl. Southa 78 A3
Whincroft Cl. Fern 165 F4
Whincroft Dr. Fern 165 F3
Whinfield Rd. Hyt 149 F4
Whinwhistle Rd. W Wel 51 D1
Whippingham Cl. Cos 157 E4
Whistler Cl. Southa 104 B2
Whistler Rd. Southa 104 B2
Whitaker Cres. Lym 198 B2
Whitby Ave. Broa 188 A1
Whitby Cl. Christ 192 B2
Whitby Cres. Broa 188 A1
Whitby Rd. M on S 213 D2
Whitchurch Ave. Broa 188 B2
Whitcombe Gdns. Ports 182 C3
White Barn Cres. Hord 197 D2
White Beam Rise. Clanf 88 B3
White Cl. Poole 205 D4
White Cloud Park. Ports 182 C2
White Cloud Pl. Ports 182 C2
White Dirt La. Horn 88 B2
White Gates. Durl 82 A3
White Hart La. Cadn 98 C4
White Hart La. Portc 156 B4
White Hart Rd. Fa Oa 57 E1
White Hart Rd. Gos 181 D2
White Hart Rd. Ports 182 A2
White Heather Ct. Hyt 126 A3
White Horse Dr. Poole 204 B3
White Horse La. Den 111 D3
White Horses. B on S 211 F4
White House Gdns. Pet 40 C3
White House Gdns. Southa 102 A3
White Knights. B on S 211 F4
White Ladies Cl. Hav 136 A1
White Lion Wlk. Gos 181 E3
White Lodge Gdns. Fare 130 C2
White Rd. Bish 56 B2
White Swan Rd. Ports 182 A3
White Way. Meons 61 D4
White's Rd. Southa 104 A3
Whitebeam Cl. Fare 154 C4
Whitebeam Cl. Wat 112 B3
Whitebeam Rd. He En 105 E3
Whitebeam Way. N Bad 54 A3
Whitebeam Way. Ver 115 D3
Whitechimney Row. Westb 137 D2
Whitecliff Cres. Poole 205 D1
Whitecliff Rd. Poole 204 C1
Whitecliffe Ave. Ports 183 D4
Whitecross Cl. Broa 188 C2
Whitecross Gdns. Ports 157 F2
Whitefield Rd. Holb 150 B2
Whitefield Rd. New M 196 A1
Whitefield Rd. Poole 205 D1
Whitehall. Christ 209 D3
Whitehaven. Horn 112 B3
Whitehayes Cl. Burt 193 E1
Whitehayes Rd. Burt 193 E1
Whitehorn Dr. Red 73 E4
Whitehorn Rd. S Hay 185 D2
Whitehouse Rd. Oakl 163 E1
Whitelaw Rd. Southa 102 A4
Whiteleaf La. Meons 86 B4
Whiteley La. Lo He 129 F3
Whiteley La. Swanw 106 B1
Whiteley Way. Lo He 129 E3
Whitemoor Rd. Brock 145 E1
Whitenap Cl. Rom 53 D3
Whitenap La. Rom 53 E3
Whiteoak Wlk. Hav 136 A3
Whites Hill. Ows 33 D2
Whites Hill. Ows 58 C2
Whites La. Faw 151 D2
Whiteshoot Hill. Red 47 F2
Whiteshoot Rd. Red 47 F2
Whiteshute La. Winch 10 C3
Whitestone Cl. Southa 101 F4
Whitewater Rise. Hyt 125 F1
Whiteways. Wi Mi 163 F3
Whitfield Park. St Le 140 A3
Whitle Cl. Westb 137 D3
Whitsbury Cl. Bour 191 E1
Whitsbury Rd. Fordi 69 F2
Whitsbury Rd. Hav 136 A3
Whitstable Rd. Cos 157 F4
Whittington Cl. Cos 133 D1
Whittington Cl. Hyt 125 F2
Whittle Ave. Lo He 129 E3
Whittle Rd. Fern 164 C4
Whittles Way. Poole 204 A1
Whitwell Rd. Ports 182 C1
Whitwell. Net 127 E4
Whitworth Cl. Gos 181 D2
Whitworth Cres. Southa 103 E4
Whitworth Rd. Gos 181 D3
Whitworth Rd. Ports 182 C4
Whitworth Rd. Southa 103 E4
Whyte Cl. Holb 150 A2
Whyteways. Eastl 56 A2
Wick Farm. Bour 209 D3
Wick La. Bour 209 D3
Wick La. Christ 209 D3
Wick La. Down 46 A4
Wicket Rd. Bour 190 B3
Wicket The. Hyt 125 F1
Wickfield Ave. Christ 209 D3
Wickfield Cl. Christ 209 D3
Wickham Rd. Bour 208 A3
Wickham Rd. Drox 85 D3
Wickham Rd. Fare 131 D3
Wickham St. Ports 182 A3
Wicklea Rd. Bour 209 D2
Wicklow Dr. N Bad 55 D3
Wickmeads Rd. Bour 209 D3
Wickor Cl. Ems 137 D1
Wickor Way. Ems 137 D1
Wicor Mill La. Portc 156 A4
Widbury Rd. Lym 198 B1
Widden Cl. Sway 172 A1
Widdicombe Ave. Poole 205 F1
Wide La. Southa 79 F3
Wide Lane Cl. Brock 145 F1
Widecombe Dr. Hyt 125 F2
Widgeon Cl. Gos 181 D4
Widgeon Cl. Southa 78 A3
Widgeon Ct. Portc 155 F4
Widlers La. Uph 58 C3
Widley Court Dr. Cos 158 A4
Widley Ct. Fare 155 D3
Widley Gdns. Wat 134 B2
Widley Rd. Cos 158 A4
Widley Rd. Ports 157 E1
Widley Wlk. Southw 133 F2
Widworthy Dr. Broa 187 F3
Wield Cl. Hav 135 E2
Wigan Cres. Hav 135 D1

Wight Wlk. Fern 165 F1
Wilberforce Cl. Winch 10 B3
Wilberforce Rd. Gos 181 E1
Wilberforce Rd. Ports 182 B2
Wild Ridings. Fare 154 B4
Wild Rose Cres. Lo He 128 C1
Wildburn Cl. Tot 76 B1
Wilde Cl. Tot 100 B4
Wildern Cl. Lo He 128 C2
Wildern La. He En 105 E4
Wilderness Hts. W End 80 B1
Wilderton Rd W. Poole 206 A2
Wilderton Rd. Poole 205 F2
Wildfell Cl. Christ 193 D1
Wildmoor Wlk. Hav 136 A3
Wildown Rd. Bour 209 D2
Wilfred Rd. Bour 207 F2
Wilkins Cl. Clanf 88 A3
Wilkins Way. Poole 204 A1
Wilkinson Dr. Bour 192 A1
Willersley Cl. Cos 133 E1
Willett Rd. Broa 162 C1
Willett Rd. Oakl 163 E1
William Cl. Christ 195 D1
William Cl. Stubb 154 B1
William Rd. Bour 207 F4
William Rd. Lym 198 C3
William St. Southa 103 E3
Williams Cl. Gos 180 B4
Williams Cl. Holb 150 B2
Williams Rd. Ports 158 A2
Willis Ave. N Bad 54 A2
Willis Rd. Gos 181 E2
Willis Rd. Ports 182 B3
Willis Rd. Southa 79 E3
Willis Way. Poole 204 A3
Willis Waye. Ki Wo 2 B3
Willow Ave. Fordi 69 F1
Willow Cl. Hav 136 A1
Willow Cl. He En 105 E3
Willow Cl. St Le 139 E2
Willow Cl. Upt 203 E3
Willow Cl. W End 80 C2
Willow Ct. Southa 78 A2
Willow Dr. Christ 209 D3
Willow Dr. Rin 141 D3
Willow Dr. Wi Mi 164 B3
Willow Gdns. N Bad 53 F3
Willow Gdns. Westb 137 D2
Willow Gr. Fa Oa 57 E1
Willow Herb Cl. Lo He 128 C1
Willow Mead. Bour 191 E2
Willow Pl. Christ 209 E3
Willow Pl. Gos 181 D3
Willow Rd. Bi Wa 83 F4
Willow Rd. Liss 21 D2
Willow Tree Ave. Wat 112 A1
Willow Tree Gdns. Fare 154 C4
Willow Tree Rise. Bour 190 A2
Willow Tree Wlk. Southa 104 A2
Willow Way. Christ 209 D3
Willow Way. Fern 165 E4
Willowdale Cl. Pet 40 A2
Willowdene Cl. Hav 135 D2
Willowdene Cl. New M 196 B2
Willows The. B on S 212 A4
Willows The. Den 110 C2
Wills Rd. Poole 205 F2
Wills Way. Rom 53 D3
Willwood Cl. Broa 188 C2
Wilmer Rd. Eastl 56 A1
Wilmington Cl. Southa 79 F2
Wilmot Cl. Bish 56 C3
Wilmott Cl. Gos 180 C3
Wilmott La. Gos 180 C3
Wilmur Cres. Poole 204 C3
Wilson Gr. Ports 182 C2
Wilson Rd. Bour 207 F3
Wilson Rd. Poole 205 E2
Wilson Rd. Ports 157 E1
Wilson St. Southa 103 E3
Wilton Ave. Southa 102 C3
Wilton Cl. Christ 192 B1
Wilton Cl. Gos 180 C2
Wilton Cres. Southa 78 B1
Wilton Dr. Wat 112 A3
Wilton Gdns. New M 195 F2
Wilton Gdns. Southa 78 B1
Wilton Pl. Ports 182 B1
Wilton Rd. Bour 207 F3
Wilton Rd. Southa 78 B1
Wilton Terr. Ports 182 B1
Wiltshire Gdns. Bran 193 F4
Wiltshire Rd. Bran 193 F4
Wiltshire Rd. Ch Fo 55 E2
Wiltshire St. Ports 182 A2
Wilverley Ave. Bour 191 F1
Wilverley Ave. Hav 136 A2
Wilverley Cl. Lym 198 A1
Wilverley Pl. Black 150 C1
Wilverley Rd. Brock 145 F1
Wilverley Rd. Brock 170 C2
Wilverley Rd. Christ 210 A4
Wimbledon Park Rd. Ports 182 B1
Wimborne Rd E. Fern 165 E3
Wimborne Rd W. Fern 164 B3
Wimborne Rd W. Wi Mi 164 B3
Wimborne Rd. Bour 190 B3
Wimborne Rd. Bour 206 C3
Wimborne Rd. Broa 162 C1
Wimborne Rd. Poole 204 B3
Wimborne Rd. Ports 183 D2
Wimborne Rd. Wi Mi 163 F3
Wimpole St. Ports 182 B3
Wimpson Gdns. Southa 77 F1
Wimpson La. Southa 101 F4
Wincanton Way. Wat 112 A1
Winchat Cl. Fare 130 B2
Winchcombe Rd. Cos 133 D1
Winchester By Pass. Comp 10 C1
Winchester By Pass. Twyf 10 C1
Winchester By Pass. Winch 11 D2
Winchester Cl. Net 127 D3
Winchester Hill. Rom 53 D4
Winchester Rd. Bi Wa 83 D4
Winchester Rd. Botl 81 F2
Winchester Rd. Ch Fo 55 F4
Winchester Rd. Durl 81 F2
Winchester Rd. Fa Oa 81 F2
Winchester Rd. Langr 39 F2
Winchester Rd. N Bad 28 B1
Winchester Rd. New M 196 B2
Winchester Rd. Ows 58 B2
Winchester Rd. Pet 39 F2
Winchester Rd. Ports 182 C4
Winchester Rd. Rom 28 B1
Winchester Rd. Rom 52 C4
Winchester Rd. Shed 83 F1
Winchester Rd. Southa 78 B1
Winchester Rd. Uph 58 B2
Winchester St. Botl 106 A4
Winchester St. Southa 102 C3
Winchester Way. Tot 100 B4
Winchfield Cl. Southa 104 A1
Winchfield Cres. Hav 135 E2
Windbury Rd. Southa 77 F1
Windermere Ave. Southa 77 F1
Windermere Ave. Stubb 154 B2
Windermere Gdns. Tot 100 C4
Windermere Rd. Bour 207 D4
Windermere Rd. Ports 157 F2
Windermere Rd. W End 80 A1
Windgreen Estate. Broa 187 F4
Windham Rd. Bour 207 E3
Windhill Field. Den 111 D2
Windmill Cl. Clanf 88 B3
Windmill Cl. M on S 213 E3
Windmill Copse. Hyt 125 F1
Windmill Gr. Portc 156 B3
Windmill Hts. Clanf 88 B2
Windmill La. Burs 105 D1
Windmill La. St Le 140 B2
Windover Cl. Southa 104 B3
Windrush Gdns. Wat 134 B4
Windrush Rd. Southa 101 F4
Windrush Way. Hyt 126 A2
Windsor Cl. Hord 196 C2
Windsor Cl. St Le 139 F2
Windsor Gate. Eastl 56 A3
Windsor Rd. Bour 207 F2
Windsor Rd. Christ 208 C4
Windsor Rd. Cos 157 F4
Windsor Rd. Gos 181 D2
Windsor Rd. Pet 40 C2
Windsor Rd. Poole 205 D2
Windsor Rd. Portc 156 B3
Windsor Way. Alderh 93 D3
Winfield Way. Ems 136 C2
Winfrith Cres. Poole 205 F4
Winfrith Way. Nur 77 E3
Wingate Dr. Southa 104 A3
Wingate Rd. Gos 155 F1
Wingate Rd. Tot 100 B4
Wingfield Ave. Christ 194 B1
Wingfield Ave. Poole 204 B3
Wingfield St. Ports 182 B4
Wingrove Rd. Ashu 100 B2
Winifred Cl. Fa Oa 57 E2
Winifred Rd. Poole 204 C3
Winifred Rd. Wat 134 C4
Winkfield Row. Wat 112 A3
Winkle St. Southa 103 D1
Winkton Cl. Burt 193 E2
Winkton Cl. Hav 135 E2
Winn Rd. Southa 79 D1
Winnall Cl. Winch 2 B1
Winnall Manor Rd. Winch 11 E4
Winnall Valley Rd. Winch 11 E4
Winnards Close. Fern 165 F1
Winnards Park. Lo He 128 B2
Winnham Dr. Portc 132 A1
Winnington Cl. Fare 130 B2
Winnington. Fare 130 B2
Winscombe Ave. Wat 112 A1
Winsford Ave. Bish 57 D1
Winsford Cl. Bish 57 D1
Winsford Cl. Christ 194 B1
Winslade Rd. Hav 135 E3
Winslade Rd. Winch 1 B2
Winsley Ave. Bour 208 B2
Winsor Cl. S Hay 185 E1
Winsor La. Cadn 99 D4
Winsor La. Ne Ma 99 E4
Winsor Rd. Cadn 75 E1
Winsor Rd. Tot 101 D3
Winsor Rd. Wat 111 E1
Winspit Cl. Hamw 203 F2
Winstanley Rd. Ports 157 E1
Winston Ave. Poole 206 A3
Winston Churchill Ave. Ports 182 B2
Winston Cl. Eastl 56 A2
Winston Cl. S Hay 184 C2
Winston Gdns. Poole 206 A3
Winston Rd. Bour 191 D2
Winston Way. Rin 141 D4
Winstone Cres. N Bad 54 A2
Winter Rd. Ports 183 D2
Winterbourne Rd. Cos 132 C1
Winterbourne Rd. Poole 204 B3
Winterbourne Rd. Rom 28 A1
Winterhayes Cl. Broa 188 C2
Winterhill Rd. Cos 157 E4
Winters Cl. Holb 150 B2
Winters Hill. Bi Wa 82 C4
Winters Hill. Co Com 58 C1
Winters Hill. Durl 82 C4
Winters Rd. Shed 84 A1
Winterslow Dr. Hav 135 F3
Winton Cl. Lym 198 C2
Winton Rd. Pet 40 C2
Winton Rd. Ports 157 F1
Winton St. Southa 103 D3
Winton Way. New M 196 A3
Wisborough Rd. Ports 182 C1
Wish Pl. Ports 182 C2
Wishart Gdns. Bour 191 D3
Witchampton Cl. Hav 136 A3
Witchampton Rd. Broa 187 F1
Withedwood Ave. Southa 102 B4
Witherbed La. Lo He 129 F3
Withermoor Rd. Bour 206 C4
Withies Rd. Gos 180 B4
Withingham Rd. Poole 205 F2
Witley Rd. Horn 111 F3
Witt Rd. Fa Oa 57 E1
Wittensford La. Cadn 98 B4
Wittering Rd. S Hay 185 F1
Wittering Rd. Southa 78 A2
Witts Hill. Southa 79 F1
Woburn Cl. Eastl 56 A3
Woburn Rd. Southa 78 B3
Wode Cl. Horn 88 B2
Wodehouse Rd. Southa 103 F2
Woking Rd. Poole 205 E2
Wolfe Cl. Winch 10 B3
Wollaston Rd. Bour 208 C2
Wollaton Cres. Fern 165 E2
Wollaton Rd. Fern 165 E2
Wollstonecraft Rd. Bour 207 F2
Wolseley Rd. Poole 205 E3
Wolseley Rd. Southa 102 B4
Wolsey Way. M on S 213 E3
Wolterton Rd. Poole 206 A3
Wolverley Ct. Southa 78 B2
Wolverton Rd. Bour 207 F3
Wolverton Rd. Hav 135 F3
Wolverton Rd. Southa 103 D3
Wonston Rd. Southa 78 A2
Wood Cl. Southa 104 B2
Wood Glade Cl. March 101 F1
Wood La. Bour 189 F3
Wood La. Bramd 15 F3
Wood La. M on S 213 E2
Wood Lark Gdns. Pet 41 E2
Wood Lawn Cl. B on S 211 F4
Wood Lodge. Tot 76 A1
Wood Rd. Ashu 100 A1
Woodacre Gdns. Fern 165 F2
Woodberry La. Ro Ca 136 C4
Woodbourne Cl. Liss 21 D2
Woodbourne Cl. Fare 130 B1
Woodbury Ave. Bour 191 F1
Woodbury Ave. Hav 159 F4
Woodbury Ave. Pet 40 C3
Woodbury Cl. Christ 192 C2
Woodcock La. Hord 197 D2
Woodcocks Cres. Bour 208 A4
Woodcot Cres. Hav 136 A3
Woodcote Dr. Upt 203 D3
Woodcote La. Stubb 155 D2
Woodcote Rd. Southa 79 E2
Woodcroft La. Wat 111 F3
Woodend Rd. Bour 206 C4
Woodend Rd. Burs 127 F4
Woodend Rd. Rin 141 F3
Wooderson Cl. Fa Oa 57 D2
Woodfield Ave. Cos 134 C1
Woodfield Dr. Winch 10 A3
Woodfield Gdns. Christ 194 B1
Woodfield Rd. Bour 190 D3
Woodford Cl. Rin 141 E4
Woodford Rd. Bour 207 E2
Woodgason La. N Hay 160 B1
Woodgreen Ave. Hav 135 E2
Woodgreen Dr. Bour 189 E2
Woodgreen Rd. Winch 1 B2
Woodgreen Wlk. Tot 76 A1
Woodhall Way. Fare 130 C2
Woodhayes Ave. Christ 194 C1
Woodhouse La. Bold 174 A1
Woodhouse La. He En 105 F4
Woodhouse La. Ro Ca 113 E2
Woodington Cl. Hav 136 A3
Woodington Rd. W Wel 51 E3
Woodland Ave. Bour 208 A2
Woodland Cl. Southa 104 B4
Woodland Cl. W Wel 51 D1
Woodland Mews. W End 80 B1
Woodland St. Ports 182 C3
Woodland View. Horn 111 F3
Woodland Way. Christ 210 B4
Woodland Way. M on S 213 E2
Woodland Wlk. Fern 165 F4
Woodlands Ave. Ems 136 C2
Woodlands Ave. Hamw 203 F2
Woodlands Cl. Bran 194 A4
Woodlands Cl. Ch Fo 30 B1
Woodlands Cl. Hyt 125 F1
Woodlands Cl. Lo He 128 C3
Woodlands Cres. Hamw 203 F2
Woodlands Ct. Hyt 125 F1
Woodlands Drove. Ashu 99 F2
Woodlands Gdns. Rom 28 A1
Woodlands Gr. Wat 134 B3
Woodlands La. Liss 21 D2
Woodlands La. S Hay 184 C3
Woodlands Rd. Ashu 99 F2
Woodlands Rd. B on S 211 F4
Woodlands Rd. Brock 172 C4
Woodlands Rd. Ne Ma 99 F2
Woodlands The. Ki Wo 2 B3
Woodlands Way. Hav 135 F2
Woodlands Way. N Bad 53 F2
Woodlands Way. New M 196 A3
Woodlands Way. Southa 102 C4
Woodlands Way. St Le 139 F2
Woodlands. Fare 131 E1
Woodlane Cl. Bramd 15 E3
Woodlea Cl. Winch 1 C1
Woodlea Gdns. W End 80 C1
Woodlea Way. Ampf 31 F1
Woodleaze Cl. Broa 188 A3
Woodley Cl. Rom 28 B1
Woodley Gdns. Lym 198 B3
Woodley La. Rom 28 A1
Woodley Rd. Gos 181 E2
Woodley Rd. Southa 103 E2
Woodley Way. Rom 28 B1
Woodlinken Cl. Ver 115 D2
Woodlinken Dr. Ver 115 D3
Woodlinken Way. Ver 115 E2
Woodmancote La. Westb 137 F2
Woodmancote Rd. Ports 183 D2
Woodmill La. Southa 79 F1
Woodmoor Cl. March 102 A1
Woodpath. Ports 182 B2
Woodpecker Cl. Hav 136 A1
Woodpecker Cl. Ver 114 C3
Woodpecker Copse. Lo He 129 D2
Woodpecker Dr. Broa 203 F4
Woodpecker Dr. March 101 F1
Woodpecker Dr. Winch 1 B1
Woodpecker Way. Eastl 55 E1
Woodroffe Wlk. Ems 136 C2
Woodrush Cres. Lo He 128 C1
Woods View Rd. Bour 206 B4
Woodsedge. Wat 135 D3
Woodside Ave. Eastl 55 F2
Woodside Ave. Lym 198 C1
Woodside Cl. Fern 165 F3
Woodside Cl. Lym 198 C1
Woodside Cl. March 101 F1
Woodside Cres. Chilw 54 C1
Woodside Gdns. Ashu 100 B2
Woodside La. Lym 198 C1
Woodside Rd. Bour 208 A2
Woodside Rd. Eastl 55 F2
Woodside Rd. Fern 165 F3
Woodside Rd. N Bad 53 F2
Woodside Rd. Poole 205 E2
Woodside Rd. Southa 103 D4
Woodside Rd. W Moo 138 B2
Woodside Way. He En 105 D3
Woodside. Chilw 54 C1
Woodside. Gos 155 D3
Woodstock Ave. Hav 112 A3
Woodstock Cl. Fare 130 C1
Woodstock Cl. He En 105 E3
Woodstock Dr. Southa 79 D1
Woodstock La. Rin 141 D3
Woodstock Rd. Burt 193 E1
Woodstock Rd. Gos 181 E2
Woodstock Rd. Hav 135 E1
Woodstock Rd. Poole 205 D1
Woodthorpe Gdns. Lo He 128 C3
Woodvale Gdns. New M 196 B2
Woodvale. Fare 130 B1
Woodview Cl. Southa 79 D3
Woodville Ave. Faw 151 D2
Woodville Dr. Ports 182 A2
Woodville Rd. Hav 135 D1
Woodward Cl. Gos 180 C2
Woofferton Rd. Cos 133 D1
Wool Rd. Poole 205 D4
Woolfield La. Frox G 18 A2
Woolford Cl. Winch 10 B3
Woolmer La. Rin 117 D1
Woolmer St. Ems 136 C2
Woolner Ave. Cos 158 A4
Woolner Ave. Pet 40 C2
Woolsbridge Rd. St Le 139 F3
Woolslope Cl. W Moo 138 C1
Woolslope Gdns. W Moo 138 C1
Woolslope Rd. W Moo 138 C1
Woolston Rd. Hav 135 E3
Woolston Rd. Net 127 E4
Woolven Cl. Poole 205 D3
Woolwich Cl. Burs 104 C1
Wootton Farm Rd. Brock 170 C1
Wootton Gdns. Bour 207 D2
Wootton Mount. Bour 207 D2
Wootton Rd. Lon S 180 A2
Wootton Rough. New M 196 A4
Wootton St. Cos 157 F4
Wootton. Net 127 E4
Worbarrow Gdns. Poole 205 E4
Worcester Pl. Lym 198 C1
Worcester Pl. Southa 104 A1
Wordsworth Ave. Bour 191 F1
Wordsworth Ave. Portc 132 C1
Wordsworth Cl. Bi Wa 83 F4
Wordsworth Cl. Winch 10 B4
Wordsworth Rd. Southa 78 B1
Worgret Rd. Poole 204 B4
Workhouse La. E Meo 38 B1
Worldham Rd. Hav 136 A3
Worrell Dr. Poole 205 E4
Worsley Rd. Ports 182 B3
Worsley St. Ports 183 D1
Worthing Ave. Gos 180 C4
Worthing Rd. Ports 182 B1
Worthington Cres. Poole 205 D2
Worthy La. Winch 1 C1
Worthy Rd. New M 196 A2
Worthy Rd. Winch 2 A1
Wortley Rd. Christ 211 D4
Wraysbury Park Dr. Ems 136 C2
Wren Cl. Christ 210 A3
Wren Cl. Rin 141 E3
Wren Cl. Winch 10 B3
Wren Cres. Poole 206 A3
Wren Gdns. Alderh 93 D3
Wren Rd. Eastl 55 F1
Wrenway. Portc 155 F4
Wrexham Gr. Horn 88 A1
Wright's Hill. Southa 104 A1
Wroxham Rd. Poole 205 F3
Wryneck Cl. Southa 78 A3
Wyatts Cl. Broa 187 E3
Wyatts La. Broa 187 E3
Wyborn Cl. S Hay 185 D1
Wych La. Gos 155 D2
Wychwood Cl. Bour 206 C2
Wychwood Dr. Black 177 F4
Wychwood Dr. Bour 206 C2
Wychwood Gr. Ch Fo 55 F4
Wycliffe Rd. Bour 206 C4
Wycliffe Rd. Southa 80 A1
Wycote Rd. Gos 155 D2
Wyeford Cl. Hav 136 A3
Wyelands Ave. Fern 164 B3
Wykeham Ave. Ports 157 F1
Wykeham Cl. Net 127 D3
Wykeham Cl. Poole 204 C4
Wykeham Cl. Southa 78 C2
Wykeham Field. Wickh 108 A2
Wykeham Pl. Lym 198 C2
Wykeham Pl. Winch 10 B3
Wykeham Rd. Net 127 D3
Wykeham Rd. Ports 157 F1
Wyld Green La. Liss 21 D3
Wylds La. Buri 65 E4
Wyllie Rd. Ports 157 F2
Wylye Cl. W End 80 A2
Wymering La. Cos 133 F1
Wymering Manor Cl. Cos 157 E4
Wymering Rd. Ports 182 C4
Wyncombe Rd. Bour 208 A3
Wyndcliffe Rd. Ports 182 C2
Wyndham Cl. Christ 195 D1
Wyndham Mews. Ports 182 A2
Wyndham Pl. Southa 102 C3
Wyndham Rd. Christ 195 D1
Wyndham Rd. Poole 205 D2
Wynford Rd. Bour 191 D2
Wynford Rd. Poole 205 E2
Wynne Cl. Broa 187 F2
Wynter Cl. Bour 207 F4
Wynter Rd. Southa 104 A4
Wynton Way. Fare 130 B2
Wynyards Gap. N Bad 53 F2
Wyre Cl. N Bad 55 D3
Wyvern Cl. Ch Fo 55 E3
Wyvern Cl. Poole 205 E4

Yaldhurst La. Lym 198 A2
Yapton St. Ports 182 B3
Yarborough Rd. Ports 182 B2
Yardlea Cl. Ro Ca 113 D1
Yardley Cl. Ports 158 B2
Yardley Rd. He En 105 E3
Yarmouth Cl. Poole 206 A3
Yarmouth Gdns. Southa 78 A1
Yarmouth Rd. Poole 205 F3
Yarrell Mead. Lym 198 A2
Yarrells Cl. Upt 203 E3
Yarrells Dr. Upt 203 D4
Yarrells La. Upt 203 E3
Yarrow Cl. Christ 210 A4
Yarrow Rd. Poole 205 D4
Yarrow Way. Lo He 128 C1
Yateley Cl. Hav 135 E3
Yaverland. Net 127 E3
Yeatminster Rd. Poole 188 C1
Yelverton Ave. Hyt 150 A4

Yelverton Rd. Bour 206 C2
Yeo Ct. Ports 183 E2
Yeomans Ind Pk. Bour 191 F1
Yeomans Rd. Bour 191 F2
Yeomans Way. Bour 191 F1
Yeomans Way. Tot 100 C4
Yeovil Chase. Southa 104 A4
Yeovilton Cl. Hord 197 F1
Yew La. New M 196 B2
Yew Rd. Southa 104 A4
Yew Tree Ave. Wat 112 A1
Yew Tree Cl. Fa Oa 57 E2
Yew Tree Cl. He En 105 D3
Yew Tree Cl. Wi Mi 163 E3
Yew Tree Dr. Swanw 129 E4
Yew Tree Gdns. Den 110 C2
Yew Tree Pl. Liss 21 D2
Yew Tree Rd. N Hay 185 D4
Yews The. Horn 112 B4
Yewside. Gos 155 F1
Yewtree La. Nur 77 D2
Yoells Cr. Wat 111 F3
Yoells La. Wat 111 F3
Yokesford Hill. Abb 27 F2
Yonge Cl. Eastl 56 A2
York Ave. New M 196 A2
York Bldgs. Southa 103 D2
York Cl. Broa 188 A1
York Cl. Christ 208 C4
York Cl. Pet 40 B2
York Cl. Southa 103 E3
York Cl. Tot 101 D4
York Cres. L on S 180 A2
York Dro. Red 73 E4
York Dro. Southa 104 A4
York Gdns. Portc 156 C3
York Pl. Bour 208 A3
York Pl. Ports 182 A3
York Rd. Bour 207 D2
York Rd. Broa 188 A1
York Rd. Eastl 80 A4
York Rd. Net 127 D3
York Rd. Southa 102 B4
Yorke St. Ports 182 B2
Yorke Way. Hamble 127 F2
Yorkwood. Liss 20 C2
Youngs Rd. Bour 190 D3
Yves Mews. Ports 182 B1

Zamek Cl. Bour 190 D3
Zetland Rd. Cos 158 B4
Zetland Rd. Gos 181 D3
Zeus La. Wat 134 C2
Zinnia Cl. Bour 190 C1